FICTION
Writer's Market

Edited by
John Brady
and
Jean M. Fredette

Writer's
Digest
Books

Cincinnati, Ohio

International Standard Serial Number 0275-2123
International Standard Book Number 0-89879-048-4

Book design by Carol Jacober

Acknowledgments

The editors of *Fiction Writer's Market* gratefully acknowledge the following publishers, authors, and agents for granting permission to reprint their articles and book excerpts:

George Antonich, "How to Turn Fact Into Fiction," *Writer's Digest*, April 1971. ⊕ *Writer's Digest*.

Jane S. Bakerman, "Such Good Writing: An Interview With Lois Gould," *Writer's Digest*, September 1980. ⊕ *Writer's Digest*.

Helene Schellenberg Barnhart, "Getting Caught in the Middle," *Writer's Digest*, January 1977. ⊕ *Writer's Digest*.

Lawrence Block, "Why Write a Novel?", from *Writing the Novel: From Plot to Print*, *Writer's Digest Books*, ⊕ Lawrence Block, 1979.

Gerald Warner Brace, "Theme," from *The Stuff of Fiction*, W.W. Norton & Company, Inc., 1969. (Reprinted with the permission of W.W. Norton & Company, Inc. Copyright ⊕ 1961 by Gerald Warner Brace; and McIntosh & Otis, Inc.)

John Braine, "Narrative Prose," from *Writing a Novel*, Coward, McCann & Geoghegan, Inc., 1974. (Reprinted with the permission of Coward, McCann & Geoghegan, Inc. and David Higham Associates, Ltd.)

Jacqueline Briskin, "Research Is a Snap," *Writer's Digest*, February 1979. ⊕ *Writer's Digest*.

Janice Young Brooks, "Tagging Your Characters," *Writer's Digest*, March 1978. ⊕ *Writer's Digest*.

Dorothy Bryant, "Writing Is Rewriting," *Writer's Yearbook* 1980. ⊕ *Writer's Yearbook*.

Pearl Buck, "Advice to Unknown Novelists," from *Writing for Love or Money*, edited by Norman Cousins, David McKay Company, Inc., 1949. (Reprinted with permission David McKay Company, Inc.)

Hallie and Whit Burnett, "Notebooks and Diaries," from *Fiction Writer's Handbook*, Harper & Row, Publishers, copyright ⊕ 1975 by Hallie Burnett. (Reprinted with permission by Harper & Row, Publishers, Inc. Excerpt from *The Notebooks of Henry James*, edited by F.O. Matthiessen and Kenneth Murdock. Copyright ⊕ 1947 by Oxford University Press, Inc.; renewed 1974 by Kenneth B. Murdock. Reprinted by permission of Oxford Press, Inc.)

Orson Scott Card, "To Make a Short Story Long . . . ," *Writer's Digest*, September 1980. ⊕ *Writer's Digest*.

C.J. Cherryh, "Arms and the Writer," *Writer's Digest*, July 1979. ⊕ *Writer's Digest*.

Diane Cleaver, "All About Agents," *Writer's Digest*, June 1980. ⊕ *Writer's Digest*.

Chet Cunningham, "The Partial Road to Selling Complete Novels," *Writer's Digest*, September 1979. ⊕ *Writer's Digest*.

Ruth Engelken, "Look . . . a Little Closer," *Writer's Digest*, July 1969. ⊕ *Writer's Digest*.

Jane Fitz-Randolph, "Patterns for Carrying Young Readers Through Your Story," from *How to Write for Children and Young Adults*, Barnes & Noble Books, 1980 (Reprinted with permission of Harper & Row, Publishers.)

Lee Floren, "The Five W's—and How!", *Writer's Digest*, July 1977. ⊕ *Writer's Digest*.

Marjorie Franco, "Fiction Is a Battleground," *Writer's Digest*, March 1973. ⊕ *Writer's Digest*.

Brian Garfield, "Ten Rules for Suspense Fiction," *Writer's Digest*, February 1973. ⊕ *Writer's Digest*.

James Cross Giblin, "Confessions of a Children's Book Editor," *Writer's Yearbook* 1977. ⊕ *Writer's Yearbook*.

James Gunn, "Where Do You Get Those Crazy Ideas?", from *Writing and Selling Science Fiction*, Writer's Digest Books, 1976. ⊕ Science Fiction Writers of America.

Charles Heckelmann, "The Six Functions of Dialogue in Fiction," from *Writing Fiction for Profit*, Coward, McCann & Geoghegan, Inc., 1968. (Reprinted by permission of the author and the author's agents, Scott Meredith Literary Agency, Inc., 845 3rd Ave., New York NY 10022.)

Vera Henry, "The Short Short," *Writer's Digest*, February 1970. ⊕ *Writer's Digest*.

Bob Jacobs, "Bradbury on Bradbury—and Beyond," *Writer's Digest*, February 1976. © *Writer's Digest*.

Eileen Jensen, "Actions Speak Louder With Descriptions," *Writer's Digest*, September 1977. © *Writer's Digest*.

Michiko Kakutani, "Portrait of the Artist as a First Novelist," *The New York Times Book Review*, June 8, 1980. (Reprinted with permission The New York Times Company.)

Stephen King, "Horror Stories and the Ten Bears," *Writer's Digest*, November 1973. © *Writer's Digest*.

Will C. Knott, "Keep the Reader Where the Action Is," *Writer's Digest*, June 1976. © *Writer's Digest*.

Manuel Komroff, "Establishing Good Writing Habits" and "Tying Up Loose Ends," from *How to Write a Novel*, Simon & Schuster, Inc., 1950. (Reprinted with permission Barthold Fles Literary Agent.)

Louis L'Amour, "Plotting and Characterization in the Western Novel," from "How to Plot an Adventure Story," and "How to Become a Character," *Writer's Yearbook* 1947, 1949. © *Writer's Yearbook*.

James D. Lucey, "Can You State Your Story in a Sentence?" *Writer's Digest*, December 1970. © *Writer's Digest*.

Ross Macdonald, "Personal Journey: A Preface to *The Galton Case*," from *Afterwords: Novelists on Their Novels*, edited by Thomas McCormack, Harper & Row, Publishers, Inc., 1969. (Reprinted with permission by Harold Ober Associates Inc.)

Somerset Maugham, "How I Write Short Stories," from *Writing for Love or Money*, edited by Norman Cousins, David McKay Company, Inc., 1949. (Reprinted with permission by David McKay Company, Inc.)

André Maurois, "The Writer's Craft," from *The Art of Writing*, E.P. Dutton, 1960. (Reprinted with permission by Georges Borchardt, Inc. Literary Agency.)

Marguerite McClain, "Slick Versus Confession," *Writer's Digest School Forum*, September/October 1980. © *Writer's Digest School Forum*.

Wright Morris, "On Being True-to-Life," from *About Fiction*, Harper & Row, Publishers, Inc., 1975. (Reprinted with permission by the publisher and Russell and Volkening, Inc. Literary Representatives.)

Flannery O'Connor, "The Nature and Aim of Fiction," from *Mystery and Manners*, Farrar, Straus and Giroux, Inc. (Reprinted by permission of Farrar, Straus and Giroux, Inc. "The Nature and Aim of Fiction," from *Mystery and Manners,* by Flannery O'Connor. Copyright © 1957, 1961, 1963, 1964, 1966, 1967, 1969 by the Estate of Mary Flannery O'Connor. Copyright © 1962 by Flannery O'Connor. Copyright © 1961 by Farrar, Straus and Cudahy, Inc.)

Jean Z. Owen, "How to Create Likable Characters in Your Fiction," *Writer's Digest*, June 1977. © *Writer's Digest*.

Mariana Prieto, "Using the Flashback in Fiction," *Writer's Digest*, May 1969. © *Writer's Digest*.

Mario Puzo, "The Making of *The Godfather*," from *The Godfather Papers*, G.P. Putnam's Sons, 1972. (Reprinted with permission by the publisher and Candida Donadio and Associates, Inc.)

Charles Thomas Samuels, "An Interview With John Updike," from *Writers at Work: The Paris Review Interviews*, Fourth Series, ed. George Plimpton, The Paris Review, Inc. © 1974, 1976. (Reprinted with permission of Viking Penguin Inc.)

Walter Sheldon, "Plotting the Novel," *Writer's Yearbook* 1973. © *Writer's Yearbook*. (Reprinted with permission by the author and the author's agents, Scott Meredith Literary Agency, Inc., 845 3rd Ave., New York NY 10022.)

William Sloane, "Scene," from *The Craft of Writing*, W.W. Norton & Company, Inc., 1979. (Reprinted with permission of W.W. Norton & Company, Inc., copyright © 1979 Julia H. Sloane.)

Mark Twain, "The Finished Book," from *Europe and Elsewhere*, 1923; © renewed 1951 by The Mark Twain Company. (Reprinted with permission of Harper & Row, Publishers, Inc.)

Eudora Welty, "Must the Novelist Crusade?", *Writer's Digest*, February 1970. © *Writer's Digest*. (Reprinted with permission by the author and her agents Russell & Volkening, Inc.)

Kathleen West, "How to Cut a Story by One-Third and Make a Sale," *Writer's Yearbook* 1972. © *Writer's Yearbook*.

Phyllis Whitney, "What Do You Mean, Gothic?", from *Mystery Writer's Handbook*, Writer's Digest Books, © Mystery Writers of America, 1976.

Lee Wyndham, "How to Organize a Book for Children and Young Adults," from *Writing for Children and Teenagers*, Writer's Digest Books, © Lee Wyndham, 1976.

Special thanks to A.D. Winans, editor of *Second Coming*, for information on small presses and little magazines; and to Gail Bason, Cathy Cooper, Fran Cummins, Barbara Lovely, Carol Rogers, and Terry Susskind for editorial assistance.

Table of Contents

Organization

The Short Short Story

The Short Story

Writers in Action: I

Story Evaluation

From Stories to Novels

The Novel

The First Novel

Endings

Agents

Markets

Contests and Awards

Writers' Organizations

Glossary

Category Index

Index to Markets

Foreword

Fiction, as Flannery O'Connor once observed, "is a self-contained dramatic unit . . . about everything human." Fiction is: doubts, fears, ambitions, dreams, ecstasies. It is history, sociology, a slice of life, a chronicle of human experience. "Fiction," says Susan Cheever, "is something you do against the world."

You against the world. You versus that blank page. You in a quiet room, or in a moving train, or at the kitchen table after the dishes have been cleared and the kids put to bed. You against the discouragements of others, the many forces Out There.

That's why we are here.

Fiction Writer's Market is a reference book and a reader for the fiction writer. It's a book of instructional and inspirational selections on writing fiction, along with an up-to-date list of publishing markets for stories and novels. It's a how-to and a where-to for fiction writers—an annual view of the field, and a reminder that there are others, too, struggling with the forces Out There. You are not alone.

Fiction Writer's Market is here at your request. Your letters to us at *Writer's Digest* and at *Writer's Market* have told us of your hopes and frustrations in your attempts to publish novels and short stories. You've asked for advice and writing tips and where to market your material. We have listened carefully, for what you say is important.

You have told us who you are. You are a dentist who writes short stories on Wednesdays and weekends. You are a young mother who sits down at a typewriter as soon as the kids are off to school. You are a journalist who writes fiction during off hours, and you are a college English major who plans to write a novel next summer. Though your backgrounds are diverse, you have a lot in common: You have chosen fiction as a hobby, a vocation, a lark, or maybe even as an obsession, and you hope to write and publish short stories and novels.

Statistics tell us that your interest in fiction is widespread and not confined to large cities or large college campuses. Enrollments continue to go up in adult education creative writing classes across the towns of America, and writing workshops and conferences are flourishing nationwide. Fiction students in the Writer's Digest Correspondence School outnumber nonfiction students two to one. So we know that fiction remains an area of high interest. And we know, too, that you are not alone.

There is no formula for acquiring writing talent or fiction technique. But those qualities that sparked your interest in fiction initially—a facility with words, a lifetime love affair with books, the restless desire to tell a story—can be fine-tuned to make you a *better* fiction writer than you perhaps are as you start through this book. Here you will find the wisdom of master writers and the know-how of proven writing teachers in chapters we have chosen to highlight skills and techniques necessary to make it in fiction writing today. The opportunities are there, too—some 800 markets that publish fiction and look at manuscripts daily.

We dedicate this book to *you*, the determined writer—from beginner to bestseller—with the sincere hope that our work, along with your own hard work at the typewriter, will lead you to even higher fields of writing achievement. Your assignment is, as ever, the fiction writer's task: an appealing character striving against great odds to attain a worthwhile goal.

Onward!

—The Editors

Fiction weather report

Despite some clouds on the horizon for the publishing business in general, the climate for fiction is surprisingly good. For decades, of course, we have heard the nagging rumors that the novel is dead, the short story is fading from the magazine world, and fiction is not what it used to be. Well, yes and no.

The novel is *not* dead, nor is the first novel in any danger of dying.

Although fiction is but a 7.2% slice of the publishing world (some 3,250 titles of more than 45,000 books published in 1979 were fiction), there were more first novels published in 1980 than in recent years—nearly 200. By October, four of those first novels had reached bestseller status. Publishers plan to issue at least the same number of novels in the year ahead—and the search for good fiction continues.

Publishers realize, too, that second novels are not possible without first novels. "You can't get a crop if you don't plant a seed," says Harold T. Miller, president of Houghton-Mifflin. Every publisher or editor hopes that the next manuscript read will be that of a new Faulkner or Roth. Thus, they are willing to search through thousands of manuscripts each year because the rewards of hitting the jackpot with a bestseller are enormous.

All books have been affected by rising costs. A few years ago a novel was a $10,000-$15,000 risk. Today that figure has grown to about $20,000-$25,000. Publishers of unknown authors are reluctant to spend large amounts on advertising and promotion. Accordingly, new novels tend to be ignored by reviewers and bookstores. Few sell as many as 3,000 copies (most to libraries), and a great number fail to earn back an average advance of $4,000. It must be noted, however, that first novels (and poetry) are not generally the biggest losers. Because they are cautiously printed and promoted, no attempt is made to overpay the author or to oversell the book. "We are motivated to publish exciting stories or books of literary merit by real writers—whether they are first novelists or not doesn't make any difference," says Robert E. Ginna of Little, Brown. But the credo of major publishing houses, as a result of the recession and other factors we will cover in a moment, is "few and safer novels."

Large publishers admit that in order to keep fiction programs ambitious it is necessary to have a secure market. Publishing novels is akin to a lottery in which an occasional title hits the mark and pays for those that do not. In other words, bestsellers, the commercial successes, may pay for art and allow an occasional benevolent publisher to "reinvest" in literature. It has been said that two of three works of fiction are not financially justifiable; the third justifies the other two.

Cautionary publishing, practiced by today's large publishing houses, results in the commercial novel. That's what the public reads. In a recent nomination for the Hemingway Award for the best first novel, ten of the 125 submissions were serious literary efforts. The rest were "consciously commercial," intended to entertain a mass audience. Similarly, serious literary work accounts for no more than 10% of all consumer book sales.

The change in publishing tactics over the last decade is graphically demonstrated in an experiment conducted by Chuck Ross discussed in *New West*. Ross retyped Jerzy Kosinski's novel *Steps*, winner of the 1969 National Book Award for fiction, and submitted it with a new title under a pseudonym to 14 publishers, including the novel's original publisher. All 14 returned it, most with a form rejection letter. Of the 26 literary agents queried, 25 were uninterested, and the 26th sent a $25 bill for the reading fee and said she doubted the manuscript could be published.

Recent successes by serious novels are scarce, but do happen. *Kindergarten*, by Peter Rushforth, was critically acclaimed. And in 1979, *The Year of the French*, the first novel by English professor Thomas Flanagan, was named the most distinguished work of fiction by the National Book Critics Circle. On the other hand, commercial first novel successes such as *Ordinary People* and *Love Story* are publishing lore. Recently *The Spike*, by Arnaud de Borchgrave and Robert Moss, earned $1 million in paperback rights; and *The Fifth Horseman*, by Larry Collins and Dominique Pierre, was sold to Paramount after its paperback sale of more than $1 million. Bestselling *Green Monday*, a 1980 novel by Michael Thomas, earned almost $375,000 in paperback; *Aztec* brought Gary Jennings $750,000 in paperback rights from Avon; and *Gorky Park* worked into a seven-figure deal for hardcover and paperback rights for Martin Cruz Smith. If the plots are commercial other media opportunities are there. *Panic on Page One* by Linda Steward was made into a movie for TV, an example of additional income for the author and publisher from the subsidiary rights.

Doctor, lawyer, indian chief

First novelists Jay Parini (*The Love Run*) and Robert Kalich (*The Handicapper*) view the status of fiction critically. Says Parini, "I am dismayed by most fiction today. Apart from a few writers, most writers fall into two mutually exclusive camps: the bestsellers and the academics. Bestsellers are largely unreadable and the academics have lost sight of E. M. Forster's great remark: 'A novel tells a story.' " Kalich spoke of his literary compromise to become published. After working 14 hours daily on his "important literary achievement," he altered and molded his novel to something salable, "a product." "I changed the novel and my soul too. In all I achieved something a lot less satisfying than when I started out. But now I am convinced that serious fiction is more difficult to sell to a publishing house than yesterday's *Daily News* tomorrow."

Some blame the fact that writers like Kalich must write "products" for the mergers and buyouts that have given conglomerates control of the book publishers. More than 300 mergers have taken place in the last two and a half decades, and, yes, corporate control of the publishing pocketbook has made everyone in the industry more interested in profit-making, and a little less interested in art-making. Yet, conglomerates may not be the villains many people would have them be. "I feel the book industry would have gone under without the infusion of money from the conglomerates," says poet/novelist Erica Jong. "Although it is not chic to say so, my own career has been helped by conglomerates. My editor at New American Library saved *Fear of Flying* from oblivion. In fact, she also encouraged me to write a book in 18th-century English (*Fanny*). She is an employee of a conglomerate and she sure as hell is not trying to get me to write like Judith Krantz."

Definitely, more than corporate control of publishers is at work against what is called "the marginal book"—that is, a book that makes marginal profits—and many novels are classified as marginal books. First is the rise of the chain bookstore, such as Little Professor, B. Dalton and Walden Bookseller. These bookstores want to fill their shelves with sure-sellers, making them less eager to carry the works of unknown authors. Because such chains now account for a large percentage of book sales many publishers are less eager to publish the works of unknown authors because they know that the major distributors may not put them in their stores.

Paperback publishers have been likewise eager to reprint only the blockbuster hardcovers, or to issue blockbuster paperback originals. This means less opportunity for marginal books in the short run—hardcover publishers, knowing that a reprint sale in which they share the profits, might be unlikely, often pass on a book they might have taken a few years ago. It also means less opportunity in the long run—much of an author's earnings comes from paperback sales, and fewer marginal books published in paperback means fewer authors making money from paperback sales.

A recent IRS ruling further dampens the market for marginal books. At one time, a publisher would routinely print books that it knew would make money over a period of years. The book would be stored in a warehouse and become a part of the publisher's "backlist." The ruling, however, made this practice less desirable. Whereas publishers could once depreciate the backlist books, the IRS ruled that they can now depreciate them only if they are sold at reduced prices or destroyed. This makes books lingering in warehouses as potential sales four and five years down the line a liability instead of an asset, and publishers in the future will hesitate to purchase a book that isn't expected to move quickly.

A further effect of the ruling is that publishers may institute a "no-returns" policy. That means that bookstores, which could take a certain number of copies of a book and return unsold copies without having to pay for them, cannot return those copies, and must pay for them. That will make bookstores additionally cautious, and leery of marginal titles.

Good things in small presses

The bottom line—a phrase now common in publishing circles—is that the commercial book publishing industry now sees profit as more compelling than literature. Not so with another segment of publishing: the small and independent literary houses that are springing up—in the US, Canada and abroad—and finding themselves in a clear field with an increasing portion of the publishing business.

Frustrated writers of serious fiction have found a home for their wide-ranging styles and themes in these small presses, a respectable alternative to the commercial market.

The difference between the major publishers and the small press is more clearly defined in philosophy than in structure and size. As Bill Henderson of Pushcart Book Press said in an interview for National Public Radio, "We are not concerned about money or profit, but about literature. The dollars come second; the talent and quality of the writing come first."

Small press publishing requires a deep-rooted commitment on the part of the editor and publisher, who handle all correspondence, read all incoming manuscripts, perform clerical duties, and plan promotion and distribution programs. "It's a dedicated lifestyle," says A.D. Winans, editor/publisher of *Second Coming*, and one that is contrary to that of the salaried editor of the major publisher. Small press efforts are often out of a basement or off a dining room table, low-budget operations that frequently depend on volunteer help or government or private grants.

Small publishing is a growing industry and a part of America's literary heritage that goes back two centuries. The list of famous writers whose work was independently or self-published is long and honorable: Thomas Gray ("Elegy Written in a Country Churchyard" 1751), Thomas Paine (*Common Sense*), William Blake, Robert Burns, Washington Irving, James Fennimore Cooper, Edgar Allan Poe, John Bartlett (*Familiar Quotations*), Walt Whitman, Mark Twain; and in the 20th century: Stephen Crane, Upton Sinclair, Zane Grey, Carl Sandburg, Ezra Pound, William Strunk Jr. (*Elements of Style*), Edgar Rice Burroughs—even James Joyce, whose *Ulysses* was too daring for commercial publishers at the outset.

As with major publishers, the independent presses have their successes, flops, and occasionally their money-earners. But this usual lack of financial rewards is justified by other rewards. As Anais Nin said of her small-press experience: "The creation of an individual work, an act of independence such as the work at the press, is a marvelous cure for anger and frustration. The insults of the publishers, the rejections, the ignorance, are all forgotten."

"Freedom of the press belongs to those who own the press," say the editors of small independent presses. Editors and writers in small operations sometimes combine their efforts in publishing, writing, printing, binding and graphics, a cooperative environment that enables the author to maintain some control over his or her book. The writer can be involved in every aspect of the book, from choosing the quality of the paper to selecting the size and style of the type, and even suggesting distribution methods.

Like the independent press, literary/little magazines usually evolve from some form of discontent, such as negligence, lack of cooperation of major publishers, or the constraints of society. The small press/little magazine editor often views the publishing world with disdain and dismay, and he may refuse to compromise his moral beliefs and seek to reform existing societal attitudes.

"Little" does not refer to size or literary content; some large magazines have small circulations and some tiny newspapers reach thousands. "Little" generally signifies the appeal of the publications to narrow segments of the general readership because they cover particular interests or causes. Most assuredly, little does *not* mean little-known; *Southern Review, Sewanee Review, Yale Review* and *Vir-*

ginia Quarterly, journals of national literary repute, are classified as literary/little. Many of the littles publish writers and writing that receive national acclaim. Short stories by Lyn Coffin and Joyce Carol Oates, for example, were selected from the pages of the *Michigan Quarterly Review* for inclusion in *Best American Short Stories 1979* and *Prize Stories 1981: The O. Henry Awards*, respectively. Realistically, however, most small magazines are run with few resources and with modest business know-how. Noncommercial by intent and altruistic by creed, the littles usually rule out hope for financial profit. For most, a good year is a break-even year.

Small magazines do have large-scale ambitions, missions that promote subjects or interests which might be neglected or forgotten. For those that survive the tough early going, ten years is the ideal life span. In the beginning years, they may lack direction but have a courageous, adolescent, even daring approach; in the middle years there is usually identity and a leveling off stage of near-security; and in the the latter years the issues lose their urgency (or funds), and become thin or outdated. A changing society and varying literary needs dictate the advent and demise of the little magazines. Fortunately, the steady arrival of new ones compensate somewhat for their impermanence. And as long as there are writers with courage and determination wishing to express themselves, there will be new little magazines and new styles, suggestions, experiments and risks in literature which the popular or academic audience cannot tolerate or accept.

The parent of all little magazines is *The Dial* (1840-1844) edited by Margaret Fuller and Ralph Waldo Emerson. It was not until the second decade of the 20th century, however, that little magazines came into their own. Margaret Anderson founded *The Little Review*, which became the forerunner of literary voices in the US and later Europe between the wars. A new era and subsequently a whole new generation of writers evolved: Gertrude Stein, Ernest Hemingway, Ezra Pound, Henry Miller, Sherwood Anderson, Dorothy Richardson, Apollinaire and Jean Cocteau. James Joyce's *Ulysses*, thoroughly rejected by US publishers, was published by Margaret Anderson in installments in the US and by Sylvia Beach in Paris in its entirety.

Commercial announcements

The small markets for fiction continue to proliferate because the commercial magazines in the last 20 to 30 years have reduced the amount of mainstream or contemporary fiction they publish. Many of the better-paying markets solicit short stories from established writers, or accept material from agents only. The fact that national magazines have held contests and given awards for fiction (*Atlantic Monthly*, *Playboy*, *Ms.*, *Seventeen*, *Redbook*, *Flare*, *Mademoiselle*), however, demonstrates a keen interest in perpetuating high-quality fiction and in seeking new writers.

John Irving's first story was published in *Redbook* in 1965. As Anne Mollegan Smith, managing editor said, "*Redbook*'s fiction editors 'discover' these talented writers by doing hard work of reading the roughly 35,000 unsolicited manuscripts that come to our offices every year. And each year *Redbook* buys at least a dozen—and sometimes as many as 20—stories from this rich resource." Lynne Sharon Schwartz, whose first novel *Rough Strife* was published by Harper & Row in 1980, sold *Redbook* a short story this way several years ago, as did Mary Gordon (*Final Payments*) and Tim O'Brien, one of whose stories from *Redbook* is in the O. Henry collection of the best short stories of the decade. Granted, it's a long-shot proposition, and an unsolicited manuscript has a difficult time getting into print, but this approach has served as a springboard for many aspiring authors.

In commerical publications the most encouraging opportunities remain with the specialized magazines and genre magazines: religious magazines, juvenile magazines, science fiction magazines and confession, mystery and other such magazines are holding steady and offer publishing possibilities to the fiction writer who can specialize.

Other commercial publications are opening their mailboxes to fiction submissions. Many city and regional publications, for instance, buy fiction related to the area they cover. Specialized publications—the motorcyle magazines, for instance—use fiction tailored to their audience. And as new publications hit the newsstands (1,362 magazines appeared during the last five years alone), the fiction outlets for writers will expand and change.

What else can the writer of fiction expect in the '80s? Change. The turmoil of the economy will put some of today's markets out of business, but, as mentioned above, other markets will likely replace them. Hundreds of companies operating today did not exist ten years ago. About 50 or more new ones are formed each year, many of which will merge with other publishers or be bought by conglomerates. More independent book packagers/producers (see glossary) will be used by the major houses as an economic and sophisticated means of advertising, promotion and distribution. Imprints of conglomerates with special lines of genre or formula fiction (gothic, mystery, science fiction) are also expected to emerge.

The small presses and little magazines will continue to grow. A.D. Winans of *Second Coming* says to expect to see more government money, which will help sustain and promote small presses and magazines. More small magazines mean more fiction markets, in addition to a greater number of short stories printed per issue. Even more encouraging is the increasing number of "little" science fiction, horror, fantasy and ethnic magazines—all demanding fiction.

Editors and publishers will find more cooperation between regional and national publishing and distribution organizations like the Coordinating Council of Little Magazines (CCLM) and the Committee of Small Magazines, Editors and Publishers (COSMEP), which will become more effective information centers for independent operations. The technology breakthroughs (typesetting and microprocessors) of the '70s will be used in the '80s to enable greater speed, craft and sophistication in format as well.

Advice from veterans

In general, the '80s will be a decade during which some of the small presses will develop a greater knowledge and understanding of the American and Canadian publishing industry, thus more effectively filling the role that conglomerates cannot always fill—supporting young individual writers and distributing their work.

Some of the changes now occurring and about to occur in the publishing industry might distress you, but they should not discourage you. Consider the attitude of novelist Robert Cormier: "I am an unfailing optimist and an ordinary human being, husband, father, living in a small town far from the marketplace. I simply wrote. And submitted. Wrote and wrote and wrote. Submitted, submitted and submitted. Sooner or later, someone notices. I adopted the attitude that editors are in the business to *buy* not reject. If they never bought, they'd have nothing to print. And would be out of a job. They need a product—why not mine if I make it good enough, giving it the best that's in me? By the best, I mean writing and rewriting—the eternal search for the one true noun, verb, adjective, adverb—cutting, tightening and when it's ready to go, doing it all over again from page one, whether it's a short story or novel. One truth I learned: There are no short cuts, no magic secrets. Writing is hard work—but hard work can be beautiful if you love it. And when others love your work, it is marvelous and the rewards are bountiful."

Here is more advice from writers who, like Cormier, worked hard to establish themselves.

Know the market: "It's important to choose your market carefully. If you aim for a definite market, make sure it's one you enjoy and respect. Otherwise, you'll write down and the smell of insincerity will taint the product." (John Updike)

"Approach the writing of fiction as a business. Write the story or novel you feel you were meant to write, and then get hard-headed about marketing that manuscript. If you have no agent, become your own. If you expect to sell in market conditions where the competition is fiercer than ever, you must submit to markets where your type of work fits the editorial needs. Don't try to write *for* a market; that is how hacks are born. But don't allow yourself, through laziness, to get into a position where, once the story is finished, you find yourself looking at the manuscript blankly and thinking 'Now what do I do with it?' " (Stephen King)

Know the field: "The beginning writer of fiction for children and young people should know the field. Read widely following the current recommendations of a good children's librarian. Styles, interests, and degrees of sophistication vary with the years." (Zilpha Keating Snyder)

Know yourself: "Write only if the passion to write can be its own reward. Otherwise the goal of publication is a snare and a delusion—too difficult for most, and not worth it to most who attain what they thought they wanted. Writing is a Chinese curse and a form of slavery. If you do it, you had better love to tell your stories. (Herbert Gold)

Accept criticism: "There are many editors, many literary agents. The opinion of each one should be taken seriously but regarded as a single opinion only. A culmination of opinions may prove useful." (Philip O'Connor)

Look ahead: "When you have written your books or story and it is going the round of publishers, be involved in the next so deeply that rejections of the first won't be upsetting." (Victoria Holt)

Stay with it: "Just keep writing. It is a truism. And it worked for me." (Jacqueline Briskin)

"Develop a thick skin and the quality of perseverance." (Isaac Asimov)

To sum up, Bill Henderson of the Pushcart Book Press says it all: "If a talented author remains unpublished and unnoticed, the fault is the author's."

Manuscript mechanics

It's a grand thing to dream of seeing a story with your byline in one of the major national or literary magazines, or to envision your novel in a publisher's catalog. The actual *writing* of it may be a bit difficult, but once you have it down in good shape on a rough draft, the rest is a snap. . .you *think*. There is still one very important—though often irksome—chore to do: preparing the final manuscript for submission to an editor.

It's irritating. It's bothersome. But it's a necessary evil and the quicker you start using the right way, the easier it is to live with.

Type of paper. One of the things to consider is the paper. It must measure 8½x11 inches. That's a standard size and editors are adamant; they don't want offbeat sizes—or colors. White is right.

There's a wide range of white, 8½x11 papers. The cheaper ones are all wood content. They will suffice but they are not recommended. Your best bet is a good 25 percent cotton fiber content paper. It has quality feel, smoothness, shows type neatly and holds up under white-outs and erasing. Editors almost unanimously discourage the use of erasable bond for manuscripts, as it tends to smear when handled. Where weight of the paper is concerned, never use onionskin or anything less than a 16-pound bond; 20-pound is preferred.

File copies. Always make a carbon or photocopy of your manuscript before you send it off to a publisher. You might even want to make several photocopies while the original manuscript is still fresh and crisp looking—as insurance against losing a submission in the mails, and as a means of circulating the same manuscript to other editors for reprint sales after the original has been accepted for publication. (Inform editors that the manuscript offered for reprint should not be used before it has first appeared in the original publication buying it, of course.) Some writers keep their original manuscript as a file copy, and submit a good-quality photocopy of the manuscript to an editor, with a personal note explaining that it is *not* a simultaneous or multiple submission. They tell the editor that he may toss the manuscript if it is of no interest to him, and reply with a self-addressed postcard (also enclosed). This costs a writer some photocopy expense, but saves on the postage bill—and may speed the manuscript review process in some editorial offices.

Type characters. Another firm rule: For manuscripts, always type double space, using either elite or pica type. The slightly larger pica type is easier to read and many editors prefer it, but they don't object to elite. They *do* dislike (and often will refuse) hard-to-read or unusual typewritten characters, such as script, italics, Old English, all capitals, unusual letter styles, etc.

Page format. Do not use a cover sheet; nor should you use a binder—unless you are submitting a play or television or movie script. Instead, in the upper left corner of page one list your name, address and phone number on four single-spaced lines. In the upper right corner, on three single-spaced lines, indicate the approximate word count for the manuscript, the rights you are offering for sale, and your copyright notice (Copyright 1981 Joe Jones). It is *not* necessary to indicate that this is page one. Its format is self-evident.

On every page after the first, type your last name, a dash, and the page number in the upper right corner (page sixteen, for example, would be: Jones—16). If you are typing a novel, indicate the chapter sequence as well as page number on each page in the top right location, beginning each chapter halfway down on a new page one. Chapter three, page five would have the following "slugline": Jones—III/5. Then drop down two double-spaces and begin copy.

How to estimate wordage. To estimate wordage, count the exact number of words on three interior pages of your manuscript (in manuscripts up to 25 pages), divide the total by 3 and multiply the result by the number of pages (your first and last pages are likely to be less than full). Carry the total to the nearest 100 words. For example, say you have a 12-page manuscript with totals of 265, 316 and 289 words on the three inside pages. Divide your total of 870 by three to get 290. Now multiply 290 x 12 pages and you get 3,480. Your approximate wordage, therefore, will be 3,500 words. On manuscripts over 25 pages, count five pages instead of three, then follow the same process, dividing by five.

Now, flip the lever to double-space and center the title in capital letters halfway down the page. To center, set the tabulator to stop in the exact left-right center of the page. Count the letters in the title (including spaces and punctuation) and back-space half that number. Centered one double-space under that, type "by" and centered one double-space under that, your name or pseudonym.

Margins should be 1¼ inches on all sides of each full page of typewritten manuscript. Paragraph indentation is five or six letter spaces, consistently.

Now after the title and byline block, drop down three double-spaces, paragraph indent and start your story; or if you are typing a novel, center the words Chapter One on this line, then double space twice, indent and begin your novel.

Concluding page. Carry on just as you have on the other pages after page one. After your last word and period on this page, however, skip three double-spaces and then center the words "The End" or, more commonly, the old telegrapher's symbol of —30— meaning the same thing.

Special points to keep in mind. Always use a good dark black (*not* colored) typewriter ribbon and clean your keys frequently. If the enclosures in the letters a,b,d,e,g, etc. get inked-in, your keys need cleaning. Keep your manuscript neat *always*. Occasional retyping over erasures is acceptable, but strikeovers are bad and

Jones--2

Begin the second page, and all following pages, in this
manner--with a page-number line (as above) that includes
your name, in case loose manuscript pages get shuffled
by mistake.

Joe Jones
1234 My Street
Anytown, U.S.A. 12348
Tel. 123/456-7890

About 3,000 words
First Serial Rights
©Copyright 1981
Joe Jones

YOUR STORY OR NOVEL TITLE HERE

by

Joe Jones

The story begins here--about halfway down the first
page. It should be cleanly typed, double-spaced, using
either elite or pica type. Use one side of the paper
only, and leave a margin of about 1-1/2 inches on all
four sides.

NEATNESS COUNTS. Here are sample pages of a fiction manuscript
ready for submission to an editor. If the author uses a pseudonym, it
should be placed on the title page only in the byline position; the author's
real name must always appear in the top left corner of the title page—for
manuscript mailing and payment purposes.

give a manuscript a sloppy, careless appearance. Sloppy typing is viewed by many editors as an index to sloppy work habits—and the likelihood of careless research and writing. Strive for a clean, professional-looking manuscript that reflects pride in your work.

Mailing your manuscript. Except when working on assignment from a magazine, or when under contract to do a novel for a publisher, always enclose a self-addressed return envelope and the correct amount of postage with your manuscript. Manuscript pages should be held together with a paper clip only—never stapled together.

For foreign publications and publishers, including the expanding Canadian markets, always enclose an international reply coupon (IRC), determined by the weight of the manuscript at the post office. Small presses and little magazines are on low budgets, so to be safe, send a SASE or IRC with all correspondence. All postal rates in the listings are current with the early 1981 postage increase.

Most editors won't object too much if manuscripts under five pages are folded in thirds and letter-mailed. However, there is a market *preference* for flat mailing (in large envelopes) of manuscripts over four pages. You will need two sizes of large gummed or clasped mailing envelopes—9x12 for the return envelope, and 9½x12½ or 10x13 for the one used to send out the manuscript and return envelope.

Mark your envelope, as desired with FIRST CLASS MAIL, or SPECIAL FOURTH CLASS RATE: MANUSCRIPT. First Class mail costs more but assures better handling and faster delivery. Special Fourth Class mail is handled the same as Parcel Post, so wrap it well. Also, the Special Fourth Class rate only applies in the US.

For lighter weight manuscripts, First Class mail is recommended because of the better speed and handling. First Class mail is handled the same as Air Mail.

Insurance is available, but payable only on the tangible value of what is in the package, i.e., writing paper, so your best insurance is to keep a copy at home of what you send. Moreover, publishers do not appreciate receiving (and signing for unsolicited manuscripts marked Certified or Registered or Insured).

First Class mail is forwarded or returned automatically; however, Special Fourth Rate mail is not. To make sure you get your submission back if undeliverable, print "Return Postage Guaranteed" under your return address.

Cover letters. You may enclose a personal letter with your manuscript sent at the Special Fourth Class Rate, but you must also add enough First Class postage to cover the letter and mark FIRST CLASS LETTER ENCLOSED on the outside.

In most cases, a brief cover letter is helpful in personalizing the submission. Nothing you say will make the editor decide in your favor (the story must stand by itself in that regard), so don't use the letter to make a sales pitch. But you may want to tell an editor something about yourself, your publishing history, or any particular qualifications you have for writing the enclosed manuscript. If you have written to the editor earlier, he probably already has the background information—so the note should be a brief reminder: "Here is the story we discussed earlier. I look forward to hearing from you at your earliest convience."

If the manuscript is a photocopy, be sure to indicate whether or not it is a multiple submission. An editor is likely to assume it is, unless you tell him otherwise—and many are offended by writers using this marketing tactic (though when agents use it, that seems to be OK).

Mailing book manuscripts. Do not bind your book manuscript pages in any way. They should be mailed loose in a box (a ream-size stationery box is perfect) without binding. To ensure a safe return, enclose a self-addressed label and suitable postage in stamps clipped to the label. If your manuscript is returned, it will either come back in your original box, or—increasingly likely today—in an insulated bag-like mailer, with your label and postage used thereon. Many publishing houses open the box a manuscript is mailed in, and toss the box (if it has not been damaged in the mails, or in the opening already); they then read and circulate the manuscript as necessary for editorial consideration, and finally route it through the mail room back to you with a letter or rejection slip. This kind of handling makes it likely that a freshly typed manuscript will be in rough shape even after one or two submissions. So it is wise to have several photocopies made of a novel-length manuscript while it is still fresh—and to circulate those to publishers, rather than risk an expensive retyping job in the midst of your marketing effort. As mentioned above, indicate in a cover note that the submission is not a multiple submission if such is the case.

Book manuscripts can be mailed Fourth Class Manuscript Rate, but that can be slow and have an additional mauling effect on the package in the mails. When doing so, if you include a letter, state this on the outer wrapping and add appropriate postage to your manuscript postal rate. Most writers use First Class, secure in the feeling that their manuscript is in an editorial office within a few days. Some send book manuscripts using the United Parcel Service, which can be less expensive than First Class mail when you drop the package off at UPS yourself. The drawback here is that UPS cannot legally carry First Class mail, so you will have to send your cover letter a few days before giving UPS the manuscript, and both will arrive at about the same time. Check with UPS in your area to see if it has benefits for you. The cost depends on the weight of your manuscript and the delivery distance.

The tips and recommendations made here are based upon what editors prefer. Give editors what they prefer and you won't be beginning with a strike or two against you before the manuscript is even read.

The waiting game. The writer who sends off a story or book manuscript to an editor should turn immediately to other ideas and try to forget about the submission. Unless you are on assignment, or under contract to do a book—in which case a phone call to your editor saying the manuscript is in the mail is quite appropriate—it's best to use your time productively on other writing projects, and let the submission take care of itself. But one day you realize it's been too long. According to the *Fiction Writer's Market* listing, your editor responds to submissions in a maximum of four weeks—and it's been six already, and you haven't heard a word. Will inquiring about it jeopardize a possible sale? Are they really considering it, or has the editor had an accident and your manuscript is at the bottom of a huge stack of unread mail?

If you have had no report from a publisher by the maximum reporting time given in a *FWM* listing, allow a few weeks' grace period and then write a brief letter to the editor asking if your manuscript (give the title, a brief description, and the date you mailed it) has in fact reached his office. If so, is it still under consideration? Your concern at this point is the mails: Is the manuscript safely delivered? Don't act impatient with an editor—who may be swamped, or short-handed, or about to give your manuscript a second reading. The wrong word or attitude from you at this point could be hazardous to your manuscript's health. Be polite, be professional. Enclose another SASE (self-addressed stamped envelope) to expedite a reply. This is usually enough to stir a decision, if matters are lagging in an editorial office, even during rush season (which is year 'round).

If you still hear nothing from a publisher one month after your follow-up, send the editor a short note asking if he received your previous follow-up, and include a photocopy of that second letter. If, after another month, you are still without word, send a polite letter saying that you are withdrawing the manuscript from consideration (include the title, date of submission, and dates of follow-up correspondence), and ask that the manuscript be returned immediately in the SASE your original correspondence included. You are now free to market the manuscript elsewhere.

Even though matters have not worked out, and you have lost months of precious marketing time—never write in anger. Be cool, professional, and set about the business of finding another publisher for your work. The advantage of having a clean photocopy of the manuscript in your files at this point cannot be overstated. Move on to another editor or publisher with it, using a personal cover letter and the same methods outlined above. In the meantime, continue working on your own writing projects.

At times like these, the advantage of having an agent who can insulate you from such marketing discouragement is considerable. See our section on Agents for guidelines on getting and working with a literary agent, especially if you are working on book-length projects.

The business of fiction writing

Writing is an occupation with many hidden costs. In addition to the time a writer spends over a typewriter actually *writing*, many hours and miles are logged doing research, soliciting materials, conducting interviews, communicating with editors, and rounding out the corners of a manuscript. While readers, and to some extent editors, are oblivious to these background tasks, the Internal Revenue Service need not be. Such costs can become deductible writing expenses at income tax time.

For the records. Though the deadline for filing your tax return is April 15, you should maintain careful records all year. To arrive at verifiable figures, you will need two things: *records and receipts*. For tax purposes, good records are not only helpful; they are *required* by law. Receipts are the foundation that careful record keeping is built upon.

At tax time each year, a freelance writer normally reports his business activities on tax Schedule C ("Profit or Loss From Business or Profession"); the resulting figure for income is entered on Form 1040. In addition, if your writing or editing work nets you $400 or more in earnings, you must file a Schedule SE and pay self-employment tax, which makes you eligible for Social Security benefits. Furthermore, if you think your taxes from freelancing will be $100 or more, you are required to pay your taxes in quarterly installments. To do this, you file a declaration of estimated tax using Form 1040-ES ("Declaration Voucher") and use the envelopes the IRS provides to mail in your estimated taxes every three months.

It's not as complicated as it may sound, but one thing is certain: To document all these tax liabilities at the end of the year, you must have accurate records.

Tax laws don't require any particular type of records, as long as they are permanent, accurate and complete, and they clearly establish income, deductions, credits, etc. It's remarkably easy to overlook deductible expenses unless you record them at the time they are paid and keep receipts for them. Since some assets are subject to depreciation (typewriter, desk, files, and tape recorder, camera equipment for research, etc.), you also need records of the purchase prices you used to determine depreciation allowances.

Finally, you need good records in case the IRS audits you and asks you to explain items reported on your return. Memos, scribbled notes or sketchy records that merely approximate income, deductions, or other pertinent items affecting your taxes are simply *not* adequate. You must have a record supported by sales slips, invoices, receipts, bank deposit slips, canceled checks, and other documents.

Records for credit purposes. You and the IRS are not the only ones interested in the well-being of your business. Banks, credit organizations, suppliers of materials, and others, often require information on the condition of your finances when you apply for credit—if, for example, you want to buy a house.

In fact, freelance writers, in the eyes of many lending institutions, might as well be totally unemployed. Some writers have taken on fulltime jobs just to qualify for financing for a home, even when the "steady" job might produce less income than freelancing.

A simple bookkeeping system. There are almost as many different ways of keeping records as there are record-keepers to keep them. For a freelance writer, normally a simple type of "single-entry" bookkeeping that requires only one account book to record the flow of income and expense is completely adequate. At the heart of this single-entry system is the journal. It is an accounting book, available at any stationery store (the *Writer's Digest Diary* can be used, too), in which all the everyday transactions of your freelance business are recorded. Each transaction is set forth clearly, including the date, a description of the transaction, and the amount entered in the proper column—either "income" or "expense".

Income entries will include whatever funds you receive, either by cash or check. Expense entries might include payments you make for writing supplies, photocopying, postage, repairs, dues paid to writers' organizations, travel expenses, books and magazine subscriptions, photo developing and printing, etc.— whatever you have to spend as a business expense.

The receipt file. Now comes the really important part: For each income entry you make, keep a copy of a receipt, an invoice, or some other record to substantiate that entry. For each expense entry, keep a canceled check, a receipt, or some other document. By keeping your record complete with some type of document to support *every* entry, your record is foolproof.

A partitioned, envelope-type folder works well for keeping receipts in order. If a receipt does not clearly indicate which entry it refers to, make a note on it and date it before filing it. That way you can locate it quickly.

Business banking. To record income as accurately as possible, it is best to deposit all the money you receive in a separate bank account. This will give you deposit slips to verify the entries in your journal. Furthermore, you should make all payments by check, if possible, so that your business expenses will be well documented. If you have to pay cash, keep receipts on file.

Any record must be retained as long as it may be material to the administration of any law. Statutes of limitations for various legal purposes vary from state to state, but if you keep your records on file for seven to ten years, you will seldom run into difficulty. Records supporting items on a tax return should be kept for at least three years, although keeping them indefinitely is a good idea.

What's deductible. Among your deductible expenses, don't overlook the following writing-related costs:

•**All writing supplies.** A tape recorder and camera, important research tools for writers like Arthur Hailey who fictionalize special subjects about business and

Date		Description	Expense	Income
JUNE	2	2 Tape cassettes - Book research	10.40	
	4	Crosstown office Supply - 1 ream paper	6.20	
	6	Photocopying - Omni story	1.25	
	6	Postage - Story To Omni	2.65	
	10	2 Book reviews - The Central Journal		30.00
	12	Book Beast - 1981 Fiction Writer's Market	15.95	
	15	Renewal of WD subscription	15.00	
	16	Young Miss - s.f. story		150.00
	17	25 Manilla envelopes	2.25	
	20	Fee for Saturday Fiction Seminar	95.00	
	23	Book Proof reading - National Press, Inc. (35 hours)		175.00
	25	Crosstown Supply - Typewriter ribbons	15.70	
	28	Isaac Asimov's Science Fiction Magazine story		375.00
		JUNE TOTALS	164.40	730.00

FICTION FIGURES. Here is a sample expense/income sheet from a simple bookkeeping system for writers (See page 16).

industry, are tax deductible, as are paper, carbons, pens, ribbons, envelopes, copying costs, postage, photo developing and printing costs, and recording tapes.

● **Repairs and maintenance of writing equipment,** including typewriter, tape recorder and camera.

● **Courses and conferences attended to enhance you as a professional writer.** It's important to realize, though, that you can't deduct courses you take to *become* a writer. The IRS rule is that courses must be "refresher" or professionally improving in nature to count. Besides deducting the costs of these, also deduct mileage (at 18½¢ a mile)—or actual car expenses, whichever is greater; cost of tickets for public transportation; costs of hotel/motel rooms; and costs of meals.

● **Dues paid for membership in writer organizations.**

● **Home office expenses.** In the past, writers using a portion of their home dining room or living room have been allowed to deduct a percentage of home costs as "office" expenses. This is no longer allowed. To take a home office deduction today, you must have a portion of your dwelling set aside *solely for writing on a regular basis.* The same rule applies to a separate structure on your property. For example, you may not use a portion of your garage for writing and a portion for parking your car. If your car goes in, your home office expense is out.

Example: If you rent a five-room apartment for $200 a month and use one room exclusively for writing, you are entitled to deduct one-fifth of the rent which comes to $40 a month, or $480 a year. Add to this one-fifth of your heating bill and one-fifth of your electric bill and watch the deductions mount up. Keep a list, too, of long-distance phone bills arising from your writing.

If you own your home and use one room for writing, you can deduct the allocated expenses of operating that room. Among these allowable expenses are interest on mortage, real estate taxes, repairs or additions to the home, cost of utilities, home insurance premiums, and depreciation on the room.

Example: If you own a seven-room house, one room used for writing, one-seventh of the total cost of the house can be depreciated, as well as one-seventh of the above mentioned expenses.

Note: There is a limit to home office expenses. You may not exceed in deductible expenses the amount of your gross income. If you made $1,000 last year, you can't deduct any more than that in home office expenses—no matter how much they came to. Just $1,000 in this case.

● **Mileage.** Take 18½¢ a mile for the first 15,000 miles you travel on writing-related missions and 10¢ a mile for miles traveled over 15,000. Or you may take the actual cost of operating your car—gas, oil, tires, maintenance and depreciation. (See below for figuring depreciation.) Compare mileage deduction to cost deduction, and use the one that gives you the bigger break.

● **What may be depreciated.** You can count depreciation of your typewriter, desk, chair, lamps, tape recorder, files, camera equipment, photocopier, or anything else related to your writing which costs a considerable amount of money and which has a useful life of more than one year. The easiest, most common method of depreciation for the writer is the straight line method.

In straight line, you take the depreciable basis (original cost of the asset minus the "salvage value"), divide by the number of useful years, and come up with the yearly depreciation deduction. The salvage value is what you could normally sell the item for after its estimated life of usefulness to you is over.

Example: Electric typewriter, purchased January, 1981 for $350. Estimated life, five years. Salvage value at end of five years, $50. Depreciation allowable for the year ending 1981 equals $60. That's what you get when you divide the cost ($350), less salvage value ($50), by the estimated number of useful years (5).

Assets purchased later in the year must be calculated only for the months you had them.

Example: Electric typewriter purchased in May, 1981 for $350. Estimated life, five years. Depreciation allowable for the year is $40. Since the asset was yours for only eight months, you calculate depreciation by dividing 12 (months) into the yearly deduction of $60. This gives you $5 a month. This $5 multiplied by eight months gives you $40 in depreciation.

If salvage value is less than 10 percent of your depreciable basis, you can disregard it for computation. However, you can't depreciate below salvage value.

In addition to deductions and depreciations, you can make some extra gains on purchases made for your "business." For any business equipment purchased during the current tax year, the IRS allows an additional deduction. This deduction, the "investment tax credit" (ITC), is allowed for furniture, equipment, and other depreciable assets, except real estate. It is also subtracted from your total tax liability.

The maximum ITC, 10 percent, occurs when the asset's useful life is seven years or more. If the useful life is only three to five years, take one-third of that 10 percent. Example: A desk with a useful life of three to five years is bought for $100. First take 10 percent ($10), then one-third ($3.33) for the total deduction.

If the asset's useful life is five to seven years, the investment tax credit is calculated on two-thirds of the 10 percent. Thus, your $100 desk, now expected to live longer, has an ITC of $6.66. Of course, once the predicted useful life of an item goes to or beyond seven years, the maximum 10 percent of the total cost may be deducted, and the ITC for your desk would be $10.

You get the investment tax credit on eligible items no matter what time during the year they were purchased.

If after deductions you earn $400 or more, you are required to pay a Social Security tax of .081 of the first $25,900 of your earnings. And you must fill out and submit a Schedule SE (for "self-employment").

Be sure to save your rejection slips. Though they may be painful to look at, keep them in a folder—and view them as communiques from publishers. If you are subjected to a tax audit, the slips will help establish you as a working writer.

Finally, as a beginning freelancer, you may just want to turn all your tax records over to a good recommended accountant who is familiar with the freelancing business. Professional guidance, often well worth the cost, will prepare you for the following year when you can handle your taxes on your own.

Rights and the writer

Selling rights to your writing. Initially, a writer may have little say in the rights sold to an editor. The beginning writer, in fact, can jeopardize a sale by haggling with an editor who is likely to have other writers on call who are anxious to please. As long as there are more writers than there are markets, this situation will remain the same.

As a writer acquires skill, reliability, and professionalism on the job, however, that writer becomes more valued to editors—and rights become a more important consideration. Though a beginning writer will accept modest payment just to get in print, an experienced writer soon learns that he cannot afford to give away good writing just to see a byline. At this point a writer must become concerned with selling reprints of stories already sold to one market or seeking markets for the same material overseas, offering work to TV or the movies. Even for the nonfiction writer, such dramatic rights can be meaningful. The hit movie *Saturday Night Fever*, for example, began as a nonfiction article in *New York* magazine.

What editors want. And so it is that writers should strive as many rights to their work as they can from the outset, because before you can resell any piece of writing you must own the rights to negotiate. If you have sold "all rights" to an article, for instance, it can be reprinted *without* your permission, and without additional payment to you. What an editor buys, therefore, will determine whether you can resell your own work. Here is a list of the rights most editors and publishers seek.

● **First serial rights.** The word serial here does not mean publication in installments, but refers to the fact that libraries call periodicals "serials" because they are published in serial or continuing fashion. *First serial rights* means the writer offers the newspaper or magazine (both of which are periodicals) the right to publish the story the first time in their periodical. All other rights to the material belong to the writer. Variations on this right are, for example, first North American serial rights. Some magazines use this purchasing technique to obtain the right to publish first in both America and Canada since many American magazines are circulated in

Canada. If they had purchased only first US serial rights, a Canadian magazine could come out with prior or simultaneous publication of the same material. When material is excerpted from a book which is to be published and it appears in a magazine or newspaper prior to book publication, this is also called first serial rights.

● **Second serial (reprint) rights.** This gives a newspaper or magazine the opportunity to print a story after it has already appeared in some other newspaper or magazine. The term is also used to refer to the sale of part of a book to a newspaper or magazine after a book has been published, whether or not there has been any first serial publication (income derived from second serial rights to book material is often shared 50/50 by author and book publisher).

● **All rights.** Some magazines, either because of the top prices they pay for material, or the fact that they have book publishing interests or foreign magazine connections, sometimes buy all rights. A writer who sells a story to a magazine under these terms, forfeits the right to use his material in its present form elsewhere himself. If you sign a "work-for-hire" agreement, you sign away all rights and the copyright to the company making the assignment. If the writer thinks he may want to use his material later (perhaps in book form), he must avoid submitting to these types of markets, or refuse payment and withdraw his material if he discovers it later. Or ask the editor whether he's willing to buy only first rights instead of all rights before you agree to an assignment or a sale.

● **Simultaneous rights.** This term covers stories which are sold to publications (primarily religious magazines) which do not have overlapping circulations. A Baptist publication, for example, might be willing to buy simultaneous rights to a Christmas story which they like very much, even though they know a Presbyterian magazine may be publishing the same story in one of its Christmas issues. Publications which will buy simultaneous rights indicate this fact in their listings in *Fiction Writer's Market*. Always advise an editor when the material you are sending is a simultaneous submission.

● **Foreign serial rights.** Can you resell a story you have had published in America to a foreign magazine? If you sold only first US serial rights to the American magazine, yes, you are free to market your story abroad. This presumes, of course, that the foreign magazine does buy material which has previously appeared in an American periodical.

● **Syndication rights.** This is a division of serial rights. For example, a book publisher may sell the rights to a newspaper syndicate to print a book in twelve installments in, say, each of twenty United States newspapers. If they did this prior to book publication it would be syndicating first serial rights to the book. If they did this after book publication, they would be syndicating second serial rights to the book.

● **Dramatic, television and motion picture rights.** This means the writer is selling his material for use on the stage, in television, or in the movies. Often a one-year "option" to buy rights is offered (generally for 10% of the total price), and the interested party then tries to sell the idea to other people—actors, directors, studios or television networks, etc.—who become part of the project, which then becomes a script. Some properties are optioned over and over again, but fail to become dramatic productions. In such cases, the writer can sell his rights again and again—as long as there is interest in the material. Though dramatic, TV and motion picture rights are more important to the fiction writer than to the nonfiction writer, producers today are increasingly interested in "real-life" material; many biographies and articles that are slices of real life are being dramatized. Gay Talese's nonfiction book *Thy Neighbor's Wife*, for instance, earned some $2.5 million for motion picture rights alone.

Communicate and clarify. Before submitting material to a market, check its listing in this book to see what rights are purchased. Most editors will discuss rights they wish to purchase before an exchange of money occurs. Some buyers are adamant about what rights they will accept; others will negotiate. In any case, the rights purchased should be stated specifically *in writing* sometime during the course of the sale, usually in a letter or memo of agreement. *Note*: If no rights are transferred in writing, and the material is sold for use in a collective work (that is, a work that derives material from a number of contributors), you are authorizing unlimited use of the piece in that work or in subsequent issues or updates of the work. Thus, you can't collect reprint fees if the rights weren't spelled out in advance, in writing.

Give as much attention to the rights you haven't sold as you do the rights you have sold. Be aware of the rights you retain, with an eye out for additional sales.

Whatever rights you sell or don't sell, make sure all parties involved in any sale understand the terms of the sale. Clarify what is being sold *before* any actual sale, and do it in writing. Communication, coupled with these guidelines and some common sense, will preclude misunderstandings with editors over rights.

Copyrighting your writing. The new copyright law, effective since January 1, 1978, protects your writing, unequivocally recognizes the creator of the work as its owner, and grants the creator all the rights, benefits and *privileges* that ownership entails.

In other words, the moment you finish a piece of writing—whether it be short story, novel, or prose poem—the law recognizes that only you can decide how it is to be used.

This law gives writers power in dealing with editors and publishers, but they should understand how to use that power. They should also understand that certain circumstances can complicate and confuse the concept of ownership. Writers must be wary of these circumstances, or risk losing ownership of their work.

Here are answers to commonly asked questions about copyright law:

●**To what rights am I entitled under copyright law?** The law gives you, as creator of your work, the right to print, reprint and copy the work; to sell or distribute copies of the work; to prepare "derivative works"—dramatizations, translations, musical arrangements, novelizations, etc. to record the work; and to perform or display literary, dramatic or musical works publicly. These rights give you control over how your work is used, and assure you that you receive payment for any use of your work.

If, however, you create the work as a "work-for-hire," you *do not* own any of these rights. The person or company that commissioned the work-for-hire owns the copyright. The work-for-hire agreement will be discussed in more detail later.

●**When does copyright law take effect, and how long does it last?** A piece of writing is copyrighted the moment it is put to paper. Protection lasts for the life of the author plus 50 years, thus allowing your heirs to benefit from your work. For material written by two or more people, protection lasts for the life of the last survivor plus 50 years. The life-plus-50 provision applies if the work was created or registered with the Copyright Office after Jan. 1, 1978, when the updated copyright law took effect. The old law protected works for a 28-year term, and gave the copyright owner the option to renew the copyright for an additional 28 years at the end of that term. Works copyrighted under the old law that are in their second 28-year term automatically receive an additional 19 years of protection (for a total or 75 years). Works on their first term also receive the 19-year extension, but must still be renewed when the first term ends.

If you create a work anonymously or pseudonymously, protection lasts for 100 years after the work's creation, or 75 years after its publication, whichever is shorter. The life-plus-50 coverage takes effect, however, if you reveal your identity to the Copyright Office any time before the original term of protection runs out.

Works created on a for-hire basis are also protected for 100 years after the work's creation or 75 years after its publication, whichever is shorter.

● **Must I register my work with the Copyright Office to receive protection?** No. Your work is copyrighted whether or not you register it, although registration offers certain advantages. For example, you must register the work before you can bring an infringement suit to court. You can register the work *after* an infringement has taken place, and *then* take the suit to court, but registering after the fact removes certain rights from you. You can sue for actual damages (the income or other benefits lost as a result of the infringement), but you can't sue for statutory damages and you can't recover attorney's fees unless the work has been registered with the Copyright Office *before* the infringement took place. Registering before the infringement also allows you to make a stronger case when bringing the infringement to court.

If you suspect that someone might infringe on your work, register it. If you doubt that an infringement is likely (and infringements are relatively rare), you might save yourself the time and money involved in registering the material.

● **I have a story that I want to protect fully. How do I register it?** Request the proper form from the Copyright Office. Send the completed form, a $10 registration fee, and one copy (if the work is unpublished; two if it's published) of the work to the Register of Copyrights, Library of Congress, Washington, DC 20559. You needn't register each work individually. A group of articles can be registered simultaneously (for a single $10 fee) if they meet these requirements: They must be assembled in orderly form (simply placing them in a notebook binder is sufficient); they must bear a single title ("Works by Joe Jones," for example); they must represent the work of one person (or one set of collaborators); and they must be the subject of a single claim to copyright. No limit is placed on the number of works that can be copyrighted in a group.

● **If my writing is published in a "collective work"—such as a magazine—does the publication handle registration of the work?** Only if the publication owns the piece of writing. Although the copyright notice carried by the magazine covers its contents, you must register any writing to which *you own* the rights if you want the additional protection registration provides.

Collective works are publications with a variety of contributors. Magazines, newspapers, anthologies, etc., are considered collective works. If you sell something to a collective work, state specifically *in writing* what rights you're selling. If you don't, you are automatically selling the nonexclusive right to use the writing in the collective work and in any succeeding issues or revisions of it. For example, a magazine that buys your material without specifying in writing the rights purchased can reuse the story in that magazine—but in no other, not even in another magazine put out by the same publisher, without repaying you. The same is true for other collective works, so always detail *in writing* what rights you are selling before making the sale.

When contributing to a collective work, ask that your copyright notice be placed on or near your published manuscript (if you still own the manuscript's rights). Prominent display of your copyright notice on published work has two advantages: It signals to readers and potential reusers of the piece that it belongs to you, and not to the collective work in which it appears; and it allows you to register all published works bearing such notice with the Copyright Office as a group for a single $10 fee. A published work *not* bearing notice indicating you as copyright owner can't be included in a group registration.

Display of copyright notice is especially important when contributing to an uncopyrighted publication—that is, a publication that doesn't display a copyright symbol and doesn't register with the Copyright Office. You risk losing copyright protection on material that appears in an uncopyrighted publication. Also, you have no legal recourse against a person who infringes on something that is published without appropriate copyright notice. That person has been misled by the absence of the copyright notice and can't be held liable for his infringement. Copyright protection remains in force on material published in an uncopyrighted publication without benefit of copyright notice if the notice was left off only a few copies, if you asked (in writing) that the notice be included and the publisher didn't comply, or if you register the work and make a reasonable attempt to place the notice on any copies that haven't been distributed after the omission was discovered.

Official notice of copyright consists of the word "Copyright," the abbreviation "Copr." or symbol ©; the name of the copyright owner or owners; and the year date of creation (for example, "© 1981 by Joe Jones").

● **Under what circumstances should I place my copyright notice on unpublished works that haven't been registered?** Place official copyright notice on the first page of *any* manuscript, a procedure intended not to stop a buyer from stealing your material (editorial piracy is very rare, actually), but to demonstrate to the editor that you understand your rights under copyright law, that you own that particular manuscript, and that you want to retain your ownership after the manuscript is published. Seeing this notice, an editor might be less apt to try to buy all rights from you. Remember, you want to retain your rights to any writing.

● **How do I transfer copyright?** A transfer of copyright, like the sale of any property, is simply an exchange of the property for payment. The law stipulates, however, that the transfer of any exclusive rights (and the copyright is the most exclusive of exclusive rights) must be made in writing to be valid. Various types of exclusive rights exist, as outlined above. Usually it is best not to sell your copyright. If you do, you lose control over use of the manuscript, and forfeit future income from its use.

● **What is a "work-for-hire agreement"?** This is a work that another party commissions you to do, such as a special contract with an imprint for a formula novel. Two types of for-hire works exist: Work done as a regular employee of a company, and commissioned work that is specifically called a "work-for-hire" in writing at the time of assignment. The phrase "work-for-hire" or something close must be used in written agreement, though you should watch for similar phrasings.

The work-for-hire provision was included in the new copyright law so that no writer could unwittingly sign away his copyright. The phrase "work-for-hire" is a bright red flag warning the writer that the agreement he's about to enter into will result in loss of rights to any material created under the agreement.

Some editors offer work-for-hire agreements when making assignments, and expect writers to sign them routinely. By signing them, you forfeit the potential for additional income from a manuscript through reprint sales, or sale of other rights. Be careful, therefore, in signing away your rights in a "work-for-hire" agreement. Many articles written as works-for-hire or to which all rights have been sold are never resold, but if you retain the copyright, you might try to resell the story—something you wouldn't be motivated to do if you forfeited your rights to the piece.

● **Can I get my rights back if I sell all rights to a manuscript, or if I sell the copyright itself?** Yes. You or certain heirs can terminate the transfer of rights 40 years after creation or 35 years after publication of a work by serving notice to the person to whom you transferred rights within specified time limits. Consult the Copyright Office for the procedural details. This may seem like a long time to wait, but remember that some manuscripts remain popular (and earn royalties and other fees) for much longer than 35 years.

● **Must all transfers be in writing?** Only work-for-hire agreements and transfers to exclusive rights *must* be in writing. However, getting any agreement in writing before the sale is wise. Beware of other statements about what rights the buyer purchases that may appear on checks, writer's guidelines or magazine mastheads. If the publisher makes such a statement elsewhere, you might insert a phrase like "No statement pertaining to purchase of rights other than the one detailed in this letter—including masthead statements or writer's guidelines—applies to this agreement" into the letter that outlines your rights agreement. Some publishers put their terms in writing on the back of a check that, when endorsed by the writer, becomes a "contract." This is a dubious legal maneuver, which many writers sidestep by not signing the check—yet depositing it in their bank accounts with the notation FOR DEPOSIT ONLY.

● **Are ideas copyrightable?** No. Nor can information be copyrighted. Only the actual expression of ideas or information can be copyrighted.

● **Where do I go for more information about copyright law?** Write or call (not collect) the Copyright Office (Library of Congress, Washington, DC 20559; tel. 703/557-8700) for a free Copyright Information Kit. The Copyright Office will answer specific questions, but won't provide legal advice. For more information about copyright and other law, consult *Law and the Writer*, edited by Kirk Polking and Leonard S. Meranus (Writer's Digest Books).

The writer's craft

by André Maurois

---

1. The Writer's Life. The starting point of a writer's life is the sense of a vocation. The child or the adolescent feels impelled to give expression in the written word to the emotions or the ideas which people and things have aroused in him. At a very early age Marcel Proust was conscious of a desire to lay hands on an imprisoned beauty which, so he believed, was hidden under the appearance of certain objects. He had a confused notion that it was incumbent upon him to free some captive truth from confinement. At that time in his life he was as yet incapable of reaching down to truths which he felt to be lurking under the bushes, the orchards and the sunlight of La Beauce. In *Louis Lambert* Balzac gives us a portrait of himself as a youth chock-full of works clamoring to be born. Victor Hugo, Byron, Musset, Valéry all wrote poems when they were young. It occasionally happens that the vocation of letters is a late-flowering growth (as in the case of Rousseau), but when that is so, numerous attempts in secret have preceded the ultimate fulfillment.

How comes it that this vocation is present in some people and not in others? One may say in answer to that question, though without laying it down as a rule, that the need to express oneself in writing springs from a maladjustment to life, or from an inner conflict which the adolescent (or the grown man) cannot resolve in action. Those to whom action comes as easily as breathing rarely feel the need to break loose from the real, to rise above, and describe it. That is why so many of the finest writers have been the victims of ill health (Poe, Proust, Flaubert, Chekhov), men whose lives have known frustration from an early age or found their natural development impeded by some obstacle. Dickens, Balzac, Hugo, Kipling and Stendhal all had an unhappy childhood which was too soon dislocated by family

---

André Maurois was a prolific French novelist, biographer and critic. He wrote a romantic biographical series of novels on Shelley, Voltaire, Marquis de Lafayette, Hugo and others in addition to numerous novels and popular histories of the U.S. and England. He was elected to the French Academy in 1938 and died in 1967.

conflicts. With others the conflict was social or religious (Voltaire, Anatole France and Tolstoy), while in some an over-sensitive nature has been driven back on itself as the result of some invincible timidity (Merimée). I do not mean that it is enough to be maladjusted to become a great writer, but writing is, for some, a method of resolving a conflict, provided they have the necessary talent.

Sources of writing

It may be objected that many writers have been happy in their lives and endowed with a healthy temperamental balance. That, no doubt, is true, but I do not know a single instance in which that balance has not had to be achieved by a struggle from which a considerable body of work has resulted. Although after 1875, when he was an astonishingly vigorous old man with a firmly established reputation, Victor Hugo had certainly no right to complain of the way in which life had treated him, yet it should never be forgotten that a difficult youth, thwarted love affairs, and sorrows brought upon him by death and political strife had made of him a sorely troubled and tormented individual—and a poet. Chateaubriand, at the time of the Restoration, as an ambassador and a Minister, had not the same motives as once he had had for voicing melodious sorrows. Nevertheless, because he was conscious of his genius, and knew on what food it flourished, he deliberately kept the old conflicts alive, or sought new ones. Paul Valéry, as I remember him, was a man of a strong and sunny temperament, but his lined and wrinkled face was eloquent of much former pain and struggle. The only writers I have known who were perfectly contented with themselves and with the world in which they lived, were, I am sorry to say, bad writers. This is not to say that in order to write well a man must be a pessimist, but only that "optimism in an artist is something that has to be won by hard fighting" (Alain).

The need for publication

First, then, the vocation and the early attempts at authorship. Next, the problem of publication. Why is it so necessary for a writer to have a public? If his purpose is to express himself, ought it not to be enough for him that he should succeed in doing so? Is a cloud of witnesses really essential? The answer to this question is almost always in the affirmative. I say "almost" always because there have been writers of memoirs, Saint Simon, for instance, and Pepys who cared nothing for public applause. They wrote for themselves or for a posterity which they could never know. But such cases are rare. Nearly every writer wants to have readers, even though they should amount to only a small number of the elect. That is but natural. He has written with the deliberate purpose of revealing the truth about himself and about the world as he sees it. The revelation can have no point unless it reaches those for whom it is intended. To find readers who shall understand him, who may perhaps love, or at least admire him, is reassuring to an author, and if his own conflict resembles that of many of his fellow men, it may, through his efforts, become less obsessive and troublesome to them, in which case he will have the additional pleasure of having been helpful.

The aim of a writer worthy of his chosen profession is never merely to achieve Power and Glory. It does sometimes happen that these rewards come the way of those who deserve them, but many great men have been cheated of them in their lifetime. Mallarmé was the idol of a few discriminating admirers: to the wider public he was unknown. Stendhal said, with considerable perspicacity: "I shall have readers in 1860"; he has still more today, but he had few before his death.

Tolstoy, on the other hand, Balzac and Dickens, enjoyed an enormous popularity. Success proves nothing either for or against a writer. It is desirable, because it gives him an assured independence, on condition that it does not come to him through scandal, the employment of such artificial means as excessive publicity, or vulgarity. The public interest in certain literary prizes does ill-service, in the last analysis, to those who receive them. A sudden and exaggerated notoriety leaves them precisely where they were before. They may, indeed, show themselves worthy of their fame, and capable of responding to the hopes reposed in them. If, on the other hand, they drop back into obscurity, then failure is the more painful by reason of the generous promises of success so unexpectedly extended to them.

The material objective

The writer who has achieved a certain degree of celebrity will find that many additional "jobs" almost inevitably come his way in the shape of newspaper articles, lectures, talking on the radio and appearing on television. What should his attitude be? To say no to all of them, especially if he be young, would prove either an abnormal pride, or incapacity. I know that some types of mind do not take kindly to public life, but many writers are fully competent to play a part in it, and, in so far as they may usefully influence a wider public by doing so, why should they not? Valéry, certainly, treated none of the offers that came to him with contempt; in fact, he was always delighted to have the chance of writing on a theme supplied to him. Some of his best work (for example, his *Preface to Montesquieu*—an astonishing manual of pure politics) was produced on commission. Hugo's best poems are those inspired by some national or international event—which is only another form of commission. But the extra labors involved in activities of this kind must never be allowed to take up so much of the writer's time that he has not enough left to give to his main occupation, which is to write what he feels he must write. In France, especially, where literary men find themselves far more involved in public affairs than elsewhere, either because they occupy some post under Government, or, on the contrary, are active supporters of the Opposition, he must be very careful to retain a necessary freedom.

Is a writer justified in making material success the main object and aim of his work? In other words, is earning a livelihood ever a sufficient reason for turning author? It cannot be denied that the need to provide for himself and his family has proved a useful stimulant to many a man of letters. A few authors, though only a few, have accumulated enormous fortunes: Hugo, Bernard Shaw, some modern American novelists, and several French dramatists. It is easier to do so today than it once was because the possible reading public is vast and international in extent, and because literacy is far more widely spread. Balzac and Dumas, in spite of their great success, were often short of cash. Consequently, they published a great deal. That, in itself, is no crime. We should always remember that a great writer, even though circumstances keep his nose to the grindstone, may still produce masterpieces. Balzac was in urgent need of the money he was to receive for *La Cousine Bette* and *Le Cousin Pons*, but those books are no less admirable for having been written under financial pressure. The English have a word for books written to "keep the pot boiling." They call them "pot-boilers." But why should not the fire which keeps the pot simmering also keep the mind in a state of effervescence?

Values

But Power, Glory and Money are only secondary objects for the writer. No man can be a great writer without having a great philosophy, though it may often remain unexpressed. That is true even of those whose lives were far from edifying. George Sand's own life was, like that of most of us, warped, mediocre and frustrated. Yet, in *Consuelo* she could create a unique model of femininity in which every woman can find something to imitate, and every man something to understand and to love. A great writer has a high respect for *values*. His essential function is to raise life to the dignity of thought, and this he does by giving it a shape. If he refuses to perform this function, he can be a clever juggler and play tricks with words such as his fellow-writers may admire, but his books will be of little interest to anybody else. If, on the contrary, he fulfills it, he will be happy in his writing. Borne aloft by the world as relected in himself, and producing a sounding echo of his times, he helps to shape it by showing to men an image of themselves which is at once true and disciplined.

2. **The Writer's Craft.** "There is as much craft in the making of a book as there is in the making of a clock," said La Bruyere. About this one might argue up and down for a long time. Undoubtedly, the making of a book involves the learning of a craft, and one that is mastered by the exercise of writing. Few succeed at the first attempt. Those whose earliest published efforts seem to show real skill are not, as a rule, strictly speaking, beginners. They will be found to have worked long and arduously in the privacy of their study, either writing themselves or absorbing the secrets of the masters. But though authorship is a craft it differs from that of the clockmaker in that the latter assembles pieces ready to his hand in a strictly determined order, whereas the writer, in the very process of putting pen to paper, has to invent not only the constructional plan of his book but the materials which go into it. Of what a nature, therefore, should his training be?

The basic tools

A book is made up of words. The first concern of the writer-to-be is to acquire a vocabulary and to master the rules of grammar. He must have so infallible a knowledge of his native tongue and its syntactical usages that he will never run the risk of employing a word to convey a meaning other than that normally attached to it, or of constructing an unintelligible or defective sentence. I am quite prepared to have it pointed out to me that very great writers have sometimes given a new meaning to an old word, or played tricks with syntax. That is so, but such liberties, though they may win approval when they stand out against the background of a perfect norm, will seem ridiculous when taken by a beginner, for in his case they will merely give the impression of ignorance. The musical composer of genius is entitled to introduce discords into his score and to spring surprises on the ear. All the same, he must have begun by learning harmony. The good painter may distort, not because he does not know how to draw, but because, knowing perfectly well how to draw, he has a right to indulge in daring experiments.

The first essential, therefore, on which the young writer must concentrate is the acquisition of an accurate vocabulary. Should it be more than usually extensive? No general rule can, I think, be laid down. Some of the great classic writers could say everything they had to say with a very small vocabulary. No better example of this could be found than Racine. Others, on the contrary, no less great in their way, accumulated a rich treasure of solid technical terms. Chateaubriand made a practice of collecting, and restoring to their place in the language, a great number of archaisms. Balzac was fully acquainted with the turns of speech in common use among bankers, journalists, police officers, lawyers and the members of many other professions. Valéry, in his prose writings, owed much to the language of science, for the rigor of which he has a marked liking. The beginner's choice depends upon the nature of his subject. Technical phrases, admirably suited to the treating of technical matters, will seem pretentious when applied to narrative. The clear and simple words of common usage are always better than those of erudition. The jargon of the philosophers not seldom conceals an absence of thought.

Training by masters

The best training for the young writer is to be found in a reading of the masters. A close study of them will show him how a masterpiece is made. Familiarity with the methods of the great will provide him with great examples. At first he will read for pleasure, like any young enthusiast with a taste for books. Then, having become familiar with this or that work, he will return to it again and again with the purpose of "taking it to pieces" and seeing just how its effects are obtained. In what way is a Balzac novel, a Chekhov story or a Shakespeare play built up? Obviously there can be no such thing as a recipe for genius. Nevertheless, the art of description, of construction and the use of dialogue can be learned. If we want to give life to our characters in the manner of Tolstoy, we shall find that he managed it by stressing gestures, tricks of behavior and linguistic mannerisms. Proust's way of moving from general ideas to individual actions deserves careful study. He had learned much from George Eliot, Dickens and Ruskin. How? By constantly reading them, by translating and annotating Ruskin, by amusing himself with the composition of "pastiches."

But is there not danger in following a master too slavishly? What we ask of a young writer is not that he should be a second Balzac, a new Dickens, but himself. The danger is, I think, imaginary. In the first place, should the young writer suddenly and miraculously produce the very novel, dealing with our contemporary society, which Balzac himself would have written had he been alive today, that would be a great and happy event. In fact, if he is truly gifted, nothing of the sort is likely to happen. He will have learned from his masters certain tricks of the trade, but he will use them differently. Even if he deliberately sets out to imitate them, a moment will come when, his own genius having taken charge, he will forget all about the imitation, take a good look at his subject, and handle it in his own way. Mauriac once attempted to produce a faithful imitation of Bossuet. The result was good Bossuet, but, all of a sudden, it also became first-rate Mauriac. Nobody expects us to write as though no one had ever written before we came upon the scene. In literature everyone is somebody's spiritual child. Musset owed a great deal to Byron, who, in his turn, owed a great deal to Voltaire, who had incurred a debt to Swift. What matters is that the beginner, by studying other men's styles, should ultimately develop a style of his own.

Style

But what, precisely, is style? It is the hallmark of an individual, which shows clearly in his use of language and in his view of life. Every man has a temperament which is personal to himself. But most men are incapable of impressing their temperaments on what they write. For most, the act of writing is something outside their usual competence. Consequently, they lack that flexibility which would allow them to give free rein to their instincts and their passions. As soon as they get a pen between their fingers, they find that nothing comes but a flood of commonplace clichés. They are used to reading bad prose, and cannot break free from it. Saint-Simon, who was a master of language and wholly indifferent to popular applause since he was writing only for himself, could give full play to his furies and his memories. The supremely right adjective came to him simultaneously with the thought he wished to express, or, rather, a cascade of adjectives which gradually encircled it. Passionately intent on what he was feeling and wanted to record, he did not much worry about the form in which it should be presented. He took the first word that occurred to him, no matter how trivial, with the result that he hit on those astonishing "finds," those powerful images which both suprise and flay. So torrential is the movement of his prose, that the incidents flood the page. Circumstances come into his mind even while he is in the act of writing, but the very disorder in which they jostle gives life to his words. The touchy duke shows through the writing. That is what style means.

There are as many variants of style as there are men of originality who know how to write. Chateaubriand was no less passionate than Saint-Simon, but he could exercise greater self-control, and he wrote to be read. His style shows traces of the great classic age. It was only toward the end of his life that he freely abandoned himself to his genius. Freely?—yes, but with this reservation, that he was fully conscious of the self-portrait he was painting. Saint-Simon let himself go: Chateaubriand watched himself letting himself go. If, now and again, he fell into an easy negligence he was perfectly well aware of what he was doing, and was careful to enshrine it in one of those long, sonorous, violoncello passages of which he was a master. He knew, none better, what images could best set his pages singing, and played tunes on many of his favorite themes—old age saddened by regret for past loves: the approach of death: the vanity of fame: the moon which brought to his mind the trees of Combourg. Even God, even the Cross, were but so many adjuncts to the sublimity of his personal drama, and all these things, which make his style, are the man himself.

I knew Rudyard Kipling well. When listening to his talk one was immediately reminded of his way of writing, of his mannerisms, of that air he had of insinuating more than he said: "What I am going to tell you would appear to be impossible: but that is how men are, and I know men"—all the while maintaining a zone of mystery, for he had to perfection the art of leaving motives in shadow, at the same time saying just enough to enable one to make a pretty shrewd guess at what they had been. Lying in the grass, with his head supported on his hand, and those astonishingly alert eyes under wild and bushy brows, he *lived* Kipling. I remember him talking to me one day, round about 1930, about Germany, which was already becoming dangerously transformed, and suddenly saying: "A people always ends by resembling its shadow . . . "—a typically Kiplingesque oracle, the veiled warning coupled with a refusal to elucidate its meaning, a distant echo of those Indian sages and those Old Testament prophets who were his masters. That was how he thought and how he wrote.

Individual expression

Some may think that this definition of style as the hallmark of a temperament stamped on the material in hand is over-romanticized, and attaches too much importance to the individual. The great classic writers, it will be said, sought rather to proclaim universal truths than to leave their imprint on them. But this view will not stand up to examination. Nothing is less like the style of Racine than the style of Corneille. We have only to read one single line of Pascal to recognize its author. Any schoolboy in a junior form could distinguish a passage of dialogue in Moliere from a scene by Beaumarchais or Marivaux. Bossuet and Voltaire are both classical writers, but they have nothing in common except the precision of their language. There does, no doubt, exist a sort of classical perfection which has no recognizable face of its own, and is, so to speak, anonymous, but it is to be found only in uninspired writers who are not, strictly speaking, writers at all.

Alain laid it down that in anything worth calling style two conditions must be fulfilled: grace and ease in the movement of the prose, and, in the work itself, its visible trace. Grace and ease can be acquired as a result of that double training to which I have already referred: reading and working. A certain degree of modesty must also be linked with them. He who takes too much obvious trouble to write well falls below the highest level. Flaubert in his letters, where he is being himself without effort, is better than the Flaubert of the novels, in which every sentence has been so frequently worked over that the style loses all natural movement and becomes rugged or clumsy. Let me, once again, quote Alain: "Style, like good manners, should never be self-conscious, but must express a free improvisation in a way that laborious application can never achieve." The resistance of the material will do the rest, as can be seen in hand-wrought iron-work or sculptured stone. That is why, as we realize in classical tragedy, style is the outcome of constraint.

It is useless to advise a writer who is seeking to express himself to be a Kipling, a Chateaubriand, a Flaubert or, indeed, anyone but himself. But it is not easy to be oneself. Many writers have died without ever finding their true selves, or, at least, without succeeding in imparting their selves to their style. This is sometimes due to lack of culture and of skill in the handling of words, though sometimes, on the contrary, to an excess of culture. They have admired so many styles that they have failed to form one of their own. What advice, then, should be given to the beginner? That he should remain a rough diamond? No, for the rough diamond has no lustre. The source of light is doubtless in it, but it remains invisible. My own advice would be to seek out those masters who best suit the young learner, those for whom he feels a natural sympathy and, having found them, to be assiduous in his study of their work. Mauriac has never given up reading Chateaubriand and the Pascal of the *Lettres Provinciales*. Others may seek their nourishment in Voltaire or Anatole France, and others still in Hemingway or Stendhal.

The beginning

Nulla dies sine linea. The aspiring author, whether genius or not, should never let a day pass without writing at least a few lines. The habit of writing is a good one, always on condition that one sets down on paper what one *really* wants to say, and does not fall a victim to the allurements of the easy cliché. Journalism can easily become a danger if it is not conducted with passionate sincerity. There is an art of saying nothing which is the very reverse of style. Journalism undertaken in the manner of Paul-Louis Courier or Diderot is, on the contrary, a wonderful training-school of good and succinct writing. Goethe's advice—start with short pieces—is, I think, excellent. The very fact of carrying through a piece of work *to the end* is of great encouragement to the beginner. To embark up a "saga-novel" at twenty would be doubly foolish. At that age few men have the necessary technical skill or a sufficient first-hand experience of life on which to draw. Writing should never be allowed to become a substitute for living. Style cannot breathe in a void. It should not be forgotten that Dickens was at one time a reporter, Balzac a lawyer's clerk and Chekhov a country doctor. Art is different from life but cannot exist without it.

"The business of getting going," says Alain, "should be reduced to a minimum," by which he meant that one should never spend months and years in planning how to start on a book. I have known writers, or, rather, men who wanted to be writers, whose whole life has been wasted in deciding to take the first step. "I still lack certain important elements," they say, "before I can begin my novel," or "I am burning to get on with this biography but there are still several essential documents on which I haven't, so far, been able to lay my hand." So, time goes by, and nothing is done. Once the choice of a subject has been made, one must jump into a book as one jumps into water. If one goes on testing the temperature with one's toe one will never learn how to swim. Once the plunge is taken, the swimmer will soon learn to adapt himself to cold and currents. The initial decision is what matters, for, without it, no work will come to anything. Once begun, the book will "serve as its own model," or, more precisely, the author, sitting down at his desk in the morning and reading over what he has written the previous day, will feel instinctively how he must go on, and, not infrequently, will surprise himself.

The first thing that a certain Scots professor used to say to his students when they handed in their essays was: "Did it never occur to you to tear up the first page?" Without reading it, he could guess that it was bad, because beginnings are the most difficult things to manage successfully. "It is there," said Chekhov, "that we do most of our lying." Before we are properly warmed up, we run the risk of being flat and pedantic. Speaking personally, I am never quite sure how I am going to begin, but, once afloat, instinct takes over the controls. That is why so many of the great masters make an abrupt opening. They fling the reader straight into a dialogue between characters about whom he knows nothing. It is for him to strike out and find his own way. The Scots professor was right. It is an admirable rule to "cut" the first page which is almost certain to be groping, slow and didactic, as well as wholly unnecessary for the intelligent reader.

The ending

As to the art of concluding, that depends on the nature of the subject. If the whole purpose of a book has been to argue a thesis, it should end, as Beethoven ended, with a passage of affirmation in which the musical material was resolved. In biography and history it is well to gather all the *motifs* in the final pages, after the manner, say, of Wagner. In the case of a novel, or any imaginative work, especially if the tone is poetic, my own preference is for ending with a touch of symbolism which shall leave the reader brooding. A fine novel, a well-written story, "proves" nothing. Certain characters have played their parts, life goes on, and the final passage may be allowed to remain with one foot in the air, as is the case with some of Chopin's conclusions. But there is no absolute rule in such matters, and there are epic novelists who like to end on a powerful crescendo, as Ravel does in *Bolero*, or Dvorak in the *New World Symphony*. Composition has features which are common to all the arts, and the author can learn as much about his business in the concert hall as in the library.

3. Periods and Forms. I have said that a writer is a man who, more than anyone else, feels a need to express himself. But the *form* of that expression will differ in different periods. Had Valéry been born in the sixteenth century he would have written ballads: in the thirteenth, mystery plays. Art and religion are, in their origins, allied. There is a close connection between sacred books and epics. The Bible is an epic. Homer was a religious poet who gave to the Greeks their essential myths. The poet is a magician. He has his incantations and his spells. Whenever poetry takes on new life it turns back to its source, that is to say, to the magic of words.

The theatre too, as everybody knows, originated as a place in which a representation of the religious mysteries was given. That is clearly visible in the practice of Ancient Greece where the play was at once a ritual and a State ceremony. We see the same form of drama reappearing in the Middle Ages with the enacting of the Passion in the open spaces in front of cathedrals. Tragedy, the form most in favor with the French writers of the seventeenth century, bears traces of this double origin, with Greek drama preponderating. Racine owed much to Sophocles and Euripides. What matters most to us is that Racine utilized the tragic convention for the purpose of getting himself into focus and of depicting the passions of his day. Period determines form: The writer uses it.

In the same age the moralist was in high favor. Court and City alike, comprising, as they did, a leisured elite, delighted in analyzing the varying shades of sentiment, and formulating their findings in Maxims and Characters. What a man of our own day would express in the novel, La Rochefoucauld stated in concise epigrams. The new freedom of thought which came with the eighteenth century changed the moralist into a philosopher. Tragedy became platitudinous and withered away. The great writers of the time were those who devoted themselves to the exposition of ideas, science and history. Simultaneously, the novel gradually became a popular means of expression (*La Nouvelle Héloise, Les Liaisons Dangereuses, Le Paysan Perverti*). In England, books like *Tom Jones* and *Clarissa Harlowe* were treading the same road.

The writers of the eighteenth century, however, still looked on the novel as a minor form of literature. Voltaire took more pride in his tragedies than in *Candide*. It was not until the dawn of the nineteenth century that the composition of novels became a sufficient activity in itself. With Balzac, Flaubert, Maupassant and the great Anglo-Saxon, Russian, Spanish and Italian story-tellers, fiction grew to be *the* form of expression *par excellence*, a means to the dissemination of ideas among the general public. Now, in the twentieth century, the predominance of the novel is unlikely to be challenged until such time as the emergence of some new form of expression shall make it obsolete.

Let us now study briefly the technique best suited to two specific departments of literature: fiction and biography.

4. The Novelist. The production of fiction, which has reached vast proportions in all countries, is what attracts and holds the attention of the public. The reputation of a great novelist easily out-distances that of the historian or the essayist, though not, perhaps, that of the dramatist. The Nobel Prize will go to ten novelists for every *one* philosopher. I know that the imminent death of the novel as an art-form is constantly being dinned into our ears. Some of these harbingers of woe tell us that its possiblities have been exhausted, that it depended for its popularity on the existence of a bourgeois society, that only such a society provided material for the portrayal of manners, that the individual, whose passions form the stock-in-trade of fiction, is losing his importance in an increasingly authoritarian and collective world. Others think that a craving for fictional narrative is still alive and kicking but finds its satisfaction in the dramas of the screen (whether cinema or television) and that novels written to be read are already under sentence of death.

Before passing on to consider the technique of novel-writing, I wish to say a few words about this sweeping assumption. No useful purpose could be served by discussing a form of literature which is destined to disappear almost immediately. I will, therefore, say at once that I refuse to believe that there is any danger of its sad demise. Why should the novel depend upon the existence of a bourgeois society—which, by the bye, still lives on even if its health gives cause for anxiety? Collective thought has not yet destroyed individual passions, even in collectivist civilizations. Novels are still being written in the U.S.S.R. and some of them are good. The demand in Russia for French fiction is very much in evidence. We are told that the Russian sales of *Le Rouge et le Noir* now amount to more than seven million copies, and that of a book which is a masterpiece of fiction. As to the dramas of the screen, they, I am convinced, can never take the place of novels in the eyes of ardent and searching readers. There is something scrambled and hustled about a portrayal of dramatic happenings which lasts, at the most, for two hours. The cinema is a far greater threat to the theatre. It may have a specific beauty of its own, but it does not permit that constant re-reading, that meditative brooding, those turnings-back to passages heavily charged with meaning, which form the special pleasure of the novel-reader.

It is further declared that even if the novel does continue, it stands badly in need of renewal; that the old methods of fiction which, as used by a Balzac or a Proust, have many masterpieces to their credit, have now been squeezed dry: that the younger generation will refuse to a man, as Valéry refused not so long ago, to write such sentences as: "The marquise took a chair, sat down, and said . . .": that the analysis of feelings—false at the best—must give place to concern with objects. I must confess that I have no more belief in this revolution than I have in the other. Obviously, the form of the novel changes whenever a novelist of genius appears. Proust is totally different from Balzac. But though that is true, he differs far less from George Eliot and Dickens. It may be possible, it may even be probable that the novel is finding fresh inspiration in the technique of the screen: that dialogue is supplanting the author's comments on the action of his story (Compton Burnett, Claude Mauriac): that the "interior monologue" (what the characters think, not what they say) has now a recognized place in the technique of fiction (Nathalie Sarraute): that concentration on external objects is the sole means of expressing the interior world—but these variants will not change the essential nature of the novel.

Subject

Almost all the great novels have as their *motif*, more or less disguised, the "passage from childhood to maturity," the clash between the thrill of expectation, and the disillusioning knowledge of the truth. Proust extracts the very essence of this movement when he shows us a young boy confronted by a world of things, attaching to *names* ideas which, later, he will have to root up one by one before he can make the names coincide with a perceived reality. Swann is in love with an Odette who exists only in his imagination. The transformation of this fictitious Odette into the formidable Odette of flesh and blood is, in itself, a subject for a novel. Natasha, in *War and Peace*, passes from mistake to mistake. One of our novelists, Michel Butor, sets before us a youthful Frenchman arriving in an English town. He cannot understand it; to him it seems monstrous. The subject of the novel is the hero's coming to grips with the real nature of the town. *Lost Illusions* is the undisclosed title of every novel. By this I do not mean that the mental development of the protagonist necessarily proceeds from illusion to cynicism. One can love a real woman after having loved her imagined counterpart. Similarly, one can adapt oneself to a society which, previously, one held in contempt. Another blanket title which would fit all the finest novels is *The 'Prentice Years*.

But if the main subject of fiction is always of the same general nature, every gifted writer chooses the variant which will allow him to express his own personal view of it. There are autobiographical novels, though they are so only in part. The really great novel, on the contrary, tends to be the exact negative of its author's life. "The characters crowd onto the page," writes Mauriac, "there to accomplish all those things which the personal destiny of the author has kept at bay. All temptations overcome, all frustrations of love, combine to produce the embryo of a being who slowly takes on form and substance until, at last, he emerges into the light of day, uttering his newborn cry. The road never trodden by the father, the child will surely tread." That is true enough, but the choice of a subject is, all the same, linked with the secret desires of the writer, and this explains how it is that the greatest novelists never cease, under a variety of masks, from writing the same book. Fabrice and Julien Sorel are two aspects of the man Stendhal would have liked to be: Mme de Renal and Clélia Conti, of the woman he would have liked to love. In Mauriac the conflict is always between Faith and Flesh. The truth is that, from the immense spectacle of the world, each novelist retains the one adventure which enables him to give expression to his own essential self, just as the painter sees in nature only pictures painted in *his* manner.

Viewpoint

The subject once decided upon, what part, in treating it, is played by the observing eye, what by the inventive imagination? Most novelists base their work on a *milieu* with which they are thoroughly familiar. Balzac's world is vast because life had brought him into close contact with many different types of men. Fictional characters are not portraits, but they are transpositions of real people. We are told that Rastignac was M. Thiers, and Micawber, Dickens' father. We may, however, be sure that many of the peculiarities of those characters were borrowed from other models. The Duchesse de Guermantes was Mme Straus, but she was also Mme de Chevigné. The really good novel is never a *roman a clef*. Nevertheless, it needs the support of reality, and the background of an actual society, otherwise it will not stand firm. If a novel is to come to life it must make contact with the facts of a society, its operative influences, its external relations, its politics and its rituals. The pastoral idyll is always a defective novel, because the lovers live their lives in isolation, as though situated in some enchanted bubble.

On the other hand, the external world in a novel must be seen through the eyes of its hero. In that form of novel which we call our life, we circle round many human beings, we see them under a succession of different lights, we are witnesses of the changes which take place in them, and it is thus that they hold our attention. Similarly, in a well-written, well-constructed work of fiction, the world presented will be three-dimensional only if it circles round the reader as well as round the hero. There are many different ways of writing novels. The story may be told directly by the author speaking as eyewitness of the action, in which case his surprises must be our surprises. The hero, on the other hand, may be the narrator, speaking in the first person, and this is the easiest method because in it the confidential tone comes naturally. Finally, the novel may be written "from the point of view of God". Of this type, *War and Peace* is a good example. In it the world revolves round several different persons, and the reader sees it now through the eyes of Prince André, now through those of Pierre Bezoukhov, now through Natasha's.

To be more precise: in the great novels of the world the characters fall into two main types—objects and subjects. A novel presents us with the picture of an individual life in such a way that we get to know it as well as we know our own. This life belongs to the "subject" (or to more than one subject), and all the other characters who make their appearance in the course of the narrative are objects only. Old Grandet is an object to his daughter. But *she* is a subject, and that is why the book is called *Eugénie Grandet*. Balzac's famous descriptions, which some critics find too long, are the visions of a subject-character, and, as such, are made vividly alive. What is described is not Grandet's house *in itself*, but Grandet's house as seen by Eugénie and her cousin, Charles.

It may be objected that some novels are purely imaginary (fantasies, philosophic tales, prophetic imaginings, science fiction). That is a mistaken view. The more different the world described is from day-to-day life and the experience of the reader, the greater the need for factual precision and an illusion of solidity. *Gulliver's Travels* can make even absurdity *seem* true. Voltaire's *Micromégas* brings Fontenelle to mind, and *Candide*, Leibnitz. The novelist who relies wholly on invention is not a realist, but he must provide his fantasy with a substratum of reality.

5. The Biographer. The biographer has two duties: he must be a portrait painter and an historian. As the former, he must provide a portrait which shall be "like," and, at the same time, a good piece of painting in itself. As the latter, he must assemble a number of genuine facts, arrange them intelligibly, and give to his work an artistic form. A biography should give us "the faithful picture of a human being on his way through life": and when I say faithful, I mean to say that the biographer must base his work on solid documentation, and organize his findings in such a way as to produce a good book.

Research

How is he to get at, and arrange his facts? First, by reading all that has been written about his hero, his hero's friends and enemies, and the period in which all of them lived. Next, he must seek out material which has never before been made public. There is always something new to be found, since the great public libraries and numerous private collections are very far from having been exhausted. He should, too, visit the places associated with his hero's life, and, if he has been dead for only a short time, hunt up and question those who knew him. Finally, he must weigh the written against the spoken evidence with a critical eye, comparing one with the other. He must so throughly soak himself in the contents of his documents as to be able, if necessary, to write without further reference to them.

Having assembled his facts, he must arrange them chronologically, taking care to observe the following rules: (1) The reader must not be swamped under a flood of documentation. What is redundant should be suppressed, and, where possible, the contents of this or that document carefully summarized. Except where a letter is of capital importance, a few lines should suffice to convey its "gist", (2) Great attention should be paid to such small details as will make the characters live—the most important being habitual tricks, gestures and turns of speech. (3) A proved fact must never be suppressed because it falsifies the biographer's preconceived idea of his hero. He must, on the contrary, constantly be at pains to retouch his picture, as a portrait painter does, adding something here, modifying something there, coming closer and closer to the truth. (4) In certain cases (happily rare), the existence of relations or close friends of the subject may necessitate a few omissions. But, though it is permissible not to tell the *whole* truth about a man, what is told must be true.

Interpretation

The invention of facts not justified by documents or by living witnesses is strictly forbidden. To attribute to one's subjects thoughts which cannot be proved, to present the reader with imaginary dialogues, is to be guilty of an infringement of the laws of biography, which are those of history. Fictional biography is a bastard literary form. On the other hand, a well-written biography should to this extent resemble a novel, that the reader should be enabled to watch the hero's progressive discovery of the world. Not only is that in accordance with the standards of serious history, but it is very necessary. It should be obvious that, for instance, Disraeli as a young man did not see English society in the same way as did Disraeli the aging Prime Minister. It is for the biographer to discover, in the writings of his hero, in the evidence of his hero's contemporaries, in the memoirs of the time, the traces of this progressive development.

Interpretation of the available facts should be undertaken with the utmost care and be solidly supported. It is often indispensable. Was Balzac really in love with Mme Hanska, or did she behave very badly to him? Did George Sand exercise a pernicious influence on Musset and Chopin, or did she, on the contrary, contribute to the maturing of their genius? Did Bonaparte, in the days of the Consulate, behave as a tyrant or as a wise friend to genuine liberty? The reader wants an answer to these questions. So far as he can, the author will provide the facts and leave the reader to draw his own conclusions. Should he feel bound to intervene where the truth is in doubt, he must indicate all the possible hypotheses. Lytton Strachey was a master at the biographical game, at saying whether the truth lay here, or, more probably, there. He excelled at enveloping in a luminous fog the obscure points which are to be found in every life, in art no less than in real life.

Moral worth

Should biography have a moral value? Yes, to the extent that all great art has a moral value. I do not mean that it should take the form of a deliberate lesson in vice and virtue. But biography may well have a beneficial effect upon the reader. "Here," he will think, "is a man, or a woman, who was very like me in more ways than one, exposed, just as I am, to the exigencies of passion and to the frustrations of existence. Nevertheless, he (or she) succeeded in making something great and lovely of life." A true portrait should be reconciliation with the sitter. A great biography should, like the close of a great drama, leave behind it a feeling of serenity. We collect into a small bunch the flowers, the few flowers, which brought sweetness into a life, and present it as an offering to an accomplished destiny. It is the dying refrain of a completed song, the final verse of a finished poem. Such a biographer as Strachey showed himself to be the equal of a great musician or a great poet. Therein lies the technique of biography, and, indeed, of all art.

On being true-to-life

by Wright Morris

From Homer to the present, the need to tell it like it is a line of descent of both fiction and nonfiction, the skeptics among the listeners being the first to recognize that fiction is a form of artful lying. This reader saw through much that he heard about Odysseus, and he sees through much that he reads about Herzog. A major problem of craft is how "to take such a reader in." How to make fiction, that is, true-to-life.

From the first it was recognized that the *lower* the life, the truer it seemed. Even Dante, out of his mind for heaven, sensed that hell was more photogenic, both hell and purgatory providing a better mirror for life on earth. Neither is hell so long absent from common daily experience that the writer should lack a public. The craft of fiction is that branch of the arts where what the author *perceives* is more important than what he observes. This is a nice, but crucial, distinction, like the one that separates the men from the boys.

Truth in the eye of the reader

That April is the cruelest month startled most readers, lying outside the range of their weather observations, but some accept it as true-to-life perception. As simple as it seems, the question still arises: What is true-to-life? *Whose* life, for example?

Dear Dr. Schoenfeld:
I am a 13 year old chick, who 4 days ago lost my virginity. The dude I balled and I were very stoned, and I didn't come. Do you think I should get a VD test?

Wright Morris is a writer of novels, short stories and critical essays. He has been compared to Sherwood Anderson in his treatment of the quality of American life in such novels as My Uncle Dudley, The Man Who Was There, Works of Love, Deep Sleep *and* Life Among the Cannibals. *He is a contributor to major magazines and a university lecturer.*

That is an inquiry in the morning paper. We can assume it is true to the person who wrote it: A writer of fiction would quote it verbatim. How improve, he would ask, on life itself? At this point, and on this level, the vernacular seems to achieve the representation of the facts the writer desires.

Then the 47-year-old housewife of a $500 a month San Jose shoe salesman took a deep breath and talked about the checkered past of her "good daughter," who gave birth to an illegitimate son when she was 19, turned topless dancer before she was 20, fell in with motorcycle gang members believed to associated with the Manson family, and now stands charged with murder. "I can't blame her for what's happened—not really," her mother said.

This too is a report from the newspaper, unsullied by the craft of fiction. Is this an instance of life imitating art? The writer of black humor could contribute little to the portrait. For writing of comparable interest we have to turn to "good" fiction. Here is J.D. Salinger's Holden Caulfield:

If you really want to hear about it, the first thing you'll probably want to know is where I was born, and what my lousy childhood was like, and how my parents were occupied and all before they had me, and all that David Copperfield kind of crap, but I don't feel like going into it, if you want to know the truth.

Do we want to know the truth? This fictional comment shares with the nonfiction I've quoted the vernacular tone of the *real* experience, of the true-to-life. Why is it that with each passing year the real seems to be nearer the bottom of the barrel? Is it a matter of taste, a matter of talent, or is it chiefly a matter of language that whacking off comes easier to Alex Portnoy than it did to Holden Caulfield? What is it, if not the language, that makes his remarkable complaint so attractive? He really tells us very little, but he tells us all about whacking off. Only the vernacular would prove to be equal to his awesome task. Only the reader of considerable sophistication would know that the candor of Holden Caulfield differs from that of the young lady writing to Dr. Schoenfeld, but it is not a difference that will turn her from life to literature for advice. It is Dr. Schoenfeld's opinion she wants, not that of J.D. Salinger. Since we lack a bonafide detached reality to which we might turn as a basis of judgment, we are left with a true-to-life established by life, with strong fictive elements, and a true-to-life established by fiction, with strong lifelike elements. Which is the *truer* remains a matter of the reader's taste.

Language leads

Although bad fiction appears to rule our lives, and proves to be more influential than "good" fiction, the writer and reader of good fiction sustain the illusion that fiction is truer to the life that "matters," the rest of life being real enough but lacking consciousness of what it is, and what it might be. Mike Hammer is real, in his fashion, but only good fiction knows what is real about him, and what is false. The daily use and abuse of the "vernacular tongue," its artful honing by both those who use it and those who write it, has blurred the once clear-cut distinction between life and its mirrored reflection. The world and its image are seen as one. The "style" that gives us this assurance is a craft achievement so invisible it appears to be absent, persuading the reader that life and the lifelike, with a little patience, will appear as one. The look of life, the tone and timbre of life, is increasingly one seamless vernacular fabric, comprehending how we sound: "The dude I balled";

how we think: "If you really want to hear about it"; and how we think we feel: "The great thing is to last and to get your work done and see and hear and learn and understand" (Hemingway). When this tone is persuasive, artfully artless, we are easily convinced that the lifelike is true-to-life.

"The Americans," Whitman prophesied, "are going to be the most fluent and melodious-voiced people in the world—and the most perfect users of words. The new world, the new times, the new vistas need a new tongue . . . what is more, they will have a new tongue—will not be satisfied until it is evolved." This new tongue is approaching its moment of triumph, but it has consequences Whitman did not imagine. We have the new world, the new times, the new vistas, but the grain of the vernacular *naturally* slopes downward. It is the fountainhead of what comes naturally, but it is reluctant to respond to effort. The writer feels that, the reader feels it, and the writer is reluctant to go against it. The language leads, and the writer follows where it leads.

How did this come to pass? Aren't we the dreamers who taught the world to fly?

There is a lag of thirty years between Whitman's exhortation and the voice of Huck Finn.

> Two or three days and nights went by; I reckon I might say they swum by, they slid along so quiet and smooth and lovely. Here is the way we put in the time.

Here the language leads the writer, and the reader, into territory that is new. The writer himself is uncertain of the terrain, and the spell of enchantment he is under. Is it a real world, really true-to-life, or a fantasy true to Huck Finn only? The point is not resolved, nor does the author comprehend the novelty of the situation. He is a sensible writer of frontier humor, well known for a story about a leaping frog. He is profoundly moved to write about the past, but never long clear *how* to write about it. Over the seven-year period of composition his point of view and "voice" vacillated, appropriate to a person whose voice was about to change. Although the narrative wavers, Huck Finn is the first of the American boys to tell the adults how it really is.

A writer half Twain's age, but more certain of his intent, wrote about a youth's initiation to war.

> Once the line encountered the body of a dead soldier. He lay upon his back staring at the sky. He was dressed in an awkward suit of yellowish brown. The youth could see that the soles of his shoes had been worn to the thinness of writing paper, and from a great rent in one the dead foot projected piteously. And it was as if fate had betrayed the soldier. In death it exposed to his enemies that poverty which in life he had perhaps concealed from his friends.

There is nothing here of lyrical charm: The writer's eye is for paradox and details. The young author had never experienced a war, but he thought it an interesting challenge to describe one as if he had. Huck Finn, remembered by a man who was aging, and *The Red Badge of Courage*, conjured up by a youth whose writing preceded his experience, had in common a language appropriate to their separate needs.

Simple words and common rhythms

Two years after Crane died, in exile in England, Gertrude Stein left Baltimore to settle in Paris. Living in Paris may have helped her to see clearly the life she knew in Baltimore.

Anna looked very well this day. She was always very careful in her dress and sparing of new clothes. She made herself always fulfill her own ideal of how a girl should look when she took her Sundays out. Anna knew so well the kind of ugliness appropriate to each rank of life.

Would we say that this language leads the writer, or that what is new in the language is being led? We sense, immediately, that it serves a new and inscrutable purpose.

Sometimes the thought of how all her world was made, filled the complex, desiring Melanctha with despair.

The content of this statement would prove to be inseparable from the manner of speaking. *Feeling* is what matters, and Gertrude Stein's craft is the first to limit itself to that subject. Of all fiction, it is the least concerned with data, major issues, speculation, epic or mythic, or other vast manipulations to make the modern world possible in art, characteristic obsessions of her male contemporaries.

Some of the early readers of Stein's fiction thought the author well-intentioned but perhaps simple-minded, not grasping what it is that constitutes literature. Those who grasped what Stein was up to experienced a peculiarly intense captivity. Sherwood Anderson and Hemingway were among the first to spread the virus of her infection. It might not be clearly grasped *what* she was doing, but how she was doing it proved to be contagious. Simple words, the rhythms of common speech deliberately made uncommon, apprehend a way of feeling, a way of seeing, and in the fullness of time a way of being, a life style. Predictably, we can say with hindsight, this all-American celebration was appropriately staged in exile. The triumph of Stein is that of the emerging vernacular. Joyce, Mann, and Proust mark a summing up, *Three Lives* an inexhaustible beginning. In fifty years she is still little read, but she is known around the world through her converts. At long last (it appeared), what had begun with Homer, and persisted through numberless mutations, would quite logically achieve its flowering in the barbaric yawp of the new world, a babble of tongues its writers of talent would make melodious. The ultimate realism, the ultimate true-to-life, and the ultimate public for this production was merely a matter of telling it like it is while writing as you pleased.

A volume by that title, *I Write As I Please*, was actually published in the early thirties, reporting on the author's travels in communist Russia. At the same time, a Frenchman, writing as he pleased, published his travels in *Journey to the End of the Night*. The American sought to describe the facts of life, the Frenchman the other side of life. No parallel journey was taken by an American—with the exception of Agee's *Let Us Now Praise Famous Men*—but the American writer believed life would be different: the Frenchman knew it would not.

Perception more than observation

The American language was well prepared for Céline, but not the American mind. His surreal blend of fiction, fantasy, and fact, the hallucinated aspect of his daylight vision, were experienced by Americans as shock waves from a remote continental disturbance, not part of the new wave of the future.

In the great hazy desert around a town, where its luxury, ending in rottenness and slime, is proved to be a lie, the town presents its posterior among the dustbins for all who wish to see. There are some factories one avoids walking past: they give out every sort of smell, some of them almost unbelievable, and the surrounding air can stink no more. Close by, a little traveling fair moulders between two tall chimneys of unequal height, its wooden horses too costly for rachitic urchins, picking their noses, who sometimes for weeks on end long to ride them, attracted, repelled and fascinated all at once by their abandoned air, poverty, and the music.

That is a barbaric yawp Whitman did not dream of shouting over the roofs of the world.

We shall never be at peace [Céline said] until everything has been said, once for all time . . . .

Whether true or not, this statement left a memorable impression on many writers, some of them American. In its simplicity it acquired the weight and persuasion of a doctrine. Céline had in mind the human condition, as distinct from the literary situation: What he had to say proved to be too strong for American tastes. It gave little thought to form, and explicitly violated existing notions of style. Céline is not the first writer of genius to abandon literary preconceptions and replace them with his own model of the true-to-life. The writer's passion for life, free of fictive intervention, derives from the example of all writers of fiction who achieve a new picture of the facts. Céline did. Great writers of fiction do: It is a function of their talent. It will not prove to be true that everything has been said, but we shall not be at peace without it. True-to-life becomes fiction where it perceives more than it observes.

Lecture on the nature and aim of fiction

by Flannery O'Connor

I understand that this is a course called "How the Writer Writes," and that each week you are exposed to a different writer who holds forth on the subject. The only parallel I can think of to this is having the zoo come to you, one animal at a time; and I suspect that what you hear one week from the giraffe is contradicted the next week by the baboon.

My own problem in thinking what I should say to you tonight has been how to interpret such a title as "How the Writer Writes." In the first place, there is no such thing as *the* writer, and I think that if you don't know that now, you should by the time such a course as this is over. In fact, I predict that it is the one thing you can be absolutely certain of learning.

But there is a widespread curiosity about writers and how they work, and when a writer talks on this subject, there are always misconceptions and mental rubble for him to clear away before he can even begin to see what he wants to talk about. I am not, of course, as innocent as I look. I know well enough that very few people who are supposedly interested in writing are interested in writing well. They are interested in publishing something, and if possible in making a "killing." They are interested in being a writer, not in writing. They are interested in seeing their names at the top of something printed, it matters not what. And they seem to feel that this can be accomplished by learning certain things about working habits and about markets and about what subjects are currently acceptable.

Flannery O'Connor had her first story published at 21 while attending the Writers Workshop at the University of Iowa. She spent the next five years writing her highly praised novel, Wise Blood. *Her literary output was great despite the debilitating disease lupus which took her life at 39. She traveled, lectured, wrote essays, letters, novels, and many short stories for major magazines and literaries.* The Complete Stories of Flannery O'Connor *received the National Book Award for fiction in 1971. This selection is one of the author's lectures.*

Appealing through the senses

If this is what you are interested in, I am not going to be of much use to you. I feel that the external habits of the writer will be guided by his common sense or his lack of it and by his personal circumstances; and that these will seldom be alike in two cases. What interests the serious writer is not external habits but what Maritain calls, "the habit of art"; and he explains that "habit" in this sense means a certain quality or virtue of the mind. The scientist has the habit of science; the artist, the habit of art.

Now I'd better stop here and explain how I'm using the word *art*. Art is a word that immediately scares people off, as being a little too grand. But all I mean by art is writing something that is valuable in itself and that works in itself. The basis of art is truth, both in matter and in mode. The person who aims after art in his work aims after truth, in an imaginative sense, no more and no less. St. Thomas said that the artist is concerned with the good of that which is made; and that will have to be the basis of my few words on the subject of fiction.

Now you'll see that this kind of approach eliminates many things from the discussion. It eliminates any concern with the motivation of the writer except as this finds its place inside the work. It also eliminates any concern with the reader in his market sense. It also eliminates that tedious controversy that always rages between people who declare that they write to express themselves and those who declare that they write to fill their pocketbooks, if possible.

In this connection I always think of Henry James. I know of no writer who was hotter after the dollar than James was, or who was more of a conscientious artist. It is true, I think, that these are times when the financial rewards for sorry writing are much greater than those for good writing. There are certain cases in which, if you can only learn to write poorly enough, you can make a great deal of money. But it is not true that if you write well, you won't get published at all. It is true that if you want to write well and live well at the same time, you'd better arrange to inherit money or marry a stockbroker or a rich woman who can operate a typewriter. In any case, whether you write to make money or to express your soul or to insure civil rights or to irritate your grandmother will be a matter for you and your analyst, and the point of departure for this discussion will be the good of the written work.

The kind of written work I'm going to talk about is story-writing, because that's the only kind I know anything about. I'll call any length of fiction a story, whether it be a novel or a shorter piece, and I'll call anything a story in which specific characters and events influence each other to form a meaningful narrative. I find that most people know what a story is until they sit down to write one. Then they find themselves writing a sketch with an essay woven through it, or an essay with a sketch woven through it, or an editorial with a character in it, or a case history with a moral, or some other mongrel thing. When they realize that they aren't writing stories, they decide that the remedy for this is to learn something that they refer to as the "technique of the short story" or "the technique of the novel." Technique in the minds of many is something rigid, something like a formula that you impose on the material; but in the best stories it is something organic, something that grows out of the material, and this being the case, it is different for every story of any account that has ever been written.

I think we have to begin thinking about stories at a much more fundamental level, so I want to talk about one quality of fiction which I think is its least common denominator—the fact that it is concrete—and about a few of the qualities that follow from this. We will be concerned in this with the reader in his fundamental human sense, because the nature of fiction is in large measure determined by the nature of our perceptive apparatus. The beginning of human knowledge is through the senses, and the fiction writer begins where human perception begins. He appeals through the senses, and you cannot appeal to the senses with abstractions. It is a good deal easier for most people to state an abstract idea than to describe and thus re-create some object that they actually see. But the world of the fiction writer is full of matter, and this is what the beginning fiction writers are very loath to create. They are concerned primarily with unfleshed ideas and emotions. They are apt to be reformers and to want to write because they are possessed not by a story but by the bare bones of some abstract notion. They are conscious of problems, not of people, of questions and issues, not of the texture of existence, of case histories and of everything that has a sociological smack, instead of with all those concrete details of life that make actual the mystery of our position on earth.

The Manicheans separated spirit and matter. To them all material things were evil. They sought pure spirit and tried to approach the infinite directly without any mediation of matter. This is also pretty much the modern spirit, and for the sensibility infected with it, fiction is hard if not impossible to write because fiction is so very much an incarnational art.

Detail over grand ideas

One of the most common and saddest spectacles is that of a person of really fine sensibility and acute psychological perception trying to write fiction by using these qualitites alone. This type of writer will put down one intensely emotional or keenly perceptive sentence after the other, and the result will be complete dullness. The fact is that the materials of the fiction writer are the humblest. Fiction is about everything human and we are made out of dust, and if you scorn getting yourself dusty then you shouldn't try to write fiction. It's not a grand enough job for you.

Now when the fiction writer finally gets this idea through his head and into his habits, he begins to realize what a job of heavy labor the writing of fiction is. A lady who writes, and whom I admire very much, wrote me that she had learned from Flaubert that it takes at least three activated sensuous strokes to make an object real; and she believes that this is connected with our having five senses. If you're deprived of any of them, you're in a bad way, but if you're deprived of more than two at once, you almost aren't present.

All the sentences in *Madame Bovary* could be examined with wonder, but there is one in particular that always stops me in admiration. Flaubert has just shown us Emma at the piano with Charles watching her. He says, "She struck the notes with aplomb and ran from top to bottom of the keyboard without a break. Thus shaken up, the old instrument, whose strings buzzed, could be heard at the other end of the village when the window was open, and often the bailiff's clerk, passing along the highroad, bareheaded and in list slippers, stopped to listen, his sheet of paper in his hand."

The more you look at a sentence like that, the more you can learn from it. At one end of it, we are with Emma and this very solid instrument "whose strings buzzed," and at the other end of it we are across the village with this very concrete clerk in his list slippers. With regard to what happens to Emma in the rest of the novel, we may think that it makes no difference that the instrument has buzzing strings or that the clerk wears list slippers and has a piece of paper in his hand, but

Flaubert had to create a believable village to put Emma in. It's always necessary to remember that the fiction writer is much less *immediately* concerned with grand ideas and bristling emotions than he is with putting list slippers on clerks.

Now of course this is something that some people learn only to abuse. This is one reason that strict naturalism is a dead end in fiction. In a strictly naturalistic work the detail is there because it is natural to life, not because it is natural to the work. In a work of art we can be extremely literal, without being in the least naturalistic. Art is selective, and its truthfulness is the truthfulness of the essential that creates movement.

Symbols

The novel works by a slower accumulation of detail than the short story does. The short story requires more drastic procedures than the novel because more has to be accomplished in less space. The details have to carry more immediate weight. In good fiction, certain of the details will tend to accumulate meaning from the story itself, and when this happens, they become symbolic in their action.

Now the word *symbol* scares a good many people off, just as the word *art* does. They seem to feel that a symbol is some mysterious thing put in arbitrarily by the writer to frighten the common reader—sort of a literary Masonic grip that is only for the initiated. They seem to think that it is a way of saying something that you aren't actually saying, and so if they can be got to read a reputedly symbolic work at all, they approach it as if it were a problem in algebra. Find *x*. And when they do find or think they find this abstraction, *x*, then they go off with an elaborate sense of satisfaction and the notion that they have "understood" the story. Many students confuse the *process* of understanding a thing with understanding it.

I think that for the fiction writer himself, symbols are something he uses simply as a matter of course. You might say that these are details that, while having their essential place in the literal level of the story, operate in depth as well as on the surface, increasing the story in every direction.

I think the way to read a book is always to see what happens, but in a good novel, more always happens than we are able to take in at once, more happens than meets the eye. The mind is led on by what it sees into the greater depths that the book's symbols naturally suggest. This is what is meant when critics say that a novel operates on several levels. The truer the symbol, the deeper it leads you, the more meaning it opens up. To take an example from my own book, *Wise Blood*, the hero's rat-colored automobile is his pulpit and his coffin as well as something he thinks of as a means of escape. He is mistaken in thinking that it is a means of escape, of course, and does not really escape his predicament until the car is destroyed by the patrolman. The car is a kind of death-in-life symbol, as his blindness is a life-in-death symbol. The fact that these meanings are there makes the book significant. The reader may not see them but they have their effect on him nonetheless. This is the way the modern novelist sinks, or hides, his theme.

The kind of vision the fiction writer needs to have, or to develop, in order to increase the meaning of his story is called anagogical vision, and that is the kind of vision that is able to see different levels of reality in one image or one situation. The medieval commentators on Scripture found three kinds of meaning in the literal level of the sacred text: One they called allegorical, in which one fact pointed to another; one they called tropological, or moral, which had to do with what should be done; and one they called anagogical, which had to do with the divine life and our participation in it. Although this was a method applied to Biblical exegesis, it was also an attitude toward all of creation, and a way of reading nature which included most possibilities, and I think it is the enlarged view of the human scene that the fiction writer has to cultivate if he is ever going to write stories that have any chance of becoming a permanent part of our literature. It seems to be a paradox that the larger and more complex the personal view, the easier it is to compress it into fiction.

Self-contained dramatic unit

People have a habit of saying, "What is the theme of your story?" and they expect you to give them a statement: "The theme of my story is the economic pressure of the machine on the middle class"—or some such absurdity. And when they've got a statement like that, they go off happy and feel it is no longer necessary to read the story.

Some people have the notion that you read the story and then climb out of it into the meaning, but for the fiction writer himself the whole story is the meaning, because it is an experience, not an abstraction.

Now the second common characteristic of fiction follows from this, and it is that fiction is presented in such a way that the reader has the sense that it is unfolding around him. This doesn't mean he has to identify himself with the character or feel compassion for the character or anything like that. It just means that fiction has to be largely presented rather than reported. Another way to say it is that though fiction is a narrative art, it relies heavily on the element of drama.

The story is not as extreme a form of drama as the play, but if you know anything about the history of the novel, you know that the novel as an art form has developed in the direction of dramatic unity.

The major difference between the novel as written in the eighteenth century and novel as we usually find it today is the disappearance from it of the author. Fielding, for example, was everywhere in his own work, calling the reader's attention to this point and that, directing him to give his special attention here or there, clarifying this and that incident for him so that he couldn't possibly miss the point. The Victorian novelists did this, too. They were always coming in, explaining and psychologizing about their characters. But along about the time of Henry James, the author began to tell his story in a different way. He began to let it come through the minds and eyes of the characters themselves, and he sat behind the scenes, apparently disinterested. By the time we get to James Joyce, the author is nowhere to be found in the book. The reader is on his own, floundering around in the thoughts of various unsavory characters. He finds himself in the middle of a world apparently without comment.

But it is from the kind of world the writer creates, from the kind of character and detail he invests it with, that a reader can find the intellectual meaning of a book. Once this is found, however, it cannot be drained off and used as a substitute for the book. As the late John Peale Bishop said: "You can't say Cézanne painted apples and a tablecloth and have said what Cézanne painted." The novelist makes his statements by selection, and if he is any good, he selects every word for a reason, every detail for a reason, every incident for a reason, and arranges them in a certain time-sequence for a reason. He demonstrates something that cannot possibly be demonstrated any other way than with a whole novel.

Art forms evolve until they reach their ultimate perfection, or until they reach some state of petrifaction, or until some new element is grafted on and a new art form made. But however the past of fiction has been or however the future will be, the present state of the case is that a piece of fiction must be very much a self-contained dramatic unit.

Plunge into reality

This means that it must carry its meaning inside it. It means that any abstractly expressed compassion or piety or morality in a piece of fiction is only a statement added to it. It means that you can't make an inadequate dramatic action complete by putting a statement of meaning on the end of it or in the middle of it or at the beginning of it. It means that when you write fiction you are speaking *with* character and action, not *about* character and action. The writer's moral sense must coincide with his dramatic sense.

It's said that when Henry James received a manuscript that he didn't like, he would return it with the comment, "You have chosen a good subject and are treating it in a straightforward manner." This usually pleased the person getting the manuscript back, but it was the worst thing that James could think of to say, for he knew, better than anybody else, that the straightforward manner is seldom equal to the complications of the good subject. There may never be anything new to say, but there is always a new way to say it, and since, in art, the way of saying a thing becomes a part of what is said, every work of art is unique and requires fresh attention.

It's always wrong of course to say that you can't do this or you can't do that in fiction. You can do anything you can get away with, but nobody has ever gotten away with much.

I believe that it takes a rather different type of disposition to write novels than to write short stories, granted that both require fundamentally fictional talents. I have a friend who writes both, and she says that when she stops a novel to work on short stories, she feels as if she has just left a dark wood to be set upon by wolves. The novel is a more diffused form and more suited to those who like to linger along the way; it also requires a more massive energy. For those of us who want to get the agony over in a hurry, the novel is a burden and a pain. But no matter which fictional form you are using, you are writing a story, and in a story something has to happen. A perception is not a story, and no amount of sensitivity can make a story-writer out of you if you just plain don't have a gift for telling a story.

But there's a certain grain of stupidity that the writer of fiction can hardly do without, and this is the quality of having to stare, of not getting the point at once. The longer you look at one object, the more of the world you see in it; and it's well to remember that the serious fiction writer always writes about the whole world, no matter how limited his particular scene. For him, the bomb that was dropped on Hiroshima affects life on the Oconee River, and there's not anything he can do about it.

People are always complaining that the modern novelist has no hope that the picture he paints of the world is unbearable. The only answer to this is that people without hope do not write novels. Writing a novel is a terrible experience, during which the hair often falls out and the teeth decay. I'm always highly irritated by people who imply that writing fiction is an escape from reality. It is a plunge into reality and it's very shocking to the system. If the novelist is not sustained by a hope of money, then he must be sustained by a hope of salvation, or he simply won't survive the ordeal.

Contact with reality and mystery

People without hope not only don't write novels, but what is more to the point, they don't read them. They don't take long looks at anything, because they lack the courage. The way to despair is to refuse to have any kind of experience, and the novel, of course, is a way to have experience. The lady who only read books that improved her mind was taking a safe course—and a hopeless one. She'll never know whether her mind is improved or not, but should she ever, by some mistake, read a great novel, she'll know mighty well that something is happening to her.

A good many people have the notion that nothing happens in modern fiction and that nothing is supposed to happen, that it is the style now to write a story in which nothing happens. Actually, I think more happens in modern fiction—with less furor on the surface—than has ever happened in fiction before. A good example of this is a story by Caroline Gordon called "Summer Dust." It's in a collection of her stories called *The Forest of the South*, which is a book that repays study.

"Summer Dust" is divided into four short sections, which don't at first appear to have any relation between them and which are minus any narrative connection. Reading the story is at first rather like standing a foot away from an impressionistic painting, then gradually moving back until it comes into focus. When you reach the right distance, you suddenly see that a world has been created—and a world in action—and that a complete story has been told, by a wonderful kind of understatement. It has been told more by showing what happens around the story than by touching directly on the story itself.

You may say that this requires such an intelligent and sophisticated reader that it is not worth writing, but I'm rather inclined to think that it is more a false sophistication that prevents people from understanding this kind of story than anything else. Without being naturalistic in the least, a story like "Summer Dust" is actually much closer in form to life than a story that follows a narrative sequence of events.

The type of mind that can understand good fiction is not necessarily the educated mind, but it is at all times the kind of mind that is willing to have its sense of mystery deepened by contact with reality, and its sense of reality deepened by contact with mystery. Fiction should be both canny and uncanny. In a good deal of popular criticism, there is the notion operating that all fiction has to be about the Average Man, and has to depict what used to be called "a slice of life." But if life, in that sense, satisfied us, there would be no sense in producing literature at all.

Conrad said that his aim as a fiction writer was to render the highest possible justice to the visible universe. That sounds very grand, but it is really very humble. It means that he subjected himself at all times to the limitations that reality imposed, but that reality for him was not simply coextensive with the visible. He was interested in rendering justice to the visible universe because it suggested an invisible one, and he explained his own intentions as a novelist in this way:

> . . . and if the [artist's] conscience is clear, his answer to those who in the fullness of a wisdom which looks for immediate profit, demand specifically to be edified, consoled, amused; who demand to be promptly improved, or encouraged, or frightened, or shocked or charmed, must run thus: My task

which I am trying to achieve is, by the power of the written word, to make you hear, to make you feel—it is, before all, to make you *see*. That—and no more, and it is everything. If I succeed, you shall find there, according to your deserts, encouragement, consolation, fear, charm, all you demand—and, perhaps, also that glimpse of truth for which you have forgotten to ask.

A gift for fiction

You may think from all I say that the reason I write is to make the reader see what I see, and that writing fiction is primarily a missionary activity. Let me straighten this out.

Last spring I talked here, and one of the girls asked me, "Miss O'Connor, why do you write?" and I said, "Because I'm good at it," and at once I felt a considerable disapproval in the atmosphere. I felt that this was not thought by the majority to be a high-minded answer; but it was the only answer I could give. I had not been asked why I write the way I do, but why I write at all; and to that question there is only one legitimate answer.

There is no excuse for anyone to write fiction for public consumption unless he has been called to do so by the presence of a gift. It is the nature of fiction not to be good for much unless it is good in itself.

A gift of any kind is a considerable responsibility. It is a mystery in itself, something gratuitous and wholly undeserved, something whose real uses will probably always be hidden from us. Usually the artist has to suffer certain deprivations in order to use his gift with integrity. Art is a virtue of the practical intellect, and the practice of any virtue demands a certain asceticism and a very definite leaving-behind of the niggardly part of the ego. The writer has to judge himself with a stranger's eye and a stranger's severity. The prophet in him has to see the freak. No art is sunk in the self, but rather, in art the self becomes self-forgetful in order to meet the demands of the thing seen and the thing being made.

I think it is usually some form of self-inflation that destroys the free use of a gift. This may be the pride of the reformer or the theorist, or it may only be that simple-minded self-appreciation which uses its own sincerity as a standard of truth. If you have read the very vocal writers from San Francisco, you may have got the impression that the first thing you must do in order to be an artist is to loose yourself from the bonds of reason, and thereafter, anything that rolls off the top of your head will be a great value. Anyone's unrestrained feelings are considered worth listening to because they are unrestrained and because they are feelings.

Competence and vision

St. Thomas called art "reason in making." This is a very cold and very beautiful definition, and if it is unpopular today, this is because reason has lost ground among us. As grace and nature have been separated, so imagination and reason have been separated, and this always means an end to art. The artist uses his reason to discover an answering reason in everything he sees. For him, to be reasonable is to find, in the object, in the situation, in the sequence, the spirit which makes it itself. This is not an easy or simple thing to do. It is to intrude upon the timeless, and that is only done by the violence of a single-minded respect for the truth.

It follows from all this that there is no technique that can be discovered and applied to make it possible for one to write. If you go to a school where there are classes in writing, these classes should not be to teach you how to write, but to teach you the limits and possibilities of words and the respect due them. One thing that is always with the writer—no matter how long he has written or how good he is—is the continuing process of learning how to write. As soon as the writer "learns to write," as soon as he knows what he is going to find, and discovers a way to say what he knew all along, or worse still, a way to say nothing, he is finished. If a writer is any good, what he makes will have its source in a realm much larger than that which his conscious mind can encompass and will always be a greater surprise to him than it can ever be to his reader.

I don't know which is worse—to have a bad teacher or no teacher at all. In any case, I believe the teacher's work should be largely negative. He can't put the gift into you, but if he finds it there, he can try to keep it from going in an obviously wrong direction. We can learn how not to write, but this is a discipline that does not simply concern writing itself but concerns the whole intellectual life. A mind cleared of false emotion and false sentiment and egocentricity is going to have at least those roadblocks removed from its path. If you don't think cheaply, then there at least won't be the quality of cheapness in your writing, even though you may not be able to write well. The teacher can try to weed out what is positively bad, and this should be the aim of the whole college. Any discipline can help your writing: logic, mathematics, theology, and of course and particularly drawing. Anything that helps you to see, anything that makes you look. The writer should never be ashamed of staring. There is nothing that doesn't require his attention.

We hear a great deal of lamentation these days about writers having all taken themselves to the colleges and universities where they live decorously instead of going out and getting firsthand information about life. The fact is that anybody who has survived his childhood has enough information about life to last him the rest of his days. If you can't make something out of a little experience, you probably won't be able to make it out of a lot. The writer's business is to contemplate experience, not to be merged in it.

Everywhere I go I'm asked if I think the universities stifle writers. My opinion is that they don't stifle enough of them. There's many a bestseller that could have been prevented by a good teacher. The idea of being a writer attracts a good many shiftless people, those who are merely burdened with poetic feelings or afflicted with sensibility. . . .

Now in every writing class you find people who care nothing about writing, because they think they are already writers by virtue of some experience they've had. It is a fact that if, either by nature or training, these people can learn to write badly enough, they can make a great deal of money, and in a way it seems a shame to deny them this opportunity; but then, unless the college is a trade school, it still has its responsibility to truth, and I believe myself that these people should be stifled with all deliberate speed.

Presuming that the people left have some degree of talent, the question is what can be done for them in a writing class. I believe the teacher's work is largely negative, that it is largely a matter of saying "This doesn't work because . . ." or "This does work because . . ." The *because* is very important. The teacher can help you understand the nature of your medium, and he can guide you in your reading. I don't believe in classes where students criticize each other's manuscripts. Such criticism is generally composed in equal parts of ignorance, flattery, and spite. It's the blind leading the blind, and it can be dangerous. A teacher who tries to impose a way of writing on you can be dangerous too. Fortunately, most teachers I've known were too lazy to do this. In any case, you should beware of those who appear overenergetic.

In the last twenty years the colleges have been emphasizing creative writing to such an extent that you almost feel that any idiot with a nickel's worth of talent can emerge from a writing class able to write a competent story. In fact, so many people can now write competent stories that the short story as a medium is in danger of dying of competence. We want competence, but competence by itself is deadly. What is needed is the vision to go with it, and you do not get this from a writing class.

Establishing good writing habits

by Manuel Komroff

Beginning each day

One of the great problems which confronts the novelist is how to start writing at the beginning of the day. It is not easy to sit down at a desk and face a blank piece of paper and expect words to flow. You do not want ordinary words. You ask for good words—words that make sense and words that continue the flow and beat of your story.

It is a strange sight to behold a novelist sitting before a blank piece of paper. His mind is blank. His eyes look out blankly and see nothing. Soon he starts fiddling with the typewriter ribbon or wire clips. He looks about and decides to sharpen pencils and fill fountain pens. He loses confidence in himself. He will do anything that will delay the words from attaching themselves to the paper. Why?

There are a number of reasons why this happens. The words are not there. They are not in his head. He cannot hear them. Nor are they in his mouth. He cannot say them. Nor does he see clearly before his eyes a picture or scene from his novel which he can describe.

This is a daily problem which every novelist must face. Young writers often feel that their inexperience prevents them from getting started easily. But experienced writers are not immune from this torturing difficulty.

Somerset Maugham said that he had two methods of overcoming this difficulty. While in his bath in the morning he tried to think out the first two sentences which helped him get started. But often this did not work. Then he resorted to a second method to conquer that first blank page. He started writing anything at all that entered his head, any sort of rubbish which might have helped fill part of the page. And suddenly, after about half a page was filled, something happened. The

Manuel Komroff, a native New Yorker, wrote 130 short stories and 13 novels in his lifetime. He was an editor for a publishing company and a teacher at Columbia University.

subconscious came forward and the thing was there. The real writing had begun. He then crossed out that half-page of rubbish and continued.

Conrad was not able to get started quite so easily. In fact, he often had a most desperate time, as you can read in one of his letters to his devoted friend Edward Garnett.

> I sit down religiously every morning, I sit down for eight hours every day—and the sitting down is all. In the course of that working day of eight hours I write three sentences which I erase before leaving the table in despair . . . . Sometimes it takes all my resolution and power of self-control to refrain from butting my head against the wall. I want to howl and foam at the mouth but I daren't do it for fear of waking that baby and alarming my wife. It's no joking matter. After such crises of despair I doze for hours still half-conscious that there is that story I am unable to write. Then I wake up, try again—and at last go to bed completely done up. So the days pass and nothing is done. At night I sleep. In the morning I get up with the horror of that powerlessness I must face through a day of vain efforts.

Unfinished business

If this happens to trained and experienced writers, it also happens to those of little experience. It presents a major writing problem. But it is not a hopeless problem, and it need not be as desperate as Conrad makes it out to be.

There are certain psychological principles which will be found useful if employed. For instance, finished business can be forgotten, but unfinished business remains uppermost in one's mind. It is as though the mind were trying hard to complete the thing which you did not finish. The unfinished part of your story will churn away in your brain, not the finished parts. This is most natural, and if you recognize this principle you may make it work for you. If unfinished business remains uppermost in the mind, why not leave your writing unfinished at the end of the day so that your mind may continue to dwell upon it overnight? Then, when you return to your work the next morning, you will know exactly how to continue.

This sounds fine, but is it really possible? Does it work? How?

The device is very simple. At the end of the day stop writing before you have completed that part of the story which you have clearly in mind. Stop quite a distance before you reach a chapter ending. Stop in the middle of a paragraph. And stop in the middle of a sentence.

In other words, you must purposely create interruption so that your work hangs unfinished, allowing your mind its usual play with unfinished business. Therefore it is best not to try to reach the end of a chapter before closing down for the day. There is, of course, a tendency to do this, for all the necessary things that would finish the chapter are clearly in mind. But wait. These things will still be in your mind on the following day. And if you drive on and conclude the chapter everything will be wound up, and the episode finished. After any conclusion a start is difficult.

The best place to stop, the very best, is right in the middle of a sentence. The next day, an unfinished sentence will finish itself quite easily. The idea of the sentence will be easily recaptured. And from this idea the next sentence is sure to follow. Your story is immediately in movement. This at once is encouraging and gives you confidence. The paragraph is soon finished and before long the chapter is done.

In this way the drive will be on. And in the forward rush, with creative steam, at pressure, and with fear put aside, the chances are that you will jump into the new chapter with full vigor, without timidity and in full control of all the forces necessary for your fiction.

Therefore, mad as it may sound, be sure to stop before you finish. If you do this you will find that more than half the battle of that agonizing problem of starting each new day will be solved.

In your own words

There are several other things which will help you get those sticky words flowing.

It is a good idea not to read over what you have written on the same day. It is better to rinse out the eye so that you can view your work with fresh vision. A fresh eye will see many mistakes. Another reason for not reading your day's work at once is the fact that words and ideas when read too often become worn and stale. They lose their sharp imprint and their sound becomes a little dulled. But reading them fresh the next morning, you will be reading them for the first time. They pick up your story and carry it along. And then suddenly you come to that place, the middle of an interrupted sentence, that may read: "Jack and Jill . . .," and it is very easy indeed to continue, for the thought is already there, and your ears are filled with the words, your own words, written the day before. "Jack and Jill went up the hill." And from that moment on you are off. The hurdle has been jumped.

Your own words are important. They are the words which you find will best express your thoughts. To get the sound of your own words into your ears and into your mouth is most essential. Even when you read words silently you seem to hear them in your ears and form them in your throat and mouth.

Your own words help you get started. And your own words are the ones which can best move your story ahead. The words of another author will not work for you. Therefore, the advice which was often given to writers, to read a page or two of the Bible or Shakespeare each morning, is very misleading. It was assumed that the writer, in difficulty, by reading a page or two of a good book would stimulate himself and induce a flow of words from within himself. Several writers I know have tried this method, but the results are disastrous.

In themselves the words of Shakespeare and the words of the Bible are supreme. But they are the instrument to give sound and articulation to the thoughts of Shakespeare and the Bible. They would not articulate the things you have to say. Your instrument may not be so well tuned as Shakespeare's, but it is the only one you have. And your own words are the only ones which can carry your ideas and further your story.

Another thing to avoid is the kind of advice which was given André Maurois by his writing master. He was advised to sit down and copy *Madame Bovary*, word for word, from the very beginning. He was assured that before he was finished with this task he would be an accomplished novelist. Needless to say, he never followed this stupid advice.

From Flaubert you can learn a good deal about Flaubert. But it is not important that you should write like Flaubert. It is more important that you should write like yourself. And you will never write like yourself if you take Flaubert's words and his cadences, which he used to express his ideas, and try to make them express your ideas.

The words of other authors may be finer words than your own, but stick to your own. Together with the unfinished sentence, rudely interrupted, your own words read over with a fresh eye will help you over that most trying moment, the start of the day's work.

Daily output

Some novelists spend only a few hours a day at the task of writing, while others put in many hours. Some find it better to work in the mornings when they are fresh, while others like the quiet of the hours at night. There is really no rule that applies to everyone.

Balzac usually spent twelve hours at his writing desk, from midnight until noon. Hawthorne felt he could compose best only in winter. He once wrote to a friend: "I am never good for anything in the literary way till after the first autumnal frost, which has somewhat such an effect on my imagination that it does on the foliage here about me—multiplying and brightening the hues." About two to four hours was Hawthorne's limit of work. After that he found that the mood upon which he depended was likely to vanish as he became tired.

Somerset Maugham also believed in a short working period. "Three hours of writing a day is enough. Darwin, I read somewhere," continued Maugham, "never worked more than three hours a day. If he could revolutionize the whole theory of evolution by working that length of time, three hours certainly should be long enough for me to write . . . . It takes too much out of you to write longer. Anyhow, a writer works all the time when he is away from his desk, absorbing impressions and making notes for writing he will do later."

Is three hours really enough? It depends upon what you can produce in the average three hours. If you can write the equivalent of a typewritten page or a little more in a single hour, then three hours will give you about a thousand words. This is not many words. And somehow or other a typewriter seems unnecessary for so few pages, say four, in three hours. One could almost write this number of words with a burnt match.

But let us see the amazing result that comes from steady accumulation. If you work steadily every day, and in each three-hour period produce about a thousand words, at the end of a year you will have three full-length novels, each 120,000 words in length. Perhaps three novels are two too many!

The power of accumulation

Balzac worked for twelve hours each day. He made many revisions and rewrote many pages. He even made extensive revisions in his proofs. All this took time and he worked very hard. It is true that there were some weeks and sometimes even months in the year when he left his desk and went traveling. But on the whole he worked very steadily year in and year out. And the accumulation produced an amazing result. He published over ninety volumes in twenty-seven years. This is a staggering amount.

Yet, if you analyzed it you would find that ninety volumes in twenty-seven years is roughly about three each year. And as French novels are often quite short—I would estimate his to average about fifty thousand words each—his production would, over the long span of years, average about 425 words each day. He wrote with a quill pen which he dipped in a pewter inkwell. This number of words today would fill only about a typewritten page and a half.

Such is the power of accumulation! This average page and a half each day added up to 90 volumes in 27 years.

At what conclusion do we arrive? A simple one: if you want results, employ the power of accumulation. Work every day. And every day you work try to accomplish at least that page and a half, a good page and a half, the very best you can produce.

The hours, however, are not so important as the quality of the ideas and words. And there are some novelists who never manage a disciplined routine. They will loaf about for months and suddenly with a great burst of energy will work madly for three or four months, and emerge with a fine novel. Sinclair Lewis was said to work in this manner. And so it is not possible to make a rule for working hours. Mathematical calculations seem a little removed from novel writing. In a way they are not too important. The important thing is the quality of the product. A writer without imagination, without inner feeling, is merely a laborer painfully arranging words on sheets of paper.

Between novels the writer will take time out to lie fallow and to rest up and brood about another book. This time should also be used for reading and research.

Charting accomplishments

It is clear that some writing routine must be established in order to produce that accumulation of effort and pages which will bring the novel to a successful termination. A stab at writing today and a lick-over next week will get you no-where.

To carry on, day after day, requires a certain amount of discipline. Hawthorne stayed in his room all morning. If he found he was unable to write, he spent the time reading. He records in his notebook: "This forenoon I began to write, and caught an idea by the tail, which I intend to hold fast, though it struggles to get free. As it was not ready to put on paper, I took up the *Dial*. . . ."

Balzac believed in sitting at his desk and using his time in a number of ways. He believed in strict discipline. "It is impossible for me to work when I have to break off and go out. I never work merely for one or two hours at a stretch." And Jack London imposed upon himself a kind of punishment. No matter what appointments he had made, he did not leave his house until he had done his 1,000 words for the day. Often, if he was really eager to go somewhere, he would get up extra early and get his 1,000 words done quickly. He would do them anyhow, good or bad, but they were done before he could bring himself to leave.

My own habits are a combination of discipline and laxity. There are whole months of moping around the house, and then suddenly a day arrives, and from that day on I will try to do 2,000 words a day. This is a lot of words and I do not always manage to accomplish so many, but I set 2,000 as the goal for the day's work. To help this along I use a calendar, and next to every day I place the number of words produced. A zero looks bad; a 500 does not look too good; but a 1,500 or a 2,000 is encouraging. During the first month of work I have very low scores on my calendar. There have often been three or four zeroes in a row. But this has been followed by good runs, a succession of days when the work flowed without interruption.

And in these periods, when the fiction is really flowing, there are some very fortunate days when, with little effort, I have been able to exceed that 2,000 mark, the goal for the day. Sometimes with luck one can do double this amount. But I have also noted that after a very productive day in which one seems to have exceeded all bounds, the next day, or sometimes even two or three days, will be quite blank. And nothing is more agonizing than a blank day. Having learned this lesson, I remain content with 2,000 words, and do not try to push much beyond this mark.

Discipline

To accomplish 2,000 words a day means that you must exclude almost everything from your life except eating and sleeping and thinking about your novel. For the day is not done when the words are done. These sometimes are written in two or three hours, though sometimes I have been at it six and eight or more hours. After your daily stint is done, the next day's work must be organized.

When you are working hard and steadily, and trying to hold the heat necessary for the creative flight, you find you will need a good deal of time away from your desk to brood, arrange, rub out, invent, add pieces and mold a hundred little things. You will probably need all the time when you are not writing, and even part of the night. Before you close your eyes you will be thinking about your scenes, your people, their actions, their words, the words they have already spoken, and the words you will want to record on the following day.

And the very moment you awake, your mind will be filled with these very same thoughts. Sometimes, oddly enough, a problem or difficulty which worried you before you closed your eyes will have solved itself by morning. How this happens is quite mysterious. Perhaps the characters have had something to say about their own destiny, and while you slept . . . I do not pretend to know, but whatever it is, when this thing happens, everything is all right; you are in the fever of work. And the chances are that you will accomplish something genuine, and possibly something of permanent value.

It is best not to attempt to read fiction by other novelists while you are writing fiction. Before you begin your novel it might be a very good idea to read as much as you like. Sir Walter Scott read hundreds of books, histories, essays and fiction, while he was mulling over a new novel. But as soon as he began writing he stopped reading.

Read a novel in bed at night and you will find it harder to begin writing on your own in the morning. This is quite easily explained. If your mind were on your own work at night, then the chances are that your work would still be in your mind in the morning. If, on the other hand, your mind is diverted at night to some other subject, then in the morning you will have the task of bringing it back to your own work. The outside reading has caused a mental interruption.

Discipline is necessary for the novelist in order to drive through against many diverting influences. You must learn to concentrate on your own writing and adjust your life so that it contributes to this most important task.

The fever of work

When the fever of work is upon you, the world that you have created and all its people will try to crowd out the world you are living in. They will take over your life. There is no cure for it but to resign yourself to that other world.

From this moment on, your work becomes something different. It is no less difficult; it is quite pleasant. There is a drive behind it and the drive pushes you on. You have less resistance to the labor. In fact, there is a pleasant compulsion about it. You may be compelled to rise from bed in the middle of the night to go to your desk and change a line or two in one of your pages. At any other time you would certainly resent this inconvenience, but not now. In the fever of work all kinds of wonderful thoughts crowd into your steaming mind. And many of these must be speared at once. Keep pencil and paper next to your bed to record any of these random ideas.

Anatole France had a system quite his own. He kept a pot under his bed, and often during the night he would light the lamp and scribble a line on a bit of paper. It was easy to file these scraps in the pot right within reach beneath the bed. When the pot was full he would bring the scraps of paper into his study. These little scraps of paper contributed to such novels as *Penguin Island, Revolt of the Angels* and *Thais*.

Such midnight interruptions may sound like an invasion of one's personal comfort. They are. But you will not object to them. They are part of your own world, the world of your creation, invading that other world, the world of mere existence. These worlds are related; but they are also worlds apart. You have endured the world of reality for years. But now you have another world in which to live, the world of your imagination. The sheer novelty of the thing makes it attractive. And the fact that it is your own world, grown from your seed, will cause you to nurture it.

By writing possessed

During this time you will find it will take you longer to fall asleep. But during those quiet moments of repose, in a half-dream state of drowsiness, the world of your creation will come vividly alive. The characters of your novel will stand out boldly before you and act up in a most audacious manner. They will live again through some of the scenes you have already recorded. And you will also see them act out new scenes which you may want to record. They will confront each other, quarrel with each other and then suddenly forgive and forget. They will make love and confess to you. They will come to you for advice and lay their troubles at your feet. They are without fear and in your presence without shame. And occasionally they may even turn on you and pointing an accusing finger cry out: "You! You made me like this! You wanted me depraved! You got me into this mess! Now you get me out."

When this happens it really means that your characters have come alive. You will not dismiss them too easily. They have serious claims on you. They are now part of your life and living in your home. You must listen to them. For their accusations are not unjust, and you will have to do something for them.

In these wonderful days, when your people take over your home, they also take over a good part of your life and work. You will find that during this time you work long hours willingly, and accomplish many pages. Your people help you. There is a compulsion that drives you on and you are willing to be driven on.

There is a pleasant desperation about the whole business. The conflict of a dual existence no longer seems to bother you, for more and more are you living in that other world. And all those marvelous characters of your creation are now with you. They are supporting you and you are supporting them. The ordinary things of life are not very important now. You are working in a fever and that deep wonderful subconscious is churning up that mysterious well which Renan described as containing "a thousand years of reveries." In other words, you are possessed. And you are writing well. The angels are on your side. You cannot fail.

How real may a character become? Almost as real as anything born in our humdrum factual world.

Balzac had a habit of speaking about his characters to his intimates as though they really existed. He would, for instance, say: "I had a letter from Colonel Chabert this morning. You know, he's found a lawyer at last who will handle his case. The lawyer is a rather shady character; I happen to know him. I wish he were more respectable. But he believes in the Colonel and is advancing him money for new clothes. And today they are going to send a letter to the Colonel's former wife. I must be sure to tell them to register this letter. You know what she is like? She might deny receiving it. Never in my life did I know a woman who could lie so easily. The evil is so deeply rooted in her nature that I am certain she will win out in the end, and the poor Colonel . . . Well, anyway, he has a lawyer now. At last!"

Balzac's characters were real to him. They were alive. They fully occupied his mind. And they are alive when you read of them today a century later in the printed pages of his novels.

Balzac was no exception. When Thackeray was writing *The History of Pendennis*, his daughter once discovered him with his eyes laden with tears. "I have just killed off Helen," he said sadly in explanation.

Imagine the state of Dickens' home on the night that Little Nell died. Many letters had come to his desk from people reading the book in its monthly installments, all begging him to spare the life of Little Nell! But no. Little Nell had to die. And on the Sunday following the publication of the chapters describing her end, all the churches of London announced her death with the tolling of their bells.

No greater tribute was ever paid to a character in a novel. And perhaps one can even say that no greater tribute was ever paid a novelist. For the person of his creation became not only real to him, but real to a vast public. Little Nell belonged to the people of London. And when she died, they mourned.

Bad days and blocks

Every novelist has a bad day now and again when it seems quite impossible for him to make any progress. Sometimes, he has even two or three bad days in a row.

The reason for these bad days is sometimes inexplicable. Do what you may, not a word can you squeeze from your dry mind. You have seen how Conrad describes this agony. Now, what is there to do?

There is a lot that can be done. The first thing is to stand by. Hold the fort. There may be an attack at any moment. And you must be on hand. Do not go to a ball game. And do not go to the movies for inspiration.

Stay close to the desk. Hold to that self-imposed discipline. It is a good idea to sit close to the writing section of your table or desk and examine the material you have at hand related to the work in progress. Not only will your desk book suggest things which possibly you have omitted, but it may suggest a scene which you might begin at once. Also, a critical examination of your chart of character appearances will show you exactly where you have left your people. And you might discover that now is the very moment for that character, the one who promised so much in an early chapter, to reappear. Or by the process of compounding, which we will soon describe, you may discover that a certain combination of characters has not yet happened to come together. And perhaps now would be the time. All this you can see very clearly by examining your chart of character appearances. This may help break the deadlock.

But even if nothing should come of it, the time thus employed is not wholly wasted, for it has all been concentrated on the work at hand. And critical study will make you more familiar with the problems before you.

When all this has been faithfully done, and still there is no possibility of your dragging out a single string of words from your enfeebled mind, then I would suggest that you go back and read over your last written pages, a good number of them, say 30 or 40. The trouble may lie further back than you know. Some false note may have crept in and caused your story to veer in its direction. At any rate, even if you cannot locate the trouble, reading over your own work is a good thing to do. Your own words, your deep individual inner voice is good to hear. This thing which I call your own "silent sound" is more likely to stir up a feeling for writing than anything else in the whole world. One's own words often prove intoxicating.

You should not consider yourself really stuck unless a whole week or more has passed without your having made any progress in spite of earnest efforts. Then things are really bad.

Is there anything that can possibly be done to overcome this desperate situation? Yes. The diary method will accomplish wonders. It has worked for me and it has worked for a number of my friends. And what it has done for us it may also do for you.

The great virtue of this device is that it accomplishes its results not from the advice of an outsider, not from a doctor who treats sick novels, but from the inner force of your own story material. Its honesty is its great virtue.

Real people

Here is how it works.

First of all, make a list of your important characters. Let us assume these characters are: Mary, John, Pop Hubbard, who is Mary's father, Mother Hubbard, Joe and a redhead named Alice. These are the six main people in your novel.

Now buy for yourself, at the stationer's, some small notebooks, the kind that are inexpensive and will fit into your pocket. You will need one for each character, and an extra one besides. The extra one is very important. Mark each notebook with the name of one of your characters. And for each character start a personal and intimate diary.

It is to be assumed, of course, that these people have already appeared in your novel, that some of them have been together and that they have already had some activity. Some of them know each other. Certainly Mary knows her father and mother and she probably also has met John. Therefore, it is not necessary to go back to the very start of the novel, but allow your diaries to begin with the last scene which you were able to write before that agony of being stuck came upon you.

The past you know, and each of your characters knows his own past, as you have already recorded it. The present starts with your last scene. The future, with a little patience, is certain to unfold.

You assume that your people are real people. They too are in a hole, and will be just as anxious to get out as you are anxious to get them out. And so they will all go to work. And they will work hard. Each records what happened on that last day, the day of which you have already written. And each records it in the first person, from an internal point of view. Each records intimately what he has seen or heard, and also his innermost feelings.

You are certain to discover at once that each has confessed in his diary a little more than you narrated in your last chapter or episode. And those characters who did not appear in your last chapter—they too will be working on their diaries and record for you exactly where they were on this day and what they were doing.

Here at once a new and unexpected note has entered your story. Your own people tell you something about which you never thought of inquiring. This excursion that they made to the neighboring town, or wherever it was they went on this day, may or may not be important.

Now when you have finished the account of this single day for each of your half-dozen people, and done it as well as you could, then you start recording the next day of their lives. And when all six characters have accounted for the next day, through their inner thoughts and actions confessed in the diary, then it is time to take up that extra book which, you remember, I said would be quite important.

In this blank book, which you might mark "God," you will assume full omniscience and look down from Olympian heights. You will look down on your people and record, not what they said they did, but what you actually saw them do. You will have sly remarks and opinions on their actions, their speech, and even their secret thoughts. You know their past better than they do, you know their present, you can see the dilemma and storm which is coming, and you have a pretty good idea as to what will happen on the following day. But you will restrain yourself and allow your characters to act out the next day for themselves before you remark about it.

You see at a glance how important this extra diary is. And you see also that in two days, with some hard work, you have established each of your characters as a living person and even added an outside viewpoint, a kind of commentator or narrator who sees all, hears all and has a philosophy about the whole business.

The third day you will record in the same manner as you have recorded the previous two. And on the fourth day, or fifth day, something quite astonishing is very likely to happen. The whole thing will suddenly begin to take shape. The dark cloud will break and a flood of light pour through. Your first impulse will be to throw away the diaries and get back to the actual pages of the novel. But on second thought you will discover that the little diaries contain valuable things, and these, whole pages and pages, scenes and dialogues, you will want to save for the actual pages of your book.

This method you will find will overcome that great difficulty of being stuck. It will do it quite easily and in short time. Sometimes only two days of diary writing will be necessary. Never have I known it to go on for longer than a week.

Notebooks and diaries

by Hallie and Whit Burnett

There is little difference between keeping a notebook and a diary, for the writer. Granted, the diary is often confessional and private, and the notebook more often records the thoughts, aphorisms, and perhaps travel notes less subjectively observed. In the end the impulse is to put down feelings, opinions, the effects of other individuals on our lives or on the world around us. Virginia Woolf in her *Writer's Diary*, for example, tells only a little more about her personal life and the demands of her society than Henry James in his more obviously literary *Notebooks*, in which he also records names of guests at dinner parties, and the world of his time, while clearly developing his ideas for his stories and novels step by step.

Virginia Woolf wrote from Juan les Pins in May 1933: "Yes, I thought, I will make a note of that face—the face of the woman stitching a very thin, lustrous green silk at a table in a restaurant where we lunched at Vienne. She was like fate—a consummate mistress of all the arts of self-preservation: hair rolled and lustrous; eyes so nonchalant; nothing could startle her; there she sat stitching her green silk with people going and coming all the time; she not looking; yet knowing, fearing nothing; expecting nothing—a perfectly equipped middle-class Frenchwoman." Virginia Woolf was preparing for her work as much as Henry James in his *Notebooks*.

On a January Saturday in 1895 James wrote:

Saturday, January 12th, 1895. Note here the ghost-story told me at Addington (evening of Thursday 10th), by the Archbishop of Canterbury: the mere

---

Hallie and *Whit Burnett*, *well known fiction experts, drew on their long experience as co-editors of* Story Magazine *in their varied careers. Whit Burnett was a reporter, city editor, instructor in advanced short story writing at Columbia University, and writer and editor of more than 35 books. Hallie Burnett is the author of seven books and co-editor of 12 anthologies. She has taught creative writing at Sarah Lawrence College and Hunter College.*

vague, undetailed, faint sketch of it—being all he had been told (very badly and imperfectly), by a lady who had no art of relation, and no clearness: the story of the young children (indefinite number and age) left to the care of servants in an old country-house, through the death, presumably, of parents. The servants, wicked and depraved, corrupt and deprave the children; the children are bad, full of evil, to a sinister degree. The servants *die* (the story vague about the way of it) and their apparitions, figures, return to haunt the house *and* children, to whom they seem to beckon, whom they invite and solicit, from across dangerous places, the deep ditch of a sunk fence, etc.—so that the children may destroy themselves, lose themselves, by responding, by getting into their power. So long as the children are kept from them, they are not lost; but they try and try and try, these evil presences, to get hold of them. It is a question of the children 'coming over to where they are.' It is all obscure and imperfect, the picture, the story, but there is a suggestion of strangely gruesome effect in it. The story to be told—tolerably obviously—by an outside spectator, observer.

Not until three years later, in 1888, did James write *The Turn of the Screw*, which appeared in a *Collier's Weekly* of that year. Remember James's incisive formula on how to create a sense of evil: "Make him [the reader] think the evil, make him think it for himself, and you are released from weak specifications."

Aphorisms and observations

A notebook or a diary need not be written in every day, although some pattern of recording is desirable.

Some write in notebooks only when they are away from home, traveling, recording new impressions for which ordinarily no hook of memory might be found. Some write only when they are not working. George Sand wrote in her journals when she was not in love; when she was "normal"—that is, "desperately in love"—she wrote her novels.

Others wait until the love affair is ended—"emotion remembered in tranquility," as Wordsworth has said.

At certain periods in our lives we find ourselves more introspective, having recognizably literary thoughts and conclusions and no one to share them with; at other times we may simply record events, trusting to memory to bring back the whole of the picture (but memory does not always humor us).

The notebook, being private, permits us to draw no morals, obey no rules, censure no extravagances. We write for ourselves only and need show no one what we have written. Sometimes, years later, a notebook will be published to the benefit of other writers; sometimes, like my Aunt Margaret's diary, it will be kept for a lifetime, recording weather, events of the day, family events, and then at the end no one cares and the journal is thrown in the fire.

For the writer, first impressions are to be seized upon, and the act of writing in a journal often ensures that these impressions are permanently recorded. We write a quick paragraph about a character, and do not look at this again; but years later we may find we have written about her, described her, so we think, from some image in our mind—then find we have simply used from memory the description we recorded long ago.

Van Wyck Brooks has said that the "writer is important only by dint of the territory he colonizes," and his colonizing for a writer simply means that he has put down impressions and observations in words which are his own.

Self-criticism: "At forty," wrote Virginia Woolf in her diary, "I am beginning to learn the mechanism of my own brain—how to get the greatest amount of pleasure out of it. The secret: I think always so to continue that work is pleasant."

Observations of life: Coleridge in his notebooks observes the behavior of children, reports his dreams, and queries about natural phenomena, making as well philosophical and psychological speculations. He also records "recipes for beef stew, and details of an illness."

Chekhov, on the other hand, makes aphorisms:

"Women deprived of the company of men pine; men deprived of the company of women become stupid."

"A woman is fascinated not by art, but by the noise made by those who have to do with art"(sic!).

"N. has written a good play; no one praises him or is pleased. They all say: 'We'll see what he writes next.'"

"A man married to an actress, during a performance of a play in which his wife was acting, sat in a box with beaming face and from time to time got up and bowed to the audience."

How much Anton Chekhov actually used the notes in stories and plays is less easy to determine than with some writers, such as Arnold Bennett, who not only wrote out his plots in his journals, but frequently scolded himself for wasting his time. But it does not matter. We may not know how or if we shall use this notebook writing in our stories or novels, but making recording a habit will add another tool to our powers of expression, our uses of observation, and the total value of the material we accumulate.

Mark Twain, Katherine Mansfield, Stendhal (Henri Beyle), André Gide, Anthony Trollope—all these and many others have left behind some of their most piquant words in notebooks, journals, and diaries, and sometimes in letters, all of which show the writers' minds most intimately at work.

Better, of course, to write our own observations if we intend being writers; but to stimulate our thoughts and creative juices it helps to read these others, to feel a kinship with Virginia Woolf when she wrote: "December 28th, 1945. It's all very well to write that date in a nice clear hand, because it begins this new book."

A unique production was Dostoevsky's *Diary of a Writer*, described by Pushkin as:

His mind's dispassioned observations
And doleful records of his heart.

In his published diary Dostoevsky wrote down everything: the political situation, appreciation and criticism of other writers, reminiscences. Treasure such observations as:

Take a Russian drunkard and compare him, let us say, with a German drunkard: the Russian is more abominable than the German; still, the German drunkard is unmistakably more stupid and ridiculous than the Russian. The Germans are pre-eminently a self-conceited people; they are proud of themselves. In a drunken German these fundamental national traits increase with the measure of beer consumed. He gets home drunk as a fiddler, and yet proud of himself. The Russian toper likes to drink from grief, and to weep. And even while he assumes bold airs, he does not triumph, but is merely turbulent. Invariably, he will recall some offense and will start reproaching the offender, whether or not he be present. Insolently, he will, perhaps, argue that he is something next to a general; he swears bitterly and, if people refuse to believe him, he will finally sound an alarm and cry out for help. Still, the reason why he is so ugly and why he cries out for help is that, in the innermost part of his tipsy soul, he is unquestionably convinced that he is no "general" at all, but merely a nasty sot, and that he has become filthier than a beast.

But I am a novelist, and it seems that one "story" I did invent myself. Why did I say "it seems," since I know for certain that I did actually invent it; yet I keep fancying that this happened somewhere, once upon a time, precisely on Christmas Eve, in *some* huge city during a bitter frost.

On Sundays, toward evening (on weekdays they are not seen at all) a great many of these absolutely sober people engaged all week in work, go out into the streets. Precisely, they come out for a walk. I have noticed that they never go on the Nevsky: mostly, they stroll near their homes, or they walk along "leisurely," returning with their families after visiting some people. (It seems there are also a great many married workers in Petersburg.) They walk along sedately and with awfully serious faces, as if it were not just a walk, conversing very little with each other, especially husbands with their wives— almost silently, but invariably in their holiday clothes.

Their clothing is old and bad—on women, it is many-colored: but every-thing is cleaned and washed for the holiday, intentionally—perhaps, for this hour . . . .

The most annoying part is that they really and seriously imagine, it seems, that by strolling in this manner they are providing themselves with genuine Sunday recreation.

Quick takes and quotes

From the Notebooks of F. Scott Fitzgerald:

Then there's Emily. You know what happened to her; one night her husband came home and told her she was acting cold to him, but that he'd fix that up. So he built a bonfire under her bed, made up of shoes and things, and set fire to it. And if the leather hadn't smelled so terrible, she'd have been burned to death.

We can't just let our worlds crash around us like a lot of dropped trays.

In the deep locker-room of the earth.

Days of this February were white and magical, the nights were starry and crystalline. The town lay under a cold glory.

New York's flashing, dynamic good looks, its tall man's quick-step.

All of a sudden the room struck like a clock.

He passed an apartment house that jolted his memory. It was on the outskirts of town, a pink horror built to represent something, somewhere, so cheaply and sketchily that whatever it copied the architect must have long forgotten.

The restaurant with a haunted corner.

Observations in this author's notebook after completing some short stories:

One must have an *arresting first paragraph*. A fumbling, or too wordy first paragraph can tire the reader before he begins; worse still, he may miss some valuable information.

Let your mind be *working on your title* as you go along.

Tell yourself the story first, as far as you are able. But do not complete too thoroughly, for then you will have the feeling it has already been done.

Do not resist the suddenly *irrational* in a story: that's imagination at work.

Find the *key emotion*: this may be all you need know to find your short story.

Search for repetition of *words*. The mind has a curious obsession at times with single words.

Trust: the *length* of a story follows naturally its development, if you relax. One need not be arbitrary about word length.

Pace. Keep the pace, never let the attention wander. Like a public speaker, keep on talking even if you are not quite sure of what you are going to say. The subconscious helps. Anything is better than a sudden drop in temperature, a lack of sweat from start to finish, or at any point in between.

Tension: must be held at all times in the short story.

Ending. Know when you have reached the right moment to stop. Use instinct here; develop your sensitivity to the end of a thought, to the climax and its significance. This is no more than developing your wit. There are several lengths at which to snip off your narrative, but only one will fit *that* story.

Read back, read back, read back. Go over work coldly, mercilessly for sentimentality, lush writing, grammatical errors, tedious dialogue, lack of wit, repetition, phrases and clauses out of place . . . . But also go over it emotionally, sensitively, *feelingly*, mindlessly, for that is how your reader will expect it to hold him.

Speak your prose.

Turbulence and triumphs

From students' notebooks, Sarah Lawrence College, 1961. Reprinted from *Story*:

When one is young and susceptible to poetic letters from delightfully neurotic young men, one must be careful to distinguish between those who write beautiful things and those who write things beautifully.

Nothing is good in excess, including moderation.

There is no greater fanatic than the man who stands solidly in the middle of the road.

It's not that I don't like him; but when we're together, I'm bored with myself.

Too many women I know are oval and round: I want to be a thousand corners, a geometric dream of squares and lines, corners never blunted, never sanded. I want to be a line that goes on and on and turns and moves to right and left and up and down and forward; knowing where I'm going, but sometimes going somewhere else, to some new corner, darker, greater, not a circle, softly twisting, mincing, this way, that, ending up just where it started.
                                                                        —Nancy Weber

I am sitting in the room again, surrounded by things that have been in it my whole three years at school. There really is a large part of me here, although sometimes I have a hard time trying to find it. And then that wretched girl, who didn't understand, came in the other day, and said: "Your room looks just the same way it did the first time I met you. Haven't you ever thought of changing it?" How could I tell her I hadn't found myself in it yet? I bet she hasn't found herself in her room; that must be why she changes it all the time.

Change is excitement, be it for bad or good.

Another long subway ride back to the middle of town. There was a woman sitting at the end of the car dressed from bottom to top in heavy black wool clothes. She could have been riding through Russia; especially with the babushka on her head, pulled almost over her eyes. The leatherlike texture of her face was everywhere covered with wrinkles and lines. She was so incongruous in that modern-day coach, beside the freshly painted teenagers, in their light cotton dresses, who stood at the other end snickering about a sign over their heads . . . .

We could *write* of that night, but it would never be the same as it is when we *think* about it.

                                                                        —Pamela Howard

We marched into N.Y. all dressed alike—tights, black skirts, etc . . . . I don't know why we're here, although it is quite pleasant. It's raining outside. Dodo is wearing a wedding ring—I wonder why. We're all sitting here listening to "The Man with the Golden Arm," and reading love comics . . . .

She was so conscious of his physical handicap that she handicapped herself . . . .

The reason why it's nice to be an adult is that there aren't any more grown-ups around.

—Sally Clay

No desire is as pressing as the desire to desire.

The plebe at West Point is like a gray rug with a black stripe: stepped on, crushed and dull.

—Meredith Monk

How to organize a book for children and young adults

by Lee Wyndham

No matter how brilliant your mental faculties, you cannot carry in your mind the multitude of details that go into the writing of a full-length book.

You have a larger cast of characters whose main problem is more complex. There are secondary themes involving additional people who are involved with the main problem. And there are more scenes—and more word space for you to move around in, which is part of the fun of writing a book. You don't feel cramped by the number of words in which to tell your tale.

At the same time, the sheer quantity of the words you are allowed can prove awesome to someone who has written only short stories. I grew up to full-length books by writing three, four, and five-part serials. Learning how to think these through, outline and synopsize them helped me to develop an organized book plan.

Is your idea book-worthy?

Before embarking on a book project, test your idea for its worth. *Is it big enough for a book?*

It would be difficult to stretch a girl's concern with "a date for the junior prom" into a full-length book, but with a fresh twist the idea might make a fine short story. On the other hand, the story of a girl who comes to New York to make a career in fashion could scarcely be covered in 3,000 words. It *requires* book-length treatment.

How to think BOOK

Full-length junior books usually run from 20,000 to 60,000 words, depending

---

The late **Lee Wyndham** *was an author, critic, lecturer, teacher, freelance editor and writing consultant. She wrote over 50 books and published more than 200 short stories, articles and serials in 30 national magazines. Her long and varied career began as a result of a broken leg, during which time she wrote her first book.*

on the age level you're aiming for. But don't let the number of words terrify you. Don't even think of the number of pages you must produce if such thoughts bother you. Instead, consider the ten to twelve pages you have been accustomed to write for a short story. That's about the length of a chapter: 2,500 to 3,000 words. *Think of your book a chapter at a time.* Even if you plan 20 chapters, by writing one chapter a week you will have a book in 20 weeks. Viewed in this way the whole prospect becomes less frightening.

Your current project

Once you have chosen your book project, label a file folder with the working title of your project. Into this folder put all the odds and ends pertaining to it—newspaper clippings, articles, pictures, brochures, and notes that you don't know what to do with—yet. Collect any books, magazines or other reference material that you'll need close to your working area. A small bookcase on wheels or a serving table with two or three tiers is handy for this purpose.

Your work book

Select a loose-leaf notebook of a convenient size, with large rings so that you can put lots of paper into it. My favorite takes 6 by 9½ inch fillers. Use linen tabs that you can cut yourself, or notebook dividers that come in different colors to index the various departments.

Below is a description of how I divide my work book, but you may decide to label and organize the sections differently. Every professional writer eventually develops his own system for ordering his work.

Tab 1. Title—I use a page to list titles as they come to mind, even when I begin with one; along the way something better may present itself.

Then I use a page for a variety of pertinent data:

a. *Deadline:* the date when I hope to have the manuscript completed. Under any circumstances, it is psychologically advisable to establish a deadline for yourself. Like a professional, you work toward a definite goal.

b. *Length:* Skipping a couple of lines, I set down the number of words this book should have: 30, 40, 50, 60,000. This is to plant the figure in my subconscious, but not to brood upon. Some of my editors like short books, others long ones. The average is about 200 pages and about 50,000 words.

c. *Theme:* Again skipping a few lines, I leave a space to write in theme—when it is clear to me.

d. *Chapters:* The number of chapters I expect to have—usually I aim for twenty, but the result may be as few as eighteen or as many as twenty-two.

e. *Date when actual writing is begun:*

f. *Date when first draft is finished:* (As a matter of statistics, it is interesting to have a record of how long it has taken you to write your various books. Besides, after you are published, people will ask you.)

If you are very methodical, you may want a separate page for a work log, a record of your day-by-day output. This may be simply a date and the number of words written on that day, with a total for the week.

What should be your quota? That depends on you—your creativity, your experience—not to mention your typing skill. Usually I can do better than 2,000 words a day, and once I wrote a 40,000-word book in ten days, but that was a kind of miracle! (In nonfiction I work much more slowly. And Elizabeth George Speare, two-time winner of the Newbery award, told me that she considers herself lucky if she gets 500 words done in a day. Each of us must work at our own pace.)

How many hours should you spend writing? That again depends on your personal makeup and circumstances. Many literary successes in the juvenile and adult fields actually write only three hours a day. But as Somerset Maugham once commented:

> . . . the author does not only write when he is at his desk; he writes all day long, when he is thinking, when he is reading, when he is experiencing; everything he sees and feels is significant to his purpose and, consciously or unconsciously, he is forever storing his impressions.

Tab 2. Plot—the story plan. When this is clear to me, I type it in here in synopsis form. To me, the synopsis is what the preliminary sketch is to an artist. I set down only the essential features of my story in a brief, general account. But long before I write even a trial synopsis, I start working in the other sections of my work book.

Tab 3. Situation—The several pages included in this section usually get written first, for here I put down the things that happen before my story actually takes off. These are the circumstances that *cause* my main character to take action: the difficulties that set up a pattern of discontent, the desire or challenge to accomplish some aim. These are the bits and pieces from which my beginning will spring.

And here lies a *difference between the short story and the book:* In the short story the problem is stated at once and the main character goes to work on it immediately. But in the full-length book the reasons which lead up to the problem are usually built up first; then the problem is stated, and the main character proceeds to solve it.

Tab 4. Problem(s)—Here I detail the main problem of my main character—the thing the story is about—the thing he or she must solve through personal effort and against almost overwhelming odds. Please notice the *almost.* No matter how serious the problem, or how close to life-or-death the struggle, the problem should be one the main character *can* do something about. In stories for young people, our characters are not usually allowed to beat their heads against the granite walls of impossible odds. There should be a chink in the wall of opposition which the main character can find and widen for the triumphant leap to victory. (There are, of course, occasional and acceptable "unhappy" endings.)

Into this section I also put all sorts of incidents and other problems and complications and developments that might be used in the course of the story. Not chronologically, but just as they occur to me. Some of these will be used, some discarded, but all are useful in getting me wound up in my story. These are the items I refer to constantly as I begin to develop my story. I take the pages out of the loose-leaf binder, shuffle them about, and whenever I use an item, I cross it out, thus reducing the bulk of notes.

Tab 5. Chapters—In this section I write down the numerals from one through twenty (or whatever number of chapters I think I'll have), with a few lines between on the page and a *wide,* two-inch margin at the left. (The margin is for a specific purpose, so keep it in mind.) Next to the numerals I shall eventually put either a chapter heading or a working title to serve as a clue to what the chapter is about, should I need to look up some point in the manuscript.

Then I allow a page for each individual chapter, where I can put down what might happen. But until my plot is set these ideas are very tentative, subject to change or discard. Once the plot is set, I become more positive about the chapter happenings—but not inflexible. Characters have a way of taking over the story, once you breathe life into them. They can work out their own destinies, a phenomenon of which the author should take advantage.

I do not include any dialogue unless it is something especially witty that I don't want to forget.

While setting down chapter incidents, I try to think in terms of drama, scene interest, setting, action, emotion. I write in detail about a third or even half of the chapters before beginning to write the story. The last half can be outlined later, based on how the book evolves. But of course, before I ever get to this writing stage, I must know the ending and the probable climax scene. Otherwise there cannot be a complete plot outline to work from.

Although chapter titles are almost always used in books for young children, they are not necessary for teenagers. Whenever you do use them, don't give away the story through chapter headings which are too revealing, such as "Kip Finds the Treasure," or "Judy Wins the Prize." Even the youngest child is annoyed when suspense is ruined in this way.

Time—In your planning, decide on the length of time your story will cover. *Make this as short as possible, because a short period (or a time limit to accomplish what must be done) intensifies interest and drama.* It also automatically affects the pace in which you write. A brisk pace conveys the sense of immediacy, of urgency, and is always preferable to the slow, leisurely one.

Books for young people should not have long time lapses covering years in the main character's life. A month, a year, one summer, even a period of a few days is far more likely to hold the reader's interest. The exception applies to career books, where the main character's success must be kept within the realm of plausibility. Too rapid a success for your hero will make your story unbelievable.

Be sure to establish the historical period in which your story takes place—past, present, or future (as in a fantasy); and the chronological time that will be involved, as "from May to December." Jot down the time covered in every chapter; the season, the month, the day of the week, even the hour(s), if pertinent. *Making the reader aware of the passage of time adds to the reality of your story.*

For a quick check of the time involved at any point, note it in the *wide* margin to the left of your numerical chapter listing, or use an extra work book page to list the time sequences as your story develops. In that case make an extra tab and put this just before the chapter tab so you can find it easily. The important thing is not to slip into Friday if your action is taking place on Tuesday, or into May if your action is still taking place in April.

Historicals—If yours is a story about a period in history, you must be especially careful of the chronology. In this case, put in a tab labeled *Historical Chronology* and consult it frequently during the planning and writing.

Tab 6. Characters—As my characters evolve, I make a list of them in order of their importance, choosing their names with the greatest of care and juggling these until I feel they are exactly right for the people in *this* story.

Then I assemble them into family groups on another page, for easy reference. Next I allow a page or more for each important character's delineation. Half a page may do for minor story actors. At the top of each character's page, I tabulate pertinent data such as age, coloring, eyes, hair, build, physical characteristics—so that I can find them quickly if I should forget what someone on page 75 looks like when I want to insert a bit of description to refresh the reader's memory.

Then I jot down chronology of birth, and anything important that might have happened to the story actors to color their personalities, create their social attitudes, establish their goals, and in short, make them what they are at the opening of the story.

Finally I write the individual character sketches which I hope will change my "types" into flesh-and-blood people, with problems, goals, emotions, and reactions to all the other characters around them. It is important to know exactly what each character thinks and feels about every other character in the story. In each character sketch I immerse myself in that particular person and view the rest of his world through his eyes.

Working with the characters in this way can be most fruitful plot-wise. Each one can make a spontaneous contribution—and with the *Problems(s)* and *Situations* sections in the work book, none of these ideas will be lost.

Tab 7. Background—Here I note down everything that I'll need for the setting of my story in general, and for the individual chapters and scenes. This may include layout sketches of grounds, streets, towns, topography of the land, house-plans— the arrangement and furnishings of rooms—the things of life.

Tab 8. Research—The importance of this section cannot be over-emphasized. It is what makes your story "authentic," whether the setting is in the immediate present or the very distant past. Usually, I prefer to use a separate notebook. However, if comparatively few notes are required for a project, the research can go directly into the work book, along with a page for bibliography and one for authorities, listing all the books and people I may have consulted while preparing to write.

Tab 9. Check—Even the most careful research can leave a trail of question marks in the actual writing. Rather than stop the creative flow to look anything up or re-check a fact that I've put down somewhere, I make a note in this section and find the answer at a more convenient time. Once I write the question down, it no longer nags and I can go on with the work I should be doing.

Tab 10. Inserts—This is for additional useful information that I think of after I have started the actual writing. Background details, some bits of character business, anything at all that I may want to put already written into the story is safe here until I'm ready to use it.

Tab 11. Words and Phrases—This, too, is a "safe deposit" section—for anything that might add sparkle to my writing: figures of speech, which do not always occur to the writer at the moment he needs them; bits of dialogue that can make the characters sound more witty; quotations; etc.

. . . And one to grow on!

There is one more section—at the *back* or my work book. It is a duplicate set of the front tabs, for the capture of any ideas I may get for my *next* project while working on *this* one. As a professional writer, I always have plans for at least one book beyond the one in work. Whenever I finish the current project, I simply move the back section into the front, and make ready another set of tabs for the project to follow.

The work book is not only a more efficient project organizer, but it is also an idea generator. By providing yourself with definite sections to work in, you always have a place to put down whatever comes into your mind. As you write in the different sections you can *see* and *feel* your story grow and develop and quicken with life. The characters clamor to be released to their adventuring, and at last *you* are ready and eager to let them—and *write!*

The short short

by Vera Henry

The short short story is like the heart of an artichoke. The incidents leading up to the event, the long passages of description, all the unnecessary words and gestures have been peeled away. What is left should be pure story.

It has a beginning which lures the reader like a sideshow barker. It has a middle which develops the story and a conclusion that should not leave the reader feeling he has been cheated. It should have not only form, but content. It is not to be confused with the anecdote. An anecdote or vignette is the sort of thing people tell at parties. It may be interesting enough, but it is incomplete. It is a fragment—the handle of a cup.

The short short story is exactly that—a miniature story that is a whole. Within the limits of two thousand words or less, it attempts to throw a bright revealing light upon a situation and the people involved in that situation. The conclusion curves like a ring back toward the beginning.

The short short must be compact. It covers a brief period of telescoped time. It uses as few scenes and characters as possible. Every word must have a purpose. It does not need to be meager. The strong words, the vivid description and simile can say as much as paragraphs. Dylan Thomas did that with phrases like—"the snow-bandaged town"—"a small, dry, egg-shell voice"—"boys catlicked their hands and faces"—"trams that hissed like ganders."

It helps to envision the short short as if it were a play being produced by a director on a low budget. Without sacrificing quality, he tries to keep the action limited perhaps to a single set or two. He uses only absolutely essential characters.

Vera Henry has contributed over 300 short stories and articles to major magazines, many of which have been reprinted in anthologies and translated into foreign languages. She has also written adult and juvenile novels, which were made into TV and radio plays. A teacher of creative writing and lecturer at writers' conferences, Mrs. Henry is also a Writer's Digest Correspondence School instructor.

Two or three are perhaps most satisfactory. Too many can confuse the reader. There is not room for the sound development of several characters. For this reason the characters used must not be overly similar. Their traits should contrast or conflict. Even the names should begin with different letters and the sounds vary.

Which subjects are best?

Not all story ideas are suitable to the short short. Some are too strong to be confined within such tight limits. The story with a complicated plot or one that depends on a detailed knowledge of the background does not belong here. The O'Henry surprise twist is not used as often now but it is sometimes effective in short short form, if the conclusion comes naturally and without distortion. Suspense stories that demand a fast, smashing pace can be done as short shorts. So can humor, or the warm story with strong reader identification but too frail a plot to spin out into a longer length.

In the April, 1980 *Redbook*, there is a short short story, "At the Center A Memory," by Margaret A. Robinson. This is the story of a college student who is unable to accept the reality of her father's death. His funeral seems unreal. When she returns to college she keeps expecting a phone call or letter from him. She thinks she sees him on the street.

She goes home at Easter. The house seems just the same. She looks at her parents' big bed that had room for her brother, herself and the Sunday papers. She remembers her father would have only white sheets and shirts. She opens the closet to inspect his clothes. They are gone, his side of the closet empty.

At her cry, her mother hurries into the room. She says for weeks she couldn't get rid of the clothes, thinking somehow he would need them. Then finally she thought they weren't doing anyone any good there. "So—well I—"

She holds out her arms and the daughter runs to her and finally is able to weep.

The theme is one with which many readers can identify. This brief, short short form is very successful in throwing a brilliant light upon a warm family relationship and the devastation of grief. There is no action, yet it fulfills the definition of a story—something of importance has happened—something has been resolved. There is change. The main character is not the same at the conclusion of the story as at the beginning.

Since the story has no plot in the usual sense, if it had been dragged out to a longer length, the strong emotional impact would have been lost. Rather than share a powerful experience, the reader might have become numb with words.

This story, dealing with death and grief, would have had trouble finding a market a few years ago. The writer must at all times keep in touch with current trends. Story styles and content change constantly. The fiction writer must not only be familiar with the current market, he must be a prophet who senses a coming trend even before it happens. He does this by constantly reading newspapers and magazine articles and listening to the sounds and trying to interpret the vision of the world around him.

The short short is a good length for the beginning writer. Its form is relatively simple. The prospect of trying a full-length novel or even a twenty-page short story can be overwhelming. The short short running anywhere from four to eight pages seems as easy (although it's not!) as a letter to home. It has the advantage, however, of being easier to sell. There are a great many markets for this length, ranging from the high-paying slicks like *Redbook* through the various religious magazines and other specialized publications.

Where does the story start?

The beginner's most serious problem seems to be knowing when and where to start the short short. Unless he has had considerable experience, a short short written in chronological order, commencing at the point where things begin to happen, is the simplest and most effective.

Writing rules are made to be broken but the writer must first know those rules and when and how they can be changed.

The flashback is seldom a satisfactory technique in the short short. It breaks the story unity and confuses the reader. Rather than distract attention with a large indigestible hunk of flashback, the writer can gradually feed in the needed background information. Dialogue can also eliminate the need for a flashback by furnishing information while giving immediacy to past events.

Here is the opening from an *Ellery Queen* story of my own.

"How was the funeral?" Mr. Leary asked, putting down his cutting knife and surveying with distaste the fifteen dollar a yard white living room carpeting which he was listlessly installing.

Estelle, the hefty maid, produced a bottle of gin and handed him a generous drink. "The way they rushed it through, you'd have thought the old lady had to catch a train to heaven, or wherever she went. They didn't waste no time or tears—cheapest kind of casket—no music—and had her cremated next day. If you ask me it shows a lack of respect."

This was a grimly humorous murder story. The cutting knife and the new carpet are important factors in the story so were introduced promptly.

It would of course have been possible to use a flashback. I might have written:

With a shudder Estelle remembered the strange happenings the day the rich old woman died. She remembered the way Margo, the daughter, had first called the contractor to order a new swimming pool and then phoned the doctor and the undertaker to say the old lady was dead.

Dialogue kept the story in the present. The use of a flashback and the necessary transition would have changed the entire mood.

A good many short shorts cover a single scene. Some cover a longer period of time, but use as few changes of scene as possible.

This story covered several weeks, but had only two scenes. Here again dialogue quickly covers the events concerning the second mysterious death.

"Cheers," said Mr. Leary accepting the proffered drink. "I just heard the news when I came back from vacation. How was *this* funeral?"

"It was real nice," Estelle said dreamily. "You should've seen the crowds and all those police and newspapermen. Margo looked as natural as life. She wore her second best wig, but you couldn't tell the difference in the coffin."

This suspense story depends throughout on characterization and dialogue before it reaches it biter-bit conclusion, with Harry, the husband, convicted, not for the murder he did commit, but for the accidental death of his wife.

"What They Don't Know Won't Hurt Them" was a short short. It had a plot.

Something of importance was resolved and there was a revelation of character. If it had been an anecdote it might have read something like this:

> Sampson was perhaps the luckiest beagle in the world. Certainly he was much luckier than his master. Harry was in jail, charged with the murder of his wife, Margo. Margo had been an heiress who recently inherited from her mother.
>
> Ordinarily the police would have sealed up the house where a crime had been committed. This would have left poor Sampson homeless. The court therefore decided to allow Sampson to remain in comfort in his old home with the maid, Estelle, to care for him.
>
> So, while Harry led a dog's life in jail, Sampson and Estelle were living up the life of—the life of Harry.

While this little anecdote contains most of the information that was in the short short, it obviously would not have sold. There is no plot or conflict. It has no theme and nothing of importance has been resolved.

What about the "no-plot" story?

A good many young writers have been driven to despair and confusion by *New Yorker* stories. This is a highly specialized, limited field, that contradicts much of what the beginner has been told about short story writing. The plot situations are not strong in the conventional sense. It is as if the reader is a passenger on a train that has paused on a siding. He can see into a brilliantly lighted room. He hears the dialogue and knows the thoughts of its occupants. He probably does not know what has happened to these characters in the past nor what will become of them in the future. For one brief, blinding instant he has witnessed the interplay of human relationships, a revelation or development of character. Many *New Yorker* stories seem to be fragments of novels. The reader may not know the past and future of the characters, but the writer knows all about them. It is this and the excellent writing that make them noteworthy.

The plotted short short

The short short must get off to a fast start. Mystery writer Dan Marlowe says it is necessary to jump off the gangplank right into the middle of the story. He says he has never written one yet in which it hasn't developed that on the second or third draft, he finds himself eliminating the three or four introductory paragraphs which at first seemed necessary.

Summed up then, the short short is a true story form dealing with an event that matters. It is compact, uses few characters and scenes and starts as close as possible to its conclusion. It springs from the heart of the situation rather than goes into detail to explain. It deals with the problem of the moment.

Its characters should be vivid and vital—dull characters make dull stories. The self-pitying spinster, the neglected parent, the unfortunates dying of incurable diseases, deserve our compassion in real life, but they are not good story material.

The short short may mystify, shock, amuse, inform and entertain. It must never bore nor meander vaguely along.

It knows where it is going and it gets there fast.

How I write short stories

by W. Somerset Maugham

When I began to write short stories I was fortunately in a position of decent independence and I wrote them as a relief from work which I thought I had been too long concerned with. Most of them were written in groups from notes made as they occurred to me, and in each group I left, naturally enough, to the last those that seemed most difficult to write. A story is difficult to write when you do not know *all* about it from the beginning, but for part of it must trust to your imagination and experience. Sometimes the curve does not intuitively present itself and you have to resort to this method and that to get the appropriate line.

I beg the reader not to be deceived by the fact that a good many of my stories are told in the first person into thinking that they are experiences of my own. This is merely a device to gain verisimilitude. It is one that has its defects, for it may strike the reader that the narrator could not know all the events he sets forth; and when he tells a story in the first person at one remove, when he reports, I mean, a story that someone tells him, it may very well seem that the speaker, a police officer, for example, or a sea captain, could never have expressed himself with such facility and with such elaboration. Every convention has its disadvantages. These must be as far as possible disguised and what cannot be disguised must be accepted. The advantage of this one is its directness. It makes it possible for the writer to tell no more he knows. Making no claim to omniscience, he can frankly say when a motive or an occurrence is unknown to him, and thus often give his story a plausibility that it might otherwise lack. It tends also to put the reader on intimate terms with the author. Since Maupassant and Chekhov, who tried so hard to be objective, nevertheless are so nakedly personal, it has sometimes seemed to me that

---

Somerset Maugham *used his unhappy experiences as an orphan and medical student for his best known novel* Of Human Bondage. *He went on to write a steady stream of novels, essays, plays and short stories, fulfilling his boyhood ambition to become an author. The celebrated play,* Rain, *was based on his most famous short story,* "Miss Thompson." *The English writer died at 91 in 1965.*

if the author can in no way keep himself out of his work it might be better if he put in as much of himself as possible. The danger is that he may put in too much and thus be as boring as a talker who insists on monopolizing the conversation. Like all conventions this one must be used with discretion.

Working notes

In early youth I had written a number of short stories, but for a long time, twelve or fifteen years at least, occupied with the drama I had ceased to do so; and when a journey to the South Seas unexpectedly provided me with themes that seemed to suit this medium, it was as a beginner of over forty that I wrote the story which is now called "Rain." Since it caused some little stir, the reader of this article will perhaps have patience with me if I transcribe the working notes, made at the time, on which it was constructed. They were written in hackneyed and slipshod phrases, without grace; for nature has not endowed me with the happy gift of hitting instinctively upon the perfect word to indicate an object and the unusual, but apt, adjective to describe it. I was travelling from Honolulu to Pago Pago and, hoping they might at some time be of service, I jotted down, as usual, my impressions of such of my fellow-passengers as attracted my attention. This is what I said of Miss Thompson:

> Plump, pretty in a coarse fashion, perhaps not more than twenty-seven. She wore a white dress and a large white hat, long white boots from which the calves bulged in cotton stockings.

There had been a raid on the red light district in Honolulu just before we sailed and the gossip of the ship spread the report that she was making the journey to escape arrest. My notes go on:

> *W. The Missionary.* He was a tall thin man, with long limbs loosely jointed, he had hollow cheeks and high cheek bones, his fine, large, dark eyes were deep in their sockets, he had full sensual lips, he wore his hair rather long. He had a cadaverous air and a look of suppressed fire. His hands were large, with long fingers, rather finely shaped. His naturally pale skin was deeply burned by the tropical sun.

> *Mrs. W. His Wife.* She was a little woman with her hair very elaborately done, New England; not prominent blue eyes behind gold-rimmed pince-nez, her face was long like a sheep's, but she gave no impression of foolishness, rather of extreme alertness. She had the quick movements of a bird. The most noticeable thing about her was her voice, high, metallic, and without inflection; it fell on the ear with a hard monotony, irritating to the nerves like the ceaseless clamor of a pneumatic drill. She was dressed in black and wore round her neck a gold chain from which hung a small cross. She told me that W. was a missionary on the Gilberts and his district consisting of widely separated islands he frequently had to go distances by canoe. During this time she remained at headquarters and managed the mission. Often the seas were very rough and the journeys were not without peril. He was a medical missionary. She spoke of the depravity of the natives in a voice which nothing could hush, but with a vehement, unctuous horror, telling me of their marriage customs which were obscene beyond description. She said, when first they went it was impossible to find a single good girl in any of the villages. She inveighed against dancing.

I talked with the missionary and his wife but once, and with Miss Thompson not at all. Here is the note for the story:

A prostitute, flying from Honolulu after a raid, lands at Pago Pago. There lands there also a missionary and his wife. Also the narrator. All are obliged to stay there owing to an outbreak of measles. The missionary finding out her profession persecutes her. He reduces her to misery, shame, and repentance, he has no mercy on her. He induces the governor to order her return to Honolulu. One morning he is found with his throat cut by his hand and she is once more radiant and self-possessed. She looks at men and scornfully exclaims: dirty pigs.

Personal portraits

The reader may have observed that in the original note of "Rain" the narrator was introduced, but in the story as written omitted. "Rain" was invented by the accident of my happening upon persons here and there, who in themselves or from something I heard about them, suggested a theme that seemed suitable for a short story. This brings me to a topic that has always concerned writers and that has at times given the public, the writers' raw material, some uneasiness. There are authors who state that they never have a living model in mind when they create a character. I think they are mistaken. They are of this opinion because they have not scrutinized with sufficient care the recollections and impressions upon which they have constructed the person who, they fondly imagine, is of their invention. If they did they would discover that, unless he was taken from some book they had read, a practice by no means uncommon, he was suggested by one or more persons they had at one time known or seen. The great writers of the past made no secret of the fact that their characters were founded on living people. We know that the good Sir Walter Scott, a man of the highest principles, portrayed his father, with sharpness first and then, when the passage of years had changed his temper, with tolerance; Henri Beyle, in the manuscript of at least one of his novels, has written in at the side the names of the real persons who were his models; and this is what Turgenev himself says: "For my part, I ought to confess that I never attempted to create a type without having, not an idea, but a living person, in whom the various elements were harmonized together, to work from. I have always needed some groundwork on which I could tread firmly."

Recollections and references

With Flaubert it is the same story; that Dickens used his friends and relations freely is notorious; and if you read the "Journal" of Jules Renard, a most instructive book to anyone who wishes to know how a writer works, you will see the care with which he set down every little detail about the habits, ways of speech and appearance, of the persons he knew. When he came to write a novel he made use of this storehouse of carefully collected information. In Chekhov's diary you will find notes which were obviously made for use at some future time, and in the recollections of his friends there are frequent references to the persons who were the originals of certain of his characters. It looks as though the practice were very common. I should have said it was necessary and inevitable. Its convenience is obvious. You are much more likely to depict a character who is a recognizable human being, with his own individuality, if you have a living model. The imagination can create nothing out of the void. It needs the stimulus of sensation. The writer whose creative faculty has been moved by something peculiar in a person (peculiar perhaps only to the writer) falsifies his idea if he attempts to describe that person other than as he sees him. Character hangs together and if you try to throw people off the scent, by making a short man tall for example (as though stature had no effect on character), or by making him choleric when he has the concomitant traits of an equable temper, you will destroy the plausible harmony (to use the beautiful phrase of Baltasar Gracian) of which it consists. The whole affair would be plain sailing if it were not for the feelings of the persons concerned. The writer has to consider the vanity of the human race and the *Schadenfreude* which is one of its commonest and most detestable failings. A man's friends will find pleasure in recognizing him in a book and though the author may never even have seen him will point out to him, especially if it is unflattering, what they consider his living image. Often someone will recognize a trait he knows in himself or a description of the place he lives in and in his conceit jumps to the conclusion that the character described is a portrait of himself. Thus in my story called "The Outstation" the Resident was suggested by a British Consul I had once known in Spain and it was written ten years after his death, but I have heard that the Resident of a district in Sarawak, which I described in the story, was much affronted because he thought I had had him in mind. The two men had not a trait in common.

I do not suppose any writer attempts to draw an exact portrait. Nothing, indeed, is so unwise as to put into a work of fiction a person drawn line by line from life. His values are all wrong, and, strangely enough, he does not make the other characters in the story seem false, but himself. He never convinces. That is why the many writers who have been attracted by the singular and powerful figure of the late Lord Northcliffe have never succeeded in presenting a credible personage. The model a writer chooses is seen through his own temperament and if he is a writer of any originality what he sees need have little relation with the facts. He may see a tall one short or a generous one avaricious; but, I repeat, if he sees him tall, tall he must remain. He takes only what he wants of the living man. He uses him as a peg on which to hang his own fancies. To achieve his end (the plausible harmony that nature so seldom provides) he gives him traits that the model does not possess. He makes him coherent and substantial. The created character, the result of imagination founded on fact, is art, and life in the raw, as we know, is of this only the material.

Complaint of competency

The odd thing is that when the charge is made that an author has copied this person or the other from life, emphasis is laid only on the less praiseworthy characteristics of the victim. If you say of a character that he is kind to his mother, but beats his wife, everyone will cry: Ah, that's Brown, how beastly to say he beats his wife; and no one thinks for a moment of Jones and Robinson who are notoriously kind to their mothers. I draw from this the somewhat surprising conclusion that we know our friends by their vices and not by their virtues. I have stated that I never even spoke to Miss Thompson in "Rain." This is a character that the world has not found wanting in vividness. Though but one of a multitude of writers my practice is doubtless common to most, so that I may be permitted to give another instance of it. I was once asked to meet at dinner two persons, a husband and wife, of whom I was told only what the reader will shortly read. I think I never knew their names. I should certainly not recognize them if I met them in the street. Here are the notes I made at the time:

A stout, rather pompous man of fifty, with pince-nez, gray-haired, a florid complexion, blue eyes, a neat gray moustache. He talks with assurance. He is resident of an outlying district and is somewhat impressed with the importance of his position. He despises the men who have let themselves go under the influence of the climate and the surroundings. He has travelled extensively during his short leaves in the East and knows Java, the Philippines, the coast of China and the Malay Peninsula. He is very British, very patriotic; he takes a great deal of exercise. He has been a very heavy drinker and always took a bottle of whiskey to bed with him. His wife has entirely cured him and now he drinks nothing but water. She is a little insignificant woman, with sharp features, thin, with a sallow skin and a flat chest. She is very badly dressed. She has all the prejudices of an Englishwoman. All her family for generations have been in second-rate regiments. Except that you know that she has caused her husband to cease drinking entirely you would think her quite colorless and unimportant.

On these materials I invented a story which is called "Before the Party." I do not believe that any candid person could think that these two people had cause for complaint because they had been made use of. It is true that I should never have thought of the story if I had not met them, but anyone who takes the trouble to read it will see how insignificant was the incident (the taking of the bottle to bed) that suggested it and how differently the two chief characters have in the course of writing developed from the brief sketch which was their foundation.

"Critics are like horseflies which prevent the horse from ploughing," said Chekhov. "For over twenty years I have read criticisms of my stories, and I do not remember a single remark of any value or one word of valuable advice. Only once Skabichevsky wrote something which made an impression on me. He said I would die in a ditch, drunk." He was writing for twenty-five years and during that time his writing was constantly attacked. I do not know whether the critics of the present day are naturally of a less ferocious temper; I must allow that on the whole the judgment that has been passed on my own stories when from time to time a collection has been published in book form has been favorable. One epithet, however, has been much applied to them, which has puzzled me; they have been described with disconcerting frequency as "competent." Now on the face of it I might have thought this laudatory, for to do a thing competently is certainly more deserving of praise than to do it incompetently, but the adjective has been used in a disparaging sense and, anxious to learn and if possible to improve, I have asked myself what was in the mind of the critics who thus employed it. Of course none of us is liked by everybody and it is necessary that a man's writing, which is so intimate a revelation of himself, should be repulsive to persons who are naturally antagonistic to the creature he is. This should leave him unperturbed. But when an author's work is fairly commonly found to have a quality that is unattractive to many people it is sensible of him to give the matter his attention. There is evidently something that a number of people do not like in my stories and it is this they try to express when they damn them with the faint praise of competence. I have a notion that it is the definiteness of their form. I hazard the suggestion (perhaps unduly flattering to myself) because this particular criticism has never been made in

France where my stories have had with the critics and the public much greater success than they have had in England.

Painting life's pictures

The French, with their classical sense and their orderly minds, demand a precise form and are exasperated by a work in which the ends are left lying about, themes are propounded and not resolved and a climax is foreseen and then eluded. This precision on the other hand has always been slightly antipathetic to the English. Our great novels have been shapeless and this, far from disconcerting their readers, has given them a sense of security. This is the life we know, they have thought, with its arbitrariness and inconsequence; we can put out of our minds the irritating thought that two and two make four. If I am right in this surmise I can do nothing about it and I must resign myself to being called competent for the rest of my days. My prepossessions in the arts are on the side of law and order. I like a story that fits. I did not take to writing stories seriously till I had had much experience as a dramatist, and this experience taught me to leave out everything that did not serve the dramatic value of my story. It taught me to make incident follow incident in such a manner as to lead up to the climax I had in mind. I am not unaware of the disadvantages of this method. It gives a tightness of effect that is sometimes disconcerting. You feel that life does not dovetail into its various parts with such neatness. In life stories straggle, they begin nowhere and tail off without a point. That is probably what Chekhov meant when he said that stories should have neither a beginning nor an end. It is certain that sometimes it gives you a sensation of airlessness when you see persons who behave so exactly according to character and incidents that fall into place with such perfect convenience. The storyteller of this kind aims not only at giving his own feelings about life, but at a formal decoration. He arranges life to suit his purposes. He follows a design in his mind, leaving out this and changing that; he distorts facts to his advantage, according to his plan; and when he attains his object produces a picture and sets it before you. You can take it or leave it.

WRITERS IN ACTION: I

Bradbury on Bradbury— and beyond

by Bob Jacobs

Ray Douglas Bradbury has been called the world's greatest living science fiction writer. Entering a genre of bug-eyed-monsters and old-time western adventure yarns loosely disguised as space operas, he was instrumental in raising the level of writing and conception to that of a respected literary form. His love of graceful language and his stories with people rather than spaceships at the heart have had a profound influence on nearly every contemporary science fiction writer. Undoubtedly the form would remain the bald and laughable man of pulp if Waukegan's Bradbury had not been enticed into it by the glowing tales of Edgar Allen Poe and Jules Verne in 1932.

He credits *The Wizard of Oz* with triggering his love of writing and of science fiction at the same time. He devoured Baum, Burroughs, Wells, Prince Valiant and Buck Rogers; those last two he consumed from the Sunday comic section of the papers he sold.

In Los Angeles he was befriended by sf writer Henry Kuttner. Bradbury says Kuttner steered him toward a meaningful career by telling him, "Ray, stop running around bothering people with your ideas. Stop tearing at every sleeve you find and shouting in people's ears about your grand ideas. Go home, get your typewriter out, and *write*! You can't *say* you want to be a writer, you have to *write* to be a writer!"

His output is as phenomenal as his perpetual youth. For 43 years he has written at least ten pages a day, six days a week. His books include *The Martian Chronicles, The Illustrated Man, The October Country, Dandelion Wine, A Medicine for Melancholy, Something Wicked This Way Comes, The Anthem Sprinters, I*

Bob Jacobs, *a freelancer and teacher, has written and directed Hollywood TV specials and commercials. His most recent credits include a TV movie,* When the Going Gets Tough, *and a full length film,* Nashville With a Bullet *(from a novel by Barry Sadler and Billy Arr). He is associate professor of radio-TV-film at the University of Wisconsin—Oshkosh and recently completed his first novel.* Season of the Beast.

Sing the Body Electric, S Is for Space, R Is for Rocket, Dark Carnival, When Once in the Dooryard Elephants Bloomed, and *The Last Circus, many of which have been adapted to screen and stage worldwide (such as The Martian Chronicles,* a recent NBC mini-series) and/or translated into foreign languages. Among the most popular writers in France, Great Britain, Germany, Italy, Brazil and Argentina, he was the only American author invited by the French government to celebrate Jules Verne's birthday fete in 1978. He was also invited to tour Russia where he was almost as popular as the cosmonauts.

More than a science fiction writer, Bradbury is a poet, playwright, lecturer, city planner, "straight" novelist and lyricist. He also won an Academy Award nomination for his screenplay adaptation of *Moby Dick.*

Looking like a cross between Leonardo da Vinci and a koala bear, Bradbury sat on the floor of his living room in Los Angeles during this interview, blazing away at every conceivable topic with an intensity and vigor beyond belief. His advice to the writer? "Don't talk about it; *write.*"

Bradbury is a writer possessed by fantasies and energy, driven "to write everything I can."

"Time runs out for us very soon," he says, "and if we don't hurry and get our work done, we die and leave nothing behind to show that we were here."

JACOBS: It's nearly as hard to tag a neat label on science fiction these days as it is on you, Ray. It's practically unrecognizable now from those early days of "bug-eyed-monsters" and cowboys in space suits. What changes have you seen? Why did you go into it?

BRADBURY: Science fiction was, for a long time, sort of nuts and bolts fiction. When we grew up with it back in the twenties, we were pleased to have people going off to land on the moon or on Mars—*going* anywhere. This was primitive science fiction. All the authors vied with each other to invent weird creatures and, in doing so, they neglected human beings.

Well, that all began to change in the late thirties when John W. Campbell became the editor of *Astounding.* About this time, I got my career started in *Weird Tales,* strangely enough, writing weird fantasy stories which the editors didn't want to publish because they were unusual, too. Then I began to write stories like "The Million Year Picnic," "King of the Great Spaces" and various other Martian stories, and the editors thought they were peculiar because they dealt with human beings. Now, I wasn't the *first* person in the field to deal with human beings, of course. Wells had done it, Heinlein and others had done it, influenced by John W. Campbell. But, I think I *was* the first to write about very *small* human beings with very small problems relative to the machines that confronted them; and in some cases, not dealing with machines at all!

I liked to deal with concepts like, what would it be like to be the average woman on the night before she goes off to Mars to join her husband? That hasn't got anything to do with science fiction in the old sense at all. You don't confront the planets, you don't confront a machine, you confront an ancient concept; the wife of the Viking, the wife of the Greek who wandered, the mistress of Ulysses, you name it. I was actually falling back, without knowing it, on Greek and Roman and Norse mythology; on the lonely stories of the wanderers and the human beings. I didn't realize how deeply I'd been influenced by these myths, but I did, indeed, go back to them in my intuition; which made my stories hard to label and to sell!

But now we've all grown older and we realize that the label "science fiction" should not narrow us to speaking merely of science as mechanics and technologies. Science fiction deals with any "idea" which is not yet born, which wants to come to birth. That has to do with philosophy, too. You can point at Plato's *Republic* and call it science fiction. Science fiction has to do with dreaming futures for ourselves, and that's what Plato was doing in those dialogues.

We Americans have been science fiction writers from the beginning of our revolution. We came here and settled on an isolated "planet"—the United States. Through this isolation we were able to experiment with a science fictional concept which is "democracy": a thing which has not yet birthed itself completely, and never will! It's a continuing process and it's uprooting everything continually. It doesn't allow an elitist group to remain in charge too long. That's fine, because I hate elitist groups. I'm an elitist myself, but when the time comes for me to be shoved out of the way, I'll be shoved, and rightfully so. Maybe I will have gained too much power by then.

The greatest thing about the science fiction field in the last 40 or 50 years is the fact that there is no elite. Heinlein isn't telling everyone how to write. I'm not telling everyone how to write. Sturgeon isn't. Harlan Ellison isn't. Arthur Clarke isn't. They go their own ways and we have respect for each other and there's very little hatred.

JACOBS: None at all? No jealousies?

BRADBURY: There may be some, but I've sensed very little of it.

Yesterday's taboo, today's story.

JACOBS: The term "speculative fiction" has been coined since so much of the current stuff has little to do with science and technology as such. Do you think the new term is a more valid one?

BRADBURY: It's a good word. There are all kinds of terms. Call it what you want, but anything that even guesses ten minutes ahead or supposes new ways of birthing ourselves still fits. It's fantastic to consider that there isn't a major problem—in fact, I defy you to name a problem in the world at this very instant—that isn't science fictional! Women's Lib couldn't exist without the effects of a science fictional device called "The Pill." If you'd written about that 30 years ago, number one, you'd never have had them published, and number two, no one would have believed them.

JACOBS: When you first started writing, one of the strict taboos in science fiction was even so much as a "damn" or a "hell," much less any talk of The Pill or sex. Now we have science fiction stories dealing very frankly with sex, sexual problems, current social scenes, and characters use all sorts of four-letter expletives when the story calls for them. What do you feel about this "moral revolution" in literature?

BRADBURY: Well, that's all come about through the change in the greater society. Most of it happened during the last ten years or so. Even pornography is a very necessary part of our lives. Now it's come out in the open. OK, maybe we've gone a little overboard here and there, but I think it's mainly to the good. On the positive side of the ledger you have Man and Woman facing up to their sexual natures. I think it's tremendously important. We have so much to give on the level of sheer lust and on the level of pure love.

We haven't *begun* to talk about it yet. We just started the dialogue. In America we are such a frozen people in so many directions. We've been *afraid* to name our emotions, to name our loves. Men especially are afraid to cry. I've set a task for myself to teach men to cry and to laugh better and to create better and to love better. I can only see this as a huge improvement. We have to feel our way for awhile and then suddenly we'll take a huge leap forward. We'll *dare* to name our emotions to one another. Your friend will say, "Hey, has that happened to you?" and you'll say, "Yeah, that's happened to me." "Well, do you ever cry in the shower?" "Yeah, it's a great place to cry!" Well, once that's out, you can get more men to crying and I think it's only going to *improve* our culture.

JACOBS: That's one thing Women's Lib has going for it, don't you think?

BRADBURY: Yeah. I argue with Women's Lib about a lot of things, but this is one area in which I *totally* agree. They'd like to teach men to cry because in our culture we're not supposed to. It's not "manly." Well, that's a lot of crap! We're *identical* to women, absolutely identical, in our need to release tensions. That's why I write as I do. I've often been accused of being too emotional and sentimental, but I believe in *honest* sentiment, and the need to purge ourselves at certain times, which is *ancient*. Men would live at least five or six more years and not have ulcers if they would cry better. A woman can say to another woman, "I love you," but it takes a *long* time for a man in a friendship to look at another man and say, "Hey, I love you." Maybe never. Science fiction is deeply involved in these problems, too.

JACOBS: Much of this new morality you're talking about is reflected in young people today, many of whom grew up under the influence of science fiction. Has the genre influenced the morality, do you think, or vice versa?

BRADBURY: It's a combination. I think people like Heinlein, from what I hear from younger people, certainly had a *huge* influence. I know I've had an influence in other directions.

JACOBS: Are you referring to Heinlein's *Stranger in a Strange Land?*

BRADBURY: Yes, that particularly of Heinlein's, but some other things as well. My books are not full of that particular kind of problem, because I guess I'm very much at ease with myself. I don't have any sexual hangups that I know of. I'm very open and accepting. First of all, I've been around the art world all my life, around booksellers and artists and dancers and actors and writers, and past the age of 25 if you haven't seen everything and felt relaxed about it, you ought to just give up! So I haven't felt any *need* to write in other directions, although I might someday.

Exorcising demons

JACOBS: Do you write only what you have a personal need to write?

BRADBURY: Yeah . . . whatever my subconscious needs to write. If I need to kill someone, then I kill them in a story. That's helpful to me and to whoever reads the story. They can commit murder and release that terrible thing. The old cathartic thing applies more today than ever before.

JACOBS: There's a great deal of talk these days about ending violence on TV, in books and movies, because vicarious violence is "bad" for people. What do you think about the advocates of that kind of thinking?

BRADBURY: I think they're on the wrong track. You've got to choose, you see. If you want to destroy your cities, the best way to destroy them is to be antiviolent in your arts. Because then you'll just repress the whole thing and it will break out in reality. You'll have murder, rape, robbery, *realized.* You have to do it one way or the other, because you have to recognize that we *are* violent creatures. If you don't give me the right to act it out inside my head, with a painting or a short story or novel or film, then I'm going to go out and enact it in real life. Read people like

Bronowski and the human situation as described by him. When you build a city within that city, and outside the gates howls the "demon dog of destruction." Now, you've got to invite him inside the city and tame him with your arts. If you try to shut out this dog of violence, he's going to knock down the walls and destroy the whole city. You'll go mad if you don't face it on one level or the other. We put away so much murder, so much violence. We save up things against our bosses and people who've hurt us because we're being "civilized." But, you can only put away so much, and then it has to come out. As long as it isn't violence to the point of sickness, it has to be good for us.

JACOBS: Many of your own stories have dealt with terror, death and violence, especially the ones collected in *Dark Carnival*. Are those reality or fantasy? How do they help us?

BRADBURY: Those are fantasy. They are helping us to accept our fantasies so that we won't feel guilty about them. We all have lists of people we would like to kill, starting when we were children, when the first competition comes into the family. When I was six and my sister was born, I was displaced and wished her dead. The next thing I knew, she was. She died of pneumonia when I was seven. A child may not even know that he remembers wanting that competition dead . . . and then God very conveniently provides bacteria and gets rid of the competition, and you triumph. For a little while you say, "Hey, wow! She's gone!" Then you suddenly remember that she's not coming back *ever*, and it hurts and you have mixed feelings of sorrow and guilt; who knows how deeply these feelings run? The purpose, then, of a *good* horror story is to exorcise these demons, is to bring them out and say, "Look, you're no different from anyone else." We've all had these feelings about our brothers, our sisters, our mothers and fathers; I mean these are *clichés*. They were invented by the Greeks and they must have thought about them before they wrote them down. Later on they were written about by Shakespeare who *invented* Freud! It's the sort of thing which Jung refers to as the history of racial memory—the "collective unconscious" of mankind. So, a good horror story takes that raw material and says, "OK, everyone, we're gonna have a real gangbusting time tonight! We're gonna break open the top of your skull and show you that you have a skeleton inside your body or that you *wanted* to kill your father or your sister or your best friend!" I remember when I was 12, there was a boy in junior high school with me who was beautiful. He ran as swift as the wind. One day he stepped on a nail and had to have his foot cut off, and all of us boys celebrated. You see, that's *grim*. That's a terrible *truth* to face up to. But that's what all the old fairy tales, the really good ones, are about. Balder in Norse mythology is the story of John Kennedy: the hubris of beauty. The gods are jealous and they send the blind man in with his sprig of thistle. The thistle flies to the mark and Balder falls dead. John Kennedy was the same thing. I'm sure Oswald was eaten up with jealousy for the beautiful god, over and above any qualities as President. See, I can talk about all this now because luckily, I didn't know what I was doing when I wrote my earlier fictions.

JACOBS: Weren't you aware at all of these intellectual considerations?

BRADBURY: No, thank Christ because they would have all been lousy! The only good writing is intuitive writing. It would be a big *bore* if you knew where it was going. It has to be exciting, instantaneous and it has to be a surprise. Then it all comes blurting out and it's beautiful. I've had a sign by my typewriter for 25 years now which reads, "DON'T THINK!" I just act and react and emotionalize and all good stuff comes out. Nobody's ever thought their way to anything in literature, even "big brains" like George Bernard Shaw. Go through some of his notes on how he did his plays. He gets his characters rolling and they begin to talk and they take over the play and write it for him. That's not thinking with a capital T, it's intuitive creation! It's the life force finding its own root system and declaring itself.

JACOBS: Who are some other intuitive writers you admire?

BRADBURY: Kazantzakis, Shakespeare, the great poet Dylan Thomas. I went into my living room about 25 years ago and found my four-year-old daughter listening to a record by Dylan Thomas: "A Child's Christmas in Wales." I thought my wife had put it on and I came into the room and found my four-year-old daughter standing there listening. She looked up and saw me there and said, "*He* knows what he's doing." And I said, "Yes, my dear . . . he *does*." There's so much beauty in Dylan Thomas that's meaningless! It's the clanging of syllables, the sound of words, the mouthing of tongues . . . it's *gorgeous!* I don't know what it's all about, it's just gorgeous. He had an ear and a tongue. He listened and he spoke and that's what writing is about. Gerard Manley Hopkins is the same way. There's a helluva lot of him that makes no sense, but the sense of beauty and of being alive? Discovering the *miracle* of being alive? My God! He's locked into that poetry of his forever. He'll be around ten thousand years from tonight because he was beautiful.

Imagination, intuition, emotion.

JACOBS: When you're writing, do you see things happening?

BRADBURY: Absolutely. You have to live in a cloud of emotions. You rev yourself up. Give yourself time in the middle of the afternoon, or when you're waking up early in the morning, when you're in that kind of wonderful, euphoric state in-between, on the verge of dreams when you get a kind of nuclear bombardment of all kinds of fragments of ideas jumping around inside your head and hitting each other. They begin to fuse and detonate each other. It's a very hard thing to describe. You don't have any control over your mind at a time like that and you don't want it, see? Let it run wild! Then watch it remotely at the bottom of your skull. Look up at all those things running around wild, then jump up and run over to the typewriter and feed them in!

JACOBS: And don't think about them, eh?

BRADBURY: No! You cannot write by thinking. You have plenty of time to think in between times. The period in between is when you *stuff* your eyeballs, when you read diversified multitudes of material in every field. I absolutely demand of you and everyone I know that they be widely read in every damn field there is; in every religion and every art form and *don't* tell me you haven't got time! There's plenty of time. You need all of these cross-references. You never know when your head is going to use this fuel, this food for its purposes. Stuff yourself with serious subjects, with comic strips and motion pictures and radio and music; with symphonies, with rock, with everything! What we often forget is that thought is to be used to correct life. It's *not* a way of life! If you make thought the center of your life, you're not going to live it. So, what you have to do is be this kind of hysterical, emotional, vibrant creature who lives at the top of his lungs for a lifetime and then corrects around the edges so that he doesn't go insane or drive his friends mad. Thought is the skin around the organ. The organ is full of blood and a beating heart, a soul and the exhaltation of being alive!

JACOBS: When did you start writing?

BRADBURY: In 1932, when I was 12. But I started writing out of love, which is a completely different thing from competition. I saw that the world was competitive in other areas and I chose not to compete. I withdrew into my interior world, my world of writing, where I could be excellent all to myself. I made people come to me on my terms, you see, rather than going to them on theirs.

I don't like to compete. It doesn't mean anything to me to beat someone. In the field of ideas, there's plenty of room for all of us. We're all building on the same foundation. If someone will just let me into the club to have tea with George Bernard Shaw, I'll be very happy, you know? If I come out at the end of my life and someone *breathes* my name in the same rarefied atmosphere with Shaw or with Shakespeare, my God! Just to be allowed into the club! So, you're really not competing that way. You just want to be allowed in.

JACOBS: Do you think of yourself or these other writers as inventors of ideas, or are you tapping something which exists independently and which creative people have the ability to perceive?

BRADBURY: You're not inventing things because I really feel that it's all there. You're finding ways to speak basic truths which have been spoken before. You're trying to find fresher ways for your generation, or sometimes finding insights to the future which you feel are important. For instance, even the Church itself has taken a long look at many of its dogmas and is changing them in light of new insights. I think they're fools if they go too far, because there's a lot of mystery there. There are mysteries at the heart of everything, so why should the Church, of all our institutions, give up mystery? Every science is based on mystery. Locked into everything is mystery. We then try to find, in any given age as writers; the truths that we grew up with. You cannot grow up in a period and not be a child of your time. You may be stupid and not realize it and not speak of it because you're blocking yourself from seeing this truth because you're trying to sell the "commercial" story. But if you look into your secret self which is the amalgam of the time in which you grew up, you can't help but benefit from it.

What we're trying to get down to is the secret of our loves and our hates; our sexuality and our murderousness. How much of our murderousness and our violence is genetic; how much of it is caused by our environment. The more I look at environment versus genetics, the more I'm flabbergasted! Why are some people automatically so fantastically evil? We don't know. I have no glib answer, but I don't believe environment has as much to do with it as we say. I lived in tenements thirty years ago in a chicano district, and I've lived with families that should have *all* been corrupt. They should have all been evil and said, "Why bother? Let's go out and steal everyone blind," but they didn't! Now there's a mystery for you, huh? What happened within the heart of *that* family to make it work better? What kind of love was functioning to protect it? Why is there always that one boy in the middle of all this who turns into a monster; at the heart of all that love, with everything in his favor? We don't *know* the answer, and these are the eternal mysteries.

Ray Bradbury, inc.

JACOBS: How do you think your environment has affected your writing?

BRADBURY: I grew up in Waukegan until I was 14 or so, and from then on, here in L.A. When you ask about environment in terms of a writer, I've always believed that environment hasn't got a damned thing to do with anything! If you want to write, you write. I saw reality very clear when I was very young; 10, 11, 12 years old. I didn't care for the male animal. We're *not* a very nice sex. Men and boys are real destroyers, and I didn't like growing up in a destructive environment where I had the hell beat out of me all the time. I wasn't very good at fighting and I wasn't very good at running and I didn't like it! Being a boy from say, the age of 11 to 15 is *really* hell on wheels! I wouldn't go back there for anything.

In fact, I wrote a short story about this called "The Playground," in which a father remembers how hellish it was to be a boy of a certain age. When his son is born, he wants to protect him from this. He makes a deal and transfers at the end of the story. His son becomes the father and he becomes the son and he's locked into being a three-year-old. He has to go through all that hell all over again. It's a horror story of magnificent dimensions! Boys are dreadful.

All this talk about freedom is pure crud from young people. They're kidding themselves. They're all absolutely totalitarian. All young people are that from the time they're three until they're 22. If you're not a brown monkey with all the others, if you don't dress the same way, you're a "fag." If you don't think "this way," you're a jerk. If you don't think some other way, they beat the hell out of you. If you diversify in *any* direction, or if you let them see that you have an I.Q.—if you *dare* let anyone know that you're brighter than they are and you're too *dumb* to realize how bright you are . . . huh?! The paradox, right? If you're dumb enough to let your brightness out, they *kill* you! They slaughter you. They pull your skin off. And if this sounds paranoid, it's because it is! Paranoia is based on reality, and the reality of the 12- or 14-year-old is, "Just don't show it around us, Buster. You be bright on your own terms." So I went off and hid and became a writer. Now, you've asked about my environment; that's it. My environment, what affected me as a writer, was the lousy world of the 12-year-old boy who wanted me to *conform*. This hasn't anything to do with the great wide world out there. It has to do with the male animal, the "machismo" or whatever you want to call it. If you don't join the gang, if you don't play baseball or football, if you don't run fast enough, if you think too much, you're in big trouble. So I pulled away and formed my own world: Ray Bradbury, Incorporated! I stuck up my finger at them and I said, "Screw all of you! I'm going my way. I'm quitting this part of the human race until I get big enough so you'll all have to come back and tip your hats!" Girls *never* know this. It's terrible.

Calling on recall

JACOBS: In one of your stories called, "The Small Assassin," you seem to be terribly bitter not only about adolescence, but about infancy as well. It's about a six-week-old baby who murders his mother and father. Would you like to explain that?

BRADBURY: Well, first of all, I recall being born.

JACOBS: You recall being born?

BRADBURY: I have total recall from the moment of birth on. But I got to thinking about it again when my first daughter was born. We brought her home from the hospital and she'd been home about two weeks. One night she woke up crying. We got out of bed to check her and she was dry and she wasn't hungry and there were no pins sticking her, so I looked at Maggie, my wife, and said, "Hey, wait a minute. I remember something like this. You know what she's going through?" Maggie said, "What?" I said, "Well, she's having a nightmare. It's obvious!" Maggie stopped and thought for a minute and said, "What can she have a nightmare about? She's only two weeks old. She hasn't had any experience." Well, she'd had the biggest experience you can have—the experience of being born! You have another one later in life when you die. Those are the two biggest experiences, and then the third one is living.

JACOBS: What are some of the things you remember?

BRADBURY: I remember everything about my infancy. The "camera angle" from my crib, the pain of being born, of being circumcised. I remember the doctor's face, the hospital lights, the scalpel as well as the flavor of my mother's milk; and she only nursed me for three days. I remember being extruded forth out into the world and the shock of this, as if it were a plot of some kind. So all this feeds into "The Small Assassin." See, again we're going back to the racial mind, the Jungian thing. We resent being evicted from a nice, easy job. Being an embryo is a great job, you know? We'd all like to have that kind of easy, floating, nine months of peaceful sleep and half-waking. And suddenly you're ejected and you have to find a job in the world. Naturally you want to kill whoever's responsible.

I also have total recall for films I saw when I was three. It's lucky, but that's why I think I'm a particular kind of a good writer. I grew up just sponging in motion pictures: all the horror films when I was a kid, then all the Edgar Allan Poe short stories, the L. Frank Baum *Oz* books, and the comic strips. There's a fantastic mulch in my head of total recall which I can summon forth anytime I need it, combined with what I've learned from Shakespeare and Gerard Manley Hopkins and Robert Frost and Dylan Thomas and other people. Now that's the kind of brain to have in your head: a combination of *all* these things.

JACOBS: You seem to have diminished your output of short stories in favor of other forms of writing—plays, screenplays and so on. Does this indicate a conscious shift in direction for you?

BRADBURY: Whatever calls you, you have to answer. I've done quite a few short stories the last few years, not as many as in the past, but I've been doing so *much* poetry. Really, poetry has dominated my life in the last few years. My first book is called, *When Elephants Last in the Dooryard Bloomed.* I chose a facetious title because I don't believe in being serious about anything. I think life is too serious to be taken seriously! I hate serious people, God, what bores! Anyway, I've done all these poems and I've *finally* learned to write really good poetry. I know it! Some of it is so beautiful that it changes other people's lives as well as my own. Then I *know* it's good.

I wrote one for my father and my love for him. It's about my sense of him being alive in me today. He's been dead 16 years and there isn't a day I haven't missed him. But the great thing is, you look at the backs of your hands and the knuckles and the hairs and he's *there*! He's in the cells, he's in the blood. I sense a proximity here of his flesh and mine that's fantastic. It's mystical! You don't want to get fancy about it because then you destroy it. It's a great comfort. That's where immortality is—in the blood. You don't have to ask for the other thing. I am my father's older self and he was my younger self. The two of us are twins. Well, that's immortality! What more do you want?

Men with dangerous toys

JACOBS: We know that life is temporary and completely absurd, as writers from Aristophanes to Beckett have pointed out. Still, we find so many bestsellers written about all those soul-searching pessimists and ersatz-tragic heroes. What are your feelings about these books?

BRADBURY: Well, we hate the long-faced people, the self-destroyers. They're the professional New York despairers. They've got a little plastic wailing wall they carry with them everywhere. They pound their heads against it and predict the end of the world and I say, "That's funny!" I learned about the end of the world when I was 13. Some group announced in the papers, as they do every few years, that the world was coming to an end. So, my brother and I decided that we'd get together a picnic lunch and go see it. So we got up early and made some ham and pickle sandwiches and took a couple of Nehi's with us and went out into the country and hiked around waiting for the world to come to an end. We wondered if it was going to be fire and everything would go, "skizz," you know, or a big wave comes in on the shore, a big 90-foot tidal wave, wow, great, y'know? And about noon we got hungry and ate the first sandwiches and we still believed it might happen. Around about four o'clock we drank the last of the Nehi and at five we went home and I've never believed in the end of the world since!

JACOBS: The machines notwithstanding, eh? You have the reputation of distrusting machines, and it is true you refuse to learn how to drive a car. What's the true story on that?

BRADBURY: Oh, that's one of those things that's being misinterpreted. People try to romanticize you if you're not careful. I don't distrust machinery. I distrust people. When I was younger I may have thought in that direction for a little while. It's sort of common among young people to say, "Ohmigod, we're being computerized out of existence!" But that's not true. We're being dehumanized out of existence by human beings. You always look behind the machine to see who's driving the car! The worst thing in the history of the world is the invention of the automobile, mainly because it put a device like that in the hands of so many maniacs and morons who then proceed to go out and kill two million people!

I've tried for twenty years at least to say I'm *not* afraid of machines. I'm not afraid of the computer. I don't think the robots are taking over. I think the men who *play* with toys have taken over. And, if we don't take the toys out of their hands, we're fools. Just watch men playing with toys and then you get afraid of men. That's where my fear is. I believe we're in charge and have to stay in charge.

The coming of age of sf

JACOBS: So you write about people

BRADBURY: I write about people and people rebelling against the use of machines in certain ways. That's why I formed my own rapid transit citizen's group ten years ago, to try to build a decent rapid transit system to compete with and to do away with the automobile; or at least to juxtapose it with something that is reasonably operative. The trouble with the car is that it's so hypnotic and so beautiful because it operates one-to-one: one person, one device. It gives a man the sense that he's free, even though he isn't. He feels as if he were—from his boss or his wife or his friends who hate him at the moment. That's a hard thing to work against. The only way you can do it is give him theatre. If he's on a freeway and there are 10,000 cars ahead of him and he sees a monorail streaking overhead at 80 miles an hour, *that's* theatre! That's where architecture and city planning enter the world of the stage.

We're going to go through a fantastic and vital theatricality in the next 40 years. The small towns of America have been dying slowly, and now we're going to watch the large cities die one by one, strangling themselves. And then the small town will reappear. We'll look at these experimental cities which various people are putting up and see which one is really operable, humanly speaking, and then we'll build hundreds of cities having 30,000 people apiece, all over the land. The small town will come back. Why? Not because I say it should, but because we'll *need* it to come back. We'll build such beautiful small towns again, with everything locked into them. Each town will have its own radio station, its own television station, its own traveling ballet and theatre company, its own university. Then you can just watch the big cities fall over and die like mammoths. Some of them will survive. I think L.A. has a chance because it is so diversified. It isn't a large city at all. It's 80 small towns. Chicago will be torn down and rebuilt and half the population will disappear. New York will be torn down if it takes a hundred years to do it, and the people will be distributed in small communities. It will be done because we'll know that it's either that or suicide.

JACOBS: We've really gotten into a lot more than science fiction and advice to writers, haven't we?

BRADBURY: Hey, I tell you, when you grow up in science fiction you grow up in everything! It's the greatest and only field *worth* growing up in. It's the total field. As a result of reading science fiction when I was eight, I grew up with an interest in music, architecture, city planning, transportation, politics, ethics, aesthetics on any level, art . . . it's just *total*! It's complete commitment to the whole human race on all the earth. That's what science fiction is about. The irony is that it's been made such fun of when it always has been the only relevant fiction that we ever had. It's 10,000 per cent more relevant when compared to the average American novel today, which is so "in" it's out. The typical description on the flyleaf of the modern American novel reads, "A New York Jewish intellectual, aged 41, discovers that death means him and can't decide whether to go back to his wife, his mistress or his boyfriend." That's the plot and you say, "Oh, no, I don't want to read *that* again! He's going to do the Thomas Wolfe bit? He's gonna discover life? He's gonna go home again? He's gonna find the 'meaning of life' and agonize and it's gonna be the 'Great American Novel'?"

You *can't* try for that, you see? You must never name the goal. You must never tell us the target you're hitting for. You must automatically go toward it without ever naming it. That's true for *all* fiction. When you write a story and you want to show a man hating something, you don't say, "He hated it." You show him going through all the feelings that surround hatred; slamming doors and knocking books over and hitting children. But you never name the thing he's doing. So, when you write the "Great American Novel," hopefully to Jesus you won't *tell* me you're writing it!

JACOBS: When you first started, there were numerous magazines buying short stories. Many of them have gone out of business, others have changed format. What is the real potential for a young science fiction writer to make it today?

BRADBURY: Well, there are about a dozen big magazines around, and there weren't more than that when I was young—that is, not really good ones. We had *Astounding Science Fiction* and *Amazing Stories* and *Wonder* and one or two others. The magazines never paid much and they still don't. Today you have *Astounding* which is *Analog*, and the *Magazine of Fantasy and Science Fiction* which has been around for over 20 years and which is still a damn good magazine.

And now you have *Omni*. There are three or four others, but even better than when I was a kid, there are hardcover books being published. Twenty-five years ago, you couldn't buy one if you wanted to. There were some little semivanity publishing houses like Gnome Press. My first book was by what amounts to a vanity publisher. I got $400 for it for five years work. Figure that out by the year! *Dark Carnival* was published by Arkham House in a 3,000 copy edition which took eight years to sell out. Now, that's all changed; *another* revolution! Your young writer now has every publisher in America looking for good science fiction novels, which they will publish without calling them science fiction. *The Andromeda Strain* was published not under a science fiction label, but under Michael Crichton—a *Novel*. No one used those "dirty words," science fiction. A lot of other big novelists have come into the science fiction field since that time, including people like Morris West. There are numerous hardcover science fiction titles published every year, which means income for a young writer if he has the stuff. Then there are paperback collections of short stories and novels published every year. There are two or three thousand paperback novels in print right now.

Quality from quantity

JACOBS: Do you really believe the short story writer has a chance then?
BRADBURY: God, yes! There's a dearth of good short story writers in this country right now. Not many people are doing it. So chances of survival are very good depending on the individual talent. If you're no good, there's no hope for you. It's as simple as that. I can offer an example of someone I thought was going to have a rough time and not make it for years. His name is Richard Bach. I've known him for over 12 years and he was a student of mine. He wrote some very pleasant things but nothing really great. I read *Jonathan Livingston Seagull* and criticized it and sent it back to him for rewriting and cutting and it got published. We both thought it was going to have a pleasant sale of maybe five or eight thousand copies, and the next thing we look around it's sold ten *million* copies! So, it's a complete surprise and you never know about things like that. Occasionally we all hit on universal themes which people are so hungry for they simply must have them.
JACOBS: In many creative writing classes, students are advised to slant articles and stories at certain markets in order to be more "commercial." Do you believe in that?
BRADBURY: The best way to destroy yourself is to slant. Writers who are "slanters" are just sunk. If anything happens to one magazine or one source, they're destroyed. Most television writers during the last strike were absolutely demolished by the situation. They'd never learned how to write a novel or a short story and late in time, there they were, out on the street, starving.

The best thing a writer can do is to educate him—or herself in all the *real* forms of writing. Unless you're a genius, you can't write for the screen or television straight off. A lot of that kind of writing can appear to be good, but people are flim-flammed by special effects. Your director can make you look great. You can get Rod Steiger in to cover all your sins for you. Laurence Olivier can come and do a small role and make it seem terrific! And it isn't at all. It's the performance.

Young writers shouldn't kid themselves about learning to write. The best way to do that is to train yourself in the short story. Read every damn one that's ever been written, and there aren't that many really good ones. You must live feverishly inside a library. Colleges are not going to do you any good unless you are born, raised and live in a library every day of your life. There hasn't been a day, I swear, since I was ten that I haven't been either in a library or in a bookstore. If you don't love bookstores and libraries so that you want to just breathe them in and push them out your ears, stay out of writing. Don't go anywhere near literature because you're going to fail and deserve to fail!

JACOBS: You're terribly prolific, but a lot of writers produce one book in a lifetime. Would you advise young writers to spend all their time polishing one piece or to go for quantity?

BRADBURY: It simply follows that quanity produces quality. Only if you do a lot will you ever be any good. If you do very little, you'll never have quality of idea or quality of output. The excitement and creativity come from a whole lot of doing, hoping you'll suddenly be struck by lightning. If you only write a few things, you're doomed. The history of literature is the history of prolific people. I always say to students, give me four pages a day, *every day*. That's three or four hundred thousand words a year. Most of that will be bilge, but the rest . . . ? It will save your life!

Can you state your story in a sentence?

by James D. Lucey

If you are like the majority of writers, you probably have a fairly good idea of what a story will be about when you first sit down to write. You could, if necessary, state the idea in a few sentences that sketch your general intentions as to plot, characters, emotional problems, and so forth. The story-in-a-sentence technique is simply a refinement on such—often vague—intentions.

A story should be fairly strong and interesting even when reduced to the minuscule dimensions of a single sentence. For example:

> A private detective's partner is murdered; in the course of solving the murder the detective falls in love with a woman he must send to prison, for he knows from the first that she is the murderess.

The above may not seem quite like your memory of *The Maltese Falcon*. However, this is probably because no two persons will condense a published story into the same story-line. One reader will see it as a series of connected events—a plot. Another one, looking at the same story, may view it as the unfoldment of a character problem. Another will see atmosphere and still another, theme. Since, in addition to the gist of the plot, one or more of these other elements must be in every story-in-a-sentence, there will be a certain amount of variation.

Unifying force

A story can be reduced to a sentence only by first finding its basic concept. That is, we must ask, What is the one inseparable element that controls the action of the story?

When this question is properly answered, you can reduce any story of any

James D. Lucey held a number of media-related jobs in addition to his military service while writing novels and for magazines, a career begun in 1948. He wrote Shackle *and adult westerns, and under the pseudonym Matthew James he published* The Adventures of Davy West.

length to its basic essentials. *For every work of art is unified*, and it is the story's unifying element that we are seeking. Even *Gil Blas*—that most picaresque of picaresque novels—which seems to be nothing but a long series of seemingly disconnected incidents in the life of a rogue—is actually unified by the hero's continuous effort to find an easy-money way to security.

Usually, the unifying force is motivational in nature—Ulysses seeking a way home, Ruth governed by family affection and loyalty, Huck Finn trying to preserve his vagabond way of life.

Often, however, the unifying concept is much more complex—Don Quixote in a world of genuine wrongs seeking honor and glory through the righting of wholly imaginary evils; Sam Spade in love with a woman whom he knows all along his duty and honor will force him to prove guilty of murder.

Once having learned to write story sentences, you will find a number of practical ways to put them to use.

They offer a method for variations on plots. For instance, in Poe's *Ulalume* a man's reaction to the loss of his fiancée causes him to forget her until he finds himself at her tomb. Bret Harte, with the simplicity of genius, parodied this in his *Willows* by changing "fiancée" to "credit," and "tomb" to "saloon": A man's reaction to the loss of his credit causes him to forget it until he finds himself in the same saloon.

You will use the story-in-a-sentence much more often, however, for detecting errors in plotting. Perhaps no plotting error is commoner than the substitution of a sketch or inflated anecdote for a story. I remember one of the kind that went like this:

> A bomber crashes and traps a crewman inside so that he cannot get loose; to keep him from burning to death in the almost instantaneous fire, the hero shoots him.

We have a genuine human interest problem here and a solution of sorts. But the hero is really no more than a *deus ex machina* for a single situation and response. Most "non-stories" reduce to a story in a sentence that is as obviously defective as the one above. Because their authors are unable to refine plots to their essentials, the vital ingredients that are missing remain hidden beneath a blur of developing action, character and emotion.

Plotted sentences

The true "slice of life" tale is fully rounded. (A story is "rounded out" and distinguished from anecdote by an interrelation between beginning and ending situations and responses.) For instance, in Paul Horgan's *Black Snowflakes*, the ending situation and response parallels the initial situation and response:

> A youngster does not understand what death is and does not realize his grandfather is dying—nor grieve for him soon after, when told his grandfather is gone; but, months later, when a favorite horse dies and the boy sees actual death, he is assailed by a storm of grief for the horse—and for his grandfather as well.

Nor need complexity prevent good plotting. Some of our most famous stories and novels work out highly complicated plots *within* their basic simplicities. Beginners' involved stories, on the other hand, are often so intricate that the reader

seldom achieves a real grasp of the affair. There are too many interacting characters, too many cross-purposes, too many scenes.

The net effect is usually one of cold narration of plot without human interest.
Such overplotted affairs cannot be reduced to unifying sentences that are satisfying. The test sentence, after all, is allowed to have but a single semicolon; whereas
such yarns as these require two . . . three . . . four. . . .

A story is actually a fairly simple thing: human interest situation—response—
solution (good or bad). All the rest is in the telling. Because of this basic simplicity,
genuine stories, no matter how involved, can be reduced to a single unifying
sentence. Consider that long and quite complex novel, *Tom Jones*:

> An orphan believes himself unworthy of the girl he loves; driven from
> his home and forced to seek his fortune, he unwittingly proves himself by his
> actions to be fully worthy of her in his character and, finally, in his lineage.

The telling of the tale takes about 1,000 printed pages . . . the whole of a
man's life from birth to marriage. Yet the unifying sentence given above is, I
believe, more or less a fair summary of the basic story.

A plot, after all, is one thing; a story something else entirely. A story is not
found in situation and it is not in a solution. *It is in the response.* It is not in Tom, the
orphan, driven from his home; and it is not in the discovery of his blue blood. It is
in the way he achieves adulthood and shows himself to be a worthy man.

When you have used the story-in-a-sentence technique long enough, ideas
will begin coming to you in the form of plotted sentences.

The story-in-a-sentence is a sort of Litmus paper with which you can pretest
your story before you write it. It is not a pH paper; it will not tell you the approximate degree of the acidity you seek, it will not distinguish the best from the good.
Properly used, however, it will separate the genuine story from all base substitutes.

To make a short story long

by Orson Scott Card

In the Munich Olympics in 1936, the Germans were very clever. They didn't let the equestrians from other nations see the course the horses would have to race. At one point in the course, after the normal obstacles that all the horses easily coped with, there was a fence. And beyond the fence was a strip of water dozens of yards across, far too wide for any horse to jump.

When the non-German equestrians reached that obstacle, they all tried to jump, of course, and floundered. But the German rider, knowing all about it, had his horse daintily step over the fence and walk gently through the water with perfect form.

It was cheating. But it's the kind of thing many of us face when we try to switch from writing short stories to writing novels. We're used to coping with 3,000 or even 10,000 words. But suddenly there yawns before us a huge expanse of words—100,000 or more. And when we try to leap over it as we would with a story, we end up with a soaking, as often as not.

Six months after I got my first check for a short story sale, I took stock of my earnings. I had sold a total of four stories in that time, for which I had been paid a total of $980. This was still $20 less than my monthly salary at my magazine editing job.

It didn't look like I would be able to go freelance very soon, not on short story sales alone. If I wanted to be a fulltime writer, I was going to have to write a novel.

So I sat down at the typewriter and began writing. I was confident. After all, what was a novel, if not a short story that had more things happen before the end? So, page by page, my first novel flowed from my typewriter. It was a science fiction epic that spanned a thousand years and dealt with the lives of 20 characters.

And it only lasted for 120 pages.

Orson Scott Card, a former magazine editor, is a fulltime writer specializing in science fiction. He has sold five novels in addition to the many short stories he has published in Omni, Analog, New Dimensions *and other publications.*

I began to suspect there was more to writing a novel than just "having more things happen."

Longer is shorter

Most of us who write fiction begin with short stories. There are several practical reasons for this: Short stories look easier to write. If you write a bad one that never sells, you have lost only 20 pages' work, not 300. And, perhaps the most common reason of all, short stories are what your college creative writing teacher wanted to see, and now you're in the habit.

How do you make the leap from short stories to novels? That intimidating stack of blank pages you have to fill is enough to frighten off most would-be novelists. But if you're one of the rare ones who is determined to go ahead, there are some things you can do to help yourself over the hurdle.

How do I know the arcana of switching to the novel form? I learned from experience. I wrote some bad novels. And each one's flaws taught me how to write the next one better.

That first novel, that 120-page thousand-year epic. I knew something was terribly wrong with it. So I took it to a friend, a fine editor who had been criticizing my short stories for me. He read it; he returned it to me silently.

"Well?" I asked.

"Um," he said. "Sure is long."

Long? A hundred and twenty pages? "The problem is it's too short."

"No," he insisted. "The problem is it's too long. It's absolutely boring. From page three on, I could hardly get through it."

The novel began like any of my short stories. I jumped into the main character's problem with both feet, and tried to make him personally interesting. It worked fine.

But on page three, I started really getting into the plot. I introduced two more characters and moved my protagonist into a life-and-death struggle. By page five, he had resolved that problem and was off on another adventure. By page ten, he had saved the world. By page 30, he had saved another world.

I wasn't writing a novel at all. I was writing a plot outline. I was so keenly aware of how much storyline I had to cover that I had raced ahead and not paused to give the reader time to absorb anything.

Short stories are designed to deliver their impact in as few pages as possible. A tremendous amount is left out, and a good short story writer learns to include only the most essential information—only what he needs to create mood, get the facts across, and prepare the reader for the climax.

But novels have more space, more time. When a reader sits down with a book he is committing several hours of his life to reading it. He will stay with you for much more peripheral material; he expects, in return, that you will provide him with a fuller experience than he could possibly get from a short story.

In my first draft of my first novel, I had written the dullest of *history*—a bare retelling of events.

When I set out to write the second draft, I knew I had to write biography—a detailed exposition of what my characters thought and said and did, and what in their past made them act that way.

My second draft was more than 300 pages long, and included only half the plot of the first draft. But it was a much better book. That is, it could be read by a person who actually stayed awake without liberal doses of NoDoz.

My friend read it again, and came back much happier. "It still isn't very good, but at least it's *shorter* this time."

Card's Law of Novel-Writing: Longer is shorter.

Don't get buried in plot

One of the things that fooled me on that first draft was the idea that if a novel is ten times the length of a short story, it must have ten times the plot. But that is rarely the case.

Think of John Fowles's novel *Daniel Martin*—629 pages of always excellent, often brilliant prose. Yet the plot, the actual, essential plot, could have been expressed in a 40-page novelette. I suspect it would be a mediocre story at best, but it could easily be done, because not that much happens on the direct plot line. Reduced to its absurd minimum, *Daniel Martin* is the story of a financially successful screenwriter who returns to England at the request of a dying friend with whom he feuded years ago. The friend's wife was the woman the screenwriter really loved and wanted to marry back in their days at Oxford. The dying friend reveals that he knew his wife had an affair with the screenwriter, and wants the two of them to get together after his death. Having delivered his message, the friend kills himself, and the screenwriter and the woman he once loved do indeed fall in love again, much to their own surprise.

Sounds like a melodramatic little story, doesn't it? And it might have turned out that way—except that stories and novels are not just devices for recounting plot.

When I first plotted that first novel of mine, I was thinking of a short story as a sort of thread through time, a few events long; I thought of a novel as simply a longer thread to fill up the pages. My metaphor was all wrong, however. Writing is not just one-dimensional.

So when you sit down to plot your novel, don't try to come up with ten times the number of events you usually put in a story. You will usually want more events than in a story, of course, but you should still leave yourself plenty of leisure to explore from character to character, from thought to thought, from detail to detail. A novel need not cover a thousand years or 48 characters or the Renaissance in Italy; you have the freedom to use the novel form to write about a single life or a single year or a single incident. Despite the deceptively simple plot of *Daniel Martin*, or perhaps because of it, Fowles was able to take his readers by surprise, bringing us to love the seemingly jaded and shallow narrator as he reluctantly showed us his true self a layer at a time.

Gulps and swallows

My first novel went through several more drafts, and I thought I had finally found a system for coping with its length. I was a short story writer, wasn't I? So why not cut up the plot into five or six novelettes? They would all lead to a climax at the end, and yet I would be on familiar ground, writing 30 or 40 pages in each section, just like a story.

Well, it worked—and it didn't. I sold the novel, and people even bought copies of it and read it, and some liked it. But the critics didn't, and much as it pains me to say, they are fundamentally right. Because that little trick of cutting the novel up into short stories simply doesn't work.

A novel isn't a half-dozen short stories with the same characters. The seams invariably show. Why? Because a novel must have integrity. The novel, no matter how dense and wide-ranging it might be, must have a single cumulative effect to please the reader. Every minor climax must point toward the book's final climax, must promise still better things to come.

But in my first novel (all right, I'll name it: *Hot Sleep*), instead of a series of minor climaxes leading toward the final climax of the book, I had six completely unrelated climaxes. In the first short story, my protagonist, as a child, faces a terrible dilemma that shapes his whole future. But when I start the second story, years have passed and those earlier events are not very important anymore—it's hard to see any real effect they might have on the events of the rest of the novel. And at the end of the second story, all but one of the major characters lose their memories in a disaster in space, and to all intents and purposes the third part of the book is another entirely new beginning. All the reader's emotional investment is gone, and he has to begin all over again. No wonder some readers got impatient!

In a way, however, my instinct was correct. You can't write a novel all at once, any more than you can swallow a whale in one gulp. You do have to break it up into smaller chunks. But those smaller chunks aren't good old familiar short stories. Novels aren't built out of short stories.

They're built out of scenes.

Lights! camera! action! cut!

Think of the way a movie works. A new setting is almost always introduced with an establishing shot, showing the audience what characters are present and where they are. Almost every time the film skips from one place to another without actually following the character there, the audience is given some time to get its bearings.

Then, as the film progresses, the camera cuts from one point of view to another, or follows as the characters travel from one place to another. The camera is able to focus on a particular thing that a character is looking at—or that the character is unaware of. But all through a single action, the camera keeps our attention tightly focused on the important matters. Then, when that scene ends, there is another establishing shot; another line of action begins.

As you see the story unwind on the screen, you aren't really aware that between each new setting there are really *many* scenes, small bits of action leading to a single, small climax or revelation. After all, neither novelists nor filmmakers show *everything* that happens. Tremendous amounts of detail are skipped over, left out—hinted at, perhaps, but never shown. All of the action is compressed into the events that *are* shown. While a filmmaker must compress everything into two hours or so, a novelist has a great deal more freedom. Within reasonable limits, you can include all the pertinent information, and the reader will be right there with you.

Like a filmmaker, however, you must present that information carefully. You can't just list the events and motives and speeches of the characters—that's history. Bad history, in fact. Instead, you present the information dramatically, through characters who have understandable desires and who are carrying out understandable actions, and with a structure that helps the reader notice and understand and feel what you want him to.

And the structure you use is composed of hundreds of different scenes, of varying lengths and varying degrees of importance, each one a single continuing action.

A single, continuing action may be, for instance, a sword fight that begins with an insult at a party and continues all over the palace until one man finally gasps with a sword in his chest and the hero, panting, watches his enemy die.

A single, continuing action may be a man standing at the window of an apartment in a tall building, looking out over a city, watching a helicopter land, regretting his decision not to be aboard it.

A single, continuing action may be a journey across the United States, summarized by telling, in two paragraphs, the routine of a single day of travel; that summary is extended to cover all the days of travel.

Each such scene is a unit, designed to have its own effect on the reader; when the scene ends, the reader knows something more—and feels something more.

How is that different from writing a short story? Ideally, a short story is an indivisible unit—every sentence in it points toward the single climax that fulfills the entire work. One moment in the story controls all the rest. But in a novel, that single climax is replaced by many smaller climaxes, by many side trips or pauses to explore. If you keep shaping everything to point to that one climax, your reader will get sick of it after a hundred pages or so. It will feel monotonous. To keep the reader entertained (i.e., to keep him reading) you must give him many small moments of fulfillment along the way, brief rewards that promise something bigger later.

How does this work in a particular novel? Let's go through chapter 27 of a recent bestseller, Stephen King's *The Stand*. After each scene number, the number of paragraphs in the scene appears in parentheses, followed by a synopsis of the scene:

1. (4) Protagonists Larry and Rita have noticed that the electricity is beginning to go off, and the smell of the decaying bodies is terrible; Larry is afraid New York will soon be unlivable.
2. (2) Flashback: They found the body of a man they had been aware of, murdered. It affected Rita deeply.
3. (20) Dialogue: Larry and Rita eat breakfast, and Larry makes the decision to leave.
4. (8) Rita suddenly rushes to the bathroom, vomits. She is fast becoming unable to cope with the disaster.
5. (3) Flashback: Rita is not as strong as Larry had thought at first.
6. (1) Larry wonders if he can take care of her.
7. (13) Dialogue: She decides to go with him, even as he comes to resent her more because of her weakness.

At this point, King takes a larger break. There is a line space, and suddenly we are with Larry and Rita as they walk along the streets of New York. In those first seven scenes, there is a definite sense of building toward a single climax, the moment in scene seven where Larry catches himself hating her. King writes: "Then he felt the familiar surge of self-contempt and wondered what the hell could be the matter with him."

" 'I'm sorry,' he said. 'I'm an insensitive bastard.' "

It is a pivotal moment for Larry; it is the reason why he takes responsibility for her even though he hates the thought of taking her along. It explains his motive. It also sets us up for later tension in later scenes, and finally, in a small way, it leads us to the climax of the novel.

Yet each of the small scenes leading to that climax had a closure of its own. Scene one closes with Larry's dark dream of a black thing that wants him. Scene two closes with the observation that seeing the dead man had made a powerful change in Rita. Scene three ends with a startling change—after a peaceful conversation, Rita suddenly has an expression on her face that scares Larry. Scene eight ends with the startling revelation that Rita is pathetically eager to do whatever she thinks Larry wants her to do. And so on.

Every scene advances the reader toward the minor climax in the seventh scene. Each scene conveys the necessary information and then closes in a way that increases the tension, the reader's expectation of a climax. And the scenes vary— first bare exposition in the author's voice, then a flashback in Larry's mind, then dialogue between Larry and Rita, then physical action as Rita rushes to the bathroom to vomit, then flashback, then reflection, and then dialogue again.

It is as if King had cut from camera to camera, showing us the continuing action from different points of view, revealing bits of information that together built to a whole—the superscene that ends with the line space. And the chapter is composed of five superscenes of varying length that, together, tell a complete episode. The chapter as a whole cements Larry and Rita together in our minds, despite the tension between them. We end up understanding and liking both. They have managed to get out of New York alive, but we know their adventures are just beginning.

Cliffhangers

These are the gulps you can use to down a whole novel. You never sit down to write 300 or 500 or 1,000 pages. You sit down to write a series of scenes that create a superscene with its own minor climax; you then add superscenes together to create the climax that completes the chapter.

Yet, while each closure, each minor climax, each chapter climax is fulfilling to the reader, none of them is *completely* fulfilling. Inherent in every climax is the promise of more tension and greater fulfillment later. In its crudest form, this is the cliffhanger technique—putting the protagonist into an awkward dilemma and then leaving him hanging there while the reader waits to buy the next day's installment. Such obvious tricks irritate most readers; but the technique, in more subtle form, is essential to creating a novel as a whole. After all, what is a novel if not the writer's attempt to involve the reader emotionally in a dilemma and keep him involved until its resolution? In your short stories, you could hold off until your single climax because the reader would stay with you for such a brief time; but in a novel, the reader's patience is not infinite.

Of course, I seriously doubt that Stephen King sat down and planned out each of those seven scenes. I wonder if he even outlined chapter by chapter. The selection of what scenes to present is art; it is felt, not intellectualized. For me, most of those decisions are unconscious. It feels right to include this scene; it feels right to interrupt the action here for a flashback that reveals important information; it feels right to describe this particular setting in loving detail.

You *can* consciously plan, however, to keep yourself aware of the possibilities open to you, so that you use all your tools. You can concentrate on the scenes and superscenes at hand, instead of letting the climax of the novel, hundreds of pages away, distract you from what you are creating now.

And, while you aren't writing short stories anymore, you *have* cut that whale of a novel into pieces small enough that you, like the reader, can forget about the hundreds of pages ahead and concentrate on only the few pages needed to reach the climax of this particular scene.

As a friend of mine once said, "I'd a lot rather fight two tons of tiny lizards than a two-ton fire-breathing dragon."

The second will be better than the first

Novels and short stories are different art forms. They have a lot more in common than do, say, novels and paintings, or even short stories and poems. Yet you are crippling yourself if you try to write a novel under the impression that it's just more of the same thing you have been doing with short stories.

Even if you keep in mind all the things I have pointed out, you will probably find new mistakes or problems I haven't mentioned. After all, there were some things I did *right* in my first novels that you might do wrong. And undoubtedly there are some things I'm *still* doing wrong that I haven't caught yet—and therefore can't warn you about.

Each novel you write, however, will make the next one easier. I'm not talking about mere confidence, either, though finishing one novel will certainly make the next one seem less intimidating. Whether or not you notice what you're learning, you *are* learning. When I was an eight-year-old, first throwing a ball at a basketball hoop, I missed time and time again. But gradually I began to be able to hit the backboard every time, and eventually I got good enough to have the ball come somewhere near the basket on every shot. Though I'm still a miserable basketball player, I did unconsciously learn and improve. In writing novels, of course, each shot takes a long time, and you aren't able to see so easily whether you missed or not. But your brain is still plugging along, learning to become comfortable with the form.

Too comfortable, sometimes. I studied Spanish for eight years and was pretty good in it—but then I lived in Brazil for two years, and spoke Portuguese the whole time. Those languages are so similar that by the end of those two years, I literally could not speak Spanish at all, Portuguese had taken over.

I find a similar thing happening to me now. With five novels under my belt, I find it increasingly hard to use that similar but still different "language" of short stories. I keep forgetting that I don't have hundreds of pages to work with; my most recent 30-page story finally ended at 130 pages, and even at that I felt that I had left out two-thirds of what should have been in it. In other words, my short story came out as a novel whether I wanted it to or not.

Anybody have any advice on how a novelist can learn to write short stories?

Why write a novel?

by Lawrence Block

If you want to write fiction, the best thing you can do is take two aspirins, lie down in a dark room, and wait for the feeling to pass.

If it persists, you probably ought to write a novel. Interestingly, most embryonic fiction writers accept the notion that they ought to write a novel sooner or later. It's not terribly difficult to see that the world of short fiction is a world of limited opportunity. Both commercially and artistically, the short-story writer is quite strictly circumscribed.

This has not always been the case. Half a century ago, the magazine story was important in a way it has never been since. During the '20s, a prominent writer typically earned several thousand dollars for the sale of a short story to a top slick magazine. These stories were apt to be talked about at parties and social gatherings, and the reputation a writer might establish in this fashion helped gain attention for any novel he might ultimately publish.

The change since those days has been remarkable. In virtually all areas, the short fiction market has shrunk in size and significance. Fewer magazines publish fiction, and every year they publish less of it. The handful of top markets pay less in today's dollars than they did in the much harder currency of fifty or sixty years ago. Pulp magazines have virtually disappeared as a market; a handful of confession magazines and a scanter handful of mystery and science-fiction magazines are all that remain of a market once numbered in the hundreds. Whole categories of popular fiction have categorically vanished; the western, the sports story, the light romance—these were once published in considerable quantity, twelve or fifteen

Lawrence Block, *author of more than 100 books, specializes in mystery and suspense fiction. His novel* Deadly Honeymoon *was made into a movie, and film rights have been purchased for several other of his books. His novel* Ariel *was a Book-of-the-Month Club selection, and his short fiction has appeared in major mystery and suspense magazines and in the* Best Detective Stories of the Year. *Block writes a monthly column on fiction for* Writer's Digest.

stories per magazine, and now they have simply gone the way of the dodo and the passenger pigeon.

The remaining pulps are scarcely worth writing for. Consider the plight, for example, of the writer of detective fiction. Twenty years ago, the two leading magazines in the field paid five cents a word for material, and their rejects sold quite readily to any of a batch of lesser markets. Now, at a time when the erstwhile nickel candy bar has gone to a quarter, those two magazines still pay the same nickel a word—and only a single cent-a-word publication exists to skim the cream of the stories they reject.

Long distance satisfactions

The outlook is not much more promising for writers of "quality" fiction. Very few magazines publish stories of literary distinction and pay a decent price for the privilege. After a piece has made the rounds of *The New Yorker*, *Atlantic*, *Harper's*, and a few others, its author is reduced to submitting it to the small literary magazines that pay off in contributor's copies or, at best, token payment. It is not merely impossible to make a living in this fashion; it is very nearly impossible, over the course of a year, to cover one's mailing expenses.

On the other hand, one can make a living writing novels.

I'm not going to make you drool by rattling on about the stratospheric sums certain writers have received of late for their novels. The earnings of best sellers, the fortunes paid for film and paperback rights, have relatively little to do with the average writer, be he neophyte or veteran. James Michener once remarked that America is a country in which a writer can make a fortune but not a living—i.e., a handful of successful writers get rich while the rest of us can't even get by. There's some truth in this—the gap between success and survival is, I submit, an unhealthily yawning one—but there's some hyperbole in it as well. A writer can indeed make a living in America; if he's a reasonably productive novelist, he can make a living verging on comfortability.

Financial considerations aside, I have always felt there are satisfactions in the novel which are not to be found in shorter fiction. I began as a writer of short stories, and to have written and published a short story was an accomplishment in which I took an inordinate amount of pride. But genuine literary achievement, as far as I was concerned, lay in being able to hold in my own hands a book with my own name on the cover. (I was to hold a dozen of my own books before one of them was to bear my own name, as it turned out, but that's by the way.)

Short story writing, as I saw it, was estimable. One required skill and cleverness to carry it off. But to have written a novel was to have achieved something of substance. You could swing a short story on a cute idea backed up by a modicum of verbal agility. You could, when the creative juices were flowing, knock it off start-to-finish on a slow afternoon.

A novel, on the other hand, took real work. You had to spend months on the thing, fighting it out in the trenches, line by line and page by page and chapter by chapter. It had to have plot and characters of sufficient depth and complexity to support a structure of sixty or a hundred thousand words. It wasn't an anecdote, or a finger exercise, or a trip to the moon on gossamer wings. It was a *book*.

The short story writer, as I saw it, was a sprinter; he deserved praise to the extent that his stories were meritorious. But the novelist was a long-distance runner, and you don't have to come in first in a marathon in order to deserve the plaudits of the crowd. It is enough merely to have finished on one's feet.

Space for skills and ideas

These arguments presented above would all seem to urge the writer to turn eventually to the novel. But it's my contention that the beginner at fiction ought to focus his attention on the novel not sooner or later but right away. The novel, I submit, is not merely the ultimate goal. It is also the place to start.

At first, this may well seem illogical. We've just seen the short story likened to a sprint, the novel to a marathon. Shouldn't a marathon runner work up to that distance gradually? Shouldn't a writer develop his abilities in the short story before attempting the more challenging work of the novel?

Certainly a great many of us do begin that way. I did myself, as far as that goes. In my earliest efforts, it was extremely difficult for me to sustain a prose narrative for the 1,500 words necessary to constitute a proper short short. Over a period of time I became increasingly at ease writing full-length short stories, and then I finally wrote my first novel. Other writers have followed a similar path, but perhaps as many have leaped directly into the novel without any serious effort at short stories. There doesn't seem to be any traditional path to follow in becoming a writer. Whatever road leads to the destination turns out to have been the right road for that particular traveler.

With the understanding, then, that all roads lead to Rome, here are some of the reasons why I believe a writer is best advised to begin with a novel.

Skill is less at a premium

This may seem paradoxical—why should a novel require less skill than a short story? You'd think it would be the other way around.

Don't you have to be a better craftsman to manage a novel? I don't think so. Often a novelist can get away with stylistic crudity that would cripple a shorter piece of fiction.

Remember, what a novel affords you as a writer is *room*. You have space to move around in, space to let your characters develop and come to life, space for your story line to get itself in motion and carry the day. While a way with words never hurts, it's of less overwhelming importance to the novelist than the sheer ability to grab ahold of the reader and make him care what happens next.

The bestseller list abounds with the work of writers whom no one would want to call polished stylists. While I wouldn't care to name them, I can think offhand of half a dozen writers whose first chapters are very hard going for me. I'm perhaps overly conscious of style—writing does radically change one's perceptions as a reader—and I find their dialogue mechanical, their transitions awkward, their scene construction clumsy, their descriptions imprecise. But if I can make myself hang on for the first 20 or 30 or 40 pages, I'll lose my excessive awareness of the trees and start to perceive the forest. The author's pure storytelling ability grips me and I no longer notice the defects of his style.

In shorter fiction, the storyline wouldn't have this chance to take over. The story would have run its course before I ceased to notice the author's style.

Similarly, some novels triumph over the style in which they are written because of the grandeur of their themes or the fascination of their subject matter. The epic novel, presenting in fictional form the whole history of a nation, catches the reader up because of the sheer power of its scope. Leon Uris's *Exodus* is a good example of this type of book. And Arthur Hailey's books exemplify the novel that conveys an enormous amount of information to the reader, telling him almost more than he cares to know about a particular industry. This is not to say that these novels, or others of their ilk, are stylistically clumsy, but merely to point out that style becomes a considerably less vital consideration than it must be in short fiction.

The idea is less important

I've known any number of writers who have postponed writing a novel because they felt they lacked a sufficiently strong or fresh or provocative idea for one. I can understand this, because similar feelings delayed my own first novel. Logic would seem to suggest that a novel, by virtue of its length, would require more in the way of an idea than a short story.

If you're having trouble coming up with ideas, you may well be better off with a novel than with short stories. Because each short story absolutely demands either a new idea or a new slant on an old one. Often the short story amounts to very little more than an idea fleshed out and polished into a piece of fiction. This is particularly likely to be the case with the short short, which is typically not much more than a 1,500-word preamble leading up to a surprise ending, an idea thinly cloaked in the fabric of fiction.

Novels, on the other hand, are time and again written with no original central idea to be found. Every month sees the publication of new gothic novels, for example, and the overwhelming majority of them hew quite closely to a single plotline—a young woman is in peril in a forbidding house, probably on the moors; she is drawn to two men, one of whom turns out to be a hero, the other a villain. Another category, the historical romance of the *Love's Tender Fury* variety, has an initially innocent heroine getting ravished in various historical periods and with varying degrees of enjoyment.

Westerns typically adhere to one of five or six standard plotlines. Similarly, there are a handful of basic book types in the mystery and science fiction fields. And, in the world of mainstream fiction, consider how many novels each year deal with nothing more original than the loss of innocence.

This is not to say that the novel does not demand ingenuity. It is this quality which enables the novelist to take a standard theme and hang upon it a book which will seem quite fresh and new to everyone who reads it. As he writes, characters come to life, scenes acquire dimension upon the page, and a wealth of original incident serves to make this particular book significantly different from all those other novels to which it is thematically identical.

Sometimes these elements of characterization and incident which make a novel unique exist in the forefront of the author's mind when he sits down to the typewriter. Sometimes they emerge from his creative unconscious as he goes along.

Easy to learn and earn

I enjoy writing short stories myself. They offer me considerable satisfaction, for all that their production is economically unsound. I very much enjoy being able to sit down at the typewriter with an idea fully formed in my head and devote myself to a day's work of transforming that idea into a finished piece of fiction.

The enjoyment's so keen that I'd do this sort of thing more often—except that each story requires a reasonably strong central idea, and the idea itself gets used up in the space of a couple of thousand words. I simply don't get that many ideas that I find all that appealing.

Ed Hoch makes a living writing nothing but short stories, and he manages this superhuman feat because he seems to be a never-ending fount of ideas. The development of short story ideas and their speedy metamorphosis into fiction is what gives him personal satisfaction as a writer. I sometimes find myself envying him, but I know I couldn't possibly come up with half a dozen viable short story ideas every month the way he does. So I take the easy way out and write novels.

You can learn more

Writing has this in common with most other skills: we develop it best by practicing it. Whatever writing we do helps us to become better writers.

It has been my observation, however, that there is no better way to learn how to write than by writing a novel. I learned quite a bit by writing short stories. I learned much much more when I wrote my first novel, and I have continued to learn something or other with virtually every novel I have written since.

Short story writing taught me quite a bit about effective use of the language. I learned, too, how to construct a scene and how to handle dialogue. Everything I learned in this fashion was valuable.

When I wrote a novel, it was as if I were working out now with heavy weights; I felt growth in muscles I had not previously been called upon to use at all.

Characterization was at once a very different matter. Before my characters had existed to perform specific functions and speak specific lines. Some were well drawn, some were not, but none had the sort of fictive life that transcended their role on the page. When I wrote a novel, the characters came to life for me. They had backgrounds, they had families, they had quirks and attitudes that added up to more than the broad lines of caricature. I had to know more about them in order to make them maintain vitality over a couple of hundred pages, and thus there was more substance to them. This is not to say that my characterization in my earliest novels was particularly good. It was not. But I learned immeasurably from it.

I learned, too, how to deal with time in fiction. My short stories had often consisted of a single scene, and rarely of more than three or four scenes. The novels I wrote seemed to cover a matter of days or weeks, and of course consisted of a great many scenes. I learned to deal with any number of technical matters— viewpoint shifts, flashbacks, internal monologues, etc.

You can earn while you learn

It's curious how many writers tend to expect instant gratification. We've barely rolled a sheet of paper into the typewriter and right away we expect to see our efforts on the bestseller list.

It seems to me that other artists are rather less impatient of tangible success. What painter expects to sell the first canvas he covers? More often than not he plans to paint over it once it's dried. What singer counts on being booked into Carnegie Hall the first day he hits a high note? Every other artistic career is assumed to have an extended and arduous period of study and apprenticeship, yet all too many writers think they ought to be able to write professionally on their first attempt, and mail off their first stories before the ink is dry.

There must be reasons for this. I suppose the whole idea of communication is so intrinsic a part of what we do that a piece of writing which goes unread by others is like Bishop Berkeley's tree falling where no human ear can hear it. If nobody reads it, it's as if we hadn't even written it.

Then too, unpublished writing strikes us as unfinished writing. An artist can hang a canvas on his own wall. A singer can croon in the shower. A manuscript, though, is not complete until it is in print.

At first glance this desire to receive money and recognition for early work would look like the height of egotistic arrogance. It seems to me, however, that what it best illustrates is the profound insecurity of the new writer. We yearn to be in print because without this recognition we have no way of establishing to our own satisfaction that our work is of any value.

I would not for a moment advise a new writer to expect to get any recognition or financial gain out of a first novel. Unless you are fully prepared to spend months writing a book with no greater reward than the doing of it, you would very likely be better off getting rid of your typewriter and taking up some leisure pastime which places less of a premium on achievement.

This notwithstanding, there is no gainsaying the fact that any number of first novels are published every year. Publishers typically bitch about the difficulty of breaking even on a first novel, conveniently ignoring the several first novels per season to achieve bestseller status. True, most first novels are not published. True too, most that are sell very poorly. The wonder is that any are published at all.

Thus it is possible to make certain gains, in money and in recognition, while acquiring those skills which can only be acquired through experience. And this sort of paid apprenticeship is far more readily accessible to the novelist than the short story writer.

It wasn't always this way. When the newsstands teemed with pulp magazines, the pulps were precisely where the new writer earned a living—albeit a precarious one—while developing his skills and refining his technique. A similar kind of magazine apprenticeship is standard procedure to this day in the field of nonfiction; article writers earn while they learn by writing for house organs and trade journals before they are ready to write either nonfiction books or articles for more prestigious magazines.

Author's apprenticeship

Some of the surviving fiction magazines are certainly open to new writers— *Ellery Queen's Mystery Magazine*, for example, makes a special point of publishing first stories, having printed over 500 maiden efforts to date. But ever since the decline of the pulps in the 1950s, there has not been sufficient depth to the magazine fiction market for a writer to serve out his apprenticeship there.

In contrast, the market for original paperback fiction continues to be quite strong, and quite receptive to the work of beginners. The relative viability of the various categories of category fiction—suspense, adventure, western, science fiction, gothic, light romance, historical romance—runs a cyclical course, but there are always several categories which constitute a healthy market.

I served my own novelistic apprenticeship in the field of paperback sex novels. In the summer of '58, I had just finished my first novel and was wondering what to do next. My agent was marketing the book; I had no idea whether it would sell or fail completely.

The agent got in touch with me to say that a new publisher was entering the field of sex novels. Did I know what these books were? Could I read a few and try one of my own?

I bought and skimmed several representative examples in the field. (If I had all of this to do over again, I'd spend more time on this analysis.) I then sat down at the typewriter with the assurance of youth and batted out three chapters and an outline of what turned out to be the start of a career.

I didn't know how many sex novels I was to write in the years to follow. For quite a while I was doing a book a month for one publisher with occasional books for other houses as well, along with a certain amount of more ambitious writing. I suppose I must have turned out a hundred of them. Maybe not—I really don't know, and my copies of most of the books were lost in the course of a move some years ago. Let's just agree that I wrote a lot of them and let it go at that.

I learned an immeasurable amount from doing this. Bear in mind that these books were written in more innocent times; while they were the most inflammatory reading matter then on the market, they can barely qualify as soft-core pornography by contemporary standards. Unprintable words were not to be found, and descriptive passages were airbrushed like an old-fashioned *Playboy* centerfold.

The books had a sex scene per chapter, but the scene couldn't take up the whole chapter. There was plenty of room left for incident and characterization, for dialogue and conflict and plot development—room, in short, for a story to be told with periodic interruptions for sexual titillation. Without the sex, surely, the books would have had no reason for existence; the stories in the main were not strong enough to carry the books unassisted. (Though I can think of one or two exceptions, books where a character took over and came to life, so that the sexual episodes seemed almost like annoying interruptions. But this was rare indeed.)

This was a wonderful apprenticeship for me. I was by nature a fast writer, gifted with the ability to write smooth copy in a first draft; thus I could produce these books rapidly enough to make a satisfactory living. (They did not pay much, nor were there royalties to be had or subsidiary income to anticipate; it was indeed like working for the pulp magazines, with all sales outright.)

I learned a tremendous amount about how to write fiction, learning by the irreproachable method of trial and error. I could fool around with multiple viewpoint, with various sorts of plot structure, could in fact try whatever I wanted as long as I continued to write the books in English and keep the action coming. I got any number of auctorial bad habits out of my system. And, as I've said, I earned while I learned.

I'm acquainted with quite a few writers who started out by cultivating this particular secret garden. There were a number who never went on to anything else; they earned some easy money at sex novels until the novelty wore off, but lacked the particular combination of talent and drive which it evidently takes to establish a writing career. The rest of us moved on, sooner or later, to other things. I don't know anyone who doesn't regard the experience as valuable.

In my own case, I suspect I found the sex-novel groove too comfortable and stayed with it too long, past the point where it was able to teach me much. I probably should have tried stretching my literary muscles a little sooner. On the other hand, I was painfully young then in virtually every possible way. The sex books put bread on the table and gave me the satisfaction of regular production and regular publication at a stage when I was incapable of writing anything much more ambitious. I can hardly regret the time I devoted to them.

Is the sex novel field a good starting place for a beginner today? I'm afraid not. Their equivalent in today's market is the mechanical, plotless, hard-core porn novel, written with neither imagination nor craft and composed of one overblown sex scene after another. The books I wrote were quite devoid of merit—let there be no mistake about that—but by some sort of Gresham's Law of Obscenity they've been driven off the market by a product that is indisputably worse. Any dolt with a typewriter and a properly dirty mind could write them; accordingly, the payment is too low to make the task worth performing. Finally, the books are published by the sort of men who own massage parlors and peep shows. You meet a better class of people on the subway.

There's no need, though, to be nostalgic for the old days, be they the old days of pulp magazines or the old days of soft-core sex novels. There always seems to be an area in which to serve out a writer's apprenticeship; for the foreseeable future it's almost certain to be a novel of some sort.

Surprises at the typewriter

The suggestion that a beginner ought to begin as a novelist is a radical one. The natural response is to offer some immediate objections. Let's consider some of the most obvious ones.

Isn't it harder to write a novel than a short story?

No. Novels aren't harder. What they are is longer.

That may be a very obvious answer, but that doesn't make it any less true. It's the sheer length of a novel that the beginning writer is apt to find intimidating.

As a matter of fact, you don't have to be a beginner to be intimidated in this fashion. My suspense novels generally stop at 200 pages or thereabouts. On the several occasions when I've begun books I knew would run two or three times that length, I had a lot of trouble getting started. The very vastness of the projects put me off.

What's required, I think, is a change in attitude. To write a novel you have to resign yourself to the fact that you simply can't prime yourself and knock it all out in a single extended session at the typewriter. The process of writing the book is going to occupy you for weeks or months—perhaps for years.

But each day's stint at the typewriter is simply that—one day's work. And that's every bit as true whether you're writing short stories or an epic trilogy. If you're writing three or six or ten pages a day, you'll get a certain amount of work accomplished in a certain span of time—whatever it is you're working on.

I remember the first really long book I wrote. When I sat down to begin it I knew I was starting something that had to run at least 500 pages in maunscript. I got a good day's work down and wound up knocking out 14 pages. I got up from the typewriter and said, "Well, just 486 pages to go"—and went directly into nervous prostration at the thought.

The thing to remember is that a novel's not going to take forever. All the old clichés actually apply—a journey of a 1,000 miles begins with a single step, and slow and steady honestly does win the race.

Consider this: If you write one page a day, you will produce a substantial novel in a year's time. The writer who turns out one book a year, year in and year out, is generally acknowledged to be quite prolific. And don't you figure you could produce one measly little page, even on a bad day? Even on a *rotten* day?

When I write a short story I can hold the whole thing in my head when I sit down at my desk. I know exactly where I'm going and it's just a matter of writing it down. I don't have that kind of grasp on a novel.

Of course you don't. Nobody does. But there are two things to keep in mind.

First of all, recognize that the total control you have over short stories may be largely illusory. What you really have is confidence—because you *think* you know everything about the story by the time you set out to write it.

But, if you're like me, you keep surprising yourself at the typewriter. Characters take on a life of their own and insist upon supplying their own dialogue. Scenes that looked necessary at the outset turn out to be superfluous, while other scenes take a form other than that you'd originally intended for them. As often as not, midway through the story you'll think of a way to improve elements of the plot itself.

This happens to a much greater extent in novels. And it should. A work of fiction ought to be an organic entity. It's alive, and it grows as it goes. Even the most elaborately outlined novel, even the product of those authors who write outlines half the length of the final book, must have this life to it if it is going to live for the reader. The writing of fiction is never purely mechanical, never just a matter of filling in the blanks and tapping the typewriter keys.

A timely investment

A second thing to realize is that you do not have to grasp the whole book at once because you are not going to be writing the whole book at once. Novels are written—as life is lived—One Day At A Time. I've found that all I really have to know about a book in order to put in a day's work on it is what I want to have happen during that day's writing.

I get in trouble when I find myself starting to project. As soon as I step back and try to envision the novel as a whole, I'm likely to be paralyzed with terror. I become convinced that the whole thing is impossible, that there are structural flaws which doom the entire project, that the book can't conceivably resolve itself successfully. But as long as I can get up each morning and concentrate exclusively on what's going to happen during that particular day's stint at the typewriter, I seem to do all right—and the book takes shape, page by page and chapter by chapter.

Many of the books I write are mystery novels of one sort or another. Books of this type have two storylines which unfold simultaneously. First, there's what happens before the reader's eyes from the first page to the last, the record of action as perceived by the viewpoint character or characters. Underlying this plot is the mystery storyline itself, that which is happening (or has happened previously) and is withheld from the reader until the book's climax.

Years ago, I took it for granted that a writer had to have both of these storylines fully worked out in his head before putting a word on paper. I've since learned that it's occasionally possible to write an elaborately complicated mystery novel without knowing the identity of the villain until the story is almost at an end. In *Burglars Can't Be Choosers*, I was within two or three chapters of the finish before a friend's chance remark enabled me to figure out whodunit; I had to do some rewriting to tie off all the loose ends, but the book worked out fine.

Suppose I spend a year writing a novel and it proves to be unsalable. I can't risk wasting that much time, so wouldn't it be safer to stick to short stories?

Would it? Let's assume that you could write 12 or 20 short stories in the time it would take you to write a novel. What makes you think you'd have a better chance of selling them? The nature of the market is such that you'd probably have a better chance placing one novel for publication than one out of 20 short stories. And, assuming you wouldn't sell either the novel or the short stories, why would a batch of unsalable short stories feel less like a waste of time than an equally unsalable novel?

Nevertheless, the fear of wasting one's time keeps a lot of people from writing novels. But I don't think the fear is justified even when it proves true.

So what if a first novel's unsalable? For heaven's sake, most of them are, and why on earth should they be otherwise?

Any of several things may happen to the person who produces an unsalable first novel. He may discover, in the course of writing the book, that he was not cut out to be a novelist, that he doesn't like the work or doesn't possess the talent.

I don't know that it's a waste of time to make this sort of discovery.

On the other hand, the author of an unpublishable first novel may learn that writing is his métier, that he has a burning desire to continue with it, and that the weaknesses and flaws which characterized his first book need not appear in the ones to follow. You might be surprised to know how many successful writers produced hopelessly incompetent first books. They were not wasting their time. They were learning their trade.

Consider Justin Scott, whose first novel I read in manuscript several years ago. It was embarrassingly bad in almost every respect, and hopelessly unpublishable. But it did him some good to write it, and his second novel—also unsalable, as it happened—was a vast improvement over the first.

He remained undiscouraged. His third novel, a mystery, was published. Several more mysteries followed. Then he spent over a year writing *The Shipkiller*, a nautical adventure story on a grand scale which brought a six-figure paperback advance, sold to the movies for a handsome sum, and did well enough in the stores to land on several of the bestseller lists.

Do you suppose Justin regrets the time he "wasted" on that first novel?

Maybe I haven't started a novel because I'm afraid I wouldn't finish it.

Maybe so. And maybe you wouldn't finish it. There's no law that says you have to.

Please understand that I'm not advocating abandoning a novel halfway through. I've done this far too often myself and it's something I've never managed to feel good about. But you do have every right in the world to give up on a book if it's just not working, or if you simply discover that writing novels is not for you.

As much as we'd all prefer to pretend our calling is a noble one, it's salutary to bear in mind that the last thing this poor old planet needs is another book. The only reason to write anything more extensive than a shopping list is because it's something you want to do. If that ceases to be the case you're entirely free to do something else instead.

I'm inclined to hope you *will* complete your first novel, whatever its merits and defects, whatever your ultimate potential as a novelist. I think the writing of a novel is a very valuable life experience for those who carry it through. It's a great teacher, and I'm talking now about its ability to teach you not about writing but about yourself. The novel, I submit, is an unparalleled vehicle for self-discovery.

But whether you finish it or not remains your choice. And failing to begin a task for fear of failing to complete it doesn't make abundant sense, does it?

OK, I'm convinced. I'm going to sit down and write a novel. After all, short stuff isn't significant, is it?

It isn't, huh? Who says?

I'll grant that commercial significance singles out the novel, and that long novels are automatically considered to be of more importance than short ones. I'll admit that, with a handful of exceptions, short story writers don't get much attention from literary critics. And I won't deny that your neighbors will take you more seriously as a writer if you tell them you've written a novel. (Of course if that's the main concern, just go ahead and tell them. You don't have to write anything. Lie a little. Don't worry—they won't beg to read the manuscript.)

But as far as intrinsic merit is concerned, length is hardly a factor. You've probably heard of the writer who apologized for having written a long letter, explaining that he didn't have the time to make it shorter. And you may be familiar with Faulkner's comment that every short story writer is a failed poet, and every novelist a failed short story writer.

I'm not sure the desire to be significant is a particularly useful motive for writing anything. But length is no guarantee of significance and brevity no hallmark of the trivial. Sonnet, short story, thousand-page novel—write whatever it is you want to write, and that's the long and short of it.

Must the novelist crusade?

by Eudora Welty

Not too long ago I read in some respectable press that Faulkner would have to be reassessed because he was "after all, only a white Mississippian." For this reason, it was felt, readers could no longer rely on him for knowing what he was writing about in his life's work of novels and stories, laid in what he called "my country."

Remembering how Faulkner for most of his life wrote in all but isolation from critical understanding, ignored impartially by the North and South, with only a handful of critics in forty years who were able to "assess" him, we might smile at this journalist as at a boy let out of school. Or there may have been an instinct to smash the superior, the good, that is endurable enough to go on offering itself. But I feel in these words and others like them the agonizing of our times. I think they come of an honest and understandable zeal to allot every writer his chance to better the world or go to his grave reproached for the mess it is in. And here, it seems to me, the heart of fiction's real reliability has been struck at—and not for the first time—by the noble hand of the crusader.

It would not be surprising if the critic I quote had gained his knowledge of the South from the books of the author he repudiates. At any rate, a reply to him exists there. Full evidence as to whether any writer, alive or dead, can be believed is always at hand in one place: any page of his work. The color of his skin would modify it just about as much as would the binding of his book. Integrity can be neither lost nor concealed nor faked nor quenched nor artificially come by nor outlived, nor, I believe, in the long run denied. Integrity is no greater and no less today than it was yesterday and will be tomorrow. It stands outside time.

Eudora Welty is a major novelist, critic, and chronicler of life in the South. She received the Pulitzer Prize in 1973 for The Optimist's Daughter *and has written many novels and short stories for magazines and literaries which have earned her numerous awards. Although she wrote the above article during the tumultous days of the civil rights movement in the late '60s, the tenets on fiction writing which she supplied are equally applicable today.*

The heart of fiction

The novelist and the crusader who writes both have their own place—in the novel and the editorial respectively, equally valid whether or not the two happen to be in agreement. In my own view, writing fiction places the novelist and the crusader on opposite sides. But they are not the sides of right and wrong. Honesty is not at stake here and is not questioned; the only thing at stake is the proper use of words for the proper ends. And a mighty thing it is.

Because the printed page is where the writer's work is to be seen, it may be natural for people who do not normally read fiction to confuse novels with journalism or speeches. The very using of words has these well-intentioned people confused about the novelist's purpose.

The writing of a novel is taking life as it already exists, not to report it but to make an object, toward the end that the finished work might contain this life inside it, and offer it to the reader. The essence will not be, of course, the same thing as the raw material; it is not even of the same family of things. The novel is something that never was before and will not be again. For the mind of one person, its writer, is in it, too. What distinguishes it above all from the raw material, and what distinguishes it from journalism, is that inherent in the novel is the possibility of a shared act of the imagination between its writer and its reader.

"All right, Eudora Welty, what are you going to do about it? Sit down there with your mouth shut?" asked a stranger over long distance in one of the midnight calls that I suppose have waked most writers in the South from time to time. It is part of the same question, Are fiction writers on call to be crusaders? For us in the South who are fiction writers, is writing a novel *something we can do about it*?

It can be said at once, I should think, that we are all agreed upon the most important point: that morality as shown through human relationships is the whole heart of fiction, and the serious writer has never lived who dealt with anything else.

And yet, the zeal to reform, which quite properly inspires the editorial, has never done fiction much good. The exception occurs when it can rise to the intensity of satire, where it finds a better home in the poem or the drama. Large helpings of naiveté and self-esteem, which serve to refresh the crusader, only encumber the novelist. How unfair it is that when a novel is to be written, it is never enough to have our hearts in the right place! But good will all by itself can no more get a good novel written than it can paint in watercolor or sing Mozart.

Observation and inner truths

Nevertheless, let us suppose that we feel we might help if we were to write a crusading novel. What will our problems be?

Before anything else, speed. The crusader's message is prompted by crisis; it has to be delivered on time. Suppose John Steinbeck had only now finished *The Grapes of Wrath*? The ordinary novelist has only one message: "I submit that this is one way we are." This can wait. When we think of Ibsen, we see that causes themselves may in time be forgotten, their championship no longer needed; it is Ibsen's passion that keeps the plays alive.

Next, we as the crusader-novelist shall find awkward to use the very weapon we count on most: the generality. On fiction's pages, generalities clank when wielded, and hit with equal force at the little and the big, at the merely suspect and the really dangerous. They make too much noise for us to hear what people might be trying to say. They are fatal to tenderness and are in themselves nonconductors of any real, however modest, discovery of the writing's own heart. This discovery is the best hope of the ordinary novelist, and to make it he begins not with the generality but with the particular in front of his eyes, which he is able to examine.

Taking a particular situation existing in his world, and what he feels about it in his own breast and what he can make of it in his own head, he constructs on paper, little by little, an equivalent of it. Literally it may correspond to a high degree or to none at all; emotionally it corresponds as closely as he can make it. Observation and the inner truth of that observation as he perceives it, the two being tested one against the other: to him this is what the writing of a novel is.

We, the crusader-novelist, having started with our generality, must end with a generality; they had better be the same. In the place of climax, we can deliver a judgment. How can the plot seem disappointing when it is a lovely argument spread out? It is because fiction is stone-deaf to argument.

The ordinary novelist does not argue: he hopes to show, to disclose. His persuasions are all toward allowing his reader to see and hear something for himself. He knows another bad thing about arguments; they carry the menace of neatness into fiction. Indeed, what we as the crusader-novelist are scared of most is confusion.

Great fiction, we very much fear, abounds in what makes for confusion: it generates it, being on a scale which copies life, which it confronts. It is very seldom neat, is given to sprawling and escaping from bounds, is capable of contradicting itself, and is not impervious to humor. There is absolutely everything in great fiction but a clear answer. Humanity itself seems to matter more to the novelist than what humanity thinks it can prove.

When a novelist writes of man's experience, what else is he to draw on but the life around him? And yet the life around him, on the surface, can be used to show anything, absolutely anything, as readers know The novelist's real task and real responsibility lie in the way he uses it.

Writing from within

Situation itself always exists; it is whatever life is up to here and now, it is the living and present moment. It is transient, and it fluctuates. Using the situation, the writer populates his novel with characters invented to express it in their terms.

It is important that it be in their terms. We cannot in fiction set people to acting mechanically or carrying placards to make their sentiments plain. People are not Right and Wrong, Good and Bad, Black and White personified; flesh and blood and the sense of comedy object. Fiction writers cannot be tempted to make the mistake of looking at people in the generality—that is to say, of seeing people as not at all *like us*. If human beings are to be comprehended as real, then they have to be treated as real, with minds, hearts, memories, habits, hopes, with passions and capacities like ours. This is why novelists begin the study of people from within.

The first act of insight is to throw away the labels. In fiction, while we do not necessarily write about ourselves, we write out of ourselves, using ourselves; what we learn from, what we are sensitive to, what we feel strongly about—these become our characters and go to make our plots. Characters in fiction are conceived from within, and they have, accordingly, their own interior life; they are individuals every time. The character we care about in a novel we may not approve of or agree with—that's beside the point. But he has got to seem alive. Then and only then, when we read, we experience or surmise things about life itself that are deeper and more lasting and less destructive to understanding than approval or disapproval.

The novelist's work is highly organized, but I should say it is organized around anything but logic. Just as characters are not labels but are made from the inside out and grow into their own life, so does a plot have a living principle on which it hangs together and gradually earns its shape. A plot is a thousand times more unsettling than an argument, which may be answered. It is not a pattern imposed; it is inward emotion acted out. It is arbitrary, indeed, but not artificial. It is possibly so odd that it might be called a vision, but it is organic to its material: it is a working vision, then.

A writer works *through* what is around him if he wishes to get to what he is after—no kind of proof, but simply an essence. In practice he will do anything at all with his material: shape it, strain it to the breaking point, double it up, or use it backwards; he will balk at nothing—see *The Sound and the Fury*—to reach that heart and core. But even in a good cause he does not falsify it. The material itself receives deep ultimate respect: it has given rise to the vision of it, which in turn has determined what the novel shall be.

Commitment to convictions

The ordinary novelist, who can never make a perfect thing, can with every novel try again. But if we write a novel to prove something, one novel will settle it, for why prove a thing more than once? And what then is to keep all novels by all right-thinking persons from being pretty much alike? Or exactly alike? There would be little reason for present writers to keep on, no reason for the new writers to start. There's no way to know, but we might guess that the reason the young write no fiction behind the Iron Curtain is the obvious fact that to be acceptable there, all novels must conform, and so must be alike, hence, valueless. If the personal vision can be made to order, then we should lose, writer and reader alike, our own gift for perceiving, seeing through the fabric of everyday to what to each pair of eyes on earth is a unique thing. We'd accept life exactly like everybody else, and so, of course, be content with it. We should not even miss our vanished novelists. And if life ever became not worth writing fiction about, that, I believe, would be the first sign that it wasn't worth living.

With a blueprint to work with instead of a vision, there is a good deal that we as the crusader novelist must be at pains to leave out. Unavoidably, I think, we shall leave out one of the greatest things. This is the mystery in life. Our blueprint for sanity and of solution for trouble leaves out the dark. (This is odd, because surely it was the dark that first troubled us.) We leave out the wonder because with wonder it is impossible to argue, much less to settle. The ordinary novelist thinks it had better be recognized. Reckless as this may make him, he believes the insoluble is part of his material, too.

The novelist works neither to correct nor to condone, not at all to comfort, but to make what's told alive. He assumes at the start an enlightenment in his reader equal to his own, for they are hopefully on the point of taking off together from that base into the rather different world of the imagination.

It's not only the fact that his world is bigger and that fewer constrictions apply that may daunt us as crusaders. But the imagination itself is the problem. It is capable of saying everything but no. In our literature what has traveled the longest way through time is the great affirmative soul of Chaucer. The novel itself always affirms, it seems to me, by the nature of itself. It says what people are like. It doesn't, and doesn't know how to, describe what they are *not* like, and it would waste its time if it told us what we ought to be like, since we already know that, don't we? But we may not know nearly so well what we are as when a novel of power reveals this to us. For the first time we may, as we read, see ourselves in our own situation, in some curious way reflected. By whatever way the novelist accomplishes it—there are many ways—truth is borne in on us in all its great weight and angelic lightness, and accepted as home truth.

Passing judgment on his fellows, which is trying enough for anybody, is frustrating for an author. It is hardly the way to make the discoveries about living that he must have hoped for when he began to write. If he does not pass judgment, does this mean he has no conscience? Of course he has a conscience; it is, like his temperament, his own, and he is one hundred percent answerable to it, whether it is convenient or not. What matters is that a writer is committed to his own moral principles. If he is, when we read him we cannot help but be aware of what these are. Certainly the characters of his novel and the plot they move in are their ultimate reflections. But these convictions are implicit; they are deep down; they are the rock on which the whole structure of more than that novel rests.

Indeed, we are more aware of his moral convictions through a novel than any flat statement of belief from him could make us. We are aware in that part of our mind that tells us truths about ourselves. Yet it is only by way of the imagination— the novelist's to ours—that such private neighborhoods are reached.

A private address

There is still to mention what I think will give us, as the crusader-novelist, the hardest time: our voice will not be our own. The crusader's voice is the voice of the crowd and must rise louder all the time, for there is, of course, the other side to be drowned out. Worse, the voices of most crowds sound alike. Worse still, the voice that seeks to do other than communicate when it makes a noise has something brutal about it; it is no longer using words as words but as something to brandish, with which to threaten, brag, or condemn. The noise is the simple assertion of self, the great, mindless, general self. And for all its volume it is ephemeral. Only meaning lasts. Nothing was ever learned in a crowd, from a crowd, or by addressing or trying to please a crowd. Even to deplore, yelling is out of place. To deplore a thing as hideous as the murder of three civil rights workers, demands the quiet in which to absorb it. Enormities can be lessened, cheapened, just as good and delicate things can be. We can and will cheapen all feeling by letting it go savage or parading in it.

Writing fiction is an interior affair. Novels and stories always will be put down little by little out of personal feeling and personal beliefs arrived at alone and at firsthand over a period of time as time is needed. To go outside and beat the drum is only to interrupt, interrupt, and so finally to forget and to lose. Fiction has, and must keep, a private address. For life is *lived* in a private place; where it means anything is inside the mind and heart. Fiction has always shown life where it is lived, and good fiction, or so I have faith, will continue to do this.

A Passage to India is an old novel now. It is an intensely moral novel. It deals with race prejudice. Mr. Forster, not by preaching at us, while being passionately concerned, makes us know his points unforgettably as often as we read it. And does he not bring in the dark! The points are good forty years after their day *because of the splendor of the novel*. What a lesser novelist's harangues would have buried by now, his imagination still reveals. Revelation of even the strongest forces is delicate work.

Indeed, great fiction shows us not how to conduct our behavior but how to feel. Eventually, it may show us how to face our feelings and face our actions and to have new inklings about what they mean. A good novel of any year can initiate us into our own new experience.

From the working point of view of the serious writer of fiction, nothing has changed today but the externals. They are important externals; we may have developed an increased awareness of them, which is certainly to the good; we have at least the same capacity as ever for understanding, the same eyes and ears, same hearts to feel, same minds to agonize or remember or try to put things together, see things in proportion with. While the raw material of our fiction is changing dramatically—as indeed it is changing everywhere—we are the same instruments of perceiving that we ever were. I should not trust us if we were not. And we do not know what is to be made out of experience at any time until the personal quotient has been added. To convey what we see around us, whatever it is, so as to let it speak for itself according to our lights is the same challenge it ever was, not a different one, only perhaps made harder by the times. Now as ever we must keep writing from what we know; and we must really know it.

No matter how fast society around us changes, what remains is that there is a relationship in progress between ourselves and other people; this was the case when the world seemed stable, too. There are relationships of the blood, of the passions and the affections, of thought and spirit and deed. There is the relationship between the races. Now can one kind of relationship be set apart from the others? Like the great root system of an old and long-established growing plant, they are all tangled up together; to separate them you would have to cleave the plant itself from top to bottom.

Passion: the chief ingredient

What must the Southern writer of fiction do today? Shall he do anything different from what he has always done?

There have already been giant events, some of them wrenchingly painful and humiliating. And now there is added the atmosphere of hate. We in the South are a hated people these days; we were hated first for actual and particular reasons, and now we may be hated still more in some vast unparticularized way. I believe there must be such a thing as sentimental hate. Our people hate back.

I think the worst of it is we are getting stuck in it. We are like trapped flies with our feet not in honey but in venom. It's not love that is the gluey emotion; it's hate. As far as writing goes, which is as far as living goes, this is a devastating emotion. It could kill us. This hate seems in part shame for self, in part self-justification, in part panic that life is really changing.

Fury at ourselves and hurt pride, anger around too often, outrage at being hated need not obscure forever the sore spots we Southerners know better than our detractors. For some of us have shown bad hearts. As in the case of our better qualities, we are locally blessed with an understanding and intimate knowledge of our faults that our worst detractors cannot match, and have been in a less relentless day far more relentless, more eloquent, too, than they have yet learned to be.

I do not presume to speak for my fellow Southern writers, a group of individuals if there ever was one. Yet I would like to point something out; in the rest of the country people seem suddenly aware now of what Southern fiction writers have been writing about in various ways for a great long time. We do not need reminding of what our subject is. It is humankind, and we are all part of it. When we write about people, black or white, in the South or anywhere, if our stories are worth the reading, we are writing about everybody.

In the South, we who are now at work may not learn to write it before we learn, or learn again, to live it—our full life in the South within its context, in its relation to the rest of the world. "Only connect," Forster's ever wise and gentle and daring words, could be said to us in our homeland quite literally at this moment. And while the Southern writer goes on portraying his South, which I think nobody else can do and which I believe he must do, then if his work is done well enough, it will reflect a larger mankind as it has done before.

And so finally I think we need to write with love. Not in self-defense, not in hate, not in the mood of instruction, not in rebuttal, in any kind of militance, or in apology, but with love. Not in exorcisement, either, for this is to make the reader bear a thing for you.

Neither do I speak of writing forgivingly; out of love you can write with straight fury. It is the *source* of the understanding that I speak of; it's this that determines its nature and its reach.

We are told that Turgenev's nostalgic, profoundly reflective, sensuously alive stories that grew out of his memories of early years reached the Czar and were given some credit by him when he felt moved to free the serfs in Russia. Had Turgenev set out to write inflammatory tracts instead of the sum of all he knew, could express, of life learned at firsthand, how much less of his mind and heart with their commitments, all implicit, would have filled his stories! But he might be one of us now, so directly are we touched, with a hundred-plus years gone by since they were first published.

Indifference would indeed be corrupting to the fiction writer, indifference to any part of man's plight. Passion is the chief ingredient of good fiction. It flames right out of sympathy for the human condition and goes into all great writing. (And of course passion and the temper are different things; writing in the heat of passion can be done with extremely good temper.) But to distort a work of passion for the sake of a course is to cheat, and the end, far from justifying the means, is fairly sure to be lost with it. Then the novel will have been not the work of imagination, at once passionate and objective, made by a man struggling in solitude with something of his own to say, but a piece of catering.

Light on the past and present

To cater to is not to love and not to serve well either. We do need to bring to our writing, over and over again, all the abundance we possess. To be able, to be ready, to enter into the minds and hearts of our own people, all of them to comprehend them (us) and then to make characters and plots in stories that in honesty and with honesty reveal them (ourselves) to us, in whatever situation we live through in our own times; this is the continuing job, and it's no harder now than it ever was, I suppose. Every writer, like everybody else, thinks he's living through the crisis of the ages. To write honestly and with all our powers is the least we can do, and the most.

Time, though it can make happenings and trappings out of date, cannot do much to change the realities apprehended by the imagination. History will change in Mississippi, and the hope is that it will change in a beneficial direction and with a merciful speed, and above all bring insight, understanding. But when William Faulkner's novels come to be pictures of a society that is no more, they will still be good and still be authentic because of what went into them from the man himself. Mankind still tries the same things and suffers the same falls, climbs up to try again, and novels are as true at one time as at another. Love and hate, hope and despair, justice and injustice, compassion and prejudice, truth-telling and lying work in all men; their story can be told in whatever skin they are wearing and in whatever year the writer can put them down.

Faulkner is not receding from us. Indeed, his work, though it can't increase in itself, increases us. His work throws light on the past and on today as it becomes the past—the day in its journey. This being so, it informs the future too.

What is written in the South from now on is going to be taken into account by Faulkner's work; I mean the remark literally. Once Faulkner had written, we could never unknow what he told us and showed us. And his work will do the same thing tomorrow. We inherit from him, while we can get fresh and firsthand news of ourselves from his work at any time.

A source of illumination is not dated by what passes along under its ray, is not qualified or disqualified by the nature of the traffic. When the light of Faulkner's work will be discovering things to us no more, it will be discovering *us*. Even we shall lie enfolded in perspective one day; what we hoped along with what we did, what we didn't do, and not only what we were but what we missed being, what others yet to come might dare to be. For we *are* our own crusade. Before ever we write, we are. Instead of our judging Faulkner, he will be revealing us in books to later minds.

Advice to unborn novelists

by Pearl Buck

The first piece of advice I shall give a novelist is to take the greatest care about where he is born. Other people may be born anywhere and it makes very little difference to anybody. But to a novelist it matters a great deal, because all his experience in life from his very earliest years is his material from which he must draw all his life long, and to start in the wrong country is most unfortunate for him, and handicaps him irreparably. I take myself as an example. I was born in America, but at the age of three months I was taken across the Pacific in a market basket.

I have been continually hampered by that fact. For it is the greatest disadvantage to a novelist to spend his pre-writing years outside of his own country. I shall never forget how handicapped I was when I first began to send out small tentative essays and stories. Back they came to me, always with the same regret—"We are not interested in anything about China." The manuscript of my little preliminary book I sent first myself to a publisher, only to have it come flying back—"regret the American public is not interested in anything on China." Here was I, compelled by my very nature to write stories, and yet the English speaking people, *my* people, did not want the only thing I knew to write about. I sent the little manuscript to an agent, expecting nothing, and I am sure that out of all the many publishers to whom he sent it not one who refused it did not include as at least one of his chief reasons against it that it dealt with Chinese subjects. When by some miracle it found a publisher, it was because he saw through the Chinese material and sensed

Pearl Buck (1892-1973) received the Pulitzer Prize for The Good Earth *in 1932. In 1938 she became the first woman to win the Nobel Prize for literature. Among her best works are the biographies of her missionary parents,* Fighting Angel *and* The Exile *(both 1936). Although she is known for her writing on China, where she grew up and lived much of her adult life, Pearl Buck wrote about American life in children's books, biographies, novels and an autobiography.*

the possiblity that the writer was primarily interested not in the Chinese people, but in people and writing about them.

One cause: humanity

My books have been called foreign not only in their material, but in their very speech. People say they are written in a style like that of the Bible. The style is not Biblical, it is Chinese. For of course when I wrote in China of Chinese things about Chinese, I used the Chinese tongue.

This brings me to another piece of advice. Never, small unborn novelist, learn first to speak in a language which is not your own. For I made that great mistake. After outgrowing the market basket, I naturally learned to talk and I talked Chinese. The first curls of my tongue and lips were made about Chinese vowels and consonants, and my first sentences were in Chinese idioms. The consequence is that when I am writing about Chinese people the story spins itself in my mind entirely in Chinese, and I literally translate it as I go. The phrases for which I am praised or blamed are idiomatic Chinese phrases, and I do not even know many times whether they are good English. I know that so long as I live I shall have difficulty with prepositions, because the Chinese language has very few, and English is simply prickly with them.

The point I am trying to make to the unborn novelist is, if he is to lead a comfortable life, that he belongs somewhere, and that he write about his own. Yet I begin to have premonitions that there is no real comfort anywhere for the novelist. I call to mind now two reviews I have read in the last few days of a recent book, unfortunately mine, in which the endeavor was made to portray very briefly through the eyes of a reticent Chinese student four or five Americans. I thought them interesting and likable people—a landlady, very good-natured although overweight as many landladies seem to be the world over, a dreaming, sensitive, religious-minded professor and his kindly Christian wife, and their daughter, a keen, intelligent, rather moody young librarian in a university. But the reviewer says with great indignation, "At least the author might have chosen the best types to represent out of her own country." It is the old familiar accusation, "Why don't you use your writing for the glory of Jesus Christ, for the glory of China, for the glory of America"—always some glory or other! The one inexorable answer of any novelist who at least desires above all else to be a true artist as far as he is able, is that he will not use any little ability he has for the glory of any religion or any cause or any country or any people or anything. He will let his writing flower as it will, and his only cause be humanity, whatever its color or creed, whether it be good or evil. He will portray human beings only as he sees them. His sight may be partial or it may be warped or it may be defective in many ways, because he also is no more than human, but if he be artist he will still write only what he really sees and knows, as he sees it. He cannot follow any other sight or hearsay, nor will he tolerate the guidance of a cause, however Christian, righteous, moral or communist it may be.

It may be then that all my advice to the unborn novelist is worthless. The truth is that he will never quite belong in the world, however carefully he chooses his native land. For it is not true that he is only human—he is always a little fey—a little just off the human. He will live much of his life bemused by his companions, his actual flesh and blood companions who are always more to him than mere flesh and blood, and besides them, he will have all the people whom he shapes from them, his book people, his real people. And because he lives in two worlds and never quite in either, is never quite upon this planet, and yet can never get wholly away from it, he will never know how to answer the questions people will surely ask him about his books—strange, definite, hard questions.

Stout heart and conviction

They will ask him, "Do you take your characters from life?" How can he answer? He knows what they mean. They mean, "Did you lift such and such a character from an actual setting? Is it Mrs. This, or is it Dr. That?" Well, of course, it is not either. It is not an actual person, for how could an actual person fit into the covers of a book? The book is not a continent, not a definite geographical measure, it cannot contain so huge a thing as an actual full-size person. Any person has to be scaled by eliminations to fit the book world. Of course, it is true that many of his characters do come from ideas given him by factual people, slight pictures he sees as he passes. The way a woman leans her head upon her hand habitually may suggest to him some other woman of his own mind, and he may clothe that dream woman with the same eyes and hair, and bestow upon her certain gestures and ways that are that factual woman's also. But he never, I think, exactly reproduces any character or any situation. His own imagination, his own emotions, the peculiar need of the situation in his book, shape and remold and inform all he takes from the actual world about him. It is true that even his imagined people, however, must have their start in actual life, because the novelist cannot imagine life quite without actuality as one cannot imagine music who has never heard a note of music.

What is real, anyway? Not what happens outside a person. I have spent my life in the midst of the most foolishly extraordinary external circumstances. I have seen the crude happenings of nature in famine and flood, and I have seen the crude happenings of men in wars and conflicts and oppressions. I have made long journeys in sedan chairs and in oxcarts and on horseback and in airplanes. But there is nothing instrinsically interesting in such things except as they happen to some person. It is only what happens inside a person that is really drama and really exciting. It brings one back to the old question of whether there can be a noise if there is no one to hear it. Does anything happen if it does not happen to someone? The novelist at least must believe that it does not.

And this little novelist must be born with one thing more. He must have a stout heart. He cannot be afraid of anyone. He cannot care for what anyone thinks. He must care for everyone, because every human being has for him especial interest. A novelist above all men must like people, and yet he must not let any human being shape his course or direct his art. He must let no approbation deceive him, nor any criticism dishearten him. Above all, he must seek to please no one. Not even the critics? Not even the critics!

For let no simple-minded, newly born novelist think that with the publishing of his book his trouble is ended. There is that horrible day of publication, which is really for him a day of judgment, when the critics in the newspapers sharpen their carving knives and leap upon their prey, determined to send him to heaven or to hell. I do not know how to advise this young novelist, how to prepare him against that dreadful day.

For it was a matter of some astonishment to me that even at first I did not mind them as much, apparently, as first novelists usually do. That very first day when a kind friend came in with a crumpled newspaper in her hand and said with a preparatory, consolatory air, "Now you must not think they all feel as this one does—remember he is very young—and his reviews are very much based on his personal prejudices," and all those things which kind friends do say to a novelist when a critic has given the beloved book a bad review. Well, I braced myself, and read the review, and it was very unfavorable. But somehow, I did not mind. It seemed as though I had heard it all before—all the accusations and denunciations, all the reiterating of a violent personal creed, to which I had no objection, but with which I did not agree—for myself.

Painful perception, acute joy

Well, the point of it is that I must advise the little unborn novelist when his first book is published and his second and his third even to the end, that he must not allow himself to be cast down by critics patterned into creeds of varying political religions, any more than he must allow himself to be weakened by the fulsome praise of critics too loose and too little discerning, so that by their over-praise he relaxes his own high standard, which is to know what he wants to do, and do it to the height of his ability, and let the result stand.

The truth is, of course, that amazingly few literary critics are able to obey that simple basic rule of all criticism, to ask what does this novelist want to do, and has he done it? The critic has no right to say, "I don't like this book because I don't agree with the author's point of view or his choice of people—in other words, I don't like his theology because it is not mine. I believe in immersion and he doesn't, and he's wrong."

It may very well be that the little novelist decides after all this that it is better not to be born a novelist at all, and he had better be born something else. My final advice to him, then, is that if he can bear to be born something else, he had better be. But if, like some of his fellows, he had rather never live than not be a novelist and a teller of tales, then let him come with the stoutest joy, for the heartiest life in the world awaits him. He will suffer ten times as much as anyone else, because he will be born cruelly sensitive to every impact upon him, to the touch of every person, of everything, of every happening. He will suffer a hundred times to another's once, because he suffers not only through the medium of his own one life, but through the lives of every person he creates. He will see ugliness beyond his endurance, because he cannot help seeing everything. To feel—to see—are his nature, even as it is his nature to create. But he will see beauty, too, as none other can see it. He will feel joy as none other can feel it, love will be to him a radiance greater than the sun, and appreciation will find him somehow if he does his work to his honest best and it will be sweeter than honey to him. If his every sense is heightened to an agony of perception, it is justly heightened, and joy is acute, too. And his will be that acutest joy of all, that rare, strange, secret, inexplicable ecstasy of joy, the joy of a god who one day took earth into his hand and created a man and a woman, and saw them live.

Portrait of the artist as a first novelist

by Michiko Kakutani

Living in a small, cheerless flat and working at a dreary job, the eager young novelist harbors intimations of glamor and success: He will write his *Bildungsroman*, perfect his art and become a respected artist. Such is the portrait of the writer as a young man that emerges in the latest novels of William Styron and Philip Roth. In *Sophie's Choice*, Stingo, a callow Southerner not unlike the young Styron, comes to New York, where he reads manuscripts for a publisher by day and dreams by night of becoming "a writer with the same ardor and the soaring wings" of Melville or Flaubert. In *The Ghost Writer*, Nathan Zuckerman, an aspiring author who resembles the young Roth in his desire to escape the banality of his middle-class youth, quits his job selling magazine subscriptions and sets out to visit the secluded home of an older writer, hoping to find in the Master a spiritual father for his own Dedalean quest.

By now, of course, both Roth and Styron are themselves masters. And even as they set down stylized recollections of their own apprenticeships, a new generation of writers has come of age. Now in their 20s and 30s, these new writers share the same expectations and uncertainties as their predecessors. What is different is that during the last two decades, the whole literary enterprise has become increasingly institutionalized. Always wary of the uncommercial author, publishers have become more and more concerned with profit margins and hence more dubious than ever about the unknown writer; at the same time, a formal apprentice system composed of creative-writing courses, government grants and teaching jobs has developed to nurture and support the growing number of would-be authors.

The elusive goals: acceptance and acclaim

How does a novelist establish a reputation today? For some, the confluence of

Michiko Kakutani joined The New York Times *as a reporter of news and culture in 1980. Previously she worked as a staff writer for* Time *magazine and* The Washington Post *after her graduation from Yale in 1976.*

talent and good fortune makes for early success. Lisa Alther made a bright debut with *Kinflicks*, as did Ron Hansen with *Desperadoes* and Jayne Anne Phillips with *Black Tickets*. Mary Gordon started her writing career as a poet, never expecting that her first attempt at fiction, *Final Payments* would receive both critical and popular acclaim. "It took me very much by surprise," she says, recalling the "tasteless" television advertisements for her novel. "I was always concerned with being a perfect writer. I wanted a tremendous *succes d'estime,* but I thought that meant working very hard in solitude and never knowing if anyone would care at all."

For others, though, the machinery of success works more slowly. Scott Spencer, whose third novel *Endless Love* was recently nominated for an American Book Award, started writing over a decade ago. "Perhaps because I came from the Midwest, I had an extraordinary idealism about writers," says the 34-year-old author. "I never wanted to do anything else, and I didn't pursue my education (beyond college) because I didn't want to have many escape routes. I was really quite fanatic in my belief that there was only one life for me."

A story of obsessive passion told in lyrical prose, *Endless Love* was preceded by *Last Night at the Brain Thieves Ball* and *Preservation Hall* which elicited respectable reviews but only modest commercial success. During those early years, Mr. Spencer ghost-wrote short stories for women's magazines, served as an evaluator for federally financed education programs, and worked as a clerk in an employment agency. He wrote most of *Endless Love* during a three-year period in which his family lived in a small house in New Hampshire and subsisted on his unemployment compensation and his wife's income as a short-order cook. The book has now been optioned as a movie, and its earnings have already surpassed the total of $50,000 that Mr. Spencer made in his last ten years of work. The money has enabled him to buy certain things he did without for years: several new suits and a Volvo station wagon.

Mr. Spencer is among the more fortunate ones. Many young writers spend years, even decades, working for considerably more modest rewards: a fellowship perhaps, or an encouraging review. Publication by a commercial house is difficult in itself. Julia Markus, for instance, began writing over a decade ago and accumulated more than 70 rejection slips before her third book, *Uncle,* was discovered in a pile of unsolicited manuscripts and chosen for the $10,000 Houghton Mifflin Literary Fellowship Award in 1978. Her first novel was never published; the second she printed herself.

Cost conscious and commercial

The writing of fiction has always been something of a marginal enterprise, and the decreasing number of magazines that pay well for it has only made matters worse. During the '20s, F. Scott Fitzgerald managed to cultivate a readership as well as support his unprofitable novels by selling short stories to many publications; today only a fraction of those periodicals exists. The odds of selling a story to one of the few remaining slicks that accept fiction—*The New Yorker, The Atlantic, Harper's, Playboy, Penthouse, Esquire*—are now formidable indeed, and young writers are increasingly turning to academic quarterlies and small magazines for publication.

To complicate the situation, first novels are usually high-risk investments, and high risks, say many editors, are harder to take these days. Given a poor or merely unexceptional track record with a first novel, many authors face even greater difficulties in selling their second and third. Such writers do not represent "a discovery" to publishers, but rather a liability: Their works have been tested and found wanting in the bookstores.

Further, it is more difficult than ever for publishers to make money with unknown writers. Library sales, which flourished during the late '60s thanks to funds allocated by the federal government, have declined. The current emphasis on so-called "blockbusters" means that there is less money left for uncommercial titles. And adequate distribution has become more and more problematic. As a result, many first novels do not even sell out their first printing of 5,000 to 10,000 copies, and in a shrinking mass paperback market they often do not get the chance to earn back their publishing costs in subsidiary rights. "The uncertainty in publishing today," says Aaron Asher, the editor-in-chief of Farrar, Straus & Giroux, "obviously hits hardest at the little known writers and writers whose books are not perceived to be for a large audience."

Given the current economics of publishing, many houses simply decline to give unsolicited manuscripts a reading, and will almost perfunctorily dismiss any fiction proposal by an unknown author. A good agent can often obtain a better hearing for a writer's work, but most aspiring authors find that agents are reluctant to take them on until they have already established a reputation. Consequently, young writers are often left with as many rejection slips from agents as from editors.

"The industry is always looking for the next John Irving," says Ted Solotaroff, an editor at Harper & Row, noting that his house publishes about eight of the more than 500 fiction manuscripts it receives a year. "I've been pretty much able to publish the young writers I *really* believe in. What suffers is the good novel, not the first-rate one. Three or four years ago I'd have gone along with a book that had flaws if I believed in the writer—in his promise, his talent, his perseverance to write other things. I don't find myself doing that now. I have to confine myself to books I'm completely enthusiastic about."

Cost-conscious as they are, publishing houses must always consider the popular appeal of any new author they take on, and the majority of first novels that get published, it seems, *are* decidedly commerical works (*Scruples*, after all, was a first novel). The judges for last year's Ernest Hemingway Foundation Award, given annually for a first book of fiction, estimated that of the 125 submissions they received (from both commercial and small press houses), only one in 12 represented literary works; the rest were intended for a mass audience.

Communication, then craft

Curiously enough, many of the "serious" novels written by younger authors today are also relatively accessible works with conventional narratives that stand in marked contrast to the more rarefied, experimental work of, say, William H. Gass or Donald Barthelme. There is an apparent emphasis on narrative and lucidity, a desire to tell a story, even to entertain. As Vance Bourjaily of the Iowa Writers Workshop observes, "the kind of dense prose that makes for difficulty doesn't seem to appeal to the younger people today; they don't seem interested in experimentation. It's as though writing novels were simply an exercise in communication."

Tim O'Brien, for one, is eager to write a bestseller. "I realized I wanted to reach a lot of people," says the 33-year-old author, who won a National Book Award last year for *Going After Cacciato*. "I don't want to be studied in English classes; I want to be read." A political science major at Macalester College in Minnesota, Mr. O'Brien says that as a student, he never thought about a writing career because he had nothing particular to say. Then, in 1968, he was drafted. What he saw in Vietnam left an indelible impression on him, and he began to write.

After writing *If I Die in a Combat Zone*, a straightforward, nonfiction account of his time in Vietnam, Mr. O'Brien joined *The Washington Post*. He felt constrained by reporting, however, and began working on *Northern Lights*, a conventional first novel about growing up in a small town. By 1974 he had left *The Post* and was writing, *Going After Cacciato*, a novel set in Vietnam. "I came to writing because I'd seen guys die and I wanted to tell how it was in the most direct, blunt way I could," Mr. O'Brien recalls. "I didn't give a damn about language or elegant sentences. I just had something I cared very deeply about, and I wanted to get the stuff across to other people. The craft came later."

Autobiographical influence

For Mr. O'Brien's friend John Irving, the craft came first. The author of *The World According to Garp* knew from the time he was 14 that he wanted to be a writer, and he set about learning the skill as methodically as he went about training to wrestle. In college, he wrote every day, mechanically learning how sentences worked, and later spent two years at the Writers' Workshop in Iowa, where he finished *Setting Free the Bears*. "I was writing it chiefly with the priority of finishing it," he recalls. His next two novels— *The Water-Method Man* and *The 158-Pound Marriage*—elicited a modest response; the fourth was *Garp*.

Although the author adamantly denies any autobiographical impulse, a certain resemblance between Mr. Irving and his hero Garp remains obvious—both are writers of fiction, both are wrestlers, both grew up in New England prep school towns. There has always been a tendency among younger writers, of course, to rely heavily on the facts and observations of their own lives; as they achieve a mature voice, that impulse is usually either abandoned or transformed into an emotional and geographical terrain of the author's own making. Yet Mary Gordon, who has drawn at length upon her own severe Catholic upbringing for both *Final Payments* and her next novel, *The Mercy Seat*, believes that for most writers such regional and ethnic themes are of diminishing significance.

"I'm a bit of an anachronism," explains the 30-year-old writer, who grew up attending Irish Catholic schools in Valley Stream, L.I. and in Queens. "The kind of intense religious life I was exposed to was more typical of a generation before me. I think I was lucky in having such a peculiar upbringing. Because backgrounds seem to be more and more homogeneous and less eccentric now, it's harder for most people to have such ready-made subjects to write about."

Individual literary efforts

If younger fiction writers share any theme at all, it is that vague '60s notion of impermanence, whereby backgrounds become gratuitous and tradition itself is abjured. This is not subversion in the political sense—indeed politics seem curiously absent in these books—but the spiritual detritus of an era of change. Many of these writers, after all, were members of the counterculture, although most seem to have maintained a certain distance from their contemporaries. Miss Gordon demonstrated with the other Columbia and Barnard students on Morningside Heights, but always worried about getting home to her mother's house in time for dinner. Mr. O'Brien worked for Eugene McCarthy and protested the war—until he was drafted and went to Vietnam. Jayne Anne Phillips, who is now 27, spent a year working as a waitress in such communities as Berkeley, Calif., and Boulder, Colorado, "where people were vegetarians and went to craft fairs," then went off to the Iowa Writers Workshop to write *Black Tickets*, a collection of short stories focused, she says, on "relationships that were changed by the mobility and rootlessness" of the times.

In her latest novel, *Falling in Place*, Ann Beattie also depicts the dislocations of spirit that afflict her peers, and like so many of her own characters who drift vaguely into love or work, Miss Beattie seems to have achieved her own reputation as a representative literary voice almost in spite of herself. "I never had a burning ambition to be a writer," says the 32-year-old author. "I started writing because I was bored with graduate school—in some kind of attempt to care about literature again, I guess I started writing it. Years ago when I might have done something else, I just didn't pursue it, and now I don't know what else to call myself except a writer."

While still in graduate school at the University of Connecticut, Miss Beattie started publishing short stories in such publications as the *Texas Quarterly* and *Western Humanities Review*. In 1973, after she had received some 20 rejections from *The New Yorker*, Roger Angell, the magazine's fiction editor, discovered one of her stories in the "slush" pile of unsolicited manuscripts. She has been a regular contributor there ever since.

Having recently moved into New York City from the suburbs of Connecticut, Miss Beattie and her husband, a musician, now live in a modest two-room apartment in Chelsea, where she writes on an electric typewriter on a small desk in the living room. Months may pass, she says, in which she does no writing at all, but once she starts a story, she works 18 hours a day, writing as fast as she can type—some 70 words a minute.

Miss Beattie claims that few of her friends are writers and that she prefers it that way. It is a sentiment apparently shared by many of her contemporaries, who seem to have lost the communal spirit of their predecessors. In the '50s, writers frequently moved within the same circles, their work was grounded in a shared legacy of modernism, and New York was clearly the nexus of literary life. Today, no such center exists—anywhere. Few of the new young writers regularly read one another's work; fewer still actually meet their literary contemporaries. As Barry Hannah, the author of *Airships*, says, "I have no idea what's going on in New York, except what I read in the slicks." Mr. Hannah lives in Tuscaloosa, Alabama; Stephen Goodwin, in Washington, D.C.; Lisa Alther, in Hinesburg, Vermont; Mary Gordon, in Poughkeepsie, New York; Jayne Anne Phillips in Provincetown, Massachusetts. John Irving and Tim O'Brien, who live several blocks from one another in Cambridge, Massachusetts, visit perhaps once every three months.

Technically superior generation

This extraordinary dispersion has to do, in part, with the proliferation of writing programs around the country. Whereas previous generations of writers tended to learn their craft at newspapers or simply by reading the works of the old masters before migrating to New York, would-be authors today can receive a master's degree in creative writing at schools around the country, then go on to teaching careers themselves. They need not seek out a Master as did Roth's young Zuckerman; instead, they may become disciples of older, established writers within academia—as did Stephen Goodwin, who studied with Peter Taylor at the University of Virginia.

"It was an old-fashioned notion that you would do pretty much what the Master did," says the author of *Kin* and *The Blood of Paradise*, recalling how similar his early stories were to his mentor's. "You couldn't help but want to be like him, and later, it was a little hard to get out from under his shadow." After leaving the University of Virginia, Mr. Goodwin began teaching at a local college in Virginia, set up housekeeping in a small backwoods cabin—much in the way that his hero did in *The Blood of Paradise*—and began to work on developing his own voice. By teaching and writing an occasional article for *The Washington Post* or *Country Journal*, he has been able to live "a pleasantly marginal existence" while working on his novels.

By furnishing a hermetic environment of study and a formal system of apprenticeship, writing programs free the young writer from the responsibility of having to invent his own career as so many authors did in the past. Instead of taking a menial job, the aspiring novelist can now survive comfortably at a university with a little help from grant programs and lecture circuits. It is precisely this aspect of the new apprenticeships, though, that disturbs many older writers and editors. The proliferation of writing programs, they argue, tends to create an insulated world devoid of authentic experience and offers false encouragement to would-be authors of mediocre talents, fostering what the novelist Reynolds Price calls "a subculture of semi-failed writers who take in one another's laundry. It gives them a sense they're writers before they've ever written anything serious," he says. "The old-fashioned thought is that you'd better go off and sit in your room and write—not postpone it by sitting in class with other writers."

But whatever their other effects, writing programs have no doubt contributed to the high degree of technical facility achieved by this new generation of authors. In virtually all their books, there exists an emphasis on precision, a respect for control. It is her fine sense of language and her eye for social detail that help Mary Gordon to maintain that delicate balance of intellect and emotion in *Final Payments*, just as it is her almost grudging use of words in *Uncle* that enables Julia Markus to give the shape and resonance of a man's entire life in all of 170 pages. And in *The Blood of Paradise*, Mr. Goodwin transforms an otherwise conventional story about a young man and his family through the calculated economy of his prose.

While their voices and their subject matter remain as disparate as the circumstances of their lives, it is evident that these new writers share both an appreciation and working knowledge of craft. "I think this generation of novelists is technically far superior to the generation before it," says John Gardner, the prolific author of *On Moral Fiction* and such novels as *October Light* and *Freddy's Book*. "Never before in history have we seen so many people who are so good at what they do. The question that remains is whether that technique is accompanied by a vision—a vision that will endure."

Research is a snap

by Jacqueline Briskin

The light was flat in the corner of the carriage museum where the hack stood.

Bert, my husband, advised. "There's not enough contrast. And the tongue of the wagon is in the frame. You'll get a rotten picture."

But I had already pressed the button. "It's just perfect," I said.

We both were right.

My photography would come in last in any contest, yet it was precisely what I needed. As soon as Bert brought it out of his darkroom, it was pinned on the immense bulletin board that fills one wall of my writing room. I squinted at the hidden recesses of the carriage . . . . Mmm, I thought. The picture had become an important part of the photographic research for my novel *Paloverde*, which McGraw-Hill would publish on completion.

Years ago, when I started writing, I thought that research of every kind was strictly for nonfiction writers. But as I began sending out short stories, I noted that the ones that didn't come back in their self-addressed, stamped envelopes, the stories that were published, had one thing in common. I had recently spent time at their location.

And with that I perceived an important truth.

My readers had many ways of spending their leisure, and if I wanted them to believe in people and stories invented in the curve of my skull, I had to present them with an enticing and alluring effect of reality. My characters had to exist in a world that had the textures of reality. In other words, I finally understood what I had been told from the first day I started to write.

Don't tell your story. Show it.

Jacqueline Briskin is the author of numerous short stories and four novels, three of which, California Generation, Rich Friends *and* Paloverde, *were on the bestseller lists.* Paloverde *was a featured alternate of the Literary Guild and a main selection of the Doubleday Book Club. The author's books have been translated into 17 foreign languages.*

Seeing is reliving

This discovery hit me while I was writing about two boys and a girl in the summer between high school and college. The three were surfers. We live in Southern California. I spent several mornings at the beach, early, when surfing is permitted. I took along a camera. I snapped a few abysmally bad color photographs. But I pinned them up, and each time I glanced at them I would recapture the feel of morning-cool sand, hear the laughing camaraderie of the surfers, see them balance or fall from their fiberglass boards, see the curling waves with strands of seaweed encased in luminous blue-green water.

A lens can capture only the visual, yet as I glanced at my photographs all the sensory details of those mornings flooded back. And this personalized computer tape inside each human mind is why a billion cameras are taken on a billion vacations.

The story sold to *Seventeen*. It was my first sale to a mass market. And it was the first time I was translated. The story was printed in England, Germany, Holland and Denmark.

After that my 35mm camera became my most important research tool. Sometimes Bert would come along because he's a far better photographer than I am. Often, though, I would have to insist he take a certain picture. He couldn't see anything worthwhile. But for me there was a vague, undefinable *some*thing.

Which brings me back to the dusty carriage museum.

The old hack had a quality that haunted me.

Paloverde, my first historical novel, involved more research than I had ever done. It is a three-generational saga of the tangled destinies, loves and fortunes of a fictional Los Angeles family called Van Vliet. And I knew that something important would happen to one of the Van Vliets in the mysterious recesses of that hack.

Sure enough, it is where Bud Van Vliet proposes to Amelie Deane. The scene is long, evocative, and even now, as I type this page, I find myself turning to the photograph to see where Amelie and Bud are sitting, and how he, in his desperation, has moved to the traditional suitor's pose, kneeling awkwardly in the narrow space as the high wheels rattle over the unpaved streets of Los Angeles.

Striking oil

A lot of other photographs are on my bulletin board.

The frame house where the Van Vliets first live, with its spoolwork veranda and shingles carved of indestructible sequoia—I can run up those four steps, fling open the front door and know the furnishing in every room, including that odd-shaped bedroom. I have never been inside that particular house, but I have photographed other varnished, curlicued Victorian interiors.

I never outline a plot. Before I start to write, however, my characters are clear. Once I am "inside" the novel, they make their destinies known to me.

Much of the story of *Paloverde* evolved from the long weekends my husband and I spent exploring and doing research. I needed to find out about railroads. We drove up to the Mother Lode Country to see a collection of antique trains still in use. Yes, I know there are excellent books with photographs of old trains, but would those photographs recall to me the heat of the steam, the acrid odor of grease and overheated metal, the blinding sun on the silvered edge of wheels, the shuddering of a wooden platform as the train pulls in?

This time, however, the benefits went deeper than sensory details. Once I had explained that I was working on a historical saga about Los Angeles and was currently on a section about the railroad, the men in the roundhouse took an interest in me.

A grayhaired engineer helped me onto the cab to look at an ancient locomotive. The firebox was blazing. "This old General burns coal," he said. "But there's no coal here in the West. We have lots of oil. And back in the '90s some smart boy figured out how to use oil in the firebox."

My mind jumped. Burning oil rather than coal was a practical idea that would appeal to an ambitious, success-haunted man like Bud Van Vliet. The conversion would, in part, be the basis of the great fortune he amasses.

The fortune is built on oil. Paloverde Oil.

Oil, in actuality, was discovered within one mile of downtown Los Angeles. The original well was not sunk by conventional drilling but was dug by hand, and I knew that Bud's brother, an impoverished visionary, would dig *his* well by hand.

As far as I could ascertain, none of the Los Angeles Central Oil Field wells were still in existence.

Needing to get a feel of the topography, we tracked down the location of the first well. But as we drove we could see that the original hills had been leveled for the Hollywood Freeway. Despairing of ever finding the location of that first well, we parked and walked under the freeway on Glendale Boulevard. "I can't imagine there's a marker," I sighed.

We turned a corner. And there it was. Not the original derrick. (I had to go to Santa Paula to get pictures of an old, brea-soaked wooden derrick.) But there stood a producing well marked *Los Angeles #1*. It was still pumping as it had been since 1892! "There's the start of Paloverde Oil," I whispered.

And my skin prickles with the same awe each time I look at the photograph.

Photos and festivities

My pictures are not uniform. Some are in black and white, others in color, some are small, others very large.

During the three years it took me to write and research *Paloverde*, I took maybe 200 shots. Most of them were meaningful only to me. Missions. Old trolley cars. Derelict houses. Wildflowers. A lizard. Rare old maps. And, of course, a paloverde tree.

The Van Vliets' maternal ancestors, who (fictionally) owned much of the land that became Los Angeles, named their vast rancho after a paloverde tree growing near their house. Paloverdes are rare in the Los Angeles area. Native to the desert, they put out very few leaves. They store moisture in their wood. The trunks and branches are a bright green. My photograph of this strange-looking, vivid tree, so significant to the novel, is an 8x10 color print.

The old maps were found in various libraries. I was graciously given permission to photograph them. Bert made enlargements for me. The map of Los Angeles in 1885 is in six pieces, glued on a cardboard four feet square.

My favorite pictures are of a fandango, an old-fashioned, California-style dancing party.

A fandango is central to the plot of the novel. The tragic schism in the Van Vliet family occurs because 3Vee (Vincent Van Vliet) is secretly in love with Amelie, his brother Bud's wife. At a fandango, 3Vee gets drunk and leads Amelie away from the festivities to confess this love. Then, in his turmoil of drunken misery, he rapes her, a completely out-of-character action that haunts his generation, and the next.

Each summer the Aman dancers of Los Angeles recreate a fandango at an old adobe house, the Leonis Adobe, in the San Fernando Valley. Between us, Bert and I got some spectacular shots of the whirling senoritas in their lacy mantillas. Alas, though, much as I would love to share these pictures, to print them would be an invasion of privacy. I neglected to get releases. (You can profit by my experience: If there is the least chance your photograph might be published, do, do, do get a release.)

As *Paloverde* moves to the twentieth century, the third generation of Van Vliets takes center stage. The hero of this section of the novel is Kingdon Van Vliet, a movie star aviator. Again, I could have relied on pictures in books and magazines. Instead, I sought out old planes. Jennies, Nieuports. Spads. And I have memories that include wind shivering on canvas wings and black streaks left by exhaust. As I pinned my new treasures on the bulletin board, I filed away my old photographs methodically.

Paloverde takes place from 1884 to 1922, and the historical events, tastes, foibles of each of these years are filed chronologically on maybe 2,000 cards. The small photographs go with these cards. The large photographs are kept in a tin case with the folded maps, newspaper clippings and pamphlets.

So much research.

There is a danger of getting so submerged that the imagination refuses to work. And imagination, ultimately, is the only spark that brings fiction to life.

As I typed the final draft, I took out my photographs.

They evoked the usual flood of sensory images. But what amazed me was the subtle alteration, the way each had become part of the fabric of the novel.

For example, the hack I had photographed in flat light is forever to me the secret enclosure where Bud Van Vliet convinces Amelie Deane to marry him.

I had succeeded.

The photographs were no longer research. They had become part of *Paloverde*, part of my created reality and—hopefully—part of my readers' lives.

How to turn fact into fiction

by George Antonich

Since that awesome day I sold my first story for $50, then spent $300 celebrating, my wife has never been one to let my expenditures go unchallenged. On a recent budget-cutting kick, she informed me that since we already subscribed to our local small town newspaper, my prized San Francisco *Chronicle* would have to be dropped.

With a bellow of righteous anger, I sat down to prove with figures that it was my most valuable writing tool. My résumé   surprised even me. Last year the paper cost me less than $50. From its pages I culled plot ideas for over 50 short stories, 32 of which I sold for an average of 5.25¢ per word. The *Chronicle* stayed. Instead, my beer ration was cut.

Author Max Shulman once said, "The writer who waits for inspiration will starve to death." I agree. As a *commercial* freelancer averaging almost three sales per month, I can't afford to wait for The Muse to strike in a blinding flash of light. I stress the word commercial because one of its meanings dearest to me is: *having financial gain as an object.* Writing in the book of Proverbs, another freelancer advised, *". . . open your eyes, and you will have plenty of bread."*

To you searchers after story ideas, I say: Open your eyes to the never-ending supply being provided daily in every newspaper. Oh, I know touting newspapers as idea sources has become almost a cliché. Yet nowhere have I seen an author take some of his news-inspired plots and follow their metamorphosis from stark fact to salable fiction. That is what I'll attempt to do.

George Antonich spent the last dozen of his years as a fulltime writer of short stories and mysteries, one of which was chosen for the Best Detective Stories of 1974. *He also wrote the comic strip* Abel N. Reddy, *sold jokes and filler items to magazines and TV scripts to programs in the '60s. A former Army man, he bartended part-time while writing "to keep touch with people, learn how they talked and know what they were thinking."*

Hot tip

For example, what does the following news item, quoted in its entirety, mean to you as a writer?

Laguy, France
A man trying to gas himself here forgetfully lit one last cigarette, caught his clothes on fire in the resultant explosion, and drowned in a barrel of water where he jumped to extinguish the flames.

Reuters

To me, the item was fascinating. I began immediately to suppose—my favorite method of working out a plot idea. Suppose the man had publicly declared his intention of doing away with himself? Suppose he had actually undertaken this desperate course of action? So far, so good—but for salable fiction we need *conflict*. Suppose a large amount of money was involved in the form of an insurance policy, with a suicide clause which would nullify payment to his heirs? Suppose, at the coroner's inquest, opposing factions fought bitterly to establish the actual cause of death? Did the man in fact commit suicide, or was his death accidental?

As a result of my supposing, I came up with a 5,000-word short story titled, "Cause of Death." It sold first time out to *Alfred Hitchcock's Mystery Magazine* and it brought me a check large enough to cover my *Chronicle* subscription for the next six years.

Does that sound too simple? It is, really. I did not, of course, sit down at once and dash off a story about a Frenchman who had goofed his own suicide. About France, I know nothing. I had to have locale I was familiar enough with to sound convincing to the editor. Yes, the editor—not the reader. The editor knows what his readers want. My job is to please him.

On hand I had some umpteen thousand words about an Indian trading post in Arizona, prepared for an article that never sold. Waste not, want not! My suicide-villain became the owner of a thriving curio and art shop. Married to an Indian girl, Miles Rigby was a doomed man. In addition to having an inoperable brain tumor, he suffered from severe emphysema from too much smoking, a fact about which his wife never ceased to nag him.

Their marital relations disintegrating, and knowing he was going to die any-how, Rigby decides to kill himself to make certain that she will not get his insur-ance money. To this end, he goes to his studio behind the main house, turns on the gas jets, and informs his wife over the intercom that he is destroying himself. There is a mysterious explosion and Rigby is found dead in the swimming pool—truth being much too strange for fiction, the barrel of water seemed a bit too much to swallow.

The insurance company representative, intent on proving suicide, clashes with the narrator-hero, who is also the coroner. The hero wants to prove accidental death so the widow will get the insurance money.

Here, the choice of a rural locale proved invaluable. Since I am not a legal brain, I could not conduct a coroner's inquest in the grand manner of Perry Mason. Being the only doctor around, my hero was appointed coroner. It's his first experi-ence at conducting such an affair. My story opens:

I brushed away pesky rivulets of desert-hot sweat trickling down into my eyes, rapped my gavel, and faced my twelve good neighbors in the jury box. "An inquest," I explained, "is a judicial inquiry conducted by a coroner—that's me. Together with a jury—that's you-all—we look into the cause of the sudden or violent death of a person." I paused to throw out a lopsided grin to put them at ease. Serving for the first time, they were all scared stiff.

After an opening like that, no reader in his right mind is going to expect a brilliant legal battle. If my characters make technical errors along the way, they will be forgiven.

The inquest turns into a duel between Jake Tobey, the insurance man, and the coroner. The vital question is: How did Miles Rigby's body end up in the swimming pool?

"The explosion (explains the coroner) was too slight, and the pool too far away from the studio to have anything blown into it."

"Then how in hell's name," Tobey screeched, "did Miles Rigby get there?"

I shrugged, then waited for what I thought was just long enough. "Mister Tobey," I asked, "how do *you* figure he got there?"

"He ran there!" Tobey cried. "I figure he did it just as I said. He lit a match and caused an explosion. His clothes caught fire and he ran to the pool."

I dropped it on him then. "For what reason, Mister Tobey?"

"Why, to put out the damn flames!" Tobey yelled.

After this exchange, one of the jurors stands up:

Doke Tinney scratched at his gray-thatched head. "If that's the case," he said, "then Rigby wasn't tryin' to kill hisself—he was doin' his damndest to save hisself!"

I pumped my head in agreement. "You're right, Mister Tinney. Miles Rigby's last act was one of self-preservation. No matter what his intentions might have been *only seconds before*, his last and final act on this earth was an attempt to preserve his own life. In my official opinion, that rules out suicide."

The jury, naturally, brings in a verdict of accidental death—and the widow collects *double indemnity!* Later, in the coroner's office, he talks with the widow. My story ends:

"I thought sure Mister Tobey would question me further on my last conversation with Miles . . . "

"Tobey," I said, "is an idiot. Besides, what could he possibly have learned by further questions?"

Faye Raven paused and blushed prettily. "I would have had to admit that I'd fallen back into my nagging ways with Miles."

"What do you mean?"

Faye Raven smiled. It was an odd sort of smile. I couldn't rightly tell if it was one of regret, or one of great personal satisfaction. "Before Miles turned off the intercom that night," she said, "I couldn't resist warning him for the last time, *not to smoke!*"

That ending would have been impossible without planting ahead of time that

Faye Raven's nagging only made her husband smoke more. Did she, on this final occasion, do it on purpose—or was it just force of habit? Who knows?

Finding fiction from funerals

While news items are the major source of plot ideas, they are by no means the only section of a newspaper rich in material. A few years ago an issue of the *Mike Shayne Mystery Magazine* carried my story, "A Short Bier." It came about after I read a daily feature called, "The Question Man," wherein a roving reporter queries pedestrians. The question that day was: "Were you a problem child?" One long-haired, hippie type answered, "Yes. I'd go through the woods feeling trees, rocks and leaves. I would feel all this electricity going through me. I'd rearrange the forest. Neaten it up. I'd see a log out of place and fix it."

Oh wow! That answer really got to me. I loved it. But I could not for the moment come up with a suitable place to use it. Later, I read a feature story, "Contessa's Fun Funeral." In it, an Italian Contessa, mad about funerals, decided to hold her own while she was still alive.

Putting the two items together, I came up with a little old lady who is considered a bit fey by everyone except her not-too-bright nephew—the narrator. She has a younger brother who wants to gain control of her property on which to build a shopping center. She refuses to sell. She and the nephew are having themselves a ball planting flowers and bushes and generally enjoying life. My story opens with the teenage nephew speaking:

Dumb as I was, I could see plain as rainwater in a barrel that my safe little world was in for a big shakeup when my Aunt Gussie started drinking her home-brew beer warm, right from the bottle—and going to funerals. I mean, she'd go to anybody's funeral, anytime, anyplace.

The greedy brother is embarrassed by her indiscriminate funeral attending. When she announces that she is going to have her own funeral the following weekend, the brother decides to have her committed as incompetent. To this end, he invites a crooked judge to come see for himself how weird she has become. The brother, Claude, says:

"Let's forget about funerals for the moment." He turned, smirking, to face Aunt Gussie. "Do you remember this afternoon? You told me you and Buddy were going into the woods for a little hike, to tidy things up a bit? What did you mean by that?"

"Poor Claude," Aunt Gussie said. "With all your fine college education, you've learned nothing. Yes, I go into the woods very often. I go to touch the trees, the rocks and leaves. I delight in feeling the vibrations of living things go through me. Whenever necessary, I rearrange the forest. I neaten it up after careless hikers disturb its symmetry. I see a log or a rock out of place and I fix it."

There was a long moment of dead silence. Then Judge Riley said, "Augusta, you—you get vibrations from the trees?"

When it appears certain that the brother will have Aunt Gussie committed, Buddy decides to take matters into his own hands. He had been warned by his aunt that certain plants were poisonous. Before Claude can sign the commitment papers, the nephew will kill him off. At the last moment, Aunt Gussie reaches out to drink some of the liquor spiked for Claude. Buddy stops her, confessing to her and Claude that he has put poisonous juices into Claude's brandy. Aunt Gussie says:

"Poison?" She sniffed at my hands. She was quiet for a time, then she cried, "Oh, Buddy, what have you done? That oleander is a deadly poison?"
"*Oleander?*" Claude's voice was a shrill screech.

Claude is dead by the time a doctor is summoned. His death, unexplicably, is attributed to heart failure. This is cleared up at the end. Buddy is speaking:

Another thing that puzzled me considerable was the fact that Aunt Gussie had told Claude I'd crushed up them oleander leaves. I mean, after sniffing my hands the way she had, she must have known it just wasn't so.
Dumb as I was, I'd crushed up the jasmine leaves!

Again, this ending would have been impossible had not the nephew's "dumbness" been planted from the very first word of the story.

A comic source of tragedy

Are you still unconvinced that your newspaper is a veritable gold mine? Perhaps you read only the comics. Fine. I enjoy them, too. A July issue of *Alfred Hitchcock's Mystery Magazine* carried my story, "A Shocking Affair." The inceptive situation came from the comics—from Gus Arriola's great strip, *Gordo*. For some time I'd read dozens of items concerning rock guitarists who'd been electrocuted when their instruments short-circuited.

Nothing seemed to jell in my mind until I read the Gordo strip. It consisted of only three short panels. In the first panel Gordo is reading *from a newspaper* about a young boy who electrocuted himself on stage with his guitar. Pepito asks him "How many have *you* had busted over your head, serenading other guys' girls?" Gordo replies, "You're right! They can lead to murder or marriage!"

With that I was off and running! I made my narrator the middle-aged owner of a beer-dancehall in backwoods Florida, the father of a luscious young daughter. Two men vied for her hand. One was meek and slightly built Cecil Pettibone. The other was Brutus Taggart, called The Brute. A guitarist, The Brute led a rock band. On the night the action begins, Cecil is behind a rough bar, ankle deep in water from the washtubs used to ice the beer they sell. He is wearing protective rubber boots. He cannot get away from his job to dance with Mavis, so she asks The Brute for a dance. Angered and humiliated, Cecil goes to The Brute's precious guitar and bangs on it as if trying to destroy it. The Brute not only beats up Cecil, but presses his hands against the hot side of a potbellied stove. Patching Cecil up, Mavis puts a pair of her dishwashing rubber gloves over his injured hands.

Later, when two revenue men come in to arrest The Brute for operating an illegal still, he kills one of them, takes Mavis as a hostage, and commands Cecil to gather up his gear.

Cecil nodded dutifully, then went to unplug the amplifier and wind up the cord. When he finished, he picked up the guitar and the sound box and started toward the front door. Then, quick as a rabbit, instead of going on out, he ducked under the bar plank.

Again, Cecil starts to bang away at The Brute's precious guitar. Enraged, Taggart drops Mavis and leaps over the bar to retrieve his instrument.

Then all hell broke loose. With the guitar in his hands, The Brute's big body began to quiver and shake. It looked to me like the sparks was flying thick and fast as lightning on the swamps. The Brute tried to rid himself of the guitar, but it stuck to him like a tick to a hound. In one final spasm, his huge body stiffened and he fell to the floor. Then Cecil calmly walked over and unplugged the outfit from the wall socket.

When Taggart's body has been removed, an official comments, "You are a lucky man, Cecil. If he hadn't snatched that short-circuited guitar away from you when he did, it might be you burned to a crisp."

Cecil grinned and came out from behind the bar. He stomped his rubber-booted feet to shake loose the water. He put out one rubber-gloved hand to give me back my penknife—with little pieces of frayed wire still sticking to it.

"You might say that," he commented to the lawman. "Yes, sir—you might say I was very lucky."

Plant of action

Again, I cannot stress too much the necessity of planting ahead of time. In the course of the *action*, without pausing to belabor the point, it was brought out why Cecil was wearing rubber boots and rubber gloves, thus insulating him against the guitar he'd purposely short-circuited to save his sweetheart and rid himself of his enemy.

When I first started clipping the various items I intended to use, I went to a great deal of trouble to start an elaborate filing system. Each item was very carefully labeled and put into a folder marked, *CRIME, LOVE, CHARACTER, SETTING, THEME, SEX, GIMMICKS*, etc. It wasn't long, however, before I had to discard this system. I found I was wasting precious hours trying to decide which category to write about. To eliminate this bottleneck, I emptied out the largest drawer in my desk and dumped all the items into it. Now when I've finished a story and mailed it off, I no longer puzzle over what to do next. I simply reach into my drawer and whatever item I grab is IT for the next story.

I mentioned that I'd written over 50 stories last year, but sold only 32 of them. In going over my files, I found that ALL my rejections fell into two categories. Either the story I'd written was too recognizable, or it was too gimmicky.

By "too recognizable" I mean the piece had been headline news all over the world. No matter how I tried, I could not hide the bones of the original, true story. Those stories "too gimmicky" concerned some bizarre method of murder, or some too-complicated swindle perpetrated. In such stories, I became so involved with the mechanics of the gimmick, I neglected character, atmosphere, emotion, and theme.

For me, the best story idea-producing newspaper items are ones like the suicide-type piece. It tells only enough to whet the appetite. It names no names, gives no motives, offers no solutions or final outcomes. It serves as a perfect springboard for one's own creative imagination to run amuck. Had this been reported in greater detail it might have been useless to me, for it would have satisfied me and failed to spur me on to fill in the missing elements of every good story—*who, what, when, where,* and *why*?

To me these newspaper items are the things from which stories are made—and sold. They can be for you, too, if you approach them with a searching mind and a great, hungry curiosity. If *anything* about a news story stirs you, clip it, study it, question it, gnaw at it the way a dog gnaws at a bone. Eventually you will reach the marrow.

Plotting the novel

by Walter Sheldon

I have an automatic plotting machine that costs less than a dollar. It works beautifully and has kept me writing and selling books for years, almost without pause. The remarkable thing about it, I think, is that any individual, using the machine's basic principles, can build his own version of it, best adapted to his own temperament and view of his crazy world.

Its component parts are (1) a composition book of almost any kind, (2) a sheaf of small slips of paper or file cards, and (3) a container to put the file cards in such as a box, a flowerpot, or the pocket of an old raincoat.

The idea for this machine originated well over 20 years ago when I was corresponding with John D. MacDonald, and when both of us were making a living writing for the old pulp magazines. In those days John D. was already a dazzling ball of fire and I, astonished at his ability to turn out something like 20 pages of manuscript a day, asked him if he had some kind of plot formula that enabled him to do this. He thought my question absurd, and perhaps it was. He explained that he never plotted in advance, but let the story form itself as he wrote. Story elements, he said, were in a kind of hopper tapering down to a point where they came out. If you tried to grab them all at once they'd jam, but if you picked them out one by one they'd come in proper sequence.

I suppose John D. still does it this way. In spite of this, I have the feeling that he goes through the same process I'm about to outline, except that he can do it mentally. Which is fine. Said Kipling: "There are six and forty ways of composing tribal lays, and every single one of them is right."

In my case, the automatic plotting machine keeps me from losing items from

---

Walter Sheldon has used his extensive experience in the Far East in the military, as a foreign correspondent, and as a political analyst for the background of his novels, mysteries and nonfiction books on Japan. Under various pseudonyms he has written westerns and 200 short stories for major magazines.

the midden of my mind, which is as disorderly as my desk-top and my habiliment. But the process of plotmaking is, I believe, basically the same for any writer, no matter what actual gestures he applies to it. It consists primarily of gathering material from sources outside his head, then rearranging it in his head so that it becomes that curiously satisfying thing we call a story.

Suppose we follow the method I used in the case of one of my books, *The Red Flower Kill*, an adventure-intrigue novel set during the Viet Nam War. You may be interested in writing things on a higher (or even a lower) plane than adventure-intrigue novels, but I think you'll find that the basic principles apply to almost any kind of book-length fiction.

Plotting step #1

All I knew in the beginning was that I wanted to do a story laid in Thailand, which I had recently visited. And where were my impressions of Thailand? In my head? Well, yes, to a degree—but also in that composition book that is one of the component parts of the automatic plotting machine.

The composition book is used in Step One of the method. I have it handy wherever I go, and in it, from time to time, I jot observations, impressions, stray thoughts, and even, saints preserve us all, snatches of poetry. It is not a diary, which demands an entry every day, but a simple journal in which you write things when you feel like it. Great for killing time when suffering from insomnia or waiting for planes. I have at least two dozen such notebooks now, filled over the years.

And so, needing something to get me started on a story about Thailand, I turned to the journal and looked over some of the entries. Here is the one that fired up the automatic plot machine and started it chugging:

Bangkok, Aug. 18. A clean, open city a world away from the dark, sad air of Phnom Penh. Towering spires of the wats, water buffalo driven by small boys in the numerous canals called *klongs*. Nearly all Thais serve some time as monks in the wats during their lives, and I understand there are even a few foreigners, Americans among them, who have become monks temporarily in order to study Buddhism—

Zap! Step #2

Did you catch it? An idea for the book right there. A character, possibly even my central character. Now, a thing like that I could remember quite easily, but I jotted it down just the same on a small file card—for that is Step Two of the handy dandy automatic method, and may not be eschewed or the entire schmeer falls apart. I said a file card, which I find durable and easy to carry around, but slips of paper or the backs of old envelopes would do as well; the important thing is that the little notes you write yourself as part of Step Two *must be separate*, and not in bound form, so that they can be shuffled later, as you will see.

Here's what I wrote on that first note for the new book:

CHARACTER. A young American studying Buddhism in a wat in Thailand. Shaved head, yellow robe, begging bowl, the whole bit. Maybe he's ex-combat man (intelligence?) from Vietnam, puzzled, disillusioned, seeking truth. Call him Ben Hardin.

Notice that I title the entry "CHARACTER." Character is certainly one of the elements of a story, and possibly the most important. Probably most writers think of story elements in different ways, or give them different names. For what it's worth, some of the story elements I tend to think of are:

Characters, Motivations (closely allied to Characters), Developments (the happenings that move the story along), Past Incidents (those necessary to explain the present state of affairs), Situations, Conflicts, Mission (the central drive of the story, like finding a treasure, catching a whale, making it with the loved one, etc.), Subclimaxes, the Climax, and the Outcome. The story's more inactive elements might be: Local Color, Technical Data (how you really go about catching a whale, for instance), Bits of Business, Dialogue, Spin-off Ideas (for future stories), and Miscellaneous for jottings that don't fit any of the other categories. I'm not even sure that slugging the notes this way is necessary; I'm just in the habit of doing it that way. The notes themselves—separately jotted, mind you—are the important thing.

I had one note, then—my first—and it happened to fall under the heading of Character, although it might well have been any of the other elements. I dropped it into a little box where all the notes eventually would go. And for the time being, forgot it.

Not long afterward I ran into a Treasury man who knew all about narcotics, and who told me that since authorities had been cracking down on the Turkey-Marseilles smuggling route, narcotics might well begin to come from Thailand where the tribesmen grow opium in the hills. That meant another card.

SITUATION: Increase in narcotics traffic from Thailand. Chinese behind opium production in hills for profit and as morale-weakening weapon. U.S. and maybe U.N. authorities want to stop. Some big Stateside operator behind this, working with Chicoms?

The next night I had dinner in a pizza joint. The proprietor—an acquaintance of mine—was incensed because a dining-magazine writer had characterized him as "right out of The Untouchables." He was, too; striped zoot-suit, accent and all, and the writer had meant to make him seem delightful rather than sinister, but the man was ready to call the Antidefamation League, and maybe did, for all I know. But here, in the flesh, was the big Stateside operator I was looking for, so I made out a CHARACTER card on him and gave him the name of Julius Drago.

A word of caution

You will, of course, take many characters from real life, but don't depict them too photographically. If the real-life person is fat, make him thin; if he's hairy, make him bald. It's even better to make your fictional characters composites of several real-life persons, often with a bit of yourself thrown in. Above all, don't make puns or anagrams on their real names. Otherwise you may find yourself gathering inspiration for your next novel as the defendant in a courtroom.

It was now about two weeks since I'd dropped that first card in the box and by this time the cards were coming fast and furiously. There's not enough space here to show all the cards, nor can I remember exactly what triggered off each idea (I seem to get a lot during morning ablutions, for some reason), but to demonstrate how it goes, here are a few random samples:

CHARACTER: A completely amoral Thai, former worker on U.S. base, who dodges sideways for a living, and prides himself in being able to procure anything. Accosts hero on street and disappointed when hero doesn't want girl. "You want boy instead, maybe?" Since legitimate Thai surname is Cat, let's call him, phonetically. Charley Alpha Tango. Maybe Charley Tango for short.

The character Charley was based on a Korean houseboy I'd put into my journal years before, and he turned out to be one of the happier creations in the book.

Knowing that narcotics would be featured in the book, I did some reading on the subject and came up with several additional notes, among them this one: Tech Data . Heroin actually greater in bulk than morphine from which it is made. About a 10 percent gain. But raw opium even bulkier.

Something clicked in my mind and I went back to an old journal entry I'd made years before. It said that to gain foreign exchange the Chinese were manufacturing heroin—Luck Street brand, made in Tientsin—and sending it out into the world. I thought about that, then wrote: SITUATION. Chinese actually manufacturing heroin in a secret plant in north Thailand (abandoned temple?) and fella in charge of operation is skilled chemist, maybe with rank of colonel. This suggested the Chinese colonel's character—young, educated, good English—and I built it up a bit and made a CHARACTER card on him, calling him Colonel Wu. I also looked up some data on temples in the jungle, abandoned or otherwise, and made out a LOCAL CHARACTER card for that particular scene.

See what was happening? The notes in the box were beginning to breed other notes!

Another progeny:

MISSION: Because our hero speaks fluent Thai he is asked to assist in an anti-narcotic operation upcountry. Probably he's a former intelligence officer who, shocked by Vietnam, has dropped out of the world to seek truth in the temple. But if he's a drop-out why agree to rejoin the world and undertake the assignment?

Which called for:

MOTIVATION. Ben Hardin in temple because back in States his girl friend died from overdose of heroin or maybe withdrawal symptoms when trying to kick habit. He thus hates narcotics and would agree to mission.

Next step:

Now I was starting to think of some female interest for the story, partly because it's a must for this genre, and partly because I enjoy working in a bit of sex and love interest, and I wondered what sort of a woman might strike some entertaining sparks with Ben. I suddenly recalled a man I knew who was a wealthy Texan, his wealth both inherited and made on his own. He'd told me that when he was 12 years old his father had had him make out his own income tax return, capital gains and all. These characteristics, transferred to a woman, might make an interesting gal, and one who would orchestrate nicely with Ben. I outlined VERNA STILES briefly on a card marked CHARACTER and tucked it away. Why was she in Thailand? It came to me in the shower one morning:

SITUATION. Wealthy Verna Stiles married her doctor-husband, Jonathan Stiles after meeting him at a party for the publishing of his book, "Jungle Doctor." Now he's back in Northern Thailand "treating impetigo on the heads of native children, or whatever he does" again, refusing to come home or even discuss their marriage satisfactorily by mail. She has jetted to Bangkok to go upcountry, find him at his clinic, surprise him and clear the air.

This kicked off an all-important, special card called:

OPENING. Ben, in shaved head and yellow robe, is out begging for his morning meal, as per custom, when he runs into Verna Stiles, sightseeing before she heads upcountry. She is intrigued with him, and he, in spite of his vows, feels his blood getting redder over her.

I don't remember how long it was before I felt I had enough cards on hand to begin the story. Three weeks, for a guess. I cannot tell you exactly how to detect the point when you're ready, but your subconscious will probably let you know. You may get a kind of itchy feeling. Up to now, you've been working on Step Two, which is making your notes as fast as they come to you and putting them into a loose pile somewhere. You've saved even farfetched ideas, and you expect to throw a lot away eventually. Don't work out anything in *too* much detail; that will discharge the energy and excitement you'll need for the actual writing.

The rough outline

And here you are, at Step Three. You now examine all your cards or scribbled notes. Shuffle those you wish to keep into a rough narrative order. What you now have is a kind of shorthand plot that reads, from note to note, almost like a narrative outline of the story. What's more, *it's a unified narrative that would have been difficult to devise all at one sitting*.

There will be some holes in the narrative, and not everything will be connected with smooth finality. Don't worry about it. The thing will pull together as you write it. You'll encounter two odd phenomena: although you've gone to all the trouble to compile your pile of notes, you'll find yourself referring to them infrequently, possibly not at all; in addition, the story may well start to write itself in a slightly different way as you go along, taking unexpected twists and turns. If these delight you, they will delight the reader.

In the case of *The Red Flower Kill* one happy serendipity was the outcome, different from the one I'd planned, that suddenly popped into being about halfway through the story. The original plot had gone something like this:

Studying Buddhism in Thailand, Vietnam veteran Ben Hardin is asked by wealthy Verna Stiles to guide her in the jungle while she attempts to contact her husband, Dr. Jonathan Stiles. A U.S. Embassy security man then asks him to do an additional chore. They've lost touch with their agent in the north—a Thai schoolteacher—who has been trying to learn about Chinese-sponsored narcotics production there. Ben is to identify himself by a Thai proverb and bring back whatever data the agent has gathered. Ben receives permission from the abbot to go out into the world again for this purpose, but feels he must still abide by the ten vows, which prohibit such sins as touching money, touching women, and the lesser peccadilloes of lying, stealing and killing.

During expedition preparations in Bangkok, Ben and Verna encounter an Amercian, Julius Drago, who is the very cliché of a Capone-era gangster; he and his two hoods annoy Verna in a restaurant and Ben trades blows with one—breaking a vow. They learn that Drago has been deported from the US but are not sure what he's doing in Thailand.

On the train upcountry, Ben is mysteriously drugged and his compartment searched. Also on the train they are accosted by seedy freelance correspondent Albert Nebel who wants to join them to report on the guerrilla situation upcountry. Ben does not like the arrogant Nebel, but Verna invites him to come along.

Staging at Chiang Mai, Thailand's northern city, Ben meets Charley Tango, but refuses his services as a guide and general factotem. Shopping for jade in an alley, however, Ben is attacked by unseen assailants, and rescued by Charley. Then, at the hotel, he finds Albert Nebel shot and dying in his room. Nebel mutters something unclear about the big operator behind a multimillion dollar narcotics enterprise.

Ben, Verna, and Charley hastily depart Chiang Mai before the police can delay them because of Nebel's death. On the jeep drive northward, Verna frankly tempts Ben and he finds it increasingly difficult to keep that particular vow.

At the remote clinic they learn that Jonathan Stiles is off on a village trip and are greeted by his assistant, Tari, a young widow from Bangkok. Thrown alone with her, Ben at last breaks the vow of celibacy. From her he learns that the schoolteacher-agent he seeks is at the village where Stiles has gone. They all proceed there and find the village smoking from a guerrilla attack and the agent badly wounded. The agent explains that he's learned that Colonel Wu is running a narcotics operation from an abandoned temple in the area, but he was too closely watched to send this information back by radio. Also, in the attack, Dr. Stiles has been captured and taken away by Colonel Wu.

Ben and Charley set off through the jungle and reconnoiter the abandoned temple, hoping to learn what's happened to Dr. Stiles. They manage to rescue Stiles from a cell and walk him back to the village, learning that he's a secret alcoholic, also that Wu captured him because he feared he knew too much. But, at the village, Wu and his soldiers reappear and recapture everyone. Stiles is killed in the gunplay.

Now Ben, Verna, Charley, and Tari are all captives at the abandoned temple. To their surprise, Julius Drago appears, apparently doing business with Wu. Drago fancies Tari and she submits to him for the express purpose of stealing his pistol. The pistol enables Ben to engineer an escape and blow up the installation's gasoline dump as they flee.

Back in Bangkok, Ben makes his report to the security people, decides to return to the temporal world and tries to decide whether he wants to do it with Verna or Tari.

The plot changes

That (if you're still with us after that bare-bone reading) was roughly the original plot. The new outcome that generated itself about halfway through went like this:

In Bangkok, Ben calls on Verna in her hotel room and has a magnificent roll in the hay with her, shedding all his vows—except the one about killing. Verna then reveals that she is the big operator behind the narcotic enterprise: Drago was trying to muscle-in on her; Nebel was her on-site representative, but was weak and had to be killed. She wants Ben to join her so that they can make beautiful money together.

Shocked, Ben refuses. With a sigh she says he'll have to go, too, knowing as much as he does now, and pulls a pistol. There is a struggle and Verna is shot. Ben showers to wash away the blood and goes out to look for Tari.

Perhaps, in outline form, the story is less than gripping. It's not the bare-bone plot that makes a good story, anyway; it's the flesh you put on them. Such things as characterization, dialogue, background, interesting information (the book was almost a course in Theravada Buddhism), and plain, old-fashioned good writing, if possible. But you must have that framework to build upon, and whether you do it by means of notes, or keep it all in your head, the process is the same: raw material is gathered, rearranged, and put together again as a story. The key to doing it is to keep those elements separate and not try to put them all together neatly at the first sitting.

I hope I haven't made all this sound like, "Look, Ma, no hands!" It's still hard work; the hardest I know, and after 35 years of it I still look for excuses not to write. But, ambivalently, I still enjoy it when I do.

By now some of you are probably saying that this is all well and good for somebody who can travel to Thailand and have drinks with narcotics agents. I'm stuck, you're saying, perhaps, at this dull job in this dull town where nobody's interesting and nothing ever happened.

The non-exotic novel

All right, let's look at a really fine writer who does things with those dull towns and dull people. John O'Hara mined excitement in rural and urban Eastern Pennsylvania for his entire career. Just for fun, let's imagine how one of his books might have been created by the automatic plotting machine. I doubt that he ever used one—yet, surely, he went through the gathering and rearranging process, as all fiction writers must.

One of my favorite O'Hara books is a little gem called *The Farmers Hotel*. I can see him passing one day through a little backwater village (equidistant from Allentown and Bethlehem, he says), seeing an old hotel there, stopping off for a cool drink, chatting with the proprietor and perhaps a few others of the village's 352 souls, and then, as he drives off, finding the germ of a story growing in his mind.

If he used my dollar plotting machine he might even stop the car right there and write down his first note:

SITUATION: Ira Studebaker, a widower and retired fruit dealer, buys old Farmers Hotel in small town not so much to make money as to dispense real old-fashioned hospitality. It's something to do: an expression of Ira's essential warmth as a human being.

As the hours and then the days passed, other elements would come to the author in their random fashion and some of them might look like this:

CHARACTER: A cheap and flashy "showbiz" manager who takes two girls to outlying towns for stag shows. He's in love with one girl, but, unfortunately, the girls are in love with each other.
BIT OF BUSINESS: Tradition says when a hotel first opens the proprietor throws away the key as fast as he can toss it. Might make a nice scene.
CHARACTERS: A fashionable couple in riding clothes driving in the country to have an extramarital affair for both.
SITUATION: Snowstorm hits the area and everybody is stranded in the newly-opened hotel.

COMPLICATION: The cheating wife has told her husband she's visiting a friend in Norristown, but she can't get there, and husband will be calling there soon. He will suspect hanky-panky.

CHARACTER: A coarse and brutal truck driver—very big man—who comes into conflict with the fashionable boy friend when he makes a pass at his married girl friend.

After stewing over these and a few other elements for awhile—possibly as he was already writing the story—O'Hara might then have pulled from the air his:

OUTCOME: Aided by the warm and gentle Ira, the cheating couple finally drive off, hoping to get to Norristown by a series of clear roads. Then the state trooper brings word that the truck driver has ambushed them, crashing into their car and setting it afire, and they are dead. There's no way now to hush it up. Ira says maybe the truck driver didn't mean to do it. His black companion and assistant says he thinks too much good of people. The night trails off and Ira falls asleep in his chair, while gazing at the old-fashioned stove.

It doesn't sound like much in outline form, for it's a story whose effect comes from mood, character, the beautiful O'Hara crystalline writing style, and the subtle implications—gently understated and marvelously *shibui*—of its theme. This supports the idea that just because you have a narrative outline doesn't necessarily mean that you've got a good story. Yet it fits the pattern of material drawn from life, rearranged, and set down again as a work of art. And it *could* have been developed with notes or file cards just as more tightly plotted entertainments can be.

The seeds of future books

I said earlier that my peculiar plotting method not only helps develop a work in progress but often plants the seeds for works to follow. A weary old pro, who writes for beans in the pot, has got to keep going this way, or there won't be any more beans.

The Red Flower Kill, whose growth we followed, was actually the second in a series of books for Gold Medal, with the titles involving both a color and the word "kill." I'd given the first two less flamboyant titles to begin, but when the editor changed the titles I figured it was my business to write books and his to make them salable. With two of the "color-kill" books in the bag (*The Blue Kimono Kill*, and *The Red Flower Kill*), I was now invited to do another, and, like any author, tyro or pro, I didn't have an idea in my head to start.

I looked over some of the notes I hadn't used in *The Red Flower Kill*. Among them was one that said: MISSION: Maybe an old British warship has been sunk off the coast with a load of gold aboard—might make a nice complication.

It had been strictly superfluous for the Thailand story, but I now dropped it into an empty box as a possible starting point for a new book. Not long afterward, I had some green turtle soup for dinner and, with the spoon halfway to my mouth, suddenly thought: "Hey! Why not *The Green Turtle Kill?*" I jotted that down and put it in the box.

The subconscious wheels began to turn. How could that title possibly be connected with the story? I thumbed through my journal. One entry—made some time before in Korea—mentioned Admiral Yi's "turtle ships," supposed to be the world's first armored craft, that drove off a Japanese invasion in the 16th century.

Hmm. If that armor was bronze, a sunken turtle ship would be green by now, wouldn't it? And suppose some people were really looking for a load of gold on a modern sunken warship, but used an archaeological expedition seeking the historic turtle ships as a cover story? Hmm.

File cards, plot elements, shuffle, shuffle—and *The Green Turtle Kill* was soon pouring out of the typewriter.

Now, I don't really expect a sudden run on file cards and composition books in stationery stores all over the country after this article appears. The cards and notebooks are merely the physical devices I use because they work for me. A writer who wants to use the basic method will be just as well off developing his own physical devices, or perhaps not using any. The important thing is to understand the storymaking process—gathering, rearranging, then writing—and to realize that a story comes to you in bits and pieces *in no logical order*, so that somewhere along the line these bits and pieces have to be winnowed down and then shuffled into the sequence you desire. This applies, I suspect, to everything from comic book scripts to Pulitzer Prize winners.

I have used my adventure-intrigue as examples because they are firmly plotted and illustrate the process in sharp, clear lines. I have actually used the process for more sophisticated works: three non-genre novels, and, to a degree, for five successful nonfiction books.

From talking to those who would write, but haven't managed to finish a work yet, let alone get it published (research shows this to be 98.6 percent of the population), I gather that most of them start out with great fire and enthusiasm, but soon bog down. When that happens, it's because your subconscious—which is much smarter than you are—knows what you're doing isn't solid and sets up blocks to keep you from doing it. You can outsmart your subconscious by using my automatic dollar plotting machine, or a suitable variant of it.

I have a stock answer for people who ask where I get ideas for stories. "I steal them," I say, "sometimes from life." Perhaps that's not very kind, but it saves a lot of unnecessary explanation. So get used to stealing your material—*preferably* from life.

The five w's-and how!

by Lee Floren

One evening, some years ago, an elderly gentleman stood in a California bookstore thumbing through western magazines, studying story illustrations and scanning lead paragraphs. I watched covertly, for I'd long wondered why a reader picks one magazine over another.

My heartbeat quickened. From the rack he took *Western Action,* whose gaudy cover carried the words: *West of Barbwire*, by Lee Floren.

Would he buy my novel?

He pondered over *Western Action* a long moment, then restored it to its former resting place. He looked through other western magazines, then returned to *Western Action* and carried it to the cash register.

He'd bought my novel.

I met him at the door.

"Excuse me, sir. I'm curious as to why you bought that particular magazine. I wrote the lead novel. That's my name on the cover. I'm Lee Floren."

"You—wrote this story?"

"Yes."

"Another California liar."

He gave me a scathing look. Without another word, he brushed past me. Since then I've seen others reading words I'd written, but I have discreetly kept my big yap nailed shut.

I don't know why that old gentleman bought *West of Barbwire,* but I think one reason was because the novel's first paragraph held the Five W's;

Lee Floren recently signed a contract for his three-hundredth western novel. Known mainly for westerns under his own name and various pseudonyms, Floren has also written historical, light-romantic novels plus short stories during the 35 years of his fulltime writing career. Able to enjoy the freedom his work affords, the author lives in Mexico.

Who
Where
When
What
Why
And, sometimes, **How**

Kipling summed up the Five W's when he wrote:

> I have six honest serving men;
> They taught me all I knew;
> Their names are Where and What
> and When
> And How and Why and Who.

The Five W's—and How—are not new. Newspapers have used them for years in story leads. They can make a strong narrative hook. And a good narrative hook can drag your reader immediately into your story, for it whets curiosity. *What* will happen next to *Who?*. The *Who* is usually the lead—or an important—character in your story.

Grabbing the reader

I did not stumble onto these long-recognized helpers accidentally. I was introduced to them years ago by one of journalism's great teachers, the late A.L. Stone of the University of Montana.

Sometimes I don't use these six in the lead paragraph of a short story, but most of the time I do. Let's look at the lead paragraph of *West of Barbwire.*

> The stage driver drove like a maniac, long whip popping, four sweaty horses lunging against collars, the June dust of Montana hanging in the hot afternoon behind the lumbering Concord. Attorney Ric Nelson, blond head close to the dirty window, glimpsed a deep rut crossing the prairie road ahead and hollered, "Hang on, everybody!"

Where is the *Who?*
Ric Nelson, of course, for in a western story, the first name the reader encounters invariably is the name of the protagonist.
The *Where?*
The prairie of Montana. And notice I wrote *Montana* and not *Montana Territory.* Western readers are almost all up on their western history. Montana became a state in 1889. Therefore my reader will automatically set the time of *West of Barbwire* after that date. This explains the *When.*
Now as to *What.* Ric is in a stage coach. Apparently he is going from one pioneer point to another. Were I to rewrite this lead behind the first sentence I would add "bound for Sagebrush," thus clearly identifying Ric's destination.
What could also apply to Ric's profession, the Law. *Why* is self evident, and can be explained in *What's* explanation.
Notice I opened on action, for action is a necessary ingredient in a western novel. Long whip popping. Horses lunging. Concord rocking. A huge rut ahead. "Hang on, everybody!"
Now let's look at the use of the Five W's in one of my light love novels,

Hollywood Nurse, written under the name Marguerite Nelson and published by Macfadden Books.

> The new Cadillac glided to a halt behind Lime Valley General Hospital whose low roof could be dimly seen over the tip of the California orange grove. Cynthia glanced hurriedly at her watch under the dash light and reached for the door handle. Ralph's big hand caught hers.
> "What's the rush, Sweetheart?"
> "Ralph, it's twenty-two to midnight, and I have to be at my nursing station at twelve sharp!"
> "You've got plenty of time."

Who is our heroine, Cynthia Nelson, who has already told our reader she is a nurse, which also covers the *What.* Another *Who* is Ralph, who evidently is one of Cynthia's close boy friends.

Where is California. *When,* 22 minutes until midnight. *What* is happening? Cynthia has to go to work. Ralph is detaining her.

How is it going to turn out? It looks as though Ralph and Cynthia are close to a lover's quarrel, does it not?

The *How* entices the reader. You have to grab your reader's attention first, then present a problem—and *How* will it end? induces him to read on.

Now let us look for the Five W's—and perhaps How—in the lead paragraph of *Deadly Doctor,* a book starring the Butcher, which I wrote under the house-name of Stuart Jason for Pinnacle Books.

> Midnight found the Butcher crouching beside a service station's office watching the apartment house across the street. And around the Butcher's six-foot three-inch muscular frame raged the sandstorm Southern California calls a Santa Ana.

Who? The Butcher. And I bring him in on a note of suspense, crouched as he is in a howling sandstorm watching an apartment. Can't you just see him—big, tough—one hand close to his shoulder holster?

Where? Southern California. *When?* Midnight. *What?* Watching an apartment, plainly going to cause trouble—and possibly kill—its occupant, which also answers *why.*

How is it going to end?

Again, the reader is pulled into the story and wants to know *how* it will end.

The interweaving of the Five W's is deliberate. Often their arrangement requires writing and rewriting the lead many times. Sometimes I spend more time writing a correct lead than I do writing a complete chapter of the novel. Sometimes I rewrite the lead *after* I have finished the novel. I can honestly say that I have never written a lead that completely satisfied me.

The following lead is one I wrestled for some time before getting it into a somewhat satisfactory form. It is from my historical novel published a few years ago by Popular Library, *Muskets on the Mississippi,* under the name Matthew Whitman Harding.

> Fort Dearborn squatted dark and ominous under Illinois thunderheads that June night in 1830 when Luke Abbott slowly and wearily walked up the gravel path leading to the log cabin in which he had been born twenty-four years before.

This lead consists of 40 carefully chosen words. The *Who,* of course, is Luke Abbott, 24 years old. *Where?* Fort Dearborn, Illinois. *When?* June, 1830. *What?* Returning home, slowly and wearily. Why is he tired, such a young man as he?

How could a man that young get so weary? Where has he been—and what has he done—to be so tired? The narrative hook has snagged my reader. Curiosity urges him to continue reading.

Researching the story

Perhaps the reader remembers that Alfred Lord Tennyson, Edgar Allan Poe and Rail-Splitter Abe were born the same year, 1809. 1830 minus 24 would make Luke born in 1806. He'd be three years older than Abe Lincoln.

A sudden thought. Why not bring Abe into this next paragraph to give the yarn more authenticity?

So the next paragraph reads:

A broad-shouldered blond giant whom some claimed as tall—if not taller than that political upstart Abe Lincoln—Luke paused momentarily before his door, long musket at rest stock-down as his blue eyes studied the dozen houses huddled close to Fort Dearborn's protection—for Sac and Fox Indian trouble lay like a heavy blanket over this northern Illinois area.

The idea for *Muskets* came from my reading about the Black Hawk Rebellion, as it is called in history. It was no rebellion. It was plain murder of an Indian tribe, squaws, papooses and warriors.

It is a sordid tale of how the whites robbed an Indian tribe and then deliberately killed its members. I decided I would try to portray the Indians' problem through the eyes of a sympathetic and knowledgeable white.

First, I had to select a protagonist—thus, tall Luke Abbott. Furthermore, I had to present a problem for him to solve, and this turned out to be an attempt to stop the oncoming killings.

If research is not appealing, then don't tackle the historical novel, for it has to run along historical lines, with a few fictional incidents to give it added color and conflict.

Luke's job was to bring peace between red man and white. Did he succeed? If so, *How* did he accomplish his goal? Did he fail? If so, *How* did he fail?

In popular fiction, each protagonist—male or female—must have a worthwhile goal to struggle toward—or you have no story. Thus I fall back on my long-time fiction formula: An appealing character struggles against great odds to attain a worthwhile goal. If the protagonist has no worthwhile goal to attempt to attain, you have no story—you have merely slice-of-life writing.

The Five W's—and How—in your lead give direction to your fiction. If you doubt their pulling ability, please return to the lead paragraph of this article.

There they are, all five of them!

Scene

by William Sloane

The keystone of all fiction is the scene. The fictional scene is the mode or way in which the writer speaks to the reader. The fictional scene is the way in which the story happens. It is also the way in which the reader experiences the novel or story. In its pure essence, a work of fiction is a sequence of scenes from page one to the end. But life does not come to us packaged in a series of scenes. It is up to the writer to package it. In a brilliant passage in his later introduction to his first novel, *Roderick Hudson*, Henry James tries to explain how the writer translates the material of life into the convention of scene:

> Really, universally, relations stop nowhere, and the exquisite problem of the artist is eternally but to draw, by a geometry of his own, the circle within which they shall happily *appear* to do so. He is in the perpetual predicament that the continuity of things is the whole matter, for him, of comedy and tragedy; that this continuity is never, by the space of an instant or an inch, broken, and that, to do anything at all, he has at once intensely to consult and intensely to ignore it.

James goes on to describe, by a metaphor, the way in which he worked at this problem:

> . . . a young embroiderer of the canvas of life soon began to work in terror, fairly, of the vast expanse of that surface, of the boundless number of distinct perforations for the needle, and of the tendency inherent in his many-colored flowers and figures to cover and consume as many as possible of the little holes. The development of the flower, of the figure, involved thus an im-

William Sloane was an editor, publisher and teacher for over 40 years until his death in 1974. His contemporaries considered him an expert in the practical and literary demands of publishing and a fine writer of both nonfiction and fiction. His novels include To Walk the Night *and* The Edge of Running Water.

mense counting of holes and a careful selection among them. That would have been, it seemed to him, a brave enough process, were it not the very nature of the holes so to invite, solicit, to persuade, to practice positively a thousand lures and deceits. The prime effect of so sustained a system, so prepared a surface, is to lead on and on; while the fascination of following resides, by the same token in the presumability *somewhere* of a convenient, or a visibly-appointed stopping-place.

What is a scene? A scene is a unit of events which has a beginning, a middle, and an end, and it contains nothing except characters in action. In the theater, which resembles fiction in that the entire substance of a play is what goes on between people, a scene begins each time the curtain rises or a character comes on stage or goes off stage. A scene ends when the curtain falls or when the onstage cast is diminished or augmented.

This is almost directly applicable to fiction. But in fiction it is vital to know what a scene is *not*. It is not the author telling the reader something, like, say, how the sunset looked. Looked to whom? In short, scene is not briefing. Scene is not a tone poem intended to evoke a mood or to stimulate poetry in prose. Scene is not material written for its own sake—a clever aside for the fun of it, a comment on the way life is. Scene is not material written prior to the necessary start of the action or following after the interaction of the characters has been completed. If a piece of fiction contains passages with such characteristics, these passages are unfictional at least and probably nonfictional.

Many unsuccessful writers have difficulty believing the simple point of *showing*, not *telling*. They believe in a sort of Divine Right of Kings by which the fiction writer can choose whether he is going to show or to tell. No such right exists. Once I was sitting on my terrace with Shane Stevens, novelist, critic, Bread Loaf Fellow. He was explaining to me that my cat, which he was stroking, was actually a duck in a catsuit zippered over her.

"You're not listening," he accused me.

I explained that I was trying to think out my next fiction lecture, and the next.

"Where are you going to begin?" he inquired.

I told him with scene, and that I thought everything in fiction had to be conveyed to the reader by way of scenes.

He scratched the duck-cat behind her ears. "You better believe it," he said.

What Shane and I had created was a scene that *shows* what we both meant better than any amount of explanation possibly could. More seriously, let me remind you of what we all subconsciously know. The scenes of fiction are what readers remember when they are not remembering the characters. "I'll never forget that scene in *David Copperfield*," they say. Or, "That was a great scene where Tom got the other fellow to whitewash the fence." Admittedly, it is trouble for the writer to find the scenes he needs and to load them with the ammunition of his fiction, but it can be done. There is nothing that belongs in fiction at all that cannot be conveyed to the reader by way of a real and lively scene.

The number of possible scenes is infinite, of course, but the writer needs to know two things in order to *select* the ones best suited to his purpose. These two things have to be *found out*, and they are so often mishandled by unsuccessful writers that every editor gets a kind of second sight about them. The instant he is sure the writer has failed to meet these two requirements, he will reject the manuscript.

First, the author has to know what his book is about. Maybe the reader doesn't need to realize this overtly, but he has to feel he is finding out. If the author doesn't know, or knows mistakenly—which is very often the case—the book or story will fail. All too many stories and novels are inert. Mostly, this inertness occurs because the author doesn't know what his story is—or is simply infatuated with the sound of his own writing voice.

Contributory and related action

The writer must know also *what happens* in his book. If he does he is past the second hurdle. No piece of fiction can survive the dullness of nothing happening. There can be no end to a thing that never started.

Once you know what your book is about and what happens in it, at least in general, you are in a position to find your first scene. The first scene will contain the moment in the "time" of your fiction in which the happening, the action, becomes sufficiently inevitable to put the writing into motion and aim it down the right path. The right path is the path into *what* happens and *how* what happens ends.

Knowing what happens in your book will also enable you to determine what the final scene should be, because once what is to happen in the book has *happened*, you stop. You stop! No epilogues, no postmortems.

Like the magnificent Frost essay on the dynamics of a poem—"like a piece of ice on a hot stove the poem must ride on its own melting"—a work of fiction consumes its own materials. Make sure it does or you will suffer the fate of Sisyphus.

The fiction writer must select his scenes with the utmost care because any work of fiction is an act of enormous compression and condensation. No novel is ever "true to life." No story either. Its truths and its effects are those of seeming, not of fact—if fact is ever ascertainable. The writer is, if you like, rationed as to words and pages with which to put this semblance of reality into dramatic form.

I don't presume here to try to teach anyone how to select a scene. There are certain kinds of scenes that cannot be written by a particular writer, and he has to find a new way of saying what he wants to say. I don't think anyone could teach Jane Austen how to write a thunderously huge scene like one of Thomas Mann's in *The Magic Mountain*. I don't think it could be done. No one would want to either, but the point is that every writer has to work within the frame of his own material. For the beginning writer, it is important to select scenes that he can handle. If yours is a historical novel try not to have a log cabin raising unless you know how they were actually built. Do not attempt scenes of madness unless you know what you are talking about—it is fascinating to speculate who "sat" for King Lear.

Even more important, the writer must know exactly what each scene accomplishes in and for the novel. Whether or not any one scene can be called "obligatory," nothing in a novel can exist unrelated to the rest. No scene can be put into a novel, and read by the reader, without coloring the reader's mind from that point on to the end; all the preceding scenes are the parents and ancestors of the next one. The experience of fiction is accumulative as well as sequential. All scenes are contributory on most of the various levels of the novel. List, if you must, what each scene does for the action, for the characterizations, for the foreshadowing, for the reader's entire experience of your fiction. Lay the scenes out in front of you and look at them in as relaxed a way as you can and see what they say back to you. But keep in mind that a scene that shows the reader nothing except a couple of characters being all too forgettable is not a scene but a fictional entry.

Scenes are something like miniature stories. They have in them the germ of the entire story or book, and they are like the larger whole in other respects. Scenes have a beginning and an ending, like any complete story. Each scene has a means of perception. Occasionally more than one, but rarely. Each scene has a setting—it takes place somewhere. Each scene poses the same problems that the story or novel poses. It must establish the reader as fast as possible. It must give evidence as soon as possible that it intends to continue the contract with the reader.

The scene at work

Scenes are constructed as invisibly as possible, just as the entire novel or short story is constructed. As with the first and last scene, every single scene commences, after the writer has selected or "found" the scene, at the moment when it becomes necessary to the action of the story. The scene ends when its point has been made, even though the characters are still talking their heads off. It is the death of good scene writing to add anticlimactic material.

Scenes need to be economical and even spare in their construction. No characters not germane to the purpose of the scene should be included as window dressing: "It was a lovely old spoon which had come to her years ago from Aunt Martha's estate." This is all right if the spoon with its genealogy is necessary to project character or action or whatever, and is not just something with which tea is being stirred.

Scenes move in terms of action, of character change and development, in terms of the passage of time—a sunken sub with the air running out, the ticking clock, so favorite a dramatic device, a symbol in itself of motion and consumption—and above all, in a rather mysterious fashion, they derive much of their motion from the reader. This last is something like the learning process and we know little about it except that the reader experiences a sense of accumulation, of growth as he is reading.

Scenes have a lot of work to do. Not only do they have to advance the work of fiction in terms of action, character, and theme, but they require a solution to the problem of transitions. These fictional scene dividers may be of an infinite variety and should, of course, be made as inconspicuous as possible. When transitions become an integral part of the action they do many things. They show the passage of time: "Three hours later we were still at it." They interpret the setting as part of the action: "The big room, when she entered, was being made ready for the solemn occasion." They even characterize: "In his usual aimless fashion he had neglected to provide for their arrival." Scenes can be constructed so that no transition is needed. If the reader can find his way quickly enough into the new scene he will have made his own transition.

There is, of course, no prescription for the number of scenes in a novel or a story. The freedom of fiction is to be its own length. Some short stories, especially very short ones, may comprise only a single scene, though the singleness is often more apparent than actual. Most modern novels use a great many scenes, particularly when the cast of characters is large. Varying the length of the scenes and the number of characters in them will avoid monotony. It is fatally easy to fall into the trap of two-character scenes, one after another.

In the passage from Henry James cited earlier, to him, apparently, the number of possible scenes in a novel is as nearly infinite as the holes in a huge canvas, the canvas of life itself. He is right about that, obviously so. But first you have to see the canvas, and then you have to notice the holes, and then you have to plan the embroidery, select the holes needed for the pattern, thread the needle, and commence. The trouble with most new writers is that the whole canvas is not there, by implication, and there isn't much variety in the threads. The new writer also tends to lean too heavily on his favorite colors, to miss some holes and put too much thread through some of the others, creating bumps. Even worse, some will have borrowed their patterns, and not enough of them will have gone to look at the Gobelins and the fabrics of Peru and Byzantium.

The necessary confrontation

Every year I receive one or more manuscripts that are not written in scenes. With some exceptions they bear certain marks of kinship, one with another. They contain numerous prose essays and explanation, which in nonfiction would not be interesting or accurate enough. There is a great deal of interior monologue by the central character. And in general they read like thinly disguised autobiography. This is not meant condescendingly. What I mean is that the avoidance of scene usually indicates fictional material insufficiently digested, a piece of writing begun before it had been sufficiently ruminated.

To use an example available to everyone, in Fitzgerald's young autobiographical novel, *This Side of Paradise*, the fictional continuum lapses into scene, frequently in fragments of dialogue, rather than develops into scene. These lapses most often occur when a confrontation is needed. Confrontations are difficult to the point of impossiblity in a fictional continuum treatment.

Thus far I have not discussed this notion of confrontation. In the selection of scenes, I believe it to be a prime consideration. By confrontation I mean a meeting between apparently incompatible elements: two armies, two kinds of love, good and evil, fire and flood, pilot and storm, mongoose and snake, parent and child, cops and robbers, honor and treachery, money and need—the list is as large as mankind has managed to become old. My reading of unsuccessful manuscripts proves nothing, but it suggests that this element of confrontation is the heart of almost all good scenes. Even in scenes of anguish with a single character, there is the Devil in opposition. The confrontation has to be felt, or experienced, in each scene directly by the character with whom the reader is identifying himself, but also shown to be felt by the other party or parties to it.

The entire matter of the story of the Good Samaritan takes place between Jesus and the lawyer in thirteen verses of St. Luke's account, but it will repay any fiction writer's prolonged study.

And, behold, a certain lawyer stood up, and tempted him, saying, Master, what shall I do to inherit eternal life?

He said unto him, What is written in the law? how readest thou?

And he answering said, Thou shalt love the Lord thy God with all thy heart, and with all thy soul, and with all thy strength, and with all thy mind; and thy neighbour as thyself.

And he said unto him, Thou has answered right: this do, and thou shalt live.

But he, willing to justify himself, said unto Jesus, And who is my neighbour?

And Jesus answering said, A certain man went down from Jerusalem to Jericho, and fell among thieves, which stripped him of his raiment, and wounded him, and departed, leaving him half dead.

And by chance there came down a certain priest that way: and when he saw him, he passed by on the other side.

And likewise a Levite, when he was at the place, came and looked on him, and passed on the other side.

But a certain Samaritan, as he journeyed, came where he was: and when he saw him, he had compassion on him.

And went to him, and bound up his wounds, pouring in oil and wine, and set him on his own beast, and brought him to an inn, and took care of him.

And on the morrow when he departed, he took out two pence, and gave them to the host, and said unto him, Take care of him; and whatever thou spendest more, when I come again. I will repay thee.

Which now of these three, thinkest thou, was neighbour unto him that fell among the thieves?

And he said, He that showed mercy on him. Then said Jesus unto him, Go, and do thou likewise.

Notice that there is no plot, as such, only a confrontation, but what a confrontation. Though extremely short, this story of Jesus and the agent-provocateur lawyer consists of two scenes, one framing the other. Yet if you think of the St. Luke Gospel as a work of fiction about a religious leader destroyed by the society he feels impelled to save, consider some of the dividends from this scene-within-a-scene: a foreshadowing of the end of Jesus' ministry; a terrific intensification of the irony of the execution of Jesus; a superb, brief, incisive addition to the characterization of Jesus; the lawyer as a reflection of the establishment; society as a member of the cast (men put Jesus to death). It is really unnecessary to elaborate further upon this particular demonstration of the power of the scene, except to remark that everything the scene means is right in there, and nothing else is.

Fiction is a battleground

by Marjorie Franco

When my daughter was ten years old, she made a discovery. "There is always something to worry about," she said, having solved one problem only to be met by another. She faced a sobering truth. Life is full of conflict and "they lived happily ever after" is a myth. Psychoanalyst Carl G. Jung said it more profoundly. "Life is a battleground. It always has been, and always will be; and if it were not so, existence would come to an end." And so would fiction.

The task of the short story writer is to transfer real life problems into story material, remembering always that fiction is true to life in essence but not in actuality. The average person in an average day faces a variety of problems about which he may or may not make decisions. The car won't start; should I take a bus? My child is sick; should I call the doctor? My friend, or fellow worker, has hurt my feelings; should I confront him, or simply brood? Problems have a way of piling up without order and often we seem to be caught in a network of unrelated conflicts.

Focus: One real problem

In order to make a short story work, the writer makes a distinction between what "really happened" and what part of it belongs in his story. He takes an idea from real life—life is a springboard—embodies it in a character and creates a fictional world in which that idea can stand apart and be seen clearly by the reader.

The writer enters into a partnership with the reader. He deals all the cards in the beginning. Every change or surprise has to have its roots. Everything is characteristic (as opposed to real life) and in a series of scenes, through detail and action,

---

Marjorie Franco, a frequent contributor to Redbook, McCall's, Good Housekeeping *and other magazines, has freelanced for 15 years. In 1979 she published a juvenile novel* So Who Hasn't Got Problems?, *and at present is writing an adult novel and short fiction. She has taught short story classes at the Indiana University Writers Conference and the Midwest Writers Conference at Ball State University.*

the writer reveals what came before as he builds tension to a climax and eventual resolution. Conflict is at work in every paragraph. Wherever you slice it, you get the story.

If the writer does his job well, the reader will do his. He will "believe in" the character and the story, no matter how far-fetched they may be. However, the demands made upon the reader are only as valid as the writer's skill in making them. "Yes, that's the way it sometimes happens," the reader might think, though it didn't happen exactly that way. He will identify, positively or negatively, with the character, pick up the clues, feel the tension, find some meaning in the events and some satisfaction in the denouement. We believe, don't we, in Kafka's insect in "Metamorphosis"?

When the writer fails to do his job and writes the way it "really happened" he cheats the reader. When he fails to focus on one problem, the reader might well ask "What is this story about? What does the sick child have to do with the friend who insulted you? Who cares if you can't get your car started? You don't need to take the bus to call the doctor. Why are you giving me all these false clues that don't mean anything? How can I trust you? How can I be your partner if you trick me?"

New writer vs. timeless plots

The new writer may be surprised to learn that, despite the many conflicts which can confront an individual, there are only three generic plots in commercial fiction: man against man, man against himself, and man against nature. But rules can be confusing, or meaningless, without examples. To avoid becoming confused, a writer should read the fiction of other writers, paying close attention to the opposing forces in the story. Seeing the rules in operation will fix them more permanently in his mind.

Time is essential in building conflict, and here the writer manipulates, compresses, flashes forward or backward. He makes great leaps over months, or years; he slows down for scenes and closeup. In a story called "The Getaway" by Carol Adorjan, a mother of two-year-old twins is badgered by her husband to go away with him for a weekend. She is harried and fragmented by the demands made on her by the twins, but she makes excuses for not going away—they are sick so how can she leave? When finally she feels that she is losing her identity, she realizes that she must go. The story takes place over five days.

I mention this story because the author is a personal friend of mine and I am familiar with the real life events that served as a springboard. The author is indeed the mother of twins, and many of the incidents in the story actually did happen. But not in five days, and not in the sequence in which they appear. Carol had discussed the story idea with me months before she wrote it. She had to select, organize and invent. She had to ask herself "What if?" What if the incidents pile up in a short space of time at the same time the twins are getting sick, and at the same time the husband is pressuring the wife to go away? Would the pressures from two different directions deepen the complication and cause the wife to make some evaluation about herself? Her role? Her identity? How could she reveal the significance of the conflict and, therefore, the meaning of the events? In this story the fragmentation of time gives consistency to the human experience. The reader can identify.

Openings to conflict

This is a good time to talk about openings. A story opens at a moment of crisis in the life of the character, a conflict that leads to the problem. My car won't start and in thirty minutes I have to be at a meeting that will decide my future. Time and conflict create tension and force a decision. Perhaps all my life I have never allowed enough time for things that matter and now I stand to lose a once-in-a-lifetime opportunity. Or, perhaps I recognize my flaw (I can't be on time) but feel my assets make up for it (I get more work done than anyone else). My problem then could be one of acceptance. Have my efforts at being a good worker compensated for my flaw? Can I convince my boss of my value even though I am late for the meeting?

In my first published story ("I Am A Gentle, Peaceful Man," *Redbook*) the conflict hinges around the problem of unconditional acceptance in a marriage. I opened with the character sitting in his office looking out the window. I described everything he saw out that window: a city park, men at work on a new building, etc., none of which had anything to do with the story. When finally I got around to the conflict I had used up several pages and a lot of precious story time. My editor told me to cut five pages and start with the problem. It was major surgery to cut away that opening. I loved it. I still love it. But it didn't belong.

Instead, I opened with the problem. It is the narrator's birthday. His wife, a musician, is about to give him a banjo (which he doesn't want) because everyone else in the family plays a musical instrument. The gift appalls him.

> The excellent Stroganoff, the loud singing and the vigorous blowing of candles made it the gayest of dinners. Eileen, who likes birthdays, seemed to find particular pleasure in this one—my thirty-third. Not even Sebastian's upset glass of milk intruded upon her splendid mood. Contentedly nourished, I carried my slice of cake—large enough to accommodate a yellow rose and the first two letters of "Happy"—into the living room. I am a quiet, easygoing sort of man, so the four boys pushing around my chair, carefully counting my few strands of gray hair while I ate my cake, did not disturb me.

The stage is set for the next line:

> Eileen swept into the room, carrying a large, rectangular box like a sorceress about to spring her magic tricks.

Strife in life and death

Even after years of practice, starting a story can be difficult for me. Though I no longer use up several pages before getting to the conflict, I often rewrite the first page eight or nine times. Openings are of great importance. If an opening isn't interesting, if it doesn't show or hint at conflict, the reader might not turn that first page, might never know the fascinating things that happen later.

I've done a series of stories for *Redbook* about a couple whose names are Genevieve and Alexander. Here is the opening for "Genevieve's Birthday Money," August, 1977.

> After being married to Alexander for more than ten years, I had learned that imperfections tend to hold a marriage together. Implicit in the "I do" is the promise not to be perfect. Total contentment could drive a person mad. Better to put up with imperfections, I say, unless, of course, they're carried to extremes.
>
> Alexander has an imperfection (I almost said "fetish") that borders

dangerously on the extreme. What's more, he insists on sharing it with me. It's called "seeing the leaves," a passion that seizes him at a particular time every fall.

These stories are about marriage, about ordinary people with whom readers can identify, and in this one, Alexander's passion for seeing the leaves leads to "one of those rare moments in a marriage when both partners see each other with perfect understanding."

Another story in the series, "Alexander's Life and Death Struggle," March 1980, opens like this:

> Alexander's father died suddenly. Alexander took it hard and that made it hard on the rest of us, which shows how death shakes up a family.
>
> His mother was a strong woman, and though her husband's death was a shock and though she went through all the stages of grief—disbelief, confusion, exaggeration, forgetfulness—she arrived with serenity at acceptance. What helped her, I think, was her seeming absence of guilt as well as her previous experience with losing a loved one.
>
> Alexander had had little experience with death. He didn't know firsthand that complicated relationships never die; they simply change. So after his father died, Alexander declared him a saint.

In this story, all of Alexander's relationships are in conflict. His struggle is with acceptance of his father's death, but involves, also, the acceptance of life.

After all the cards are dealt in the beginning, the writer is concerned with keeping the tension going. For example, a look through Frank O'Connor's "My Oedipus Complex" shows a master at work. There is conflict in every paragraph. Taking the viewpoint of a little boy, he says his father was in the army all through the war and "I never saw much of him, and what I saw did not worry me." Then later, "The war was the most peaceful period of my life." When his father came home for good "he put on his best blue suit, and Mother was as pleased as anything. I saw nothing to be pleased about—." With the father home, occupying much of the mother's time and attention, the tension continues to build until "Father and I were enemies, open and avowed." Finally, with sound logic (because he knew his characters) Frank O'Connor resolves the conflict. The picture changes with the arrival of a new baby in the household. The mother's attention turns to the baby, and father and son, now both neglected, finish as allies.

Building private battles

How much does an author need to know about people? Everything—within his powers of observation and experience. Human beings are complex, problem solving creatures who reveal themselves, not so much by what they say, but by what they do. Drama lies in action. Action is stimulated by conflict. Conflict moves the plot. The plot is nothing but a way of solving the problem.

A short story writer cannot be expected to solve the world's problems. Nor does he aim that high. But he can show a particular character in the grip of a particular problem, and perhaps, through his insight, he can touch a kind of universality. His efforts, if he is serious, are a means of explaining the world around him, of capturing a meaning out of ordinary events. His deep interest in people enables him to test human traits as his character wrestles with a problem. Then, as a result, the reader will go along with him and experience something from the "expanded moment."

"Life is a battleground" and the writer's mind is his own private battleground. His life is his material, after all. Before he can explain the world around him he needs to experience the world in his own way. Writing is a process of discovery, of gaining insight, and every writer is unique. Each has his own vision. He grows in realization by what he sees and hears and by how much of his deeper self rises up to cause a change. A writer thinks differently than other people. From the countless ideas and impressions which are constantly bombarding him, he must make his selections. What is significant? What problem in the life of a person, or a character, is important? What is relevant to today's world? How can I articulate a vague feeling or idea? Do I know what I mean only after I have said it? Pasteur said "Chance favors the prepared mind." It may not be easy to think like a writer, but it is never dull.

Conflict is never dull. Caught in the grip of conflict, a character can't stand still. Either he grows, or he dies. Fiction is a battleground, and so is life. My ten-year-old daughter was disillusioned when she realized that there is always something to worry about, but I think she took an important step toward maturity.

Tagging your characters

by Janice Young Brooks

Jack Benny's tag was his habit of slowly folding his arms, cocking his head to one side and drawling, "Well." Jimmy Carter's tag was his lavish dental display and soft southern accent.

Character tags are those external aspects—either visual or aural—that set one character apart from another. Whether the details are of physical appearance, clothing or speech, they should be vivid and symbolic—for they are the permanent or habitual qualities of your characters that identify them and make them memorable.

Character *tags* are not character *traits*, though they often enhance or reflect traits:

> Grandmother always had a jigsaw puzzle set up somewhere, and she would sit for hours aimlessly pushing the pieces around. She never seemed to care if she finished the puzzles. They merely provided an excuse to sit and think about how her life had turned out.

The *tag* is Grandmother's habit of sitting over half-finished puzzles. The *trait* is her introspective, solitary nature. Character tags can also contrast with traits, but should be used sparingly this way. An example: the kind, gentle woman with the unexpectedly shrill voice. A little of this, however, goes a long way.

Several years ago I began a list of tags, of the ways people look and sound. My catalog of tags breaks into five general categories: Body, Speech, Face, Movement and Clothing.

BODY

Size—*Rachel was a diminutive old woman with a skeletal structure like an arrangement of dried twigs—angular and incredibly fragile.*

Janice Young Brooks is a novelist who has written historical fiction under her own name, and who has co-authored a series for Dell under the pseudonym Valerie Vayle. Series titles include Lady of Fire, Seaflame, *and* Oriana.

Shape—*His Hawaiian shirt emphasized his beer belly, and his shorts revealed spindly legs. Jim thought immediately of a brightly painted barrel on stilts.*

Posture—*She was a tall girl who adopted a fashionable slouch to disguise the fact. Unfortunately, this only made her look like a tired giraffe.*

Carriage—This has to do with general movement rather than specific mannerisms or gestures.

Even in broad daylight, he moved as if darting from shadow to shadow.

Proportions—Is your character top heavy, long-legged, pear-shaped, obese, cadaverous . . . ?

Gwen's outdated bouffant hairdo made her look like a flagpole with an eagle's nest on top.

VOICE AND SPEECH

Speed—*Lavinia always feared that she might grow old and die waiting for Fred to get to the end of a sentence.*

Voice quality—*Lady Priscilla's voice was so shrill and piercing that her merest whisper seemed to penetrate the thick stone walls of the castle.*

Accent—It is generally better to suggest an accent by word choice rather than try spelling it phonetically.

"I brung this here horse from down home," he drawled.

Accents can be national or regional, genuine or assumed.

"Y'all come back," Juilet said in the lilting southern accent she had adopted in youth and stubbornly clung to through 40 years residence in Chicago.

Vocabulary and educational level—Remember that your characters must speak with their own vocabulary, not yours. A college professor and a ghetto child are bound to sound different. (Mrs. Malaprop, in *The Rivals*, is a classic example of vocabulary as a character tag.)

She looked like a young Elizabeth Taylor, but when she opened her mouth the resemblance came to a slamming halt. She had the vocabulary of a bad-tempered stevedore, and she used it with a fluency that was amazing in one so young.

Speech impediments—Like accents, these can be tricky. Try to avoid resorting to phonetic spelling. Readers have to read aloud to make sense of it, and you risk losing their interest. Better to suggest it obliquely:

"That's not the point!" Mrs. Wilson said juicily.

Marian had stood too close. "I guess not," she said, trying to wipe the minuscule drops of moisture off her face without being obvious about it.

Or simply describe the impediment:

His speech had a strange, baby-talk quality. Diane decided that it was the R's and L's in the language that did him in.

Speech patterns—This is the way people put their sentences together.

"Saw the girl," he admited. "Yesterday. Didn't like her. Too fat. Like 'em thin. Sexier that way."

Sound level—*"I'm right here, Jean," I said "You don't need to scream." "I'm not screaming," she screamed.*

Other—Does your character have a pet subject he keeps coming back to or some other vocal habit?

Mary had a habit of humming quietly while she worked. She had a melodious voice, and the tune was cheerful. New workers found it rather pleasant the first day, vaguely irritating on the second and downright maddening by the third. There was a large turnover in Mary's department which the office manager couldn't understand.

FACE

General configuration—*His face had the sad, pushed-in look common to old boxers who are has-beens without ever having been somebodies.*

Eyes—Think about spacing, color, size. Are they shifty, blinky or sleepy looking? *His eyes were the icy blue of a clear winter morning and just as pitiless.*

Eyebrows—Thin, surprised, shaggy? *She wore her hair pulled back so severely that her eyebrows looked like they were fighting to get free of their moorings and fly off in opposite directions.*

Nose—*Mrs. Exeter's nose was large, well-shaped and ideal for sticking into other people's business.*

Mouth—*Her teeth were lovely—white and straight, but they looked like they belonged to a much larger person.*

Hair—*She stood there rigidly. With her slim body and red-gold hair she looked like a small defiant candle.*

Other—Complexion, make-up, chin, forehead, scars, moles, tics, etc.

MOVEMENT

This is an enormous category, and, rather than subdivide it, let me give a few examples and suggest you additionally look at one of the many books on body language.

At intervals she put her index finger to the bridge of her nose, a reminder of those awful glasses she used to wear before she got her contacts.

She never walked if she could ride. If she was offered the choice between standing and sitting she sat. The only physical activity she liked was making love, and she did even that lethargically.

Remember: Character tags are those actions which are habitual or continual. This is *not* a character tag:

He thumped his chest with a hammy fist. "Me, I believe in first things first."

This *is:*

He was always thumping his chest with a hammy fist and saying things like, "Me, I believe in first things first," or, "Me, I got scruples."

CLOTHING

There are those who believe that the clothing people wear says a great deal about their personalities. Fit, color, style and condition of clothes can make a character vivid.

I peered into the mirror critically. John said that pantsuits made me look like the matron in an English mental hospital. I decided that he was right. Back to dresses!

The Duke of Somerset kept tossing back his ermine-trimmed cape the way a vain woman does long hair.

It seems to me now that Mama always wore white in the summer—white duck pants, white eyelet peasant blouses, white bathing suits with white caps. It made her seem cool and elegant while the rest of us sweated and felt vulgar for it.

This is not intended as a comprehensive list of tags. You have undoubtedly thought of others already. Inventing your own examples is a good exercise. And when you're hung up for ideas, these vignettes might well suggest stories to you.

How to create likable characters in your fiction

by Jean Z. Owen

Although most fiction editors report they need upbeat stories with likable protagonists, many writers—especially beginners—continue to submit only sour, downbeat material. Why? Try my little experiment and see. Note your emotional reactions as you appraise these situations:

A. While driving through the suburbs, you notice a moving van parked in a driveway; movers are carrying furniture into the house. A pleasant-faced young housewife comes down the street. She holds a home-baked cake. Obviously, she is bringing a gift to welcome the new neighbors.

B. A good-looking young man is waiting, along with several other persons, to board a crowded bus. When it appears there won't be room for everyone, he pushes ahead of an elderly woman, who must now wait for the next bus.

Now assay your responses. You may be one of the few persons who feel more strongly about the good character, but it's not likely. Most readers react far more intensely toward the rude, pushy young man. In real life, he might be able to cancel out this impression and win eventual approval—but not in a story. In fiction, that one act locks in his characterization for the duration.

Real but not lifelike

But it's not that easy when you are dealing with a likable character. Not only is reader reaction less intense, but a permanent characterization is more difficult to

---

Jean Z. Owen has used her nurse's training for much of the background in her 200 pieces of fiction (short stories, novelettes, magazine-length novels and one hardcover novel) and many nonfiction books and articles for major magazines. She lectures frequently at writers' conferences and workshops and is currently at work on two novels.

establish. If handled inexpertly by the writer, the unselfish, friendly gesture can make the reader wary. Perhaps the woman is calling on the new neighbors to snoop or gossip. Perhaps she's a neurotic Goody Two-Shoes. Perhaps she wants a favor in return. Is she so foolish as to use a cake to try to buy the new neighbors' approval? Is she really as generous as she pretends to be?

It takes real craftsmanship to nip these suspicions and make the reader feel more than lukewarm acceptance of the character. The inexperienced writer is tempted to abandon his "good guy" story and retreat to the less demanding depiction of a villainous protagonist. But he need not do so. Anyone who can master the other storytelling fundamentals can learn to portray likable characters—and produce salable fiction. Here are some tips:

Create your own characters. Sometimes a new writer assumes that if he uses a popular real-life person for a model, his protagonist will automatically have the same appeal. This is a delusion. A stronger, more appealing character will evolve if the author builds him from imagination, using bits of characterization from several sources.

Here's an example from one of my early unsold stories. I patterned my 60-year-old protagonist after a vital, beloved woman I knew and admired:

> Everyone in town liked "Mrs. M.," as they all called her. She had sparkling blue eyes and a bright smile and she was always giving away armloads of flowers she had raised in her garden. No one had ever heard her complain or say an unkind word about anyone.

As you read this excerpt, you undoubtedly agreed with the editors who rejected the story; the description of Mrs. M. is flat. The writing is so lackluster you may have difficulty believing that even now, as I copied those old sentences, my eyes blurred with tears and my throat tightened with emotion. The words make Mrs. M. come to life for me vivid and compelling way because I still look at her through the lenses of memory and affection—lenses the reader is not wearing.

Now compare the description of Mrs. M. with that of a similar character I constructed entirely from imagination for a story that *did* sell—not only to *Good Housekeeping* but to the movies:

> Mrs. Hoyle's gray curls bounced merrily as she approached the desk and peered through her bifocals at the anemic, watery-eyed hotel clerk. "I see your cold is better, William," she said.
>
> "Yes, ma'am."
>
> "It's the goose grease, I trust you're still wearing the red flannel?"
>
> Willie's gaze shifted around the lobby before he hooked his forefingers in the front of his shirt and pulled it open, exhibiting an area of red cloth.
>
> "Good." There was maternal approval in Mrs. Hoyle's voice. "You'd better come up to my room tonight and let me rub your chest again. One can't be too careful."
>
> "Yes, ma'am," Willie said again and watched the little old lady as she turned and waddled across the lobby to her favorite chair by the window.
>
> A moment later, Lily, the streetwalker, went past. Mrs. Hoyle tapped on the glass, beamed, and waved a cheery greeting. "Lovely girl," she murmured to no one in particular.

After the story was published, I was deluged with calls and letters from persons who wanted to know where I had gotten the idea for Mrs. Hoyle. They were certain I had known their dear aunts, mothers or grandmothers.

Injecting qualities

Why are made-up characters more true-to-life than characters derived from life? Perhaps, because flesh-and-blood people are not always as consistent as fictional characters must be. Perhaps because, in order to depict emotion, the writer must step inside the character's mind. If you are portraying an actual person, the feeling that you are intruding on his privacy may hamper you. (This fear of intrusion can exist even if you are writing about a stranger, a dead person, or someone who will never know he was used as a pattern.) But undoubtedly the *biggest* handicap in adapting your characters from life is that your feelings give you a bias that can distort your objectivity and insight.

Have your character try to solve his own problems. Without a problem there is no conflict; without conflict there is no plot. Most writers, even beginners, are aware of this fact, so they make certain their story gets off to a good start by thrusting the protagonist into a sticky situation. But then, too often, the writer permits the character to sit down and do nothing but feel sorry for himself until a twist of fate bails him out of his difficulty.

Any person (real-life or fictional) who puts forth no effort to resolve his problems is dull, tiresome and disgusting. Conversely, we feel sympathy and admiration for anyone who tries to extricate himself from his dilemma, even if he fails. To keep him likable, keep him slugging!

Don't soften your character with adverbs. A fiction editor told me that whenever he suggests to a writer that his protagonist be made more appealing, rarely will the revised manuscript show improvement.

He said, "Too many writers merely go through the manuscript and insert adverbs—she said *kindly*, she listened *sympathetically*, she volunteered *graciously*—in a misguided attempt to emphasize the fact that the character is an admirable person."

This never works. An occasional adverb can be valuable; but an excess of adverbs gives the story unrealistic, melodramatic overtones.

A writer takes a shortcut toward selling when he learns not to "paint" a character's appearance and gestures and speech but to inject likable qualities into the protagonist's *personality*. This injection is not confined to a single description, a single scene; it embraces the entire story. For the purpose of illustration, however, here are two treatments of an isolated episode:

Poor: "All right, sir," Donald told his employer respectfully. "Maybe," he went on patiently, "there will be an opening in the art department next year." He strugged his shoulders dejectedly and walked hurriedly out of the office.

Better: "All right, sir." Donald was amazed that his voice could sound so calm—even respectful, when he was seething with anger. "Maybe there will be an opening in the art department next year." Another year—a lifetime away. How could he even hope to show anyone what he could do as long as he was a square-peg artist stuck in the round hole of accounting? His frustration swelled suddenly into rage. Holding back the bitter words that would have finished his chances, he turned and hurried out of the office.

In passing, you might note two additonal things about those examples. One, the attribution *he went on patiently* is an awkward break in the quotation in the first treatment; it does not mark a natural pause in the quote. (Read it aloud and see.) When the attribution is omitted in the second treatment, the quote reads more smoothly. Two, you often profit from turning an adverb into a verb. *He hurried* is more terse and dramatic than *he walked hurriedly*.

Traits in conflict

Give your protagonist two outstanding traits. The dominant trait, of course, should be highly admirable. The secondary trait (which opposes the dominant) should be less likable; sometimes it can even be a character flaw.

If the dominant trait of our cake-giving heroine was a generous, impulsive nature, her secondary trait would be something that made it difficult for her to show others her true self. For instance, shyness would act as a foil to her generous impulses and create an inner struggle. And the harder the protagonist must struggle, the greater the chances are that the reader will like him.

Caution: The secondary trait must never denigrate the character or cancel out the dominant trait. To be likable, a character may be mistaken, but not stupid. Yearning, but not grasping. Sexy, not lascivious. Eager, not brash. Brave, not foolhardy. Trusting, not gullible. Soft-hearted, not soft-headed.

The easiest and most satisfactory way to balance these two traits is to show them in conflict with each other. To do this, step inside the character's thoughts and emotions.

Poor: The pleasant-faced, shy young woman walked toward the house the new neighbors were moving in. She carried a home-baked chocolate cake, and her hands trembled slightly as she moved reluctantly toward the front door.

Better: I can't. Paula told herself. I can't go up those steps or ring that bell. No one takes food to new neighbors any more. Why am I always doing something like this? Why can't I learn to do things Edith's way? Edith wouldn't be caught dead doing a funky thing like taking anyone a chocolate cake to strangers.

Let your character argue with himself. Have him scold himself, make resolutions he knows he'll break:

"I'm through kidding myself," Bob said. "I've had my last drink. From now on, I'm on the wagon." But even as he spoke, Bob felt his fingers slide into his pocket to touch the coins that, five minutes from now, would pay for a quick one at Dunnigan's Bar. Just one drink, to help him get through the evening. And that would be the last time. Sure, it would.

Let your character display her doubts and hangups:

Someone would surely ask her to dance. Amy assured herself as she slipped the new pink dress over her head. People were always telling her she was pretty—but *was* she? She stared at her reflection in the mirror. No, I'm not, she thought. I'm not one bit pretty. I can't even pretend I am. No one will want to dance with me. But I'm going to be there, anyway. I'll stick it out if it kills me. And no one will know I'm not having fun.

Let your character castigate herself; let her occasionally pat herself on the back. Show her fears and hopes and angers. Describe her emotions as she fails and scoops together her shattered self-respect and broken dreams:

"Well," Fred said, not quite looking at her. "I've got to split. Be seein' you, kid."

"Of course. Soon. Good-night, Fred," Sally answered, careful to keep her voice light, casual, so he wouldn't know she was hurting inside. She'd lost him, she knew. Love had come her way and somehow she had blown it. The other girls would know; everyone would pity her.

Sally took a deep breath as she watched Fred turn the corner and go out of sight. I'll show them, she told herself staunchly. Love will come again . . . *I know* it will come again. And next time I'll be smarter; I'll know how to handle it. But I wish . . . oh, I wish it had been Fred.

By showing your character's inner conflicts, you're almost certain to establish reader identification; these emotions reflect the small, silent dramas we experience daily. This is what your readers want to find when they buy a magazine and turn to your story.

Whenever I urge students to become skilled in creating likable protagonists, someone is sure to point out that *un*-likable story-people sometimes appear in print as the principal characters, too.

Of course they do! But because they are more difficult to sell, you can bet the author weighed the material carefully before deciding that that particular story could be told *only* via that particular viewpoint. Which brings us to the final guideline:

Check your story for proper point of view. Remember—the Cinderella story would have been a bitter (and probably unsold) tale had it been told from the viewpoint of one of the stepsisters. Or your favorite story—the one that kept you reading eagerly to the end—had the story been presented from the villain's point of view.

Take a fresh look at some of the sour, downbeat stories in your reject file. You may be surprised to find you have some truly fine stories there, marred by the wrong viewpoint. Dig them out; try the *good* character as your protagonist. It won't be easy, but you may be amazed at the way this enhances the story's salability.

Once you master the technique, you may find tremendous satisfaction in breathing life into a fictional *friend* for your reader. Give him someone to love, someone who marches to the drumbeat *he* hears.

Put a lift in your stories. Your fan mail will warm your heart. And your bank account will swell with joy.

Theme

by Gerald Warner Brace

In a letter to a friend in 1888, Chekhov wrote: "It seems to me that the writer of fiction should not try to solve such questions as those of God, pessimism, and so forth. His business is but to describe those who have been speaking or thinking about God and pessimism, how, and under what circumstances." A few months later he wrote to the same friend: "You are right in demanding that an artist should take an intelligent attitude to his work, but you confuse two things: *solving a problem* and *stating a problem correctly*. It is only the second that is obligatory for the artist."

Perhaps in this context even the word "problem" is suspect. Chekhov was not really interested in problems, in the intellectual or philosophical sense, and he was right in assuming that it is not an artist's business to solve them anyway. In fact, he goes on to say that in this world no one can make anything out, not even Socrates or Voltaire.

A more useful word for the writer might be *predicament*, or one of the synonyms cited by Webster: *dilemma, quandary, plight, fix, jam,* and *pickle*. These terms and all that they imply provide the true stuff of drama and fiction, and the writer's main job is to recognize what the circumstances are and how they are involved in the actions and reactions of individual characters. There may be no solution, in any philosophical sense. There may be an end of effort, a win or loss, a recognition, an unveiling or unmasking, a temporary stasis, but in art there are no final solutions.

Yet, Chekhov notwithstanding, writers are forever preoccupied with ideas, even with what they hope are solutions to the puzzles of existence. They do write about God and pessimism; they offer opinions not only on how men have lived but

Gerald Warner Brace *died in 1978 after a long career as an educator and an author. He taught at Boston University, where in 1967 he won the Shell Award for Distinguished Writing, and wrote both nonfiction and novels about life in New England, which had the predominant themes of reason and self control.*

on how they may or should live. They offer themes and theses, sometimes strongly and dogmatically projected.

Individual definitions

Who can say what theme in art really is? We may call it the unifying idea, but that does no more than substitute one abstract term for another. Is theme a "philosophy"? Is it a moral? Is it a universal truth? Is it no more than the "momentary stay against confusion" that Robert Frost proposes? Must every good piece of fiction have a theme? Does a writer evolve his theme with conscious and rational purpose or does he simply tell his story as it comes in hopes that it will achieve the larger significance that everyone looks for in art? If he is wise enough to write good fiction at all, he is presumably wise enough to evaluate his materials with persuasive consistency.

Yet when we look at the themes of great literature we find some notions that are neither sensible nor profound. Samuel Richardson's novels are based on the proposition he enunciates as follows: "There is but one word necessary to explain that other precious word, *honor*. . . .It is *matrimony*." The tenet seems absurdly literal and morally provincial, yet the novels are accepted as great—*Clarissa*, in fact, is regarded by many as one of the greatest of all novels. The poet William Blake, now ranked among the highest, considered man's reasoning faculty to be evil. Meredith regarded nature as beneficent. Hardy regarded nature as inimical. D.H. Lawrence had a Blake-like faith in man's "unconscious" responses, and celebrated the blood as the true source of his virtue. Critics who would normally regard this as nonsense none the less find much to admire in Lawrence; F.R. Leavis, in fact, considers him the ablest English novelist of our age.

One of F. Scott Fitzgerald's well-known stories is "The Rich Boy," and the theme of it is quite explicit. The boy, whose name is Anson Hunter, is brought up to enormous wealth. His father is one of the great railroad tycoons, and his own habits through school and college and into early maturity are conditioned by his unlimited wealth. It is Fitzgerald's thesis that Anson Hunter, or any other similar rich boy, is rendered unfit for normal life. He can't work like other men. He can't engage in ordinary social relationships. He can't even love and marry happily. That, in brief, is Fitzgerald's "theme" about the very rich. Yet we see on every hand the extraordinary good and useful and successful careers of men of similar background and wealth, including most notably Averell Harriman, who has spent most of his life in effective public service, and who inevitably suggests the prototype for Anson Hunter. Fitzgerald's theme, in other words, is not reliable.

This, at least, is the literal view of it. But the fact seems to be that artists as a rule have little philosophical standing. No serious history of ideas, so far as I know, pays attention to Shakespeare, or to Dickens or Joyce or Faulkner. The tragedy *King Lear* may be the most powerful ever written, but any reasonable justification of its theme runs into difficulties. The motive of blessed innocence in *Pickwick* is delightful but will hardly bear analysis. Artists, it seems, use ideas not because they are "true" in reason or logic but because they have dramatic and imaginative potential: More than that, they display the actual follies and ordeals of mankind. For some writers, for Richardson, say, with his fixed and convinced moral position, the idea is so demanding that it barely lets him function as an artist at all, and we feel that *Clarissa* bursts into dramatic life almost in spite of its author. And in such writers as Hardy and Lawrence the push of literal theme is at times intrusive and deadening. At the poignant end of *Tess*, who wants to hear about the President of the Immortals? For the most part, theme is an adventurous hypothesis, a possibility full of human meanings, a vision, a hope, a beguilement, a chain of supposes. In our study of poetry we are warned against translating the "meaning," or the theme, into a literal summary. If we try to paraphrase Wordsworth's "Ode," for example, and explain that babies come from heaven, the argument seems preposterous, but if we let the poetry re-create in us the instinctive delights of childhood and youth in spring we not only enjoy it but are beguiled into believing in the divinity it imagines. The good writer, in proposing a theme, does not argue it—if he is wise he does not even insist on it; he *supposes* it, he speculates on it, he sees its possibilities, he discovers angles and contingencies in it that others may have overlooked, he perceives not *the* truth in it, but aspects and facets of truth. We may agree that Fitzgerald's rich boy contradicts some of the actualities we happen to know of, but the question of what unlimited wealth can do to the individual remains open, as it were. The idea is a valid one. The possibilities are full of significance. Wealth is power, and power corrupts, so we are told. The world's tragedies from the time of Sophocles up to now offer us variations on the theme—not in the way of literal history or revealed truth but as imagined human probabilities.

Light thread or heavy chain

A theme gives a writer a certain technical advantage. It offers a path to follow, a connection between start and finish. It can be, in the lightest sense, a thread hardly noticed in a story's progress, or it can be a chain rather too formidable for the dramatic illusion. Mark Twain wrote *The Mysterious Stranger* to demonstrate that all men are helpless victims of a nature which is ruthless and even diabolic. The "chain" of his thesis is very strong indeed, and reduces his drama to a sequence of illustrations arranged as confirmations. In an ordinary writer the effect would be too obviously forced, the chain is heavy and insistent, but Twain's convictions are so brilliantly and bitterly projected that the story triumphs over its own artifices. It is a cynical parable, an apologue rather than a valid drama, and we must give it a place apart in our critical designations, but its very difference may be a warning to other writers: We read it with more of a sense of sorrow for Mark Twain than for mankind. It is not possible to advise any writer as to how seriously he should or should not take his convictions—or his self; the dedicated moralist or polemicist can be very formidable, and may be a major prophet, but more often he is a bore, or he corrupts his art with dogma and prejudice, or he imprisons himself in the iron framework of his own theory, as Hawthorne said of some of his Concord neighbors. We see always how good art conceals itself, how it proceeds by indirections and beguiles by apparent innocence, and in no area is this illusion of spontaneous vitality more necessary than in the area of theme or thesis. Art, Conrad said, appeals to temperament, and temperament is not amenable to persuasion. It does not want an argument or a scolding; it wants chiefly to *see*, and to make its own decisions and evaluations about what is going on. The right use of theme can be likened to the steel re-enforcement in prestressed concrete; it is not visible, the casual observer does not know it is there, but it binds the structure into a unit of formidable strength.

The necessary concealments may be achieved in various ways. Perhaps the safest is to say nothing about theme at all, to proceed with an effect of beguiling innocence. Everyone is pleased with Joel Chandler Harris's story of Brer Rabbit and the Tar Baby; it is obviously and delightfully a good story, a triumph, in fact, and much of its strength lies in the theme we are hardly aware of as we read it. On the surface it is simply a preposterous duel between two mortal enemies. Our hero is Brer Rabbit, who is cocky and vain ("as sassy as a jay-bird"), and our villain is Brer Fox, who tends to be heavy and a bit slow on the uptake, and who represents, in his own mind at least, respectability and convention. Brer Rabbit is certainly due for his comeuppance, and Brer Fox at least knows that the way to trap him is through his own vanity. The plot is precise and tricky, and very effective. It derives from character, as good plots should. But of course Brer Rabbit emerges in triumph, his way of life is vindicated, wit is worth more than muscle, sassiness is infinitely more admirable than respectability. At the end the idea is implicit in the sound and rhythm of the words, in what we must call the poetry, or even the pure music. " 'Bred en bawn in a brier-patch, Brer Fox—bred en bawn in a brier patch.' En wid dat he skip out des es lively ez a cricket in de embers." The "thesis" is evident when you see it and state it, but nothing in the story argues it or pretends to advocate it or even to take it seriously. It is a silly story after all. And perhaps any notion that a cocky little adventurer like Brer Rabbit should be admired above respectable folks is not worth very much—perhaps it is irresponsible. But of course any effort to translate the story into rational discourse is futile: Brer Rabbit exists, exactly as Falstaff and others do, as a human experience, and no one who sees and hears him ever forgets. Perhaps he "symbolizes" the delightful rascality that we all cherish, but we don't admit to taking such things very solemnly. But who can resist the triumphant and immortal image of that actual rogue, that "monstrous soon critter," sitting cross-legged on a chinkapin log combing the pitch out of his hair with a chip? The art of fiction can do no better than that.

Effective irony

A major classic way of concealing theme is by irony, which of course can operate in many ways. In *Jonathan Wild*, Fielding pretends that the evil gangster is a great man, and treats him with mock respect. In *Joseph Andrews* there is a scene where some huntsmen set their dogs on the good Parson Adams for the sport of it and are scolded by the master of the hounds—not for torturing a clergyman but for letting the hounds learn bad habits by pursuing human vermin. Thackeray of course used a similar ironic method: He pretends to admire the successful rascals of the fashionable world and mocks the dullness and simplicity of the virtuous; in *Vanity Fair* he scolds and abuses his nonhero William Dobbin, though it is evident that Dobbin's deplorable behavior represents chiefly courage, loyalty, and unselfishness.

But irony has two edges, and the writer who takes it up as a deliberate policy may himself be hurt. Or he may be unaware of the implications. Even the great Thackeray puzzles and annoys his readers by an ambivalence which he seems hardly aware of: His policy of irony may be quite explicit and understandable, but the characters themselves transcend the "policy" and leave us with the uneasy feeling that the author is not really in control of his own drama. His *theme* is on one level, his human actualities seem to be on another. Becky Sharp represents all that is unscrupulous and selfish, but when Thackeray calls her his heroine we know that he halfway means it. His policy did not allow for the almost autonomous strength of his imagination—a problem, indeed, that many an author has had: The Satan of *Paradise Lost* becomes the "hero" in spite of Milton's rational intentions; such characters as Lovelace in *Clarissa* and Heathcliff in *Wuthering Heights* assert their everlasting vitality regardless of the thematic scheme. We even use the word irony in such connection: It is ironic, we say, that Soames Forsyte in Galsworthy's *Sága* began as the villain and ended as the hero, though the irony that we see was not apparent to the author. Most writers discover, in fact, that their best characters have a will and a destiny of their own, and any effort to make them conform to a prearranged theme tends to deprive them of their native vitality.

Symbols, subtle and explicit

Theme is most often conveyed by symbols, sometimes explicity, as in a parable, sometimes so subtly that the unwary reader fails to perceive it at all. But artists almost inevitably think in terms of symbols: The images that they conjure up are not idle fancies, but are representations of universal experience. Brer Rabbit's brier patch is a symbol. So is the ship in Conrad, and the sea and the Congo River. In Hawthorne's fiction, everything is symbolic—woods, flowers, houses, costumes, even the ancestral hens in *The House of the Seven Gables*. The novels most admired in our times are those in which the symbolism is obscure and subtle, and advanced courses in the universities are given in "the difficult novel," with particular reference to Joyce and Faulkner and Proust. The influence of academic critics is so strong, in fact, that difficulty and even obscurity are counted as virtues. And since most writers in our time are college or university graduates, the symbolic (and difficult) mode is in fashion.

When great difficulties are overcome, the resulting success is clearly very great. Faulkner's *Light in August*, for example, is filled with motives and themes and symbols which blend into a powerful dramatic whole: it is the kind of book which contains "levels of meaning," and at the same time generates an effect of spontaneous and urgent life. Its "difficulties" intensify its triumph.

But when symbolism is arbitrarily applied or insisted on, or when it remains an author's secret or exists as a hidden acrostic that the reader must search for and solve, or when its chief business is to provide a motive for academic dissertations, or even when it becomes a thing-in-itself to be abstracted from the work as a whole, then it has no honest dramatic function.

No one can tell, not even the writer himself, how an idea can best be projected in terms of human drama. The imagination *sees* what it wants to create. Or it hears, or feels, or even tastes and smells. The writer is swept almost bodily into his imagined scene, and is carried with it to a conclusion that he has not quite foreseen. Characters take charge and settle their destinies in unexpected ways, and the writer's theoretical wisdom, his theme or thesis, is constantly tested in the actual drama that seems to unfold according to its necessities. Thackeray, for one, always implied that his characters were a stubborn and willful lot, and went their own way regardless of his intentions. Katherine Mansfield was astonished at the reality of her imagined scenes. Faulkner evaded all questions about his themes and purposes; he was not a man of letters, he said, but merely a writer. Any good novelist can testify to the life-force that seems to generate, not in him the creator but in the lives he is imagining. *Uncle Tom's Cabin* is a powerful tract and polemic, but it lives as a novel, it projects its people and scenes with graphic and dramatic vitality. The world was astonished that so gentle and ladylike a New Englander as Harriet Beecher Stowe could have written it, and one of her brothers feared that it would work harm to her Christian character: "Dear soul," she responded, "he need not be troubled. He doesn't know that I did not write that book . . . No, I only put down what I saw . . . it all came before me in visions, one after the other, and I put them down in words." True imaginative power seems to many writers to be divine in its origin, but Rudyard Kipling had another word for it: he called it his Demon.

Using the flashback in fiction

by Mariana Prieto

We have all heard the phrase, "The past is prologue." Certainly this applies to the writing of the flashback.

Sequence can sour. The "flashback" can keep the story fresh and interesting. But it must be deftly mixed in. Like the pieces in an intricate mosaic, we must fit the flashback in so that it blends with the rest of the story.

To refresh our memory on the definition of a flashback, it is an interruption in the story line or plot, to show events or situations prior to those just presented. It does just what it is called. It flashes back to a previous time so that the present becomes easier for the reader to understand.

You, the author, should know the past of your lead character and what made him react as he does, what got him to where he is in the story. Some writers like to write out definite "past history" and then condense it into a brief flashback. You must be clear in your own mind about the past, even making a diagram or chart, if you are using it in longer form, in a novel. But not all of the "past" that you know needs to be contained in the flashback. You must be *selective* about what you choose and consider it well. Be sure that it is important to the present story line.

Relevant information

I'm sure we all have friends who include in their conversation long explanations about past events. Many times they have no direct bearing on the subject and we are inclined to want to say, "Please go on with it."

Mariana Prieto has 15 juvenile and two adult novels and over 800 nonfiction and fiction magazine articles to her credit. She has taught creative writing at the University of Miami, has lectured at writers' conferences and can write in Spanish as well as English. Presently she teaches writing in adult education programs where she seeks in her students "that special sense of awareness, a perception that comes with observation, interpretation and consciousness."

This is how a reader feels if the flashback is too long. He wants to flip the page and go on reading the story.

This is why we must be very careful about flashbacks and not let them become "flopbacks" that can cause our story to "flop" and sag and fall apart.

The short story should *begin* at a high point, a dramatic scene, if possible. If it is necessary for the reader to know how the character got in this situation or what went before, that led up to this situation, then we must introduce a flashback. This device helps clarify the situation. The flashback should carry the reader back and give him relevant information that leads up to where the story opened.

Sometimes a sentence will serve as sufficient flashback, other times a paragraph is needed. Beware: Do not let the flashback be so long that it outbalances the rest of your story.

In a short story the span of time should be short. Therefore the flashback technique is important to maintain this brevity of time. The writer can thus give an account of past events that have bearing on the story and bring the reader up to the present situation without transferring from the present. This is where practice, polishing and craftsmanship are important. Try to analyze your material for pace. We live in a fast-paced world and no amount of material, no matter how important, must seem to slow the rhythm and movement of the story line.

A story without a flashback would lack dimension because it would all be one time element.

In writing a children's story, the flashback is important. However, with children, one must be very exact and sure that the children understand that they are going back as, "at supper yesterday" or "only two days ago he had seen Jane's dog."

Also make it plain when you bring them back to the present action.

In my own story, "A Kite for Carlos," I used this technique.

"Tell me grandfather, about when you were a little boy and learned to fly kites in Spain," Carlos begged.

So his grandfather told him again about the kites he had made. Then how he and his family had moved to Cuba where he made more kites and later how they had moved again. This time to the United States.

This flashback was necessary to the story and in one paragraph gave the life background of the grandfather and acquainted the reader with Carlos' ancestry.

This was the "tell me" technique in order to get into the flashback. Another familiar device used to lead the reader back, is music. A melody can set the character's thoughts back in time and introduce the recounting of that time. A bird song or a shrill voice can set into motion the recall process of a character and smoothly introduce the flashback. In "October Song" by William Sanson (McCall Corp.), music was the device used for the leadback, as:

Humoresque cosseted her. Awful tearoom stuff, she thought, but gave in and listened to its soothing tinkle of security. Like the sunny cream walls, like the chintzes, it took her back to the simpler '30s, when the children were babies and they had all lived and laughed together in an ample gabled house in Surrey. Life then had seemed to have a future. Fir trees in the garden, mud-guards glinting on the gravel drive, tradesmen at their entrance, a cook in the kitchen . . . .

Well, now it was a three-roomer in Kensington, the war survived, the children dispersed and bringing up children of their own.

The transition to the present is smoothly accomplished and information about the present setting is given.

Action, dialogue, recall

Francoise Sagan in her short story, "Help or Something," (1967, Vogue) again gives us an example of clever handling of necessary information. She does it this way:

> That spring we were in Normandy and living in a sumptuous house, all the more sumptuous for our having, after two years of inundations, had the roof repaired. The sudden absence of pans set out strategically under the beams, the absence at night of ice-cold droplets of water on our peaceful, sleeping faces, the absence of a spongy carpet underfoot intoxicated us.

A writer with less craftsmanship might have told these problems in sequence and it would have been dull reading, like the recitation of a tiresome relative. As it is, she opens on the happy note that the roof is repaired, then flashes back to the problems that preceded it, the absence of which accounts for their present happiness.

In my writing classes, I keep telling my students that just because a thing really happened, it isn't necessarily interesting. At least not always if told in the exact sequence of the happening. We must, as writers, select the sequence that will prove most interesting to the "other fellow." We must whet his appetite, gain his attention and then go on from there. This is why it is better to open on a high note, then go back and explain, if explanation is necessary.

Here we have an example from a story published in *Redbook*, the title "Breaking Free," by Ralph McInery. This shows a flashback as presented in a first person story. The narrator gives us the information plus some insight into his own character.

> I nodded. I had never known her husband—he had died when Jane was in her early teens—but I had difficulty imagining Mrs. Reynolds as shattered as my mother now was. Not that my mother's condition could be described as desolate sorrow. My father's fatal attack had taken him in the bed of another woman, one my mother had known about. Whatever check there had been on her drinking had died with my father.

Here is an example of a very short flashback from one of my published adult stories, "The Tinsel Star" in *The Magnificat*.

> As she patted the baby, her eyes caught the gleam of the star in the sapphire ring on her finger. She had accepted that ring as she accepted all Eric's gifts and love, with no intention of return.

This brief passage shows that the character had been selfish in the past as she was now in the present.

Speech, action, dialogue, recall, all can be paths that lead into the smoothly presented flashback. The reader should not be jolted by it, or into it.

No break in the story flow should be occasioned by the flashback and certainly a reader should not have to go back and read it to understand it.

Flashbacks can be presented in segments in the longer story. The entire flashback need not be given all at one time but rather as it contributes to the story progress. Too long a glimpse into the past can cloud the reader's understanding of the present.

Think of newspaper headlines. They give the exciting part of the story to the reader, then after he is "hooked," they tell what leads up to the headline. In other words, they resort to flashback technique.

Even the clever conversationalist uses flashbacks to hold his listeners. He opens with, "My house burned down," and the listener listens.

"Why?" the listener asks. "What caused it?"

Just as the reader wants to know what went before, what led up to the present situation or involvement.

Yes, life is full of flashbacks; we can't escape or deny them. But we can by studying the technique of other writers, learn how to introduce them skillfully.

I urge you to become flashback conscious. When you come to a flashback in a story, red pencil it. After you have finished reading the story, put it away and see if you can recall the flashback. Even write it and see if you can remember the introductory sentence that moulded it smoothly into the story.

A flashback, like a girdle, should be stretched just to cover the necessary area, and it can be done. Try a carefully fashioned flashback and see!

Narrative prose

by John Braine

My working rule with narrative prose is the same as for dialogue: If it can't be read aloud, it's no good. I don't mean by this that your narrative is supposed to represent actual speech. But your prose must have the rhythms of speech. Otherwise it becomes arid and obscure and intellectualized. It may, by any other test than the ear, be brilliant; but it won't do for a novel. For though it doesn't have to pretend to be otherwise than written, still, behind every novel is a man telling us a story face-to-face.

As I've said before, no one can teach you how to write a story. You can, however, be taught to write decent prose, which is simply clear and understandable prose. This doesn't necessarily mean absolutely bare prose. It doesn't mean that your prose can't be complex. It doesn't mean that you're not allowed metaphor. There are no limits to what you can do, to the tricks you can play with words, as long as you remember, in Flaubert's words, that if your prose doesn't follow the rhythms of the human lungs, then it isn't worth a damn. If you doubt this, then look at the prose of Shakespeare or Webster or Donne, which is very specifically meant to be spoken aloud.

Another rule—and I'm aware that it's a counsel of perfection—is to do without adjectives. If you do use one, let it be the least expected one. For when you eliminate adjectives, then you're forced to find the right verb and the right noun. Verbs and nouns together are naked and active; the putting together of a noun and a verb means, as often as not, that you've used the first noun which came into your head, and that the noun could only be given color and life by sticking on an

---

John Braine once said of his writing, "I'm a novelist and only a novelist." Known for his critically acclaimed novel Room at the Top, *Braine is also a British journalist and writer of nonfiction. His other works include* The Queen of a Distant Country, The Crying Game, The Jealous God, From the Hand of the Hunter *and* The View From Tower Hill.

adjective. The strength of English is its huge variety of synonyms; the word which expresses precisely the shade of meaning which you need is always there if you look for it. To reject adjectives means that you have no option but to look for it.

You must also reject clichés. They don't say anything and, in any case, are almost always used inaccurately. When something is described as being as white as snow, for example, the comparison is made without considering the fact that snow isn't always the same shade of white. And blood isn't always the same shade of red or grass the same shade of green. Describe the color of a material as being the bright frothy red of arterial blood, and the cliché is no longer a cliché. To be exact, to take the trouble mentally to use one's five senses is to eliminate the cliché.

Language of metaphor

And that is all there is to metaphor. You take your images from your own experience, from the life around you. A metaphor isn't an ornament, a decoration attached to a plain statement. It's the only possible way of describing what you have to describe. This is most of all true when you're describing a state of mind:

> I felt a certain reaction to what she said, but I am a slow-thinking man, and it occurred to me simultaneously that of all natural forces, vitality is the incommunicable one. In days when juice came into one as an article without duty, one tried to distribute it—but always without success; to further mix metaphors, vitality never "takes." You have it or you haven't it, like health or brown eyes or honor or a baritone voice. I might have asked some of it from her, neatly wrapped and ready for home cooking and digestion, but I could never have got it—not if I'd waited around for a thousand hours with the tin cup of self-pity. I could walk from her door, holding myself very carefully like cracked crockery, and go away into the world of bitterness, where I was making a home with such materials as are found there—and quote to myself after I left her door:
> *"Ye are the salt of the earth. But if the salt hath lost its savour, wherewith shall it be salted?"*
> Matthew 5-13. (F. Scott Fitzgerald, "The Crack Up").

I've chosen this extract from Scott Fitzgerald's "The Crack-Up" because the writer's only concern here is to describe his personal situation. If he could have expressed himself by means of plain statement, he would have done so. But the words to express his state of mind don't exist. (Perhaps they exist in the vocabulary of psychology, but he wasn't a psychologist.)

Metaphor, for the creative writer, isn't an extension of language. It is almost another language. I'm even wrong to use the term "plain statement." If, paradoxically, metaphor isn't plain statement, then it fails. If it has no relevance to the story, then it fails. If it holds up the story, then it fails.

There are, of course, too many rules here to keep in the mind all at once. The overall rule in the writing of a novel is to keep it in the concrete, to avoid the abstract. All my rules have been taken from others; I have devised none myself. This rule for writing good prose was lifted straight from Stuart Chase's *The Tyranny of Words* (Harcourt, Brace & World, Inc., 1938). This has been the most important book in my life. It isn't for me to say whether my work has any lasting merit, but if I have been able to make a living as a professional novelist, it has been entirely due to reading Chase's book at a formative age. Before I read it I knew that I wanted to write, but I didn't know what writing was about. I wanted to write well, but I didn't know how to set about learning how to write well. I wanted a style of my own, but I thought that style was a sort of conjuring trick.

I believe that I had good natural taste; I divided novels in particular into dead and alive. I couldn't say why, and didn't realize that if I couldn't judge other people I couldn't judge myself. I'm sure that I believed in inspiration, that the ability to write would be given me without my taking any conscious thought about it. What saved me, what made me instantly grasp the truth of Chase's arguments, was that I have an essentially earth-bound mind and a devouring interest in the material world. Ideas mean nothing to me unless I can perceive their connection with the material world.

I shall not attempt to summarize Chase's book; you must read it for yourself. But its essence is the examination of the relationship between word and referent. The referent is

the object or situation in the real world to which the word or label refers. A beam of light comes from a moving animal to my optic nerve. The animal, which I recognize through prior experience with similar animals, is the referent. Presently I add the label and say, "That's a nice dog." Like the term "semantics," I shall use the term "referent" frequently in the following pages. Indeed the goal of semantics might be stated as "Find the referent." When people can agree on the thing to which their words refer, minds meet. The communication line is cleared.

Chase goes on to define three groups of words or, as he puts it, labels:

1. Labels for common objects, such as "dog," "chair," "pencil." Here difficulty is at a minimum.

2. Labels for clusters and collections of things, such as "mankind," "consumers' goods," "Germany," "the white race," "the courts." These are abstractions of a higher order, and confusion in their use is widespread. There is no entity "white race" in the world outside our heads, but only some millions of individuals with skins of an obvious or dubious whiteness.

3. Labels for essences and qualities, such as "the sublime," "freedom," "individualism," "truth." For such terms, there are no discoverable referents in the outside world, and by mistaking them for substantial entities somewhere at large in the environment, we create a fantastic wonderland. This zone is the especial domain of philosophy, politics, and economics.

We normally beg the hard question of finding referents and proceed learnedly to define the term by giving another dictionary abstraction, for example, defining "liberty" by "freedom"—"thus peopling the universe with spurious entities, mistaking symbolic machinery for referents." We seldom come down to earth, but allow our language forms or symbolic machinery to fashion a demonology of absolutes and high-order abstractions, in which we come to believe as firmly as Calvin believed in the Devil. (*The Tyranny of Words*).

As a novelist, your words should all come from the first group. (I am, of course, talking here specifically about narrative.) This is, of course, a counsel of perfection, as is dispensing with adjectives. But the test is simple: If you can't find a referent for the word, then you're writing nonsense. It might be splendid as philosophy but you're not a philosopher. It isn't your job to think in the abstract.

The test becomes second nature. So does the decision as to when it's not necessary to apply it—or, for that matter, possible. You can't really find any referents for thoughts, unless it's minute electrical charges. You can't really find any referents for states of mind like happiness or depression, or for qualitites like good or evil. You can, however, present your character's thoughts exactly as you imagine that they really are, no matter how shocking or incongruous. Whether or not it's possible to find an absolutely accurate image for the state of mind, it is most definitely possible to describe exactly the circumstances of the person concerned; and if this is done properly, a simple statement is often enough. This is irrespective of the correspondence of the circumstances to the state of mind; as often as not, to choose a very simple example, it's the contradiction of the circumstances by the state of mind, as with someone feeling depressed on a fine day, which describes the state of mind fully, but in only a few words. The sun shines on and the birds sing through the depression; fine day and depression are in the same world. Let your main effort go into describing what you can describe. All that matters is the physical world and what happens in it.

Level of prose

It was when I discovered *The Tyranny of Words* that I ceased to worry about evolving an individual style. I had the dim idea of creating something out of Hemingway, Joyce, Lawrence, and Dos Passos; I even used to copy out passages from them to imagine myself in their shoes, have some of their talent rub off on me. I realized after reading *The Tyranny of Words* that this was adolescent and egoistic. The function of prose is to convey meaning to as many readers as possible. Style, in the sense of being unmistakably oneself, is a by-product. The more one consciously strives for it, the further away one will go from it.

Along with the search for the referent came the growing conviction that what the average reader didn't find easy to read was bad prose. Rarely, if ever, bad because too clever, too complex; but bad because not properly worked out, bad because words were used without the author knowing what they really meant. And so I drew up another childishly simple working rule: Don't use any word if you're not sure about its meaning.

At the same time—and as this book proceeds, the contradictions mount up— you mustn't write down to your audience, mustn't be afraid of the most complex constructions, recondite metaphors, the rarest words, as long as they're the only ones which will express exactly what you mean. I'm convinced—and again have only my instincts to back me—that good writing can be understood and enjoyed even when words are used which aren't known to the general public. As long as you, the writer, know what they mean, the public will know.

I see as my audience everyone of average intelligence from 16 onwards. Since at this age most children are capable of coping with Shakespeare and Chaucer and the New Mathematics, I see no reason why they shouldn't comprehend me. If I set my sights any lower, I shouldn't enjoy writing.

I shall not list the faults you should avoid because that would be merely negative. And I couldn't make the list comprehensive under 40,000 words. Nor shall I state what is correct English usage: Sir Ernest Gowers and H.W. Fowler, among others, have done it for me. I can only make a general statement here: It's always better to be correct. Even if, to choose only one example, everyone else uses "decimate" as meaning reduction by nine-tenths, you must use it as meaning reduction by a tenth. I don't mean that you must be pedantic, but simply that you mustn't be sloppy.

Absolute clarity

The question still arises, after you've followed all my working rules, of how you can judge whether your prose is as good as it should be. One answer is that you don't ask yourself the question; ask yourself only functional, *working* questions—does my prose do what it has set out to do?

As long as you don't ask yourself about the merits of your prose, you'll be told the answer. Follow my rules—I realize how arrogant this claim must sound—and you'll be told not only about your prose, but about the novel itself.

This knowledge came to me with a passage in the last chapter of *Room at the Top*:

I ordered a bottle of IPA and a gin-and-it. Time was beginning to move too quickly, to slither helplessly away; each minute I looked at my watch it was ten minutes later; I knew that I'd only that minute met Mavis, but that minute was anything up to a year ago; as I drank the sharp summer-smelling beer the floor started to move again. Then every impression possible for one man to undergo all gathered together from nowhere like a crowd at the scene of an accident and yelled to be let in: time dancing, time with clay on its hobnailed boots, the new taste of the beer and the old taste of brandy and rum and fish and cornflour and tobacco and soot and wool scourings and Mavis' sweat that had something not quite healthy about it and her powder and lipstick—chalk, orris-root, pear-drops—and the hot hand of brandy steadying me again and just as it seemed that there wasn't to be any other place in the world but the long room with the green *art moderne* chairs and glass-topped tables, we were out in the street with our arms round each other's waists and turning in and out of narrow streets and alleys and courts and patches of waste ground and over a footbridge with engines clanging together aimlessly in the cold below as if slapping themselves to keep warm and then we were in a corner of a woodyard in a little cave of piled timber; I took myself away from my body, which performed all the actions she expected from it. She clung to it after the scalding trembling moment of fusion as if it were human, kissing its drunken face and putting its hands against her breasts.

There were houses very near on the dirt road at the top of the woodyard; I could hear voices and music and smell cooking. All around were the lights of the city; Birmingham Road rises from the centre of Leddersford and we were on a little plateau about halfway up; there was no open country to be seen; not one acre where there wasn't a human being, 200,000 separate lonelinesses, 200,000 different deaths. And all the darkness the lights had done away with, all the emptiness of fields and woods long since built over, suddenly swept over me, leaving no pain, no happiness, no despair, no hope, but simply nothingness, the ghost in the peepshow vanishing into the blank wall and no pennies left to bring him out again.

The answer came with the sentence beginning "And all the darkness. . . ." I knew when I read it over that my prose was the best that I could do, that it presented my characters and my world with absolute clarity. The novel all hung together, it was a unity. But I can't put into words exactly what I felt, except, quite simply, that I knew that it would be all right.

This moment only comes once, and it can come at any point in the book. It cannot be induced by any means, and it's best not to hope for it. To have its possibility in your mind is almost to scare it away. It will inform you that you're going in the right direction or that you have gone in the right direction. I won't tell you how to recognize it because I can't. But you can't mistake it; there is no other experience to match it.

Arms and the writer

by C.J. Cherryh

Even for an ugly thought, my teacher said, *it is never necessary to choose an ugly word.*

We were in Latin class, not journalism; we were translating Vergil into English prose. It was my translation under criticism.

Mentally I objected to the thought. It nagged at me as things will that contradict some basically held belief. I kept picking it up again, worrying at it, trying to understand in what sense I had been criticized.

I was a closet writer at the time, desperate, determined—unpublished. *Show reality*, I had been taught by my English instructors, *and make it ugly if need be.*

Days later I looked at my translation. Vergil's words had sung, rhythmic and full of grace: the fall of Troy—murder, treachery, tragedy—a tale full of potential ugliness. I considered his rendering of it. I looked then at my own—lame, patched and faulted: same subject, but assuredly the hand of a student, not a master.

I began from that understanding, and rewrote.

Word power

I learned what the Roman knew, this man who lived when tales were sung—learned how words should fit in rhythm, should play on every sense at once.

I *looked around*, I might then have said, *and saw that the place was in ruins. The pillars had fallen at the bedroom doors and there were Greeks where there wasn't any fire.*

C.J. Cherryh is a classicist and a writer whose credits include 15 science fiction novels, nine of which have been selections of the Science Fiction Book Club. In 1977 she won the John W. Campbell Award for the best new science fiction writer in the field; in 1978 she was nominated for the Nebula Award given by the Science Fiction Writers of America; and in 1979 she won the Hugo Award at the World Science Fiction Convention in England.

Vergil said: *At those fifty chambers, full of the hope of children yet unborn, the columns wrought in foreign gold, the spoils of war—had fallen. Greeks held what the fire had missed.*

I saw the hall, felt the implication of power, of wealth, of ruin . . .in that order, as Vergil intended. The word *fallen* was at the end; the rhythm, irretrievable in English, led like a cadence to that final, fatal word. Vergil chose words emotionally and visually charged: *the hope of children; foreign gold* . . .master-phrases intimating the duration of dynasty and the scope of empire. The old adage—*Show, don't tell*—took on new meaning for me. Vergil had not interrupted the action with a paragraph describing Troy's former power and wealth: He had slipped the idea into my mind in two words. *The spoils of war* . . .here he made no heavy-handed discourse on ironies and the transitory nature of power: A phrase planted the thought. *Had fallen*—a dark word against the bright. Then follow the garish images of the enemy and the consuming fire, linked in their destructiveness.

I kept trying to touch my wife's ghost and put my arms about her, I would have written. *But it slipped out of my hands three times and faded out of sight.*

Vergil's words: *Three times I tried to put my arms about her; three times from my helpless, reaching hands her image fled, equal to the gentle winds, and very like a fleeting dream.*

The man has seen his wife's ghost in the streets of Troy; he has not known until now that she has been killed. *Helpless, reaching hands:* I felt what he felt, understood his effort, strong man that he was. I saw his wife and felt her character in the manifestation itself: *equal to the gentle winds.* And at the last came that image of despair, the vanished dream that had been their life: *Fleeting*, the image of brevity and loss, as if she were already slipping from his mind.

Images organized

Vergil taught me to see and feel with an artist's eye: That came first—to know that a single well-chosen word can carry a paragraph of explanation.

I learned to see a scene slowly, from its sensory beginning—to stand in a character's tracks and inhale deeply, to look about me and see the meaningful details of my surroundings.

Consider a coastline, pitching, seen from the deck of a ship. Feel the waves, the boards underfoot. Inhale; taste the air. Listen to the sounds of the ship, the creaking of ropes, the groan of timbers, the slap of water against the hull. Is the ship moving? You hardly need to say; describe sensations well, and the reader will know. What is the focus of interest? That shore: a light; perhaps another ship. What is the mood? Step by step, the reader knows

Now think of a dozen good words and the questions they arouse. Cold. Near-dark. Sleet. Restless. Knife-edged wind. Light. What direction, left side of face or right? Firelight on canvas, on planking. Anxiety. Dawn. Others stirring, the creak of boards. Who? Trust? Anxiety? What relationship with these men?

On such sensations a scene is built. Such impressions can be conveyed in the midst of action, moving the story along without delay; I avoid the word *was* in descriptions wherever possible.

Once I might have written: *The coast was in sight. The ship was at anchor, and the sea was very rough because it was windy and it was snowing. Ivar was cold.*

Now: *Thule lay to starboard, a shadowy line across the dark and heaving waters, dimly visible through the blowing sleet. Ivar put his chilled fingers against his lips and blew on them to warm them, his frosting breath torn by the wind.*

In the first rendition, sensations are not organized. The first impression is that of tranquility, a ship at anchor, a state of rest. Then we come to the storm. Finally, there is Ivar, so vaguely described that he might be floating between ship and coast, for all the reader can tell.

In the second version I planted the following information, in order: The land is Thule; we are seeing it from a ship; it is dusk or dawn; there is wind; it is storming and cold; our viewpoint character is Ivar; he is male; he is bare-handed; he is out in the open; he is standing in an uncomfortable and exposed place; and by implication he would have reason for doing so. Furthermore, he has to be on that ship. I have not used the verb *was* once in all that description.

Information in rhythm

Next comes the matter of rhythm. *ARMS and a MAN sing I,* Vergil began his tale. The important words surfaced, first and centrally in the rhythms of his native tongue, limning *WAR* with all its connotations, and, most importantly, a *MAN,* with all that word implies: magnificently simple.

English tends to group words in threes (excluding such small, swallowed sounds as pronouns and articles) and emphasizes most strongly the first and last word of each such thought-group; furthermore, the first and last word of any clause will receive even stronger emphasis, hitting the eye first or leaving it last. That is a natural rhythm within the sentence, and therefore any insertion or break that creates a new phrasing will create a change in emphasis.

"I warned you not sit on that chair," I said.

The reader tends to pick up *warned* and *chair.*

"I warned you," I said, "not to sit on that chair."

Now the reader picks up more information. The emphasis picks up both the interaction of I-*you*, while *warned* is clearly heard—and puts *not-sit . . .on-chair* in clear focus. There is nothing wrong with either sentence: The choice of emphasis is in the hands of the writer.

Consider this example: *It was dark and vast.* The adjectives do not receive equal consideration in that order. Shift it about. *Dark it was, and vast.* Now the first-last rhythm picks them up . . . and the broken nature of the second triad *and vast . . .* leaves a rhythm-stopping attention on that last word—a useful device when the writer wants to make a word stand out.

Important pieces of information can be lost if they are allowed to rest in the middle of a long thought-group, or if important words are buried in a string of words of identical rhythm. Read it aloud. If the emphasis could possibly be misconstrued at a crucial point, then it will be, by some reader. Rewrite until the words that must be heard are in emphatic position.

Negatives make positive

There was hardly any light in hell, the student might have said, *and they didn't see any people. It wasn't colorful and it wasn't very interesting.*

Vergil: *Darkly they went through the murk of that lonely night, through vacant halls of hell and realms of emptiness, as down some forest path under the baleful light of the changing moon, when God hides the sky in shadow and dark Night steals the color from things.*

Ah, negatives: Quoth the Roman (or at least he might have said): *Say only what you want the reader to see.* Say *THERE WAS HARDLY ANY LIGHT* and the reader sees light, quite the opposite of the effect you want. Say *PEOPLE* and he sees people, even if you tell him there were none. Sometimes this can be a useful effect—carefully applied—calling up ghosts of things not present; but the mind generally balks at negatives. The reader wants to believe, but suddenly he's sorting through forbidden images like rags in a drawer, having to discard almost every piece of information in the sentence. Not this, not this, not this: He's seeing everything he's discarding, of course, and still hunting for precisely what it is he's allowed to keep.

Remember also, quoth the Roman, *that the first impression and the last are strongest.* Begin with *NOT THIS* and end with *NOT THIS EITHER*, and the reader grows desperate.

Guide the reader surely and firmly, revealing only what should be seen, everything in its due course, precisely as he would become aware of it if he were there, within the flesh and bone of the viewpoint character. This is the essence of viewpoint—that through the viewpoint character we lead the reader step by step down the path, letting him believe, accustoming him to feel, to see, to react *in the sequence we choose.*

Read your work aloud. Consider the sequence of sensations. Eliminate the awkward, the unfortunate sound, the unintended connection of images. Edit until it sings.

Even for an ugly thought, it is never necessary to choose an ugly word.

It is not reality that should be rejected, but the abrupt, the jolting, the inept word—that lames the line and renders the image ineffectual. The ancient storyteller sang, seized the senses, led his hearer by careful intent.

To paraphrase another that Vergil would have known: *What comes to effect not by chance, but by the writer's plan—is art.*

Look . . . a little closer

by Ruth Engelken

To keep from stereotyping your own descriptions, broaden your terminologies. What can you say about an eye beside the fact that it is blue, gray, green hazel, brown, violet or chameleon? You might consider the eye's shape—round, almond, slanted (oriental), elongated, slatted, and so forth. How are the eyes placed—close-set, wide-set or regularly spaced? Are they deep-set under beetle brows or do they protrude like a bug's? Most likely, neither is the case, but it pays to be aware of differing ocular structures. What about the size of the eyes? Are they large, small or medium with expanded, contracted, or average pupils? Their condition, too, demands attention. Are they healthy eyes—clear, sparkling, with white membrane surrounding the iris? Or are they "sick" eyes—rheumy, bloodshot, mattery, or with yellowed membrane? What about the area surrounding the eyes? Is it dark-ringed or puffy? Are the lids encrusted, or tinted, or outlined? What about the lashes and brows? Are the former long or short, thick or thin, curled or straight, dark or pale, false or nonexistent? Are the latter straight or curved, scraggly or plucked, penciled or plain, pointed a la Fu Manchu or winged a la Marlene Dietrich? Do they start over the tear duct or do they cover the bridge of the nose, punctuating the face with a long, hairy dash?

Willa Cather in "Paul's Case" took care to describe Paul's eyes:

> His eyes were remarkable for a certain hysterical brilliancy, and he continually used them in a conscious, theatrical sort of way, peculiarly offensive in a boy. The pupils were abnormally large, as though he were addicted to belladonna, but there was a glassy glitter about them which that drug does not produce.

Ruth Engelken has been an editorial assistant of Writer's Digest, a writing teacher at the University of Cincinnati, and a freelance writer for almost twenty years. Her short stories and articles have appeared in scores of magazines and newspapers. In addition, she has written three juvenile books and one adult biography.

Vladimir Nabokov in "Pnin," likewise, paid special attention to Liza's eyes.

Actually her eyes were of a light transparent blue with contrasting black lashes and bright pink canthus, and they slightly stretched up templeward, where a set of feline little lines fanned out from each.

Pictorial prose

Beginning writers generally find the nose even more difficult to describe than the eyes, the lashes and brows. I suspect that the problem stems from two sources: the novice's unfamiliarity with names for basic nasal shapes and the limited color range that can be applied to the nose. Chaucer already put a wart on the Miller's nose, Rostand elongated Cyrano's breathing apparatus to ridiculous proportions, and Dickens reddened the beak of Mr. Macawber; what terms remain to define a nose? Many. Let's look first at some basic shapes and perhaps some clue figures that will help you remember them. Broadly speaking, noses are aquiline (hooked like an eagle's—witches); Roman (having a prominent bridge—Dick Tracy); patrician (aristocratic looking); retroussé (turned up); bulbous (shaped like a bulb—W.C. Fields); ski-shaped ("bridgeless" with curved tip—Bob Hope); pug (short, broad, somewhat turned up like the dog's of the same name); flattened (like the prizefighter's); straight; broad; thin; fleshy; or broken. In addition to the shape, of course, the color ranges on the spectrum from off-whites through pinks, reds, and purples (and all the synonyms therefor). The nose's condition also supplies adjectives—pocked, blue-veined, swollen, runny, mottled.

Clever writers have displayed ingenuity in describing noses: James Joyce speaks of "the wings of the nose." Nabokov gives Pnin a "fat glossy nose" and later he has him "put on his heavy tortoise-shell reading glasses, from under the saddle of which his Russian potato nose smoothly bulged." Again, he gives to an old man "a tumefied purple nose resembling a huge raspberry. . . ."

The writer wishing to describe lips thinks first of color and looks toward the red-purple segment of the color wheel—or at least he did until recently. Now, with the off-shades of lipstick so popular, he may select subtle corals and browns and frost them with gloss. The lips can be full or thin, the Cupid's-bow strongly defined (like Theda Bara's from the days of the *femme fatales* or nonexistent (like Katharine Hepburn's and Bette Davis'), and the cut of the lips (or more accurately, the mouth) can be wide or narrow.

Descriptions of ears, hair, neck, arms, feet, stance, body build, tone of voice, and type of gesture have all been used as character clues by one writer or another. Certainly one of the reasons why beginning writers are urged to read widely is to learn how top professionals write pictorially. Studying the prose of accomplished writers reveals the fact that the most ordinary subject may be made extraordinarily interesting.

Actions speak louder with descriptions

by Eileen Jensen

The pitchfork of fiction has three tines:
    Make me *know*.
    Make me *see*.
    Make me *feel*.
The center prong is the most useful because when you see, you *know*, and when you know, you *feel*, and when you feel, you *believe*.

As a writer, you have an obligation to make your readers believe. That's what makes them turn the page instead of the television knob. You must involve them emotionally by giving them strong visual evidence of what is going on in your story. Don't tell them, show them. Prod their imagination. Prick their memory. Goad them into action by creating scenes in which they can participate fully.

Popular fiction writers impale the reader at three points through:
    Action verbs
    Action scenes
    Action descriptions

Action verbs are the easiest. Why let your character merely *talk* when it might be better to *shout, whisper, giggle, wink,* or *spit*? Don't let him *walk* when he could *run, skip, slouch, saunter, sashay,* or *take the steps two at a time.* That heroine in tears—is she *crying*? Or is she *bawling*? Chances are she's a different woman, depending on the action in your verb. Let that action reflect character, and you're way ahead of your readers. They'll follow you with interest because something lively is going on, and they want in on it.

When I first began to write and sell fiction, I had a miserable time with the verb *think*. My characters always were *thinking* things over—and as Miss Piggy

Eileen Jensen, a resident of Indiana, writes regularly for major magazines. She has sold short stories to Redbook, Cosmopolitan, Saturday Evening Post, Playboy, McCall's, Good Housekeeping *and* Ladies' Home Journal.

might carol, it was BOOOOORRRrrrringggg.

In looking through my early notes I came across a 15-year-old list of words I had jotted down as alternatives to *think*. It reads: *meditate, speculate, contemplate, ponder, muse, mull over, study, worry, fret, brood, reason, guess, reflect,* and *ruminate.*

In 15 years, I never have used the word *ruminate*. It conjures in my mind the placid picture of a cow chewing her cud. Still, this is a useful list. You can find one in any thesaurus, of course, but it is the act of creating your own list, copying it, posting it at eye level in front of your typewriter—it is all this action which puts the words into your subconscious.

If you are a beginning writer, start now to add to your own stock of action verbs. After your skills improve, you can throw the list away.

World for your words

Action scenes are more work and more fun. I find them easy to write because of my early training as a playwright. I visualize my characters. I see them move. I know what they are wearing. I hear their voices as the story unfolds. They enter and exit as on a stage set. I am convinced that almost anyone who is creative and who will make the effort can learn to think in this delightful, three-dimensional way.

To do it, imagine your people moving about in your head instead of writing them flat on paper. If you have a static scene with two people sitting there talking to each other, use your action verbs. Better yet, get one of your characters up on her feet. Give her something interesting to do. Engage her in some kind of highly visual activity. Ideally, this activity reflects character or moves the plot along. With luck and skill, it does both.

A man comes home from work. He opens the front door and greets his wife. *Dull.* But supposing a man comes home from work, opens the front door, and bangs it against a stepladder on which his wife is precariously perched, hanging wallpaper. Contrived. But suppose a paperhanger who has been promising his wife for six months that he would hang new paper in their front hall comes home from work, opens the door and finds her hanging that wallpaper . . . .

Let me give you a simple example from one of my own stories which was published in the *Ladies' Home Journal.* The scene is essentially a dialogue between Eric and Gerard, two brothers who share a bachelor apartment in a building they own. They have invited their wealthy Aunt Abigail to dinner. I made the scene visual by giving appropriate action to Eric, a gourmet cook whose elaborate food nauseates the older brother Gerard, an accountant and health food nut.

Gerard comes home to dinner unexpectedly after quarreling with his woman friend, a pretty widow in the apartment upstairs. Remember that this is nothing more than two men talking. The curtain rises. Enter, Gerard, the narrator:

> The apartment smelled of bay leaf and wine. Eric came out of the kitchen with a ladle in his hand. "What's the matter, old chap? You look gray around the edges." He was wearing his chef's hat. "Did Francine throw you out?"
>
> "As a matter of fact, Eric, she did." I hung up my coat. "She called me a robot."
>
> "You have a good thing going with the widow. Don't blow it."
>
> I sniffed. "What's cooking?"

"Abigail's favorite." He waved the ladle, and I followed him to the kitchen.

I lifted the pot lid on a bubbling stew, Boeuf Bourguignonne. "I'm desperate enough to eat it." I slumped on a stool. "Eric, do I strike you as a reasonable man?"

"Reasonable? Man, you're so reasonable you're rigid." He rinsed some fresh mushrooms at the sink. I nibbled a raw one.

They continue to talk. Eric sets the table. He swings the salad basket. The doorbell rings. He slides a pan of garlic bread into the oven. Aunt Abigail arrives. Eric trundles out the bar cart. He chunks ice into the glasses. . . .

None of this is world-shaking. But it is highly visual, and it draws the reader into the action. I like to think that my reader came to this party, smelled the food, sipped a cocktail, participated in all that went on here. And the dinner party was not contrived. It subsequently resolved the plot by revealing to Gerard, through the behavior of his guests, the arid quality of his bachelor existence.

If you will go back and read the above dialogue minus the action, you will see how flat the scene falls.

Teachings of TV

Readers are restless. They want to move. Hollywood is famous for bringing couples together in action—colliding, quarreling, stalled in an elevator, popping up out of a manhole—anywhere! This can become contrived, but the unusual scene rivets attention.

Are you old enough to remember a film in which Rosalind Russell met Jack Carson at a holiday ball? He was wearing a lighted Christmas tree on his head. As I recall, his hair caught fire from the flaming candles (it actually was a St. Cecilia's crown), and she shoved him into a fountain to quench the blaze. Love at first dunk. Now, *that's* visual.

Think of Rhett Butler rearing up out of that sofa after overhearing Scarlett's quarrel with Ashley. Forty years later, on television, it still takes your breath away.

Contemporary novelists go to kinky extremes. Consider Lisa Alther's *Kinflicks*. She shows you a young married couple, nude, climbing up on two chairs to hang from a rafter in their living room, handcuffed together, coupling in mid-air in pursuit of the ultimate orgasm. In the scramble, the chairs are accidentally kicked away leaving the naked lovers stranded, dangling below the ceiling. Neither can reach the key to the handcuffs. He finally inches along the beam and manages to dial a telephone with his bare toe. Friends are summoned. The rescue party arrives in the living room. They stare up at the couple.

I see it. Don't you?

Action is so important in the competitive entertainment market of today that motion pictures put it ahead of the title. Clint Eastwood starred in a picture in which his wife was raped and his children murdered *before* the movie title appeared on the screen. Think of Liza Minnelli's *Lucky Lady* or *A Star is Born*, with Kris Kristofferson stoned, singing, brawling, racing about in the lancing spotlights—in action before the title credits roll. In fact, it's difficult today to name a motion picture which doesn't put the action up front.

Television taught us this lesson with the highly successful "tease"—that brief taste of the most dramatic moment, which they pitch into our living room before the commercial airs and the story begins. This technique is valuable.

"It's so cold that—"

Finally, let's consider the third prong of the action trident: *action descriptions*. These add a sophisticated dimension to your prose. You achieve the effect by substituting action for your ordinary adjectives and adverbs.

An example from the story cited earlier:

Gerard, the stuffy accountant who is employed in the computer center at Dunn, Dunn & Olson, describes women in the office as he sees them.

> Unlike numbers, women do not add up. Don't misunderstand me. I like females. Their eyes are lustrous and their contours are pleasing. But at DD&O they come late for work. They spill face powder. They lose the key to the toilet. They lunch out of paper bags in order to save money with which to purchase false eyelashes. They marry. They quit. They cry. I am helpless when they cry. . . .

The interesting thing here is that while describing the women, Gerard reveals himself.

The same thing occurs when Gerard describes Eric:

> Eric is ten years my junior, and we share an apartment in a building we own in New York City. In the mornings, Eric refuses to get out of bed until he checks his horoscope. He wears his hair long and his pants snug. His socks may be red or plaid, or worse, mismatched. Eric doesn't care. He whistles in the shower. He lends people money. And he cooks. Gourmet. Coq au Vin. Escargots. Tournedos Rossini. Indescribable odors permeate our apartment. I am a vegetarian . . . .

When Gerald describes the pleasant widow he is courting, it goes like this:

> Francine treats me as if I were a precocious boy with big feet, a good appetite, and a knack for mathematics. She calls me Jerry (which no one else does) and we play checkers (a game I always win) and we converse in Morse code (a skill she taught me). She encourages me to stretch out on the sofa with my head in her lap. It is surprising how pleasant such a simple gesture can be . . . .

Francine invites him to Philadelphia to meet her parents. Gerard describes how

> her father poured champagne as if this were an occasion, and everybody kept smiling, and offering toasts, and patting me on the back. . . .

Consider the way I describe, through Francine's eyes, the three single women in Eric's life:

> that hot-eyed ballet dancer who leaves her pink shoe ribbons lying about the apartment like crumbs marking a trail. And that long-legged librarian who pretends a burning interest in his books. There's a fashion model, too—a gaunt rangy type who wears designer labels and full makeup to the laundry room in the basement . . . .

This lively kind of writing comes from skills developed through practice. You probably won't be able to do it immediately, but you can begin to learn the technique with one simple exercise.

Take a verb or an adverb and substitute an appropriate action for the word.

I did that earlier in this article where I made the statement that "after 25 years it still was exciting." When I went back to rewrite (I always rewrite) I struck out the word *exciting* and used action instead.

You can take this very word *exciting* and use it for a writing exercise of your own. Make a list of how many active ways you can show excitement. When you're excited, what happens? You may *breathe fast, gasp, drop something, begin to sweat, faint, wet your pants*, whatever.

Television writers do this exercise all the time. Stand-up comics pay their writers big money to do it. Haven't you heard Johnny Carson saying, "How cold was it? It was so cold that—"

It was so hot that—
It was so crowded that—
He's so stingy that—
I was so scared that—
She is so mean that—

Fill in the action which reveals the word. That's all there is to it!

In fiction you go one step farther. You process that action through the filter of the narrator's personality and vocabulary. This requires more than craft. This requires talent, imagination, creativity and discipline. When you have polished your skills to the point where you can write this kind of revelatory action, your story expands like a mushroom cloud. The fallout settles into the consciousness of your reader. They see, they feel, they know. Knowing, they believe.

I made them believe Gerard—half bore, half saint, half child, all man. That's one-and-a-half, larger than life—and that's what a fictional character must be.

Hoist him on your pitchfork. Flip him over. What makes him special? Your reader will delight in your story if you wield your fiction tools with zest. Get in there and dig. You may turn up pay dirt.

The six functions of dialogue in fiction

by Charles N. Heckelmann

Dialogue can be defined simply as a written record of conversation between two or more people. It is, literally, a talking together. And it is one of the most important elements in any short story or novel. The author who is blessed with a perceptive ear for human speech patterns and rhythms and who can transmit them to the reader through the medium of his fictional characters can truly be said to have a lot going for him. Consider the six functions of dialogue in fiction:

1. To delineate characters (the speaker or main viewpoint character as well as other characters with whom the protagonist comes in contact).
2. To convey emotion or feeling.
3. To lend forward progression or movement to the narrative.
4. To provide important information that is integral to the plot.
5. To add vividness and color and to act as an aid in establishing locale.
6. To break up long passages of exposition or straight narrative for the purpose of establishing greater readability and to lend a greater eye appeal to the printed page.

Most successful authors actually combine several of the functions at one time in their conversational passages. In other words, there is no conscious attempt to do just one thing at a time. Dialogue should not interrupt the narrative. Rather, it should push the story along, providing information that is not given by means of exposition, helping reveal the characters' emotional reactions to events and spoken statements, while also adding to the complete flesh-and-blood portrait of the men and women in the story.

Descriptive and dramatic

In the following passages involving a meeting between a married couple and a

Charles N. Heckelmann has been a book editor of publishing firms, a newspaper editor and a sportswriter. A frequent contributor of short fiction to magazines, he has also written nonfiction books and numerous novels and westerns.

private detective with respect to a blackmail attempt upon the woman, I have combined the five *major* functions of dialogue in one sequence:

Craig Evans was waiting for Karen and Joe Hyde when the headwaiter brought them to the dimly lit booth at the far corner of the small side street restaurant.

"I've been waiting almost a half hour," said Evans.

"We're sorry, Mr. Evans," said Joe Hyde. "The delay was unavoidable."

Evans looked up at the headwaiter and waved him away. "We'll call when we're ready to order." When the headwaiter had gone off, he turned to Karen. "All right, Karen. Let's have it. What happened?"

Hyde held up his hand, his pale, smoothly shaved face flushing. "There's no need to be abrupt, Mr. Evans. And we can dispense with your familiarity."

Evans laughed, but the widening wedge of his lips could hardly have been called a smile. His slate-blue eyes held no warmth. "Let's get down to business, Hyde," he said, his sharp glance riveting the older man. "I've got a lot of things on my mind. I'm not interested in your wife—only her problem."

Hyde's flushed features quivered with quick outrage. He was about to make an angry retort, but Karen placed a trembling hand on his arm and spoke directly to Evans. "Oh, Craig! I'm so frightened. I got another phone call right before we left the apartment."

Evans' lip flattened out. "From the same guy who called last week?"

"Yes," she whispered, running a thin hand through her soft blond hair. "It—it sounded like him." She halted and craned her head around to stare at the other tables. Only three tables were occupied and none near their booth. "Craig, this place gives me the creeps. Can't we go someplace else? It's so dark and dismal and that—that headwaiter keeps looking over here."

Evans placed a calloused hand over hers, then removed it when he saw Hyde staring at him. "Forget it, baby," he said. "This is a good spot. The owner knows me, and we won't be disturbed."

"Craig," she said, her lower lip quivering, "I'm afraid to go anywhere. I've got a feeling I'm being watched. Maybe those two men at that corner table are working for those—those hoodlums who are trying to bleed Joe and me."

Evans turned idly, looked at the two men she indicated. Both of them appeared to be occupied with eating their dinner and were deep in conversation. He laughed again, harshly and without mirth. "Turn it off, Karen. I know them both. One's a reporter for the *Tribune*; the other is a public relations guy."

"Craig, you've got to help me," she begged.

"All right. All right. Tell me what the guy said."

She looked at Hyde before answering. "He—he said he wanted ten thousand dollars by Friday."

"So he upped the ante?"

"Yes."

"And you still don't know what's behind the threat?"

Karen reached for the glass of water in front of her and took a sip. Then she said, "He warned me if he didn't get the money he'd give out a story to all the newspapers that I used to work in a striptease joint on Bourbon Street in New Orleans."

Evans grinned. "Is that true, Karen?"

She colored. Hyde answered for her. "It's true enough, if the information gives you any pleasure."

"Go on," snapped Evans.

"What do you mean?" asked Hyde.

"Oh, hell. Stop playing games. Karen's not the first dame who was a stripper before she got respectable and married into money. So what's the pitch?"

"I recently decided to run for the city council," said Hyde. "If news about Karen being a stripper gets out, I won't have a chance of making it."

"So pay the ten grand."

"No. That will be only the beginning."

Evans nodded. "You're smarter than I thought. So you want to fight them?"

Karen turned to her husband. "Joe, are you sure you want—"

"Yes, I'm sure."

"All right," said Evans. "But you both could have saved a lot of time if you'd told me what was behind it the first time Karen came to see me."

Fifty / fifty

Rather than employ several short examples, I purposely took one longer scene that would combine the various functions of conversation. If you study the sequence carefully, you will see (aside from the few brief descriptive and emotional touches) how the spoken words of these people reveal some insight into their character. Craig Evans is obviously a hard-edged individual, unsentimental, cold and precise. He wastes no time, and he says what he thinks. Hyde is a bit stiff and formal, and people like Evans annoy him. Despite her background, Karen is apparently gentle and soft—or rendered so by the circumstance of blackmail in which she finds herself.

The conversation also reveals Karen's fear for herself—a fear that is physical in its application. Joe Hyde is disturbed by the situation, annoyed with Evans, and possibly a little jealous because of Evans' familiarity with Karen. Evans shows a cold-blooded, almost emotionless reaction to what is said. He is impatient, more than anything else.

The dialogue also provides new information, revealing that the blackmailer has called again, has asked for additonal money and given a deadline for delivery. We also learn that Karen has been a stripper and that her husband plans to enter politics. From the way the characters talk, we gather this is information new to Craig Evans. The information serves to advance the plot, and the revelation that Hyde doesn't plan to give in provides a new dramatic development—a step forward in terms of action.

Finally, Karen's remarks about the restaurant add a little color, supplying an inkling of the dismal quality of their surroundings. We know they're in a cheap little bistro which is obviously not well lighted and quite plain in decor.

Let me point out that dialogue cannot be expected to reveal character, portray emotion, supply valuable information, and advance the plot all by itself. Dialogue is merely a contributing factor, an aid—one of the various tools the author has at his disposal to accomplish these ends. There are other ways of portraying character and emotion and keeping the story moving. Dialogue is just another element—among many—that adds to the total picture, the composite of action, complication, conversation, motivation, basic theme, and setting that goes to make up a story or novel.

The final function of dialogue—that of breaking up long passages of exposition or narration—is a purely mechanical one. Dialogue inevitably aids readability. Books with page after page of exposition, unleavened by conversation, can get ponderous and tedious. Dialogue enlivens the story, gives it vividness and color and sprightliness. And it's a great touchstone for revealing hidden wells of emotion in people. It gives spark to people and events and, if kept to essentials, speeds the story along. And from a solely practical point of view of eye appeal, a book page containing conversational passages is more attractive than one filled with solid lines of exposition. A story with no dialogue at all can be said to have three strikes on it. And one with very little conversation isn't much better off. A good, safe average is 50 percent dialogue to 50 percent narration and action, but if you can use even higher percentage of conversation without sacrificing other important elements in your story, all well and good.

Talk "in character"

An important adjunct of writing effective dialogue is the ability to observe and absorb the speech patterns and rhythms of people around you. All of us have little quirks or mannerisms that are revealed in our spoken words. Some people are long-winded and devious. Others are abrupt and laconic (like the people who never bother saying "good-bye" when terminating a telephone conversation). Some individuals salt their words with a great deal of slang or crude expressions. Others are sophisticated and worldly. Still others are hesitant and unsure, guilty of wrong word usage, or are continually fumbling for the proper words to express their thoughts.

In any event, as a writer charged with the responsibility of telling a story through the medium of people, you must have a keen ear for all modes of speech so that the words you put in the mouths of your characters will ring true and lifelike. If your story deals with labor union troubles on the New York docks and your key characters are stevedores, you obviously cannot have them talking like college professors. Dockwallopers will necessarily have limited vocabularies, will use much slang and profanity, and will be direct and blunt in everything they say. And if you are dealing with adolescents in a tough city ghetto, their dialogue must match the customary speech patterns, the colorful and rough slang idiom of youngsters operating in that milieu. The same precautions will hold true for any segment of men and women around which you happen to build your narrative. Your characters must speak and act like ordinary men and women in their particular social stratum of real life would speak and act.

Not only must your fictional people speak naturally—and without stiffness or artificiality—but they must also stay "in character." This simply means that if you have portrayed your heroine as being a gentle, soft-spoken, cultured young woman, you cannot show her going around shouting her lungs out and acting like a scolding old woman. To be sure, she can be angry and exhibit displeasure at events that may occur, but it isn't "in character" for her to perform like a shrew or termagant. And a tough private detective, accustomed to speaking in a flip, laconic fashion, can't—without your showing some logical and convincing reason for the transformation—suddenly begin to converse in the hesitant, soft-spoken fashion of a timid, reticent Mr. Milquetoast.

Be natural

Another danger to avoid is triteness of clichéd   expressions. A trite statement is an utterance that lacks freshness and originality or has become overfamiliar owing to repeated usage. I am referring now to such phrases as "busy as a bee," "last but not least," "like a bolt from the blue," and "strong as an ox." We all have heard these expressions so frequently that we are sick of them. Unless you are dealing with a character who has a fetish for using such expressions and this quirk of his can be integrated logically into the plot, you should shun them and concentrate on letting your fictional creatures speak with as much freshness and originality as your own creative powers will permit.

I have placed sharp emphasis on the requirement for an author to be certain that his characters speak naturally and realistically, as well as within the limits of the psychological, social, and emotional profiles. However, this advice must not be followed too literally. For example, most conversations in real life begin with a great deal of nonessential utterances. There are greetings, comments about the weather, queries about the health of members of the family, a recent vacation trip or a planned holiday, perhaps some idle scuttlebutt about neighbors or business associates. This is even true of men having a business lunch or dinner. They will talk about a lot of tangential subjects that may be mutually interesting to them before they get down to the actual transaction that is the reason for their meeting.

It would be foolhardy for an author to go through this kind of maneuver each time he described a confrontation between two or more people. The result would be a needless and interest-destroying padding of the narrative. When you are writing fiction, you must keep the dialogue natural and real, and you must learn the art of condensation and compression. Employ only the essential elements of any conversation. Stick to the highlights, to the factors that have real significance to the individual scene and thus will contribute to the forward progression of the plot. The dialogue you use must perform one or more of the several functions already outlined and thus keep the story moving. Many of the inconsequential gambits, the idle chitchat, that mark so many real-life conversations, must be abandoned.

On the reverse side of the coin, however, do not become overzealous in your attempt to compress your fictional conversations to the point that your people appear to be talking like animated telegraph keys.

Who said?

Whenever there is a discussion about fiction writing and the talk shifts to the problems of handling dialogue, you can usually count on someone bringing up the dilemma about the use of that little word "said." In some of the old pulp magazine tales many authors went out of their way to avoid using the word and substituted all kinds of colorful and graphic alternates. In recent years, however, it is the accepted custom to rely pretty much on "said" to convey conversation. Actually, there is no better word, and it is used from 80 to 90 percent of the time. After all, the essential thing is to identify who is talking and to convey the essence of what is being spoken. You don't need a lot of fancy words such as "murmured," "shouted," "whispered," "grated," "recounted," "declared," "stated," "shrieked," "bellowed," "asseverated," and the like.

This does not mean that, on occasion, you can't employ an alternate word where it is imperative to indicate a change of mood or a sudden flare of emotion. By all means go ahead and use a word like "grumbled" if one of your characters is a chronic complainer and in a long dialogue sequence you want to insert an occasional variation. The same is true of any other word that you might wish to use to break up the continual use of "said." Also, remember that the word does not have to be used with each line of conversation. If you study some of the examples I have used, you will see that many times I have not used any word to indicate who is speaking simply because the identity of the speaker is clear. In many long passages involving a verbal exchange between two characters, it is not necessary to insert a "said Johnson" or "he said" or "said Anne" more frequently than every five or six paragraphs. The main consideration is to keep the focus clear, to be sure the reader always knows who is talking.

As another variation from the use of the word "said," you can often include a brief line of description that will convey some emotional reaction on the part of one of the characters. Then you lead right into the conversation without any specific helping word to indicate the character is speaking.

For example:

"No one is trying to railroad you," said Bryant, pounding his desk with a meaty fist, "but you are going out of here."
Chalmers sneered,"Sure, so you can give my job to your son-in-law."

This is an easy way of giving a little variety to the scene, avoiding excessive use of "said" while also not falling prey to some of the luridly graphic words that tend to make your prose sound "purple." You can also add an emotional touch by the restrained use of an occasional adverb with the verb indicating speech. This permits you to convey emotion and color. Thus, a character who is obsessed with rage could have his statement tacked on to "said angrily" or "said viciously." Adverbs such as "fearfully" or "vaguely" or "dismally" might be used to convey a particular feeling experienced by an individual. And of course, in an extreme situation—one of high tension or travail or terror or consuming rage—a colorful word like "howled" or "bellowed" or "screeched" can be used. But for average, day-by-day usage in fiction, stick to "said." You can't go wrong with it.

For uses of indirect dialogue

Indirect dialogue, in which the reader is told—rather than shown in a direct, onstage fashion—what a particular character is saying also has its place in fiction writing. However, its usage is fairly limited, and it can never be an adequate substitute for fully developed conversation.

Generally, there are four occasions when indirect dialogue can be employed. The first instance involves the avoidance of repetition when it is necessary for one character to tell another about some bit of action that has already taken place in full view of the reader. Instead of the particular character repeating all the dialogue that may have occurred between another character and himself to a third party, he merely summarizes in narrative form the gist of the earlier conversation.

A second function of indirect dialogue is to supply some bit of information that may not be significant enough to warrant a rendering in full dialogue. For example, somewhere in your story it might be necessary for one person to instruct another in a specific assignment. Taking the time to detail this instruction through the byplay of conversation would use up valuable verbiage, so you might just say:

After the board meeting broke up, Waring spent fifteen minutes with his secretary explaining to her precisely what corporate records should be gotten out of the files and photostated for submissions to Compton Broadcasting Company.

The third function of indirect dialogue is purely mechanical—to provide a break or hiatus in a long dialogue sequence. Sometimes an extended passage of this kind will become tedious unless it is leavened in some way. Therefore, you can select some unimportant item of conversation and relay it indirectly to the reader. You can even go further and incorporate the nucleus of several exchanges between two people in a few summarized lines and then shift back into live conversation.

The fourth function of indirect dialogue is to use it as a means of compression and control. Many times, when authors get rolling in a scene in which verbal exchanges predominate, they tend to pad out the situations. They forget to stick to essentials and highlights. They put in a lot of trivia. This will often occur in what appear to be very crisp and tight scenes where the dialogue is a little more than a brief phrase or just a short sentence and the words are hammered back and forth between characters like a Ping-Pong ball. When this happens, you have a choice of deleting some of the trivia or telescoping the scene by means of occasional deft insertions of a line or two in indirect dialogue.

"Special" dialogue

If you plan to write about people in any special segments of our society, then you will perforce have to employ some of the jargon they customarily speak. To do so will give your dialogue a greater semblance of reality. It will be more alive. Yet restraint must be exercised lest you overload your story with this kind of shoptalk to the point where you alienate your audience. Use enough of the jargon so your fictional characters will speak like their real-life counterparts, but don't let it dominate the dialogue so that understanding and reader identification are lost.

Keep the reader where the action is

by Will C. Knott

Beginning fiction writers are often advised to stick with a single point-of-view to achieve both unity and reader identification. And this is still good advice. In the more than 30 teenage novels I published over the past 12 years, I did just that; and readers' comments indicated that I had succeeded in achieving the unity I wanted and the reader identification so essential at that level.

But in writing western and adventure novels, I find myself switching viewpoints constantly—and enjoying every minute of it. Over the years, while sticking to the assigned point-of-view, I had been nagged by the realization that there was a great deal going on offstage that this restricted viewpoint simply would not allow me to fully dramatize. Furthermore, the characterizations of my protagonist and my minor characters lacked heft—especially those of the minor characters, who were seen only through the eyes of my protagonist.

For these reasons, then—to be where the action was, and to add depth to the characterizations—I turned to the multiple viewpoint.

Ace paperbacks published a western of mine, *Vengeance Seeker #1*. In the short italicized prologue to the novel, a young boy, to be later known as Wolf Caulder, is severely wounded and left for dead by five riders who have ridden onto his father's ranch and robbed and killed his parents.

Although Caulder is to be the hero of the novel, the book opens not with him but with one of those five raiders, a deputy sheriff named Hogan. The man moves into a saloon. In his conversation with the bartender, he learns that Caulder, who has already killed three of Hogan's buddies, is now in town looking for him. Hogan ducks out through the rear of the saloon, intent on fleeing the territory that night.

The second chapter opens with Caulder high above the trail, watching Hogan ride out of town. Earlier, Hogan had learned that Caulder had visited the town in a deliberate effort to flush Hogan. Now Caulder follows him, confronts him. There is

---

Will C. Knott has written numerous western novels under his own name and various pseudonyms. He has also authored many teenage novels and two textbooks.

an exchange of gunfire that kills Hogan and seriously wounds Caulder as the second chapter ends.

Wolf in the barn

Again the viewpoint shifts from Caulder, and the third chapter begins:

> Ellen Bowman paused in the doorway. She was certain of it this time. A horse was nickering softly, anxiously, from somewhere in back of the carriage barn, and that was not where Abe had left the horses. . . .

A moment later, Ellen Bowman finds the wounded Caulder in her barn.

> In the dim light provided by the single, dirt-smeared window behind the stall, she could see that he was a frighteningly ugly man, taller than her by more than a foot, with one eye and the right side of his face cruelly scarred, his face lean and drawn and paler than moonlight.
> The ghost of a smile flickered across his broken visage. Slowly—the movement obviously causing him great discomfort—he motioned to her with the gun, indicating she should turn and go back out while he followed. . . .

When Caulder collapses a moment later, Ellen sends her husband into town for the doctor. The reader goes with him and is present when the sheriff gets wind of Caulder's presence at Ellen's spread. The sheriff leaves at once to ride out to tell a blind rancher—Sanderson—that Caulder is in the area. Sanderson, the leader of that band which attacked Caulder's ranch ten years earlier, had been waiting for Caulder to show, and at once makes his plans against Caulder.

Only after this scene—the beginning of the fourth chapter—does the reader return to Caulder's point-of-view as an old grizzled ranch hand leans over him and pokes for the slug still lodged in his side.

Meanwhile, back at the . . .

This shifting of the viewpoint continues throughout the novel—though to a lesser extent, now that the situation confronting Caulder has been made clear to the reader. This, of course, is one of the many advantages gained by shifting viewpoints. No longer locked into the mind of the protagonist, the reader can be shown those forces building against the hero, enhancing the sense of menace and certainly the suspense. Note, for example, how shifting the point-of-view builds suspense in this scene, taken from the final chapter:

> As Tyson tried to get up, Wolf looked down at the slowly twisting form and remembered Ellen. And Bob Bowman fleeing before Ruel on his stumps. . . .Wolf stepped back and kicked the man in the face and left him on his back in the grass, mewling helplessly.
> Turning carefully, Caulder started for the house. He walked slowly. The ground had become unsteady under his feet. He realized dimly that he could well pass out before he got to the house.
> Turning from the study window, Tara cried, "He's still coming!"
> "Yes, of course he is," said Sanderson. "Now leave that window and get out of here. I'll handle Caulder myself."
> "No! I won't leave you!"
> "This is my fight, woman! Get out of here!" He pulled her still closer to

him, not caring how cruelly his powerful fingers closed about her wrists. "Do this for me, Tara!"

When she did not answer, the blind man pushed her abruptly from him. "Get out! Do as I say!"

Sanderson heard the sob that broke from his daughter's throat, and then the sound of her stumbling backward across the room. She reached the door, flung it open, and ran out.

As he heard her go, Sanderson's face lit grimly, and he reached for the right-hand drawer and lifted from it his well-oiled Colt, leaving the holster and cartridge belt in the drawer. Placing the Colt on the top of the desk, he closed the drawer, then fitted his hand almost lovingly around the butt.

Had the viewpoint remained exclusively with Caulder as he made his way across the yard and into the house, this scene showing the blind rancher in terrible conflict with his daughter—and then waiting alone for Caulder's approach—would have been lost, and with it, a great deal of the suspense.

Obviously, then, the multiple viewpoint *does* keep the reader where the action is and does much to impart suspense and immediacy to the narrative.

As seen by Ruel

The other reason for using the multiple viewpoint is to deepen the characterizations—not only that of the novel's protagonist, but also those of his adversaries. It is a fact that if those forces moving against your protagonist are not shown to be sufficiently dangerous—if the men he must defeat are not seen as entirely ruthless—the hero loses much of his dimension, and his eventual victory, much of its excitement.

With this in mind, consider Ruel Tyson, the hired gun Caulder must get by before he can reach Sanderson:

As Nat tried to get out of bed, Ruel swore, withdrew the gun from the blanket and struck Nat across the right cheekbone, opening a deep gash clear to the bone. Nat crumpled back onto the cot, barely conscious.

He groaned as Ruel pulled the bandage off his wound. The doc had sewed the wound crudely but effectively. Poking the six-gun's barrel well into the wound, Ruel ripped upward. The stitches came out and a dark flood followed after. . . .Ruel thrust the barrel still further into the freshly opened wound and fired. The explosion filled the tiny room with a deafening whomp. Ruel withdrew his Colt, wiped the barrel on the blanket, and returned once more to the door to look out. The bunkhouse was still empty. He holstered his Colt and carefully folded the blanket. . . .

Not long after, Ruel knocked on Sanderson's door. Opening it, he saw Sheriff Gulch and the foreman standing by Sanderson's desk. The owner of the Diamond T was staring in his direction, his blind eyes narrowed with concern.

"That you, Tyson?" the man wanted to know.

"It's me, Mr. Sanderson," Ruel replied. He smiled thinly at the blind man. "I came to tell you. Nat Love just died. He bled to death in the bunkhouse."

With some satisfaction, Ruel noted the grim approval that split Sanderson's gaunt face.

How else but in this fashion could the reader gain a true appreciation of Ruel Tyson's ruthless nature?

Multiple viewpoint then, allows the writer to characterize more vividly those outside his protagonist's purview. But it also enables the writer to add a few brush strokes to the hero himself by showing the concern, the affection, the apprehension his presence arouses in others. In the first chapter, Hogan's reaction to the news that Caulder had been in town looking for him certainly did much to characterize not only Hogan, but also Caulder. Later, Ellen's view of him in the barn told us as much about Caulder as it did about Ellen.

And here is the blind rancher. Sanderson just after he has learned that Caulder is at Ellen Bowman's ranch:

Tara had described Caulder to him as exceedingly ugly—an outsized, cruelly marked apparition. Not only was it the eye patch and the deep scar that ran back from the blind eye, but the crooked, yet powerful set to his broad shoulders.

How many bullets had they sent into that crazy kid? He stirred uneasily at the thought. They'd shot him twice; once in the left shoulder and the second time in the back. That first slug would account for the crooked shoulder, then. But what could account for the astonishing persistence, the satanic implacability that had already seen to the execution of four hard men—and that now brought Caulder here to his door, ready to strike him down as well?

Sanderson spun quickly in his swivel chair. The sun had abruptly lost its warmth. He took the cigar from his mouth and tried to find the ashtray. It was there, but he couldn't find it. Becoming more irritated with each second, he began to slap about the desk top with his left hand. In his haste, he knocked the ashtray—and something else—off the desk. At once he exploded in rage and hurled his cigar across the room.

He clung to the sides of the desk in an effort to pull himself together. It was the little things. Always the little things—like finding his boots in the morning, or putting a cup back on its saucer—that nagged at him, that nibbled away at his patience and set him to seething in wild, disabling fury at his blindness.

Calmer now, he got up from his chair. . . .

Two men—Sanderson and Caulder—have been characterized in this brief scene: Caulder, through the thoughts and memories of Sanderson; and Sanderson himself, by his reaction to those musings.

Broad characters

What I have termed multiple viewpoint is not what is generally referred to as omniscient viewpoint, or worse, author intrusion. This is because once the writer shifts his viewpoint, he stays resolutely within that person until the viewpoint shifts again. Furthermore, the writer is careful when he changes viewpoint to indicate not only that he has done so, but also to give some clear indication into whose personality he has taken the reader:

As Sanderson heard Ruel's footsteps die away, he stared into the eternal night that hung before him. He was willing, it seemed, to ally himself with any man, willing to commit any crime to accomplish Caulder's defeat. He smiled bleakly and closed his eyes against the darkness that now seemed to be seeping into the very marrow of his bones.

Ruel entered the small room and pulled the door shut behind him. Nat Love, stretched out on a narrow cot, put down the dime novel he was reading and looked up in surprise at Ruel's entrance.

"Hi, Nat," said Ruel, lifting his six-gun from its holster. "Got yourself a nice private room in here, eh?"

And again:

. . . Weed scrambled down behind the boulder and checked to make sure his six-gun was loaded. Then, leaning his head back against the rock, he listened. Caulder was down there still, waiting. Weed could almost feel the son of a bitch.

Just below Weed on the narrow ledge, Caulder lay prone and looked up at the boulder behind which Weed was crouching. Though one of Weed's bullets had caught him in the fleshy portion of his right shoulder. . . .

We've already seen that the single, restricted point-of-view gains for the writer both unity and reader identification. How then does one compensate for this loss?

The writer simply accepts some dilution of effect in return for the sense of immediacy one achieves and for the depth in characterization that should result. It is a trade-off. Furthermore, the writer can do much to avoid this dilution of effect if he makes sure that whenever he shifts viewpoint, what happens to this new character is of vital concern to the lead and is a dramatic contribution to the novel's momentum. Indeed, unless the shift accomplishes this, the change in viewpoint is unwise.

The multiple viewpoint then is an excellent way to broaden your characterizations and keep your reader on top of the action. Why not try it with your next novel, and revel in the range and excitement it adds to your story and the dimension it imparts to your people?

Writing is rewriting

by Dorothy Bryant

"Writing is rewriting." I don't know who first said that. Everyone, I guess. Everyone who's ever seriously tried to write says it sooner or later.

Writers are fond of comparing the writing of a novel to the gestation and birth of a child. The only thing wrong with the metaphor is that it is not carried far enough. The planning stages are rather like a pregnancy, and the writing of the first draft is like the labor of childbirth: intense, joyful, exciting, painful and exhausting.

But finishing the book, bringing it through rewriting to completion, is more like raising the born child to adulthood: a long, time-consuming, often tedious and exasperating job that requires more patience and devotion than we thought we were capable of. Conceiving and giving birth does not make a woman a mother. A mother is the person who, after birth, puts in those long, caring years. Finishing a first draft doesn't make you a novelist. Anyone can do the rough draft of a novel, and it probably won't look much worse than the first draft of any great novel you care to name. The difference between "anyone" and a serious writer is rewriting, rewriting, and more rewriting, sometimes over a period of years.

This may discourage most beginners. But the serious novelist reads these words with cautious yet growing elation. "Do you mean that the first draft of (fill in the title of your favorite great novel) looked as bad as mine does?" Probably. "Does that mean that if I rewrite and rethink and rewrite, I can write a novel as good as that?" Possibly. Not likely. But possibly. We serious writers remember Einstein's "Genius is the infinite capacity for taking pains" and, grinning over our gritted teeth, decide that we can work as hard as anyone.

Dorothy Bryant began writing in 1960 while teaching in San Francisco area schools and colleges. Her earlier novels include Ella Price's Journal and The Kin of Ata Are Waiting for You. Miss Giardino, The Garden of Eros, and Prisoners plus a nonfiction manual, Writing a Novel, were published by her own publishing house, Ata Books (1928 Stuart St., Berkeley, California 94703).

Scheduled inspiration

It used to be the almost world-wide custom that after the birth of a baby the mother was exempt from all duties, except nursing, for six weeks. She was waited on, pampered, indulged and encouraged to be irresponsible and lazy.

The same period of time seems to be the minimum rest period for a manuscript: six weeks or more in which you don't write in it, read it, or if possible even think about it. One reason for this layoff is that you need to get distance from it. You should aim to get so far away from it that when you look at it again, it will seem almost as if you are reading the work of someone else.

The second reason for a layoff is that physically and spiritually you are empty, exhausted. Before you can get back to work rewriting your infant book, you need a period of recovery.

Ideally you'd spend a couple of days sitting in the sun talking with warm, intelligent friends, followed by a few weeks of comfortable travel. Then . . . but *you* can go on filling in this dream. Lacking the money or the time for such an idyll, most of us have to make do with other changes. Probably you've let so many things go that catching up with the rest of your life will provide plenty of change: getting reacquainted with your family and friends, catching up on domestic chores, reading. (Some writers find it hard to read while working on a novel.)

Adventures are even more conducive to recovery, so try to do something different: a walk you've never taken before, a trip to the zoo, an art exhibit, or any place that's off your usual rounds. During one period of my life, when I was broke and busy with job and kids, I could take only an hour or so at a time for "adventures" that would speed recovery. So I answered want ads: "Antiques for sale," or "Apartment for rent," (in a part of town I hardly knew) or "Moving, selling record collection." (That one turned out to be a Persian trapeze artist who was going to Africa on tour. He served me a cup of tea while we listened to some records, and we had a long talk about the decline of the circus in America.) Answering ads took me, at no cost, into unfamiliar settings and occasionally into situations almost as foreign as those I might encounter on a long trip.

If you are a compulsive writer like me, you may find that two weeks of no writing is the absolute maximum before a case of high anxiety threatens to wipe out the rest and change benefits. The answer is to write something else, a short story, a review (Virginia Woolf rested by doing some of the best critical writing we have), long journal entries, letters to neglected friends, a few notes on books you plan for the future—anything as long as you don't touch The Novel until you are, as an editor once put it, "well rinsed."

If you have a family and a job, you will find that writing is impossible during certain periods like Christmas holidays or inventory days at work. There is no escape from these enforced layoffs, which are all the more exasperating because they're nobody's fault. But one way of living with them is to schedule rewriting stints around them, using them as rest and change periods.

Am I seriously suggesting that artistic inspiration can be put on a schedule? Well . . . uh . . . yes, sometimes it can, especially if the only alternative is letting it wither away.

Policing the manuscript

I always read the whole manuscript through fairly quickly before I choose what to work on. This is no time to get bogged down in correcting the spelling. What I want is a general sense of how it moves and where it doesn't. As I read I pencil notes in the margin to remind me of my initial reaction as reader-critic. Often these notes are in the form of questions: *Would she have said it that way? Cut this? Credible? Introduce sooner?*

Gradually or suddenly I become aware of parts that don't fit together, of huge gaps where something is needed to connect things. I may put in an extra sheet of paper on which I outline these bigger problems. In the second part of the book, I will find things not prepared for in the first part, or I may find that something I started in the first part was allowed to fade away later. I make notes of everything, surveying the manuscript like a policeman at the site of a collision. I try to list the damages coolly, in the cop's mood of alert but routine investigation, though part of me feels like the driver who caused the accident, standing there in the midst of broken glass, partly in shock, partly furious at my wrong turning.

Too often we think of criticism as purely negative, telling us only what's wrong. Or we think of the critic as passing down a sweeping verdict on the whole book: good or bad. That's because we read "good" or "bad" reviews that hand down a verdict based on careless reading or ignorant bias. These reviews are not written by *critics.*

The rare, real critic is generous. She will unerringly spot a weakness, but she delights in finding strength, celebrating good writing and praying for its increase. You must be that rare, complete critic, identifying all the weak spots but paying special attention to the strong ones.

As you read through your first draft, you will come to places where you forget you are reading and you enter the world of the book. These are the parts that work! Maybe for a couple of pages. Maybe for only a couple of lines. But they take you in, they live, and you know that these parts can stand as they are. What you have to do is to make the rest of the book come up to them. You examine these good parts and wonder how you did them; you can't remember! Sometimes, you can't even remember having written them.

Examining the "good parts" may give you mixed feelings of elation and despair, because you wonder how you can consciously *make* good writing happen. But you should pay some attention, show respect, because these good parts are the keys to what you do well. They are the signposts that point you in the right direction toward developing your voice, your style.

I don't often use the word style because most beginning writers think of style as some kind of elegance or grace they must impose on their material. Your style is just you. You cannot learn it, copy it, or invent it out of nothing. You can only discover it, first recognizing it in these occasional "good parts," then nourishing it and helping it grow.

I don't mean that when you do something well, you should keep doing it over and over, never trying a new challenge. Your style is deeper than that; it is your special strength that supports your attempts to do many things.

Making change

What do you do first? Overhaul the third chapter? Change that word? Redo that character in the beginning to match what she became in the middle? Give the central character two children instead of three? Cut out that whole scene?

When I think of the process of working over a manuscript, I think of my father, who has been a natural mechanic from the time he was big enough to hold a wrench. He made our living fixing cars, but he could fix anything. Long after I left home, I was always bringing him my car and every small appliance that broke down, with total faith that, "Pop will fix it."

He would take a strange machine apart and silently contemplate it for a while. Then would come a series of grunts and mumbles, to himself and to the machine, as he began to tinker with it. He tried this and that, never in a hurry, rearranging parts, improvising new parts from the wires, washers and other bits and pieces stored in the garage. Then, after minutes, hours or days, he would bring it to me and say, "Now try it." And, of course, it worked perfectly, even better than before, because he had probably oiled and cleaned it as well.

Good rewriting demands this kind of easy, unhurried tinkering with words. Each unsuccessful try eliminates another wrong solution and leads you to the right one. I can't emphasize too strongly how important this is, the fact that writing leads to writing, that failed attempts lead to eventual success, that the solution to a rewriting problem is made up of all the attempts that led nowhere.

The trouble is that when you're just beginning to write, you may believe that words committed to paper are sacred, fixed, immutable. But you're not dealing with a finished, printed, copyrighted book, only with an idea, a pile of words that will change many times before they take shape as a book.

Written and rewritten

I wish I could give you an authentic sample of my own rewriting, step by step, but I doubt that I could ever salvage the real thing. Those facsimiles you sometimes see of a famous writer's manuscript, with scribbled corrections, don't begin to show the think-scribble-retype-patch-up process as it really takes place. Out of curiosity I once tried to keep every version of one short story, to keep track of its formation. But I gave up when I found myself getting lost in a mass of tattered scraps. I'm puzzled when I hear writers say they keep working manuscripts for collectors' archives; if I did, I'd soon be buried under a mountain of paper.

However, I did keep the rough first draft manuscript of my novel, *Miss Giardino*, so I can offer you a sample from that. And, while I can't show the stages it passed through, I'll try to recall some of them and explain how it became the final version.

The first draft:

"Then let me ask you one more question," said Maria. "Does it help if I tell you that you were the best teacher I ever had? If I say, in spite of what happened between us, I learned more from you than from anyone, that I found myself using methods I learned in your class, and that they're still good. Does it help, in your feeling about Camino and all those years, when I tell you that?"

Anna smiled, then took a deep breath. "A little, but . . ." She shook her head slowly. "No, it doesn't really touch anything deep, it doesn't change anything, if that's what you mean."

"That's what I was afraid you'd say," said Maria. "That's why I . . . tell me, why didn't you leave teaching?"

"Leave teaching?" Anna looked at Maria without comprehension. "I can't imagine doing anything else. Teaching was what I did well. It was my work. From the first moment I walked into a classroom, when I was a child, I knew that was where I belonged."

"You can say that, and at the same time think about what it did, what teaching does to your life?"

Now Anna felt very impatient. "It is quite possible to hold in the mind two ideas which cannot be reconciled. One: I have hated teaching more than I loved it. It has hurt me and taken much from me and given back little. Two: It is my work. It is what I do. If I were to live my life again, I would have to be a teacher again." She said it as though pronouncing sentence on herself. She could see the slight shake of Maria's head that showed her retreat from this. She pointed her finger at Maria, in the same way she had often pressed an important point in the classroom, drilling it into them whether they liked it or not. "Take care how you reject an idea that doesn't please you. That's how you stop thinking, and once you stop thinking, you stop being human."

Maria surprised her by laughing. "Oh, I used to love it when you stood in front of the class that way. It was frightening but thrilling too."

Anna dropped her hand into her lap. She felt ridiculous.

"I guess I've tired you," said Maria.

Anna shook her head. "You've just reminded me of many things, many more things. You see, I keep trying to remember what happened to me the other night. It is blacked out, blocked. But I keep remembering things from years ago. Things I'd rather not remember. Those are the things that tire me."

"Sorry," said Maria. "We were going to talk about your . . injury, and we went all around again and back to teaching."

Anna laughed. "That's what Arno . . . an old friend of mine . . . used to complain of. He said you couldn't have two teachers in a crowded room without the conversation turning to teaching . . . that teachers could talk about nothing else."

Maria stood up. "I've got to go . . . pick up my son at nursery school."

"I'm glad to have seen you again, Maria." Anna stood, took her hand and shook it. "No matter what I said . . . it meant a good deal to me, this visit. I'm only sorry that I wasn't able to be of more help in talking to you about your problems."

Their eyes were on a level now and Maria looked into hers steadily as she said, "Miss Giardino, I've never spoken to you without learning something."

Rewritten and rewritten

Clearly, a lot of fat must be trimmed from this. The first thing I eliminated, as I remember, was Anna's speech about her hate-love relation to teaching. That was implied everywhere in the book and could be adequately summed up by a simple, "Teaching was my work." I threw out the reference to Arno's statement, which also was intrinsic to the book. Then I eliminated Anna's reference to the mysterious incident she was trying to remember. I had already sprinkled enough reference to it throughout the book.

It was a harder decision to get rid of Anna's fingerpointing gesture. I loved that part. I could just see her doing it, and I loved defusing it with Maria's delighted laugh. But I finally concluded that there were too many statements of Anna's austerity. If the reader were to be able to sympathize with her, and if Anna were not to sink into stereotype, some of these gestures would have to go.

After redoing this scene a few times, and after working on the end of the book, I began to feel that Miss Giardino's final decision about her life carried her austerity too far. I had left her too much alone at the end. It was in character for her to choose the hard, independent, austere way, but it was not in keeping with her change that she should drop back into the isolation she had suffered for several years. So I went back into other scenes, adding a few more letters received from former students. In the final scene I spread these letters out on a table where Anna was seated, answering them, a hint of renewed contacts with people. Then I added her mention of a dinner date with Maria, hinting that the young former student might become her friend. To support this, I had to go back to the earlier scene between them, adding a hint of future contact between them, with Maria's statement that she wants to see Anna again. This statement also added some warmth to Anna, indicating Maria not only respected her but also liked her. Anna's surprise at this possibility made her, I hoped, even more likable. So here's the final version:

> "Then let me ask you one more queston," said Maria. "Does it help if I tell you that you were the best teacher I ever had? If I say, in spite of what happened between us, I learned more from you than from anyone else, that I use methods I learned in your class, and they're still good. Does it help, in your feeling about Camino and all those years, when I tell you that?"
>
> Anna smiled and took a deep breath while she thought. "I'd like to say that makes it all worthwhile. But . . ." She shrugged. "Did knowing you were in the right help after the car had run over you?"
>
> "Then I just can't understand why you didn't leave teaching."
>
> Anna hesitated, almost stammering at such a strange question. "Teaching was my work."
>
> Maria waited as if Anna must have more to say. But what else was there to say? Finally Maria stood. "I have to pick up my son at nursery school."
>
> "I'm glad you came, Maria." Anna stood and extended her hand. Their handshake was firm, as if sealing an agreement. "No matter what I said, it meant a great deal to me, your visit. I'm only sorry that I wasn't able to be of more help, to tell you something useful."
>
> Maria looked steadily into Anna's eyes as she said, "Miss Giardino, I've never spoken to you without learning something. May I come again?"
>
> Anna was surprised. "Why, yes. If you really want to."
>
> "I really want to."

Re: rewriting

All you need are patience, a pair of scissors, and a roll of scotch tape. Yes, at last I can give you one definite, universal rule for writing: Don't make additions and changes in the margin or on the back of the page. Cutting and splicing, rather than scribbling and squeezing in, your changes postpones having to type a clean copy just to be able to see what you are doing.

Start wherever you can, fixing a little problem first, perhaps, to give you courage to tackle a big one. Then fix up whatever you disturbed by fixing, because rewriting leads to more rewriting.

Rewriting is tedious, especially if you do it well. You will miss the excitement of writing the first draft. The exhilaration and spontaneity are gone. But so is the tension, the fear that you'll lose it, abort the novel before you're halfway into it. This means less energy is drained in rewriting, and you may find you can work for longer periods without anxiety, without feeling your nerves stretched like rubber bands at the snapping point. Interruptions won't bother you as much, nor will working for short periods more than once a day (if necessary because of other demands on you) rather than the longer sessions of first draft writing. Often, in rewriting, you'll find the solution to a problem while you're doing something else, not even thinking about the book, and you can make a note of it and do the change whenever it's convenient, with no danger of losing impetus.

Rewriting involves a lot of time during which you may seem to be getting nothing done. Not true. You are rethinking. Robert Frost said his famous "Stopping by Woods on a Snowy Evening" came to him spontaneously, as if dictated, fully formed, written out in a few minutes and never revised. I have heard similar accounts of the creation of some short stories and even, occasionally, a novel. It is possible. Even remembering that the inspired, perfect work usually comes "spontaneously" after years of daily uninspired work, like the basketball player's perfect toss that came after thousands of tries, I do believe a novel could be written that would require almost no revision. But not often.

Getting caught in the middle

by Helene Schellenberg Barnhart

Story beginnings can be deceptively easy to write. Buoyed by inspiration, words come faster than you can tap them out. You skim along under full sail.

But along about page five or six, something terrible happens. Like Coleridge's Ancient Mariner, you sit as idle as a painted ship upon a painted ocean. You're becalmed!

Take courage. You're only stranded temporarily in the middle story—a familiar predicament. And the means for getting underway again is already at hand. In fact, it's in your story beginning.

How can that be? Let's look at the ingredients of a short story:

1. A character who wins the reader's sympathy is
2. Faced with a single problem that
3. He must solve *despite obstacles*;
4. After a struggle, the problem is resolved and the character is changed.

If you've established those first two elements in your opening—and sketched in a believable background—then you've already planted the seeds for your middle story, which puts your character through the obstacle course (the third element).

By planning your story in this logical manner, you can find drama in even a story as bald and overlooked as "Cinderella." Here's the opening of "Cinderella"— boiled down to its essentials, without any color or dressing:

> Once upon a time there was a little girl named Cinderella. Her mother had died, so she came to live with her stepmother and three stepsisters. In Cinderella's new home, it was her duty to spend her days tending the furnace.

Helene Schellenberg Barnhart used her teaching/writing expertise in producing five young adult novels, numerous short stories, confessions, articles and newspaper features. Her first publication was in the confession market, a source of good writing fundamentals, she feels. Between her adult education classes in writing and her lectures at workshops, she is at work on a historical novel and a mystery.

Although she was grateful to have any home at all, she was often lonely. She longed to be in the bright, cheery part of the house, laughing and talking about parties attended, as her stepmother and stepsisters did.

Hope's eternal spring

Even without the fiction writer's usual enlivening devices—dialogue, scene-setting, whatever—that's a good beginning. We win the reader's sympathy by showing Cinderella as a half-orphan. And we plant the problem by comparing Cinderella, who tends the furnace, to her stepmother and stepsisters, who laugh and party.

Our second paragraph builds on this:

One day, Cinderella overheard her stepmother and stepsisters chattering happily about the pretty new gowns they had bought to wear to the ball the prince was giving at the palace.

If only I could go, Cinderella thought. But the prince would never invite a cinder girl to the ball. And even if he did, how could she go? She had nothing to wear. Tears streaked her sooty face as she gazed down at her ragged dress.

Still, Cinderella dreamed of going to the ball. She imagined herself dressed in a beautiful silk gown, dancing with the handsome prince.

Now our opening meets the requisites: An appealing character is faced with a problem she must resolve herself. Out of the struggle emerges the Cinderella theme: Hold on to a dream despite adversity; goodness has its own reward. That's a universal theme—and it could be the basis for *your* Cinderella story.

A motherless girl, loneliness, a dream—these, too, are universals planted in the Cinderella opening. They provide the threads for the exciting middle and satisfying ending. How? Through the powerful device of reversal. Rags turn to silk. Transportation appears. Loneliness is exchanged for love and happiness.

But we could call up countless pumpkins and mice in the story middle and still fail, if we don't first win the reader's sympathy in the opening. In a poor lead, for instance, we might show Cinderella hating her stepmother and resenting the favors heaped on her stepsisters. In real life, of course, people *do* hate and resent those who wrong them—but they still enjoy their friends' sympathy. But in fiction, such a character—unless deftly handled—will have trouble winning the reader's sympathy. Why? *Because a short story presents a character in relation to one situation only.* In real life, we know people in many roles—as co-worker, parent, spouse; we see someone fail miserably in one role, but shine in another. In a short story, there is rarely a second view.

An opening might also fail if it dwells on sunsets and Axioms of Life instead of establishing an intriguing character with an intriguing problem. Read your opening critically. Does it merely set the stage instead of putting a character into *action*? If so, don't despair: Even the best writers get carried away with their poetic but unnecessary descriptions. Cut the fat out of the opening; bring the character into the first line, if you can. Once you've hooked the reader with the plot, he'll stay with you when you paint that sunset in the middle story.

Making trouble

OK: You've tightened your opening, and it now establishes your character and his problem without any stalling. Now you can deal with the middle story itself, and plant obstacles in the path of your character. The average story (3,500 to 4,000 words) should have three to five strong obstacles to thicken the plot.

Let's return to "Cinderella." Cinderella's problem is the ball. She wants to go. But three obstacles intially face her:

She has no invitation.
She has no suitable clothes.
She has no transportation.

Your obstacles should be just as clearly defined as these, and consistent with your opening. Outline each obstacle on an index card, if that would help. Then ask yourself these questions: Does this obstacle really contribute to the story? Does it throw light on the character, or on the story's theme?

Those first three obstacles in "Cinderella," for instance, prove one thing about the character: She is impoverished. They also develop the story's theme that goodness has its own reward; after all, they are overcome—for the moment, at least—by the fairy godmother, who cherishes Cinderella's goodness. But suppose that we rewrote the middle of the story, and confronted Cinderella with a different obstacle. In our version, Cinderella *has* an invitation, suitable clothes and transporation, thanks to her loving godmother; but the night before the ball, Cinderella has a terrible argument with her stepsisters and runs away from home, only to find herself lost by morning. That's certainly an obstacle. And it lends suspense to the story, which is one of the main functions of an obstacle. But it's still a failure, because it's inconsistent with the characterization of Cinderella—as a sweet, docile girl—in the opening. Follow through on that obstacle course, and—unless you rewrite the story from the beginning—you'll hit middle story sag. That's why it's helpful to have a firm grip on your character *before* you begin your story. Your opening should then be clear and purposeful, and you'll have no problem deciding which obstacles are consistent with your character and his problem.

Another tip: Never resolve one obstacle before you have begun another. Once an obstacle is overcome, suspense dies. To keep the suspense going, keep the obstacles coming.

In "Cinderella," those first three obstacles are disposed of in short order when the fairy godmother transforms a pumpkin and six mice into a coach with horses, and Cinderella's rags into a gown of gold and silver. (When Cinderella can arrive at the ball in such beauty and finery, she really doesn't *need* an invitation.) But then the fairy warns the ecstatic girl, "Do not stay a moment after midnight. If you do, your coach will turn back into a pumpkin, your horses into mice, and your riches into rags." And Cinderella has a new obstacle.

Present the past

In addition to obstacles, your story middle usually contains a flashback—that is, a glimpse into the past that—provides motivation for the present story action. For example, Cinderella might overhear her stepsisters twittering about the ball, and then go into a flashback about the day she met the handsome prince four years ago, while she was selling apples on the street. . . . If deftly handled, that flashback would show the reader *why* Cinderella longs to attend the ball—and meet the prince again.

But again—a flashback is only a *glimpse*. Keep it short and pertinent to the story problem. You can keep on course by blocking out each flashback on a sheet of paper, and determining what motivation it should illustrate.

Watch your transitions going into and coming out of flashbacks. Return your reader to the exact time and place in which you left him when you went into flashback. Notice how the past perfect ("had") tense serves as a glide into the past:

> Standing at the kitchen window, Lucy saw the black storm clouds forming. She shivered. It was just such a day five years ago that Tom had been killed. She remembered how excited he'd been about the new car.
>
> "Don't go today," she pleaded . . . .

From here you go into how and why Tom *did* go, and how his death changed her life:

> After the police left, Lucy began dumping out the ashtray they had filled. Tom didn't like cigarette smoke. Abruptly she set the ashtray down and went to the kitchen window and stood there for a long moment, watching the unmoving clouds. Tom liked to stand here, just before dinner, just dreaming. Then the full weight of his death struck her and she began to cry, for the first time in she didn't know how many years, but even as she cried she had vowed: *I'll never marry again. Never. Nobody could mean as much to me as Tom.* The clouds had begun to gather . . . .
>
> Now turning her back on the darkening sky, Lucy told herself she must not let her imagination run wild. The storm clouds were beyond her control. But she could control her own emotions. Today, stormy or clear, was the beginning of her new life—the day of her second wedding.

Caution: Don't begin your flashback until your critical opening situation is fully developed. The reader must be hooked by what is happening *now*. Once he can identify with the main character and understand the problem clearly, he will *want* to know more about the cause for the present dilemma. But if you present a flashback hard on the heels of a skimpy and underdeveloped opening, the reader will be confused, and think, "What has all this to do with the situation?"

In the story of a girl who feels her life is threatened by an unknown killer, you might dramatize the threat in your opening with an on-stage incident that terrifies the girl. Develop the scene fully. Then go into a flashback showing that this was not the first time strange things had occurred. There was the first night in the apartment when . . .

Odds and endings

Ultimately, of course, your flashbacks and obstacles—and, for that matter, your openings and middle story—should culminate in the ending. This is an article about the middle story, so we can't delve too deeply into the problems of the ending. But let's look briefly at how the middle story can contribute to two moments in the finale—the *dark moment* and the *crisis*.

Your heroine almost surrenders in the dark moment. The odds are great. Remember Cinderella? At the ball, the clock strikes twelve. She is late in making her exit. She loses the glass slipper, the magic symbol. Back she goes to ashes and rags. What could be darker?

And what could be more effective? At the peak of her success, just as her obstacles seem overcome, Cinderella tumbles back down to where she started, because of the biggest obstacle of all—the time limit that her godmother imposed. That's the secret to a memorable dark moment: Just before your character triumphs, reassert his obstacles. Throw the hero back into the dungeons. The loss of the glass slipper lends irony to Cinderella's dark moment, and that can be effective, too.

Now comes the crisis. Your hero makes a final effort to overcome the biggest obstacle in the story. In a commercial story, the character wins, or gains some insight that makes the problem bearable.

Cinderella's final effort is not so much *doing* as *being*. In the beginning, she is shown as a shy girl with faith. The author draws from this characterization again in the crisis: Cinderella returns to the cinders, gently bearing her stepsisters' taunts, and secretly hoping still for the prince. Her dreams are rewarded when the prince announces that he will marry the girl whose foot will fit the little glass slipper, which he found on the palace steps after the ball.

So you need not drag new elements into your ending. Faith, hope, and a glass slipper—these were the threads that the author plucked from the beginning and middle of "Cinderella" to draw the story to a satisfying close. And you can do the same.

Smooth sailing

Admittedly, the story middle is the hardest part of a story to write. You must have strong obstacles. You must keep your flashback tight and relevant. Above all, perhaps, you must make sure that the elements of your middle story are consistent with your opening, and clear the way for your ending.

Good story middles depend not so much upon inspiration as upon a thorough knowledge of story structure. This is where we separate the sailors from the landlubbers.

The next time your story middle has you at sea, take a sounding on your beginning. Make sure it's structurally solid. Then draw from it the ingredients you'll need for your middle. If you've written a good beginning, you won't run dry. Your sails will catch the wind. You'll be writing again. And the once-distant shore, the end, will be in sight.

How to cut a story by one-third and make a sale

by Kathleen West

A 1,500-word story I mailed to a children's magazine brought this response:

Dear Mrs. West:
We like your story "A Thief in the Neighborhood," but we rarely print anything over 1,000 words in length.

We assume that you have a copy of this story. Please let us keep the original until we get your 1,000-word version at your earliest convenience. If you shorten it to our satisfaction, within this length, we would want to accept it.

Cordially,
Editor-in-Chief
Highlights for Children

Could I cut a third of my story without changing its effect and appeal? To some, this may seem an easy task, but when you're a beginning writer, and this is only the second acceptance you've had, it's formidable.

I wasn't quite sure how to wave a magic wand and make 500 words disappear, but it didn't take long to find that editing involves no magic at all—just work. One key question became my guideline: Is this word or phrase or sentence absolutely essential to the understanding of the story? I didn't find 500 words to delete the first time I worked through the manuscript—not the second, or even the third. There were days when I didn't go near it. The little darling sat patiently on a shelf while I pretended it didn't exist.

But one week and five readings later, it was finished.

Cutting words, then . . .

Eliminating single words is a good place to begin. For instance: "John was

Kathleen West has published short stories and articles for Writer's Digest. She is a resident of California.

scared, ~~really scared.~~" It's just as effective to say, "John was scared."

"With a big swing of his foot, Mark kicked the camera down the sidewalk."

"He bought a ~~brand~~ new camera."

After single words come small phrases—twelve in all were discarded. "Let me have it," ~~the boy named~~ Mark yelled.

"Suddenly there was a loud crash ~~on the sidewalk.~~"

"John looked down ~~at the ground~~ to see his camera smashed."

Next, complete sentences were axed. "John looked down to see his camera smashed, the parts sprawled on the pavement. He felt sick. ~~He looked up at the four boys.~~ 'I tried to tell you the camera was mine,' he said. 'My brother gave it to me.'" It doesn't really matter whether John spoke while looking at the ground or at the boys. The reader can picture it whichever way he chooses—and it gave me seven less words.

"~~He remembered how hard Rick, his brother, had worked to save the money for that camera. And now it was smashed.~~" The reader knows how John treasured the now-broken camera (he felt sick). In the next paragraph John tells the boys, "My brother gave it to me." That's really all we need to know about the brother. His name and how he got the camera aren't important to the story, so these sentences were repetitious and came out.

I even found an entire paragraph, worth 35 words, that left the story better for its being dropped. Ten-year-old John has been accused of stealing a boy's camera. Since John is new in the neighborhood, and has a camera just like the lost one, the boys think he is a thief. Even though John didn't steal the camera, and the boys broke his own, he still wants to be accepted by them. So he goes to the bank, withdraws some of the money he was saving for a camping lantern, and buys another camera just like the one that was lost. We arrive at this point in the story to find John returning home. He has decided to hide the new camera in the boys' clubhouse, hoping they will find it, think it is the lost camera, and realize he isn't a thief.

Eliminating paragraphs

The paragraph I eliminated said: "He got back to his neighborhood just in time to see the four boys getting into a car driven by one of the boys' father. They were in swimming trunks and headed for the beach." By deleting this, not only was I 135 words ahead, but suspense is added because now the reader doesn't know where those boys are, and there is a chance they may find John sulking around their clubhouse and then—more trouble.

When I reached this stage in chopping, I was still 250 words long, but there were three sections which could be completely rewritten. One of them described John going to the bank to withdraw his money. It took thirteen lines and 156 words. It showed him filling out a withdrawal slip, handing it to the teller, receiving money, counting it, and almost changing his mind. Lots of unimportant details. The rewrite covers only six lines and 78 words, saving me 78 words but still saying all that is needed to carry along the story.

"The next morning he walked uptown to the bank. He didn't really want to take any money out of his account because he'd been saving to buy a new lantern to use on the family's camping trips. But he knew it was the only way he could square things. He took out nine dollars and went down the street to the camera shop and bought a new camera, just like the one that had been stolen."

Condensing the close

The clincher, which finally brought me below the 1,000-word mark, was the ending. In its original form it was 509 words. The mother of Mark, the boy whose camera was supposedly stolen, discovered his camera in his closet, buried under a baseball glove. She brought the camera to her son who was with his friends and John. They had just discovered the camera in the clubhouse and were apologizing to John for thinking he was a thief. Now there were two cameras, and a mystery.

Mark's mother launched into a 126-word explanation of what she thought John did. To be truthful, it was preachy.

In the revised ending, Mark's mother simply brings the camera to him, and he and the other boys figure out what John did. The mother's role is minor and shouldn't have much dialogue anyway. The conflict is between the boys, and it is better they discover the answers themselves.

With the new ending I gained 179 words—I was home free! Cutting single words, short phrases, complete sentences, whole paragraphs, and rewriting sections had brought it under 1,000 words, and it was a far better story. Now, what would *Highlights* think?

I barely breathed during the next two weeks. Then one day it came:

Dear Mrs. West:
We like your version of "A Thief in the Neighborhood" and wish to purchase it . . . ."

The partial road to selling complete novels

by Chet Cunningham

I sell books by writing partials. First I have the idea, work out the story line and major characters, involve them all in a horrendous amount of trouble and strife—and then write five or six scintillating chapters that leave an editor begging for more.

Does it work? You bet.

Does it fail? You bet.

Not too many seasons ago, I found myself sadly staring at three brown envelopes in the morning's mail. I had sent the same partial—for a novel about a family in years just before the American Revolution—to six paperback houses. So far I had received negative replies from two editors, and now . . . the envelopes, please.

The third editor said no, too. If I changed the lead to a woman and did a new partial, she said she'd take a look.

The fourth editor said this field was saturated and I should forget the novel.

The fifth editor returned the manuscript with a printed, informal rejection slip. Not even a note. She told me, in effect, to go have chopped cold turkey for lunch.

The telephone rang and I grabbed it before the first sound had finished. If it's bad news, I want to get it over with fast. I said hello and waited.

"Hello, Chet Cunningham please."

"Yes, speaking."

"Oh, this is Susan Calderella from Tower Publications in New York. I have the partial you sent us about *The Patriots*, and we want to talk to you about it.

"We like your outline very much but we have one small problem," she said. "We just don't publish books that long. We can't take on a huge 180,000-word novel."

Chet Cunningham is a fulltime writer in San Diego. He specializes in historical and men's action novels, most of which he has sold with partials.

"Oh, you want me to make it shorter?" I asked the question not really knowing if my brain had connected to my voice yet. I don't get many calls from editors in New York.

"What we were wondering was, could you divide the story? Perhaps you could make it into three parts. If you could do that we could talk about doing three books of 60,000 words each."

Could I? Could I hit my qwertyuiop from six inches? I said I thought I might be able to divide it somehow with some extra work, and we talked about money. By the time our bargaining had finished, I had a verbal contract for three 60,000-word books at $1,500 each. That's not a fortune, but $4,500 buys a lot of typewriter ribbons and hamburgers.

The partial way

That was back in 1976, and subsequently the three books have come out from Tower: *The Patriots*, 1976; *The Seeds of Rebellion*, 1977; *Beloved Rebel*, 1978.

That's how the partial idea works for me. I've sold 67 books: softbacks, hardbacks, novels, juveniles, how-to's, gothics, historicals, historical romances and men's action books—and most on the basis of a partial.

Will this work for all types of books? No. And some writers I know won't do a partial for *any* kind of book. But for me it's the most logical way to sell what you write. By sending a partial you give the editor a chance to help mold the final story along the lines he likes, or that he thinks he can get approved by his editorial board, and that he thinks his house can sell profitably.

The first book I did with a partial was a fact juvenile; and it was not a choice, but a matter of necessity. My agent had been talking with an editor at G.P. Putnam's Sons who said he had a hole in a series of books he was doing, and he needed someone to write a juvenile about cars. I had been writing in the fact automotive field for ten years, so my agent called me. I said of course I could do it. I had the job if I could come up with five or six pages of outline about the proposed book, and two sample chapters. This was my introduction to the partial way of writing, and I've been using it ever since. The juvenile came out in 1973 from Putnam's as a hardback called *Your Wheels: How to Keep Your Car Running*. During the next five years I kept earning royalties from that book, and it served as a door opener as I sold two more hardback juveniles to the same publisher—both on partials.

Yes, you're right. Many types of books can't be done this way. The heavy think piece, where the author isn't quite sure what he's going to say, or how his logic is going to develop until he does the actual writing, is not a partial book candidate. But most novels can be written this way.

A friend of mine says a partial is harder to write than simply doing the whole book. He may be right. But for me it's easier to come up with a partial and to follow the plot through in skeletal form, than it is to try to plot out a novel as I go along.

I don't "whip out" a partial. Starting any book is a time for hours of pondering and experimenting, of trial and error with characters, incidents, situations, backgrounds, locations and themes. But once you've got this done, and know what you're writing about, and what the central core of your novel is, and you've created people to move your story along, you have completed the hardest work of novel writing—and the most exciting part! This is the work that will ultimately show whether you have a worthwhile, marketable story.

Pay-as-you-write plan

A partial is simply shortstopping the novel process about a quarter of the way through. You create the story idea, the people, the themes, and the plot outline. Then write the first five or six chapters, and polish the rest of a chapter-by-chapter outline. Now you have a marketable piece of writing that has taken you about a month of time.

An experienced editor can look at this much of a novel and know if it will work as a book and sell for that house. Understand, we're not talking about the Great American Novel, or a bestseller, or *literature*; rather, it's the work-a-day commercially successful writer who can earn $25,000 a year writing several such novels.

The beauty of working with partials is that when you sell one you sign a contract, and you get half of the advance. This is the pay-as-you-write plan, one of the best basic reasons writers try to get a book contracted before it is written. They don't waste time by writing a book that won't sell; and, more importantly, they get half the advance to help finance the grocery bills while they're writing the epic.

Writing a partial is an exercise in salesmanship. Someone said a partial has to be twice as good as a complete book. You have to start out fast, then explode into action. You have only 70 pages to hook you editor and make him want to buy the book—so he can find out how the rest of it comes out.

Parts of the partial

Enough theory. Let's take a look at my four-step formula for writing partials that sell books.

1. Write a short cover letter and attach your credits.
2. Write the first four chapters of your book. Don't send a first draft. Make it the very best writing you can do: It should sing, be terse, flowing, with fine characterization, exciting plot. Each chapter is 12 to 18 pages long, depending on your style and type of book.
3. Now do the rest of your novel in a chapter-by-chapter outline. Write one page, double spaced, for each chapter in the rest of the book. Write in present tense (Now the hero *goes* to the bank, *steals* the telephone, and *calls* the F.B.I.). Spell out the major plot as it develops, bring in new characters, and show changes in familiar ones. This might run another 15 chapters, so you write it in 15 more pages.
4. Now you have a partial manuscript of 60 to 90 pages that is all set to go out to an editor.

Here is an excerpt from the partial I used to sell *The Patriot* series:
Chapter 1: Boston's Street Brawl Martyrs

March 5, 1770:
As often happened in those days in Boston town, a gang of hecklers had gathered near the Customs House, and began throwing insults and jeers at the 12-man contingent of English Redcoat troopers who stood guard. Not a day wen' by that the members of the Twenty-Ninth Regimental Guard didn't take their share of abuse from the colonials. The soldiers had first arrived in Boston in September 1768, after the board of Custom Commissions sent wild tales of riots, plunder and anarchy that put their very lives in jeopardy.

During the winter snowballs and insults were the lot of the guards, but after 18 months they had grown used to it. Today the snowballs came in larger sizes and the crowd of ruffians at the corner had grown to two dozen. It appeared not only to be saucy boys there, but mulattoes and jeering lowborn as well pelting ice balls at the Redcoats. The usual ranks were swelled by a few Negroes, Irish Teagues, known troublemakers and outlandish jack-tars. The troops were avoiding the snowballs the best they could when their commanding officer, Captain Preston, came around the corner on his usual inspection tour.

The snowball that soared high over the crowd was packed hard with slush from the Boston street where the warm March sun was melting the snow. The ice ball slammed hard into the face of a Redcoat private, jolting him off his feet and breaking his jaw. He slumped into the snowy slush in surprise with a cry of pain and alarm.

A young Negro ran forward from the now jeering crowd and threw a bottle at the formation. He was joined by others who advanced into easy range and launched a shower of ice balls, sticks, bottles and small stones at the Lobsterbacks. One soldier caught a bottle and threw it back at the crowd. The action brought a swift and stinging rebuke from his sergeant.

The hecklers heard it and hooted.

"Don't be nasty, Redcoat. You pay attention to your nice sergeant there," a jeering call came form the throng. Now dozens of snowballs and sticks flew at the troopers who tried to dodge them, but quiet orders were given to stand fast, and they held their formation.

"Hey, a bottle of rum says I can hit the bloody captain there in three tries," one of the jack-tars called. The sailor's first ice ball fell short of its mark, splattering at the officer's feet. The second went wide, and the British officer bristled.

"Take firing positions . . . move!" The command shrilled through the suddenly quiet March air.

Plunging right along

From that point the action of the first chapter continues in full blown prose at my polished best. The second and third chapters followed the first with no unusual break, as if the editor were reading the regular manuscript. Because all were relatively high in action, setting the storyline and introducing several of the important leading characters, I decided that three would be enough. They also detailed the life and times of that pre-Revolution era and got the story off to a good start.

To make a sale with a partial, you must move your story quickly and with great promise of more action to come. Always try to end each chapter on a high point, one that will make the editor want to find out what comes next. In *The Patriots*, the last chapter in my partial wound up this way:

Ben Rutledge settled back in his chair to read the latest edition of the *Boston Gazette*. As usual it was filled with interesting and important political maneuverings. A moment later Martha brought a sailor into the study, his round hat in his hands, pitch odor ripe on his pants, and an expression of fear and awe on his rough face.

"Begging your pardon, Mr. Rutledge, Sir. But Captain Nelson says you should come right down to his ship."

Ben lifted his brows. "Why, man?"

The sailor turned and found Mrs. Rutledge listening. "I wasn't supposed to say unless I had to, sir. Captain Nelson it is. He done shot one of them British Customs Commissioners!"

This ending of the partial, while not exactly a cliff hanger, was enough to urge the reader and the editor on to the next chapter. Even *touching* a Port Customs Commissioner in 1768 was a serious offense, and shooting one was a hanging felony of the first order.

Outlining the rest

Now you want to let the editor know where the book is going next and how you're going to get there. Do this with a reading outline.

I suggest you write one page of double-spaced copy for each chapter planned for the book. This accomplishes several things.

If you haven't worked out a firm plot for the whole of your story, it forces you to do so. In some cases you may find that you don't have a novel at all. In other situations you may find that the story you thought you were telling isn't the real central narrative in the book, and you need to go back and write an entirely new opening. It also lays out, in easy-to-understand form, the germ of your book, the skeleton of the plot, and shows character development and how the hero accomplishes—or doesn't accomplish—his task.

When writing the outline for one of my partials, I always put two or three lines of capital-lettered words at the start of the outline section so the editor is certain to know that what follows is an outline, not the rest of the finished book.

THE NOVEL, THE PATRIOTS, CONTINUES HERE IN OUTLINE FORM. THIS IS TO GIVE YOU A QUICK STUDY OF THE REMAINDER OF THE NOVEL. THE FOLLOWING IS THE GENERAL DIRECTION THE BOOK WILL TAKE, BUT SOME OF THE DETAILS MAY BE CHANGED OR REARRANGED IN THE ACTUAL WRITING.

The Patriots then continues in outline:

Chapter 4:
Ben Rutledge and the sailor ride back to the ship as fast as they can. They find the Captain and the wounded Customs Commissioner. Captain Nelson explains what happened, and soon Dr. Joseph Warren puffs up to give medical aid. He announces that the commissioner is not mortally wounded, the ball from the flintlock pistol went through the chest high and missed all vital organs.

As they talk they discover the commissioner was trying to seize the ship on false grounds so he could make a profit on it and he was already half drunk. They urge the commissioner to drink more to help him relieve the pain, and soon he is so drunk he passes out. They take him to a brothel where one of the girls will cooperate.

They take him by carriage to the girl's crib. The doctor stays until the head port commissioner comes and the girl convinces him that she shot the man by accident when he wanted some "special" favors. The girl says he was so drunk he could hardly perform as it was. The girl entices the head commissioner and he decides the shooting was an accident.

The next day in his office Ben worries about his financial health. The Townshend Act passed by Parliament is big trouble for Ben. The colonies agreed not to import certain items taxed under the new law. These include tea, glass, paper and paint. Suddenly Ben's import tonnage is cut by half. Ben worries about this as he watches the economy of Boston slow down to half its usual vigor.

Ben's teenage daughter is growing up, and learning about sex from her cousin. They whisper their limited knowledge and even more limited contacts. Harriet yearns for a real sexual experience, but is frightened of the idea at the same time.

When you come to the last chapter of the book, write the one-page outline and stop. Your partial is completed. Whether it sells now is up to the editor. You have done your best.

What editors want

What are you selling? You are selling the editor on the idea that here is an outstanding book that her company must have and must publish. How do you hook this editor, who knows all the tricks, who is wallowing in good manuscripts up to her eyebrows, and now has at last focused her bifocals on your brilliant prose? The basics: good writing, good characters, good story sense, good plotting and a humdinger of a problem.

Characters are the most important element in any work of fiction. Get your characters introduced and established quickly. Few of us remember the plot of *Gone With the Wind*, but who can forget Scarlet O'Hara or Rhett Butler? Just knowing that I have only 60 pages to sell the editor often gives me that incentive I need to cut through all the non-essentials and get into the story quickly, cleanly and with a purpose that is easy to spot and with which readers will identify.

Some writers say they don't like outlines because they cut off their creative juices when they are doing the finished writing on the chapter. Balloonsticks and pollywog gills. The outline is a minimum in plot or fabric of your story, and any writer worth his IBM is going to make changes in outline and story as he writes. You may kill off a character, create new ones not even mentioned in the outline, and the story may come out much different than you anticipated. Editors understand this and applaud it, because it means that the final story will turn out even *better* than the outline suggested.

For me the creation of an outline is one of the most difficult, but one of the most rewarding, creative aspects of writing a novel. I love it.

Multiple partials

When your partial is all typed, with cover sheet in place, your credit sheet inside, go to your favorite speedy printer with a good photocopying machine, and have six copies made on plain 20-pound bond. Six? Right, six.

I never send out an original. Why? I sent one novel to New York from California. It was rejected, and the editors, overlooking my return 4th-class postage, sent it by United Parcel Service. UPS proudly delivered to me a padded envelope with three pages of the manuscript inside and the side seam of the envelope split from top to bottom. Two hundred and seventeen pages were missing. It takes me four days to retype 220 pages, or it costs me $220 to hire them done. That's why I no longer send originals.

When you have six copies ready, file your original for future use, and pick out six publishers to try first. Yes, six all at once. It's called multiple submissions and it is not a dirty term or bad practice. Ten years ago publishers scolded us for doing this. Today many editors admit that they expect writers to multiple submit.

The turnabout occurred when photocopying machines became so good that it is now hard to tell a duplicate from the original. Many writers advise an editor with a cover note when they are sending a multiple-sub; but I feel that a note like that will kill your chances with some editors. So I never tell them it's a multiple-sub, and if an editor wants to buy my book, there is a negotiation and contract procedure during which such topics can be raised and discussed.

Multiple submissions are simply good merchandising. You send out a partial, say, to Avon. Avon says no thanks, but it takes two months. If you got two-month service from six different publishers, one at a time, with your original, it would take you a year to cover all six. By sending out six partials at once you can cover the same publishers in two months, and get your product to 18 publishers in only six months! This is especially important if you have a subject that is topical or tied in with the news. In a year the idea might be so out of date, the book would not be worth publishing.

Partial for you?

Can you expect a contract if you haven't published before? That depends on many factors. First, the partial must be outstanding, or must fill in a hole, or fit into a genre that is needed at the moment. Then the editor must believe that you can and will finish the book. Most unpublished writers have trouble selling an outline, so if you have sold articles or stories be sure to list them on a separate sheet and send it along with the partial. I always put my credits right under the title page of the book where the editor can't overlook them.

Any way that you can assure an editor that you are a writer who can produce, that you can write, that you have special knowledge in your field, the easier it will be for her to give you the go-ahead and with a contract. Even if you don't have credits, you still must present the most professional-looking package you can. The editor will notice this. If she can't quite see her way to contract for the book, she may write and tell you she likes the book idea and that she wants you to be sure to send the completed book to her.

This way she protects herself in not buying a pig in a new-writer poke, and she encourages you to finish the book and send it to her first. If it is good, she still has the chance to buy it. At the same time you have made an important contact, you have an editor's name. She will remember you and the partial when you send it back completed.

Is there a drawback to writing partials and spreading several of them into the market? Yes, but it's a nice kind to have. I did a number of partials during the last months of 1977 and first months of 1978. Then in March the floodgates opened.

In one week I received contracts for seven books. I spread out the due dates as best I could and had only one conflict, which I solved before the deadline. I don't know if I want seven contracts hanging over my head again, but it certainly helps out with the budget!

Are partials the way for you to go? Only you can answer that question. But if you haven't tried it, why not give it a fling, especially if you're in the middle professional ranks and have some credits.

I'm totally sold on the partial as the only way to write and sell a book. I don't have two years to play with an idea and come up with a book that may not sell after I finish it. For the conscientious, hard-working, mid-level selling pro, it pays to be partial to partials.

Confessions of a children's book editor

by James Cross Giblin

"May I send you my manuscript?"

That question ends many of the 500 queries we receive each year in the children's book department at Clarion Books/Houghton Mifflin. To over three-quarters of them, we write a polite but firm no, softening the blow with a phrase like "unfortunately your project doesn't sound suitable for our list." At other publishers, the percentage of rejection is probably as high or even higher.

Why do children's book editors say no to the majority of queries they receive? Is it because of the way the letters are written, or what they reveal of the contents of the manuscripts—or both? Why do editors rarely say *why* a project doesn't seem suitable? Do they really feel most such projects are unsalvageable?

To answer these questions, let's look at four hypothetical queries. Two concern picture books, the third relates to a work of fiction, and the last to a nonfiction project. While they by no means cover all types of children's books being published today, they do provide a typical sampling of the queries that reach the desks of children's book editors in every mail. Here is one describing a fantasy picture book:

> I have just completed a 30-page picture book story in verse about Little Grape, who runs away from home because he doesn't want to be pressed into wine. He joins a flea circus and becomes a star acrobat. When the circus performs in Little Grape's home town, all his surviving relatives come to see him and are so proud. Here's a sample stanza from the text:
>
> Mama Grape, Mama Grape, what do I see?

James Cross Giblin is editor and publisher of Clarion Books/Houghton Mifflin, a children's book imprint of Houghton Mifflin Company. He lectures frequently to writers' groups and has published numerous articles in magazines on editing and writing. Currently he has turned to writing for children and has completed The Scarecrow Book (1980) *and* The Skyscraper Book (1981).

> Our own Little Grape, So bold,
> yet so wee

An art teacher friend of mine has painted six sample watercolor illustrations for the story that I can send you along with the manuscript. May I hear from you soon?

It's not the time to rhyme

What would this author hear from us? We'd wish him good luck in placing his project elsewhere, and he would probably get a similar response from most editors. Why? Because several points in his letter reveal that he isn't knowledgeable about picture books. For instance, a 30-page manuscript is much too long for picture book treatment. Most published picture book texts are two to five typewritten pages long.

The fact that the story is in verse doesn't sound promising, either. Perhaps because the books of Dr. Seuss have been so successful, many beginning picture book authors seem to believe that their work will stand a better chance of winning acceptance if it is written in verse. Not true—especially if the rhyming is as forced as it is in the sample stanza from this manuscript.

The story line appears to present problems, too. Fantasy can be freewheeling, but it must establish its own convincing logic. A grape that has the ability to run away from the bunch and then to become the star of a flea circus would seem to be stretching any system of logic to its limits, no matter how exciting and unusual the grape's adventures may be.

This author, like many others, obviously thinks that editors want to see illustrations with picture book story submissions. In fact, most editors prefer *not* to look at sample illustrations until they've read a story and seen possibilities in it for their list. Even then they may well decide that they would rather work with an artist of their own choosing. For book illustration requires highly specialized training in the techniques of reproduction that many otherwise talented artists have not had.

Is there *anything* in this query that we and other editors would respond to favorably? Yes—the author's imagination. Then why wouldn't we tell him so instead of simply writing him a polite but general note of rejection? Because book publishing is a business; most editorial staffs are small, and must deal with a pressing load of work.

This situation is often as frustrating for editors as it is for writers. Editors are always on the lookout for promising new talent and wish they had more time to encourage beginning authors. If an editor did have the time, here's what he or she might tell the author of the picture book about the runaway grape:

> Clearly you have an active imagination, but we think you could come up with a more likely central character for your story than a grape. How about a rabbit, a bee, a bird, or even an earthworm—some creature that can logically move?
>
> Judging by the sample stanza you sent us, we'd suggest that you tell the story in poetic prose rather than in verse, and we would recommend that it be no longer than five or six typewritten pages, to allow more room for illustrations. We'd also prefer seeing the story by itself first, rather than with sample illustrations.

An episode, not a story

Now here's a query about another kind of picture book story, one drawn from everyday life:

Last month a handsome stray cat appeared on our porch one afternoon. My young son and I fed it some milk and he played with the animal until suppertime. After supper, when he went outside again, the cat had disappeared. I have written up this episode and think it would appeal to all children who love animals and would like to have a pet. May I send my story to you?

The author herself gives us the best reason for declining this manuscript when she calls it an "episode." From her description, the piece has no apparent story line; the cat simply arrives on the porch in the afternoon and disappears in the evening. No doubt the author's son was drawn to the animal, but there's no indication that his personality underwent any growth or development as a result of his meeting the cat. There was hardly time for that.

To this author, we might write:

While undoubtedly genuine, your manuscript doesn't sound as if it contains the necessary action, suspense and character interest to make a satisfying picture book story. Using the basic situation as a springboard, why don't you let your imagination go and try to invent a story that incorporates these vital elements?

Truth is stronger than fiction

The next mail brings this query about a book for older readers:

For over ten years I have been carrying on a pen-pal correspondence with a Japanese family, and have learned many interesting things about their daily lives, activities and holidays. Now I have written a novel entitled *Around the Year with a Japanese Family* in which I weave in much of the information that I've gathered. It's really nonfiction, but I thought children would enjoy reading it more if it were presented in fictionalized form. For illustrations I have over 75 color snapshots of my pen pals and their friends, with many famous and colorful spots in Japan shown in the backgrounds. I hope you will want to read my manuscript, and look forward to hearing from you.

At first glance, this query might seem to contain the most possibilities of the three we've read so far. But on closer scrutiny, it, too, appears to have serious flaws. Evidently the author has never been to Japan, yet she intends her book to convey an authentic flavor of Japanese life. A more serious weakness is her decision to present what she admits is nonfiction in a fictional framework. Although she may not be aware of it, the day of Johnny and Janey going with Uncle Tim to visit a berry farm or a garbage disposal plant is virtually over. Authors today are employing lively, straightforward approaches to their juvenile nonfiction ideas and avoiding contrived fictional setups.

This author is unaware of another book publishing reality of she suggests that color snapshots would make effective illustrations for her project. Even if the snapshots were outstanding, few juvenile nonfiction book budgets today can support the cost of full color illustrations.

However, this query does have an appealing warmth and a sincerity that deserve encouragement. Here's what we might write to its author, if we had a spare five minutes at the end of the day:

> Since you've not been to Japan yourself, why not explore the material from your own, American point of view? You could convey the pleasure one derives from being a pen pal, the knowledge one can gain about life in another country, the feelings one can share with friends halfway around the world. And we definitely feel that it would be more effective if you presented the material as nonfiction.

Thorough, realistic and professional

In the next morning's mail might come this query concerning another project for older readers:

> I have spent the last three years researching the life of Mary Todd Lincoln, and have just completed a biography of her for ages ten to 14. Much has been written for this age group about Abraham Lincoln, of course. But after checking the latest editions of the *Subject Guide to Books in Print*, and talking with our local public and school librarians, I could find only two other books about Mrs. Lincoln, and both were published quite some time ago.
>
> In my manuscript I have tried to deal honestly with the complexities of Mrs. Lincoln's character, and have not concealed or whitewashed the neurotic side of her personality. I have previously published several articles and stories in children's magazines (and she lists them), but this is my first attempt at a book. Would you like to see my manuscript?

Yes, chances are that we would write this author to send along her manuscript. What made us respond favorably to her query? First, her thoroughness and professionalism: Not only has she done a great deal of research on her book, but she has also investigated the competition it will encounter in the marketplace. Second, her awareness: Obviously she has a realistic and responsible attitude toward Mrs. Lincoln, which is more likely to find acceptance among critics and young readers today than an idealized treatment would. Finally, the modest yet confident tone of her letter appealed to us and made her seem like an author who would be pleasant to work with.

Important questions for success

Of course a favorable response to a query is no guarantee that a manuscript will be accepted for publication. Writing an effective letter and bringing characters, events or topics to life in a manuscript are two very different things. But a query can be the first successful bridge of communication between an author and an editor.

So there they are: Queries about four children's book manuscripts, only one of which we would ask to see. Looking back at the questions that were raised in the beginning, it's clear that it wasn't the form of the letters that made the difference, but rather what they revealed of the content of the manuscripts. And where three out of the four authors seemed to go wrong was in the basic creative decisions they had made before they even started to write.

In order to avoid making similar mistakes, here are some questions that you might ask yourselves before you embark on a new children's book project:

If it's a fantasy picture book idea, does the story line have a consistent logic of its own?
If it's an idea for a realistic picture book, will it result in a complete and satisfying whole with action, suspense, and a beginning, middle and an end? Or will it merely be an incident that requires further fleshing out?
Whether fantastic or realistic, will the story be more effectively told in prose or in verse? Can the material be approached from more than one angle? If so, which would be the freshest and most appropriate one?
Does research in a library or bookstore reveal that the idea is likely to meet stiff competition from existing books? If it does, how can this competition best be overcome?

Finally you should ask yourself, "What special insights and knowledge can I and I alone bring to this project?" There's probably no story idea or nonfiction topic that some author somewhere hasn't already written about. But that author wasn't you.

Once you've answered these and other questions that occur to you as honestly and fully as you can, why not write a query to yourself describing the idea for the book in detail. Then ask yourself the last and hardest question: "If I were an editor, would I want to see this manuscript?"

If the answer is yes, then full steam ahead. But if it's no, you'd better take the idea back to your desk for further questioning and development. Time spent now on rethinking and reshaping the idea until it satisfies *you* will probably spare you a lot of disappointments later when you send out your queries to children's book editors. It may even ensure a response of, "Yes, why don't you send along your manuscript," instead of "Sorry, but this doesn't sound like something that would be right for our list."

Patterns for carrying the young reader through your story

by Jane Fitz-Randolph

Good plotting, good characterization, strong emotional appeal and suspense, and good writing are all essential to successful stories for children and young adults. So is just plain basic skill in fiction writing. Mastering a few techniques that apply to all fiction presentation, whether for children or adults, can put you on the right track.

Viewpoint

The technique that causes the most difficulty and is most often bungled by beginning writers—and more advanced writers too—is handling viewpoint. Yet viewpoint need not be difficult.

With so few exceptions that they are hardly worth mentioning, stories for young readers are told from the single viewpoint, either first person or third person. This means simply that the writer will go into the mind and feelings of only one character, almost always the main character; the writer *becomes* the viewpoint character, seeing and hearing what that character sees and hears, thinking as he thinks, feeling as he feels, experiencing the events just as the viewpoint character lives and experiences them.

The advantages of this technique are so strong that any deviation from it—into multiple viewpoint or omniscient author viewpoint, which are found in a few adult short stories and most adult novels—will almost certainly weaken a story so that it will fail. Very rarely, there is a story that really can't be told from the single viewpoint; if ever you find such a story published, save it and study it, for it must be

Jane Fitz-Randolph has co-authored two science books, Time and Clocks in the Space Age *and* From Sundials to Atomic Clocks, *with James Jespersen. A teacher of adult and juvenile writing courses in the University of Colorado's Continuing University Studies program, she frequently participates in writers' workshops and seminars. Her other credits include children's films, filmstrips and short stories. She is currently at work on a book on telecommunications.*

a very good story indeed, unusually strong in other respects, to have succeeded in spite of the viewpoint weakness.

The most important advantage of the single viewpoint is that it establishes immediately and then sustains a sense of reader identity. Because the *writer* has identified with the viewpoint character, the reader also identifies with the character, living the events of the story with him, feeling the same suspense, excitement, fear, relief, triumph that the viewpoint character feels. The reader experiences the events as they unfold, never for a moment feeling that he is simply himself, separate from the story, being *told* a story *about* the viewpoint character—which may have happened sometime in the past—by still a third person, the author.

The single viewpoint is both natural and realistic. In real life, one person cannot know what another thinks or feels, cannot know how something looks or tastes or smells to someone else, cannot know what is going on or being said in some place where he is not present. So the reader, once he identifies with the viewpoint character, is only annoyed or derailed if the subjective thoughts and feelings of some other character or of the author—things the main character could not possibly know—are introduced.

The same is true of scenes in which the main character is not present, though of course the main character, and the reader along with him, may *speculate* about these things, just as we all do in real life.

Once they understand the principle, most writers do not find the single viewpoint difficult, and are immediately aware of any deviation from it in their own or published stories.

Should you choose first- or third-person viewpoint for your story? Some writers find one easier, others the other; actually it's mostly a matter of practice, and you should learn both. Readers under 12 or 13 generally prefer third-person stories, whereas older readers often enjoy the intimacy and informality, the close identity with the subjective thoughts and feelings of a first-person character. But you will find both viewpoints for readers of all ages.

Both have advantages and limitations. It's almost impossible to write about a first-person "hero," for whatever he tells of his exploits and ingenuity seems like bragging. A similar limitation becomes apparent when he tries to describe himself or his possessions. On the other hand, if the main character is in some way inept, a blunderer, or in a position of disadvantage through no fault of his own, the choice of first-person viewpoint can often help to create reader sympathy, whereas a third-person viewpoint might make him seem pathetic. If a character honestly recognizes his deficiencies and can accept them with grace and humor, showing good sportsmanship in spite of difficulty and defeat, he can become a most appealing first-person main character.

Another situation for which first-person treatment is effective is one in which the viewpoint character tells an entertaining, usually humorous account of another character who is really the main character. In such a story, usually the viewpoint character's goal is to help the main character solve *his* problem or reach *his* goal. For example, a story of a school election might be about Joan's campaign, told in the first person by her campaign manager, Frank. Frank's problem is to help Joan solve her problem, which is to be elected.

Staying inside the viewpoint character

A few comments about the common errors made in working with third-person viewpoint should help you to use it with finesse: First, remember that you cannot go into the thinking or subjective feelings of anyone but the viewpoint character. You must not say, for example, "The boys' hearts were hammering against their ribs." Instead, say, "Rob's heart hammered against his ribs. He looked at Marty and knew he was scared, too."

The viewpoint character may *surmise* what someone else thinks or feels. You might write, "Tim had tried all day to get up enough courage to ask, 'May—may I go with you on the elk hunt this year?' 'You might help the burro carry our gear,' Uncle Hank said, laughing. Uncle Hank thought he was joking."

"Uncle Hank thought he was joking" does not really go into Uncle Hank's thoughts; it is simply the conclusion Tim draws from what his uncle says and does. Second, you cannot have a scene in which the viewpoint character is not present. You cannot say, "After Jack had gone to bed, Mother and Daddy sat up late talking." And conversely, you should not withhold from the reader anything known to the viewpoint character; you should not say, "Suddenly Lisa had a wonderful idea. 'I know it will work,' she said aloud, and ran to her room. . . .That evening, when the family gathered for dinner . . ." Usually you should let the reader in on what she has planned, so that the reader can enjoy the anticipation with her. Similarly, if the viewpoint character has been working to solve a mystery, you would not write, "Sammy looked down at his feet, and there it was, lying right in the dust before him—the one clue that might help. He stooped, picked it up quickly, and dropped it in his pocket." If Sammy knows what it is, the reader should be told, too.

Third, be very careful about describing the appearance of your viewpoint character, especially the facial expression and the eyes. If you say, "Emily's smile faded and her eyes grew sad," obviously you are not in Emily's viewpoint, but in the viewpoint of someone looking *at* her; Emily is not aware of this change in her facial expression, and would not thus describe herself if she were. Instead, stay "inside" Emily: "Suddenly Emily felt all alone again, and tears were close to the surface." Similarly, if you say, "Emily was a picture of grace as she danced in the blue taffeta dress," you are outside Emily's viewpoint. Instead, you might say, "Emily caught a glimpse of her reflection in the glass of the French doors as they danced past. The blue taffeta is just right, she thought happily." Or you could use dialogue: " 'That dress is perfect for you, Em,' Myrna said. 'It just matches your eyes and makes your hair even more golden.' "

If you are ever in doubt about these points, simply transpose momentarily into first person, and you will see immediately whether you're at fault. You would never say, "I was furious; my eyes became pinpoints of anger." If it's absurd in first person, it is equally absurd to assign it to a third-person-viewpoint character.

Fourth, avoid author intrusion; think of your story as a play on a stage, where everything must be conveyed by the action and dialogue of the characters, and you, the author, can tell nothing. This will keep you from ever being tempted to say something like "This was the naughtiest thing she had ever done." There simply isn't anybody on stage to make such a remark. It will also keep you from getting ahead of your story: "Little did they know when they left home that before nightfall . . ." It will keep you from saying, "Paul was so busy tacking up the decorations that he didn't see Andy and Myrna come into the gym," or, "Jan was so miserable that she didn't notice the bright sun." What your viewpoint character fails to see or hear or notice will have to be left out.

Finally, avoid ever addressing the reader as "you": "Marie ran to the back porch to feed Muff, and what do you think she found?" This is another form of author intrusion that immediately destroys reader identity, reminding the reader that he's simply reading *about* the character. And avoid epithets to refer to the characters, especially to the viewpoint character. To the writer, it seems as if he is repeating a character's name endlessly, and trying to avoid this, the beginning writer will refer to the character as "the older boy," "the young cowboy," "the redhead," and so on. Actually, such epithets draw attention to themselves far more than even a great deal of repetition of the name, because the name is natural and the epithet is not; the characters in the story—especially the main character—do not think of themselves or one another as "the older boy" or "the young cowboy." So use only the character's name or a pronoun to refer to him.

Study viewpoint techniques in the best published stories. Note really fresh and clever devices authors have used to handle difficult problems. E.L. Konigsburg found an ingenious way to use a double viewpoint legitimately in her Newbery Award-winning book *From the Mixed-Up Files of Mrs. Basil E. Frankweiler*. The whole book is a letter, written by Mrs. Frankweiler to her attorney, in which she tells of the children's adventure; she has had both Claudia and Jamie tape-record their account of their activities, so she has the subjective account of each, and quite naturally relates both in her letter. If you understand what you are doing and why, viewpoint will not give you any trouble.

Scene building

Whether your story is a 300-word incident for preschoolers or a teenage novel, it will be told in a series of scenes; and learning to think of a story in terms of scenes will help you plan and write good stories. Each time there is a change in setting or time, or a major personnel change, the scene changes. Each scene is like a miniature story, complete with its own problem, crisis, and climax. The main character enters the scene with a purpose, makes some effort to achieve it, and is either successful or defeated. Thus each scene moves the plot forward and adds to the suspense, with the main character sometimes gaining a bit on his ultimate goal, sometimes being thrust back.

The scene breakdown for "The Mystery of the Fourth-Floor Cat," one of my own stories, goes like this:

Scene I: Nine-year-old Shelly's Christmas, two days away, looks bleak. She should be happy about the new bunk beds already delivered and set up; but Smudge, her cat, has been missing for five days. She's asked every one of their fourth-floor neighbors, but no one has seen Smudge. Defeat.

Scene II: Shelly sees Mike, a neighbor, enter through the stairs door, and when she realizes people use this door all the time, she thinks Smudge could be far away. Defeat. But Mike tells her about the radio pet patrol and suggests Shelly call there for help. Hope.

Scene III: Shelly's mother is sure the cat got out into the hall and has been stolen, but reluctantly agrees to call the pet patrol when Shelly pleads. Shelly writes the radio announcement, and Mother phones it to the patrol. Success.

Scene IV: Shelly hears the announcement read, the next morning. Hope.

Scene V: Shelly is wrapping presents on Christmas Eve, the last a catnip mouse. Still no word of Smudge. Defeat. Black Moment.

Scene VI: The delivery man who brought the beds comes with Smudge. He explains he's had the cat for nearly a week, after finding it in his van, but had no idea where it came from until he heard the radio announcement. Smudge had crept into one of the mattress cartons. Shelly knows it's the best Christmas ever. Success.

Breaking the story down this way into scenes gives you smaller pieces to work with—something you can handle—instead of trying to shape and mold the whole unwieldy mass of the story. It helps you hew to your story line. Most stories, especially those by beginning writers, tend to grow too long, both for the market and for the story they tell. Outlining your story in scenes, either before you write it or when revising and polishing, will often show you where to cut. Perhaps you can start it at a later point, with some of what you now have in the beginning worked into dialogue later on. Often you'll find you can cut out an entire scene, combining what it achieves from a plot standpoint with what happens in another scene.

Cutting, shaping, tightening invariably results in a better, more compact, faster-moving story. It ensures your story against sagging because of scenes that don't build toward the climax. There should never be a single scene or episode that is not essential to the working out of the plot.

When you write your scene—and when you revise and polish it—concentrate on the action. Use only what information and description are necessary, and weave these in with the action and dialogue. Two or three well-presented details usually provide enough for the reader to go on and fill in other details for himself.

Think about the time span covered by your story. To achieve unity, coherence, and suspense, it should be as short as the story material permits. Keep scenes compact, time lapses between scenes as short as possible. A short story rarely covers more than a week or so. Many cover only a day or two, and some of the best take place in an hour or two.

In most respects the scenes in a story are very similar to the scenes of a play, and thinking in terms of scenes will help you to write both. Make it a general rule to give the opening and closing lines of each scene to your main character; be *sure* to give the opening and closing lines of the *story* to the main character. Give him the spotlight with every important entrance and exit he makes.

Transitions

How do you move smoothly from one scene to the next? The secret of making adroit transitions is to find or provide a common denominator between the scene you are completing and the one you are about to start. For example, one scene may end with Myra saying to her friend, "We'll meet at my house after dinner." And the next scene might open: "Myra had cleared the table and laid out the poster materials when the doorbell rang."

Another device is to end one scene with a question and start the next with the answer to the question: "And even if he did manage to talk Dad into letting him use the station wagon, how was he going to get nine boys and their instruments, including Bill's drums, into it?" The next scene, which might be a day later, could open: "Steve and Bill had rearranged the instrument cases six different ways and were unloading for a seventh try when Larry drove up in his brother's VW."

Sometimes you can cover elapsed time with a quick montage: "Two Cokes and an ice-cream soda later, Louella was still sitting there in the booth trying to compose an acceptable letter."

By giving attention to skillful scene transitions in published stories in the best magazines and analyzing how the author achieved them, you will find ways to adapt these methods to your own writing. Work to develop a variety of devices and methods, so that readers will not become conscious of a repetition of just a few devices used over and over.

Story opening

Even seasoned writers often wonder why story openings have to be so troublesome. There aren't any real "rules" to help with openings, and often one simply has to try several different approaches before finding the best one; sometimes it's well to wait until the story is all written before making a final decision.

The first problem is deciding *where* to begin. Since all stories for children and all but a very few for teenage readers are told chronologically without flashback or retrospect such as is used in many adult stories, the decision is simplified somewhat: you begin at the beginning. But novice writers tend to start *before* the story begins, with explanations of who the character is and how he happens to be in this situation. For example, if Mary is spending the summer with Uncle Ben on his farm, the inexperienced writer will start with Mary packing her bag, going to the airport, saying good-by to Mother, being met by Uncle Ben, and so on. The story isn't even started yet and half the allowable wordage is gone. The story should start with Mary at the farm facing her problem, whatever it is.

The all-important aim of the opening is to "hook" readers immediately and hold their attention. The best way to do this is to introduce the main character and his situation and problem as promptly as possible. The author should also indicate why the problem will be difficult to solve and why the solution is important to the main character. At the same time, the writer should make the reader like the main character and care what happens to him.

To do all this in the first few sentences demands that the story open with the main character doing something interesting. His action should characterize him a bit and at least hint at the story problem; it can be developed more fully as the story progresses. Of course the action must happen in some setting, so that the reader sees the character "on stage"—in the living room, walking along the street, on the playgound, or wherever he is.

The character may be alone or with others. Having others present makes dialogue possible, which always adds interest. But the writer must be sure to make clear the relationship of those present and show clearly which is the main character and from whose viewpoint the story will unfold. The main character should be the first one mentioned, and is usually the first to speak.

Right from the start, the main character should feel some emotion, and the reader should understand clearly what the emotion is and identify with it. The beginning should arouse curiosity and promise dramatic action. Remember that the reader isn't interested in description and information. He wants a story, an emotional experience; he wants to feel excitement, suspense about what will happen next. So avoid static, explanatory details in the opening; any *necessary* explanatory details can wait until later, where they can be woven in unobtrusively with action and dialogue.

Study the openings of stories in current young people's magazines. Stop at the end of 50 or 60 words and ask yourself, What makes the reader want to go on reading? If you find openings you think are weak, study them to understand why; see if you could improve on them. This practice will help you greatly in writing good openings for your own stories.

Title

Sometimes a title comes easily, sometimes hard. Often the title is the last thing about a story to be decided—after it's all written, perhaps. And then after all your struggle to come up with a good title, an editor may decide something else would be better.

But try to think of at least a working title when you first start to write, for this helps you to crystallize your story, your theme; it helps you to shake down your story material and decide exactly what story you wish to tell.

Your title, together with the opening sentences of your story, should say, Pay attention; here's something you want to know about. Try to find a title that arouses curiosity and that's fresh and provocative. "Billie's Bad Day," "Susan Learns a Lesson," "A Present for Mother," and so on have been worn threadbare.

Think of your title apart from the story, as it would appear in a table of contents. Would it make a reader want to turn immediately to the story to see what it's about? The "brainstorming" technique of writing quite rapidly a dozen or more possible titles—even those you know aren't right but may lead to something that *is* right—often produces something good. Alliterative titles can be appealing: "Lucy's Lucky Lollipop" or "The Serendipity Social." A phrase from the story may suggest or provide a good title.

Be sure your title doesn't telegraph your punch by giving away the outcome of the story. "Andy's Home Run" or "A Scholarship for Josey" lets the reader know in advance just how the story will end.

Editors do sometimes change a title if it's too similar to another in the same issue of the magazine or to the title of another story they've recently published—or in the case of a book, if it's too similar to a title recently used by another publisher. Or sometimes an editor wants to give a story a slightly different emphasis. For this reason, if you've been able to think of more than one good title, you may wish to let the editor know; it's quite appropriate to type, immediately under the word count in the upper right part of page 1, "Alternate Title(s)" and then list one or two other possible titles.

A good title helps to sell a story, so give it the thought it deserves.

You will find in published stories plenty of examples of exceptions to and violations of all the principles outlined here. This does not mean the principles are invalid; it means only that the stories succeeded *in spite of* these aberrations, not because of them. Either the story had something the editor liked well enough to buy in spite of the weaknesses, or she took it because she *needed* a Valentine story—or a baseball story or a summer camp story—and nothing better came in. But *you* want to be a real craftsman; your aim is to do things right, not to see what you can get away with. So don't be influenced by examples of technical flaws you find in published material into thinking it's really all right to do these things. Set your standards high, and don't be satisfied with anything less than meeting them.

Ten rules for suspense fiction

by Brian Garfield

The English call them thrillers and in our clumsier way we call them novels of suspense.

They contain elements of mystery, romance and adventure but they don't fall into restrictive categories. And they're not circumscribed by artificial systems of rules like those that govern the whodunit or the Gothic romance.

The field is wide enough to include Alistair Maclean, Allen Drury, Helen MacInnes, Robert Crichton, Graham Greene, Arthur Hailey and Donald E. Westlake. (Now THERE'S a parlay.) The market is not limited by the stigmata of genre labels and therefore the potential for success of a novel in this field is unrestricted: *Day of the Jackal*, for instance, was a first novel.

Game's object: to perch the reader on edge, keep him flipping pages to find out what's going to happen next.

Game's rules are harder to define; they are few, and these are elastic: The seasoned professional learns the rules mainly in order to know how to break them to good effect.

But such as they are, the rules can be defined as follows.

1. *Start with Action; explain it later.*

This is an extension of Raymond Chandler's famous dictum: When things slow down, bring in a man with a gun. To encourage the reader to turn to page two, give him something on page one: conflict, trouble, fear, violence. I realize you've got a lot of background that needs to be established, leading up to the first moments of overt conflict; but you can establish all that in Chapter Two. Flash back to

Brian Garfield, author of 65 books and stories for six movies, began writing at age 12 and published his first novel at 21. He received the MWA "Edgar" award for his novel Hopscotch *in 1976 and co-wrote and co-produced the 1980 Walter Matthau-Glenda Jackson movie of the same name. His most recent book is* The Paladin, *a novel which has been on the British bestseller list. Garfield is currently working on several films and a novel set in East Africa.*

it if you need to. But in Chapter One get the show on the road.

2. *Make it tough for your protagonist.*

Give him a worthy antagonist and make things look hopeless. Don't drop convenient solutions in his lap. The tougher the opposition, the more everything is stacked against him, the better.

3. *Plant it early, pay it off later.*

Don't bring in new characters or facts at the end to help solve the protagonist's dilemma. He must work out his own solution based upon a conflict which is established early in the story. No cavalry to the rescue, and no sudden unearthing of a revealing letter written before he died by a character who was dispatched 'way back in Chapter Three. (Unless, of course, you established in Chapter Four that such a letter exists, and followed that revelation with a race between the protagonist and his enemies to see who'll get the letter first.) *No* cavalry to the rescue.

4. *Give the protagonist the initiative.*

All good dramatic writing centers upon conflict: interior (alcoholism; oedipal conflicts) or exterior (a dangerous enemy; an alien secret police force). Only in *poor* gothic fiction is the protagonist habitually and tearfully and hand-wringingly at the mercy of evil opposing forces which push him/her around at will. *The best story is usually that in which the protagonist takes active steps to achieve a goal against impossible odds, or to prevent opposing forces from overcoming him or his loved ones.* The protagonist may begin by reacting, but in the end he must act from his own initiative.

5. *Give the protagonist a personal stake.*

No longer is it acceptable for the hero to solve a mystery just because it presents an interesting puzzle. The more intimate his involvement in the main conflict of the story, the better. He himself, or his aims, should be in jeopardy: his own life or his loved ones should be in danger, or his best friend has been murdered, or he is the kind of character whose values and principles won't let him sit by and allow injustice to destroy the people around him. Whatever the conflict is, if he loses, it's going to cost him horribly; that's the essence.

6. *Give the protagonist a tight time limit; and then shorten it.*

This doesn't always work because the logic of many stories prohibits it; don't use it unless you can work it in believably. But when time is a factor, and when the brief span of time in which he must resolve the conflict is then shortened, you have gone a long way toward heightening the suspense.

7. *Choose your character according to your own capacities as well as his.*

Don't use as your protagonist an accomplished professional spy unless you are prepared to do the research and groundwork necessary to create such a character convincingly. It is better, particularly when approaching the early stages of your own professionalism, to stick to the familiar. Some of the most successful suspense-novel protagonists—many of Eric Ambler's, for instance—are ordinary innocent people caught up in dangerous webs. The indignant honest idealist makes a good protagonist because his innocence makes the professional opposition all the more frightening. Yet a plot-structure for this character is often difficult to contrive because in spite of his naiveté he has to be clever and resourceful enough (*not* lucky) to prevail over his awesome enemies. The other face of this coin, of course, is the professional-crook-as-protagonist; he's easy to identify with because he's an outcast, an underdog, one man using his wits to survive against society's oppressive machinery; but the pitfalls of this genre are treacherous and unless you know criminal procedure and feel comfortable competing with Anthony Burgess and Richard Stark, it's better to avoid the crook-hero in the beginning.

8. *Know your destination before you set out.*

The prevailing weakness of many suspense stories which are otherwise successful is the let-down the reader experiences at the end: the illogical and disappointing anti-climax. It isn't enough to set up intriguing conflicts and obey all the other rules if you haven't got an ending that fulfills the promise of the preceding chapters. It becomes disgustingly obvious when a writer has confronted his hero with thrilling obstacles only to paint himself into a corner. Presented with his own unsolvable cliffhanger he is reduced to bringing in *deus ex-machina* to solve the hero's problems for him. It is not necessary to tie up all loose ends but the climax should resolve the principal conflict one way or another. (In recent years, to avoid the traditional clichés of virtue-triumphant or ironic-downfall, several talented novelists have resorted to obscure endings which no reader can possibly decipher. I rather hope the fad is dying out; whatever the reasons behind it, it demonstrates lazy thinking and infuriates the reader.) The best key to a good ending is to know what the ending will be before you start writing the book. Whether you write a preliminary outline or not, you should know where the journey will end, and how.

9. *Don't rush in where angels fear to tread.*

I admit this one is a catch-all. Essentially I mean that it is wise to observe not only what the pros do but also what they *avoid* doing. The best writers do not jump on bandwagons; they build new ones. The pro doesn't write a caper novel about the world's biggest heist unless he's convinced he can write an unusual story with a unique and important twist. Otherwise he risks unfavorable comparison with the classics in that sub-genre. "Why bother with it if it's not as taut as *Rififi* and not as funny as *The Hot Rock*?" Yet this should not be taken to mean every writer must obey faddish advice such as, "Spy fiction is dead," or, "Historical novels are *out* this season." There is no such thing as a "dead" genre because the human imagination is limitless and there is never a dearth of new ideas, new twists, new talents. The question is, is this idea strong enough and important enough to make this story sufficiently different from its predecessors to merit publication? If a novel is good enough it will find a publisher whether it is a hard-boiled detective story, a western, a spy novel, a historical adventure, or a novel about bug-eyed monsters from Mars. If it isn't good enough the publisher may reject it by saying that such novels are out of style, but this is merely a euphemism.

10. *Don't write anything you wouldn't want to read.*

This one sounds self-evident but I've met several young writers who decided they wanted to start out by hacking their way through gothics or westerns just to learn the ropes, because those categories looked easy to imitate. Nuts. If you start out that way you'll end up a hack. Now if you like to read westerns, then write a western. But don't write in a genre for which you have contempt. If you don't like gothics but insist on writing one, your contempt will show; you can't hide it. You'll end up by "writing down" and the reader will resent your attitude. I don't say you can't sell books this way; God knows people do, all too often; but if you thoroughly enjoy sea stories—even if you don't know a thing about nautical life—you're better off attempting to write a sea story because you'll go into it with enthusiasm, you'll make it a point to learn the terminology and the life, and you'll write a far better book.

A personal journey: a preface to *The Galton Case*

by Ross Macdonald

Detective story writers are often asked why we devote our talents to working in a mere popular convention. One answer is that there may be more to our use of the convention than meets the eye. I tried to show in an earlier piece ("The Writer as Detective Hero," *Essays: Classic and Contemporary*, ed., R.W. Ltd, Lippincott, 1967, pp. 307-315) how the literary detective has provided writers since Poe with a disguise, a kind of welder's mask enabling us to handle dangerously hot material.

One night in his fifth year when we were alone in my house, my grandson Jimmie staged a performance which demonstrated the uses of disguise. His main idea seemed to be to express and discharge his guilts and fears, particularly his overriding fear that his absent parents might punish his (imperceptible) moral imperfections by never coming back to him. Perhaps he had overheard and been alarmed by the name of the movie they were attending, *Divorce American Style*.

Jimmie's stage was the raised hearth in the kitchen, his only prop a towel. He climbed up on the hearth and hid himself behind the back of an armchair. "Grandpa, what do you see?"

"Nothing."

He put the towel in view. "What do you see now?"

"Your towel."

He withdrew the towel. There was a silence. "What am I doing with my towel?"

I guessed that he was doing something "wrong," and that he wanted me to suspend judgment. "You're chewing it," I said boldly.

Ross Macdonald, lives in California where he writes mystery novels including the series with detective hero Lew Archer, a name synonymous with his own. Macdonald was a school teacher, a Navy man and an instructor in adult education writing classes. He has written short stories and nonfiction on crime writing in addition to such novels as The Blue Hammer, Lew Archer, Private Investigator, The Barbarous Coast, The Galton Case *and many others.*

"No. But I have it in my mouth."

My easy acceptance of his wickedness encouraged him to enact it before my eyes. His head popped up. He was completely hooded with the towel, like a miniature inductee into the Ku Klux Klan.

"I'm a monster," he announced.

Then he threw off the towel, laughing. I sat and watched him for a time while the hooded monster and the laughing boy took alternate possession of the stage. Finally, soothed and purged by his simple but powerful art, Jimmie lay down on the cushioned hearth and went to sleep.

Oedipal roots

His little show speaks for itself, and needs no Aristotle. But let me point out some connections between his monodrama and my detective fiction. Both draw directly on life and feed back into it. Both are something the artist does for his own sake. But they need an audience to fulfill even their private function, let alone their public ones. Disguise is the imaginative device which permits the work to be both private and public, to half-divulge the writer's crucial secrets while deepening the whole community's sense of its own mysterious life.

I was forty-two when I wrote *The Galton Case*. It had taken me a dozen years and as many books to learn to tell highly personal stories in terms of the convention I had chosen. In the winter of 1957-1958 I was as ready as I would ever be to cope in fiction with some of the more complicated facts of my experience.

Central among these was the fact that I was born in California, in 1915, and was thus an American citizen; but I was raised in Canada by Canadian relatives. After attending university in Canada, I taught high school there for two years. In 1941, in one of the decisive moves of my life, I came back to the United States with my wife and young daughter, and started work on a doctorate in English at the University of Michigan.

It was a legitimate move, but the crossing of the border failed to dispel my dual citizen's sense of illegitimacy, and probably deepened it. This feeling was somewhat relieved by a couple of years in the Amercian Navy. After the war I closed a physical circle, if not an emotional one, by settling in California, in Santa Barbara. At the same time I took up my lifelong tenancy in the bare muffled room of the professional writer where I am sitting now, with my back to the window, writing longhand in a Spiral notebook.

After ten years this writing routine was broken by circumstances which my later books more than adequately suggest. My wife and I lived in the San Francisco area for a year, and then came back to Santa Barbara. We rented a house on a cliff overlooking the sea and lived in it for a winter and a summer.

The Pacific had always lapped like blue eternity at the far edge of my life. The tides of that winter brought in old memories, some of which had drifted for forty years. In 1919, I remembered, my sea-captain father took me on a brief voyage and showed me a shining oceanic world from which I had felt exiled ever since, even during my sea duty in the Navy.

Exile and half-recovery and partial return had been the themes of at least two earlier books, *Blue City* and *The Three Roads* (which got its title from *Oedipus Tyrannus*). I wrote them in 1946, the year I left the Navy and came back to California after my long absence. These novels borrowed some strength from my return to my native state but they missed the uniquely personal heart of the matter—matter which I will call Oedipal, in memory of that Theban who was exiled more than once.

In the red Spiral notebook where I set down my first notes for *The Galton Case*, Oedipus made an appropriately early appearance. His ancient name was surrounded by a profusion of ideas and images which I can see in retrospect were sketching out the groundwork for the novel. A crude early description of its protagonist turns up in two lines of verse about a tragicomic track meet:

A burst of speed! Half angel and half ape,
The youthful winner strangles on the tape.

Two lines from another abortive poem—
Birds in the morning, scattered atomies: The voice is one, the voice is not my own.

were to supply an important detail to the closing page of the completed novel. The morning birds appear there as reminders of a world which encloses and outlasts the merely human.

Personal dilemmas

A third and final example of these multitudinous early notes is one for an unwritten story—"'The Fortieth Year' (downgrade reversed by an act of will)"—which recalls my then recent age and condition and suggests another character in the novel, the poet Chad Bolling. This middle-aged San Francisco poet is at the same time an object of parody and my spokesman for the possibilities of California life. Bolling's involvement in the Galton case takes him back to a sea cliff which he had visited as a young man, and he recovers some of a young man's high spirits:

He flapped his arms some more. "I can fly! I breast the windy currents of the sky. I soar like Icarus toward the sun. The wax melts. I fall from a great height into the sea. Mother Thalassa."

"Mother who?"

"Thalassa, the sea, the Homeric sea. We could build another Athens. I used to think we could do it in San Francisco, build a new city of man on the great hills. A city measured with forgiveness. Oh, well."

Not long after this outburst, Bolling sits down to write his best poem in years, as he says. While I am not a true poet, I am content to have Bolling represent me here. He shows the kite-flying exuberance of a man beginning a lucky piece of work, and speaks unashamedly for the epic impulse which almost all writers of fiction try to serve in some degree.

It was a complex business, getting ready to write even this moderately ambitious novel. Dozens of ideas were going through my mind in search of an organizing principle. The central idea which was to magnetize the others and set them in narrative order was a variation on the Oedipus story. It appears in the red notebook briefly and abruptly, without preparation: "Oedipus angry vs. parents for sending him away into a foreign country."

This simplification of the traditional Oedipus stories, Sophoclean or Freudian, provides Oedipus with a conscious reason for turning against his father and suggests that the latter's death was probably not unintended. It rereads the myth through the lens of my own experience, and in this it is characteristic of my plots. Many of them are founded on ideas which question or invert or criticize received ideas and which could, if brevity were my forte, be expressed in aphorisms.

Neither plots nor characters can be borrowed, even from Freud or Sophocles. Like the moving chart of an encephalograph, the plot of a novel follows the curve of the mind's intention. The central character, and many of the other characters, are in varying degrees versions of the author. Flaubert said that he was Madame Bovary, William Styron that he became Nat Turner. The character holding the pen has to wrestle and conspire with the one taking shape on paper, extracting a vision of the self from internal darkness—a self dying into fiction as it comes to birth.

My mind had been haunted for years by an imaginary boy whom I recognized as the darker side of my own remembered boyhood. By his sixteenth year he had lived in fifty houses and committed the sin of poverty in each of them. I couldn't think of him without anger and guilt.

This boy became the central figure of *The Galton Case*. His nature and the nature of his story are suggested by some early titles set down in the red notebook: "A Matter of Identity," "The Castle and the Poorhouse," "The Impostor." He is, to put it briefly and rather inexactly, a false claimant, a poorhouse graduate trying to lie his way into the castle.

"The Castle and the Poorhouse," old-fashioned and melodramatic as the phrase is, accurately reflects the vision of the world which my adult imagination inherited from my childhood. It was a world profoundly divided, between the rich and the poor, the upright and the downcast, the sheep and the goats. We goats knew the moral pain inflicted not so much by poverty as by the doctrine, still current, that poverty is always deserved.

In the first winters of the Depression in Ontario, skilled factory workers were willing to put in a full week on piecework for as little as five dollars. The year I left high school, 1932, I was glad to work on a farm for my board alone. Healthy as that year of farm life was, it was a year of waiting without much hope. I shared with many others the dilemma of finding myself to be at the same time two radically different kinds of people, a pauper and a member of the middle class. The dilemma was deepened by my fear that I'd never make it to college, and by my feeling of exile, which my mother had cultivated by teaching me from early childhood that California was my birthplace and natural home.

Such personal dilemmas tend to solidify along traditional philosophic lines. In a puritanical society the poor and fatherless, suffering the quiet punishments of despair, may see themselves as permanently and justifiably damned for crimes they can't remember having committed.

Personal vs. artistic

The Platonic split between more worthy and less worthy substances, idea and matter, spirit and flesh, widens under pressure. The crude pseudo-Darwinian dualism of my own phrase, "half angel and half ape," suggests an image of man not only divided but at war.

The Galton Case was an attempt to mend such gross divisions on the imaginative level. It tried to bring the Monster and the Laughing Boy into unity or congruence at least, and build a bridge, or a tunnel, between the poorhouse and the castle.

The castle is represented by the Galton family's Southern California estate, described as if it was literally a medieval demesne: "The majestic iron gates gave a portcullis effect. A serf who was cutting the lawn with a power-mower paused to tug at his forelock as we went by." The old widow who presides over this estate had quarreled with her son Anthony some twenty years ago, and Anthony had walked out and disappeared. Now Mrs. Galton has begun to dream of a reconciliation with her son. Through her attorney she hires the detective Lew Archer to look for him.

My earliest note on Anthony Galton will give an idea of his place in the story. A very young man and a poet, Anthony deliberately declassed himself in an effort, the note says, "to put together 'the castle and the poorhouse.' He changes his name [to John Brown] and became a workingman . . . . Married under his pseudonym, to the common law wife of a man in jail," he was murdered when the other man got out.

About one-third of the way through the novel, the detective Archer is shown an incomplete set of human bones which prove to be Anthony Galton's. At the same time and the same place—not many miles up the coast from the Northern California town where I was born—Archer finds or is found by a boy who represents himself as Anthony's son and calls himself John Brown. The rest of the novel is concerned with this boy and his identity.

Perhaps I have encouraged the reader to identify this boy with me. If so, I must qualify that notion. The connections between a writer and his fiction, which are turning out to be my present subject, are everything but simple. My nature is probably better represented by the whole book than by any one of its characters. At the same time John Brown, Jr.'s life is a version of my early life: The former could not have existed without the latter.

The extent of this symbiosis can be seen in the two false starts I made on the novel, more clearly than in the finished product, where personal concerns were continually reshaped by overriding artistic needs. The most striking fact about these early versions is that they begin the story approximately where the completed novel ends it. Both Version One and Version Two, as I'll call them, are narrated by a boy who recalls aspects of my Canadian boyhood. The other characters including the father and mother are imaginary, as they are in the published novel.

In Version One the narrator's name is Tom. He lives on the poorer side of London, Ontario (where I attended university and in a sense graduated from the "poorhouse" of my childhood). Tom has finished high school but has no prospects. At the moment he is playing semi-pro pool.

He is challenged to a game by an American named Dawson who wears an expensive suit with a red pin-stripe in it. Tom wins easily and sees, when Dawson pays, that his wallet is "thick with money—American money, which always seems a little bit like stage money to me." From the standpoint of a poor Canadian boy, the United States and its riches seem unreal.

Tom has a taste for unreality. He has done some acting in high school, he tells Dawson.

> *"Did you enjoy acting?"*
> *Did I? It was the only time I ever felt alive, when I could forget myself and the hole I lived in, and turn into an imaginary character. "I liked it, yeah."*

Tom is not speaking for me here. I don't like acting. But it is probably not a coincidence that the American, Dawson, is a Ph.D. trained, as I was trained at the University of Toronto, "in the evaluation of intelligence."

Dawson is testing the boy's memory and acting ability and talking vaguely about hiring him, as Version One died in mid-sentence on its thirteenth page. This version suffered from lack of adequate planning, and from the associated difficulty of telling the boy's complicated story in his own simple person. Neither structure nor style was complex enough to let me discover my largely undiscovered purposes.

But immediately I made a second stab at having the boy narrate his own story. His name is Willie now, and he lives in Toronto, almost as if he was following in my footsteps. He has an appointment with an American, now named Mr. Sablacan, who is waiting for him at the Royal York Hotel.

Symbiotic split

Willie never gets there. All of Version Two takes place in his home, in the early morning. This rather roughly written six-page scene breaks the ground for my book and introduces some of its underlying themes: the hostility between father and son, for instance, here brought to an extreme pitch:

> The old man was sitting at the kitchen table when I went down. He looked like a ghost with a two-day beard. The whole room stank of wine, and he was holding a partly empty bottle propped up between his crotch.
> . . . I kept one eye on him while I made breakfast . . . . He wouldn't throw the bottle as long as it had wine in it. After that, you never knew.

The shades of Huck Finn and his father are pretty well dispelled, I think, when the boy's mother comes down. She approaches her drunken husband "with that silly adoring look on her face, as if he was God Almighty giving her a break just by letting her live. 'You've been working and thinking all night,' she said. 'Your poor head needs a rest. I'll fix you a nice cup of tea . . . .' "

Later, she stops an argument between the father and the boy by silencing the father.

> He sat in his chair and looked down into his bottle. You'd think from the expression on his face that it was a telescope which let him see all the way down to hell. All of a sudden his face went slack. He went to sleep in his chair. The old lady took the bottle away from him as if he was a baby . . .
> . . . I sat and ate my breakfast in silence. With the old man propped up opposite me, eyes closed and mouth open, it was a little like eating with a dead man at the table.

My story had begun to feed on its Oedipal roots, both mythical and psychological. Relieved by the mother of his crotch-held bottle, the father has undergone symbolic death. The short scene ends with the boy's determination to get away not only from his father but from his mother:

> She'd go on feeding me until I choked. She'd be pouring me cups of tea until I drowned in the stuff. She'd give me loving encouragement until I suffocated.

Version Two was a good deal more than a false start. Swarming with spontaneous symbolism, it laid out one whole side, the sinister side, of the binocular vision of my book. In fact it laid it out so completely that it left me, like Willie, nowhere to go but away. I couldn't begin the novel with the infernal vision on which part of its weight would finally rest; the novel must converge on that gradually. But by writing my last scene first, in effect, and facing its Medusa images—

poverty and family failure and hostility—my imagination freed itself to plan the novel without succumbing to the more obvious evasions.

Even so, as I was trying to finish the first draft, I got morally tired and lost my grip on my subject, ending the book with a dying fall in Nevada. My friend John Mersereau read this draft—entitled, appropriately, "The Enormous Detour"—and reminded me that a book like mine could not succeed as a novel unless it succeeded in its own terms as a detective novel. For my ending I went back to Version Two, which contains the dramatic essence of the final confrontations. Willie's scene with his parents served me well, leading me into the heart of my subject not just once but again.

Alter egos

A second break-through at the beginning, more technical and less obviously important, came with my decision to use the detective Archer as the narrator. This may seem a small matter, but it was not. The decision on narrative point-of-view is a key one for any novelist. It determines shape and tone, and even the class of detail that can be used. With this decision I made up my mind that the convention of the detective novel, in which I had been working for fifteen years, would be able to contain the materials of my most ambitious and personal work so far. I doubt that my book could have been written in any other form.

Miss Brigid Brophy has alleged against the detective story that it cannot be taken seriously because it fails to risk the author's ego and is therefore mere fantasy. It is true as I have noted that writers since Poe have used detectives like Dupin as a sort of rational strong point from which they can observe and report on a violent no-man's-land. Unfortunately this violent world is not always fantastic, although it may reflect psychological elements. Miss Brophy's argument disregards the fact that the detective and his story can become means of knowing oneself and saying the unsayable. You can never hit a distant target by aiming at it directly.

In any case I have to plead not guilty to unearned security of the ego. As I write a book, as I wrote *The Galton Case*, my ego is dispersed through several characters, including usually some of the undesirable ones, and I am involved with them to the limit of my imaginative strength. In modern fiction the narrator is not always the protagonist or hero, nor is the protagonist always single. Certainly my narrator Archer is not the main object of my interest, nor the character with whose fate I am most concerned. He is a diliberately narrowed version of the writing self, so narrow that when he turns sideways he almost disappears. Yet his semi-transparent presence places the story at one remove from the author and lets it, as we say (through sweat and tears), write itself.

I remember the rush of invention that occurred when the emotional and imaginative urges, the things *The Galton Case* was to be about, were released by Willie's scene with his parents, and channeled by my decision to write the book from Archer's point of view. The details came unbidden in a benign avalanche which in two or three days filled the rest of the red notebook. The people and the places weren't all final, but they were definite enough to let me begin the wild masonry of laying detail on detail to make a structure. (Naturally many of the details came in already organized gestalts: people in relationship, events in narrative order.)

Detective novels differ from some other kinds of novel, in having to have a rather hard structure built in logical coherence. But the structure will fail to satisfy the mind, writer's or reader's, unless the logic of imagination, tempered by feelings and rooted in the unconscious, is tied to it, often subverting it. The plans for a detective novel in the making are less like blueprints than like travel notes set down as you once revisited a city. The city had changed since you saw it last. It keeps changing around you. Some of the people you knew there have changed their names. Some of them wear disguises.

Take for exmaple Dr. Dawson who lost a game of pool to Tom in Version One and became, in Version Two, a Mr. Sablacan waiting for Willie at the Royal York. In my final notes and in the novel itself he has become Gordon Sable, identifiable with his earlier personae by his name and by the fact that, like Dr. Dawson, he wears a suit with a wicked red pin-stripe in it. His occupation has changed, and his function in the novel has expanded. Gordon Sable is the attorney who hires Lew Archer on Mrs. Galton's behalf to look for her lost son Anthony.

Archer and Gordon Sable know each other. The nature of their relationship is hinted at by a small incident on the first page of the novel. A line of it will illustrate some of the implications of style, which could be described as structure on a small scale. Archer sits down on a Harvard chair in Gordon Sable's office and then gets up. "It was like being expelled."

In a world of rich and poor, educated and disadvantaged, Archer's dry little joke places him on the side of the underdog. It suggests that he is the kind of man who would sympathize with the boy impostor waiting in the wings. And of course it speaks for the author—my own application for a graduate fellowship at Harvard was turned down forty years ago—so that like nearly everything in fiction the joke has a private side which partly accounts for its having been made. The University of Michigan gave me a graduate fellowship in 1941, by the way, and my debt to Ann Arbor is duly if strangely acknowledged in the course of John Brown, Jr's story.

Deeper dimensions

Detective stories are told backward, as well as forward, and full revelation of the characters and their lives' meanings is deferred until the end, or near the end. But even deeper structural considerations require the main dynamic elements of a story to be laid in early. For this and other reasons, such as the further weight and dimension imparted by repetition, it is sometimes a good idea to let a character and his story divide. One part or aspect of him can perform an early function in the story which foreshadows the function of his later persona, without revealing too much of it.

John Brown, Jr., as I've already said, doesn't enter the story until it is one-third told. I decided, though hardly on the fully conscious level, to provide John with a stand-in or alter ego to pull his weight in the early part of the narrative. When I invented this other boy, and named him Tom Lemberg, I had totally forgotten that Tom was the name of the boy in Version One who beat Dr. Dawson at pool. But here he is in the novel: an earlier stage in the development of my boy imposter. A specimen of fiction, like a biological specimen, seems to recapitulate the lower stages of its evolution. I suspect Tom had to be brought in to validate my novel, proving that I had touched in order all the bases between life and fiction. At any rate the book comes alive when Archer and Tom Lemberg, two widely distinct versions of the author, confront each other in Chapter Five.

This confrontation with Tom of course prefigures Archer's confrontation with the boy impostor John. Tom serves an even more important purpose at the beginning of the book, when he is held responsible for the murder of Peter Culligan. The structure of the story sufficiently identifies Culligan with the wino father, so that Culligan's death parallels and anticipates the final catastrophe. Like the repeated exile of Oedipus, the crucial events of my novel seem to happen at least twice. And like a young Oedipus, Tom is a "son" who appears to kill a "father," thus setting the whole story in circular motion.

I have told a little too much of that story for comfort, and a little too much of my own story. One final connection between the private story and the public one should suffice. When Archer opens the dead Culligan's suitcase, "Its contents emitted a whiff of tobacco, sea water, sweat, and the subtler indescribable odor of masculine loneliness." There were the smells, as I remembered and imagined them, of the pipe-smoking sea-captain who left my mother and me when I was about the age that grandson Jimmie was when he became a monster in my poor castle, and then a laughing boy, and fell asleep.

What do you mean, "gothic"?

by Phyllis Whitney

The American Heritage Dictionary puts it very well: "Of or pertaining to a literary style of fiction prevalent in the late 18th and early 19th centuries which emphasized the grotesque, mysterious, and desolate." Remember all those desolate moors in *Wuthering Heights*? Remember the hidden mad woman in *Jane Eyre*, and the sense of brooding mystery in both novels? Those were gothics, built on the foundation of the earlier *Castle of Otranto*.

Today a modern emergence of the gothic has developed into a genre of its own. Another name for it is the romantic suspense novel, which some of us prefer. Daphne duMaurier unquestionably started the modern version with *Rebecca* and *My Cousin Rachel*, and she has made her own public bows to Jane Eyre and Mr. Rochester. However, there was no great stir in the genre until the early '50s when Mary Stewart and Victoria Holt, encouraged by women who had the foresight to believe there was a good market for this type of book, made spectacular successes with *Nine Coaches Waiting*, *Mistress of Mellyn*, and other titles, building toward the explosion which was to follow.

Nevertheless, my own books, and the other occasional romantic suspense novels appearing in hardcover, were mostly ignored and seldom appeared in softcover. Then in 1960 one softcover editor, starting a romantic suspense series, called his books "gothics" and lightning struck. The softcover field opened up to all of us because readers out there wanted more, and they are still wanting more all these years later.

Phyllis Whitney, author of Spindrift *and more than 55 books, attributes some of her great success to a basic formula: write eight pages a day of emotional stories of women in peril. An average press run on a typical Whitney gothic is 800,000 copies, giving credence to her statement, "I'm an entertainer." She continues to write one juvenile and one adult book a year.*

Credible crises

The well-written gothic is clearly one of the most lucrative and enduring lines in all hard- and softcover fiction. Where the standard murder mystery is fortunate if it sells 7,500 copies in hardcover, a first-rate gothic in the hands of an established and skillful writer will sell 100,000 in hardcover and millions in softcover. Hardcover success is vital: it brings major bookclub exposure (and money!), as well as newspaper and magazine review coverage. But there is also a strong welcome for the *good* softcover original if it is not one of the cheaper imitators, which never sell as well.

Gothics are thriving in the British markets too, and in all languages around the world. They are written mainly by women for women, but a remarkable number of men readers also enjoy them, as I know from my own fan mail, and a number of men writers have hidden behind feminine names to cash in on what began as a success created and developed by women. A few men have even been brave enough to write them under their own names.

There is an excellent reason for the extraordinary popularity of romantic suspense. Exciting storytelling is perennially popular, and story is the essence of the gothic. The story must never be predictable, but build through an ever-deepening series of credible crises—often emotional—to an overwhelming climax and a genuine suprise at the conclusion that may fool even the seasoned mystery writer. Its appeal is honest entertainment and once-upon-a-time story magic, and readers surfeited with phony sex and violence welcome it. For gothics, like any other successful fiction, require absolute emotional involvement on the part of the reader with characters whose very real problems must be satisfyingly resolved.

Not that there isn't sex in these books. It smoulders in *Jane Eyre*, but it is subtle, not explicit: the imagination can often do a better job with the implied than with what is spelled out. Violence has its place, but not violence for its own sake, and its bloodier aspects are usually kept offstage. Anticipated terror is the bedrock of the story, and its promise must be fulfilled in a dramatic climax where death threatens. The "chase" scene is almost always essential, even more than it may be in a straight mystery.

As in the gothics of the last century, backgrounds are tremendously important. Often the setting is a real place. Foreign backgrounds are much in demand, as are interesting parts of the United States that have some exotic or different atmosphere to offer. As an American writer in a field crowded by English writers, I decided to make a virtue of background and atmosphere. I began to use foreign settings from the viewpoint of an American heroine, and readers seemed to like it. When I write about a place that is new to me, I read extensively about it before I travel there. Then I make copious notes on-scene and take color snapshots. When I write, it is always from the viewpoint of strangers to the locality—that being my own legitimate viewpoint—though of course people of the locality come into the story. On the other hand, if you can't make a trip to far places, the background can often be acquired through careful research. Superficial research always shows, I'm afraid.

Sensory details are important—what the main character can see, hear, smell, taste, touch. Not only the outdoors, but houses, rooms, furniture, clothes— everything that makes up *particular* background details—are richly presented, and enjoyed by feminine readers.

Period lends itself nicely to the genre, but it can be equally compelling in modern dress if the brooding old house, the atmosphere of mystery, the sense of a terrible unknown threat are there.

Emotional mysteries

Of course we have romance, and the hero often looks to Mr. Rochester, Heathcliff, and Maxim de Winter as his ancestors. The writer plays variations as far as possible, and sometimes this brooding, dark-browed figure is the hero, and sometimes he's the villain, but we like to have him there. (On occasion he can even be blond!) He's apt to be pretty much a chauvinist, neatly captured by the spunky heroine.

One difference between the romantic suspense story and the standard mystery is that the police seldom put in an appearance. There may well be a murder in the past or in the present—and the fear of violence is always there—but if the police are called in, we don't dwell on procedure or on the details of detecting. It is the "civilians," not the police, who matter, and they don't sit around examining clues in the usual sense. Sometimes it is convenient to have the murder look like an accident, or even have it take place before the story begins, so we can get away from police business that may hold up the forward action. Gothics are true mysteries, but they are never detective stories. If there is any detecting, it's apt to be in the hands of a lady whose standing is strictly amateur, and she is usually out to solve the mystery of her own predicament.

The basic difference between the romantic suspense novel written for women, and the suspense novel intended primarily for men is that the male reader wants hard, fast, violent action and emotional turmoil may leave him cold. The female reader is often more interested in psychological conflict and the interplay of character. A suspenseful scene can take place between two people sitting in a drawing room if there is an honest confrontation involving an issue of substance, and if there is real uncertainty about its outcome. Of course there are scenes of exciting action in gothics too, but they are interspersed with people-conflicts that may not be merely physical. Happenings grow out of what the people are, as in all good fiction, rather than from outside elements.

The heroine usually starts out in a moment of crisis in her life, facing serious trouble and with a big problem to be solved. There must be something of importance at stake. She is often arriving in a new place with which she is unfamiliar—a place that is clearly to decide her future destiny. But beware of that plane about to land. We've all used that too many times.

In a sense, the gothic heroine is your truly liberated woman. Jane Eyre was fighting for independence and social change long before Gloria Steinem. Our heroine is courageous, struggling valiantly against great odds, although of course she may have moments of fear and trembling when she is quite willing to fall into the rescuing arms of the hero. Who of us isn't?

Headstrong heroines

Which brings us to the everlasting pitfall that lies in the path of the gothic writer: how to get the heroine *into* trouble without having her seem foolhardy by rushing into situations of danger—as she must do—when if she had any sense she'd stay quietly at home and mind her own business, giving us no story at all. Personally, I fret under this objection of some critics. My heroines *are* reckless, headstrong, and determined to fight for what they want. I'd like to claim equal rights for them with the male heroes of suspense novels who are always going off alone into dangerous situations without anyone complaining. But there it is—discrimination— and so you'd better give that girl an awfully good reason for doing what she does and make it clear that she really isn't an idiot.

The heroine must be admirable, appealingly vulnerable to honest emotional stress—in a word, a true individual, or your reader won't care what happens to her. Though happy endings are in order, since this is intentional escape fiction, your heroine must deserve her reward at the end of the story, whatever it is. And she had better have her own goals and solve her own problems, even if the hero comes along at the climax to rescue her physically.

First person telling is favored to a great extent by most readers. Though there is no taboo against third person if you prefer it, the sense of reader participation is greater in the first person. Real feeling, real emotion can usually be better conveyed when an "I" is talking. Readers also prefer a single viewpoint: jumping from one character to another can break the line of emotional suspense in the genre, perhaps more than in others. But anything goes if you do it well.

As for technique, all the tricks and devices and efforts to fool the reader of any mystery story can and should be used. There must be suspense and a sense of immediacy in every chapter. Trouble is always *now*, and it must deepen in intensity. Obviously, characterization should have as much dimension as you can bring to it, and the writing should be the best of which you are capable. The gothic is for fun, it is entertainment, but the successes in the field are well written and please even the discriminating reader. In its own palatable way, the genre may even have some comment to make from time to time of current or past society.

To write gothics successfully, I believe you must enjoy reading them. These are not books you can write with tongue in cheek and one hand lashed behind your back, patronizing your reader. Respecting what you and others write in your own field, respecting your reader, is probably Rule One for any writer.

Will the gothic last? Well, it's been around almost as long as the novel itself, and within the boundaries of that mysterious and desolate landscape endless variations are possible. The rewards for the writer are satisfying: loyal readers and generous checks.

Horror stories and the ten bears

by Stephen King

At parties, people usually approach the writer of horror fiction with a mixture of wonder and trepidation. They look carefully into your eyes to make sure there's no overt bloodlust in them, and then ask the inevitable question: "I really liked your last story . . . where do you get your ideas?"

That question is common to any writer who works in a specialized genre, whether it's mystery, crime, western or science fiction. But it's delivered in different tones for different fields. It's directed to the mystery writer with real admiration, the way you'd ask a magician how he sawed the lady in half. It's directed to the science fiction writer with honest respect for a fellow who is so farseeing and visionary. But it is addressed to the horror writer with a sense of fascinated puzzlement—the way a lady reporter might ask mild-mannered Henri Landru how it feels to do away with all those wives. Most of us, you see, look and seem (and *are*) perfectly ordinary. We don't drown houseguests in the bathtub, torture the children, or sacrifice the cat at midnight inside of a pentagram. There are no locked closets or screams from the cellar. Robert Bloch, author of *Psycho*, looks like a moderately successful used car salesman. Ray Bradbury bears an uncomfortable resemblance to Charles M. Schulz, creator of *Peanuts*. And the writer generally acknowledged to be the greatest master of the horror tale in the twentieth century, H.P. Lovecraft, looked like nothing so much as a slightly overworked accountant.

Constructive therapy

So where do the ideas—the *salable* ideas—come from? For myself, the answer

---

Stephen King has parlayed America's love/hate conflict with horror stories into a successful enterprise. His books Carrie *and* The Shining *were both adapted for movies, and* Firestarter *has been on the bestseller lists. In 1980 he completed the screenplay for* The Stand *and* Danse Macabre, *a nonfiction study of horror in the media. King has also written many short stories with a horror theme.*

is simple enough. They come from my nightmares. Not the night-time variety, as a rule, but the ones that hide just beyond the doorway that separates the conscious from the unconscious. A good assumption to begin with is what scares you will scare someone else. A psychologist would call these nightmares phobias, but I think there's a better word for our purposes.

Joseph Stefano, who wrote the screenplay for *Psycho* and who produced a mid-'60s television series called *The Outer Limits*, calls these fears "bears." It's a good term for the aspiring writer of horror fiction to use, because it gets across the idea that general phobias have to be focused on concrete plot ideas before you can hope to scare the reader—and that's the name of the game. So before we go any further, let's take a few bears—ones we're all familiar with. You may want to rearrange some of the items on my list, or throw out a few and add some of the skeletons in your own closet. But for purposes of discussion, here is my own top ten:

1. Fear of the dark
2. Fear of squishy things
3. Fear of deformity
4. Fear of snakes
5. Fear of rats
6. Fear of closed-in places
7. Fear of insects (especially spiders, flies, beetles)
8. Fear of death
9. Fear of others (paranoia)
10. Fear *for* someone else

The bears can be combined, too. I took a #1 and #10 and wrote a story called "The Boogeyman," which sold to *Cavalier* magazine. For me, fear of the dark has always focused on a childhood fear: the awful Thing which hides in the closet when you're small, or sometimes curls up under the bed, waiting for you to stick a foot out under the covers. As an adult looking back on those feelings (not that we ever conquer them completely—all those of you out there who don't have a bedroom lamp within reach of your hand please stand up), it seemed to me that the most frightening thing about them was the fact that grown-ups don't understand them very well—they forget how it is. Mother comes in, turns on the light, smiles, opens the closet (the Thing is hiding behind your clothes, well out of sight—it's sly) and says, "See, dear? There's nothing to be afraid of." And as soon as she's gone, the Thing crawls back out of the closet and begins to leap and gibber in the shadows again. I wrote a story about a man who finds out that his three children, who have all died of seemingly natural causes, have been frightened to death by the boogeyman—who is a very real, very frightening monster. The story takes a child-hood fear and saddles an adult with it, puts him back into that dreamlike world of childhood where the monsters *don't* go away when you change the channel, but crawl out and hide under the bed.

Once, when thinking of a story, I decided that the scariest things going would be rats—great big #5's, breeding in the darkness under a deserted textile mill. In this case, I began with the fear and built the plot (including the deserted mill) to fit it. The story climaxed with the main character being overwhelmed by these giant rats in the dark and enclosed subcellar of the mill (slyly hedging my main bet by working in a generous dose of #1 and #6). I felt sorry for the poor guy—the thought of being overrun by giant rats frankly made my blood run cold—but I made $250 on the sale and managed to take one of my own pet fears for a walk in the sun at the same time. One of the nice things about working in this field is that, instead of paying a shrink to help you get rid of your fears, a magazine will pay you for doing the same thing.

Weary werewolves

George Langlahan, a Canadian author, wrote a novelette called *The Fly*, using a #7 bear, made a sale to *Playboy*, and has since seen his bear made into three movies—*The Fly, The Return of the Fly*, and *The Curse of the Fly*. The late John W. Campbell wrote a cracking good horror story in the early '50s called "Who Goes There?" using a #2 bear which turns out to be a sort of walking vegetable from another planet. The story was turned into a classic horror movie called *The Thing*. Hollywood has always understood the principle of working from the bear out—surrounding a basic fear with a plot, rather than the other way around. Edgar Allan Poe wrote the same way, and suggested again and again in his literary essays that the only way to write a short story was to begin with the effect and then work your way out.

The would-be writer of horror stories may be tempted to stop right here and say: That's a lousy list of bears, fella. There isn't a werewolf or a vampire to be had. True enough. Not even an escaped mummy hunting for tanna leaves. My humble advice is to leave these bears to their well-deserved rest. They've been done to death. There are undoubtedly a few twists left in the Old Guard, but not many. Even the endlessly proliferating comics market is turning away from them in favor of more contemporary subjects.

Another caution is in order at this point: Don't think that because you have selected a scary bear, the rest of the story will be a snap. It won't be. Horror isn't a hack market now, and never was. The genre is one of the most delicate known to man, and it must be handled with great care and more than a little love. Some of the greatest authors of all time have tried their hands at things that go bump in the night, including Shakespeare, Chaucer, Hawthorne ("My Kinsman, Major Molinaux" is a particularly terrifying story, featuring a #9 bear), Poe, Henry James, William Faulkner ("A Rose for Emily"), and a score of others.

So where is the horror market today? For straight fiction, it's mainly in the men's magazines. But the writer who feels he can approach *Playboy* or *Cavalier* or *Penthouse* with 1930s-style blood-pulp-and-sex meller is going to find the market has progressed beyond that to a reasonable point of sophistication—good for the professional who wants to work seriously in the genre, bad for the amateur who thinks he can mix a couple of sea monsters with an Atlantic City beauty contest and come up with a few hundred bucks. Here are a few practical hints on selling horror to the men's magazines:

1. **Don't feel obligated to add sex to your story if there isn't a sex angle there to begin with.** We've both been to the corner drugstore and know that pin-ups are a stock in trade, along with articles that deal with the sex life of the American male. But a fair proportion of the fiction steers clear of women entirely, dealing with "escape" subjects instead: survival situations, science fiction, crime, suspense . . . and horror.

2. **Read the market**. To be perfectly blunt, your chances of selling a story to a men's magazine you haven't read are probably no more than 2%, even if your story

is another "The Lottery." Get rid of the idea that all men's magazines are the same. Find out who is buying stories from two to four thousand words, who is buying out-and-out fantasy, who has a penchant for psychological horror, who is publishing good stories by people you never heard of.

3. Take a hard, critical look at your own story. Try to decide if it's better, worse, or about equal to the fiction being published in the magazine you're considering. The realization that your brainchild may not be up to *Playboy*'s standards may be a bitter pill, but it's better than wasting postage in a lost cause—especially when you could be selling your story to another editor.

4. Throw away Poe and Lovecraft before you start. If you just screamed in agony, wait a minute and let me expand a little on this one. If you're interested in the horror story to begin with, you were (and possibly still are) an avid reader of Edgar Allen Poe and Howard Philips Lovecraft. Both these fine writers were rococo stylists, weaving words into almost Byzantine patterns. Both wrote some excellent short-short stories ("The Tell-Tale Heart" by Poe can be read in ten minutes, and Lovecraft's "In the Tomb" is not much longer—yet the effect of both stories is never forgotten), but both did their finest work in longer form. The men's magazines usually don't buy novelettes. The average length of accepted fiction is 2,500-4,000 words. Neither will they buy much, if any, fiction written in the styles of Poe or Lovecraft. In spite of the antique charm both hold for modern readers, most editors regard the style as outdated and bankrupt. If you're still screaming and cradling your wounded manuscripts, I'm sorry. I'm only telling the truth. If it's Poe or Lovecraft, send it to a fanzine and be content with your contributor's copies.

A great many writers begin with the mistaken notion that "the Lovecraft style" is essential to success in the field. Those who feel this way no doubt pick up the idea by reading the numerous Lovecraft-oriented anthologies on sale. But anthologies are not magazines, and while the idea is no small tribute to H.P.L.'s influence on the field, it's simply not so. If you're looking for alternatives (ones that are adaptable to the men's magazine format), I'd recommend John Collier, Richard Matheson, Robert Bloch (who began as a Lovecraft imitator and has made a successful switch to a more modern style), and Harlan Ellison. All of these writers have short story anthologies on the market, and a volume of each makes a wonderful exercise book for the beginner.

5. When your story is ready for rewrite, cut it to the bone. Get rid of every ounce of excess fat. This is going to hurt; revising a story down to the bare essentials is always a little like murdering children, but it must be done. If the first draft runs 4,000 words, your second should go about 3,000. If the first is around 3,000, you can still probably get down to about 2,500 by tightening up the nuts and bolts. The object here isn't to shorten for the sake of shortening but to speed up the pace and make the story fly along.

To market, to market

Many men's magazines, a few smaller and more specialized publications and a number of literary/little magazines are excellent markets for the beginning horror writer. They often need lots of material, and most of them could care less if you're an unknown. If your story is good, and if you pick the right market, you can make a sale.

Some of the possible horror markets in magazines (mostly men's) include: *Dude, Gallery, Gent, Hustler, Mink, Nugget, Penthouse, Playboy, Rustler* and

Starwind. Check the *Fiction Writer's Market* index for a more complete list, including smaller and/or non-paying publications, and be sure to look up each one's individual specifications before submitting a manuscript. *Penthouse, Playboy* and *Hustler* all pay well enough to attract "name" authors much of the time, and they do accept freelance on occasion. Probably the most useful thing I can say is don't bypass them if you think your story is really top-drawer stuff. Start at the top. You may find a healthy check from one of the best markets in your mailbox some morning.

Remember, people, as human nature dictates, have always loved a good horror story, and in these days when short magazine fiction has taken a backseat to nonfiction, it's good to know that, in this field at least, the beast is still alive and kicking. And snarling. And drooling. . . .

Plotting and characterization in the western novel

by Louis L'Amour

In the '40s, before Louis L'Amour achieved his great success as a western writer, he wrote two articles in which he explained his tenets for writing adventure stories. The following is a summary of his advice on plotting and characterization, basic reasons why L'Amour, next to Harold Robbins and Irving Wallace, is America's most widely printed novelist.

—The Editors

1. It is essential the adventure story begin with action or the events immediately preceding action.

In a fight you walk out and sock the other guy on the chin. That's exactly what you do in a story. Once a man is struck on the chin he is under no misapprehension. He's in a fight, and he knows it. So walk out in your story and hit your readers on the chin with the first paragraph.

You don't walk out and start telling the crowd all the events that led up to the fight. If you did, you'd get hit first and be counted out before you started. That is exactly what happens to writers who waste paragraphs at the beginning of a story building up to what is going to happen. Your reader is not interested in your telling him about what is going to happen. He wants to know what is happening now!

2. In the first paragraph, or as soon thereafter as possible, introduce your lead character and bring him on in action.

This action must be a part and parcel of the story. Don't have him busy with something that has nothing to do with the story. It is also advisable to present the

Louis L'Amour, author of over 80 novels under his own name and pseudonyms, was born in North Dakota, where his experiences in varied jobs served as background lore for his westerns. A self-educated, encyclopedic researcher, L'Amour is a renowned storyteller who has chronicled the pains and joys of a growing nation in such western classics as Hondo, How the West Was Won *and* The Quick and the Dead.

situation, or part of it, or a hint of it, in the first paragraph.

For several months *Popular Western* carried stories of mine about a Texas Ranger known as Chick Bowdrie. The following opening is my own use of introducing the lead character in the first paragraph and bringing him on in action. Frankly, I think I've done this better in other stories, but it is an illustration:

> The slim, broad-shouldered young man with the dark Apache face was riding warily. Only a moment before he had been dozing in the saddle, weary after the long miles behind, and then a sudden tensing of the hammer headed roan he was riding snapped him out of it.

Not only have you met the lead character, but he is brought on in action, and a dangerous situation is pending.

In another story of this series the lead character is introduced in the second paragraph, but here is the opening:

> There were two bullet holes in the bank window and the blood was still on the hitching rail where the cashier had fallen while trying to get in a last shot. Lem Pullitt had died there on the ground, but not before telling how he had been shot when his hands were up.

As you see, while the lead character is not introduced until the next paragraph (and he is brought on in action) this first paragraph puts you right in the middle of something.

3. The Opening introduced your lead character and brought him on in action. Your Situation introduces the other characters and sets forth the circumstances that pose the problem.

The situation of a story comprises two things, actually. To me it includes both the locale of the story—the immediate locale, that is—and the situation in which the characters find themselves.

To expand a bit, it is the situation of the characters in reference to each other, and to their physical environment.

The second paragraph of the story above brings Chick Bowdrie on the scene and brings him on in action. In the third paragraph, the situation is set forth and the problem presented:

> "It smells," he muttered, striking a match on the rail. "Somebody wanted him to die, or else the hombre was a cold-blooded killer. I don't savvy why, but she smells."

Bowdrie's problem is to find out what was wrong, and exactly what happened.

The situation will occasionally be set forth immediately; in other cases it will develop and become more clearly outlined as the story moves along. If you haven't presented your opposing character (the term *opposing* seems more fitting here than the word *villain*, as in many stories the opposing character, the one who opposes the hero, is not a villain) in the opening paragraph, it is well to get him on the scene at once.

If you have presented your situation as it should be, *the problem will be the natural result.*

Therefore, you must move from your situation into your problem as from cause to effect. The one is the natural, unavoidable result of the other.

It seems peculiar, but many beginning writers do not realize that a story must have a problem. It must be *about* something, and something must be solved by its action.

In other words, your lead character becomes aware of a situation that is painful or dangerous to him or to someone he loves or respects. He sets out to change that condition, to remove the pain or the danger and its cause. It is the process of doing this that makes the story.

Your problem must be of life and death importance to the lead character. Moreover, you must make him *feel* its importance. That is why most crime stories involve a murder. The average reader cannot be too much impressed by the absolute necessity of capturing a thief. There has to be a reason for your hero to stick his neck out. Nobody goes around walking into punches or ducking bullets for fun.

Right here is where I want to say something about suspense. That is the most important word in a writer's book. Your reader must be led to expect something to happen, he must be kept waiting (not too long) holding his breath, while that something is about to happen.

Your hero is an attractive, appealing person. This must be so. Being so, the reader's heart is with him. His pulse beats more rapidly as the hero nears danger, fear comes to the reader as well.

Now your hero has his problem. Here is where you need your suspense and lots of it. There must be danger. There must be menace. In his first attempt to cope with the problem, he may fail. This is always an advantage in creating suspense as it makes the solution of the problem more remote. It increases the lead character's desperation, and as a result, your own anxiety.

4. To heighten suspense, always express yourself in terms of feeling, of sight, sound and smell.

Prof. Walter Campbell of the University of Oklahoma School of Writing insisted that every sentence should contain both a *fact* and a *feeling*. Here are illustrations from my own work:

Chick *rode* with *caution.*

Chick *glanced* up and felt *a queer, cold feeling* flow over him.

The *wind* was an *icy blast* that *stung* their faces with frozen snow.

At times of great emotion or great danger the pace of life seems too slow, you become more sensitive to things. After a sudden fracas is over, you look around startled, and if there is a clock near, you'll be suprised to see what apparently took so long has happened in only a minute or two.

To create suspense the writer must do that same thing for his reader. Even as the man's whole mind is so keyed up that events seem to plod during moments of danger, so the writer must take the reader over his feelings and emotions. Your protagonist, your hero, must smell the damp earth, feel a faint breeze on his cheek.

5. Every line should point toward the end of the story, and nothing should be written that doesn't build toward the climax.

Someone said, Jack Woodford, I think, that if you had to describe a sunset, put it in a footnote. Nothing more intelligent has ever been said about writing fiction.

6. Get into your story, keep it moving in every line, and never let your reader's interest wane.

It is better to build everything, every emotion, every action in a steadily rising tempo.

This is a point I nearly forgot when doing a fight story called "The Greatest Fighter in the World." I had two of the best fighters in the world, a middle and a light heavyweight, fighting a battle without a referee. A grudge fight, but with rounds, seconds and a bell. But there was no limit, and they were fighting strictly for murder. If I do say so myself, it was a honey of a scrap.

Rarely do I get carried away with anything I'm writing myself. In that fight I certainly did. I finished it off, then had to go look in the mirror to see how many teeth I'd lost in the process. But suddenly I was faced with an awful realization! That fight wasn't the climax of the story. To keep interest mounting, to keep the story building to a climax, and to prevent the reader from feeling that the last fight in the story was an awful letdown, I would have to write the last one much better!

The point is, don't shoot the works in the beginning and have nothing left for the final rounds. You must bring your story to a smashing climax, so be careful to build gradually toward that climax.

7. Make your summary brief; at the end, a snap line. If possible, leave them with a smile, laugh, or a chuckle.

If you have written a satisfactory climax, your end will come naturally.

Finally, throughout your story, remember a very important point: Every story is a story of character. Five methods are usually used to express and develop character in fiction, and might be described as character development by Explanation, Speech, Action, Reaction, and Effect.

1. Explanation. In delineating the character by explanation, the author himself explains the character by a description of his appearance, dress, mannerisms, attitude, speech and background or any part of these phases.

Although all of us use this first method of presenting characters—by describing them ourselves for the reader—it is a method which the beginner frequently overuses. The beginner does this so often that the editor considers it his hallmark.

Here is a paragraph from my story "Old Doc Yak," published in *New Mexico Quarterly Review*:

> He was a man without humor. He seemed somehow aloof, invulnerable. Even his walk was pompous and majestic. He strode with the step of kings and spoke with the voice of an oracle, entirely unaware that his whole being was faintly ludicrous, that those about him were always suspended between laughter and amazed respect.

Another danger to be avoided in presenting character by this method is a letdown after presentation. For instance, the above character must immediately speak and act to illustrate the author's description.

Brevity is the quality most to be sought in illustrating a character by explanation.

2. Speech. Character is illustrated through speech. "As a man speaketh, so is he." By dialogue the story is advanced while the speech itself describes your character.

Certain actions or speeches such as the Lone Ranger's "Hi, ho, Silver!" or Sherlock Holmes's "Elementary, my dear Watson" are now symbols known to millions.

The characterization of Holmes is also established by his playing of a violin while solving crimes, his deer stalker's cap and his pipe. Your reader learns much about your character from his words, but he will also learn from his dress and from his actions, and the effect he has upon those around him.

3. Action. We know people by their responses to situations. Character may be betrayed by small things as well as great. Little, unconscious gestures or mannerisms may reveal a feeling or an uncertainty.

Every action, no matter how seemingly unimportant, is an expression of character. The failure to act may be a more perfect illustration of character than an action.

In real life, character is a variable and plastic thing, yet not so much so as is often believed. For the purpose of the novel the writer may use a variable character. In a short story it's a dangerous thing to do, for the secret of the short story is single effect, and the writer has no time within the limitations of the form to present many variations in character.

The dominant character trait and the single effect are the standard techniques of the shorter forms of fiction.

4. Reaction. We may illustrate character by showing the reactions of the character to people and situations. Here, in a quotation from a *Saturday Evening Post* serial "Murder For Millions," is an excellent paragraph of characterization by Nancy Rutledge:

> Father. Everlastingly, father. Sometimes Chad *hated* Horace Trimbal even more in death than in life. Almost he could hear Horace's chuckle, malicious and a little dry.

The first three words are an obvious expression of irritation, sharpened by the word *hated*, betraying his true feeling for the old man he has murdered but whose spirit persists in confronting him on every hand.

5. Effect. Many characters are most plainly seen through their effect upon those around them.

An example of this is my own story "Dutchman's Flat" which appeared in *Giant Western*. The protagonist does not show himself in person until the very end of the story. Until that time he is seen entirely through the eyes of others. Lock, a stranger in the country, has killed a man friendly to the local ranchers and they are out to find him and hang him if he is not killed in being taken.

They believe him to be a no-good specimen and possibly a rustler. They also believe that he shot their friend in the back. As they ride along, following his trail, the true pattern of Lock's character becomes manifest. He is no tenderfoot; he thinks of his horse; at one point he could have killed several of them and he did not. Later, they find a spring he had walled up. It is not the act of a shiftless man, but of one who thought of others, of one who planned ahead. Gradually, despite themselves, they began to have a grudging admiration for him. He deliberately makes pursuit easy, he prepares a fire for them, leads them to water, he deliberately breaks branches and drops them in the trail, and he marks arrows in the sand. It irritates them, angers some of them, but despite that the feeling gradually works into their minds that Lock is not the sort of man to shoot another in the back, and before their final meeting with him they are ready to listen to his side of things.

The five methods of characterization listed do not give the writer a knowledge of character. For that he must go to school to life itself. There is no other way.

If you devote a lot of time to the study of characters, someday you may overhear someone talking of you, and they will say, "Him? Oh, he's a character!"

Where do you get those crazy ideas?

by James Gunn

Science fiction is often called a literature of ideas. No one should be surprised, then, to learn that the most important part of writing a science fiction story is getting a good idea; and that the question laymen always ask science fiction writers is, "Where do you get those crazy ideas?"

That's us—the people with the crazy ideas. It's no use saying, "You mean crazy ideas like atomic energy, space travel, overpopulation, pollution, automation, catastrophes, holocausts, technological change, evolution, and all the other limitless possiblities in a universe which may be infinite and possibly eternal?" It doesn't even do any good to ask, "How can you keep from having crazy ideas when you are living in a world that is changing while you look at it? How can you avoid wondering what will happen next when life is one surprise after another? How can you avoid speculating about the direction change is heading and where it will take us and how this will affect the way people live and feel and behave?"

So I just shrug and say, "Oh, crazy ideas come easy when you're in the business."

This business—crazy ideas—has become the last frontier of the short story writer. Anyone who wants to begin writing by selling short stories, which is much the easiest way to begin, had better try to write science fiction, because that's one of the few markets left. There may be about three detective magazines still, but one of the biggest markets for short fiction in this country still is the half dozen or so science fiction magazines and the ten to 20 or more original science fiction anthologies.

James Gunn has taught fiction writing and the literature of science fiction at the University of Kansas. He is widely known in the science fiction field for his nonfiction articles, novels, novelettes, and short stories, many of which have been reprinted internationally and dramatized on radio and TV. He is a past president of the Science Fiction Writers of America.

Even in the field of the novel, science fiction has passed the western and is creeping up on the mystery.

Moreover, science fiction always has been peculiarly receptive to the beginning writer.

Write 'em down—fast

If people persist in asking where I get my crazy ideas, I usually dig deeper into what some authorities call creativity and what I call habit. Noticing the fictional possibilities in the information that flows into my head has become a pattern of behavior: "What a great idea for a story!"

Ideas, of course, are not unique to science fiction. Every story, of any kind, demands an idea, though it may be less specific, less speculative. Students in my fiction writing classes with some writing experience generalize their complaint. "I can't come up with anything to write about," they say. That's another way of asking, "How do you get an idea?"

That's such a preposterous complaint that I usually begin by saying to them the same thing I say to the laymen: "How do you avoid getting ideas?" I have card files stuffed with ideas for stories, and desk drawers jammed with story ideas jotted down on odd scraps of paper. I'll never have time to get to all of them, not even to ten percent of them. The problem of every real writer is not getting ideas but finding the time to write.

I admit that this answer is a bit unfair. It wasn't always this way with me. I tell my students about the second time I turned to freelance writing. It was more serious this time: now I had a wife and a child; I wasn't experimenting but trying to make a career of it. I returned from a trip to New York City where I had been talking to editors; I had a couple of story ideas and a panicky feeling that I might never have another. That was the moment when I began jotting down every idea that occurred to me. Soon I had a stack of them and I never panicked again. About that.

That leads me to a point I should make early: write ideas down. A few words are enough. The idea that comes to you at an odd moment, as you are reading or watching something happen outside your window or listening to a lecture or lying awake in bed at night or dreaming, the idea that seems so magnificent and unforgettable, will vanish within hours, even minutes, never to be recalled—unless it is written down. All of them will not seem as wonderful when reread; many golden ideas turn into lead with the passage of time; but some will retain that magic ability to recreate excitement every time the author touches them. Those are the ones with the basic quality every idea for fiction should have: of impelling the writer toward the typewriter to turn them into story. Excitement, a glow in the stomach, a fire in the head—that's how a writer recognizes a good idea.

On speculation

But where does he get the idea in the first place? Since he is a writer, he reads—no one who isn't in love with reading should consider writing as a career or even an avocation—and he gets ideas as he reads. It doesn't matter whether it is fiction or nonfiction, a newspaper, a magazine or a book.

In science fiction, speculation about new developments in the hard or soft sciences is the source of many story concepts. Once this kind of speculation was more prevalent in the general magazines such as *Scientific American, Time,*

Newsweek, Saturday Review, or *Psychology Today*; the scientific journals were likely to leave the speculation to others. This is changing as science becomes more aware of its responsibilities and more willing to consider the consequences of its discoveries. An experienced science fiction writer can build his own speculative world on a bare description of some discovery, but most of us can benefit from the informed projections of other, more experienced minds.

Once scientists were not much good at speculation. To know too much about a subject inhibits the ability to think wild thoughts. But recent discoveries have shaken up the conservatives who used to feel that they knew not only most of what was known but at least the general nature of what could be known about their disciplines. New and unexpected breakthroughs in astronomy and physics, chemistry, biology and other sciences have loosened the chains of reality that bound the scientific imagination. Today the craziest ideas are being thought by astrophysicists such as Carl Sagan and Freeman Dyson.

Larry Niven got the basic idea for *Ringworld* from speculations by Dyson that a truly advanced civilization would be able to use all the energy radiated by its sun; it would be able to reconstruct the planets of that sun into a sphere completely enclosing the sun. The inhabitants would live on the inside of the sphere and not only enjoy all of the sun's energy but a vastly increased living area. Dyson's point was that such civilizations would be invisible in the visual spectrum, but would radiate the sun's energy as heat in the infrared; thus we might be able to detect advanced civilizations by picking up strong infrared where we could see no star.

The concept of the gigantic living space captured Niven's imagination. He changed it, however, into a gigantic ring—a slice from Dyson's sphere—a million miles wide and encircling the sun.

My novel *The Listeners* was inspired by reading Walter Sullivan's *We Are Not Alone*, a historical survey of efforts to communicate with other worlds and an account of speculation by astronomers, beginning in the late '50s, about the possibility of picking up communications from other intelligent creatures in the universe.

Mining stories from stories

A writer can even get ideas from encyclopedias, almanacs or statistical reports. I was reading an article about "Feeling" in the *Encyclopaedia Britannica*; it developed into an analysis of the various ways to be happy and ended with the final sentence, "But the true science of applied hedonics is not yet born." That statement expanded into my novel *The Joy Makers*.

I got the idea for a fantasy story called "The Beautiful Brew" from a Virgil Partch cartoon that showed two men looking at a mug of beer on which the foam has shaped itself into the bust and head of a girl. The caption was something like: "That guy really puts a head on a glass of beer."

Other people's stories also can be a rich source of ideas. The first few paragraphs of a popular story are intended to intrigue the reader, to draw him into the story; in addition they suggest what the story is going to be about, and in the best-crafted stories they *tell* the reader what is going to happen, how the story is going to end, but in such a way the reader doesn't understand. Often then, after reading the first few paragraphs of a story, I find myself thinking ahead; sometimes I'm wrong about how the story will develop, but then I have a story idea of my own. Or, as it often happens in science fiction, the reader may find himself disagreeing with the author's solution to a basic concept and use the author's situation to reach a different resolution, sometimes exactly the opposite, as Robert Heinlein's *Starship Troopers* inspired Gordon Dickson to write *Naked to the Stars* and Harry Harrison, *Bill, the Galactic Hero.*

Or the writer may take the emotional impact of a story and translate that into other situations, as I tried to do with the ending of Graham Greene's *The Heart of the Matter* in an otherwise totally dissimilar story called "The Power and the Glory."

Firsthand experience—first-rate source for ideas

Sometimes a writer may approach the problem of idea from the angle of story, that is, from the interrelationships of people. A human problem often can be intensified in a science fiction situation, or it can be considered more dispassionately in a cooler environment than our hot contemporary scene with all of its instant preconceptions and prejudices.

Thus a story of lovers may achieve new levels of emotion if they are separated by time rather than distance, as in Robert Heinlein's *The Door Into Summer*; or if one is a human being and the other is an android, as in Lester del Rey's "Helen O'Loy" or J.T. McIntosh's "Made in U.S.A." The generation gap may become more significant if parents are discovered plotting against their children, as in my story "The Old Folks," or if the son is a superman, as in Henry Kuttner's "Absalom"; and the problems of parenthood can be dramatized more effectively if the infant is an omnipotent superman, as in Kuttner's "When the Bough Breaks."

Possibilities such as these can occur to a writer while he is reading other kinds of literature, or while glancing over the feature and human interest stories in the day's newspaper. Such capsule stories about real human beings suggest to the writer what he can never satisfactorily invent: the fantastic variety of situations into which men and women can involve themselves, and the fantastic variety in which men and women exist.

Finally, the writer can get ideas from observation—by watching people, by listening to conversations, by absorbing the anecdotes of friends or relations . . . . Or, best of all, from personal experience, which is the writer's unique source of inspiration. It is all he ever has in the end, even in science fiction. One of my best-known stories, "The Misogynist," was based on my own experience with women. On an index card one day in 1950, I jotted down, "Women are aliens." Six months later, when I had come up with a viewpoint character and a way of handling the narration, I had a unique story.

A twist on the future

Science fiction has a great deal of concept sharing. It is a close community of writers, even of readers, and one writer will construct his story on another writer's premises or extrapolations. "Science fiction builds upon science fiction," Donald Wollheim wrote in his personal history of science fiction, *The Universe Makers.* Simply rewriting an old idea is worse than nothing; a writer must bring to his story some new vision, some different twist, which will reinvigorate the concept. Science fiction demands novelty; that is both its distinction for the reader and its problem for the writer.

Novelty is not always easy. In my illustrated history of science fiction, *Alternate Worlds,* I encompass all of the themes of science fiction in 14 phrases; 1)far traveling; 2)the wonders of science; 3)man and the machine; 4)progress; 5)man and his society; 6)man and the future; 7)war; 8)cataclysm; 9)man and his environment; 10)superpowers; 11)superman; 12)man and alien; 13)man and religion; and 14)miscellaneous glimpses of the future or the past. Within these broad categories, however, lie an infinity of unique perceptions about man and his racial possibilities.

Science fiction is "origin of species fiction," wrote English critic Edmund Crispin, and almost all of the concepts of science fiction have racial implications. Trivial topics have little success. Novelty and meaning, meaning and novelty—a new idea, a different perspective, significance . . . . The demands that science fiction makes on writers drain them, sometimes drive them into writer's blocks.

And yet a writer who is good enough can pick up an old idea and make it as good as new. Heinlein did that with a 1951 novel called *The Puppet Masters*, which took the old theme of invasion by alien monsters, made them parasites, and created an effective new story. In his collection of novellas, *Born With the Dead*, Robert Silverberg made brilliant new use of three old ideas: the revivification of the dead, the sun stopped in the heavens, and euthanasia.

Get fresh

Originality, however, is safest for the beginning writer. If he should be so incautious or so unaware as to submit a story about flying saucers, visitors from other worlds who turn out to be our ancestors, World War III, or even time travel, he is likely to receive in the return mail only a printed rejection slip, or at best a note reading, "Heinlein did it better." Young writers naturally begin with imitation; they get turned toward writing because they love reading and admire the work of particular writers. But the novice must break with the past; he must do his own thing rather than pale or inept reworkings. The new writer is wise to avoid ideas that end with classic revelations: the alien castaways on Earth who turn out to be Adam and Eve, the catastrophe that turns out to have destroyed Atlantis, the character sent to Earth (or out of the future) to save it from destruction who turns out to be Christ or Mohammed or Buddha . . . . David Gerrold wrote *The Man Who Folded Himself*, Michael Moorcock wrote *Behold the Man*, and most of us have tried our hand at old themes and done them badly or well, but the beginning writer should leave that practice for his more experienced, later incarnation. Harlan Ellison could take the old theme of the omnipotent computer that rebels against its human masters, that becomes a tyrannical God, and make it new again in "I Have No Mouth and I Must Scream"; that is no job for a novice.

The beginning writer should try to find a new perception. John Campbell, the late, long-time editor of the magazine that was born as *Astounding* and became *Analog*, said twenty years ago: "The reader wants the author to do one of two basic things—and prefers the author who does both. The author's function is to imagine for the reader, of course—but he must either (a) imagine in greater detail than the reader has, or (b) imagine something the reader hasn't thought of. Ideally, the author imagines something new, in greater detail."

Get a fresh idea. That demands a considerable familiarity with science fiction, of course, in order to identify what has been done before. A good place to start is the *Science Fiction Hall of Fame*, Volumes I and II, but there are other good anthologies. A hopeful writer of science fiction should have read everything he could find—short stories, novels, magazines, books . . . . Then he may be ready to distinguish the old from the new, the bad from the good.

Detail work

Once the writer has a fresh idea, he should explore its implications; he should imagine it in depth, the way Hal Clement imagined the "whirligig world" of extremely high gravity where his *Mission of Gravity* took place; or Frederik Pohl and Cyril Kornbluth imagined the world controlled by advertising agencies that they created in *The Space Merchants*. Then the writer must imagine people trapped in that world, up against things, forced to do things they don't want to do or can't do, trying to adjust or trying to change the conditions.

In Tom Godwin's touchstone story "The Cold Equations," the pilot of an emergency delivery ship is forced to eject an innocent girl stowaway into airless space because otherwise the ship would crash and its essential cargo be lost. Where did he get that crazy idea? Perhaps by considering the traditional story in which women and children are saved first, no matter what the cost.

In John W. Campbell's novelette "Who Goes There?" a group of Antarctic scientists discover buried deep in the ice an alien monster that has the power to absorb any protoplasm and imitate it perfectly. Where did Campbell get the idea? He had written "The Brain Stealers of Mars" a few years before; it concerned the ability of Martian creatures to read minds and turn themselves into confusing duplicates. Campbell returned to the idea in "Who Goes There?" with a different setting and one small alteration: The imitated protoplasm must first be eaten.

Robert Heinlein's "Universe" begins with the idea of a spaceship which is a world in itself. Murray Leinster had described one in his "Proxima Centauri," but Heinlein added the facts that the ship must travel for generations to reach its goal and that a mutiny had destroyed awareness of mission and meaning until the survivors consider the ship to be the entire universe and their remembered history as parable.

In "A Martian Odyssey" Stanley Weinbaum asked whether aliens had to be unfriendly, and if an intelligent alien could not learn to communicate quickly with a reasonably intelligent human.

We know where Isaac Asimov got the idea for "Nightfall," the classic story in which a world is surrounded by six suns and a moon so that night falls only once every 2,050 years, at which time the inhabitants of that world go mad and burn their civilizations to make light. John Campbell challenged Asimov with a quotation from Emerson (Asimov used it as an epigraph to his story): "If the stars should appear one night in a thousand years, how would men believe and adore, and preserve for many generations the remembrance of the city of God!"

Murray Leinster took the old idea of "First Contact" with aliens and pointed out that it need not be a deadly encounter, no matter how much is at stake, even racial survival, if a trade-off can be conceived that is more profitable than conflict.

We might speculate that Arthur Clarke got the idea for "The Nine Billion Names of God" when he learned that Tibetan monks are trying to enumerate all the names of God as they spin their prayer wheels; when they have done so, the world will end. In Clarke's story they obtain a computer to do the job in 100 days instead of 15,000 years.

In 1941 Lester del Rey asked himself what would happen if something went wrong in an atomic factory; his answer was "Nerves." Cyril Kornbluth noted in 1951 that successful people were limiting their families, and unsuccessful people were not; he foresaw "The Marching Morons." In 1947 Jack Williamson wondered what a perfect machine would do to humanity, and visualized it doing everything so much better that mankind was left "With Folded Hands."

Horace Gold, founding editor of *Galaxy*, suggested to Fred Pohl that the problems of poverty might some day be supplanted by the problems of affluence; if you were poor you would have to consume more, and if you were rich you could afford to live simply. When Pohl solved the fictional problems, he wrote "The Midas Plague."

Character under stress

Not all stories can be reduced to this kind of simple summary, just as not all ideas can be traced to a single source. Many stories are either more complex or dependent upon mood or description or style. But somewhere there is an idea lurking behind the finished product, even if it is only an idea for a setting where something important or exciting must happen, or a character to whom something must happen, or a situation that places a character under stress.

Fiction, John Ciardi once said, is character under stress. It doesn't matter whether you start with the character and develop the stress that will peculiarly test that character, or if you start with the stress and invent a character who will be peculiarly tested by it.

My own definition of a short story is: "a piece of prose narrative about a human problem which is complicated by events and resolved satisfactorily." The problem must be *human*, or, in stories with protagonists who are animals or aliens, problems that we can imagine as human, with which we can identify; otherwise readers are uninvolved and uninterested. There must be a *problem*, or it is only a sketch or a description or an essay; to use the term "short story" for slice-of-life pieces only confuses matters, for then we must find another name for the narrative in which a problem occurs that a protagonist must solve; moreover, the two kinds of writing have different impacts upon the reader. The problem must be *complicated*—made more difficult, more urgent—and by *events*, not just reflection, because this process intensifies our concern about the person with the problem and builds up to a final payoff of satisfaction. The problem must be *resolved*, or we feel that the writer has promised us something he did not deliver; and it must be resolved *satisfactorily*—that is, the problem posed must be the one resolved, and the resolution must satisfy the promises the rest of the story has made.

The beginning writer will start with no idea, no problem, no sympathetic character; the events of his narrative will be haphazard rather than directed at complicating the story's problem, if there are any events; and if he has a resolution, it will not resolve the problem posed, or it will resolve it in a way that is cheap, easy, or out of character.

Acting it out

How, then, does the beginning writer recognize a good idea when it comes to him? First of all by its originality, second by the excitement it engenders in him to get to a typewriter, third by its ability to attract good characters, to collect places where the idea must happen, to end somewhere, to put characters under stress, to force characters to act, and finally to resolve itself.

A good idea becomes good fiction when it states itself in terms of human conflict; up to that time it is merely an interesting observation, such as "women are aliens," or "the advertising agencies are taking over the world," or "only persons willing to perform military service should be permitted to vote."

A person with a file drawer full of good ideas is not yet a writer; he must turn those ideas into stories. That requires some uncommon attributes. We hear, for instance, that writers are sensitive. Some are; some aren't. But every good writer is conscious of sensory stimuli. He is visually alert and aware of sounds and smells and tastes and the feel of things. He puts these things into his stories, when they are appropriate, when he is striving for verisimilitude, because he knows that no place exists in reality or in fiction without appearance, without sound and smell—and some cannot exist without taste or feel.

In addition, the writer must have certain skills, not only in the use of words but in the techniques of fiction. He should know the difference between summary and drama, what Carolyn Gordon and Allen Tate call the panorama and the scene. Panorama is the broad view generally encountered in a summary of events or in exposition; it is sometimes necessary but usually nondramatic. Scene is the close-up; it shows things happening before the reader's eyes; it is drama, and everything else is only preparation for it. Often the beginning writer summarizes everything, and ends up with a scenario. The experienced writer visualizes the action of the story happening in front of him like a stage play, and reports it to the reader as it happens. He writes in scenes; as Henry James urged, he doesn't tell—he shows.

The writer gets involved. Harlan Ellison says that when he is writing a story he paces around and acts out all the parts. I find myself gesturing and speaking bits of dialogue. Anyone passing by must think us strange indeed.

Take care with your characters

It helps a beginning writer to see the story's action as a struggle between a sympathetic character and his or her opposition, whether it is another character or a natural obstacle or conditions. Usually a character must accomplish something or take an action that is important to him. His coping, or being unable to cope, with the situation is what creates reader interest; the sophistication of the story emerges through the ingenuity of the situation, the cleverness of the resolution, the verisimilitude of the details, the subtlety of the presentation, the appropriateness and the wit of the language, and the validity of the observations of life and character.

I stress sympathy in character because too many beginning writers present characters who are at best passive and at worst unlikable or incompetent or uncaring or dull; we cannot become interested in them because we know from the beginning that they don't want anything we want, or if they do then they won't get it and the resolution will be obvious or omitted or invalid. I don't mean, of course, that they must be "nice" people or even "good" people; but they must be people whose problems we can imagine being involved in, no matter how outlandish, and whose responses to those problems we can understand. We can even use a character we dislike, whom we want to see fail, but he must be threatening someone we care about.

I also stress the importance of the action the character must take. Too often beginning writers set a task that is unimportant, often easily accomplished, for the characters; they don't care much about it, and the reader cares nothing at all.

Honor thy contract

Reader involvement is the only way to create a successful story. The writer establishes an implicit contract with every person he can induce to read his story:

you invest your money and your time, and I will entertain you in a certain way; I will show you a person whose situation will intrigue you, and I will show you that person coping or failing to cope with that problem in a way that will provide you with a pleasant suspense and a final satisfaction that is your reward for reading.

One reason fiction has been dying is that too many readers have been disappointed too often. They have become disillusioned by broken contracts.

All of this doesn't mean formula writing; or it means formula only insofar as life itself is a formula. Our main business in life is success, however we measure it; sometimes success is just survival, sometimes getting what we want or love and avoiding what we dislike or hate; sometimes it is finding what is important and real in life. But it all begins with birth and progresses through various stages until death ends it, and the various combinations are limited in broad outline. They move naturally—in a formula, if you will—through growing up, into adulthood and responsibility, to independence and the effort to get an appropriate share of the world's goods, to romance and the problems with love that does not endure, to the deterioration of the body and the mind which extends through middle age into senility. In between we have various subthemes such as the difficulties of communication, the search for meaning, and the battle between tradition and change. A formula is something that, like human experience, is infinitely repeated.

Heinlein has said that there are only three basic plots: 1)boy meets girl, the romance; 2)the little tailor, the character who must solve a problem; 3)the person who learns better, the character who believes one thing about himself or his world and learns that he has been wrong.

Plots can be sliced in other ways, depending upon the element one chooses to emphasize. One is the story of the child developing into an adult, the rite of passage; another, the revelation of the true nature of life or oneself, the story of sudden truth. And most stories involve several plot types: a romance within a problem story, for instance, and possibly the man who learns better as well.

What distinguishes a story from a sketch is that in a story something changes. Usually someone changes; but sometimes it is only his circumstances, as in the case of many adventure heroes—Conan or James Bond or Kimball Kinnison. But even in the most adventurous of stories, usually the protagonist has been changed by his experience, if only to the extent of satisfying, for the moment, his desire for adventure.

Checklist

Final recommendations for the beginning writer:

1. Begin with a worthwhile idea, preferably one that is fresh and new, but at least one that hasn't been exhausted.

2. Create characters who can ideally dramatize your idea. Make them suffer; make their suffering move them to action.

3. Plan out a scheme of action—a plot—that will present all the scenes necessary to show the characters working out their problem(s).

4. Omit everything that doesn't advance the plot—unnecessary scenes or casual conversation or pointless characters. Everything must work; everything must contribute. Ask yourself: If I leave this out, will it matter? If the answer is now, leave it out. Like a sculptor who creates a statue out of a block of stone by chipping away everything that isn't statue, remove everything from what you have written that isn't story.

5. Start your story in the middle of things, as Homer began the *Iliad*. This is the point where the problem of the story is stated; where characters are shown in the grip of the situation. Then, if you must, backtrack to exposition. Exposition is dead material, however, and is best integrated into the action of the story.

6. Avoid clichés in plot, characterization and phrasing. This is difficult for the beginning writer, because every writer begins as a reader in love with someone else's ideas. Learning to avoid the trite is half the task of learning to write.

7. Write in scenes; visualize them completely; bring in other sensory detail when possible.

8. Dramatize everything you can; try to eliminate everything that isn't dramatic.

9. Revise.

10. Submit what you have written for publication. Heinlein said this a long time ago; it's still true. You must aim at publication.

And if you find a new way to get crazy ideas, please let me know.

Slick versus confession

by Marguerite McClain

Like kids who unexpectedly say the darnedest things, story ideas can come at the darnedest times. A neighbor's chance remark over coffee, a tiny news item that pops into your vision as you are taking out the trash, a sudden insight into a personal problem while you are waiting for the traffic light to change can all fuel the inspirational rocket.

But before taking off into creative space it is necessary to aim at a specific market. A submission that fails to make contact with a slick magazine does not on the second try hit target at *True Story*.

A writer friend who had published in the women's "slicks" submitted one of her slick magazine story rejects to a confession magazine. It was a first person story, told from the point of view of a woman who is having an affair with a married man while at the same time maintaining a close friendship with his wife. Skillfully written, technically perfect, with an intriguing emotional problem—how could it miss?

The manuscript *did* make it up to the editor, who returned it with a note saying that she had enjoyed reading the story but that it was unsuitable for her magazine. She didn't explain why, but to anyone familiar with the requirements of the confession market the reasons were evident.

First of all, the story lacked confession *tone*. The narrator presented her situation without apology, making no effort to motivate her participation in an adulterous relationship. It is quietly implied in the story that love is reason enough to disregard moral principles.

Not so with the confession reader, who *must* condone the narrator's fall from

Marguerite McClain has had a long career in the confession field and sells consistently to the top confession magazines. She sold her first story at 20, and since then has published over 1,000 juvenile, suspense, fiction and nonfiction stories and articles. She has conducted a confession workshop at the University of Florida, and is an instructor in the Writer's Digest Correspondence School.

grace. It can't be written off as merely a sign of human weakness. In a confession story the narrator would have once been engaged to the man who is now her lover. They became separated through some twist of fate, but the narrator feels they still "belong to each other." It is unimportant that there is no logic to her rationaliza-tion. To the confession reader, fancy is bred in the heart, not in the head.

There would also have been an emotionally satisfying reason why the narrator is such a close friend of the wronged wife. Perhaps the wife is an alcoholic whose other women friends have deserted her. Without the narrator's frequent compan-ionship she would have no one of her own sex to turn to in order to ease her loneliness.

To the beginning confession writer this all sounds pretty corny. Most writers have been influenced by the current sophisticated approach to sexual mores and are therefore not particularly shocked at morally questionable situations. Toler-ance has replaced condemnation.

Confession "rules"

In the confession magazine, however, there is still the distinct line between good and evil. The transgressor must rationalize her actions (how can it be wrong to give him the sexual love he doesn't find at home?). She must suffer the pangs of guilt throughout the course of her wrongdoing, realize the error of her ways in a dramatic scene, and take her punishment.

There can be that well-known exception to the rule. But in taking a fast mental review of the stories I have written over the years I can't think of any deviations in the formula story. (There is also the non-formula story that we will touch upon later.) Motivation, guilt and punishment may be soft-pedaled as a concession to the times, but they're still there.

The confession reader is looking for a less sophisiticated treatment than is found between the covers of the slick women's magazine, where even the whole-some family type story places an emphasis on materialism. (Slick story Daddy is a lawyer; confession story Daddy drives a truck.) In my friend's story the woman narrator was an ad executive, who had stayed single through choice. Her lover was a bank director, and the two held their clandestine meetings in exclusive New York City bars as well as her Park Avenue apartment.

Confession lovers rendezvous in shabby little taverns and motels (at least those who are conducting shabby little affairs). At story end the narrator winds up with a shattered ego, a broken heart, and in one of my stories that I recall, a battered body.

In this particular story of mine, the married lover's two teenage children had caught on to the affair and gone to the narrator's apartment, where they proceed to beat the living daylights out of her. And did this victim of violence press charges against her attackers, thereby bringing the whole mess into the open and destroy-ing her lover's business, marriage, etc? What do *you* think?

Naturally she did what any typical confession narrator would do—she packed her suitcases and left town, sadder but infinitely wiser. And the confession reader could tell herself that she could understand why the poor thing had acted that way around a married man, only of course, it had been wrong, but now she's learned her lesson—and the sanctity of the home remains secure.

But back to my friend's story. The narrator, in addition to her lack of guilt regarding her affair, went through no period of suffering, and reaped no punishment. In the "turnover" (that scene in the story that causes a change in the main character's thinking thus "turning" the story) the wife confides to narrator her suspicions that husband is having an affair. Does her best friend think these suspicions could be true?

Best friend knows full well they're true. But there is no admission of guilt. In true slick story fashion, she keeps this knowledge to herself. She does, however, deem it prudent to call an end to the relationship with her married lover. At story end she is thinking a bit wryly that a certain era of her life is over.

The bare outline gives no indication of the beauty and sensitivity of the treatment of this story. It eventually was published in a local magazine that featured "quality" writing.

This does not mean that confession editors don't appreciate good writing. But their standards of excellence do not coincide with the standards of other publications. There are no subtleties, no characters whose actions are interpreted by the reader. Everything is "spelled out," leaving no doubt as to the story meaning.

While the subject matter in both slick and confession is similar, a serious problem (such as divorce, desertion or rape) is more apt to be handled as a nonfiction piece in the women's slicks. For example, in the May 1980 issue of *McCall's* is an article under the heading, "Sexual Freedom: The Medical Price Women Are Paying," dealing with the recent changes in sex attitudes and how they have affected women's health. In the confession magazine the same information would be detailed in a story, with the narrator relating her sexual experiments and how this experimentation has affected her emotionally and physically.

There would be the narrator's admission of guilt stemming from these numerous sexual episodes, and the realization at story end that the new so-called freedom may carry a costly price tag.

This is the *sin, suffer and repent* pattern that is the basis of the formula story and that is followed in the majority of the confessions. There is also, however, the non-formula story in which the narrator is coping with a problem that has come about through no fault of her own. A woman whose teenage son is on drugs does not have to assume the blame for his addiction. Her story will concern her struggle to help him rid himself of the drug habit. In essence—*This was my problem, and this is how I solved it.*

Short story vs personal experience article

Here again is the type of problem that would most likely be presented as an article in the slicks, either as a discussion of teenage drug abuse in general, or as a true, bylined piece of nonfiction. (Occasionally this *it-happened-to-me* type of nonfiction is published anonymously to protect the characters involved. Anonymity is granted if the subject matter is sensational. Example: "I Married A Bisexual." In this event, the slick article is much like the confession "story," with allowances made for the difference in the treatment.)

The slick article, for example, is less likely to be scened. More information will be given in straight narration. The wife narrator and her husband may be college graduates living on the "right" side of town.

The narrator will view her problem from a more objective viewpoint, depending upon the situation itself for reader sympathy. She may solve her problem undramatically through the aid of a psychiatrist, or she may tell the reader she has learned to accept it, something the confession narrator would never do.

In the confession story there will be a dramatic scene in which the problem is solved to the reader's satisfaction. Most important, while the confession story sounds authentic and is built upon actual facts, the slick article is told precisely as it happened, with no deviation from actuality in order to give the story emotional impact.

Scenes and dialogue may be used sparingly in the personal experience slick article, but as a rule they serve only to illustrate a certain facet of the problem. In the confession story the wife of the bisexual, in a fit of self-pity, may take refuge in an affair. This sexual episode will add additional spice to an already "spicy" story, but does nothing to enhance the reader's knowledge of the problem of bisexuality, and how to deal with it.

While the confession narrator does not need to assume responsibility for her son's drug addiction, she does hold herself liable for an accident to a younger child who has been left alone in the house. Here the narrator is guilty of negligence, and she admits that guilt in order to gain reader sympathy. She suffers for this negligence and expresses the hope that her story will serve as a warning to other mothers of young children. (In the slick magazine this warning would be contained in an article under a heading such as "Killer In Your Kitchen," and would deal with the household hazards to children in general, with perhaps one example to illustrate the point.)

A story can range in mood from farce to tragedy. The confession magazine does not publish the farcical approach to a problem. Satire is not wanted. Humor is welcomed, however, and some very funny stories appear in confession magazines. The humor story must, of course, fit the general confession criteria, and be built around a situation with which the reader can identify.

A very funny story that appeared in a slick magazine concerned a woman's determination to learn conversational Spanish from her Mexican maid. The average confession reader does not have a maid. The average slick may not have one either, but she is able to identify with a character who is on a higher status level than her own. (It is because of this ability that the slick stories are filled with doctors and heiresses and weekend trips to Cannes.) The humorous confession story is built around a familiar, usually domestic, situation. The May 1980 issue of *Modern Romances* carried the story of a little girl with her imaginary playmate. While this was whimsy on the part of the little girl, the problem was real to her mother who tells the story. However, the problem is not too serious, or beyond resolving. When a puppy is brought home the little girl pushes her imaginary playmate out the door, telling her never to come back.

The slick magazines, as a rule, do not delve as deeply into tragedy as do the confessions. In the middle range, between the extremes of tragedy and farce, a story idea may be written to fit one market or the other, and the decision as to which market it will be should be made before a word is set down on paper.

Which market for your story?

Here are some factors to consider in making your decision:

A confession story is "easier" to write.

The slick story is told more subtly. It takes a skilled writer to achieve that deceptively simple style. There may be a whisper of conflict, where in the confession story it would be a shout. While a sentence taken out of context may be nearly identical to one out of a confession story, the slick story as a whole is more delicately constructed.

Slick characters are more disciplined emotionally. A frown can denote as much conflict as does a slammed fist in the confession. The dialogue is in equally low key. "That was the summer we toured Germany," the husband remarks at a dinner party honoring his second wife's birthday, and second wife feels the momentary bleakness at the realization that he is referring to his first wife and their children.

In the confession story, the incident would go something like this: *I hated it when Mike got on the subject of his first wife and their kids. But here he was at the neighborhood cookout, going on and on about Billy making the winning home run in the Little League playoff and how Joan had run right out on the field and hugged him. Maybe it was small of me to feel that way, but I couldn't help it.*

Many writers become self-conscious when attempting the slick story, trying too hard to be witty and sophisticated. The result is often a stiff and pompous piece of work that never gets off the ground.

On the other hand, the knowledge that the confession market does not expect sophistication and wit can release a writer from these self-imposed inhibitions, substituting the freedom to turn out an honest and moving story.

There is a more receptive market for the confession story. The May 1980 issue of *McCall's* lists two stories in its table of contents; May 1980 *Modern Romances* lists ten. In the confession marketplace the writer is not competing with top names. As bylines are not used, the name of a seasoned professional carries no clout.

What about the sex-oriented confession magazine? Like sex itself it seems to be here to stay. The criticism can be made, and often is, that the sensational confession magazines, with their lurid titles and suggestive illustrations, pull down the image of the entire confession market.

This is unfortunate. The "clean" confession magazines, and they are in the majority, cannot dictate the editorial policies of other publishers.

The writer who wants to produce the honest and worthwhile confession story will find a receptive market. Macfadden takes pride in the caliber of its stories, and there are other confession publishers with the same high standards.

The best advice for the new confession writer is to study the format of the various markets, and let your conscience, and your own standards of good taste determine what you write.

Of course, the slick market pays more. And there is the prestige that goes along with the appearance of your story in a slick publication. "I can live for two months on a good compliment," Mark Twain said, and the writer who has sold to a leading slick market can feed his ego for a much longer period.

But remember that an inner glow of satisfaction can accompany the sale of an inspirational or documentary confession. Both of them offer help to the reader. A letter to the editor saying, "This story changed my life" can do happy things to the soul. Ask any confession writer!

The making of *The Godfather*

by Mario Puzo

I've written three novels. *The Godfather* is not as good as the preceding two; I wrote it to make money. My first novel, *The Dark Arena* (1955), received mostly very good reviews saying I was a writer to watch. Naturally I thought I was going to be rich and famous. The book netted me $3,500 and I still didn't know I had a whole fifteen years to wait.

My second novel, *The Fortunate Pilgrim*, was published ten years later (1965) and netted me $3,000. I was going downhill fast. Yet the book received some extraordinarily fine reviews. *The New York Times* called it a "small classic."

Anyway, I was a hero, I thought. But my publisher, Atheneum, known as a classy publishing house more interested in belles-lettres than money, was not impressed. I asked them for an advance to start on my next book (which would be a *BIG* classic), and the editors were cool. They were courteous. They were kind. They showed me the door.

Well, we had another talk. The editors didn't like the idea behind my new novel. It sounded like another loser. One editor wistfully remarked that if *The Fortunate Pilgrim* had only had a little more of that Mafia stuff in it maybe the book would have made money. (One of the minor characters was a mob chief.)

I was 45 years old and tired of being an artist. Besides, I owed $20,000 to relatives, finance companies, banks and assorted bookmakers and shylocks. It was really time to grow up and sell out, as Lenny Bruce once advised. So I told my editors okay, I'll write a book about the Mafia, just give me some money to get started. They said no money until we see a hundred pages. I compromised. I wrote a ten-page outline. They showed me the door again.

Mario Puzo was a freelance writer of articles, short stories and reviews, an editor, and the author of two highly praised but little read novels, The Dark Arena *and* The Fortunate Pilgrim, *before the great success of* The Godfather. *Since then he has written the novel* Fools Die, *and screenplays for* The Godfather, The Godfather: Part Two, Earthquake *and* Superman.

There is no way to explain the terrible feeling of rejection, the damage, the depression and weakening of will such manipulation does to a writer. But this incident also enlightened me. I had been naive enough to believe that publishers cared about art. They didn't. They wanted to make money. (Please don't say, "No kidding.") They were in business. They had a capital investment and payrolls to meet. If some lunatic wanted to create a work of art, let him do it on his own time.

I had been a true believer in art. I didn't believe in religion or love or women or men, I didn't believe in society or philosophy. But I believed in art for 45 years. It gave me a comfort I found in no other place. But I knew I'd never be able to write another book if the next one wasn't a success. The psychological and economic pressure would be too much. I had never doubted I could write a bestselling commercial novel whenever I chose to do so. My writing friends, my family, my children and my creditors all assured me now was the time to put up or shut up.

I was willing, I had a ten-page outline—but nobody would take me. Months went by. I was working on a string of adventure magazines, editing and writing freelance stories. I was ready to forget novels except maybe as a puttering hobby for my old age. But one day a writer friend dropped into my magazine office. As a natural courtesy I gave him a copy of *The Fortunate Pilgrim*. A week later he came back. He thought I was a great writer. I bought him a magnificent lunch. During lunch I told him some funny Mafia stories and showed him my ten-page outline. He was enthusiastic. He arranged a meeting for me with the editors of G.P. Putnam's. The editors just sat around for an hour listening to my Mafia tales and said go ahead. They also gave me a $5,000 advance and I was on my way, just like that. Almost-almost, I believed that publishers were human.

"Chooch" nor mooch

I'm ashamed to admit that I wrote *The Godfather* entirely from research. I never met a real honest-to-god gangster. I knew the gambling world pretty good, but that's all. After the book became famous, I was introduced to a few gentlemen related to the material. They were flattering. They refused to believe that I had never been in the rackets. They refused to believe that I had never had the confidence of a Don. But all of them loved the book.

In different parts of the country I heard a nice story: that the Mafia had paid me a million dollars to write *The Godfather* as a public relations con. I'm not in the literary world much, but I hear some writers claim I must have been a Mafia man, that the book could not have been written purely from research. I treasure the compliment.

After three years of work, I finally had to finish *The Godfather* in July, 1968, because I needed the final $1,200 advance payment from Putnam to take my wife and kids to Europe. My wife had not seen her family for twenty years and I promised her that this was the year. I had no money, but I had a great collection of credit cards. Still I needed that $1,200 in cash, so I handed in the rough manuscript. Before leaving for Europe, I told my publisher not to show the book to anybody; it had to be polished.

My family had a good time in Europe. American Express offices cashed five-hundred-dollar checks against their credit cards. I used their offices in London, Cannes, Nice and Wiesbaden. My children and I gambled in the poshest casinos on the French Riviera. If just one of us could have gotten lucky, I would have been able to cover those checks that American Express airmailed back to the

United States. We all lost. I had failed as a father. When we finally got home, I owed the credit card companies $8,000. I wasn't worried. If worse came to worst we could always sell our house. Or I could go to jail. Hell, better writers had gone to jail. No sweat.

I went to New York to see my agent, Candida Donadio. I was hoping she'd pull a slick magazine assignment out of her sleeve and bail me out as she'd often done in the past. She informed me that my publisher had just turned down $375,000 for the paperback rights to *The Godfather*.

I had given strict orders it wasn't to be shown to even a paperback house, but this was no time to complain. I called my editor at Putnam, Bill Targ, and he said they were holding out for $410,000 because $400,000 was some sort of record. Did I wish to speak to Clyde Taylor, their reprint rights man, who was handling the negotiations? I said no; I said that I had absolute confidence in any man who could turn down $375,000. I hung around New York, had a very late lunch with Targ, and over our coffee he got a call. Ralph Daigh of Fawcett had bought the paperback rights for $410,000.

I went up to the adventure magazine office to tell all my friends. We had some drinks and then I decided to get home to Long Island. While waiting for my car, I called my brother to tell him the good news. This brother had ten percent of *The Godfather* because he supported me all my life and gave me a final chunk of money to complete the book. Through the years I'd call him up frantic for a few hundred bucks to pay the mortgage or buy the kids shoes. Then I'd arrive at his house in a taxi to pick up the money. In rain or snow he never took a taxi, but he never complained. He always came through. So now I wanted him to know that since my half of the paperback rights came to $205,000 (the hardcover publisher keeps half), he was in for a little over twenty grand.

He is the kind of guy who is always home when I call to borrow money. Now that I had money to give back, he was naturally out. I got my mother on the phone. She speaks broken English but understands the language perfectly. I explained it to her.

She asked, "$40,000?"

I said no, it was $410,000. I told her three times before she finally answered. "Don't tell nobody."

My car came out of the garage and I hung up. Traffic was jammed, and it took me over two hours to get home out in the suburbs. When I walked in the door, my wife was dozing over the TV and the kids were all out playing. I went over to my wife, kissed her on the cheek, and said, "Honey, we don't have to worry about money anymore. I just sold my book for $410,000."

She smiled at me and kept dozing. I went down to my workroom to call my brothers and sisters. The reason for this was because every Italian family has a "chooch," a donkey. That is, a family idiot everybody agrees will never be able to make a living and so has to be helped without rancor or reproach. I was the family "chooch" and I wanted to tell them I was abdicating the family role.

I called my older sister.

"Did you hear?" I said.

My sister's voice was pretty cool. I started getting annoyed. Nobody seemed to think this was a big deal. My whole life was going to change, I didn't have to worry about money. It was almost like not having to worry about dying. Then my sister said, "You got $40,000 for the book. Mama called me."

I was exasperated with my mother. After all those explanations she had gotten it wrong. Her 80 years were no excuse. "No," I told my sister, "it was $410,000."

Now I got the reaction I wanted. There was a little scream over the phone and an excited minute of conversation. But I had to get back to my mother. I called and said, "Ma, how the hell could you get it wrong? I told you five times that it was $410,000 not $40,000. How could you make such a mistake?"

There was a long silence and then my mother whispered over the phone, "I no maka a mistake. I don't wanta tell her."

Well, it's a nice happy ending. But nobody seemed to believe me. So I called Bill Targ and drew an advance check for $100,000. I paid my debts, paid my agents' commissions, paid my brother his well-deserved 10 per cent and three months later I called my publishers and agent for more money. They were stunned. What about the huge check I had just gotten three months before? I couldn't resist. Why should I treat them any differently than I had treated my family all those lean years? "A hundred grand doesn't last forever," I said.

At least I could be a publisher's "chooch."

A big mistake

By then *The Godfather* had earned over $1 million but I still wasn't rich. Some of the money diverted to trust funds for the kids. There were agents' commissions and lawyers' fees. There were federal and state income taxes. All of which cut the original million to less than half. But before I grasped all this I had a great time. I spent the money as fast as it came in.

I loved the money, but I didn't really like being "famous." I found it quite simply distressing. I never much liked parties, never liked talking to more than two or three people at one time. I dislike interviews and having my picture taken (with reason).

I got conned into doing the *Today* show by an editor at Putnam's who said, "How do you know you don't like it when you've never done it?" That sounded reasonable. I did it. I hated it. So I was never tempted when offers came from other talk shows. I don't think it was a reverse snobbism. Or a phony kind of humility. It's just damn uncomfortable. And nearly every writer I've seen on TV has seemed foolish; it's not a writer's medium.

Interviews came out sounding like someone I didn't even know; and I couldn't even blame the interviewers. I did make those dumb statements, but I didn't say them like that. So I quit on TV and all publicity, including interviews.

In the meantime I had made what turned out to be a very big mistake. Before publication, when I had the first 100 pages of *The Godfather* done, the William Morris Agency approved a contract with Paramount for the book for a $12,500 option payment, against $50,000 with "escalators" if they exercised the option. I had already switched to Candida Donadio as agent, but William Morris had signed the initial book contract and so represented me in the movie deal. They advised me against taking it. They advised me to wait. That was like advising a guy underwater to take a deep breath. I needed the cash, and the $12,500 looked like Fort Knox. Let me say now that the fault was mine. And I never held it against Paramount that they got *The Godfather* so cheap.

The movie

I had read all the literature about Hollywood, how they did-in Fitzgerald.

Nathanael West, and novelists in general. So I was not interested at all in what Hollywood did to the book as a movie just so long as I didn't help them do it. But one day I picked up the paper and it said that Danny Thomas wanted to play the role of the Godfather. That threw me into a panic. I had always thought that Marlon Brando would be great. So through a mutual friend, I contacted Brando, wrote him a letter, and he was nice enough to call me. We had a talk on the phone. He had not read the book but he told me that the studio would never hire him unless a strong director insisted on it. He was nice over the phone but didn't sound too interested.

What I didn't know at this time was that Paramount had decided not to make the movie. The reason for this was that they had a movie called *The Brotherhood*—also about the Mafia—and the movie was a critical and financial disaster. When I saw *The Brotherhood*, I felt that they had given the first 100 pages of my book to a real cookie-cutter screenwriter and told him to write a switch.

When I saw the picture, I wasn't angry because I thought Paramount had hustled me. That was OK. Working for my magazines, I'd written some cookie-cutting switches in my time. But I hated the sheer stupidity of that movie, the writing, the whole concept, the whole misunderstanding of the Mafia world. What I didn't know at the time was that the financial disaster of the film made the studio brass feel there was no money in Mafia movies. It was only when *The Godfather* became a super seller that they had to make the film.

Finally Al Ruddy, the producer, was assigned to the film, and he came to New York, saw my agent and said Paramount wanted me to do the script. It would be a low budget, he said, so they couldn't offer to pay me much. I turned the offer down. They found more money and a percentage and I agreed to write the script.

Fellow novelists wondered why I wanted to make movies. I didn't like show biz. I was a novelist; I had my novels to write.

So how come? When I was poor and working at home on my books, I made my wife a solemn promise that if I ever hit it big I'd get a studio, get out from under her feet. She hated having me home during the day. I was in the way. I rumpled up the bed. I messed up the living room. I roamed around the house cursing. I came charging and yelling out of my workroom when the kids had a fight. In short, I was nerve-racking. To make matters worse she could never catch me working. She claims she never saw me type. She claims that for three years all I did was fall asleep on the sofa and then just magically produce the manuscript for *The Godfather*. Anyway, a man is bound by solemn oaths. Now that I was a big success, I had to get out of my own house during working hours.

I tried. I rented quiet elegant studios. I went to London. I tried the French Riviera, Puerto Rico and Las Vegas. I hired secretaries and bought dictating machines. Nothing happened. I needed the kids screaming and fighting. I needed my wife interrupting my work to show me her newest curtains. I needed those trips to the supermarket. I got some of my best ideas while helping my wife load up the shopping cart. But I had made a solemn promise to get out of the house. So OK. I'd go to Hollywood.

La dolce vita

It's true—success really throws a writer. For a year I wandered around having "a good time." It wasn't that great. It was OK but it wasn't great. And then remember that for twenty years I had lived the life of a hermit. I had seen a few close personal friends on occasion for dinner. I had spent evenings with my wife's friends. I had gone to movies. I had taught my children how to gamble with percentages. But mostly I had been living in my own head, with all my dreams, all my fantasies.

Also I had always been very content to be an observer at the few parties I went to over the years. I rarely initiated a conversation or a friendship. Suddenly I didn't have to. People seemed genuinely delighted to talk to me, to listen to me; they were charming to me and I loved it. I became perhaps the most easily charmed guy in the Western Hemisphere. And it helped that the people were for the most part genuinely charming people. It was easy to stop being a hermit, in fact it was a pleasure. So I had the courage to leave for Hollywood.

The deal for the script was agreeable: $500 a week expense money, nice money, up front (sure money), plus 2.5 percent of net profit. A fair deal in the marketplace of that time, especially since Al Ruddy had gotten his job by saying he could produce the picture for only a million.

But the deal was not as good as it sounded. For one thing, a suite at the Beverly Hills Hotel was $500 a week, so that wiped out the expense money right there. Plus the fact that my 2.5 percent was worth zero unless the picture became a big blockbuster like *Love Story*. The way it works is that the studio usually legally snatches all profits from anybody working on a percentage of net profit. They do this with bookkeeping. If the picture costs $4 million, they add another million for studio overhead. They charge advertising department costs to pictures that make money. They have accountants who make profits disappear like Houdini.

So I went to Hollywood absolutely sure it held no surprises for me. I was armored. *The Godfather* was their picture, *not mine*. I would be cool. I would never let my feelings get hurt. I would never get proprietary or paranoid. I was an employee.

California had a lot of sunshine and a lot a fresh air and a lot of tennis courts. (I'd just discovered tennis and was crazy about it.) I'd get healthy and skinny.

My office was fun. I loved the Paramount lot with its fake Western town, its little alleyways, its barrack-like buildings, its general atmosphere that made me feel I was in the Twilight Zone. I had my place on the third floor, out of the traffic, just as I liked it. Al Ruddy had his much more elaborate HQ down on the first floor and we both could just run up and down the stairs to see each other.

My office wasn't really that great but I didn't mind. I had a refrigerator and an unlimited supply of soda pop free. And I had an adjoining office for my secretary and a telephone with a buzzer and four lines. This was living.

So I spent the next two weeks playing tennis and seeing friends of mine from New York who had settled in California. Also I had conferences with Robert Evans, the head of production for Paramount Pictures, and Peter Bart, his right-hand man.

I had read once a *Life* magazine article on Evans, a savage putdown. So I was surprised to find that he was easy and natural. I liked Evans right off for one reason. There were five of us having a conference in his office. He had to take a private phone call. So he stepped into a little closet to take it. Now Louis B. Mayer would have told the four of us to squeeze into the closet and shut the door so that we wouldn't hear him take the call at his desk.

Some days in the sun

Evans was open to argument and he could often be swayed. He was, of course, charming but everybody in the movie business is charming, in fact, everybody in California is charming, except: Peter Bart, who has a cold intelligence and is the only uncharming guy in the movie business whom I met. He didn't say much either. The reason for this (though I didn't know it at the time) is because he likes to think things out before voicing an opinion, and he hadn't yet picked up the California trick of being charming while he was thinking.

The first conference went over very well. There were Evans, Al Ruddy, Peter Bart, Jack Ballard and myself. Ballard is a Yul Brynner-headed guy who keeps track of production costs on a movie. Self-effacing, but producers and directors shook in their boots when he totaled tabs on their costs. Evans directed the meeting. It was a general conversation with a built-in pep talk intended for me. This was going to be the big movie for Paramount. I had to come through. This picture would "SAVE" Paramount. I love that kind of stuff, it makes me feel important and I work twice as hard. (I really wanted to *"SAVE"* Paramount but I was too late. *Love Story* did it before me.) Then we talked casting. I suggested Marlon Brando for the role of the Godfather. They were kind to me but I got the impression my stock had dropped 50 points.

Al Ruddy suggested Robert Redford for the role of Michael, and I didn't care how nice a guy he was, his stock dropped 50 points. I spoke out and was pleasantly surprised when Evans and Bart agreed with me.

They had no director. I had to write the script before they got a director. Directors like to read scripts before they sign. Well, that was what I was in California for. I assured them I was one of the best technicians of the Western world. (Not bragging; technique *can* be measured. You can't brag about art.)

All this had happened at the Paramount studio's plush headquarters on Canon Drive. When Al Ruddy and I got back to his comparatively humble office on the Paramount studio lot, we were just like soldiers returning to the front lines and finally rid of the brass.

"You just do what you want to do," Ruddy said. "You're the writer. But do me a favor. Start off with a love scene between Michael and Kay." He still wanted Redford.

"Al," I said as I drank his whiskey and smoked his cigars, "you can't start *The Godfather* off with a love scene. It ain't fitting."

He recognized the tag line and he laughed. He was a New York City street guy and I felt comfortable with him.

"Listen," he said, "just try it. We can always cut it out later."

"OK," I said. I went back upstairs and read the contract and, sure enough, it said the producer can tell the writer how to write the script. I had to start off the movie with a youthful love scene. So I wrote it and it was lousy. I showed it to Al and he loved it.

That made me happy. Love my work, I love you. But I still knew he was wrong. I spent the next three days playing tennis. Hell, I spent the next two weeks playing tennis. Then I decided to go home for a couple of weeks. I missed my wife and kids.

Ruddy took the decision like a gentleman. He even kept paying me the $500-a-week expense money while I was living at home. I stayed home for a couple of weeks and did some work and then flew back to California with a stop at Las Vegas, where I lost what I had saved of my expense money.

Frankie speaking

From April to August of 1970 I commuted back and forth from New York to Los Angeles, working on the script, playing tennis, getting a taste of the social life in Hollywood. All very pleasant. The time before a writer delivers the script is sort of a honeymoon time. Love is everywhere.

I had rented a house at Malibu for one of the summer months and brought the family out from New York. I was now seriously at work after goofing off for some four months. I had a secretary typing and I was zeroed in on the script—really in the groove. But I was past my deadline for the first draft. Peter Bart knew I had been goofing off and started putting pressure on. I said OK, the end of the week. Naturally I wasn't ready at the end of the week. He insisted. There was still a final section that I wanted to rewrite and give it that extra polish and editing a solid piece of work needs. And then it wasn't finally so much that Bart or anybody else got tough; they were always courteous, always kind; it was just that all of a sudden I said to myself, "What the hell do I care? It's *not* MY movie."

So I told my secretary to just type out what I had already written. I didn't go over the last section. I then put on my bathing suit, and for the first time since I had moved into the house on the beautiful beach of Malibu, I took a dip in the ocean. I would enjoy a beautiful, luxurious swim.

Now this was very wrong of me. Instead of getting my feelings hurt, I should have just let Bart wait. Guilty conscience. I should have been more adult. It was also very wrong of me because I hate going into the ocean.

They had the script and everybody liked it. Of course, by contract, I had to do a revision. This was in August, 1970. Meanwhile, in the following months, while they looked for a director, I had a few adventures. The most interesting was with Frank Sinatra, rated as one of the ten most famous people in the world, a guy who had been my idol from afar. Despite this I had never wanted to meet him or be introduced. I just believed he was a great artist (singing, not acting) and that he had lived a life of great courage. I admired his sense of family responsibility, especially since he was a Northern Italian, which to a Southern Italian is as alien as being an Englishman.

In *The Godfather* the singer named Johnny Fontane has been assumed by many people to be based on Frank Sinatra. Before the book came out, my publisher got a letter from Sinatra's lawyers demanding to see the manuscript. In polite language we refused. However, the movie was another story. In the initial conferences with Paramount's legal staff they showed concern about this until I reassured them the part was very minor in the film.

Now the thing was, in my book I had written the Fontane character with complete sympathy for the man and his lifestyle and his hang-ups. I thought I had caught the innocence of great show-biz people, their despair at the corruption their kind of life forces on them and the people around them. I thought I had caught the inner innocence of the character. But I could also see that if Sinatra thought the character was himself, he might not like it—the book—or me.

But of course some people wanted to bring us together. At Elaine's in New York one night Sinatra was at the bar and I was at a table. Elaine asked if I would object to meeting Sinatra. I said OK with me if it was OK with him. It was not OK with Sinatra. And that was perfectly OK with me. I didn't give it another thought.

A year later I was working on the script in Hollywood. I rarely went out in the evening but this particular night I was invited to my producer's friend's birthday party at Chasen's. A party for twelve given by a famous millionaire. Just an agreeable dinner. Everybody had been so charming to me the past six months I had gotten over some of my backwardness. So I went.

The millionaire turned out to be one of those elderly men always trying to be youthful. He wore red slacks and a miniature Stetson and had that five-martini affability I dread more than anything else in the world. As we were having a drink at the bar, he said Sinatra was having dinner at another table and would I like to meet him. I said no. The millionaire had a Right-Hand Man who tried to insist. I said no again. We finally went to dinner.

During the dinner there was a tableau of John Wayne and Frank Sinatra meeting in the space between their two tables to salute each other. They both looked absolutely great, better than on the screen, twenty years younger than they really were. And both were beautifully dressed, Sinatra especially. It was really great to see. They were beribboned kings meeting on the Field of the Cloth of Gold.

The food brought me back to reality. It was lousy. Christ, I'd eaten better in one-arm Italian joints all over New York. This was the famous Chasen's? Well, OK, the fancy French restaurants in New York had been a disappointment, too. I was glad when we were finished and I started to leave.

But on the way out the millionaire took me by the hand and started leading me toward the table. His Right-Hand Man took me by the other hand. "You gotta meet Frank," the millionaire said. "He's a good friend of mine."

We were almost to the table. I still could have wrenched loose and walked away, but it would have been an obvious snub. It was easier, physically and psychologically, to be led the few remaining steps. The millionaire made the introduction. Sinatra never looked up from his plate.

"I'd like you to meet my good friend, Mario Puzo," said the millionaire.

"I don't think so," Sinatra said.

Which sent me on my way. But the poor millionaire didn't get the message. He started over again.

"I don't want to meet him," Sinatra said.

Meanwhile I was trying to get past the Right-Hand Man and get the hell out of there. So I heard the millionaire stuttering his apologies, not to me, but to Sinatra. The millionaire was actually in tears. "Frank, I'm sorry. God, Frank, I didn't know, I'm sorry—"

But Sinatra cut him short and his voice was now the voice I had heard while making love as a kid, soft and velvety. He was consoling the shattered millionaire. "It's not your fault," Sinatra said.

I always run away from an argument and I have rarely in my life been disgusted by anything human beings do, but after that I said to Sinatra, "Listen, it wasn't my idea."

And then the most astounding thing happened. He completely misunderstood. He thought I was apologizing for the character of Johnny Fontane in my book.

He said, and his voice was almost kind, "Who told you to put that in the book, your publisher?"

I was completely dumbfounded. I don't let publishers put commas in my books. That's the only thing I have character about. Finally I said, "I mean about being introduced to you."

Time has mercifully dimmed the humiliation of what followed. Sinatra started to shout abuse. I remember that, contrary to his reputation, he did not use foul language at all. The worst thing he called me was a pimp, which rather flattered me since I've never been able to get girl friends to squeeze blackheads out of my back, much less hustle for me. I do remember his saying that if it wasn't that I was so much older than he, he would beat the hell out of me. I was a kid when he was singing at the Paramount, but OK, he looked twenty years younger. But what hurt was that here he was, a Northern Italian, threatening me, a Southern Italian, with physical violence. This was roughly equivalent to Einstein pulling a knife on Al Capone. It just wasn't done. Northern Italians never mess with Southern Italians except to get them put in jail or deported to some desert island.

Sinatra kept up his abuse and I kept staring at him. He kept staring down at his plate. Yelling. He never looked up. Finally I walked away and out of the restaurant. My humiliation must have showed on my face because he yelled after me, "Choke. Go ahead and choke," the voice frenzied, high-pitched.

Incidents like this send the writer scurrying back to his workroom for safety. Make no mistake, writers become writers to avoid the pains and humiliation of the real world and real people. I started rewriting the script, playing tennis and reading quietly at night in my suite. If I was going to be a hermit, the Beverly Hills Hotel was a great hut.

I felt depressed too, because I thought Sinatra hated the book and believed that I had attacked him personally in the character of Johnny Fontane. But a few weeks later, when Francis Coppola was named as director of the film, he, too, had an incident with Sinatra. They ran into each other in a L.A. club one night, and Sinatra put his arms around Coppola's shoulders and said, "Francis, I'd play the Godfather for you. I wouldn't do it for those guys at Paramount, but I'd do it for you."

Stars and gripes forever

Some very famous directors turned *The Godfather* down because it offended their social consciences, because "it glorified the Mafia and criminals." I understood them. My first novel was called degenerate and dirty by a few critics, though others praised it as art. By now the only opinion about my work I worried about was my own. And I was a tougher critic than most, so my feelings were rarely hurt. What I didn't know was that there was some argument about making the movie as a cheapie and cashing in on the book's sales record.

Finally they decided to go all the way. Bart had written a critique of my first-draft screenplay that made a lot of sense, and also made up for his lack of California charm. In fact I found that most of the time I could get straight answers when I asked him questions. It was Bart who came up with the idea of using Francis Coppola as the director. When Al Ruddy told me the news, I had not yet met Coppola, but I knew him by reputation. He was considered a highly skilled screenwriter and later in the year was to win an Oscar for collaborating on the screenplay of *Patton*. (He and his collaborator never met.)

"The one thing Francis and I want you to understand," Ruddy told me, "is that there is no intention of his rewriting your script. Francis just wants to direct and everybody is happy with your work."

I knew *immediately* that I had a writing partner.

Sure enough. He rewrote one half and I rewrote the second half. Then we traded and rewrote each other. I suggested we work together. Francis looked me right in the eye and said no. That's when I knew he was really a director.

I liked him. And he earned his half of the screen credit. And I was glad to see him get it. I could blame all the lousy dialogue lines on him and some of the lousy scenes. He was never abrasive; we got along fine, and finally there was a shooting script.

The fun was over. Now everybody got into the act. Stars, agents, studio heads and vice-presidents, the producer, the associate producer, songwriters and assorted hustlers. Now I knew it wasn't my movie.

The big question: Who was to play the Godfather? I remembered what Brando had told me so I had a little talk with Francis Coppola one afternoon. He listened and said he liked the idea. I warned him that *everybody* hated the idea. Some were afraid Brando would make trouble, that he was weak at the box office, and a million other reasons. I figured this young director couldn't put on the necessary muscle.

Francis Coppola is heavy-set, jolly, and is usually happy-go-lucky. What I didn't know was that he could be tough about his work. Anyway he fought and got Brando. And, incidentally, Brando never gave any trouble. So much for his reputation.

The casting began. Actors would come in and talk to Coppola and exert all their art and skills to make him remember them. I sat in on some interviews. Coppola was cool and courteous to these people, but for me it was simply too painful. I quit. I couldn't watch them anymore. They were so vulnerable, so open, so naked in their hope for lightning to strike. It was at this time that I realized that actors and actresses should be forgiven all the outrageousness and tyrannies of their stardoms. Not to say you have to put up with it. But the one incident that made me check out of the casting stuff was when a quite ordinary, nice-looking girl came into the office and chatted with everybody and announced she was trying to get a part. I asked her which part. She said, "Appolona."

The part of Appolona is a young Sicilian girl who is described in the book as very beautiful. I asked this nice girl why she thought she wanted the part. She answered, "Because I look just like Appolona." This is when it dawned on me that all actors and actresses were crazy.

Finally everything moved to New York. Coppola started shooting screen tests. Now the big problem was to find someone to play Michael, really the most important part in the film. At one time Jimmy Caan seemed to have the role. He tested well. But he tested well for Sonny, the other Godfather son, and tested well for Hagen. Hell, he could have played all three of them. Suddenly it looked like he wouldn't get any of them.

Robert Duvall tested for Hagen and he was perfect. Another actor was perfect for Sonny. That left Jimmy Caan for Michael but nobody was quite satisfied. Finally the name of Al Pacino came up. He had scored a smashing success in a New York play but nobody had seen him on film. Coppola got hold of a screen test Pacino had done for some Italian movie and showed it. I loved him. I gave Francis a letter saying that above all Pacino had to be in the film. He could use it at his discretion.

But there were objections. Pacino was too short, too Italian looking. He was supposed to be the American in the family. He had to look a little classy, a little Ivy league. Coppola kept saying a good actor is a good actor.

Pacino tested. The cameras were running. He didn't know his lines. He threw in his own words. He didn't understand the character at all. He was terrible. Jimmy Caan had done it ten times better. After the scene was over I went up to Coppola and I said: "Give me my letter back."

"What letter?"

"The one I gave you saying I wanted Pacino."

Coppola shook his head. "Wait a while." Then he said, "The self-destructive bastard. He didn't even know his lines."

They tested Pacino all day. They coached him, they rehearsed him, they turned him inside out. They had it all on film. After a month of testing they had everybody on film. It was time to show it all in the Paramount screening room in the Gulf and Western Building.

What goes on in the screening room is instructive. I had been amazed at how well the scenes played live, but they were not so effective on camera. There were tests of the girls who had tried for the part of Kay, the young-girl role. There was one girl who wasn't right for the part but jumped off the screen at you. Everybody commented on her and Evans said, "We should do something with her—but I guess we never will." The poor girl never knew how close she came to fame and fortune. Nobody had the time for her just then. Hell, I did but I wasn't a mogul.

Some of the tests were terrible. Some of the scenes were terrible. Some were astonishingly good. One scene Francis had used was a courtship scene between Kay and Michael. Francis had written it so that at one point Michael would kiss Kay's hand. I objected violently and Francis took it out. But in the tests every actor who tested kissed Kay's hand or nibbled on her fingers. Francis called out teasingly, "Mario, I didn't tell them to do that. How come they all kiss her hand?"

I knew he was kidding but it really irritated me. "Because they're actors, not gangsters," I said.

The irritation was not casual. I'd felt that Coppola in his rewrite had softened the characters.

On screen Pacino still didn't strike *anybody*—excepting Coppola—as right for the part of Michael. Coppola kept arguing. Finally Evans said, "Francis, I must say you're alone in this." Which I thought was the nicest "no" I'd ever heard. We would have to keep hunting for a Michael.

I had to go away for a week. When I came back, Al Pacino had the part of Michael, Jimmy Caan had the part of Sonny. The guy who had had the part of Sonny was out. Jack Ryan, who tested better than anybody for the important role of Carlo Rizzi, was out. Even though he supposedly had been told he had the role. Ryan was so stunning in his tests of the part that I did something I had never done. I sought him out to tell him how great he'd played the part. He was replaced by a guy named Russo who had some sort of radio show-biz background in Las Vegas. I never found out what happened. I would guess Coppola and the Paramount brass horse-traded.

The magic act

Though the script was done, I was still on the payroll as consultant for $500 a week. Now the Italian-American Civil Rights League began to make noises. Ruddy asked me if I would sit down with the League to iron things out. I told him I would not. He decided he would and he did. He promised them to take out all references to the Mafia in the script and to preserve the Italian honor. The League pledged its cooperation in the making of the film. *The New York Times* put the story on page one and the next day even had an indignant editorial on it. A lot of people were outraged as hell. I must say Ruddy proved himself a shrewd bargainer because the word "Mafia" was never in the script in the first place.

At about this time I quit the picture as a consultant, not because of any of this, but simply because I felt I was in the way. Also, in most of the arguments I had lately been siding with management, rather than the creative end. Which made me very nervous.

The shooting of a motion picture is the most boring work in the world. I watched two days' shooting; it was guys running out of houses and into cars that screeched away. So I gave up. The picture went comparatively smoothly and I lost track of it. It was not my movie.

Finally, the movie was ready to be cut and edited. The cutting of the film had always struck me as primarily a writing job. It is very much like the final draft of a piece of writing. So I really wanted to be in on the cutting.

I saw two rough cuts of the movie and said what I had to say. Again everybody was courteous and cooperative. My movie agent, Robby Lantz, said I was treated as well as any new writer had been in Hollywood. So then, why was I still dissatisfied? Quite simply because it wasn't my movie. I was not the boss. But then really it wasn't anybody's movie. Nobody had really gotten his way with the picture.

I had wanted to bring some friends to see the cut and Al Ruddy said, "No, not yet." I asked Peter Bart and he said, "No, not yet." I asked Bob Evans and he said yes, if the picture wasn't being pulled apart for scoring and dubbing and never mind how legitimate that excuse is. It was the second-best nicest "no" I'd heard. The whole business was that they didn't want strangers to see it. Or maybe because I was opposed to the ending they used. I wanted an additional 30 seconds of Kay lighting the candles in the church to save Michael's soul but I was alone on this. So I said the hell with it, if my friends couldn't see it with me, I didn't want to see it. Again kid stuff.

I wish like hell the script was half as good as the acting, even though half of the script is mine. Brando is very fine. So is Robert Duvall. And so is Richard Castellano. In fact all three, I think, have a shot at the Academy Award. And they are good. But the great bonus was Al Pacino.

As Michael, Al Pacino was everything I wanted that character to be on the screen. I couldn't believe it. It was, in my eyes, a perfect performance, a work of art. I was so happy I ran around admitting I was wrong. I ate crow like it was my favorite Chinese dish. Until Al Ruddy took me aside and gave me some kindly advice. "Listen," he said, "if you don't go around telling everybody how wrong you were nobody will know. How the hell do you expect to be a producer?"

While all this was going on, interviews and stories would appear in various publications. Always causing trouble. One interview I have to admit depressed me. Francis Coppola explained he was directing *The Godfather* so that he could get the capital to make pictures he really wanted to make. What depressed me was that he was smart enough to do that at the age of 32 when it took me 45 years to figure out I had to write *The Godfather* so that I could do the other books I really wanted to.

I had a good time. I didn't work too hard (script-writing is truly not as hard as writing a novel). My health improved because I got out in the sunshine and played tennis. It was fun. There were a few traumatic experiences but all usable in a novel and as such to be accepted and even savored.

It always takes me a year or two to catch on to things, which happens to be a good thing for me as a novelist but complicates my daily life. So I just now realize that, though I was treated very well by Evans and Bart and Ruddy at Paramount, they really magicianed me. One day I'd be at the very center of power and seemingly in on all decisions. Then suddenly they could make me disappear, *Twilight Zone* fashion. And they always made me disappear when they were doing something they felt I wouldn't like. Which was in a way considerate, of course, but left me in the dark as to what really happened on the shooting of *The Godfather*.

The sequel

The Godfather will undoubtedly be the biggest grosser of all time. But all this is not as great as it sounds. Success always causes trouble. Paramount decided they would do a movie sequel and I had to write the screenplay (my lawyers making sure that nobody would be allowed to turn it into a novel). *The Godfather, Part II*, as it is called was as ambitious a picture as the original using a lot of the stuff and characters that we had to leave out of *Godfather I*. For instance, in the novel there was an incident about a baby thrown into the furnace, but Coppola refused to have it in the movie. I told him I have never heard a complaint about the baby incident. It was the horse that made them flinch.

As for me, I'm resigned to the fact that I'm no longer a novelist. I have become a junior partner in the Godfather business.

WRITERS IN ACTION: II

Such good writing: an interview with Lois Gould

by Jane S. Bakerman

Lois Gould's novels feature wit and humor that belie the extreme seriousness with which she regards writing. She has worked with words for most of her life. At 15 she worked on a magazine during the summer "in a totally non-editing capacity, but it was still word-centered." She later went on to do editorial work, eventually becoming executive editor of *Ladies' Home Journal*; she has also worked for a newspaper.

Her nonfiction books range from the early *The Childbirth Challenge* (with W.L. Fielding) and *So You Want to Be a Working Mother!* to *Not Responsible for Personal Articles*, a 1978 collection of essays, many of which first appeared in *The New York Times*.

In between, she has written novels that have made a major impact on the contemporary literary scene. *Such Good Friends* (1970) is the story of a young woman who discovers her dying husband's infidelities. *Necessary Objects* (1972) scrutinizes sisters who devote their lives to intensive consumerism; fittingly, they are the heirs to a vast department store. *Final Analysis* (1974) depicts the heroine's long therapy, which includes an affair with her analyst. Gould's fourth novel marked a major shift in style. *A Sea-Change* (1976) is a myth about the birth of an androgynous world; it records the transformation of a "model woman" into a kind of goddess who achieves total control over her life and alters the lives of her loved ones.

Add to those *X: A Fabulous Child's Story* (1978), which first appeared in *Ms.* and was later released as a book, and you have an impressive list of successful

Jane S. Bakerman teaches in the English Department at Indiana State University, specializing in American literature, women's studies and detective fiction. She has done a number of interviews with prominent novelists, several of which have appeared in Writer's Digest, *and is currently working on a book about Daphne du Maurier. Partial funding for this interview was provided by the Indiana State University Research Committee.*

works that prove that their author is not afraid to experiment, to push her craft to new limits.

A native New Yorker, a characteristic which she shares with most of her characters, Lois Gould now lives in a comfortable town house across the street from the East River. She shares her home with her husband, Robert, a psychiatrist; two sons; and a calico cat that is featured in one essay in *Not Responsible for Personal Articles*. Gould recently welcomed WD interviewer Jane S. Bakerman to her hours. "The home's first floor is mainly given over to a comfortable, long, narrow room, a combination sitting-dining area, which opens at the front from the kitchen and at the back into a plant-filled courtyard," reports Bakerman. Sipping diet root beer, we settled on a king-sized couch, loaded with what seemed like hundreds of handsome, small pillows that match the tapestried panels on the wall.

Whether we were talking about the weather (good), the house (the Goulds renovated it themselves), or her work, she gave serious attention to the questions and thought to her answers. Gould's voice is soft and quiet; she speaks deliberately, using light inflections to emphasize a point and sometimes coloring her comments with the humor and irony that mark her writing.

Necessary decisions

Bakerman: Did you always plan to be a novelist?

Gould: I had no sense as a child that I could write a novel. A novel was something that people who had been to war or to whorehouses—preferably both—wrote because those were the two central experiences of human life—as I had been taught. Any novelists who had not done both of those things—what could they have to write about?

Bakerman: What *did* you want to be?

Gould: My first really burning ambition, which came on me when I was five, was to be a tap-dancer. It was only after my parents *wrested* me out of tap-dancing at the age of 11, on the grounds that it was not "seemly" for a young lady growing up to be doing that sort of thing instead of dancing with fellows, that I gave up the ambition. It simply stopped and I was heartbroken.

Bakerman: Then what?

Gould: The only other thing that I did very seriously was draw. I felt very intimidated about doing that because my mother, a designer, had been an artist in her youth, and she was really quite cutting about whatever ability I showed. I felt very sure that I didn't want to get into her territory.

So I got into words. Nobody else seemed to notice that or to care, but I was very serious about it. I thought at first that I wanted to be a poet, and then I wanted to be a playwright. I never thought, then, about novels at all.

Bakerman: Once you had moved into fiction, did you have instant confidence in your work?

Gould: The terror of trespassing was very, very great. I sat for a long time constantly rewriting 30 pages of *Such Good Friends*. My husband said, "You've got to show it to someone; you cannot sit there for the rest of your life with those 30 pages."

The highest point of elation came when an editor said, "I want to talk to you about your book and arrange to publish it."

Bakerman: How did you feel about the warm public reception of *Such Good Friends*? Was it exciting?

Gould: Yes, but it was unreal. I was never really aware that the book was an enormous success as it was being published. It was spectacular but seemed very distant from me and had nothing to do with what I was looking for. What I was looking for was an "A" from an imaginary English teacher, and I essentially still haven't gotten that.

Bakerman: How did your boys feel when they were little? Did they think, "Oh good, Mom's writing again; we'll have to protect her time?"

Gould: Never. Never. I've never had any respect from anyone as to my time. At first, we had a dining room table at which I sat and worked. At mealtimes I had to clear the pages all away, and I had no place to put them. They sat in piles on the floor while the meal went on. And the next day I had to fish them all out and arrange them in the same piles so that I could go on.

Bakerman: Do you still set up your work space on the dining room table?

Gould: No, I work in bed. Or on a couch with a lot of pillows, but I don't seem to be able to sit up very long. I haven't been able to sit up very long in years. And I do fall asleep a lot, which reminds me of pregnancy. I feel very lethargic and sluggish. But something is going on in my head even when I do fall asleep, and I console myself with the idea that I'm not really sleeping; I'm gestating.

Bakerman: Do you begin at the beginning and write straight through chronologically?

Gould: Yes, and I do most of my writing and revision in longhand. I have such a dread of sitting up and working a machine. I never learned to type very well, so I only want to type it once. I work lying down with pad and pens. I try to distract myself with different colored pens and different colored pieces of paper so I don't always have to stare at that white sheet. This way, I feel in control.

Not responsible for personal laundry

Bakerman: Do you write at a steady tempo?

Gould: I'm not very good at the beginning of a book and I dread it. I feel terribly dead, and I feel dead for a long time, but I begin to come alive as it works on the page.

Then I get tremendous spurts of adrenaline toward the middle as it's moving and as it's taking some kind of shape, and I can believe that it's true.

Toward the end, I can work 12 and 14 hours a day, which is a lot, but it only takes place over a short period; it may, in fact, be just a matter of weeks.

When it's over, I am carried along by this buoyant wave of adrenaline for days, a week, maybe—this terrific natural high that you work yourself into. But, whether it's a feeling of accomplishment or whether it's relief, I don't really know.

Bakerman: What do you do about blockages in the middle of a work?

Gould: Sit and let it lie there for a while and go out and take a walk. The stoppage may last for a month or two. They're not painful to me. I just know, "Look, it's not going; I'll do something else." I scrub floors; I tend to have terrible attacks of housewifism which seem terribly filled with drudgery and horrible overtones of guilt, but they are just as cathartic as going to a bar is for male writers.

Bakerman: How do you manage all the daily domestic demands and write too?

Gould: In the last two books, I've had to leave at a certain point toward the end where I am so totally *in* the book that I can't come out of it. I can't deal with "We're out of eggplant" or the fact that somebody has no shirts or whatever. I can't answer their questions; I don't know what they're saying to me, and I have to leave.

So I go to the country. I like working in this kind of bleak, punitive environment where I am alone; I am cut off from the world, getting the feeling of total solitude: no car, no way out—just me and this thing. It's very productive.

Bakerman: Which comes first, character or situation?

Gould: That's happened to me different ways with each book. With *Necessary Objects*, for instance, I knew the people; I had no idea what I was going to do with them; and in fact, it wasn't very important what I did with them. I just wanted to group them and show them—take them apart and put them together again. So whatever the action was in the book was very minor.

With *A Sea-Change*, I knew the story, but I didn't know the people. I knew what was going to happen, but what I had to find out was what the people were going to be like—what would they do and say and feel.

Necessary objectives

Bakerman: How did you go about figuring out what the people were like?

Gould: It's difficult to explain. It's almost, I guess, what writing science fiction must be, where you begin with a premise of an imaginary occurrence on another kind of world, and you must invent the people to fit that world. Then you must find some connection between the emotions that *you* know and the emotions that those people in that place must feel while undergoing a totally foreign event, an otherworldly event, a supernatural event. And that's what I had to learn. I knew that the people would begin in very familiar forms, and that they would have to undergo an enormous upheaval, emotional and physical and social. What would it feel like if it were me or people that I knew? I had to learn all of that as I went along.

Bakerman: You also had to figure out what sort of event would allow for the emotional eruptions when they came?

Gould: Right. I stumbled on it after struggling for a very long time, struggling to find some way to express what I needed, something to express the inner turmoil. When I realized that it had to be almost a cataclysm that occurred without as well as within, that's how I came to use a storm. The storm answered a great many problems; it came to be, in effect, a major character in the book.

Bakerman: A symbol—even if you don't say to yourself, "Now I am creating a symbol."

Gould: Right. You don't say that. You begin to see it, and say, "Hey, this expresses what I need to express, and isn't that neat, or isn't that a relief, or isn't that spectacularly wonderful that there are in fact existing forms of events or of character-expression that can say what needs to be said?" It's really looking for modes of language that will convey what you need to put across.

Bakerman: Is that "inspiration"? Does "inspiration" have any meaning for you?

Gould: Yes, but I don't know what inspiration is. There is a certain point where something is coming together, and it begins to work systematically. It's a moment that enables me to begin visualizing a specific scene. The first page then has its life and from then on, you are there . . . and you can't leave. I don't know if that's inspiration; that's just sweat. Too much, sometimes. . . .

Bakerman: Do you have vivid mental pictures of your characters?

Gould: I'm really very fuzzy on that. I don't describe people very much; I don't put down much about their physical attributes. I don't see them that way. I see what they say, and I see how they feel, and I see how they move, but I don't see what they're wearing or the color of their hair or anything like that.

As a reader, I get upset when authors pin things down too much for me; I don't want them to do that. I'm also irritated especially when they do it with brand names, which pinpoint it too specifically with regard to the place and time. That limits the book and makes it live only in that moment. Then it becomes a newspaper story, and it's not what I think of as universal or timeless.

Bakerman: Do you borrow any characters directly from life?

Gould: I'm sure there are aspects of people I have known that show up in the most unlikely places, just as there are aspects of me that do. I see myself in almost every character, and when I'm looking for some specific trait (which may be a horrible one), I'll find a piece that'll match it. If I can't find it in me, I'll find it in somebody else. If I need it, I'll take it from wherever it was born.

Dialogue comes back to me—memorable phrases that I don't even know the origin of, but while I'm engaged in some real experiences of life, I'm not taking mental notes. The characters all talk in some perversion of *my* voice—which is dangerous because sometimes you end up making all your characters sound alike.

Such good training

Bakerman: Has your work as a journalist helped your fiction?

Gould: That's good training. The ability to write quickly on demand and to maintain one's style in a deadline situation is very good discipline. It's like scales on the piano, I think. On the other hand, it makes me write shorter books than other people! Also, I wrote my earliest books surrounded by people, children, the tritest household work—and I don't know that I could have marshaled that kind of concentration had I not learned in a newspaper office to work with teletype machines going and everyone else talking and telephones ringing.

Bakerman: Why did you give up editorial work, which you liked?

Gould: The journalism was easy and was a pattern that had been established by other writers. The point was that it was supposed to be a logical progression toward fiction; yet, the longer one put fiction off, the more difficult the leap seemed. But there are biological time clocks that one sets for oneself in all things, and I guess I did that. I felt that I had to have my first baby by the time I was thus-and-so. These were all self-imposed limits and deadlines from within. And I met them. I felt that I had to have a hardcover book before I began having babies, and I did all of that out of a compulsion, some sort of emotional need, and I did fiction the same way. I had already done two nonfiction books, and there was no way I could go on with those because I considered them essentially expanded journalistic exercises—and that was not a real test.

Bakerman: Did you just stop doing journalism?

Gould: Well, I was on leave from a magazine; I had been executive editor and was having a very rough year; I had started a book (*Such Good Friends*) and wanted to stay with it, but I was taking an enormous leap, and I had no idea that there was any kind of net that I was going to land in on the other side.

Bakerman: How do you feel about doing journalistic writing now?

Gould: When I was doing a column for the daily *Times* (after *A Sea-Change* was published), it was very hard and it was very good. It was another set of mental muscles. I liked the instant reader response. I was writing on a weekly basis and people would comment. That kind of interaction is much closer to what one has on other jobs than novel writing.

Bakerman: You don't get the same response to a book?

Gould: With a book, you have spent possibly two years of your life agonizing over the idea and another year writing it, and then ten months more waiting for it to be published, and then another six months before anybody who's read it comes up to you and says, "Boy, I was moved. It did something for me" or "I was touched," or something. By that time, it's three years since it's left your head, and you don't even know what they're responding to, so you feel no immediate joy.

Final analysis of *A Sea Change*

Bakerman: Do you keep some sort of ideal reader in mind as you write?
Gould: No . . . it's for the inner ear . . . what sounds right. The rhythm of the speech pattern, the cadence; those are what I'm working for, and they are all very private and have nothing to do with how somebody else is going to see it.

Of course, there comes a time in the process of writing, where you look at it, and you say, "Oh my God! What are people going to think of this?" But usually you don't do anything about that; you just have that terrible, stabbing thought and go on.

And I get panic-stricken at the idea of what some people are going to think— all kinds of people: my family, critics, people like that. But I never think about the reader. I always think that the reader is on my side, and all those other people are on the other side.
Bakerman: When you abandoned the realism of your earlier novels and turned to the fantasy—the myth-making—of *A Sea-Change*, did the shift affect you?
Gould: It felt as if I had burned my bridges and my passport and I was in this other kind of territory that was much stranger and more frightening, and the question is, where does one go, if one has the requirement of never receding and doing another contemporary, familiar landscape? I have to "go somewhere else" after this.

Sometimes it takes me a very long time to *recover* from either the impact of the specific book or the desolation one feels if it hasn't gone the way one wants it to after publication. I was very unhappy after *A Sea-Change*. It took me a long time to come out of writing that book. It affected me very deeply.
Bakerman: In what way?
Gould: There were a lot of negative reviews and a lot of reviews that did not speak to the question of whether I was a writer, or whether I was a good writer, or whether I had done a good job, and I was very disappointed in that whole aspect of it. I felt that if one is being reviewed, then that means that there is this august figure like Edmund Wilson in a book-lined study, puffing away contemplatively on his pipe, and saying, "Yes, this writer can do thus-and-so, but on the other hand. . . ." But there were no such reviews, and there were, in fact, no such critics.

But I have been flirting with a new novel for some months, for which I am now about to begin the research. I signed a contract to do it and nothing else till I've done it.
Bakerman: How do you arrive at a contract?
Gould: Usually there's a conversation between me and my editor, and then I usually write a short memo, a couple of pages, to my agent, saying that this is the book I'm considering. Then that is given to the editor or editors; then they discuss it, and then contract discussions take place between the publisher and the agent for the terms.
Bakerman: Does the contract itself have any significance to you apart from the financial one?

Gould: For me—I think for many writers—the solemnity of the vow that is implicit in the contract is a cathartic experience and a spur and a permission. It permits one to say the book is real, to believe in it. There's someone waiting for it, which means that there's a point in one's spending all one's time and energy and stomach lining and heart on this particular project because someone cares. If you're just fooling around in your own lonely room, and the world doesn't care if it's completed, you tend, *I* tend, not to believe in it all.

Such good rewards: elation and ecstasy

Bakerman: What advice would you give to the unpublished writer?

Gould: The small satisfactions have to mean a great deal to make one survive the other stuff. There are a lot of people who can stay the route for one book. I think that there are very few people who can stay the route for a career as a writer because it is incredibly painful and lonely. I mean, you are not "Queen for a Day" as it looks like you are.

You read once in a while that somebody has signed a million-dollar contract, and what that represents is the hard- and softcover rights, and you prorate it over the eight years that it took the person to write the book, and then pay out the taxes and pay the agent and all that stuff, and that person is making $40,000 a year like any executive in a modest-sized company . . . but no one ever thinks about prorating.

Bakerman: What are some of those small satisfactions you spoke about?

Gould: The sense of elation at the accomplishment of a phrase or a paragraph. If you tried to prorate that, it would come out to about 15 minutes of ecstasy about every three years, and I don't know that that's enough to sustain most of us. But on the other hand, if you look at the average worker in other fields, in sort of drudgery kinds of jobs, there is no satisfaction, ever. The only elation they feel is, "I got through another week, and here's my paycheck."

Bakerman: People who don't write don't know what hard work it is, do they?

Gould: No, everyone assumes that everyone can write. The publishing industry at the present time is doing its best to create that impression. They now have an attitude that is very much like show business, which is we'll get new stars every year, new faces, fresh products . . . put them on the market shelves, send this one around on the tour. And then we have another hot topic, we have the fact that we've broken another taboo. Now we have a movie star's daughter who has talked about her movie star mother, and tomorrow we have somebody talking about incest in their family.

It's like what yellow journalism used to be. But they're talking about books, and once the assumption is made that everyone can write a book, that everyone has a story, you devalue the craft, the skill—and the point.

Bakerman: And the point is that you're creating something of substance? Something lasting?

Gould: But one reads these awful stories about poor bindings and how the book comes apart. Even if it's kept, the book is going to come apart before you die, and you question in ways that you never questioned before whether the value of your work is sufficient to demand what you have to give that work.

You feel as if you are writing for something that is designed to be destroyed immediately or to self-destruct—and then what is the point of writing? It seems as if you might just as well be writing for television, where people see it tonight and forget about it tomorrow morning.

When we all wanted to become writers, that was not what it was about. It was about writing your name on the cave and leaving a mark after you die.

Bakerman: How do you feel about the fact that people label some of your marks on the cave as "feminist literature"? Does it bother you?

Gould: Not if people mean the same thing by the term that I would mean by it, which is *humanist* in the sense that there is no qualitative difference or inferiority or superiority in one sex or the other. Unfortunately, you have to be called a feminist to elevate the concept of women to the idea of full humanity, and so that's what the term means. I think that any work that centers on this question of elevating the female to the full human or to the center or to the foregound is going to be called feminist for a long time.

Fabulous child and adult stories

Bakerman: Are there special problems for women writers?

Gould: One of the problems of women writers is that they are doubly isolated: they are isolated as women and as family people, and they are isolated as writers. And so this lemming-like attraction that housewives feel for the career of writing is really not an answer to their lives. What they need is to get into a situation where they have to interact with other adults. I think it's the wrong thing for writing now to be touted as the great solution to independence for women.

Bakerman: *X: A Fabulous Child's Story* was a big departure from your writing for adults. Was writing a children's story different? For instance, did you limit your vocabulary or did you pay the children the compliment of just being yourself?

Gould: I never watched my vocabulary while writing it; I wrote it as if I were talking to my own family, including the adults. I must say it's the thing that took me the least time of anything I've ever written, but I didn't know for sure that it was addressed to children. I've been told that it isn't, that any age person can read it without feeling that it's for another age group, which is fascinating.

Bakerman: Was it fun?

Gould: It was terrific fun, and I was exhilarated about it. My husband read it the day that I finished it—I don't really think it took me more than a couple of days—and he was so excited. He said, "It's the best thing you've ever done, and it's really important!" And it was thrilling because it worked so well for him. Then my children read it, and my older son—I don't remember how old he was when I finished it—said, "If they make a movie of it, I want to play X!"

Bakerman: Do you have a favorite among your books?

Gould: Oh, no. I like each of them for different things. It's like children; you never ask anybody which is their favorite child. I think that *Necessary Objects* was the most difficult kind of traditional novel, and I was very proud of getting all the threads together and braiding them and so forth. With *A Sea-Change*, I felt that I had taken this major step which put me in a whole new place as a writer, and so I valued it for that. *Final Analysis* I loved because of how it read, the humor in it, and the breezy style; it had a voice I like. They are all different facets of one's own personality.

Bakerman: Where would you like to go from here?

Gould: I don't know—if I get through this next book alive and not bleeding, I really am going to sit back and think very hard before I start another. It does not become less painful. I am having more pain with this than I remember having with any other book. They say it's like labor pain; you never remember what it's like until you're having it, but with childbirth I think it gets easier with successive children—but it's not the same with a book. With labor, you believe it will end or you recognize the territory, but each territory here, as we said before, is different, so I don't know; I really don't know.

A final analysis of new fiction

Bakerman: What other options are you considering?

Gould: I'm fascinated now creatively with visual media though so many writers are terrified of or contemptuous of things like television commercials and fiction that's written in that form. I think that the television commercial is a full-blown cultural phenomenon that is not even recognized as an art form in this culture—and it should be! It's a fusion of the creative fictional art and the modern technology that is beyond us, we who are rooted to the word on the page. It is yet another language that has evolved without us, and it has tremendous impact.

Bakerman: And it intrigues you as fiction?

Gould: I watch sometimes a commerical for a fragrance, which to me is the purest form of fiction because there's no product—the fragrance doesn't exist when the commercial is written, and no one has smelled it, and it doesn't remind anyone of anything—they simply begin as fiction writers begin, with a concept. And without words, this remarkable phenomenon is achieved, and I am stunned by how effective it is.

But word-people are contemptuous of it, and I think at their peril. That is why they've lost a great deal of their audience. That audience which responds to television no longer can glue its eyes to a page with gray type, and we're going to lose them completely if we don't understand that. We need to listen to them and to watch them because otherwise we're going to lose them very quickly.

Bakerman: If, apart from your books, you could send a message to your readers, what would it be?

Gould: Oh, gee . . . I think the fascinating thing about being a writer is that you speak to people who live with you in your world, and then you can find connections between them and yourself and the world that is and was and might be, and that there is something underneath the words that creates a thread, a bond, that is very strong. And I think that's why good books do not lose their power.

Tying up loose ends

by Manuel Komroff

Happy is the writer when he reaches the concluding pages of his novel. But at this point certain problems confront him.

Great care should be exercised to allow nothing, absolutely nothing, to hold back that feverish downhill rush of the narrative to the last lines of the work in progress. Care also must be exercised at this terminal state of the novel because of the importance of last words. The lines at the end of a book take on a special accent of their own. They represent a summing up, a conclusion, a rounding out or a final tying together of the narrative. Here, too, the philosophy or special meaning of the narrative is often reinforced with a final scene designed to linger in the reader's mind.

At this point the novelist feels that the reader has been terribly good to have stayed with him so long. He will want to satisfy his reader and leave no loose ends dangling in the air. Everything promised must be delivered. All loose ends must be tied up and disposed of in a satisfactory manner. Every character must be accounted for, so that the reader is not left questioning.

Thus by the raising of the black flag in the prison yard the reader learns that Tess of the D'Urbervilles has mounted the scaffold and paid with her life. The "sport with Tess" is done. This is the end. The life narrative is concluded by death. No more adventures are possible.

As for Mr. Pickwick, his adventures require some concluding remarks so that the reader will finally stop asking, "And then what happens?" Or, as Dickens himself says in the very last pages of this novel:

> It is the fate of all authors or chroniclers to create imaginary friends, and
> lose them in the course of art. Nor is this the full extent of their misfortunes;

Manuel Komroff, a native New Yorker, wrote 130 short stories and 13 novels in his lifetime. He was an editor for a publishing company and a teacher at Columbia University.

for they are required to furnish an account of them besides.

In compliance with this custom—unquestionably a bad one—we subjoin a few biographical words, in relation to the party at Mr. Pickwick's assembled.

These words are followed by eight short paragraphs disposing of the characters who have, for so many pages, amused the reader. The reader learns (1) that Mr. and Mrs. Winkle moved into a new house (2) that Mr. and Mrs. Snodgrass settled in Dingley Dell and cultivated a small farm (3) that Mr. Tupman "took lodgings at Richmond" (4) that Mr. Bob Sawyer accompanied by Mr. Allen sailed for India and (5) that Mrs. Bardell now earns a good profit letting rooms to single gentlemen, and her attorneys Messrs. Dodson and Fogg "continue in business, from which they realize a large income."

But the best is kept for the end. Dickens still has to account for Sam Weller, his father, and Pickwick himself. "Sam Weller kept his word, and remained unmarried, for two years." But then he marries Mary, who becomes Mr. Pickwick's housekeeper. The elder Mr. Weller retires and has independence from his income. Mr. Pickwick himself spends his days in great comfort, an honored gentleman, for "he is known by all the poor people about, who never fail to take off their hats, as he passes, with great respect." And now that the Pickwick Club has been dissolved, so that the reader can expect no further adventures. Mr. Pickwick employs his long leisure hours arranging the minutes which he will present to the secretary of his once famous organization.

This is an example of tying up the loose dangling ends. No vexing point remains for the reader to question. The adventures are ended by dissolving the club.

Summing up

So many loose ends which require to be tied in the last chapter present a difficulty and also a weakness of the novel as a form. Dickens himself recognized this weakness when he refers to this custom as "unquestionably a bad one." It is bad, though necessary. It is bad when, as in the case of *The Pickwick Papers*, a whole catalogue of characters must be listed. It is better when few characters remain at the very end to be accounted for. The picaresque novel, which is also episodic, seems to suffer from this defect.

Don Quixote employs a similar technique in its concluding chapter. The main characters of this episodic novel are quickly accounted for in the last pages. Don Quixote, you are certain, can never ride again for in the final pages you stand beside his bed and witness his last hours and his famous parting with the lovable Sancho, who cries out all in tears:

. . . don't die this bout, but take my counsel, and live on a many years; 'tis the maddest trick a man can ever play in his whole life, to let his breath sneak out of his body without any more ado, and without so much as a rap o'er the pate, or a kick in the guts. . . .

But Don Quixote brushes him aside and continues dictating his will, in which he mentions all the main characters in the book and in remembering them he also reminds the reader of the parts they played in the narrative now being concluded. In this way a quick review is accomplished. Such a concluding chapter as this suggests a kind of summary.

Recapitulation is often employed by the novelist in the last summing up. It serves as a slight reminder of where the reader has been and some of the more important emotional experiences which he has had. When these are added quickly together, the piling up has an emotional weight which is often most impressive.

In this way does the soldier in *The Red Badge of Courage* review briefly some highlights of the battle in the last pages of this novel.

> He had been where there was red of blood and black of passion, and he was escaped. His first thoughts were given to rejoicings at this fact.
> Later he began to study his deeds, his failures, and his achievements. Thus, fresh from scenes where many of his usual machines of reflection had been idle, from where he had proceeded sheeplike, he struggled to marshal all his acts.
> At last they marched before him clearly.

Then when these are reviewed a note of exaltation and prophecy seems to come forward and provide an artistic end to the novel.

> He had been in touch with the great death, and found that, after all, it was but the great death. He was a man.
> . . . Yet the youth smiled, for he saw that the world was a world for him, though many discovered it to be made of oaths and walking sticks. He had rid himself of the red sickness of battle. The sultry nightmare was in the past. He had been an animal blistered and sweating in the heat and pain of war. He turned now with a lover's thirst to images of tranquil skies, fresh meadows, cool brooks—an existence of soft and eternal peace.
> Over the river a golden ray of sun came through the hosts of leaden rain clouds.

In this manner is the reader returned from war to peace. He is returned from the experience of battle to the early pages of the novel which showed the youth on the farm.

That long awkward concluding catalogue of characters, so necessary to *The Pickwick Papers* and *Don Quixote*, is very often avoided in novels that employ fewer characters. These manage to dispose of their characters, one at a time, before they reach the concluding pages. In this way a certain freedom is obtained. The novelist is then free to use his last pages for more important matters.

Patterns beginning to end

The ending of a novel is closely related to the beginning of the novel. If the direction has been downward, as in the pattern of a tragic novel, it should continue its downward path to the very end. To attempt a sudden final upswing would be out of keeping with the substance of the narrative. A tragic novel must end on a note of tragedy. A comic novel must end with a note of comedy. Pickwick is consistently Pickwickian to the very end. The pattern is maintained throughout. The ending of a novel should be consistent with the over-all plan.

Added meaning is often given a novel by a final note of symbolism or prophecy.

The reader sees Lord Jim at the end in a noble light. While "he passes away under a cloud" he could not "in the wildest days of his boyish visions" have dreamed of "such an extraordinary success!" This is in preparation for that note of symbolism and prophecy which now enters the last page of the novel. The reader sees Jim as "an obscure conqueror of fame, tearing himself out of the arms of a jelous love" to go to his death "and celebrate his pitiless wedding with a shadowy ideal of conduct." To this symbol the narrator suggests a prophecy. Lord Jim's memory will linger on, for "there are days when the reality of his existence comes to me with an immense, with an overwhelming force. . . ."

A note of symbolism also concludes *Moby Dick*. As the entire crew of the boat, except for the narrator Ishmael, are dragged to the bottom of the sea by the evil white whale, the reader encounters a deeply moving passage of symbolic significance. As the ship is sinking with all its noble souls, an arm reaches out of the water to nail the flag fast to the mast. The captain and crew do not surrender, but go down with colors flying. At this moment a large sky-hawk is entangled in the flag and is nailed through.

> . . . and so the bird of heaven, with archangelic shrieks, and his imperial beak thrust upwards, and his whole captive form folded in the flag of Ahab, went down with his ship, which, like Satan, would not sink to hell till she had dragged a living part of heaven along with her, and helmeted herself with it. . . and the great shroud of the sea rolled on as it rolled five thousand years ago.

Such an ending seems entirely satisfactory for a novel which is charged throughout with mystical symbolism, though so deep a symbolism may not suit a more realistic narrative.

Yet, symbolism and prophecy may be joined to a realistic novel if the novel has been planned from the start as a realistic presentation of an idea which is symbolic.

Satisfaction

The modern French novelist Albert Camus had such an intention at the very outset of his novel *The Plague*. In this novel the reader is given a realistic picture of a small town in French Africa suddenly stricken with bubonic plague. This disease is carried by rats. The beginning of the book shows us the dead rats, on stairways, in courtyards and in numerous places. The city is then quarantined and life—all life—is surrounded by death. The reader begins to understand that this realistic picture has been designed to tell a little more than a factual account. He seeks a deeper meaning. Soon he gathers that this city represents all society. The illness is war; the disease, fascism.

When the siege of the city is lifted and the reader reaches the last page of *The Plague*, the symbolism and prophecy are clearly stated. They are reserved as a summing up for the last paragraph of the novel.

> And, indeed, as he listened to the cries of joy rising from the town, Rieux remembered that such joy is always imperiled. He knew what those jubilant crowds did not know but could have learnt from books: that the plague bacillus never dies or disappears for good; that it can lie dormant for years in furniture and linen-chests; that it bides its time in bedrooms, cellars, trunks, and bookshelves; and that perhaps the day would come when, for the bane and the enlightening of men, it would rouse up its rats again and send them forth to die in a happy city.

Now the reader knows that the disease is never really conquered, and in a note of prophecy he is is warned that war and fascism may again break the peace of civilization.

But unless the novelist has a definite philosophy, one that is sustained by his narrative, the sudden introduction of a note of symbolism and prophecy at the end of his novel will be incongruous. To try to strain for a symbol which hardly exists in the narrative at once adds a false note and leaves the reader in a very doubtful mood.

Moll Flanders can end her adventures very nicely without any suggestion of symbolism or prophecy. "We are now grown old; I am come back to England, being almost seventy years of age. . . ." And here she intends to pass the remainder of her years "in sincere penitence for the wicked" life she has led. The reader is content, and there is no need for symbolism or prophecy to enter such a clear and definite conclusion. She has sinned. She is seventy. She is sorry. We are satisfied.

The finished book

by Mark Twain

Do you know that shock? I mean, when you come, at your regular hour, into the sick room where you have watched for months, and find the medicine bottles all gone, the night table removed, the bed stripped, the furniture set stiffly to rights, the windows up, the room cold, stark, vacant—and you catch your breath. Do you know that shock?

The man who has written a long book has that experience the morning after he has revised it for the last time, seen the bearers convey it from the house, and sent it away to the printer. He steps into his study at the hour established by the habit of months—and he gets that little shock. All the litter and the confusion are gone. The piles of dusty reference books are gone from the chairs, the maps from the floor; the chaos of letters, manuscripts, notebooks, paper knives, pipes, matches, photographs, tobacco jars, and cigar boxes is gone from the writing table. The furniture is back where it used to be in the long ago. The housemaid, forbidden the place for five months, has been there, and tidied it up, and scoured it clean, and made it repellent and awful.

I stand here this morning, contemplating this desolation, and I realize that if I would bring back the spirit that made this hospital homelike and pleasant to me, I must restore the aids to lingering dissolution to their wonted places, and nurse another patient through and send it forth for the last rites, with many or few to assist there, as may happen; and that I will do.

Mark Twain (Samuel Clemens) was a humorist, satirist, lecturer, critic and one of America's most beloved writers. From his childhood and riverboat experiences in Missouri and travel experiences abroad he captured the mood and spirit of his time in such classics as Roughing It, Tom Sawyer, Life on the Mississippi, The Adventures of Huckleberry Finn, Puddn'head Wilson *and* A Connecticut Yankee in King Arthur's Court. *Many consider Mark Twain the father of American literature.*

All about agents

by Diane Cleaver

About two years ago, Robert Wilson, a writer in Detroit, sent me a proposal for a novel called *Crooked Tree*: He enclosed the first three pages of the prologue and a single-spaced outline in the midst of which he included paragraphs from different chapters as the story progressed. I couldn't tell much from the proposal, but I did like his letter and I was intrigued by the prologue. It had tone and texture, and it evoked feelings. I said I would read the complete manuscript. He didn't want to send the manuscript because it wasn't "in shape" yet, but I told him even if I could sell the novel from the proposal, which I doubted, it would sell for much less than it would if we sold it based on the completed manuscript. I felt if anyone even came near $2,500 we would be lucky.

Wilson sent me the manuscript rough and unedited. I read it one Sunday afternoon and began to get the feeling in the pit of my stomach: *This is really something.* A couple of months later I sold it to Putnam's for six figures. Then I sold the movie rights, and foreign rights have gone to England, Spain, France and Holland.

Could Wilson have reached his level of success if he had tried to sell the book himself? Maybe. But I think that I as his agent sold *Crooked Tree* more easily, more efficiently and more profitably than the author could have done himself. I don't mean to boast when I say that, because my point is that in most cases an agent will help make a writer's career easier and more profitable. That's the agent's job.

Basically, an agent is the writer's business partner, the liaison between you and your editor. The agent sells your books, negotiates royalty advances and other deals for you, and handles your contract negotiations. The agent takes care of any

Diane Cleaver is a literary agent with Sanford J. Greenburger Associates in New York City. Previously she was an editor at Doubleday, Straight Arrow, Scribners and Simon & Schuster. "I don't think anyone grows up thinking she is going to be an agent," she reflects. "It's a profession that might be defined as a byproduct of experience."

problems or negotiations that don't specifically concern the manuscript (and some that do), so that your dealings with your editor can focus on the writing, which is, after all, the most important part of a publishing deal. In other words, the agent serves as your link to the publishing industry. In fact, as publishing has changed— bigger companies, increased competition for books, higher costs everywhere—it has evolved that the agent is often the *only* permanent force in an author's career.

An author once could find an editor and publisher and stay with them forever. Editors, an author's real connection with the publisher, change jobs more often now; there's no security that the editor who signed you up will be the editor who publishes you. And companies don't stick with their authors through thick and thin, through good books and bad, through profit and loss. Authors frequently change publishing houses. Agents, whether with a company or on their own, are independent. They work for themselves, they are not likely to change jobs, they grow with their authors. Moreover, they know the publishing business. They know what companies have money and are operating from a position of strength, and what companies are about to go broke or are over-inventoried in certain categories. Agents know what publishers are buying, what kinds of books they do well with, the style of the houses, the range of advances, how large the publisher's list is, and whether they have good sales and promotion departments. And agents know editors' tastes and what they respond well to. For instance, when writer Diane Simmons submitted her novel, *Let the Bastards Freeze in the Dark*, to me, I immediately thought of Larry Freundlich at Wyndham Books. I have known Freundlich for some time—we worked at Doubleday together—and I have a good idea of what his tastes are. The personality of *Let the Bastards Freeze in the Dark* matched Freundlich's personality, so I sent the book to him first. He bought it.

Authors can pick up marketing information like this, but it takes time and energy that should be put into writing. Understanding publishing and how to work effectively in that world is the *agent's* job.

Publication problems

Another important role of the agent is maintaining smooth relations between the author and the editor. For example, money is a prime cause of friction between author and editor. An editor's responsibility and priority is the manuscript. If an author and editor negotiate a contract together they can become upset before they even approach the manuscript. Perhaps an argument will arise not because of the advance itself, but because the author wants his sister-in-law, a painter, to do the dust jacket. That's likely to be a marketing decision, not the editor's. The agent can cope with the realities of the author's sister-in-law, or discuss the reprint split up front before the editor is ready to make his final offer. If an author is upset with a publisher and an editor is irritated with the author, the manuscript can suffer. An agent's role is mediating the problems of publication.

Selling books and making deals are essential functions of agents, but the agent's importance to a writer doesn't stop there. For example, agents have the responsibility to help their clients realize their ideas, to find ideas for them, and to guide them toward the right projects and, equally important, away from those not to pursue. Ideas often need focusing and I can sometimes help that process by asking the right questions. Focus makes the difference between a salable and unsalable idea.

Agents, however, don't do everything. I can't, for example, write your proposal or book, or teach you how to write a salable novel. What I should be able to do is see the possibilities in ideas and manuscripts, ask the right questions, and make suggestions. I have read hundreds of manuscripts and proposals in which the author assumes that the reader knows as much as he does about it. Half the book is still in the author's head. Things that seem obvious to authors are not always obvious to readers. I try to pinpoint the weak spots.

Trust, ego and commitment

As an agent, I have a great interest in making my writers' work salable and in helping them succeed. The success of the author is the success of the agent, and this correlation makes the writer-agent relationship intimate and tenuous.

It's intimate whether or not the author and agent are the best of friends (although, even if you don't meet often, there must be respect, liking and admiration on both sides) because a book is not just a product to be marketed: It's personal; it involves ego and commitment.

The relationship is tenuous because it's based so much on trust; the agent trusts the writer to execute his ideas, the author trusts the agent to direct and support, and to make every effort to sell those ideas—that book—to absolutely the best advantage. Without trust and support on both sides, agent and writer can lose faith and interest very quickly.

Authors sometimes believe that agents, like publishers, are interested only in big books and big money. They worry that agents aren't going to care about them and their work, that the agent didn't try hard enough, or that the manuscript isn't selling because the agent doesn't know what she's doing. Sometimes these things are true, but mostly agents don't take on books they don't like or don't think they can sell; they want a reasonable advance as much as the author.

I think too that authors often feel tenuous with agents because they know agents have other clients, that sometimes an author's book is not always his agent's priority. The author has spent a lot of time on his manuscript; it's his priority every day, whether it's being written, being read, in the hands of an agent, with a publisher, or being published. Agents can't be so single-minded. My aim is to give each manuscript the attention necessary to sell it, even if the attention is sometimes brief. I try to be there at the right time with the right call, note or response to a writer, or a nagging call to a publisher; to keep my manuscripts circulating; to urge publishers to respond. Because there are hundreds of things to follow through on all of the time I write myself hundreds of notes about when to follow up on this or when to call about that. During one day I probably talk to 60 or 70 people—writers, publishers, people with ideas, others wanting information. Fortunately, my mind can jump around and concentrate on each call or conversation or manuscript for however long it takes. Because I'm caught up with many different books and writers and editors doesn't mean I can't do a good job for each book, each writer. But I must have the trust and support of the author to do that job.

Commission rates

Some agents won't take on authors without a signed written agreement. Other agents believe agreements aren't that important, that if an agent and author aren't getting along there's no point in working together. I agree with that, but I also realize that agreements offer protection. Agents do get burned by authors. We have all worked with authors over extensive periods of time, shaping the proposal and talking to publishers, only to have the author, with his material in shape and salable, dump the agent and make a deal himself. Authors don't pay agents for any direction or assistance until a contract is made. We don't make money unless we sell manuscripts, and we can work with someone a long time before that happens. Once a book is sold, there's no problem; the agent's clause becomes part of the publisher's contract and states that all monies earned on that particular book go through the agent.

Agents earn their money by deducting commissions from these sales. Most of us don't charge for reading or working with you before we sell your books. There is no reason why you should pay an agent for "reading and evaluation." If an agent is interested, either from your letter of inquiry or sample chapters, she will read, and often comment on, your manuscript free of charge.

Commission rates are changing. Until recently the standard rate was 10%. Many agents, and I'm one of them, now charge a 15% commission. There are lots of 10% agents; some are long-established and have been able to maintain effective selling with a 10% commission. The 10% agent is still the rule rather than the exception, but I think that is changing and as newer agents come along, and the marketplace changes, even some of the most established literary agents will be forced to raise their commissions. I have heard of one agent charging 12% and another who goes as high as 20% (but that's *very* rare). More agents are charging 15% because overhead is increasing. Our agency, for example, could not supply the services we do for less than 15%. Our mail and messenger expenses alone are enormous. We don't charge authors when we telephone them long distance. We don't charge them for foreign submissions. If we sell, we're covered; if we don't, we're out of pocket. A 15% commission makes us more effective as selling agents because we have the staff and facilities to work efficiently.

The agreement and disagreement

Be careful when confronted with agreements to be sure you're not signing away 10% or 15% of everything. If you're writing a novel, for example, but also sell regularly to magazines and place those stories yourself, you may not want to pay an agent's commission on that work. Or you might not want to be committed to an agent for two or three years. A writer who was dissatisfied with her agent recently asked me to represent her. She wrote her agent, informing him that the relationship was terminated. When I read the agreement she and her agent had signed, however, I discovered that she was bound to the agent until November because the contract has a self-renewing clause, something the writer hadn't realized when she first signed the agreement. I think agreements on a book-by-book basis are best; they protect the agent's immediate interest but don't tie the author to a relationship that one day might not be happy and mutually productive.

Market analysis

Now, let's take a closer look at exactly what an agent does to earn her commission.

First and foremost, agenting is selling. Once I decide I like a manuscript and want to represent it, I must think about how to sell it. There are several things to consider when analyzing the potential market for a book:

Who is the audience for the book? Is it for a special audience, or will readers in general be interested it it?

What publishers would reach the right audience? It's obvious that I'm going to stay away from a paperback house that specializes in gothic romances if I have a war novel.

Within the publishing houses that might be interested, which editor will respond most enthusiastically? Even though a publishing house as a whole has a specific "taste" in books, to which editors try to conform, individual tastes will vary widely anyway. I want to find the editor whose tastes match the book I'm selling.

What format (hardcover, etc.) best serves the book, and what publishers specialize in that format? If, for instance, the book has strong sales or literary potential, I will take it to hardcover publishers because it will get review attention and stands a decent chance of a good reprint sale. If it's a genre fiction book with a more established audience, or if I don't believe it will get major review attention, I may go straight to a paperback original house (though I might go to a hardcover publisher, depending on the book.)

What are the subsidiary rights possibilities? Does the book have, for example, a good possiblity of being made into a movie? If it does, it has greater sales potential.

How many copies do I think it will sell? Based on what I know about sales of similar books, I will estimate how many copies of this particular book will sell. If I think it will sell 50,000 copies, my options are unlimited; everyone wants to publish a book that sells that well. If I think it will sell 10,000 copies, I will probably turn to a smaller publisher or an editor who will love this book and give it the special care it will need.

How much will I sell it for? I estimate this figure based on my answers to all the above questions, and on the sale price of similar books. If I know a book has great potential, I will set a high selling price and go to the publishers that can afford and are willing to pay the price.

Sometimes I answer my own questions incorrectly. For instance, sometimes I believe a book will sell for $25,000, and I'm only able to sell it for $15,000. Sometimes, though, it works the other way. When I sold Jessie Ford's *Love, Remember Me* (a first novel, by the way), Ballantine Books bought it for $2,500 *more* than I had estimated. I was particularly delighted because it's unusual for me to estimate on the low side. Obviously, Ballantine knows their market a little better than I do: They made a splash with the book—a large print order, floor displays and promotion, and now eagerly await her second novel.

One on one

How one actually *sells* a manuscript varies from book to book. Sometimes I read a manuscript and think of one editor immediately, and will make a single submission. Sometimes I think of several editors who would like it and then often I will make a multiple submission. I have to act on my knowledge of the book, the book's potential market, and what I know about editors and their publishers. I rely on information I have gathered by talking with editors about their needs over the phone and over lunch, by studying each publisher's catalogs, by studying publishers' ads and other information in industry trade publications like *Publishers Weekly*.

A multiple submission is a proposal (and sometimes a manuscript) that goes to several editors; it *doesn't* mean an auction. Publishers make an offer and I accept the best one.

There was a time when publishers didn't like multiple submissions. They resented agents pushing for faster answers, and they didn't like being placed in the position of competing with other publishers. These attitudes are changing, however, to everyone's benefit. Authors get faster answers and publishers get a chance to see many more manuscripts in which they might be interested than they did before. Publishers still don't react favorably to authors conducting their *own* multiple submissions, though.

Most of my submissions go through the mail, with one exception: I would never submit an "auction" book through the mail. An auction is a multiple submission with a deadline for responses and the understanding that the publishers involved are competing with each other, with me as the agent mediating. When I'm auctioning a book, I first call the editors, then send a copy of the manuscript to them by messenger. Some editors will stop by my office to pick up the book if they're in the neighborhood. I give the publishers the minimum bid I will accept, and I will take bids until the deadline, called the *closing date*. If a publisher's bid is topped by another publisher, the first has the right to make a counterbid. I keep all interested publishers informed of the current high bid via the phone.

Multiple submissions are very common, auctions rarer. I must be sure that I have something everyone will want—because of the stature of the author, the brilliance of the manuscript, the timeliness of the subject, and the commercial value of the book—before I conduct an auction for it. Nothing is more embarrassing than holding an auction that no one wants to participate in.

Bob Wilson's *Crooked Tree* was sold through an auction, and I think we got a better deal on it because of that. The publishers involved knew that *Crooked Tree* was a good book, and would have paid healthy advances for it. But because they could see exactly how much other publishers were willing to invest in the book, and were afraid to lose a valuable property, they were willing to raise their offers to make sure they landed the book. Besides, auctioning a book makes editors look at it differently; they know an agent won't bother auctioning a run-of-the-mill property.

Advance warning

Selling the book is only the beginning. The next step is negotiating the advance and contract, and an agent can usually get a much better deal than an unagented author can get. Before becoming an agent, I worked as an editor at several large publishing houses, including Doubleday and Simon & Schuster. I discovered very quickly that, in general, authors were paid modest advances, that very little attention was paid to most books, and that once a book was sold to a publisher an author had very little to say about what happened to it.

Over the years as an editor I worked with dozens of authors and became convinced that not only were those with agents financially better off, but that their books also were published better. It's not that publishers are out to take advantage of writers, but they *are* out to make the best deal they can on their terms. The less money they pay an author, the more profit they will make. The publisher, for example will resist paying an author $10,000 and offer $7,500 even though he knows it's worth the higher figure. Nine times out of ten the author will accept the lower figure. An agent will be much firmer than the author and nearly always get the $10,000. And very often an agent won't have to push too hard, because the publisher will come to the agent with an offer of $10,000 in the first place, realizing the agent's stronger bargaining power.

One bestselling author I know began her career with a book she sold herself for $2,500. Her publisher had, as sales rose, increased her advances for succeeding books, offering her $70,000 for her fourth. Then she got an agent who knew the author was worth more than the advance offered, and demanded more. The publisher thought the agent was way off-base, but four weeks later came back with an offer for more than $600,000. Their view of the author's work also changed; they had to follow through on what a $600,000 commitment meant: They had to advertise and promote the book rigorously to sell enough copies to recover their investment. Because of that, the author hit the bestseller list and the publisher recouped its investment through bookstore sales and a large reprint sale—which was enchanced by the agent selling a miniseries to television. Today that author is over the million-dollar advance mark.

Author advantages

Often publishers don't say, "I'll offer you this much"; they say, "How much do you want?" I don't, most of the time, give an on-the-nose-figure; I give a range because both the publisher and I need room to negotiate. I try not to be unrealistic about advances to either the author or publisher. I don't want to promise the author more than I think the book will sell for, and I don't want to ask the publisher for an advance so large that the book won't be worth his while to publish it.

Books don't have fixed prices; it's a fluid market and I try to use it to the author's advantage. The successful negotiation is one in which each party comes away believing that he has won a prize. The editor should feel that he wasn't pushed to the wall, and the author and agent should know they received a fair price.

The advance is only part of the negotiation. It is the obvious part and the key to whether you are finally going to settle with each other. If the advance satisfies both sides, the agent is in a stronger position to negotiate all the other rights—splits on reprints, royalties and options, or approvals on subsidiary sales.

An author selling directly to a publisher has little negotiating power. The publisher handles all rights on behalf of the author and tells you what the splits are.

Most publishing contracts are fairly standard. Publishers usually split reprint rights (paperback reprint of a hardcover book, usually), book club rights and second serial rights (magazine or newspaper excerpts after publication) with the author—a 50/50 split is standard. The split on reprint rights is a point of negotiation, though some publishers will not budge on the 50/50 split, but many will. It is possible on some contracts to get a 60/40 or a 55/45 split at a certain point. For instance, a publisher might agree to split money made on reprint sales 50/50 until $100,000 is made, and then give the author 55% after that.

First serial rights are the rights to sell excerpts or condensations of the book to a magazine or newspaper before publication. Usually the amounts involved are modest, but excerpts give the book exposure. Some agents put more stress on these rights than others. Sometimes a publisher will ask for first serial or foreign rights, or a share in any movie deal.

The world market

Foreign rights are usually sold through subagents in a foreign market, and, depending on the arrangement, an American usually leaves all the negotiations up to the subagent. They know their market, the publishers and the prices. Not every book is right for foreign audiences; some are inherently American in content and form.

I can help the subagents I work with when foreign publishers visit New York.

Foreign editors make periodic trips to call on American publishers and agents to get an idea of what's happening in the coming year, what rights haven't sold abroad yet. When I meet with a foreign editor I tell him about the books I have sold and why he might be interested, and tell him he can get the manuscript through my subagent. Or, if he has time and I have a spare manuscript, he can read it while in New York. When he goes home, he can negotiate the sale with my subagent.

Whatever the interests and strengths of American literary agents, authors are usually well-represented in foreign markets. If a sale is possible, it will be made, although for smaller advances. Our agency has agents all over the world and I regularly keep in touch with them through phone calls, telexes and letters, telling them what I have sold, to whom, why it might interest them—as much information as I can give to help them sell in their territories.

There are lots of other details in contracts: author's warranty, discount and special sales royalties, out-of-print clauses, payment schedules, option on next work—all points to discuss and negotiate. Sometimes, although this is a tough one, an agent can have some kind of advertising budget, guaranteeing that a set amount will be spent to advertise the book, written into the contract. This is passionately resisted by publishers and usually they prevail. Sometimes in a big auction one publisher will win over another, when they have both offered similar advances, by agreeing to a predetermined amount to be spent on advertising.

This happened to *The Bidders*, by John Baxter. Several publishers were interested, but the deal was clinched for Lippincott when they included a $25,000 advertising budget in their contract. Advertising commitments are sometimes used in negotiating for a book by an established author, even when it's not an auction.

After selling the book and negotiating the deal, the agent's third major function is to serve as a liaison between writers and editors, and to keep both informed and happy. An editor at Doubleday a few years ago always told her authors as they signed the contract, "You love me now, but wait until we publish your book." Often authors become upset with publishers—not enough is being done, the copy editor changed the sense of something, the jacket is terrible, why is it taking so long? Then after publication there aren't any copies of the book in the local bookstore; the author's aunt called from Kalamazoo and can't find the book either; another author was on television, why isn't he?; where are the reviews?

Often the agent can explain to the author what's happening, or, for serious problems, get answers from the publisher and affect what is happening—like making sure the book is in the author's hometown and Kalamazoo, and reassuring the author that the entire publishing industry is not conducting a campaign designed to ruin his life. The relationship between author and editor should be smooth and supportive, not overwhelmed by problems that can reflect on the book.

It's also the agent's role to keep the names of authors in the minds of editors. I talk about what my authors are writing, what they have sold, what I'm selling, what the reviews have said, who bought the paperback rights, vague ideas that seem to have possiblities. Who knows what may happen in the future, what my writers will be up to next, what editors will be looking for? We broadcast as much information as we can about whom we represent and what they're doing.

Hooray for Hollywood?

Movie rights, particularly on certain novels, are potentially the most financially rewarding for an author. Although Hollywood and New York publishers are currently having a hot romance and we all read about the big book deals becoming big film deals or television miniseries, a lot of it is pie-in-the-sky. Most movie deals, whether feature or television, are option deals: The producer will pay the writer $3,500, for example, for the right to decide about using the book for a film. The producer has paid $3,500 for a one-year *option* on the book, and if he actually decides to produce the film, he will pay much more money, perhaps up to $35,000. The $3,500 option against a $35,000 pick-up price is in the range of most deals for two-hour television movies; a $10,000 option against a $100,000 pick-up price is typical for a feature movie deal.

I have been involved with big book, big film deals. Film rights to Robert Wilson's *Crooked Tree* went for $250,000, for instance. But I'm more often involved with what can be termed "normal" film rights dealings. My sale of Madeena Spray Nolan's *The Gift* to TV, for instance, was an option deal to a studio. They are in the process of developing the property—finding a director, a scriptwriter, trying to put the pieces together. And I've recently optioned for *Selma, Lord, Selma*, a love story written by Sheyann Webb and Rachel West Nelson and published by the University of Alabama. It will probably be produced as a docudrama, and is hardly the glittery project many writers imagine a Hollywood deal to be.

Also to be negotiated are matters of sequels and remakes, foreign distribution, running time (the longer the film, the more the book author is paid)—all of which can mount up if the option is picked up, if the film is made, and if it hits.

Hollywood *is* part of what's happening to publishing—big books, big money. Several publishing houses are connected to film companies—Gulf and Western owns Simon & Schuster, Pocket Books and Paramount; MCA (Universal) owns Putnam, Berkley and Jove; Warner Bros. has its own film and book divisions. The big studios and smaller production companies have New York story editors who concentrate on publishing. They all want to see any and all manuscripts before any of the other movie people do. They see agents, they see editors, they have contacts in book clubs, in production departments, in subsidiary rights departments. If they can't get a manuscript from one source, they track it through another. Which means it's very hard for anyone to keep control of what studio or what producer or what story editor saw a manuscript when. This can create a problem if a studio sees a pirated manuscript and turns it down. The word goes around pretty fast, and, as everyone's looking for the same thing—the big book that'll be a big movie—it can't be any good if somebody already turned it down.

This is Hollywood and publishing at its most frustrating. Sometimes a producer does fall in love with a book and wants to take an option, or even, on rare occasions, to buy it, and then he will go out to find backing.

Most New York agents work with Hollywood agents when they have a book that seems like a movie possibility and when their doors haven't been beaten down by the New York story editors or studios or producers. Most of us know producers or other movie people, but getting around in Hollywood is as complicated as getting around in New York publishing.

Landing an agent

By now you should agree with me that an agent can go far in advancing your career, and that you should get one. Finding an agent that suits you can be very difficult, however; or it can be surprisingly easy. Here are a few tips to get your started.

If you know other writers, ask them who their agents are and how they feel about them. Perhaps they will let you use their names by way of introduction to the agents. These are the sorts of contacts you can develop by joining writers' clubs and organizations.

You can sometimes get in touch with an agent by attending writers' conferences, which often feature agents as speakers. Carry samples of your work to the conference. You probably won't get a chance to show the agent the samples, but you can try. Besides, you can at least introduce yourself to the agent so she will have a face to associate with your name when you later write her a query letter.

If you contribute regularly to a magazine, or have built a rapport with an editor in some other way, ask the editor if he can recommend any agents. Magazine editors buy material from agents regularly—usually book excerpts for their pages—and are often in a position to be helpful.

Another way to get an agent is to submit your book to the publishers yourself. When a publisher is interested enough to make you an offer, ask the editor to recommend an agent, or approach an agent yourself. Most publishers won't mind your bringing in an agent at the last minute; in fact, most will prefer working with an agent over working with the author directly. One of my new clients used just that route: She approached me after a publisher had made her an offer, and I have agreed to represent her.

Sometimes editors read manuscripts they like or think promising but for one reason or another can't take on. They recommend agents to writers.

And agents find writers. Sometimes articles will strike the right chord and we think there might be a book in that story, or we read a distinctive short story and think the author might be working on a novel.

If an agent doesn't write to you, and you don't know any other writers, and you don't have a distant relative with connections in the publishing industry, and you don't have an offer from a publisher (and even if you do), the approach used by Colleen McCullough, author of *The Thorn Birds*, is as good as any. McCullough found her agent in *Literary Market Place*. She chose Frieda Fishbein because she was preparing fish that night, and wrote Fishbein a query letter. The decision was whimsical, but indeed fortuitous for both of them.

Write to an agent or several agents, telling them about your book, who you are and why you're qualified to write it, and why you want to write it. *Don't send your manuscript.* Please enclose a self-addressed envelope with suitable postage for a reply. Ask if they will consider your work. If they won't, you will find out much faster than if you send a complete manuscript, which will have to take its turn with a lot of other manuscripts; and it might not get read at all. I receive at least 15 manuscripts a week from new writers. Because of commitments to writers I already represent, it takes a while to read new material. I'm always way behind. And guilty. Most agents and editors don't read in the office; we read at nights and weekends. Many agents don't accept unsolicited manuscripts or new authors at all and sometimes we're just too busy with the authors we already have to consider new clients.

Some writers think that if only an agent could read the full manuscript, she would be convinced that the manuscript was salable. Sometimes that's true, but usually it's not. I can tell well enough from a letter whether your book is something I want to know more about. If there's enough to capture my interest, I will ask to read a proposal, or perhaps two or three chapters. If I'm still interested I will ask to read the complete manuscript. If I don't think I'm the right agent for you, at the very least you will get a letter saying so and you can cross me off your list.

That letter of inquiry is important because it gives an initial impression, however limited and subliminal it is; it might prompt me to ask for more. Letters of inquiry should be direct and factual. Here's an example of a good query letter that interested me, and eventually led to my taking on the letter's author, Jessie Ford, as a client.

> Dear Ms. Cleaver:
> I am inquiring about your interest in and requirements for representing me for a historical romance I have written entitled *Love Remember Me.*
>   *Love Remember Me* is complete at 707 ms pages, and is a novel set in Europe, Louisiana and California, with the most significant action occurring just prior to the opening of the Civil War. The historical portion of the story deals with pro-Southern leanings and intrigues in California during that era.

Here Ford included two paragraphs describing the novel's two protagonists—Louisa Boyd Hudson and Aaron Sumner—and detailing the events that shape the protagonists' lives, and therefore the novel. Ford continues:

>   The essential romantic conflict of the novel centers on Aaron's ambivalent feelings for Louisa, his doubts and fears, his refusal to communicate his love for her, and on Louisa's misery as a result. The couple come close emotionally and back away, torturing themselves and each other with the kind of skill at which lovers are often so adept.
>   This is my first novel—actually my first venture (adventure) into professional writing.
>   Please advise me of what your requirements are in order for you to review my novel, and under what terms you would accept the ms for marketing. I have enclosed a self-addressed, stamped envelope for your reply. Thank you.

I sold the book to Ballantine.

Some agents will ask you to send along some sample chapters rather than the entire manuscript—three chapters are usually requested. If so, send the *first* three chapters, not chapters five, seven and ten. A book evolves, and by the end of chapter three, whether it's fiction or nonfiction, I should know your point of view, the focus of your book, who the characters are, what the situation is, and what elements combine to make this book unique and worth looking at further. By sending disparate chapters you do yourself a disservice by not allowing me to take part in the evolution of your ideas, which is what reading is all about.

Prejudices and passions

If I don't ask to see some of your work, it might be because the idea doesn't seem well thought-out, or because the topic doesn't interest me. If you write only articles, poetry or short stories, you are not likely to find (or even need) an agent to represent you. Magazine and journal editors buy from such writers and specialists regularly and directly. Literary agents cannot make enough profit on 10% or 15% of a $500 or $1,000 magazine sale to expend the effort. If you have done a story series (and it has been published), however, you may have the makings of a book proposal on the same theme. An agent might be interested in hearing about that. Most agents only deal with authors working on book projects exclusively.

Agents will take you on if they have the time, like your ideas, and believe that you can write the book you propose—and that they can sell it. Much of publishing is based on personal opinion and agents have as many opinions, prejudices and passions as do editors and publishers and authors. I know I do. To work well with an author, I must have confidence in his abilities and respect his point of view. To sell and negotiate effectively, I must have confidence in what I'm selling. That confidence is, ultimately, based on the quality of the manuscript and my own opinions about it.

Most agents have stories about manuscripts they didn't take on because they didn't like them or see them as possibilities, only to watch them become successful with another agent. And that's all right.

There's also the other side of the coin when an agent takes on a book and then can't find the right publisher immediately. It sometimes seems that the author and agent are the only two people in the world who have faith in the book. If agents didn't believe in the books they represent, they would give up submitting them very quickly. Selling a book takes doggedness and passion and that's what agents must have. For example, Philip Spitzer, a dedicated agent who cares about writers, represents author William Schnurr, whose book *Johnny Death* was turned down by 30 publishers before Pocket Books took it.

Clients and contacts

When you finally find an agent who suits you, remember one thing: An agent won't solve all your problems. *You* must still write the book. Moreover, simply having an agent doesn't guarantee that your book will be sold quickly, or at all. Give your agent enough time—and enough trust—to do her job effectively. I work with 60 authors, and that seems to be a typical client list. I try to get in touch with each one every month or so. If your agent doesn't contact you that often, drop a note every couple of months asking where the manuscript is. If it's sitting in the agent's office, it's temporarily worthless. Also, some agents don't return phone calls; they should, because the agent-author relationship must be strong and open.

We need each other. Authors need agents because agents can make a profound difference to a writer's career, and because they need a voice in publishing. It's a fact, and not really a sad one, that once an author has finished his manuscript and mailed it off, it is, for all intents and purposes, no longer his. It belongs to his agent, to his editor and publisher, to the marketplace. Other people will discuss the work, make decisions about it, act on those decisions; none of them is going to *feel* that work as much as the author did; his part is over and the best thing he can do is sit down in front of the typewriter and begin the next book.

With a good agent behind you, though, you don't have to exist in the vacuum created by writing "the end" to something you have spent two years working on. You can know that someone is defending your interests, is concerned about your career as a writer, and is going to make as much money as she possibly can on your behalf.

And agents need authors, because without you we would have nothing to believe in, nothing to hustle like mad for. The story of Bob Wilson is a good example of a beneficial agent-author relationship. If he hadn't contacted me, he may never have sold his proposal, he may not have earned a six-figure advance, and the book might not have sold to the movies. And I most assuredly would not have earned a five-figure commission.

Agents who handle fiction

Many writers—among them, novelists John Updike and Joseph Wambaugh—prefer not to have an agent. They do their own deal-making, hire an attorney for contract review, and keep the 10%—or, increasingly, the 15%—for themselves. Others find an agent invaluable and cannot function in the manuscript-marketing world without one. Still others cannot find an agent at all. They lack the credits, the contacts . . . whatever it takes to get an agent's sincere attentions.

Getting an agent

If you are hunting for an agent, the search won't be easy. But if you have good ideas (preferably book-length ones), and if you are persistent, the search can be successful. The most direct approach is to contact an agent by mail with a brief query letter (not to exceed two single-spaced typewritten pages) in which you describe your work, yourself, and your publishing history. For fiction, a few sample chapters (up to 50 typed double-spaced pages) will tell an agent whether the book is no or go. Your letter should be personalized—not a photocopied form letter with the agent's name typed in; and *always include SASE* with enough postage for a reply plus return of materials. If you don't hear from an agent within six weeks, send a polite note asking if the material has been received—and include a photocopy of your original query plus materials and another SASE. If you hear nothing within four months, send a note withdrawing the material—and contact another agent using the same method, immediately.

Agents and the market today

Literary agencies generally come in three sizes: small (handling up to 60 clients), medium (up to 100), and large (over 100). An agent should not be measured by the number of clients, or even by the number of sales made in a given time period, but rather by the number of deals and dollars that really account for writing success. Agents work for *additional* sales of your manuscripts. No good agent will be satisfied selling your novel to a hardcover publisher, for instance;

he'll invest some time in selling it to a paperback house, to a movie producer, to a newspaper syndicate for serialization, to a book club, to a foreign publisher. To do this, the agent exercises energy, ideas, connections and business experience the writer probably doesn't have.

Most agents do not handle magazine articles, short stories, poetry, or essays. There is not enough revenue generated from such sales to make them worth an agent's time. Most writers develop their own rapport with the people who edit such publications and sell to them directly. Later, when a writer is doing books, his agent may handle such small sales—as a professional courtesy, not an income maker. If you are writing genre fiction—such as mysteries, science fiction or romances—you may have to get a couple of book sales behind you before an agent will handle your work. Most publishers who do genre fiction are generally receptive to hearing from authors directly anyway.

Some agents specialize. A list of play agents, for example, is available from The Dramatist Guild, 234 W. 44th St., New York City 10036 (include SASE when making the request). Agents who handle screenplays are listed in the *Screenplay Sales Directory* (published by Joshua Press, 8033 Sunset Blvd., Suite 306, West Hollywood, California 90046; write for price information on current edition). Most of the agents in the list that follows are members of the Independent Literary Agents Association (Box 5257, FDR Station, New York City 10022), or the Society of Authors' Representatives (40 E. 49th St., New York City 10016). The SAR publishes a pamphlet called "The Literary Agent," which explains the role of the agent and how to get an agent, and lists the current SAR membership. The pamphlet is free, *if* you send SASE (#10 size envelope) with the request. Also available from SAR (for $1.65 in U.S. postage stamps *only*; they do not accept checks) is a packet that includes copies of two model contracts (one for US book publication, the other for foreign translation rights). Write to Jeanne Boose, executive secretary at SAR, who adds: "The model contracts were prepared by SAR committees and are recommended by this association. The contracts' contents reflect the views of a majority of our membership, but members are in no way bound to use them. It should be pointed out that whatever form is used, modifications and changes are always involved."

The fee-charging agent

In "The Literary Agent" pamphlet, the SAR stresses what an agent *cannot* do: Agents can't "sell unsalable work; teach a beginner how to write salable copy; act as editor of the writer's work; solve the author's personal problems or lend money; be available outside of office hours except by appointment; or perform the functions of press agent, social secretary or travel agent." In other words, having an agent is *not* the final solution to your writing problems. An agent can aid and simplify your career, but ultimately your career is in your hands.

One of the SAR bylaws states that its members may not charge "reading fees"—that is, fees to read and consider a submission. Some agents, however, do charge fees, claiming that reading new material consumes so much time that might otherwise be spent selling books, they have to charge the fee or stop reading unsolicited material altogether. Here are some questions to ask about reading fees:

Is it a one-time fee, or will you have to pay again on subsequent submissions?
Will you have to pay the fee again when resubmitting a revised manuscript?
Will the fee be refunded if the agent decides to represent you?

Will the agent waive the fee if you have already had work published, or if you have particular expertise in the area you are writing about?

What do you get for the fee? Just a reading, or some criticism and analysis?

Agents may offer suggestions on how a book might be rewritten to be made salable, but under no circumstances do legitimate agents charge a fee for editing your manuscript. *Editing should be done by editors—after the book is sold.*

Remember, though, that most agents *don't* charge a reading fee, and you should try to work with those agents first.

The pseudo-agent

Do not confuse true literary agents with other individuals or "agencies" that advertise as "consultants" offering manuscript criticism or "literary services" for a fee that may cover a critique, an edit, or a rewrite of your manuscript. Ask anyone who claims to be an "agent," or who uses agent-like phrasing ("We like your manuscript and we think it is marketable—of course, some revisions will be neces sary to make it professionally acceptable," etc.) when discussing a fee of any sort, to give you a list of *recent* book sales. If an agent type has not sold three books to established publishing houses in the previous year, he is probably out of the publishing market midstream. Make sure you can afford such literary services offered you. Fees may range from several hundred to several *thousand* dollars—and there is no guarantee that the arrangement will result in a sale to recoup your investment. Such firms and individuals may make their profits from reading and criticism and editing fees—not from sales to publishers.

Contract considerations

Be careful, too, in signing any contract with an agent. Many legitimate agents conduct business with a handshake, believing that a contract will neither solidify a good relationship nor help a bad one. They want to be free to drop (or add) clients as relationships develop. Other agents—and many pseudo-agents—require a contract that should be studied carefully with an attorney before signing. Know what rights the agent is handling for your material, and check that no charges are made for services that you do not fully understand and agree to. Some agencies charge for criticism or impose a "marketing fee" for office overhead, etc. If you pay such a fee, you are entitled to see any correspondence that such a marketing endeavor would produce.

Legitimate agents will discuss marketing problems a manuscript might be having. If you have any doubts about where (or whether) your manuscript is being marketed, ask to see the mail between your agent and the publishers he claims to be showing your work to. If you have paid a marketing fee, it is illegal for the agent to withhold a prepaid service longer than three months—unless the customer is allowed to cancel the order and get a refund. An agent who breaks this law can be sued by the writer.

The best way to avoid such complications—legal or otherwise—is by selecting your agent carefully. Here is a listing of agents who handle fiction and who do not charge reading fees:

Carol Abel, 160 87th St., New York City 10024.
Dominick Abel, Inc., 498 West End Ave., New York City 10024.
Edward J. Acton, 17 Grove St., New York City 10014.
Bret Adams, Ltd., 36 61st St., New York City 10021.

Audrey R. Adler Literary Agency, 1001 Connecticut Ave. NW, Suite 710, Washington, D.C. 20036.

Maxwell Aley Associates, 145 E. 35th St., New York City 10016. Contact: Ruth Aley.

Julian Bach Literary Agency, Inc., 747 3rd Ave., New York City 10017.

The Balkin Agency, 403 115th St., New York City 10025.

Virginia Barber Literary Agency, Inc., 44 Greenwich Ave., New York City 10011.

Bill Berger Associates, Inc., 444 E. 58th St., New York City 10022.

Lois Berman, 250 W. 57th St., New York City 10019.

Ron Bernstein, 200 W. 58th St., New York City 10019.

Blassingame, McCauley & Wood, 60 E. 42nd St., New York City 10017.

Georges Borchardt, Inc., 136 E. 57th St., New York City 10022.

Brandt & Brandt Literary Agents, Inc., 1501 Broadway, New York City 10036.

The Helen Brann Agency, Inc., 14 Sutton Place S., New York City 10022.

Curtis Brown, Ltd., 575 Madison Ave., New York City 10022.

James Brown Associates, Inc., 25 W. 43rd St., New York City 10036.

Ann Buchwald, 4327 Hawthorne St. NW, Washington, DC 20016.

Knox Burger Associates, Ltd., 39½ Washington Square S., New York City 10012.

Cantrel-Colas, Inc., 229 E. 79th St., New York City 10021.

Collier Associates, 280 Madison Ave., New York City 10016.

Liz Darhansoff, 52 E. 91st St., New York City 10028.

Joan Daves, 59 E. 54th St., New York City 10022.

Lois de la Haba, 142 Bank St., New York City 10014.

Anita Diamant, 51 E. 42nd St., New York City 10017.

Jonathan Dolger Agency, 49 E. 96th St., Apt. 9B, New York City 10028.

Candida Donadio & Associates, Inc., 111 W. 57th St., New York City 10019.

Joseph Elder, 150 W. 87th St., #6-D, New York City 10024.

Ann Elmo Agency, Inc., 60 E. 42nd St., New York City 10017.

Patricia Feeley, 52 Vanderbilt Ave., New York City 10017.

Barthold Fles Literary Agency, 507 5th Ave., New York City 10017.

The Fox Chase Agency, Inc., 419 E. 57th St., New York City 10022.

Max Gartenberg, Literary Agent, 331 Madison Ave., New York City 10017.

Frances Goldin, 305 E. 11th St., New York City 10003.

Arnold Goodman, 500 West End Ave., New York City 10024.

Sanford J. Greenburger Associates, 825 3rd Ave., New York City 10022.

Blanche C. Gregory, Inc., 2 Tudor City Place, New York City 10017.

Maxine Groffsky, 2 5th Ave., New York City 10011.

Helen Harvey, 410 W. 24th St., New York City 10011.

Alexandria Hatcher, 150 W. 55th St., New York City 10019.

Mary Jane Higgins, 106 Spooner Rd., Chestnut Hill, Massachusetts 02167.

John Hochmann, 505 Park Ave., New York City 10022.

Bernice Hoffman, 215 W. 75th St., New York City 10023.

Richard Huttner Agency, Inc., 330 E. 33rd St., New York City 10016.

Hutto Management, Inc., 110 W. 57th St., New York City 10019.

International Creative Management, 40 W. 57th St., New York City 10019.

JCA Literary Agency, Inc., Suite 1401, 200 W. 57th St., New York City 10019.

Lucy Kroll Agency, 390 West End Ave., New York City 10024.

The Lantz Office, Inc., 114 E. 55th St., New York City 10022.

Lenniger Literary Agency, Inc., 437 5th Ave., New York City 10016.

Robert Lescher Literary Agency, 155 E. 71st St., New York City 10021.
Ellen Levine Literary Agency, Inc., 370 Lexington Ave., New York City 10017.
Wendy Lipkind, 225 E. 57th St., New York City 10022.
Literistic, Ltd., 32 W. 40th St., New York City 10018.
The Sterling Lord Agency, Inc., 660 Madison Ave., New York City 10021.
Barbara Lowenstein, 250 W. 57th St., Suite 502, New York City 10019.
Gerard McCauley Agency, Inc., 209 E. 56th St., New York City 10022.
Kirby McCauley, 310 E. 46th St., New York City 10017.
McIntosh & Otis, Inc., 475 5th Ave., New York City 10017.
Carol Mann, 519 E. 87th St., New York City 10028.
Denise Marcil, 316 W. 82nd St., New York City 10024.
Elaine Markson Literary Agency, Inc., 44 Greenwich Ave., New York City 10011.
Harold Matson Co., Inc., 22 E. 40th St., New York City 10016.
Helen Merrill, 337 W. 22nd St., New York City 10011.
Robert P. Mills, Ltd., 156 E. 52nd St., New York City 10022.
William Morris Agency, Inc., 1350 Avenue of the Americas, New York City 10019.
Jean V. Naggar Literary Agency, 420 E. 72nd St., New York City 10021.
Harold Ober Associates, Inc., 40 E. 49th St., New York City 10017.
Phoenix Literary Agency, 150 E. 74th St., New York City 10021.
Arthur Pine Associates, Inc., 1780 Broadway, New York City 10019.
Aaron M. Priest, 150 E. 35th St., New York City 10016.
Susan Ann Protter, 156 E. 52nd St., New York City 10022.
Paul R. Reynolds, Inc., 12 E. 41st St., New York City 10017.
Barbara Rhodes, 140 West End Ave., New York City 10022.
Flora Roberts, Inc., 65 E. 55th St., New York City 10022.
Marie Rodell-Frances Collin Literary Agency, 156 E. 52nd St., New York City 10022.
Howard Rosenstone & Co., Inc., 1500 Broadway, New York City 10036.
Jane Rotrosen, 318 E. 51st St., New York City 10017.
Russell & Volkening, Inc., 551 5th Ave., New York City 10017.
Gloria Safier, Inc., 667 Madison Ave., New York City 10021.
John Schaffner Agency, 425 E. 51st St., New York City 10022.
Susan F. Schulman Agency, 165 West End Ave., New York City 10023.
Arthur Schwartz, 435 Riverside Dr., New York City 10025.
Rita Scott, Inc., 25 Sutton Place S., New York City 10022.
Phyllis Seidel, 164 E. 93rd St., New York City 10028.
James Seligmann Agency, 280 Madison Ave., New York City 10016.
Charlotte Sheedy Literary Agency, 145 W. 86th St., New York City 10024.
Evelyn Singer Literary Agency, Box 1600, Briarcliff Manor, New York 10510.
Elyse Sommer, Inc., Box E, 962 Allen Lane, Woodemere, New York 11598.
Philip G. Spitzer Literary Agency, 111-25 76th Ave., Forest Hills, New York 11375.
Gloria Stern, 1230 Park Ave., New York City 10028.
Gunther Stuhlmann, Author's Representative, Box 276, Becket, Massachusetts 01223.
Al Tafoya, 655 6th Ave., #212, New York City 10010.
Roslyn Targ Literary Agency, Inc., 250 W. 57th St., New York City 10019.
Susan Urstadt, 125 E. 84th St., New York City 10028.
Wallace & Sheil Agency, Inc., 177 E. 70th St., New York City 10021.
Writer's House, Inc., 132 W. 31st St., New York City 10001.
Mary Yost Associates, Inc., 75 E. 55th St., New York City 10022.

Literary/little magazines

Literary/little magazines have long been an acceptable and recommended avenue for the beginning writer to break into print. Because they are independent of the financial pressures of big business, little magazines are free to experiment and develop new styles, thus helping to nurture literary growth not always accepted as "salable" in consumer magazines. This independent, often happy-go-lucky editorial spirit and energy result in great diversity in the hundreds of small publications that feature fiction. They not only demonstrate individuality in styles and subjects, but also in audience direction and presentation.

In definition there is a fine line between literary and little magazines. Literaries, often associated with a college and usually directed to an educated, academic or even intellectual audience, may be little, too—in size, management and budget. Likewise, independently-owned magazines for a special interest group may accept literary fiction. Therefore these terms are used loosely and interchangeably.

Whereas category, mainstream or formula fiction are the accepted styles in most commercial or "slick" publications, the littles will accept these styles and also invite new ideas in serious literary or experimental fiction—such as a one-page novel or a prose poem. Little magazines sometimes develop around a specific theme—a social or political topic which the editors may espouse, or a general interest subject such as dreams, wine, horror, music, photography, sex or basketball. Or there may be no particular theme at all. Publications may be directed to fellow writers, feminists, gays, chess players, prisoners, doll lovers, the deaf, the Alaskans of the Far North or the American Indians of the Southwest. Contributors often are a part of a special interest group; for example, a senior citizen magazine requires that its writers be over 50; and a children's magazine desires short stories from 8- to 12-year-olds.

The graphics and formats are as different as their titles. There are journals, reviews, tabloids, and even tape cassettes. Some are large, others small; some reputable, others questionable; some slick, a few downright shoddy. But diversity means opportunity. Today there are not only little speciality magazines for every reader, but for every writer as well, regardless of experience.

The littles may not be for everyone, though. Generally they are *not* an alternative market for a previously rejected manuscript. Small magazine editors demand clean professional work, and they are careful in their selection. One editor of a literary magazine reads 5,000 mss a year to find the approximate 35 he will publish.

For the money-oriented writer, the literaries offer little incentive. Pay is low to negligible and often in contributor's copies only or perhaps a gratis subscription. Payment may depend on availability of funds, private donations or grants; and as the monies fluctuate so do the magazines' needs, their direction, even frequency of publication. Unable to keep up with inflation, many little mags go out of business each year.

Once aware of the pitfalls of the literary/little market, however, the writer will find great advantages. Because the staff is invariably small, the short story may bypass a reader and go directly to the editor-in-chief. Editors, usually writers themselves, are often willing to help the young or inexperienced author. A personal note with friendly but constructive advice and even recommendations for revision might accompany a rejected manuscript. Once published in a literary, the writer will have the satisfaction of reaching dedicated interested readers and occasionally even editors of major magazines and publishing houses who scout small magazines for talent.

Literary/little magazine editors are specific in what they like to see in a manuscript. Some recommendations for meeting their needs:

1. Aspire to write for literary magazines *only* if they are your preferred reading field.

2. Ask for sample copies (free-$12 in cost) and *study* them. It is very important to know the theme, tone and subjects desired of each magazine. Do not send blindly; blind submissions will meet with blind results 99% of the time.

3. Query only if requested. The majority of editors prefer to see the entire manuscript of a short story. A short cover letter may accompany the manuscript.

4. Do not ask for writing help when submitting a manuscript. Although some editors offer a word or two of encouragement *voluntarily*, most do not have the time to critique a manuscript.

5. Write and write; then rewrite and rewrite. Polish and tighten your manuscript. Prepare and proof your work carefully; be your own editor before submitting. Ask yourself: "Would *I* buy this?"

6. Know what to expect in payment and rights. Magazines vary in business and ethics.

7. *Always* include a self-addressed stamped envelope (SASE) with sufficient postage, and if writing for a foreign market, enclose international reply coupons (IRC) from the post office. (Canadian editors have a large supply of useless American stamps.)

Competition in the littles is, of course, not as fierce as in the commercial markets, but it is still keen. Although the magazines differ in philosophy and appearance, their editors are all looking for those special ingredients found in a quality short story: talent, originality and craftsmanship.

And, if at last your manuscript is accepted by a literary/little magazine, remember that you are in good company—Flannery O'Connor, John Gardner, Ernest Hemingway, Gail Godwin, Joyce Carol Oates, Ann Beattie, George V. Higgins and many other well known writers have all contributed to the littles—and the littles have contributed to *them*.

ABBA, Abba Books & Broadsides, 3913 Wilbert Rd., Austin TX 78751. Editor: Eutychus Peterson. Literary journal of fiction, nonfiction, poetry and book reviews for seminarians and theologians. Estab. 1976. Circ. 350.
Needs: Religious/inspirational. "No sentimental ankle-deep religious slush, or how I prayed away a mole from my left instep. Keep too your cute stories about devils and angels. Also, note the differences between church life, ethics, and theology. I deal only in the last." Length: 1,000-5,000 words.
How to Contact: Send complete ms with brief biography with SASE. Reports in 3 weeks on queries and mss. Sample copy $5. Free guidelines with legal-sized SASE.
Payment: $10-50. Free author's copy. $5 charge for extra copy.
Terms: Pays on acceptance for all rights.
Tips: "We accept mss handwritten, typed, anything readable. But if you haven't impressed your freshman English instructor, you'll have to be a saint to reach me."

ABBEY, White Urp Press, 5011-2 Green Mountain Circle, Columbia MD 20144. Editor: David Greisman. "Unassumed intelligence in a publication of finite production for the type of person who knows the pure poetry of Molson Ale." Quarterly. Estab. 1970. Circ. 200.
Needs: Literary, contemporary, science fiction and regional (appreciation of Maryland). Nothing political! Anything espousing a cause. Anything purposefully explicit." Accepts 3-6 mss/year. Length: 1,000-2,000 words.
How to Contact: Query with SASE. Reports in 1 month on queries, 2 months on mss. Sample copy 50¢.
Payment: 1-2 free author's copies.
Terms: Acquires one-time rights.
Tips: "Plug in the typewriter. Buys stamps. Don't imitate Thomas Hardy. Drink less than Behan or Thomas. Tell stories like Frederic Raphael."

AFTA—The Magazine of Temporary Culture, AFTA Press, Inc., 47 Crater Ave., Wharton NJ 07885. (201)366-1967. Editor: Bill-Dale Marcinko. "We are basically a review magazine of books and media—TV, films, science fiction, rock music. Our audience is primarily young adults who are very interested in pop culture and social issues. Most of our readers are attending college or are college graduates." Quarterly. Estab. February 1978. Circ. 20,000.
Needs: Contemporary, psychic/supernatural, science fiction, fantasy, horror, women's, feminist, gay/lesbian, mystery and humor. "Fiction should be of a rather emotional, honest tone, rather than 'light' or 'literary.' We like stories with irony, satire, and a humorous, perhaps even morbid, character. No religious, erotic, pornographic or romantic work will be considered." Buys 2-3 mss/issue. Length: 1,000-5,000 words.
How to Contact: Query with SASE. Reports in 1 week on queries, 2 weeks on mss. Sample copy $3.
Payment: Free author's copies.
Terms: Acquires one-time rights.
Tips: "Be honest, simple, direct, and don't write about what you haven't experienced in some way. Have a particular feeling, tone, and thrust to your work that is clear as the work progresses."

ALBATROSS MAGAZENE, T.A.C., Box 2046, Central Station, East Orange NJ 07019. Editor: S.M. Franchild. Lesbian satire magazine. Published irregularly. Estab. October 1974. Circ. 1,000-5,000.
Needs: Psychic/supernatural, science fiction, fantasy, horror, feminist, gay/lesbian, erotica, humor and juvenile. No long, boring pieces.
How to Contact: Query with SASE. Reports in 1 month on queries and mss. Sample copy $3.50.
Payment: Free author's copies.
Terms: Acquires one-time rights.

THE ALCHEMIST, Box 123, Lasalle, Quebec, Ontario, Canada H8R 3T7. Editor: Marco Fraticelli. Fiction Editor: Guy LaFlamme. "We publish prose in every issue with no prejudices in regard to style, but we tend to favor the experimental rather than the traditional." Published irregularly. Estab. 1974. Circ. 500.
Needs: Literary. Buys 1 mss/issue.
How to Contact: Send complete ms with SASE. Reports in 1 month on queries and mss. Free sample copy.
Payment: Free author's copies.
Terms: Pays on publication. Rights remain with author.

ALDEBARAN, Roger Williams College, Ferry Rd., Bristol RI 02809. (401)255-1000. Co-Editors: Jack Chielli, Darlene Mikula. Literary of prose and poetry for a general audience. Published annually or twice a year. Estab. 1970.
Needs: Will consider all fiction. Short stories preferred.
How to Contact: Send complete ms with SASE. Reports in 1 month. Sample copy 50¢ with SASE.
Payment: 2 free author's copies.
Terms: Pays on publication.

ALPHA, Box 1269, Wolfville, Nova Scotia, Canada B0P 1X0 (902)542-2476. Editor: Penny L. Ferguson. Estab. 1976. Published 3 times/year.
Needs: Contemporary, literary, experimental, faction, adventure, mystery, spy, historical, western, war, gothic, romance, science fiction, fantasy, horror, humor/satire. No pornographic.
How to Contact: Submit complete ms for short stories with SASE. Simultaneous and photocopied submissions OK. Reports slowly on mss.
Payment: 2 free author's copies.
Tips: "Fiction has become (as has our society) much more open about topics once considered taboo (ie. homosexuality, sexuality). There are a greater number of markets open to writers today. A writer can usually find a market *suitable* to his material. This is an important factor young writers often overlook."

THE ALTERNATE, Alternate Publishing, 15 Harriet St., San Francisco CA 94103. (415)864-3456. Editor: John W. Rowberry. Gay lifestyle/new magazine. Monthly. Estab. 1978. Circ. 45,000.
Needs: Literary, contemporary, science fiction, men's, gay/lesbian, erotica, mystery, serialized novels, translations and works in progress. No run-of-the-mill sexual escapades, coming out stories, or stories not related to readership. Buys 1-2 mss/issue, 12-20 mss/year. Length: 50,000 words maximum.
How to Contact: Query with clips of published work. Reports in 1 week on queries, 1 month on mss. Sample copy $2. Free guidelines.
Payment: $50-200.
Terms: Pays on publication for first, first North American serial and one-time rights.
Tips: "Read the publication, be familiar with contemporary gay fiction in general. We are interested in a writer's *best* work, and he or she should feel that the submission is a cut above most of the material read." A fiction contest each year; details announced in the magazine. *The Alternate* runs pieces by gay writers of note. Competition is very hard and rejections run 20 to 1.

AMERICAN FIDDLERS NEWS, American Old Time Fiddlers Assoc., 6141 Morrill Ave., Lincoln, NE 68507. (402)466-5519. Editor: De DeRyke. "We cover anything about the violin/fiddle in the world. We appeal to fiddlers, fiddling lovers and those wanting to learn about fiddling. There is nothing like it anywhere." Quarterly. Estab. January 1965. Circ. 5,000.

Needs: "The only 'fiction' we would consider is 90%+ truth with just a few details missing and filled in with an educated guess. The whole thing should not exceed two single-spaced typed pages. Preferably stories about experiences with fiddling—not just from a dancer's point of view but something from the fiddler's point of view. The fiddler must always be treated with respect." Length: 750-1,000 words.
How to Contact: Send complete ms with SASE. Reports in 1 month. Free sample copy with 9x12 SASE.
Payment: Free author's copies.
Tips: "Writer must really know subject or have advisor who knows subject. Writer must write easy-to-read style—no large words. We stress a common person approach and style; 'nothing university professor-ish' as it doesn't go. Keep it simple and plain."

AMERICAN LITERARY REVIEW, American Literary Review, 21 Woodman St., #6, Jamaica Plain MA 02130. (617)522-8748. Editor: Lee Bates. "Literary magazine of fiction, poetry, new journalism, artwork, photos, puzzles, interviews, etc. for people interested in lively writing and unusual graphics. The magazine is read because it contains well-written material and is attractively designed." Published 3 times/year. Estab. January 1979. Circ. 500.
Needs: Literary, contemporary and translations. No overly political material. Buys 2 mss/issue, 6 mss/year. Length: 5,000-15,000 words.
How to Contact: Send complete ms with SASE. Reports in 4-5 months on mss. Sample copy $3 and free guidelines with legal-sized SASE.
Payment: 2 free author's copies. $1.50 charge for extras.
Terms: Acquires first rights (rights revert to author on publication).
Tips: "Write something that catches the reader's attention and sustains interest throughout. Keep rewriting over and over; that's the key to success. Please be patient with late replies; the volume of submissions is tremendous, and we are only 2 people doing the best we can."

AMERICAN MAN, Box 693, Columbia MD 21045. (301)997-1373 (after 6 PM). Editor: Richard Haddad. Fiction Editor: Kathleen Beechem. Magazine of issues, poetry, health, books in relation to the contemporary man and his role in society today for those with a personal or professional interest in sex-role issues. Quarterly. Estab. 1980. Circ. 500.
Needs: "Subject matter must be related in some way to the male sex-role or the male experience. Any category OK except feminist." Buys 1 ms/issue; 4 mss/year. Length: 2,000-3,000 words.
How to Contact: Send comple ms with SASE. Reports in 2 months. Sample copy $3.50 and free guidelines.
Payment: 2 free author's copies. Pays on publication for one-time rights.
Tips: "Get a flavor for our publication before submitting ms. Most new contributors do not readily understand our theme."

ANOTHER CHICAGO MAGAZINE (ACM), Thunder's Mouth Press, 1152 S. East Ave., Oak Park IL 60304. (312)524-1289. Editor: Lee Webster. Fiction Editor: Dawn Webber. Estab. 1977.
Needs: Contemporary, literary, experimental, feminist, gay/lesbian, ethnic, humor/satire, translations and political/socio-historical.
How to Contact: Unsolicited mss. acceptable with SASE. Sample copies are available for $2.50 ppd. Reports in 6 weeks on queries and mss.
Payment: Contributor's copies.
Tips: "Write and submit, constantly and continuously. Get used to rejection slips, and don't get discouraged. Keep query and introductory letters short. Make sure ms has name and address on it, and that it is clean, neat and proofread. We are looking forward to publishing full length fiction mss in late 1981."

THE ANTIGONISH REVIEW, St. F.X. University, Antigonish, Nova Scotia, Canada B2G 1C0. 867-2221. Editor: R.J. MacSween. Literary magazine for the educated and creative. Quarterly. Estab. 1970. Circ. 500.
Needs: Literary, contemporary and translations. No erotic or political material. Buys 6 mss/issue. Length: 3,000-5,000 words.
How to Contact: Send complete ms with SASE. Reports in 6 weeks on queries and mss. Free sample copy.
Payment: 2 free author's copies.
Terms: Acquires first rights.
Tips: "Learn the fundamentals and do not deluge an editor."

ANTIOCH REVIEW, Antioch Review, Inc., Box 148, Yellow Springs OH 45387. (513)767-7386. Editor: Robert S. Fogarty. Fiction Editor: Nolan Miller. "Literary and cultural review of contemporary issues in politics, American and international studies, literature for general readership. Quarterly. Estab. January 1941. Circ. 4,000.
Needs: Literary, contemporary, translations and experimental. No children's, science fiction or popular market. Buys 3-4 mss/issue, 10-12 mss/year. Length: 12,000 words maximum.
How to Contact: Send complete ms with SASE. Reports in 2 months. Sample copy $2.50; free guidelines.
Payment: $10/page. 2 free author's copies. $2.10 charge for extras.
Terms: Pays on publication for first and one-time rights (rights returned to author on request).
Tips: "Our best advice, always, is to *read* the *Antioch Review* to see what type of material we publish."

APALACHEE QUARTERLY, D.O.B. Press, Inc., Box 20106, Tallahassee FL 32304. (904)224-0478. Editor: P.V. LeForge. Fiction Editor: D.M. Morrill. Contemporary journal of fiction poetry and drama for educated readers from 20-45. Quarterly. Estab. 1972. Circ. 400.
Needs: Literary and contemporary. "All categories of fiction are considered as long as the works aspire toward the very pinnacles of art. Dostoevsky wrote a mystery; the Brontes wrote gothic romances; I.B. Singer writes ethnic stories; Rechy gay stories; Lessing and Pynchon have delved into science fiction. Yet these writers have transcended these 'sub-genres.' We encourage writing in all areas, but if the writing is thin, send it to a magazine that will appreciate it more than we will." Buys 5 mss/issue, 20 mss/year. Length: 1,000-6,000 words.
How to Contact: Send complete ms with SASE. Reports in 1 month. Sample copy $1.50, includes postage.
Payment: 2 free author's copies. $1 charge for extras.
Terms: Acquires first rights.
Tips: "Write 4 hours every day. Read 100 pages every day. Work diligently, but learn the fundamentals of fiction (point of view, motivation) as soon as possible. Show your work to as many people as possible. If you're rejected more than five times, it may be time to consider revising. We sometimes sponsor regional or statewide contests, depending on grant money."

AQUILA MAGAZINE, ROQ Press, 116 Old Mill Rd., Apt 6, State College PA 16801. (814)237-7509. Editor: Bob Quarteroni. Fiction Editor: Bill Blair. Academic journal of poetry and short fiction. Published 3 times/year if possible. Estab. 1975. Circ. 400.
Needs: Literary, contemporary, religious/inspirational, psychic/supernatural, science fiction, fantasy, horror, men's, women's, gothic and humor. "We are interested in almost anything unusual and original; we also like nature writing of the Annie Dillard or John McPhee type. No long, introspective mss." Buys 1-2 mss/issue. Length: 1,500 words.
How to Contact: Query with clips of published work with SASE. Reports in 1 month on

queries, 2 months on mss. Sample copy $2.
Payment: Free author's copies.
Terms: Pays on publication for first rights.
Tips: "Come up with something fresh and different. I'm always looking for something, anything new. If I find a writer I like, I'll devote a whole issue to him or her." Possible contest and special issues devoted to single authors in 1981.

ARBA SICULA, ARBA Sicula, Inc., Box D, Brooklyn NY 11204. (212)331-0613. Editor: Alissandru Caldiero. Bilingual ethnic literary review (Sicilian-English) dedicated to the dissemination of Sicilian culture. Published 2-4 times a year. Estab. 1979. Circ. 1,000.
Needs: Accepts ethnic literary material consisting of various forms of folklore; stories both contemporary and classical. Material submitted must be in the Sicilian language with English translation desirable.
How to Contact: Send complete ms with SASE. Reports in 2 months. Sample copy $5 with 8½x11 SASE and 90¢ postage.
Payment: 1-2 free author's copies. $4 charge for extra copies.
Terms: Acquires all rights.
Tips: "This review is a must for those who nurture a love of the Sicilian language."

THE ARGONAUT, Box 7985, Austin TX 78712. (512)478-2396. Editor: Michael Ambrose. "*The Argonaut* is a fantasy magazine, by which we mean stories in the genres of science fiction, mystery, occult adventure; the word 'fantasy' carries few restrictions here. Our readership is primarily college-educated and mature. Many are themselves writers of fantasy, collectors of first editions, etc. *Argonaut* readers want original, literate, unusual stories." Semiannually. Estab. March 1972. Circ. 200.
Needs: Science fiction, fantasy, horror, mystery, occult adventure. "As indicated above, such categories do not constrain the writer to remain rigidly within the traditions of fantasy, science fiction, or horror; well-written stories in the detective, mystery, and adventure fields are also welcome. No heroic fantasy in rank imitation of the Robert E. Howard school, or wide-eyed Tolkienesque fantasies. In general, nothing that has been said before and better." Buys 8-10 mss/issue, 20-25 mss/year. Length: 1,500-6,000 words.
How to Contact: Send complete ms with SASE. Reports in 3 weeks. Sample copy $1.50.
Payment: .005¢/word. Free author's copy. $1.50 charge for extras or 5 copies or more at 40% discount.
Terms: Pays on acceptance for first North American serial rights.
Tips: "Know the fields of fantasy and science fiction thoroughly and remember, most of it has already been done in one form or another. Read the professional magazines, sample *The Argonaut* and other small press magazines before submitting anything. Be professional—lightly-photocopied mss and faded ribbons are a waste of the editor's eyes and time. Don't submit more than one ms at a time, and keep trying when rejected. *The Argonaut's* infrequent publishing schedule lets me be very selective of the stories I receive. It takes more than a polished style with no originality of idea, or all idea with no style on the other hand, to get me interested."

ARIZONA QUARTERLY, The University of Arizona, Tucson AZ 85721. (602)626-1029. Editor: Albert F. Gepenheimer. Quarterly. Estab. March 1945.
Needs: Literary, contemporary and translations. Length: 3,000-4,000 words.
How to Contact: Send complete ms with SASE. Reports in 1 month. Free sample copy.
Payment: Subscription and 20 author's copies.
Terms: Acquires all rights.
Tips: Contest with annual award for best short story of the year.

THE ARK RIVER REVIEW, The Ark River Review, Inc., Box 14, Wichita State University, Wichita KS 67208. (316)689-3130. Editors: Anthony Sobin and Jonathan Katz. "We are a literary magazine publishing only three-writer issues in poetry and fiction. We present large selections of an individual's work, usually by writers who have yet to publish a book with a major house. Our audience tends to be made up of well-educated people over 21, especially in the university community. The review is well known as a magazine of sophisticated and leading-edge fiction and poetry." Publishes 2 double issues/year. Estab. 1971. Circ. 1,000+.

Needs: Literary and contemporary. Chapbook-sized collections of short fiction (or novellas if self-contained). Total of 130 typewritten pages up to one-third of which may have been previously published in magazine form. "We are not as particular about the content as the way it is written and the general quality and sophistication of the piece. No *ordinary* fiction of any genre, science fiction or satire." Buys 3 mss/issue. Length: 75-130 pages.

How to Contact: Order sample fiction issues and then submit full ms with SASE. Reports in 1 week to several weeks and months if a finalist on mss. Sample copy $2.50 (specify fiction). Free guidelines with legal-sized SASE.

Payment: $250. 10 free author's copies.

Terms: Pays on publication for all rights (we will grant any reprint request made by the author, free).

Tips: "Our criteria are that you demonstrate an understanding of the literary tradition and advance upon what's already been done. We prefer to take a chance with something really new rather than print what is highly competent but ordinary. See back issues for best indication. We tend to be very receptive to writers who are underpublished because their material has been too unusual for the audiences of widely distributed magazines. Be warned, however, that our standards are high and the competition for these three spots is very tough."

AURA Literary/Arts Review, University of Alabama in Birmingham, 117 Campbell, University Station, Birmingham AL 35294. (205)934-3216. Editor: Pamela Johnston Horn. Fiction Editor: Laurie Youngers. "We publish various types of fiction with an emphasis on short stories. Our audience is college students, the university community and literary-minded adults, the arts community." Published semiannually. Estab. 1974. Circ. 1,000.

Needs: Literary, contemporary, science fiction, men's, women's, feminist and ethnic (black). No mss longer than 5,000-6,000 words or pornographic material. Buys 2-3 mss/issue. Length: 2,000-6,000 words.

How to Contact: Send complete ms with SASE. Reports in 2 months. Free sample copy with 9x12 SASE and 68¢ postage.

Payment: Free author's copies.

Terms: Pays on publication for first North American serial rights.

Tips: "If it's fiction and shows evidence of craft, we will consider it. No simultaneous submissions; please include biographical information."

BACHY: A Journal of the Arts in Los Angeles, Papa Bach Editions, 11317 Santa Monica Blvd., Los Angeles CA 90025. Editor: Leland Hickman. International journal of fiction, poetry, art and photography. Bold, eclectic, purist and corrupt material. Unknown writers and well-known. Audience is college-educated, nationwide, international. Triquarterly. Estab. 1972. Circ. 1,000.

Needs: Literary, contemporary, feminist, gay/lesbian, ethnic and translations. General orientation is for artistic noncommerical work. "No trash. Do no submit anything that would not find acceptance in any literary magazine aspiring to excellence." Buys 4-6 mss/issue, 12-18 mss/year.

How to Contact: Send complete ms with SASE. Reports in 3 months. Sample copy $3.50 with 8½x11 SASE and 90¢ postage.

Payment: Free author's copies (1/page plus one). Negotiable charge for extras.

Terms: Pays on publication for one-time rights (rights revert to authors).

Tips: "Read the magazine first. If the writer is not committed to his art for a *lifetime*, he or she should not count on being accepted."

BACK BAY VIEW, Back Bay View, Inc., 33 Karen Dr., Randolph MA 02368. (617)986-5704. Editor: Charlotte Boehm. Fiction Editor: Gerald B. Macaulay. Managing Editor: Alicia Holmes. "*Back Bay View* is a literary and fine arts magazine that stresses publication of new fiction and poetry as well as high quality graphics. We emphasize creativity, innovation, and high literary standards. *Back Bay View* reaches a largely urban and educated audience in the New England area. Because of the Northeast's huge academic population, interest and participation in the fine arts run high." Estab. 1976. Circ. 5,000.
Needs: Literary and contemporary. "Of course, good fiction transcends categories and genres; if a work is well conceived and well written, specific categories will be irrelevant. We do not particularly wish to see journal entries, self-analyses, or 'do-it-yourself' verbal therapy. Please do not send mss in which endings are unresolved or stories in which nothing occurs (long descriptions are boring)." Length: open.
How to Contact: Send complete ms accompanied by contributor's note with SASE. Reports in 1 month on mss. Sample copy $1.50.
Payment: 2 free author's copies. $1.50 charge for extras.
Terms: Acquires first rights.
Tips: "Write for a sample copy or buy a copy of *Back Bay View* and *read* it. A thorough reading will inform a potential contributor of the standard and quality of our fiction. *Know* the publication to which you are submitting your work. Occasionally, *Back Bay View* will run a poetry or fiction competition. Prizes are usually publication or the opportunity to read one's work publicly."

BACKCOUNTRY, Cheat Mountain Poets, Box 390, Elkins WV 26241. (304)636-6236. Editor: Michael Mazzolini. Poetry and short fiction, graphics and photo journal for mixed audience. Published semiannually. Estab. 1977. Circ. 1,000.
How to Contact: Send complete ms with SASE. Reports on deadline on mss. Sample copy 50¢.
Payment: 3 free author's copies.
Tips: "Read a sample of our publication before sending in mss. We have an occasional contest with cash prizes."

THE BARAT REVIEW, Barat College, 700 Westleigh Rd., Lake Forest IL 60045. (312)234-3000. Editor: Lauri S. Lee. "*The Barat Review* is a journal of literature and the arts, printing the finest in contemporary fiction. The avant-garde is our focus. Our audience is sophisticated and well-educated, composed to a great extent of writers and academicians in the arts and liberal arts. They look to this journal for fiction which is fresh and actively experimental, but solidly constructed." Semi-annual. Estab. 1966. Circ. 2,000.
Needs: Literary, women's and translations. "Use of language which is not precise or energetic is something which we particularly don't want to see. Also, the traditionally-told tale, with sequential plot structure and narrative, is not of much interest. Buys 2 mss/issue, 4 mss/year.
How to Contact: Send complete ms or query with clips of published work with SASE. Reports in 1 month on queries and mss. Sample copy $4.50.
Payment: 10 free author's copies. In some case payment, which varies according to each author; up to $100/story. 40% discount for extras.
Terms: Pays on acceptance for first North American serial rights.
Tips: "Definitely read a recent issue of the magazine for first-hand exposure to the quality of fiction which we publish."

BARE WIRES, A Harmless Flirtation with Wealth, 2343 Burgener Blvd., San Diego CA 92110. (714)276-6120. Editor: Helen McKenna.
Needs: Literary, women's, feminist, gay/lesbian, humor/satire, short, clever puzzles and cartoons. "We want very short pieces. No war, gore, porn or religious mss."
How to Contact: Query with SASE. Simultaneous and photocopied submissions OK.

Reports in 2 weeks on queries, 1 month on mss. 6 author's copies.
Tips: "Read a lot and learn to appreciate quality. Query first."

THE BELLINGHAM REVIEW, 412 N. State St., Bellingham WA 98225. Editors: Peter Nicoletta and Knute Skinner. Fiction Editor: Richard Dills. "A literary magazine featuring original short stories, novel excerpts and poetry of palpable quality." Semiannual. Estab. 1977. Circ. 500.
Needs: Literary, contemporary, psychic/supernatural, science fiction, fantasy, horror, feminist, gay/lesbian, erotica, gothic, mystery, humor, ethnic, serialized novels, condensed novels and translations. Buys 1-2 mss/issue. Length: 5,000 words.
How to Contact: Send complete ms. Reports in 2 months. Sample copy $2.
Payment: 2 free author's copies plus 2-issue subscription. $1.50 charge for extras.
Terms: Acquires first North American serial and one-time rights.

THE BERKELEY MONTHLY MAGAZINE, The Boston Monthly Magazine, 910 Parker St., Berkeley CA 94710. (415)848-7900. Editor: Salli Gaddini. Estab. 1970.
Needs: Contemporary, literary, experimental, adventure, historical, western, war, women's and humor/satire.
How to Contact: Send complete ms with SASE. Photocopied submissions OK. Reports in 6 weeks on ms.
Terms: Pays $120-140 for first serial rights.

BEYOND BAROQUE, Beyond Baroque Foundation, 681 Venice Blvd., Venice CA 90291. (213)822-3006. Editor: Manuel "Manazar" Gamboa. "Contemporary poetry and fiction with an emphasis on Third World and bilingual works. Quarterly. Estab. 1968. Circ. 6,000.
Needs: Literary. "No genre fiction categories, unless *very* good."
How to Contact: Send complete ms or query with clips of published work with SASE. Reports in 3 weeks on queries, 3 months on mss. Free sample copy.
Payment: 15 free author's copies.
Terms: Acquires first North American serial rights.
Tips: "Send mss and we will read. Especially interested in clean, direct interesting writing that is *not* self-confessional. Pay attention to language."

BLACK FORUM MAGAZINE, Black Forum Magazine, Box 1090, Bronx NY 10451. Editor: Revish Windham. Fiction Editor: Horace Mungin. Literary magazine of short stories, articles, poetry, reviews, interviews, puzzles, etc., for students, writers and adults 18 and over. Annually. Estab. November 1979. Circ. 4,000.
Needs: Literary and ethnic (black). Buys 2 mss/issue, 2 mss/year. Length: 500-1,000 words.
How to Contact: Send complete ms with SASE. Reports in 2 months on mss. Sample copy $1.25; free guidelines with legal-sized SASE.
Payment: $15 minimum for stories.
Terms: Pays on publication for first rights.
Tips: "Read previous issue—important."

BLACK JACK, Seven Buffaloes Press, Box 249, Big Timber MT 59011. Editor: Art Cuelho. "Main theme: Rural. Publishes material on the American Indian, farm and ranch, American hobo, the common working man, folklore, the Southwest, Okies, Montana, humor, Central California, etc. for people who make their living off the land. The writers write about their roots, experiences and values they receive from the American soil." Annual. Estab. 1973. Circ. 500.
Needs: Literary, contemporary, western, adventure, humor, American Indian, American hobo and parts of novels and long short stories. "Anything that strikes me as being amateurish, without depth, without craft, I refuse. Actually I'm not opposed to any kind of writing, if the author is genuine and has spent his lifetime dedicated to the written word." Buys 5-10

mss/year. Length: 3,500-5,000 words (there can be exceptions).
How to Contact: Query for current theme with SASE. Reports in 1 week on queries, 2 weeks on mss. $1 off sale price to writers for sample copy with 6½x9½ SASE and 80¢ postage.
Payment: Pays 1-2 free author's copies.
Terms: Acquires first North American serial rights and reserves the right to reprint material in an anthology or future *Black Jack* publications.
Tips: "Enthusiasm should be matched with enough skill as a craftsman. That's not saying that we don't continue to learn, but every writer must have enough command of the language to compete with other proven writers. Save postage by writing first to the editor to find out his needs. A small press magazine always has specific needs at a given time."

BLACK MARIA, Black Maria Collective, Box 25187, Chicago IL 60625. "Women's creative writing that is women identified. Poetry, fiction, articles, essays. For feminists for enjoyment, enlightenment, consciousness raising, living in a liberated way in the midst of oppression and finding sources of power." Annually. Estab. 1971. Circ. approximately 800.
Needs: Literary, feminist, and gay/lesbian. "Images of women should be strong and creative. We do not consider material written by men or with male viewpoints, book length material, or subjects that are violent or denigrate women."
How to Contact: Send complete ms with SASE. Reports in 2-6 months. Sample copy $1.50 with 8½x11 SASE and 60¢ postage.
Payment: 2 free author's copies.
Terms: Acquires first rights.
Tips: "The motivation should be communicating with other women. We prefer giving exposure to heretofore unpublished women. *Black Maria* has a political philosophy that is apparent in issues so it helps to be familiar with our publication. Writers should submit work with the understanding that we are a volunteer collective and cannot respond and evaluate submissions within the time frames of commercial, mainstream publications."

THE BLACK REVIEW, Blackberry Press, Box 9405, Baltimore MD 21228. Editor: Carole Y. Lyles. Literary magazine devoted entirely to work by Afro-American and Afro-Caribbean or African writers. Biannual. Estab. October 1978. Circ. 500.
Needs: Literary and black ethnic. No true confessions, inspirational, pornographic or science fiction. Buys 10 mss/year. Length: 2,500 words.
How to Contact: Send complete ms with SASE. Reports in 2 months on mss. Sample copy $3 with 8x11 SASE with 48¢ postage.
Payment: 2 free author's copies.
Terms: Acquires one-time rights.
Tips: "Each issue features short stories, novel excerpts, essays and book reviews from writers from all over the country and Africa. All of the material is published for the first time. We accept materials on a continuing basis, and we will respond to everyone who submits work to us."

THE BLACK SCHOLAR, The Black World Foundation, Box 908, Sausalito CA 94966. (415)332-3130. Editor: Robert Allen. Fiction Editor: Conyus Calhoun. Magazine on black culture, research and black studies for Afro-Americans, college graduates and students. "We are also widely read by teachers, professionals, and intellectuals, and are required reading for many black and Third World Studies." Bimonthly. Estab. 1969. Circ. 25,000.
Needs: Literary, contemporary, men's, women's, juvenile, young adult and ethnic. No religious/inspirational, psychic, etc. Length: 2,000-5,000 words.
How to Contact: Query with clips of published work with SASE. Reports in 3 weeks on queries, 1 month on mss. Free sample copy with SASE.
Payment: 12 author's copies and 1 year's free subscription to *TBS*.
Terms: Pays on publication for all rights.

BLITZ, Alternative Research, Box 1294, Kitchener, Ontario, Canada N2G 4G8. (519)743-5043. Co-ordinator: Kenneth Guse. Theme—alternative movement resources, whole range from spiritual, political and otherwise. Publishes poetry, short stories, art, satire, "written or comic-form for editors, librarians, autonomous leftists, liberation movement people, utopians, info-maniacs, iconoclasts, survivalists, holistic-attitude people, naturalists, who read to get a wide range of information all in the same place and an integrated view of life." Quarterly. Estab. March 1979. Circ. 1,500.
Needs: Psychic/supernatural, fantasy, men's, women's, feminist, gay/lesbian, erotica, humor, utopian, alternative futures, counter-culture, new age/spiritual, radical left, pagan, and so on. "All categories from an 'alternative' perspective, generally though not always." Length: 4,000 words maximum.
How to Contact: Send complete ms or query with clips of published work with International Reply Coupons or SASE. Reports in 1 month on mss. Sample copy sometimes free, depending on money situation, with envelope to hold 8½x11 magazine with 2 International Reply Coupons.
Payment: Free author's copies.
Terms: Acquires simultaneous rights.
Tips: "Send us the ms for consideration; it's especially good if it's in an unusual style and/or about subject matter generally not treated."

BLUE HORSE PUBLICATIONS, Box 6061, Augusta GA 30906. Editor: Jacqueline Bradley. Fiction Editor: Patrick Kelly. "*Blue Horse* prints both chapbooks and anthologies in limited edition with colophon for the collector of the unusual in literature for academic, scholarly persons and the laymen-public who have not lost their senses of wit." Annually and special editions. Estab. 1964. Circ. 700.
Needs: Literary, fantasy, erotica, gothic and humor. "*Blue Horse* began in 1964 at the University of Florida as an 'in' publication satirizing literature in style and manner and with an introduction in Sanskrit to '. . . confuse the simple.' " People who believe in Causes should not try to unload their lack of taste and judgment via the pages of *Blue Horse*. Generally, the work of Louis Ebert suits us; for poetry/fiction/short, short works, see Lynne Savitt and Lyn Lifshin. Unless written satirically: no sophomoric love stories; no personal suffering; no inspiration; no searching for roots; no gay or other political writing; no religious or born-again warblings. We would like to see more art work and some erotic writing which women seem to do best." Buys 12 mss/issue. Length: 500-1,500 words.
How to Contact: Send complete ms with SASE. Reports in 1 month on mss. Free sample copy with 8x10 SASE and free guidelines.
Payment: $25 maximum and sometimes only contributor's copies.
Term: Payment on acceptance and rights to author.
Tips: "Many are called but few are chosen. The writing of satire is a gift, not an achievement and is not taught in any school and seldom practiced on the public. If you have it, we'll print it. Unless a writer has written awhile, there is no avoiding the 'pitfalls' and the vicissitudes of writing. Clarification: We print as original ideas as we can get that are well-written. The writer knows he is in good company in *Blue Horse*."

BOSS, Boss Books, Box 370, Madison Square Station, New York NY 10159. (212)683-3274. Editor: Reginald Gay. Lively journal interested in latest fiction and in experimental work for a young audience especially writers and potential writers. Also a large university readership. Annually. Estab. 1966. Circ. 1,000.
Needs: Literary, contemporary, gay/lesbian, erotica, black and Hispanic ethnic and translations. No mystery or western. Accepts 1-2 mss/issue. Length: 5,000-8,000 words. "We would be very interested in very short, almost prose-poem fiction."
How to Contact: Query with clips of published work or if suitable send ms with SASE. Reports in 3 weeks on queries, 2 months on mss. Sample copy $4.50.
Payment: 2 free author's copies. 20% discount for extras.

Terms: Negotiates rights.
Tips: "Consider the type of material we publish. It would be quite clear that, e.g., a story with a romantic theme would have to be a knockout in expression. There seem to be more outlets for fiction than competent writers to fulfill those outlets. Too many beginning writers do not seem to struggle to refine their work. The main reason for publishing in a small independent magazine is the prestige of being in a lively periodical, especially true for the very unpublished. Otherwise, why not try to get paid for it? Many grants require quite a list of published work; an appearance in a small magazine may lead to a reprint in wider-circulation press for substantial pay."

BOX 749, The Printable Arts Society, Inc., Box 749, Old Chelsea Station, New York NY 10113. Editor: David Ferguson. "We publish fiction and poetry of every length and any theme; satire, belles-lettres, plays, music and any artwork reproducible by photo-offset. We have no particular stylistic or ideological bias. *Box 749* is directed to people of diverse backgrounds, education, income and age—an audience not necessarily above or under-ground. Such an audience is consistent with our belief that literature (plus art and music) is accessible to and even desired by a larger and more varied portion of society than has generally been acknowledged." Annually. Estab. 1972. Circ. 5,000.
Needs: Literary, contemporary, science fiction, fantasy, humor and ethnic translations. "Fiction in any of the categories here, could be art. If so, we would consider it for publica-tion. We ask that all translations be accompanied by 'translation history' of the work: Has this work ever been translated into English? If so, when? By whom? Where did the transla-tion appear?" Buys 10-15 mss/issue, 10-15 mss/year.
How to Contact: Send complete ms with SASE. Reports in up to 3 months or longer on mss depending on length. Sample copy $2.50 with 9x12 SASE and postage for special 4th class book (and ms) rate (about 80¢).
Payment: 3 free author's copies. Charge for extras: regular $2.50 cover price plus postage, unless buying in bulk.
Terms: Acquires all rights, but we reassign rights to author after publication.

BROADSHEET MAGAZINE, Broadsheet Magazine, Ltd., Box 5799, Auckland, New Zealand. 794-751AUCK. Editor: Sanda Coney. Feminist magazine of news, reviews, inter-views, fiction and poetry for people interested in feminism. Monthly. Estab. June 1972. Circ. 10,000.
Needs: Women's, feminist and gay/lesbian. Length: 2,500 words.
How to Contact: Send complete ms with SASE. Reports in 1 month on mss. Sample copy $1.
Payment: No payment.

BROWNING SOCIETY NOTES, Browning Society, Fitzwilliam College, Cambridge, En-gland. (0223)358657 ext. 63. Editor: John Woolford. Magazine with the life and works of Robert and Elizabeth Browning for mainly academics and others specifically interested in Robert and Elizabeth Browning. Published 3 times/year. Estab. 1970. Circ. 220.
Needs: "We could only consider works directly connected with the Brownings, e.g. paro-dies, imitations, short stories about their lives, prose poems spoken 'by' them or about them or in deliberate and explicit relation to their works. Our brief extends no further, but we will gladly consider works along these lines." Length: 5,000 words.
How to Contact: Send complete ms. Reports in 1 week on ms.
Payment: Free contributor's copies.
Terms: Acquires first rights.

BUG TAR, Bug Tar Press, Box 1534, San Jose, CA 95109. (408)248-7220. Editor: Scott Mace. Fiction Editor: M.A. Olds. "*Bug Tar* explores the question: Is mankind becoming a large insect colony? Not literally, of course, but intellectually and spirtually. Anything that touches upon the loss of individuality, society's increasing regimentation, and other, larger human themes is welcome. But our fiction is also personal and human, not expository or experimental. All approaches—humorous, grotesque, what have you—are explored. *Bug Tar* is for all who wish to think, question and not be merely entertained." Quarterly. Estab. August 1977. Circ. 50.

Needs: Literary, contemporary and humor. No experimental fiction, autobiographical or Marxist. Buys 4 mss/issue. Length: 5,000 words, maximum of 20,000.

How to Contact: Send for sample issue first with SASE. Reports in 1 month on queries, 2 months on mss. Free sample copy with 9x6 SASE and 65¢ postage.

Payment: Contributor's copies. 75¢ charge for extra copies.

CALLIOPE, Creative Writing Program, Roger Williams College, Bristol, RI 02809. (401)255-2378. Advisory Editor: Martha Christina. "We are an eclectic little magazine publishing contemporary poetry, fiction, interviews, and reviews of other little magazines for those who appreciate fine contemporary writing." Published semiannually. Estab. December 1977. Circ. 300.

Needs: Literary, contemporary, men's, women's, feminist, humor and experimental/innovative. "We are receptive to a wide variety of subject matter but insist on high quality work in the above categories. We try to include 1 piece of fiction in each issue." Length: no limit.

How to Contact: Send complete ms with SASE. Reports immediately to 3 months on mss. Sample copy $1.

Payment: 2 free author's copies. $1 charge for extras.

Terms: Rights revert to author on publication.

Tips: "We are not interested in reading anyone's very first story. If the piece is good it will be given careful consideration. Reading a sample copy of *Calliope* is recommended."

CALYX, A Journal of Art & Literature by Women, Calyx, Inc., Box B, Corvallis OR 97330. (503)753-9384. Editors: B. Baldwin, M. Donnelly. Publishes prose, poetry and art. Looking for quality work. Triannually. Estab. June 1976. Circ. 2,000.

Needs: Prose of no exact specification. Buys 2-3 mss/issue, 9 mss/year. Length: 5,000 words maximum.

How to Contact: Send ms with SASE and biographical notes. Reports in up to 6 months on mss. Sample copy $3.50.

Payment: "Dependent on grants for per page rate amount."

Terms: Pays on publication for one-time rights and copyright by *Calyx*.

CANADIAN AUTHOR & BOOKMAN, Canadian Authors Association, 24 Ryerson Ave., Toronto, Ontario, Canada M5T 2P3. Fiction Editor: Geoff Hancock. Managing Editor: Sybil Marshall. "We are mainly a craft magazine for Canadian writers, publishing articles that tell how to write and where to sell. We publish half-a-dozen poems and one short story per issue as well as the craft articles. We aim at the beginning or newly emerging writer who reads us to find out how to create the salable article (story or poem) and reap the benefits of his seminal imagination and feverish activity." Quarterly. Estab. 1921. Circ. 4,000.

Needs: Literary, contemporary, science fiction, fantasy, horror, men's, women's, feminist, gothic, romance, western, mystery, adventure and humor. "No porn, near-miss inspirational, personal essays masquerading as short stories, formula writing with tired blood or whatever else is trite, banal, or just dull." Buys 1 ms/issue, 4 mss/year. Length: 2,000-3,500 words.

How to Contact: Send complete ms with SASE. Reports in 1 month on mss. Sample copy $1.

Payment: $125. Free author's copy.

Terms: Pays on publication for first rights.

Tips: "Send Geoff Hancock a story that will dominate memory and you are in business. He reads with an eye for originality, flair, and imaginative work. He asks, whatever the form or procedure of the story, that it succeed in the author's intention. To write good stories, you must read great stories, and read them from the inside out. The writer's strategy must be examined, from the overall structure, to the rise and fall of the sentences, to the placement of the punctuation. For more specific information send $1 to Canadian Authors' Assoc. with your request for a copy of *CA&B*, Nov. 1979 and read "The Green Glad Bag Review" by Geoff Hancock."

CANADIAN FICTION MAGAZINE, Box 946, Station F, Toronto, Ontario, Canada M4Y 2N9. Editor: Geoffrey Hancock. "This magazine is a quarterly anthology devoted exclusively to the contemporary creative writing of writers and artists in Canada and Canadians living abroad. Fiction only, no poetry. The ideal reader of *CFM* is a writer or somebody interested in all the modes, manners, voices, and conventions of contemporary fiction." Quarterly. Estab. 1971. Circ. 1,800.
Needs: Literary. "Theme, style, length, and subject matter are at the discretion of the author. The only requirement is that the work be of the highest possible literary standard. Each issue is approximately 148 pages. Buys 10 mss/issue, 35 mss/year. No restriction on length.
How to Contact: Send complete ms with SASE or IRC. Reports in 6 weeks on mss.
Payment: $10/page plus one year subscription.
Terms: Pays on publication for first North American serial rights.
Tips: "It is absolutely crucial that three or four issues be read. We sell back issues up to 1976 for $3; current issue $5.50 (postage included). Some double issues are $7.85. *CFM* publishes Canada's leading writers as well as those in early stages of their careers. This is a professional literary magazine. A wide knowledge of contemporary literature (in English, and in translation) plus expertise in creative writing, modern fiction theories, current Canadian literature, and the innovative short story would be of great help to a potential contributor. *CFM* is an independent journal not associated with any academic institution. Each issue includes French Canadian fiction in translation, interviews with well known Canadian writers on the techniques of their fiction, forums and manifestoes on the future of fiction, as well as art work and reviews. $250 annual prize for the best story submitted in either French or English. Previous winners include John Metcalf, Mavis Gallant, Leon Rooke, W.P. Kinsella, Anne Copeland."

CEDAR ROCK, Cedar Rock Press, 1121 Madeline, New Braunfels TX 78130. (512)625-6002. Editor: David C. Yates. Fiction Editor: Pat Ellis Taylor. "We publish quality fiction and poetry, as well as essays pertaining to literature. We direct our publication to intelligent and sensitive persons, not necessarily college-educated." Quarterly. Estab. January 1976. Circ. 1,200.
Needs: Contemporary, psychic/supernatural, science fiction, fantasy and adventure. "Fiction should be readable. We prefer stories with plot, with strong characterization, with a beginning, a middle and an end. No stories without plot and form, pornographic or gothic." Buys 2-3 mss/issue, 8-12 mss/year. Length: 1,000-3,500 words.
How to Contact: Send complete ms with SASE. Reports in 1 month on mss. Sample copy $1.50. Free guidelines with legal-sized SASE.
Payment: $5-150. Free author's copy. $1.50 charge for extras.
Terms: Pays on acceptance for first North American serial rights.
Tips: "Look at back issues. Write stories with strong characterization. Keep submitting. Important: Send fiction to our fiction editor, Pat Ellis Taylor, Box 14122, Dallas TX 75204. Do not send it to our central office."

CHANGIN', Changin' Magazine, 833 Koman Dr., Paramus NJ 07652. Fiction Editor: Carol Weissbein. "A magazine for Bob Dylan fans which publishes articles related to Bob Dylan in some way—reviews, interpretations, listings, interviews; fiction relating to Bob Dylan (rock music, related topics). For his fans to keep up with his career and to keep in touch with other fans. Quarterly. Estab. 1976. Circ. 1,000+.

Needs: Contemporary. Does not want "anything that could not be construed as somehow, at least remotely, related to Bob Dylan or of special interest to his fans." Length: 700-2,800 words.

How to Contact: Query. Reports in 1 month on mss and 2 months on mss. Sample copy $1.50.

Payment: 2 free author's copies. $1.50 charge for extras.

Terms: Acquires all rights.

Tips: "Be a clear-writing, clear-thinking Bob Dylan fan."

CHANNEL X, Padre Productions, Box 1275, San Luis Obispo CA 93406. (805)543-5404. Editor: Lachlan P. MacDonald. Fiction Editor: Mack Sullivan. "*Channel X* is a paperback fiction anthology featuring vignettes, short shorts and brief experimental forms of fiction. All stories have a twist, a bizarre note, or break taboos of one kind or other. It is for the viewer of TV who wants quick fiction that engages his attention briefly and stays in the mind and for the short-attention-span yet sophisticated reader." Annually. Estab. 1980.

Needs: Literary, contemporary, fantasy, adventure, humor and young adult. "We are also publishers of novels in the categories checked above. No juvenile mss except adventure for ages 10-14. No long stories." Buys 40-60 mss/year. Length: 100-1,200 words.

How to Contact: Send complete ms with SASE. Reports in 2 months on mss.

Payment: Pro-rated royalties on each edition. Free author's copies. Full rate for extras.

Terms: Pays on publication for first North American serial rights, book rights and radio-TV rights.

Tips: "Make every word count. Rewrite, polish. Type clearly. Innovate. Think of the reader. Avoid photocopies, unclean typewriter keys, spelling errors (they kill it right there). *Channel X* is dedicated to reviving and vitalizing the short short form of fiction that will be remembered by readers of the American vignettes, Mark Hellinger, etc. and fans of *Cruel Shoes* and of contemporary writers like Hugh Fox."

THE CHARITON REVIEW, Northeast Missouri State University, Kirksville MO 63501. (816)665-5121, ext. 2156. Editor: Jim Barnes. "We demand only excellence in fiction and fiction translation for a general and college audience." Semiannually. Estab. 1975. Circ. 700+.

Needs: Literary, contemporary and translation. Buys 3-5 mss/issue, 6-10 mss/year. Length: 3,000-6,000 words.

How to Contact: Send complete ms with SASE. Reports in 1 month on mss. Sample copy $2 with SASE.

Payment: $5/page. Free author's copy. $2 charge for extras.

Terms: Pays on publication for all rights; rights returned on request.

Tips: "Write well and study the publication you are submitting to. We are interested only in the very best fiction and fiction translation. We are not interested in slick material. We do not read photocopies or carbon copies. You send the original; you keep the copy."

CHELSEA, Chelsea Associates, Inc. Box 5880, Grand Central Station, New York NY 10163. (212)988-2276. Editor: Sonia Raiziss. "We have no consistent theme except for single special issues. Otherwise, we use general material of an eclectic nature: poetry, prose, artwork, etc. for a sophisticated, literate audience interested in avant-garde literature and current writing both national and international." Annual. Estab. 1958. Circ. 1,000+.

Needs: Literary, contemporary and translations. No humorous, scatological, purely confessional, child/young-adult experiences. Length: not over 25 printed pages.

How to Contact: Query with SASE. Reports in 3 weeks on queries, 2 months on mss. Sample copy $3 plus postage.

Payment: 2 free author's copies.

Terms: Pays on publication for one-time rights.
Tips: "Familiarize yourself with issues of the magazine for character of contributions. Mss should be legible, clearly typed, with minimal number of typographical errors and cross-outs, sufficient return postage and if a covering letter is included it should be short, to the point with a few major credits and publications."

CHICAGO REVIEW, Chicago Review, Box C, University of Chicago, 5700 S. Ingleside, Chicago IL 60637. (312)753-3571. Editor: Bill Monroe. Fiction Editors: Jan Deckenbach and Sarah E. Lauzen. Magazine for a highly literate, largely academic audience. Quarterly. Estab. 1946. Circ. 2,000.
Needs: Literary, contemporary, science fiction, fantasy, satire and experimental. Accepts 5 mss/issue, 18 mss/year. No preferred length.
How to Contact: Send complete ms with SASE. Reports in 4 months on mss. Sample copy $3.75. Free guidelines.
Payment: 3 free author's copies and subscription. 40% discount for extras. "We have an annual award and prize for our best fiction."

CHOCK MAGAZINE, 172 Romford Rd., London, England E9 6HY. Editor: Ian Durant. Published 3 times/year. Estab. 1978.
Needs: Literary, contemporary, Third World, experimental, translations. "No adventure, mystery, spy, historical, western, war, romance, juvenile."
How to Contact: Send complete ms. Reports in 6 weeks.
Payment: Free author's copies by agreement.

CHUNGA REVIEW, The Chunga Press, Box 158, Felch MI 49831. (906)246-3562. Editor: M. Felten. "A publication to bridge the gap between the Jaws II mentality and the university press. We like to publish fiction that is 'not suitable' to anyone else's needs. Our audience grows nauseous in large bookstores. They have read Joyce and Salinger on the subway and corn flake boxes." Quarterly. Estab. 1978. Circ. 250+.
Needs: Literary, contemporary, fantasy, feminist and humor. "No kitty-cat stories, genre fiction, contemplative pieces about naked people in the ocean or anything that you are satisfied with." Buys 2-3 mss/issue. Length: 5,000 words.
How to Contact: Send complete ms with SASE. Reports in 1 month on mss. Sample copy $1.25.
Payment: Contributor's copies.
Terms: Pays on publication for first rights.
Tips: "Write it for yourself, whatever it is. Scan your *Fiction Writer's Market*. If you become discouraged because it doesn't seem to belong anywhere, mail it to us. Look for the unusual and read it to a friend; if he or she stabs you or kisses you—send it to us. If your friend falls asleep, don't send it to us."

CIMARRON REVIEW, Oklahoma State University, 208 LSE, Stillwater OK 74078. (405)624-6573. Editor: Neil John Hackett. Managing Editor: Jeanne Adams Wray. "Poetry and fiction on contemporary themes; personal essay on contemporary issues that cope with life in the 20th century for educated literary cognoscenti. We work hard to reflect quality." Quarterly. Estab. 1967. Circ. 500.
Needs: Literary and contemporary. No collegiate reminiscences or juvenile. Accepts 5-6 mss/issue, 20-24 mss/year.
How to Contact: Send complete ms with SASE. Reports in 1 month on mss. Free sample copy with 6½x9½ SASE and 40¢ postage.
Payment: 2 free author's copies. $1.50 charge for extras.
Terms: Acquires all rights on publication.

CITY MINER, City Miner Magazine, Box 176, Berkeley CA 94701. (415)841-1511. Editor:

Michael Helm. "Anthology with focus on Northern California writers and themes. Emphasis on first person stories, articles and essays. Must be well-written and thought provoking for a literary audience." Annual. Estab. 1976. Circ. 4,000.

Needs: Contemporary, erotica, humor, folklore and urban. Length: 2,000-5,000 words.

How to Contact: Send complete ms with SASE. Reports in 1 month on mss. Sample copy $1 with SASE and 68¢ postage.

Payment: Annual royalty. Free author's copy. 40% discount on extras.

Tips: *City Miner* suspended publication as a quarterly magazine in 1980. Will accept fiction for annual anthology.

CLIFTON MAGAZINE, Communications Board, 204 Tangeman University Center, Cincinnati OH 45221. Editor: Chris O'Dell. Fiction Editor: David Montagno. "*Clifton* is the magazine of the University of Cincinnati, presenting fiction, poetry, and feature articles of interest to the university community. It is read by a highly literate audience of students, academics and professionals looking for original and exciting ideas presented in our award winning format." Quarterly. Estab. 1972. Circ. 10,000.

Needs: Literary, contemporary, science fiction, fantasy, feminist, gay/lesbian, erotica, humor and ethnic. "Will consider anything we haven't read a thousand times before. We try to have no preconceptions when approaching fiction. No semi-autobiographies of sensitive young people finding themselves." Accepts 1-2 mss/issue, 5 mss/year. Length: 30,000 words.

How to Contact: Send complete ms with SASE. Reports in 1 month on mss. Sample copy $1. Free guidelines with legal-sized SASE.

Payment: 5 free author's copies.

Terms: Acquires first rights.

Tips: "*Clifton* often publishes work by unpublished authors, and is quite open to any fiction just as long as it doesn't bore us. We have previously published Allen Ginsberg, Richard Price, and James Wright, as well as unpublished writers who now are professionals. We look forward to continuing the publication with both young and established writers."

THE COE REVIEW, Student Senate of Coe College, 1220 1st St., Cedar Rapids IA 52402. Editor-in-Chief: Jerry Farnsworth; Fiction Editors: Sean Hennessey and James Meyer. Annual anthology of "quality experimental writing in both poetry and fiction. Especially directed to an academic or experimental literary audience that is concerned with current literature." Annual. Estab. 1972. Circ. 500.

Needs: Literary, contemporary, psychic/supernatural, science fiction, fantasy, men's, women's, feminist, gay/lesbian, erotica, quality ethnic, serialized and condensed novels, translations. "We publish students, unsolicited professional, and solicited professional mss. *The Coe Review* is growing and it is our goal to become nationally acknowledged in literary circles as a forerunner in the publication of experimental writing. We support writing workshops and invite both writing professors and student writers to submit." No "religious propaganda, gothic, romance, western, mystery or adventure. We avoid 'sap' and predictability." Buys 8-10 mss/issue. Length: 500-4,000 words.

How to Contact: Send complete ms with SASE. "Mss sent in summer will possibly not be returned until fall depending on availability of a fiction editor in summer." Sample copy $3 with SASE plus $2.75 postage.

Payment: $25-$100 for solicitations. 1-2 free author's copies. $5 charge for extras.

Terms: Pays on publication for all rights "but possibly sooner with solicited mss. Upon request we will reassign rights to the author."

Tips: "We desire material that seeks to explore the vast imaginative landscape and expand the boundaries thereof. We use the I CHING symbol or 'breakthrough' to exemplify this intention. Study experimental writers such as Borges, Vonnegut, Brautigan, J. Baumbach and E. Gorman. Avoid sentimentalism. Do not be afraid to experiment or to write intelligent fiction." Plans to sponsor a contest for students of Coe College and a nationwide contest for writing workshops.

COEVOLUTION QUARTERLY, Point Foundation, Box 428, Sausalito CA 94965. Editor: Stewart Brand. Assistant Editor: Stephanie Mills. "*CQ* is unique and trustworthy" and the types of material published include "excellence, learning, authenticity. Eclectic." Audience is curious and self-reliant. Quarterly. Estab. 1974. Circ. 41,000.
Needs: "We'd prefer fiction which can't be categorized. Quality is more important than type." Buys 1-2 mss/issue. Length: 1,000-15,000 words.
How to Contact: Send complete ms with SASE. "We don't like queries." Reports in 2 months. Sample copy $4.
Payment: $100-$300. 5 free author's copies plus a year's subscription.
Terms: Pays on publication for first rights.
Tips: "What's good? New, not read a hundred times before, not an imitation of old *CQ* articles, often a personal passionate statement. Consider yourself to be writing a letter to an intelligent, uninformed friend about something that is interesting/important to you. We often print things that everyone, including the author, thought were too odd to be printed anywhere. Remember that we print all lengths from a paragraph to many pages, so don't puff a good, short idea into four tedious pages. And please don't try to please us by creating something you think we'll like. Being hustled is boring. We'd rather print true love—yours for your subject. All things are possible and may be printed. We have no editorial policy for or against any subject matter."

COFFEE BREAK, Coffee Break Press, Box 103, Burley WA 98322. (206)857-4329. Editor/Publisher: D.M. Nicolai. Fiction Editors: C. Parkhurst, Kate Bourg. "Our slogan is: A magazine to brighten commuting time, coffee breaks and other hum-drum lulls." It is a family magazine with short fiction, articles, how-to's cartoons and poetry for adults and children. Family readership. Quarterly. Estab. 1977. Circ. 5,000.
Needs: Literary, contemporary, psychic/supernatural, science fiction, fantasy, horror, men's, women's, romance, western, mystery, adventure, juvenile, young adult, and especially humor. "Our editors are looking for quality and freshness, new ideas, excellent fiction, new forms, fillers and humor for adults and juveniles. We need mss in good taste but not sugar coated. Our editorial policy is flexible. A sparkling style will help. We will accept any manuscript that is skillfully constructed by a writer who has bothered to apply knowledge and craftsmanship, especially if it is coupled with fresh ideas. No religion, erotica, politics or pornography." Length: 1,500 words maximum.
How to Contact: Send complete ms with SASE. "No queries for fiction." Reports in 6 weeks. Sample copy $1. Free guidelines with legal-sized SASE.
Payment: $5-$25 or 10 free author's copies. No charge for extras "within reason."
Terms: Pays on publication for one-time rights.
Tips: "Ask for editorial comments. You will be pleasantly surprised to find that our editors take the time to write personal replies and comments to anyone who wants them. Read at least one copy of *Coffee Break* before submitting a ms. We try not to be subjective in our selections but a clever writer will soon learn what we prefer. Do not submit a ms with the same plot that you found in our last issue. Many new writers start with *Coffee Break*. Many professionals stay with us."

THE COFFEEHOUSE, Wire Press, 3448 19th St., San Francisco CA 94110. Editor: Dino Siotis. "Theme is contemporary Greek Arts and Letters. Mostly we publish Greek short stories, fiction and poetry in English translation. Our audience is comprised of people who are interested in what's happening in Greece today concerning arts and letters." Semiannual. Estab. October 1975. Circ. 1,000.
Needs: Greek ethnic, literary, translations. "We publish only works by Greeks, Greek-Americans and Americans if the subject of their writing has to do with the theme of the

magazine." Accepts 2 mss/issue, 4 mss/year. Length: 1,000-1,500 words.
How to Contact: Query with SASE. Reports in 1 month. Sample copy $2.
Payment: Pays in contributor's copies.

COLUMBIA: A MAGAZINE OF POETRY & PROSE, 404 Dodge Hall, Columbia University, New York NY 10027. Editors: Bonnie ZoBell, Nancy Schoenberger. Fiction Editor: John Soat. "We are not looking for a set formula—just good writing. Short stories, parts of novels, translations, interviews, and poetry are all welcome." Semiannual or annual.
Needs: Literary and translations but "although we only mention 2 categories, we will consider anything of literary merit." Accepts 3 mss/issue, 3-6 mss/year ("depending on how many issues published").
How to Contact: Send complete ms with SASE. Reports in 2 months.
Payment: 2 free author's copies. $3 charge for extras.
Tips: "We will consider all mss. $100 Carlos Fuentes Award for Best Fiction."

COMBINATIONS, A JOURNAL OF PHOTOGRAPHY, Combinations Press, Rt. 1, Box 83, Greenfield Center NY 12833. (518)584-4612. Editor/Publisher: Mary Ann Lynch. "*Combinations* is a nonprofit art and literary publication directed toward photographers and artists interested in photography as well as to educators and the general public with an interest in the medium." Quarterly. Estab. 1977. Circ. 1,000.
Needs: "Short fiction only, must pertain to photography in some way." Accepts 6-12 mss/year. Length: 750-5,000 words.
How to Contact: Send complete ms with SASE. Reports in 1 month on mss. Sample copy $4.50. Free guidelines with legal-sized SASE.
Payment: 2 free author's copies. Charge for extras, discounts available.
Terms: Acquires one-time rights.
Tips: "Read back issues. In addition to our quarterly journal, we will be publishing anthologies of works involving photography, which may be longer in length (up to 10,000 words). In all cases, we are interested in previously unpublished works only and it is part of our agreement with the author that *Combinations* will be acknowledged as first publisher in the event works are reproduced elsewhere."

THE COMMUNICATOR, Box 2140, Springhill, Nova Scotia, Canada. B0M 1X0. Editor: Bob Eby. "We are a prisoner-published magazine operating in Springhill Penitentiary and material we publish should relate to the experience of imprisonment, justice, etc. Poetry, short fiction and articles. Audience: prisoners across North America, friends of prisoners, and interested parties. We consider ourselves one of the best magazines of this type anywhere." Bimonthly. Estab. 1972. Circ. 1,000.
Needs: Prison-related material. No self-pitying or religious stances or appeals to authority. Accepts 1 mss/issue. Length: 2,000 words maximum.
How to Contact: Send complete ms. Reports in 1 month. Free sample copy.
Payment: 3 free author's copies and one year's subscription.
Terms: Acquires one-time rights.
Tips: "Say something different or from a different approach. Grab the reader's sense of the perverse or unusual. Don't send middle of the road material. Take a point of view whether or not you agree with it. Be aware of the inherent bias of the publication you are after. Especially interested in people who have done time or have a loved one who has. We advocate self-support and alternatives to incarceration."

COMPASS POETRY & PROSE, Compass, Box 51, Burwood, NSW, Australia 2136. (02)747-1592. Co-editors: C. Mansell, S.D. Thwaites. Quarterly. Estab. 1978. Circ. 1,000.
Needs: Literary, contemporary, science fiction, fantasy. No poorly constructed stories. Buys 3 ms/issue. Length: 2,000-3,000 words.
How to Contact: Send complete ms with SASE or IRC. Reports in 2 months on mss.

Sample copy $2 (Australian).
Payment: $5/page and 2 free author's copies. $2 charge for extras.
Terms: Buys first rights (Australian).
Tips: "Subscribe first."

CONCEPTIONS SOUTHWEST, UNM Student Publications, UNM Box 20, University of New Mexico, Albuquerque, NM 87131. (505)277-5656. Editor: Leslie A. Donovan. Publishes "all forms of creative expression from the UNM community and its faculty, students, staff and alumni. *CSW* is directed to all those interested in the creative arts here in the Southwest. This audience is concerned with the work being done and looks to *CSW* to present that material in a single body." Annual. Estab. Spring 1978. Circ. 1,000.
Needs: "We will consider any and all fiction categories as long as the author is or has been connected with the UNM community. We will consider almost any word length. Anything exceptionally long may be excerpted with author's approval."
How to Contact: Query with ms. Reports in 3 weeks on queries, 1 month on mss. Sample copy $2.75.
Payment: 1 free author's copy. $2 charge for extras plus 75¢ postage and handling.
Terms: Acquires one-time rights.
Tips: Submit "typed, double-spaced mss with SASE attached to work for easiest and speediest processing."

CONFRONTATION, Long Island University, English Dept., 1 University Plaza, Brooklyn NY 11201. (212)834-6170. Editor: Martin Tucker. Fiction Editor: Ken Bernard. "We like to have a 'range' of subjects, form and style in each issue and are open to all forms. Quality is our major concern. Our audience is literate, thinking college students, educated and self-educated lay persons." Semiannual. Estab. 1968. Circ. 2,000.
Needs: Literary, contemporary, science fiction, fantasy, horror, men's, women's, feminist, gay/lesbian, erotica, confession, gothic, humor, translations. No "proseletyzing" literature. Buys 10 mss/issue, 20 mss/year. Length: 500-2,000 words.
How to Contact: Send complete ms with SASE. Reports in 6 weeks on mss. Sample copy $1.50.
Payment: $15-$100. 1 free author's copy. Half price charge for extras.
Terms: Pays on publication for all rights "with transfer on request to author."

CONFRONTATION/CHANGE REVIEW, 1107 Lexington Ave., Dayton OH 45407. Editor: F.M. Finney. "A journal of political economy and Americana (including Caribbean) fiction and poetry. Readership is college level, literary and just 'plain readers.' Style is designed to allow readers to enjoy material." Published 3 times/year. Estab. 1976. Circ. 1,910.
Needs: Literary, contemporary, fantasy, black ethnic. No gay/lesbian, women's liberation or alternative life style pieces at this time. Buys 2 mss/issue, 6 mss/year. Length: 1,500-3,000 words.
How to Contact: Send complete ms with SASE. Reports in 1 month. Sample copy $1.25 with SASE.
Payment: $50 maximum, usual or 3 free author's copies.
Terms: Pays on publication for first North American serial rights.

CONNECTICUT ARTISTS MAGAZINE, Connecticut Artists Publication, Box 131, New Haven CT 06501. Editor: David Alvarez. Fiction Editor: Donald Faulkner. "We publish distinguished fiction of all types from Connecticut writers, both new and established. We are read by an educated, professional audience made up of persons interested in the Connecticut arts scene. Many of our readers are artists." Quarterly. Estab. 1977. Circ. 10,000.
Needs: Connecticut writers only. Literary, contemporary, science fiction, mystery, and rarely excerpts from novels. "We are always open to new ideas and approaches to fiction, as well as solid work in traditional areas. No overly experimental, erotic or political subjects."

Accepts 1-2 mss/issue, 4-5 mss/year. Length: 500-7,000 words.
How to Contact: Send complete ms with SASE. Reports in 1 month. Sample copy $2.
Payment: Free author's copies.
Terms: "Reassigns rights after publication."
Tips: "Write stories that have a beginning, a middle and an end. Characters and plot should work to a cohesive end. Avoid sentimental, overly-autobiographical material and stories other people have written better."

COTTONWOOD REVIEW, Cottonwood Review Press, Box J, Student Union, Kansas University, Lawrence KS 66045. Editors: Denise Low and Melanie Farley. Fiction Editor: James Carothers. "*Cottonwood Review* is a literary magazine that publishes new and well known writers. We have no theme aside from quality. For readers of fine literature, poetry and fiction in the Midwest and the nation." Semiannual. Estab. 1965. Circ. 800.
Needs: Literary, contemporary, men's, women's, translations. "We are not interested in contrived, slick material. Accepts 2-3 mss/issue, 6 mss/year. Length: 500-3,000 words.
How to Contact: Query, send complete ms. SASE for query, ms. Reports in 1 month on queries, 2 months on ms. Sample copy $2.50.
Payment: 2 free author's copies. $2.50 charge for extras.
Terms: Acquires one-time rights.
Tips: "Read sample issues."

CREACION, Editorial Creación, Apartado III, Estación G, Ponce Puerto, Rico 00732. (809)844-4194. Editors: Cirilo Toro Vargas and Hector J. Martell. Stresses fiction, poetry, essays, graphics, biographies and interviews of Latin Americans; interested in literature from Latin American authors. Annual. Estab. 1975. Circ. 1,000.
Needs: Literary, Puerto Rican ethnic and children's literature. Submit fiction in Spanish only. Length: 2,500 words maximum.
How to Contact: Query with SASE. Reports in 4 months. Free sample copy for 9x8 SASE.
Payment: 5 free author's copies. 50¢ charge for extras.

CREAM CITY REVIEW, University of Wisconsin-Milwaukee, Box 413, Milwaukee WI 53201. Editor: Ned Williams. Fiction Editor: Tom Wilkinson. "We publish traditional and innovative poetry, fiction and nonfiction. Themes vary with editorial staff changes each year." Audience is literate and regional. Semiannual. Estab. 1975. Circ. 700.
Needs: Literary, contemporary, fantasy, translations. Accepts 6-8 mss/issue. Length: 1,000-5,000 words.
How to Contact: Send complete ms with SASE. Reports in 2 months. Sample copy $3. Free guidelines.
Payment: 1 free author's copy.
Terms: Acquires first rights.

CREATIVE PITTSBURGH JOURNAL, Creative Pittsburgh, Box 7346, Pittsburgh PA 15213. Managing Editor: G. Ulrich Musinsky. Fiction Editor: H. Kermit Jackson. Magazine of character pieces which are in-depth analyses of people in a particular situation for a general audience who enjoys reading fiction and is interested in people and their concerns. Published 3 times/year. Estab. April 1976. Circ. 1,000.
Needs: Literary, contemporary, psychic/inspirational, science fiction, fantasy, horror, men's, women's, romance, western, mystery, adventure, humor, all ethnic, translations. "*Creative Pittsburgh* will soon be going to single issues of fiction published once a year. Some will be resembling a prose anthology with illustrations in book format." Accepts 3-5 mss/issue, 8-12 mss/year. Length: 1,000-5,000 words (2,500 preferred).
How to Contact: Send complete ms with SASE. Reports in up to 6 months on mss. Sample copy $2.75 with 7x10 envelope.
Payment: 2 free author's copies. Negotiates charge for extras.

Terms: Acquires all rights.
Tips: "If you feel confident about your story, its development, characters, plot, and you believe it is the best you have written, there's a good chance we'll take it. Prefer originals but copy okay if not submitted elsewhere. Be sure story is complete and not a sketch; experimental work no good if it can't be understood. Story must be tightly written, no excessive words, etc."

CROP DUST, Crop Dust Press, Rt. 2, Box 392, Bealton VA 22712. (703)439-2140. Editor: Edward C. Lynskey. Rural and city landscapes for the university and general writing community. Semiannual. Estab. Spring 1980. Circ. 500.
Needs: Literary and contemporary, all types of fiction. Accepts 5 mss/issue, 10 mss/year. Length: 500-5,000 words.
How to Contact: Send complete ms. Reports in 3 months. Sample copy $1.50. Free guidelines with legal-sized SASE.
Payment: 1 free author's copy.
Terms: Acquires first North American serial rights, which revert to author on publication.
Tips: "Read a copy of the magazine before submitting. Send only one story. Short stories fare better with editors in our publishing space." Future contests planned.

CROSS CURRENTS, Westlake Technology, 2200 Glastonbury Rd., Westlake Village CA 91361. Editor: Linda Brown Michelson. "*Crosscurrents* is a magazine of the West which offers another corner for today's artistry. This is not a limitation but a slant. We publish short fiction, poetry, graphic arts, and nonfiction. We direct our publication toward an educated audience which appreciates good writing, good art and enjoys a periodic sampling of current trends in these fields." Quarterly. Estab. March 1980. Circ. 500.
Needs: Most all categories except heavy erotica, juvenile and young adult. "We try to remain open to as many types of fiction as possible. Good writing is what we look for and consider first. Limitations as to type are few." Buys 3-5 mss/issue, 15 mss/year. Length: 8,000 words maximum.
How to Contact: Send complete ms with SASE. Reports in 6 weeks on mss. Sample copy $2.50.
Payment: $35 minimum.
Terms: Pays on acceptance for first North American serial rights.
Tips: "We are constantly on the lookout for new talent and welcome the beginner. Look at a sample issue to see what we publish. Include a short letter with your ms to let us know who you are. Good quality photocopies fine, but no simultaneous submissions." Sponsors fiction contest.

CROTON REVIEW, Croton Council on the Arts, Inc. (non-profit organization), Box 277, Croton on Hudson NY 10520. Editors: Ruth Lisa Schechter, Lawrence Alson, Dan B. Thomas. An award-winning publication based on excellence of literary content. Publishes contemporary, original, quality writing and poetry, as well as art. Annual. Estab. 1978. Circ. 2,000.
Needs: Literary, contemporary, men's, women's. "No trite or hackneyed themes. Avoid clichés." Approximate length: 8-16 double spaced pages.
How to Contact: Send complete ms with brief biography. SASE. Reports in 6 weeks. Sample copy $1 with SASE.
Payment: 2 free author's copies.
Tips: "Subscribe and read the *Croton Review*. Originality desirable. Our contributors submit from all over the US. New and well known writers are invited. All submissions are read carefully. The editorial board consists of writers and editors."

C.S.P. WORLD NEWS, Edition Stencil, Box 2608, Station D, Ottawa, Ontario, Canada K1P 5W7. Editor: Guy F. Claude Hamel. Publishes poetry and fiction for a general reader-

ship. Monthly. Estab. 1962.
Needs: Literary. "I'll look at anything." Buys 2 mss/year. Length: 1,000-1,200 words.
How to Contact: Query first or query with clips of published work. SASE for query, ms. Reports in 3 weeks. Sample copy $1.50 with legal-sized SASE.
Payment: Negotiates pay for fiction. 2 free author's copies. $1.50 charge for extras.
Terms: Pays on acceptance on a work-for-hire basis.
Tips: "Be yourself and research well."

CUMBERLAND JOURNAL, Box 2648, Harrisburg PA 17105. Editor: George Myers, Jr. Publishes literary biography and innovative cultural criticism for serious fiction readers, artists and critics. Quarterly. Estab. 976. Circ. 400.
Needs: Literary, men's, women's, confession, adventure, translations. Length: 1,000-18,000 words.
How to Contact: Query or send complete ms. SASE for query, ms. Reports in 2 weeks. Sample copy $3.
Payment: Free author's copies.
Terms: Acquires first rights or first North American serial rights.
Tips: "Purchase sample copy to see what we publish."

CUMBERLANDS, formerly *Twigs*, Pikeville College, College Box 2, Pikeville KY 41501. (606)432-9227. Editor: Leonard Roberts. A "little magazine, light, somewhat experimental, with articles, fiction, art, Appalachian settings, etc. for not only the young and college age readers but practicing writers and poets who read it to find new and challenging material, humor and magic (in our folktales)." Published 3 times/year. Estab. 1979 (*Twigs*-1965). Circ. 500.
Needs: Literary, contemporary, psychic/supernatural, fantasy, men's, women's, mystery, adventure, humor. "No explicit sex, horror, pulp western or romance, gay, freakish." Accepts 3-4 mss/issue. Length: 1,500-2,500 words.
How to Contact: Send complete ms with SASE. Reports in 1 month. Sample copy $1 with 9x12 SASE plus 80¢ postage. Free guidelines.
Payment: 1-2 free author's copies plus $25 award/volume for best contribution. Half price charge for extras.
Terms: Acquires first rights.
Tips: "Send third draft of short piece which you feel good about. We will read and do minor editing; we like to see corrections made by author. Avoid humorless long, creeping, awkward discourses with poor or no dialogue or with no defined point of view."

DARK HORSE, Box 36, Newton Lower Falls MA 02162. Managing Editors: June Grass, Erika Mumford. Estab. 1974.
Needs: "Literate, contemporary, very high quality fiction. No science fiction, mystery, juvenile. With those exceptions, will consider anything that meets standards of quality."
How to Contact: Submit complete ms with SASE. Reports in 3 months on ms. Simultaneous submissions OK.
Payment: Pays $25 for outright purchase and 4 free author's copies. Sample copy $2.
Tips: "Stories should be no longer than 15 double-spaced typewritten pages."

DE COLORES JOURNAL, Pajarito Publications, Box 7264, Albuquerque NM 87104. Editor: Jose Arimas. "Chicano literature for college audiences." Quarterly. Estab. 1972. Circ. 10,000.
Needs: Chicano ethnic, literary, contemporary, psychic/supernatural, science fiction, fantasy, men's, women's, feminist, romance western, mystery, adventure, humor, juvenile, young adult, serialized and condensed novels and translations. No religion or confession. Buys 15 mss/issue. Length: 2,000-10,000 words.
How to Contact: Query with SASE. Reports in 2 weeks on queries, 2 months on mss.

Sample copy for $3 with 6x9 SASE.
Payment: Free author's copies.
Terms: Payment is on publication for first rights.
Tips: "Write, write, write. Then rewrite, rewrite, rewrite."

DENVER QUARTERLY, University of Denver, Denver CO 80208. (303)753-2869. Editor: Leland H. Chambers. "We publish fiction, articles and poetry for a generally well-educated audience primarily interested in literature and the literary experience. They read *DQ* to find something a little different from a strictly academic quarterly or a creative writing outlet." Quarterly. Estab. 1966. Circ. 450.
Needs: Literary, contemporary and translations. "No superficial, sleazy, cute, tricky or incompetently crafted fiction." Buys 1-2 mss/issue, 5-8 mss/year.
How to Contact: Send complete ms with SASE. Reports in 2 months on mss. Sample copy $2 with SASE.
Payment: Pays $5/page. 2 free author's copies plus 5 tear sheets.
Terms: Acquires first North American serial rights.
Tips: "Write intelligently and sensitively. Photocopy OK."

DESCANT, Department of English, Texas Christian University, Fort Worth TX 76129. (817)921-7240. Editor: Betsy Colquitt. "*Descant* uses fiction, poetry, essays. No restriction on style, content or theme. It is a little literary magazine, and its readers are those who have interest in such publications." Quarterly. Estab. 1955. Circ. 500.
Needs: Literary and contemporary. No genre or category fiction. Length: 1,500-5,000 words.
How to Contact: Send complete ms with SASE. Reports usually within 6 weeks on ms. Sample copy $2.
Payment: 4 free author's copies. $2 charge/extra copy.
Terms: Acquires first North American serial rights.
Tips: "Submit good material. Even though a small publication, *Descant* receives many submissions, and acceptances are few compared to the total number of mss received. We offer a $100 annual prize for fiction—the Frank O'Connor Prize. Award is made to the story considered (by a judge not connected to the magazine) to be the best published in a given volume of the journal."

DESCANT, Box 314, Station P, Toronto, Ontario, Canada M5S 2S8. (416)766-9241. Editor: Karen Mulhallen. High quality poetry and prose for an intelligent audience who wants to see good, new poetry and prose. Triannual. Estab. 1970. Circ. 1,000.
Needs: Literary, contemporary, psychic/supernatural, science fiction, fantasy, horror, men's, women's, feminist, gay/lesbian, erotica, confession, gothic, romance, western, mystery, adventure, humor, young adult, ethnic, serialized and condensed novels and translations. "Although most themes are acceptable, all works must have some literary merit."
How to Contact: Send complete ms with SASE. Reports in 3 months on mss. Sample copy $2 with 9x11 SASE and IRC (32¢ Canadian postage.)
Payment: Pays in free author's copies and 1 year subscription. $2 charge for extra author's copies.
Terms: Acquires one-time rights.
Tips: "Edit yourself first. Do not send numerous submissions at once. Send only a few, at most, of your best works. Rewrite your material until you are convinced it is the best that can be done on that theme. Know the journal you submit to; each one has a personality."

DIANA'S ALMANAC, Diana's Bimonthly Press, 71 Elmgrove Ave., Providence RI 02906. (401)274-5417. Editor: Tom Ahern. Anthology of contemporary American literature, literature in translation, and illustrated artists' narratives. "*Diana's* is read by people interested in innovative design and is directed to those well-informed about contemporary concerns in

literature." Annual. Estab. 1972. Circ. 1,100.
Needs: "No mass-market, popular or derivative fiction." Buys 2-3 mss/issue. Length: 5,000-30,000 words.
How to Contact: Query with clips of published work with SASE. Reports in 1 week on queries and mss. Sample copy $5.
Payment: Pays $150 minimum and 10 free author's copies.
Terms: Pays on publication for one-time rights.
Tips: "Be sure your work makes a difference."

DOUBLE HARNESS MAGAZINE, DM/AVED, 9 Bradmore Rd., Oxford, England 0X2 6QN. Editor: Andrew Cozens. Literary magazine with socio-political side interests for a literary audience. Annual. Estab. August 1979. Circ. 750.
Needs: Literary, contemporary, men's, women's, feminist, gay/lesbian, erotica, confession, gothic, humor, serialized novels and translations. No romance. Length: 500-8,000 words.
How to Contact: Query with clips of published work. Reports in 1 month on both queries and mss. Free sample copy.
Payment: Unlimited amount of free author's copies.

DREAMS UNLIMITED, Box 247, Middleton WI 53562. (608)238-6575. Editor: Elizabeth Lowe. "We publish (or plan to publish) dream-based or dream-related short stories—preferably utilizing an actual dream or dreams of the author. Dream poetry will also be considered. (The bulk of the list is nonfiction informational and self-help materials on dreams.) Directed to people interested in dreams from a psychological, humanistic, psychic or new age perspective." Estab. 1979.
Needs: Contemporary, religious, psychic/supernatural, science fiction, fantasy, feminist, gay/lesbian, erotica, gothic, romance, western, mystery, adventure, humor, ethnic (author's choice) and experimental psychological. "No subject matter which seems unlikely to yield dream-based fiction, hard-core or anarchist." Buys 4-10 mss/year. Length: 1,000-10,000.
How to Contact: Query with a discursive letter telling about your dream and the story you have in mind with SASE. Reports as soon as possible but no longer than 1 month on queries, 2 months on mss. Publication list enclosed with response to queries.
Payment: Pays $50 maximum, in royalties or copies (negotiated).
Terms: Negotiates rights.
Tips: "Have a dream. Record it. Plan how that dream could be used in or as a basis of a story. Share your dream and ideas with me. If it's appealing, we can take it from there. New writers are especially welcome. If you wish to create a fictional dream, read enough dream literature to understand actual dream composition. *Dreams Unlimited*, an alternative press publishing specifically and solely on dreams, is committed to a brief (10,000 words or less) and readable format. Depending on the length of the short story, one story could take up an entire booklet, or a booklet could be comprised of two or more stories by the same or different authors."

DREAMWEAVER MAGAZINE, Dreamweaver, 50 Seymour Ave., Toronto, Ontario, Canada M4J 3T4. (416)466-6728. Editors: Harry Posner and Nick Trusolino. Associate Editor: Steve Solomon. "We explore the world of sleep and dreams including articles focusing upon current sleep and dream research, the world of children, symbols, dream interpretations, etc. Aimed at professionals in mental health fields, university educated individuals (18-39) and any who take an interest in dreaming and sleep. Our magazine is both informative and entertaining." Quarterly. Estab. April 1980. Circ. 4,000.
Needs: Literary, contemporary, psychic/supernatural, science fiction, fantasy, horror, feminist, gay/lesbian, erotica, gothic, western, mystery, adventure, humor and translations. "Almost any genre is acceptable, as long as the theme of the story relates *directly* to *any* aspect of the world of sleep or dreams." Buys 1 ms/issue, 4 mss/year. Length: 2,000-2,500 words.

How to Contact: Send complete ms with SASE or IRC. Reports in 3 weeks on mss. Free sample copy.
Payment: Pays $50-70 or 3¢/word.
Terms: Pays on publication for all rights.
Tips: "Keep writing and keep submitting. Eventually you will hit us where it counts. Always make copies of the story—never send an original."

EARTHWISE QUARTERLY, Earthwise Publications, Inc., Box 680536, Miami FL 33168. (305)688-8558. Editor: Barbara Holley. Fiction Editor: Kaye Carter. "A quarterly journal mainly of poetry and interviews. We are aiming for larger issues with more space for fiction, articles, etc. We have various quarterly themes, usually announced at start of year. We have an eclectic audience of mainly poets, some artists, authors. We aim for quality literature and are attaining a fine reputation. We also publish a quarterly newsletter announcing contests, markets, etc." Quarterly. Estab. 1978. Circ. 350.
Needs: Literary, contemporary, psychic/supernatural, science fiction, fantasy, gothic, romance, western, mystery, adventure, humor and any ethnic. Please query on translations. Nothing morally or ethically pornographic. Buys 1-2 mss/issue, 4-6 mss/year. Length: 900-1,200 words.
How to Contact: Query with clips of published work with SASE. Reports in 1 month on queries and mss. Sample copy $2.
Payment: Pays $5-25.
Terms: Pays on publication for first North American serial rights.
Tips: "We like light, amusing or warm stories for *Earthwise*. We much prefer the well done story even if a bit longer. Cameos or vignettes are also acceptable. No submissions are read from June 30 through September 5th each year."

EERIE COUNTRY, Weirdbook Press, Box 35, Amherst Branch, Buffalo NY 14226. Editor: W. Paul Ganley. "Latter day pulp magazine of supernatural horror and fantasy of lesser known writers for literate fans of horror/supernatural." Published irregularly. Estab. 1976. Circ. 150.
Needs: Psychic/supernatural, fantasy, horror and gothic (not modern). No psychological mystery or physical horror (blood), traditional stories, science fiction, or reincarnation stories or swords and sorcery without a supernatural element.
How to Contact: Send complete ms with SASE. Reports in 2 months on mss. Sample copy $1.50. Free guidelines with legal-sized SASE.
Payment: Pays ¼¢/word and free author's copy.
Terms: Acquires first North American serial rights plus rights to reprint entire issues.

EMPTY WINDOW REVIEW, New Wave Press, Box 442, Iowa City IA 52244. Editor: Michael Cummings. "The theme is to promote all types of new literature including poetry, fiction, drama, translations and reviews of all types. Our audience includes those with cultivated literary tastes, as well as the general public." Quarterly. Estab. July 1980.
Needs: Literary, contemporary, psychic/supernatural, science fiction, fantasy, horror, erotica, western, mystery, serialized and condensed novels and translations. Buys 2-3 mss/issue. Length: 100-4,000 words; prefers 1,000.
How to Contact: Send complete ms with SASE. Reports in 1 month on ms. Sample copy $1 with 9x12 SASE and 40¢ postage.
Payment: Pays with 3 free author's copies. 50¢ charge for extra copies.
Terms: Pays on publication (rights revert to author upon publication).
Tips: "Send a compact, well-typed piece of fiction. Write about only those topics you really understand. Don't follow too closely in another writer's footprints. Try to find your own voice and vision."

EPOCH MAGAZINE, 245 Goldwin Smith Hall, Cornell University, Ithaca NY 14853.

(607)256-3385. Editors: Jas McConkey, Walter Slatoff and C.S. Giscombe. "Top level fiction and poetry for people who are interested and capable of being entertained by good literature." Published 3 times a year. Estab. 1947. Circ. 1,000.

Needs: Literary, contemporary and ethnic. "So many categories seem insufficient to describe the kind of fiction we're looking for. We have not, for example, specified the category of western because I'm afraid of being inundated with a lot of the pale and mindless action/adventure/horse-opera stuff I see in the popular western magazines at the newsstands. We would be thrilled, though, to publish the work of a young Walter Van Tilberg Clark."Buys 4-5 mss/issue. Length: 10-30 typed, double-spaced pages.

How to Contact: Send complete ms with SASE. Reports in 2 weeks-2 months on mss. Sample copy $2 with 6x7 SASE and 90¢ postage.

Terms: Pays on publication for first North American serial rights.

Tips: "We *strongly suggest* that potential contributors either examine a copy of *Epoch* at the library or purchase one from us before submitting work."

EUREKA REVIEW, Orion Press, 90 Harrison Ave., New Canaan CT 06840. Editor: Roger Memmott. A journal of fiction, poetry and art; eclectic in subject matter for a literary audience. Annual. Estab. 1975. Circ. 600.

Needs: Literary, contemporary, science fiction and humor. No sentimental or pseudo-academic material. Buys 8-12 mss/issue. Length: 1,000-7,500 words.

How to Contact: Send complete ms with SASE. Reports in 2 months on mss. Sample copy $1.50.

Payment: Pays with 2 free author's copies. $1.50 charge for extras.

Terms: Pays on publication for first North American serial rights.

EVENT, Douglas College, Box 2503, New Westminster, British Columbia, Canada V3L 5B2. Editor: Leona Gom. Fiction Editor: Maurice Hodgson. Primarily a literary magazine, publishing poetry, fiction, reviews, plays and graphics for creative writers, artists, anyone interested in contemporary literature. Semiannual. Estab. 1970. Circ. 250.

Needs: Literary, contemporary, science fiction, fantasy, feminist, gay/lesbian, adventure and humor. No technically poor or unoriginal pieces. Buys 4-10 mss/issue. Length: 4,000 words.

How to Contact: Send complete ms with SASE. Reports in 1 month on mss. Sample copy $2.50.

Payment: Pays $20 minimum plus free subscription and 2 author's copies.

Terms: Pays on publication for first North American serial rights.

Tips: "*Read* our magazine first; and read a lot of contemporary literature."

EXIT, A Journal of the Arts, Rochester Routes/Creative Arts Projects, 50 Inglewood Dr., Rochester NY 14619. (716)436-0178. Editor: Frank Judge. "Our magazine has no theme and no particular bias but *quality*; there are some restrictions on length and content, as detailed below. We assume our readership is the 'lit mag' audience; we've had nothing to disprove this assumption so far." Published 3 times/year. Estab. 1976. Circ. 1,000.

Needs: Literary, contemporary, science fiction, fantasy, erotica, mystery and translations. "Science fiction, fantasy, erotica and mystery submissions should have a 'literary' slant giving a broader appeal than that of the respective forms; query preferred for these categories." No religious/inspirational, psychic/supernatural, men's, women's, feminist, gay/lesbian, confession, gothic, romance, western, adventure, humor, juvenile, young adult, ethnic and serialized or condensed novels. Buys 1-2 mss/issue. Length: 2,000 words maximum.

How to Contact: Send query or complete ms with SASE. Reports in 3 weeks on queries, 1 month on mss. Sample copy $2.50.

Payment: 2 free author's copies. $1 charge for extras.

Terms: Pays on publication for second serial and first North American serial rights.

FELLOWSHIP IN PRAYER, Fellowship in Prayer, Inc., 20 Nassau St., Suite 250 E., Princeton NJ 08540. (609)924-0880. Editor: Paul Griffith. Magazine with prayer and meditation theme. Monthly. Estab. 1949. Circ. 4,000.
Needs: Religious/inspirational. Buys 1-2 mss/issue. Length: 1,500 words.
How to Contact: Send complete ms with SASE. Reports in 2-3 weeks on mss. Free sample copy.
Payment: Pays .05¢/word and up for quality work. 6 free author's copies.
Terms: Pays on publication for first rights.

FEMINIST STUDIES, Feminist Studies, Inc., c/o Women's Studies Program, University of Maryland, College Park MD 20742. (301)454-2363. Editor: Claire G. Moses. Fiction Editor: Rachel Blau Duplessis. Editorial Assistant: D. Johnson-Clagett. Journal of feminist issues. A forum for analysis, debate and exchange. Audience consists of Women's Studies faculty, students, anyone interested in feminist issues and research. Published 3 times/year. Estab. 1972. Circ. 5,000.
Needs: Women's, feminist, gay/lesbian and Thirld World women's writing.
How to Contact: Send complete ms with SASE. Reports in 1 month on mss. Free guidelines.

FICTION INTERNATIONAL, St. Lawrence University, Canton NY 13617. (315)379-5961. Editor: Joe David Bellamy. Assistant Literary Editor: Julia Fitzgerald. "For readers interested in the best writing by talented writers working in new or old forms in especially fruitful new ways; readers are interested in contemporary literary developments and possiblities. Previous contributors include Russell Banks, T. Coraghessan Boyle, Rosellen Brown, Jerry Bumpus, David Madden, Joyce Carol Oates, Ronald Sukenick, Gordon Weaver and Robley Wilson, Jr." Annual. Estab. 1973. Circ. 2,500.
Needs: Literary and contemporary. Buys 12-16 mss/issue. No length limitations but rarely uses short shorts or manuscripts over 30 pages. Portions of novels acceptable if self-contained enough for independent publication. Unsolicited mss will be considered only from Sept. through Dec. of each year.
How to Contact: Send complete ms with SASE. Reports in 1-3 months on mss. Sample copy $5.
Payment: Varies.
Terms: Pays on publication for first and first North American serial rights.
Tips: "Study the magazine. Highly selective. Not an easy market for unsophisticated writers. Annual St. Lawrence Award for Fiction, a $1,000.00 prize given for an outstanding first collection of short fiction published in North America. Sponsors the annual *Fiction International*/St. Lawrence University Writers' Conference, held at the university's conference center at Saranac Lake in the Adirondacks and featuring writers such as Margaret Atwood, Russell Banks, E.L. Doctorow, Gail Godwin, Daniel Halpern, Joyce Carol Oates, Robie Macauley, Annie Dillard and James Tate."

THE FIDDLEHEAD, University of New Brunswick, PO Box 4400, Fredericton, NB E3B 5A3. (506)454-3591. Editor: Roger Ploude. Fiction Editor: Ted Colson. Literary magazine with poetry, short stories, book reviews and sketches. Quarterly. Estab. March 1980. Circ. 1,100.
Needs: Literary. Buys 4-5 mss/issue, 20-25 mss/year.
How to Contact: Send complete ms with IRC and SASE. Reports in 1-2 months on mss. Sample copy $2.50.
Payment: Pays $5/printed page-$50. Free author's copy. $2.50 charge for extras.
Terms: Pays on publication for first North American serial rights.

FIFTH SUN, Quincunx Press, 1134-B Chelsea Ave., Santa Monica CA 90403. (213)828-2918. Editor: Max Benavidez. "Revelations into the cultural crossroads of the North American continent. Stories and excerpts which confront hypocrisy and intolerance in interpersonal, intergroup and international relationships. Also interested in fiction which deals with identity crisis. Audience is mostly artists, writers, academics with a sprinkling of general readership. It is read by those who desire a perspective often lacking in most outlets." Annual. Estab. 1978. Circ. 450-500.

Needs: Literary, contemporary, science fiction, fantasy, horror, men's, women's, feminist, gay/lesbian, erotica, humor, condensed novels and experimental. "We will also consider any worthwhile fiction regardless of category. No male-oriented sex fantasy or pornography lacking any social worth." Accepts 4-5 mss/issue. Length: 750-3,000 words.

How to Contact: Query with clips of published work with SASE. Reports in 1 month on queries, 2 months on mss. Sample copy $2 with 8½x11 SASE and $1 postage.

Payment: 5 free author's copies. $1 charge per extra copy.

Terms: Pays on publication for all rights (sometimes), first rights and one-time rights.

FIGHTING WOMAN NEWS, Fighting Woman News, Box 1459, Grand Central Station, New York NY 10163. Editor: Valerie Eads. Fiction Editor: Muskat Buckby. "Women's martial arts, self-defense, combative sports. Articles, reviews, etc., related to these subjects. Well-educated adult women who are actually involved with martial arts read us because we're there and we're good." Quarterly. Estab. 1975. Circ. 5,600.

Needs: Science fiction, fantasy, feminist, adventure and translations. "No material that shows women as victims, incompetents, stereotypes or 'fight scenes' written by people who don't know anything about fighting skills. " Length: 2,500 words.

How to Contact: Query with clips of published work with SASE. Reports as soon as possible on queries and mss. Sample copy $2. Free guidelines with legal-sized SASE.

Payment: Pays in 5 free author's copies. Cover price plus postage charged for extras.

Terms: Pays on publication for one-time rights.

Tips: "Study the fiction of C.J. Cherryh, James Tiptree, Jr., Ursula Le Guin, André Norton, F.M. Busby, Chelsea Quinn Yarbro, etc. Read the journals *Windhaven* and *Janus*. Read Homer, Virgil, Tolkien, etc. See Samurai movies, Chinese swordswoman movies, old swashbuckler movies. Study feminist journals and newspapers. If you don't practice any martial art, get started—fencing at the 'Y' or an acting school will do just fine. If, after all that, you still want to write for a feminist martial arts magazine that pays in copies . . . welcome. It never hurts to read the magazine you want to write for."

FIRELANDS REVIEW, Cambric Press, Firelands Campus/BGSU, Huron OH 44839. Editor: Joel Rudinger. Annual. Estab. 1972. Circ. 1,000.

Needs: Good quality fiction of any type. Buys 10 mss/issue. Length: 1,000-3,000 words.

How to Contact: Send complete ms with SASE. Reports in 1 month on mss. Sample copy $2.50.

Payment: 2 free author's copies. $2 charge for extras.

Terms: Pays on publication for first North American serial rights. Copyright reverts to author upon publication.

Tips: No previously published work. Simultaneous submissions acceptable, if indicated.

FLOATING ISLAND, Floating Island Publications, Box 516, Point Reyes Station CA 94956. Editor: Michael Sykes. Anthology with poetry, prose, photography and graphic arts. Short fiction, journals, essays and explorations. For artists and writers, libraries, small press bookstores, poetry centers, colleges and institutions. The emphasis is literary, artistic and non-commercial. Published 2-3 times/year. Circ. 2,000.

Needs: Literary, contemporary, psychic/supernatural, science fiction and fantasy. Buys 4-5 mss/issue. Length: short.

How to Contact: Query with SASE. Reports in 2 weeks on queries, 2 months on mss. Sample copy $6.95 with $1.30 postage.

Payment: 2 free author's copies. $5 charge for extras.

Terms: Acquires simultaneous rights.

FLORIDA ARTS GAZETTE, INC., Box 397, Fort Lauderdale FL 33302. (305)463-6891. Editor: Kirt M. Dressler. Fiction Editor: Ginger Curry. "We are a news-magazine just beginning to consider short fiction."
Needs: Contemporary, mystery, historical, ethnic (Cuban, Haitian and black), science fiction, fantasy, humor/satire and art-related. No pornographic material.
How to Contact: Query with SASE. Simultaneous and photocopied mss (good quality) are OK. Reports in 1 month on queries and mss.
Payment: 5 free author's copies.
Tips: "The *Florida Arts Gazette* sponsors an annual short story contest. Send SASE for rules. We definitely plan to pay for fiction pieces in future. We are particularly interested in short fiction (around 2,000 words) about the arts and or by visual artists, dancers, poets, writers, actors, musicians, etc., who can write and especially by resident writers of Florida."

FOCUS: A JOURNAL FOR LESBIANS, Daughters of Bilitis Boston, O.C.B.C., 1151 Massachusetts Ave., Cambridge MA 02138. Editor: Paula Bennett. Magazine with literature and art relevant to and for lesbians. Bimonthly. Estab. 1970. Circ. 300.
Needs: Lesbian. "All categories are 'acceptable' to us as long as they are oriented toward a lesbian audience. No pornography, anything by, for or about men." Buys 3-4 mss/issue, 24 mss/year. Length: 2,000-4,000 words.
How to Contact: Send complete ms with SASE. Reports in 2 months on mss. Sample copy with SASE and 30¢ postage.
Payment: Free author's copy. $1.35 charge for extras.
Terms: Pays on publication for first rights.
Tips: "Try us. Be neat and professional. Proofread. Type double-spaced and have something to say. We have an annual prose contest each summer with a $35 award."

FORESIGHT, Foresight, 29 Beaufort Ave., Hodge Hill, Birmingham, England B34 6AD. (021)783-0587. Editor: John Barklam. Fiction Editor: Judy Barklam. Magazine with "new age material, world peace, psychic phenomena, research, occultism, spirtualism, mysticism, philosophy, etc. For psychic enthusiasts, people with an open mind who take pleasure in their search for truth." Published every 2 months. Estab. August 1970. Circ. 800.
Needs: Psychic/supernatural. Length: 300-1,500 words.
How to Contact: Query with clips of published work with SASE. Reports in 2 weeks on queries, 1 month on mss. Sample copy $1.
Payment: Free author's copy. 75¢ charge for extras.
Tips: "Send original, exciting material with a good strong, topical theme, relating to the present times."

FORGE, Forge Press, Inc., 47 Murray St., New York NY 10007. Editor: Christopher Parker. "Current poetry, fiction and thought for literary, academic, students, writers and general public." Quarterly. Estab. 1980. Circ. 1,000.
Needs: No pornography. Buys 2 mss/issue, 8 mss/year.
How to Contact: Query with clips of published work with SASE. Reports in 1 month on queries, 2 months on mss. Sample copy $3 with 6x9 SASE and 58¢ postage. Free guidelines with legal-sized SASE.
Payment: Free author's copies.
Terms: Pays on publication for first rights.
Tips: "Be aware of the changes occuring in our culture."

FORMAT: ART & THE WORLD, Seven Oaks Press, 405 S. 7th St., St. Charles IL 60174. (312)584-0187. Editor: Ms. C.L. Morrison. "Magazine of art, survival information for contemporary artists, essays, interviews, poetry, articles and short fiction with useful information for artists." Monthly. Estab. September 1978. Circ. 1,000.
Needs: Survival-oriented; stories related to art, artists, economics or current events.

Length: 1,500 words maximum.
How to Contact: Send complete ms with SASE. Reports in 3 weeks on ms. Sample copy $1.
Payment: Pays $5-15. 6 free author's copies. 80¢ charge for extras.
Terms: Pays on publication for simultaneous rights.
Tips: "Write honestly about something you know with insight and understanding."

FORMS: The Review of Anthropos Theophoros, AT Press, Box 3379, San Francisco CA 94119. Editor: Emily McCormick. Publication promoting excellence in all forms of art; short stories, poems, book reviews, essays, political-theological and philosophical opinion for a literate audience. Quarterly. Estab. 1976. Circ. 500.
Needs: Literary, contemporary, religious, humor and translations. No science fiction. Buys 5-7 mss/issue. Length: 10,000 words maximum.
How to Contact: Send complete ms with SASE. Reports in 2-4 months on mss. Sample copy $1.
Payment: Offers 2 free author's copies (more by arrangement).
Terms: Acquires one-time rights.

FOUR QUARTERS, LaSalle College, 20th and Olney Ave., Philadelphia PA 19141. (215)951-1171. Editor: John C. Kleis. Magazine of poetry, fiction, nonfiction for mainly academic audience. Quarterly. Estab. November 1951. Circ. 750.
Needs: Literary and contemporary. Buys 5 mss/issue, 20 mss/year. Length: 2,000-5,000 words.
How to Contact: Send complete ms with SASE. Reports in 4-6 weeks on mss. Sample copy $1 and free guidelines.
Payment: Pays $25 and 3 free author's copies. $1 charge for extras.
Terms: Pays on publication for all rights.
Tips: "Technical mastery gets our attention and respect immediately. We admire writers who use the language with precision, economy, and imagination. But fine writing for its own sake is unsatisfying unless it can lead the reader to some insight into the complexity of the human condition without falling into heavy-handed didacticism."

THE FRONT MAGAZINE, Front Press, Box 1355, Kingston, Ontario, Canada K7L 5C6. Editor: Jim Smith. Magazine of experimental, adventurous explorations into the nature of fiction for anyone who might enjoy it. Published sporadically. Estab. 1975. Circ. 500.
Needs: Literary, contemporary, science fiction, fantasy, horror, feminist, gay/lesbian, erotica, humor, serialized novels, translations and absurdist. No formula fiction or "realistic" fiction. Buys 2-3 mss/issue, 10 mss/year.
How to Contact: Send complete ms with SASE. Reports in 2 weeks on mss. Sample copy $3 with 9x12 SASE and 3rd class IRC.
Payment: Pays in 5 free author's copies.
Terms: Pays on publication for first rights.
Tips: "Concentrate on your writing and don't worry about breaking into a magazine. Always include a SASE or IRC (International Reply Coupons). No handwritten mss."

GALAXY, Galaxy Magazine, Inc., 339 Newbury St., Boston MA 02115. Editor: Floyd Kemske. Science fiction magazine publishing nonfiction science, science fiction and science fiction commentary for college age readers. They respond to the "adventure of the future." Bimonthly. Estab. October 1950. Circ. 50,000.
Needs: Science fiction. No fantasy, psychic/supernatural or juvenile. Buys 30-35 mss/year. Length: 1,000-10,000 words.
How to Contact: Send complete ms with SASE. Reports in 3 weeks. Sample copy $1.50 and free guidelines.
Payment: Pays $100-250 and 3 free author's copies.
Terms: Pays on publication for first world serial rights plus a few nonexclusive options.

Tips: "Get to know science fiction and observe the classical elements of storytelling craft. Science fiction is scientifically credible (although it need not be especially technical) and has very little to do with phenomenology, telepathy, UFOs, Bermuda Triangle anecdotes, and stories of the paranormal have little appeal to science fiction readers. It is difficult to find effective science fiction humor, although we always need it."

GARGOYLE MAGAZINE, Paycock Press. Box 57206, Washington DC 20037. (202)333-1544. Editor: Richard Peabody. Estab. 1976. Published 3 times/year.
Needs: Contemporary, literary, experimental, humor/satire and translations. "We like fiction in the 2-10 typed page range, with an emphasis on the short short story. We generally print 3-6 stories an issue."
How to Contact: Submit complete ms with SASE. Photocopied submissions OK. Reports in 1-2 months on mss.
Payment: Free author's copy.
Tips: "Small magazines are deluged with mss these days. Writers should keep in mind that rejection doesn't mean a story is bad, only that the magazine editor doesn't want to, or can't, use it. You have to learn to endure."

GAY COMMUNITY NEWS, National Gay News, Inc., 22 Bromfield St., Boston MA 02108. (617)426-4469. Editor: Richard Burns. Managing Editor: Amy Hoffman. "*Gay Community News* is the national newsweekly dedicated to providing thought-provoking coverage of the lesbian and gay male experience in America. The *National Gay Task Force* has called *Gay Community News* 'the primary news source for anyone concerned with what is being done to and by lesbians and gay men everywhere in this country.'" Weekly. Estab. June 1973. Circ. 25,000.
Needs: Fantasy, feminist, gay/lesbian and humor. "Most of the fiction we publish is satire or humor. No poetry." Buys 1 ms/issue. Length: 5-10 pages.
How to Contact: Either query first or send complete ms. Reports in 2 weeks on queries, 3 weeks on ms. Free sample copy and guidelines.
Payment: 10 free author's copies.
Terms: Pays on publication for first rights.
Tips: "Read our magazine first to get an idea of what it is we do. Triple space mss, submit clean copy (typed) along with a cover letter, and perhaps some background on yourself."

GAY SUNSHINE JOURNAL, Gay Sunshine Press, Box 40397, San Francisco CA 94140. (415)824-3184. Editor: Winston Leyland. "An intellectual gay culture/literary journal, published quarterly. We publish short fiction, poetry, interviews, essays and articles directed at a highly literate readership nationwide, mainly gay." Quarterly. Estab. 1970. Circ. 5,000.
Needs: Literary, contemporary, men's, gay, erotica, ethnic (Latin American) and translations. Fiction must have a bearing on a gay theme/consciousness. Length: Maximum of 20 typed double-spaced pages.
How to Contact: Query with clips of published work. Reports in 2 weeks on queries, 1 month on mss. Sample copy $2.50.
Payment: Free author's copies (amount of copies negotiable) plus nominal cash payment or books.
Terms: Pays on publication for first North American serial rights.

THE GAYOSO STREET REVIEW, Box 11736, Memphis TN 38111. Editors: Gloria Baxter, Jack Baxter and Charlotte Schultz. Journal of poetry, fiction, plays, condensed novels and interviews for a regional audience. Published 3 times/year. Estab. April 1980. Circ. 500.
Needs: Literary and contemporary. Manuscripts will be accepted from around the country, but primary focus will be on the works of local and regional writers. Length: 3,000-7,500 words.

How to Contact: Send complete ms with SASE. Reports in 2 months on mss. Sample copy $2.

Payment: Pays in 2 free author's copies. $2 charge for extras.

Terms: Acquires first rights and first North American serial rights..

GLOBAL TAPESTRY JOURNAL, BB Books, 1 Spring Bank, Longsight Rd, Salesbury, Blackburn, Lancs, England BB1 9EU. 0254-49218. Editor: Dave Cunliffe. "Post-underground with avant-garde, experimental, alternative, counterculture, psychedelic, mystical, anarchist, etc., fiction used for a bohemian and counter culture. Magazine has readership ranging from academics to New Wave punks. Only present United Kingdom literary magazine of its kind." Quarterly. Circ. 1,000.

Needs: Literary, contemporary, science fiction, fantasy, erotica, confession, translations and novel extracts. "The mystical material we do use is largely Buddhist, Taoist, Tantric, occult. We do use creative prose which blurs the distinction between fiction and reportage." No romance, western, mystery and detective. Uses 2 mss/issue. Length: 500-2,000 words.

How to Contact: Send complete ms with SASE, IRC. Reports as soon as possible. Sample copy $1.20.

Payment: Free author's copy. Half the cover price for extras charge.

Terms: Pays on publication for one-time rights.

Tips: "This specialized publication needs to be studied. We are interested in honest, uncontrived writing. Don't copy established authors. We don't require reflected Kerouac, Burroughs, Miller. Prefer the genuine article. This is a little magazine (edited, typeset, printed, distributed, etc., by one person) published by a small press with no outside funding. Therefore, its quarterly frequency often breaks down, due to available time and finance being limited."

GOETHE'S NOTES, Goethe's Press, 2319 E. Park Place, Milwaukee WI 53211. (414)332-6286. Editor: Jesse Glass Jr. "We try to present the best small press writing that we can find for readers who are interested in the ultra-new in poetry, graphics, and prose." Quarterly. Estab. 1974. Circ. 100-500.

Needs: Literary. No short/experimental. Buys 3-4 mss/issue.

How to Contact: Send complete ms with SASE. Reports in 1 month on mss. Sample copy $2.

Payment: 3 free author's copies. Regular price charged for extras.

Terms: Pays on publication for one-time rights (rights revert to author on publication).

Tips: "Read the magazine before submitting. We are a small press and exist on a shoestring budget. We cannot offer slick production for those who publish in *Goethe's Notes*, but we do guarantee talented company, and an intelligent audience."

GOLDEN ISIS, Wilva, PO Box 3717, Granada Hills CA 91344. Editor: Gerri Nova. Theme: mystical, cosmic, surrealistic and occult. Short fiction and poetry. For persons who enjoy mystical and cosmic subculture literature. They read the publication because they can find fiction and poetry that express unique modes, and ideas not found in most publications." Quarterly. Estab. 1980. Circ. 350.

Needs: psychic/supernatural, science fiction, fantasy, horror, mystery and humor. "Horror and mystery are acceptable so long as the descriptions of violence and gore are not overdone. We also try to avoid material that is vulgar or in bad taste. We do not want anything pornographic or religious." Buys 2 mss/issue. Length: 300-500 words.

How to Contact: Send complete ms with SASE. Reports in 1 month on both queries and mss. Sample copy $1.95 and free guidelines.

Terms: Acquires first North American serial rights.

Tips: "We would like to see a story with a good hook, good characterization, and impact ending. Do not send anything trite and overused. Two important things to avoid in fiction writing are a confused ambiance and predictable ending."

GOTHIC, Gothic Press, 4998 Perkins Rd., Baton Rouge LA 70808. (504)766-2906. Editor: Gary W. Crawford. "Macabre fiction in the tradition of Poe, Lefanu, etc. A literate and scholarly audience with a serious interest in gothic fiction for critics and collectors of this fiction." Semiannual. Estab. June 1979. Circ. 1,000.
Needs: Psychic/supernatural, fantasy, horror, gothic and translations. No science fiction. Buys 6 mss/year. Length: 3,000-20,000 words.
How to Contact: Send complete ms with SASE. Reports in 2 months on mss. Sample copy $3.25 with free guidelines.
Payment: Pays 1¢/word and higher to authors with agents. Free author's copy. $1.95 charge for extras.
Terms: Pays on publication for first North American serial rights.
Tips: "*Gothic* invites fiction mss that derive directly from or are influenced by the tradition of the gothic novel. We interpret Gothicism very broadly as a spirit or impulse incarnating supernatural horror, the macabre, the numinous, dark fantasy, mental aberration and psychic disintegration, dread of the unknown and the unknowable. Prospective contributors should be critically aware of Gothicism in all its variations, from the gothic novels of Radcliffe, Maturin, and Lewis, through the English and American authors of Dark Romanticism and ghost tales, such as Hawthorne, Poe, Lefanu, Henry James, and M.R. James, to the twentieth-century masters of cosmic paranoia and demon gods, such as Machen, Blackwood, Lovecraft, or such modern Gothicists of mental aberration and disintegration as Faulkner, Carson McCullers, Flannery O'Connor, and Robert Bloch. Contributors should regard Gothicism as an imaginative flame that is still penetrating the darker side of human existence. We are particularly open to experimental variations of gothic themes."

THE GRAMERCY REVIEW, The Gramercy Review, Box 15362, Los Angeles CA 90015. Editors: Dennis Bartel and Mark Heyman. Contemporary poetry and fiction for college educated (those interested in writing and mainline development in the arts). Quarterly. Estab. July 1977. Circ. 1,100.
Needs: Literary, contemporary, religious/inspirational, science fiction, humor and translations. No exploitive or workshop fiction. Buys 1-2 mss/issue, 6-8 mss/year. Length: 10,000 words maximum.
How to Contact: Send complete ms with SASE. Reports in 2 months on mss. Sample copy $2 with 9x6 SASE and 80¢ postage.
Payment: Pays $10-50.
Terms: Pays on publication for first rights.

GREAT RIVER REVIEW, Box 14805, Minneapolis MN 55414. (612)378-9076. Editors: Jean Ervin and Chet Corey. Literary publication of fiction, poetry, art and book reviews. Semiannual. Estab. 1977.
Needs: Contemporary and experimental. No mass-circulation style fiction. Buys 6-7 mss/issue. Length: 2,000-10,000 words.
How to Contact: Send complete ms with SASE. Sample copy $3.
Payment: Pays $20-$50.
Terms: Pays on publication. Photocopied submissions OK.
Tips: "Priority to midwestern writers and mss with strong sense of the Midwest." Award for best fiction each issue.

GREEN'S MAGAZINE, Green's Educational Publications, Box 313, Postal Substation 40, University of Regina, Regina, Saskatchewan, Canada S4S 0A2. Editor: David Green. "A family magazine with a carefully balanced array of short fiction and poetry, intended to be exemplary in a variety of high-standard styles for a general audience." Quarterly. Estab. 1972. Circ. 600.
Needs: Literary. Buys 12 mss/issue. Length: 1,000-2,500 words.
How to Contact: Send complete ms with SASE or IRC. Reports in 2 months on mss.

Sample copy $2 and free guidelines with legal-sized SASE.
Payment: Pays $10-25. 2 free author's copies. $2 charge for extras.
Terms: Pays on publication for first North American serial rights.
Tips: "Study the magazine. We will not read photostats or other copies."

GREENSBORO REVIEW, University of North Carolina, Dept. of English, Greensboro NC 27412. (919)379-5459. Editor: Tom Kirby-Smith. Fiction Editor: Pamela Postma. Literary magazine featuring fiction and poetry for readers interested in contemporary literature. Semiannual. Circ. 500.
Needs: Contemporary and experimental. Buys 3-4 mss/issue, 8 mss/year. Length: 6,000 words maximum.
How to Contact: Query and send complete ms with SASE.
Payment: Pays in contributor's copies.
Terms: Acquires first North American serial rights. Byline given. Photocopied submissions OK. Acceptances in September and January only.

THE GUERNICA REVIEW, Guernica Editions, Box 633, Station N.D.G., Montreal, Quebec, Canada H4A 3R1. Editor: Antonio D'Alfonso. Fiction Editor: Umberto Claudio. A new publication for prose, criticism and interviews that deals with current issues on literature, film, politics for poets and artists and interested non-elitist people. Quarterly. Circ. 500-1,000.
Needs: No "concrete, experimental for experimental sake" type material. Length: 500-2,000 words.
How to Contact: Query first with SASE. Reports in 2 weeks on queries, 1 month on mss. Free sample copy with SASE.
Payment: 2 free author's copies.
Terms: Acquires one-time rights.
Tips: "Perseverance, intelligent hard work pay off. Try to base yourself on tradition, instead of contemporary art. Let modernism come from the past. Avoid arrogance, anything that smells too stiff or is not open-minded enough."

GUSTO MAGAZINE/Press, Box 1009, 2960 Philip Ave., Bronx NY 10465. (212)931-8964. Editor: M. Karl Kulikowski. "A literary magazine, primarily of poetry, but we publish about 10 short stories a year for creative writers." Quarterly. Estab. August 1978. Circ. 500.
Needs: Literary, contemporary and humor. "Any good fiction has a chance with us. We are an open door. Our only bias is against adolescent porn." Buys 10 mss/year. Length: 500-5,000 words.
How to Contact: Send complete ms and only one short story at a time with SASE. Reports in 2 weeks on mss.
Payment: "We do not pay."
Terms: Acquires one-time rights.
Tips: "At *Gusto* we are eclectic; we are always looking for good writers with good material. We have a Discovery Series, wherein we publish books of short stories for writers on a royalty basis. We published one such book in 1979 and another in fall 1980. We will start a Regional Series with the next book, regional, in that the writer of the book has a book of short stories (or a book of poetry) written on one region (or one city) in the country."

HAPPINESS HOLDING TANK, Stone Press, 1790 Grand River, Okemos MI 48864. Editor: Albert Drake. Primarily a magazine of poetry, articles, reviews, and literary information for poets, students, teachers, other editors and lay people. "I think a good many people read it for the literary information, much of which isn't available elsewhere." Published irregularly. Estab. Oct. 1970. Circ. 300-500.
Needs: Literary. "We publish a limited amount of fiction: very short stories, parables, prose poems, fragments, episodes. Not a good market for traditional fiction." Accepts 4-5 mss/

year.

How to Contact: Query. SASE for query, ms. Reports in 1 week on queries, 3 weeks on mss (except during summer). Sample copy $1 plus 68¢ postage.

Payment: 2 free author's copies.

Terms: Acquires one-time rights with automatic return of all rights to author.

Tips: "Be more careful about what you send out. Rewrite. Tighten. Compress. Read it aloud."

HARVARD ADVOCATE, Harvard Advocate Trustees, Inc., 21 South St., Cambridge MA 02138. (617)495-7820. Editor: Charles H.C. Gerard. Fiction Editor: Larry Shapiro. "We publish only work of Harvard affiliates—i.e., alumni, faculty, undergraduates, and staff. We generally focus on fiction, poetry, photographs, drawings, and criticism. Readership is primarily students and readers who live in and around Boston and New York. Limited national circulation." Quarterly. Estab. 1866. Circ. 15,000-20,000.

Needs: Literary, feminist, gay/lesbian, translations, art criticism, fiction fragments. Length: 7,000 words maximum.

How to Contact: Send complete ms with SASE. Reports in 1 month on mss. Free sample copy.

Payment: 10 free author's copies. $2 charge for extras.

Tips: Harvard affiliation required. "There are no specific sorts of fiction we favor except as the staff's taste might dictate year by year."

HEIRS MAGAZINE, Heirs, Inc., 2868 Mission St., San Francisco CA 94110. (415)824-8604. Editor: Alfred Durand Garcia, Jill Immerman. Estab. 1968. Circ. 6,000.

Needs: Literary, experimental, contemporary, multi-cultural ethnic, translations. Buys 6 mss/issue. Length: 3,000 maximum.

How to Contact: Send complete ms with SASE. Reports in 6-8 weeks on mss. Sample copy $4.

Payment: Token payment plus copies. 40% discount on extra copies.

Terms: Pays on publication for all rights.

HERESIES: A Feminist Publication on Art/Politics, Heresies, Box 766, Canal St. Station, New York NY 10013. "We are a feminist collective. Each issue is put together by a separate group of women which forms the editorial collective." Nationwide readership gathered from alternative bookshops and women's spaces. Quarterly. Estab. January 1977. Circ. 8,000.

Needs: Women's, feminist and lesbian.

How to Contact: Query. Reports in 1 month on queries. Free guidelines.

Payment: Small payment post publication and free author's copies.

Tips: "Check back issues for special themes and content. Since each issue has its own guidelines, be specific. We only accept mss directed to special issues which are noted in the back of each publication."

HIGH PERFORMANCE, Astro Artz, 240 S. Broadway, 5th floor, Los Angeles CA 90012. (213)687-7362. Editor: Linda Frye Burnham. "A documentary magazine about performance art (live works by visual artists or happenings) including fiction and poetry by visual artists. Avant-garde art audience and general public interested in esoteric activity." Quarterly. Estab. Feb. 1978. Circ. 5,000.

Needs: "We are only interested in fiction by those who work primarily in visual art. This is not to say that the story/poem must be visual or illustrated. No very long works." Buys 1 ms/issue, 4 mss/year. Length: 1,000-20,000.

How to Contact: Send complete ms and resumé. SASE for ms. Reports in 3 months on mss. Sample copy $3.50.

Payment: $25-$50. 2 free author's copies. $2 charge for extras.

Terms: Pays on publication for one-time rights.
Tips: "Get MFA in art. Type. Double-space. Learn to spell. It is truly essential for anyone interested in submitting work to get a look at our publication and have an understanding of contemporary art, especially performance art."

HOB-NOB, 715 Dorsea Rd., Lancaster PA 17601. Editor/Publisher: Mildred K. Henderson. "*Hob-Nob* is a small amateur publication currently with a literary emphasis in original prose and poetry. This publication is directed toward amateur writers and poets, but many of them would like to be professional. For some, appearance in *Hob-Nob* is simply an opportunity to be published somewhere, while others possibly see it as a springboard to bigger and better things." Annual. Estab. Fall 1969. Circ. 100-200.
Needs: Literary, contemporary, religious/inspirational, psychic/supernatural, science fiction, fantasy, romance, mystery, adventure, humor, young adult, very brief condensed novels, excerpts from novels, short stories in installments. "No erotica, works with excessive swearing or blatantly sexual words, gross violence, etc." Accepts 4-10 mss/issue. Length: 500-1,000 (longer if serialized).
How to Contact: Send complete ms with SASE. Reports in 2 weeks. Sample copy for 54¢ postage.
Payment: 1 free author's copy. $1 plus 54¢ postage for extras.
Terms: Acquires first rights.
Tips: "Read over your work before handing it in and see whether it makes sense. Get someone else to read it, if possible. Number pages. Include name and address on at least the first page, and name on others. State 'original and unpublished.' " Has had contests for prose and poetry in past years. There may be an extra issue occasionally like the "Holiday Special" in 1980.

HOME PLANET NEWS, Box 415, Stuyvesant Station, New York NY. Co-editorial Directors: Donald Lev and Enid Dame. Fiction Editor: Robin Lamiere, 1408 Coney Island Ave., Brooklyn NY 11230. Quarterly. Estab. 1978.
Needs: Literary, contemporary, experimental, feminist, gay/lesbian, ethnic, science fiction, humor/satire, translations. No "dreams, journals or anything racist, sexist, 'age-ist', or anti-semitic. No plotless stories or those in which the author looks down on or 'hates' the characters." Length: "The shorter the better (1,200 words or less)."
How to Contact: Send complete ms. Reports in 6 weeks.
Payment: Pays in author's copies.
Tips: "Don't use footnotes. A short cover letter is better than an essay explaining the work submitted. Be objective about your work and ask 'What has happened?' , 'To whom?' , 'Has any change occurred? or any insight been granted, if not at least to the character, to the reader?' And don't tell—in the cover letter—what's wrong with the story."

HOO-DOO MAGAZINE, Energy Earth Communications, Box 1141, Galveston TX 77553. (713)762-8018. Also publishes *Synergy Magazine*. Editor: Ahmos Zu-Bolton. Fiction Editor: Harryette Mullen. Publishes "good fiction and poetry" with an open theme. Quarterly. Estab. 1974. Circ. 10,000.
Needs: Literary, science fiction. Accepts 7-10 mss/year.
How to Contact: Send complete ms with SASE.
Terms: Pays on publication for first rights.
Tips: "Send us something good, something new."

HOR-TASY, Ansuda Publications, Box 123, Harris IA 51345. Editor/Publisher: Daniel R. Betz. "*Hor-Tasy* is bringing back actual *horror* to horror lovers tired of seeing so much science fiction and SF passed off as horror. We're also very much interested in true, poetic pure fantasy. Directed toward horror fans sick of SF."
Needs: Fantasy and horror. "Pure fantasy: Examples are trolls, fairies, mythology. The

horror we're looking for comes from the human mind—the ultimate form of horror. It must sound real—so real that in fact it could very possibly happen at any time and place. We must be able to feel the diseased mind behind the personality. No science fiction in any way, shape, or form. We don't want stories in which the main character spends half his time talking to a shrink. We don't want stories that start out with: 'You're crazy,' said so and so." Plans to accept 6 mss/issue.

How to Contact: Query or send complete ms with SASE. Reports in 1 day for queries. "If not interested (in ms), we return immediately. If interested, we may keep it as long as 6 months." Query for sample copy. Guidelines for legal-sized SASE.

Payment: 2 free author's copies. Charge for extras: Cover price less regular discount rates.

Terms: Acquires first North American serial rights.

Tips: "*Hor-Tasy* is a unique publication. Get a copy before submitting. Only unpublished work will be considered."

THE HOT SPRINGS GAZETTE, The Doodly-Squat Press, Box 40124, Albuquerque NM 87196. (505)243-4301. Editor: Eric Irving. "A small press magazine specializing in material about hot springs. Kind of a cross between *The Sierra Club Bulletin* and *High Times*." Published irregularly. Estab. 1977. Circ. 1,000.

Needs: "We will accept quality prose or poetry that concerns wilderness experience." Length: 50-2,000 words.

How to Contact: Send complete manuscript with SASE. Reports in 3 weeks. Sample copy $2.

Payment: Free lifetime subscription.

Terms: Acquires all rights.

Tips: "Find some hot springs. Send for a copy."

HUDSON REVIEW, 65 E. 55th St., New York NY 10022. Managing Editor: Richard B. Smith. Literary articles, translations and reviews. Quarterly.

Needs: Quality fiction; no designated categories. Length: 10,000 words maximum.

How to Contact: Send complete ms with SASE. Reports in 6-8 weeks.

Payment: Pays 2½¢/word.

Terms: Pays on publication.

THE HUNGRY YEARS, Box 7213, Newport Beach CA 92660. (714)548-3324. Editor/ Publisher: Les Brown. "*The Hungry Years* is entirely freelance and welcomes all material for consideration. No restriction for style or genre. Good taste recommended. All ages read this magazine. Basically, it's a forum for new creative talent for artists and writers." Quarterly. Estab. 1978. Circ. 500-1,000.

Needs: Literary, contemporary, psychic/supernatural, science fiction, fantasy, horror, serialized and condensed novels. "Nothing pornographic or religious." Accepts 1 ms/issue; 4 mss/year. Length: 2,500-10,000 words.

How to Contact: Send complete ms with SASE. Reports in 6 months. Sample copy $1. Free general guidelines.

Payment: 1 free author's copy. Additional copies on request.

Terms: Acquires one-time rights.

Tips: "Inquire first; maintain your own carbons; acquire an agent."

THE ICELANDIC CANADIAN, The Icelandic Canadian Club, 1-67C Gertrude Ave., Winnipeg, Manitoba, Canada R3M 2M9. Editor-in-Chief: Axel Vopnfjord. Editor: Paul A. Sigurdson. Literary promoting knowledge of Icelandic culture, activities and accomplishments of American and Canadian people of Icelandic lineage. For people interested in Iceland and Icelandic culture. Quarterly. Estab. 1944. Circ. 1,300.

Needs: Literary, contemporary, adventure, humor, ethnic (Icelandic) and translations. No

erotic or avant- garde. Buys 1 ms/issue, 4-6 mss/year. Length: 2,000-4,000 words.
How to Contact: Send complete ms with International Reply Coupons. Reports in 2 months on mss. Sample copy $2 with 7x10 SASE, IRC.
Payment: Free author's copy with $2 (Canadian) charge for extras.
Terms: Acquires one-time rights.
Tips: "Write an authentic story about Icelandic people. Stories must have family appeal and avoid too much crude language."

ILLUMINATIONS, Illuminations Press, 2110 9th St., Apt B, Berkeley CA 94710. (415)849-2102. Editor: Norman Moser. "Entirely eclectic in re: styles, characters, subjects, etc. for literate professionals (especially those in the arts), educated people and others." Published occasionally. Estab. 1965. Circ. 1,000.
Needs: Literary, contemporary, religious/inspirational, humor, nature. "Only current project that possibly includes fiction, and even this is still tentative, is an anthology (possibly with poetry) of material using nature images in a mystical way." No science fiction, romance or confessions. Accepts 2-3 mss/issue. Length: 5,000 words maximum.
How to Contact: Query OK. SASE for query, ms. Reports in 1 month on queries. Sample copy $2.50 with 9x12 SASE.
Payment: Free author's copies ("except for occasional prizes/awards").
Tips: "Use simple and lucid style. Not too self-conscious with easy, natural flow, sharp dialogue. Don't make ms too long and rambling. We don't have university or well-heeled private backers."

IMAGE LITERARY MAGAZINE, Kendrick Publishing House, 3322 Isabelle, Inkstar MI 48141. Editor: Sue Carolyn Smith. "A literary reflection of today's lifestyles. Prose and poetry. Directed toward those who enjoy reading relevant and entertaining material but haven't time for novels." Bimonthly. Estab. May 1980. Circ. 3,000.
Needs: Literary, contemporary, religious/inspirational, romance, mystery, adventure, humor, serialized novels. "No violence, explicit sex, or profanity." Buys 3-4 mss/issue. Length: 1,000-2,000 words.
How to Contact: Send complete ms or query with clips of published work. Reports in 2 weeks on queries, 2 months on mss. Sample copy $1.50 with legal-sized SASE.
Payment: $25-$75.
Terms: Pays on acceptance for first rights, second serial (reprint) rights or first North American serial rights.

IMAGE MAGAZINE, Cornerstone Press, Box 28048, St. Louis MO 63119. (314)752-3703. Editor: Anthony J. Summers. "*Image* uses only the best material it receives from all over the world. There is no definite theme, but we prefer material to be well-written with no sloppy attempts at creativity. It must be a bit different, off the wall. Directed toward college students, free thinkers, writers, poets, editors, teachers. They read it to be educated, amused, entertained, to cause them to think and see life in a different perspective." Published 3 times/year. Estab. 1970. Circ. 600.
Needs: "We are willing to take a chance with anybody, anything. No murder mysteries or anything sloppy." Buys variable amount of mss/issue.
How to Contact: Query. SASE for ms. Reports in 2 weeks on queries, 3 weeks on mss. Sample copy $1 with SASE plus 47¢ postage.
Payment: $10-$100 or 2 free author's copies. $1 charge for extras.
Terms: Pays on publication. Negotiates rights with author.
Tips: "Buy a sample copy and see what we use. I look for the well-written ms free from the errors of illiteracy."

IMPEGNO '80, Casella Postale, n. 30. Mazara Del Vallo, Sicily, Italy 91026. (0923)945492. Editor: Rolando Certa. Emphasizes "poetry, prose, essays, theater, narrative, book reviews, art criticsm, sociology for intellectuals, poets, students, etc. who want to know what is going on in cultural quarters in Sicily and the southern countries of Europe." Quarterly. Estab. 1971. Circ. 1,500.

Needs: Literary, contemporary, humor, translations, narrative, book reviews. "No pseudo-cultural literature efforts." Length: 500-1,500 words.

How to Contact: Send complete ms. Reports "as soon as possible." Free sample copy.

Payment: Up to 5 free author's copies.

Terms: "We leave publishing rights to the author."

Tips: "Study others, literature, and contemporary writers. Do not be in a hurry to see yourself in print. Before publication, reflect. We are interested in an international cultural exchange between ourselves and others in the world."

IMPULSE MAGAZINE, Impulse Publishing Co., Box 901, Station Q, Toronto, Ontario, Canada M4T 2P1. (416)368-7511. Editors: Eldon Garnet and Shelagh Alexander. "Theme is art and culture with an emphasis on technology of the future and its relation to the artist. We publish experimental/innovative fiction, interviews for an audience of 18 to 35 years old. They read *Impulse* to keep informed of the changes now happening in the art and science field." Quarterly. Estab. summer 1971. Circ. 10,000.

Needs: "Experimental, innovative writing. We are also a visual publication and would appreciate any accompanying photos, illustrations, etc. No plays." Accepts 4-5 mss/issue, 15-20 mss/year. Length: 250-2,000 words.

How to Contact: Send complete ms with SASE. Reports in 1 month on mss. Sample copy $2.

Terms: Acquires first rights.

Tips: "Keep trying. Avoid too lengthy a ms."

IN A NUTSHELL, Hibiscus Press, Box 22248. Sacramento CA 95822. Editor: Margaret Wensrich. "Mainstream publication of short stories, poetry, pen and ink drawings for people who like to read, who look below the surface, and who think." Quarterly. Estab. Winter 1975. Circ. 5,000.

Needs: Literary, contemporary, science fiction, men's, women's, gothic, romance, western, mystery, adventure, humor. "We judge each story on its own merit. Craftsmanship is essential. No articles, personal experiences, etc. or excerpts from novels." Buys 2-3 mss/issue, 8-12 mss/year. Length: 1,000-3,500 words.

How to Contact: Send complete ms with SASE. Reports in 1 month. "We may hold a ms longer if we want to read it another time before reaching a decision." Sample copy $2.50. Free guidelines for legal-sized SASE.

Payment: $10-$25 and 2 free author's copies.

Terms: Pays on publication for first rights.

Tips: "Send clean copy and enclose a SASE of a size that fits your ms. Cover letter not necessary for us. Ms stands or falls on its own merit. Send a legal-sized SASE for a free copy of 'Improve Your Writing By Reading.'"

INDIANA WRITES, Indiana Writes, 110 Morgan Hall, Bloomington IN 47401. (812)337-3439. Editor: Anneke Campbell. Publishes poetry, prose. Quarterly. Estab. 1976.

Needs: Literary. Accepts 2-3 mss/issue.

How to Contact: Query or send complete ms with SASE. Reports in 2 months. Sample copy $2. Free guidelines.

Payment: 2 free author's copies. $2.50 charge for extras.

Terms: Acquires first rights.

INKY TRAILS PUBLICATIONS, Box 345, Middleton, ID 83644. Editor/Publisher: Pearl Kirk. Magazine consisting of poetry, art, fillers, quotes, fiction and TV or radio scripts. Published 3 times/year. Estab. 1967. Circ. 300.

Needs: Literary, contemporary, religious/inspirational, psychic/supernatural, fantasy, romance, western, mystery, adventure, humor, juvenile, young adult. "Would like to have some art with mss for illustrations and novels to run in several issues. No filth or four letter words." Length: 3,500 words maximum.
How to Contact: Send complete ms with SASE. Reports in 2 months. Sample copy $3 with 10x13 SASE plus 70¢ postage. Free guidelines for legal-sized SASE.
Payment: 2 free author's copies. Occasional cash ($15/first, $10/second place) awards.
Terms: "All rights stay with the writers as long as *Inky Trails* is given credit for first printing."
Tips: "Have a title, start with characters and conflict. Let the characters come alive with emotion, and write about something familiar. Solve the problem or conflict. Surprise endings are good. I use all types of good clean material. Awards given at end of year but recipient must be a subscriber."

INLET, Virginia Wesleyan College, Norfolk VA 23502. Editor: Joseph Harkey. "A small literary magazine publishing poetry and short fiction for people of all ages." Annual. Estab. 1970. Circ. 700.
Needs: Literary, contemporary, science fiction, fantasy, humor. "Our main interest is well-written fiction." Accepts 2-5 mss/issue. Length: 500-1,500 words but "will consider up to 3,000."
How to Contact: "Mss are read September through March only." Send complete ms with SASE. Reports in 2 months. Sample copy 75¢. Addressed labels welcomed.
Payment: 2 free author's copies. Negotiates charge for extras.
Tips: "Write carefully and present a neatly typed ms with SASE. Send an example of your best work; short shorts preferred."

IO, North Atlantic Books, 635 Amador St., Richmond CA 94805. (415)236-1197. Editor: Richard Grossinger. "Themes change by issue. Readership is literary, academic, interdisciplinary." Published irregularly. Estab. 1964. Circ. 1,500.
Needs: "We will accept topics only on baseball and basketball. We do not accept conventional short stories and the usual sort of fiction; we are looking only for unusual pieces. Please see issues before sending queries." Buys 8-10 mss/year. Length: 600-3,000 words.
How to Contact: Query. SASE for query, ms. Reports in 1 week.
Payment: Variable. 1 free author's copy. 60% of cover charge for extras.
Terms: Pays on publication for one-time rights.
Tips: "Read our magazine. We do not want inquiries from people who have not seen our publication."

IRON MAGAZINE, Iron Press, 5 Marden Ter., Cullercoats, North Shields, Tyne & Wear NE30 4PD, UK. (0632)531901. Editor: Peter Mortimer. "Literary magazine which publishes contemporary fiction, poetry, articles and graphics. We seek an audience sympathetic to new literature or, in some small way, hope to create one." Quarterly. Estab. April 1973. Circ. 900.
Needs: Literary, science fiction, humor, translations. "Generally we are open to all styles of fiction if we feel the author is serious about intentions (though he or she may, of course, be humorous in application). We are not interested in the 'mechanical' type of story specifically written with an automatic market in mind, such as teenage romance stories or others which seem to fit a well-worn framework and offer the reader little which is new." Accepts 4 mss/issue, 14 mss/year. Length: 7,000 words maximum.
How to Contact: Send complete ms with SASE. Reports in 3 weeks. Sample copy $2 with SASE plus 2 op (UK) or 2 IRC coupons (USA).
Payment: 1 free author's copy. $2 charge for extras.
Terms: "Copyright remains with author."
Tips: "We advise authors to see the magazine initially and make themselves familiar with

our approach to publishing fiction. No lengthy letters of why the story is so good (we'll make up our own minds). No more than two pieces of fiction to be submitted at the same time."

JAM TO-DAY, Jam To-day, Box 249, Northfield VT 05663. Fiction Editor: Judith Stanford. Co-editors: Don Stanford and Floyd Stuart. Forum for serious nonacademic poetry and fiction by unknown and little-known contemporary writers. Annually. Estab. 1973. Circ. 400.
Needs: Literary, contemporary, science fiction and feminist. No light fiction, word-play fiction, highly allusive or allegorical fiction. Buys 1 ms/year. Length: 1,500-4,000.
How to Contact: Send complete ms with SASE. Reports in 2 months on mss. Sample copy $2.50.
Payment: $5/printed page.
Terms: Pays on publication for first rights.

JEOPARDY, Western Washington University, Humanities Bldg., Bellingham WA 98225. (206)676-3118. Editor: Rudy Yuly. Poetry and fiction. Readership: College students, educators, writers and anybody else who is interested. Annual or biannual.
Needs: "Quality is our only criterion. If it reads well, has something to say, shows strong attention to detail (spelling, grammar, punctuation) and doesn't treat itself as God's gift to writing we'll like it." Accepts up to 20 mss/year. Length: 15,000 words maximum "unless it's great."
How to Contact: Send complete ms with SASE. Reports in 2 months on mss. Sample copy with 9½x11 SASE plus 80¢ postage.
Payment: 3 free author's copies.
Terms: Acquires all rights. Rights returned on request.
Tips: "Write about the world. Show a grasp of the English language. Be honest. Don't be afraid to edit your stories. If you feel half-interested in the story, don't submit it to us."

JOHN O'HARA JOURNAL, John O'Hara Journal, Inc., Box 106, Pottsville PA 17901. Editor: Vincent D. Balitas. Publishes literary criticism, original poetry and short fiction, book reviews for a mixed audience—working class, educators, professionals, poets and "fictionists." Semiannual. Estab. 1978. Circ. 500.
Needs: Literary, contemporary, fantasy, men's, women's, feminist, gay/lesbian, gothic, western, mystery, adventure, translations, experimental, traditional and post modern. No restrictions as to style, theme, content or form. Length: 2,500-7,500 words.
How to Contact: Send complete ms with SASE. Reports in 1-2 months on mss.
Payment: 3 free author's copies. Charges cost of issue and postage for extras.
Terms: "Each issue—copyrighted as a periodical. Individual contributors, however, retain ownership. We ask only that notice of first appearance be given with successive printings."
Tips: "Conceive carefully and execute. Write (type) cover letter. Type all material. Send SASE with everything. We try to publish high quality literature and criticism."

"JOINT" CONFERENCE, King Publications, Box 19332, Washington DC 20036. (202)234-1681. Editor: Kathryn E. King. "This is an inmate-written literary magazine using short fiction for prisoners and those who like to keep up with inmates' work." Annual. "Expect to publish on quarterly basis soon." Estab. 1974. Circ. "Subscribers: 110, readership in prisons: several thousand."
Needs: Literary, contemporary, science fiction, fantasy, gay/lesbian, romance, western, mystery, adventure, humor, ethnic (black, American Indiana, Hispanic). "While this magazine prints work only by prisoners, the material does not have to relate to prisons. As a matter of fact, I prefer that it does not because most 'prison' writing tends to get into a rut. No porno, semi-porno, or overly political writing." Buys 5-6 mss/issue, 20-25 mss/year (when published quarterly). Length: 1,500-5,000 words.
How to Contact: Send complete ms. "If an inmate can send SASE, it would help. Slow to

report on mss because this is a one-person operation." Free sample copy and guidelines.
Payment: $15-35 and 1 free author's copy. $2 charge for extras.
Terms: Pays on acceptance for one-time rights.
Tips: "Writer must be in prison or jail when he contacts me initially and should have a clear and vivid writing style. I don't care about spelling and grammar errors or what a ms looks like when it is submitted. Most are handwritten (prisoners often have difficulty getting access to typewriters) and some of the best work I've ever received came in on blue-lined paper. I will correct spelling and grammatical errors. I just want well-written material."

JOURNAL FANTOME, Fantome Press, 720 N. Park Ave., Warren OH 44483. Editor/ Publisher: C.M. James. "A review of the macabre in the arts and letters for people interested in macabre aspects of literature, film, and graphics arts." Annual. Estab. 1979. Circ. 500.
Needs: Fantasy, horror. "While we are primarily interested in reviews, we will consider very short works of prose. No material without macabre aspect." Accepts 10-20 mss/year. Length 10-1,000 words.
How to Contact: Query. SASE for query, ms. Reports in 6 months. Free sample copy for legal-sized SASE.
Payment: 5 free author's copies. 50% discount on extras.
Terms: Acquires first North American serial rights.
Tips: "Be brief and succinct. Study the market carefully."

THE JOURNAL OF THE NORTH AMERICAN WOLF SOCIETY., North American Wolf Society, Rt. 2, Troy Pike, Versailles KY 40383. (606)873-6450. Editor: Sandra Gray Thacker. "Our emphasis is wildlife education with specific priority on wild canids, their necessity and value to natural ecosystems, etc. We publish articles under our 'Post Scripts' section which are devoted to creative ecological fiction. The *Journal's* view is that our readers are intelligent activists who need to receive valid information." Readership: "Professional biologists/zoologists/ethologists, lay conservationists, federal and state wildlife personnel, universities, etc. Informed, active participants in the area of wildlife conservation. They read it because it maintains high standards of credibility and nationality." Published 3 times/year. Estab. 1974. Circ. 400+.
Needs: "Predator conservation with specific themes relative to wild canids: wolf, coyote, fox, or their prey. We are especially interested in historical approaches. All submissions should be based on sound ecological/biological fact. No overly emotional, fantasy articles which do not reflect the true character or existence of wild canids or their prey." Accepts 1 ms/issue, 3-4 mss/year. Length 2,000-4,000 words (prefers 2,000).
How to Contact: Send complete ms with SASE. Reports in 1 month. Sample copy $2. Free guidelines.
Payment: 5 free author's copies. $2 charge for extras.
Tips: "We are interested in well-researched folkloric scenarios, factual bases, etc., all with a strong ecologic message. We are not interested in personal philosophizing or overly emotional dissertations. The *Journal* has enjoyed, and worked very hard for, a reputation of objectivism and high credibility, which is very important to the continuation of our work, and our effectiveness in wildlife conservation. We welcome new writers who also place a high priority on the credibility of their work."

JUICE, Juice Press, 1015 Rose Ave., Oakland CA 94611. Editors: Brekke/Morse. Fiction Editor: Stephen Morse. "We publish fiction, art and poetry generally not published in the mainstream for readers who tend to be sophisticated, college educated with an appreciation for the unusual." Published irregularly. Estab. 1975.
Needs: Literary, contemporary, psychic/supernatural, science fiction, fantasy, horror, men's, women's, feminist, gay/lesbian, erotica, western, adventure, humor. "Generally open to anything that is both original and well written. Not interested in ordinary anything." Accepts 3-6 mss/issue. No preferred length.

How to Contact: Send complete ms with SASE. Reports in 1 month. Sample copy $1.
Payment: 2 free author's copies. $1 charge for extras.
Terms: Acquires all rights.
Tips: "Read a copy of *Juice*. Get a feel for what we're doing. If you like what you read then submit. We are very open. Do not send photocopies unless you also send a letter/note indicating that the ms is not being considered by another publication. We won't read it otherwise. We, as editors, will take the time to comment on individual submissions if requested. But you must have patience as our time is in short supply. If you want a quick response, don't ask for comments."

JUMP RIVER REVIEW, Jump River Press, Inc., 819 Single Ave., Wausau WI 54401. (715)842-8243. Editor: Mark Bruner. "We are a nonprofit literary quarterly with an interest in any form of written art. Specific interests: myth, folklife, enchantment." Readership: "Directed to writers and anyone interested in contemporary literature of quality." Quarterly. Estab. August 1979. Circ. 400.
Needs: Literary, contemporary, psychic/supernatural, fantasy, horror, erotica, ethnic, translations, myth, folklore. "No religiosity, purple sentiment, confessionals or cute bunny rabbit stories. No self-centered streams of consciousness." Accepts 2 mss/issue, 8-10 mss/ year. No preferred length.
How to Contact: Query or send complete ms with SASE. Reports in 1 week. Sample copy $2.50.
Payment: Copies.
Terms: Acquires one-time rights.
Tips: "Do not send a pretentious cover letter. If you're a young writer, mention that—it might help and get you feedback. Remember that the sensory image is all important—show your fiction instead of telling it." Occasional award and cash incentives.

JUST PULP, THE MAGAZINE OF POPULAR FICTION, Hidden People Press, Box 243, Narragansett RI 02882. (401)751-2101. Editor: Thomas R. Rankin. Fiction Editor: Robert E. Moore. "Designed as a vehicle of popular entertainment and aimed at those readers who find the standard 'little' magazines stuffy and the other available 'pulps' too restrictive in content. For a general, educated audience who appreciates good fiction." Quarterly. Estab. 1976. Circ. 600.
Needs: "We publish all types of fiction and insist only that the stories be well plotted and fully developed. To be considered, erotica must have a lot more going for it than what titilates the eye." Buys 7 mss/issue. Length: 1,000-15,000 words.
How to Contact: Send complete ms with SASE. Reports in 2 months on mss. Sample copy $2.
Payment: ¼¢/word and 1 free author's copy.
Terms: Pays on publication for all rights "but reassigns after publication."
Tips: "Write with an eye to the wind and a firm hand on the tiller. Do not send 3x5 SASE with 20¢ stamp on it and expect the return of 30 page ms."

KALLIOPE, A JOURNAL OF WOMEN'S ART, Florida Junior College at Jacksonville, 101 W. State St., Jacksonville FL 32202. Editor: Betty Bedell. Fiction Editor: Chris Durham. A literary and visual art journal for women, *Kalliope* "celebrates women in the arts by publishing their work and by providing a medium of communication through which they may share ideas and opinions." Short stories, poems, plays, essays, criticism, reviews, drawings, photos. For people interested in visual and verbal art by women. Published 3 times/year. Estab. fall 1979. Circ. 1,000.
Needs: "Literary, contemporary, science fiction, fantasy, women's with a historical perspective, past, present and future. We are not lesbian/feminist. No non-professional, sentimental, rambling junk, porno or special pleading." Accepts 1-2 mss/issue. No preferred length—"just short fiction."

How to Contact: Send complete ms with SASE. Reports in 3 months on ms. Sample copy $2.50 with 6x9 SASE plus $1.25 postage.
Payment: 3 free author's copies. $2.50 charge for extras.
Terms: Acquires first rights. "We accept only unpublished work. Copyright remains with author."
Tips: "Read our magazine. The work we consider for publication will be well written and the characters and dialogue will be convincing and have strength and movement. We like a fresh approach and are interested in new or unusual form. Create characters capable of living, characters we can care about."

KANSAS QUARTERLY, Kansas Quarterly Association, Denison Hall, Kansas State University, Manhattan KS 66506. (913)532-6716. Editors: Harold Schneider, Ben Nyberg, W.R. Moses. "A literary and cultural arts magazine publishing fiction and poetry. Special material on selected, announced topics in literary criticism, art history, folklore, and regional history. For well-read, general and academic audiences." Quarterly. Estab. 1968. Circ. 1,300.
Needs: Literary, contemporary, science fiction, fantasy, men's, women's, feminist, gay/lesbian, confession, gothic, romance, western, mystery, adventure, humor, ethnic. "We consider most categories as long as the fiction is of sufficient literary quality to merit inclusion. We avoid translations and parts of novels, but do not absolutely refuse them." Accepts 25-30 mss/year. Length: 350-12,000 words.
How to Contact: Send complete ms with SASE. Reports in 3 months on mss. Sample copy $3.
Payment: 2 free author's copies and annual awards to stories.
Terms: Acquires all rights. "We reassign rights on request at time of republication."
Tips: "Send story after consulting magazine." Sponsors awards.

KARAMU, English Dept., Eastern Illinois University, Charleston IL 61920. (217)581-5614. Editor: Bruce Guernsey. Fiction Editors: Victor Bobb and John Kilgore. "We have no theme as such; our wish is simply to publish the best poetry and fiction submitted to the magazine." For a literate, college-educated audience. Annual. Estab. 1967. Circ. 600.
Needs: Literary, contemporary, gothic, humor. Accepts 4-5 mss/issue. Length: 3,000-10,000 words.
How to Contact: Send complete ms with SASE. Reports in 2 months on mss. Sample copy $1.50.
Payment: 2 free author's copies. Half price charge for extras.
Tips: "Send for a sample copy, read it, and send a complete ms if your stories seem to match our taste. Please be patient—we sometimes get behind in our reading."

KAYAK, Kayak Books, Inc., 325 Ocean View Ave., Santa Cruz CA 95062. Editor: George Hitchcock. Theme: primarily poetry; some off-beat fiction. Readership: poets, writers. Quarterly. Estab. 1964. Circ. 1,300.
Needs: Literary, fantasy. "We are interested only in short parables, tales or fantasies of high literary quality. No straightaway realism." Accepts 2-3 mss/issue.
How to Contact: Send complete ms with SASE. Sample copy $1.
Payment: 2 free author's copies.
Terms: Acquires first rights.
Tips: "Read the magazine first."

KONGLOMERATI, Konglomerati Florida Foundation for Literature and the Book Arts, Inc., Box 5001, Gulfport FL 33737. (813)323-0386. Editors: Richard Mathews and Barbara Russ. "A finely printed letterpress showcase for contemporary literature. We publish intelligent and beautiful writing, including experimental and avant-garde as well as traditional forms." Readership: general, college educated, "persons with an interest in fine typography

and printing, collectors of contemporary literature and fine printing."
Needs: Literary, contemporary, science fiction, fantasy. "Literary quality is more important than category. We want the best fiction we can find regardless of form or subject." Buys 1-2 mss/issue, 2-6 mss/year.
How to Contact: Query or send complete ms with SASE. Reports in 6 weeks on queries, 2 months on mss. Sample copy $7.50 plus $1.30 for postage and packing.
Payment: $5-$10/printed page and 3 free author's copies.
Terms: Buys first rights.
Tips: "Send us your best story. Be courteous to and patient with overworked editors. Wait a little while after a rejection slip before submitting again to the same place unless the editor asks to see another story."

LAKE STREET REVIEW, Lake Street Review Press, CD/DM Books, Box 7188, Powderhorn Station, Minneapolis MN 55407. Editor: Kevin FitzPatrick. "A Minneapolis-St. Paul literary magazine which focuses on the work of writers and artists that live or have lived in this area. Readers are interested in contemporary writing by writers who have some connection with the Minneapolis-St. Paul area." Biannual. Estab. 1976. Circ. 500.
Needs: Literary, contemporary. Accepts 5 mss/issue. Length 500-4,000 words.
How to Contact: Send complete ms with SASE. Reports in 1 month on mss. Free sample copy with 7½x11 SASE plus 60¢ postage.
Payment: 2 free author's copies.
Terms: Acquires first rights.
Tips: "Send for a sample copy and read what we have recently printed."

LATIN AMERICAN LITERARY REVIEW, Latin American Literary Review, Baker Hall, Carnegie-Mellon University, Pittsburgh PA 15213. (412)578-2896. "A journal in English devoted to the literature of Latin America and Latin American minorities in the US. Our publication is directed primarily to an audience of young adults and adults with an interest in Latin American literature." Biannual. Estab. 1972. Circ. 1,000.
Needs: Literary, contemporary, ethnic (Hispanic, Latin American, chicano). No "themes not pertaining to the focus of our journal." Accepts 3-5 mss/issue. No preferred length.
How to Contact: Send complete ms with SASE. Reports in 2 months. Sample copy if requested.
Terms: "Rights are relinquished by author upon publication of ms."
Tips: "The fiction which appears in the *LALR* is usually translations of works originally written in Spanish by established authors." *LALR* is associated with the Latin American Literary Review Press (Box 8316, Pittsburgh PA 15218) which publishes novels in Spanish and Portuguese and English translations."

LAUREL REVIEW, West Virginia Wesleyan College, Dept. of English, Buckhannon WV 26201. (304)473-8006. Editor: Mark DeFoe. Fiction Editor: Jeanne DeFoe. "We publish poetry and fiction of high quality, from the traditional to the avant-garde. We are eclectic, open, and flexible. Good writing is all we seek. We try to encourage writers from Appalachian America although we publish material from across the country, Canada, and the world." Biannual. Estab. 1960. Circ. 500.
Needs: Literary, contemporary, humor, ethnic (Appalachian). Accepts 2 mss/issue, 4 mss/year. Length: 2,000-10,000 words.
How to Contact: Send complete ms with SASE. Reports in 2 months on mss. "Sometimes slow!" Sample copy $1.50.
Payment: $10 maximum. 2 free author's copies.
Terms: Pays on publication for first rights.
Tips: "Hang in there. Write, learn, read, read, read. Also read a copy of *Laurel Review*."

LEBEACON REVIEW, Le Beacon Pressé, 621 Holt, Iowa City IA 52240. Editor-in-Chief: K. Gormezano. Publishes the work of new and unknown writers and artists in poetry, fiction and graphics for a college educated audience up to age 35. Quarterly. Estab. January 1980. Circ. 200.
Needs: Literary, contemporary, science fiction, fantasy, horror, men's, women's, erotica, western, mystery, adventure, humor, translations and short shorts. Buys 10-20 mss/year. Length: 25-1,000 words.
How to Contact: Send complete ms with SASE. Varied reporting time. Sample copy $1 with size #10 SASE.
Terms: Acquires one-time rights.
Tips: "Send us your shortest works with name and address on all sheets."

LETTERS MAGAZINE, Box 786, New York NY 10007. (212)732-0475. Editor: Carole Bovoso. Co-Editor: James Lecesne. Estab. 1974. Circ. 6,500.
Needs: Literary, women's, feminist, gay/lesbian, humor/satire, translations, men's. No pornography, confessions, religious, or western.
How to Contact: Send inquiries or complete ms with SASE.
Payment: 2 free author's copies. .05¢ a word.

LETTERS MAGAZINE, Maine Writers Workshop, Mainspring Press, Box 82, Stonington MA 04681. (207)367-2484. Editor: Helen Nash. "Accepts only high quality material in all ethical fields of literature." Readership: General public. Quarterly. Estab. 1975. Circ. 3,500.
Needs: Literary, science fiction, mystery. "No porno, confessions, etc." Buys 5-10 issues/ year. Length: 500-1,000.
How to Contact: Query with SASE or send complete ms with SASE. Reports in 1 month on queries. Free sample copy and guidelines.
Payment: Varies.
Terms: Pays on publication for all rights.

LILITH MAGAZINE, Lilith Publications, Inc., 250 W. 57th St., New York NY 10019. Editor: Susan Weidman Schneider. "A Jewish feminist magazine for Jewish women/all women/all Jews." Quarterly. Estab. 1976. Circ. 10,000.
Needs: Literary, women's, feminist, gay/lesbian, juvenile, young adult, ethnic (Jewish), translations. Buys 1 ms/issue. Length: 1,200-2,000 words.
How to Contact: Send complete ms with SASE. Reports in 3 months on mss. Sample copy $2.50.
Payment: $25 minimum. 5 free author's copies. $2 charge for extras.
Terms: Pays on publication for all rights.

THE LITERARY MONITOR, 1070 Noriega Ave., #7, Sunnyvale CA 94086. Editor: Gary Lagier. Theme: review/resource/commentary magazine for poets, writers, editors, publishers, teachers, librarians, reviewers. Bimonthly. Circ. 14,000.
Needs: Literary, contemporary, science fiction, humor, translations. No religious material. Accepts 6 mss/issue. Length: 2,500 maximum (prefers 1,000) words.
How to Contact: Send complete ms with SASE. Reports in 2 weeks on mss. Sample copy $3 with 9x12 SASE plus $1.05 postage.
Payment: 1 free author's copy. $3 with 9x12 SASE plus $1.05 postage for extras.
Terms: Acquires first world serial plus non-exclusive reprint rights.

Tips: "Read an issue. Too many people are throwing together short stories, etc. and calling them 'finished.' Avoid excessive number of handwritten corrections and predictable plots."

THE LITTLE MAGAZINE, Box 207, Cathedral Station, New York NY 10025. Editor: David G. Hartwell. Fiction Editor: Felicity Thoet. Readership: readers of little magazines. Quarterly. Estab. 1966. Circ. 1,000.
Needs: Literary, science fiction, fantasy, horror. Accepts "no set amount—but few" mss/issue. Length: 4,000-5,000 words.
How to Contact: Send complete ms. SASE for ms. Reports in "approximately 6 weeks on mss." Sample copy $2.
Payment: 2 free author's copies. Extra copies "by arrangement."
Terms: Acquires first North American serial rights.
Tips: "Try hard but read the magazine first. No multiple submissions or poorly written mss. We return mss not properly prepared."

LIVE WRITERS! LOCAL ON TAP, La Reina Press, Box 8182, Cincinnati OH 45208. (513)579-8798. Editor/Publisher: Lupe A. Gonzalez. Fiction Editor: Karen Feinberg. "We are interested in the human condition from the point of view of Southern Ohio writers. Short fiction and poetry ranging from humorous to serious are published. For college-educated adults and those seeking alternative vehicles of literature. This audience enjoys 'discovering' writers in their own area and they want to express their support." Quarterly. Estab. March 1980. Circ. 400-500 "and increasing."
Needs: Literary, science fiction, feminist, mystery, humor, ethnic (native and Latin American and others). No religious, inspirational, romance, or confessions. Accepts 2-3 mss/issue, 8-12 mss/year. Length: 650-1,000 words.
How to Contact: Send complete ms with SASE or "query if you wish." Reports in 6 weeks on mss. Sample copy $2.50.
Payment: Free author's copies.
Terms: Makes assignments on a work-for-hire basis.
Tips: "Read the classics and the contemporary works that appeal to you. Try to write what you observe, experience and know about as if you're writing to a best friend who doesn't know the details. Remember the five senses. Hone the basic writing tools, use the dictionary and please check your spelling. We give suggestions and comments we feel helpful to the writers whose work we reject. We point out where they miss the mark with us, what we think are their strong and weak points. We want writers to know why their fiction is being rejected. It takes more of our time and energy, but it seems to have improved the quality of mss we receive."

LOONFEATHER:/Minnesota North Country Art, Box 48, Hagg-Sauer Hall, Bemidji State University, Bemidji MN 56601. (218)755-2813. Editor: William D. Elliott. A literary journal of fiction, poetry and photography. Mostly a market for North Central Minnesota, Minnesota, and Midwest writers. Published 3 times/year. Estab. Fall 1979. Circ. 2,000.
Needs: Literary, contemporary, serialized novels. Accepts 2 mss/issue, 6 mss/year. Length: 600-1,500 words (prefers 1,500).
How to Contact: Send complete ms with SASE. Reports in 1 month. Sample copy $2.
Payment: Free author's copies.
Terms: Acquires one-time rights.
Tips: "Send carefully crafted but experimental and literary fiction. No long mss."

LOST AND FOUND TIMES, Luna Bisonte Prods, 137 Leland Ave., Columbus OH 43214. (614)846-4126. Editor: John M. Bennett. Theme: Experimental, avant-garde and folk literature, art. Published irregularly. Estab. 1975. Circ. 300.

Needs: Literary, contemporary. Prefers short pieces. Accepts approximately 2 mss/issue.

How to Contact: Query with clips of published work. SASE for query, ms. Reports in 1 week on queries, 2 weeks on mss. Sample copy $1.50.

Payment: 2 free author's copies.

Terms: Rights revert to authors.

LUDDS MILL, Eight Miles High Products, 44 Spa Croft Rd., Teall St., Ossett, W. Yorkshire WF5 0HE, UK. Wakefield 275814. Editor: Andrew Darlington. "Alternative culture in the Bohemian tradition, experimental but accessible, direct, exciting, 'beat,' 'hipster,' 'punk,' etc. Aimed at late-teens, twenties, plus anyone with a mental orientation open to 'alternative' culture. Dada, surrealism, anarchist-left, pre-raphaelite, 60s underground, beat generation, etc." Biannual. Estab. 1971. Circ. 1,500.

Needs: Literary, contemporary, science fiction, feminist, gay/lesbian, erotica, condensed novels, experimental fiction. "Emphasis is not on commercial quality, but on originality, ability to excite, experiment with artistic integrity." Length: 10,000 maximum.

How to Contact: Send complete ms with SASE, IRC. Reports in 1 month. Sample copy $2 with SASE plus A4 envelope.

Payment: Free author's copies.

Terms: All rights remain with contributor.

Tips: "Get in contact. Send selection of work with brief biographical note/friendly letter. If work is not suitable we will supply address list of alternatives. Check requirements of magazine before submitting material. Keep mss circulating."

LYNN VOICES, BLT Press, 72 Lowell St., Peabody MA 01960. (617)531-7348. Editor: Peter Bates. Fiction Editor: Bill Costley. "A community tabloid publishing satire, poetry, fiction, photos, and raw drawings that focus on the grit and grime of survival in the city. For the dispossessed, the down-and-outers, the fixed-income strata, the industrial worker, the trade unionist, the feminist, and social radical." Biannual. Estab. June 1980. Circ. 15,000.

Needs: Literary, contemporary, fantasy, humor, ethnic (black, Latino), satire. "Please no tripped-out, God and doom-dwellers, reactionary, or racist." Accepts 1 ms/issue, 2 mss/year. Length: 1-500 (prefers 500) words.

How to Contact: Query. SASE for ms. Reports in 1 month on queries, 2 months on mss. Sample copy 25¢ with large manilla SASE plus 40¢ postage.

Payment: Free author's copies.

Terms: Acquires simultaneous rights.

Tips: "Please, be at least 40% satirist and deal with social issues (jobs, government, sexism, racism). Move out of the lyrical and into the dramatic. Stop thinking about yourself. Put distance between yourself and reader."

MAELSTROM REVIEW, Box 4261, Long Beach CA 90804. (213)597-9663. Editor/Publisher: Leo Mailman. "Poetry, fiction and reviews with contemporary fiction format, but not too experimental, for literary, college-educated, or student readership." Semiannual. Estab. 1972. Circ. 400-700.

Needs: Literary, contemporary. "No highly romantic, gothic, religious, political, or highly experimental material." Accepts 2-3 mss/issue, 5-6 mss/year. Length: 2,000 words, 10-20 ms pages.

How to Contact: Send complete ms with SASE. Reports in 2 months on mss. Sample copy $2.

Payment: 3-5 free author's copies "with eligibility for annual award and payment." Half price charge for extra copies.

Terms: Acquires all rights.

Tips: "Buy a sample issue and read the fiction before submitting. Mss accepted are eligible for best short story award of year in *Maelstrom Review*."

MAGIC CHANGES, Celestial Otter Press, Box 152, Mt. Prospect IL 60056. (312)884-6425. Editors: John Sennett and Don Bullen. "Theme: arts renaissance. Material: poetry, songs, fiction, stories, reviews, art, essays, etc. For the entertainment and enlightenment of all ages." Quarterly. Estab. December 1979. Circ. 2,000.
Needs: Literary, psychic/supernatural, science fiction, fantasy, erotica. "Fiction should have an artistic slant." Accepts 2-3 mss/issue, 8-12 mss/year. Length: 3,000 words maximum.
How to Contact: Send complete ms with SASE. Reports in 1 month. Sample copy $4.
Payment: 1-2 free author's copies. $4 charge for extras.
Terms: Acquires first North American serial rights.
Tips: "Write well. Read poetry." Sponsors contest. Offers critiquing service.

MAGICAL BLEND, Box 11303, San Francisco CA 94101. Editor: Katherine Zunic. Fiction Editor: Michael P. Langevin. "Presents the world as a magical land where peace and harmony reign. We print fantasy, positive occultism, comics, graphics, poetry, and articles on magic for liberal, open-minded people who enjoy a blending of creative works and might even use magic in their own lives. Ages 18-40." Quarterly. Estab. Spring 1980. Circ. 4,000.
Needs: Psychic/supernatural, fantasy, adventure. "We also feature specialized issues, for example: sea mammals, health. No dark or dismal portrayal of life." Accepts 4 mss/issue, 15 mss/year. Length: 500-3,000 words.
How to Contact: Send complete ms with SASE. Reports in 1 month on mss. Sample copy $3. Guidelines for legal-sized SASE.
Payment: 3 free author's copies. Half price charge for extras.
Terms: Acquires one-time rights.
Tips: "We like fiction that takes our readers to beautiful worlds and ends happily. Share your fantasies, dreams and stories of magic with us."

MAIZE, NOTEBOOKS OF XICANO ART AND LITERATURE, Maize, Box 8251, San Diego CA 92102. (714)455-1128. Editors: Xelina and Alurista. "Works of Third World social consciousness: fiction, poetry, drama, graphics, art, line drawing, photos, literary criticism. Readers: Third World and chicano. *Maize* provides a long overdue outlet for abundant material." Quarterly. Estab. 1977. Circ. 1,000.
Needs: Literary, contemporary, men's, women's, erotica, humor, ethnic. Wants to see "that literature which relates to the social concerns of Third World people—their culture and lives." No scientific material. Accepts 2 mss/issue. Length: 1,500-4,000 (prefers 3,000) words.
How to Contact: Send complete ms with SASE. Reports in 2 months on mss. $4/sample copy.
Payment: 3 free author's copies. $2 charge for extras.
Terms: Acquires first rights.
Tips: "Aim toward the consciousness of Third World people. Remain honest and simple."

THE MALAHAT REVIEW, University of Victoria, Box 1700, Victoria, B.C., Canada V8W 2Y2. Editor: Robin Skelton. "An international literary quarterly of life and letters. Publishing first in English, fiction, poetry, criticism, essays, and art for public and university libraries, colleges and senior high schools, and individuals with literary interests." Quarterly. Estab. 1967. Circ. 800.
Needs: Literary, contemporary, science fiction, men's, women's, humor, translations. No horror, romance or juvenile. Buys 4 mss/issue, 50 mss/year. Length: 4,000-5,000 words.
How to Contact: Query or send complete ms. SASE for query, ms. "Work not returned without Canadian stamps or International Reply Coupons." Reports in 1 week on queries, 2 months on mss. Free sample copy with 10½x7½ SASE plus $1 postage.
Payment: $25 per thousand words and 2 free author's copies. $3 less 33% discount for extras.
Terms: Acquires first world serial rights. All rights revert to author after publication.
Tips: "Be sure to keep your own duplicate of ms."

MAMASHEE, Sydenham Press, R.R. 1, Inwood, Ontario, Canada N0N 1K0. Editor: Margaret Drage. "Any theme which concerns the so-called serious writer with emphasis on quality poetry, short fiction, and essays. Limited literary-minded readership—limited but we hope not elitist. Readers enjoy contemporary prose and poetry by new and established writers." Quarterly. Estab. 1976. Circ. less than 200.
Needs: Literary. "Some experimental fiction." Accepts 2 mss/issue. Length: 1,000-2,000 words.
How to Contact: Send complete ms with SASE. Reports in 3 months on ms. Sample copy $1.50 plus 70¢ postage.
Payment: Free author's copies.
Terms: Acquires one-time rights.
Tips: "Study the little magazines which are available in public and college libraries and read anthologies of quality contemporary fiction. Edit stories for spelling or grammatical errors. New writers often forget to put their names and addresses on the mss which may get lost. Have patience. Most editors of little magazines are doing this work on a part-time voluntary basis and they handle mss as quickly and carefully as possible. Although *Mamashee* is essentially a Canadian publication we welcome submissions from any country as long as they are accompanied by SASE or IRC. We try to maintain a standard of quality work and attempt to present variety."

MANGO, Mango Publications, Box 28546, San Jose CA 95159. Editors: Lorna Dee Cervantes, Orlando Ramirez and Adrin Rocha. "A literary/art magazine; chicano emphasis, multicultural in actuality. High quality literature only; need not be obviously political or ethnic. For readers who want to keep abreast of current trends in the field of chicano/Third World literature." Annual. Estab. 1976. Circ. 1,000.
Needs: Literary, contemporary, science fiction, fantasy, men's, women's, feminist, gay/lesbian, erotica, chicano/Latino ethnic, translations, bilingual (English/Spanish), Spanish. "We rarely use highly experimental fiction. We do not want to see material on Mexico, Mexicans or any other Latin peoples or cultures written by Anglos." Accepts a variable number of mss/issue. Length: 5,000 words maximum.
How to Contact: Send complete ms. Query on longer mss. SASE for query, ms. Reports in 3 weeks on queries, 2 months on mss. Sample copy $2.50.
Payment: 4-5 free author's copies.
Terms: Acquires first rights.
Tips: "Read our publication before submitting. We will consider longer fiction for chapbooks and books up to 200 pages in length written by chicano authors. Query first, with sample."

MARK TWAIN JOURNAL, Kirkwood MO 63122. Editor: Cyril Clemens. Semiannual. Estab. 1936.
How to Contact: Query first. Reports in 2 weeks. "We occasionally use fiction." Sample copy $1 with SASE.
Payment: Free author's copies.

THE MASSACHUSETTS REVIEW, Memorial Hall, University of Massachusetts, Amherst MA 01003. Editors: John Hicks and Robert Tucker. Quarterly.
Needs: Short stories.
How to Contact: Send complete ms. No ms returned without SASE. Reports promptly. Sample copy $3.
Payment: Pays $50 maximum.
Terms: Pays on publication for first North American serial rights.
Tips: "Shorter rather than longer stories preferred (20-25pp.). Avoid submitting material during summer months."

MATI, Ommation Press, 5548 N. Sawyer, Chicago IL 60625. Editor: Effie Mihopoulos. "Primarily a poetry magazine but we do occasional special fiction and science fiction issues." Quarterly. Estab. 1975. Circ. 1,000.
Needs: Literary, contemporary, science fiction, feminist, translations. No mystery, gothic, western, religious. Length: 1-2 pages.
How to Contact: Send complete ms with SASE. Reports in 1 week. Sample copy $1.50 with 9x12 SASE (preferred) plus 80¢ postage.
Payment: 1 free author's copy. Special contributor's rates available for extras.
Terms: Acquires first North American serial rights. "Rights revert to author but *Mati* retains reprint rights."
Tips: "We want to see good quality writing and a neat ms with sufficient return postage; same size return as outside envelope and intelligent cover letter. Editor to be addressed as 'Dear Sir/Ms' instead of 'Dear Sir' when it's a woman editor."

MATRIX, Champlain College, Box 510, Lennoxville, Quebec, Canada J1M 1Z6. Editor: Phil Lanthier. Fiction Editor: Marjorie Retzleff. "A literary magazine with Canadian and American content. We specialize in long poems and experimental fiction for readers and writers usually in, or on the fringes of, the academic world." Biannual. Estab. 1975. Circ. 800.
Needs: Literary. Buys 3-4 mss/issue. Length: 1,000-5,000 words.
How to Contact: Send complete manuscript with SASE. Reports in 1 month on mss. Free sample copy.
Payment: $15-$125. Contributors copies $1 each.
Terms: Pays on publication for first North American serial rights.
Tips: "Use strong dialogue, good endings. Avoid hackneyed themes."

M 'GODOLIM, LeBeacon Pressé, 621 Holt, Iowa City IA 52240. Editor: Shabtui Gormezano. Publishes the works of Jewish writers and artists for a Jewish-oriented audience. Quarterly. Estab. June 1980. Circ. 200.
Needs: Literary, contemporary, religious/inspirational, science fiction, fantasy, horror, feminist, mystery, adventure, humor, ethnic (Jewish) and translations. Buys 10 mss/year. Length: 25-1,000 words.
How to Contact: Query and send complete ms with SASE. Reporting time varies on both queries and mss. Sample copy $1 with size #10 SASE.
Terms: Pays on publication for one-time rights.

MIDATLANTIC REVIEW, Box 598, Baldwin Place NY 10505. Fiction Editor: Stephen Baily. Theme: Serious fiction. Quarterly. Estab. 1975. Circ. 1,000.
Needs: Literary. Accepts 3-5 mss/issue. Length: 4,000 words maximum.
How to Contact: Send complete ms with SASE. Reports in 2 months on mss. Sample copy $2.
Payment: 2 free author's copies.
Terms: Acquires one-time rights.

MIDSTREAM-A MONTHLY JEWISH REVIEW, The Theodor Herzl Foundation, 515 Park Ave., New York NY 10022. (212)752-0600. Editor: Joel Carmichael. Fiction Editor: Debra Berman. Theme: articles, essays, poetry, reviews dealing with world and cultural subjects of Jewish interest. "We are aimed at those who wish to keep abreast of developments in world and cultural Jewish affairs." Monthly. Estab. 1955. Circ. 15,000.
Needs: Literary, religious and Jewish ethnic. Buys 1 ms/issue. Length: 1,000-4,000 words.
How to Contact: Send complete ms with SASE. Reports in 1 month. Free sample copy.
Payment: 5¢ per word and 3 free author's copies.
Terms: Pays on publication for first rights.

MINOTAUR, Minotaur Press, 2419 24th Ave., San Francisco CA 94116. (415)661-4035. Editor/Publisher: Jim Gove. Fiction Editor: Chris Leddy. Associate Editor: Charles Mitchell. "Contemporary poetry, short fiction, articles on the literary scene, reviews. We tend to favor experimental work but we are not exclusive about it. Readers are those who probably write or study contemporary literature." Quarterly. Estab. 1976. Circ. 500.
Needs: Literary, contemporary. "No genre fiction." Accepts 1 ms/issue. Length: 2,000 maximum.
How to Contact: Send complete manuscript with SASE. Reports in 3 weeks. Free sample copy with 6½x9½ SASE with 33¢ postage.
Payment: Free author's copies.
Terms: Acquires first rights.
Tips: "For us, fiction, to be considered, must be literate and probably have enough of an experimental element to be difficult to publish elsewhere."

MISSISSIPPI REVIEW, University of Southern Mississippi, Southern Station, Box 5144, Hattiesburg MS 39401. (601)266-4169. Editor: Frederick Barthelme. Associate Editor: Elizabeth Inness-Brown. Literary publication for those interested in contemporary literature—writers, editors who read to be in touch with current modes. Semiannual. Estab. 1972. Circ. 1,500.
Needs: Literary, contemporary, fantasy, erotica, humor, translations, experimental, avant-garde and "art" fiction. No juvenile. Buys varied amount of mss/issue. Length: 100 pages maximum.
How to Contact: Send complete ms with SASE including a short cover letter. Reports in 3 months on mss. Sample copy $4.50.
Payment: Pays with 6 free author's copies. Charges cover price for extras.
Terms: Pays on publication for first North American serial rights.

MISSISSIPPI VALLEY REVIEW, Western Illinois University. Dept. of English, Simpkins Hall, Macomb IL 61455. Editor: Forrest Robinson. Fiction Editor: Loren Logsdon. "A small magazine, *MVR* has won nine Illinois Arts Council awards in poetry and fiction. We publish stories, poems, and reviews." Biannual. Estab. 1971. Circ. 400+.
Needs: Literary, contemporary.
How to Contact: Send complete ms with SASE. Reports in 3 months.
Payment: 2 free author's copies.
Terms: Individual author retains rights.
Tips: "We prefer to receive one story at a time."

THE MISSOURI REVIEW, University of Missouri, 231 Arts & Science, English Dept., U. of Mo., Columbia MO 65211. (314)882-6421. Editor: Larry Levis. Fiction Editor: Speer Morgan. Theme: fiction, poetry, criticism, essays, reviews, interviews. "All with a distinctly contemporary orientation. For writers, academics, others. We present non-established as well as established writers of excellence and offer a forum for modern critical theory." Published 3 times/academic year. Estab. 1977. Circ. 750.
Needs: Literary, contemporary; open to all categories except gay/lesbian, juvenile, young adult. Buys 2-3 mss/issue, 6-9 mss/year. No preferred length.
How to Contact: Send complete ms with SASE. Reports in 1 month. Sample copy $1.
Payment: $5-10/page.
Terms: Pays on publication for all rights.
Tips: "Practice writing and wait three years to try to break into a publication."

THE MOONSHINE REVIEW, Moonshine Cooperative, Rt. 2, Box 488, Flowery Branch GA 30542. Editors: Tom Liner and Dan Ward. Theme: "Experimental—poetry, fiction, ink drawings, reviews, what-you-will. Audience is generally young, literate, interested in what's happening now in writing." Annual. Estab. 1978. Circ. 300.

Needs: Literary, contemporary, fantasy, humor, translations, experimental. "No pornography, religious tracts, feminist rantings (don't preach here.)" Accepts 1 mss/issue. Length: 2,000 words maximum.
How to Contact: Query, send complete ms. "Query is better on fiction for us." SASE for query, ms. Reports in 1 month. "Sometimes longer on mss." Sample copy $2.
Payment: 3 free author's copies. $1 charge for extras.
Terms: Acquires first North American serial rights.
Tips: "We are especially interested in the beginner but our room for fiction is very limited. It should be original, unusual and good."

MOOSEHEAD REVIEW, Moosehead Press, Box 169, Ayer's Cliff, Quebec, Canada J0B 1C0. (819)838-5921 (4801). Editors: Robert Allen, Hugh Dow, Steve Luxton, Jan Draper. "A small literary and political periodical." Biannual. Estab. 1978. Circ. 500.
Needs: Literary, science fiction, translations, literary theory (especially Marxist). Accepts 2-3 mss/issue, 4-6 mss/year. No preferred length.
How to Contact: Send complete ms with SASE. Reports in 6 weeks. Sample copy $3.
Payment: 3 free author's copies.
Terms: Acquires one-time rights.
Tips: "We are a very competitive market. Only top quality fiction is considered, but we do not judge by reputation. A first story has as much chance as a story by a well-known writer."

MOUNTAIN REVIEW, Box 660, Whitesburg KY 41858. (606)633-4811. Editor: René Hansel Stamper. Magazine dealing with history, preservation, present and future Appalachian areas. Audience consists of Appalachians of all ages, backgrounds and those interested in mountain life. Quarterly. Estab. 1974. Circ. 2,000.
Needs: Open to all writing by Appalachian writers, including, but not limited to themes just dealing with some aspect of mountain life. Length: 1,000-3,000 words.
How to Contact: Send complete ms with SASE. Reports in 3-6 months. Sample copy $1.50.
Terms: Acquires all rights; copyright reverts to the author after publication. Byline given. Photocopied submissions OK. Seasonal material 4 months in advance.

MUNDUS ARTIUM, A Journal of International Literature And Arts, University of Texas at Dallas, Box 688, Richardson TX 75080. Editor: Rainer Schulte. Literary review of nonfiction, poetry, fiction with bilingual format for all levels, "except the scholarly, footnote-starved type." Semiannual. Estab. 1967. Circ. 2,000.
Needs: Stories must be experimental and fantasy or translations. Length is open.
How to Contact: Send complete ms with SASE. Reports in 3 months. Sample copy $3.50.
Payment: Pays $5 minimum.
Terms: Pays on publication for all rights. Photocopied submissions OK.

MUSCADINE, 1111 Lincoln Pl., Boulder CO 80302. (303)443-9748. Editor: Lucille Cyphers. "Writers must be over 60 years of age. Everyone enjoys *Muscadine* as a glimpse of oldsters' rich experiences and creativity." Bimonthly. Estab. 1977. Circ. 400.
Needs: Literary, contemporary, psychic/supernatural, science fiction, fantasy, men's, women's, western, mystery, adventure, humor, juvenile, ethnic (all). No horror, erotica, novels. Length: 350-1,200 words.
How to Contact: Send complete ms with SASE. Reports in 1 month on mss. Sample copy $1.
Payment: 1 free author's copy. $1 charge for extras.
Terms: Acquires first rights.
Tips: "We give priority to beginners. Try to stay off trite themes. Express it your way. It might have the freshness we value—the common touch. The more skilled writers have to compete for space. Brevity is a priority. Mss don't have to be typewritten."

THE NANTUCKET REVIEW, Box 1234, Nantucket MA 02554. Co-Editors: Richard Cumbie and Richard Burns. "We are a general literary magazine ascribing to no specific school(s) of literature. We publish primarily fiction (60%) and poetry (40%), but also satire, essays, cultural articles for those interested in new writing, students, writers. They read us to see work by new writers side-by-side with work by established writers." Published 3 times/year. Estab. 1974. Circ. 600.
Needs: Literary, feminist, translations. "It's difficult for us to rule out some types of fiction. *The Man From Laramie* and *The Ox-Bow Incident* are both 'western' stories, for example, but stories like the former wouldn't be of much interest to us, while those like the latter would be. We are interested in serious (that is not to say, humorless) fiction. " Length: 1,500-6,000 words.
How to Contact: Send complete ms with SASE. Reports in 2 months. Sample copy with 6x9 SASE plus 56¢ postage.
Payment: $5-$25 ("occasional payment becomes more frequent") and 2 free author's copies. $1.50 charge for extras.
Terms: Pays on publication for first North American serial rights.
Tips: "Read an issue of the magazine before submitting fiction to us. It's a constant complaint among editors that they receive many mss totally unsuited to their publications. Any writer serious about his craft and eager to publish can, for $15-$20 (or less, depending on library availability), examine a dozen magazines he wishes to try with stories. Be neat. Always, if you feel compelled to do multiple submissions, inform the editor when you submit. Please don't submit stories of more than 6,000 words."

NEBULA MAGAZINE, Nebula Press, 970 Copeland, North Bay, Ontario, Canada P1B 3E4. Editor: Ken Stange. Fiction Editor: Gil McElroy. Theme: literary. Readership: well-read. Quarterly. Estab. 1975. Circ. 750.
Needs: Literary—"but open to all genres if treated maturely. No poorly written mss." Accepts about 6 mss/year. No preferred length.
How to Contact: Send complete ms with SASE or IRC. Reports in 1 month. Sample copy $2.
Payment: 2 free author's copies.
Terms: Acquires first rights.
Tips: "Read us first." Sometimes sponsors grants.

NEW AMERICA, c/o Dept. of American Studies, University of New Mexico, Albuquerque NM 87131. (505)277-4452. Editors are rotating. "A journal of American and Southwestern culture. Our material includes fiction, poetry, photography, and graphic art exploring American and Southwestern culture. Our audience is very diverse. Past themes have been geared toward those interested in SW culture, American studies, chicano literature, Native American literature, photographers, energy buffs, etc. Our aim is to reach a larger audience by having different themes." Semiannual. Estab. 1974. Circ. 700.
Needs: Literary, contemporary, men's, women's, gay/lesbian, ethnic (chicano, Native American), and Southwestern American studies. "We solicit different material for each specific issue." No preferred length.
How to Contact: Query. SASE for query, ms. Reports in 1 week on queries, 3 months on mss. Sample copy $3.50.
Payment: 1 free author's copy. 40% discount for 10 or more extras.
Terms: Buys all rights.

NEW EDINBURGH REVIEW, EUSPB, 1 Buccleuch Pl., Edinburgh 8 Scotland, (031) 667-5718. Editor: James Campbell. Features, fiction, poetry, reviews for a general readership. Quarterly. Estab. 1969.
Needs: Literary, contemporary, ethnic, translations only. Buys 2 mss/issue, 8 mss/year. Length: 1,000-4,000 words.

How to Contact: Send complete ms. SASE or IRC for ms. Reports in 3 weeks. Sample copy available for fee.
Payment: Negotiates pay for fiction. 1 free author's copy.
Terms: Pays on publication for first rights.
Tips: "Read our magazine before submitting."

NEW ENGLAND SAMPLER, Seacoast Press, Rt. 1, Box M119, Brooks ME 04921. (207)525-3575. Editor/Publisher: Virginia M. Rimm. "An upbeat family magazine featuring old-time New England values and heritage. We use historic and humorous material, nature articles, interviews, poetry, book reviews, ESP experiences, fiction, off-beat places to visit, etc. Audience consists of well-educated rural families, senior citizens, middle-aged adults. We reflect the values with which these segments were raised, and we try to provide a feeling of hope rather than hopelessness. They read us because we give them a 'lift.' " Monthly. Estab. August 1980. Circ. 1,000.
Needs: Inspirational, psychic, science fiction, fantasy, gothic, mystery, adventure, humor, juvenile, nature and outdoor. "We use only wholesome material suited to a family audience. No angry, anti-establishment articles; no erotic, gay/lesbian, feminist, ethnic or confession themes. We want general inspirational material, not denominational work. New England slant required." Accepts 6-8 mss/year. Length: 2,500-3,500 words.
How to Contact: Query on fiction. SASE for query, ms. Reports in 2 weeks on queries, 1 month on mss. Sample copy $1. Free general writer's guideline.
Payment: 1-4 free author's copies. $1 charge for extras.
Terms: Acquires first rights.
Tips: "Send for sample copy and free guidelines. Remember, we're a New England regional with an upbeat format aimed at the family audience. Pick a subject with strong New England flavor, write in lively, fast-paced fashion with good plot and characterization. Be fresh and original. Don't use subject matter incompatible with our format and purpose. We judge our material only by the quality of the workmanship. We're a new magazine and our entire staff works without pay. We want to build and grow and need professional calibre writing. We hope in time to be able to pay. Since we're new, we're a good place for would-be professionals to break into print."

THE NEW KENT QUARTERLY, Campus Printing, 239 Student Center, Kent State University, Kent OH 44240. Editor: Nancy Henkel. "The magazine is a creative arts outlet for the university community and other interested artists. We publish poems, prose, and photography for the general public." Biannual. Circ. 300.
Needs: Literary. Length: 1,600 words maximum.
How to Contact: Send complete ms with SASE. Reports in 1 month. Sample copy $1 with SASE.
Payment: Pays in contributor's copies.
Terms: Acquires all rights.

NEW LAUREL REVIEW, New Laurel Review, Box 1083, Chalmette LA 70044. (504)271-4209. Editors: Alice and Calvin Claudel. Journal of poetry, fiction, critical articles and reviews. "We have published such nationally known writers as Guy Owen, Jesse Stuart, H.E. Francis, Tonita Gardner, Dorothy Stanfill, and Jim Barnes (translations)." Readership: "Literate, adult audiences as well as anyone interested in writing with significance, human interest, vitality, subtlety, etc." Biannual. Estab. 1970. Circ. 500.
Needs: Literary, contemporary, fantasy, translations. No "dogmatic, excessively inspirational or political" material. Accepts 1-2 mss/issue. Length: about 10 printed pages.
How to Contact: Send complete ms. SASE for query, ms. Reports in 1 month. Sample copy $2.
Payment: 2 free author's copies.
Terms: Acquires first rights.

Tips: "Write fresh, alive 'moving' work. Not interested in egocentric work without any importance to others. Be sure to watch simple details such as putting one's name and address on ms and clipping all pages together. Caution: Don't use overfancy or trite language."

NEW MEXICO HUMANITIES REVIEW, New Mexico Tech, Box A, NMT, Socorro NM 87801. (505)835-5445. Editor: John Rothfork. Review of poetry, essays and prose of Southwest. Readership: academic but not specialized. Published 3 times/year. Estab. 1978. Circ. 600.
Needs: Literary. "No formula." Buys 12-15 mss/year. Length: 6,000 words maximum.
How to Contact: Send complete ms with SASE. Reports in 2 months. Sample copy $2.
Payment: $5/page. 1 year subscription.
Terms: Pays on publication for one-time rights.

NEW ORLEANS REVIEW, Box 195, Loyola University, New Orleans LA 70118. (504)865-2294. Editor: John Biguenet. Publishes poetry, fiction, translations, photographs, nonfiction on literature, film and general culture. Readership: those interested in current culture, literature. Published 3 times/year. Estab. 1968. Circ. 1,500.
Needs: Literary, contemporary, translations. No special categories designated. Buys 9-12 mss/year. Length: Under 40 pages.
How to Contact: Send complete ms with SASE. Reports in 1 month. Sample copy $2.50. Free guidelines.
Payment: "Rates are changing."
Terms: Pays on publication for first North American serial rights.

THE NEW RENAISSANCE, 9 Heath Rd., Arlington MA 02174. Fiction Editors: Louise T. Reynolds and Harry Jackel. "An international magazine of ideas and opinions, with a classicist position in literature and the arts. Publishes a variety of quality fiction, always well crafted, sometimes experimental. Generally for the literate reader. *tnr* is unique among literary magazines for its marriage of the literary and visual arts with articles and essays on current events. We publish the beginning as well as the established writer." Biannual. Estab. 1968. Circ. 1,300.
Needs: Literary, humor, translations, off-beat, quality fiction and, occasionally, experimental fiction. "We don't want to see heavily plotted stories with one-dimensional characters or academic fiction. *tnr* is interested in fiction that has something to say, that says it with style or grace and that speaks in an individualized voice." Buys 3-5 mss/issue, 6-10 mss. year. Length: 3-38 pages.
How to Contact: Send complete ms with SASE. Reports in 6 months. Sample copy $1.90 (specify fiction issue).
Payment: $18.50-$50. 1 free author's copy. $3.50 each for 1-2 copies, $3 each for additional copies.
Terms: Pays on publication for all rights.
Tips: "Read an issue or two very carefully to see our tone and philosophy and send us the very best story you have. We are not interested in imitative or derivative fiction. Beginning and new writers should first of all, be readers of fiction and, ideally not merely readers of contemporary or even just modern work. Study the market and submit only if you respect the magazines."

THE NEWSCRIBES INC., c/o P. Scarpa, 140 Bay Ridge Pkwy., Brooklyn NY 11209. Editor: Peter Scarpa. Fiction Editor: Thomas Lane. Poetry, short stories, novel excerpts, and some essays. Readership: all types. Quarterly or biannual. Estab. 1976. Circ. 500.
Needs: Literary, contemporary, science fiction, fantasy, serialized novels. No preferred length.
How to Contact: Send complete ms with SASE. Reports in 3 weeks.
Payment: Free author's copies.
Terms: "All rights to the author."

NIR/NEW INFINITY REVIEW, Infinity Publications, Box 804, Ironton OH 45638. (614)533-9276. Editor: James R. Pack. Manuscript Editor: Ron Houchin. Theme: "Material by new and unknown writers—fiction; experimental, avant-garde, visual poetry; creative photography; surrealistic and visionary art." Readership: Famous people awarded lifetime merit subscriptions for contributions made in the arts, literature, science, etc., that advance new perspectives and challenge the mysterious and unknown. Quarterly. Estab. 1974. Circ. 500.
Needs: Contemporary, psychic/supernatural, science fiction, fantasy, mystery, humor. No religious, romance, gothic, feminist, gay/lesbian, erotica. Accepts 2-4 mss/issue. Length: 500-2,000 words.
How to Contact: Send complete ms with SASE. Reports in 10 weeks. Sample copy $2. Free guidelines.
Payment: 2 free author's copies. 75¢ charge for extras.
Terms: Acquires first North American serial rights.
Tips: "We are looking for writers with 'pizazz and verve' (creative energy and personal integrity), so the clearer and more direct the ms the better. Good English usage is a must. Avoid excessive use of profanities. Be original. Strive for a new perspective."

NIT & WIT, 1908 W. Oakdale, Chicago IL 60657. (312)248-1183. Editor: Leonard J. Dominguez. A literary arts magazine of dance, music, criticism, film, poetry and reviews. Quarterly. Estab. 1977. Circ. 5,000.
Needs: Literary, contemporary, the arts, psychic/supernatural, fantasy, adventure, humor, translations. No science fiction. Accepts 4 mss/issue, 12 mss/year. Length: 1,500 words.
How to Contact: Send complete ms with SASE. Reports in 2 months on mss. Sample copy $1.50. Guidelines for legal-sized SASE.
Payment: Free author's copies.
Terms: Acquires first rights.

NORTH AMERICAN MENTOR MAGAZINE, John Westburg, 1745 Madison St., Fennimore WI 53809. (608)822-6237. Editor/Publisher: John Westburg. "We publish short fiction, poetry, essays, including criticism, philosophy, social sciences, humanities in general. We are eclectic, cosmopolitan, and international. Mature readers, most with college education or equivalent. Many are professional writers, professional persons in other fields, including education, law, medicine, religion, engineering, government, military." Quarterly. Estab. 1974. Circ. 500+.
Needs: Literary, contemporary, science fiction, fantasy. "Undesirable fiction would be that which is from the viewpoint of a religious true believer, a political ideologue or person with a loud message or sales pitch. We frown upon raw sex, sensationalism, minority causes, abuse of any race or nation, use of obscenity and vulgarity." Accepts 1-3 mss/issue, 6-8+ mss/year. Length: 3,500 words (prefers 1,500).
How to Contact: Send complete ms with SASE. Reports in 6 months. Sample copy $4.
Payment: Free author's copies.
Terms: Acquires all rights. "We reject mss offering only first North American rights or one-time rights. We must acquire all rights, but we do, upon request, grant permission without charge for publication elsewhere."
Tips: "We would consider any kind of fiction that is well-written, well-organized, with a beginning, middle, and ending, good characterization, good description, and reasonable action. We are still looking for a modern Charles Dickens who can combine all those qualities with a keen wit and insight to character. We have yet to find the ideal story, and we are still looking for it, one with clarity, good characterization, description, action, wit, unity, plot, and a good point to it. Modern writers would do well to study the 19th century English short story writers to emulate them in modern or contemporary scenarios."

THE NORTH AMERICAN REVIEW, University of Northern Iowa, Cedar Falls IA 50614.

Editor: Robley Wilson, Jr. Theme: quality fiction. Quarterly. Estab. 1815. Circ. 3,100.
Needs: "We print quality fiction of any length and/or subject matter. Excellence is the only criterion." Buys 30-40 mss/year. No preferred length.
How to Contact: Send complete ms with SASE. Reports in 2 months. Sample copy $1.50.
Payment: $10/printed page. 2 free author's copies. $1.50 charge for extras.
Terms: Pays on publication for first North American serial rights.
Tips: "We stress literary excellence and read 5,000 mss a year to find an average of 35 stories that we publish. The fiction department is closed from May 1 to October 1 annually, during which period we do not read mss."

NORTH COUNTRY ANVIL, North Country Anvil, Inc. Box 402, Winona MN 55987. Editor: Reggie McLeod. "We publish a variety of material, including articles on lifestyles, social issues, the arts, the environment and fiction. Our audience is made up of people concerned with our themes. Though we include articles from all over the country our readers are mostly in the upper Midwest." Bimonthly. Estab. 1972. Circ. 2,000.
Needs: Literary, contemporary, fantasy, horror, humor. "No stories taking place in Los Angeles or New York City." Accepts 1 ms/issue, 6 mss/year. Length: 1,000-2,000 words.
How to Contact: Send complete ms with SASE. Reports in 2 months. Sample copy $1.50.
Payment: 3 free author's copies plus 1 year subscription. $1 charge for extras.
Terms: Acquires one-time rights.
Tips: "Give the reader some new insights and food for thought concerning society or human nature. Address yourself to an intelligent audience, but keep it simple."

NORTHEAST JOURNAL, Box 235, Annex Station, Providence RI 02901. Editor: Miles D. Parker III. "A journal concerned with publishing a diverse selection of contemporary literature. The primary focus is on poetry, prose and reviews. The average reader is probably a writer or teacher." Biannual. Estab. 1969 (under name of *Harbinger*). Circ. 600.
Needs: "We will consider any work of quality which can stand on its own outside a specialized format." Length: 4,000-10,000 words.
How to Contact: Send complete ms with SASE. Reports in 6 months. Sample copy with 9½x6½ SASE plus $1 postage.
Payment: 2 free author's copies plus 1 year subscription.
Terms: Acquires all rights (negotiable).
Tips: "Just send work--clean, proofed copy."

NORTHWARD JOURNAL, Penumbra Press, Box 340, Moonbeam, Ontario, Canada P0L 1V0. Editor: John Flood. "A magazine of northern arts which publishes northern (thematically) artwork, poetry, fiction, drama." Quarterly. Estab. 1974. Circ. 2,000.
Needs: Literary, ethnic (native peoples). "Note that work must be of the North (Far North)." Buys 6-10 mss/year. Length: 1,500-2,500 words.
How to Contact: Send complete ms with biography. SASE (Canadian stamps) or IRC for ms. Reports in 2 months on mss. Sample copies available.
Payment: $50 and 1 free author's copy. $5 less 40% discount for extras.
Terms: Pays on publication for first North American serial rights.
Tips: "Read and know the magazine. Read as much as you write."

NORTHWEST REVIEW, 369 PLC, University of Oregon, Eugene OR 97403. (503)686-3957. Editor: John Witte. Fiction Editor: Deb Casey. "A general literary review, featuring poems, stories, essays and reviews with a Northwest slant, international scope. For a literate audience in avant-garde as well as traditional literary forms; interested in the important younger writers who have not yet achieved their readership." Published 3 times/year. Estab. 1957. Circ. 2,000.
Needs: Literary, contemporary, translations, experimental. Accepts 3-5 mss/issue, 10-20 mss/year. Length: "Ms longer than 25-30 pages is a disadvantage."

How to Contact: Send complete ms with SASE. Reports in 2 months. Sample copy $2.
Payment: 3 free author's copies. $2 charge for extras.
Terms: Acquires first rights.
Tips: "Persist. Copy should be clean, double-spaced, with generous margins. Careful proofing for spelling and grammar errors will reduce irksome slowing of editorial process."

NOSTOC MAGAZINE, Arts End Books, Box 162, Waban MA 02168. (617)965-2478. Editor: Marshall Brooks. "We publish the best of what we receive. Biannual. Estab. 1973. Circ. 500.
Needs: "We are open-minded." Prefers brief word length.
How to Contact: Query. SASE for ms. Reports in 1 week on queries, 1 month on mss. Sample copy $1.50.
Payment: Free author's copies.
Terms: "Copyright; rights revert to author."
Tips: "All you've got to do is write naturally. Request a sample copy before submitting."

NOT GUILTY (!), The Not Guilty Press, Box 2563, Grand Central Station, New York NY 10163. Editor/Publisher: Derek Pell. "Devoted to absurdist writing and art. Pataphysics and voodoo. Published irregularly. Estab. 1975. Circ. 500.
Needs: Erotic fiction. Accepts 30-40 mss/issue. No preferred length.
How to Contact: Query. SASE for query, ms. Reports in 2 weeks.
Payment: 2 author's copies.
Terms: Acquires first rights.
Tips: "Always enclose SASE. Nothing angers an editor of a little magazine more than to receive a 200 lb. ms (unsolicited) without envelope and proper return postage. *Not Guilty* has always been open to new talent, but we do expect potential contributors to be interested enough to read a copy of the magazine first. Recent contributors: Ahern, Codrescu, Edson, Eluard, Gogarty, Nations, Payack, Sanders, Vance, and Woods."

OBSIDIAN: BLACK LITERATURE IN REVIEW, English Dept., Wayne State University, Detroit MI 48202. (313)577-3213. Editor: Alvin Aubert. Works in English by and about black writers worldwide. Readership: "General ethnic/small press who read *Obsidian* to keep in touch with contemporary black writing." Published 3 times/year. Estab. 1975. Circ. 500 "and slowly growing."
Needs: Ethnic (black). Accepts 7-9 mss/year. Length: 1,500-10,000 words.
How to Contact: Send complete ms with SASE. Reports in 2 months. Sample copy $2.
Terms: Acquires one-time rights.

OCCASIONAL REVIEW, Realities Library, 1976 Waverly Ave., San Jose CA 95122. Editor: R. Soos. Reviews and interviews. Readership: "Directed toward persons looking to buy small press material." Published irregularly. Estab. 1979. Circ. 600.
Needs: Literary, science fiction. "I am specifically looking for fictional interviews with historic poets; however, I will consider other fiction." Accepts 1 ms/issue. Length: 5,000 words maximum.
How to Contact: Query with proposal. SASE for query, ms. Reports in 2 weeks. Sample copy $1.
Payment: 5 free author's copies. 50¢ charge for extras.
Terms: Acquires first rights.
Tips: "Read. Read—Richard Grayson, Franz Kafka, Mark Twain, etc. Be prepared by knowing what is going on and then write. Fiction is not reality."

OCCIDENT, 103 Sproul Hall, University of California, Berkeley CA 94720. Fiction Editor: John Talbot Hawkes. Literary. Quarterly. Estab. 1881. Circ. 1,500.

Needs: Literary, men's, women's, feminist, gay/lesbian, translations. Length: 10,000 words maximum.
How to Contact: Send complete ms with SASE. Reports in 2 months on mss. Sample copy $2.
Payment: 5 free author's copies. $2 charge for extras.
Terms: Acquires first rights.

THE OHIO JOURNAL, Department of English, Ohio State University, 164 W. 17th St., Columbus OH 43210. Editor: William Allen. Theme: "general interest: fiction, poetry, interviews, book reviews, nonfiction, and photo essays. For an educated audience, knowledgeable in literature and the arts, but not of an academic nature." Biannual. Estab. 1973. Circ. 1,000.
Needs: "Any subject." Accepts 1-5 mss/issue. Length: 4,000 words maximum.
How to Contact: Send complete ms with SASE. Reports in 2 months. Sample copy $2.
Payment: Free author's copies. $2 charge for extras.
Terms: "Will reassign rights in exchange for mentioning material first published in *O.J.*"
Tips: "Each contribution is automatically entered into competition for the annual President's Awards: $100 for fiction and $100 for poetry."

OLD HICKORY REVIEW, Jackson Writers Group, Box 1178, Jackson TN 38301. (901)422-2860. Editor: Charles T. Stanfill. Fiction Editor: Dorothy M. Stanfill. Publishes contemporary poetry and fiction of eclectic styles; accepts submissions from all over USA. Biannual (spring and fall). Estab. 1969. Circ. 500.
Needs: Literary, contemporary, fantasy, science fiction. "We like regional contemporary themes with real characterizations if well written. We welcome humor. No pornography." Length: 2,000-3,000 words (prefers 2,500).
How to Contact: Send complete ms with SASE. Reports in 3 weeks. Sample copy $2.
Payment: 2 free author's copies. $2 charge for extras.
Terms: Acquires all rights. "We will assign permission to reprint any time."
Tips: "Try to write honestly about what you know well. Avoid pitching too high at first. Learn the markets by sending out and getting back rejections and buying copies of magazines."

OSIRIS, Box 297, Deerfield MA 01324. Editor: Andrea Moorhead. Fiction Editor: Robert Moorhead. "An apolitical, international journal which prints original texts in English, French, Spanish, and Italian. Material tends to be non-narrative. For an urban intellectual audience. Cuts across cultural boundaries." Semiannual. Estab. 1972. Circ. 1,000.
Needs: Literary, contemporary, experimental fiction in English, Spanish or French. No science fiction material. Length: 1,100-3,000 words.
How to Contact: Query with SASE. Reports in 1 week. Sample copy $1.
Payment: 3 free author's copies. $2 charge for extras.
Terms: "Inquire."
Tips: "Send piece after piece. Do not be offended by rejection slips."

OUTERBRIDGE, The College of Staten Island (CUNY), (A323), 715 Ocean Terr., Staten Island NY 10301. (212)390-7654. Editor: Charlotte Alexander. "We are a national literary magazine publishing mostly fiction and poetry. To date, we have had two special focus issues (the 'urban' and the 'rural' experience; 'Southern' in 1981). For anyone with enough interest in literature to look for writing of quality and writers on the contemporary scene who deserve attention. There probably is a growing circuit of writers, some academics, reading us by recommendations." Biannual. Estab. 1975. Circ. 500-700.
Needs: Literary. "No *Reader's Digest* style; that is, very popularly oriented." Accepts 4-5 mss/issue, 8-10 mss/year. Length: 10-25 pages.
How to Contact: Query. Send complete ms. SASE for query, ms. Reports in 2 weeks on

queries, 2 months on mss. Sample copy $2 for single and $4 for double issues.
Payment: 2 free author's copies. Charges ½ price of current issues for extras to its authors.
Terms: Acquires one-time rights. Requests credits for further publication of material used by *OB*.
Tips: "Read our publication first. Don't send out blindly; get some idea of what the magazine might want. A *short* personal note with biography is appreciated."

PACIFIC POETRY AND FICTION REVIEW, Campanile Press, San Diego State University, San Diego CA 92182. Editor: Dawn Kolokithas. "There is no designated theme. We publish high quality fiction and poetry: academic work meant for, but not restricted to, an academic audience." Biannual. Estab. 1974. Circ. 1,000.
Needs: "We do not restrict or limit our fiction in any way other than quality. We are interested in all fiction, from the very traditional to the highly experimental. Acceptance is determined by the quality of submissions." No preferred length.
How to Contact: Send original with 2 copies. SASE for ms. Reports in 2 months on mss. Sample copy $4.
Payment: 1 free author's copy. $4 charge for extras.
Terms: "Rights revert to author."
Tips: "The more professional a ms is, the better the chance for publication."

PARABOLA, The Society for the Study of Myth and Tradition, 150 5th Ave., New York NY 10011. (212)924-0004. Editor: D.M. Dooling. Fiction Editor: Susan Bergholz. "Mythology, folklore, comparative religion—stories, parables, fairytales retold, original fiction, poetry. We have an open cross-cultured, intelligent but not scholarly approach. Audience is educated, professional, informed book readers interested in stories, myths, folklore, psychology, comparative religion and the arts." Quarterly. Estab. 1976. Circ. 15,000.
Needs: Literary, contemporary, science fiction, fantasy, men's, women's, translations. No humor, romance, erotica, western, inspirational, gothic, horror. Buys 5 mss/issue. Length: 1,000-5,000 words.
How to Contact: Send complete ms with SASE. Reports in 2 months. Sample copy $6.50. Free guidelines.
Payment: $25-$100.
Terms: Pays on publication for first rights, second serial rights, one-time rights.
Tips: "Read previous issues to understand our flavor and direction."

PARAGRAPH: A QUARTERLY OF GAY FICTION, The Antares Foundation, Box 14051, San Francisco CA 94114. Editor: N.A. Diaman. "Quality prose fiction about the lesbian and gay male experience for a predominantly gay audience—both women and men." Quarterly. Estab. 1978.
Needs: Gay/lesbian. "Open to almost any genre as long as it deals in some way with the lesbian or gay male experience. No pornography or propaganda." Accepts 6 mss/issue. No preferred length.
How to Contact: Send complete ms with SASE. Reports in 2 months. Sample copy $3.
Payment: 2 free author's copies. $3 charge for extras.
Terms: Acquires first rights.
Tips: "Read an issue of the magazine first to get an idea what we have published. The first paragraph of a story is very important in drawing the reader into the work. It must attract curiosity, hold attention, impress the reader. Read! Read! Read! Know literature. Understand grammar, syntax, paragraph construction and polish your work before submitting it. Give to the story the integrity it asks of you by being potential art. Avoid the didactic narrative so common to 'movement writing.' We are looking for serious quality fiction, but less that story on the traumas of being gay or explaining what gay is, than the celebration of the complexity of gay life."

THE PARIS REVIEW, 45-39 171st Place, Flushing NY 11358. (212)539-7085. Editor: George A. Plimpton. Fiction Editor: David Evanier. "Fiction and poetry of superlative quality, whatever the genre, style or mode. Our contributors include the most prominent, as well as little-known and previously unpublished writers. Recent issues have included the work of Thomas Disch, Ray Russell, Joseph Brodsky, Sena Jeter Naslund, Bart Midwood, Helen Chasin, Peter Handke, C.W. Gusewelle, Thom Gunn, Jerome Charyn, Phyllis Janowitz and Andre Dubus. 'The Art of Fiction' interview series includes the most important contemporary writers discussing their own work and the craft of writing in general."
Needs: Serious, intense, committed work of boldness and originality, combining excellence of form and content. Buys 2-3 mss/issue. No preferred length.
How to Contact: Send complete ms with SASE. Reports in 2 months on ms. Sample copy $4.20.
Payment: $75-$200. 2 free author's copies. Regular charge for extras.
Terms: Pays on publication for first North American serial rights.
Tips: "Electricity, intensity, the unmistakable roundedness of a fully-realized work of art are what we are seeking. *The Paris Review* has the widest circulation of all the small presses. We are devoted to helping talented, original writers find larger audiences. The Aga Khan Fiction Prize is awarded annually to the best piece of previously unpublished fiction by a relatively unknown writer."

PASSAGES NORTH, Wm. Bonifas Fine Arts Center, Escanaba MI 49829. (906)786-3833. Editor: Elinor Benedict. "The purpose of *Passages North* is two-fold: To stimulate and recognize writing of high quality in the Northern Michigan region and to bring to the same region writing of high quality from other parts of the nation and beyond." Readership: general and literary. Semiannual. Estab. October 1979. Circ. 500.
Needs: Short fiction, sketches. "High quality is our aim. Subjects and genre are open. No excerpts of novels, unless they stand alone in a coherent way. No 'pop' or formula stories." Accepts 6-8 mss/year. Length: 300-2,000 words.
How to Contact: Send complete ms with SASE. Reports in 1 week to several months on mss. Sample copy $1. Guidelines for legal-sized SASE.
Payment: 3 free author's copies. $1 charge for extras.
Terms: Copyrighted; rights revert to author on publication.
Tips: "Be aware of what is happening in contemporary poetry and fiction. Strive for writing that makes readers see, feel, imagine, and experience."

THE PAWN REVIEW, The Pawn Review, Inc., 1162 Lincoln Ave., #227, Walnut Creek CA 94596. Editors: Michael Anderson and Thomas Zigal. "No theme in particular; we publish quality short stories, poetry, photos and articles and reviews by authors from every region, but we have a preference for young Texas writers." Readership: "libraries (which maintain literary magazine collections); individuals and writers (who are interested in contemporary Southwest literature); college English teachers (who read our reviews and articles)." Biannual. Estab. 1976. Circ. 700.
Needs: Literary, contemporary, science fiction, erotica, humor, translations. No religious or juvenile. Accepts 10-12 mss/year. Length: 1,000-25,000 words.
How to Contact: Query or query with clips of published work. SASE for query, ms. Reports in 2 weeks on queries, 2 months on mss. Sample copy $3.
Payment: 1 free author's copy. 25% discount for extras. "We currently are paying authors with CCLM grant: $7-$10/story."
Terms: Acquires first rights. Copyright reverts to author upon publication.
Tips: "We require traditional stories—in the sense that plot and characters interweave to create a unified narrative; otherwise, subject matter and form run from traditonal to avant-garde. Read a copy of the magazine. Avoid overly dramatic or overworked plots and obtuse, trite or arcane images. Strive for clean narrative line and revealing (but not obvious or overstated) characterization. Read the contemporary *and* early masters of short fiction."

PHANTASM, Heidelberg Graphics, Box 3606W, Chico CA 95927. Editor: Larry S. Jackson. "A multi-cultural eclectic magazine publishing current literary events, fiction, poetry, translations, features, guest columns, contemporary art, national literary announcements, photos, book reviews and editorials. The publication is directed toward a literate audience which is primarily comprised of educators, poets, writers, and small press editors. They read *Phantasm* for its exclusive articles, creative writing and literary news." Bimonthly. Estab. 1976. Circ. 1,000.
Needs: Literary, contemporary, men's, women's, feminist, gay/lesbian, erotica, western, mystery, adventure, humor, ethnic (all), translations. Buys 2 mss/issue. Length: 800-5,000 words.
How to Contact: Send complete ms with SASE. Reports in 2 months. Sample copy $2.
Payment: $2 plus 1 free author's copy. Cover price charge for extras.
Terms: Pays on publication for first rights.
Tips: "We do not publish reprints nor do we consider mss simultaneously submitted to other publishers."

PHOEBE, George Mason University, 4400 University Dr., Fairfax VA 22030. Editor: Tim Darby. "A literary magazine publishing well-written short stories of the usual kind; submissions accepted from outside the university. Directed to students at the university and distributed free on campus." Quarterly. Estab. 1970. Circ. 2,500.
Needs: Literary, contemporary, humor. "No action/adventure, science fiction, murder/mystery/detective/spy stories." Length: 6,000 words maximum.
How to Contact: Send complete ms with SASE. Reports in 2 months. Sample copy $3.
Payment: 2 free author's copies. $3 charge for extras.
Terms: Acquires one-time rights.
Tips: "Write well, don't pad, have believable (or unbelievable but entertaining) characters one may want to get involved in."

THE PHOENIX, Morning Star Press, RFD Haydenville MA 01039. Editor: James Cooney. Associate Editors: Louise Michel, Rosa Luxemburg, Emma Goldman. Theme: "A literary magazine actively engaged in spreading mutiny against the ancient crime of war. In alliance with all who defend individual conscience and resist social injustice and an ally of everyone struggling for human rights and the idealities of democracy." Subscriptions come from public libraries and libraries of universities, colleges, and high schools. Quarterly. Estab. 1938. Letterpress printing; thread sewn binding; issues of 352 to 384 pages. Sample issue, $3. Special lowered rates for those who cannot afford regular rates. Free subscriptions to prison libraries, state hospitals and mental institutions.
Needs: Traditional forms of literature: stories, diaries, serialized novels. No length limitations. Complete contents of each issue covered by the *Arts & Humanities Citation Index*.
How to Contact: Send SASE with ms or with inquiry. Reports within 1 to 4 weeks.
Terms: Acquires copyright for protection of all published materials but arranges permission for author to reprint in collections, anthologies, etc.
Tips: "Write truthfully. Write in the way Vincent Van Gogh painted; in the way Franz Schubert wrote music; in the way Bartolemeo Vanzetti & Rosa Luxemburg wrote their letters from prison."

PIEDMONT LITERARY REVIEW, Piedmont Literary Society, Box 3656, Danville VA 24541. (804)799-9049. Editor: Don Conner. "The theme of our publication is human expression through the written word. We publish short stories, essays, and articles. Our publication is directed toward all lovers of literature regardless of their stature in life." Quarterly. Estab. 1976. Circ. 250.
Needs: Literary, contemporary, science fiction, fantasy, humor. No overt sex. Accepts 12-15 mss/year. Length: 1,500 words maximum.
How to Contact: Send complete ms with SASE. Reports in 3 months on mss. Sample copy

$1.50. Guidelines for legal-sized SASE.
Payment: 1 free author's copy. $2.50 charge for extras.
Terms: Acquires one-time rights.
Tips: "Be human. Robots and plastic people turn us off. 'Robots, insensitive and cold, bend plastic people to fit their molds.' Pay close attention to grammar and form. Borrow inspiration from others, not words or ideas." Annual contest.

PIERIAN SPRING, Pierian Press, Box 5; Brandon University, Brandon, Manitoba, Canada R7A 6A9. Editor: Dr. Robert W. Brockway. Fiction Editor: Linda West. "We publish short fiction and poetry, mostly mainstream rather than avant-garde, and try to assist new writers as well as established. Directed toward those who like comprehensible verse and stories with plot and characterization. Most of our readers are writers themselves, but we are attracting others." Quarterly. Estab. 1968. Circ. 300.
Needs: Literary. "The theme of the story could be almost anything, as long as the story has literary quality. We don't like plotless or aimless fiction, stream-of-consciousness, or incomprehensible material. No translations, juveniles." Length: 1,500-3,500 words.
How to Contact: Send complete ms with SASE. Reports in 3 months on mss. Sample copy $1. Free guidelines.
Payment: 3 free author's copies. $1 charge for extras.
Terms: Acquires one-time rights.
Tips: "Get a sample copy and try us. We have a $25 first prize every issue for best short story (and poem), and a book prize for second best."

PIG IRON, Pig Iron Press, Box 237, Youngstown OH 44501. (216)744-2258. Editor: Jim Villani. Fiction Editor: Rose Sayre. "Contemporary literature by new writers, especially concerned with surreal, experimental, fantasy, psychological and satirical material. For college educated young adults—upwardly mobile." Semiannual. Estab. 1975. Circ. 1,000.
Needs: Literary, fantasy. No mainstream. Buys 1-5 mss/issue; 2-10 mss/year. Length: 15,000 maximum.
How to Contact: Send complete ms with SASE. Reports in 3 months. Sample copy $2.50.
Payment: $2/printed page. 2 free author's copies. $2 charge for extras.
Terms: Pays on publication for first North American serial rights.
Tips: "Disregard past models."

THE PIKESTAFF FORUM, Box 127, Normal IL 61761. Also publishes *The Pikestaff Review*. (309)452-4831. Editors: Robert D. Sutherland and James Scrimgeour. "Both *The Pikestaff Forum* and *The Pikestaff Review* are general literary magazines publishing poetry, prose fiction, drama. Readership: "General literary with a wide circulation in the small press world. Readers are educated (but not academic) and have a taste for excellent serious fiction." Published irregularly—"whenever we have sufficient quality material to warrant an issue." Estab. 1977. Circ. 1,000.
Needs: Literary, contemporary with a continuing need for good short stories or novel excerpts. We welcome traditional and experimental works from established and non-established writers. We look for writing that is clear, concise, and to the point; contains vivid imagery and sufficient concrete detail; is grounded in lived human experience; contains memorable characters and situations; and lifts us right out of our chairs. No confessional self-pity or puffery; self-indulgent first or second drafts; sterile intellectual word games or five-finger exercises or slick formula writing, genre-pieces that do not go beyond their form (westerns, mysteries, gothic, horror, science fiction, swords-and-sorcery fantasy), commercially-oriented mass-market stuff, violence for its own sake, or pornography (sexploitation)." Accepts 1-4 mss/issue. Length: From 1 paragraph to 4,000 or 5,000 words.
How to Contact: Query. Send complete ms. SASE for query, ms. Reports in 3 weeks on queries, 3 months on mss. Sample copy $1.
Payment: 3 free author's copies. Cover price less 50% discount for extras.

Terms: Acquires first rights. Copyright remains with author.
Tips: "Read other authors with an appreciative and critical eye; don't send out work prematurely; develop keen powers of observation and a good visual memory; get to know your characters thoroughly; don't let others (editors, friends, etc.) define or 'determine' your sense of self-worth; stick to your guns. Don't be easily discouraged; if you have an eggshell ego you're in for trouble; be willing to learn; outgrow self-indulgence. Develop discipline. Show, don't tell; and leave some work for the reader to do."

PIKESTAFF REVIEW, Box 127, Normal IL 61761. Also publishes *The Pikestaff Forum*. (309)452-4831. Editors: Robert D. Sutherland and James Scrimgeour. Estab. 1977. Circ. 1,000.
Needs: Literary, contemporary. Accepts 1-4 mss/issue. Length: from 1 paragraph to 4,000 or 5,000 words.
How to Contact: Query. Send complete ms. SASE for query, ms. Reports in 3 weeks on queries, 3 months on mss. Sample copy $2.
Payment: 3 free author's copies. Cover price less 50% discount for extras.
Terms: Acquires first rights. "Copyright remains with author."
Tips: See *The Pikestaff Forum*.

PLAINSWOMAN, INC., Plainswoman, Inc., Box 8027, Grand Forks ND 58202. (701)781-4234. Editor: Karla Spitzer. Ficton Editor: Joan Eades. "A feminist, informational publication which publishes fiction and poetry by women or fiction and poetry which deals emphathetically with women by men." Readership: "Mainly women and girls of the Great Plains area who want information concerning women's issues nationally and regionally and like to read fiction and poetry reflecting women's experiences and rural life." Bimonthly. Estab. 1977. Circ. 540.
Needs: Men's, women's, feminist.
How to Contact: Send complete ms with SASE. Reports in 2 weeks. Sample copy $1.
Payment: Acquires all rights.

PLOUGHSHARES, Ploughshares, Inc., Dept. M, Box 529, Cambridge MA 02139. Editor: DeWitt Henry. "Our theme is new writing (poetry, fiction, criticism) that addresses contemporary adult readers who look to fiction and poetry for help in making sense of themselves and of each other." Quarterly. Estab. 1971. Circ. 3,000.
Needs: Literary. "No genre (science fiction, detective, gothic, adventure, etc.), popular formula or commercial fiction whose purpose is to entertain rather than to illuminate." Buys 20+ mss/year. Length: 2,000-6,000 words.
How to Contact: "Query for best time to submit and examine a sample issue." SASE for query, ms. Reports in 3 weeks on queries, 3 months on mss. Sample copy $3.
Payment: $5/page to $50 maximum, plus copies.
Terms: Pays on publication for first North American serial rights.
Tips: "Be familiar with our fiction issues, fiction by our writers and by our various editors (e.g. Rosellen Brown, Tim O'Brien, Jay Neugeboren, Jayne Anne Phillips) and more generally acquaint yourself with the best short fiction currently appearing in the literary quarterlies, and the annual prize anthologies (*Pushcart Prize, O'Henry Awards, Best American Short Stories*). Don't, in submitting, look for help in writing. The professional question is: Can you use this, yes or no? Also realistically consider whether the work you are submitting is as good as or better than—in your own opinion—the work appearing in the magazine you're sending to. What is the level of competition? And what is its volume (in our case, we accept about 1 ms in 200). Never send 'blindly' to a magazine, or without carefully weighing your prospect there against those elsewhere. Always keep a copy of work you submit, and if you don't hear back in reasonable time, withdraw your submission and keep it circulating."

PRAIRIE SCHOONER, University of Nebraska, English Department, 201 Andrews Hall,

Lincoln NE 68588. (402)472-1800. A general literary of stories, poems, essays for a general educated audience who reads for pleasure. Quarterly. Estab. 1927. Circ. 1,500.
Needs: Literary, contemporary, humor, translations. Accepts 4-5 mss/issue. Length: 6,000 words maximum.
How to Contact: Send complete ms with SASE. Reports in 2 months on mss.
Payment: 2 free author's copies, 10 offprints.
Terms: Acquires all rights.
Tips: "Read *Prairie Schooner*. Annual prize of $100 for best fiction.

PRIMAVERA, University of Chicago, 1212 E. 59th St., Chicago IL 60637. (312)752-5655. Editor: Janet Ruth Heller. Fiction Editor: Mary Biggs. Literature and graphics by women: poetry, short stories, essays, photos, drawings. Readership: "a high school (and above) audience who is interested in women's ideas and experiences." Annual. Estab. 1975. Circ. 1,000.
Needs: Literary, contemporary, science fiction, fantasy, feminist, gay/lesbian, humor. "We dislike slick stories packaged for women's magazines." Accepts 6-10 mss/issue. Length: 25 pages maximum.
How to Contact: Send complete ms with SASE. Reports in 5 months on mss. Sample copy $3.90. Guidelines for legal-sized SASE.
Payment: 2 free author's copies. $2.50 charge for extras.
Terms: Acquires first rights.
Tips: "Read the magazine. We publish a wide variety of stories. We like new ideas and techniques."

PRISM INTERNATIONAL, 1874 E. Mall #204, University of British Columbia, Vancouver, B.C., Canada V6T 1W5. (604)228-2514. Editor: John Simmons. Fiction Editor: Bill Gaston. "A journal of contemporary writing—fiction, poetry, drama and translation. *Prism*'s audience is world-wide, as are our contributors." Readership: "Public and university libraries, individual subscriptions, bookstores—an audience concerned with the contemporary in literature." Published 3 times/year. Estab. 1959. Circ. 1,000.
Needs: Literary, contemporary or translations. "Most any category as long as it is *fresh*; e.g., religious/inspirational seldom is, whereas gothic, fantasy, romance, humor, etc. could be. No overtly religious, overtly theme-heavy material or anything more message or category-oriented than self-contained." Buys approximately 25 mss/year. Length: 5,000 words maximum "though flexible for outstanding work."
How to Contact: Send complete ms with International Reply Coupons. Reports in 3 months. Sample copy $4.
Payment: $10/printed page 1 free year's subscription. $4 charge for extras.
Terms: Pays on publication for first North American serial rights.
Tips: "On the one hand, don't try to imitate another writer's style—come up with your own; on the other hand, don't forget that fiction is primarily concerned with the telling of a story, regardless of aesthetic decisions. (Neither of these means not to read contemporary fiction.) Avoid writing three words in a row which have been seen in a row before. Don't forget the SASE, in this case with Canadian stamps or International Reply Coupons."

PROP, Workspace Loft, Inc., 845 Park Ave., Albany NY 12208. (518)489-5059. Rotating editors. "A journal devoted to the informal exchange of ideas that take visual or literary form, or that can only be expressed by a combination of both." Readership: "art and free form literature-oriented." Quarterly. Estab. March 1979. Circ. 1,000.
Needs: Literary, contemporary, fantasy. Length: 1,200 words maximum.
How to Contact: Send complete ms with SASE. Reports in 2 months on mss. Sample copy $1.
Payment: 1 free author's copy. $1 charge for extras.
Terms: Rights remain with author.

Tips: "Our motto is 'Normal Art in a Normal World.' If you agree with this, send us contributions. Be patient if mss are returned. We have a rotating editorship with different tastes. The shorter the better. Mss over the maximum length have no chance."

PROSPICE (WORDS/MUSIC), Aquila Publishing/C.R. Green (Publishers) Ltd., Box 1, Portree Isle of Skye, Scotland 1V51 9BT. Editor/Managing Director: J.C.R. Green. Theme: Literary which introduces new way of talking about the "language" of music for writers, linguists, musicians, composers. Biannual. Estab. 1974. Circ. 5,000.
Needs: Literary, contemporary, translations. Short stories or prose pieces. No "popular" type material. Accepts 10 mss/year. Variable length.
How to Contact: SASE or IRC for query, ms. Reports in 1 month on queries, 2 months on mss. Sample copy $4.
Payment: Free author's copies. Amount "depends on length of submission."
Terms: Makes assignments on a work-for-hire basis.

PTERANODON MAGAZINE, Lieb/Schott Publication, Box 229, Bourbonnais IL 60914. Editors: Lieb/Schott. A literary magazine containing short stories and poetry. Aimed toward poets and writers. Published 3 times/year. Estab. January 1979. Circ. 500.
Needs: Literary, contemporary, science fiction, fantasy, gothic, romance, western, mystery, adventure, humor. Accepts 1-3 mss/issue. Length: 1,200 words preferred.
How to Contact: Send complete ms with SASE. Reports in 3 weeks. Sample copy $2.50. Free guidelines.
Payment: 1-3 free author's copies. $2.50 charge for extras.
Terms: Acquires one-time rights.

THE PUB, Ansuda Publication, Box 123, Harris IA 51345. Editor/Publisher: Daniel R. Betz. "We use fiction different from that published by most other magazines. We allow the author to express his inner concerns and feelings in prose form. We prefer mystery, adventure, science fiction, 'true-to-life.' We don't direct *PUB* to any particular audience. Our readers enjoy it and believe in what we publish and are doing. The majority are college-educated. However, many are blue collar workers." Published 3 times/year. Estab. January 1979. Circ. 200.
Needs: Literary, psychic/supernatural, science fiction, fantasy, horror, mystery, adventure, serialized and condensed novels. "We are looking for honest, straightforward stories. No love stories or stories that ramble on for pages about nothing in particular. Accepts 1-4 mss/issue. Length: No requirement.
How to Contact: Send complete ms with SASE. Reports in 1 month on mss. Sample copy $1. Guidelines for legal-sized SASE.
Payment: 2 free author's copies. Cover price less regular bulk discount for extras.
Terms: Acquires first North American serial rights and second serial rights on reprints.
Tips: "Read the magazine—that is *very* important. If you send a story close to what we're looking for, we'll try to help guide you to exactly what we want."

PULP, 720 Greenwich St., New York NY 10014. Editor/Publisher: Howard Sage. Theme: fiction, poetry, international and intercultural relations for writers/readers interested in various styles of fine writing on all subjects. Biannual. Estab. 1975. Circ. 2,000.
Needs: Literary, ethnic (all), serialized novels, translations (send original). Accepts 8 mss/year. Length: 2,500-7,500 words.
How to Contact: Send complete ms with SASE. Reports in 1 month. Sample copy $1 cash.
Payment: 2 free author's copies. 50¢ charge for extras.
Terms: Acquires first North American serial rights.
Tips: "Brief biography should accompany all submissions. See sample before submitting."

PURPLE PATCH, 106 Walsull Rd., West Doromurch, West Midlands, England. Editor:

Geoff Stevens. "Middle of the road poetry, short stories, reviews, creative writing." Readership: poets, writers, teachers, and students. Quarterly. Estáb. 1976. Circ. 200.
Needs: Literary, contemporary, humor. Length: 12,000-15,000 words maximum.
How to Contact: Send complete ms with SASE or IRC. Reports in 1 month. Sample copy with 6x4 SASE plus IRC.
Terms: Acquires all rights.
Tips: "We aim to help young and new writers as well as the established ones. Will consider anything as long as it is good. We try to be friendly but constructive. Submit sincere, concise, strong, descriptive writing. Shock tactics do not usually impress, but we are open minded to anything that is well written and/or unusual."

QUARTERLY WEST, University of Utah, 312 Olpin Union, Salt Lake City UT 84112. (801)581-3839. Editor: Michael Dobberstein. Fiction Editor: Brian Bedard. "We try to publish a variety of fiction by writers from all over the country. Our publication is aimed primarily at an educated audience which is interested in contemporary literature and criticism." Semiannual. Estab. 1976. Circ. 800.
Needs: Literary, contemporary, translations. Buys 4-6 mss/issue, 10-12 mss/year. No preferred length.
How to Contact: Send complete ms. Cover letters welcome. SASE for query, ms. Reports in 2 months; "sooner, if possible."
Payment: $25-$100.
Terms: Pays on publication for first North American serial rights.
Tips: "Write a clear and unified story which does not rely on tricks or gimmicks for its effects. Don't send more than 2 stories at a time."

QUIXOTE, Quixote Press, Box 70013, Houston TX 77007. Editor: Morris Edelson. Fiction Editor: Melissa Bondy. Theme: "anti-capitalist satire, humor, fiction." Readership: "the disaffected, the discontented. Misery loves company." Monthly. Estab. 1965. Circ. 500.
Needs: "Unconventional material." Accepts 10 mss/year. Length: "shortish."
How to Contact: Query. Reports in 2 weeks. Sample copy $1.50.
Payment: 5 free author's copies.
Terms: Acquires one-time rights.
Tips: "Read our publication. Talk to working class and disenfranchised people. Write about something you care about. We are eclectic but exclude usually the merely clever. We do, however, print the best of what we get, so we often relax from our puritanical leftism."

RAGGED READIN', G.F. Edwards, Box 1461, Lawton OK 73502. (405)248-6870. Editor: G.F. Edwards. A magazine to "encourage book reading and collecting. We publish anything that is book related. For book collectors and sellers." Quarterly. Estab. 1976. Circ. 510.
Needs: Literary, science fiction, fantasy, horror, mystery, adventure, humor, young adult. "No pornographic material." Buys 4 mss/issue, 16 mss/year. Length: 200-1,500 words.
How to Contact: Query. SASE for ms. Reports in 2 weeks on queries, 2 months on mss. Free sample copy.
Payment: 30¢/column inch and 5 free author's copies. Cover price charge for extras.
Terms: Pays on publication for second serial and one-time rights.
Tips: "Look over a copy before submitting material."

RAINCOAST CHRONICLES, Harbour Publishing, Box 119, Madeira Park, B.C., Canada V0N 2H0. Editor: Howard White. Theme: "history and culture of the British Columbia coast." Readership: "primarily residents of the region." Annual. Estab. 1972. Circ. 5,000.
Needs: Literary, adventure, humor. "No fiction not set specifically in a coastal environment." Buys 1-2 mss/issue. Length: 5,000 words maximum.
How to Contact: Query. SASE for query, ms. Reports in 1 month on queries, 2 months on mss. Sample copy $3.95.

Payment: 5¢/word.
Terms: Pays on publication for first North American serial rights.

RARA AVIS MAGAZINE, Books of a Feather Press, Box 3095, Terminal Annex, Los Angeles CA 90051. Fiction Editors: J. De Angelis and A. Rodriquez. A journal of prose and poetry. Estab. 1978.
Needs: Literary, contemporary, experimental, women's, feminist, gay/lesbian, ethnic (chicano), translations.
How to Contact: Send complete ms or query with SASE. Reports in 6 weeks on queries, as soon as possible on mss.
Payment: 2 free author's copies.
Tips: "Read our magazine *first*."

RED CEDAR REVIEW, Red Cedar Press, Dept. of English, Morrill Hall, Michigan State University, East Lansing MI 48824. (517)355-9656. Editor: Paul Murphy. Theme: "literary—poetry, fiction, book reviews, one-act plays, interviews, graphics." Biannual. Estab. 1961. Circ. 500.
Needs: Literary, science fiction. Accepts 3-4 mss/issue, 6-10 mss/year. Length: 500-7,000 words.
How to Contact: Send complete ms with SASE. Reports in 2 months on mss. Sample copy $1.
Payment: 3 free author's copies. $2.50 charge for extras.
Terms: Acquires all rights.
Tips: "Read the magazine and good literary fiction. Annual creative writing contest for MSU students only."

REVISTA/REVIEW INTERAMERICANA, Interamerican University Press, Box 3255, San Juan PR 00936. (809)763-9622. Editor: John Zebrowski. Fiction Editor: Consuelo Villegas. "A scholarly journal oriented to Puerto Rican, Caribbean and Hispanic subjects. Poetry, short stories, reviews. For educated laymen and professionals, including academics and scholars who read us because we're the foremost such journal in this field." Quarterly. Estab. 1971. Circ. 1,200.
Needs: Literary, contemporary, ethnic (Puerto Rican, Hispanic, Caribbean), translations, scholarly, experimental. "We are bilingual and seek mss in either English or Spanish." Accepts 1-2 mss/issue, 4-8 mss/year. Length: 4,000-5,000 (prefers 1,500-2,000) words.
How to Contact: Query. Send complete ms with SASE. Reports in 1 week on queries, 3 months on mss. Free sample copy.
Payment: 25 free author's copies.
Terms: Acquires all rights. "We will revert copyright and pay 50% of reprint rights."
Tips: "Originality, good writing, clean copy are important. We are always short of good fiction and poetry and are always looking for new writers in either Spanish or English."

RFD, Box 127 E, Bakersville NC 28705. Fiction Editor: Ron Lambe. "Published by and for gay men who share a country or rural consciousness. We seek fiction, poetry and articles dealing with gay men living in a non-urban environment. Gay men read the magazine mainly for contact with other gay men in the country and relief from a feeling of isolation." Quarterly. Estab. 1974. Circ. 1,200.
Needs: Gay, adventure. "No sexist or racist material or anything not dealing with gay men or a non-urban consciousness."
How to Contact: Send complete ms with SASE. Reports in 2 months on mss. Sample copy $2 with 9x12 SASE. Free guidelines.
Payment: 2 free author's copies. $2 charge for extras.
Terms: Acquires simultaneous rights.
Tips: "Write for guidelines or read some back issues."

RHINO, The Poetry Forum, 77 Lakewood Pl., Highland Park IL 60035. Editors: Suzanne Brabant and Elizabeth Peterson. "Exists for writers of short prose and poetry—for new writers whose eyes and ears for language are becoming practiced, and whose approaches to it are individualistic. Aimed toward the poetically inclined." Annual. Estab. 1976. Circ. 500.
Needs: "Short prose (sometimes referred to as prose poems—approx. 200 to 500 words). We aim for artistic writing; we also accept the well-written piece of wide or general appeal." Length: 200-750 words.
How to Contact: Send complete ms with SASE. Reports in 1 month on mss. Sample copy $2.
Payment: 1 free author's copy.
Terms: Acquires one-time rights.
Tips: "We recommend you know how to construct a variety of idiomatic English sentences; take as fresh an approach as possible toward the chosen subject; and take time to polish the ms for its keenest effect. We 'read' mss between March 1-June 30. Our publication appears the first week in October of each year."

ROCKBOTTOM MAGAZINE, Mudborn Press, 209 W. De la Guerra, Santa Barbara CA 93101. Editor: Erasmus (Sasha) Newborn. Theme: "contemporary (as opposed to modern) belles-lettres, with emphasis on autobiography. Our basis is humanism in writing; includes translations. For people under 40 (in mind) who wear soft shoes and carry knapsacks: post-moderns. *Rockbottom* is a noncommercial outlet for contemporary writing." Published 3 times/year. Estab. 1976. Circ. 600.
Needs: Literary, contemporary, translations, journals, letters. "We are looking for unique work that is both innovative and readable. Intelligence and the creative use of it are more important to us than any school or topic. We do good work, we expect our authors to do the same. No genre, slick, pulp, ho-hum, inspirational, dull material." Accepts 5 mss/year. Length: 100-90,000 words.
How to Contact: Query with 1-page sample. SASE. Reports in 3 weeks on queries, 2 months on mss. Sample copy $3 with 6x9 SASE plus book-rate postage.
Payment: Short pieces: 2 free author's copies, 50% discount for extras. Book length: contract with 5-10% royalties (average print run 1,000).
Terms: Acquires all rights for book-length; first rights for short pieces.
Tips: "Buy a sample copy. Study the market; most rejections from here are for inappropriate material."

ROOM OF ONE'S OWN, Growing Room Collective, Box 46160, Station G, Vancouver, B.C., Canada V6R 4G5. Editors: Gayla Reid, Margo Dunn, Carroll Klein, Jean Wilson, Eleanor Wochtel. Feminist literary: fiction, poetry, criticism, reviews. Readership: general, non-scholarly. Quarterly. Estab. 1975. Circ. 1,000.
Needs: Literary, women's feminist, lesbian. No "sexist or macho material." Buys 3 mss/issue. Length: 3,000 words preferred.
How to Contact: Send complete ms. SASE or International Reply Coupon for query, ms. Reports in 3 months. Sample copy $2.50 with SASE, IRC.
Payment: $10 plus 2 free author's copies and subscription. $2 charge for extras.
Terms: Pays on publication for first rights.
Tips: "Write well and unpretentiously."

SACKBUT REVIEW, Sackbut Press, 2513 E. Webster Pl., Milwaukee WI 53211. Editor: Angela Peckenpaugh. "Poems, essays, fiction, prose poems for general reading public and writers breaking into small press scene who read for entertainment." Quarterly. Estab. 1978. Circ. 300.
Needs: Literary, contemporary, fantasy, feminist, translations, prose poetry. No "fiction pieces that push way beyond traditional form rendering them somewhat indecipherable.

Nothing that projects a message of extreme depression." Accepts 4 mss/year. Length: 500-1,200 words.
How to Contact: Send complete ms with SASE. Reports in 1 month. Sample copy $1.50.
Payment: Free author's copies.
Terms: Acquires first rights.
Tips: "Read a sample of a prose issue (published annually in the summer) and send something that doesn't depart from my taste. Only send prior to the summer issue. *Sackbut* is a very small magazine with a limited budget and a small circulation. Be aware of this before submitting mss."

ST. MAWR, St. Mawr of Vermont, Box 356, Randolph VT 05060. Editor: J.H. Kennedy. "A tape cassette periodical with emphasis upon experience in jazz sub-culture for persons interested in oral literature and/or jazz music." Quarterly. Estab. 1977.
Needs: Literary, music. "Submissions must be on tape cassettes." Accepts 3 cassettes/issue, 12/year. Length: 500-3,000 words.
How to Contact: Submit tape cassette of reading with SASE. Reports in 2 weeks on mss. Sample copy for 6x9 SASE, tape cassette and 30¢ postage.
Payment: 2 free author's copies. Half price charge for extras.
Terms: Acquires first rights.

SALOME: A LITERARY DANCE MAGAZINE, Ommation Press, 5548 N. Sawyer, Chicago IL 60625. Editor: Effie Mihopoulos. "*Salome* tries to bring together all the arts with a prime focus on literature and dance for all those interested in the arts." Quarterly. Estab. 1976. Circ. 1,000.
Needs: Literary, contemporary, science fiction, fantasy, women's, feminist, gothic, romance, mystery, adventure, humor, serialized novels, translations. "We seek mss relating to the dance. The theme doesn't have to be specifically about dance (one of the characters can be a dancer or choreographer; one of the characters might have a friend who is, etc.) but there must be some sort of dance relation. We seek dance-related fiction of all kinds and lengths, including prose poems." Accepts 20 mss/year. No preferred length.
How to Contact: Send complete ms with SASE. Reports in 1 week. Sample copy $4. 9x12 SASE with 80¢ postage preferred.
Payment: 1 free author's copy. Contributor's rates for extras upon request.
Terms: Acquires first North American serial rights. "Rights revert to author but we retain reprint rights."
Tips: "Write a well-written story or prose poem relating to dance. See a sample copy. Specify fiction interest."

SALT LICK, Box 1064, Quincy IL 62301. Editor: James Haining. A journal of new literature and art. "We publish the best material received regardless of form, style, or content." Published irregularly. Estab. 1969. Circ. 1,500.
Needs: Literary, contemporary, religious/inspirational, psychic/supernatural, science fiction, fantasy, horror, men's, women's, feminist, gay/lesbian, erotica, gothic, adventure, humor, juvenile, young adult, ethnic (open), serialized and condensed novels, translations. Accepts varying number of mss/issue. No preferred length.
How to Contact: Send complete ms with SASE. Reports in 3 weeks. Sample copy $3.
Payment: Free author's copies.
Terms: Acquires first rights, second serial rights.
Tips: "Think. Write what you want to read."

SAMISDAT, Box 129, Richford VT 05476. Editor: Merritt Clifton. Fiction Editor: P.J. Kemp. "*Samisdat* creates the culture of the future. Our stories, poems, and essays discuss the gradual but inevitable and necessary trend toward self-reliance, conservation, live-and-let-live politics, and Transcendentalist philosophy. We're outlaws and activists who direct our

publication to reading eco-freaks, war-resisters, back-to-the-earthers, unschoolers, atheists, anarchists, libertarians—individualists who extend a willing hand from choice, not because Big Brother says so. They read us because we live out the beliefs we espouse and set a good, honest example of the possibilities." Published irregularly. Estab. 1973. Circ. 300-500.
Needs: Literary, contemporary, psychic/supernatural, science fiction, feminist, gay/lesbian, erotica, gothic, western, humor. "We don't use anything belonging to narrow genre confines. Our most frequent fiction contributors write war-stories, gothics, outdoor stories, contemporary, psychic, and religious/inspirational—but the common denominator is that we all write about life, for the living, for those of us daring to choose our own destinies. No material modeled after anything seen in slicks or on bestseller lists. We'll consider anything genuine." Accepts 3-10 mss/issue, 15-50 mss/year. Length: 1,500-5,000 words.
How to Contact: Send complete ms with SASE. Reports in 3 weeks. Sample copy $2.
Payment: 2 free author's copies. Cover price less discount for extras.
Terms: Acquires first rights, one-time rights.
Tips: "Read *Samisdat* first. If you belong here, you'll know it instinctively. Be willing to rewrite and rethink. We prefer short mss. Anything over 3,000 words is usually padded and verbose. We will reprint submissions if so designated. We work hard to help writers and expect writers to work equally hard toward helping themselves. Have a particular reason for submitting to us. We tend to introduce half a dozen new writers per issue. In addition to the magazine we also publish occasional novels and a great many single-author chapbooks presenting longer selections from regular magazine contributors. No photocopies."

SAN JOSE STUDIES, San Jose State University Foundation, 125 S. 7th St., San Jose CA 95152. Editor: Selma Burkom. "A journal for the general, educated reader. Covers a wide variety of materials: fiction, poetry, interviews, interdisciplinary essays. Aimed toward the college-educated common reader with an interest in the broad scope of materials." Tri-annual. Estab. 1975. Circ. 500.
Needs: Literary, contemporary, men's, women's, humor, ethnic (black/Jewish, etc.). Accepts 1-2 mss/issue, 3-6 mss/year. Length: 2,500-5,000+ words.
How to Contact: Send complete ms with SASE. Reports in 2 months.
Payment: 2 free author's copies.
Terms: Acquires first rights.
Tips: "We seldom print beginning writers of fiction." Annual $100 award for best story, essay or poem.

SCHOLIA SATYRICA, University of Southern Florida English Dept., Tampa FL 33620. (813)974-2421. Editor: R.D. Wyly. Fiction Editor: John Iorio. Theme: satirical fiction and poetry for writers and readers interested in modern satire. Biannual. Estab. 1975. Circ. 250.
Needs: Humor, satirical fiction only. Accepts 6 mss/issue, 12 mss/year. Length: 4,000 or less.
How to Contact: Send complete ms with SASE. "Because subscriptions do not cover publication costs, we charge a $1 reading fee to read a ms; or, if the writer subscribes ($3.50/year), there is no reading fee." Reports in 2 months.
Payment: 2 free author's copies. $1 charge for extras.
Terms: Acquires first rights.
Tips: "We stress wit and stylistic excellence. Verbose, drawnout mss immediately returned. Most writers waste words (and space). We are not interested in writing that is not succinct. Also, poor grammar and spelling are simply inexcusable."

SECOND COMING, Second Coming, Inc., Box 31249, San Francisco CA 94131. Editor/Publisher: A.D. Winans. "An international literary quarterly. Publishes only first class prose and fiction from professional writers for a literary audience." Biannual. Estab. 1971. Circ. 1,000+.
Needs: Literary, science fiction, humor. "We do not buy the common or trite story outlines

and first person confessional stories seen elsewhere." Accepts 2-6 mss/issue. Length: 1,500-4,000 (prefers 3,000) words.

How to Contact: Query. Send complete ms. SASE for query, ms. Reports in 1 month. Sample copy $3.

Payment: Free author's copies. Occasionally pays $25 on publication.

Terms: Acquires first rights.

Tips: "See a sample copy of magazine. Be previously published in other literary journals before contacting us. We are a small publishing house, but our reputation is world-wide and we have published some of the best writers practicing their trade today."

SECOND GROWTH: APPALACHIAN NATURE & CULTURE, East Tennessee State University, Box 24,292, ETSU, Johnson City, TN 37614. (615)929-4339. Editor: Frederick O. Waage. Theme: "Environmental and cultural writings of all kinds related to Appalachian area of US for a regional audience seeking information and enjoyment." Quarterly. Estab. 1979.

Needs: Literary, contemporary, adventure, humor, ethnic (regional). "No real limitation on genre but must be of high literary quality." Accepts 1-2 mss/issue. Length: 4,000 words maximum.

How to Contact: Send complete ms with SASE. Reports as soon as possible. Free sample copy for 8½x11 SASE with 60¢ postage.

Payment: 2 free author's copies.

Terms: Acquires first rights.

THE SECOND WAVE, Box 344, Cambridge A, Cambridge MA 02139. Editors: Collective Members. Publication for women interested in feminist issues. Irregular publication. Estab. 1971. Circ. 2,500.

Needs: Women's and feminist. No fiction glorifying traditional women's roles and lifestyles or liberal feminist work (women suceeding in male-defined roles). Buys 2-3 mss/issue. Length: varied.

How to Contact: Query or send complete ms with SASE. Reports in 2 weeks on queries and 1-3 months on mss. Sample copy $2 with 80¢ postage.

Payment: Pays with 2 free author's copies. $2 charge for extras.

Terms: Acquires first rights.

Tips: "Would like to see fiction by women dealing with women's struggles for liberation, women's relationships with other women, rural women, working women, etc. Experimental, mainstream, science fiction, fantasy are all welcome."

SEEMS, Lakeland College, Sheboygan WI 53081. (414)565-3871. Editor: Karl Elder. "We publish fiction and poetry for an audience which tends to be highly literate. People read the publication, I suspect, for the sake of reading it." Published irregularly. Estab. 1971. Circ. 250.

Needs: Literary. Accepts 6-8 mss/issue. Length: 5,000 words maximum.

How to Contact: Send complete ms with SASE. Reports in 2 months on mss. Sample copy $2.50.

Payment: 2 free author's copies. $2.50 charge for extras.

Terms: "Rights revert to author."

Tips: "Read the magazine in order to help determine the taste of the editor."

SEQUOIA MAGAZINE, Storke Publications Bldg., Stanford CA 94305. "Publishes poetry, prose, fiction, interviews with selected authors, b&w photography and artwork; 90% freelance; student writing welcome. *Sequoia* prints fiction and poetry to be read by those outside as well as within the Stanford community. Many of our readers are authors themselves; others are interested in our magazine because of the well-known writers and inter-

viewees featured in past issues." Published 3 times/year. Estab. 1956. Circ. 100.
Needs: "Literary excellence is the primary criterion. We'll consider anything but prefer literary, contemporary, men's, women's, ethnic, translations, and satire." Length: 8,000 words or 20 pp. maximum.
How to Contact: Send complete ms with SASE. Reports in 3 months "during academic year." Sample copy $1.
Payment: 1-2 free author's copies. Contributor's rates on request.
Terms: Acquires all rights.
Tips: "Be persistent. Don't allow your fiction to rely on shock value. Don't submit to a student-run publication during the summer; we generally close down then. In the past, we've had theme issues (translation, student writing) which naturally affect what's selected for a given issue."

THE SEWANEE REVIEW, University of the South, Sewanee TN 37375. (615)598-5931, Ext. 245. Editor: George Core. "A literary quarterly, publishing original fiction, poetry, essays on literary and related subjects, book reviews and book notices for well-educated readers who appreciate good American and English literature." Quarterly. Estab. 1892. Circ. 3,400.
Needs: "Literary, contemporary. No translations, juvenile, gay/lesbian, erotica." Buys 4-8 mss/year. Length: 6,000-7,500 words.
How to Contact: Send complete ms with SASE. Reports in 1 month on mss. Sample copy $4.50.
Payment: $10-$12/printed page. 2 free author's copies. $4.50 charge for extras.
Terms: Pays on publication for first North American serial rights and second serial rights by agreement.
Tips: "Send only one story at a time, with a serious and sensible cover letter."

SEZ/A MULTI-RACIAL JOURNAL OF POETRY & PEOPLE'S CULTURE, Shadow Press, USA, Box 8803, Minneapolis MN 55408. (612)870-0899. Editor/Publisher: Jim Dochniak. "Minnesota's only multi-cultural literary magazine. It places special emphasis on supporting writing which is class-conscious, deals with current social concerns, and, in some way, helps readers focus on building a new human culture. Publishes poetry, journal/diary excerpts, reportage, interviews, articles dealing with current social/cultural concerns and reviews, in addition to fiction. *Sez* is geared toward readers who may not necessarily read or appreciate academic, obscure, or self-indulgent art for art's sake journals. Our audience, therefore, is one which believes that art is for humanity's sake, an audience which reads clear, understandable writing that is meaningful to their lives." Published irregularly. Estab. 1978. Circ. 1,500.
Needs: Literary, contemporary, men's, women's, feminist, gay/lesbian, ethnic (all), folklore, reportage, political. "We favor first-person, subjective narrative in any form. No material that is self-indulgent, cynical, racist, elitist, sexist or degrading." Accepts 1-2 mss/issue. Length: 250-2,500 words.
How to Contact: "Request sample copy with query." SASE for query, ms. Reports in 1 month on queries, up to 6 months on mss. Sample copy $1.50.
Payment: Free author's copies. Cover price less 50% discount for extras.
Terms: Acquires one-time rights.
Tips: "Study sample issues; query with list of possible writing ideas or projects. We try to support younger and unknown writers. Quality is very important. We favor writers and writing from and about the upper Midwest region and writing from Third World writers. Each issue is often focused on a particular theme and, therefore, writers should inquire before sending. Writers east of the Hudson are discouraged from sending."

SHADOWGRAPHS, Shadowgraph Press, Box 546, Newburyport MA 01950. Editor: Richard Summers. "Art literature showcase publishing poetry, fiction, prose, photography, etching, and drawing for writers and artists and/or their public." Published 2-3 times/year. Estab. July 1979. Circ. 500.

Needs: Literary, contemporary, surrealism. "We do not wish to read unfinished work." Accepts 2-3 mss/issue, 5-7 mss/year. Length: 1,500-3,500 (prefers 2,500) words.

How to Contact: Send complete ms and biographical information with cover letter. SASE. Reports in 2 months on mss. Sample copy $2.50.

Payment: 2 free author's copies. $1.50 charge for extras.

Terms: Acquires one-time rights.

Tips: "Look over a sample copy carefully. Get to know us as editors of not *just* fiction. Send us your 'better than life' work. Work must be previously unpublished."

SHEBA REVIEW-THE LITERARY MAGAZINE FOR THE ARTS, Sheba Review, Inc., 2631 Sue Dr., Jefferson City MO 65101. Editor: S.D. Hanson. Theme: to promote the arts and artists in the Midwest; poetry; literary and journalistic prose. For those interested in cultural (artistic) concerns. Biannual. Estab. 1978.

Needs: Literary, contemporary, religious/inspirational, psychic/supernatural, science fiction, fantasy, humor, ethnic, translations. No pornographic material.

How to Contact: Send complete ms with SASE. Reports in 8 months on mss.

Payment: Free author's copies.

Terms: Acquires one-time rights.

Tips: "Review a sample copy prior to submissions." Sponsors contests.

SHENANDOAH: THE WASHINGTON AND LEE REVIEW, Washington and Lee University, Box 722, Lexington VA 24450. (703)463-9111, Ext. 283. Fiction Editor: James Boatwright. Poetry Editor: Richard Howard. "We are a quarterly literary review publishing fiction, poetry, essays, and reviews." Estab. 1950. Circ. 1,200.

Needs: Quality fiction.

How to Contact: Send complete ms with SASE.

Payment: "By arrangement." 2 free author's copies. 75¢ charge for extras.

SIGNALS, Alpha Epsilon Rho, USC College of Journalism, U of South Carolina, Columbia SC 29208. (803)777-6783. Editor: Joe Misewicz. "Geared to articles, mainly nonfiction, about the radio-TV film business, industry, personalities; for university students majoring in broadcasting and professionals employed in radio-TV-film." Quarterly. Estab. 1977. Circ. 2,000.

Needs: Men's women's, humor. "We are not really seeking fiction pieces as much as in-depth nonfiction."

How to Contact: Query. SASE for query, ms. Reports in 3 weeks on queries, 2 weeks on mss. Sample copy with 9x14 SASE plus 50¢ postage.

Payment: 2 free author's copies. $2 charge for extras.

Terms: Acquires first rights.

SILVERFISH REVIEW, Silverfish Press, Box 3541, Eugene OR 97401. (503)344-3535. Co-Editors: Rodger Moody and Randall Roorda. High quality literary material for a general audience. Published 3 times/year. Estab. 1979. Circ. 500.

Needs: Literary. Accepts 1-2 mss/issue.

How to Contact: Send complete ms with SASE. Reports in 1 month on mss. Sample copy $1 with SASE and 80¢ for postage.

Payment: 3 free author's copies.

Terms: Pays on publication; rights revert to author.

THE SILVER UNICORN, Rt.3, Box 181, Richland Center WI 53581. Editor: Hans-Peter Werner. Publishes fantasy and fantasy-related fiction and poetry, as well as art. Some reviews of books. Audience is college-age, mostly avid readers of fantasy and science fiction;

many write or draw in the genre. Semiannual. Estab. 1980. Circ. 75.

Needs: Literary, contemporary, psychic/supernatural, science fiction, fantasy, horror, mystery and adventure. Prefers material with a literary slant, but any good story that is fantasy-related will be considered. No gay/lesbian, erotica, juvenile or translations. Buys 4-5 mss/issue. Length: 2,000-3,000 words preferred.

How to Contact: Send complete ms with SASE. Reports in 1 month on mss. Sample copy $1.

Payment: Free author's copy. $1 charge for extras.

Terms: Pays on publication for first North American serial rights.

Tips: "The emphasis is on characters and action and a well-developed plot. Style should be natural. Believability is essential. Finally, we're looking for the unusual, but not the profane."

SING HEAVENLY MUSE!, Sing Heavenly Muse, Box 14027, Minneapolis MN 55414. (612)822-8713. Editor: Sue Ann Martinson. Women's poetry, prose and artwork specifically for a female literary audience. Semiannual. Estab. 1978.

Needs: Literary, contemporary, fantasy, women's, feminist, mystery, humor, ethnic and translations.

How to Contact: Reports in 1-3 months for queries and mss. Sample copy $2.50.

Payment: 2 free sample copies.

Terms: Pays on publication for first rights.

Tips: "We make specific comments on all mss with suggestions."

SLICK PRESS POETRY/FICTION MAGAZINE, 5336 South Drexel, Chicago IL 60615. Editor: Linda Williams. "To publish unknown writers/artists in the form of chapbooks and to encourage them to broaden their creativity for an audience that can react/relate to images on the page." Quarterly. Estab. 1976. Circ. 2,000.

Needs: Contemporary, fantasy, horror and romance. No fiction longer than 3 pages.

How to Contact: Query first with SASE. Reports in 1 week on queries, 2 weeks on mss.

Payment: Free author's copy.

Terms: Accepts publisher/author six-month rights which revert to author.

Tips: "Write as you talk; make images tight enough to jump off page. Be most concerned about what you have to say."

THE SMALL POND MAGAZINE, Box 664, Stratford, CT 06497. (203)378-4066. Editor: Napoleon St. Cyr. "Features contemporary poetry, the salt of the earth, peppered with short prose pieces of various kinds. The college educated and erudite read it for good poetry, prose and pleasure." Triannual. Estab. 1964. Circ. 300.

Needs: "Rarely use science fiction or formula stories you'd find in *Cosmo, Redbook, Ladies Home Journal*, etc." Buys 10-12 mss/year. Length: 200-2,500 words.

How to Contact: Send complete ms with SASE. Reports in 2 weeks-1 month on mss. Sample copy $2.

Payment: 2 free author's copies. $2/copy charge for extras.

Terms: Pays on publication for all rights.

Tips: "Send for a sample copy first. All mss must be typed. Name and address and story title on front page, name of story on succeeding pages."

SNAPDRAGON, English Dept., University of Idaho, Moscow ID 83843. (208)885-6937. Editors: Ron McFarland, Margaret Newsome and Tina Foriyes. "Poems, artwork, photos and stories are the types of material published for a largely local, Northwest audience of mostly college students or graduates who know the contributors or have been contributors themselves." Biannual. Estab. 1977. Circ. 200.

Needs: Literary, contemporary. "We will consider whatever we see. We don't invite special types of work. No gay, feminist, erotica, science fiction (except literary) or juvenile." Buys 2

mss/issue, 4 mss/year. Length: 200-5,000 words.
How to Contact: Send complete ms with SASE. Reporting time varies on mss; if sent in September or early March there is a rapid response. Sample copy $1.50 and 80¢ for postage.
Payment: Free author's copy, occasionally small cash payments.
Terms: Pays on publication for one-time rights.
Tips: "Be honest, proofread your work, don't overwrite. Write a sound conventional story (without clichés) before you try experimental modes."

SNOWY EGRET, 205 S. Ninth St., Williamsburg KY 40269. (606)549-0850. Editor: Humphrey A. Olsen. Fiction Editor: Dr. William T. Hamilton. Natural history and material related to natural history. Semipopular. Semiannual. Estab. February 1922. Circ. 400.
Needs: Literary and translations, stories that are natural history related. Buys 1-2 mss/issue, 3-4 mss/year. Length: 3,000-10,000 words.
How to Contact: Query with SASE. Reports in 2 weeks on queries, 2 months on mss. Sample copy $2.
Payment: Pays $2/magazine page. Free author's copy. $1.50 per copy up to 5 extra.
Terms: Pays on publication for first North American serial rights.
Tips: "Write the kind of fiction we are looking for. Be sure material is related to natural history and has the element of surprise."

SOJOURNER, Sojourner, Inc., 143 Albany St., Cambridge MA 02139. (617)661-3567. Editor: Martha Thurber. Fiction Editor: Dorinda Hale. "We are the New England women's journal of news, opinions and the arts. We publish nonfiction, fiction, poetry, reviews (books, music, theatre, dance and cinema) on topics of interest to women." Monthly. Estab. Sept. 1975. Circ. 30,000.
Needs: Literary, contemporary, religious/inspirational, psychic/supernatural, science fiction, fantasy, women's, feminist, gay/lesbian, gothic, romance, western, mystery, adventure, humor, juvenile, young adult, ethnic and translations (unpublished works). "We consider for publication any fiction that is not racist, sexist or homophonic." Length: 8-10 pages, double-spaced, 60 characters wide.
How to Contact: Send complete ms with SASE. Sample copy $1.25. Free guidelines.

SOME OTHER MAGAZINE, Robert Richman, 47 Hazen Ct., Wayne NJ 07470. Editors: Robert Richman and Barry Schwabsky. Fiction, confession and poetry magazine for literary types. Biannual. Estab. December 1978. Circ. 200.
Needs: Literary, contemporary, erotica, confession and translations. Buys 1 ms/issue, 2 mss/year. Length: 500-1,000 words.
How to Contact: Send complete ms with SASE. Reports in 1 month on mss. Free sample copy.
Payment: Pays in contributor's copies.
Terms: Pays on publication; rights revert to author.
Tips: "Be bold, funny, parodic. Avoid seriousness. Don't be shocking or avant-garde just for the sake of being so."

SONORA REVIEW, University of Arizona, Department of English, Tucson AZ 85721. Editor: Steven Schwartz. Fiction Editors: Carol Nowotny-Young, Frank Miele and Rick Kaneen. *The Sonora Review* publishes short fiction and poetry of high literary quality. Semiannual. Estab. August 1980. Circ. 500-700.
Needs: Literary. "We are open to a wide range of stories with accessibility and vitality being important in any case. We're not interested in genre fiction, formula work." Buys 4-6 mss/issue. Length: open, though prefers work under 25 pages.
How to Contact: Send complete ms with SASE. Reports in 1 month on mss. Sample copy $3.
Payment: 3 free author's copies. $2 charge for extras. Annual cash prizes.

Terms: Acquires first North American serial rights.
Tips: "We ask that writers send us mss they have confidence in. All mss are read carefully and we try to make brief comments if time permits. Our hope is that an author will keep us interested in his or her treatment of a subject by using fresh details and writing with an authority that is absorbing."

SORCERER'S APPRENTICE, Flying Buffalo, Inc., Box 1467, Scottsdale AZ 85252. Editor: Elizabeth Danforth. Magazine devoted to role-playing games and fantastic literature for those who enjoy science fiction, fantasy, dedicated lovers of war games. Quarterly. Estab. 1979. Circ. 3,000.
Needs: General fantasy, heroic fantasy, swords and sorcery, possibly science fiction. "We don't want anything that could possibly be considered mainstream fiction. No fictionalized games you have played; no religion or pornography." Buys 1 ms/issue. Length: 1,000-5,000 words.
How to Contact: Send complete ms with SASE. Reports in 1 month on mss. Sample copy $2.25 with 3rd class SASE ($1 postage).
Payment: Pays 1-5¢/word.
Terms: Pays on publication for first North American serial rights. Simultaneous and photocopied submissions OK.
Tips: "Our primary interest is new slants on gaming, especially fantasy role-playing gaming. Must be acquainted with games such as Tunnels and Trolls, Dungeons and Dragons, etc. Competition here is tough. Established writers take precedence over beginners."

SOUNDINGS EAST, English Dept., Salem State College, Salem MA 01970. (617)745-0556. Advisory Editor: Claire Keyes. "No theme necessarily. Mainly a college audience, but we also distribute to libraries throughout the country." Biannual. Estab. 1973. Circ. 2,000.
Needs: Literary and contemporary. No juvenile. Publishes 2 mss/issue. Length: 2,500-10,000 words. "We are open to short pieces as well as to long works."
How to Contact: Send complete ms with SASE only between September and March. Reports in 2 months on mss. Sample copy $1.
Payment: 2 free author's copies.
Terms: All publication rights revert to authors.
Tips: "The writer should read a few of our issues to get a sense of the range of fiction we publish. The mss should be clean-that is, clearly typed with no hand-written revisions."

SOURCE, Queens Council on the Arts, 161-04 Jamaica Ave., Jamaica NY 11432. (212)291-1100. Editor: Conciere Taylor. Fiction Editor: Dennis Straus. A literary magazine of fiction, poetry, criticism, essays, book reviews, interviews, etc., for college educated, those interested in quality writing. Annual. Estab. 1976. Circ. 600.
Needs: Literary, contemporary, feminist, gay/lesbian and translations. "We will take horror, fantasy, science fiction, if they are done in a literary vein. We are not interested in slickly done magazine style fiction. No gothic or romance." Length: 2,500 words maximum.
How to Contact: Send complete ms with SASE. Reports in 4-6 months on mss. Sample copy $1.50.
Payment: Free author's copy. $1 charge for extras.
Terms: Acquires one-time rights.

THE SOURCE: A Supportive Magazine, Vanilla Press, 2400 Colfax Ave. S., Minneapolis MN 55405. (612)374-4726. Editor: Jean-Marie Fisher. Fiction Editor: Nell Morningstar. "Self-help/humanist concerns; a directory of helping services in the upper Midwest. Persons interested in alternatives to living/lifestyles read our magazine for its refreshing point of view." Monthly. Estab. 1978. Circ. 30,000.
Needs: Literary, contemporary, some psychic/supernatural, men's, women's, feminist, gay/lesbian, humor, ethnic and serialized novels. "Must fit the format of the magazine in

content, i.e., humanist. Rarely do we accept so-called 'art for art's sake.' No preachy, egocentric, abstruse, pseudointellectual, violence-is-the-answer, sex-is-the-whole-answer, non-Midwestern regional inside jokes that would leave Midwestern readers with their noses pressed against the window." Length: 1,000 words or booklength.

How to Contact: Query with sample page that need not be returned with SASE. "Don't send us a ms if you can't bear to wait." Sample copy 50¢.

Payment: Pays $20-25 per appearance.

Terms: Pays on publication for first rights on short stories.

Tips: "Author's direction is next to impossible to discern if our publication has not been read (recent issues). New material only (no reprint). Interested in the innovative, but author should ask himself/herself: Do I really buy this myself, and why?"

SOUTH CAROLINA REVIEW, Clemson University, Clemson SC 29631. (803)656-3457. Editor: R.C. Calhoun. Managing Editor: F.L. Day. Semiannual. Estab. 1967. Circ. 500.
Needs: Literary, contemporary, humor and ethnic.
How to Contact: Send complete ms with SASE. Reports in 1 month on mss. Sample copy $1.
Payment: Pays in contributor's copies.

SOUTH DAKOTA REVIEW, University of South Dakota, Box 111, University Exchange, Vermillion SD 57069. (605)677-5220. Editor: John R. Milton. Emphasis is on the West and its writers, but will accept mss from anywhere. Issues are generally fiction and poetry with some literary essays. Specific needs vary according to budget and other conditions. The magazine is directed toward a literary audience, who reads the magazine because of its quality. Quarterly. Estab. 1963. Circ. 800.
Needs: Literary, contemporary.
How to Contact: Send complete ms with SASE. Reports in 3 weeks on mss. Sample copy $1.50.
Payment: Amount of free author's copies varies with length of ms. $1.50-$2 charge for extras.

SOUTHERN HUMANITIES REVIEW, Auburn University, 9090 Haley Center, Auburn AL 36830. Co-Editors: D.K. Jeffrey and Barbara A. Mowat. "We publish poetry, fiction, reviews, and articles on topics in the humanities. Our fiction has ranged from very traditional in form and content to very experimental. Literate, college-educated audience. We hope they read it for enlightenment and pleasure both." Quarterly. Estab. 1968. Circ. 750.
Needs: Literary, contemporary, fantasy, humor, translations and parts of novels. "We have very few limits. We'll read everything." Accepts and prints 2 mss/issue, 8 mss/year. Length: 500-5,000 words.
How to Contact: Send complete ms with SASE. Reports in 1 month on mss. Sample copy $2.
Payment: 5-10 free autror's copies. $2.50 charge for each extra.
Terms: Pays on publication for first rights.
Tips: "Send us the ms with SASE. If we like it, we'll take it or we'll recommend changes. If we don't like it, we'll tell the author why and send it back. Read the journal. Send a typewritten, clean copy carefully proofread. We also award annually the Hoepfner Prize of $100 for the best essay or short story of the year."

THE SOUTHERN REVIEW, Louisiana State University, Drawer D, University Station, Baton Rouge LA 70893. (504)388-5108. Editors: Donald E. Stanford and Lewis P. Simpson. A literary publishing critical essays, poetry and fiction for the highly intellectual audience. Quarterly. Estab. 1935. Circ. 3,000.
Needs: Literary and contemporary. "We emphasize style and substantial content. No mystery, fantasy or religious mss." Buys 3-4 mss/issue. Length: 2,000-10,000 words.

How to Contact: Send complete ms with SASE. Reports in 2 months on mss. Sample copy $2.00.
Payment: Pays $12-20/printed page. 2 free author's copies.
Terms: Pays on publication for first North American serial rights. "We transfer copyright to author on request."
Tips: "Develop a careful style with characters in depth."

SOUTHWEST REVIEW, SMU Press, Southern Methodist University, Dallas TX 75275. (214)692-2263. Editor: Margaret L. Hartley. Fiction Editors: Margaret L. Hartley and Charlotte T. Whaley. "*Southwest Review* embraces almost every area of adult interest, with emphasis on short fiction, poetry, literary criticism, essays on contemporary affairs, and book reviews. The majority of our readers are college-educated adults, who wish to stay abreast of the latest and best in contemporary fiction, poetry, literary criticism, and books in all but the most specialized disciplines." Quarterly. Estab. 1915. Circ. 1,250.
Needs: Literary and contemporary. "No sentimental, religious, western, poor science fiction, pornographic, true confessions, mysteries, juvenile, serialized novels or condensed novels." Length: 3,000-5,000 words.
How to Contact: Send complete ms with SASE. Reports in 3 months on mss. Sample copy $1. Free guidelines.
Payment: Pays ½¢/word, plus 4 free author's copies.
Terms: Pays on publication for one-time rights.

SOUTHWESTERN REVIEW, University of Southwestern Louisiana, Box 44691, Lafayette LA 70504. (318)264-6908. Editor: Steve Glassman. Fiction Editor: Mary Jo Pendleton. "Fiction of all sorts but restricted to local authors." Semiannual. Estab. 1975. Circ. 4,000.
Needs: Literary. Buys 10-20 mss/year. Length: 1,500-3,500 words.
How to Contact: "Query first. God only knows when we can report." Free sample copy with 9x11 SASE.
Payment: 2 free author's copies.
Terms: Acquires first rights.
Tips: "It is unlikely we will take your ms unless you are from our region. But who knows? You might have something we think our readers will find interesting. That something will have to be a local theme, topic, etc."

THE SPIRIT THAT MOVES US, The Spirit That Moves Us, Inc., Box 1585, Iowa City IA 52244. (319)338-5569 and 354-7061. Editor: Morty Sklar. Publishes fiction, poetry and essays. "We want feeling and imagination for lovers of real, not academic writing, those who care for work coming from the human experience." Semiannual. Estab. 1975. Circ. 800.
Needs: Literary and contemporary (not academic), men's, women's, feminist, gay/lesbian, humor, ethnic and translations. No sensational or academic. Buys 1-2 mss/issue. Length: 7,000 maximum words.
How to Contact: Query or send couple of pages of ms and SASE. Reports in 1 week on queries, 1 week to 1 month on mss. Sample copy $2.
Payment: 2 free author's copies. 40% discount on extras.
Terms: Pays on publication for first rights.
Tips: "We will consider any style, school, or what have you, as long as the work has those qualities. We're small but good and well-reviewed. Send the work you love best. Write from yourself and not from what you feel is the fashion or what the editor wants. This editor wants what you want if it has heart, guts, imagination and skill. Read a copy of the magazine you'll be submitting work to. Don't rely on your writing for money unless you're in it for the money. Have time to write, as much time as you can get (be anti-social if necessary). We have published a 504 page volume of fiction, poetry, essays and graphics entitled *Editor's Choice: Literature & Graphics From The US Small Press, 1965-1977*. If anything can succinctly express our taste and needs, it will."

STAND, US address: c/o 16 Forest St., Norwell MA and 19 Haldane Terrace, Newcastle upon Tyne, Newcastle, England 812614. Editors: Jon Silkin and David McDuff. Fiction Editors: Lorna Tracy (England) and Jim Kates (US). "Our audience is the common reader, in the sense that Virginia Woolf and Samuel Johnson used the term. Presumably readers' minds and sensibilities are stimulated and that is why they read the magazine." Quarterly. Estab. 1952. Circ. 4,500.

Needs: Literary, contemporary and translations. "We're all for humor if it provokes *thoughtful* laughter. We are just as interested in work by women as by men and work that makes a subtle argument for a case. Don't want propaganda, mindless violence or any 'throw-away' stories, any tricky endings, or dreary 'social realism,' or dreary 'art-about-art,' for that matter. No formula fiction; what we want is good writing, with a high degree of internal organization. Plots and 'themes' don't interest us." Buys 15-20 mss/year. Length: 10,000 words.

How to Contact: Send complete ms with SASE. Reports in 2 weeks on mss. Sample copy $2.50.

Payment: Pays $25/1,000 words. Free author's copy. $2.50 less 1/3 charge for extras.

Terms: Pays on publication for first North American serial and first British serial rights.

Tips: "Write well and honestly. Study this magazine before sending work; don't send us work that's been taken by some other publication, or that is under consideration elsewhere. We report promptly. Use the American address."

STARDANCER, 415 3rd St., #3, Brooklyn NY 11215. (212)768-7841. Co-Editors: Chael Graham and Michael S. Prochak "We publish essentially new and evolutionary art. Mostly poetry and criticism. For students, forward thinkers and lovers of literature, writers and others who crave the new, the powerful, and the lasting human quality in writing." Biannual. Estab. 1976. Circ. 500.

Needs: Literary, contemporary and translations. Interested in prose poems and experimental fiction as well as worthy traditional forms. "Nothing derivative, trite, formulaic, or muttered." Buys 1-2 mss/issue. Length: 5,000 words.

How to Contact: Query with SASE. Reports in 1 month on queries, 2 months on mss. Sample copy $4.

Payment: Pays $10.

Terms: Pays on publication for first rights.

Tips: "Read a copy carefully and have clear purpose to your writing. We abhor commercialism and literary jingoism. Be craft-wise. No mss read without query. Be sure you know where you've submitted and why."

STONE SOUP, THE MAGAZINE BY CHILDREN, Children's Art Foundation, Box 83, Santa Cruz CA 95063. (408)426-5557. Editor: Gerry Mandel. Theme: Stories, poems, book reviews, and art by children up to age 12. Readership: children, librarians, educators. Published 5 times/year. Estab. 1973. Circ. 8,000.

Needs: Literary, contemporary, science fiction, fantasy, feminist, mystery, adventure, juvenile. Accepts approx. 15 mss/issue. No preferred length.

How to Contact: Send complete ms with SASE. Reports in 2 months on mss. Sample copy $1.50. Free guidelines.

Payment: 2 free author's copies. $1 charge for extras.

Terms: Acquires all rights.

STORY QUARTERLY, Story Quarterly, Inc., 820 Ridge Rd., Highland Park IL 60035. (312)831-4684. Co-Editors: F.R. Katz, Janine Warsaw, Dolores Weinberg. A magazine devoted to the short story and committed to a full range of styles and forms. Also features interviews with writers. Readership: "literate readers and writers of short fiction who read us for our quality and variety." Published irregularly. Estab. 1975. Circ. 3,000.

Needs: Literary, contemporary, women's, humor, self-contained novel excerpts. "No slick women's magazine material with contrived endings. No science fiction, religious, psychic, horror, romantic, juvenile, or young adult material." Accepts 12-15 mss/issue, 30-50 mss/year. Length: 5,000 words maximum.

How to Contact: Send complete ms with SASE. Reports in 2 months on mss. Sample copy $3.00 with #75 clasp envelope plus 80¢ postage.

Payment: 3 free author's copies. $2 charge for extras.

Terms: Acquires one-time rights. Copyright reverts to author after publication.

Tips: "Have sensibility, a mastery of language and technique, relationships, and a non-imitative, fresh voice."

STRAIGHT AHEAD INTERNATIONAL, Time Capsule, Incorporated, Box 1185, New York NY 10116. (212)675-7197. Editor: Martha Cochrane. Theme: "fiction, poetry, articles, profiles, book reviews, novel excerpts by women of all ages; also photographs, line drawings. Work from all countries/continents for people of all ages, races, worldwide." Quarterly. Estab. Spring 1980. Circ. 10,000.

Needs: Literary, contemporary, fantasy, women's, feminist, gay/lesbian, erotica, confession, romance, western, mystery, adventure, humor, juvenile, young adult, ethnic (all), serialized and condensed novels, translations. No science fiction, diatribes. Accepts 10 mss/issue, 40 mss/year. Length: 500-3,500 words.

How to Contact: Send complete ms with SASE. Reports in 1 month. Sample copy $1 with 10x13 SASE.

Payment: 1 free author's copy. $1 charge for extras.

Terms: Acquires one-time rights.

Tips: "A showcase and forum for beginning as well as established women writers and artists. Work should be clearly written with passion and integrity and address itself to real people in real human situations. No self-conscious esoteric literary work directed at a small audience will be published." Sponsors contests.

STROKER MAGAZINE, 129 2nd Ave. #3, New York NY 10003. Editor: Irving Stettner. "An un-literary literary review interested in sincerity, verve, beauty, humor and anger. For an intelligent audience—non-academic, non-media dazed—in the US and throughout the world." Published 3-4 times/year. Estab. 1974. Circ. 500.

Needs: Literary, contemporary. No academic material. Length: "3-5 pages preferred but not essential."

How to Contact: Send complete ms with SASE. Reports in 6 weeks. Sample copy $1.50.

Payment: 2 free author's copies. $1 charge for extras.

Terms: Acquires one-time rights.

THE SUN, The Sun Publishing Company, Inc., 412 W. Rosemary St., Chapel Hill NC 27514. (919)942-5282. Editor: Sy Safransky. "A magazine of ideas. We publish all kinds of writing—fiction, articles, poetry. Our only criteria are that the writing make sense and enrich our common space. We direct *The Sun* toward interests which move us, and we trust our readers will respond." Monthly. Estab. 1974. Circ. 10,000.

Needs: Open to all fiction. Accepts 1 ms/issue. Length: 5,000 words maximum.

How to Contact: Send complete ms with SASE. Reports in 1 month. Free sample copy.

Payment: 5 free author's copies and a complimentary subscription.

Terms: Acquires one-time rights.

SUN DOG, Florida State University Poetry Arts Coop, 330 Williams, Florida State University, Tallahassee FL 33706. (904)644-4230. Editor: Eugenie Nable. Fiction Editor: Laura Newton. Theme: "The illimitable vision of human possibility in poetry, fiction, photography, and graphic art for a small press audience." Biannual. Estab. Spring 1979. Circ. 2,500.

Needs: Literary, contemporary. "No pornography/gratuitous violence." Accepts 3-5 mss/issue. Length: 2,000-5,000 words.

How to Contact: Send complete ms with SASE. Reports after February 1 for spring issue. Sample copy $3.
Payment: 1 free author's copy. $3 charge for extras.
Terms: Acquires one-time rights which then revert to author.

SUN & MOON: A JOURNAL OF LITERATURE & ART, Sun & Moon Press, 4330 Hartwick Rd. #418, College Park MD 20740. (301)864-6921. Editor/Publisher: Douglas Messerli. Publishes "high quality contemporary—primarily experimental—fiction, poetry, art, criticism, and drama. Our major audiences are contemporary writers, critics, artists, university professors and students." Published 3 times/year. Estab. 1976. Circ. 700.
Needs: Contemporary, feminist, gay/lesbian, confession, translations. "We publish all types of fiction, including parts of novels, epistolary works, travel guides, anatomies, and other genres. However, we are primarily interested in serious contemporary (i.e. postmodern) fiction. We are not interested in traditional modern fiction unless it is of exceptionally high quality." Accepts 3-4 mss/issue, 9-12 mss/year. No preferred length.
How to Contact: Do not query. Send complete ms with SASE. Reports in 3 weeks. Sample copy $4.50 with SASE plus 80¢ postage.
Payment: 2-3 free author's copies. Cover price less 20% discount for extras.
Terms: Acquires first North American serial rights.
Tips: "We are open equally to all writers, established or beginning."

SUNRISE, RAS Communications, #204-3620 52nd Ave., Red Deer, Alberta, Canada T4N 4J5. Editor/Publisher: Randy Stables. "No specific theme. Magazine of poetry, fiction, art, and cartoons for an audience of writers, poets, artists, and others interested in literary and visual art." Annual. Estab. 1978. Circ. 200.
Needs: Literary, contemporary, science fiction, fantasy, gothic, western, mystery, adventure, humor, juvenile, young adult, serialized and condensed novels, translations, experimental fiction. Accepts 3 mss/issue, 12 mss/year. Length: 500-4,000 words.
How to Contact: Send complete ms with SASE. Reports in 2 months on mss. Free sample copy.
Payment: 1 free author's copy. $2 charge for extras.
Terms: Acquires simultaneous rights, first rights, second serial rights, first North American serial rights.
Tips: "Write a good strong, well-researched story."

SUN TRACKS: AN AMERICAN INDIAN LITERARY SERIES, Sun Tracks, Department of English, University of Arizona, Tucson AZ 85721. Co-Editors: Larry Evers and Cynthia Wilson. "We publish material that comes from or draws on native American literary traditions. For a literary audience, those interested in American Indian affairs." Annual. Estab. 1971. Circ. 1,500.
Needs: Ethnic (American Indian) only. No preferred length.
How to Contact: Query. SASE for query, ms. Reports in 2 weeks on queries, 1 month on mss. Sample copy $10.
Payment: 2 free author's copies. Charge for extras: "our cost."
Terms: Acquires first rights.

SYNERGY MAGAZINE, Energy Earth Communications, Box 1141, Galveston TX 77553. (713)762-8018. Editor: Ahmos Zu-Bolton. Fiction Editor: Harryette Miller. News-oriented publication which also publishes literary pieces. Quarterly. Estab. 1974. Circ. 10,000.
Needs: Literary. Buys 1-2 mss/issue; 4-6 mss/year.
How to Contact: Send complete ms with SASE. Sample copy for $3.50.
Payment: Varies.
Terms: Pays on publication for first rights.
Tips: "Send good literary mss, something new."

SYZYGY, Cincinnati Women's Press, 3901 Ledgewood Dr., Cincinnati OH 45229. Editor: Dorothy Weil. "All themes acceptable. Short prose fiction only. For a literate audience, interested in development of fiction and new writers." Biannual. Estab. 1976. Circ. 500.
Needs: Literary, contemporary, fantasy, men's, women's, feminist.
How to Contact: Send complete ms with SASE. Reports in 3 months. Sample copy for fee and SASE.
Payment: 2 free author's copies. $3 charge for extras.
Tips: "Write a good story. We are interested in quality."

TAMARISK, 319 S. Juniper St., Philadelphia PA 19107. (201)327-7469. Editors: Dennis Barone and Deborah Ducoff-Barone. "A literary magazine of fiction, poetry, photography, reviews for an educated literary audience." Biannual. Estab. 1975. Circ. 300.
Needs: Literary. Accepts 1-2 mss/issue, 2-4 mss/year.
How to Contact: Query only. Reports immediately. Sample copy $1 with 8x11 SASE plus 28¢ postage.
Payment: 3 free author's copies. $1 charge for extras. "We usually pay small amounts."
Terms: Acquires one-time rights.
Tips: Looks for clarity and innovation in mss.

TEMPEST, Earthwise Publications, Inc., Box 680536, Miami FL 33168. Editor: Barbara Holley. Fiction Editor: Kaye Carter. A journal with avant-garde theme. Biannual. Estab. 1979. Circ. 200.
Needs: Science fiction, mystery. No pornography or religious submissions.
How to Contact: Query with clips of published work. SASE for query, ms. Reports in 1 month. Sample copy $2.
Payment: $5-$25.
Terms: Pays on publication for first North American serial rights.
Tips: "No mss from June 30-Sept. 5, please."

THE TEXAS REVIEW, Sam Houston State University Press, Huntsville, TX 77341. (713)294-1423. Editor: Paul Ruffin. Fiction Editor: Phillip Parotti. "We publish top quality poetry, fiction, articles, interviews, and reviews for a general audience." Semiannual. Estab. 1976 (as *Sam Houston Literary Review*). Circ. 500.
Needs: Literary, contemporary. "We are eager enough to consider fiction of quality, no matter what its theme or subject matter. No juvenile fiction." Accepts 4 mss/issue. Length: 500-10,000 words.
How to Contact: Send complete ms with SASE. Reports in 2 months on mss. Sample copy $2.00.
Payment: Free author's copies plus one year subscription.
Terms: Acquires all rights.
Tips: "We publish many new writers."

13TH MOON, 13th Moon, Inc., Drawer F, Inwood Station, New York NY 10034. (212)569-7614. Editor: Ellen Marie Bissert. "*13th Moon* is a literary magazine publishing quality fiction by women with a feminist perspective. The audience is intelligent, sophisticated, and interested in women's issues and culture." Biannual. Estab. 1973. Circ. 4,000.
Needs: Feminist, lesbian, Third World, working class, "No traditional, commercial women's fiction." Accepts 2 mss/issue; 4-10 mss/year. Length: 4,000-15,000 words.
How to Contact: Send complete ms with SASE. Reports "between 1 week and 6 months depending on mss." Sample copy $2.25 plus $1 postage.
Payment: Free author's copies.
Terms: Acquires first rights.
Tips: "Read the magazine before submitting work."

THE THREEPENNY REVIEW, Box 335, Berkeley CA 94701. (415)849-4545. Editor: Wendy Lesser. Publishes "literature and performing arts reviews, essays, fiction, poetry, and other reviews for a wide-ranging audience including anyone interested in the arts." Quarterly. Estab. winter/spring 1980. Circ. 10,000.
Needs: Short fiction. Accepts 1 ms/issue; 4 mss/year. Length: 3,000-5,000 words.
How to Contact: Query. SASE for query, ms. Reports in 2 weeks on queries, 2 months on mss. Sample copy $1 with 9x12 SASE plus 70¢ postage. Guidelines for legal-sized SASE.
Payment: 10 free author's copies. $1 charge for extras.
Terms: Acquires first rights.

THUNDER MOUNTAIN REVIEW, Thunder City Press, Box 11126, Birmingham AL 35202. Editor/Publisher: Steven Ford Brown. "A magazine of poetry, translations and reviews; will concentrate on special kinds of fiction, especially experimental and the prose poem form, etc. For the college level, university, literary type audience, the general public in the future." Biannual. Estab. 1979. Circ. 500.
Needs: Literary, contemporary, translations. "No junk or beginner pieces." Accepts 1 ms/issue, 1-2 mss/year. Length: 10,000 words maximum.
How to Contact: Query. SASE for query, ms. Reports in 2 weeks. Sample copy $3.
Payment: Free author's copies.
Terms: Acquires first North American serial rights.
Tips: "Read the magazine and be an accomplished writer. It is hard to break in the first time. There really is a need for good fiction these days and many editors are unable to find it." Sometimes sponsors awards.

TIME TO PAUSE, Inky Trails, Box 345, Middleton ID 83644. Editor: Pearl Kirk. A review of prose and poetry. Biannual. Estab. 1970. Circ. 150.
Needs: Literary, contemporary, religious/inspirational, psychic/supernatural, fantasy, romance, western, mystery, adventure, humor, juvenile, young adult, novels. No horror, gay/lesbian, erotica, profanity. Accepts 5-8 mss/year in *Time to Pause* and *Inky Trails*. Length: 5,500 words maximum.
How to Contact: Send complete ms with SASE. Reports in 6 weeks. Sample copy $3 with 9x12 or 10x13 SASE plus 70¢ postage. Guidelines for legal-sized SASE.
Payment: Free author's copies plus occasional cash awards.
Terms: All rights stay with the writer as long as *Time to Pause* is given credit for 1st printing. Fiction contest each year; cash awards.

TOTAL ABANDON MODERN ARTS MAGAZINE, Total Abandon Publishers, Box 1207, Ashland OR 97520. (503)482-5598. Editor/Publisher: Rick Stanek. Theme: "Avant-garde, experimental, progressive, political, erotic, conceptual, abstract, surreal, dada, constructivist, occult, unusual, punk. Readership: "Young artists, non-commercial oriented artists, open-minded, non-righteous, non-ethical artists, and people who will give credence and space to this kind of work." Quarterly to semiannual. Estab. 1977. Circ. 1,000.
Needs: Literary, contemporary, erotica, translations, occult, experimental prose, satiric, anthropological. No "western, religious, any fiction that is not stretching the limits of all we have seen so far in the literary tradition. Let us be modern and transcend patterns." Accepts 3 mss/issue, 8 mss/year. Length: 500-4,000 words.
How to Contact: Send complete ms with SASE. Reports in 3 months on mss. Free sample copy with 10x13 SASE plus $1 postage.
Payment: 5 free author's copies. $1.50 charge for extras.
Terms: Rights revert to author.
Tips: "Send several different works in the above mentioned modes. Don't bother to submit if your work is not pushing the established norms for creative writing or is not high energy. Include a cover letter which talks about yourself on a personal level, your artistic philosophy. Solicit criticism and be open to its harsh reality. Fruits follow to be reaped."

TOUCHSTONE LITERARY QUARTERLY, Houston Area Writers' Workshop, Box 42331, Houston TX 77042. (713)461-6201. Senior Editor: Marge Baron. "*Touchstone* is sponsored by a group of professional writers as a service project to provide a market for and encourage poetry and short fiction. We also publish letters and, once a year, reviews. Our audience is primarily writers of all ages and friends and relatives of writers. Our readers are ardently devoted to us because our only aim is to promote and encourage good writing." Quarterly. Estab. 1976. Circ. varies to 1,000.
Needs: Literary, contemporary, humor. "We do not rule out anything if it is good. No pornographic material." Accepts 2 mss/issue, 8 mss/year. Length: 1,000-2,500 words.
How to Contact: Send complete ms with SASE. Reports in 3 weeks on mss. Sample copy $1.75.
Terms: Acquires one-time rights.
Tips: "Don't try to decide, by reading the magazine, what kind of fiction we want. Just be your own original self, and send us your best. Our senior editor writes a personal note with every returned ms, but if you ask for a detailed critique, you will get one. Then try us again. Don't skimp on your postage. We are a nonprofit organization with limited budget. Of course, we don't read mss that aren't typed, double-spaced. Our magazine circulates in a number of university libraries. Our contributors are from several countries, and they have ranged from 17 to 95, from university professors to convicts on death row. Many of our contributors are the authors of published trade books. Many more are novices. Anyone with a good story is welcomed. We sponsor contests from time to time and are announced only in our magazine. We also make nominations annually for the Pushcart Prize."

TRANSLATION, The Translation Center, Columbia University, 307A Mathematics Bldg., New York NY 10027. (212)280-2305. Executive Director: Dallas Galvin. Semiannual. Estab. 1973. Circ. 2,200.
Needs: Translations only. Accepts varying number of mss/year. Length: No requirement.
How to Contact: Send complete ms with SASE. Reports in 3 months on mss. Sample copy $7.
Payment: Free author's copies.
Terms: Acquires first North American serial rights.
Tips: "We are particularly interested in translations from more obscure languages."

TRIQUARTERLY, Northwestern University, 1735 Benson Ave., Evanston IL 60201. (312)492-3490. Fiction Editors: Elliott Anderson and Jon Brent. "A general, literary quarterly of fiction. We publish short stories, novellas, or excerpts from novels, usually by American writers. Genre or style is not a primary consideration. We aim for the general reader, someone looking for good stories, told well. Many of our readers are also writers." Published 3 times/year. Estab. 1964. Circ. 5,000.
Needs: Literary, contemporary, translations. Buys 20 mss/issue, 60 mss/year. Length: No requirement.
How to Contact: Send complete ms with SASE. Reports in 1 month on mss. Sample copy $2.
Payment: $100-$500. 4 free author's copies. Cover price less 30% discount for extras.
Terms: Pays on publication for first North American serial rights.
Tips: "Read a few recent copies of the magazine to become familiar with the kinds of fiction we publish."

TWO WORLDS, Coop. Antigruppo Siciliano, via Argenteria Km4, Trapani, Sicily. Editor: Nat Scammacca. Fiction Editor: Gianni Diecidue. "We publish books of poetry (Italian and English), novels, 2 reviews, essays, art, a newspaper, anthologies, short stories, etc." Audience: "Local and national lovers of poetry, politics, prose, language." Quarterly. Estab. 1973. Circ. 2,000.
Needs: Literary, contemporary, humor, translations, history (local, Sicilian, Scots, Greek,

English, Hungarian and French). Buys 100 mss/year. Length: No requirement.
How to Contact: "Send previously published material so we can then ask for the material we want." Reports in 2 weeks. Free sample copy.
Payment: $50 minimum for short stories. Free author's copies at author's request.
Terms: "No rights."
Tips: "Ask for our 21 points of the Antigruppo which is a pluralistic guide and encouragement to write as one speaks. Don't copy anyone but oneself and write the way the language is spoken at home in your own region, not imitating others."

UMBRAL, Umbral Press, 2330 Irving St., Denver, CO 80211. Editor: Steve R. Tem. "*Umbral* prints science poems, science fiction and fantasy poems and prose poem fables. The occasional piece of fiction we publish must involve these areas, and have 'prose poem' qualities. For fantasy and science fiction fans, people interested in various kinds of fantasy-influenced poetry." Quarterly. Estab. 1978. Circ. 350.
Needs: Psychic/supernatural, science fiction, fantasy, horror only. Accepts 1 ms/issue, 4 mss/year. Length: 1,500 words maximum.
How to Contact: Send complete ms with SASE. Reports in 1 month. Sample copy $1.50.
Payment: 3 free author's copies. $1.25 charge for extras.
Terms: Acquires one-time rights.
Tips: "Study the magazine, read Russell Edson, Michael Benedict, Jack Anderson and others using the fable or prose poem form. Also know the traditions of fantasy and science fiction."

UNCLE MAGAZINE, Heart's Desire Press, Rt. 1, Box 1134, Springfield MO 65803. Editor: Ed DeBriese. Fiction Editor: John Mort. "Our magazine is for those who have given up. Humor, satire, whimsy, parody—we seek to be contrary and ornery. We hope to have more than a literary audience, but realize that *Uncle* will appeal mainly to those interested in little magazines. We believe we will appeal to those eager for a brash approach to contemporary sacred cows." Quarterly. Estab. November 1980.
Needs: "We will consider fiction from any category as long as its emphasis is humorous. We are not interested in heavily confessional material or giddy new celebrations of the Universe." Accepts 2-4 mss/issue. Length: 2,000 words maximum.
How to Contact: Send complete ms with SASE. Reports in 1 month on mss. Sample copy $1.
Payment: Free author's copies.
Terms: Acquires one-time rights.
Tips: "Keep it short, be outrageously funny and watch our contest announcements. A modest sum is awarded."

UNIVERSITY OF WINDSOR REVIEW, University of Windsor, Windsor, Ontario, Canada N9B 3P4. Editor: E. McNamara. Fiction Editor: Alistair MacLeod. Estab. 1965.
Needs: Literary, contemporary. We wish to see lots of experimental fiction. Buys 4 mss/year. Length: No requirement.
How to Contact: Send complete ms with SASE. Reports in 6 weeks.
Payment: $25.

UROBOROS, Allegany Mountain Press, 111 N. 10th Street, Olean NY 14760. (716)372-0935. Fiction Editor: Ford F. Ruggieri. "Fiction dealing with current mythological motifs, dreams, folklore, psychological insights, history of consciousness, etc. for those interested in these topics." Published irregularly. Estab. 1973. Circ. 500.
Needs: Literary, erotica, humor, experimental. "No formula hackwork." Accepts 4-6 mss/year. Length: No requirement.
How to Contact: Send complete ms with SASE. Reports in 2 months on mss. Sample copy $2.

Payment: Free author's copies. Cover price less 50% discount for extras.
Terms: Acquires first rights and one-time rights. Rights revert to author.
Tips: "Be familiar with a magazine before sending mss (saves time and money in the long run)."

URTHKIN, Box 67485, Los Angeles CA 90067. Editor/Publisher: Larry Ziman. "A yearly anthology of the best in poetry and short fiction. For a literary audience looking for the best in contemporary poetry and short fiction." Annual. Estab. 1978. Circ.300.
Needs: Literary, contemporary, science fiction, fantasy, horror, erotica, romance, adventure, humor. "No religious sentimental melodrama or mawkish nature glorifications." Length: 1,000 words maximum.
How to Contact: Send complete ms with SASE. Reports in 3 weeks.
Payment: Free author's copies.
Terms: Acquires second serial rights on reprints.
Tips: "Submit as much as you like, whatever you like, whenever you like. We reject writing not writers. Keep submitting new material."

U.S. 1 WORKSHEETS, The Princeton Packet, c/o Rod Tulloss, 21 Lake Dr., Roosevelt NJ 08555. Rotating Editors. "We publish poetry and prose of many styles for anyone interested in contemporary fiction and poetry." Biannual. Estab. 1971. Circ. 1,000.
Needs: Literary, contemporary. "We have published fiction that *might* be labelled confessional, gay/lesbian, feminist, or western." Length: Approximately 500 words.
How to Contact: Send complete ms with SASE. Reports in up to 6 months on mss. Sample copy $1 with 8x11 SASE plus 40¢ postage.
Payment: 2 free author's copies. 50¢ charge for extras.
Tips: "I think we might best be described as a publication that wants to avoid labels and stereotypes; we seek instead good writing. Write carefully rather than in over-enthusiastic haste. Don't try to be original or 'hype.' Tell a good story."

VALLEY GRAPEVINE, Seven Buffaloes Press, Box 249, Big Timber MT 59011. Editor/Publisher: Art Cuelho. Theme: "Poems, stories, history, folklore, photographs, ink drawings, or anything native to the Great Central Valley of California which includes the San Joaquin and Sacramento Valleys. Focus is on land and people and the oilfields, farms, orchards, Okies, small town life, hoboes." Readership: "Rural and small town audience, the common man with a rural background, salt-of-the-earth. The working man reads *Valley Grapevine* because it's their personal history recorded." Annual. Estab. 1978. Circ. 325.
Needs: Literary, contemporary, western, ethnic (Okie, Arkie). No academic, religious, gay/lesbian, supernatural material. Length: 2,500-10,000 (prefers 5,000) words.
How to Contact: Query. SASE for query, ms. Reports in 1 week. Sample copy available to potential contributors or writers for $1 discount off cover price.
Payment: Free author's copies.
Terms: Acquires first North American serial rights. Returns rights to author after publication.
Tips: "Buy a copy to get a feel of the professional quality of the writing. Know the theme of a particular issue. Some contributors have 30 years experience as writers; most 15 years. Age does not matter; quality does."

VIRGINIA QUARTERLY REVIEW, 1 W. Range, Charlottesville VA 22903. (804)924-3124. Editor: Staige Blackford. "A national magazine of literature and discussion. A lay, intellectual audience, people who are not out-and-out scholars but who are interested in ideas and literature." Quarterly. Estab. 1925. Circ. 4,500.
Needs: Literary, contemporary, fantasy, men's women's feminist, romance, adventure, humor, ethnic, serialized novels (excerpts), translations. "No gay/lesbian or pornography." Buys 3 mss/issue, 20 mss/year. Length: 3,000-7,000 words.

How to Contact: Query or send complete ms. SASE for query, ms. Reports in 2 weeks on queries, 2 months on mss. Sample copy $3.
Payment: $10/printed page.
Terms: Pays on publication for all rights. "Will transfer upon request."
Tips: "Because of the competition it's difficult for a non-published writer to break in." Emily Clark Balch Award for best published short story of the year.

WASCANA REVIEW, University of Regina, Regina, Saskatchewan, Canada. Editor: William Howard. Theme: "literary criticism, fiction, poetry for readers of serious fiction." Semiannual. Estab. 1966. Circ. 500.
Needs: Literary, humor. Buys 6 mss/year. Length: No requirement.
How to Contact: Send complete ms with SASE. Reports in 2 months on mss. Sample copy $2.50. Free guidelines.
Payment: $3/page. 2 free author's copies.
Terms: Pays on publication for all rights.

WASHINGTON REVIEW, Friends of the Washington Review of the Arts, Box 50132, Washington DC 20004. (202)638-0515. Fiction Editor: Patricia Griffith. "We publish fiction, poetry, articles and reviews on areas of the arts. We have a particular interest in the interrelationships of the arts and emphasize the cultural life of the DC area." Readership: "Artists, writers and those interested in cultural life in this area." Bimonthly. Estab. 1975. Circ. 10,000.
Needs: Literary. Buys 1-2 mss/issue. Length: Prefers 2,000 words.
How to Contact: Send complete ms with SASE. Reports in 1 month. Sample copy for tabloid-sized SASE.
Payment: Author's copies.
Terms: Pays on publication for first North American serial rights.
Tips: "Read our publication. Occasionally we have an all fiction issue."

WAVES, 79 Denham Dr., Thornhill, Ontario, Canada L4J 1P2. (416)889-6703. Editor: Bernice Lever. Fiction Editor: Marvyn Jenoff. "A college literary journal, printing poems, short stories, reviews with graphics by international artists and writers." Readership: English teachers, writers and fans of quality literature. Published 3 times/year. Estab. 1972. Circ. 1,000.
Needs: Literary, contemporary, inspirational, supernatural, science fiction, fantasy, horror, erotica, gothic, romance, western, mystery, adventure, humor, young adult, ethnic, translations. Also interested in "sample chapters of novels. Type of submission is not important—style and quality are. No dull plots, careless writing, cardboard characters, lecturing dialogues, stupid themes, boring cliches, etc." Accepts 3-6 mss/issue, 15 mss/year. **Length:** 1,000-5,000 words.
How to Contact: Send complete ms with SASE. Reports in 1 month on mss. Sample back issue copy $1.
Payment: 2 free author's copies. $1 charge for extras.
Terms: Acquires first North American serial rights.
Tips: "Read *Waves* in a library or buy a sample. Look at several literary magazines. Spend time being creative with the writing and inventive with language. Know contemporary writing. Develop your own voice."

WEBSTER REVIEW, Webster College, Webster Groves MO 63119. Editor/Publisher: Nancy Schapiro. "We have no specific theme. We're interested in quality fiction and in translations of international fiction." Readership: Writers, students, teachers and anyone interested in contemporary international fiction. Quarterly. Estab. 1974. Circ. 1,000.
Needs: Literary, contemporary, translations. "Not interested in popular (i.e., non-serious) work." Accepts 4 mss/issue, 8 mss/year. No preferred length.

How to Contact: Send complete ms with SASE. Reports in 1 month. Free sample copy.
Payment: 2 free author's copies. No charge for extras.
Terms: Acquires first rights.
Tips: "The competition is stiff so a writer should master his craft before attempting to publish."

WEE GIANT, Wee Giant Press, 178 Bond St. N., Hamilton, Ontario, Canada L8S 3W6. Editor: Margaret Saunders. "A little literary magazine of poetry, book reviews, fiction. Audience reads *Wee Giant* to keep up with what is going on in the wee magazine field." Published 3 times/year. Estab. 1977. Circ. 400.
Needs: Literary. Accepts 5 mss/year. Length: 2,500 words maximum.
How to Contact: Send complete ms with SASE. Reports in 3 weeks. Sample copy $1 with 9½x6⅓ SASE plus 48¢ postage.
Payment: 1 free author's copy. $1.35 charge for extras.
Terms: Acquires first North American serial rights.
Tips: "Send for a sample copy of our magazine and study it. Submit to the right market. We publish the work of unknown writers along with established writers such as John Robert Columbo."

WEIRDBOOK, Weirdbook Press, Box 35, Amherst Branch, Buffalo NY 14226. Editor: W. Paul Ganley. "Latter day 'pulp magazine' along the lines of the old pulp magazine *Weird Tales*. We tend to use established writers. We look for an audience of fairly literate people who like good writing and good characterization in their fantasy and horror fiction, but are tired of the clichés in the field." Annual. Estab. 1968. Circ. 900.
Needs: Psychic/supernatural, fantasy, horror, gothic (not modern). No psychological horror; mystery fiction; physical horror (blood); traditional ghost stories (unless original theme); science fiction; swords and sorcery without a supernatural element; reincarnation stories that conclude with 'And the doctor patted him on . . . THE END!' " Buys 8-12 mss/issue. Length: 15,000+ words maximum.
How to Contact: Send complete ms with SASE. Reports in 2 months on mss. Sample copy $3. Guidelines for legal-sized SASE.
Payment: ½¢/word minimum, and 1 free author's copy.
Terms: Pays on publication ("part acceptance only for solicited mss") for first North American serial rights plus right to reprint the entire issue.
Tips: "Read a copy and then some of the best anthologies in the field (such as Daw's 'Best Horror of the Year,' Arkham House anthologies, etc.) Occasionally we keep mss longer than planned. When sending a SASE marked 'book rate' (or anything not first class) the writer should add 'Forwarding Postage Guaranteed.' "

WEST BRANCH, Dept. of English, Bucknell University, Lewisburg PA 17837. Editors: K. Patten and R. Taylor. Theme: Fiction and poetry. Readership: "Readers of contemporary literature." Biannual. Estab. 1977. Circ. 600.
Needs: Literary, contemporary, translations. No science fiction. Accepts 3-4 mss/issue. No preferred length.
How to Contact: Send complete ms with SASE. Reports in 6 weeks on mss. Sample copy $2.
Payment: 2 free author's copies. Cover price less 20% discount for extras.
Terms: Acquires first rights.

WESTERN HUMANITIES REVIEW, University of Utah, Salt Lake City UT 84112. (801)581-7438. Editor: Jack Garlington. "Articles on various aspects of the humanities: Fiction, poetry, book and film reviews." Readership: Highly educated. Quarterly. Estab. 1947. Circ. about 1,200.
Needs: Literary, contemporary, humor, ethnic (all), serialized and condensed novels, translations. Buys 2-3 mss/issue; 8-12 mss/year. Length: No requirement.

How to Contact: Send complete ms with SASE. Reports in 1 month on mss. Sample copy $2.50.
Payment: $150 maximum.
Terms: Pays on acceptance for all rights.
Tips: "Read an issue and see what we like."

WHISPERS, Whispers Press, Box 904, Chapel Hill NC 27514. Editor/Publisher: Stuart David Schiff. "A literary journal devoted to original fantasy, terror, and horror in the tradition of Poe and Lovecraft. High quality fiction by professional authors." Readership: Literate adults. Biannual. Estab. 1973. Circ. 3,000.
Needs: Fantasy, horror. No science fiction. Buys 25 mss/year. Length: 1,000-6,000 words.
How to Contact: Send complete ms with SASE. Reports in 3 months. Sample copy $2.50
Payment: 1¢/word. 2 free author's copies.
Terms: Pays ½ on acceptance and ½ on publication for first North American serial rights.

WILDCAT, (formerly *Cryptoc*), Partners in Publishing, Box 1427, Seminole OK 74868. (405)382-3354. Editors: Peg Fielding and Joyce McKinnon. Fiction Editor: Michael Lail. "We publish all genres. Our motto is: 'Tomorrow's New Stars of Art & Story.' We are read for our wide range of genres and articles by ages 11-83." Quarterly. Estab. 1977. Circ. 1,600.
Needs: Literary, contemporary, religious/inspirational, psychic/supernatural, science fiction, fantasy, horror, men's, women's, feminist, gothic, western, mystery, adventure, humor, juvenile, young adult, translations. No "material containing sexually graphic events and/or language." Accepts 3-4 mss/issue, 12-14 mss/year. Length: No requirement.
How to Contact: Send complete ms with SASE. Reports in 3 weeks. Sample copy $1.
Payment: "We pay $6 each for Best Fiction, Best Nonfiction, Best Poet, and Best Art for each issue. Our readers vote on these categories."
Terms: Rights revert to author.
Tips: "Imagination required. We don't care for obscure stories."

THE WILLIAM AND MARY REVIEW, College of William and Mary, Williamsburg VA 23185. (804)253-4862. Fiction Editors: Stacy Puls and Andrea Talbot. Editors change annually. "We publish quality fiction, poetry, and essays. Our audience is primarily undergraduate and professional." Semiannual. Estab. 1943. Circ. 2,500.
Needs: Literary, contemporary, humor. "We have no interest in science fiction, erotica, religious parables or stories about the possibility of finding oneself through hunting and/or fishing." Accepts 7 mss/issue, 14 mss/year. Length: 5,000 words maximum.
How to Contact: Send complete ms with SASE. Reports in 2 months.
Payment: 5 free author's copies.
Terms: Acquires first rights.
Tips: "We always appreciate a story with a sense of humor."

WIND/LITERARY JOURNAL, The Wind Press, Rt. 1, Box 809K, Pikeville KY 41501. (606)631-1129. Editor: Quentin R. Howard. "Literary journal with stories, poems; book reviews from the small presses and some university presses. Readership is students, literary people, professors, housewives and others." Quarterly. Estab. 1971. Circ. 500.
Needs: Literary. "No restriction on form, content or subject." Accepts 4 mss/issue. Length: No requirement.
How to Contact: Send complete ms with SASE. Reports in 1 month. Sample copy $1.50.
Payment: Free author's copies.
Terms: Acquires first rights.
Tips: "We're constantly looking for beginning fiction writers. Diversity is one of our major editorial goals. We have published since 1971 approximately 80 beginners in fiction; 45 are publishing regularly today in many magazines. No multiple submissions please. We have no taboos, but set our own standards on reading each ms."

WISCONSIN REVIEW, Box 276, Dempsey Hall, University of Wisconsin, Oshkosh WI 54901. (414)424-2267. Editor: Perry Peterson. Literary magazine of prose and poetry. Quarterly. Estab. 1966. Circ. 2,000.
Needs: Literary and experimental. "Imaginative materials that are experimental should include explanation of writer's intent." Length: up to 5,000 words.
How to Contact: Send complete ms with SASE. Reports in 0-5 months. Sample copy $1.
Payment: Pays in contributor's copies.
Terms: Acquires first rights.

WOMEN: A JOURNAL OF LIBERATION, 3028 Greenmount Ave., Baltimore MD 21218. Contact: J. Nelson. "Issues related to women; non-sexist, feminist, non-classist." Readership: "Women, generally feminist." Published by volume. Estab. 1969. Circ. 10,000.
Needs: Contemporary, fantasy, women's, feminist, gay/lesbian, mystery, adventure, humor. Accepts 4 mss/issue. Length: 3,000 words maximum.
How to Contact: Send complete ms with SASE. Reports in 6-10 months on mss. Sample copy $1.25.
Payment: 1 free author's copy. 50¢ charge for extras.
Terms: Acquires all rights.
Tips: "We are a thematic publication. Therefore, there's a better chance if the ms is related to the issue."

WRIT MAGAZINE, 2 Sussex Ave., Toronto, Canada M5S 1J5. Editor: Roger Greenwald. "Literary magazine for literate readers interested in the work of new writers." Annual. Estab. 1970. Circ. 600.
Needs: Literary, translations, parts of novels. No other categories. Accepts 4-5 mss/year. Length: 300-20,000 words.
How to Contact: Send complete ms with SASE. Reports in 1 month—"longer May-August." Sample copy $2.50.
Payment: 2 free author's copies. Negotiates charge for extras.
Terms: Acquires first North American serial rights. Copyright reverts to author.

WRITERS FORUM, University of Colorado at Colorado Springs, Colorado Springs CO 80907. Editor: Dr. Alex Blackburn. "8-10 short stories or self-contained novel excerpts published once a year along with 25-35 poems. Highest literary quality only: mainstream, avant-garde, with preference to western themes. For small press enthusiasts, teachers and students of creative writing, commercial agents/publishers, university libraries and departments interested in contemporary American literature." Annual. Estab. 1974. Circ. 800.
Needs: Literary, contemporary, ethnic (Native American, chicano, not excluding others), novel excerpts. No "sentimental, over-plotted, pornographic, anecdotal, polemical, trendy, disguised autobiographical, fantasy (sexual, extra-terrestrial), pseudo-philosophical, passionless, placeless, undramatized, etc. material." Accepts 8-10 mss/issue. Length: 1,500-10,000.
How to Contact: Send complete ms (two copies) and letter with brief bio and relevant career information with SASE. Reports in 3 weeks on mss. Sample copy $8.95.
Payment: 1 free author's copy. Cover price less 20% discount for extras.
Terms: Acquires one-time rights. Rights revert to author.
Tips: "Read our publication. Have an experienced author recommend your ms. Be prepared for constructive criticism. Persist. Send best work only. Have a serious intention about fiction as an art. Most accepted mss tend to come from established writers or new writers who have studied in writing classes. We're open, but that's the tendency because excellence is our primary criterion. Every volume is introduced by a distinguished American author whose critical commentary can be of enormous help in encouraging writers in their careers. Furthermore our format—a 5½x8½ professionally edited and printed paperback book—lends credibility to authors published in our imprint."

WRITER'S LIFELINE, Highway Book Shop, Cobalt, Ontario, Canada P0J 1C0. (705)679-8375. Editor: D.C. Pollard. "A market newsletter for freelance writers and poets." Bimonthly. Estab. 1974. Circ. 1,000.
Needs: Short fiction articles on writers and poets. Length: 500-1,000 words.
How to Contact: Send complete ms with SASE. Reports in 1 month. Free sample copy.
Payment: One year free subscription.
Terms: Acquires one-time rights.
Tips: "Have your story deal in some way with writers and/or poets."

WRITERS NEWS MANITOBA, MWN Publications, 304 Parkview St., Winnipeg, Manitoba, Canada R3J 1S3. (204)885-2652. Editor: Andris Taskans. Fiction Editor: Kate Bitney. "Information, critical reviews, short fiction, poetry by and for Manitoba/Canadian writers and readers. Non-Canadian work also considered. For writers and readers interested in Canadian/Manitoba literature and literary activities." Published 5 times/year. Estab. 1978. Circ. 500.
Needs: Literary, contemporary, fantasy, feminist, ethnic (French Canadian, possibly others). "We will consider work on any topic (except juvenile) of artistic merit, including short chapters from novels-in-progress. We wish to avoid gothic, confession, romance and pornography." Accepts 1-2 mss/issue, 6-10 mss/year. Length: 1,500-2,500 words.
How to Contact: Send complete ms with SASE. Reports in 1 month.
Payment: 2 free author's copies. $1 charge for extras.
Terms: Acquires one-time rights. Rights revert to author on publication.
Tips: "Read our publication before submitting. Send a ms and expect possible rejection."

THE YALE REVIEW, Yale University Press, 1902A Yale Station, New Haven CT 06520. (203)436-8307. Editor: Kai T. Erikson. Fiction Editor: Sheila Huddleston. "A general interest quarterly; publishes literary criticism, original fiction and poetry, cultural commentary, book reviews for an educated, informed, general audience who seeks intelligent articles of literary criticism, cultural commentary, and substantial book reviews." Quarterly. Estab. 1911. Circ. 5,000.
Needs: Literary, contemporary. Buys 1-4 mss/year. Length: 3,000-5,000 words.
How to Contact: Send complete ms with SASE. Reports in 2 months. Sample copy $3.50.
Payment: $50-$100. 1 free author's copy. $1.75 charge for extras.
Terms: Makes assignments on a work-for-hire basis. Pays on publication for first North American serial rights.

Commercial periodicals

Commercial magazines used to be a thriving marketplace for fiction. Writers in the '30s, '40s and '50s could earn a respectable living with short story sales to *Collier's*, *Story Magazine*, *The Saturday Evening Post* and other magazines now defunct. (*Satevepost* is back, but not as the high-paying fiction market it used to be.)

Fiction writers today are likely to have better luck with publications that are smaller, more specialized, and even regional in audience appeal—some city magazines, for instance, are now using occasional fiction. Other periodicals publish genre fiction for audiences of very specific tastes, and editors at many men's, women's, mystery, science fiction, religious, confession and other magazines, often welcome the newcomer as well as the veteran fiction writer to their pages. While the checks may not be as big as the ones Scott Fitzgerald used to cash after a *Saturday Evening Post* sale, they may arrive more frequently for the writer who has a fiction specialty and who can produce a steady flow of good manuscripts.

The special-interest or genre periodicals have moved into fiction subjects and styles that were taboo in Scott Fitzgerald's time. Changes in our mores and social structure have opened up more possibilities for candid, adult-rated themes in short story writing—notably in feminist, working women's, men's and confession magazines. Other specialized publications provide opportunities for stories told in a different vein. A children's magazine may want juvenile science fiction, for example; a religious publication might need short stories of fantasy; a teen magazine may run a detective story occasionally; and ethnic, senior-citizen or regional publications may be open to fiction topics at large, provided they have meaning for their special audiences. As always, the fiction writer must *study* the various publications to determine where a particular manuscript is likely to find a receptive editor. As bestselling novelist Stephen King observed when he was getting started with story submissions to commercial periodicals, "Reading the market is essential. Go out to your local newsstand and pick up a dozen or so at a swipe. Your chances for success without reading the market first is zero." You can also find back issues of many magazines at the library before sending off your story.

Special interest magazines vary greatly among themselves in theme and format and, as a result, there may be great latitude in style—from simple and direct writing to literary quality, thereby affording more opportunities for different kinds or styles of short stories. The key to writing for a specialized market is to know your subject well. If you write a story involving biking, racquetball or computers, you must be thoroughly knowledgeable with the theme of the magazine to appeal to sophisticated readers who read the magazine because of a hobby or interest. Editors are seldom hoodwinked by a poorly researched story or a rejected manuscript with a patched plot to fit a particular theme.

Equally important is familiarity with the audience. If you write for children you must *know* and even *like* them. Likewise you must understand the audiences of other publications, by taking a rural point of view in a story for a farm magazine, for example, or by telling a story as seen through the eyes of the wife of a blue collar worker for a confession magazine.

To write credible fiction it is also important to stay current with what is going on today in subjects you approach. Just as the science fiction writer should keep abreast of changing scientific news, the contemporary teen or children's author should be aware of current fads, music, slang and dialogue.

Magazine fiction trends change frequently. Today short stories are not the only form of fiction accepted. Several commercial magazines (*Family Circle*, *Woman's Day*, *Redbook*, and even *People*) are using condensed and excerpted or serialized novels because of favorable reader response. Another trend in magazine publishing of advantage to the writer is the joint ownership of genre magazines. Thus, if a manuscript is rejected by one periodical of a group, it might be sent to one, two or three other magazines owned by the company.

What editors of all magazines want to see, despite their varied specifications, is originality, interesting characters, provocative themes, and stylish writing. Erotica does not mean poor quality; men's magazines want exceptional literary quality, too. Confession magazines, which need scores of stories and welcome freelance material, should not be thought of as an easy market, nor necessarily the way to break in, because they too require special writing skills, as do other genres. Always write your best, and never write down to a market—or your manuscripts will be turned down quickly and often.

Reasons for rejection are uniform, say the editors: The idea is overworked; it lacks emotional appeal; it is trite or unbelievable; the dialogue is dull; the manuscript is unprofessionally prepared (see *Manuscript Mechanics*); or the subject matter does not fit the magazine's needs. One magazine editor said he seldom prints short stories "due to a lack of good fiction." Fiction writers therefore have a responsibility to send the best manuscript possible to the right editor at the right publication—thereby keeping fiction alive and thriving.

ALFRED HITCHCOCK'S MYSTERY MAGAZINE, Davis Publications, Inc., 380 Lexington Ave., New York NY 10017. (212)557-9100. Editor: Eleanor Sullivan. Associate Editor: Susan Calderella Groarke. Mystery fiction magazine for mystery lovers. Published 13 times/year. Estab. December 1956. Circ. 282,000.
Needs: Mystery. No non-mystery, horror or sensationalism. Buys 8-13/issue depending on length. Length: 1,000-11,000 words.
How to Contact: Send complete ms and SASE. Reports in one month. Free guideline sheet.
Payment: 3¢/word and up on acceptance. Manuscripts submitted to *AHMM* receive an alternate reading for *Ellery Queen's Mystery Magazines*, also published by Davis.

ALIVE! for Young Teens, Christian Board of Publication, Box 179, St. Louis MO 63166. (314)371-6900. Editor: Michael Dixon. *Alive!* is a leisure reading magazine for junior high youth (12-15) in several major protestant denominations. Monthly. Estab. September 1969. Circ. 20,000. "We are one of the few magazines to slant toward the specific needs and interests of this age group, and we encourage youth participation in its creation."
Needs: Religious/inspirational, adventure, humor, young adult and ethnic. "Please deal with concerns and situations peculiar to the age group of *Alive!* readers (12-15). Stories about children or older youth have little chance of acceptance. Religious stories shouldn't be 'preachy' or with obvious moral." Buys 1-2 mss/issue. Length: 500-1,200 words.
How to Contact: Send complete ms with SASE. Reports in 3 weeks on ms. Sample copy 30¢. Free guidelines for legal-sized SASE.
Payment: 2¢/word. Free author's copy. 30¢ charge for extras.
Terms: Pays on publication for simultaneous and one-time rights.
Tips: "Keep your audience in mind—know what would interest junior high youth. We return many well written manuscripts that are too 'childish' or oriented around older teen interests. We are very strict on maximum length of stories."

ALOHA, THE MAGAZINE OF HAWAII, Davick Publishing Co., 828 Fort Street Mall, Honolulu HI 96813. (808)523-9871. Editor: Rita Gormley. "We are a regional publication dealing with the life and culture of the state of Hawaii for upper income, well-educated people around the world interested in Hawaii." Bimonthly. Estab. January 1978. Circ. 80,000.
Needs: "Themes must be Hawaii-related. Fiction dealing with the tourist's experience in Waikiki doesn't have a chance." Buys 2-3 mss/year. Length: 2,500 words minimum.
How to Contact: Send complete ms with SASE. Reports as soon as possible. Sample copy for $2.
Payment: 10¢/word. Free author's copy. $1.50 for extra copies.
Terms: Pays on publication for all rights.
Tips: Be knowledgeable on Hawaii and the people.

THE AMERICAN MIZRACHI WOMAN, American Mizrachi Women, 817 Broadway, New York NY 10003. (212)477-4720. Editor: Agatha I. Leifer. Fiction Editor: Avi Feinglass. "*The American Mizrachi Woman* is the national magazine for the major religious women's Zionist organization in the United States. Our readers are concerned with Jews the world over, Israel, aspects of Judaism and current world events affecting all three." Monthly. Estab. 1925. Circ. 55,000.
Needs: Jewish/Israeli ethnic and Jewish holiday stories. Buys 1 ms/issue, 8 mss/year. Length: 750-2,000 words.
How to Contact: Query and send complete ms with SASE. Reports in 1 month on both query and ms. Free sample copy with 10x13 SASE and 55¢ postage. Free guidelines.
Payment: Pays $50 for fiction. Free author's copy.
Terms: Pays on publication for first rights.

ANALOG SCIENCE FICTION/SCIENCE FACT, Davis Publications, Inc., 380 Lexington Ave., New York NY 10017. (212)557-9100. Editor: Stanley Schmidt. "Well-written science fiction based on speculative ideas and fact articles on topics on the present and future frontiers of research. Our readership includes intelligent laymen and/or those profession-ally active in science and technology." Monthly. Estab. 1930. Circ. 100,000.
Needs: Science fiction and serialized novels. "No stories which are not truly science fiction in the sense of having a plausible speculative idea *integral to the story*." Buys 4-8 mss/issue. Length: 2,000-80,000 words.
How to Contact: Send complete ms. Query only on serials with SASE. Reports in 3 weeks on both query and ms. Free guidelines.
Payment: 3.4¢-6.9¢/word.

Terms: Pays on acceptance for First North American serial rights and non-exclusive foreign rights.

ARARAT, Armenian General Benevolent Union of America, 628 Second Ave., New York NY 10016. (212)684-7530. Editor: Leo Hamalian. Readership consists of people interested in Armenian background, culture and history. Quarterly. Estab. 1960. Circ. 2,000.
Needs: Armenian ethnic. Prefers to be Armenian written. Buys 1-2 mss/issue.
How to Contact: Query with SASE. Reports in 1 month on query, 3 months on ms. Free guidelines.
Payment: $10-75 plus 2 free author's copies.
Terms: Pays on publication.

ARES MAGAZINE, Simulations Publications, Inc., 257 Park Avenue South, New York NY 10010. Editor: Redmond A. Simonsen. Fiction Editor: Michael Moore. "*Ares* is the magazine of science fiction and fantasy simulation. Readers enjoy both playing games and reading science fiction and fantasy. They enjoy solving problems and dealing with complex, fully detailed world constructs." Bimonthly. Estab. Feb. 1980. Circ. 13,500.
Needs: Science fiction and fantasy. "We seek action-oriented stories with strong central conflicts and interesting characters. 'Hard' science fiction, exciting science fantasy, sword & sorcery, and quest/adventure stories are needed. No scientifically inaccurate stories or serials." Buys 12-15/year. Length: 3,000-8,000 words.
How to Contact: Send complete ms with SASE. Reports in 45 days on ms. Sample copy $3. Free guidelines.
Payment: 3-6¢/word.
Terms: Pays on acceptance for First English language serial rights.
Tips: "Stories should have a beginning, middle and end; the central conflict should be resolved using elements of the world constructed. The story should have a feeling of 'strangeness.' Try to think of fresh plots, not the tired old space opera themes. Keep in touch with current trends of science to find where the future is heading. The fiction editor will attempt to point out strengths and failures of submissions."

ATLANTIC MONTHLY, 8 Arlington St., Boston MA 02116. (617)536-9500. Editor: Robert Manning. Associate Editor: Michael Curtis. General magazine for the college educated with broad cultural interests. Monthly. Estab. 1860. Circ. 340,000.
Needs: Literary and contemporary. "Seeks fiction that is clear, tightly written with strong sense of 'story' and well-defined characters." Buys 2 mss/issue. Length: 4,000-6,000 words.
How to Contact: Send complete ms with SASE. Reports in 2 months on mss.
Payment: Pays $100/page and up to $1,000 maximum.
Terms: Pays on acceptance for first and first North American serial rights.
Tips: "Read magazine with great care and write well."

ATTENZIONE, Paulucci Publications, Inc., 10 E. 49th St., New York NY 10017. Editor: Donald Dewey. Senior Editor: Gwenda Blair, Stephen Hall, Joseph Mancini. General interest magazine with emphasis on Italian and Italian-American political and social endeavors for those with interest in Italy or of Italian descent. Monthly. Estab. 1979. Circ. 160,000.
Needs: Ethnic (Italian-American). All mss must have Italian-Amercian theme. Buys 6 mss/year. Length: 3,000 words.
How to Contact: Send complete ms with SASE.
Payment: Pays $350.
Terms: Pays 2 months after acceptance for first North American serial rights.

THE AUGUSTA SPECTATOR, Harbert Publishing Co., 110 8th St., Augusta GA 30904. (404)722-3113. Publisher/Editor: Faith B. Bertsche. Regional publication, modern in outlook; short stories, poems, articles for upper income marrieds; average age 45. Published every 4 months. Estab. April 1980. Circ. 5,000.

Needs: Literary, contemporary, romance, mystery, adventure and humor. No explicit sex or violence. Buys 1-2 mss/issue. Query with SASE. Reports in 1 month. Free guidelines.

Payment: $25-50/copy.

Terms: Pays on publication for first rights.

AUTOSPORT CANADA, Wheelspin News, Inc., 3045 Universal Dr., Mississauga, Ontario, Canada L4X 2E2. (416)625-5300. Editor: Pete Chapman. Fiction Editor: Katie Champion. Theme: Motorsport and automotive general interest magazine for motorsport and automotive enthusiasts in Canada. Monthly. Estab. March 1975. Circ. 32,000.

Needs: Humor and psychological narratives of drivers. Buys 1-2 mss/year. Length: 350-2,000 words. Query with SASE. Reports in 2 weeks on queries, 3 weeks on mss. Free sample copy.

Payment: $2/column inch. Free author's copy.

Terms: Pays on publication for first rights.

BEAVER, QMG, Magazines Corp., 235 Park Ave., South, New York NY 10003. Editor: Biff Norganski. Magazine with sex themes and general interest subjects related to men for men of all ages. Monthly. Estab. 1975. Circ. 200,000.

Needs: "We want to see erotic mystery, erotic scientific fiction, erotic fantasy. No 'graffiti' (erotica by itself). Buys 2 mss/issue, 24 mss/year. Length: 2,500-3,000 words.

How to Contact: Send complete ms with SASE. Reports in 2 weeks on mss. Sample copy $2.25 with free guidelines.

Payment: Pays $400.

Terms: Pays on acceptance for all rights.

THE BEEHIVE, 201 8th Ave. S., Nashville TN 37203. Editor: Martha Wagner. "Eight page hand-out of articles and stories of interest to children in grades 5 and 6 in United Methodist Church schools." Weekly.

Needs: Juvenile. "Modern day life problems, unusual historical stories and church history. No overly didactic or moralistic material, slang or references to drinking or smoking." Length: 700 words.

How to Contact: Send complete ms with SASE. Reports in 3 months on ms. Free sample copy.

Payment: 3¢ a word.

Terms: Pays on acceptance for all rights.

Tips: "Make stories moderate in length, realistic and imaginative." Will not accept freelance materials after May 1981.

BREAD, Church of the Nazarene, 6401 The Paseo, Kansas City MO 64131. Editor: Gary Sivewright. Christian leisure reading magazine for junior and senior high students. Monthly.

Needs: Adventure. Themes should be school and church oriented. Adventure stories wanted, but without sermonizing. Buys 1,500 mss/year.

How to Contact: Send complete ms with SASE. Reports in 6 weeks on mss. Free sample copy and guidelines.

Payment: Pays 3¢/word for first rights and 2¢/word for second rights.

Terms: Pays on acceptance for first rights and sometimes second serial rights. Accepts simultaneous submissions. Byline given.

BUFFALO SPREE MAGAZINE, Spree Publishing Co., Inc., 4511 Harlem Rd., Buffalo NY 14226. (716)839-3405. Editor: Johanna V. Shotell. Fiction Editor: Gary L. Goss. "City

magazine for professional, educated and above-average income people." Quarterly. Estab. 1967. Circ. 20,000.
Needs: Literary, contemporary, men's, women's, feminist, mystery, adventure, humor and ethnic. No pornographic or religious. Buys 1 ms/issue, 4 mss/year. Length: 1,000-2,000 words.
How to Contact: Send complete ms with SASE. Reports within 1 week to 2 months on ms. Sample copy for $1 with 9x12 SASE and $1.00 postage.
Payment: $50-125. 2 free author's copies. $1 charge for extra.

CANDIAN DRIVER/OWNER, 481 University Ave., Toronto, Ontario, Canada M5W 1A7. Editor: Rolf Lockwood. Magazine for truckers and people involved in the trucking industry. Bimonthly.
Needs: Humor and short stories presenting truck driver's viewpoint. Length: 750-1,500 words.
How to Contact: Query.
Payment: Pays $75/printed page.
Terms: Pays on acceptance for first Canadian rights.

CANADIAN SKATER, Canadian Figure Skating Assoc., 333 River Rd., Ottawa, Ontario K1L 8B9. (613)746-5953. Editor: Teresa Moore. Bimonthly. Estab. 1974. Circ. 10,000.
Needs: Adventure, young adult and skating. Buys 1 ms/issue. Length: 1,200-2,000 words.
How to Contact: Send complete ms with SASE. Reports in 1 month on ms. Free sample copy.
Payment: $50-80.
Terms: Pays on acceptance for first rights and one-time rights.

CAPPER'S WEEKLY, Stauffer Communications, Inc., 616 Jefferson, Topeka KS 66607. (913)295-1108. Editor: Dorothy Harvey. A "clean, uplifting and nonsensational newspaper for families from children to grandparents." Biweekly. Estab. July 1879. Circ. 420,000.
Needs: Serialized Novels. "We only accept novel length stories for serialization. No fiction containing violence or obscenity." Buys 2-3 stories/year.
How to Contact: Send complete ms with SASE. Reports in 5-6 months on ms. Sample copy 45¢.
Payment: $150-200 for one-time serialization. Free author's copies (1-2 copies as needed for copyright).
Terms: Pays on acceptance for second serial (reprint) rights and one-time rights.

CAVALIER MAGAZINE, Dugent Publishing Corp., 2355 Salzedo St., Coral Gables FL 33134. (305)443-2378. Editor: Douglas Allen. Fiction Editor: M. DeWalt. Sexually oriented, sophisticated magazine for single men aged 18-35. Monthly. Estab. 1952. Circ. 250,000.
Needs: Science fiction, horror, men's and erotica. No material on children, religious subjects or anything that might be libelous. Buys 3 mss/issue. Length: 1,500-3,000 words.
How to Contact: Send complete ms with SASE. Reports in 3 weeks on mss. Sample copy for $3.00. Free fiction guidelines.
Payment: $200-300 per ms.
Terms: Pays on publication for first North American serial rights.

CHATELAINE, Maclean-Hunter Publishing Co., 481 University Ave., Toronto, Canada M5W 1A7. 596-5000. Editor: Mildred Istona. Fiction Editor: Barbara West. "This is a magazine for Canadian women. We present articles, fiction, service material, news and reviews relevant to their lives. Because Canada's population is relatively small we do not concentrate on a specific part of the market but address ourselves to all Canadian women, including housewives, career women, feminists, mothers, singles, etc." Monthly. Estab. March 1928. Circ. 1 million +.

Needs: Literary, contemporary, romance, mystery, adventure, humor. Buys 1-2 ms/issue, approximately 25/year. Length: 2,500-4,500 words,

How to Contact: Send complete ms with SASE. Reports in 3 weeks on ms. Free fiction guidelines.

Payment: $1,000 in Canadian currency. 2 free author's copies. $1 (Canadian) per extra copy.

Terms: Pays on acceptance for first North American serial rights in English and French.

Tips: "We're looking for good, human interest stories in which women play the leading parts, or at least share center stage with men. We are primarily interested in Canadian stories, particularly those about contemporary relationships. Stories that are too explicit sexually don't work for us, nor do avant-garde pieces, nor nostalgic reminiscences. Drug taking, four-letter words, not for us. Old-fashioned-type 'women's stories' don't appeal. We are eager to discover new talent, and to this end sponsor an annual fiction contest for only Canadian writers."

CHESAPEAKE BAY MAGAZINE, Chesapeake Bay Communications, Inc., 1819 Bay Ridge Ave., Annapolis MD 21403. (301)263-2662. Editor: Betty Rigoli. "*Chesapeake Bay Magazine* is a regional publication for those who enjoy reading about the Bay and its tributaries. Most of our articles are boating-related. Our readers are yachtsmen, boating families, fishermen, ecologists, anyone who is part of Chesapeake Bay life." Monthly. Estab. 1971. Circ. 15,000.

Needs: Fantasy, mystery, adventure, humor and historical. "Any fiction piece *must* concern the Chesapeake Bay. Only stories done by authors who are familiar with the area are accepted. No general type stories with the Chesapeake Bay superimposed in an attempt to make a sale." Buys 1 ms/issue, 8 mss/year. Length: 1,250-3,000 words.

How to Contact: Query or send ms with SASE. Reports in 1 month on queries, 2 months on mss. Sample copy $1.50. Free fiction guidelines.

Payment: $35-75. 2 free author's copies.

Terms: Pays on publication for all rights and first North American serial rights.

Tips: "Always query first. Make sure you have knowledge of the area. Send only material that is related to our market. All mss must be typed, double-spaced, in duplicate."

CHIC MAGAZINE, Larry Flynt Publications, 2029 Century Park East, Suite 3800, Los Angeles CA 90067. (213)556-9200. Editor: Donald R. Evans. "*Chic* is a major slick men's magazine for ages 18-40. It publishes erotica fiction which has a fully developed plot and characterization. Sexual activities should grow out of the plot rather than being the main theme of the story." Monthly. Estab. November 1976. Circ. 300,000.

Needs: Erotica. No incomplete mss. Buys 1 ms/issue. Length: 3,500-4,500 words.

How to Contact: Send complete ms with SASE. Reports in 1 month on ms.

Payment: $500-740. Free author's copy.

Terms: Pays on acceptance for first rights and first North American serial rights.

Tips: "*Chic* recommends that the writer read the magazine to get an idea of publishable fiction. We like to see twist endings. We would like to point out once again, that a series of sexual events strung together does not produce a short story to qualify for *Chic*. This is a common mistake made by many writers."

CHICAGO MAGAZINE, WFMT Inc., 500 N. Michigan Ave., Chicago IL 60611. (312)751-7150. Editor: Allen Kelson. Fiction Editor: Christine Newman. City magazine for well-educated professional people who are interested in the arts of the city. Monthly. Estab. October 1969. Circ. 200,000.

Needs: Literary, contemporary, men's, women's, humor, ethnic and book excerpts. Stories preferably related somehow to Chicago. No juvenile, young adult or erotic. Buys 9 mss/year. Length: 5-18 double spaced pages.

How to Contact: Send complete ms with SASE. Reports in 1 month on mss. Sample copy $2.50.
Payment: Pays $350-750 with free author's copies.
Terms: Pays on acceptance for first time North American rights.
Tips: "Submit mss with care."

CHILD LIFE, The Benjamin Franklin Literary & Medical Society, Inc., 1100 Waterway Blvd., Box 567B, Indianapolis IN 46206. (317)634-1100. Editor: John D. Craton. Juvenile magazine for youngsters ages 7-11.
Needs: Juvenile. No adult or adolescent fiction. Length: 1,800 words.
How to Contact: Send complete ms. Reports in 8-10 weeks. Sample copy 50¢. Free writer's guidelines with SASE.
Payment: 3¢/word.
Terms: Pays on publication for all rights.

CHILDREN'S DIGEST, Children's Health Publications, 1100 Waterway Blvd., Box 567B, Indianapolis IN 46206. Magazine with special emphasis on health, nutrition, exercise, and safety for 9-12 year olds.
Needs: Health-related material. "Short factual features dealing with nature, sports, historical and biographical articles. Realistic stories, adventure and mysteries. Humorous stories are highly desirable."
How to Contact: Send complete ms. Sample copy 50¢. Queries not needed. Reports in 10 weeks on mss sent with SASE.
Payment: Pays 3¢/word with 2 free author's copies. Free guidelines with SASE.
Terms: Pays on publication for all rights.
Tips: "We try to present our health-related material in a postive—not a negative—light and we try to incorporate humor and a light approach wherever possible without minimizing the seriousness of what we are saying. Fiction stories that deal with a health theme need not have health as the primary subject but should include it in some way in the course of events. Simultaneous submissions are not accepted."

CHILDREN'S PLAYMATE, The Benjamin Franklin Literary & Medical Society, Inc., 1100 Waterway Blvd., Box 567B, Indianapolis IN 46206. (317)634-1100. Juvenile magazine for children ages 5-8 years.
Needs: Juvenile with special emphasis on health, nutrition, safety, exercise. No adult or adolescent fiction. Length: 600 words.
How to Contact: Send complete ms. Reports in 8-10 weeks.
Payment: 3¢/word.
Terms: Pays on publication for all rights.
Tips: "Stories should be kept simple and entertaining."

CHRISTIAN LIVING FOR SENIOR HIGHS, David C. Cook Publishing Co., 850 N. Grove, Elgin IL 60120. (312)741-2400. Editor: John Conaway. A take-home Sunday School paper used for senior high classes. Weekly. Estab. 1895.
Needs: "Each piece must present some aspect of the Christian life without being preachy. No closing sermons and no pat answers. Any topic appropriate to senior high is acceptable." Buys 16-20 mss/year. Length: 900-1,200 words.
How to Contact: Send complete ms with SASE. Reports in 2 months on mss. Phone queries OK. Free guidelines
Payment: Pays $60-$75.
Terms: Pays on acceptance for all rights.
Tips: "Get to know as much as possible about today's senior high age student. Write from a firm evangelical conviction. We encourage teens to write to us."

THE CHURCH HERALD, The Church Herald, 1324 Lake Dr. S.E., Grand Rapids MI 49506. (616)458-5156. Editor: Dr. John Stapert. "Our publication is directed toward Reformed Protestants who are interested in issues arising in the church, ethics and theology, society and 'culture' from the audience's point of view." Biweekly. Estab. 1826. Circ. 72,000.
Needs: Literary, religious/inspirational, juvenile and young adult. Buys 100 mss/year. Length: 750-1,500 words.
How to Contact: Query with SASE. Reports in 2 weeks on query. Free sample copy with SASE.
Payment: Based on word and volume of ms.
Terms: Pays on acceptance or publication on all rights, first rights, second serial (reprint) rights and one-time rights.

THE CHURCH MUSICIAN, The Sunday School Board of the Southern Baptist Convention, 127 9th Ave. N., Nashville TN 37234. (615)251-2964. Editor: William M. Anderson Jr. "*The Church Musician* is for church music leaders in local churches—music directors, pastors, organists, pianists, choir coordinators, and members of music councils and/or other planning committees or groups. Music leaders read the magazine for spiritual enrichment, testimonials, human interest stories and other materials related to music programs in local churches." Monthly. Estab. October 1950. Circ. 20,000
Needs: Categories related toward church music. Length: 750-2,000 words.
How to Contact: Send complete ms with SASE. Reports in 2 months on ms. Free sample copy with SASE and 30¢ postage.
Payment: Maximum 3¢ per word.
Terms: Pays on acceptance for all rights.
Tips: "Avoid mushy sentiment when writing. It must be believable and, of course, practical."

COBBLESTONE, Cobblestone Publishing, Inc., 28 Main St., Peterborough NH 03458. Editor: Frances Nanklin. History magazine for children (8-13 years old). Monthly with a national distribution.
Needs: Young adult, adventures, humor, mystery, historical and western fiction including "reminiscences, plays and retold folk tales must relate to months theme." Length: 800-2,000 words.
How to Contact: Query with clips of published work. Reports on mss in 6 weeks. Sample copy $1.50. Free guidelines with legal-sized SASE.
Payment: Pays up to 20¢/word.
Terms: Pays on publication for all, first and one-time rights.
Tips: "We make some assignments on a work-for-hire basis. Request an editorial guideline sheet that explains the upcoming issue themes. Submit material 3-4 months in advance. Simultaneous and previously published submissions OK."

CO-ED, Scholastic Inc., 50 W. 44th St., New York NY 10036. Publication for girls and boys, ages 13-18. Monthly.
Needs: "We prefer stories of older (16, 17, 18 year old) teenagers which deal with contemporary problems. Characters should show growth as they confront problems with relationships with friends, family, dating. Suggested themes are finding identity, reconciling, reality and fantasy, making correct life decisions. Non-preachy themes should help initiate class discussions, since the magazine is used as a teaching tool in home economics classes. Charactacters should be well-rounded, strong, non-stereotyped and plots must be logical. No cliché type fluffy romances. Girls with conventional 'feminine' interests must be interesting, active and realistic people." Free sample copy and writer's guidelines with SASE.

COLLAGE, Collage Publications, 2444 Moorpark Ave., #214, San Jose CA 95128.

(408)279-4224. Editor: Timothy J. Seidler. Managing Editor: Lawrence S. White. "*Collage* is an entertainment magazine containing features and interviews related to the music and film industry. Our main interests lie with contemporary music. Our audience appreciates serious, in-depth writings of the music and film industry." Monthly. Estab. May 1977. Circ. 180,000.

Needs: Literary, contemporary, science fiction, fantasy, horror, mystery and humor. "We are open to any writer who has a developed style. No rambling or 'tulips-in-the field' stories." Buys 8 mss/year. Length: 2,000-3,500 words.

How to Contact: Send complete ms with SASE. Reports in 6 weeks on ms. Free sample copy.

Payment: 2¢ per word. Free author's copy.

Terms: Pays on publication for one-time rights (will reassign to writer).

Tips: "Don't be afraid (or lazy) about rewriting. Read your material as though someone else was the author. Strive to be tight in your writing. Please include phone number. Will look at photocopies."

COLORADO WOMAN, Affiliate of Titsch Publishing Co., Inc., Box 5400 TA, Denver CO 80217. (303)573-1433. Publisher: Judy Lockwood. Editor: Nancy Clark. Magazine for all women in the Rocky Mountain area; business, job market, parenting, health and fiction. Monthly. Estab. 1975. Circ. 13,000.

Needs: Women's. Buys 3-5 mss/issue. Length: 500-2,000 words.

How to Contact: Send complete ms with SASE. Reports in 1 month on mss. Sample copy $1.50.

Payment: 8¢/word.

Terms: Pays on publication. Byline given.

CONTACT, United Brethren Publications, 302 Lake St., Huntington IN 46750. (219)356-2312. Editor: C. Stanley Peters. Managing Editor: Steve Dennie. "Sunday School weekly containing articles on believable religious experiences. No tacked on morals. Our audience is adult members of the United Brethren denomination with strong evangelical viewpoints." Weekly. Estab. 1957. Circ. 6,000.

Needs: Religious/inspirational, humor and young adult. Historical fiction welcome. No pieces below high school level or anything lacking religious content. Buys 2 mss/issue. Length: 400-1,200 words.

How to Contact: Send complete ms with SASE. Reports in 2 months on mss. Free sample copy with regular SASE plus 40¢ postage. Free fiction guidelines with legal-sized SASE.

Payment: ¾-1¢/word.

Terms: Pays on acceptance for simultaneous rights, first rights and second serial (reprint) rights.

Tips: "Use dialogue, simple-to-read style, with no tacked on morals."

COSMOPOLITAN MAGAZINE, Hearst, 224 W. 57th St., New York NY 10019. (212)262-5700. Editor: Helen Gurley Brown. Fiction Editor: Nancy Coffey. Associate Fiction Editor: Mary Lou Mullen. Magazine consists of stories with male-female relationships, traditional plots, characterizations; medical, how-to pieces for single career women (18-34). Monthly. Circ. 3 million.

Needs: Contemporary, women's, romance, mystery, adventure. "Stories should include a man and a woman in a relationship or women in jobs with the woman being the protagonist. No highly experimental pieces." Buys 2 short stories plus a novel or book (never unsolicited) excerpt/issue. Length: short shorts (1,500-3,000); longer (4,000-6,000).

How to Contact: Send complete ms with SASE. Reports in 4-6 weeks on mss. Free guidelines with legal-sized SASE.

Payment: Pays $700-1,200. Short shorts $300-$600.

Terms: Pays on acceptance for first North American serial rights.

Tips: "It is rare that unsolicited mss are accepted. We prefer agents and professional writers. Research the magazine you are submitting to."

CREATIVE COMPUTING MAGAZINE, Creative Computing, Box 799M, Morristown NJ 07960. (201)540-0445. Editor: David Ahl. Fiction Editor: Ted Nelson. "*Creative Computing* is the number one magazine in applications and software for personal computers. Readers include educators, computer professionals, students, business people and home users. Content consists of articles, evaluations and profiles of software and hardware." Monthly. Estab. December 1974. Circ. 85,000.
Needs: Contemporary, science fiction, fantasy, men's, women's, humor and computer related. "Fiction does not make up a substantial portion of the magazine. This is not a highly technical journal, but, rather, a form of support for the rapidly expanding field of personal computing. We usually run 2 pieces of fiction and foolishness a month." Buys 2 mss/issue, 24 mss/year. Length: 500-3,000 words.
How to Contact: Send complete ms. Reports in 4-5 weeks. Sample copy $2.50 with SASE.
Payment: $15-400.
Terms: Pays on acceptance for all rights.
Tips: "Fiction must be specifically related to robots or computers. Interesting stories should show how computers can benefit society or be of use in the home."

CRICKET MAGAZINE, Open Court Publishing Co., Box 100, La Salle IL 61301. (815)224-6666. Editor: Marianne Carus. Magazine for children, ages 6-12. Monthly. Estab. September 1973. Circ. 150,000.
Needs: Literary, contemporary, science fiction, fantasy, western, mystery, adventure, humor, juvenile, ethnic and translations. No adult articles. Buys 10-12 mss/year. Length: 500-1,500 words.
Terms: Send complete ms with SASE. Reports in 2 months on mss. Sample copy for $1.75 with 7½x10½ SASE and 45¢ postage. Free guidelines with legal-sized SASE.
Payment: 25¢ per word. 2 free author's copies. $1 charge for extras.
Terms: Pays on publication for first North American serial rights and one-time rights.
Tips: "Do not write *down* to children. Write about familiar subjects which have been well-researched."

DASH, Christian Service Brigade, Box 150, Wheaton IL 60187. (312)665-0630. Managing Editor: Michael J. Chiapperino. "Our magazine aims to provide entertaining wholesome reading while challenging our constituency to love and serve Jesus Christ. Readers are boys, ages 8-11 years, registered in Christian Service Brigade. Published 8 times/year. Circ. 30,000.
Needs: Religious/inspirational, adventure, humor, juvenile and young adult. No stories that contain boring, pat answers. Buys 2 mss/issue, 15-20 mss/year. Length: 800-1,200 words.
How to Contact: Query with or without clips of published work with SASE. Reports in 1 week on queries, 2 weeks on mss. Free fiction guidelines with SASE.
Payment: $35-75. 2 free author's copies. $1 charge for extras.
Terms: Buys first or reprint rights.
Tips: "Make dialogue up to date and realistic; aim for conflict or suspense. Be sure to subtly teach something worthwhile. Use a gripping lead."

THE DEAF CANADIAN MAGAZINE, Deaf Canadian Readers' Association, Box 1291, Edmonton, Alberta, Canada T5J 2M8. (403)466-6707. Editor: Roger Carver. Executive Editor: David Burnett. "Magazine published for deaf persons, families, and also for teachers, physicians, psychologists, rehabilitation counselors, audiologists, speech pathologists, nurses, social workers, occupational therapists, linguists, sociologists, clergymen, and students in these disciplines. The magazine is a very valuable source of information on deafness." Monthly. Estab. September 1972. Circ. 100,000.

Needs: Fiction on deafness. "We do not want anything not related to deafness but will accept any kind of fiction provided it is written by a deaf person." Buys 4 mss/year. Length: 3,000 words.

How to Contact: Query or send complete ms with SASE (must be Canadian postage or International Reply Coupons). Reports in 1 month on queries, 2 months on mss. Sample copy $2.50.

Payment: Free author's copy.

Terms: Pays on publication for assignments on a work-for-hire basis, first rights and first North American serial rights.

Tips: "We recommend that a potential writer subscribe to the magazine to be oriented with our materialistic use ($20.00 regular subscription . . . a special price of $15.00 for any fiction writer or nonfiction writer). To writers unversed in deafness and the deaf world, our suggestion is that you try to become acquainted with its ways before trying to write anything."

DELAWARE TODAY MAGAZINE, Delaware Today, Inc., 206 E. Ayre St., Wilmington DE 19804. (302)995-7146. Editor: John Taylor. Fiction Editor: Rolf Rykken. "We are a regional, middle-class publication, a monthly state magazine, focusing on interesting news feature stories about topics and people of Delaware. Aimed primarily at the suburban-urban areas of northern Delaware, but we also cover the entire state, much of which is rural." Monthly. Estab. April 1962. Circ. 10,200.

Needs: Literary, contemporary, women's, feminist, mystery and humor. No stories about writers; "nothing anti-women, gay, black, etc. or stories in which characters are murdered, blown up in WWIII, commit suicide in the end." Buys 1 ms/issue, 12 mss/year. Length: 1,500-3,000 words.

How to Contact: Send complete ms with SASE. Reports in 1-2 months on mss. Free sample copy with SASE. Free fiction guidelines.

Payment: $100 and 2 free contributor's copies. $1 charge per extra issue.

Terms: Pays on publication for one-time rights.

Tips: "We are perhaps the only state/regional commercial monthly magazine which publishes fiction. While we publish only 12 stories a year, we provide an opening for undiscovered writers in a tight market. However, we seek stellar work—good dialogue, precise description, interesting characters in some sort of discernible conflict, with a semblance of plotting. We are prejudiced against stories about writers and the angst of writing (and filling out forms). We also have good illustrations with the stories."

DISCOVERIES, Nazarene Publishing House, 6401 The Paseo, Kansas City MO 64131. (816)333-7000. Editor: Mark A. York. *Discoveries* is a Sunday School story paper for children ages 8-11. Stories should be character building and teach Christian truths. The audience is composed of children who attend Sunday School in the church of the Nazarene. The paper is for leisure reading. Weekly. Estab. January 1976. Circ. 100,000.

Needs: Religious/inspirational, mystery, adventure and juvenile. Fiction must appeal to children ages 8-11. In a survey of our readership they listed mystery as the favorite type of fiction. No erotica, horror, gay/lesbian, fantasy, confession, gothic, etc. Buys 1-2 mss/issue, 75-104 mss/year. Length: 500-1,000 words.

How to Contact: Send complete ms with SASE. Reports in 3 weeks on mss. Free sample copy with SASE plus 15¢ postage. Free fiction guidelines.

Payment: 3¢ per word up to $30; 2¢ per word for second rights.

Terms: Pays on acceptance for first rights or whatever is offered.

Tips: "Writers should contact our office for the brochure describing our publication's needs. Stories which fit our requirements should then be submitted for consideration. Fiction should be action-oriented with a strong beginning and ending. Christian teaching should be intrinsic within the story and not added on at the end of the manuscript. It must correlate with the purposes of one of our Sunday School lessons for it to be purchased and used. Most of the stories published in *Discoveries* are fiction; we are always looking for talented authors of short stories for children that teach Christian principles. Manuscripts submitted to *Discoveries* that show merit may be purchased and edited as much as necessary to adjust them to fit the purposes of the story paper."

DISCOVERY, Dept. of Christian Education, Free Methodist Headquarters, 901 College Ave., Winona Lake IN 46590. (219)267-7161. Editor: Vera Bethel. Sunday School take-home paper for children in grades 4-5-6. Weekly. Estab. 1970. Circ. 35,000.
Needs: Juvenile. "We buy fiction involving kids 9-12 in school and play situations wherein some conflict must be solved in a manner suggesting positive attitudes and growth." No talking animals, Biblical background, informational articles parading as fiction. Buys 1 ms/issue, 52 mss/year. Length: 1,000-1,200 words.
How to Contact: Send complete ms with SASE. Reports in 1 month on mss. Free sample copy. Free fiction guidelines with legal-sized SASE.
Payment: 2¢ per word. 2 free author's copies. 10¢ charge for extra.
Terms: Pays on acceptance for simultaneous, first, second serial (reprint) and one-time rights.

DUDE, Dugent Publishing Corp., 2355 Salzedo St., Suite 204, Coral Gables FL 33134. (305)443-2379. Editor: John C. Fox. Fiction Editor: Thomas W. Austin. Men's magazine of erotic appeal (fiction and nonfiction). Bimonthly. Estab. 1958. Circ. 100,000.
Needs: Literary, contemporary, psychic/supernatural, science fiction, horror, men's erotica, western, mystery, adventure and humor. Short fiction (only), preferably but not always of a sexually-oriented nature. No material on children, religious subjects or anything that might be libelous. Length: 1,000-2,000 words.
How to Contact: Send complete ms with SASE. Reports in 1 month on mss. Sample copy $3.00. Free fiction guidelines with legal-sized SASE.
Payment: $100-125/copy. Free author's copy. Pays on publication for first rights.

EASYRIDERS MAGAZINE Entertainment for Adult Riders, Box 52, Malibu CA 90265. (213)889-8701. Editor: Lou Kimzey. Men's magazine with bike related material: how-to's, travel, new equipment information, fiction for adult men who own or desire to own expensive custom motorcycles, rugged individualists who own and enjoy their choppers. Monthly. Circ. 482,702.
Needs: Men's and adventure. Only interested in hard-hitting rugged fiction. Length: 2,000-3,500 words.
How to Contact: Send complete ms with SASE. Reports in 3 weeks on mss. Sample copy 25¢.
Payment: Pays 10¢/word; payment depends on quality, length and use in magazines.
Terms: Pays on acceptance for all rights.
Tips: "Gut level language accepted; dope or sex scenes OK but are not to be graphically described. As long as the material is directly aimed at our macho intelligent male audience, there should be no great problem breaking into our magazine. Before submitting material, however, we strongly recommend that the writer observe our requirements and study a sample copy."

EBONY JR!, Johnson Publishing Co., Inc., 820 S. Michigan Ave., Chicago IL 60605. (312)322-9272. Editor: Marcia V. Roebuck. Fiction Editor: Mary C. Lewis. "A magazine designed to highlight the outstanding experiences of blacks, both past and present, as well as to improve children's learning skills, particularly in language arts. Directed to children ages 6-12, with special attention to black children of those ages. Due to the content emphasis on black history and current events as they relate to blacks, *Ebony Jr!* provides a good learning tool." Monthly; bimonthly June/July and August/September. Estab. May 1973. Circ. 90,000.

Needs: Contemporary, science fiction, fantasy, western, mystery, adventure, humor, juvenile, ethnic (black) and condensed novels. "All categories must be geared with our audience in mind. No articles using characters with stereotypical images of blacks, or women; violence and/or death unnecessarily; or stories poking fun at culture's traditions." Buys 2-3 mss/issue, 20-30 mss/year. Length: 400-1,500 words.

How to Contact: Query or send complete ms with SASE. Reports in 3 weeks to 3 months on queries and mss. Sample copy 75¢. Free guidelines with legal-sized SASE.

Payment: $75-150. Free author's copy. 75¢ charge per extra copy.

Terms: Pays on acceptance for all rights, second serial (reprint) rights and first North American serial rights.

Tips: "Purchase at least one sample copy and peruse fiction therein carefully for style, content, characterizations; query first giving specific idea as well as indication of deadline for submission. Request writer's guidelines; if rejected, continue to submit ideas/queries. Follow up on your submissions (don't be discouraged by any initial rejections) with further ideas. Don't send in a manuscript without doing research on the publication first." *Ebony Jr!* sponsors an annual writing contest for children ages 6-12. This contest involves short story entries; contest is announced in the October issues (1st and 2nd prize winners' stories are published in the October issue).

ELITE, Playpen Enterprises, 234 Eglinton Ave. E., Suite 401, Toronto, Ontario, Canada M4P 1K5. (416)487-7183. Editor: D.S. Wells. Fiction Editor: K. Lynn. Men's magazine with general and erotic material, ages 18-40. Monthly. Estab. February 1974. Circ. 200,000.

Needs: Contemporary, fantasy, men's, erotica and humor. Buys 2 mss/issue, 24 mss/year. Length: 2,000-3,500 words.

How to Contact: Send complete ms with SASE. Reports in 1 month on mss. Sample copy $1 with 9x12 SASE plus 63¢ postage. Free fiction guidelines. Payment: $75-150.

Terms: Pays on publication for one-time rights.

ELLERY QUEEN'S MYSTERY MAGAZINE, Davis Publications, Inc., 380 Lexington Ave., New York NY 10017. (212)557-9100. Editor: Ellery Queen. Managing Editor: Eleanor Sullivan. Magazine for lovers of mystery fiction. Published 13 times/year. Estab. 1941. Circ. 400,000.

Needs: "We accept only mystery." Buys 10-15 mss/issue. Length: up to 9,000 words.

How to Contact: Send complete ms with SASE. Reports in 1 month on mss. Free fiction guidelines.

Payment: 3¢ per word and up.

Terms: Pays on acceptance for first North American serial rights.

Tips: "Read the magazine; know what we publish. We have Department of First Stories and publish at least one first story an issue—i.e., the author's first published fiction. A story submitted to *EQMM* receives an alternate reading for *Alfred Hitchcock's Mystery Magazine* if it is rejected by *EQMM*."

ESQUIRE, 13-30 Corp., 2 Park Ave., New York City NY 10016. (212)561-8100. Editor: Phillip Moffitt. Fiction Editor: Rust Hills. Male-oriented magazine with good modern American writing for young professional men 21-40. Estab. 1933.

Needs: Literary, contemporary, short stories. No erotica, horror, religious or inspirational. Buys 1 ms/issue. Length: 5,000-7,000 words.

How to Contact: Send complete ms with SASE. Reports in 1 month on mss.

Payment: Varied.

Terms: Pays on acceptance for varied rights.

Tips: "Send a clearly typed proofread story with plain straightforward cover letter. Never send a query for fiction mss."

ESSENCE, 1500 Broadway, New York NY 10036. (212)730-4260. Editor: Daryl Alexander. Fiction Editor: Rosemary Bray. General interest magazine with historical, how-to, humor, financial, health, education, beauty, travel subjects for black women. Monthly. Estab. May 1970. Circ. 600,000.
Needs: Fantasy, romance, adventure, humor, experimental and condensed and serialized novels. Buys 33 mss/year. Length: 1,500-3500 words.
How to Contact: Send complete ms with SASE. Reports in 2 months on mss. Sample copy $1. Free guidelines.
Payment: Pays $300.
Terms: Pays on acceptance. 25% kill fee and byline given.
Tips: "We're looking for fiction about contemporary black women, the challenges they face, their joys and sorrows; upbeat material if possible."

EVANGEL, Dept. of Christian Education, Free Methodist Headquarters, 901 College Ave., Winona Lake IN 46590. (219)267-7161. Editor: Vera Bethel. Sunday School take-home paper for distribution to young adults who attend church. Fiction involves young couples and singles coping with everyday crises, making decisions that show growth; ages 25-35 year olds. Weekly. Estab. 1896. Circ. 35,000.
Needs: Religious/inspirational. "No fiction without any semblance of Christian message or where the message clobbers the reader." Buys 1 ms/issue, 52 mss/year. Length: 1,000-1,500.
How to Contact: Send complete ms with SASE. Reports in 1 month on ms. Free sample copy. Free fiction guidelines with legal-sized SASE.
Payment: $20 or 2¢ per word. 2 free author's copies. 10¢ charge for each extra.
Terms: Pays on acceptance for simultaneous, first, second serial (reprint), first North American serial rights and one-time rights.
Tips: "Choose a contemporary situation or conflict, create a good mix for the characters (not all-good or all-bad heroes and villains). Don't spell out everything in detail; let the reader fill in some blanks in the story. Too much detail is boring. Keep him guessing."

FACE-TO-FACE, United Methodist Publishing House, 201 8th Ave. S., Nashville TN 37202. (615)749-6225. Editor: Rev. Eddie L. Robinson. Religious-oriented magazine for teens, ages 15-18. Quarterly. Estab. 1968. Circ. 15,000.
Needs: Literary, contemporary and religious/inspirational. Fiction should deal with major problems and concerns of older teens, such as finding one's own identity, dealing with family and peer group pressures, and so forth. No straight moral fiction or stories with pat answers or easy solutions used. Story must fit themes of issue. No serials. No other subjects considered. Buys 4-6 mss/year. Length: 1,000-4,000 words.
How to Contact: Send complete ms with SASE. Reports in 2 months on mss. Free sample copy with 9x12 SASE and 55¢ postage. Free fiction guidelines.
Payment: 4¢ per word. 2 free author's copies.
Terms: Pays on acceptance for all rights.

FAMILY CIRCLE, Family Circle, 488 Madison Ave., New York NY 10022. Editor: Arthur Hettich. Books and Fiction Editor: Constance Leisure. Service magazine, mostly how-to articles on food, crafts, work, money saving, health and beauty for women, ages 20-70+. They read it for information, advice and to find out how to do everything better. Published every 3 weeks. Estab. 1930. Circ. 8 million.
Needs: Family-oriented, contemporary, inspirational, women's, confession, romance, mystery, humor, ethnic, serialized and condensed novels. "We do get most of our fiction by excerpting or condensing books now. The readers seem to like this more than traditional short stories." Buys 10 mss/year. Length: 700-5,000 words.
How to Contact: Send complete ms with SASE. Reports in 2 months on mss. Free guidelines.
Payment: Pays $500. 10 free author's copies.

Terms: Pays on acceptance for all, first, second, one-time rights.
Tips: "Read the magazine. Make sure the story says something. So many writers don't make a point. A short story is like a poem—it needs shaping and definition."

FAR WEST, Wright Publishing Co., Inc., Box 2260, 2949 Century Place, Costa Mesa CA 92626. (714)545-2118. Editor: Scott McMillan. Associate Editor: Dee Anderson. Western fiction, from the period 1820 to the turn of the century; settings generally located west of the Missouri River; for the traditional western fiction reader. Quarterly. Estab. March 1978. Circ. 125,000.
Needs: Western. No excessive use of violence, heavy sex, no poetry (westerns) at this time being accepted. No range romances. Buys 12 mss/issue, 50 mss/year. Length: 2,000-35,000 words.
How to Contact: Send complete ms with SASE. Reports in 2 months on mss. Sample copy $2.50 with 9x12 SASE with free guidelines.
Payment: Pays $50-$700.
Terms: Pays on publication for all rights and by contract with author.
Tips: "Be familiar with western technology, terms used in stories such as guns, horses, saddles, etc. Avoid over-use of western phraseology ('Wal, pardner, y'all')."

FARM WIFE NEWS, Box 643, Milwaukee WI 53201. (414)272-5410. Managing Editor: Ruth Benedict. General interest publication with focus on subjects of daily interest to the farm woman for national farm and ranch women of all ages. Estab. 1970. Circ. 350,000.
Needs: Contemporary, humor. Themes should relate to country living. Buys 20-30 mss/ year. Length: 1,000 words.
How to Contact: Query or send complete ms. Reports in 6 weeks on queries and mss. Sample copy $1 with free guidelines.
Payment: Pays $55-$150.
Terms: Pays on publication. Byline given. Submit seasonal material at least 6 months in advance. No photocopied submissions.
Tips: "We are always looking for good freelance material. Topic, subject should be approached from a rural woman's point of view or appeal to the farm wife."

FIRST CLASS, Western Airlines, 141 El Camino, Beverly Hills CA 90212. (213)273-1990. Editor: Frank M. Hiteshew. General interest magazine of Airline Passengers Association for first class passengers all over the world. Bimonthly.
Needs: Contemporary, romance and humor. Light, positive, upbeat stories relating to travel anywhere. No plane crash stories. Length: 2,000 words.
How to Contact: Query with SASE. Reports in 3 months on mss.
Payment: Pays 10¢/word.
Terms: Pays on publication for all rights.
Tips: "Due to lack of good fiction, we seldom print short stories. Byline given. Photocopied submissions OK. 50% kill fee. Submit seasonal stories one year in advance of issue date."

FLARE, 481 University Ave., Toronto, Ontario, Canada M5W 1A7. (416)596-5453. Editor: Keitha McLean. Associate Editor: Rona Maynard. Magazine of fashion, beauty and lifestyle for women from 18-34. Published 10 times/year. Estab. 1979. Circ. 163,000.
Needs: No designated categories. Length: 5,000 words.
How to Contact: Send complete ms with International Reply Coupon. Sample copy 60¢ with free guidelines.
Payment: Pays $400 minimum.
Terms: Pays on acceptance for first North American serial rights. Byline given. Seasonal material 3 months in advance. Simultaneous, photocopied and previously published submissions OK.

Tips: "Canadian writers only. We promote new Canadian literary talent, which we find through an annual competition announced each fall."

FLORIDA SINGLES MAGAZINE AND DATE BOOK, Box 83, Palm Beach FL 33480. Editor: Harold Alan. Magazine dealing with all aspects and problems of "singles" (children, dating, etc.) for single, divorced, widowed, separated persons. Bimonthly. Estab. 1978. Circ. 10,000.
Needs: "We will look at any ms that is related in general to the single life." Length: 800-1,400 words.
How to Contact: Send complete ms with SASE. Reports in 2 weeks on mss. Free sample copy.
Payment: Pays $10-$30 ($30 for first time in publication; $15 for each time reprinted in other magazines).
Terms: Pays on publication for second serial and one-time rights. Simultaneous and photocopied submissions OK.

THE FRIEND, Church of Jesus Christ of Latter-day Saints, 50 E. North Temple, Salt Lake City UT 84150. (801)531-2210. Managing Editor: Lucile C. Reading. Children's magazine directed toward ages 12 and under. Monthly except for a combined August/September issue. Estab. January 1971. Circ. 210,000.
Needs: Literary, contemporary, inspirational, adventure, humor, and juvenile. Buys 8-10 mss/issue. Length: 1,000-2,000 words.
How to Contact: Send complete ms with SASE. Reports in 1 month on ms. Free sample copy and guidelines.
Payment: 5¢ and up per word.
Terms: Pays on acceptance for first rights.

GALLERY MAGAZINE, Montcalm Publishing Corp., 800 2nd Ave., New York NY 10017. (212)986-9600. Editorial Director: Eric Protter. Executive Editor: Joseph Spieler. Sophisticated men's magazine similar to *Playboy*; general interest, how-to's, humor, interviews, investigative reports and fiction for men between 18 and 35 years old. Monthly. Estab. November 1972. Circ. 650,000.
Needs: Literary, science fiction, fantasy, horror, erotica and humor. No romance. Buys 1-2 mss/issue, 20-24 mss/year. Length: 3,500-6,000 words.
How to Contact: Query or send complete ms with SASE. Reports in 1 month on queries, 6 weeks on mss. Sample copy $2.95.
Payment: Pays $250-$750 (special arrangements with established name writers).
Terms: Pays half on acceptance and half on publication for first North American serial rights. Byline given.
Tips: "Submit seasonal/holiday stories six months in advance. Photocopied mss accepted."

THE GAMBLING SCENE, Box 4483, Stanford CA 94305. Editor: Michael Wiesenberg. Magazine for readers interested in gambling and gaming, particularly that of cardrooms and casinos of the West. Monthly. Estab. 1978. Circ. 10,000.
Needs: Gambling-related subjects. Nothing derogatory to gambling, overly sexual, sexist or discriminatory. Buys 2-3 fiction mss/year. Length: 300-1,800 words.
How to Contact: Send complete ms with SASE. Reports on mss in 1 month or mss may be held for later use. Sample copy $1.
Payment: 2-5¢/word.
Terms: Pays on publication for second serial (reprint) rights and first North American serial rights.

GENT, Dugent Publishing Corp., 2355 Salzedo St. Suite 204, Coral Gables FL 33134. (305)443-2378. Editor: John C. Fox. Fiction Editor: Thomas W. Austin. "Men's magazine designed to have erotic appeal for the reader. Our publications are directed to a male audience, but we do have a certain percentage of female readers. For the most part, our audience is interested in erotically stimulating material, but not exclusively." Monthly. Estab. 1959. Circ. 175,000.

Needs: Literary, contemporary, psychic/supernatural science fiction, horror, men's, erotica, western, mystery, adventure and humor. *Gent* specializes in D-Cup cheesecake, and fiction should be gauged accordingly. "Most of the fiction published includes several sex scenes, although on occasion we do use stories without prurient interest. No fiction that concerns children, religious subjects, or anything that might be libelous." Buys 3 mss/issue, 36 mss/year. Length: 2,000-3,500 words.

How to Contact: Send complete ms with SASE. Reports in month on mss. Sample copy $2.50. Fiction guidelines free with legal-sized SASE.

Payment: $100-150. Free author's copy.

Terms: Pays on publication for first North American serial rights.

Tips: "Since *Gent* magazine is the 'Home of the D-Cups,' stories and articles containing either characters or themes with a major emphasis on large breasts will have the best chance for consideration. We advise would-be contributors to obtain and study a sample copy first."

GOLF JOURNAL, United States Golf Assoc., Golf House, Far Hills NJ 07931. (201)234-2300. Editor: Robert Sommers. Managing Editor: George Eberl. "The magazine's subject is golf—its history, lore, rules, equipment, and general information. The focus is on amateur golf and those things applying to the millions of American golfers. Our audience is generally professional, highly literate, and knowledgeable; presumably they read *Golf Journal* because of an interest in the game, its traditions, and its noncommercial aspects." Published 8 times a year. Estab. 1949. Circ. 120,000.

Needs: Humor. "Fiction is very limited. *Golf Journal* has had an occasional humorous story, topical in nature. Generally speaking, short stories are not used much. Golf jokes will not be used." Buys 10-12 mss/year. Length: 1,000-2,000 words.

How to Contact: Send complete ms with SASE. Reports in 2 months on mss. Free sample copy with SASE.

Payment: $150-300. 1-10 free author's copies.

Terms: Pays on acceptance.

Tips: "Know your subject (golf); edit your copy thoroughly; familiarize yourself first with the publication."

GOOD HOUSEKEEPING, 959 Eighth Ave., New York NY 10019. Editor: John Mack Carter. Fiction Editor: Naome Lewis. Homemaking magazine of informational articles, how-to's for homemakers of all ages. Monthly. Circ. 5 million.

Needs: Contemporary, women's, gothic, romance, western and adventure and mother-child stories. Buys 2 short stories/issue. Length: 1,000-4,000 words. Novel condensations to 20,000 words.

How to Contact: Query and send complete ms with SASE. Reports in 3 weeks on both queries and mss.

Payment: Pays standard magazine rates.

Terms: Pays on acceptance for periodical publishing rights, second serial and first North American serial rights.

GRIT, 208 W. 3rd St., Williamsport PA 17701. (717)326-1771. Editor: Terry L. Ziegler. Fiction Editor: Mrs. Frances Noll. Tabloid; newspaper which presents positive inspirational features, human interest, patriotic stories for general readership of all ages in small town and rural America. Weekly. Circ. 1,200,000.

Needs: Stories should be wholesome with interesting plots and believable characters. Writ-

ing should be simple and down-to-earth. No explicit sex, profanity, drugs or immorality. Length: 15,000-30,000.
How to Contact: Query or send complete ms with SASE. Reports in 2-4 weeks on queries and mss. Sample copy $1 with free guidelines.
Payment: Variable rates.
Terms: Pays on acceptance. Buys reprint and original material. Byline given.

GULFSHORE LIFE, Gulfshore Publishing Co., Inc., 3620 Tamiami Trail, N., Naples FL 33940. (813)262-6425. Editor: Merrie Pate. Seasonal magazine about people, sports, homes, boats, features of interest to winter residents, year-round residents and visitors of Southwest Florida. Published October through June. Estab. 1970. Circ. 18,000.
Needs: Stories must have Florida setting. Buys mss for annual fiction writer's contest; deadline is March 1; 3,000 word limit.
How to Contact: Send complete ms with SASE beginning January 1. Reports after contest judging.
Terms: Pays on publication for first-time rights. Byline given. Photocopied and simultaneous submissions OK.

HADASSAH MAGAZINE, 50 W. 58th St., New York NY 10019. Executive Editor: Alan M. Tigay. General interest magazine primarily concerned with Israel, the American Jewish community and American current affairs for members of Hadassah. Monthly except combined June/July and August/September issues. Circ. 370,000.
Needs: Ethnic (Jewish). Length: 3,000 words maximum.
How to Contact: Send complete ms with SASE. Reports in 6 weeks on mss.
Payment: Pays $300 minimum.
Terms: Pays on publication for US publication rights.
Tips: "We get too many 'I Remember Mama' stories. Write a good short story with strong plot showing positive Jewish values."

HARPER'S MAGAZINE, 2 Park Ave., Room 1809, New York NY 10016. Editor: Lewis H. Lapham. Magazine for well-educated, widely read and socially concerned college-aged and older, those active in political and community affairs. Monthly. Circ. 325,000.
Needs: Contemporary and humor. Stories on contemporary life and its problems. Length: 1,000-5,000 words.
How to Contact: Query through agent. Reports in 6 weeks on queries.
Payment: Pays $500-1,000.
Terms: Pays on acceptance for rights though they vary on each author and material. Negotiable kill fee and byline given.

HARVEY FOR LOVING PEOPLE, Harvey Shapiro Inc., 450 7th Ave., Suite 2305, New York NY 10001. (212)564-0112. Editor: Harvey Shapiro. Managing Editor: Ray Schultz. Magazine dedicated to the enrichment of loving relationships between couples, offering sexually informative material in graphically erotic manner. "Our readership consists of people interested in highly informative sex-related information." Monthly. Estab. December 1979. Circ. 300,000.
Needs: Gay/lesbian and heterosexual-erotica. No material accepted that is not sexually oriented. Buys 2-3 mss/issue. Length: 1,000-1,500 words.
How to Contact: Query with SASE. Reports in 2 weeks on queries, 1 week on mss.
Payment: $75-100
Terms: Pays on publication for all rights.

HEAVY METAL, National Lampoon, Inc., 635 Madison Ave., New York NY 10022. (212)688-4070. Editor: J. Simmons. *Heavy Metal* is an adult illustrated fantasy magazine for science fiction, fantasy and comics fans. Monthly. Estab. April 1977. Circ. 200,000.

Needs: Science fiction and fantasy. "Though we don't publish fiction per se, we will look at fiction to turn into illustrated strips."
How to contact: Query and send complete ms. Reports on queries and mss in 2 weeks. Sample copy $2. Free fiction and art guideline.
Payment: Negotiable.
Terms: Pays on publication for all rights for 18 months.

HERS, I.P.C. Magazines, Ltd., King's Reach Tower, Stamford St., London, England SE1 9LS. Editor H. Dawson. Fiction Editor: Ms. J. Meek. Fictionalized true-life magazine with stories dramatic and slightly sexual in content and written in the first person style. For young women (19-26) either married with young children or dating. Low to middle socio/economic background. Monthly. Estab. 1968. Circ. 140,000.
Needs: Psychic/supernatural, men's, women's, confession, young adult and ethnic. No romantic, third person stories or overtly pornographic material. Buys 11 mss/issue. Length: 1,000-5,000 words.
How to Contact: Query and send complete ms with International Reply Coupons. Reports on queries in 3 weeks, 2 months on mss. Free fiction guidelines.
Terms: Pays on acceptance for first British serial rights.
Tips: "Know your characters and have the story outline clear in your mind from beginning to end before you start. Keep stories dramatic and/or emotional and the principal female characters young; avoid characters with teenage children. The material must relate to the reader's lifestyle."

HI-CALL, Gospel Publishing House, 1445 Boonville Ave., Springfield MO 65802. (417)862-2781 ext. 1208. Editor: Dr. Charles W. Ford. Ass't. Editor: Tom Young. Take-home Sunday School paper for teenagers (12-17). Weekly. Estab. 1954. Circ. 160,000.
Needs: Religious/inspirational, romance, western, mystery/suspense, adventure, humor, young adult with a strong but not preachy Biblical emphasis. Length: up to 1,800 words.
How to Contact: Send complete ms with SASE. Reports in 3 weeks on mss. Free sample copy and guidelines.
Payment: Pays 1-2¢/word.
Terms: Pays on acceptance for one-time rights. Simultaneous and previously published submissions OK.

HIGHLIGHTS FOR CHILDREN, 803 Church St., Honesdale PA 18431. (717)253-1080. Editor-in-Chief: Walter Barbe. Editor: Kent L. Brown Jr. Address fiction to: Constance McAllister, Associate Editor. Published 11 times/year. Circ. 1.2 million.
Needs: Juvenile (2-12). "We are eager for easy stories for very young readers but realize that this is the most difficult kind of writing. No war, crime or violence." Buys 6-7 mss/issue. Maximum length: 900 words.
How to Contact: Send complete ms with SASE. Reports in 2 months on mss. Free guidelines with legal-sized SASE.
Payment: Pays 8¢/word.
Terms: Pays on acceptance for all rights.
Tips: "It is not our policy to consider fiction on the strength of the reputation of the author. We judge each submission on its own merits. Like stories with real-life children, unusual fiction, vivid and full of action for boys and girls. Need winter, urban, horse, mystery and humorous stories. Moral teaching should be subtle."

HOME LIFE, The Sunday School Board of the Southern Baptist Convention, 127 9th Ave., N., Nashville TN 37234. (615)251-2271. Editor: Reuben Herring. A Christian family magazine. "Top priorities are strengthening and enriching marriage; parenthood; family concerns and problems; and spiritual and personal growth. Most of our readers are parents between the age of 25-50. They read it out of denominational loyalty and desire for Chris-

tian growth and discipleship." Monthly. Estab. January 1947. Circ. 790,000.
Needs: Contemporary, religious/inspirational, humor and young adult. "We do not want distasteful, risque or raunchy fiction. Nor should it be too fanciful or far-fetched." Buys 1-2 mss/issue, 12-24 mss/year.
How to Contact: Query or send complete ms with SASE. Reports in 1 week on queries, 2 weeks on mss. Free sample copy with 9x11½ SASE and 70¢ postage.
Payment 3½/word (for published copy). 3 free author's copies.
Terms: Pays on acceptance for all rights, first rights and first North American serial rights.

HUDSON VALLEY MAGAZINE, 16 School St., Yonkers NY 10701. (914)963-8411. Editor/Publisher: Angelo R. Martinelli. "General interest magazine with an editorial thrust toward leisure activities and folklore of this historical, beautiful town and country region of New York, West Connecticut and Western Massachusetts. Appeals to people of all ages and both sexes. Readership is upscale in education and income." Monthly. Estab. 1971. Circ. 27,000.
Needs: "We seek good objective fiction of interest to Hudson Valley residents." Length: 1,000-2,000 words.
How to Contact: Send complete ms with SASE. Reports in 1 month on mss. Sample copy $1.00 with free guidelines.
Payment: Pays 3¢/word.
Terms: Acquires all rights. Simultaneous and photocopied submissions OK.

HUMPTY DUMPTY'S MAGAZINE, Children's Health Publications, Benjamin Franklin Literary & Medical Society, Inc., 1100 Waterway Blvd., Box 567B, Indianapolis, IN 46206. Editor: Christine French. Children's magazine stressing health, nutrition, hygiene, exercise, and safety for children ages 4-7. Monthly except bimonthly April-May, June-July and August-September. Circ. 500,000.
Needs: Juvenile health-related material. No inanimate talking objects. Rhyming stories should flow easily with no contrived rhymes. Buys 1-3 mss/issue. 600 words maximum.
How to Contact: Send complete ms. SASE. Reports in 8-10 weeks. Sample copy 50¢. Editorial guidelines with SASE.
Payment: Pays 3¢/word for stories plus 2 author's copies.
Terms: Buys all rights.
Tips: "Although brief, stories should have a beginning, middle and end. In contemporary stories, characters should be up-to-date, with realistic dialogue. We prefer that the main character solves his or her own problems."

HUSTLER MAGAZINE, Larry Flynt Publications, 2029 Century Park East, Los Angeles CA 90067. (213)556-9200. Editor: Bruce David. Fiction Editor: Richard Warren Lewis. Adult men's magazine. Monthly. Estab. 1974. Circ. 1.9 million.
Needs: Literary, contemporary, psychic/supernatural, science fiction, horror, men's, erotica and adventure. Buys 1 ms/issue. Length: 4,000-4,500 words.
How to Contact: Send complete ms with SASE. Reports on mss in 2 months. Free fiction guidelines.
Payment: $1,000 minimum. 2 free author's copies.
Terms: Pays on acceptance for negotiable rights depending on agreement with writer.
Tips: "Use an IBM Selectric typewriter; set margins at 15x70. Avoid first person singular."

IDEALS MAGAZINE, Ideals Publishing Corp., 11315 Watertown Plank Rd., Milwaukee WI 53226. (414)771-2700. Editor: James A. Kuse. *Ideals* is a family-oriented magazine with issues corresponding to seasons and based on traditional values. Published 8 times a year. Estab. 1944. Circ. 700,000.
Needs: Religious/inspirational, men's, women's, humor, juvenile, seasonal/holidays, nostalgia and travel. No lewd or risque fiction. Buys 4-5 mss/issue, 40 mss/year. Length: 500-2,500 words.

How to Contact: Send complete ms with SASE. Reports in 2 months on mss. Free sample copy with 8½x11 SASE and $1.35 postage.
Payment: Varies.
Terms: Pays on publication for one-time rights.

IN TOUCH, Wesleyan Publishing House, Box 2000, Marion IN 46952. (317)674-3301. Office Editor: Sandy Metz. Publication for teens, ages 13-18. Weekly.
Needs: Religious/inspirational. Stories should have definite Christian emphasis and character building values but not be preachy. Setting, plot and action should be realistic. Length: 1,200-1,600 words.
How to Contact: Send complete ms with SASE. "Queries are not encouraged." Reports in 6-8 weeks on mss. Free sample copy.
Payment: Pays 2¢/word.
Terms: Pays on acceptance. Byline given.

INSIGHT, Young Calvinist Federation, Box 7244, Grand Rapids MI 49510. (616)241-5616. Editor: John Knight. Fiction Editor: Martha Kalk. "*Insight* magazine is designed to help young people recognize Christ as Lord, and to prepare them to serve Him always and everywhere. Our readership is made up of young people 15 to 21 years of age in American and Canadian urban and rural areas." Published 10 times per year. Estab. 1919. Circ. 22,000.
Needs: Literary, contemporary, religious/inspirational and young adult and teen. Buys 1 ms/issue, 10 mss/year. Length: 900-2,000 words.
How to Contact: Send complete ms with SASE. Reports in 1 month on mss. Free sample copy with 9x12 SASE and 50¢ postage. Free fiction guidelines with legal-sized SASE.
Payment: $35-100.
Terms: Pays on publication for simultaneous, first, second serial (reprint) and one-time rights.
Tips: "Short stories should lead our readers into a better understanding of how their Christian beliefs apply to their daily lives. The events and the characters must be lively, and so must the dialogue. Anything unrealistic or overly sentimental cannot be used. Quality is a high priority; the pieces must be well-written and professional."

INTIMATE ROMANCES, Rolat Publishing Corp., 667 Madison Ave., New York NY 10021. Editor: Ilene Dube. Contemporary women's magazine on romance and erotica. "We are primarily read by teenagers and young working class women wanting to learn about sex. We do, however, have readers of all ages and calibers. We are seeking to expand our readership to all groups of women with liberal, open-minded attitudes about sex." Monthly. Circ. 100,000.
Needs: Psychic/supernatural, fantasy, horror, feminist, gay/lesbian, erotica, confession, gothic, romance, mystery, adventure and humor. "We are interested in supernatural, horror, and science fiction and fantasy to the extent that it qualifies as a romance or confession. All themes can be worked into the confession genre by a good writer. No stories condemning premarital sex or abortion or those with religious overtones or morals. No stories that do not accept liberated, contemporary women." Buys 7-8 mss/issue. Length: 3,000-7,000 words.
How to Contact: Send complete ms with SASE. Reports in 1-2 months on mss. Free fiction guidelines with legal-sized SASE.
Payment: $125.
Terms: Pays on acceptance for all rights.
Tips: "Study our magazines (not other confession magazines) for style, language, tone, and type of story. Stories should have strong emotional conflict. If including a sex scene, it should be described in a soft and tender manner. Realistic dialogue is an important ingredient. We are constantly deluged with material, so it is a very competitive market. Contrary to popular belief, we are not a good place for beginners to break in. Though we do not care if

an author has previous publishing credits, we are interested in well-written quality material. Writing confession stories is a specialized craft in which not many people succeed. However, there is some good news: We are always interested in fresh new ideas and themes, and are willing to work with a new writer who offers these." Also publishes *True Secrets* and *Intimate Secrets*.

INTIMATE SECRETS, Rolat Publishing Corp., 667 Madison Ave., New York NY 10021. Editorial Director: Ilene Dube. "Rolat Women's Group includes *True Romances, Intimate Secrets*, and *Intimate Romances*. The guidelines for all 3 magazines are the same." See *Intimate Romances*.

INTIMATE STORY, Ideal Publishing Corp., 2 Park Ave., New York NY 10016. (212)683-4200. Editor: Janet Wandel. "*Intimate Story* is a modern confession magazine. Its fiction is sex-oriented, centered around conflicts and problems within the family, between men and women, challenges facing women alone, etc. It also uses general, human interest fiction. Our audience is primarily blue-collar women of a wide age range. This magazine provides inexpensive entertainment on a variety of subjects of interest to women." Monthly. Estab. 1948. Circ. 200,000.
Needs: Psychic/supernatural, women's, erotica (mild), confession, romance and young adult. Does not want anything outside the realm of possibility, material that is negative or depressing, or hard-core porn. Buys 10 mss/issue. Length: 2,000-7,000 words.
How to Contact: Send complete ms with SASE. Reports in 3 months on mss.
Payment: 3¢/word up to a maximum of $160.
Terms: Pays on publication for all rights.
Tips: "Carefully read the most recent issue of *Intimate Story* you can find. It's your best guide to acceptable subject matter and writing style. Know specifically the type of magazine you're submitting to; send suitable material. Be patient about responses to queries and submissions. Please don't ask for detailed explanations as to why a manuscript has been rejected."

ISAAC ASIMOV'S SCIENCE FICTION MAGAZINE, Davis Publications, Inc., Box 13116, Philadelphia PA 19101. Editor: George Sithers. Magazine consists of science fiction stories for adults and young adults. 13 issues a year. Estab. 1977. Circ. 150,000.
Needs: Science fiction. No horror or psychic/supernatural. Buys 10 mss/issue. Length: up to 20,000 words.
How to Contact: Send complete ms with SASE. Reports in 1 week on mss. Free fiction guidelines with legal-sized SASE.
Payment: 5¢/word for stories up to 7,500 words long, 3¢ a word for stories over 12,500 long, $375 for stories between those limits.
Terms: Pays on acceptance for first North American serial rights plus specified foreign rights, as explained in contract.

JACK AND JILL, The Benjamin Franklin Literary & Medical Society, Inc., 1100 Waterway Blvd., Box 567B, Indianapolis IN 46206. (317)634-1100. Editor: William Wagner. Children's magazine of articles, stories and activities with a health, safety, exercise or nutritionally oriented theme, ages 7-10 years. Monthly except April/May, June/July, August/September. Estab. 1938. Circ. 600,000.
Needs: Science fiction, mystery, adventure, humor and juvenile. No religious or non-health-related subjects. Length: 500-1,500 words.
How to Contact: Send complete ms with SASE. Reports in 10 weeks on mss. Sample copy 50¢. Free fiction guidelines.
Payment: 3¢/word.
Terms: Pays on publication for all rights.
Tips: "Try to present material in a positive—not a negative—light. Use humor and a light approach wherever possible without minimizing the seriousness of the subject."

JUNIOR TRAILS, Gospel Publishing House, 1445 Boonville Ave., Springfield MO 65802. (417)862-2781. Editor: Charles Ford. Elementary Editor: John Maempa. A Sunday School take-home paper of nature articles and fictional stories that apply Christian principles to everyday living for 9-12 year old children. Weekly. Estab. 1920. Circ. 115,000.
Needs: Contemporary, religious/inspirational and juvenile. Adventure stories are welcome. No Biblical fiction or science fiction. Buys 2 mss/issue. Length: 1,000-1,200 words.
How to Contact: Send complete ms with SASE. Reports in 1 month on mss. Free sample copy and guidelines.
Payment: 1½-2¢/word. 3 free author's copies.
Terms: Pays on acceptance for first rights.
Tips: "Know the age level and direct stories relevant to that age group.

KINDERGARTNER, Graded Press, 201 8th Avenue South, Nashville TN 37202. Editor: Sonia Aguila. Magazine of poetry, creative activities and stories for kindergarten age children. Quarterly.
Needs: Juvenile. Contemporary and Biblical stories for children. Buys 2-4 mss/issue. Length: 250-300 words.
How to Contact: Query and send complete ms with SASE. Reports in 2 months on mss. Free sample copy with SASE. Free fiction guidelines with legal-sized SASE.
Payment: 3¢/word plus 2 free author's copies.
Terms: Pays on acceptance for all rights.

LADIES' HOME JOURNAL, Publishing Co. (division of Charter Corp.), 641 Lexington Ave., New York NY 10022. Editor: Lenore Hershey. Fiction/Books Editor: Phyllis Levy.
Needs: Book mss and short stories are accepted only through an agent. Return of unsolicited material cannot be guaranteed. "We do not have the facilities that permit proper handling."

LIVE, The Gospel Publishing House, 1445 Boonville, Springfield MO 65802. Editor: Kenneth D. Barney. A Sunday School take-home paper of articles and stories of believable characters working out their problems according to Bible principles for adults (30 years on up). Weekly. Circ. 224,000.
Needs: Religious/inspirational. No controversial stories about such subjects as race, feminism, war, capital punishment, or homosexuality. Buys 2 mss/issue. Length: 1,200-2,000 words.
How to Contact: Send complete ms with SASE. Reports in 6 weeks on mss. Free sample copy with SASE. Free fiction guidelines.
Payment: 2¢/word (first rights); 1½¢/word (second rights).
Terms: Pays on acceptance for one-time rights.

LIVING MESSAGE, The Anglican Church of Canada, Box 820, Petrolia, Ontario, Canada N0N 1R0. (519)882-2497. Editor: Rita Baker. "*Living Message* calls forth from its readers a Christian response to family and social concerns. Encourages and aids the ministry of clergy and lay people. Especially interested in human rights. Our readers are committed Christians, especially of the Anglican Church (Episcopal). Readers want to know about Anglican work in all areas of the world. They want to know how they can minister to people in local communities." Monthly except July and August. Estab. 1889. Circ. 14,000.
Needs: Literary, contemporary and humor. "We do not require religious/inspirational stories. No sentimental writing; no moralizing please!" Buys 1 ms/issue. Length: 1,000-1,500 words.
How to Contact: Send complete ms with International Reply Coupons. Reports in 1 month on ms. Free sample copy.
Payment: $15-25. 2 free author's copies. Extras are free on request.
Terms: Pays on publication for second serial (reprint) and first North American serial rights.

Tips: "Don't write long letters to the editor. Make sure you study the market; read the whole magazine, not just the fiction. We receive very few good stories. If you can write simply, with insight and sensitivity, let us see your work."

LIVING WITH TEENAGERS, Baptist Sunday School Board, 127 9th Ave. North, Nashville TN 37234. (615)251-2273. Editor: E. Lee Sizemore. Magazine especially designed "to enrich the parent-teen relationship with reading material from a Christian perspective" for Southern Baptist parents of teenagers. Quarterly. Estab. October 1978. Circ. 35,000.
Needs: Religious/inspirational and parent-teen relationships. Nothing not related to parent-teen relationships or from a Christian perspective. Buys 2 mss/issue. Length: 600-2,400 words.
How to Contact: Query with clips of published work or send complete ms with SASE. Reports in 1 month on both queries and mss. Free sample copy with 9x12 SASE and 30¢ postage.
Payment: 3½¢/published word. 3 free author's copies
Terms: Pays on acceptance for all and first rights.

THE LOOKOUT, Standard Publishing, 8121 Hamilton Ave., Cincinnati OH 45231. (513)931-4050. Editor: Mark A. Taylor. Inspirational/motivational publication "for Christian adults who need to be informed, to get tips for building Christian marriages and families, to find help in living a Christian life in a secular world." Weekly. Estab. 1894. Circ. 160,000+.
Needs: Religious/inspirational, men's, women's and young adults. No predictable, preachy material. Taboos are blatant sex, swear words, drinking alcohol. Buys 1 ms/issue. Length: 1,200-2,000 words.
How to Contact: Send complete ms with SASE. Reports in 2 months on ms. Sample copy 50¢. Free guidelines with legal-sized SASE.
Payment: 3¢/word for first rights. Free author's copies.
Terms: Pays on acceptance for simultaneous, first, second serial (reprint), first North American serial and one-time rights.
Tips: "No queries please. Send us a believable story which is inspirational and helpful but down to earth."

THE LUTHERAN JOURNAL, Outlook Publications, Inc., 7317 Cahill Rd., Minneapolis MN 55435. (612)941-6830. Editor: Rev. A.U. Deye. A family magazine to provide wholesome and inspirational reading material for the enjoyment and enrichment of Lutherans. Quarterly. Estab. 1936. Circ. 112,000.
Needs: Literary, contemporary, religious/inspirationl, men's, women's and young adult. Must be appropriate for distribution in the churches. Buys 2-4 mss/issue. Length: 1,000-2,500 words.
How to Contact: Send complete ms with SASE. Free sample copy with SASE.
Payment: $10-20. 6 free author's copies.
Terms: Pays on publication for all and first rights.

MADEMOISELLE MAGAZINE, Condé Nast Publications, Inc., 350 Madison Ave., New York NY 10017. (212)880-8579. Editor: Amy Levin. Fiction Editor: Audrey Leung. Fashion magazine for women from 18 to 28 with articles of interest to women; beauty and health tips, features, home and food, fiction. Audience interested in self-improvement, curious about trends, interested in updating lifestyle and pursuing a career. Monthly. Estab. 1935. Circ. 800,000.
Needs: Literary, contemporary, men's, women's, feminist, gay/lesbian, ethnic and excerpts fiom novels. Buys 1 ms/issue, 12/year. Length: 2,000-4,600 words.
How to Contact: Send complete ms with SASE. Reports in 6 weeks. Free fiction guidelines.
Payment: $100 minimum.

Terms: Pays on acceptance for second serial (reprint) and first North American serial rights.
Tips: Read as much as you can: fiction, nonfiction, magazines.

MAGOOK, Magook Foundation, 25 Hollinger Rd., Toronto, Ontario, Canada M4B 3G2. (416)755-8195. Editor: Marilyn Day. Fiction Editor: Madeline Kronby. Canadian magazine/book of children's fiction; illustrations, poetry, games and stories for children of 5-12. Quarterly. Estab. 1977. Circ. 50,000.
Needs: Literary, contemporary, psychic/supernatural, science fiction, fantasy, mystery, adventure, humor, juvenile and serialized novels. Buys 4 mss/issue, 16 mss/year. Length: 1,000-3,000 words.
How to Contact: Send complete ms with SASE. Reports in 2 months on mss. Sample copy $2.25; free guidelines.
Payment: Pays $25-1,000 and 5-15 free author's copies. 50% charge for extras.
Terms: Pays on publication for all rights.
Tips: "We only publish Canadian writers."

MAINE LIFE, Maine Life Press, Inc., Sedgwick ME 04676. (207)359-2280. Editor: Tom Schroth. "Theme is found in the title of our magazine—'*Maine Life*, past, present and future. The people and places of Maine.' Our readers are people who love Maine and its remote environment, what it was like and is like now." Monthly. Estab. 1945. Circ. 20,000.
Needs: "Rather free, innovative or traditional material welcomed, but nothing risque, please. No erotic, too romantic love stories or personal crises." Buys 2-3 mss/year. Length: 1,000-4,000 words.
How to Contact: Send complete ms with SASE. Reports in 3 weeks on mss. Free sample copy with SASE.
Payment: $30. 2 free author's copies. $1 charge for extras.
Terms: Pays on publication for first rights.
Tips: "Hold out very little hope of acceptance. Submit only when convinced the fiction might be appropriate for our mostly nonfiction magazine."

MATURE LIVING, Sunday School Board of the Southern Baptist Conv., MSN 140, 127 Ninth Ave. N., Nashville TN 37234. (615)251-2191. Editor: Jack Gulledge. Fiction Editor: Zada Malugen. "Our magazine is Christian in content and the material required is what would appeal to 60+ age group (mainly Southern Baptists): inspirational, instructional, nostalgic, humorous. Our magazine is distributed mainly through churches (especially Southern Baptists churches) that buy the magazine in bulk and distribute it to members in this age group." Monthly. Estab. April 1977. Circ. 196,000.
Needs: Contemporary, religious/inspirational, humor and senior adults. Avoid all types of pornography, drugs, liquor, horror, science fiction, stories demeaning to the elderly. Buys 1 ms/issue. Length: 400-1,400 words (prefers 875).
How to Contact: Send complete ms with SASE. Reports in 1 month on mss. Free sample copy. Free guidelines.
Payment: $14-49. 3 free author's copies. 75¢ charge for extras.
Terms: Pays on acceptance for all and first rights.

MATURE YEARS, United Methodist Publishing House, 201 Eight Ave. S., Nashville TN 37202. (615)749-6438. Editor: Dr. Ewart Watts. Fiction Editor: Daisy D. Warren. Magazine helps persons in and nearing retirement to appropriate the resources of the Christian faith as they seek to face the problems and opportunities related to aging. Quarterly. Estab. January 1953.
Needs: Religious/inspirational. "We don't want anything poking fun at old age, saccharine stories or anything not for older adults." Buys 1-2 mss/issue, 4-6 mss/year. Length: 1,000-2,000 words.
How to Contact: Send complete ms with SASE. Reports in 2 months on mss. Free sample

copy with 10½x11 SASE and 67¢ postage.
Payment: 4¢/word.
Terms: Pays on acceptance for all and first rights.

McCALL'S, The McCall's Publishing Co., 230 Park Ave., New York NY 10169. (212)551-9500. Editor: Robert Stein. Fiction Editor: Helen DelMonte. General women's magazine for "adult women of considerable literary sensibility who are interested in every facet of family life as well as the world around them." Monthly. Estab. April 1876. Circ. 6,200,000.
Needs: Literary, contemporary, humor and novel excerpts. "No vague mood pieces; character sketches that aren't real stories; slick, formula stories; stories that are heavily contrived; depressing stories that offer no redeeming catharsis; stories that have no discernible point." Buys approximately 30 mss/year. Length: 1,500-5,000 words.
How to Contact: Send complete ms with SASE. Reports in 1 month on ms. Free guidelines.
Payment: $1,000-3,000.
Terms: Pays on acceptance for first North American serial rights.

MESSENGER OF THE SACRED HEART, Apostleship of Prayer, 833 Broadview Ave., Toronto, Ontario, Canada M4K 2P9. (416)466-1195. Editor: Rev. F.J. Power, S.J. Fiction Editor: Mary Pujolas. Magazine for Canadian and US Catholics who are interested in the Apostleship of Prayer as a way to lead a Christian life. Monthly. Estab. 1891. Circ. 23,000.
Needs: Religious/inspirational, psychic/supernatural, science fiction, romance, western, mystery, adventure and humor. No gay/lesbian, erotica, confession or feminist stories. Buys 1 ms/issue. Length: 1,800-2,200 words.
How to Contact: Send complete ms with SASE or International Reply Coupons. Reports in 1 month on mss. Free sample guide with SASE or IRC.
Payment: 2¢/word. 3 free author's copies.
Terms: Pays on acceptance for first North American serial rights.
Tips: "Use a dictionary to ensure words are used correctly. Develop a plot that does not peter out but reaches a climax. Do not preach but get the message across through plot and characters. A light touch and a sense of humor helps."

METRO, THE MAGAZINE OF SOUTHEASTERN VIRGINIA, Metro Magazine, Inc., Box 1995, Norfolk VA 23501. (804)622-4122. Editor: William H. Candler. General interest and regional magazine of lifestyles and important issues on Southeastern Virginia for urban adults. Monthly. Estab. 1970. Circ. 20,000.
Needs: Uses occasional fiction if exceptional by local author or about the local region.
How to Contact: Query or send complete ms with SASE. Reports in 6 weeks on both queries and mss. Sample copy $1.79; free guidelines.
Payment: Pays negotiable kill fee; byline given. Submit seasonal stories 6 months in advance.
Terms: Pays on publication for all rights.

MIKE SHAYNE MYSTERY MAGAZINE, Renown Publications, Inc., Box 178, Reseda CA 91335. (213)782-2502, Editor: Charles E. Fritch. A mystery/suspense magazine for mystery lovers of all ages. Monthly. Estab. 1956. Circ. 80,000.
Needs: Offbeat crime fiction. "Elements of psychic/supernatural, science fiction, fantasy, horror, gothic, mystery, adventure and humor might be acceptable *But* the major classification of mystery/suspense should not be overpowered by these other elements. No standard situations such as would-be spouse killers; routine cop investigations; cliché private eye yarns; hitpersons; little old ladies being threatened; nice guys clobbered just for plot purposes." Buys 5-8 mss/issue. Length: up to 3,500 words.
How to Contact: Send complete ms with SASE. Reports in 1 month on mss. Sample copy $1.50.

Payment: 1½¢/word.
Terms: Pays on publication for non-exclusive world magazine serial rights.
Tips: "Make it short and unusual; avoid standard situations. Learn the craft first, then submit mss."

MINK, 234 Eglington Ave. E., Suite 401, Toronto, Ontario, Canada N4P 1K5. (416)487-7183. Editor: David S. Wells. Fiction Editor: Karen Lynn. Magazine with erotica and general interest stories entertaining men between 18-40. Monthly. Estab. 1979. Circ. 100,000.
Needs: Contemporary, fantasy, horror, men's, erotica, mystery, adventure and humor. "We are always open to new ideas." Buys 2 mss/issue. Length: 2,000-3,500 words.
How to Contact: Send complete ms with SASE. Reports in 3 weeks to 1 month on mss. Sample copy $1 with 8x12 SASE. Free guidelines with legal-sized SASE.
Payment: $75-150.
Terms: Pays on publication for one-time rights.

MODERN MATURITY, American Association of Retired Persons, 215 Long Beach Boulevard, Long Beach CA 90801. (213)432-5781. Editor: Hubert C. Pryor. General interest magazine for readership over 55 years of age. Bimonthly.
Needs: Nostalgic, upbeat stories. Buys 2-3 mss/year. Length: 1,000-1,500 words.
How to Contact: Send complete ms with SASE. Reports in 2 weeks. Free sample copy with SASE.
Payment: $200 and up.
Terms: Pays on acceptance for all rights.

MS MAGAZINE, 370 Lexington Ave., New York NY 10017. (212)725-2666. Managing Editor: Suzanne Levine. Fiction Editor: Phyllis Rosser. Consciousness-raising magazine for "feminists of all ages," those committed to exploring new lifestyles and changing roles in society. Monthly. Estab. 1972. Circ. 400,000.
Needs: Literary, contemporary, psychic/supernatural, science fiction, fantasy, women's, feminist, gay/lesbian, mystery, adventure, humor, juvenile, young adult and ethnic. Also needs stories about women from all backgrounds or of progressive child rearing. No pornography or derogatory attitudes toward women or children, nor "Hemingway" or right wing political stories. Buys 1 ms/issue. Length: 2,500-3,000 words.
How to Contact: Send complete ms with SASE. Reports in 3 weeks to 1 month on mss.
Terms: Pays on acceptance for first North American serial rights.
Tips: "We seek good writing."

NATIONAL DOLL WORLD, House of White Birches, 303 Cook Ave., Brooksville FL 33512. Editor: Barbara Hall Pedersen. Magazine for doll hobbyists and collectors. "We use articles about doll makers, antique dolls, modern dolls, miniatures, etc., which doll collectors, doll makers, doll artists read for instruction, information and entertainment." Bimonthly. Estab. April 1976. Circ. 50,000.
Needs: Inspirational, psychic/supernatural, fantasy and humor. Only doll-related fiction considered. No sex, horror or drug-related subjects. Buys 3-4 mss/year. Length: 800-1,500 words.
How to Contact: Send complete ms with SASE. Reports in 2 months on mss. Free sample copy with 9x12 SASE and $1.00 postage.
Payment: $35-75.
Terms: Pays on acceptance for all rights.
Tips: "Write a seasonal story about dolls, about 1000 words. Illustrate it with pen and ink drawings. Remember to submit 10 months early for holidays."

THE NATIONAL SUPERMARKET SHOPPER, The American Coupon Club, Inc., Box

1149, Great Neck NY 11023. (516)466-6970. Editor: Ruth Brooks. Magazine informing shoppers on how to save money on their grocery bills, through coupons, refunds, and smart shopping. Monthly, Estab. July 1978. Circ. 50,000.

Needs: Fantasy, women's, confession, romance, mystery and humor. But the action must take place in the supermarket, at the dinner table, etc. Buys 6-8 mss/year. Length: 1,000-2,500 words.

How to Contact: Send complete ms with SASE. Reports in 1 month on ms. Free sample copy.

Payment: 5¢/published word.

Terms: Pays on publication for all rights.

NEW ALASKAN, R.W. Pickrell Agency, Rt. 1 Box 677, Ketchikan, AK 99901. (907)247-2490. Editor: Bil Ostlund. Magazine with both fiction and nonfiction dealing with the history and lifestyle of Southeast Alaska. Monthly. Estab. 1964. Circ. 7,000.

Needs: Adventure and humor. "We accept only stories dealing with Southeast Alaska." Buys 12 mss/year. Length: 1,000-5,000 words.

How to Contact: Send complete ms. Reports in 2 months on mss. Sample copy $1 with 8x13 or larger SASE with 66¢ postage.

Payment: 2¢/word.

Terms: Pays on publication for first, second serial (reprint) and one-time rights.

THE NEW YORKER, The New Yorker, Inc., 25 W. 43rd St., New York NY 10036. (212)840-3700. Editor: William Shawn. A quality magazine of interesting, well-written stories for a literate audience. Weekly. Estab. 1927.

Needs: No fables or short anecdotal fillers. Buys 1-2 mss/issue.

How to Contact: Send complete ms with SASE. Reports in 6-8 weeks on mss.

Payment: Varies.

Terms: Pays on acceptance.

Tips: "Be lively, original, not overly literary. Write what you want to write, not what you think the editor would like."

NORTHWEST SKIER AND NORTHWEST SPORTS, Western Ski Promotions, Inc., Box 5029, University Station, Seattle WA 98105. (206)634-3620. Editor: Grant Alden. Tabloid of winter skiing in the Northwest US and Western Canada and summer sports activities available to Northwest audience. Audience is comprised of skiers—"75% have been reading *NWS* over five years and are earning over $30,000 per year." Biweekly (September-March), monthly (April-August). Estab. October 1958. Circ. 15,000.

Needs: Skiing in Northwest. Buys 2-3 mss/month. Length: 750-1,500 words.

How to Contact: Query with clips of published work. Reports in 1 month on queries and mss. Sample copy $1 with large SASE and 65¢ postage.

Payment: $1.25-$1.50/inch. 5 free author's copies. 50¢ charge for single extras or half price for ten or more extras.

Terms: Pays on publication for one-time rights.

NUGGET, Dugent Publishing Corp., 2355 Salzedo St., Suite 204, Coral Gables FL 33134. (305)443-2378. Editor: John C. Fox. Fiction Editor: Thomas W. Austin. Men's magazine designed to have erotic appeal for a large male audience. Bimonthly. Estab. 1956. Circ. 100,000.

Needs: Literary, contemporary, psychic/supernatural, science fiction, horror, men's, erotica, western, mystery, adventure and humor. Offbeat, fetish-oriented material should encompass a variety of subjects. Most of fiction includes several sex scenes. No fiction that concerns children or religious subjects, or material that is unnecessarily abstract or in an overly mannered style. Buys 3 mss/issue. Length: 1,500-2,500 words.

How to Contact: Send complete ms with SASE. Reports in 1 month on ms. Sample copy

$2.50. Free guidelines with legal-sized SASE.
Payment: $100-125. Free author's copy.
Terms: Pays on publication for first rights.
Tips: "Keep in mind the nature of the publication which is erotically-oriented. Subject matter can vary, but prefer sexual themes."

OMNI, Penthouse International, 909 3rd Ave., New York NY 10022. Editor: Ben Bova. Fiction Editor: Robert Sheckley. Magazine of science and science fiction with an interest in near future; stories and articles of what science holds, what life and lifestyles will be like in areas affected by science for a young, bright and well-educated audience between 18-30. Monthly. Estab. October 1978. Circ. 1,000,000.
Needs: Science fiction and fantasy. No sword and sorcercy or other genres. Buys 3 mss/ issue, 36 mss/year. Length: 7,500 words maximum.
How to Contact: Send complete ms with SASE. Reports in 1 month on mss. Free guidelines with legal-sized SASE.
Payment: Pays $800-1,250; 2 free author's copies.
Terms: Pays on acceptance for first North American serial rights with exclusive worldwide English language periodical rights and nonexclusive anthology rights.
Tips: "Buy a copy and study our magazine. We are not the same as other science fiction magazines. Young authors should read a lot of the best science fiction and short stories today. Don't rewrite *Star Wars*. We are looking for strongly written stories dealing with the next 100 years."

ORANGE COAST MAGAZINE, O.C.N.L., Inc., 2041 Business Center Dr., Irvine CA 92715. (714)752-9376. Editor: Janet Eastman. "Regional publication dealing with the quality of life in changing, growing Orange County. For intelligent, active and educated readers, devotees of the good life." Monthly. Estab. January 1974. Circ. 40,000.
Needs: Literary, contemporary, romance, western, mystery, adventure and humor. No science fiction. Buys 2-3 mss/year. Length: 2,250-2,500 words.
How to Contact: Send complete ms with SASE. Reports in 3 weeks on mss. Sample copy $2. Free guideline with legal-sized SASE.
Payment: $100-150.
Terms: Pays on publication for first North American serial rights.
Tips: "We are very enthusiastic if a writer sends *good* fiction. Avoid writing about Orange County unless you have an intimate knowledge of it."

OUI MAGAZINE, 8560 Sunset Blvd., Los Angeles CA 90069. (213)652-7870. Editor: Mort Persky. Magazine for college age males and older. Monthly. Estab. 1972. Circ. 1 million.
Needs: Contemporary, fantasy, men's, mystery, humor. Buys 1 ms/issue, 12 mss/year. Length: 1,500 words.
How to Contact: Send complete ms with SASE. Reports in 6 weeks on mss.
Payment: Pays $750-1,000.
Terms: Pays on acceptance for first rights.

OUR FAMILY, Oblate Fathers of St. Mary's Province, Box 249, Battleford, SK, Canada S0M 0E0. (306)937-2131. Editor: Reb Materi, O.M.I. Magazine primarily for Catholic families who want information, inspiration and encouragement in Christian living. Monthly. Estab. 1949. Circ. 14,500.
Needs: Religious/inspirational. "The material we use must have Christian content and values. No science fiction or adult sex stories." Buys 3 mss/month. Length: 1,200-2,500 words.
How to Contact: Send complete ms with SASE. Reports in 1 month on ms. Sample copy $1. Free guidelines. Payment: 3-5¢/word. 2-4 free author's copies. $1 charge for extras.

Terms: Pays on acceptance for simultaneous, second serial (reprint) and first North American serial rights.

Tips: "Base your story on an actual Christian experience, a personal experience or one you have come to know. Obtain our guide and study it to understand the policy we follow consistently."

OUTSIDE, Mariah Publication Corp., 3401 W. Division St., Chicago IL 60651. (312)342-7777. Fiction Editor: Michelle Stacey. Magazine emphasizes general interest subjects on outdoor life; how-to's, profiles, new products, personal experiences and short stories for campers, hikers and lovers of outdoors. Bimonthly. Estab. February 1976. Circ. 200,000.

Needs: Fantasy, adventure and humor. Length: 1,000-4,000 words.

How to Contact: Query with clips of published work. Reports in 1 month on queries. Sample copy $2; free guidelines.

Payment: Pays $250-1,000.

Terms: Pays on publication for all, first and first North American serial rights and assignment on a work-for-hire basis.

PENTHOUSE, Penthouse International, Ltd., 909 Third Ave., New York NY 10022. (212)593-3301. Editorial Director: James A. Goode. Fiction Editor: Kathryn Green. A men's entertainment magazine featuring high quality sophisticated articles of interest to men between the ages of 18-34. Exposés, humor, interviews, fashion and fiction. Monthly. Estab. 1965. Circ. 5,350,000.

Needs: Contemporary, psychic/supernatural, science fiction, horror, men's, erotica, western, adventure and first serial excerpts from novels. No stories with women's point of view, plotless sexual encounters or extreme avant-garde fiction. Buys 12 mss/year. Length: 3,000-6,000 words.

How to Contact: Query with SASE. Reports in 3 weeks on queries, 1 month on mss.

Payment: $750 minimum.

Terms: Pays on acceptance for first English language rights and sometimes world rights.

Tips: "Send us well-written stories, neatly typed and of interest to our audience. We are always looking for new fiction talent."

PERSONAL COMPUTING, Hayden Publishing Company, Inc., 50 Essex St., Rochelle Park NJ 07662. (201)843-0550. Editor: J.S. Mulholland, Jr. Fiction Editor: Don Wood. "We publish computer programs that our readers can use on their microcomputers at business, office, home and school, plus articles of related interest. Our audience consists of consumers who want to use personal (micro) computers for practical applications. Our readers are *not* computer professionals; we are a *consumer*, not trade, magazine." Monthly. Estab. 1977. Circ. 40,000.

Needs: Science fiction, and humor. All fiction must relate to the theme of personal (small, micro) computers. "We do not want to see anything that does not involve computers and computing." Buys 4-5 mss/year. Length: 500-3,000 words.

How to Contact: Send complete ms with SASE. Reports in 3 weeks on mss. Write: c/o Circulation Director for sample copy $3.

Payment: $20 minimum. 5 free author's copies. $3 charge for each extra.

Terms: Pays on acceptance for all rights.

Tips: "Avoid computer clichés (such as 'computer takes over world') and gee-whiz hardware. Show us fresh, insightful ideas on how computers—especially personal computers—will affect people and society. Be original. Follow accepted ms standards. Make your work look professional. While not the most important criterion, neatness *does* count."

PERSONAL ROMANCES, Ideal Publishing Co., 2 Park Ave., New York NY. (212)683-4200. Editor: Ronnie Mann. Confession and romance for mostly women readers. Monthly.

Needs: Contemporary, psychic/supernatural, fantasy, women's, feminist, confession, gothic and romance. Buys 4 mss/issue. Length: 2,000-6,000 words.
How to Contact: Send complete ms with SASE. Reports in 2 months on mss. Free guidelines with legal-sized SASE.
Payment: Pays 3¢/word up to $160 maximum.
Terms: Pays on acceptance for all rights.
Tips: "We want first person stories told in up-to-date terms by young marrieds, singles and teens revealing their emotional, sexual and family conflicts and their search to resolve personal problems."

PILLOW TALK, Carla Publishing, 215 Lexington Ave., New York NY 10016. Editor: I. Catherine Duff. Magazine offering self-help and advice to the lovelorn, etc. Articles on meeting people, improving relationships, expanding sexualtiy for male/female, ages 18-35. Readers are looking for ways to improve their lives. Monthly. Estab. 1975. Circ. 200,000.
Needs: Erotica only. Buys 1 ms/issue. Length: 1,500-2,000 words.
How to Contact: Send complete ms with SASE. Reports in 1 week. Sample copy $1.75. Free guidelines with SASE.
Payment: $50-150. Free author's copy.
Terms: Pays on publication for all rights.
Tips: "Read us, slant erotica to our format, send complete ms. *No other fiction except titillating erotica.*"

PLAYBOY MAGAZINE, Playboy Enterprises, Inc., 919 N. Michigan Ave., Chicago IL 60611. (312)751-8000. Editor: Arthur Kretchmer. Fiction Editor: Alice K. Turner. Entertainment magazine for a male audience. Monthly. Estab. December 1953. Circ. 5,700,000.
Needs: Literary, contemporary, science fiction, fantasy, horror, men's, western, mystery, adventure and humor. No pornography or fiction geared to a female audience. Buys 1-3 mss/issue, 22 mss/year. Length: 1,000-10,000 (average 6,000) words.
How to Contact: Send complete ms with SASE. Reports in 1 month on mss. Free guidelines.
Payment: $2,000 minimum.
Terms: Pays on acceptance for all rights.

PLAYERS MAGAZINE, Players International Publications, 8060 Melrose Ave., Los Angeles CA 90046. (213)653-8060. The "basic black" *Playboy* magazine with profiles, reviews, sports, travel, and general interest for the black male. Monthly. Estab. 1973. Circ. 400,000.
Needs: Science fiction, fantasy, erotica, adventure, historical, humor and experimental. "No crime or prison-type stories. We get 'tons' of those." Length: 1,000-4,000 words.
How to Contact: Send complete ms. Reports in 3 weeks.
Payment: Pays 10¢/word.
Terms: Pays on publication for all rights.
Tips: "We want to see stories that are light-hearted and positive."

PRIME TIMES, National Association for Retired Credit Union People, Inc., (NARCUP), Editorial Offices: Suite 503, 433 W. Washington Ave., Madison WI 53703. Managing Editor: Glenn Deutsch. Magazine for people 50 and older who (once or) currently belong to a credit union, who care to "redefine retirement and aging." Each edition based around a general theme: health, energy, retirement communities, money management, etc. Readers share the common bond of CU membershp and the CU philosophy: "Self reliance and cooperative credit: People of even meager means can pool their resources to pull themselves up." Quarterly. Estab. 1979. Circ. 50,000.
Needs: Literary, contemporary, men's, women's, feminist, erotica, romance, mystery, adventure, humor and ethnic (US Hispanic and black). "*Protagonist* must be 50 or older."

Buys 1 ms/issue, 4 mss/year. Length: 1,500-2,500 words.
How to Contact: Send complete ms or query with clips of published work with SASE. Reports in 2 weeks on queries, 1 month on mss. Free sample copy with 9x12 SASE (five 1st class stamps). Free guidelines.
Payment: $150-500. 3 free author's copies. $1 charge for each extra.
Terms: Pays on publication for first, second serial (reprint) and first North American serial rights.
Tips: "Our dream would be to always publish John Updike—quality writing about characters who are 50 and older. We are very happy to feature second serial work as long as it hasn't appeared in another *national* 'maturity market' publication."

RACQUETBALL ILLUSTRATED, CFW Enterprises, 7011 Sunset Blvd., Hollywood CA 90028. (213)467-1300. Editor: Ben Kalb. "General feature magazine on instruction, interviews, medical advice all related to racquetball and racquetball players of all levels; mostly for the 21-45 age group. Monthly. Estab. June 1978. Circ. 100,000.
Needs: Literary, contemporary and humor. "Must have racquetball theme to it." Buys 6 mss/year. Length: 2,000-2,500 words.
How to Contact: Query and send complete ms with SASE. Reports in 1 month on queries. Sample copy $1.50.
Payment: $100-300.
Terms: Pays on acceptance for first rights.

R-A-D-A-R, Standard Publishing, 8121 Hamilton Ave., Cincinnati OH 45231. (513)931-4050. Editor: Dana Eynon. "*R-A-D-A-R* is a take-home paper, distributed in Sunday School classes for children aged 8-11. The stories and other features reinforce the Bible lesson taught in class. Boys and girls who attend Sunday School make up the audience. The fiction stories, Bible picture stories, and other special features appeal to their interests." Weekly. Estab. 1877.
Needs: "No talking animal stories, science fiction, Halloween or first-person stories from an adult's viewpoint. Stories should contain Christian teaching or moral values." Length: 900-1,100 words.
How to Contact: Send complete ms with SASE. Reports in 1 month. Free sample copy and guidelines.
Payment: 1½-2¢/word. Free author's copy.
Terms: Pays on acceptance for first and second serial (reprint) rights.
Tips: "Send for sample copy, guidesheet, and theme list. Study them carefully and follow instructions."

RANGER RICK'S NATURE MAGAZINE, National Wildlife Federation, 1412 16th St. NW, Washington DC 20036. (703)790-4217. Editor: Trudy Farrand. Fiction Editor: Lee Stowell Cullen. "*Ranger Rick* emphasizes conservation and the enjoyment of nature through full-color photos and art, fiction and nonfiction articles, games and puzzles and special columns. Our audience ranges in ages from 4-12, with the greatest number in the 7 to 10 group. We aim for a fourth grade reading level. They read for fun and information." Monthly. Estab. January 1967. Circ. 850,000.
Needs: Science fiction, fantasy, mystery, adventure, humor and juvenile. "Any kind of interesting stories for kids about nature. Science fiction which carries a conservation message is always needed, as are adventure stories involving kids with nature or the outdoors. Moralistic 'lessons' taught children by parents or teachers are not accepted. Human qualities are attributed to animals only in our regular feature, 'Ranger Rick and His Friends.' " Buys 1 ms/issue, 12 mss/year. Length: 900 words maximum.
How to Contact: Query with clips of published work with SASE. Reports in 2 weeks on queries, 2 months on mss. Free sample copy. Free guidelines with legal-sized SASE.
Payment: $300 maximum/full-length ms.

Terms: Pays on acceptance for all rights.
Tips: "Read past issues to learn preferred style and approach; write naturally with no affectation; keep reader in mind at all times without being condescending. Think of your own childhood and include the best from it."

REDBOOK, The Redbook Publishing Co., 230 Park Ave., New York NY 10169. Editor: Sey Chassler. Associate Fiction Editor: Jacqueline Johnson. *Redbook's* readership consists primarily of young American women 18-34 years of age, most married, some single, many mothers of young children, many working outside the home. *Redbook* readers are well-educated, progressive in their attitudes toward the roles and opportunities open to them as women and concerned with larger social issues as well as with their homes, their personal relationships and their health and appearance." Monthly. Estab. 1903. Circ. 4,500,000.
Needs: *"Redbook* takes fiction very seriously, which may be why *Redbook* was the first magazine to win the National Magazine Award for fiction *twice*. We publish three short stories in every issue (except in August, when our special fiction issue features eight or nine stories), as well as a condensed complete-in-the-issue novel. We are looking for fiction that will appeal to vital, thinking, contemporary young women. Stories need not be about young women exclusively; we also look for fiction reflecting the broad range of human experience. We are interested in new voices and buy around a quarter of what we publish each year from our unsolicited submissions. But standards are high; stories must be fresh, felt and intelligent; no straight formula fiction, surprise endings, highly oblique or symbolic stories without conclusions, please." Length: 15-20 manuscript pages for short stories, 5-10 pages for short shorts.
How to Contact: Send complete ms with large SASE. Reports in 6-8 weeks. Free guidelines with legal-sized SASE.
Terms: Pays on acceptance. Buys first North American serial rights.
Tips: "Short short stories are always in demand. We wish we saw more of the following: intelligently humorous stories (not anecdotes), stories about women in situations other than the home, in jobs other than the traditionally female ones, in relationships with persons other than family, mates or lovers, stories from a sensitive, enlightened male point of view. Submit seasonal material at least three months before the appropriate issue."

REFLECTION, Pioneer Ministries, Inc., Box 788, Wheaton IL 60187. (312)293-1600. Editor: LoraBeth Norton. Assistant Editor: Lorraine G. Mulligan. "The purpose of *Reflection* is to present Christ in every phase of life through story, biography and personal experiences for girls in grades 7-12." Bimonthly. Estab. 1961. Circ. 8,000.
Needs: Literary, contemporary, religious/inspirational, science fiction, fantasy, romance, mystery, adventure, humor, juvenile and young adult. "Christian principles should be inherent in the story and not tacked on at the end." Buys 2-3 mss/issue. Length: 500-1,500 words.
How to Contact: Send complete ms with SASE. Reports in 8 weeks on mss. Sample copy $1.50 and free guidelines.
Payment: $25-55.
Terms: Pays on acceptance for assignment on a work-for-hire basis, first and second serial (reprint) rights.

ROAD KING MAGAZINE, William A. Coop, Inc., 233 E. Erie, Chicago IL 60611. (312)664-2959. Editor: William A. Coop. "Leisure-reading publication for long-haul, over-the-road professional truckers. Contains short articles, short fiction, some product news, games, puzzles and industry news. Truck drivers read it while eating, fueling, during layovers and at other similar times while they are enroute."
Needs: Science fiction, fantasy, men's, western, mystery, adventure, humor. "No erotica or violence." Buys 1 ms/issue, 4 mss/year. Length: 2,000-2,500 words.
How to Contact: Send complete ms with SASE. Reports in 2 months on mss. Sample copy

with 6x9 SASE with 68¢ postage.
Payment: $100 maximum.
Terms: Pays on acceptance for all rights.
Tips: "Remember that our magazine gets into the home and that truckers tend to be Bible belt types. Don't phone. Don't send mss by registered or insured mail. Don't try to get us involved in lengthy correspondence. Be patient. We have a small staff and we are slow."

ROAD RIDER, Road Rider Magazine, Box 678, South Laguna CA 92677. Editor/Publisher: Roger Hull. Managing Editor: Dave Petersen. "Our magazine is a source of information and entertainment 'for the touring motorcyclist since 1969' and relates in one way or another to road and street motorcycling." Monthly. Estab. August 1969. Circ. 35,000+.
Needs: Road/street cycling only. "We do not accept the same old stuff, stuff written by non-cyclists, stories with no credibility or pretentious in any way." Buys 2-3 mss/year. Length: 2,000 words maximum.
How to Contact: Send complete ms with SASE. Reports in 1 month on mss. Sample copy $1.50.
Payment: $75 (first timers).
Terms: Pays on acceptance for all rights.
Tips: "Reading a copy won't be all that much help since we rarely print fiction. It is essential that road motorcyclists/motorcycles be a prominent part of the story—not just window dressing—so non-cyclists are discouraged from submitting. Never submit in duplicate; humorous material (within our specifications) stands the best chance here. Cannot emphasize too strongly—don't try to fool us on cycle knowledge; we're experts. We print very little fiction because there is very little new and fresh which meets our requirements. We like good humor; always looking for it. But too many writers—again, particularly non-cyclists—seem to think crashing a cycle is funny. Usually we disagree. We are a difficult market to crash with fiction."

ROMANTIC TIMES, Romantic Times, Inc., 163 Joralemon St., Suite 1234. Brooklyn Heights NY 11201. (212)875-5019. Editor: Kathryn Falk. A newspaper for readers of romantic fiction. "We are looking for short stories, novels, serials for the historical, contemporary, regency and romantic suspense genres. For readers of romantic fiction, primarily women. They read the publication for the latest book reviews, profiles of the authors, articles about romantic fiction, publishers' trade talk and a how-to section." Bimonthly. Estab. January 1981. Circ. 20,000.
Needs: Gothic, romance, serialized and condensed novels, regency and historical. No erotica or soft-core pornography. Buys 2 mss/issue. Length: varied.
Terms: Query with clips of published works with SASE. Reports in 1 month on queries. Sample copy $2.
Payment: Pays $50-200.
Terms: Pays on acceptance for second serial rights.
Tips: "We are looking for intelligent stories for intelligent women. Mss should include the following elements: 1) strong character development, 2) accurate and detailed historical description, 3) realistic plots, 4) vicarious female reader identification, 5) romantic sex. Women who read romantic fiction are looking for romantic and adventurous escape for a few hours.

RUSTLER, Elite Rustler Mink, Inc., 234 Eglington Ave. E., Suite 401, Toronto, Ontario, Canada M4P 1K5. Editor: David S. Wells. Fiction Editor: Karen Lynn. Entertaining erotic men's magazine with general interest articles and fiction for males between 18-40 interested in sex and other controversial subjects. Monthly. Estab. 1978. Circ. 100,000.
Needs: Contemporary, fantasy, horror, men's, erotica, mystery, adventure and humor. Buys 2 mss/issue, 24 mss/year. Length: 2,000-3,500 words.
How to Contact: Send complete ms with International Reply Coupons for US authors. Reports in 1 month on mss. Sample copy $1 with 8x12 SASE. Free guidelines.

Payment: $75-150.
Terms: Pays on publication for one-time rights.

RV'N ON, 10417 Chandler Blvd., N. Hollywood CA 91601. Editor: Kim Ouimet. "We publish an entertaining but informative mini-newspaper for recreational vehicle owners. Adding fiction in '81 will be a new feature. Our audience is made up of people who own RVs or are just interested in camping and travel. They are involved in all walks of life." Monthly. Estab. June 1979. Circ. 500.
Needs: Contemporary, science fiction, fantasy, horror, gothic, western, mystery, adventure, humor, juvenile and young adult. "We plan to run a fiction piece in several parts unless the story is told in only a few paragraphs. No handwritten material." Buys 3 mss/year, then serializes into parts. Length: 300-1,000 words.
How to Contact: Query with SASE. Reports in 1 month on queries. Sample copy 65¢.
Payment: .03/word-$15.
Terms: Pays 30 days after publication for first North American serial rights; may later make a reprint deal on a percentage basis.

ST. ANTHONY MESSENGER, St. Anthony Messenger, 1615 Republic St., Cincinnati OH 45210. Editor: Jeremy Harrington, O.F.M. "*St. Anthony Messenger* is a Catholic family magazine which aims to help its readers lead more fully human and Christian lives. We publish articles which report on a changing church and world, opinion pieces written from the perspective of Christian faith and values, personality profiles, and fiction which entertains and informs." Monthly. Estab. 1893. Circ. 320,000.
Needs: Contemporary and religious/inspirational. "We do not want mawkishly sentimental or preachy fiction. Stories are most often rejected for poor plotting and characterization. No fetal journals, no rewritten Bible stories." Buys 1 ms/issue, 12 mss/year. Length: 2,500-3,000 words.
How to Contact: Send complete ms with SASE. Reports in 1 month on mss. Free sample copy and guideline with legal-sized SASE.
Payment: 10¢/word maximum. 2 free author's copies. $1 charge for extras.
Terms: Pays on acceptance for first North American serial rights.

SAN GABRIEL VALLEY MAGAZINE, Miller Books, 2908 W. Valley Blvd., Alhambra CA 91803. (213)284-7607. Editor: Joseph Miller. "Regional magazine for the valley featuring local entertainment, dining, sports and events. We also carry articles about successful people from the area. For upper middle class people who enjoy going out a lot." Bimonthly. Estab. 1976. Circ. 3,000.
Needs: Contemporary, inspirational, western, adventure and humor. No articles on sex or ERA. Buys 2 mss/issue, 20 mss/year. Length: 500-2,500 words.
How to Contact: Send complete ms with SASE. Reports in 2 weeks on mss. Sample copy $1 with 9x12 SASE.
Payment: 5¢/word. 2 free author's copies.
Terms: Payment on acceptance for one-time rights.
Tips: "Write a good story with positive attitudes."

SATURDAY EVENING POST, Curtis Publishing, 1100 Waterway Blvd., Indianapolis IN 46202. (317)634-1100 Editor: Dr. Cory Servaas, M.D. Senior Editor: Janet Kioski. Magazine with articles on general interest, health care, personalities, book reviews and games for conservative middle age, middle income, college-educated audience. Published 9 times/year. Estab. 1728. Circ. 600,000.
Needs: Religious/inspirational, science fiction, gothic, romance, western, mystery, adventure and humor. No explicit sex, profanity, perversion, ethnic humor or anti-traditional family life. Buys 1 ms/issue. Length: average of 2,500 words.
How to Contact: Send complete ms with SASE. Reports in 1-8 weeks.

Payment: Pays average of $250.
Terms: Pays on publication for all rights.
Tips: "We want positive stories about romance, family and love, people winning out in the end. Humor has a better chance. Keep it simple."

SATURDAY NIGHT, New Leaf Publications Limited, 69 Front St. E., Toronto, Ontario, Canada M5E 1R3. Editor: Robert Fulford. "Intelligent commentary and analysis of the political, economic, entertainment, and literary scenes in Canada for fairly well-educated Canadians." Monthly. Estab. 1887. Circ. 120,000.
Needs: Literary and contemporary. Buys 1 ms/issue, 12 mss/year. Length: 1,500-4,000 words.
How to Contact: Send complete ms with SASE. Reports in 1 month on mss. Sample copy $1.50.
Payment: $1,200 maximum.
Terms: Pays on acceptance for first North American serial rights.
Tips: "*Saturday Night* publishes high quality writing by new or established writers."

SCANDINAVIAN REVIEW, American-Scandinavian Foundation, 127 E. 73 St., New York NY 10021. (212)879-9779. Editor: Nadia Christensen. "Contemporary Scandinavian articles, illustrative graphics, fiction and poetry in translation, reviews of books, films, music for well-educated general public with interest in Scandinavian life and culture." Quarterly. Estab. 1910. Circ. 6,500.
Needs: Ethnic (Scandinavian) and translations in English. Nothing without a Scandinavian connection. Buys 1-2 mss/issue. Length: 2,500 words.
How to Contact: Send complete ms with SASE. Reports in 1 month on mss.
Payment: $40-80 plus 2 contributor's copies.
Terms: Pays on publication for all, first and second serial (reprint) rights.

SCHOLASTIC SCOPE, Scholastic, Inc., 50 W. 44th St., New York NY 10036. Editor: Katherine Robinson. National publication on subjects of general and human interest; profiles of teenagers who have overcome obstacles or done something unusual; short stories and plays for teens. Weekly. Circ. 1,100,000.
Needs: Stories about the problems of teens (drugs, prejudice, runaways, failure in school, family problems, etc.); relationships between people in family; job, and school situations. Looking for material about American Indian, chicano, Mexican-American, Puerto Rican and black experiences and other ethnic groups. No crime stories. Length: 400-1,200 words.
How to Contact: Send complete ms with SASE.
Payment: Pays $150 minimum.
Terms: Acquires all rights; byline given.
Tips: "Strive for directness, realism and action in dialogue rather than narrative. Characters should have depth. Avoid too many coincidences and random happenings."

SECRETS, Macfadden Women's Group, 215 Lexington Ave., New York NY 10016. (212)983-5644. Editor: Jean Press Silberg. Fiction and nonfiction confession magazine for blue-collar women with families; ages 18-35. Monthly. Estab. 1936.
Needs: Women's interest and confession. Themes involving family, marriage, work; should be relevant to readers' lives. First person narrator may be male or female. Stories should be realistic and strongly plotted. Buys 150 mss/year. Length: 2,000-8,000 words.
How to Contact: Send complete ms with SASE. Reports in 2 months on mss. No photocopied or simultaneous submissions. Seasonal stories should be submitted 4-5 months in advance.
Payment: Pays 3¢/word.
Terms: Pays on publication for all rights.

SEEK, Standard Publishing, 8121 Hamilton Ave., Cincinnati OH 45231. Editor: R.W Baynes. "Inspirational stories of faith-in-action for Christian young adults; a Sunday School take-home paper." Weekly. Estab. January 1970. Circ. 60,000.
Needs: Religious/inspirational. Buys 50 mss/year. Length: 500-1,500 words.
How to Contact: Send complete ms with SASE. Reports in 2 weeks on mss. Free sample copy and guidelines.
Payment: 1-2½¢/word.
Terms: Pays on acceptance for first rights.
Tips: "Write a credible story with Christian slant—no preachments; avoid overworked themes such as joy in suffering, generation gaps, etc."

SEVENTEEN, Triangle Communications, 850 3rd Ave., New York NY 10022. (212)759-8100. Editor: Midge Richardson. Fiction Editor: Catherine Winters. A service magazine with fashion, beauty care, pertinent topics such as trends in dating, attitudes, experiences and concerns during the teenage years. Monthly. Estab. 1944. Circ. 1½ million.
Needs: Literary, contemporary, religious/inspirational, science fiction, fantasy, feminist, romance, western, mystery, adventure, humor, young adult and ethnic. No overworked themes, clichés, stories concerning the seamier side of nature, vulgar language, violence or racial slurs. Buys 1-2 mss/issue. Length: 3,000 words.
How to Contact: Send complete ms with SASE. Reports in 2 months on mss. Free guidelines.
Payment: Pays average of $500.
Terms: Pays on acceptance for one-time rights.
Tips: "Read back issues of the magazine; study the craft, know the market, pay attention to grammar, spelling, character and plot development."

SMILE AND CHUCKLE, INC., Smile and Chuckle, Inc., 108 S. Iris St., Alexandria VA 22304. (703)370-2085. Editor: Dan Boger. Humor tabloid distributed to residents in the regional area. Estab. 1979. Circ. 11,000.
Needs: Humor. No sex, violence, controversial or political subjects.
How to Contact: Query and send complete ms with SASE. Phone queries OK. Reports in 2 weeks on queries, 2 months on mss. Free sample copy and guidelines with legal-sized SASE. Seasonal material 2 months in advance. Simultaneous and photocopied submissions OK, if indicated.
Payment: Pays 5¢/word.
Terms: Pays on publication for all rights.

SPRINT for Junior Highs, (formerly *Looking Ahead*), David C. Cook Publishing Co., 850 N. Grove, Elgin IL 60120. Editor-in-Chief: David C. Cook III. Editor: Kristine Tomasik. "*Sprint* provides a Christian perspective on life for junior high Sunday School students. We are looking for high-quality fiction with believable, real characters and dialogue. The Christian viewpoint should be integrated into the story, not a moral tacked onto the end of it." Weekly. Estab. for over 100 years.
Needs: Religious/inspirational, adventure, humor and young adult. Preachy, patronizing or implausible fiction is not acceptable. Buys 20-30 mss/year. Length: 1,000-1,200 words.
How to Contact: Send complete ms with SASE. Reports in 2 months on mss. Free sample copy with business SASE and 20¢ postage.
Payment: $60-75.
Terms: Pays on acceptance for all rights.
Tips: "Please read us first and be sure you understand our market. Be your own toughest judge of a story. Ask yourself, 'Would a teen be simply unable to put this story down?' "

STARWIND, the Magazine of Science Fiction and Fantasy, Starwind Press, Box 3346, Ohio State University, Columbus OH 43210. Editor: Kathy McCarron. "Most of our readers are people between the ages of 15 and 30 who are interested in science fiction or writers who are trying to break into the market." Semiannual. Estab. 1974.

Needs: Psychic/supernatural, science fiction, fantasy and horror. No specialty fiction, such as westerns, confession, etc., not related to science fiction or fantasy. Buys 10 mss/issue, 20 mss/year. Length: 1,000-10,000 words.

How to Contact: Send complete ms with SASE. Reports in 3 weeks on mss. Sample copy $2; free guidelines with legal-sized SASE.

Payment: ½-1¢/word.

Terms: Pays on publication for first North American serial rights.

Tips: "We prefer the shorter-length stories (up to 5,000 words) to longer stories; a longer story generally must be better than a shorter one of similiar quality. We accept a lot of humorous stories and 'social' science fiction and buy very little sword-and-sorcery. We appreciate a good submittal format. We will critique the story for 25¢."

STORY FRIENDS, Mennonite Publishing House, 616 Walnut Ave., Scottdale PA 15683. (412)887-8500. Editor: Marjorie Waybill. Sunday School publication which portrays Jesus as a friend and helper. Nonfiction and fiction for children 4-9 years of age. Weekly.

Needs: Juvenile. Stories of everyday experiences at home, in church, in school or at play, which provide models of Christian values. "It is important to include relationships, patterns of forgiveness, respect, honesty, trust and caring. Prefer exciting yet plausible short stories which offer different settings, introduce children to wide ranges of friends and demonstrate joys, fears, temptations and successes of the readers." Length: 300-800 words.

How to Contact: Send complete ms with SASE. Seasonal or holiday material should be submitted six months in advance. Free sample copy.

Payment: Pays 2½-3¢/word.

Terms: Pays on acceptance for rights. Not copyrighted. Byline given.

STRAIGHT, Standard Publishing Co., 8121 Hamilton Ave., Cincinnati OH 45231. (513)931-4050. Editor: Dawn Brettschneider. Publication helping teens to cope with problems by using Christian principles. Distributed through churches and some private subscriptions. Quarterly in weekly parts. Estab. October 1951. Circ. 140,000

Needs: Contemporary, religious/inspirational, romance, mystery, adventure, humor, juvenile and young adult all with Christian emphasis. "Stories must have character building elements and interesting, well-constructed plots. Problems should be dealt with positively, showing a Christian teen's response. Nothing preachy or in poor taste, no suggestive stories, moral situations dealt with distastefully or language used abusively." Buys 3 mss/issue, 150 mss/year. Length: 1,200-2,500 words.

How to Contact: Send complete ms with SASE. Reports in 6 weeks on mss. Free sample copy with 6x9 SASE and 40¢ postage. Free guidelines.

Payment: 2¢/word.

Terms: Pays on acceptance for first and one-time rights.

Tips: "Don't try to be a writer that you are not—write naturally, not stylistically."

STUDENT LAWYER, American Bar Assoc., 1155 E. 60th St., Chicago IL 60637. (312)947-4087. Editor: A.J. Buckingham. "Magazine for law students as part of their law student division/ABA membership. Features legal aspects, trends in the law, social/legal issues and lawyer profiles. Monthly (September-May). Circ. 42,000.

Needs: "All stories have to have a legal/law/lawyer/law school element to them. No science fiction." Buys 2 full length, 2-3 short humorous pieces/year. Length: 1,000-3,000 words.

How to Contact: Send complete ms with SASE. Reports in 1 month on mss. Sample copy $1.

Payment: $75-300.

Terms: Pays on acceptance for all rights.

SUNDAY DIGEST, David C. Cook Publishing Co., 850 N. Grove Ave., Elgin IL 60120. (312)741-2400. Editor: Gregory D. Cook. Associate Editor: Janice Kluck. "A magazine distributed weekly to adults in Sunday Schools. We are a nondenominational, evangelical Christian magazine for adults between the ages of 35 and 70 for inspiration and understanding of their Christian faith." Quarterly.
Needs: Religious/inspirational. Only accepts Christian themes. Length: 300-2,000 words.
How to Contact: Send complete ms with SASE. Reports in 1 month on mss. Free sample copy with 6x9 SASE and 40¢ postage.
Payment: $25-200.
Terms: Pays on acceptance for all rights (with author's desires).
Tips: "Write believable fiction with an implicit—not tacked-on or phony Christian emphasis. Most Christian fiction is poorly done—it is often simplistic, with undefined characters or poorly developed plot."

SUNSHINE MAGAZINE, Henrichs Publications, Box 40, Litchfield IL 62056. "Family publication with inspirational short stories generally based on true life experiences. Humorous, at times and uplifting. *Sunshine* is also produced in large print format. Audience ranges in age from preschool through the 90s. Stories are brief and inspiring and can be read quickly." Monthly. Estab. 1924. Circ. 120,000.
Needs: Literary, inspirational, men's, women's, gothic, humor and juvenile. No religious subjects dealing with heavily depressing material, sex or violence. Buys 8-11 mss/issue. Length: 600-1,200 words.
How to Contact: Send complete ms with SASE. Reports in 2 months on mss. Sample copy 50¢. Free guidelines with legal-sized SASE.
Payment: $10-100. Free author's copy. 35¢ charge for extra copy.
Terms: Pays on acceptance for first North American serial rights.

SUSQUEHANNA MAGAZINE , Susquehanna Times & Magazine, Inc., Box 75A, R.D.1, Marietta PA 17547. (717)426-2212. Editor: Richard S. Bromer. Publisher: Nancy H. Bromer. "Regional, general interest for Lancaster County, Pennsylvania, and Southeastern Pennsylvania. Emphasis on local history, culture, ecology, etc., for upper middle, better educated, family/community oriented, intellectual audience." Monthly. Estab. 1976. Circ. 6,000.
Needs: Regional. "We print very little fiction. When we do, it has a very definite tie to our regional distribution." Length: 1,200-3,000 words.
How to Contact: Query with clips of published work with SASE. Reports in 1 month on both queries and mss. Sample copy $1.50.
Payment: $25-75. Pays on acceptance; negotiable rights.
Tips: "Become familiar with our publication for style, topics, format, etc., to submit appropriate material."

SWANK MAGAZINE, Swank Corp., 888 Seventh Ave., New York NY 10106. Senior Editor: Larry McClain. "Men's sophisticate format. Sexually-oriented material as well as investigative reporting, humor, fiction, interviews, etc. Presumably our reader is after a mix of erotic material and lifestyle information." Monthly. Estab. 1952. Circ. 350,000.
Needs: High-caliber erotica and medium-length humor pieces. Fiction generally has an erotic theme; writers should try to avoid the clichés of the genre. Buys 1 ms/issue, 12/year. Length: 3,000-4,000 words.
How to Contact: Send complete ms with SASE. Reports in 1 month on mss. Sample copy $3 with SASE.
Payment: $250-750. Free author's copy.
Terms: Pays on acceptance for second serial (reprint) and first North American serial rights.
Tips: "Research the men's magazine market. Try to write lucid, intelligent material which will sell us on the project."

TAR HEEL: The Magazine of North Carolina, New East Corp., Box 7286, Greenville NC 27834. (919)758-1288. Editor: James E. Wise. "Regional magazine for North Carolinians and people who wish they were. Travel, investigative, interview, homes and gardening, historical and nonfiction. Audience is North Carolinians (25-45), college educated, middle and upper middle income who read *Tar Heel* for entertainment." Monthly. Estab. 1972. Circ. 25,000.
Needs: Literary, science fiction, fantasy, horror, mystery, adventure, humor and historical with North Carolina settings. "No down-homey, neo-dialect stories, harking over the good old days or woman-meets-man, Harlequin Romance stuff. Would love to see a good mystery that could be serialized over 3-4 issues." Buys 9-10 mss/year. Length: 2,000-2,500 words.
How to Contact: Send complete ms. Reports in 2 weeks on mss. Sample copy $2.
Payment: $40-100. 2 free author's copies. $1 charge for extras.
Terms: Pays on publication for all rights.
Tips: "Read the magazine, including the nonfiction, to get a feel for what we're trying to do to avoid wasting our time and your postage."

'TEEN MAGAZINE, Petersen Publishing, Co., 8490 Sunset Blvd., Los Angeles CA 90069. Editor: Roxie Camron. Copy Editor: Sarah Lancaster. "The magazine contains fashion, beauty, and features for the young teenage girl. The median age of our readers is 16. Our success stems from our dealing with relevant issues teens face, printing recent entertainment news and showing the latest fashions and beauty looks." Monthly. Estab. 1957. Circ. 1 million.
Needs: Romance, mystery, humor and young adult. Every story, whether romance, mystery, humor, etc., must be aimed for teenage girls. The protagonist should be a teenager, preferably female. No experimental, science fiction, fantasy or horror. Buys 1 mss/issue, 12 mss/year. Length: 2,000-4,000 words.
How to Contact: Send complete ms with SASE. Reports in 2 months on mss. Free sample copy with 9x11 SASE; free guidelines.
Payment: Pays $100.
Terms: Pays on acceptance for all rights.
Tips: "Try to find themes that suit the modern teen. We need innovative ways of looking at the age-old problems of young love, parental pressures, making friends, being left out, etc. Today's teens do more than go to the prom. No prom stories, unless it's about more than just getting a date. Also, trying out for cheerleader and getting a date with the football captain are tired plots. Mss must be typed neatly and double spaced. Handwritten mss will not be read."

TEENS TODAY, Church of the Nazarene, 6401 The Paseo, Kansas City MO 64131. (816)333-7000. Editor: Gary Sivewright. Sunday School take home paper for junior and senior high students involved with the Church of Nazarene who find it interesting and helpful to their areas of life. Weekly. Circ. 50,000.
Needs: Contemporary, religious/inspirational, romance, humor, juvenile, young adult and ethnic. "Nothing that puts teens down or condemns lifestyle not in keeping with denomination's beliefs and standards." Buys 1-2 mss/issue. Length: 1,500-2,500 words.
How to Contact: Send complete ms with SASE. Reports in 6 weeks on mss. Free sample copy and guidelines.
Payment: Pays 3¢/word and 2¢/word on second reprint.
Terms: Pays on acceptance for first and second serial rights.
Tips: "Study sample copies. Don't be too juvenile. Target on a higher quality of writing than what we are presently receiving and publishing."

TRAILS, Pioneer Ministries, Inc., Box 788, Wheaton IL 60187. (312)293-1600. Editor: LoraBeth Norton. Assistant Editor: Lorraine G. Mulligan. *Trails'* purpose is to present

Christ in every phase of life through story, biography and personal experience for girls in grades 1-6. Bimonthly. Estab. 1961. Circ. 20,000.

Needs: Literary, contemporary, religious/inspirational, science fiction, fantasy, romance, mystery, adventure, humor, juvenile and young adult. "No stories with a tacked-on moral. Christian principles should be inherent in the stories." Buys 2-3 mss/issue. Length: 500-1,500 words.

How to Contact: Send complete ms with SASE. Reports in 2 months on mss. Sample copy $1.50 with free guidelines.

Payment: $25-55.

Terms: Pays on acceptance for assignments on a work-for-hire basis, first and second serial (reprint) rights.

TRUE LOVE, Macfadden Women's Group, 215 Lexington Ave., New York NY 10016. (212)340-7500. Editor-in-Chief: Florence J. Moriarty. Editor: Lois E. Wilcken. "The main theme is romance, especially young romance. Family and problem stories constitute secondary themes. All stories are told in first person. Most end with a moral lesson learned by the narrator. Audience consists of young blue-collar housewives." Monthly. Circ. 200,000.

Needs: Romance. No pornography, violence or any other sexually explicit material. Buys 10-12 mss/issue, 120-150 mss/year. Length: 2,000-8,000 words.

How to Contact: Send complete ms with SASE. Reports in 2 months on ms. Sample copy $1.50.

Payment: 3¢/word. Free author's copy. $1.50 charge for extra copies.

Terms: Pays on publication for all rights.

Tips: "Try broad, universal themes at first, especially young love and its problems. Main characters should be sympathetic, multi-dimensional. Keep the story's resolution upbeat. Keep the tone conversational and real. Avoid stories outside the possible experience of a young blue-collar housewife."

TRUE SECRETS, Rolat Publishing Corp., 667 Madison Ave., New York NY 10021. Editorial Director: Ilene Dube. For women 15-35. Circ. 170,000. Rolat Women's Group includes *True Secrets, Intimate Secrets* and *Intimate Romances*. The guidelines for all three magazines are the same. See *Intimate Romances*.

TURTLE MAGAZINE, The Benjamin Franklin Literary & Medical Society, Inc., 1100 Waterway Blvd., Box 567B, Indianapolis IN 46206. Editorial Director: Beth Wood Thomas. Magazine of picture stories and articles for preschool children, 2-6 years old.

Needs: Juvenile (preschool). Length: 8-12 lines for picture stories; 500 words for bedtime or naptime stories. Special emphasis on health, nutrition, exercise, safety.

How to Contact: Send complete ms. Reports in 8-10 weeks on mss. No queries.

Payment: .03/word.

Terms: Pays on publication for all rights.

Tips: "Keep it simple and easy to read. Vocabulary must be below first grade level."

VENTURE, Christian Service Brigade, Box 150, Wheaton IL 60187. Managing Editor: Michael J. Chiapperino. "Our magazines aim to provide entertaining, wholesome reading, while challenging our constituency to love and serve Jesus Christ. CSB is a boys' organization that operates through evangelical churches across North America. When a boy registers in CSB, he automatically receives a subscription to one of our magazines." Published 8 times/year. Circ. 15,000.

Needs: Religious/inspirational, adventure, humor, juvenile and young adult. "No stories that are full of boring, pat answers." Buys 2 mss/issue, 15-20 mss/year. Length: 800-1,200 words.

How to Contact: Query or query with clips of published work with SASE. Reports in 1 week on queries, 2 weeks on mss. Sample copy $1. Free guidelines with legal-sized SASE.

Payment: $35-75. 2 free author's copies. $1 charge for extra copies.
Terms: Pays on publication for first or reprint rights.
Tips: "Query first, make dialogue up-to-date and realistic; aim for a conflict or suspense. Subtly teach worthwhile lessons."

THE VINE. The United Methodist Church, 201 8th Ave. S., Nashville TN 37202. (615)749-6369. Editor: Betty M. Buerki. Publication of the United Methodist Church of biographies, articles and stories for children in grades 3-4. Weekly.
Needs: Juvenile. Length: 500-800.
How to Contact: Send complete ms with SASE. Reports in 1 month on mss. Free sample copy.
Payment: Pays 4¢/word.
Terms: Pays on acceptance for all rights.
Tips: "Should make a point about values but without sounding moralistic. Also accept stories written just for fun. Mss will be purchased through April 1981."

VISTA, Wesleyan Publishing House, Box 2000, Marion IN 46952. Managing Editor: Cindy Holloway. Publication of the Wesleyan Church for adults. Weekly. Circ. 63,000.
Needs: Short on fiction; could use more humor. "Humor is an excellent way to convey spiritual instruction in palatable form." Length: 1,500-1,800 words.
How to Contact: Send complete ms. Reports in 6 weeks.
Payment: Pays 2¢/word.
Terms: "Not copyrighted. Along with mss for first use, we also accept simultaneous submissions, second rights and reprint rights. It is the writer's obligation to secure clearance from original publisher."
Tips: "Stories should have definite Christian emphasis and character-building values without being preachy. Setting, plot and action should be realistic."

WESTCHESTER ILLUSTRATED, 16 School St., Yonkers NY 10701. (914)472-2061. Editor: Stephen H. Acunto. Regional and general interest magazine with emphasis on life in Westchester County, New York for active, sophisticated, college-educated readers, 25-49 years of age. Monthly. Estab. 1976. Circ. 37,000.
Needs: Good objective fiction; all categories open. Length: 800-1,500 words.
How to Contact: Send complete ms. Reports in 5 weeks on mss. Sample copy $1.50; free guidelines.
Payment: Varies.
Terms: Acquires all rights.

WESTERN PEOPLE, Western Producer Publications, Box 2500, Saskatoon, Saskatchewan, Canada S7K 2C4. (306)665-3500. Editor: R.H.D. Phillips. Managing Editor: Mary Gilchrist. "*Western People* is for and about Western Canadians, a supplement of the region's foremost weekly agricultural newspaper. Includes fiction, nonfiction (contemporary and history) and poetry. Readership is mainly rural and Western Canadian." Weekly. Estab. August 1978. Circ. 135,000.
Needs: Contemporary, adventure, humor and serialized novels. Buys 50 mss/year. Length: 750-2500 words (unless for serialization).
How to Contact: Send complete ms with SASE. Reports in 3 weeks on mss. Free sample copy with 9x12 SASE. Free general guidelines with legal-sized SASE.
Payment: $150 maximum (more for serials).
Terms: Pays on acceptance for first and first North American serial rights.
Tips: "The story should be lively, not long, related in some way to the experience of rural Western Canadians."

THE WESTERN PRODUCER, The Western Producer, Box 2500, Saskatoon, Saskatchewan, Canada S7K 2C4. (306)665-3500. Editor: R.H.D. Phillips. Managing Editor: Clarence Fairbairn. "Material of interest to rural residents of Western Canada. Farm families read *The Western Producer* because it's a complete package of information." Weekly. Estab. 1922. Circ. 135,000.

Needs: Men's, women's, western, mystery, adventure, humor, juvenile and serialized novels. "Stories should be of interest to farm families of all ages." Buys 50+ mss/year. Length: 750-1,500 words.

How to Contact: Send complete ms with SASE. Reports in 2 weeks on mss. Free sample copy with 8x12 SASE. Free guidelines.

Terms: Pays on acceptance for first rights.

Tips: "Read the story twice more before sending it; don't underestimate a rural audience."

WESTERN'S WORLD, Western Airlines, 141 El Camino, Beverly Hills CA 90212. (213)273-1990. Editor: Frank M. Hiteshew. Inflight magazine of general interest, travel and dining entertainment for airline travelers. Bimonthly. Circ. 250,000.

Needs: Contemporary, fantasy, romance and humor. Short stories should relate to geographic area served by Western Airlines (now includes Miami and London). Light, upbeat and positive tone. No plane crashes or stories of the Old West (writers are often misled by title). Length: 2,000 words.

How to Contact: Query with SASE. Reports in 3 months on mss.

Payment: Pays 10¢/word.

Terms: Pays on publication for all rights.

Tips: "We rarely print fiction because we seldom see good strong stories." Byline given and 50% kill fee.

WIND, The Wesleyan Church, Box 2000, Marion IN 46952. (317)674-3301, ext. 146. Editor: Stanley K. Hoover. Magazine for teens. Monthly. Circ. 7,000.

Needs: Religious/inspirational short stories. Buys 5-10 mss/year. Length: 1,000 words.

How to Contact: Query or send complete ms with SASE. Reports in 3 weeks on queries and mss. Free sample copy and guidelines.

Payment: Pays 2¢/word for first rights and 1¢/word for second rights.

Terms: Pays on publication for first and second serial rights. Byline given.

Tips: "Submit seasonal material at least 3 months in advance. We do not use a great amount of fiction but will occasionally print a piece that fits a theme. Be realistic. Even problems that are solved can leave a scar."

THE WISCONSIN RESTAURATEUR, M/S Publishing, 121 W. Main, Madison WI 53703. (608)257-9069 or 251-3663. Editor: Jan LaRue. Published for foodservice operators in the state of Wisconsin and for suppliers of those operations. Theme is the promotion, protection and improvement of the foodservice industry for foodservice students, operators and suppliers. Monthly except November/December combined. Estab. 1933. Circ. 3,100.

Needs: Literary, contemporary, science fiction, men's, women's, western, mystery, adventure, humor, juvenile and young adult. "Only exceptional fiction material used. No stories accepted that put down persons in the foodservice business or poke fun at any group of people. No off-color material. No religious. No political." Buys 1-2 mss/issue, 12-24 mss/year. Length: 500-2,500 words.

How to Contact: Send complete ms with SASE. Reports in 2 weeks on mss. Free sample copy with 8½x11 SASE. Free guidelines. Free author's copy. 50¢ charge for extra copy.

Payment: $2.50-20.00.

Terms: Pays on acceptance for first and first North American serial rights.

Tips: "Make sure there is some kind of lesson to be learned, a humorous aspect, or some kind of moral to your story."

WOMAN'S DAY, CBS Publications, 1515 Broadway, New York NY 10036. (212)975-4321.

Editor: Geraldine Rhoads. Fiction Editor: Eileen Herbert Jordan. A strong service magazine, geared to women, with a wide variety of well-written subjects (foods, crafts, beauty, medical, etc.). Publishes 15 issues/year. Estab. 1939. Circ. 8½ million.
Needs: Literary, contemporary, religious/inspirational, fantasy, women's, feminist, humor and juvenile of high quality. No violence, crime, totally male-oriented or period stories.
How to Contact: Send complete ms with SASE. Reports in 4 weeks. Free guidelines.
Payment: Pays top rates.
Terms: Pays on acceptance.
Tips: "Read the magazine and keep trying."

WONDER TIME, Beacon Hill, Press of Kansas City, 6401 Paseo, Kansas City MO 64131. (816)333-7000. Editor: Evelyn Beals. Hand-out story paper published through the Church of the Nazarene Sunday School; stories should follow outline of Sunday School lesson for 6-7 year olds. Weekly. Circ. 60,000.
Needs: Religious/inspirational and juvenile. Stories must have controlled vocabulary and be easy to read. No fairy tales or science fiction. Buys 1 ms/issue. Length: 600 words.
How to Contact: Send complete ms. Reports in 6 weeks on mss. Free sample copy with SASE.
Payment: Pays 3¢/word.
Terms: Pays on acceptance for first rights and will buy reprints.
Tips: "Control vocabulary. Study children to know what children are interested in; stories should deal with children's problems of today and must be tastefully handled."

WORKING FOR BOYS, Xaverian Brothers, Box A, Danvers MA 01923. (617)774-2664. Editor: Bro. Alphonsus Dwyer. "We publish articles of human interest, nature, biography, travel, religion, how-to, sports, etc., for elementary school children and their parents." Published 3 times/year. Estab. 1884. Circ. 16,000.
Needs: Literary, religious/inspirational, adventure, humor and juvenile. Buys 25 mss/year. Length: 800-1,200 words.
How to Contact: Query and send complete ms with SASE. Reports in 2 weeks on queries and mss. Free sample copy. Free guidelines.
Payment: 4¢/word.
Terms: Pays on acceptance.

WORKING MOTHER, McCall's Publishing, Co., 230 Park Ave., New York NY 10069. (212)551-9412. Editor: Vivian Cadden. Assistant Editor: Kathy Minton. Magazine about working mothers read by working mothers. Bimonthly. Estab. October 1978. Circ. 300,000.
Needs: Contemporary, women's and juvenile. Length: 2,500-3,000 words.
How to Contact: Send complete ms with SASE. Reports 1 month. Sample copy $1.50.
Payment: Average $500. Free author's copy.
Terms: Pays on acceptance for all rights.
Tips: "The stories we like most feature a working mother as the central character."

WORLD OVER, Board of Jewish Education, 426 W 58th St., New York NY 10019. (212)245-8200. Editor: Stephen Schaffzin. Fiction Editor: Linda Schaffzin. Administrative Assistant: Eva de Ponceau. Children's magazine for Jewish children between 8-13 years. Monthly. Estab. 1939. Circ. 50,000.
Needs: Religious/inspirational, ethnic (Jewish), translations. Buys 1-2 mss/issue. Length: 500-750 words.
How to Contact: Send complete ms with SASE. Reports in 2 months on mss. Free sample copy with SASE. Free guidelines with legal-sized SASE.
Payment: $50-125. 3 free author's copies. 25¢ charge for each extra copy.
Terms: Pays on acceptance for first rights.

YANKEE MAGAZINE, Yankee, Inc., Dublin NH 03444. Editor: Judson D. Hale. Fiction Editor: Deborah Stone. Entertaining and informative New England regional of current issues, people, history, antiques, crafts for general reading audience. Monthly. Estab. 1935. Circ. 850,000.
Needs: Literary. Fiction is to be set in New England or compatible with the area. No religious/inspirational, formula fiction or stereotypical dialect, novels or novellas. Buys 1 ms/issue, 12 mss/year. Length: 2,000-4,500 words.
How to Contact: Send complete ms with SASE. Reports in 3 weeks on ms. Free sample copy and guidelines. Payment: $500-750.
Terms: Pays on acceptance for first rights.
Tips: "Read previous 10 stories in *Yankee* and keep writing until you write well. Emphasis should be on character development rather than plot. Fiction must be realisitc and reflect life as it is—complexities and ambiguities inherent." Fiction prize awarded to best story published each year.

YOUNG AMBASSADOR, Good News Broadcasting Co., 12th & M St., (Box 82808), Lincoln NE 68501. (402)474-4567. Editor: Melvin A. Jones. Managing Editor: James D. Wallace. "It's designed to aid the spiritual growth of young teen Christian readers through the presentation of Biblical principles and content." 11 issues/year. Estab. 1946. Circ. 80,000.
Needs: Religious/inspirational. "We must have a Bible based spiritual lesson. We will not purchase anything which does not have more than merely a moral perspective. It should be clear in the story that characters have a personal relationship with Jesus Christ. Also, stories should have a contemporary setting and should feature teens in the 14-16 year range." Buys 3-4 mss/issue, 35-40 mss/year. Length: up to 2,000 words.
How to Contact: Send complete ms with SASE. Reports in 2 months on mss. Free sample copy and guidelines.
Payment: 4-7¢/word for unassigned fiction. More for assignments.
Terms: Pays on acceptance for first and second serial (reprint) rights.
Tips: Teen fiction writers under 18 may enter annual contest.

YOUNG AND ALIVE, Christian Record Braille Foundation, Inc., 4444 S. 52nd St., Lincoln NE 68506. Editor: Richard Kaiser. Magazine for blind and visually impaired young adults; published in braille and large print for an interdenominational Christian audience. Monthly.
Needs: "Need all forms of stories, including serials, parables, satires; stories usually based on tension or conflict provoked by the clash of Christian principles and people, situations, or ideas which are in opposition. We seek interesting, credible stories of an interesting manner with themes familiar to Christian youngsters." Length: 1,800-2,000 words.
How to Contact: Query with SASE. Free guidelines.
Payment: Pays 3-5¢/word.
Terms: Pays on acceptance.

THE YOUNG CRUSADER, National Women's Christians Temperance Union, 1730 Chicago Ave., Evanston IL 60201. (312)864-1396. Editor-in-Chief: Mrs. Kermit S. Edgar. Managing Editor: Michael C. Vitucci. Character building material showing high morals and sound values; inspirational, informational nature articles and stories for the 6-12 year olds. Monthly. Estab. 1887. Circ. 10,000.
Needs: Juvenile. Stories should be naturally written pieces not saccharine or preachy. Buys 4-5 mss/issue, 60 mss/year. Length: 600-800 words.
How to Contact: Send complete ms with SASE. Reports in 6 months on mss. Free sample copy with SASE
Payment: Pays 1¢/word and free author's copies.
Terms: Pays on publication. "If I like the story and use it, I'm very lenient and allow the author to use it elsewhere."

YOUNG MISS, Parents Magazine Enterprises, 685 Third Ave., New York NY 10017.
Editor: Suzanne Kennedy Flynn. Magazine that provides interesting, helpful and thought-
provoking material for preteen and teenage girls. Published 9 times/year.
Needs: Contemporary, science fiction, romance, mystery, humor and young adult. No
sensational sex. Buys 1-3 mss/issue. Length: 2,000-2,300 words.
How to Contact: Send complete ms with SASE. Reports in 1 month on mss. Sample copy $1
with free writer's guidelines.
Payment: $100-150. 2 free author's copies.
Terms: Pays on acceptance for all rights, assignment on a work-for-hire basis and first
rights.

Small press

Small presses are publishers independent in spirit that resist commercial pressure. They include self-publishers, Mom and Pop operations, cooperatives, interest groups, and university presses that publish experimental and contemporary fiction. Numbering in the thousands, they have grown and developed amazingly in the last 15 years, demonstrating that the small press is a recognized and important outlet for literary fiction.

Inadequate funding, along with distribution and promotion problems, account for the volatility of the small press market, and many such presses simply cannot survive. Regional and national support groups, such as CCLM and COS-MEP (see glossary) have helped substantially with grants and donations, which not only keep the presses running but also encourage others to spring up. An estimated 50 new presses (for nonfiction and poetry along with fiction) go into business each month and press births exceed deaths by ten to one.

Despite the increasing number of new small presses, however, many more manuscripts than can be published flood in. One university press, for instance, publishes only five novellas of the 200 manuscripts received annually.

Small presses have definite specifications that you should respect. Their manuscript-handling policies may be based on economics. A one- or two-person staff may mean that the manuscripts pile up. Readers who screen manuscripts are generally not employed (except by the occasional university press), and decisions may take up to a year because of the heavy volume and thorough search for high-quality material. For most small presses, unsolicited submissions in any other field *not* designated in the following listings will present problems. Editors simply do not have time or money to handle them, and the manuscripts might be tossed out. Because of the uncertainty of funding, many editors cannot plan their title lists too far in advance.

Follow these instructions when approaching the independent presses:

●Study the listing and its individual specifications very carefully. Time, effort and money can be saved if you know exactly what a certain press needs. Request a book catalog, if available, and review the titles and subjects published.

●If required, send an outline/synopsis, plus sample chapters in *sequential* order: one, two, three, as opposed to sending the first, the seventh and the last chapters.

●In queries or cover letters (if required), don't tell the editor how great your novel is; let your work speak for itself. Your letter may include a few words about your literary background and publishing history, but only if it pertains to the manuscript.

●Read as much as possible. Study the masters in fiction and the contemporary champions that the small presses admire. Spend time in the library or bookstore to stay in touch and know what is current.

●Imitate your betters; imitate what works. But don't copy; don't *plagiarize*. Even if a small press is new to the publishing business, it still wants professional, high-quality fiction, "strong individual voices" from those who have served a "literary apprenticeship." Natural talent and aptitude are like a rough diamond; they are useless in the raw. Skills and techniques must be practiced.

●Write out of love and belief. As one editor says, "Make whatever you write worthy of the life of the tree that is your paper."

●Be patient. Do not expect a quick reply. Even university presses are small operations, often understaffed; and other independent presses may be run by one or two editors, who, in order to keep their businesses going, hold down other jobs.

●Do not be dismayed over difficulties in getting work into print. Even Hemingway had great frustrations finding a publisher when he began to write. View rejection simply as a rite of passage in the publishing process. In some cases, getting a manuscript published by the right press may take as much time and energy as the writing itself.

●Include SASE or International Reply Coupons (IRC) with all correspondence with small presses, which simply are not financially equipped to return submissions without sufficient postage. One editor says graphically that if he receives an unsolicited manuscript without a SASE, he will line his catbox with it.

●Be realistic in your financial expectations. Small presses offer excellent opportunities for publishing serious fiction, but·payment may be no more than a few contributor's copies.

Because small presses vary greatly in their business policies and ethics, be fully aware of rights and terms before signing a contract. There are no *standard* publishing terms, and definition is often a matter of semantics. Be aware of the variables as terms may be broad: "By arrangement and mutual agreement"; "We'll award honorarium if grant money is available"; "Fees and arrangements are negotiable"; and "We'll work things out with the author if we like the work." These arrangements must be defined *before* the contract is signed.

Small press publishers are frequently involved in subsidy arrangements (see glossary), wherein you may pay partial or complete publishing expenses, which can range from several hundred to several thousand dollars. Under a subsidy plan, there may be royalty returns until all the money is refunded; or the contract may require an investment that will be returned through sales; or the author may never see his invested money again. Some small press publishers are gradually moving to non-subsidy contracts as their businesses develop and grant money becomes available.

There are also cooperative groups that you may be invited to join. As a fee-paying member, you have some control over the editing, layout, printing, distribution and promotion of his books; or, on an individual basis, you may be asked to pay for "extra services," which may mean contributing to promotion and distribution costs.

Some writers have chosen to publish interchangeably with commercial publishers and small presses. Others have found the small press a springboard to publication by commercial magazines and publishing houses. And still others find that they prefer an independent press because of the individual attention they receive.

Whatever the publishing arrangement, a thoroughly researched market is the recommended one. Shop around; compare terms and possible fees to find the fairest and most beneficial deal. Before signing a contract or agreeing to the publishing of your book, check to see how long the press has been in business, how many titles it released last year, how much experience the editors have had. Understanding exactly what the terms are for a book manuscript will help make the publishing experience happy and fulfilling. The press might be small, but the pleasure you get from working with it will not.

ALLEGANY MOUNTAIN PRESS, 111 N. 10th St., Olean NY 14760. (716)372-0935. Imprints include Uroboros Books. Editorial Director: Ford F. Ruggieri. Estab. 1972. Publishes hardcover and paperback originals. Number of titles: 1 in 1980; 2 planned for 1981.
Needs: Literary, experimental, erotica, humor/satire. "We want to see fiction with a serious literary intent. Though we are interested in books that will sell, we are not interested in 'bestsellers' if it means pandering to bad taste. Previously we have only published poetry in book form, mainly because we haven't received the kind of ms we'd like to publish in the novel."
How to Contact: Submit outline/synopsis with 2-3 sample chapters. No simultaneous submissions; photocopied submissions OK. Reports in 1 week on queries, 6 weeks on mss.
Terms: Pays in 50 author's copies and 10-15% royalties. Advance: 50 copies of book. Book catalog for 6x9 SASE plus 38¢ postage.
Advice: "Study the market you're aiming for and look to the people who have written the best things in that field as a guide."
Comments: "Don't waste your time or money sending us pop or hack type fiction. We will only consider work that we believe will have a significant cultural impact."

AND BOOKS, 702 S. Michigan, South Bend, IN 46618. Editorial Director: Janos Szebedinsky. Estab. 1977. Publishes paperback originals. Number of titles: 2 in 1979, 4-6 in 1980; 10+ planned for 1981.
Needs: Experimental, practical mystery, erotica, fantasy, horror, juvenile and young adult (animal), translations. "No romance."
How to Contact: Submit outline/synopsis with sample chapters. SASE for ms. Simultaneous and photocopied submissions OK. Reports in 2 weeks on queries, 6 weeks on mss.
Terms: Pays 5-10% royalties; no advance. Book catalog for legal-sized SASE plus 38¢ postage.
Advice: "There is a good possibility that satire and humor mixed with science fiction will be a welcome change."
Comments: "Self-publish your work and prove it to be of public value. Impatience is the usual pitfall of the writer."

ANGEL PRESS, PUBLISHERS, 171 Webster St., Monterey CA 93940. (408)372-1658. Editorial Director: André D'Angelo. Estab. 1962. Publishes hardcover and paperback originals. Number of titles: 1 in 1980.

Needs: Feminist, gay/lesbian, erotica, religious/inspirational, satire, controversial.
How to Contact: Query. SASE for ms. Simultaneous and photocopied submissions OK. Reports in 2 weeks on queries, several months on mss.
Terms: Negotiates royalties. Free book catalog.
Advice: "All beginning writers should get professional criticism from knowledgeable editors before submitting a ms. A professional opinion carries a lot of weight in deciding what to publish."
Comments: "All submissions must be accompanied by a complete resume of the writer's writing background and an analysis of the potential market. Furthermore, we need to know what the author intends to do to promote sales: radio, shows, public appearances, etc."

APPLE-WOOD PRESS, Box 2870, Cambridge MA 02139. (617)964-5150. Editorial Director: Phil Zuckerman. Estab. 1976. Publishes hardcover and paperback originals. Number of titles: 2 in 1979, 3 in 1980; 3 planned for 1981.
Needs: Literary. "Could be in any category but must be literary." Recently published *Shipping Out*, by Michael Stephens (avant-garde fiction); *P-town Stories*, by R.D. Skillings (vignettes about a small town); *Candace & Other Stories*, by Alan Cheuse (short stories and a novella set in the South).
How to Contact: Query with SASE. Simultaneous and photocopied submissions OK. Reports in 2 weeks on queries, 2 months on mss.
Terms: Pays in 12 author's copies and 10-15% royalties; no advance. Book catalog for legal-sized SASE plus 38¢ postage.
Comments: "Major publishers no longer publish serious fiction. Young writers should familiarize themselves with small, literary houses. Have patience. Enclose a cover letter."

APPLEZABA PRESS, 410 St. Louis, Long Beach CA 90814. Editorial Director: Shelley Hellen. Estab. 1977. Publishes paperback originals. Number of titles: 1 in 1979, 1 in 1980; 1 planned for 1981.
Needs: Contemporary, literary, experimental, faction, feminist, gay/lesbian, erotica, fantasy, humor/satire, translations, short story collections. No gothic, romance, confession, inspirational. Recently published *The Cure*, by Gerald Locklin (satire).
How to Contact: Submit complete ms with SASE. No simultaneous submissions; photocopied submissions OK. Reports in 2 months.
Terms: Pays in author's copies and 10-15% royalties; no advance. Free book catalog.
Advice: "Write legibly. Cover letter with previous publications, etc. is OK, but I'm put off by the type of letter that goes to the effect: 'If you publish this ms, the both of us will get rich,' etc."
Comments: "We have been receiving material that is satirical, black humor almost slapstick. We publish only book length material."

THE ARCANE ORDER, 2904 Rosemary Ln., Falls Church VA 22042. (703)536-6408. Imprints include Jacksonville Poetry Quarterly. Editorial Director: L.J. Mather. Estab. 1950. Number of titles: 4 in 1980; 4 planned for 1981.
Needs: Erotica, psychic/supernatural, religious/inspirational, fantasy.
How to Contact: Submit complete ms with SASE. Simultaneous and photocopied submissions OK. Reports in 6 weeks.
Terms: "We do not pay."
Advice: "Make as many contacts as possible. Believe in Murphy's Law and read Isaiah 57:20-22."

ARIADNE PRESS, 4817 Tallahassee Ave., Rockville MD 20853. President: Carol F. Hoover. Estab. 1976. Publishes hardcover originals. Number of titles: 1 planned for 1981.
Needs: Contemporary, literary, adventure, mystery, spy, historical, war, women's, feminist, humor/satire. "No short stories, only novels." Recently published *Lead Me to the Exit*, by

Ellen Moore (a woman's changing role).
How to Contact: Query with SASE. Simultaneous and photocopied submissions OK. Reports in 2 weeks on queries, 1 month on mss.
Terms: Pays 10% in royalties; no advance.
Comments: "Try major publishers first. This is a shoestring operation, producing some 1,200 copies/book. Our aim is to publish first-rate, readable fiction which has not been accepted by major markets."

BENINDA BOOKS, Box 9251, Canton OH 44711. Editorial Director: George P. Argiry. Estab. 1977. Publishes paperback originals. Number of titles planned: undecided.
Needs: Adventure, mystery, western.
How to Contact: Query with SASE. No simultaneous or photocopied submissions. Reports in 2 weeks.
Terms: Pays 10% maximum in royalties; no advance. Free book catalog.

BICENTENNIAL ERA ENTERPRISES, INC., Box 1148, Scappoose, OR 97056. Contact: Cathy Lee. Estab. 1978. Number of titles: 1 planned for 1981.
Needs: Adventure, mystery, spy. "No low class, poorly written, dumb, sex junk."
Terms: No advance.

THE BIELER PRESS, 4603 Shore Acres Rd., Madison WI 53716. (608)222-3711. Contact: Gerald Lange. Estab. 1975. Publishes hardcover and paperback originals and paperback reprints. Number of titles: 1 in 1979, 4 in 1980.
Needs: Contemporary, literary, experimental, fable, science fiction, fantasy, horror. Recently published *Initiation*, by Jean Follain (chapbook); *Everything That Has Been Shall Be Again*, by John Gilgun (hardcover and paperback original).
How to Contact: Query. SASE for query and ms. Simultaneous and photocopied submissions OK. Reports in 1 week on queries, irregularly on mss.
Terms: Pays 10% in author's copies (original), 10% in royalties (reprint); no advance. Free book catalog.
Advice: "Be committed to your work, not your publishing credits."
Comments: "Avoid impersonal correspondence. We expect to establish a good relationship with our authors as we work closely with them on a book's production. We are not submitted a great deal of fiction. Especially interested in the modern fable."

THE BLACKHOLE SCHOOL OF POETHNICS, Box 555, Port Jefferson NY 11777. Editorial Director: Grinley Nash. Estab. 1978. Publishes various forms of books. Number of titles: 4 in 1980.
Needs: "Minimal, having to do with what wasn't known and perhaps now is and will change life for everything but humans." Recently published *Nothing Left to Fake*, by Graham Everett (4 page novel); *Rent*, by Ed Harson (fictional poems); *Manaqua 6 P.M.*, by Ernesto Cardenal and J. Cohen (program); *Lights*, by E. Cardenol and J. Cohen (broadsheet).
How to Contact: Submit outline/synopsis with SASE. No simultaneous submissions. Photocopied submissions OK "if they're vital to the ms." Reports "when we want."
Terms: Pays "a share after bills"; no advance.
Comments: "Verbosity is a trend today. Avoid great expectations."

BROKEN WHISKER STUDIO, Printers Row, 711 S. Dearborn, Loft 505, Chicago IL 60605. (312)969-8311. Editorial Director: Joan H. Lee. Estab. 1976. Publishes paperback originals. Number of titles: 2 in 1979, 2 in 1980; 3 planned for 1981.
Needs: Contemporary, literary, experimental.
How to Contact: Submit complete ms with SASE. No simultaneous submissions; photocopied submissions OK. Reports in 1 month on mss.

Terms: Pays in author's copies and royalties. "We use a negotiable contract." Rarely offers advance. Free book catalog.
Comments: "We publish *short* fiction that is no more than 150 pages. Novellas, short stories, poetry, juveniles. We use art work, are interested in combinations (syntheses) of visual and verbal. Interested in material for chapbooks, broadsides, and poemcards."

CALAMUS BOOKS, Box 689, Cooper Station, New York NY 10003. Imprint includes Gay Presses of New York. Editorial Director: Larry Mitchell. Estab. 1977. Publishes paperback originals. Number of titles: 2 in 1979.
Needs: Gay/lesbian. "We will publish any type of fiction as long as it is gay/lesbian. No fiction about heterosexuals." Recently published *Queer Free*, by Alabama Birdstone (gay fantasy novel).
How to Contact: Query or submit complete ms. SASE for query and ms. Simultaneous and photocopied submissions OK. Reports in 6 weeks.
Terms: Pays in 20 author's copies and 7-8% royalties. Offers $200 advance. Free book catalog.

CARPENTER PRESS, Rt. 4, Pomeroy OH 45769. Editorial Director: Robert Fox. Estab. 1973. Publishes paperback originals. Number of titles: 3 in 1979, 2 in 1980; 2 planned for 1981.
Needs: Contemporary, literary, experimental, science fiction, fantasy. "Literary rather than genre science fiction and fantasy." Recently published *The Runner*, by Brian Swann (experimental short stories); *The Holy City*, by Matthew Paris (novel-science fiction parody); *O Rosie*, by Daniel Lusk (experimental novel).
How to Contact: Query with SASE. Unsolicited mss are returned unopened. Simultaneous and photocopied submissions OK. Reports in 1 week.
Terms: Pays in author's copies or 10% royalties. "Terms vary according to contract." No advance. Free book catalog.
Advice: "Don't try to impress us with whom you've studied or where you've published."
Comments: "Read as much as you can so you're not unwittingly repeating what's already been done. I look for freshness and originality rather than superlative technique. I wouldn't say that I favor experimental over traditional writing. Rather, I'm interested in seeing how recent experimentation is tying tradition to the future, and to the work of writers in other countries."

THE CENTER FOR STUDY OF MULTIPLE GESTATION, 333 E. Superior St., Suite 463-5, Chicago IL 60611. Executive Director: Donald Keith. Estab. 1977. Publishes hardcover and paperback originals.
Needs: "Will only consider mss related to twins, triplets or other multiples. Do not send anything that is not related. None will be returned or acknowledged."
How to Contact: Query. Simultaneous and photocopied submissions OK. Reports in 6 weeks.
Terms: Pays 10-15% royalties; no advance. Book catalog for legal-sized SASE.
Comments: "Do not send unless it has been queried first. Do not query unless it's about our subject! Do your homework. Edit the work before you send it out. Send neat and readable material. Unsolicited mss in other fields will be disposed of and unanswered."

CHALLENGE PRESS, 1107 Lexington Ave., Dayton OH 45407. (513)275-8637. Imprint includes *Confrontation/CHANGE Review*. Editor: F.M. Finney. Estab. 1976. Publishes hardcover originals and reprints. Number of titles: 1 in 1980; 2 planned in 1981.
Needs: Literary, faction, mystery, historical, ethnic (black), historical. "No historical-Southern fiction".
How to Contact: Query with SASE. Simultaneous and photocopied submissions OK. Reports in 2 weeks on queries, 6 weeks on mss.

Terms: Pays 15-40% royalties and by outright purchase of $1,000 maximum; no advance. Book catalog for 7x10 SASE.
Advice: "We are a small operation; therefore do not expect a 'quick' reply. We are reasonable and encourage simultaneous submissions."
Comments: "We expect a shift to two extremes—the historical novel and science fiction for young adults."

CHAPMAN, 52 Bath St., Edinburgh, Scotland EH15 1HF. Imprints include Lothlorien. Editorial Director: Joy M. Hindry. Estab. 1970. Number of titles: 3 in 1979, 3 in 1980; 3 planned for 1981.
Needs: Contemporary, literary, experimental. "No novels."
How to Contact: Query or submit complete ms. SASE for query, mss. Reports in 2 weeks.
Terms: Pays 5 pounds/printed page; offers advance.

CHARISMA PRESS, St. Francis Seminary, Box 263, Andover MA 01810. Editorial Director: Fr. Lucius Annese. Publishes hardcover and paperback originals and reprints. Number of titles: 1-2 in 1980; 2-3 planned for 1981.
Needs: Literary. "Ours is a public purpose. We publish books by members of Charisma Press. For nonmembers we help writers to write step-by-step. For this purpose we have Charisma Press Institute consisting of two parts, the *basics* and the *advanced*. The texts we use are *Writing Skills* and *Write and Publish* both by the Director of Charisma Press, Fr. Lucius Annese. Persons interested in this educational service may contact us. No irreligious, uninspiring, unedifying material considered."
How to Contact: Query. SASE for query, ms. No simultaneous submissions. Photocopied submissions OK. Reports in 2 weeks on queries, 1 month on mss.
Terms: "We do not pay." Free book catalog.
Advice: "Avoid inconsistencies, prejudice, and unreality."
Comments: "Realism and nature, direct and simple, are the current formulas. Be compact and let each word count. I encourage writers."

CHEAPO PRESS, formerly Phyroid (sic) Press, 50 Buckland Rd., Maidstone, Kent, England ME16 0SH. Editorial Director: Billy Childish. Estab. 1976. Publishes paperback originals and reprints. Number of titles: 10 in 1979, 15 in 1980; 15 planned for 1981.
Needs: Contemporary, literary, humor/satire, extracts from work to be published. "Query with sample of work; we are not so narrow-minded as to reject whole subjects at a time." Recently published *Cheapo Review*, by C. Thomson and others; *Gazunda 3*, by R. Earl and others; *Merz*, by Billy Childish (all paperbacks).
How to Contact: Query or submit outline/synopsis with 2 sample chapters. SASE, IRC for query, ms. Simultaneous and photocopied submissions OK. Reports in 1 month on queries, 6 weeks on mss.
Terms: Pays in 1 author's copy—"perhaps more if required." No advance. We do not pay. Book catalog for "A4" SASE plus 4 International Reply Coupons.
Comments: "Today we see less humor and more preoccupation with self, misery or escapism; few take a positive approach to anything. Bear in mind that all our work is cheaply produced, haphazardly distributed and that the print-run is only about 200. We can't afford to publish any more than extracts of work or very, very short stories. Other than that, if you can put up with anarchist approaches to publication, you will not be ripped off. We publish mostly poetry."

CHOCK PUBLICATIONS, 172 Romford Rd., London E9 6HY England. Imprints include *Chock Magazine*. Editorial Director: Ian Durant. Estab. 1981. Publishes paperback originals. Number of titles: 1 or more booklets planned for 1981.
Needs: Contemporary, literary, experimental, Third World literature. No adventure, mystery, spy, historical, western, war, romance, confession, women's, juvenile and young adult.
How to Contact: "Submit short synopsis, including comments on style."SASE, IRC for

query and ms. Simultaneous and photocopied submissions OK. Reports in 6 weeks.
Terms: Pays in authors copies; no advance. Book catalog for A5 SASE with "enough International Reply Coupons."
Comments: "Have perseverence, a strong blue pencil, self critical attitude. Avoid overwriting, lack of subtlety, illegibility."

CHTHON PRESS, 77 Mark Vincent Dr., Westford MA 01886. Imprints include Nonesuch Publications and Spindle City Editions. Publisher: Paul J.J. Payack. Estab. 1973. Publishes paperback originals.
Needs: Experimental, science fiction, metafiction only. Recently published *CPU Wars*, by Charles Andres (paperback).
How to Contact: "By invitation only." Simultaneous and photocopied submissions OK. Reports in 6 weeks.
Terms: Pays by standard royalty contract. Free book catalog.
Comments: "Find your 'voice' and once you've found it write and write and write. But this is only half the task. It is the author's duty to make sure his work is available to the populace. Therefore, submit your work to every publisher you can think of and view rejections simply as part of the publication process."

COLORADO STATE REVIEW PRESS, Colorado State University, English Dept., 322 Eddy, Fort Collins, CO 80521. Imprint includes *Colorado State Review* (magazine). Editorial Director: W. Ude. Estab. 1977. Publishes paperback originals. Number of titles: 1 in 1979, 1 in 1980; 1 planned for 1981.
Needs: Contemporary, literary, experimental. "Short fiction only. No material which lacks serious literary intent. We probably will not be publishing novels." Recently published *Skin and Bones*, by Robert Abel (short stories).
How to Contact: Query. "We solicit mss only from those writers who have published in our magazine, *Colorado State Review*". No simultaneous or photocopied submissions. Reports in 6 weeks on mss.
Terms: Pays in author's copies (50 on printing of 500); no advance.
Advice: "Write the story or book first—then worry about money and your 'career,' if you must. Don't send us any mindless popular formula fiction—we're apt to be insulting in our response."
Comments: "We see a return to meaning—a retreat from the 'beautiful artifact' extremes of post-modernism, and even in the US, a fair amount of magical realism. We plan to do only one collection of stories each year and will usually prefer to solicit mss from those authors who have published in our literary magazine."

CO-OP BOOKS (PUBLISHING) LTD., 50 Merrion Sq., Dublin, 2, Ireland. Administrator: John Meehan. Estab. 1976. Publishes hardcover and paperback originals and paperback reprints. Number of titles: 7 in 1979, 8 in 1980; 10 planned for 1981.
Needs: Contemporary, literary, experimental, historical, women's, feminist, gay/lesbian, ethnic (Irish), humor/satire. No faction, adventure, mystery, spy, western, war, gothic, romance, confession, erotica, psychic/supernatural, religious/inspirational, science fiction, fantasy, horror, juvenile and young adult, sports, animal, spy/adventure, historical, fantasy/science fiction, easy-to-read, translations. Recently published *The Feast of Michaelmas*, by Adrian Kenny; *Identity Papers*, by Anthony Cronin; *The Happy Elephants*, by Peter O'Connor (novels).
How to Contact: Query or submit outline/synopsis and sample chapters. SASE, IRC for query, ms. No simultaneous submissions; photocopied submissions OK. Reports in 2 weeks on queries, 3 months on mss.
Terms: Pays 5-10% in royalties; no advance. Book catalog for 6½x8½ SASE plus 60p-airmail to USA).
Comments: "Bear in mind that the outlets for fiction published in Ireland are very limited

and therefore Irish writers will be given greater consideration. Only in very exceptional circumstances could we depart from this."

CROSS-CULTURAL COMMUNICATIONS, 239 Wynsum Ave., Merrick NY 11566. (516)868-5635. Editorial Director: Stanley H. Barken. Estab. 1971. Publishes hardcover and paperback originals. Number of titles: 50 folios/3 anthologies/1 novel in 1979, 14 chapbooks in 1980; 20 chapbooks planned for 1981.
Needs: Contemporary, literary, experimental, ethnic, humor/satire, juvenile and young adult folktales, translations. "Main interests: bilingual short stories and children's folktales, parts of novels of authors of other cultures, translations, American fiction. No fiction that is written originally in American English with a focus that is not directed toward other cultures in our multi-cultural/multi-lingual society." Recently published *Modern Yugoslav Satire*, by Branko Mikasinovich (anthology: satire/translations from Yugoslavia); *50 Dutch & Flemish Novelists*, by Joost de Wit, Stanley H. Barkan (novels/translations from Holland and Flanders-excerpts); *An Anthology of Modern Swedish Literature*, by Per Wastberg, ed. (short story excerpts, novel excerpts); *Due Mondi*, by Nat Scammacca (nonfiction—novel, Italian).
How to Contact: Query with SASE. "Note: Original language ms should accompany translations." Simultaneous and photocopied submissions "of good quality" OK. Reports in 1 month.
Terms: Pays "sometimes" 10-25% in royalties and "occasionally" by outright purchase, in author's copies—"10% of run for chapbook series," and "by arrangement for other publications." No advance. Book catalog for 5½x8½ SASE plus 40¢ postage.
Advice: "Write because you want to or you must; satisfy yourself. If you've done the best you can in that subject, style, and circumstance, then you've succeeded. Authentic creative expression should be your goal. You will find a publisher and an audience eventually."
Comments: "Generally, we have a greater interest in nonfiction-novels and translations. Short stories and excerpts from novels written in one of the traditional neglected languages are preferred—with the original version (i.e., bilingual). Our kinderbook series will soon be in production with a similar bilingual emphasis, especially for folktales, fairy tales, and fables."

THE CROSSING PRESS, 17 W. Main St., Trumansburg NY 14886. Editor: Elaine Gill. Publishes paperback and hardcover originals. Estab. 1966.
Needs: Literary, contemporary, women's, feminist, gay/lesbian.
How to Contact: Query. Reports in 1 month. Free book catalog.
Payment: 7½-10% royalties.

CURBSTONE PRESS, 321 Jackson St., Willimantic CT 06226. Imprints include Augustinus/Curbstone. Director: Alex Taylor. Estab. 1975. Number of titles: 2 in 1980.
Needs: Contemporary, literary, experimental, faction, historical, women's, feminist, gay/lesbian, ethnic, translations. Recently published *Centralia Dead March*, by T. Churchill (documentary novel); *The Box*, by V. Kaplan (short stories).
How to Contact: Submit outline/synopsis and sample chapters or submit through agent. SASE for query, ms. No simultaneous submissions; photocopied submissions OK. Reports in 1 week on queries, 6 weeks on mss.
Terms: Pays in author's copies (10%); no advance. Free book catalog.
Comments: "Our authors have usually established a reputation in magazines. If an author has not published individual pieces in literary magazines or journals, he would be well

DECEMBER PRESS, 6232 N. Hoyne, 1C, Chicago IL 60659. (312)973-7360. Editor: Curt Johnson. Estab. 1958. Publishes paperback originals. Number of titles: 2 in 1979, 1 in 1980; 1 planned for 1981.
Needs: Literary and experimental. Recently published *In Empty Rooms*, by Henry H. Roth

(short stories); *Abstract Relations*, by Thomas E. Connors; and *Why Girls Ride Sidesaddle*, by Dennis Lynds.
How to Contact: Query and send complete ms with SASE. Photocopied submissions OK; no simultaneous submissions. Reports in 1 month on queries, 6 weeks on mss.
Terms: Pays in 3 author's copies. No advance. Book catalog for #10 SASE.

DEINOTATION-7 PRESS, Box 194, Susquehanna PA 18847. Author/Publisher: Al Stella. Estab. 1978. Publishes paperback originals. Plans to publish 2 titles in 1981.
Needs: Contemporary.
How to Contact: Submit through agent only. Simultaneous and photocopied submissions OK. Reports in 1 week on queries and quite awhile on mss.
Terms: Pays in appropriate amount of author's copies. No advance. Book catalog with #10 SASE and 26¢ postage.
Comments: "You gotta hang in there. The writer can avoid pitfalls by keeping in mind the deep, underlying purpose of Deinotation-7 Press."

DIMENSIONIST PRESS, 5931 Stanton Ave., Highland CA 92346. (714)862-4521. Editor: Arnold Arias. Estab. 1978. Publishes paperback originals. Plans to publish 1 title in 1981.
Needs: Literary, experimental, psychic/supernatural, science fiction, fantasy, juvenile and easy-to-read.
How to Contact: Query and send complete ms with SASE. Simultaneous and photocopied submissions OK. Reports in 2 weeks on queries and mss.
Terms: Negotiates terms with author. No advance.
Comments: "Dimensionist Press represents a new movement in the arts, *Dimensionism*. A Dimensionist strives to evoke or describe a visionary-mystical experience or future world or extra-dimensional realm in art, music, or literature."

THE DRAGONSBREATH PRESS, R1, Sister Bay WI 54234. Editor: Fred Johnson. Estab. 1973. Publishes paperback and hardback originals. Number of titles: 2 in 1980; 3 planned for 1981.
Needs: Contemporary, literary, experimental, adventure, mystery, western, erotica, science fiction, fantasy, horror and humor/satire. "No novels, but rather short stories or novellas."
How to Contact: Query and send complete ms with SASE. Simultaneous and photocopied submissions OK. Reports in 2 weeks on queries, 1 month on mss.
Terms: Negotiates terms with author. No advance.
Comments: "This is a small press working with the book as an art form producing hand-made limited-edition books combining original artwork with original writing. Since we work with hand-set type and have limited time and money we are not interested in novels, but prefer shorter writing suited to handwork and illustrating."

EDUCATION GUILD, Box 205, Saddle River NJ 07458. (201)327-8486. Imprints include Teacher Update. Assistant Editor: M. Bennett. Estab. 1976.
Needs: "We have not yet published a work of fiction, but will consider all submissions."
How to Contact: Query or submit: complete ms, outline/synopsis and sample chapters or submit through agent—all with SASE. Simultaneous and photocopied submissions OK. Reports in 1 month on queries and mss.
Terms: Pays in royalties and outright purchases. $100 advance. Free book catalog.

FANTOME PRESS, 720 N. Park Ave., Warren OH 44483. Imprint includes *Journal Fantome*. Editor/Publisher: C.M. James. Estab. 1976. Publishes limited edition folios. Published 6 titles in 1979.
Needs: Gothic, erotica, science fiction and fantasy. "No other subjects accepted." Recently published *Antarktos*, by H.P. Lovecraft; *The Riddle*, by Joseph Payne Brennan; and *When Chaugnar Wakes* by Frank Belknap Long.

How to Contact: Query and send complete ms with SASE. Simultaneous and photocopied submissions OK. Reports in 6 weeks on queries and mss.
Terms: Negotiates terms with author. No advance. Free book catalog with SASE and 20¢ postage.
Comments: "Avoid sending material outside of our genre."

FICTION COLLECTIVE, INC., c/o George Braziller, One Park Ave., New York NY 10016. Co-Directors: Thomas Glynn and Harold Jaffe. Estab. 1975. Publishes hardback and paperback originals. Currently 32 titles in print.
Needs: Contemporary, literary and experimental. "Primarily interested in new fiction and all that term implies. Recently published *Emergency Exit*, by Clarence Major; *Chez Charlotte and Emily*, by Jonathan Baumback; and *Long Talking Bad Conditions Blues*, by Ronald Sukenick.
How to Contact: Query. Simultaneous and photocopied submissions OK. Reports in 1 month on queries, 6 weeks on mss.
Terms: The collective is a publishing cooperative. No advance. Free book catalog.

FRED A. FLEET, II, 151 N. Lincoln St., Washington PA 15301. Publishes hardcover and paperback originals and paperback reprints. Number of titles: 2 in 1980; 5 planned for 1981.
Needs: Contemporary, experimental, adventure, romance, psychic/supernatural, fantasy and humor/satire.
How to Contact: Submit complete ms with SASE. Simultaneous and photocopied submissions OK. Reports in 1 week on queries, 1 month on mss.
Terms: Pays 5-10% royalties. No advance.
Comments: "Supernatural material is on the rise as is light, easy-to-read romance. Watch what is selling in the bookstores. Buy a couple of those books, and then prepare your mss. We are small but we read everything that comes in. We are looking for good writers and we are willing to work with you."

FOLDEN EDITIONS, 103-26 68th Rd., Forest Hills NY 11375. (212)275-3839. Associate Editor: Perry Aldan. Editorial Director: Dr. Daisy Aldan. Fiction Editor: Diana Cohen. Estab. 1959. Publishes hardback and paperback originals. Number of titles: 2 in 1979, 1 in 1980; 2 planned for 1981.
Needs: Contemporary, literary, women's, fantasy and translations. No obscene erotica, horror, violence, crime, sport or science fiction. Recently published *A Golden Story*, by Daisy Aldan (novella) and *The Fall of Antichrist*, by Albert Steffen (play translated by Dora Baker).
How to Contact: Query with SASE. Photocopied submissions OK; no simultaneous submissions. Reports in 1 week on queries and mss.
Terms: Pays in 10 free author's copies. "We are a small press. If we get a grant, we will pay the author."
Comments: "There is a big market for books of superficial sensationalism, violence and sex. We exist to counteract this, to influence once more the taste of readers for good literature. Do not debase your art, your dignity, or in other words, the word, for money. Have a sense of responsibility for what you write and for the welfare of the world. Make sure there are no errors in spelling, grammar, etc. Avoid obscenities, clichés. Ask yourself if what you are writing will add to or detract from the reader's experience of writing as an art. We are interested only in quality literature."

FRONT PRESS, Box 1355, Kingston, Ontario, Canada M5A 2R9. Editor: Jim Smith. Estab. 1975. Publishes paperback originals. Number of titles: 2 in 1979, 3 in 1980; 10 planned for 1981.
Needs: Contemporary, literary, experimental, erotica, science fiction, humor/satire and

translations. No conventional formula. Recently published *Surface Structures*, by Jim Smith (poetry).
How to Contact: Submit complete ms with SASE. Photocopied submissions OK; no simultaneous submissions. Reports in 2 weeks on mss.
Terms: Pays in 10 author's copies. No advance.
Comments: "Experiment."

GAY SUNSHINE PRESS, Box 40397, San Francisco CA 94140. (415)824-3184. Imprint includes *Gay Sunshine Journal*. Editor: Winston Leyland. Estab. 1970. Publishes hardcover and paperback originals. Number of titles: 4 in 1979, 4 in 1980; 5 planned for 1981.
Needs: Literary, experimental, gay and translations. "We desire fiction on gay themes of *high* literary quality and prefer writers who have already had work published in literary magazines." Recently published *Now the Volcano*, edited by Winston Leyland. "We also include some short fiction."
How to Contact: Query with SASE. Reports in 2 weeks on queries, 1 month on mss.
Terms: Negotiates terms with author.
Comments: "Before submitting a ms to a publisher, ask competent people in your own city for an appraisal of the literary quality of your work. No sophomoric writing. Avoid sending in a ragged ms."

GLUXLIT PRESS, Box 884, Redlands CA 92373. Publisher: Bud Long. Estab. 1977. Number of titles: 2 in 1979, 1-2 in 1980.
Needs: Contemporary, literary, adventure, mystery, spy, historical, western, war, romance, ethnic (deafness), science fiction, horror, humor/satire and juvenile and young adult. "Only the above mentioned are acceptable." Recently published *The Year 2079, Any Price You Wish*, and *The Case of the Lombard Street Murder*, by Bud Long.
How to Contact: Query. Photocopied submissions OK; no simultaneous submissions. Reports in 1-2 months on mss.
Terms: Pays 10% in royalties and by outright purchase of $10-$500. No advance.
Comments: "Detective fiction is not popular with small presses, at least with people our books reach. If the writer is deaf, we are interested. Important, Gluxlit Press accepts fiction and other mss from deaf writers only—we do not publish books by people with normal hearing."

GOETHE'S PRESS, 254 N. Gorsuch Rd., Westminster MD 21157. (301)848-3690. Imprint includes *Goethe's Notes*. Editor/Publisher: Jesse Glass, Jr. Estab. 1974. Publishes paperback originals. Number of titles: 2 in 1980; 2 planned for 1981.
Needs: Literary and experimental (short). "No long works, if not solicited."
How to Contact: Submit complete ms with SASE. Simultaneous and photocopied submissions OK. Reports in 1 month on queries and mss.
Terms: Pays with 3 author's copies. No advance.
Comments: "First, buy a sample copy. See what we're doing. We are a small press publisher and work on a shoe-string budget. We publish a magazine and chapbooks of poetry and prose."

JCR GREEN (PUBLISHERS) LIMITED, Box 1, Portree, Isle of Skye, Scotland 1V51 9BT. Imprints include Aquila Publishing, Club Leabhar and J.C.R. Green Ass. Managing Director: JCR Green. Estab. 1968. Publishes hardcover and paperback originals. Number of titles: 6 in 1979, 10 in 1980 and 15 planned for 1981.
Needs: Contemporary, literary, experimental, adventure, mystery, spy, historical, erotica, psychic/supernatural, science fiction, fantasy, horror, humor/satire, translations and short stories. No romance, westerns, gothic, feminist, war, confession, women's, gay/lesbian, ethnic, religious/inspirational or juvenile/young adult. Recently published *In Search of Jasper McDoom*, by Stephen Wade (short stories), *The Miserable Child And Her Father*, by

Dinah Brooke, (literary novel, hardback) and *Belladonna*, by Paul Matthews, (short stories, paperback).
How to Contact: Query and send complete ms with SASE. No simultaneous submissions, photocopied submissions OK. Reports in 1 month on queries, 6 weeks on mss.
Terms: Pays 10-15% in royalties and in short chapbook copies. No advance. Free book catalog with 9x6 SASE and 4 International Reply Coupons.

GRIFFON HOUSE PUBLICATIONS, Box 81, Whitestone NY 11357. (212)767-8380. President: Frank Grande. Estab. 1976. Publishes paperback originals and reprints. Number of titles planned for 1981 is undecided.
Needs: Contemporary, literary, experimental, ethnic (open) and translations.
How to Contact: Query with SASE. No simultaneous submissions; photocopied submissions OK. Reports in 1 month on queries, 6 weeks on mss.
Terms: Pays in 6 free author's copies. No advance.

GROUND UNDER PRESS, 2913 Shattuck Ave., Berkeley CA 94705. Editor/Publishers: Tobey Kaplan and A. Dibz. Estab. 1978. Publishes paperback originals and reprints. Number of titles: 2 in 1979, 3 in 1980; 3 planned for 1981.
Needs: Contemporary, literary, experimental, women's, feminist, gay/lesbian, fantasy, humor/satire and translations. Recently published *Light Tracks*, by A. Dibz (chapbook of prose-poems).
How to Contact: Query and submit outline/synopsis and sample chapters with SASE. Simultaneous and photocopied submissions OK. Reports in 6 weeks on queries, 2 weeks on mss.
Terms: Pays in author's copies. No advance. Free book catalog.
Advice: "Don't send complete mss. I do this on my own time so I don't have a lot of time to read through what may be excellent. Send query first!"
Comments: "Autobiographical work tends to be best when it is somewhat fictionalized. Write and get responses/critiques. Read a lot."

GUERNICA EDITIONS, Box 633, Station N.D.G., Montreal, Quebec, Canada H4A 3R1. Imprint includes *The Guernica Review*. President and Poetry Editor: Antonio D'Alfonso. Fiction Editor: Umberto Claudio. Estab. 1978. Publishes hardcover and paperback originals and reprints. Number of titles: 4 poetry in 1980 and plans 4 in 1981.
Needs: Contemporary, literary, romance, confession, women's, feminist, gay/lesbian, erotica, psychic/supernatural, religious/inspirational, humor/satire, juvenile and young adult and translations.
How to Contact: Query with SASE. No simultaneous submissions; photocopied submissions OK. Reports in 2 weeks on queries, 6 weeks on mss.
Terms: Pays 2-3 author's copies. "We will be paying in the near future." No advance. Free book catalog.
Advice: "Have perseverance, intelligence, courage. Guernica was established for writers who have not been published in the way they thought they should have been. We want writers who know the value of their work. Avoid arrogance."
Comments: "We will accept any writer who has been published in magazines but who has not been published in book form."

HARIAN CREATIVE PRESS, 47 Hyde Blvd., Ballston Spa NY 12020. Imprints include The Harian Press, Barba-Cue Special Serials. President/Executive Editor: Dr. Harry Barba. Estab. 1967. Publishes hardcover and paperback originals. Number of titles: 2 in 1979, 3 in 1980 and plans 3-6 in 1981.
Needs: Contemporary, experimental, romance, science fiction, fantasy and translations. No obscenity, pornography for its own sake, or violence. Recently published *The Day The*

World Went Sane by Harry Barba (science fiction); and *Love, In the Persian Way*, by H. Barba (Baroque novella).
How to Contact: Query or submit outline/synopsis and sample chapters (2-3) with SASE. Simultaneous and photocopied submissions OK. Reports in 1 month on queries, 6 weeks on ms.
Terms: Terms are negotiated; no advance. Free book catalog with 9x11 SASE.
Advice: "Keep a good job and write when you can find the time. Writing is a salubrious act. The benefits are not just monetary; they are emotional and intellectual. But money is also important. We look for functionally suitable style—manner married to matter."

HOLMGANGERS PRESS, 22 Ardith Ln., Alamo CA 94507. Publisher: Gary Elder. Estab. 1974. Publishes paperback originals. Published 1 title in 1980; undecided for 1981.
Needs: Contemporary, literary, experimental, historical, western, juvenile and young adult, animal, and translations. Will not accept any but the above subjects. "We published one novel and one book of short stories in 1975; one experimental fiction chapbook on 1976; two novels in 1977."
How to Contact: Query with SASE. No simultaneous submissions; photocopied submissions OK. Reports in 1 week on queries, 6 weeks on mss.
Terms: Pays 10% of gross after recovery of costs. No advance. Free book list for legal-sized SASE and 38¢ postage.

HOUSE OF ANANSI PRESS LIMITED, 35 Britain St., Toronto, Ontario, Canada M5A 1R7. (416)363-5444. Publisher: Ann Wall. Estab. 1967. Publishes paperback originals; sometimes releases in hardcover first. Number of titles: 3 in 1979, 2-3 in 1980; 2-3 planned for 1981.
Needs: From Canadian authors: contemporary, literary, experimental, women's, ethnic (women) and translations (from French Canada only). No formula or genre fiction. Recently published *The "Jimmy" Trilogy*, by Jacques Poulin, translated by Sheila Fischman; *The Hockey Sweater and Other Stories*, by Roch Carrier, translated by Sheila Fischman (short stories); and *Five Legs/Communion*, by Graeme Gibson, introduction by Leon Edel, (novel).
How to Contact: Query with SASE or IRC. Simultaneous and photocopied submissions OK. "However, the writer should be careful to inform us that it is a multiple submission, and to tell us what the deadline for offers is." Reports in 2 weeks on queries, 1 month sometimes sooner on mss.
Terms: Pays 15% maximum in royalties. Advance varies greatly depending on type of book and on how well-known the author is already. Also can offer subsidy through the Ontario Arts Council. Free book catalog.
Advice: "Try to get very clear in your mind what it is you are writing: If it is commercial, genre fiction, then do it as well as you can, keeping in mind the conventions required by what you are doing. If attempting to produce literature, then don't expect to get rich from it, but keep writing it anyway. The most rare bird there is, is a literary novel or book of stories that sells extremely well. The writer should keep in mind that we publish Canadian authors only, and that we publish only well-written literary work. (If everybody kept that in mind our unsolicited ms pile would diminish considerably.)"
Comments: "We see a trend toward more and more 'commercial' fiction, escape fiction, and away from fiction which requires that the reader think a bit. In what is submitted to us we see the same sort of mix as always, with a lot of 'young man writes a novel' novels by young men (or young women . . .). General level of writing seems to be improving over the last few years, though."

ILLUMINATIONS PRESS, 2110 9th St., Apt. B, Berkeley CA 94710. (415)849-2102. Publisher: N. Moser. Estab. 1965. Publishes paperback originals occasionally.
Needs: Contemporary, literary, experimental and humor/satire. Material dealing with

nature and mysticism (using nature images, in other words) for possible anthology in '81-2.
How to Contact: Query with SASE. Simultaneous and photocopied submissions OK. Reports in 1 month on queries, 6 months on mss.
Terms: Pays 1 or more author's copies usually. No advance. Free book catalog with $1.95 postage.
Advice: "Keep language simple. Don't try to change the world in fiction. Write what you know and feel for sure. Avoid excessively complicated language or poor characterizations."
Comments: "Trend is away from the narrative (beginning, middle, end, etc.) As years go by, I like the trend less and less."

IN BETWEEN BOOKS, Box T, Sausalito CA 94965. (415)388-8048. Contact: Karla Andersdatter. Estab. 1973. Publishes paperback originals. Number of titles: 1 in 1979 and 1 in 1980.
Needs: Fantasy. Open to most children's subjects if queried first. Recently published *Marissa The Tooth Fairy*, by Karla Andersdatter (children's fantasy).
How to Contact: Query. No simultaneous submissions. Photocopied submissions OK. Reports in 6 weeks on queries.
Terms: After first printing, pays 10% in royalties. Negotiable author's copies. No advance. Free book catalog.
Advice: "Read a lot. Avoid cutsey-wootsey, goodie-goodie 'fantasies.' "
Comments: "Golden Books has taken over. Commercialism is rampant. I like quality and a fresh unique style. Write on two levels so adults get the 'message' too."

INTERMEDIA PRESS, Box 3294, Vancouver, British Columbia, Canada V6B 3X9. (604)879-0471. Editorial Director: Edwin Varney. Estab. 1973. Publishes hardcover and paperback originals. Number of titles: 3 in 1979, 2-3 in 1980; 3 planned for 1981.
Needs: Contemporary, literary, experimental, historical, women's, humor/satire and translations. "No historical romance. Literary quality only." Recently published *Tea With The Queen*, by Nellie McClung (humorous); *Stories For Late Night Drinkers*, by Michel Tremblay (short fiction); and *Tales of Solitude*, by Margaret Rose (translation) and Yvette Naubert (author) (short stories).
How to Contact: Query or submit through agent with SASE. Photocopied submissions OK. Reports in 2 weeks on queries, 6 weeks on mss.
Terms: Pays 7-10% in royalties. No advance (only to established writers). Book catalog for $1.
Comments: "We have a decided inclination to Canadian fiction and resent submissions that ignore the fact that we are a Canadian publisher. By all means, study successful writers, but don't crank out imitations, or if you do, don't send them to us. We want strong individual voices. Don't submit American mass market thrillers, spy, detective, softcore, etc. Query first."

JELM MOUNTAIN PUBLISHING, 209 Grand, Laramie WY 82070. (307)742-8053. Imprint includes Jelm Mountain Press. Editor: Jean Jones. Estab. 1976. Publishes paperback originals. Number of titles: 3 in 1979, 3 in 1980; 1 planned for 1981.
Needs: Historical, western and fantasy. No types not related to western or frontier living, whether placed in the past, present or future. Recently published *Whispers on The Wind*, by Richard Heasler (Indian-fantasy); *Carmela*, by Carlos Mellizo (Spanish/English novel); and *Wyoming Sun*, by Edward Bryant (science fiction fantasy).
How to Contact: Query and submit outline/synopsis and sample chapters with SASE. Simultaneous and photocopied submissions OK. Reports in 2 week on queries, 4 weeks on mss.
Terms: Pays 5-15% in royalties and 10 author's copies. No advance. Free book catalog with SASE.
Advice: "Be serious, learn the fundamentals of writing, keep your mind on the story and not on how popular or rich it will make you."

Comments: "Our editor prefers an up-beat approach—meeting life's challenges! Our press is small enough to give writers, especially novices, a lot of attention, but we hope they are willing to help by being able to pay for extra services."

LAKES & PRAIRIES PRESS, 6334 N. Sheridan Rd. 4-D, Chicago IL 60660. Editor: Edward Haggard. Publishes trade and paperback books. Estab. 1974.
Needs: Literary, contemporary, feminist, young adult, serialized and condensed novels.
How to Contact: Query. SASE for query, ms. Reports in 3 weeks on queries, 2 months on mss.
Terms: Pays in author's copies.
Comments: "Lakes & Prairies Press is a spin-off small book press from *Lakes & Prairies, A Journal of Writings*, which is no longer published. The first book appeared in fall 1980 and is a volume of poetry. We are devoted to the publication of short stories and short novels. We are not interested in writing of a strictly commercial/slick intent and inspiration. That is not to say we are indifferent to quality prose that may also have commercial appeal; such work is perfectly acceptable."

LAME JOHNNY PRESS, Box 66, Hermosa SD 57744. Editorial Director: Linda M. Hasselstrom. Estab. 1970. Publishes hardcover and paperback originals and paperback reprints. Number of titles: 2 in 1979.
Needs: Historical, western. "I accept on quality, not quantity. I want fiction of and for Great Plains, no gothic, romance, fantasy, and especially no so-called 'contemporary' explorations of the author's navel and psyche." Recently published *The Indian Maiden's Captivity* and *The Heart of the Country*, by E.R. Zietlow (western historical fiction).
How to Contact: Query. No simultaneous submissions; photocopied submissions OK. Reports in 1 month on queries, usually 1 month on mss.
Terms: Pays 10% of print run in author's copies and 30-50% in royalties. No advance. Book catalog for legal-sized SASE with 38¢ postage.
Advice: "Write what you know. Avoid self-analysis."
Comments: "More self-contemplation is evident in style today."

LAPIS EDUCATIONAL ASSOCIATION, INC., 18225 Gottschalk, Homewood IL 60430. Editorial Director: Karen Degenhart. Estab. 1977.
Needs: Contemporary, literary, experimental, psychic/supernatural, religious/inspirational. "Jungian psychology focus only. We very rarely publish fiction."
How to Contact: Query. SASE for query, ms. Simultaneous and photocopied submissions OK. Reports in 2 weeks on queries, "indefinite" on mss.
Terms: "We do not pay. Authors must be fee paying members of this association to be published but may join after submitting ms. Don't have to join to submit ms." No advance. Free book catalog.
Advice: "Don't hope for too much. Our budget is under $1,000/year."

LAUGHING BEAR PRESS, Box 23478, San Jose CA 95153. Imprint includes *Laughing Bear* quarterly magazine. Editor: Tom Person. Estab. 1976. Publishes paperback originals.
Needs: Literary, experimental, mystery, spy, western, gothic, science fiction, fantasy, horror. "Not interested in anything over 50,000 words at this time. Styles are open, but I lean away from religious, confession, or psychic material."
How to Contact: Query. Simultaneous and photocopied submissions OK. Reports in 2 weeks on queries, 1 month on mss.
Terms: Pays in at least 10 author's copies.
Advice: "First learn to write a sentence that is a story in itself; then move out to the one page story, the short story, the serial, and finally the novel. Read the best—and the worst. Learn from the shortcomings of others. Become a critic. Become a storyteller before you try to

write a story. And listen to your voice in the telling. Use it in your writing."

Comments: "I think there is a strong trend back toward the detective, gothic, and western story. But with new twists. The story form acts as a solid base for innovation. The reader has a familiar skeleton for reference. In an unstable society, the familiar becomes important and, if utilized well, popular. Laughing Bear Press has published mostly poetry in the past, but as I am becoming more involved in writing fiction myself, we will become more involved in publishing it."

LIBERATOR PRESS, Box 7128, Chicago IL 60680. (312)663-4329. Editorial Director: R. Burns. Estab. 1976. Publishes cloth and paperback originals and reprints. Number of titles: 2 in 1979, 3 in 1980; 7 planned for 1981.
Needs: Contemporary, literary, ethnic, historical, war, women's, feminist. No romance or science fiction. Recently published *Trouble On the Hill*, by Michael Glenn (short story collection).
How to Contact: Query. Simultaneous and photocopied submissions OK. Reports in 1 week on queries, 6 weeks on mss.
Terms: Pays 8-15% in royalties; offers advance. Free book catalog.

LIBRA PRESS, Box 341, Wataga IL 61488. (309)375-6682. Editor: Jim McCurry. Book series publishing poetry, fiction, reviews when available, graphics—any genre of writing. Estab. June 1975.
Needs: Literary, contemporary, religious/inspirational, psychic/supernatural, science fiction, fantasy, novels and translations. No cinematic, soap-opera fiction. Length of ms is flexible.
How to Contact: Query with clips of published or unpublished work with SASE.
Payment: Half the press run number of copies. Negotiable.
Terms: Pays on publication for power of copyright belonging to individual author.
Tips: "Work on writing, not getting published. Work on living, not getting rich and famous. Surrender attachments."

LIBRARY RESEARCH ASSOCIATES, Rt. 5, Box 41, Dunderberg Rd., Monroe NY 10950. Editorial Director: Matilda A. Gocek. Estab. 1968. Publishes hardcover and paperback originals. Number of titles: 2 planned for 1981.
Needs: Historical of New York State only. Recently published *By Faith Alone*, by Doris Crofut (hardcover trade).
How to Contact: Submit outline/synopsis and sample chapters with SASE. No simultaneous submissions; photocopied submissions OK. Reports in 6 weeks.
Terms: Pays in royalties; no advance. Book catalog for legal-sized SASE with 20¢ postage.
Advice: "Do not ask me to evaluate your work as a matter of course. Do not cost me more than my time to read the material."
Comments: "There is a gradual return to a good story line less dependent upon violence and explicit sex. I am looking to develop a line of fiction titles based on actual events or people in New York State. Fictionalized biographies based on fact would be welcomed, particularly of women in New York, any period."

LIBRE PRESS, INC., Suite 529, Connell Bldg., Scranton PA 18503. (717)348-1010. Imprint includes *The Metro*. Editorial Director: Joseph Skorupg. Estab. 1970. Publishes paperback originals. Number of titles: 6 in 1979, 6 in 1980; 6 planned for 1981.
Needs: Contemporary, literary, experimental, humor/satire, arts and cultural development. Will accept short story anthology.
How to Contact: Query or submit outline/synopsis and sample chapters. SASE on query. All unsolicited mss are returned unopened. Simultaneous and photocopied submissions OK. Reports in 6 weeks.
Terms: Pays 1-5% royalties; no advance.

LINTEL, Box 34 St. George, Staten Island NY 10301. Editorial Director: Walter James Miller. Estab. 1977. Publishes paperback originals. Number of titles: 3 in 1979, 3 in 1980; 4 planned for 1981.
Needs: Experimental fiction, poetry. Recently published *The Fairy Tales of My Mind*, by Rebecca Rass (experimental/fantasy).
How to Contact: Query. No simultaneous submissions; photocopied submissions OK. Reports in 1 month on queries, 6 weeks on mss.
Terms: Negotiated. No advance. Free book catalog.
Advice: "Buy a photocopy machine. Write with an audience in mind."
Comments: "Subject matter is becoming drippy. Style is becoming loose. This could be a good thing, but it usually isn't. The writer should try to picture himself as the publisher receiving the ms. Does it really have any market value? Is it publishable? Is it good?"

LOLLIPOP POWER, INC., Box 1171, Chapel Hill, NC 27514. (919)929-4857. Editorial Director: Kathleen Gallagher. Estab. 1970. Number of titles: 3 in 1979, 0 in 1980; 1 planned for 1981.
Needs: Children's: pre-school and early elementary. "We publish children's books exclusively. Our publishing priorities require that a book be nonsexist and nonracist and that it offer some alternative to the sex-role stereotypes usually seen in children's books." Recently published *Maria Teresa*, by Mary Atkinson; *Jesse's Dream Skirt*, by Bruce Mack; *When Megan Went Away*, by Jane Severance (all children's books).
How to Contact: Query, submit complete ms or submit outline/synopsis and sample chapters. SASE for ms. Simultaneous and photocopied submissions OK. Reports in 2 weeks on queries, 6 weeks on mss.
Terms: "We pay a flat $200 which is split between author and illustrator."

LORIEN HOUSE, Box 1112, Black Mountain NC 28711. (704)669-9992. Contact: D. Wilson. Estab. 1969.
Needs: Experimental, fantasy, humor/satire. "No emphasized sex or horror."
How to Contact: Query or submit complete ms. SASE for query, ms. Simultaneous and photocopied submissions OK. Reports in 1 week on queries, 2 weeks on mss.
Terms: "Vanity Press unless exceptional—then direct payment." No advance. Free book catalog.
Advice: "Before sending, have 5 people read your mss, including at least two strangers, for honest opinions."
Comments: "I don't want to hear how great the piece is; I just want to know the category, approach and specific story line in a query. My publishing firm is small. Emphasis began on poetry, shifted to solar energy to pay the bills. Fiction is difficult selling for a small press, but I do want a crack at what is out there."

LYNX HOUSE PRESS, Box 800, Amherst MA 01004. Fiction Editor: Robert Abel. Estab. 1971. Publishes hardcover and paperback originals. Number of titles: 5 in 1979, 5 in 1980; 5 planned for 1981.
Needs: Contemporary, literary, ethnic (Native American). "No juveniles, translations, romance, confession, religious, supernatural." Recently published *Blount's Anvil*, by Don Hendrie, Jr. (contemporary novel); *Becoming Coyote*, by Wayne Ude (Native American novel); *A Waltz*, by Kevin McIlroy (contemporary novel).
How to Contact: Query. SASE for query, ms. Simultaneous and photocopied submissions OK, if we're advised. Reports in 2 weeks on queries, 6 weeks on mss.
Terms: Pays 10% of press run in author's copies; no advance.
Advice: "Read, absorb and don't imitate. Please do not send 1) polemical writing; 2) ragged mss; 3) long letters describing how you've tried everywhere else and we're your last hope; or 4) plotless prose with no attention to the nuances of language."
Comments: "We've noticed a kind of cheap experimentalism that some writers try to

substitute for the discipline of good fiction—traditional or experimental. We specifically publish literary fiction for a general but educated audience. We don't wish to see commercial fiction that couldn't find a publisher because the writing was inadequate."

MAINE WRITERS WORKSHOP, Box 82, Stonington ME 04681. (207)367-2484. Imprints include *Letters Magazine* and Mainespring Press. Editorial Director: H.N. Nash. Publishes hardcover and paperback originals. Number of titles: 2 in 1979, 4 in 1980; 6 planned for 1981.
Needs: Contemporary, literary, mystery, historical, science fiction, humor/satire, juvenile and young adult. "Especially high quality in these categories."
How to Contact: Submit 50 pp. ms or submit outline/synopsis with first and last chapters. SASE "with full postage or no return!". No simultaneous submissions; photocopied submissions OK. Reports in 1 month.
Terms: Pays 15% maximum royalties; no advance.
Advice: "Write, write, write, then revise even more before submissions."

MASTERS PUBLICATIONS, Box 1332, Brooklyn NY 11201. (212)596-1598. Imprints include Real Life Books, Transition Books. Editorial Director: Jim Masters. Estab. 1976. Publishes paperback originals. Number of titles: 3 in 1979, 5 in 1980; 7 planned for 1981.
Needs: Juvenile and young adult: easy-to-read. "Especially stories about children with handicaps, or children who are moving, starting school, new sibling, etc. No adult trade fiction." Recently published *Starting School* and *New Baby*, by Dr. Gil Martin (activity books).
How to Contact: Submit complete ms or outline/synopsis and sample chapters. SASE for query, ms. Simultaneous and photocopied submissions OK. Reports in 2 months.
Terms: Pays 5-15% royalties or by outright purchase. Also pays in 10 author's copies; nominal advance.
Advice: "Persist. Don't expect a reply overnight!"

METIS PRESS, INC., Box 25187, Chicago IL 60625. Editorial Director: Chris Johnson. Estab. 1978. Publishes paperback originals. Number of titles: 1 in 1979, 2 in 1980; 2 planned for 1981.
Needs: Women's, feminist, gay/lesbian. Recently published *The Secret Witch*, by Linda J. Stern (children's); *Shedevils*, by Barbara Sheen (women's short stories); *Wild Women Don't Get the Blues*, by Barbara Emrys (lesbian short stories); *Hurting and Healing and Talking it Over*, by Arny Christine Straayer (lesbian short stories).
How to Contact: Query or submit complete ms. SASE with query, ms. Simultaneous and photocopied submissions OK. Reports in 6 weeks on queries, 3 months on mss.
Terms: Pays in royalties, by outright purchase and in author's copies; no advance. Free book catalog.

M.O.P. PRESS, Rt. 24, Box 53c, Fort Myers FL 33908. (813)482-0802. Editorial Director: Shirley Aycock. Estab. 1978. Publishes chapbooks. Number of titles: 3 in 1979, 5 in 1980; 5 planned for 1981.
Needs: "Practically anything except erotica, gay, juvenile." Recently published *Winging It*, by M.O.P./sra (chapbook, poetry).
How to Contact: Query first with SASE "for lengthy ms." No simultaneous submissions; photocopied submissions OK. Reports "as soon as possible. This might be as long as 6 weeks if involved in printing when received."
Terms: "We do not pay. Order blank and/or printing quotes for SASE."
Comments: "Although mainly interested in poetry, we will consider and provide quote for printing for authors who wish to self-publish. My small operation would be limited to about 50 pages—sufficient for novelette, short story(s) or poetry, chapbook style only."

MORNING STAR PRESS, Poplar Hill Rd., West Whately, via RFD Haydenville MA 01039. Imprints include *The Phoenix*, American Novelists Cooperative, American Poets Cooperative. Editorial Director: James Cooney. Estab. 1938. Publishes hardcover and paperback originals.

Needs: All forms of literature, novels, stories, travel books, diaries. "No exclusions except works which do not intrinsically espouse human rights and democracy."

How to Contact: Query or submit complete ms with SASE. Simultaneous and photocopied submissions OK. Reports in 2 weeks on queries, 1 month on mss.

Terms: Pays 25% royalties; no advance.

Advice: "Whatever you write, do it out of belief and love; and whenever you are discouraged, read and re-read the unabridged letters of Vincent Van Gogh, one of the world's obscure great writers, just as during his entire lifetime he was an obscure and unrecognized great painter."

MOSAIC PRESS/JAZLEY EDITIONS, Box 1032, Oakville, Ontario, Canada L6J 3E9. (416)844-0963. Editorial Director: L. Shacter. Estab. 1975. Publishes hardcover and paperback originals. Number of titles: 1 in 1979, 2 in 1980; 3 planned for 1981.

Needs: Literary only.

How to Contact: Query. No simultaneous submissions; photocopied submissions OK. Reports in 2 weeks on queries, 3 months on mss.

Terms: Pays 10% royalties; no advance. Free book catalog.

MOUNTAIN STATE PRESS, University of Charleston, 2300 MacCorkle Ave. SE, Charleston WV 25304. (304)346-9471, Ext. 290. Editorial Director: Ira Herman. Estab. 1978. Publishes hardcover and paperback originals and reprints. Number of titles: 3 in 1979, 4 in 1980; 7 planned for 1981.

Needs: "We publish only material about Appalachia or material in *all* categories by Appalachian residents. No pornography, racist or sexist material. Literary quality is our basic criterion." Recently published *As I Remember It*, by Stanley Eskew (autobiographical Appalachian fiction); *A Tree Full of Stars*, by Davis Grubb (children's Christmas novel); *Tale of the Elk*, by W.E.R. Byrne (anecdotes about the Elk River region of WV).

How to Contact: Query or submit complete ms. SASE for query, ms. Simultaneous and photocopied submissions OK, if so indicated. Reports in 1 week on queries, 1 month on mss.

Terms: Pays 10-30% royalties and by outright purchase; sometimes offers advance. Book catalog for legal-sized SASE with 20¢ postage.

Advice: Study fiction writing techniques, and keep at it with a vengeance."

Comments: "Appalachian fiction is a steadily growing market. We want believable characterization and strong plots, no preaching. Book length mss only."

MUDBORN PRESS, 209 W. De la Guerra, Santa Barbara CA 93101. Imprint includes *Rockbottom Magazine*. Editorial Director: Erasmus (Sasha) Newborn. Estab. 1975. Publishes paperback originals and paperback reprints. Number of titles: 2 in 1979, 2 in 1980; 4 planned for 1981.

Needs: Contemporary, literary, experimental, faction, translations. "No third-person or constructed formula fiction." Recently published *First-Person Intense*, by S. Newborn (anthology of autobiography); *The Al Drake Issue*, by S. Newborn (featured interview, stories, photos of writer/editor); *24x12*, by M. Clifton; *Autobiographies* by R. Kostelanetz.

How to Contact: Query or submit outline/synopsis and 2 sample chapters. SASE for query, ms. No simultaneous submissions; photocopied submissions OK. Reports in 3 weeks on queries, 1 month on mss.

Terms: Pays 8% maximum royalties and in author's copies. "Other arrangements negotiable." Book catalog for 6x9 SASE.

Advice: "There are dismal prospects for the literary 'author' who expects the publisher to do all the work and shower blessings on him."

Comments: "Cover letters are appreciated with some biographical information."

THE NAIAD PRESS, INC., Box 10543, Tallahassee FL 32302. (904)539-9322. Editorial Director: Barbara Grier. Estab. 1973. Number of titles: 4 in 1979, 4 in 1980; 6 planned for 1981.
Needs: Feminist, lesbian. Recently published *Retreat: As It Was,* by Donna J. Young (fantasy-science fiction); *Black and White of It,* by Ann Allen Shockley (short stories).
How to Contact: Query. SASE for query, ms. No simultaneous submissions; photocopied submissions OK "but we prefer original mss." Reports in 1 week on queries, 2 months on mss.
Terms: Pays 15% royalties; no advance. Book catalog for legal-sized SASE.
Advice: "Work hard, pretend that your book will be read fifty years from today and try not to be an object of mirth at that remove."
Comments: "We publish lesbian/feminist fiction primarily and prefer honest work (i.e., positive upbeat lesbian characters). No breast beating or complaining."

NEW RIVERS PRESS, 1602 Selby Ave., St. Paul MN 55104. Editorial Director: C.W. Truesdale. Fiction Editors: C.W. Truesdale and Roger Blakely. Estab. 1968. Number of fiction titles: 4 in 1980; 4 planned for 1981.
Needs: Contemporary, literary, experimental, historical (especially personal), translations. "No popular fantasy/romance. Nothing pious, polemical (unless very good other redeeming qualities). We are interested in only quality literature and always have been (though our concentration in the past has been poetry)."
How to Contact: Query. SASE for query, ms. No simultaneous submissions; reluctantly accepts photocopied submissions. Reports in 1 month on queries, within 2 months of query approval on mss.
Terms: Pays in 100 author's copies; no advance. Free book catalog.
Advice: "Find a *real* subject, something that belongs to you and not what you think or surmise that you should be doing by current standards and fads. Be very patient with yourself in writing, take time, exercise care and craft, and be patient with getting published. A great deal of good energy is wasted by young (and old) writers crying over rejections."
Comments: "We are not really concerned with trends. We read for quality, which experience has taught can be very eclectic and can come sometimes from out of nowhere. We are interested in publishing short fiction (as well as poetry and translations) because it is and has been a great American indigenous form and it almost completely ignored by the commercial houses. The worst thing a writer can do, except for writing badly, is to say too much about his work—overselling it. This puts me off and is likely to make objective evaluation more difficult."

NEW SEED PRESS, Box 3016, Stanford CA 94305. (415)328-3944. Estab. 1971. Publishes paperback originals and reprints. Number of titles: 2 in 1980; 1 planned for 1981.
Needs: Feminist, gay/lesbian, ethnic, juvenile and young adult. "No adult fiction that is not for children." Recently published *My Mother and I Are Growing Strong,* by Inez Maury (paperback, ages 4-10).
How to Contact: Query or submit complete ms. SASE for ms. Simultaneous and photocopied submissions OK. Reports in 2 weeks on queries, 1 month on mss.
Terms: Pays in royalties and by outright purchase; no advance. Book catalog for legal-sized SASE.
Advice: "As we are a feminist collective publishing antiracist, antisexist books, we discourage writers from sending us 'apolitical animal-type stories' whose intent is to avoid rather than confront issues."
Comments: "We publish children's books free from stereotyping, stories with active female characters, stories that challenge assumptions about the inferiority of women and Third World peoples."

NO DEAD LINES, 241 Bonita, Portola Valley CA 94025. Editorial Director: Venetia Gleason. Estab. 1975. Publishes paperback originals.

Needs: Will consider all categories.

How to Contact: Query with SASE. Simultaneous and photocopied submissions OK. Reports in 2 weeks on queries, 1 month on mss.

Terms: Pays 10% of profits (sales minus product and promotion expenses). Free book catalog.

Advice: "Get it into print. If you can't interest the New York literary establishment, then query the small presses or publish it yourself. Go for it. Produce a small, elegant, affordable edition, and when you've made your money back, repeat the experience. Writing is to communicate."

Comments: "It is ironic that as big-time publishing houses discovered that it pays to publish more and more daring, experimental fiction, small presses are discovering the joy of publishing simple, well-told, well-crafted traditional fiction. I like both trends. No Dead Lines has not published much fiction. Mostly we publish poetry and graphics in small, limited editions. In 1977 we did a series of six fiction chapbooks."

NORDIC BOOKS, Box 1941, Philadelphia PA 19105. Editorial Director: Niels Malmquist. Estab. 1977. Number of titles: 1 in 1979; 1 planned for 1981.

Needs: Ethnic (Scandinavian), translations.

How to Contact: Query. No simultaneous submissions; photocopied submissions OK. Reports in 1 week on queries, 2 weeks on mss.

Terms: Pays by mutual agreement; no advance.

Comments: "Write before submitting."

NORO PRESS, Box 1447, San Francisco CA 94101. Editor: Geraldine Kudaka.

Needs: Literary, contemporary. Special interests in science fiction, fantasy, horror, feminist, gay/lesbian, erotica, ethnic, condensed novels, translations.

How to Contact: Query with SASE. Reports in 1 month.

Terms: Pays in free author's copies.

Comments: 1981-82 erotic issue, $2.50 per page payment plus free author copy.

OMMATION PRESS, 5548 N. Sawyer, Chicago IL 60625. Imprints include *Mati Magazine*, *Ditto Rations Chapbook Series*, *Offset Offshoot Series*, *Salome: A Literary Dance Magazine*. Editorial Director: E. Mihopoulos. Estab. 1975. Number of titles: 2 in 1979; 1 planned for 1981.

Needs: Contemporary, literary, experimental, feminist, prose poetry. Recently published *Hide & Seek*, by Rochelle Ratner; *Spirals*, by Douglas MacDonald (both poetry and prose poetry).

How to Contact: Submit complete ms. SASE for query, ms. Simultaneous and photocopied submissions OK if so indicated. Reports in 1 week.

Terms: Pays in 50 author's copies (and $100 honorarium if grant money available). Book catalog for legal-sized SASE.

PAYCOCK PRESS, Box 57206, Washington DC 20037. Imprint includes *Gargoyle Magazine*. Editor/Publisher: Richard Peabody, Jr. Estab. 1976. Publishes paperback originals and reprints. Number of titles: 2 in 1979, 2 in 1980; 2 planned for 1981. Publishes fiction and poetry volumes.

Needs: Contemporary, literary, experimental, humor/satire and translations. "No tedious academic resume-conscious writing or NEA-funded minimalism." Recently published *The Love Letter Hack*, by Michael Brondoli (contemporary/literary).

How to Contact: Query with SASE. No simultaneous submissions; photocopied submissions OK. Reports in 1 week on queries, 1 month on mss.

Terms: Pays in author's copies 10% of print run plus 50% of all sales "after/if we break even on book." No advance.

Advice: "Keep trying. Many good writers simply quit. Many mediocre writers keep writing, eventually get published, and become better writers. If the big magazines won't publish you, try the small magazines, try the local newspaper. Don't think about writing—do it. Always read your fiction aloud. If you think something is *silly*, no doubt we'd be embarrassed too. Write the kind of stories you'd like to read and can't seem to find."

Comments: "I sense a drift away from the Pynchonesque style of the last few years, away from 'mandarin narcissism,' and a return to what John Gardner and John Fowles have been espousing as 'moral fiction,' e.g.: imaginative ideas conveyed in real life terms. Maybe a return to slice-of-life stories would be a good idea for the '80s. We're pretty open-minded. We like verbal tension we can believe in. Try to write about what you know. Don't try to bluff us."

PEPPERMINT PRESS, 204 Stibbard Ave., Toronto, Ontario, Canada M4P 2C3. Imprints include Abraxas and Aura Publications. Publisher: Richard Miller. Estab. 1973. Publishes hardcover and paperback originals. Number of titles: 2-3 planned for 1981.

Needs: Erotica, science fiction, fantasy, humor/satire and juvenile and young adult (our prime interest). No experimental.

How to Contact: Query, submit complete ms, submit outline/synopsis and sample chapters (as many as the author thinks necessary) or submit through agent, all accompanied by SASE. Simultaneous and photocopied submissions OK. Reports in 6 weeks on queries, 3 months on mss.

Terms: Pays in royalties and in author's copies; both negotiable. Advance also negotiable.

Advice: "Read the competition and learn the difference between a good story and an excellent one. The same holds true for the quality of writing. A sloppy ms, poor grammar, and excessive spelling errors are not the products of careful authors."

Comments: "Our books are issued intermittently and are produced with great care and pride. We select our mss just as carefully."

PERIVALE PRESS, 13830 Erwin St., Van Nuys CA 91401. (213)785-4671. President: Lawrence P. Spingarn. Estab. 1968. Number of titles: 1 in 1980; 1 planned for 1981.

Needs: Contemporary, literary, experimental, western, women's, feminist, ethnic (any), erotica, and translations. No adventure, mystery, spy, historical, war, gothic, romance, confession, gay/lesbian, psychic, religious, science fiction, horror or juvenile. Recently published *Rice Powder*, by Sergio Galindo (novella of Mexico), *The Blue Door & Other Stories*, by Lawrence P. Spingarn (short stories).

How to Contact: Query with SASE. Simultaneous and photocopied submissions OK. Reports in 1 week on queries, 6 weeks on mss.

Terms: Pays 10-15% in royalties. No advance. Free book catalog with SASE and 26¢ postage.

Advice: "Place stories first, even in literary magazines, before submitting ms to publisher. On translated work, get clearance from original publisher before submitting. Writer should consider a subsidy plan whereby his investment is returned through sales; he should also agree to making personal appearances (lectures, TV shows, etc.) if we offer contract."

Comments: "More experimental work like *Black Tickets* is being submitted."

PERSEPHONE PRESS, Box 7222, Watertown MA 02172. (617)924-0336. Publishers: Pat McGloin and Gloria Z. Greenfield. Estab. 1976. Publishes paperback originals and reprints. Number of titles: 2 in 1979, 3 in 1980; 5 planned for 1981.

Needs: Woman-identified pioneering work and translations also about women. No heterosexual romance. Recently published *The Wanderground: Stories of the Hill Women*, by Sally Miller Gearhart (collection of thematic science fiction stories) and *The Coming Out Stories*, edited by Julia Penelope-Stanley and Susan J. Wolfe.

How to Contact: Query. No simultaneous submissions; photocopied submissions OK. Reports in 1 month on queries.

Terms: Receives 50% profit. No advance. Free book catalog.
Advice: "Get involved in writing groups and start publishing short stories in journals. Do not send ms without first sending query and receiving response. Make sure ms is clean and in orderly fashion. Should not have any sexist, homophobic, racist or anti-Jewish material in it. Persephone Press is dedicated to fostering lesbian-feminist sensibility through the publication of innovative and provocative writings by women. We are *very* interested in effective, new styles of writing."

PIG IRON PRESS, Box 237, Youngstown OH 44501. (216)744-2258. Editor: Jim Villani. Estab. 1975. Publishes paperback originals. Number of titles: 1 in 1980; 1 planned for 1981.
Needs: Contemporary, literary, experimental, science fiction, fantasy and humor/satire. "We especially want to see experimental, surreal, psychological and philosophical." Recently published *The Stolen House*, by Jack Remick (comic-fantasy about writers).
How to Contact: Submit outline/synopsis and sample chapters with SASE. No simultaneous submissions; photocopied submissions OK. Reports in 6 weeks on queries, 12 weeks on mss.
Terms: Pays 10% in royalties and 50 author's copies. No advance.

PIKESTAFF PUBLICATIONS, INC., Box 127, Normal IL 61761. (309)452-4831. Imprints include The Pikestaff Press: Pikestaff Fiction Chapbooks. Editorial Directors: James R. Scrimgeour and Robert D. Sutherland. Estab. 1977. Publishes hardcover and paperback originals. Number of titles: 1-2 in 1980; 1-2 planned for 1981.
Needs: Contemporary, literary and experimental. "No slick formula writing written with an eye to the commercial mass-market or pure entertainment that does not provide insights into the human condition. Not interested in heroic fantasy (dungeons & dragons, swords & sorcery); science-fiction of the space-opera variety; westerns; mysteries; love-romance; gothic adventure; or pornography (sexploitation)."
How to Contact: Query or submit outline/synopsis and sample chapters (1-2 chapters) with SASE. No simultaneous or photocopied submissions. Reports in 1 month on queries, 3 months on mss.
Terms: Negotiates terms with author.
Comments: "Explore the possibilities of self-publication; there are many how-to books on the market that explain the ropes. One advantage is the control you can maintain over the shape and appearance of the final product—and you're not subject to editorial whim. Always be honest and play fair with your editors; don't be afraid to assert yourself. Yet be willing to learn. Don't be superficial with your writing. Develop your craft. Have fictional characters we can really *care* about; we are tired of disembodied characters wandering about in their heads unable to relate to other people or the world about them. Avoid too much TELLING; let the reader participate by leaving something for him or her to do. Yet avoid vagueness, opaqueness, personal or 'private' symbolisms and allusions."

PIKEVILLE COLLEGE PRESS, College Box 2, Pikeville KY 41501. (606)432-9227. Director: Dr. Leonard Roberts. Estab. 1972. Publishes paperback originals and reprints. Number of titles: 2 in 1980; 1-2 planned for 1981.
Needs: Ethnic (Appalachia) and folklore. No autobiographies or explicit sex. Recently published *Quare Do's in Appalachia*, by Hiser (30 legends, paperback); and *Old Greasybeard*, by L. Roberts (50 folktales).
How to Contact: Query or submit complete ms with SASE. No simultaneous submissions; photocopied submissions OK. Reports in 2 weeks on queries, 1 month on mss.
Terms: 1-10 free author's copies. No advance. Free book catalog.

POET GALLEY PRESS, 224 W. 29th St., New York City NY 10001. Editor: E.J. Paulos. Estab. 1970. Publishes paperback originals. Number of titles: 5 in 1980; 7 planned for 1981.
Needs: Contemporary, literary and experimental. No poorly written, poorly plotted stories.

Specializes in works of American authors living outside continental United States.
How to Contact: Query. Simultaneous and photocopied submissions OK. Reports in 6 weeks on queries and mss.
Terms: Pays in royalties. No advance.

THE PRAIRIE PUBLISHING COMPANY, Box 264, Station C, Winnipeg, Manitoba, Canada R3M 387. (204)885-6496. Publisher: Ralph Watkins. Estab. 1969.
How to Contact: Query. No simultaneous submissions; photocopied submissions OK. Reports in 1 month on queries, 6 weeks on mss.
Terms: Pays 10% in royalties. No advance. Free book catalog.
Advice: "Do not be discouraged by rejections."

PRESS GANG PUBLISHERS, 603 Powell St., Vancouver, British Columbia, Canada V6A 1H2. (604)253-1224. Estab. 1972. Publishes hardcover and paperback originals. Number of titles: 1 in 1980; 3 planned for 1981.
Needs: Non-sexist children's books. Recently published *Common Ground; Stories by Women* (anthology).
How to Contact: Query if in doubt, submit complete ms or submit outline/synopsis and sample chapters with SASE and International Reply Coupons. Simultaneous and photocopied submissions OK (but we must be told). Reports in 1-2 weeks on queries, 4-6 weeks on mss.
Terms: Pays 5-10% in royalties. Terms vary and are negotiated individually. No advance. Free book catalog.
Comments: "Mss with many American places named are given low priority. Sexist or racist material not considered."

PROGRAMMED STUDIES, INC., Rt. 62, Box 113, Stow MA 21775. (617)897-2130. Director: R. Whitzon. Estab. 1975.
Needs: Experimental, confession, feminist, gay/lesbian, erotica, humor/satire.
How to Contact: Query. Simultaneous and photocopied submissions OK. Reports in 1 week to 6 months on queries.
Terms: Pays in royalties. No advance. Free book catalog.
Comments: "We'll look at fiction query letters, but we don't believe we're the right publisher for 'general' work. Fiction aimed at specific, reachable audiences will fit our needs better."

PUCKERBRUSH PRESS, 76 Main St., Orono ME 04473. (207)866-4868. Publisher/Editor: Constance Hunting. Estab. 1970. Publishes paperback originals and reprints. Number of titles: 2 in 1979, 2 in 1980; 2 planned for 1981.
Needs: Literary. No other category considered. Recently published *A Stranger Here, Myself*, by Thelma Mason (short stories); and *Between Sundays*, by Douglas Young (fictionalized sketches).
How to Contact: Submit outline/synopsis and sample chapters (2) with SASE. Simultaneous and photocopied submissions OK. Reports in 2 weeks on queries, 6 weeks on mss.
Terms: Pays 10% maximum in royalties and 10 free author's copies. No advance.
Comments: "There's less experimental subject matter, more satire; style is cleaner and revision is in. Read to find out how it's done; then do your *own* writing."

PULSE-FINGER PRESS, Box 16697, Philadelphia PA 19139. Editor: Orion Roche. Estab. 1967. Publishes hardcover and paperback originals. Number of titles: 6 in 1979, 5 in 1980; 7 planned for 1981.
Needs: Contemporary, literary and experimental. Recently published *Disco Candy*, by L.C. Phillips (stories); *Stallion's Reach*, by Ralph Brawn (novel); and *Quando Jumps*, by Sheila Rist (novel).

How to Contact: Query with SASE; all unsolicited mss are returned unopened. Simultaneous and photocopied submissions OK. Reports in 1 month on queries, 8 weeks on mss.
Terms: Pays 3-10% on royalties. Offers maximum $500 advance.
Advice: "No handwritten queries or mss. Novels should not exceed 300 typewritten pages, double-spaced. No fads or science fiction. We like strongly developed characters, plot and, above all, a sense of style (but not overblown writing)."

QUINTESSENCE PUBLICATIONS, 356 Bunker Hill Mine Rd., Amador City CA 95601. (209)267-5470. Publisher: Marlan Beilke. Estab. 1976. Publishes hardcover and paperback originals.
Needs: Literary; books only.
How to Contact: Query with SASE. Simultaneous and photocopied submissions OK. Reports in 2 weeks on queries, 1 month on mss.
Terms: Open to negotiation; no advance. Free book catalog with SASE and postage for 2 oz weight.
Advice: "Quality must be paramount throughout. Miracles occur as a result of sweat."
Comments: "We've noticed increased interest in the writing by/of/about Jack London and Robinson Jeffers. We print/publish strictly letter-press editions—handset and linotype exclusively."

RACCOON BOOKS, Suite 401, Mid-Memphis Tower, 1407 Union, Memphis TN 38104. (901)357-5441. Managing Editor: Phyllis A. Tickle. Editor: David Spicer. Estab. 1975. Publishes hardcover and paperback originals and reprints. Plans 3 titles in 1981.
Needs: Contemporary, literary and experimental. Prefers short short stories and novellas.
How to Contact: Submit complete ms with SASE. Simultaneous and photocopied submissions OK. Reporting depends on the quality of the mss.
Terms: Negotiates terms; no advance.

RAINY DAY BOOKS, 2812 W. 53rd St., Fairway KN 66205. (913)384-3126. Estab. 1975. Publishes paperback originals. Number of titles: 2 in 1980; 5 planned for 1981.
Needs: Open to any subject. Recently published *The Tragic Tale of The Dog Who Killed Himself*, by Richard W. Jennings (adult short fiction).
How to Contact: Query. Simultaneous and photocopied submissions OK. Reports in 1 month on queries.
Terms: Individually negotiated; no advance. Free book catalog.

RAS COMMUNICATIONS, #20A 3620 52 Ave., Red Deer, Alberta, Canada T4N 4J5. Imprints include Blind Eye Books and Jasmine, How-To-Do-Books. Editor/Publisher: Randy Stables. Estab. 1978. Publishes paperback originals. Number of titles: 1-5 in 1980; 5-10 planned for 1981.
Needs: Contemporary, literary, experimental, faction, adventure, mystery, spy, historical, western, war, gothic, science fiction, fantasy, humor/satire, juvenile (animal, easy-to-read), young adult, and translations. No pornographic, obscene material, or homosexuality.
How to Contact: Submit complete ms. Simultaneous and photocopied submissions OK. Reports in 1 month on mss.
Terms: Pays 10-40% in royalties and 20 author's copies; no advance.
Comments: "Write good stories which people want to read."

RIVERSEDGE PRESS, INC., Box 1547, Edinburg TX 78539. Editor: Dorey Schmidt. Assoc. Editor: Patricia De La Fuente. Estab. 1977. Plans 1 title in 1981.
Needs: Contemporary, literary, experimental, fiction, historical, feminist, ethnic (chicano), translations and the Southwest. No book-length fiction. We use short stories and short story collections.
How to Contact: Simultaneous and photocopied submissions OK. Reports in 1 month on

queries, 6 weeks on mss.

Terms: Pays from 2-15 author's copies; no advance.

Comments: "Since we publish primarily short fiction, I think our type of publication is a good training ground for ideas which might be incorporated into longer fiction later. Pedantic, moralizing, and sexist views are not welcome. Nor is extreme erotica. I am always looking for fiction that suggests that moments of satisfaction with the human condition are indeed still possible even in this 'worst of all possible worlds.' Obviously as long as people do not *all* engage in mass suicide, there is something to be said for life and humanity. Say it, in fresh ways."

R&M PUBLISHING COMPANY, INC., Box 210, Marion SC 29571. President: Mack B. Morant. Editor: Ms. Mosezelle Nichols. Fiction Editor: Bobby Roberts III. Estab. 1978. Number of titles: 5 in 1980; 10 planned for 1981.

Needs: Literary, mystery, romance, confession, women's, feminist, gay/lesbian, ethnic, psychic/supernatural, religious/inspirational, science fiction, horror, juvenile and young adult. "Any kind as long as it is well written."

How to Contact: Query or submit ms with SASE. Simultaneous and photocopied submissions OK. Reports in 1 month on queries, 6 weeks on mss.

Terms: "We will work things out with the author if we like the work." No advance. Free book catalog.

Comments: "Write what you feel, and read everything available to stay in touch with the most recent trends or societal fads."

SALT LICK PRESS, Box 1064, Quincy IL 62301. Imprint includes Lucky Heart Books. Publisher/Editor: James Haining. Estab. 1969. Publishes paperback originals. Number of titles: 1 in 1979, 1 in 1980; 2 planned for 1981.

Needs: Contemporary, literary, experimental, faction, adventure, mystery, spy, historical, western, war, gothic, women's, feminist, gay/lesbian, ethnic, erotica, psychic/supernatural, science fiction, fantasy, horror, humor/satire and translations. Recently published *A Book of Spells*, by G. Burns.

How to Contact: Submit complete ms with SASE. No simultaneous submissions, photocopied submissions OK. Reports in 1 month on mss.

Terms: Pays in author's copies; no advance.

SAMISDAT, Box 129, Richford VT 05476. Imprint includes *Samisdat Magazine*. Editor/Publisher: Merritt Clifton. Estab. 1973. Publishes paperback originals. Number of titles: 3 in 1979, 2-3 in 1980; 2-3 planned for 1981.

Needs: Recently published *How He Got The Mule*, by Doug Odom (2 short stories & poem); *The Green Chain*, by Everett Whealdon (novel); and *Betrayal*, by Merritt Clifton (novella).

How to Contact: Query or submit complete ms with SASE. Reports in 1 week on queries, time varies on mss.

Terms: No advance. Free book catalog with SASE

Comments: "We do not wish to see *any* book-length ms submissions from anyone who has not already either published in our quarterly magazine, *Samisdat*, or at least subscribed for about a year to find out who we are and what we're doing. We are not a 'market' engaged in handling books as commodities and are equipped to read only about one novel submission per month over and above our magazine submission load. Submissions are getting much slicker, with a lot less guts to them. This is precisely the opposite of what we're after. Our regular magazine contributors are providing all the book-length material we can handle right now. Read the magazine. Submit stories or poems or chapters to it. When familiar with us, and to our subscribers, query about an appropriate book ms. We don't publish books except as special issues of the magazine, and blind submissions stand absolutely no chance of acceptance at all. Submissions from people who've taken the trouble to understand us, on the other hand, have a pretty good batting average—if they're something within our technical capabilities to begin with. Our author payments for books are a paradox: At this writing, we've published exactly 100 titles over the past 8 years, 86 of which, or 86%, have earned the authors a profit. On the other hand, we've relatively seldom issued royalty checks—maybe 15 or 20 in all this time, and all for small amounts. We're also paradoxical in our modus operandi: Authors cover our cash expenses in exchange for part of the press run, but we make no money from authors and if we don't promote a book successfully, we still lose."

SCHOOL OF LIVING PRESS, RD. 7, York PA 17402. (717)755-1561. Editor: Rarihokwats. Estab. 1936. Publishes paperback originals. Plans 3 titles in 1981.
Needs: "We work only with titles that either fictionally or nonfictionally deal with human, decentralist social change. Titles for the future in planning stages."
How to Contact: Simultaneous and photocopied submissions OK. Reports in 1 week on queries, 1 month on mss.
Terms: Pays in 5 author's copies; no advance. Free brochure with SASE.
Comments: "We see a larger public interest in social change. Keep at it. Be clear, brief and illustrate with specifics. Avoid long treatises; be sure of researched facts."

SEED CENTER, Box 658, Garberville CA 95440. (707)986-7575. Editor: Sura Thurman. Estab. 1972. Publishes paperback originals and reprints.
Needs: Contemporary, literary, women's, psychic/supernatural, religious/inspirational, science fiction, fantasy, humor/satire and juvenile and young adult.
How to Contact: Query. Simultaneous and photocopied submissions OK. Reports in 2 weeks on queries, 1-3 months on mss.
Terms: Pays 8-15% in royalties; no advance. Free book catalog.

SHAMELESS HUSSY PRESS, Box 3092, Berkeley, CA 94703. (415)548-7800. Publisher: Alta. Estab. 1969. Number of titles: 4 in 1979, 4 in 1980; 4 planned for 1981.
Needs: Contemporary, literary, experimental, adventure, mystery, spy, historical, western, women's, feminist, ethnic, science fiction, fantasy, humor/satire, juvenile and young adult. "Our specialty is women's and feminist." Recently published *The Wise Queen*, by K. Simon (children's fiction).
How to Contact: Submit outline/synopsis and sample chapters. SASE for query and ms. Simultaneous and photocopied submissions OK. Reports in 6 weeks.
Terms: Pays in author's copies; no advance. Free book catalog.
Advice: "Publish yourself."

SHOAL CREEK PUBLISHERS, INC., Box 9737, Austin TX 78766. (512)451-7545. Editor: Ruth Steyn. Publishes hardback originals and reprints. Number of titles: 1 fiction/year.
Needs: Historical (Southwest regional) and juvenile picture books.
How to Contact: Query or submit complete ms. For juvenile books, submit samples of finished artwork. Simultaneous and photocopied submissions OK. Reports as soon as possible.
Terms: Pays 10% on retail price in royalties; no advance. Free book catalog.
Comments: "This is a small company where one person does everything. Therefore good editing and proofreading should be done before submitting mss."

SMALL WORLD PUBLICATIONS, Box 10632, Portland OR 97210. Editor: Rick Cooper. Estab. 1978. Publishes paperback originals. Number of titles: 1 in 1979, 1 in 1980; 2 planned for 1981.
Needs: Experimental, religious/inspirational and humor/satire. No spy, detective, horror, fantasy, sports or "anything lacking human values and substance."
How to Contact: Submit complete ms with SASE. Simultaneous and photocopied submissions OK. Reports in 6 weeks on mss.

Terms: Pays 20-25% in royalties; no advance.
Comments: "We notice too many spy and detective novels, too much loveless sex, too much fantasy. Let's see life the way it was meant to be. Positive, uplifting, fulfilling and spirited. Write about that which is closest to your heart, let the words come from your highest source of inspiration—anything but your mind. Send us what you would publish yourself if you had the money—writing that is fresh, alive, honest and classical—and you'll be in. Make whatever you write worthy of the life of the tree that is your paper."

THE SMITH, 5 Beekman St., New York NY 10038. Editor: Harry Smith. Fiction Editor: Nancy Hallinan. Managing Editor: Tom Tolnay. Estab. 1964. Publishes paperback originals. Number of titles: 3 in 1979, 3 in 1980.
Needs: Recently published *Forever and a Wednesday*, by Menke Katz (legends); *The Magic Whorehouse*, by Tom Tolnay (short stories); and *Stranger from Home*, by Elizabeth Leonie Simpson (novel).
How to Contact: Submit complete ms. Simultaneous and photocopied submissions OK.
Terms: Pays by outright purchase of $500 maximum; no advance. Free book catalog.
Comments: "No new books of fiction will be published until later in 1981."

SONO NIS PRESS, 1745 Blanshard St., Victoria, British Columbia, Canada V8W 2J8. (604)382-1024. President: Richard E. Morriss. Editor: Robin Skelton. Promotion Manager: M. Reynolds. Publishes hardback and paperback originals. Number of titles: 10 in 1979 and 10 in 1980.
Needs: Contemporary, literary and experimental. Recently published short stories by Ralph Gustafson.
How to Contact: Submit complete ms. Simultaneous and photocopied submissions OK. Reports in 1 month on ms.
Terms: Pays 10% royalties and 10 author's copies; no advance. Free book catalog.

STORY PRESS, Box 10040, Chicago IL 60610. (312)442-7295. Editor: Richard Meade. Editorial Director: Carol Evans. Estab. 1978. Publishes hardcover and paperback originals. Number of titles: 1 in 1979, 1 in 1980; 2 planned for 1981.
Needs: Contemporary, literary, women's and ethnic. "We are a literary press and are not interested in most kinds of popular fiction. We publish only collections of stories." Recently published *The Monkey Puzzle Tree*, by Florence Cohen (short stories).
How to Contact: Query with SASE. Simultaneous and photocopied submissions OK. Reports in 2 weeks on queries, 6 weeks on mss.
Terms: Pays in author's copies (10% of the press run); no advance. Free book catalog.
Advice: "Write and begin submitting to small magazines. Don't send chapters of novels or poorly prepared mss."
Comments: "We notice movement toward interior landscapes away from fiction with a clear narrative line."

SURREE LIMITED, INC., 9467 Mission Park Place, Santee CA 92071. Editor: Pete Dixon. Publishes paperback originals. Prints 90-144 titles annually.
Needs: Contemporary, gay male erotica.
How to Contact: Submit outline/synopsis and sample chapters (1-2) with SASE. Reports in 2 weeks on queries, 6 weeks on mss.
Terms: Pays by outright purchase; no advance.
Comments: "There's an increased openness and forthright treatment of all subject matter, and a willingness of major publishers to put out 'outre' material. Study the specific market and publisher you wish to submit to; gear your efforts to their individual formats."
End Small Press P-S

TALESPINNER PUBLICATIONS, INC., Box 19087, Minneapolis MN 55419.

(612)825-0087. Copy Director: Susan Talanda. Estab. 1978. Number of titles: 2 in 1979; 4-6 planned for 1981.

Needs: Juvenile and young adult: sports, animal, spy/adventure, historical, fantasy/science fiction, easy-to-read (all in the K-4th grade range only). "No adult or adolescent fiction." Recently published *Ferocious Sarah*, by Ethel M. Benson; and *The Spaghetti Tree*, by Jan Fontaine (both paperbacks).

How to Contact: Query with SASE. Simultaneous and photocopied submissions OK. Reports in 1 month.

Terms: Pays in "negotiated honorarium (cash) since we are a nonprofit press"; no advance.

Advice: "The children's market is difficult to write for, but most authors think it's a snap. Each word is important and each scene must further the action of the story. Strongly and critically edit your work. Children's fiction for the K-4th grade audience must be less than 2,500 words and about 1,500 words is still 'plenty'. Remember that our books will feature illustrations that will also help tell your story, so do not overdo details, descriptions. Avoid condescending attitudes toward both children and adult characters. Don't introduce unnecessary characters into the story. Keep the conflict clearly upfront for young readers. When dialogue can tell the story, please use it. Avoid using a narrative that tells the story passively without letting dialogue and action do the job. And even with 'message' stories, your tale has to be entertaining. Before submitting mss to us, test your story out on children in our target age group. They will be your most honest critics."

Comments: "We've observed a shift to fantasy and a disturbing lack of submissions dealing with 'real' children in 'real life' settings. We'd like to see more of that latter type of story, as well as tales showing children in other lands, cultures, and backgrounds. Fiction writers should not be afraid to submit their works to small or independent presses as opposed to the big conglomerate publishers. We independent presses are often a great way to enter the publishing field, and our press specializes in helping fiction writers get into print in the field of children's literature for the first time. As a nonprofit service, Talespinner also helps critique mss."

THIRD COAST, 146 Broad St., Lake Geneva WI 53147. Editorial Director: D.C. Kenzle. Estab. 1976. Publishes paperback originals. Number of titles: 1 in 1979, 1 in 1980; 2 planned for 1981.

Needs: Contemporary, literary, experimental (especially), women's, feminist, gay/lesbian, erotica, science fiction, fantasy, humor/satire. Recently published *Gathering: A Free Will Anthology*, edited by Linda Fry Kenzle (anthology of multimedia work).

How to Contact: Submit complete ms with SASE. No simultaneous submissions; photocopied submissions OK. Reports in 6 weeks.

Terms: Pays in author's copies; no advance.

Comments: "We are a small press currently trying to publish one anthology a year. We like the offbeat."

THUNDER CITY PRESS, Box 11126, Birmingham AL 35202. Imprint includes *Thunder Mountain Review*. Editorial Director: Steven Ford Brown. Estab. 1975. Publishes paperback originals. Number of titles: 1 in 1980; 2 planned for 1981.

Needs: Contemporary, literary, experimental, translations.

How to Contact: Query. SASE for query, ms. No simultaneous submissions; photocopied submissions OK. Reports in 2 weeks on queries, 1 month on mss.

Terms: Pays in author's copies (10%) and royalties "after we break even"; no advance. Book catalog for SASE.

Advice: "There is a place for good fiction writers in publishing today. There is so much poor writing being passed off as good fiction."

Comments: "We see an increased emphasis on fiction in translations especially from Latin American. I publish very little fiction at present but plan to expand in the future."

UNIVERSITY OF ILLINOIS PRESS, Box 5081, Station A, Champaign IL 61820. (217)333-0950. Editorial Director: Richard L. Wentworth. "Send mss to Fiction Editor." Estab. 1918. Publishes paperback originals ("simultaneous publication"). Number of titles: 4 in 1979, 4 in 1980; 4 planned for 1981.
Needs: Contemporary, literary, experimental. "No novels." Recently published *The Return of Service*, by Jonathan Baumback; *Surviving Adverse Seasons*, by Barry Targan; *The Gasoline Wars*, by Jean Thompson (all short story collections).
How to Contact: Query or submit complete ms. SASE for ms. Simultaneous and photocopied submissions OK. Reports in 1 week on queries, 4-6 months ("and sometime longer") on mss.
Terms: Pays "10% of net of first 10,000 cloth copies sold; 15% thereafter; 7½% net on first 10,000 paperback; 10% thereafter." No advance. Free book catalog.
Comments: "We do not publish novels and we have no outlet for individual short stories. We publish collections of short fiction by authors who've usually established their credentials by being accepted for publication in periodicals, generally literary periodicals. But 5 recently published novels are by authors who have had no previous book publications."

SHERRY URIE, West Glover VT 05875. Editorial Director and Fiction Editor: Sherry Urie. Estab. 1974. Publishes paperback originals and reprints. Number of titles: 2 in 1979, 1 in 1980; 3 planned for 1981.
Needs: Contemporary, literary, mystery, historical, women's, religious/inspirational. "New England settings. We will consider all types of fiction." Recently published *Green Mountain Farm*, by Elliott Merrick (Vermont adventures).
How to Contact: Submit complete ms with SASE. Simultaneous and photocopied submissions OK. Reports in 1 month on mss.
Terms: Pays by individual arrangement; no advance. Book catalog for 35¢.

WALNUT PRESS, Box 17210, Fountain Hills AZ 85268. Fiction Editor: Louise Thompson. Estab. 1976. Publishes paperback originals. Number of titles: 3 in 1979, 3 in 1980; 3 planned for 1981.
Needs: Only juvenile and young adult: animal, historical, easy-to-read. Recently published *A Tale of the Butterscotch Bear*, by Davis and Beronski; *The Merry Christmas Mice*, by Davis and Thompson; *Cook & Color with Recipe Rabbit*, by Morris et al. (children's books).
How to Contact: Query with SASE. Simultaneous and photocopied submissions OK. Reports in 1 month.
Terms: Pays by outright purchase of $100 minimum and 50 author's copies; no advance.
Advice: "Have patience and persistence."
Comments: "Juvenile mss must be clever, intelligent and suitable for the library market. Illustrations are helpful."

JOHN WESTBURG, 1745 Madison St., Fennimore WI 53809. (608)822-6237. Imprints include Westburg Associates Publishers and *The North American Mentor Magazine*. Editorial Director: John Westburg. Estab. 1964. Number of titles: 1 in 1980; 1 planned in 1981.
Needs: Contemporary, literary, experimental, adventure, historical, western, war, science fiction, fantasy, humor/satire. "We desire writing that is in good taste, for mature readers of above average education. Short stories should have action, plot, significance, depth of thought amd should be elevating rather than depressing; tragedy is welcome provided there is a true tragic flaw in the protagonist; character should be depicted in the action rather than by description. Sustained wit without sarcasm or humiliation would be welcome. Propaganda pieces, whether racial, religious, or political, are not wanted. No vulgarity, no obscenity, no blasphemy, no pornography, no 'ethnic' whatsoever that debases any nationality or race, no anti-Caucasian racism, no religious works presenting ideas of 'true' believers, no ugliness or shoddiness in human behavior, no vilification, etc. The only fiction stories that we published last year were short fiction stories in the *North American Mentor Magazine*.

These included: "Yankee Canal", by Rickie Bruce; "Change of State", by Margaret Snow; "Eugenia and the Electric Car", by Richard A. Hurley.

How to Contact: Submit complete ms with SASE. "Post office will not accept prepaid postage by metered machines. Must include return postage." Simultaneous and photocopied submissions OK. Reports in 3-6 months.

Terms: Pays in 1 author's copy; no advance. Book catalog for SASE.

Advice: "Be sure to read your ms carefully again and again before you put it in the mail. Good writing does require rereading, rewriting, and revision after revision to put it in finest order."

Comments: "A great deal of illiteracy, anti-values, anti-humanism, and cheap vulgarity seem to be current in most submissions to us. I hope this is not a trend. *The North American Mentor Magazine* is a noncommercial literary and humanities quarterly supported entirely by subsidies and subscriptions and donations. All staff are volunteer and unpaid. We have limited record-keeping facilities. Therefore, owing to the complexity of the new copyright laws, we must obtain all rights to the work we publish in order to keep the record-keeping categories to a bare minimum. However, we readily give permission to the author to publish elsewhere any of his work that we publish."

WILSON BROTHERS PUBLICATIONS, Box 712, Yakima WA 98907. (509)457-8275. Editorial Director: Robert S. Wilson. Estab. 1978. Publishes paperback originals. "We are an extremely small firm. We have published a series entitled *Trolley Trails Through the West* and a travelog entitled *Rambling Through British Columbia*. We also offer custom publishing for other authors, any type of work whether fiction or nonfiction on a limited basis. Thus far our production in that line has been nonfiction. We produce only soft cover books, usually 8½x11 though can also produce 5½x8½. Our services include editing, production of the book, and advice to the author about advertising and marketing. We do not buy mss for our own use. Author *pays entire cost* of production and books are his when completed, shipped to his request."

How to Contact: Query or submit complete ms. SASE for ms. No simultaneous submissions; photocopied submissions OK. Reports in 1 week on queries, 2 weeks (usually) on mss.

WIM PUBLICATIONS, Box 5037, Inglewood CA 90310. (213)774-5230. Editorial Director: S. Diane Bogus. Estab. 1979. Publishes paperback originals. Number of titles: 1 in 1980; 1 planned in 1981.

Needs: Feminist, gay/lesbian. No abstract experimentation or plotless work.

How to Contact: Query. SASE for query, ms. All unsolicited mss are returned unopened. Simultaneous and photocopied submissions OK. Reports in 2 weeks.

Terms: "We do not pay. We are a small press (one author)." Free book catalog.

Advice: "Trust that there *is* a publisher for your work. Work at getting better. Associate with writers. Read. Operate professionally."

Comments: "There's a trend towards documentary type fiction, more first person, more present time narratives/settings. We do not plan to publish any other than S. Diane Bogus until 1982."

WOMEN'S EDUCATIONAL PRESS, Suite 313, 280 Bloor St. W, Toronto, Ontario, Canada M5S 1W1. (416)922-9447. Contact: Lois Pike. Estab. 1972. Publishes paperback originals. Plans 1 title in 1981.

Needs: Canadian writers only. Contemporary, experimental, women's, feminist, gay/lesbian, fantasy, juvenile and young adult. "No autobiography." Recently published *The True Story of Ida Johnson*, by Sharon Riis (experimental feminist fiction).

How to Contact: Query or submit complete ms. SASE for ms. Simultaneous and photocopied submissions OK. Reports in 3 months.

Terms: Pays in negotiated royalties.

Comments: "We see too much American slick fiction, i.e., *Princess Daisy*."

YORK PRESS, Box 1172, Fredericton, N.B., Canada E3B 5C8. (506)455-6501. Editorial Director: Dr. S. Elkhadem. Estab. 1975. Publishes hardcover and paperback originals. Number of titles: 5 in 1979; 1-2 planned for 1981.

Needs: Contemporary, experimental, translations. "No mss written mainly for entertainment; i.e. those without literary or artistic merit." Recently published *Modern Egyptian Short Stories* and *Three Contemporary Egyptian Novels*, translated and edited by Saad El-Gabalawy.

How to Contact: Query. No simultaneous submissions; photocopied submissions OK. Reports in 1 week on queries, 1 month on mss.

Terms: Pays 5-10% in royalties; no advance. Free book catalog.

Comments: "We are devoted to the promotion of scholarly publications; areas of special interest include general and comparative literature, literary criticism, and creative writing of an experimental nature."

Commercial publishers

Fiction writing is competitive. Major publishers receive as many as 10,000 manuscripts a year, not to mention the number of queries they receive. The odds are against fiction writers, too; 15 nonfiction books are published for each fiction book. Yet, commercial book publishers *are* eager for material. Publishers are just as eager to find authors as authors are to find publishers.

Commercial publishers, loosely defined as those motivated primarily by profit, vary a great deal in their interests and philosophies. Many publishing houses are conservative to cautious in taste, they are reluctant to recognize good writing, and they will "try" an author only after his exposure in magazines and/or assurance of his commercial potential. "Go commercial and put aside your literary ideals," says an editor of a large established publishing house. "Phooey on trends," counters another of a smaller and newer independent commerical press that seeks "writers with vision, sensitivity and style," those without grandiose ideas of movie or TV rights. Younger publishing houses are generally more willing to give unsolicited submissions a read; some presses aren't equipped to handle much fiction; and others simply won't make the gamble. But people in all publishing circles generally acknowledge that every book that deserves to be published *will* see print.

Today category books dominate the fiction paperback book racks. More and more novels are printed in original paperback (versus hardcover), and publishers are more willing to take a chance on a genre novel than a mainstream novel. New lines of large publishers have developed new fiction lines, distributed under special imprint names. There are special lines for historical romances, ("bodice rippers"), romantic suspense, Regency romances, gothics, adventure tales, mysteries, science fiction, romantic contemporary fiction, westerns, and a new historical series aimed, for a change, toward the male reader.

That doesn't mean that the borders between the various types of fiction cannot be crossed. Science fiction books, for instance, are often published simply as novels without the "science fiction" label.

Some presses are showing a resurgence in interest in war stories—and they are encouraging WWII and Vietnam novels. Family sagas are still acceptable and feminist novels and detective stories with women as protagonists are reaching mass audiences.

The market for juvenile fiction is tighter than in recent years. Because the "baby boom" children are now young adults and older, and because federal funds to school libraries have been reduced, fewer juvenile titles are published each year. Other trends in the juvenile market: more books are written and illustrated by the same person, and there is a greater need for original animal, adventure, mystery and realisitic ficition for four- to eight-year-olds.

Publishers Weekly is a magazine that will help keep you current with the frequent changes in publishing. In August and February, PW publishes special issues examining the fall and spring lines, respectively, of most publishers. These issues are especially useful, because they are packed with information about new books, new lines of books, which houses carry genre fiction, which topics are "hot," and which have cooled. Another publication, *Library Journal*, makes available essays by first novelists on a quarterly basis, which reveal those publishing houses receptive to beginning writers.

Before you submit a manuscript, a proposal or a query, study the following listings closely and *use* the information; otherwise you can expect automatic rejection. You can't travel the route to success if you can't follow directions.

Other tips: Establish a goal. Study the paperback racks or lines of a publisher and read voraciously to familiarize yourself with the subjects and styles. Once you have chosen a publisher, address the query using an editor's name. Send adquate postage (see the "Small Press" introduction for more information).

Submitting a query or an outline/synopsis is the simplest method of contacting an editor, and the fairest method to the editor. Remember, the proposal will sell the book, so spend time on it. If you spend a year writing a book, don't waste that effort by spending only five minutes on your letter or outline. Make your proposal original both in content, and in form—no photocopies. Present your manuscript as professionally as you would present yourself. And don't let a couple of rejections discourage you; send your mansucript out again—and again.

More and more publishers are requiring that submissions be sent through an agent, but generous opportunities for unagented fiction remain. An agent is not generally required for children's books and small to medium-sized independent (and many large) publishers will read unsolicited manuscripts from the slush pile.

A manuscript might be rejected for any of a number of reasons: It might have been sent to an inappropriate publisher; the idea or subject might be overworked or insignificant; the writing might be unexciting or overwritten (purple prose); the style might be evidently imitative and unoriginal; there might not be enough descriptive images or metaphors; there might be a lack of continuity or too many erudite thesaurus-type words; the editor might like the book, but it might not "thrill" him—many reasons for selecting a manuscript are personal.

Editors further request that you do not call, come in or be pushy about your manuscript. Be prepared to wait, knowing that the route of a submission at a large publisher may be circuitous. It is intially screened by a "first reader" and passed on *if* it has possibilities. Then a market forecast is done, production costs are estimated, and the potential market for subsidiary rights and the potential return on investment are studied. The proposal is prepared and taken to a committee composed of the publisher, sales manager, marketing and publicity director, and editors. A manuscript submitted to a smaller press will, of course, not be treated so formally. The reading time will be shorter, but it *all* takes time.

The most important advice about writing a novel is to be persistent. Don't give up. Publishers *are* eager for good material, and if you maintain faith in your manuscript, you will eventually find an editor who will invest as much faith, and a healthy advance, in your book.

A & P BOOKS, 1701 Park Rd., Benicia CA 94510. Imprint includes Atlantic & Pacific Commerce Co., Inc. President: E.H. Mikkelsen. Editor: Elsie Sanchez. Estab. 1974. Publishes hardcover and paperback originals. Number of titles: 4 in 1979, 15 in 1980 and plans 35 in 1981.
Needs: Juvenile and young adult: sports, animal, historical, fantasy and translations. Serials welcomed.
How to Contact: Submit outline/synopsis and sample chapters. Simultaneous and photocopied submissions OK. Reports in 1 week on queries, 1 month on mss.
Terms: Pays in royalties and by outright purchase; also offers advance. Free book catalog.
Comments: "Keep in mind that it is our children who will make our tomorrow."

ACADEMY CHICAGO LTD., 360 N. Michigan Ave., Chicago IL 60601. Editor: Anita Miller. Estab. 1975. Publishes hardcover originals and paperback and hardback reprints. Number of titles: 5 in 1980 and plans 5 in 1981.
Needs: Mystery, feminist and translations. No experimental, religious or romance.
How to Contact: Query and/or submit outline/synopsis with SASE. No simultaneous submissions; photocopied submissions OK. Reports in 2 weeks on queries, 6 weeks on mss.
Terms: Pays 7-15% in royalties; no advance. Free sample copy with 8½x11 SASE.
Comments: "Fiction is hard to sell. We think it needs a special appeal, mystery, women, etc. We used to accept multiple submissions but will not any more."

ACE SCIENCE FICTION, 51 Madison Ave., New York NY 10010. Imprints include Ace Books, Charter and Tempo. Editor: Susan Allison. Estab. 1948. Publishes paperback originals and reprints. Number of titles: 120 in 1979, 120 in 1980 and plans 120 in 1981.
Needs: Science fiction and fantasy. No other genre accepted. Recently published: *Janissaries*, by Jerry Pournelle (science fiction); *The Patchwork Girl*, by Larry Niven (science fiction); and *Empire of the East*, by Fred Saberaagen (fantasy).
How to Contact: Submit outline/synopsis and sample chapters (3). No simultaneous submissions; photocopied submissions OK. Reports in 2 weeks on queries, 8 weeks on mss.
Terms: Pays 6-8% in royalties; by outright purchase $3,000 minimum. Free book catalog.
Comments: "Back to basics: plots with beginnings, middles, ends are 'in' as are sympathetic characters with recognizable motivation."

ACE/TEMPO BOOKS, Division of Grosset & Dunlap, 51 Madison Ave., New York NY 10010. (212)689-9200. Sr. V.P./Editor: Susanne Jaffe. Executive Editor: Sarah Ashman. Editor: K. O'Hehir. Publishes paperback originals and reprints. Number of titles: 50 in 1979, 35 in 1980; 35 planned for 1981.
Needs: Contemporary romance and juvenile and young adult. "First love romance stories for young adults." Recently published *Flash Gordon Novels*, by David Hagberg; and *One Step Apart*, by Joan Oppenheimer.
How to Contact: Submit outline/synopsis and sample chapters (4) with SASE. Simultaneous and photocopied submissions OK. Reports in 2 months on queries and mss.
Terms: Pays 4-6% in royalties; offers $2,500 in advance. Free book catalog with 9x11 SASE.
Comments: "Librarians and educators are looking for contemporary romances for young adults. Be aware of publishing trends. Study the formula of various genres or create a story

within a contemporary framework. Since we are looking specifically for romances—first love stories—the writer should realize the difference between problem novels and romances."

ADDISION-WESLEY PUBLISHING COMPANY, INC., CHILDREN'S BOOK DEPARTMENT, Jacob Way, Reading MA 01867. Managing Editor: Irma Hoijer. Estab. 1969. Publishes hardcover originals and quality paperbacks. Number of titles: 10 in 1979 and 19 in 1980.
Needs: Juvenile and young adult: sports, animal, spy/adventure, historical, fantasy/science fiction and easy-to-read. No explicit sex in categories listed. No adult fiction. Must have reasonable limits for age range. Recently published: *The Dragon and the Wild Fandango*, by P. Wolcott; *SuperDan and the Dinosaurs*, by John Kastner (cartoons); *A Show of Hands*, by Mary Beth Sullivan and Linda Bourke (sign talk); and *Once Upon a Time in a Pigpen*, by Margaret Wise Brown (picture book).
How to Contact: Submit complete ms or outline/synopsis and sample chapters with SASE. No simultaneous submissions; photocopied submissions OK. Reports in 8 weeks on mss.
Terms: Pays in royalties and gives advance. Free book catalog.

ALCHEMY BOOKS, 681 Market St. #755, San Francisco CA 94105. (415)362-2708. Editor-in-Chief: D. Mark Pittard. Managing Editor: Kenneth Park Cameron. Estab. 1975. Publishes hardcover originals. Total number of titles: 20 in 1979, 30 in 1980.
Needs: Contemporary, literary, science fiction, religious/inspirational, political, historical, humor/satire, psychic/supernatural, fantasy, easy-to-read, animal, children's. "Alchemy Books is looking for current subjects which relate to today's concerns. Thoughtful and important books with emotional content; also those which are just for fun." Recently published nonfiction: *Iran's Revolutionary Upheaval* by Sephyr Zabih; *Tarot Revelations* by Colin Wilson and Joseph Campbell; *A Comprehensive Guide for Cancer Patients* by Ernest Rosenbaum, et al.
How to Contact: Query and submit complete ms with SASE. Simultaneous and photocopied submissions OK. Reports in 1 week on queries, 2-4 weeks on mss.
Terms: Regular royalty schedule. No advance.
Comments: "Our program calls on the author to participate fully and vigorously in the promotion of his work."

ANDREWS AND MCMEEL, INC., 4400 Johnson Dr., Fairway KS 66205. Imprint includes Sheed and Ward Classics. Publishes hardcover and paperback originals. Number of titles: 5 in 1979, 4 in 1980.
Needs: Contemporary, adventure, mystery and historical. Recently published: *The Rosary Murders*, by William Kienzle (mystery); *River Notes*, by Barry Lopez (nature/fiction); and *Dutch Treat*, by Tristan Jones (World War II novel).
How to Contact: Query with SASE. Simultaneous and photocopied submissions OK. Reports in 6 weeks on queries, 8 weeks on mss.
Terms: Pays in royalties and offers advance. Free book catalog for SASE.
Comments: "This is a difficult market for new fiction. Unfortunately we feel we can publish very little of it."

APPLE PRESS, 5536 SE Harlow, Milwaukie OR 97222. (503)569-2475. Senior Editor: Judith S. Majors. Publishes paperback originals. Number of titles in 1981 depends on the economy.
Needs: Contemporary and juvenile. Especially needs mss "read for enjoyment" (nontechnical or nonerotic), those which are suitable for Christian families. Recently published: *Mr. Fix It* (juvenile humor).
How to Contact: Submit complete ms with SASE. Reports 4-6 weeks on mss.
Terms: Pays 7-10% in royalties and offers $200-500 in advance.

ARBOR HOUSE PUBLISHING COMPANY, 235 E. 45th St., New York NY 10017. Imprint includes Priam Books.Senior Editor: Jared Kieling. Publisher: Donald I. Fine. Estab. 1969. Publishes hardcover originals and Priam trade paperbacks. Number of titles: 65 in 1979, 80 in 1980.
Needs: Subjects open. Recently published *Ice Brothers*, by Sloan Wilson (novel); and *Murder in the White House*, by Margaret Truman (novel).
How to Contact: Submit through agent. Simultaneous and photocopied submissions OK (but does not prefer them).
Terms: Pays in negotiable royalties; offers advance. Free book catalog.

ARCHIVAL PRESS INC., 141 Columbia St., Cambridge MA 02139. (617)868-9788. President: Robert K. Wiener. Estab. 1977. Publishes hardcover originals, paperback originals and reprints. Number of titles: 2 in 1979, 3 in 1980; 6 planned for 1981.
Needs: "At the present time Archival Press is not looking for submissions. Our schedule is booked through the end of 1981." Books are in the areas of adventure, spy, science fiction, fantasy and humor/satire. Recently published: *Horns of Elfland*, by Charles Vess (fantasy); *Miss Fury*, by Tarpe Mills (adventure); and *Back for More*, by Berni Wrightson (science fiction/horror).
Terms: Pays 4-6% in royalties for paperback and 5-10% for hardback; offers $0-$1,000 in advance.
Comments: "Good luck. Magazine submissions appear to be the best way for a beginning fiction writer to gain experience and visibility. Please do not submit in 1981. Maybe next year we'll have expanded enough to be in a different situation."

ATLANTIC MONTHLY PRESS, 8 Arlington St., Boston MA 02116. (617)536-9500. Imprint includes Little, Brown and Co. Editor: Melanie Kroupa. Publishes hardcover originals. Number of titles: 13 in 1979, 10 in 1980; 12 planned for 1981.
Needs: Juvenile: sports, animal, spy/adventure, historical, fantasy/science fiction and easy-to-read. Recently published: *Words By Heart*, by Ouida Sebestyen; *It All Began With Jane Eyre* and *The Secret Life of Franny Dillman*, by Sheila Greenwald; and *The Muskrat War*, by Larry Callen (adventure).
How to Contact: Submit complete ms or submit through agent (but not necessary) with SASE. No simultaneous submissions; photocopied submissions OK. Reports in 1 month on mss.
Terms: Pays variable royalties and offers $1,500-3,000 in advance. Free book catalog.
Comments: "Today there is interest in young adult romance. Books for young adults should show superior story telling with strong characterization and convincing action and plot development."

AUGSBURG PUBLISHING HOUSE, 426 S. 5th St., Minneapolis MN 55438. (612)330-3432. Editor: Roland Seboldt. Estab. 1850. Publishes paperback originals. Number of titles: 3 in 1979, 2 in 1980; 4 planned for 1981.
Needs: Religious/inspirational for young readers (grades 8-12). General fiction. Recently published: *Growing Up Isn't Easy, Lord*, by Stephen Sorenson (short story devotions for boys); *Lord, I Have A Question*, by Betty Westrob Skold (short story devotions for girls); and *Change in the Wind*, by Phyllis Reynolds Naylor (short stories for teenagers).
How to Contact: Query or submit complete ms or submit outline/synopsis and sample chapters with SASE. Simultaneous and photocopied submissions OK. Reports in 6 weeks on queries.
Terms: Pays 10% in royalties and offers $500 advance. Free book catalog.
Comments: "We are looking for good religious fiction with a Christian theme for young adults."

AVALON BOOKS, 22 E. 60th St., New York NY 10022. Imprint includes Thomas Bouregy

& Co., Inc. Editor: Rita Brenig. Publishes hardcover originals. Number of titles: 60 in 1980; 60 planned for seasonal/holiday1981. Recently published: *My Love Betrayed*, by April Kihlstrom (light romance); *The Curse of Wayfield*, by Juanita T. Osborne (gothic); and *A Man Called Banker*, by Terrell Bowers (western).

Needs: "We want well-plotted, fast-moving, romances, romance-mysteries, gothics, westerns, and nurse-romances, all of about 50,000 words."

How to Contact: Query with SASE or submit complete ms with SASE. Do not telephone. Reports in 12 weeks on mss.

Terms: Offers $350 advance which is applied against sales of the first 3,000 copies of the book.

Comments: "We like the writers to focus on the plot, drama and characters, not the background."

AVON BOOKS, Camelot Books, Children's Book Imprint. 959 8th Ave., New York NY 10019. (212)262-7454. Senior Editor: Jean Feiwel. Estab. 1967. Publishes paperback originals and reprints. Number of titles: 30 in 1979, 36 in 1980; 36 planned for 1981.

Needs: Contemporary, fiction, adventure, mystery, western, juvenile and young adult: animal, fantasy/science fiction and easy-to-read. No historical. Recently published: *The Westing Game*, by Ellen Raskin (mystery); *The Watchers of Space*, by Nancy Etchemendy (fantasy); and *Good Work Amelia Bedelia*, by Peggy Parish (picture book).

How to Contact: Query or submit outline/synopsis and sample chapters (3) with SASE. Simultaneous and photocopied submissions OK. Reports in 6 weeks on queries and mss.

Terms: Pays 4-10% in royalties; offers $1,500-5,000 in advance. Free book catalog with SASE.

A & W PUBLISHERS, INC., 95 Madison Ave., New York NY 10016. (212)725-4970. Imprints include A & W Visual Library and Galahad Books. Executive Editor: Carolyn Trager. Fiction Editor: Ruth Pollack. Estab. 1972. Publishes hardcover and paperback originals and reprints. Number of fiction titles: 2 in 1980; 5-10 planned for 1981.

Needs: Open to most all subjects. No juvenile.

How to Contact: Query or submit complete ms or submit outline/synopsis and sample chapters (3) or submit through agent. Simultaneous and photocopied submissions OK. Reports in 1 week on queries, 1 month on mss.

BAKER BOOK HOUSE, CO., Box 6287, Grand Rapids MI 49506. (616)676-9185. Editor: Dan Van't Kerkhoff. Publishes hardcover and paperback originals.

Needs: Juvenile and young adult. Looking for mystery, adventure for preteens and young teens. Recently published: *Mystery at Red Rock Canyon*, by E. Vogt; *Star Eye*, by William Schmidt; *Bobby Keeps Watch*, by Hester Monsma, and *Caught in the Middle*, by Anne Schraff.

How to Contact: Submit complete ms with SASE. Simultaneous and photocopied submissions OK. Reports in 1 month on mss.

Terms: Pays 5-10% in royalties and by outright purchase $250-500; no advance. Free book catalog for SASE.

BANTAM BOOKS, INC.,, 666 5th Ave., New York NY 10103. (212)765-6500. Imprints include Skylark, New Age and Peacock Press. Editorial Director: Rollene W. Saal. Fiction Editor: Angela Rinaldi. Estab. 1945. Publishes paperback originals and reprints. Number of titles: 200 in 1979, 150-200 in 1980; 150-200 planned for 1981.

Needs: Contemporary, literary, adventure, mystery, spy, historical, western, war, gothic, romance, women's, feminist, gay/lesbian, ethnic, psychic/supernatural, religious/inspirational, science fiction, fantasy, horror, humor/satire and young adult. Recently published: *The Far Pavilions*, by M.M. Kaye (romance/historic/adventure); *The Matarese Circle*, by Robert Ludlum (suspense); and *Sophie's Choice*, by William Styron (fiction).

How to Contact: Query with SASE or submit through agent. Simultaneous and photocopied submissions OK. Reports on queries as soon as possible.
Terms: Individually negotiated; offers advance.

BEAUFORT BOOKS, INC., 9 E. 40th St., New York NY 10016. (212)685-8588. Estab. 1980. Publishes hardcover originals. Number of titles: 15 in 1980; 45 planned in 1981.
Needs: Contemporary, faction, adventure, mystery, spy, historical, war, gothic, romance, women's, psychic/supernatural, science fiction, fantasy, horror, humor/satire and juvenile and young adult: sports, animal, spy/adventure, historical, fantasy/science fiction and easy-to-read. Recently published: *Periscope Red*, by Rohmer (thriller); and *Daughters of the Law*, by Asher (young adult).
How to Contact: Submit complete ms with SASE. No simultaneous submissions; photocopied submissions OK. Reports in 6 weeks on mss.
Terms: Royalties vary with individual; advance also varies with each author. Free book catalog with 6x9 SASE (97¢ postage).
Comments: "Some publishers will not read and publish first novels—we do."

BETHANY FELLOWSHIP, INC., 6820 Auto Club Rd., Minneapolis MN 55438. (612)944-2121. Managing Editor: Carol Johnson. Estab. 1956. Publishes paperback originals. Number of titles: 5 in 1980; 5 planned for 1981.
Needs: Religious/inspirational, adventure, mystery, romantic, historical, gothic, juvenile. Recently published: *The Rahab Link*, by J. Alexander McKenzie (mystery/religious); *The Music Machine*, by Samuel Wright (juvenile fantasy); and *Love Comes Softly*, by Janette Oke (prairie romance).
How to Contact: Query or submit outline/synopsis and sample chapters (2-3) with SASE. Simultaneous and photocopied submissions OK. Reports in 1 month on queries, 6 weeks on ms.
Terms: Pays in royalties; no advance. Free book catalog with 8½x11 SASE and $1.30 postage.

JOHN F BLAIR, PUBLISHER, 1406 Plaza Dr., Winston-Salem NC 27103. (919)768-1374. Editor: George McDaniel. Editor-in-Chief: John F. Blair. Estab. 1954. Publishes hardcover originals and paperback originals. Number of titles: 4 in 1979, 4-5 in 1980; 4-5 planned for 1981.
Needs: Contemporary, literary, experimental, historical, romance, feminist, ethnic, humor/satire and young adult. Basically likes regional material dealing with Southeastern US. No confession or erotica. Recently published: *The High Pitched Laugh of a Painted Lady*, by Lewis Green (collection of short stories); *The Epic of Alexandra*, by Dorothy Dayton (children's fantasy); and *With Their Ears Pricked Forward*, by Joshua Lee (autobiographical fiction).
How to Contact: Query or submit through agent with SASE. Simultaneous and photocopied submissions OK. Reports in 2-3 weeks on queries, 8-9 weeks on mss.
Terms: Pays 10% standard royalties, 7% on paperback royalties. Royalties can go as high as 15% by special arrangement. Free book catalog.
Comments: "We are not interested in books for the very young. Currently we are saturated with historical novels. We are primarily interested in serious adult novels of high literary quality."

THE BOBBS-MERRILL COMPANY, INC., 4 W. 58th St., New York NY 10019. Executive Editor: Grace G. Shaw. Publishes hardcover originals. Number of titles: 4 in 1979, 4 in 1980.
Needs: Contemporary, faction, historical, war and women's. "We do not want any young people's books or juveniles."
How to Contact: Query with SASE or submit through agent. No simultaneous submissions; photocopied submissions OK.

Terms: Each arrangement is on an individual basis; offers advance. Free book catalog with SASE.
Comments: "Subject matter is less literary and more commercial. If the writer wishes to be published, he should study the bestseller lists and read the books on them. I'm sorry to say, however, that the chances of publishing a literary novel in the fine publishing tradition of old are very slim. Literary/serious novels do not sell and few publishers can afford to subsidize them. The best procedure is to write a short, factual query. A letter of this sort rather than a flowery statement that tries to impress has a better chance of creating interest. Writers should be advised not to call a week after submission and ask to speak to the editor. After a month, it makes sense to write a follow-up query."

BOOKCRAFT, INC., 1848 W. 2300 South, Salt Lake City UT 84119. Editor: George Bickerstaff. Publishes hardcover originals. Number of titles: 3 in 1979, 2 in 1980; 2 for 1981.
Needs: Contemporary, historical, western, romance, women's, religious/inspirational, juvenile and young adult. Recently published: *Bishop's Horse Race*, by Blaine and Brenton Yorgason (historical novel); *The Windwalker*, by Blaine Yorgason (western/historical); and *Where the Heart Leads* by Susan McCloud.
How to Contact: Query or submit outline/synopsis and sample chapters with SASE. No simultaneous submissions; photocopied submissions OK. Reports in 6 weeks on both queries and mss.
Terms: Pays royalties; no advance. Free book catalog.
Comments: "Read our fiction. Our market is the membership of The Church of Jesus Christ of Latter-day Saints (Mormons), and all stories must be related to the background, doctrines or practices of that church. No preaching, but tone should be fresh, positive, and motivational. No anti-Mormon works. Copy of information for authors supplied on request."

BOREALIS PRESS, 9 Ashburn Dr., Ottawa, Ontario, Canada K2E 6M4. Imprint includes *Journal of Canadian Poetry*. Editor: Frank Tierney. Fiction Editor: Glenn Clever. Estab. 1970. Publishes hardcover and paperback originals and reprints. Number of titles: 15 in 1979, 20 in 1980; 20 planned for 1981.
Needs: Contemporary, literary, adventure, historical, juvenile and young adult. "Must have a Canadian content or author; otherwise query first." Recently published: *Threat Through Tibet*, by Duke (adventure); *Nightmare Tales*, by Freiber (short stories); and *Laura's Gift*, by Jacobs (young adult).
How to Contact: Submit complete ms with SASE (Canadian postage or International Reply Coupons). No simultaneous submissions; photocopied submissions OK. Reports in 2 weeks on queries, 8-10 weeks on mss.
Terms: Pays 10% in royalties and 3 free author's copies; no advance. Free book catalog with SASE or IRC.
Comments: "Have your work professionally edited. We generally publish only material with a Canadian content or by a Canadian writer."

BRADBURY PRESS, INC., 2 Overhill Rd., Scarsdale NY 10583. (914)472-5100. Editor: Richard Jackson. Publishes hardcover originals. Number of titles: 19 in 1980; 20 planned for 1981.
Needs: Contemporary, adventure, science fiction, humor/satire, juvenile and young adult. "Also, stories about real kids with realistic dialogue." No fantasy or religious material. Recently published: *Starring Sally J. Freedman As Herself*, by J. Blume; *The Girl Who Loved Wild Horses*, by P. Goble; and *The Slave Dancer*, by P. Fox.
How to Contact: Send complete ms with SASE. No simultaneous submissions; photocopied submissions OK. Reports in 3 months on mss.
Terms: Pays 10% on royalties or 5% on retail price to author and 5% to artist; offers $1,000 advance. Free book catalog.

BREAKWATER BOOKS, LTD., 277 Duckworth St., Box 2188, St. John's, Newfoundland, Canada A1C 6E6. (709)722-6680. President: Clyde Rose. Estab. 1972. Publishes hardcover and paperback originals and reprints. Number of titles: 7 in 1979, 1 in 1980; undecided for 1981.
Needs: Literary, historical, ethnic (Canadian), juvenile and young adult. Recently published: *Williwaw*, by P.S. Moore (science/political fiction); *Only the Gods Speak*, by Harold Horwood (collection of short stories); and *The Bannonbridge Musicians*, by Raymond Fraser (story of two active maritimers).
How to Contact: Query or submit complete ms with SASE. Simultaneous and photocopied submissions OK. Reports in 8 weeks on queries, 6 months on mss.
Terms: Negotiable; no advance. Free book catalog.

BROADMAN PRESS, 127 9th Ave. N., Nashville TN 37234. (615)251-2433. Editorial Director: Thomas L. Clark. Publishes hardcover and paperback originals. Number of titles: 5 in 1979, 5 in 1980; 5 planned for 1981.
Needs: Adventure, historical, religious/inspirational, humor/satire, juvenile and young adult. Will accept no other genre. Recently published: *Ahaz*, by Constance Head (Biblical fiction); *Fire In The Canebrake*, by Reuben Herring (historical); and *Joanna's Miracle*, by Wm. H. Armstrong.
How to Contact: Query but decision is not made until ms is reviewed. No simultaneous submissions; photocopied submissions OK. Reports in 2 months on queries and mss.
Terms: Pays 10% in royalties; no advance. Free book catalog.

CELESTIAL ARTS, 231 Adrian Rd., Millbrae CA 94030. Imprint includes Les Femmes. Fiction Editor: David Morris. Estab. 1970. Publishes hardcover and paperback originals. Number of titles: 1 in 1979, 2 in 1980; 2-4 planned for 1981.
Needs: Contemporary, literary, experimental, adventure, historical, women's, feminist, erotica, psychic/supernatural, science fiction, horror, humor/satire. Publishes little fiction and does not plan to expand. Recently published *Jacob Atabet*, by Michael Murphy (speculative fiction); *On the 8th Day*, by Lawrence Okum (science fiction).
How to Contact: Query or submit outline/synopsis and sample chapters. SASE for query, ms. Simultaneous and photocopied submissions OK. Reports in 2 week on queries, 6 weeks on mss.
Terms: Pays royalties. Book catalog for 8½x11 SASE.
Comments: Primarily publisher of nonfiction.

CHARLES RIVER BOOKS, 1 Thompson Sq., Charlestown MA 02129. Senior Editor: B. Comjean. Assistant Editor: Dennis Campbell. Estab. 1978. Publishes hardcover and paperback originals and hardcover reprints.
Needs: Open to all categories. Recently published *It Will Take a Lifetime*, by F. Sweeny (short stories).
How to Contact: Query. Simultaneous and photocopied submissions OK. Reports in 6 weeks.
Terms: Pays 4-10% royalties; "modest" advance. Book catalog for SASE.

CHARTER BOOKS, 51 Madison Ave., New York NY. (212)689-9200. Editorial Director: Michael Seidman. Estab. 1977. Publishes paperback originals and reprints. Number of titles: 85-100 in 1980; 60-70 planned for 1981.
Needs: General mass market fiction; suspense a la Ludlum and Stephen King. No other genres. Recently published *Blindside*, by Dave Klein (mystery); *Eagles Fly*, by Sean Flannery (espionage); *A Farewell Party*, by Franklin Bandy (suspense).
How to Contact: Send partial or complete ms. Prefers partial or complete outline/synopsis. SASE. Simultaneous and photocopied submissions OK. Reports in 1 month on queries, 2 months on mss.

Terms: Negotiates contract and pays ½ in advance, ½ on delivery of original ms. Reprints: Pays ½ when agreement signed and ½ on publication. Book catalog for SASE.
Advice: "Be thorough in queries and synopses/outlines."

THE CHILD'S WORLD, INC., Box 681, Elgin IL 60120. President: Jane Buerger. Estab. 1968. Publishes hardcover and paperback originals. Number of titles: approximately 50 per year.
Needs: Juvenile: sports, animal, spy/adventure, historical, fantasy/science fiction, easy-to-read. "All of our titles are for the juvenile market. Most are only 32 pages." Recently published *It's OK to Cry*, by Leone Anderson (juvenile fiction); *Why The Cock Crows Three Times*, by Bernice Foley (juvenile folktale); *The Talking Tabby Cat*, by Jane B. Moncure (juvenile folktale).
How to Contact: Submit complete ms or submit outline/synopsis. Simultaneous and photocopied submissions OK. Reports in 1 month on queries.
Terms: Pays by outright purchase of $300-$600; no advance. Free book catalog.
Advice: "Avoid sending material for high school and adult age groups."

CLARION BOOKS/HOUGHTON MIFFLIN, 52 Vanderbilt Ave., New York NY 10017. (212)972-1190. Editor/Publisher: James C. Giblin. Estab. 1965 "as the children's book division of Seabury Press; 1979 as a new children's book imprint of Houghton Mifflin Company." Publishes hardcover originals. Number of titles: 19 in 1979, 21 in 1980; 23 planned for 1981.
Needs: Juvenile and young adult: sports, animal, spy/adventure, fantasy/science fiction, easy-to-read, humorous contemporary stories for ages 8-12 and 10-14. Recently published *Cute Is a Four-Letter Word*, by Stella Pevsner (light contemporary school and family story); *The Climb*, by Carol Carrick (picture book adventure); *Prisoners at the Kitchen Table*, by Barbara Holland (mystery suspense story).
How to Contact: Query on mss of more than 50 pages. SASE for query, ms. Reluctantly considers simultaneous submissions; photocopied submissions OK. Reports in 2 weeks on queries, 6 weeks on mss.
Terms: Pays 5% royalties on picture books; 10% on older books; offers $1,500-$2,000 advances. Free book catalog.
Advice: "It's a truism, but I really believe that the best novels come out of the author's self-knowledge of his or her own experience and background. Don't send us imitations of other writers' successes."
Comments: "We've noticed a return to lighter stories from the heavier problem novels of recent years."

CLARKE, IRWIN & CO. LTD., 791 St. Clair Ave. W., Toronto, Ontario, Canada M6C 1B8. Editorial Director: John Pearce. Estab. 1930. Publishes hardcover and paperback originals. Number of titles: 5 in 1980; 6 planned for 1981.
Needs: Contemporary, literary, adventure, mystery, spy, historical, war, women's, science fiction, fantasy, humor/satire, juvenile and young adult: sports, animal, spy/adventure, historical, fantasy/science fiction. Specializes in Canadian subjects. Recently published *Kowalski's Last Chance*, by Leo Simpson (adult literary humor); *Days of Terror*, by Barbara Smucker (young adult historical); *A Man Without Passion*, by Florence Evans (adult).
How to Contact: Query, submit outline synopsis and sample chapters or submit through agent. Simultaneous and photocopied submissions OK. Reports in 1 week on queries, 1 month on mss.
Terms: Pays in royalties; offers advance.

COKER PUBLISHING HOUSE, Box 27842, Houston TX 77007. (713)861-4882. Editorial Director and Fiction Editor: E.A. Grief. Estab. 1978. Publishes paperback originals. Number of titles: 1 in 1979, 6-10 in 1980; 6-10 planned for 1981.

Needs: Literary, experimental, fantasy. "We will also consider quality fiction (analytical and insightful) in the existential traditon of Nietzsche, Dostoevsky, Hesse, Camus, and Sartre; works similar in style and quality to Kosinsky, Wheelis, and Gardner. No romance or horror." Recently published *Bondage*, by W.L. Garrison.
How to Contact: Submit outline/synopsis and sample chapters with SASE. Simultaneous and photocopied submissions OK. Reports in 2 weeks on queries, 6 weeks on mss.
Terms: Pays in author's copies and by negotiation; no advance.
Comments: "First, one should only write if he has something to say. Second, one should write to please oneself as opposed to what is presently in vogue in fiction."

COLUMBIA PUBLISHING COMPANY, INC., Frenchtown NJ 08825. (201)996-2141. President: Bernard Rabb. Estab. 1973. Publishes hardcover originals. Number of titles: 2 in 1979, 3 in 1980; 3 planned for 1981.
Needs: Literary, experimental, historical, translations. Recently published *Cousin Drewey*, by John L. Sinclair (Southwest literary novel); *Don Juan*, by Gonzalo Torrente Ballester (literature).
How to Contact: Submit complete ms with SASE. Simultaneous and photocopied submissions OK. Reports in 6 months.
Terms: Pays in royalties; offers advance. Book catalog for 8½x11 SASE.
Comments: "Do *not* send us romantic novels, science fiction novels, spy novels, parables which will instruct the world to change its ways, gothic novels, shoot-'em-up westerns or the like. Thoughtful writers, serious writers, and writers with vision, sensitivity, and style are always welcome. If the writer thinks his work will be a blockbuster bestseller and will be a movie at MGM, chances are the work is not for us. But if the work is intended for the smaller audience of literate readers, then we would like to consider it for publication."

COMMONER'S PUBLISHING, 432 Rideau St., Ottawa, Ontario, Canada K1N 5Z1. Editor: Glenn Cheriton. Estab. 1973. Publishes paperback originals.
Needs: Literary, experimental, translations.
How to Contact: Submit complete ms. Simultaneous and photocopied submissions OK. Reports in 1 month.
Terms: Pays 10% minimum royalties.
Comments: "We are open to any quality, properly presented ms or proposal. Mss are read and evaluated by at least 3 editors and such comments may be passed on. Writers are encouraged to familiarize themselves with our style by viewing our previous works rather than requesting an explanation of our editorial policies."

CONCORDIA PUBLISHING HOUSE, 3558 S. Jefferson Ave., St. Louis MO 63118. (314)664-7000. Contact: Ms. Pat McKissack. Estab. 1869. Published 5 children's titles in 1979.
Needs: Religious/inspirational fiction "is all that we will consider." Recently published *God, Why* series: *God, Why Is She the Way She Is?*, by Linda Jacobs Ware; *God, Why Did He Die?*, by Anne Harler; *God, Why Am I So Miserable?*, by Mildred H. Arthur; *God, When Will I Ever Belong?*, by Katherine D. Marko; *I Am*, by J. Marxhausen (all children's fiction).
How to Contact: Query or submit outline/synopsis. SASE for query, ms. Simultaneous and photocopied submissions OK. Reports in 2 weeks on queries, 6 weeks on mss.
Terms: Pays 5-10% in royalties and 6 author's copies; offers $300 average advance.

DAVID C. COOK PUBLISHING COMPANY, 850 N. Grove, Elgin IL 60120. (312)741-2400. Imprints include Chariot Books. Managing Editor: Janet Hoover Thoma. Estab. 1875. Publishes hardcover and paperback originals. Number of fiction titles: 12 in 1979, 15 in 1980; 20 planned for 1981.
Needs: Contemporary, mystery, gothic, romance, religious/inspirational, juvenile and young adult: sports, animal, spy/adventure, historical, fantasy/science fiction, easy-to-read,

Recently published *Olympia*, by Elgin Groseclose (adult historical novel); *Romance at Redhaven*, by Kathleen Yapp (adult Christian romance); *Dear Angie*, by Carol Nelson; and *The Longest Highway*, by Hilary Milton (both junior novels).

How to Contact: Submit outline/synopsis and sample chapters. Simultaneous and photocopied submissions OK. Reports in 2 months on queries, 3 months on mss.

Terms: Pays 7-10% ("depending on whether it is trade, mass market or cloth") in royalties and 10 author's copies; offers advance. Free book catalog.

Comments: "We are doing a series of category books, Chimes Books, for the Christian woman. This series, including mysteries, romances, and gothics, has been very well received. The action frequently involves a love triangle (always with unmarried partners) and develops the relationship between the hero and heroine. Flashbacks are only used if they are memories—described in conversation or portrayed through the heroine's thoughts. The narrative should be sequential and straightforward. A Chime Book is primarily a romance. Suspense and mystery play a secondary role. The backdrop should be romanticized (but still authentic) in such a way that a reader is transported to a place she feels she has always wanted to visit. A familiar setting can work, but normally places most often used are the Mediterranean, New York, California, New Zealand, London, Scotland, Arizona, Brazil; the reader wants places where she/the reader can take a holiday. The occupational or professional setting should be one of the glamour industries, for instance, medicine, law, publishing, music, ranching, and so on. We prefer novels set in modern times. Chime Books are generally 10-12 chapters long, approximately 50,000-56,000 words."

COWARD, McCANN & GEOGHEGAN, INC., 200 Madison Ave., New York NY 10016. Editorial Director: Joseph A. Kanon. Estab. 1926. Publishes hardcover originals. Number of titles: 50 in 1979, 50 in 1980; 50 planned for 1981.

Needs: Contemporary, literary, biography, psychic/supernatural, popular nonfiction, horror, juvenile and young adult. "We prefer the two extremes: solid commercial fiction (bestseller potential) or fine literary fiction; preferably *not* genre fiction." Recently published *Shadowland*, by Peter Straub (horror); *King of the Jews*, by Leslie Epstein (literary), and *Rise of Theodore Roosevelt* by Edmund Morris (biography-Pulitzer Prize Winner).

How to Contact: Query, submit outline/synopsis and 1 sample chapter or submit through agent. SASE for query. Simultaneous and photocopied submissions OK. Reports in 6 weeks.

Terms: Pays 10-15% in royalties; offers advance. Book catalog for 8x11 SASE.

Advice: "It's always best to submit through an agent, but if you can't find one, check out the kind of books we publish before sending your ms to us."

CREATIVE ARTS BOOK CO., 833 Bancroft Way, Berkeley CA 94710. (415)848-4777. Imprint includes Modern Authors Monograph Series. Other imprints: Creative Arts Communications Books and Black Lizard Books. Publisher: Donald S. Ellis. Senior Editor: Barry Gifford. Estab. 1976. Publishes hardcover and paperback originals and paperback reprints.

Needs: Serious fiction. Recently published *Fathers*, by H. Gold; *The Horn*, by J.C. Holmes; and *Port Tropique*, by B. Gifford.

How to Contact: Query. Simultaneous and photocopied submissions OK. Reports in 3 weeks.

Terms: Pays 5-10% royalties on retail price and occasionally by outright purchase of $500-$10,000; offers $500 minimum advance. Free book catalog.

CROWELL AND LIPPINCOTT JUNIOR BOOKS, 10 E. 53rd St., New York NY 10022. (212)593-7011. Editorial Director: Patricia Allen. Fiction Editors: Barbara Fenton, Elizabeth Isele, Marilyn Kriney. Publishes hardcover originals. Number of titles: 60 in 1979, 55 in 1980; 55 planned for 1981.

Needs: Juvenile and young adult: sports, animal, spy/adventure, historical, fantasy/science fiction, easy-to-read, translations. "We want fiction—preschool to grade 9." Recently published *The Ape Inside Me*, by Kim Platt (young adult novel); *My Friend The Monster*, by Clyde Bulla (ages 9-11); and *Jacob Have I Loved* (young adult novel).

How to Contact: Query; submit complete ms; submit outline/synopsis and sample chapters; submit through agent. SASE for query, ms. "We read everything even if we get behind." Please identify simultaneous submissions; photocopied submissions OK. Reports in 8 weeks.

Terms: Average 10% in royalties. Royalties shared equally with illustrators. Offers advance. Book catalog for self-addressed label.

Advice: "Read widely in the field of adult and children's literature. Realize that writing for children is a difficult challenge."

Comments: Crowell and Lippincott imprints are separate but listed in joint catalog.

CROWN PUBLISHERS, INC., 1 Park Ave., New York NY 10016. (212)532-9200. Editor-in-Chief and Director Children's Book Dept.: Norma Jean Sawicki. Editor: Miriam Rinn. Publishes hardcover originals. "Occasionally publish paperbacks simultaneously with hardcover but no original paperbacks." Number of titles: 16 in 1979, 18 in 1980; 20 planned for 1981.

Needs: Humor/satire, juvenile and young adult: sports, animal, spy/adventure, fantasy/ science fiction, realistic fiction, easy-to-read, ethnic (all). Recently published *A Hunter Comes Home*, by Ann Turner; *Conrad's War*, by Andrew Davies; *Weird Henry Berg*, by Sarah Sargent.

How to Contact: Complete ms for fiction and picture books. No simultaneous submissions; photocopied submissions OK. Reports "within six to eight weeks."

Terms: Pays "advance against royalty." Free book catalog.

Advice: "Write about what you know."

DAWNE-LEIGH PUBLICATIONS, 231 Adrian Rd., Millbrae CA 94030. (415)692-4500. Distributed by Atheneum Publishers. Editor: Orly Kelly. Estab. 1978. Publishes hardcover and paperback originals and hardcover reprints. Number of titles: 12 in 1979, 8 in 1980; 14 planned for 1981.

Needs: Juvenile and young adult: animal, adventure, historical, fantasy/science fiction. "No contemporary fiction for children/YA of the genre such as 'My parents got a divorce, but I'm coping.' We specialize in fairy tales, fantasy, science fiction, etc." Recently published *Scooter & The Magic Star*, by Gardner/Smith (fairy tale); *Fantasies Two*, by Griffith (fantasy/science fiction); *Dream Feather*, by Stan-Padilla (contemporary Indian myth); *Follow the Star*, by Powers (Christmas stories); *Nativity Stories*, by Howard (Christmas stories).

How to Contact: Submit complete ms if short or submit outline/synopsis and 4 sample chapters. SASE for query, ms. Simultaneous and photocopied submissions OK. Reports in 2 weeks on queries, 6 weeks on mss.

Terms: Pays in royalties; offers small advance. Free book catalog.

Advice: "Send only your best effort; make sure it is as good as it can be before submitting. We get so many mss to plow through; many are very carelessly done. Make sure yours is original—not just a rehash of work that is already done better."

DELACORTE JUVENILE, 1 Dag Hammerskjold Plaza, New York NY 10017. See Dell Publishing Co., Inc.

DELACORTE PRESS, 1 Dag Hammerskjold Plaza, New York NY 10017. See Dell Publishing Co., Inc.

DELL PUBLISHING CO., INC., 1 Dag Hammerskjold Plaza, New York NY 10017. Imprints include Delacorte Press, Delacorte Juvenile, Delta, Dell, Laurel-Leaf, Yearling,

Purse. Estab. 1922. Publishes hardcover and paperback originals and paperback reprints.
Needs: See below for individual imprint requirements.
How to Contact: General guidelines for unagented submissions. Reports in 3 months. Photocopied and simultaneous submissions OK. Please adhere strictly to the following procedures: 1. Send *only* a 4 page synopsis or outline with a cover letter stating previous work published or relevant experience. Enclose SASE. 2. *Do not* send ms, sample chapters or artwork. 3. *Do not* register, certify or insure your letter. Dell is comprised of several imprints, each with its own editorial department. Please review carefully the following information and direct your submissions to the appropriate department. Your envelope must be marked: Attention: (One of the following names of imprints), Editorial Department—Proposal.
DELACORTE: Publishes in hardcover; looks for top-notch commercial fiction. Recently published *Class Reunion*, by Rona Jaffe; *Evergreen*, by Belva Plain. 120 titles/year.
DELTA: Publishes in trade paperback; rarely publishes original fiction; looks for useful, substantial guides (nonfiction). 60 titles/year.
DELL: Publishes mass-market paperbacks; rarely publishes original nonfiction; looks for family sagas, historical romances, sexy modern romances, adventure and suspense thrillers, psychic/supernatural, horror, war novels. Especially interested in submissions for Candlelight (light romances and regencies) and western categories. Not currently publishing original mysteries. 360 titles/year.
DELACORTE JUVENILE: Publishes in hardcover for children and young adults, grades K-12. 40 titles/year. "We prefer complete mss for fiction."
LAUREL-LEAF: Publishes originals and reprints in paperback for young adults, grades 7-12. 60 titles/year.
YEARLING: Publishes originals and reprints in paperback for children, grades K-6. 60 titles/year.
PURSE: Publishes miniature paperbacks about 60 pages in length on topics of consumer interest. No fiction.

Terms: Pays 6-15% in royalties; offers advance. Book catalog for 8½x11 SASE plus $1.30 postage (Attention: Customer Service).
Advice: "Don't get your hopes up. Query first only with 4 page synopsis plus SASE."
Comments: "Westerns and war action are on the increase. Study the paperback racks in your local drugstore. We encourage all authors to seek agents."

DELTA PRESS, 1 Dag Hammerskjold Plaza, New York NY 10017. See Dell Publishing Co., Inc.

DHARMA PUBLISHING, 2425 Hillside Ave., Berkeley CA 94704. (415)548-5407. Editorial Director: Merrill Peterson. Fiction Editors: Kimberley Bacon and Elizabeth Cook. Estab. 1972. Publishes hardcover and paperback originals.
Needs: Will consider most all subjects. "No pornographic, violent, political material. We have not published fiction in the past year, but have published children's fiction in previous years. As we receive good mss in the future in fiction of any kind, we will be open to considering this material."
How to Contact: Submit outline/synopsis and 1-3 sample chapters. SASE for query, ms. Simultaneous and photocopied submissions OK. Reports in 2 weeks on queries, 1 month on mss.
Terms: Pays per agreement negotiations; no advance. Free book catalog.
Comments: "We are a highly specialized publisher in Buddhist philosophy, psychology, art, religion, etc. We publish sophisticated, high quality work; we do our own printing as well as design, editing, etc. It is not usual for us to do fiction for the mass market or trade, but we would consider fiction within the realm of our particular publication philosophy."

THE DIAL PRESS, 1 Dag Hammarskjold Plaza, New York NY 10017. Editorial Director: J. Jursevics. Estab. 1924. Publishes hardcover and trade paperback originals. Number of titles: 65 in 1979, 65 in 1980; 70 planned for 1981.
Needs: Contemporary, literary, adventure, mystery, spy, historical, western, women's, feminist, psychic/supernatural.
How to Contact: Query, submit outline/synopsis and about 3 sample chapters of book ("*first* three chapters—not middle of book") or submit through agent. SASE preferred for return of ms. Simultaneous and photocopied submissions OK if legible. Reports in 2 weeks on queries, 6 weeks on mss.
Terms: Pays in royalties; offers advance. Free book catalog.

DODD, MEAD & COMPANY, INC., 79 Madison Ave., New York NY 10016. (212)685-6464. Fiction Editors: Alexander Burnham, Allen Klots, Mrs. Margaret Norton, Peter Weed. Estab. 1839. Publishes hardcover originals and hardcover and paperback reprints. Number of titles: 125 in 1979, 125 in 1980; 125 planned for 1981.
Needs: Contemporary, literary, experimental, faction, adventure, mystery, spy, historical, war, gothic, women's, feminist, ethnic, religious/inspirational, humor/satire, juvenile and young adult: sports, animal, spy/adventure, historical, fantasy/science fiction, easy-to-read, and translations. Recently published *The Lime Pit*, by Jonathan Valin (detective fiction); *The People From the Sea*, by Velda Johnston (suspense); *The Walker in the Shadows*, by Barbara Michaels (suspense); *The Weather in Africa*, by Martha Gellhorn (novellas); *Summer Girl*, by Caroline Crane (suspense novel).
How to Contact: Query or submit outline/synopsis and sample chapters. SASE for query, ms. "Reluctantly" considers simultaneous submissions. Photocopied submissions OK. Reports in 1 month.
Terms: Pays in royalties; offers advance. Free book catalog.
Comments: "Today's themes are based on current events and the contemporary scene."

THE DONNING COMPANY/PUBLISHERS, INC., 5041 Admiral Wright Rd., Virginia Beach VA 23462. (804)499-0589. Imprints include Starblaze Editions (science fiction & fantasy), Editor: Hank Stine; Unilaw Library (metaphysical/inspirational/religious), Editor: Richard Horwege. Estab. 1974. Publishes hardcover and paperback originals. Number of titles: 6 in 1979, 10 in 1980; 15 planned for 1981.
Needs: Psychic/supernatural, religious/inspirational, science fiction, fantasy. "We will consider all types of fiction." Recently published *Starborn*, by John Nelson (metaphysical fiction); *Apostle*, by Roger Loven; *Dominant Species*, by George Warren; *The Web of Darkness*, by Marion Zimmer Bradley (all science fiction).
How to Contact: Submit complete ms with SASE. Simultaneous and photocopied submissions OK. Reports in 1 month.
Terms: Pays 8-15% in royalties; offers negotiable advance. Free book catalog.
Advice: "It's becoming increasingly harder to publish a first novel in general fiction. It may be more prudent to pick a particular genre such as gothic, science fiction, occult, etc. and try to break in that way. Many publishers are more likely to take a chance on category fiction. Submit a readable and complete ms with SASE, and an outline of the book as well. Use original plot with dialogue to get ideas across rather than long didactic paragraphs. Be flexible in working with editors, and be prepared to wait. We are receiving more well-written material, but we are willing to see more."
Comments: "Regional books are growing in popularity, and many writers are incorporating regional themes in historical fiction and other types of regional-based fiction."

DOUBLEDAY AND CO., INC., 245 Park Ave., New York NY 10017. (212)953-4561. Imprint includes Dolphin Press. Executive Editors: Lisa Drew, Kate Medina. Estab. 1897. Publishes hardcover originals. Number of titles: 167 in 1979, about 175 including series in 1980; about 160 planned for 1981.
Needs: Will consider all genres except confession and erotica.
How to Contact: Query. All unsolicited mss are returned unopened. Simultaneous and photocopied submissions OK. Reports in 3 weeks on queries, 2 months on mss.
Terms: Pays in royalties; offers advance.
Advice: "Your letter of inquiry should be addressed to Editorial Department. First sentence should tell us whether the book is a novel, mystery or whatever and what the book's about in a clear and straightforward description. Summarize plot and background and give a sketch of major characters. If you have already been published, give us details at the end of your letter along with credentials or experience that qualify you to write your book."
Comments: "We will accept complete mss for mysteries and science fiction if addressed to appropriate editor (for example: Science Fiction Editor.)"

DOUBLEDAY CANADA, 105 Bond St., Toronto, Ontario, Canada M5B 1Y3. (416)977-7891. Managing Editor: Rick Archbold. Submissions should be sent to Janet Turnbull, editor. Publishes hardcover and trade paperback originals and reprints. Number of titles: 15 planned for 1981.
Needs: Contemporary, literary, faction, adventure, mystery, spy, historical, war, confession, women's, feminist, ethnic, psychic/supernatural, humor/satire, translations. "Encourage Canadian content or Canadian writers." Recently published *Laughing War*, by Martyn Burke.
How to Contact: Submit outline/synopsis and 2-3 opening chapters along with brief biography. Photocopied submissions OK. Reports in 2 weeks.
Terms: Pays in royalties; offers advance. Free book catalog.
Comments: "It helps if the author tells who his potential market is."

E.P. DUTTON PUBLISHERS, 2 Park Ave., New York NY 10016. Editor: Charles P. Corn. Paperback and Artbook Editor: Cy Nelson. Publishes hardcover and paperback originals. Number of titles: 8 in 1979, 8-12 in 1980; 8-12 planned for 1981.
Needs: Contemporary, literary, faction, juvenile, young adult and translations. No gothics, historicals, romance or mystery. Recently published *Bellefleur*, by Joyce Carol Oates; *Sleeping Dogs Lie*, by Julian Gloagg; and *Love*, by Susan Fromberg Schaeffer.
How to Contact: Temporarily not accepting unsolicited mss. Writers may send a query letter. Reports in 6 weeks on queries.
Terms: Rates vary individually; offers advance. Free book catalog.
Comments: "Do not overlook literary magazines and journals. They are often receptive and have more time to supply feedback."

EAKIN PUBLICATIONS, Box AG, Burnet TX 78611. (512)756-6911. Imprint includes Nortex. Editor: Edwin M. Eakin. Estab. 1978. Publishes hardcover and paperback originals and reprints.
Needs: Juvenile. Specifically needs historical fiction for school market, juveniles set in Southwest for Texas gradeschoolers. Recently published *The Death of Jimmy Littlewolf*, by Lee Templeton; *Shag Chacota*, by J. Watson; and *Seed of a New Land*, by V. Gholson.
How to Contact: Query or submit outline/synopsis and sample chapters. Simultaneous and photocopied submissions OK. Reports in 3 months on queries.
Terms: Pays 10-15% in royalties; no advance. Free book catalog on request.

ELSEVIER/NELSON BOOKS, 2 Park Ave., New York NY 10016. (212)725-1818. Editor: Virginia Buckley. Publishes hardcover young adult fiction. Number of titles: 30-35 annually.
Needs: Contemporary, experimental, adventure, mystery, historical, western, science fiction, fantasy and humor/satire.
How to Contact: Submit complete ms. Photocopied submissions OK. Reports in 4 months on mss.
Terms: Pays retail price in royalties; offers advance.

PAUL S. ERIKSSON, PUBLISHER, Battell Bldg., Middlebury VT 05753. (802)388-7303. Editor: Paul S. Eriksson. Estab. 1960. Publishes hardcover and paperback originals and reprints. Number of titles: 7 in 1980.
Needs: Mainstream. Recently published *The Silkies*, by Charlotte Koplinka (Shetland novel).
How to Contact: Submit outline/synopsis and sample chapters. No simultaneous submissions; photocopied submissions OK.
Terms: Pays 10-15% in royalties; advance offered if necessary. Free book catalog.

EROS PUBLISHING COMPANY, 9172 Eton Ave., Chatsworth CA 91311. (213)709-1160. Editor: Charles D. Anderson. Estab. 1960. Publishes paperback originals. Number of titles: 72 in 1979, 144 in 1980; 144 planned for 1981.
Needs: Contemporary, experimental, mystery, spy, historical, western, war, gothic, feminist, gay/lesbian, erotica, psychic/supernatural, fantasy, horror and humor/satire. No definite restrictions. Recently published *Murder on the Ecstasy Express*, by Norman Bates (mystery); *Dusk to Dawn*, by Jules Griffon (youth romance); *To Love A Vampire*, by Nigel Fleming (horror); and *Knockout!*, by Jake Caldwell (boxing).
How to Contact: Query with SASE. Simultaneous and photocopied submissions OK. Reports in 2 weeks on queries and ms.
Terms: Varies with line. Free book catalog.
Comments: "There's a greater leaning toward contemporary themes with quick reader identification. Query publishers first with your idea and allow them to guide you in tailoring the ms to specific needs."

EVEREST HOUSE, PUBLISHERS, 1133 Avenue of the Americas, New York NY 10036. Estab. 1977. Publishes hardcover paperback originals. Number of titles: about 40 titles/year.
Needs: Contemporary, adventure, mystery, spy, historical, political, sports, women's, ethnic and humor/satire. Must be in good taste. Recently published *Razzmatazz*, by Philip D. Wheaton (family story).
How to Contact: Query with sample outline or sample chapters. No complete mss please. Reports in 1 week on queries.
Terms: Pays standard royalties; offers varied advance.
Comments: "We're looking for quality; of course, anything publishable must be of particular merit and interestingly presented."

FARRAR, STRAUS & GIROUX, 19 Union Sq. W., New York NY 10003. Imprints include Hill & Wang and Octagon. Children's Books Editor-in-Chief: Sandra Jordan. Number of titles: 24 in 1980; 24-30 planned for 1981.
Needs: Juvenile and young adult. Recently published *A Season In-Between*, by Jan Greenberg (contemporary); *Anywhere Else But Here*, by Bruce Clements (contemporary); and *A Ring of Endless Light*, by Madeleine L'Engle (contemporary/fantasy).
How to Contact: Submit outline/synopsis and sample chapters (2). No simultaneous sub-

missions, photocopied submissions OK. Reports in 1 month on queries, 6 weeks on mss.
Terms: Pays in royalties; offers advance. Free book catalog.

FAWCETT GOLD MEDAL, Division of Fawcett Books Groups, 1515 Broadway, New York NY 10036. (212)975-7674. Senior Editors: Michaela Hamilton and Michael Ossias. Executive Editor: Maureen Baron. Estab. 1955. Publishes paperback originals. Prints 48 titles annually.
Needs: Contemporary, family saga, adventure, suspense, science fiction, fantasy, horror and young adult. "We love to see contemporary novels with a real conflict or mystery at the heart." Recently published *Sweeps,* by Bill Granger (contemporary novel); *The Voyagers,* by Vivian Lord (family saga); and *The Chinese Godfather,* by Paul Gillette (contemporary adventure/suspense).
How to Contact: Query only with SASE. If ms is requested, simultaneous and photocopied submissions OK. Reports in 1 month on queries, 6 weeks on mss.
Terms: Pays usual advance and royalties.

FAWCETT POPULAR LIBRARY, 1515 Broadway, New York City NY 10036. (212)975-4321. Imprints include Fawcett Crest, Gold Medal, Coventry, Columbine and Juniper. Executive Editor: Dudley Frasier. Editor-in-Chief: Arlene Friedman. Publishes hardcover reprints and paperback originals. Number of titles: 110 in 1979, 85 in 1980; 80 planned for 80 1981.
Needs: Contemporary, adventure, mystery, spy, historical, women's, horror and young adult. No gothic, romantic suspense, humor, religious or juvenile under 14. Recently published *Power Play,* by Kenneth Cameron (futurist); *Somebody's Darling,* by Larry McMurtry (contemporary); and *The Flash of the Firefly,* by Paris Bonds (romantic/historical).
How to Contact: Query or submit outline/synopsis and sample chapters with SASE or submit through agent. Simultaneous and photocopied submissions OK, but only from agents. Reports in 2 weeks on queries, 6 weeks on mss.
Terms: Varied terms on contracts and advances. Free book catalog with letter addressed to Reader's Service Department.

THE FIRST EAST COAST THEATRE & PUBLISHING CO., INC., Box A244, Village Station, New York NY 10014. Imprint includes First East Coast. Editor: Paul Boccio. Fiction Editors: Paul and Karen Boccio. Estab. 1979. Publishes paperback originals. Plans to publish 2 titles in 1981.
Needs: Literary and war. "Our company will not consider the 'fashion' novel. We are interested in promoting serious material; that is, fiction written in a strong, individual style, demonstrating a unique and new voice."
How to Contact: Query or submit outline/synopis and sample chapters (5) with SASE. Simultaneous and photocopied submissions OK. Reports in 2 weeks on queries, 1 month on mss.
Terms: Pays 7-12% in royalties; offers $1,000 in advance.
Advice: "Submit a professional copy to us and you will be treated like a professional. Be confident."

RICHARD GALLEN BOOKS, 32 E. 39th St., New York NY 10016. Editor-in-Chief: Judith T. Sullivan. Fiction Editor: Star Helmer. Publishes hardcover and paperback originals. Number of titles: 70 in 1979; 120 in 1980.
Needs: Women's contemporary and historical romances. Recently published *Tanya,* by M.

Bradley (historical romance); and *Caravan of Desire*, by Elizabeth Shelley (historical romance).
How to Contact: Query with SASE. Simultaneous and photocopied submissions OK. Reports in 3 weeks on queries and mss.
Terms: Pays 6-8% royalties; offers $3,000-10,000 advance.

DAVID R. GODINE, PUBLISHER, INC., 306 Dartmouth St., Boston MA 02116. (617)536-761. Imprint includes Non Pareil Books. Managing Editor: Sarah Saint Onge. Estab. 1970. Publishes hardcover and paperback originals and reprints. Number of titles: plans 50 in 1981.
Needs: Contemporary, literary, adventure, mystery, historical, ethnic, fantasy, horror, humor/satire, juvenile and young adult. Recently published *Vanishing Animals*, by Mary Morris (short stories); *Finding A Girl in America*, by Andre Dubus (short stories); and *The State of Ireland*, by Benedict Kiely (short stories).
How to Contact: Query with outline synopsis. Simultaneous and photocopied submissions OK. Reports in 3 weeks on queries.
Terms: Pays 5-10% in royalties; offers $500-1,000 in advance. Free book catalog.
Comments: "Though we don't do a lot of fiction, we are planning more. Use tactful perseverance, but not pushiness, or demands for answers to queries."

GREEN TIGER PRESS, 7458 LaJolla Blvd., La Jolla CA 92037. (714)238-1001. Imprints include Star & Elephant, Circling Suns, and Dream Pedlar. Editor: Harold Darling. Editorial Assistant: Paul Stenson. Estab. 1971. Publishes hardcover and paperback originals and reprints. Number of titles: 6 in 1979, 6 in 1980; 18 planned for 1981.
Needs: Experimental. "We are publishers of illustrated picture books. Our work tends to be imaginative or poetic in flavor, somewhat anachronistic in sentiment, and soldily visual in focus." Recently published *Caretakers of Wonder*, by Cooper Edens; and *Beauty and the Beast*, illustrated by Michael Hague.
How to Contact: Query or submit complete ms or outline/synopsis and sample chapters or submit through agent. Simultaneous and photocopied submissions OK. Reports in 2 weeks on queries, 6 weeks on mss.
Terms: A variety of arrangements is possible depending upon the capacity in which a given work is used; offers advance. Book catalog for $3.95.
Comments: "Read voraciously. Even bad books can provide much by way of negative example. Write and strive for beauty. Persevere in submitting mss. Different houses have different needs."

GREENLEAF CLASSICS, INC., Box 20194, San Diego CA 92120. Editorial Director: Douglas Saito. Estab. 1961. Publishes paperback originals. Prints 360 titles annually.
Needs: Erotica. No science fiction, fantasy, mysteries, satire, memoirs, period pieces or occult themes.
How to Contact: Query (requesting guidelines) or submit complete ms or outline/synopsis and sample chapters (3) with SASE. No simultaneous submissions. Reports in 1 week on queries, 2 weeks on mss.
Terms: Pays by outright purchase $400; no advance.
Comments: "Don't waste time submitting until you've received our guidelines. Send SASE for writer's guidelines."

GREENWILLOW BOOKS, Division of Wm. Morrow & Co., 105 Madison Ave., New York NY 10016. (212)889-3050, ext. 214. Editor-in-Chief: Susan Hirschman. Estab. 1975.

Publishes hardcover originals. Number of titles: 60 annually.

Needs: Juvenile and young adult: sports, animal, spy/adventure, historical, fantasy/ science fiction and easy-to-read. Recently published *The Road From Home*, by David Kherdian (historical biography); *The Devil on the Road*, by Robert Westall (adventure/time travel); and *Kate Crackernuts*, by K.M. Briggs (folk tale/witches).

How to Contact: Submit complete ms or outline/synopsis and sample chapters (2-3) or submit through agent with SASE. No simultaneous submissions; photocopied submissions OK. Reports in 2 weeks on queries, 6 weeks on mss.

Terms: Royalty and advance. Free book catalog.

GROVE PRESS, INC., 196 W. Houston St., New York NY 10014. Imprints include Evergreen, Black Cat and Outrider. Editorial Director: Barney Rosset. Estab. 1952. Publishes hardcover and paperback originals and reprints. Number of titles: averages 50/year.

Needs: Contemporary, literary, experimental, mystery, spy, historical, feminist, gay/ lesbian, ethnic, erotica, science fiction, humor/satire, translations and investigative journalism. No historical romance.

How to Contact: Submit outline/synopsis and sample chapters (2) or submit through agent. Must have SASE. Simultaneous and photocopied submissions OK. Reports in 1 month on queries and mss.

Terms: Pays in royalties and offers advance. Free book catalog.

HARCOURT BRACE JOVANOVICH, 757 3rd Ave., New York NY 10017. Imprint includes Let-Me-Read. Editor: Barbara Lucas. Senior Editor: Anna McBier. Associate Editor: Nancy T. Rockwell. Publishes hardcover and paperback originals and reprints. Number of titles: 18 in 1979, 21 in 1980; 19 planned for 1981.

Needs: All subjects must be for children and young adults: sports, animal, spy/adventure, historical, fantasy/science fiction, easy-to-read and translations. "We especially need books for early readers. Romance, if it is written without sensationalism is also of interest to this department. We are looking for any honestly approached and thoughtfully written ms that has some pertinence for children and young adults." Recently published *The Seance*, by Joan Lowery Nixon (mystery); *What If They Knew*, by Pat Hermes (novel); and *Working On It*, by Joan Oppenheimer (novel).

How to Contact: Submit complete ms or outline/synopsis and sample chapters (2-4) or submit through agent with SASE. No simultaneous submissions; photocopied submissions OK. Reports in 1 month on queries, 6-8 weeks on mss.

Terms: Pays 5-10% in royalties; 10 free author's copies; offers $1,000-3,000 in advance. Free book catalog.

Advice: "Suggest that potential writers keep abreast of the needs of young people and what is going on in their world, and that authors write honestly and simply. Books for early readers are very difficult to write well and are therefore in demand. Anyone who is attempting to write for children should visit the library and see what is already available. The work should be fresh, honest, and as original as the writer is capable of producing. Subject matter may be any topic that is of interest to young people or affects their lives."

Comments: "Language is less formal. Subjects are more varied. There are fewer taboos. There is a greater attempt to deal with issues that are troubling young people and more exploration of different lifestyles."

HARLEQUIN ENTERPRISES, LTD., 225 Duncan Mill Rd., Don Mills, Ontario, Canada M3B 3K9. (416)445-5860. Editor: George Glay. Estab. 1949. Publishes paperback originals and reprints. Number of titles: averages 200/year.

Needs: Mystery, historical and romance. Will accept nothing that is not related to the desired categories.

How to Contact: Send outline and first 50 pages (2 or 3 chapters) or submit through agent with IRC and SASE. Absolutely no simultaneous submissions, photocopied submissions

OK. Reports in 1 month on queries; 6 weeks on ms.
Comments: "The quickest route to success is to follow directions for submissions: query first. Before sending a ms, read as many Harlequin Romances that you can get your hands on. It's very important to study the style and do your homework first."

HARMONY BOOKS, Division of Crown Publishers, 1 Park Ave., New York NY 10016. (212)532-9200. Editor: Peter Shriver. Publishes hardcover originals. Number of titles: 1 in 1979, 1-2 in 1980; 1-2 planned for 1981.
Needs: Contemporary, literary, faction, women's, feminist, ethnic and science fiction. Recently published *Charting by the Stars*, by Linsey Abrams (woman's novel); and *Hitchhiker's Guide to the Galaxy*, by Douglas Adams (science fiction).
How to Contact: Query with SASE. Simultaneous and photocopied submissions OK. Reports in 6 weeks on query.
Terms: Advance given varies. Free book catalog.
Comments: "Be sure and send query letter."

HARPER & ROW PUBLISHERS, INC., 10 E. 53rd St., New York NY 10022. (212)593-7000. Editorial Director/Associate Publisher: Roger W. Straus III. Managing Editor: Peggy Jeanes. Estab. 1817. Publishes hardcover originals.
Needs: Open to all categories and subjects. Recently published *Man, Woman and Child*, by Erich Segal (contemporary); *Rough Strife*, by Lynn Sharon Schwartz (contemporary and literary); and *Oh My America!*, by Johanna Kaplan (literary).
How to Contact: Query with SASE. Simultaneous queries OK. Reports in 2 weeks on queries.
Terms: Pays 10-15% in royalties; offers $5,000 average in advance.

HARVEY HOUSE PUBLISHERS, 20 Waterside Plaza, New York NY 10010. Publisher: L.F. Reeves. Publishes hardcover originals.
Needs: Juvenile and young adult. "We prefer realistic fiction about contemporary problems. No science fiction, romance, fantasy, talking animals or rehashed fairy tales." Recently published *Danny*, by Gessner.
How to Contact: Simultaneous and photocopied submissions OK, if so informed. Reports in 6 weeks on queries and mss.
Terms: Pays royalties based on wholesale and retail price; offers advance depending on the ms. Free book catalog.

HEIAN INTERNATIONAL, INC., Box 2402, South San Francisco CA 94080. (415)467-0222. Editor: Karl Ray. Publishes hardcover and paperback originals. Number of titles: 12 in 1980.
Needs: Contemporary, literary, adventure, historical (Japanese or Eastern oriented), ethnic (Eastern cultures), religious/inspirational (Eastern), juvenile and young adult. Recently published *The ABC Book*, by J. Harada; and *Wally, The Whale Who Loved Balloons*, by Yuichi Watanabe.
How to Contact: Query with SASE. Simultaneous and photocopied submissions OK. Reports in 1 week on queries, 1 month on mss.
Terms: Pays in royalties. Free book catalog.
Comments: Interested in books with religious oriental theme or ones that treat man's inner search (Eastern and Western). Submit original material which is well-written and illustrated. Also original juveniles.

HERALD PRESS, Division of Mennonite Publishing House, 616 Walnut Ave., Scottdale PA 15683. (412)887-8500. Editor: Paul M. Schrock. Publishes hardcover and paperback originals. Number of titles: 9 in 1979, 7 in 1980; 8 planned for 1981.
Needs: Religious/inspirational, juvenile and young adult. Recently published *The Weight*,

by Joel Kauffmann (young adult); *River of Glass*, by Wilfred Martens (historical); and *Secret in the City*, by Marian Hostetler.

How to Contact: Query or submit outline/synopsis and sample chapters (2) with SASE. No simultaneous submissions; photocopied submissions OK. Reports in 2 weeks on queries, 6 weeks on mss.

Terms: Pays 10-15% in royalties; 12 free author's copies; no advance. Book catalog 65¢.

Comments: "We are happy to respond to book proposals from Christian authors of adult and juvenile fiction."

HILL & WANG, Division of Farrar, Straus and Giroux, Inc., 19 Union Square W., New York NY 10003. (212)741-6900. Editor: Arthur W. Wang. Publishes hardcover originals.

Needs: General, selected fiction, ethnic.

How to Contact: "Inquire before submitting." Reporting time varies.

HOLIDAY HOUSE, INC., 18 E. 53rd St., New York NY 10022. (212)688-0085. Editor: Margery Cuyler. Estab. 1935. Publishes hardcover originals. Number of titles: 29 in 1979, 30 in 1980.

Needs: Contemporary, literary, adventure, romance, gay/lesbian, ethnic and humor/satire. Recently published *Doris Fein: Superspy*, by T. Ernesto Bethancourt (thriller); *Love is Like Peanuts*, by Betty Bates (romance); and *Taking Care of Melvin*, by Marjorie Sharmat (humor).

How to Contact: Query first on picture books or submit outline/synopsis and sample chapters (3). Simultaneous and photocopied submissions OK. Reports in 1 week on queries, 1 month on mss.

Terms: Advance and royalties are flexible, depending upon whether the book is illustrated. Free book catalog with SASE.

Comments: "This appears to be a decade in which publishers are interested in reviving the type of good, solid story that was popular in the '50s. Certainly, there's a trend toward humor, formula series, romance and religion. Problem novels seem to be out."

HOLLOWAY HOUSE PUBLISHING, 8060 Melrose, Los Angeles CA 90046. (213)653-8060. Executive Editor: Robert Leighton. Associate Editor: Leslie Gersicoff. Estab. 1961. Publishes paperback originals and reprints. Number of titles: averages 25/year.

Needs: Contemporary, adventure, historical, ethnic, juvenile sports and biographies. "Black and Hispanic novels. Must be action packed—aimed at an adult market. No 'this is my story' treatments. Plots should be well-developed, characters easily identified and action graphically depicted with realistic dialogue, authentic slang, and current 'street' language." Recently published *Black Lady Luck*, by Leo Guild (fiction); *Airtight Willie and Me*, by Robert Beck (black experience); and *Bitch*, by J. Jason Grant (black experience).

How to Contact: Query with SASE. Simultaneous and photocopied submissions OK, only excellent copies. Reports in 2 weeks on queries, 6 weeks on mss.

Terms: Pays standard rate on royalties; offers advance. Free book catalog with SASE.

Comments: "We are presently interested in quality Hispanic experience novels; 85-90% should be in English. We are not interested in boring, running narratives about one's own experiences. Our Hispanic line should be exciting, dangerous and realistic. Too many writers assume that because they have worked on a book, someone should read it. Follow guidelines; query letters are usually uninformative, necessitating a letter to query the 'author's query.' A query letter should contain information enough to intrigue the editor. Query letters reading . . . 'and I'd appreciate your reading my book,' with no description, direction or outline are most often ignored. A ms will be reviewed upon arrival. If it is unacceptable for any of the above reasons, it will be returned promptly. If it is accepted for consideration, please allow at least six weeks for a decision."

HORIZON PRESS PUBLISHERS, LTD., 156 5th Ave., New York NY 10010.

(212)924-9225. Imprints include Quartet Books Ltd., The Smith. Editor: Ben Raeburn. Estab. 1950. Publishes hardcover and paperback originals. Number of titles: 18 in 1979, 22 in 1980. Recently published *A Kingdom* and *Welsh Sonata*, by James Hanley.
How to Contact: Query. Reports in 2 weeks on queries, 3 months on mss.
Terms: Standard royalties. Free book catalog.

HWONG PUBLISHING COMPANY, 10353 Los Alamitos Blvd., Los Alamitos CA 90720. (213)598-2428. Managing Editor: Sarah Keating. Fiction Editor: Wally MacGregor. Estab. 1972. Publishes paperback originals. Number of titles: 5 in 1979, 19 in 1980; 20 planned for 1981.
Needs: "At present we have no restrictions on fiction." Recently published *King Tut and the Flying Carpet*, by James & Alinecia Markham (children's fiction); *Hello Kid*, by Toivo Puustinen (adventure); and *Stories for Discussion and Delight*, by Bruce Clark (collection of famous fiction).
How to Contact: Submit complete ms with SASE. Simultaneous and photocopied submissions OK. Reports in 1 month on mss.
Terms: Pays 10-15% in royalties and arrangements are flexible; no advance. Free book catalog. Hwong sometimes publishes on a subsidy basis.

ICARUS PRESS, Box 1225, South Bend IN 46624. (219)291-3200. President: Bruce Fingerhut. Estab. 1977. Number of titles: 1-2 planned for 1981.
Needs: Contemporary, literary, historical, war, translations. No western, romance, erotica.
How to Contact: Query or submit outline/synopsis and sample chapters. SASE for query. Photocopied and simultaneous submissions OK, if so indicated. Reports in 3 weeks on queries; may take as long as 2 months on mss.
Terms: Pays 10-15% in royalties; offers "modest" advance. Free book catalog.
Comments: "We probably won't be publishing much fiction in the next year or so but we plan more for the future. With the recession it is more difficult to publish first novels. Our interest lies in works of high literary merit."

IDEALS PUBLISHING CORP., 11315 Watertown Plank Rd., Milwaukee WI 53226. (414)771-2700. Imprint includes "Good Friends" Juveniles. Editorial Director: James A. Kuse. Estab. 1947. Number of titles: 4 in 1980.
Needs: Juvenile: animal, easy-to-read. No adult fiction or any other subjects or categories.
How to Contact: Submit complete ms with SASE. No simultaneous submissions, photocopied submissions OK. Reports in 6 weeks on mss.
Terms: Varies; offers variable advance.
Advice: "Know the publisher's books before submitting."

INDIANA UNIVERSITY PRESS, 10th and Morton Sts., Bloomington IN 47405. (812)337-4203. Director: John Gallman. Estab. 1950. "No original fiction published recently. Have published translations. Little by little publishing more original fiction." Number of titles: 3-4 planned for 1981.
Needs: "Non-category" quality fiction.
How to Contact: Query first describing ms and include not more than a 10-page sample of ms. All unsolicited mss are returned unopened. No simultaneous submissions; photocopied submissions OK. Reports in 2 weeks.
Terms: Pays 6-10% of list price in royalties; occasional small advance. Free book catalog.
Advice: "Some writers write for therapeutic reasons. There's more to professional writing than that. Develop self confidence and don't listen to advice from others. Quality fiction is having a harder time getting published."
Comments: "No limit on length or narrative form. Absolutely do not want simultaneous submissions. Follow guidelines."

ISLAND PRESS, Star Rt. 1, Box 38, Covelo CA 95428. Senior Editor: Barbara Dean. Estab.

1978. Publishes paperback originals; "one out of four mss is fiction".

Needs: Religious/inspirational, regional history. "We are interested only in the unusual fiction that would merge with our primarily nonfiction list; fiction dealing with environmental consciousness or with human experience leading to personal/spiritual growth. No gothic, science fiction, romance, confession, etc." Recently published *The Christmas Coat* (story of a family discovering itself); *No Substitute for Madness*, by R. Jones (short stories); *The Search for Goodbye-To-Rains*, by P. McHugh (young man's odyssey across America to find himself).

How to Contact: Query or submit outline/synopsis and sample chapters. SASE for ms. Simultaneous and photocopied submissions OK. Reports in 3 months.

Terms: Pays 10-15% in royalties; $1,500-$3,000 advance. Book catalog for SASE.

KENAN PRESS, Division of Simon & Schuster, 1230 Avenue of the Americas, New York NY 10020. Editorial Director: Dan Green. Estab. 1980. Publishes hardcover originals. Number of titles: 4 in 1980; 15 planned for 1981.

Needs: No special categories. The only prerequisite is that the ms be literate. Recently published *My America!*, by Elliott Wagner (novel).

How to Contact: Query or submit through agent. All unsolicited mss are returned unopened. Simultaneous and photocopied submissions OK. Reports as soon as possible.

Terms: Pays in royalties; offers advance.

ALFRED A. KNOPF, 201 E. 50th St., New York NY 10028. Senior Editor: Ashbel Green. Estab. 1915. Publishes hardcover originals. Number of titles: 26 in 1979, 25 in 1980.

Needs: Contemporary, literary, mystery, spy. No western, gothic, romance, erotica, religious, science fiction. Recently published *Morgan's Passing*, by Anne Tyler (contemporary); *Kennedy for the Defense*, by George V. Higgins (contemporary); *The Begger Maid*, by Alice Munro (literary).

How to Contact: Submit complete ms with SASE. Simultaneous and photocopied submissions OK. Reports in 1 month on mss.

Terms: Pays 10-15% in royalties; offers advance.

Comments: Publishes book length fiction of literary merit by known and unknown writers.

LARKSDALE PRESS, 133 S. Heights Blvd., Houston TX 77007. (713)869-9092. Imprints include Linolean Press (religious). Publisher: James F. Goodman. Editor-in-Chief: Nancy Buquoi Adleman. Estab. 1978. Publishes hardcover and paperback originals. Number of titles: 1 in 1980; 3 planned for 1981.

Needs: No special categories desired. Recently published *Hidden Treasures*, by Beatrice Levin (short stories).

How to Contact: Query or submit complete ms to Brad Sagstetter, production editor. SASE for query, ms. Photocopied and simultaneous submissions OK, if so indicated. Reports in 1 month on queries, 3 months on mss.

Terms: Pays in royalties; no advance. Book catalog for SASE.

Advice: "We don't care who you are, or what your friends had to say about your book, or that it is being reviewed by a NY publisher or agent. Your work must stand on its own merit, even if it takes a hundred rewrites. The chief cause of failure is giving up. Be able to take criticism and keep after it."

Comments: "Larksdale will soon begin Harle House of Books, a mass market paperback romance and western series. First book to be published is *Twice the Heartache*, the story of a young mother who has to deal with a severe heart problem."

LAUREL-LEAF, 1 Dag Hammerskjold Plaza, New York NY 10017. See Dell Publishing Co., Inc.

SEYMOUR LAWRENCE INC., co-publisher with Delacorte Press, 61 Beacon St., Boston

MA 02108. (617)227-1719. Publisher/President: Seymour Lawrence. Publishes hardcover and paperback originals. Number of titles: 9 in 1980; 15 planned for 1981.

Needs: Adult fiction. Recently published *Jailbird*, by Kurt Vonnegut; *Schultz*, by J.P. Donleavy; *Neighbors*, by Thomas Berger.

How to Contact: Submit outline/synopsis and sample chapters with SASE.

Terms: Pays in royalties of 10% to 5,000 copies; 12½% to 10,000; 15% thereafter on hardcover books.

LEISURE BOOKS, Division of Nordon Publications, Inc. 2 Park Ave., New York NY 10016. Imprints include Tiara Books. Editorial Director: Milburn D. Smith. Publishes paperback originals and reprints. Number of titles: 96 in 1979, 168 in 1980; 168 planned for 1981.

Needs: Contemporary, adventure, mystery, spy, historical, western, war, gothic, romance, women's, psychic/supernatural, science fiction, fantasy, horror, humor/satire. No literary, experimental, faction, confession, feminist, gay/lesbian, ethnic, erotica, religious/inspiration, juvenile or young adult, translations. Recently published *Nicola*, by Dorothy Daniels (historical romance); *Horsethief Trail*, by J.D. Harkleroad (western); *Yesterday's Music*, by Megan Hughes (modern novel).

How to Contact: Query, submit outline/synopsis and sample chapters or submit through agent. SASE for query, ms. Simultaneous and photocopied submissions OK. Reports in 1 month on queries, 2 months on mss.

Terms: Pays 4-10% royalties; offers $1,500 advance. Book catalog for SASE.

LESTER AND ORPEN DENNYS LTD., 78 Sullivan St., Toronto, Ontario, Canada M5T 1C1. (416)863-6402. Managing Editor: Beverley Beetham-Endersby. Publishes hardcover originals and reprints.

Needs: Contemporary, literary, experimental, faction, adventure, mystery, spy, historical, western, war, women's, feminist, science fiction, fantasy, horror, humor/satire, translations, art. Recently published *Alter Ego*, by Patrick Watson (psychological thriller); *The Trial of Adolph Hitler*, by Philippe Van Rjndt (historical suspense); *Canada 1984*, by Murray Soupcoff (humor/satire).

How to Contact: Prefers partial submissions on specialized topics. Send enough material so company can judge work. Simultaneous and photocopied submissions OK. Reports in 2 weeks on queries, 8 weeks on mss.

Terms: Pays in royalties; offers advance. Free book catalog.

Advice: "The trend seems to be away from literary fiction, but we encourage the literary novel as art form."

LIBRA PUBLISHERS, INC., 391 Willets Rd., Roslyn Heights, LI, NY 11577. (516)484-4950. President: William Kroll. Estab. 1960. Publishes hardcover originals. Number of titles: 5 in 1979, 4 in 1980.

Needs: All categories considered. Recently published *Please Stand By-Your Mother's Missing*, by Tallman & Gilsenan (satire of women's movements); *Billie Is Black*, by S. Forman (adventures of black slave escapees in old West); *The Gentle Losers*, by F. Gerber (WWII experiences of Dutch under German occupation).

How to Contact: Prefers submission of complete ms but queries OK. SASE for query, ms. Simultaneous and photocopied submissions OK. Reports in 1 week on queries, 2 weeks on mss.

Terms: Pays 10-15% in royalties; no advance. Free book catalog.

Comments: "Have persistence. We prefer finished copy rather than drafts."

LIPPINCOTT JUNIOR BOOKS, 10 E. 53rd St., New York NY 10022. (212)593-7011. See Crowell Junior Books.

LITTLE, BROWN & CO., 34 Beacon St., Boston MA 02106. (617)227-0730. Fiction Editor: Sandra Thomas. Estab. 1837. Published hardcover and paperback originals and paperback reprints. Number of titles: 102 in 1979.
Needs: Contemporary, literary, faction, adventure, mystery, spy, historical, war, women's, feminist, ethnic, humor/satire, juvenile and young adult, translations. Recently published *Provenance*, by Frank McDonald (novel); *Maybe*, by Lillian Hellman; and *The Executioner's Song*, by Norman Mailer (both nonfiction).
How to Contact: Query with SASE or submit through agent. No complete mss. Simultaneous and photocopied submissions OK. Reports in 3 months.
Terms: Pays in royalties and 10 author's copies; offers advance. Free book catalog.
Comments: "We do not accept complete mss. If a query letter sparks our interest, we will request sample chapters. In this case, the author should be careful to keep a copy of his submission."

MACMILLAN PUBLISHING CO., INC., 866 3rd Ave., New York NY 10022. (212)935-2000. "Address juvenile mss to Children's Book Dept." Imprints include Collier Books, The Free Press. Editorial Director: George Walsh. Fiction Editors: George Walsh, Toni Lopopolo, Elizabeth Scharlatt, Joyce Jack, Henry William Griffin, Marion Wheeler. Publishes hardcover originals and hardcover and paperback reprints. Number of titles: 23 in 1979, 22 in 1980; 21 planned for 1981.
Needs: Will consider all categories. Recently published *Mom Kills Kids and Self*, by Alan Saperstein (mainstream fiction); *Targets*, by Don McQuinn (mainstream fiction); *The Province Puzzle*, by Vincent McConnor (detective fiction).
How to Contact: Query, submit outline/synopsis and sample chapters, submit complete ms or submit through agent. Simultaneous and photocopied submissions OK. Reports in 6 weeks.
Terms: Pays in royalties; offers advance. Free book catalog.

MACMILLAN OF CANADA, 70 Bond St., Toronto, Ontario, Canada M5B 1X3. (416)362-7651. Publisher: Douglas M. Gibson. Managing Editor: Jan Walter. Executive Editor: Colleen Dimson. Estab. 1905. Publishes hardcover originals. Number of titles: 10 in 1979, 15 in 1980; 15 planned for 1981.
Needs: Contemporary, literary, experimental, faction, adventure, mystery, spy, historical, western, war, women's, feminist, humor/satire. Recently published *The Resurrection of Joseph Bourne*, by Jack Hodgins (literary novel; won Canadian Governor-General's Award for Fiction); *From The Fifteenth District*, by Morris Gallant (literary; short stories); *Random Descent*, by Katherine Govier (literary; first novel).
How to Contact: Query or submit outline/synopsis and sample chapters. SASE for query, ms. All unsolicited mss are returned unopened. Simultaneous and photocopied submissions OK. Reports in 6 weeks.
Terms: Pays 10-15% royalties.

MADRONA PUBLISHERS, INC., 2116 Western Ave., Seattle WA (206)624-6840. President: Daniel J. Levant. Editorial Director: Sara Levant. Publishes hardcover and paperback originals and paperback reprints.
Needs: Contemporary.
How to Contact: Query with SASE. Simultaneous and photocopied submissions OK. Reports in 6 weeks.
Terms: Pays 7½-15% royalties; offers modest advances. Free book catalog.

MANOR BOOKS INC., 45 E. 30th St., New York NY 10016. (212)686-9100. Imprints include MacFadden Romances. Editor-in-Chief: Larry Patterson. Estab. 1930. Number of titles: 216 in 1979, 216 in 1980; 216 planned for 1981.
Needs: Adventure, mystery, spy, historical, western, war, gothic, romance, confession,

women's, psychic/supernatural, science fiction, fantasy, horror. No pornography, erotica, juvenile, or experimental. Recently published *The Cattle Mutilators*, by John J. Dalton (science fiction); *High Gun*, by Lee Floren (western); *Nightside*, by Thomas Collins (mystery).

How to Contact: Query or submit complete ms. SASE for query, ms. Brief biography should be included. No partials please. Simultaneous and photocopied submissions OK. Reports in 1 week on queries, 6 weeks on mss. "May take longer."

Terms: Pays in royalties; offers advance. Book catalog for legal-sized SASE.

Comments: "We are currently interested in action war novels about Viet Nam or Korea, especially those in which the central character is an enlisted man or an officer in the field. We publish books with currently accepted sexual content, but we do not buy pornography or work primarily and exclusively concerned with sex. We are a mass market paperback publisher and we are committed to a commercial line of category books."

MANYLAND BOOKS, INC., 84-39 90th St., Woodhaven NY 11421. (212)441-6768. Editorial Director: Stepas Zobarskas. Estab. 1962. Publishes hardcover and paperback originals. Number of titles: 5 in 1979, 3 in 1980; 5 planned for 1981.

Needs: Literary, experimental, faction, adventure, spy, historical, war, ethnic (all), erotica, religious/inspirational, juvenile and young adult, translations. Recently published *The House of a Stranger*, by Gerald E. Baily; *Prague Diptych*, by Marija Petrovska (novels).

How to Contact: Submit complete ms with SASE. Photocopied submissions OK. Reports in 2 months.

Terms: "Open for negotiations." No advance. Free book catalog.

RICHARD MAREK PUBLISHERS, Division of G.P. Putnam's Sons, 200 Madison Ave., New York NY 10016. (212)576-8900. Estab. 1977. Publishes hardcover originals. Number of titles: 11 in 1979, 17 in 1980; 36 planned for 1981.

Needs: Will consider all categories. Recently published *The Bourne Identity*, by Robert Ludlum; *The Entwining*, by Richard Condon; *Hardcastle*, by John Yount.

How to Contact: Query or submit through agent. SASE for query, ms. Simultaneous and photocopied submissions OK. Reports in 3 months on queries, 12 months on mss.

Terms: Pays in royalties; offers advance. Free book catalog.

MARGARET K. McELDERRY BOOKS/ATHENEUM PUBLISHERS, 597 5th Ave., New York NY 10017. (212)486-2665. Editorial Director: Margaret K. McElderry. Division estab. 1971. Publishes hardcover originals. Number of titles: 28 in 1979, 29 in 1980; 30 planned for 1981.

Needs: All categories for juvenile and young adult: picture books, contemporary, literary, experimental, adventure, mystery, science fiction, fantasy. Recently published *Galactic Warlord*, by Douglas Hill (science fiction); *Country of the Broken Stone*, by Nancy Bond (contemporary realism); *Jemmy*, by Jon Hassler (contemporary, about a half breed Indian).

How to Contact: Query or submit complete ms. SASE for query, ms. Simultaneous submissions OK only if so indicated (and preferably *not*); no photocopied submissions. Reports in 1 week on queries, 1 month on mss.

Terms: Pays in royalties; offers advance. Free book catalog.

Comments: "Fantasy and science fiction still riding high. We swing away from contemporary problem novels for young readers except when outstanding."

METHUEN PUBLISHERS, 733 3rd Ave., New York NY 10017. (212)922-3550. Managing Editor: Barbara Lagowski. Estab. 1977. Publishes hardcover originals and reprints and trade paperbacks. Number of titles: 25 in 1979, 25 in 1980; 25 planned for 1981.

Needs: Contemporary, literary, experimental, faction, adventure, spy, war, feminist, gay/lesbian, ethnic, science fiction, fantasy, humor/satire, translations, young adult: sports, animal, spy/adventure, historical, fantasy/science fiction, easy-to-read. No adult mystery, historical, western, gothic, romance, confession, women's, psychic/supernatural, religious/ inspirational, horror. Recently published *Waiting for Sheila*; *Room At The Top*; *Life At The Top*, by John Braine (all novels about young man's fame and fortune).

How to Contact: Submit complete ms or 3 sample chapters. "Query letters alone go nowhere here." Simultaneous and photocopied submissions OK. Reports in 1 month.

Terms: Pays in royalties: 10% for first 5,000 copies, 12½ for next 5,000 and 15% thereafter for hardcovers; offers advance. Free book catalog.

Advice: "Don't lose heart. Keep sending work out no matter how many rejections you get."

Comments: "We are looking for more literary type books—a blend of literary and trade. That's not to discourage purely commercial projects, though."

MILLER BOOKS, 2908 W. Valley Blvd., Alhambra CA 91803. (213)284-7607. Editorial Director: Joseph Miller. Estab. 1962. Publishes hardcover originals and paperbacks. Number of titles: 2 in 1979, 3 in 1980; 4 planned for 1981.

Needs: Considers all categories except erotica and religious. Recently published *Headless Horseman*, by Henry Boye (fiction).

How to Contact: Submit complete ms. SASE for query, ms. Simultaneous and photocopied submissions OK. Reports in 2 weeks on mss.

Terms: Pays 10-15% royalties; no advance. "Private books paid by author." Free book catalog.

Advice: "Write something original that is not about someone of stature. Do not send good reporting; this should be sent to our magazine. Write positive, not depressing or negative stories."

MOODY PRESS, 2101 W. Howard St., Chicago IL 60645. (312)973-7800. Address fiction to: Beverly J. Burch, Administrative Editor. Estab. 1894. Publishes hardcover and paperback originals and hardcover and paperback reprints. Number of fiction titles: 30 in 1979, 30 in 1980; 30 planned for 1981.

Needs: Contemporary, historical, western, religious/inspirational, young adult adventure. "No erotica, gay, psychic, fantasy, or other categories which would offend Christians." Recently published *The Secret at Pheasant Cottage*, by Patricia St. John (juvenile mystery); *The Pure Land*, by Lonnie Mings (adult novel); *Weep Not for Me*, by Gary Cohen (adult historical fiction).

How to Contact: Query or submit outline/synopsis and sample chapters with biographical sketch of author. SASE for query, ms. No simultaneous submissions; photocopied submissions OK. Reports in 2 weeks on queries, 6 weeks on mss.

Terms: "No comment." No advance. Book catalog for 8½x11 SASE plus 97¢ postage.

Advice: "Write out the outline of the story before you begin writing the text. Use lots of action (60%) and less description and conversation (20% each). Have a goal for writing before you write."

Comments: "We publish to teach and/or evangelize, not just entertain and seek books which are not only religious in nature, but are clearly Biblically based, and in which the Christian message is central to the plot, not subordinate to it."

WILLIAM MORROW AND COMPANY, INC., 105 Madison Ave., New York NY 10016. Imprints include Morrow Quill Paperbacks, Morrow Junior Books, Greenwillow Books, Lothrop, Lee & Shepard. Editor-in-Chief: Hillel Black. Editorial Director: James D. Landis. Estab. 1926. "We published 204 adult hardcover and trade paperbacks in 1979 of which approximately one third were fiction."

Needs: "Morrow accepts only the highest quality submissions in" contemporary, literary, experimental, adventure, mystery, spy, historical, war, romance, women's, feminist, gay/ lesbian, science fiction, horror, humor/satire, translations. Juvenile and young adult divisions are separate. Recently published *The Lords of Akchasaz*, by Yashar Kemal; *Mandragon*, by R.M. Koster; *The Man Who Cried*, by Catherine Cookson; *Blind Pilot*, by Ambrose

Clancy; *One Corpse Too Many*, by Ellis Peters; *A Very Private War*, by Jon Cleary.
How to Contact: Submit through agent. All unsolicited mss are returned unopened. "We will only accept queries, proposals, or mss when submitted through a literary agent." Simultaneous and photocopied submissions OK. Reports in 2 months.
Terms: Pays in royalties; offers advance. Free book catalog.
Comments: "The Morrow divisions of Morrow Junior Books, Greenwillow Books, and Lothrop, Lee and Shepard handle juvenile books."

MOUNTAINEERS BOOKS, 719-B Pike St., Seattle WA 98101. (206)682-4636. Editorial Director: John Pollock. Estab. 1906. Publishes hardcover and paperback originals and hardcover and paperback reprints all in the mountaineering field. Plans to publish fiction in 1981.
Needs: Adventure, humor/satire. "Might consider well done mss but only on outdoor/ mountaineering theme. It could be humorous and/or for juvenile audience." No mystery.
How to Contact: Query with SASE. Simultaneous ("depending on circumstances") and photocopied submissions OK. Reports in 2 months.
Terms: Pays 10-15% royalties "based on wholesale or retail price; occasionally offers advance. Free book catalog.
Comments: "We are interested in receiving more fiction."

NEW AMERICAN LIBRARY, 1633 Broadway, New York NY 10019. (212)397-8000 Imprints include Signet, Mentor, Signet Classic, Plume, DAW, Meridian, and NAL Hardcover. Fiction Editor: Ms. Pat Taylor. Estab. 1948. Publishes hardcover and paperback originals and paperback reprints. Number of titles: 120 in 1979, 125 in 1980; plans undetermined for 1981.
Needs: Contemporary, adventure, mystery, spy, historical, war, romance, confession, women's, psychic/supernatural, science fiction, horror, regency romance. "No short stories." Recently published *Sphinx*, by Robin Cook; *The Stand*, by Stephen King; *The Passionate Savage*, by Constance Gluyas.
How to Contact: Submit complete ms or submit outline/synopsis and sample chapters with SASE or submit through agent. Simultaneous and photocopied submissions OK. Reports in 3 months.
Terms: Pays in royalties and author's copies; offers advance. Free book catalog.
Comments: "We will consider unsolicited mss. However, there is a 2-3 month delay in response from time of receipt. If the writer wants us to acknowledge receipt of the ms, a SASE postcard should be enclosed."

NORDON PUBLICATIONS INC., 2 Park Ave., New York NY 10016. (212)769-7707. Imprints include Leisure Books, Tiara Books. Editorial Director: Milburn Smith. Senior Editor: Jane Thornton. Estab. 1972. Publishes paperback originals and reprints. Number of titles: 125 in 1979, 144 in 1980; 144 planned for 1981.
Needs: Contemporary, adventure, mystery, spy, historical, western, war, gothic, romance, women's, science fiction, fantasy, horror, humor/satire. No pornography. Recently published *Mothers & Lovers*, by Jeannie Sakol; *The Terror Alliance*, by Jack D. Hunter; *The Regulars*, by Stephen Lewis (novels).
How to Contact: Submit outline/synopsis and 2 sample chapters with SASE. Simultaneous and photocopied submissions OK. Reports in 6 weeks on queries, 1 month on mss.
Terms: Pays 4-8% royalties; offers $1,000-$2,000 advance. Book catalog for legal-sized SASE.
Advice: "Do not send a photocopied query letter. Please make the query letter concise. Long, involved synopses are not necessary. Let the sample chapters speak for your book. Check and recheck your spelling, grammar, and punctuation. Please be patient. Mass market houses get thousands of queries a month."

W.W. NORTON & COMPANY, INC., 500 5th Ave., New York NY 10110. (212)354-5500. For unsolicited mss contact: Sterling Lawrence. Estab. 1924. Publishes hardcover originals. Number of titles: 200 in 1980; plans undetermined for 1981.
Needs: Contemporary, adventure, mystery, spy, historical, western, war, women's, feminist, humor/satire, translations. No occult, science fiction, religious, gothic, romances, experimental, faction, confession, erotica, psychic/supernatural, fantasy, horror, juvenile and young adult. Recently published *Confessions of a Ladykiller*, by George Stade (contemporary); *The Medicine Calf*, by Bill Hotchkiss (fictionalized biography); *The Boogeyman*, by Ron Koertge (contemporary); *Off Duty*, by Andrew Coburn (suspense novel); *One Fine Day*, by Leon Arden (contemporary); and *Bachman's Law*, by Richard Thorman (contemporary).
How to Contact: Submit outline/synopsis and sample chapters. Simultaneous and photocopied submissions OK. Reports in 1 month on queries and mss. Return of material not guaranteed unless return postage is enclosed.
Terms: Pays 10% of catalog retail price on first 5,000 copies; 12½ on next 5,000; 15% thereafter in addition to 25 author's copies; offers advance. Free book catalog.
Advice: "Read the masters. To paraphrase Eliot, the minor writer borrows, the major writer *steals*. And parenthetically makes it his own. Then, get an agent."
Comments: "Unagented mss have a very hard time of it. Chances are, if your book is good and you have no agent, you will eventually succeed. But the road to success would be easier and shorter if you had an agent backing the book."

OAK TREE PUBLICATIONS, INC., 11175 Flintkote Ave., San Diego CA 92121. (714)452-8676. Editor: Cynthia Tillinghast. Publishes hardcover and paperback originals.
Needs: Juvenile and young adult. No picture books. Open to themes, subjects for juvenile (up to 12) and young adult. Recently published *Carnival Kidnap Caper*, by Dr. F. Dodson and P. Reuben.
How to Contact: Query or submit complete ms with SASE. Simultaneous and photocopied submissions OK.
Terms: Pays 10-15% in royalties; offers variable advance. Free book catalog with 9x12 SASE.

ODDO PUBLISHING CO., Box 68, Beauregard Blvd., Fayetteville GA 30214. (404)461-7627. Managing Editor: Genevieve Oddo. Publishes hardcover and paperback originals.
Needs: Recently published *The Little Dog Who Wouldn't Be*, *Robbie and the Raggedy Scarecrow*; and *Shasta and The She-Bang Machine*, by K. Oana (language arts).
How to Contact: Submit complete ms with SASE. Reports in 3-4 months on mss.
Terms: Pays in royalties for special mss only. "We judge all mss independently and pay by outright purchase accordingly." Free book catalog.
Comments: "Mss must be easy to read, general with current themes. Must be easily coordinated to illustrations. No stories of grandmother long ago, no romance, permissive or immoral words or statements."

THE PAN AMERICAN PUBLISHING COMPANY, Box 1505, Las Vegas NM 87701. Imprint includes Pan-Am Books. Editor-In-Chief: Rose Calles. Fiction Editor: Rita Vargas. Estab. 1934. Publishes hardcover and paperback originals and reprints. Number of titles: 4 in 1979, 4 in 1980; 10 planned for 1981.
Needs: Contemporary, literary, experimental, mystery, historical, romance, confession, women's, psychic/supernatural, religious/inspirational, science fiction, fantasy, horror, humor/satire and juvenile and young adult. No gay/lesbian or erotica. Recently published *Saints & Sinners*, by Marian Ackerman (historical fiction); *The Legend of La Llorona*, by Ray John de Aragon (horror); and *City of Candy & Streets of Ice Cream*, by R. John de Aragon (easy-to-read).

How to Contact: Query or submit complete ms with SASE. Simultaneous and photocopied submissions OK. Reports in 2 weeks on queries and 4-6 weeks on mss.
Terms: Pays 10% in royalties; no advance. Free book catalog.
Comments: "There has been a tremendous interest in the areas of mystery, fantasy, science fiction and horror. If the beginning fiction writer is definitely serious about the quality of his work he should be persistent. The material must be original with a unique approach in order to generate a high level of reader interest."

PARENTS MAGAZINE PRESS, 685 3rd Ave., New York NY 10017. (212)878-8612. Editor: Stephanie Calmenson. Publishes hardcover originals. Number of titles: 10 in 1979, 14 in 1980; 14 planned for 1981.
Needs: Juvenile: easy-to-read text for what are essentially picture books. No other categories are acceptable. Recently published *But No Elephants*, by Jerry Smath (picture storybook); *Sand Cake*, by Frank Asch (picture storybook); and *Detective Bob and The Great Ape Escape*, by David Harrison, pictures by Ned Delaney (picture storybook).
How to Contact: Submit complete ms with SASE. No simultaneous submissions. Reports in 6-8 weeks.
Comments: "We are looking primarily for humorous stories for our 48 page books, which are illustrated in bright, full color, and designed to *entertain* young children, age 3-8."

PELICAN PUBLISHING COMPANY, 1101 Monroe St., Gretna LA 70053 Editor: Frumie Selchen. Editorial Director: James Calhoun. Estab. 1928. Publishes hardcover reprints and originals. Number of titles: 20 in 1980.
Needs: Contemporary, literary, experimental, mystery, historical, war, ethnic, religious/inspirational, humor/satire, juvenile and young adult. No sex or violence.
How to Contact: Query or submit complete ms or outline/synopsis and sample chapters (3-5) with SASE. No simultaneous submissions, photocopied submissions OK. Reports in 2 weeks on queries; varies on mss.
Terms: Pays 10% in royalties; 10 free author's copies; advance only under special conditions. Free book catalog with SASE.

PENINSULA PUBLISHING, Box 867, Los Altos CA 94022. (415)948-2511. Editor: Charles Wiseman. Estab. 1978. Publishes hardcover and paperback originals and reprints. Number of titles: 4 in 1980; 6 planned for 1981.
Needs: Contemporary, adventure, spy, historical, western, romance, juvenile and young adult. No definitive limits established at the onset of entry into fiction. Last year published only technical books.
How to Contact: Query or submit through agent. Simultaneous and photocopied submissions OK. Reports in 1 month on queries.
Terms: Pays 10-20% in royalties; offers advance. Free book catalog.

PEREGRINE SMITH, INC., Box 667, Layton UT 84041. (801)376-9800. Imprint includes Sagamore Books. Editor: G.M. Smith. Fiction Editor: Richard Firmage. Estab. 1970. Publishes hardcover and paperback originals. Number of titles: 1 in 1979, 2 in 1980; 2 planned for 1981.
Needs: Contemporary, literary and historical. No children's, young adult or other categories. Recently published *Trout Madness*, by Robert Traver (fishing stories).
How to Contact: Query with SASE. No simultaneous submissions; photocopied submissions OK. Reports in 2 weeks on queries, 6 weeks on mss.
Terms: Negotiable royalties; no advance. Free book catalog with 6x9 SASE.

PINNACLE BOOKS, INC., 2029 Century Park E., Suite 1000, Los Angeles CA 90067. Editorial Director: Patrick O'Connor. Publishes paperback originals and reprints. Number of titles: averages 180/year.

Needs: Contemporary, mystery, war, contemporary gothic, women's, science fiction, horror, and international intrigue. No pornography or hard core. Recently published *Love's Sweet Agony*, by Patricia Matthews (historical/romance); *The Executioner*, by Don Pendleton (men's adventure); *The Hearse*, by Henry Clement (supernatural); and *Malibu Colony, by Pamela Wallace (contemporary)*.
How to Contact: Query or submit outline/synopsis and sample chapters (4) with SASE. Simultaneous and photocopied submissions OK. Reports in 2 weeks on queries, 6-8 weeks on mss.
Terms: Contracts and terms standard and competitive. Free book catalog with 4x9½ SASE.
Advice: "Secure an agent to do your submitting. If you don't have an agent, use the query form with SASE before submitting a ms. Request specific 'tip sheets' from a publisher before submitting anything. Follow each publisher's method of submission exactly to avoid confusion, delay and problem. No telephone calls, please."
Comments: "Keep abreast of current trends. Read bestsellers and try to see why they sell."

PLATT & MUNK, Division of Grosset & Dunlap, 51 Madison Ave., New York NY 10010. Editor-in-Chief: Nancy Hall. Publishes hardcover and paperback originals and reprints.
Needs: Juvenile and young adult: sports, animal, spy/adventure, fantasy/science fiction and easy-to-read. Recently published *Monsters* by Nancy Christensen; *Giants* by Doug Cushman; and *Dinosaur Mysteries*, by Mary Elting and Ann Goodman.
How to Contact: Submit complete ms with SASE. Simultaneous and photocopied submissions OK. Reports in 5 weeks on mss.
Terms: Pays by outright purchase of $1,000-$3,500; no advance.

PLAYBOY PRESS, 747 3rd Ave., New York NY 10017. Editor: Irma Heldman. Publishes hardcover and paperback originals and reprints. Number of titles: averages 120/year.
Needs: Contemporary, literary, historical, romance, women's, feminist, science fiction, fantasy and horror.
How to Contact: Query with SASE. Simultaneous and photocopied submissions OK. Reports as soon as possible.
Terms: Pays in royalties and by outright purchase; offers advance.

POCKET BOOKS, Division of Simon & Schuster, 1230 Avenue of the Americas, New York NY 10020. (212)246-2121. Editor: Marty Asher. Assistant Editor: Joan Kingsley. Publishes paperback originals and reprints. Number of titles: averages 250/year.
Needs: Contemporary, literary, faction, adventure, mystery, spy, historical, western, war, gothic, romance, women's, feminist, ethnic, erotica, psychic/supernatural, science fiction, fantasy, horror, and humor/satire. Recently published *Ghost Story*, by Peter Straub; *True Confessions*, by John Gregory Dunne; and *Good as Gold*, by Joseph Heller.
How to Contact: Query with SASE. Reports in 6 months on queries.
Terms: Pays in royalties; by outright purchase; and offers advance. Free book catalog.
Comments: "We are not interested in increasing the number of queries, only the quality of fiction."

CLARKSON N. POTTER, INC., 1 Park Ave., New York NY 10016. (212)532-9200. Distributed by Crown Publishers, Inc. Publisher: Jane West. Executive Editor: Carol Southern. Number of titles: 3 planned for 1981.
Needs: Contemporary, literary, faction, adventure, mystery, spy, historical, women's, humor/satire and translations. No lurid romance.
How to Contact: Query or submit outline/synopsis and sample chapters or submit through agent. Simultaneous and photocopied submissions OK. Reports in 2 weeks on queries, 3 weeks on mss.
Terms: Pays 10-15% in royalties; offers $5,000-$10,000 in advance. Free book catalog with SASE.

Comments: "Read the classics. Don't submit anything until it is as good as you can make it."

PRENTICE-HALL, Juvenile Division, Englewood Cliffs NJ 07632. Editor-in-Chief: Barbara Francis. Publishes hardcover and paperback originals and reprints. Number of titles: 50 in 1980.
Needs: Juvenile and young adult: gothic, humor, mainstream and mystery. Recently published *Harper's Mother*, by Wendy Simons (novel); *Face at the Window*, by Wolfgang Ecke (mystery); *The Last Puppy*, by Frank Asch (picture book); and *Scornful Simkinby*, by Lee Lorenz (picture book).
How to Contact: Submit outline/synopsis and sample chapters with SASE. Reports in 4-6 weeks on mss.
Terms: Pays in royalties; offers average advance. Free book catalog with SASE.
Comments: "New emphasis on contemporary young adult novels. Will continue with high caliber picture books. Also interested in easy-to-read and good historical fiction"

QUEENSTON HOUSE PUBLISHING, LTD., 102 Queenston St., Winnepeg, Manitoba, Canada R3N 0W5. (204)489-6862. Publisher: Joan Parr. Estab. 1974. Publishes hardcover and paperback originals. Number of titles: 2 in 1980; 4 possibly planned for 1981.
Needs: Literary and humor/satire. Nothing trendy, wants original, individualized fiction. Light entertaining material and mss with literary merit. Recently published *Corner Stone*, by Bess Kaplan (regional).
How to Contact: Query or submit complete mss with SASE. American writers send IRC's, not US stamps. No simultaneous submissions, photocopied submissions OK. Reports in 6 weeks on queries, 6 months on mss.
Terms: Pays in royalties; no advance.

RAND MCNALLY & COMPANY, Juvenile Division, Box 7600, Chicago IL 60680. (312)673-9100. Senior Editor: Dorothy Haas. Estab. 1856.
Needs: Juvenile: sports. No juvenile novels or adult fiction. "Fiction to us means a picture book only, or a word book which shows preschool words with inventive illustrations to make the book appealing." Recently published *A Mouse Family Album*, by Pamela Sampson (picture book); *The Visit*, by Joan Esley (picture book); and *Adventures of Brer Rabbit*, by Ruth Spriggs (storybook).
How to Contact: No query necessary on picture books. SASE with mss. No simultaneous submissions; photocopied submissions OK. Reports in 6 weeks on queries, 3 months on mss.
Terms: Pays in royalties and by outright purchase. Book catalog with 9x11½ SASE.

RANDOM HOUSE, INC., 201 E. 50th St., New York NY 10022. Imprints include Vintage Books, Knopf, Ballantine, Modern Library, Pantheon. Publishes hardcover and paperback originals.
Needs: "We publish fiction of the highest standards."
How to Contact: Query with SASE.
Terms: Payment as per standard minimum book contracts.

RANDOM HOUSE, INC./Juvenile Division, 201 E. 50th St., New York NY 10022. (212)751-2600. Managing Editor: Elma Otto. Publishes hardcover and paperback originals. Number of titles: 87 in 1980.
Needs: Juvenile. Good stories for preschool through 8th grade. No young adult.
How to Contact: "At present, we are only reviewing mss from published authors and agents."
Comments: "Usually most of work is generated in-house, or freelancers are commissioned for flat fee."

RED DEMBNER ENTERPRISES, CORP., 1841 Broadway, New York NY 10023. (212)265-1250. Imprint includes Dembner Books. Editor: S. Arthur Dembner. Senior Editor: Anna Dembner. Publishes hardcover originals.
Needs: Contemporary, adventure, mystery/suspense and historical. "We are prepared to publish a limited number of well-written, non-sensational works of fiction." Recently published *Like Father*, by D. Black (novel).
How to Contact: Submit outline/synopsis and sample chapters with SASE. Simultaneous and photocopied submissions OK.
Terms: Offers negotiable advance.

RESOURCE PUBLICATIONS, Box 444, Saratoga CA 95070. (408)252-4195. Publisher: William Burns. Publishes paperback originals.
Needs: Religious/inspirational/educational. "Religious fiction should be useable for sermons or classroom religious education. Material is intended to be shown to pros in the field for analogy or demonstration in teaching." Recently published *Winter Dreams and Other Such Friendly Dragons*, by Joseph Juknialis; and *In Season and Out*, by Bruce Clanton (illustrated short stories).
How to Contact: Submit complete ms with SASE. No simultaneous submissions; photocopied submissions OK. Reports in 2 months on mss.
Terms: Pays 8% in royalties; no advance.
Comments: Occasionally subsidy publishes. Does not use much fiction; prefers very short fantasy stories.

ROSS-ERIKSON, PUBLISHERS, 629 State St., Santa Barbara CA 93101. (805)962-1175. Editor: Buzz Erikson. Managing Editor: Lois Shearer. Publishes hardcover and paperback originals. Total number of titles: 40 in 1979, 51 in 1980; 58 planned for 1981.
Needs: Contemporary, literary, mystery, western, women's, feminist, gay/lesbian, ethnic. Any work in any category that is of quality. Recently published *Sicily Enough*, by Claire Rabe (women's novel).
How to Contact: Query or submit complete ms or outline/synopsis and sample chapters with SASE. No simultaneous submissions, photocopied submissions OK. Reports in 2 weeks on queries, 6 weeks on mss.
Terms: Pays 8-12% in royalties; offers occasional advance. Free book catalog with SASE.

ST. MARTIN'S PRESS, 175 5th Ave., New York NY 10010. (212)674-5151. President: Thomas. J. McCormack. Publishes hardcover and paperback originals. Number of titles: more than 150 in 1980, "the most by any American publisher.".
Needs: Contemporary, literary, experimental, faction, adventure, mystery, spy, historical, western, war, gothic, romance, confession, women's, feminist, gay/lesbian, ethnic, erotica, psychic/supernatural, religious/inspirational, science fiction, fantasy, horror and humor/satire. No plays, children's literature or short fiction. Recently published *Shadow of the Moon*, by M.M. Kaye (historical romance); and *Passion Play*, by Jerzy Kosinski (contemporary).
How to Contact: Query or submit complete ms with SASE. Simultaneous and photocopied submissions OK. Reports in 2-3 weeks on queries, 4-6 weeks on mss.
Terms: Pays standard advance and royalties.

SCHOLASTIC-TAB PUBLICATIONS, 123 Newkirk Rd., Richmond Hill, Ontario, Canada L4C 3G5. (416)883-5300. Imprint includes North Winds Press. Managing Director: W.C. McMaster. Editorial Director: F.C.L. Muller. Publishes hardcover and paperback originals and reprints. Number of new titles: 3 in 1979, 9 in 1980; 10 planned for 1981. Total of 80 titles to date.
Needs: Juvenile: mystery, sports, animal, spy/adventure, fantasy/science fiction and easy-to-read. Canadian authors only will be considered. Recently published *Beware the Fish!*, by

Gordon Korman (humor); *Not Yet Summer*, by Susan Brown (juvenile); and *Exit Barney McGee*, by Claire Mackay (young adult).

How to Contact: Query or submit complete ms or outline/synopsis and sample chapters (3). Simultaneous and photocopied submissions OK (would like to know if it is a multiple submission). Reports in 2 weeks on queries; 2 months on mss.

Terms: Pays in royalties; offers varied advance. Free book catalog.

Comments: "We're still receiving a number of 'maturing' or young adult mss, but there have been more in the areas of mystery, science fiction, fantasy. We usually consider only full-length materials, for grades K-12. Preschool titles or read-aloud titles may not be suitable; 'thin' stories with 'cute' characters aren't suitable at all."

CHARLES SCRIBNER'S SONS, 597 5th Ave., New York NY 10017. Editor: Jacek K. Galazka. Fiction Editor: Laurie Graham. Estab. 1846. Publishes hardcover originals and paperback reprints. Number of titles: 41 in 1979, 50 in 1980; 60 planned for 1981.

Needs: Contemporary, literary, experimental, faction, adventure, mystery, spy, historical, war, women's, feminist, science fiction, horror, humor/satire, juvenile and young adult. Only the above categories are accepted. Recently published *A Coat of Varnish*, by C.P. Snow (novel); *Let the Lion Eat Straw*, by E. Southerland (novel); *Innocent Blood*, by P.D. James (mystery); and *Free Flight*, by Doug Terman (thriller).

How to Contact: Submit outline/synopsis and sample chapters (2) with SASE or submit through agent. Reports in 2 weeks on queries, 1 month on mss.

Terms: Pays in royalties; offers advance.

SEAVIEW BOOKS, Division of Playboy Press, 747 3rd Ave., New York NY 10017. Editor: Charles Sopkin. Publishes hardcover reprints and originals. Number of titles: 50 in 1979, 60 in 1980; 70 planned for 1981.

Needs: Contemporary, literary, faction, historical, women's, feminist, ethnic, psychic/supernatural and western. Recently published *The Passing Bells*, by Philip Rock (historical); *Umbertina*, by Helen Barolini (ethnic); and *A Certain Slant of Light*, by Margaret Bonauno (contemporary).

How to Contact: Query or submit outline/synopsis and sample chapters (2-3) with SASE. Simultaneous and photocopied submissions OK. Reports in 1 month on queries and mss.

Terms: Pays standard rate of 10% or $5,000 in royalties; offers advance.

SILHOUETTE ROMANCES, Simon & Schuster Bldg., 1230 Avenue of the Americas, New York NY 10020. (212)245-6400. Imprint includes Silhouette Books. Editor: Karen Solem. Assistant Editor: Leslie J. Wainger. Estab. 1979. Publishes paperback originals. Number of titles: 51 in 1980; 72 planned for 1981.

Needs: Contemporary romance. No gothic, suspense or historical. Recently published *Payment in Full*, by Anne Hampson; *Playing for Keeps*, by Brooke Hastings; and *Unreasonable Summer*, by Dixie Browning.

How to Contact: Submit complete ms with SASE. No simultaneous submissions; photocopied submissions OK. Reports in 6 weeks on mss.

Terms: Pays in royalties; offers advance (negotiation on an individual basis).

Comments: "Request our tip-sheet and study our published books before submitting to make sure that the submission is a potential Silhouette. Authors should never send the only copy of a ms as we are not responsible for loss of or damage to submissions."

SIMON & PIERRE PUBLISHING COMPANY LIMITED, Box 280, Adelaide St. Postal Stn., Toronto, Ontario, Canada M5C 2J4. Imprint includes Bastet Books, Canplay Series. Editor: Marian M. Wilson. Assistant Editor: Kathryn Chittick. Estab. 1972. Publishes hardcover and paperback originals. Number of titles: averages 4/year.

Needs: Contemporary, literary, adventure, mystery, spy, historical, humor/satire, juvenile, young adult and translations. No romance, erotica or horror. Recently published *Zoom*, by

Andrew Brycht (contemporary); *Dragon Spoor*, by Jack H. Crisp (mystery/spy/adventure); and *La Sagouine*, by Antonine Maillet (historical).
How to Contact: Query or submit complete ms or submit outline/synopsis and sample chapter or submit through agent with SASE. Simultaneous and photocopied submissions OK. Reports in 1 month on queries, 3 months on mss.
Terms: Pays in royalties; no advance. Free book catalog.
Comments: "There's a greater interest in lifestyles evident today in fiction. We prefer Canadian authors. Include with submissions: professional resume listing previous publications, detailed outline of proposed work and sample chapters."

STANDARD PUBLISHING, 8121 Hamilton Ave., Cincinnati OH 45231. (513)931-4050. Director: Marjorie Miller. Estab. 1866. Publishes hardcover and paperback originals and reprints. Number of titles: averages 10/year.
Needs: Religious/inspirational and easy-to-read. "Should have some relation to moral values or Biblical concepts and principles." Recently published *What God Did for Zeke, the Fuzzy Caterpillar*, by Robert O' Rourke (children's); *The Happy Shepherd*, by Richard Baynes (children's); and *Soaring*, by Roger Elwood (experience after death).
How to Contact: Query or submit outline/synopsis and sample chapters (2-3) with SASE. Simultaneous and photocopied submissions OK. Reports in 1 month on queries, 6 weeks on mss.
Terms: Pays varied royalties and by outright purchase; offers varied advance. Free book catalog with SASE.

STEIN AND DAY PUBLISHERS, Scarborough House, Briarcliff Manor NY 10510. (914)762-2151. Imprints include Stein and Day Books, Scarborough Books, Day Books. President: Sol Stein. Vice President/Editor: Patricia Day. Executive Editor: Benton M. Arnovitz. Estab. 1962. Publishes fiction for the general reader. Number of titles: 105 in 1979; 73 in 1980.
Needs: Fiction. No westerns or romance. Recently published *Solo*, by Jack Higgins (fiction); *The People In His Life*, by Maia Rodman.
How to Contact: *Must* send query letter first with SASE; no unsolicited mss. Reports as soon as possible.
Terms: Standard.

STEMMER HOUSE PUBLISHERS, INC., 2627 Caves Rd., Owings Mills MD 21117. (301)363-3690. Imprint includes International Design Library, Stemmer House Story-to-Color. Editor: Barbara Holdridge. Publishes hardcover and paperback originals and reprints. Number of titles: averages 1/year.
Needs: Contemporary, literary, historical, war, ethnic, fantasy, juvenile and young adult. No detective or science fiction. Recently published *On the Verge*, by Dikkon Eberhart (contemporary); and *Dark Places, Deep Regions*, by Margaret Sutherland (contemporary).
How to Contact: Query or submit complete ms or outline/synopsis and sample chapters (3) or submit through agent (not necessary) with SASE. Simultaneous and photocopied submissions OK. Reports in 2 weeks on queries, 6 weeks on mss depending on backlog.
Terms: Pays 5-10% in royalties; offers small advance. Free book catalog.
Comments: "Trend today seems to be less literate work. Write to be read 50 years from today. Don't tell us how good the novel is. Perfect your grammar and spelling. Most writers seem to have read the latest paperback and swear to write something 'just as good'—but it's most often not even an improvement."

STRATFORD PRESS, INC., Distributed by Harper & Row, 9606 Santa Monica Blvd., Beverly Hills CA 90210. (213)550-8292. Editor: Ellen Shahan. Estab. 1979. Publishes hardcover reprints and originals. Number of titles: 1 in 1980; 4 planned for 1981.
Needs: Considers all subjects. Recently published *Double Crossing*, by Erika Holzer (international intrigue).

How to Contact: Query or submit outline/synopsis and sample chapters with SASE. Simultaneous and photocopied submissions OK. Reports in 3 months on queries and mss.
Terms: Each contract is structured uniquely depending upon the work, the author, etc.

SUMMIT BOOKS, Division of Simon & Schuster, 1230 Avenue of the Americas, New York NY 10020. Editor-in-Chief: James H. Silberman. Estab. 1976. Number of titles: averages 12-15/year.
Needs: General trade fiction of high literary quality. No category books. Recently published *Vida*, by Marge Piercy; *The Bleeding Heart*, by Marilyn French; and *As Summers Die*, by Winston Groom.
How to Contact: Submit outline and sample chapters. Will consider simultaneous submissions but prefer not to; photocopied submissions OK. Reports in 2 months on sample chapters.
Terms: Negotiates according to ms; offers advance occasionally.

SUN PUBLISHING, CO., Box 4383, Albuquerque NM 87196. Editor: Skip Whitson. Estab. 1974. Publishes paperback originals and reprints. Number of titles: 1 in 1979, 2 in 1980; 2 planned for 1981.
Needs: Science fiction. Limited fiction market but, "we are open to suggestions." Recently published *Etidorhpa*, by John Uri Lloyd (reprint classic).
How to Contact: Query with SASE. Simultaneous and photocopied submissions OK. Reports in 3 months on queries.
Terms: Pays 8% of retail price in royalties and by outright purchase depending on book. Will also subsidy publish; no advance. Free book list with SASE.
Comments: "We have noticed a growth in science-oriented fiction in the last 20 years. However, be prepared to print your own book. Because of the competitive market, some publishers find it risky to publish unpublished authors, so it is often difficult breaking in."

TALONBOOKS LTD., 201/1019 E. Cordova, Vancouver, British Columbia, Canada V6A 1M8. (604)255-5915. Editorial Editor: David Robinson. Estab. 1967. Publishes paperback originals and reprints. Number of titles: 4 in 1979; 5 planned in 1981.
Needs: Literary, women's, feminist, gay/lesbian, translations. Recently published *Latakia*, by Audrey Thomas (women's literary novel); *The Con Man*, by Ken Mitchell (comedy literary novel); *Prisoner of Desire*, by Britt Hagarty (prison/drugs literary novel).
How to Contact: Query, submit complete ms or submit through agent. SASE for ms. Simultaneous and photocopied submissions OK. "Not prompt with unsolicited mss unless we know the author or he has been recommended." Offers advance. Free book catalog.
Comments: "Please do not trouble us with unpublishable mss written by amateurs who have served no literary apprenticeship. Interested in serious literary fiction only."

TANDEM PRESS PUBLISHERS, Box 237, Tannersville PA 18372. (717)629-2250. Editor: Judith Keith. Fiction Editor: Elisa Fitzgerald. Estab. 1969. Publishes hardcover and paperback originals. Number of titles: averages 2/year.
Needs: Contemporary, mystery, historical, gothic, romance and women's. "We give all submissions a read." Recently published *Desires of thy Heart*, by Joan C. Cruz (historical romance); *Lucetta*, by Elinor Jones (historical romance); *Tamara*, by E. Jones (historical romance); and *Night Jasmine*, by Mary Lou Widmer (contemporary romance).
How to Contact: Query with SASE. No simultaneous submissions; photocopied submissions OK. Reports in 2 weeks on queries, 1 month on ms.
Terms: Pays in royalties; offers varied advance.
Comments: "Historical romance is difficult to sell in hardcover or in paperback because the market is glutted. Regency romance and contemporary romance are holding up well. Mysteries, too, are difficult if written by a total unknown. As a small publisher we find it best to sell works by new authors as original paperbacks for smaller advances so as to establish a

track record for them. The market is paradoxical. Hardcover sales are way down as are paperbacks. The average shelf-life of middle list paperback books is 13 days. Whatever the author receives upfront as an advance against royalties is what he essentially will earn on that particular work as returns are enormous. Concentrate on good contemporary romance because the greatest number of paperback and hardcover book buyers are women. Write your query letters with care as we often determine the quality of the writing by the letters we receive. And, once the ms is submitted, please wait to hear from us; if it is something we want, we will call you. Always include phone numbers with submissions. While the hardcover fiction market is depressed there is a good market in paperbacks, television and movies. Many times materials we receive are weak as potential books, but we then work with the author to develop the story with the possibility of selling the idea for television or movies. In this case we act as agent."

THAT NEW PUBLISHING COMPANY, 1525 Eielson St., Fairbanks AK 99701. (907)452-3007. Imprints include Alaskan House and Black Experience Library. President: W. Walker. Estab. 1977. Publishes hardcover originals. Number of titles: averages 1/year.
Needs: Humor/satire and stories of Alaska.
How to Contact: Query with SASE. Simultaneous and photocopied submissions OK. Reports in 2 weeks on queries, 6 weeks on ms.
Terms: Pays 10% in royalties; no advance. Free book catalog.
Comments: "Start with nonfiction. Don't attempt ms without knowing the real Alaska. Our philosophy is to handle Alaskan subjects from the Alaskan point of view."

THORNDIKE PRESS, One Mile Rd., Thorndike ME 04986. (207)948-2962. Senior Editor: Timothy A. Loeb. Estab. 1977. Publishes hardcover and paperback originals and reprints. Number of titles: 3 in 1979, 16 in 1980; 25 planned for 1981.
Needs: Contemporary, adventure, humor/satire, regional history and lifestyle, and outdoors. "We are not publishing children's fiction or young adult material, nor are we interested in books out of the mainstream, such as feminist or gay, for example." Recently published *Jeff White, Young Woodsman*, by Lew Dietz (mystery/adventure); *Jeff White, Young Trapper*, by L. Dietz (mystery/adventure); and *How to Talk Yankee*, by Gerald Lewis (humor).
How to Contact: Query or submit complete ms or outline/synopsis and sample chapters (3-4) with SASE. Simultaneous and photocopied submissions OK. Reports in 2 weeks on queries, 1 month on ms.
Terms: Pays 5-10% in royalties; by outright purchase $100-$1,000; offers $500 advance. Free book catalog.
Comments: "Know your market before mailing submissions. Those titles not appropriate to our line are rejected automatically. If a writer wants to be successful, he should know the product line of the firm he is submitting to and work within that framework. A little research beforehand will pay dividends in time and money saved."

TIARA BOOKS, Division of Nordon Publications, Inc., 2 Park Ave., New York NY 10016. Senior Editor: Jane Thornton. Editor-in-Chief: Milburn D. Smith. Publishes paperback originals and reprints. Number of titles: averages 48/year.
Needs: Historical, gothic, romance and women's. Any woman-oriented fiction. No male-oriented fiction.
How to Contact: Query or submit complete ms or submit outline/synopsis and sample chapter or submit through agent with SASE. Simultaneous and photocopied submissions OK. Reports in 1 month on queries, 6 weeks on mss.
Terms: Pays 4-8% in royalties; offers $1,000-$1,500 advance.
Comments: "There's an upsurge in women's fiction of all kinds in publishing today."

TICKNOR & FIELDS, Affiliate of Houghton-Mifflin, 52 Vanderbilt Ave., New York NY

10017. Editor: Joan Kahn. Estab. 1979. Publishes hardcover originals. "Plans for fiction titles are undetermined as yet as we are a young publishing house."
Needs: Open to all categories but only to "the best there is. We are very fussy." Special interest in suspense. Recently published *Floater*, by Calvin Trillin (humor); and *The Gossamer Fly*, by Meira Chand (suspense novel).
How to Contact: Submit complete ms. No simultaneous submissions (unless very special); photocopied submissions OK. Reports in 7 weeks on ms.
Terms: Pays standard amount of royalties. Offers advance depending on the book. Free book catalog with SASE and 1st class stamps.
Comments: "Read *your own book* before sending ms to us. It's incredible the number of poorly constructed mss we see. Competition is rough, but there are more opportunities with paperback originals now. Things are looking better in publishing."

TIMELY BOOKS, Box 267, New Milford CT 06776. Editor-in-Chief: Yvonne MacManus. Estab. 1978. Publishes 5½x8½ trade paperback reprints. Number of titles: 1 in 1979, 1 in 1980; 2 planned for 1981. No original mss to date, but interested.
Needs: Feminist and gay/lesbian only, at this time. Recently published *By Sanction of the Victim*, by Patte Wheat (child abuse).
How to Contact: Query with SASE. No simultaneous submissions; photocopied submissions OK. Reports in 6 weeks or less on queries.
Terms: Pays 6-10% in royalties; offers varied advance.
Comments: "Dissect bestsellers, scene by scene, to see what makes them 'work.' Read. Sloppy mss and cute letters are a total turnoff. We wish to publish quality, professional mss of interest to feminists and the gay community—fiction or nonfiction. No erotica."

TIMES BOOKS, 3 Park Ave., New York NY 10016. (212)725-2050. Vice President and Editor-in-Chief: Edward Chase. Adminstrative Editor: Hugh Howard. Senior Editor: Roger Jellinek. Publishes hardcover and paperback originals. Total number of titles: 95 in 1979; 100 in 1980; 120 planned for 1981.
Needs: Contemporary, literary, spy, historical, war, women's, humor/satire and translations. Recently published *The Clinic*, by Anthony Pietropinto (satire); *Compromising Positions*, by Susan Issacs; and *Without Fear or Favor*, by H.E. Salisbury.
How to Contact: Send complete ms with SASE. Simultaneous and photocopied submissions OK. Reports in 2-3 weeks on mss.
Terms: Pays in royalties; offers average advance. Free book catalog.

TOWER PUBLICATIONS, INC., 2 Park Ave., New York NY 10016. Senior Editor: Jane Thornton. Editor-in-Chief: Milburn D. Smith. Publishes paperback originals and reprints. Number of titles: 120 in 1979, 168 in 1980; 168 planned for 1981.
Needs: Contemporary, adventure, mystery, spy, historical, western, war, gothic, romance, women's, psychic/supernatural, science fiction, fantasy and horror. Recently published *A Star Rising*, by Jess Carr (historical); *Choices*, by Corinne Gerson (women's); and *The Phantom Lady*, by Carter Brown (mystery).
How to Contact: Query or submit complete ms or outline/synopsis and sample chapters (3) with SASE. Simultaneous and photocopied submissions OK. Reports in 1 month on queries, 6 weeks on mss.
Terms: Pays 4-8% in royalties; offers $1,500 advance. Free book catalog with SASE.
Comments: "We've noticed an upsurge of romance, contemporary women's novels, westerns. Extensive research does not make a novel. Personal experiences should be used as a springboard for plot and character development, not as their sole basis. Learn how to criticize your own work and when to seek objective advice. Literary devices should be used when appropriate and not just for the sake of seeming more 'literate.' "

TREACLE PRESS, Box 638, New Paltz NY 12561. Imprint includes Documentext. Editor:

Bruce McPherson. Estab. 1973. Publishes hardcover and paperback originals. Number of titles: 7 in 1979, 4 in 1980; 5 planned for 1981.

Needs: Literary, experimental, feminist and translations. Recently published *Conversion*, by Kelly Cherry; *Bearing Gifts*, by Jascha Kessler; and *Bastards: Footnotes to History*, by Ursule Molinaro.

How to Contact: Query with SASE. No simultaneous submissions; photocopied submissions OK. Reports in 2 weeks on queries, 1-10 weeks on mss.

Terms: Pays 6-12% in royalties; varied amount of free author's copies. Free book catalog with SASE.

Comments: "We are interested in serious fiction with particular emphasis on experimental works."

UNITY PRESS, 235 Hoover Rd., Santa Cruz CA 95065. Editor/Publisher: Craig Caughlan. Estab. 1971. Publishes hardcover and paperback originals.

Needs: Contemporary, literary and science fiction/fact.

How to Contact: Submit outline/synopsis and sample chapters (3). Simultaneous and photocopied submissions OK. Reports in 1 week on queries, 6 weeks on mss.

Terms: Pays in royalties; offers occasional advance. Free book catalog.

UNIVERSITY OF MISSOURI PRESS, 200 Lewis Hall, Columbia MO 65211. (314)882-7641. Managing Editor: Susan E. Kelpe. Publishes hardcover and paperback originals. Number of titles: averages 1-2/year.

Needs: Contemporary, literary, adventure, war, feminist, gay/lesbian, ethnic, fantasy, and humor/satire. No novels.

How to Contact: No simultaneous submissions; photocopied submissions OK. Submissions accepted February and March of odd-numbered years only.

Terms: Competition for publication only. Free book catalog.

Comments: "Publishes short fiction in Breakthrough Series, not to exceed 35,000 words."

URIZEN BOOKS, INC., 66 W. Broadway, New York NY 10017. (212)962-3413. Imprint includes Mole Editions. Editor/Publisher: Michael Roloff. Estab. 1975. Publishes hardcover and paperback originals. Number of titles: averages 5/year.

Needs: Contemporary, literary, experimental, gay/lesbian, and translations. Recently published *Detour*, by Michael Brodsky; *Blue of Noon*, by Georges Bataille (translation); and *Buried Child*, by Sam Shepard.

How to Contact: Query with SASE. Simultaneous and photocopied submissions OK. Reports in 1 week on queries, 1 month on mss.

Terms: Pays through standard royalty contracts; offers $2,000 in advance.

Comments: "First class fiction of high caliber writing."

VANGUARD PRESS, INC., 424 Madison Ave., New York NY 10017. (212)753-3906. Editor: Bernice Woll. Estab. 1926. Publishes hardcover originals. Number of titles: averages 15-20/year.

Needs: Contemporary, literary, faction, adventure, mystery, spy, war, humor/satire, juvenile and young adult. Recently published *The Butterfly World*, by Margaret Gibson (short stories); and *Unholy Loves*, by Joyce Carol Oates (novel).

How to Contact: Query or submit outline/synopsis and sample chapters (3) with SASE. Advise if simultaneous submissions; photocopied submissions OK. Reports in 2-4 weeks on queries, 8-12 weeks on mss.

Terms: Pays in royalties; offers advance, amount depending on book.

Comments: "We're always interested in new writers."

VESTA PUBLICATIONS, LTD., Box 1641, Cornwall, Ontario, Canada K0H 5V6 (613)932-2135. Editor: Stephen Gill. Estab. 1974. Publishes hardcover and paperback originals. Number of titles: 7 in 1979, 7 in 1980; 10 planned for 1981.

Needs: Literary, experimental, historical, war, gothic, romance, ethnic, religious, science fiction, juvenile, young adult and translations. Recently published *Immigrant*, by Stephen Gill; *Corey*, by Norma Linder; *The House on Dorchester Street*, by Ronald J. Corke.

How to Contact: Query with SASE. Simultaneous and photocopied submissions OK. Reports in 1 week on both queries and mss.

Terms: Pays 10-12% in royalties; no advance. Free book catalog.

Comments: "Today there is a more simple, straightforward style. Never give up and keep writing for every possible media."

VIKING PENGUIN, INC., 625 Madison Ave., New York NY 10022. Imprint includes Viking Junior Books, Studio Books. Estab. 1923. Number of titles: averages 40/year.

Needs: "All categories are open; quality fiction, in general." Recently published *Firestarter*, by Stephen King; *Burger's Daughter*, by Nadine Gordimer; and *Smash*, by Garson Kanin.

How to Contact: Submit complete ms through agent or through intermediary to specific editor. Simultaneous and photocopied submissions OK. Reports in 6 weeks on ms.

Terms: Amount and type of advance payment and royalty scale depend on the individual situation. Free book catalog.

WALKER AND COMPANY, 720 5th Ave., New York NY 10019. Imprint includes Walker Educational Book Co. (WEBCO). Editor-in-Chief: Richard K. Winslow. Adult Trade Editor: Ruth Cavin. Publishes hardcover originals and reprints. Number of titles: averages 20/year.

Needs: Mystery ('whodunits'), romance (Regency). Science fiction and horror hardcover juvenile and young adult only. Recently published *Mistress of Willowvale*, by Patricia Veryan (Regency romance); *Swan Song*, by Edmund Crispin (mystery); and *Murder, Murder, Little Star*, by Marion Babson (mystery).

How to Contact: Query or submit complete ms or outline synopis and sample chapters (2) with SASE or submit through agent. No simultaneous submissions; photocopied submissions OK. Reports in 1 month on queries, 6 weeks on mss.

Terms: Negotiable. Free book catalog with 6x9 SASE.

Comments: "In historical romances, gothics are out. In mysteries there's a return to the conventional whodunit, the English type of police procedural or 'country house' kind of murder mystery, as opposed to violent, overtly sexual, tough private eye stories."

FREDERICK WARNE AND CO., INC., 2 Park Ave., New York NY 10016. Editor: Meredith Charpentier. Parent company started in 1881 in England. Publishes hardcover originals. Number of titles: averages 15/year.

Needs: Juvenile and young adult: sports, animal, spy/adventure, historical and fantasy/science fiction. Recently published *The Last of Eden*, by Stephanie Tolan (young adult); *The Way to Windra*, by Patricia Baehr (fantasy); and *If You Say So, Claude*, by Joan Nixon/Lorinda Cauley (illustrated tall-tale).

How to Contact: Query with letter only or submit through agent. No simultaneous submissions. Reports in 1 week on queries, 10 weeks on ms.

Terms: Pays 5-10% in royalties; offers varied advance. Free book catalog.

WARNER BOOKS, 75 Rockefeller Plaza, New York NY 10019. Editor-in-Chief: Bernard W. Shir-Cliff. Estab. 1970. Publishes hardcover and paperback originals. Number of titles: averages 150/year.

Needs: "Buys mss on individual merit, not by category; wants to see all categories." Recently published *Hanto Yo: An American Saga*, by Ruth Beebe Hill (historical novel); *Paloverde*, by Jacqueline Briskin (panoramic novel); and *Dead And Buried*, by Chelsea Quinn Yarbro (horror).

How to Contact: Query with detailed letter or detailed outline, enough for editor to tell

quickly if book is in area desired; also include writing credentials. Simultaneous and photocopied submissions OK. Reports in 1 day to 5 weeks on queries.
Terms: Pays 6-10% in royalties; offers advance. Free book catalog with standard SASE.
Comments: "We were buying a lot of romance and historical but now are buying more horror. Trends change from year to year. Send good query letter."

WESTERN PUBLISHING COMPANY, INC., 1220 Mound Ave., Racine WI 53402. Imprints include Golden Books and Whitman Books. Senior Editor: William H. Larson. Estab. 1909. Publishes hardcover and paperback originals. Number of titles: averages 100/year.
Needs: Adventure, mystery, humor and juvenile: sports, animal, spy/adventure, fantasy/ science fiction and easy-to-read. Recently published *Gypsy and the Moonstone Stallion*, by Sharon Wagner (fiction); *The Giant Who Wanted Company*, by Lee Priestly; and *The Clock Book*, by Donna Kelly.
How to Contact: Query (longer works) or submit complete ms or outline/synopsis and sample chapters (2-3) with SASE or submit through agent. Simultaneous and photocopied submissions OK. Reports in 6-8 weeks on mss.
Terms: Pays by outright purchase (amount varies with format); offers advance for assignment novels only.

WESTMINSTER PRESS, 925 Chestnut St., Philadelphia PA 19107. (215)928-2723. Children's Book Editor: Barbara S. Bates. Publishes hardcover originals. Number of titles: 19 in 1980; 15 planned for 1981.
Needs: Juvenile: mystery, humor, adventure, family, science fiction, suspense for ages 8-12. No picture books or stories in rhyme. Recently published *Never Mind Murder*, by T. Wosmek (mystery); *Midnight Wheels*, by R. Hallman (suspense); and *Trouble with Leslie*, by Ellen Matthews (humor).
How to Contact: Submit outline/synopsis and sample chapters. No simultaneous submissions of complete mss; photocopied submissions OK. Reports in 3 months or less on mss.
Terms: Pays royalties but amount depends on author's experience and credentials and the number of illustrations needed; offers advance.

ALBERT WHITMAN & CO., 560 W. Lake St., Chicago IL 60606. Editor: Kathleen Tucker. Publishes hardcover originals. Number of titles: averages 17-18/year.
Needs: Juvenile only. "We like to see true-to-life, humorous and upbeat mysteries for all ages. We also want simple picture book mss about children coping with realistic situations. No young adult novels or alphabet books." Recently published *Nick Joins In*, by Joe Lasker (picture book); *Gloomy Louie*, by Phyllis Green (novel); and *Come Home, Wilma*, by Mitchell Sharmat (picture book).
How to Contact: Submit complete ms of picture book or outline/synopsis and sample chapters of novel with SASE. No simultaneous submissions; photocopied submissions OK. Reports in 2 months.
Terms: Pays varied royalties and by outright purchase; also offers advance. Free book catalog.

WILLIAM-FREDERICK PRESS, 308 E. 79th St., New York NY 10021. (212)628-1995. Imprint includes Pamphlet Distributing Co. Editorial Director: Alvin Levin. Editor: T. Reed. Estab. 1940. Publishes hardcover and paperback originals and reprints. Number of titles: 22 in 1979, 40 in 1980; 40 planned for 1981.
Needs: All categories accepted; no restrictions.
How to Contact: Query or submit complete ms. Simultaneous and photocopied submissions OK. Reports in 2 weeks on queries and ms. Request free literature.
Terms: Pays 70% in royalties; free author's copies and subsidy publication; no advance.

YEARLING, 1 Dag Hammerskjold Plaza, New York NY 10017. See Dell Publishing Co., Inc.

ZEBRA BOOKS, 21 E. 40th St., New York NY 10016. (212)889-2299. Editor/Publisher: Roberta Grossman. Fiction Editor: Leslie Gelbman. Estab. 1975. Publishes hardcover reprints and paperback originals. Number of titles: 120 in 1979, 130 in 1980; 150 planned for 1981.

Needs: Contemporary, adventure, historical, western, war, gothic, romance, confession, women's, erotica, psychic/supernatural, and horror. "Romantic suspense, no! Gothic, yes!." Recently published *Caly*, by Sharon M. Combes (horror); *Whitewater Dynasty #1: Hudson*, by Helen Lee Poole (historical); *Wild Violets*, by Ruth Baker Field (horror); and *Charge Nurse*, by Patricia Rae Walls.

How to Contact: Query or submit complete ms or outline/synopsis and sample chapters with SASE. Simultaneous and photocopied submissions OK. Reports in 3 months on queries and mss.

Terms: Pays 4-8% in royalties; offers $500 and up. Free book catalog with #10 SASE.

Advice: "Put aside your literary ideals, be commercial. Work fast and on assignment. Keep your cover letter simple and to the point. Too many times, 'cutesy' letters about category or content turn us off some fine mss."

Comments: "More involved family and historical sagas. But please do research. We buy many unsolicited mss, but we're slow readers. Have patience."

Contests and awards

Fiction contests offer opportunities for personal and financial reward as well as beneficial exposure and publicity. Here is a list of contests and awards sponsored by a wide variety of magazines, publishers and organizations that firmly believe in attracting, promoting and recognizing distinguished achievement in quality fiction.

These contests—regional, national and international—are for published and unpublished short stories and novels of all lengths and subjects. The rewards range from magazine publication and a small fee or plaque to a book contract plus a sizable sum of money.

Some contests do not invite entries from individual writers, but are included because of their national or literary merit. If you feel that your work will meet the requirements of a special competition, we suggest that you ask your publisher or agent to enter your material.

Before submitting a manuscript for consideration, be sure to study the listing and its specifications for eligibility; age, nationality, geographical location and fiction subject matter are often important criteria. Unless the contest states that the entry will not be returned, a SASE or an international reply coupon is necessary for all correspondence, including the request for an entry blank.

JANE ADDAMS CHILDREN'S BOOK AWARD, Jane Addams Peace Association and The Women's International League for Peace & Freedom, 1213 Race St., Philadelphia PA 19107. Contact: Annette C. Blank, 5477 Cedonia Ave., Baltimore MD 21206. Estab. 1953. Annual award.
Purpose: The award is made for a book that promotes the cause of peace, social justice, and world community.
Requirements: Published submissions. Announcement of the award is made Sept. 6 for a book published the previous year. Books submitted may be translated or published in English in other countries.
Award: A hand illuminated scroll; seals are placed on the book jacket by the publisher.

Honor scrolls are awarded to books that merit this recognition.
Information: Choices are made by a national committee of people concerned with children's books and their social values.

AGA KHAN PRIZE, *Paris Review*, 541 E 72nd St., New York NY 10021. Contact: George Plimpton, editor. Annual award.
Purpose: To promote younger and lesser known writers.
Requirements: Unpublished submissions. June 1 is deadline entry.
Award: $500.
Information: Contest/award rules and entry forms available with SASE. "We are looking for entries with quality."

ALBERTA CULTURE AND GENERAL PUBLISHING COMPANY LIMITED: The Search-for-a-New-Alberta-Novelist Competition, Alberta Culture, 12 Floor, CN Tower, Edmonton, Alberta, Canada T5J 0K5. Contact: John Patrick Gillese, director. Estab. 1972. Biannual award.
Purpose: To encourage the development of fiction writers living in the province of Alberta.
Requirements: The competition is open to any writer who has never before had a novel published and who is a resident of the province of Alberta. Deadline entry, Dec. 31. No SASE is necessary. Brochures and further information available.
Award: $4000. Of this, $2500 is an outright award given by Alberta Culture and $1500 is an advance against royalties given by General Publishing Co. Limited.
Information: Length may range from 60,000-100,000 words. Novels in adult category only of highest literary quality.

THE ALBERTA WRITING-FOR-YOUNG-PEOPLE COMPETITION, Alberta Culture in cooperation with Clarke Irwin Company Ltd., 12 Floor, CN Tower, Edmonton, Alberta, Canada T5J 0K5. Contact: John Patrick Gillese, director. Estab. 1980. Biannual award.
Purpose: The competition is designed to direct Alberta's writers to the challenging world of writing for juveniles.
Requirements: Unpublished submissions. Deadline entry: Dec. 31. The competition brochure and/or further information will be sent, upon request.
Award: There is a $2500 prize; an outright award of $1500 from Alberta Culture and a $1000 advance against royalties from Clarke Irwin.
Information: "We are looking for the best publishable manuscript—fiction or nonfiction—written for young readers. There are 2 categories: book mss for young adults (up to age 16) averaging 40,000 words in length; and book mss suitable for younger readers (8-12 years) running between 12,000 and 20,000 words.

AMERICAN ACADEMY AND INSTITUTE OF ARTS AND LETTERS LITERARY AWARDS, 633 W. 155th St., New York NY 10032. Contact: Carol Brennan or Joanna O'Neill. Annual award.
Purpose: To honor authors for excellence in literature and encourage them in their creative work.
Requirements: Previously published submissions. Selection is by the Academy.
Award: Prizes vary. $4,000 in 1980 to winners (3 for fiction). Special awards include: 1) Richard Hinda Rosenthal Foundation Award: $3,000 for "an American work of literary fiction published during the preceding 12 months;" 2) Sue Kaufman Prize for First Fiction: $1,000 and 3) William Dean Howells Medal for Fiction (every 5 years).

THE AMERICAN BOOK AWARD (ABA), Association of American Publishers, 1 Park Ave., New York NY 10016. Annual award.
Purpose: To honor distinguished authors in fiction; children's books, first novel, general fiction, mystery, western, and science fiction.
Requirements: Previously published submissions. Deadline entry: August 15.

Award: $1,000 for each category.
Information: Selections are nominated by publishers only.

ARIZONA QUARTERLY BEST SHORT STORY, University of Arizona, Tuscon AZ 85721. Contact: Albert Gegenheimer, editor. Annual award.
Purpose: To recognize the best short story of the year as chosen by the editorial board.
Award: Bound copy of the year's volume and appropriate certificate plus award money which may vary from year to year.

ARTISTS FOUNDATION, ARTISTS FELLOWSHIPS, Artists Foundation, Inc., 100 Boylston St., Boston MA 02116. Contact: Susan R. Channing, director. Estab. 1975. Annual award.
Purpose: To encourage artists to live and work in Massachusetts.
Requirements: All manuscripts are to be typed so there will be no indication of whether work has been previously published or not. For Massachusetts residents only, over 18, and not enrolled as students. All work to be completed within the last five years; does not need to be published. Deadline entry: March 15. Contest/award rules and entry form available with SASE.
Award: $3,500.
Information: Looking for artistic excellence. Work is judged anonymously by a panel of writers who are from out of state.

ASF/PEN TRANSLATION PRIZE, American-Scandinavian Foundation, 127 E. 73rd St., New York NY 10021. Contact: Kathleen Madden. Estab. 1980. Annual award.
Purpose: To encourage the translation and publication of the best of contemporary Scandinavian fiction and to make it available to a wider American audience.
Requirements: Previously published in the original Scandinavian language. Original authors should have been born within the past 100 years. Deadline entry: February 15. Contest/award rules and entry forms available with SASE.
Award: $500 and publication.
Information: Looking for high quality both as fiction and as translation.

THE ATHENAEUM LITERARY AWARD, The Athenaeum of Philadelphia, 219 S. 6th St., Philadelphia PA 19106. Contact: Literary Award Committee. Estab. 1950. Annual award.
Purpose: To recognize and encourage outstanding literary achievement in Philadelphia and its vicinity.
Requirements: Previously published submissions from the preceding year. Deadline entry: December. Nominations shall be made in writing to the Literary Award Committee by the author, the publisher, or a member of the Athenaeum accompanied by a copy of the book.
Award: A bronze medal bearing the name of the award, the seal of the Athenaeum, the title of the book, the name of the author, and the year.
Information: Looking for significance and importance to the general public as well as literary excellence. The Athenaeum Literary Award is granted for a work of general literature, not exclusively for fiction. Juvenile fiction is not included.

ATLANTIC FIRSTS, *Atlantic Monthly*, 8 Arlington St., Boston MA 02146. Contact: Fiction Editor. Estab. 1940 (approximately).
Purpose: To encourage submission of original fiction to *The Atlantic*, and honor unusual accomplishments.
Requirements: Unpublished submission. No deadline entry date. Awards given periodically at the discretion of the editor. Contest/award rules and entry forms available with SASE.
Award: $1,000 first prize; $750 second prize.
Information: Judged on strong story line, characterization, sophisticated use of language and distinctiveness.

AUTHOR'S AWARDS, Periodical Distributors of Canada, 322 King St. W., Toronto, Ontario, Canada M5V 1J2. Contact: Sherill Reid, awards coordinator. Estab. 1977. Annual award.
Purpose: The Author's Awards are offered in recognition of outstanding Canadian writing and design in English-language mass market magazines and paperback books.
Requirements: Previously published submissions. In the case of books, the hardcover edition may have been printed in the previous year, while all paperback books and magazine submissions must have been printed between July 1 of the previous year and June 30 of the award year. Deadline entry: July 15. Contest/award rules and entry forms available with SASE.
Award: Paperback book: 1st prize $600; 2nd prize $300. Magazine (for outstanding short stories or other works of fiction): 1st prize $400; 2nd prize $200.
Information: Quality of writing is the basic criterion.

AWP AWARD SERIES IN SHORT FICTION, The Associated Writing Programs, c/o Old Dominion University, Norfolk VA 23508. Contact: Larry Moffi, assistant director of publicity and distribution. Estab. 1977. Annual award.
Purpose: "The AWP Award Series were established in cooperation with several university presses in order to make quality short fiction (and poetry—we sponsor an Award Series in poetry, as well) available to a wide audience."
Requirements: Unpublished submissions. Deadline entry: December 31. Contest/award rules and entry forms available with SASE.
Award: The winning manuscript in short fiction is published by the University of Missouri Press. Winning author invited to read honored selection. $500 honorarium plus travel support given.
Information: No bias other than quality. $3 submission fee.

AWP AWARD SERIES IN THE NOVEL, The Associated Writing Programs, c/o Old Dominion University, Norfolk VA 23508. Contact: Larry Moffi, assistant director of publicity and distribution. Estab. 1977. Annual award.
Purpose: The AWP Award Series were established in cooperation with several university presses in order to publish and make fine fiction available to a wide audience.
Requirements: Unpublished submissions in book form. Deadline entry: December 31. Contest/award rules and entry forms available with SASE.
Award: "The winning novel ms is published by the State University of New York Press. The winning author is invited to read at the AWP Annual Meeting, a reading that carries a $500 honorarium plus travel support. In addition, AWP tries to place mss of finalists (from 3-8 in each genre) with participating presses."
Information: Looking for quality. $5 submission fee with ms.

EMILY CLARK BALCH AWARDS, *The Virginia Quarterly Review*, 1 West Range, Charlottesville VA 22903. Contact: Staige D. Blackford, editor. Estab. 1957. Annual award.
Purpose: To recognize distinguished short fiction by American writers.
Requirements: Previously published submissions in *The Virginia Quarterly Review* during the calendar year. No unsolicited stories considered. Submit a story to *VQR* for consideration.
Award: $500.
Information: Looking for originality.

LEBARON R. BARKER FICTION AWARD, Doubleday & Company, Inc., 245 Park Ave., New York NY 10017. Contact: Sally Arteseros, senior editor. Estab. 1973. Awarded at the discretion of the judges.
Purpose: To acknowledge and reward growth and development of fiction writers. In memory of LeBaron R. Barker, distinguished Doubleday editor.

Award: $2,500 prize.
Information: This award is given only to a novel published by Doubleday & Company. Authors cannot make submissions for the award. The award is given to a novel which represents a "giant step forward" for the author, a "distinct advance in the author's craftsmanship and approach to the art of fiction."

BENNETT AWARD, *The Hudson Review,* 65 E. 55th St., New York NY 10022. Annual award.
Purpose: "To recognize outstanding accomplishments in a novelist or man of letters." V.S. Naipaul was the 1980 recipient.
Requirements: Previously published submissions. Individual submissions are not invited.
Award: $12,500.

JOHN W CAMPBELL AWARD, World Science Fiction Society, c/o Howard DeVore, 4705 Weddel St., Dearborn Heights MI 48125.
Purpose: To award the best new writer in science fiction.
Requirements: Previously published submissions.
Award: Award is associated with the Hugo Science Fiction Achievement Awards (novel, novelette, short story, magazine, new author).

CANADA COUNCIL CHILDREN'S LITERATURE PRIZES, Canada Council, 255 Albert St., Ottawa, Ontario, Canada K1P 5V8. Contact: Jocelyn Harvey, senior writer. Estab. 1975. Annual award.
Purpose: "To honor the Canadian writers or illustrators of books for young people published during the preceding year."
Requirements: Published submissions only during preceding year. "All books for children published during the preceding year are considered by two juries (one for English-language works, one for French-language works). No entry forms are required."
Award: $5,000 each.
Information: Judged on excellence.

CANADIAN FICTION MAGAZINE CONTRIBUTOR'S PRIZE, *Canadian Fiction Magazine,* Box 946, Station F, Toronto, Canada M4Y 2N9. Contact: Geoffrey Hancock, editor-in-chief. Estab. 1975. Annual award.
Purpose: To celebrate the best story published in either French or English during the preceding year.
Requirements: Unpublished submissions only. All manuscripts published in *CFM* are eligible. Deadline: August 15.
Award: $250, public announcement, photograph. Prize winners are often republished in best Canadian or American magazines.
Information: "Looking for contemporary creative writing of the highest possible literary standards. Previous winners include Leon Rooke, Ann Copeland, John Metcalf, W.P. Kinsella, Mavis Gallant, and David Sharpe."

CHATELAINE FICTION COMPETITION, *Chatelaine Magazine,* 481 University Ave., Toronto, Ontario, Canada M5W 1A7. Contact: Barbara West, fiction editor.
Purpose: To award Canadian authors in short fiction.
Requirements: Canadian writers only may enter contest. Check magazine or write for rules. SASE. Deadline: April 30.
Award: 1st prize: $500 plus $1,000 for publication in *Chatelaine*; 2nd prize: $250 plus $800 if story is published; 3rd prize: $100 plus $800 if story is published.
Information: "Story should entertain or enlighten the reader while illuminating some aspect of being a woman in Canada today."

CHILD STUDY CHILDREN'S BOOK AWARD, Child Study Children's Book Award, Committee at Bank St. College, 610 W. 112th St., New York NY 10025. Contact: Josette Frank, executive editor. Estab. 1943. Annual award.
Purpose: "To honor a book for children or young people which deals realistically with problems in their world. It may concern universal, personal or emotional problems."
Requirements: Only books sent by publishers for review are considered. No personal submissions. Books must be published within current calendar year.
Award: Certificate.

THE CHRISTOPHER AWARD, The Christophers, 12 E. 48th St., New York NY 10017. Contact: Ms. Peggy Flanagan, awards coordinator. Estab. 1949. Annual award.
Purpose: "To encourage creative people to continue to produce works which 'affirm the highest values of the human spirit' in adult and children's books."
Requirements: Published submissions only.
Information: Examples of books awarded: *All Together Now*, by Sue Ellen Bridgers (ages 12 and up); *Frederick's Alligator*, by Esther Allen Peterson (ages 5-8); *What Happened in Hamelin*, by Gloria Skurzynski (ages 9-12).

CLEVELAND MAGAZINE FICTION CONTEST, *Cleveland Magazine*, 1621 Euclid Ave., Cleveland OH 44122. Contact: Michael D. Roberts, editor. Estab. 1977. Annual award.
Requirements: Unpublished submissions only. Deadline entry: Sept. 20.
Information: "Story must be set in Greater Cleveland and if possible contain a little of the true flavor of the area. The short story is not to exceed 10,000 words."

COOKE COUNTY COLLEGE SHORT STORY CONTEST (NON-STUDENT), Cooke County College, Box 815, Gainesville TX 76240. Contact: Joseph Colin Murphey, director of creative writing. Estab. 1970. Annual award.
Purpose: "To promote interest in creative writing and to become acquainted with talented writers in the area or elsewhere."
Requirements: Unpublished submissions only. Deadline entry: "about the end of March. Contest Awards Day is held around April 25th." Entry form or rules for SASE.
Award: Certificate of award. First prize, $30; second, $20; third, $10 plus publication in the college literary magazine of the winners.
Information: Looking for "short stories that have a plot, well-developed characters and themes that are subtle but universal, meaningful and profound."

CROSSCURRENTS FIRST ANNUAL FICTION AWARDS, *Crosscurrents*, 2200 Glastonbury Rd., Westlake Village CA 91361. Contact: Linda Brown Michelson, editor. Estab. 1981. Annual Award.
Purpose: "To encourage excellence."
Requirements: Unpublished submissions only. Deadline entry: Sept. 30. Entry form or rules for SASE. Contest rules will be available after May 15, 1981.
Information: Looking for "craftsmanship and substance."

THE FAULKNER AWARD, P.E.N. South, Box 3787, Charlottesville VA 22903. Contact: John Morrone, c/o P.E.N. American Center, 47 5th Ave., New York NY 10003. Estab. 1980. Annual award.
Purpose: "To award the most distinguished work of fiction published by an American writer. First award presented April 18, 1981."
Requirements: Published submissions only. Publishers submit eligible titles published the preceding year. No juvenile. Authors must be American citizens or permanent residents of the US.
Award: $2,000.
Information: This new annual award which "reflects the truly national character of our literary talent" is judged by a panel of writers' peers.

DOROTHY CANFIELD FISHER AWARD, Vermont Congress of Parents and Teachers and Vermont Department of Libraries, 138 Main St., Montpelier VT 05602. Contact: Carol Chatfield, Chairperson. Estab. 1957. Annual award.
Purpose: "To encourage Vermont school children to read more and better books, to discriminate in choosing worthwhile books to read, and to honor the memory of one of Vermont's most distinguished and beloved literary figures."
Requirements: "Publishers are sent the committee review copies of books to consider. Only books of the current publishing year can be considered for next year's award. Master list of titles is drawn up in late February or March each year. Children vote each year in April, and the award is given before the school year ends in early June."
Award: Illuminated scroll.
Information: Submissions must be "written by living American authors, be suitable for children in grades 4-8, and have literary merit. Can be nonfiction also."

FLARE, Maclean-Hunter Ltd., 481 University Ave., Toronto, Canada M5W 1A7. Contact: Barbara West, fiction editor.
Purpose: To award Canadian authors in short fiction.
Information: For Canadian writers only. Check the magazine for entry information.

FLORIDA ARTS GAZETTE FICTION CONTEST, *Florida Arts Gazette*, Box 397, Himmarshee Village, Fort Lauderdale FL 33302. Contact: Kirt M. Dressler, editor. Estab. 1980. Annual award.
Purpose: "To recognize and encourage Florida literary artists to pursue their craft; to give particular attention to the literary arts (poetry and fiction) which are usually the most under-recognized and under-funded of all the arts; to assist Florida's Department of State in its goal of making 'Florida—State of the Arts.' "
Requirements: Unpublished submissions only. Deadline entry: April 25. Entry form or rules for SASE. "All writers wishing to enter this contest *must* send SASE for rules."
Award: First prize, $50 plus publication; second prize, $25; third prize, $10; 10 honorable mention certificates.
Information: Looking "mainly for good writing and original ideas. We do look more favorably on those entries that meet the above criteria and are also about some aspect of the arts (e.g., dance, literature, music, theater, visual arts, etc.) although this is not a requirement. The *Florida Arts Gazette* is also planning an annual nationwide fiction contest. Writers should send SASE."

MILES FRANKLIN, Permanent Trustee Coy Ltd., 23-25 O'Connell St., Sydney, New South Wales, Australia. Contact: Marie Carre, assistant trust officer. Estab. 1957. Annual award.
Purpose: "Miles Franklin Award is set up in terms of the will of the late Miles Franklin (administered by Permanent Trustee Coy Ltd.) for the entry having the highest literary merit for the improvement and advancement of Australian literature. It must necessarily present Australian life in any of its phases."
Requirements: Published submissions only. Award announced as soon as possible after the end of February in following year.
Award: $3,000 Australian $.
Information: Send for rule sheet.

FRIENDS OF AMERICAN WRITERS (CHICAGO) JUVENILE BOOK AWARD, 412 N. Prospect, Park Ridge IL 60068. Contact: Mary Lou Loughlin, Juvenile Book Award chairman. Estab. 1928. Annual award.
Purpose: "To encourage and promote high standards and ideals among Midwest authors. Author must be from one of the 16 Midwest states or the locale of the book must be of that region."
Requirements: "Entrant may have no more than 6 previously published books. Books must

be published the previous year. Deadline entry: January 1. Entry form or rules for SASE.
Award: $150-$400.
Information: Looking for "excellent writing for children through young adults. Awards are in Chicago each year in April."

FRIENDS OF AMERICAN WRITERS AWARD, Friends of American Writers, 840 William, River Forest IL 60305. Contact: Mrs. N.A. Parker, chairman of award committee. Estab. 1922. Annual award.
Purpose: "To encourage good writing standards among comparatively new authors with Midwest backgrounds or by those who write about that locale."
Requirements: For 1981 published submissions only during the year 1980. "A writer should have his publisher send us two complimentary review copies as soon after publication as possible and by December 1. We will furnish information concerning requirements."
Award: First award $1,000; 2 or more lesser awards up to $300.
Information: Looking for "writing that shows promise by an author with fewer than 6 books published."

CARLOS FUENTES FICTION AWARD, *Columbia: A Magazine of Poetry & Prose*, 404 Dodge, Columbia University, New York NY 10027. Contact: John Soat, fiction editor. Estab. 1978. Annual award.
Purpose: "To recognize and promote talented writing."
Requirements: Unpublished submissions only. Deadline entry: February. Entry form or rules for SASE.
Award: $100.
Information: Looking for "originality, talent, nothing more than ability to move the reader."

GOLDEN KITE, Society of Children's Book Writers, Box 296, Los Angeles CA 90066. Contact: Sue Alexander, chairperson. Estab. 1973. Annual award.
Purpose: "To recognize an outstanding work of fiction for children written by a member of the Society of Children's Book Writers and published in the award year."
Requirements: Published submissions during January-December of previous year. Deadline entry: December 31. Entry form or rules for SASE.
Award: Statuette and plaque.
Information: Looking for quality material for children. Individual "must be a member of the SCBW to submit ms."

GOVERNOR GENERAL LITERARY AWARDS, Canada Council, 255 Albert St., Ottawa, Ontario, Canada K1P 5V8. Contact: Jocelyn Harvey, senior writer. Estab. 1937. Annual award.
Purpose: "To honor the Canadian writers of 3 English-language and 3 French-language works published during the preceding year. Awards are given in the fields of fiction, nonfiction, and poetry or drama."
Requirements: Published submissions. No entry forms are required.
Award: $5,000 each category.
Information: "All books in the 3 fields are considered by one of 6 juries (3 for French language works, 3 for English language)." Looking for excellence.

GREAT LAKES COLLEGES ASSOCIATION NEW WRITERS AWARDS, Great Lakes Colleges Association, Wabash College, Crawfordsville IN 47933. Contact: Donald W. Baker, director. Estab. 1969. Annual award.
Purpose: "To recognize good young writers, promote and encourage interest in good literature."
Requirements: Submissions previously published "during the year preceding each year's

February 28 deadline for entry, or the following spring." Entry form or rules for SASE.
Award: "Invited tour of up to twelve Great Lakes Colleges (usually 7 or 8) with honoraria and expenses paid."
Information: Looking for "quality. Entries in fiction (there is also a poetry section) must be novels or volumes of short stories already published, and must be submitted (four copies) *by publishers only*—but this may include privately published books."

GULFSHORE LIFE'S ANNUAL FICTION CONTEST, *Gulfshore Life Magazine*, 3620 Tamiami Trail N., Naples FL 33940. Contact: Merri Pate, editor. Estab. 1979. Annual award.
Purpose: "To encourage writers and to offer our readers outstanding fiction."
Requirements: Unpublished submissions only. Deadline entry: March 1. Entry form or rules for SASE.
Award: lst prize: $100 plus publication; 2nd prize: $75; 3rd prize: $50.
Information: "Story must have a Florida setting. No more than one entry per person. Submissions must not exceed 3,500 words. Open to all writers."

HARIAN CREATIVE FICTION AWARDS, Harian Creative Press & Adirondack-Metroland Writers & Educators Contest, Box 189, Ballston Spa, NY 12020. Contact: Dr. Harry Barba, publisher and executive director. Contest offered "when warranted by quality of submissions."
Purpose: "To encourage socially functional writing, socially functional literature, writing that communicates a 'moral' texture without being preachy; writing strong in characterization and plot and written in a functionally suitable style, all of which leaves the reader a little higher up as a connected human being, concerned, compassionate and resolution-oriented."
Information: Write for entry rules.

ERNEST HEMINGWAY FOUNDATION AWARD, PEN American Center, 47 5th Ave., New York NY 10003. Contact: John Morrone, coordinator of programs. Estab. 1976. Annual award.
Purpose: "To give beginning writers recognition and encouragement and to stimulate interest in first novels among publishers and readers."
Requirements: Submissions previously published during calendar year under consideration. Deadline entry: December 31. Entry form or rules for SASE.
Award: $6,000.
Information: "The Ernest Hemingway Foundation Award is given to the author of the best first-published booklength work of fiction published by an established publishing house in the US each calendar year, by an American writer."

HIGHLIGHTS FOR CHILDREN, 803 Church St., Honesdale PA 18431. Contact: Constance McAllister, associate editor.
Purpose: "To recognize quality short fiction in suspense, adventure, mystery category."
Requirements: Unpublished submissions only.
Award: $750.
Information: Ms to be approximately 1,000 words.

THEODORE HOEPTNER AWARD, *Southern Humanities Review*, 9092 Haley Center, Auburn AL 36830. Contact: David K. Jeffrey or Barbara A. Mowat, co-editors. Estab. 1970. Annual award.
Purpose: "To reward the author of the best essay or short story published in the *SHR* each year."
Requirements: Unpublished submissions only.
Award: $100.

THE 'HUGO' AWARD (Science Fiction Achievement Award), The World Science Fic-

tion Convention, c/o Howard DeVore, 4705 Weddel St., Dearborn Heights MI 48125. Temporary; address changes each year.
Purpose: "To recognize the best writing in various categories related to science fiction."
Requirements: The award is voted on by the members of the World Science Fiction Convention from previously published material of professional publications.
Award: Metal spaceship 15 inches high. "Winning the award almost always results in reprints of the original material and increased payment. Winning a 'Hugo' in the novel category frequently results in additional payment of $10,000-$20,000 from future publishers."
Information: "Some titles in the novel category have remained in print almost continously for some 20 years and are frequently reprinted in foreign editions."

INKY TRAILS FICTION OF THE YEAR AWARD, Inky Trails Publications, Box 345, Middleton ID 83644. Contact: Pearl L. Kirk, editor/publisher. Annual award.
Purpose: "To help a new writer get started to reach the better publications."
Requirements: Unpublished submissions only. "If used for magazine we will use those published. If ms is published we give credit for lst printing." Deadline entry: February 15. Entry form or rules for SASE. $3 entry fee.
Award: $15 and $10. "If there are enough entries we may raise award money."
Information: "Any subject except science fiction, horror and sexual natures. Keep it clean. For under 14 years: romance, war, love, history, personal, western, mystery, adventure, humor, juvenile, young adult, religion."

IOWA SCHOOL OF LETTERS AWARD FOR SHORT FICTION, Iowa School of Letters/ University of Iowa Press, Graphic Services Building, Iowa City, IA 52242. Contact: Shirley Boyce, sales and promotion manager. Estab. 1969. Annual award.
Purpose: "To encourage writers in short fiction (a literary genre largely neglected by commercial publishers)."
Requirements: Deadline entry: September 30. Entries must be submitted between August 1 and September 30. Entry form or rules for SASE.
Award: "$1,000 plus publication of the winning collection the following fall, and a visit to the University of Iowa Campus to be honored at a reception and generally lionized about campus."
Information: Looking for "sophistication of narrative technique, fidelity to the art of story-telling. Mss are initially read by Iowa Writers Workshop instructors and staff who look for splendor, pathos, the power to haunt, disturb, etc."

IRISH AMERICAN CULTURAL INSTITUTE FICTION AWARD, Irish American Cultural Institute, 683 Osceola Ave., St. Paul MN 55105. Contact: Dr. Erin McKiernan, president. Estab. 1980. Biannual award.
Purpose: "To stimulate writing about Irish-American life. The first award will be made in 1982."
Requirements: Previously published material from 1980 to June 30, 1982. Deadline entry: June 30 each biennium. "The book will be chosen from published books dealing with Irish-Americans in the late 18th century colonies or states. It will be the responsibility of publishers to submit their nominations (in the form of published books—proof copy acceptable if the work has not yet 'hit the streets')."
Award: $5,000 outright.
Information: "The Irish American Cultural Institute is a public foundation that already makes annual literary awards in Ireland. This new fiction award will be the first made in the US specifically for an Irish-related novel. Looking for excellence of writing and insightful understanding of the Irish-American life of the period."

JOSEPH HENRY JACKSON AWARD, The San Francisco Foundation, 425 California

#1602, San Francisco CA 94104. Contact: Susan Kelly, assistant coordinator. Estab. 1957. Annual award.

Purpose: "To award the author of an unpublished, partly completed book-length work of fiction, nonfiction, short story, or poetry."

Requirements: Unpublished submissions only. Applicant must be resident of Northern California or Nevada for 3 consecutive years immediately prior to the date for which submission is being made. Age of applicant must be 20 through 35. Deadline entry: January 15. Entry form or rules for SASE.

Award: $2,000 and award certificate.

"JOINT" CONFERENCE FICTION/POETRY CONTEST, *"Joint" Conference*, King Publications, Box 19332, Washington DC 20036. (202)234-1681. Contact: Kathryn E. King, editor/publisher. Estab. 1977. Annual award.

Purpose: "To encourage fiction and poetry writing among inmates in correctional institutions."

Requirements: Unpublished submissions only. Deadline entry: March 31. Entry form or rules for SASE.

Award: First prize: $100; second prize: $50.

Information: Looking for "good writing first and foremost. This contest is open *only* to inmates in correctional institutions. They can be released before the winning entries are judged, but they must have sent in the entries before they are released from prison."

JESSE H. JONES AWARD, Texas Institute of Letters, Southern Methodist University, Box 3143, Dallas TX 75275. Contact: Marshall Terry, secretary/treasurer. Estab. 1948. Annual award.

Purpose: "To recognize the best work of fiction by a Texan or about Texas."

Requirements: Entry form or rules for SASE.

Information: Write for rule sheet.

JANET HEIDINGER KAFKA PRIZE IN FICTION BY AMERICAN WOMEN, University of Rochester: Annual Writers Workshop & Department of English, University College, University of Rochester, Rochester NY 14627. Contact: Mrs. Anne Ludlow, assistant dean. Estab. 1976. Annual award.

Purpose: "The prize will be awarded (no more than once a year) to a woman citizen of the US who has written the best book-length published work of prose fiction, whether novel, short stories, or experimental writing."

Requirements: Previously published material during the calendar year in which it is submitted. Deadline entry: December 31. Entry forms are distributed to publishers. Entries evaluated by 5 jurors. "Works written primarily for children and vanity house publication will not be considered. Mss must be submitted by the publishers."

Information: Looking for "literary quality."

KANSAS QUARTERLY/KANSAS ARTS COMMISSION AWARDS, *Kansas Quarterly*, 106 Denison Hall, Kansas State University, Manhattan KS 66506. Contact: The editors. Estab. 1972. Annual award.

Purpose: "To reward and recognize the best fiction published during the year from authors anywhere in the US or abroad."

Requirements: "Anyone who submits unpublished material which is then accepted for publication becomes eligible for the awards." No deadline; material simply may be submitted for consideration at any time. To submit fiction for consideration, send it in with SASE.

Award: Recognition and monetary sums of $250, $150, $100.

Information: Looking for "the best that is available. Ours are not 'contests'; they are monetary awards and recognition given by persons of national literary stature. Judges have included William Inge, John Cheever, John Gardner, Kay Boyle, Anne Tyler, William Gass, David Madden."

ROBERT F. KENNEDY BOOK AWARD, Endowed by Arthur Schlesinger, Jr., from proceeds of his biography, *Robert Kennedy and His Times*. Annual award.
Purpose: To award the author of a book that best honors the causes that concerned Robert F. Kennedy.
Requirements: Previously published submissions during the calendar year.
Award: $2,500 cash prize which is awarded in the spring.
Information: Looking for "a work of literary merit in fact or fiction that shows compassion for the poor or powerless or those suffering from injustice."

JACK KEROUAC ANNUAL FICTION PRIZE, *Magic Changes*, 1923 Finchley Ct., Schaumburg IL 60194. Contact: Don Bullen and John Sennett, Editors. Estab. 1979. Annual award.
Purpose: "To encourage writers to write the finest fiction."
Requirements: Unpublished submissions only. No deadline. Entry form or rules for SASE.
Award: First, second and third cash prizes are a percentage of entry fees.
Information: Looking for short stories, short fiction. Winning entries published in *Magic Changes*.

LE PRIX LITTERAIRE ESSO DU CERCLE DU LIVRE DE FRANCE, Le Cercle Du Livre De France, 8955 Blvd. Saint-Laurent, Montreal, Quebec, Canada H2N 1M6. Contact: M. Pierre Tisseyre, president. Estab. 1949. Annual award.
Requirements: Unpublished submissions in French only. Deadline entry: July 15. Entry form or rules for SASE.
Award: $5,000.
Information: Reserved to mss in French.

MADEMOISELLE COLLEGE FICTION COMPETITION, *Mademoiselle Magazine*, 350 Madison Ave., New York NY 10017. Contact: Audrey Leung, fiction editor.
Requirements: See August *Mademoiselle* for rules or write to fiction editor. Each entry must be accompanied by entry form or by 3x5 card with name, age, college, year of graduation, home and school address.
Award: 1st prize: $700 plus publication of winning story in a future issue of *Mademoiselle*; 2nd prize: $300 cash prize. Honorable mention: special certificates.
Information: Open to undergraduate women and men currently enrolled in an accredited college or junior college. Work must be submitted before graduation. Entries will not be returned.

MAELSTROM REVIEW BEST SHORT STORY OF THE YEAR, Box 4261, Long Beach CA 90804. Contact: Leo Mallman, Editor.
Purpose: To recognize the best short story of the year published in the *Maelstrom Review*.
Requirements: Unpublished submissions.
Information: Write for entry rules.

THE JOHN H. MCGINNIS MEMORIAL AWARD, *Southwest Review*, SMU Press, Southern Methodist University, Dallas TX 75275. Contact: Margaret L. Hartley, editor. Estab. 1962. Biannual award. (One year for fiction and the next for nonfiction).
Requirements: Previously published submissions in the *Southwest Review* within a two-year period prior to the announcement of the award.
Award: $500.
Information: "Looking for stories of character development or psychological penetration rather than those depending chiefly on plot. The John H. McGinnis Memorial Award is given each year for material—alternately fiction and nonfiction—that has been published in the *Southwest Review* in the previous two years. Thus, stories are not submitted directly for the award, but simply for publication in the magazine. From among those published in each

two-year period, then, the judges select what they feel to be the best story for the McGinnis award."

MS MAGAZINE COLLEGE FICTION CONTEST, Ms. Foundation, 370 Lexington Ave., New York NY 10017. Contact: Phyllis Rosser, fiction editor.
Information: Contest announced annually in February or March issue.

NATIONAL JEWISH BOOK AWARDS, JWB Jewish Book Council, 15 E. 26th St., New York NY 10010. Contact: Ruth Frank, director. Annual award.
Purpose: "To promote greater awareness of Jewish-American literary creativity."
Requirements: Previously published submissions only by a US or Canadian author. Submissions must be during the calendar year. Awards announced in spring.
Award: $500 plus citation to publisher. William and Janice Epstein Award for Jewish Fiction (novel or short story); Charles and Bertie G. Schwartz Juvenile Award (juvenile book on a Jewish theme) and Workmen's Circle Award for Yiddish Literature (work of fiction, poetry, essays, memoirs in Yiddish).

NATIONAL MAGAZINE AWARD FOR FICTION, American Society of Magazine Editors, Graduate School of Journalism, Columbia University, Room 706, 116th St., New York NY 10027. Annual award.
Purpose: To encourage editorial vitality in magazines.
Requirements: Previously published submissions as a magazine series. Magazine is to submit entries only.
Award: Winning magazine will receive a plaque and reproduction of Alexander Calder's stabile "Elephant." Certificates to winners and finalists.

NATIONAL MEDAL FOR LITERATURE, The American Book Awards, 1 Park Ave., New York NY 10016. Contact: Bobbie Schlesinger. Annual award.
Purpose: "Prestigious literary award conferred on a living American writer for his contribution to American letters."
Award: $15,000 and a bronze medal.
Information: Award is endowed by the Guinzburg Fund, in memory of Harold K. Guinzburg, founder of Viking Press and a president of The American Book Publishers Council. Recipients include Eudora Welty, Thornton Wilder, Conrad Aiken, E.B. White, and others. Candidates nominated by special committee.

NATIONAL WRITERS CLUB ANNUAL BOOK CONTEST, National Writers Club, 1450 S. Havana, Aurora CO 80012. (303)751-7844. Contact: Donald E. Bower, director. Estab. 1974. Annual award.
Purpose: To encourage and recognize writing by freelancers in the field of the novel.
Requirements: Unpublished submissions. Deadline entry: July 1. Contest/award rules and entry forms available with SASE.
Award: $1,000 in prizes; $400 first prize.
Information: Looking for originality of idea, and freshness of writing.

NATIONAL WRITERS CLUB ANNUAL SHORT STORY CONTEST, National Writers Club, 1450 S. Havana, Aurora CO 80012. (303)751-7844. Contact: Donald E. Bower, director. Estab. 1940. Annual award.
Purpose: To encourage and recognize writing by freelancers in the short story field.
Requirements: Unpublished submissions. Write for rule sheet.

NATIONAL YOUTH WRITING COMPETITION, Interlochen Arts Academy, Interlochen MI 49643. Contact: Karen Galbraith. Estab. 1976. Annual award.
Purpose: To identify and encourage young writers.

Requirements: Contest is open to students in grades nine to twelve. Deadline entry: December 15. Contest/award rules and entry forms available with SASE.
Award: First prize $100, second prize $50 and third prize $25 with publication in the *Interlochen Review*.

NEBULA AWARD, Science Fiction Writers of America, 68 Countryside Apts., Hacketts-town NJ 07840.
Purpose: To honor outstanding writers of science fiction.
Requirements: Previously published submissions (science fiction of various lengths).
Award: Lucite trophies sculptured by Judith Blish.
Information: Candidates are voted on by members of Science Fiction Writers of America.

NEUSTADT INTERNATIONAL PRIZE FOR LITERATURE, *World Literature Today*, 110 Monnet Hall, University of Oklahoma, Norman OK 73019. Contact: Dr. Ivar Ivask, director. Estab. 1970. Biannual award.
Purpose: To recognize distinguished and continuing achievement in fiction, poetry, or drama.
Award: $10,000, and eagle feather cast in silver, an award certificate and a special issue of *WLT*.
Information: "We are looking for outstanding accomplishment in world literature. The Neustadt Prize is not open to application. Nominations are made only by members of the international jury, which changes for each award. Jury meetings are held in February of even-numbered years. Unsolicited manuscripts, whether published or unpublished, cannot be considered. Previous laureates: Elizabeth Bishop (USA), 1976, Czeslaw Milosz (Poland/USA), 1978 and Josef Skvorecký (Czechoslovakia/Canada), 1980."

THE O. HENRY AWARDS: PRIZE STORIES, Doubleday & Company, Inc., 245 Park Avenue, New York NY 10017. Contact: Sally Arteseros, senior editor. Estab. 1919. Annual award.
Purpose: To honor the memory of O. Henry, with a sampling of outstanding short stories and to make these stories better known to the public. These awards are published by Doubleday every spring.
Requirements: Previously published submissions. "All selections are made by the editor of the volume, William Abrahams. No stories may be submitted. Mr. Abrahams reads several hundred magazines (all listed in the back of the volume) to select the twenty or so finest (published) American stories."

OHIOANA BOOK AWARD, Ohioana Library Association, 1105 Ohio Departments Bldg., 65 S. Front St., Columbus OH 43215. Contact: James P. Barry, director. Estab. 1929. Annual award (only if the judges believe a book of sufficiently high quality has been submitted).
Purpose: To bring recognition to outstanding books by Ohioans or about Ohio.
Requirements: "Previously published books to be submitted on or before publication date, in two copies. Each spring a jury considers all books received since the previous jury. No entry forms, etc., are needed. We will be glad to answer letters asking specific questions."
Award: Certificate and medal.
Information: "Ms must be by an Ohioan (defined as a person born in Ohio or who has lived there for a total of at least 5 years), or about Ohio or the state's people. The submission must be of high quality."

THE OKANAGAN SHORT FICTION AWARD, *Canadian Author & Bookman*, 24 Ryerson Ave., Toronto, Ontario, Canada M5T 2P3. Contact: Geoff Hancock, fiction editor. Estab. 1979. Award offered 4 times a year.
Purpose: To present good fiction "in which the writing surpasses all else" to an appreciative literary readership, and in turn help Canadian writers retain an interest in good fiction.

Requirements: Unpublished submissions. Entries are invited in each issue of our quarterly *CA&B*. Writers are asked to submit mss only. Sample copy $1; guideline printed in the magazine. "Our award regulations stipulate that writers must be Canadian, stories must not have been previously published, and be under 3500 words. Mss should be typed double-spaced on 8⅜x11 bond. SASE requested. Award is made possible through a Capital Trust Fund (donor anonymous) and, it is hoped, will continue in perpetuity."
Award: $125 to each author whose story is accepted for publication.
Information: Looking for superior writing ability, stories with good plot, movement, dialogue and characterization.

PEN AMERICAN CENTER AWARDS, 47 5th Ave., New York NY 10003. Annual award.
Requirements: Previously published submissions. Decisions for all prizes are made by a panel of judges appointed by the Executive Board of PEN.
Award: Awards include: Ernest Hemingway Foundation Award, PEN Translation Prize: $1,000 annually; PEN Writing Awards for Prisoners: a total of $525 is awarded annually for fiction, poetry, nonfiction; and The Faulkner Award: $2,000. (See separate listings.)

JAMES D. PHELAN AWARD, The San Francisco Foundation, 425 California #1602, San Francisco CA 94104. Contact: Susan Kelly, assistant coordinator. Estab. 1935. Annual award.
Purpose: To award the author of an unpublished incomplete work of fiction, nonfiction, short story, poetry or drama.
Requirements: Unpublished submissions. Applicant must have been born in the state of California and be 20-35 years old. Deadline entry: January 15. Contest/award rules and entry forms available with SASE.
Award: $2,000 and a certificate.

PIEDMONT LITERARY SOCIETY CREATIVE WRITING CONTEST, Piedmont Literary Society, Box 3656, Danville VA 24541. Contact: John Dameron, president. Estab. 1978. Annual award.
Purpose: To promote creative writing, particularly among students and beginners.
Requirements: Unpublished submissions. Deadline entry: November or December (usually). Contest/award rules and entry forms available with SASE.
Award: Small cash prizes; publication and contributor's copies of *Piedmont Literary Review*.
Information: Looking for short short stories of high literary quality that are readable by the average educated person.

PIERIAN PRESS EDITORS' PRIZE, Box #5, Brandon University, Brandon, Manitoba, Canada R7A 6A9. Contact: R.W. Brockway, chief editor. Quarterly award.
Purpose: To encourage and reward effective writing of good quality.
Requirements: Unpublished submissions. We have guidelines that are available upon request.
Award: 1st prize $25, and 2nd prize a short story anthology. "Prizes are awarded on the basis of the best out of four published stories per issue plus one or two book prizes for runners-up. Since we have limited resources, we feel we can compensate our writers best by giving what we have to the most deserving rather than pay a derisory sum to all four of our fiction writers per issue; also the prize enables us to commend the fine writer."
Information: Looking for well-developed plot, effective writing and imaginative themes.

PLAYBOY'S ANNUAL AWARDS, *Playboy Magazine*, 919 N. Michigan Ave., Chicago IL 60611. Estab. 1956. Annual award.
Purpose: To acknowledge and award *Playboy* contributors.
Requirements: Winners are selected by the magazine staff. Only material published in the magazine during the calendar year is considered. This is not an open competition. In the

fiction category, there are awards for the Best Short Story and Best New Contributor: Fiction.
Award: $1000 and a medallion.

EDGAR ALLAN POE AWARDS, Mystery Writers of America, Inc., 105 E. 19th St., New York NY 10003. Contact: Gloria Amoury, executive secretary. Estab. 1945. Annual award.
Purpose: To enhance the prestige of the mystery.
Requirements: Previously published submissions in the calendar year. Deadline entry: December 31. Each award committee operates differently. Contact above address for specifics.
Award: Ceramic bust of Poe. Awards for: Best Mystery Novel, Best First Novel, Best Softcover Original Novel, Best Short Story and Best Juvenile Novel.
Information: Looking for excellence.

KATHERINE ANNE PORTER PRIZE FOR FICTION, *Nimrod*, Arts and Humanities Council, 2210 S. Main St., Tulsa OK 74104. Annual award.
Requirements: Accepts mss for consideration beginning December 1.
Award: $500 first prize and $250 second prize.

PRESIDENT'S AWARD, *The Ohio Journal*, Ohio State University Dept. of English, 164 W. 17th Ave., Columbus OH 43210. Contact: William Allen, editor. Estab. 1978. Annual award.
Purpose: To acknowledge and compensate the most outstanding fiction contribution of the year published in *The Ohio Journal*.
Requirements: Previously published submissions in *The Ohio Journal*. Deadline entry: August 15. Submit fiction to be considered for publication. All published fiction is automatically entered. Guidelines available. Sample copy of magazine, $2.
Award: $100.
Information: Looking for outstanding fiction.

PRIX CHAMPLAIN, Conseil De La Vie Francaise En Amefique, 59, Rue D' Auteuil, Quebec, Canada G1R 4C2. Estab. 1957. Annual award.
Purpose: To encourage literary work in novel or short story in French by Francophiles living outside Quebec and in the US or Canada.
Requirements: Previously published or contract submissions OK, no more than 3 years old previous to award. Deadline entry: Dec. 31. Author must furnish 4 examples of work, resume, address and phone number.
Award: $1,000 in Canadian currency.

PULITZER PRIZE IN FICTION, Columbia University, Graduate School of Journalism, 702 Journalism Bldg., New York NY 10027. Contact: Richard T. Baker. Estab. 1917 by Joseph Pulitzer. Annual award.
Purpose: To honor literary work by an author in fiction.
Requirements: Previously published submissions. Open to American authors of distinguished literary achievement. Deadline entry: November 1. No open nominations.
Award: $1,000.

PUSHCART PRIZE, Pushcart Press, Box 845, Yonkers NY 10701. Contact: Bill Henderson, editor. Annual award.
Purpose: To publish and recognize the best of small press literary work.
Requirements: Previously published submissions; books or short stories on any subject or short self-contained sections. Must have been published during the current calendar year. Deadline: Oct. 15. Nomination by small press publishers/editors only.
Award: Publication in *Pushcart Prize: Best of the Small Presses* plus $100 to lead story.

SIR WALTER RALEIGH AWARD, North Carolina Literary & Historical Association, 109 E. Jones St., Raleigh NC 27611. (919)733-7305. Contact: Joan C. Lashley, secretary-treasurer. Annual award.
Purpose: To stimulate among the people of the state an interest in their own literature.
Requirements: Previously published submissions only by North Carolina authors. It must be an original work published during the twelve months ending June 30 of the year for which the award is given. Deadline entry: July 15. Contest/award rules and entry forms available with SASE.
Award: Statuette of Sir Walter Raleigh.
Information: Looking for creative and imaginative quality, excellence of style and universality of appeal.

REGINA MEDAL AWARD, Catholic Library Association, 461 N. Lancaster Ave., Haverford PA 19041. Contact: Matthew R. Wilt, executive director. Estab. 1959. Annual award.
Purpose: To honor a continued (lifetime) distinguished contribution to children's literature.
Award: Silver medal.
Information: Looking for excellence.

ST. LAWRENCE AWARD FOR FICTION, St. Lawrence University/*fiction international*, St. Lawrence University, Canton NY 13617. Contact: Joe David Bellamy, editor. Annual award.
Requirements: Published submissions by an American publisher during the year previous to the award date. Deadline entry: January 31. Contest/award rules and entry forms available with SASE. Submissions (final nominations) from publishers only.
Award: $1000 cash prize.
Information: Looking for outstanding first collection of short fiction of literary merit.

SAN JOSE STUDIES BEST STORY AWARD, Bill Casey Memorial Fund, 125 S. 7th St., San Jose CA 95192. Contact: Selma Burkom.
Purpose: To recognize the author of the best story (or essay or poem) appearing in a previous volume of *San Jose Studies*.
Award: $100. Winning author to receive a year's complimentary subscription to the journal.

SAXIFRAGE PRIZE, Saxifrage, Inc., 36-C Stratford Hills, Chapel Hill NC 27514. Contact: Roger Sauls. Estab. 1980. Biannual award.
Purpose: To recognize the best book of short stories published by a small press or university press during the eligibility period.
Requirements: Previously published submissions 2 years prior to date of work. Deadline entry: May 1, (1981) of every other year. Contest/award rules and entry forms available with SASE.
Award: $1000 to author, $500 to publisher.

SEAL BOOKS FIRST NOVEL COMPETITION, Seal Books, 60 St. Clair Ave., E., Suite 601, Toronto, Ontario, Canada M4T 1N5. Contact: Editor. Estab. 1976.
Requirements: Unpublished submissions. Deadline entry: December 31. Contest/award rules and entry forms available with SASE. Applicant must be either a Canadian citizen or a Canadian landed immigrant.
Award: $50,000 plus a contract with Seal Books (the mass market imprint of McClelland & Stewart-Bantam Ltd.) that will guarantee publication of novel first in hard bound edition, then as paperback.
Information: Mss to be not less than 60,000 words. Must be double-spaced on white paper, submitted in English under author's own name.

THE SEATON AWARDS, *Kansas Quarterly*, 106 Denison Hall, Kansas State University, KS 66506. Contact: Editors. Estab. 1980. Annual award.
Purpose: To reward and recognize the best fiction published during the year from authors anywhere in US or abroad.
Requirements: Submissions may be either published or unpublished. Anyone who submits short unpublished material which is then accepted for publication becomes eligible for the awards. Seaton Awards are specifically for Kansas natives or Kansas residents. No deadline. Material simply may be submitted for consideration at any time with SASE.
Award: Recognition and monetary sums of $150, $100 and $50.
Information: Looking for the best that is available. "Ours are not contests. We give monetary awards and recognition by persons with national literary stature. Judges have included John Cheever, John Gardner, Kay Boyle, Anne Tyler, William Gass, David Madden."

SEVENTEEN FICTION CONTEST FOR TEENS, *Seventeen Magazine*, 850 3rd Ave., New York NY 10022. Contact: Cathy Winters.
Purpose: To honor best short fiction by teenage girl.
Requirements: Rules are found in the March/April issue. Contest for 13-20 year olds.

SOCIAL COMMENT ANNUAL, *Quixote Magazine*, Box 70013, Houston TX 77007. Contact: Morris Edelson, publisher. Estab. 1966. Annual award.
Purpose: "To encourage satirical or serious exposure of bourgeois lifestyle and the filing of capitalism as seen in personal experience."
Requirements: Unpublished submissions. Deadline entry: January. Send query letter describing project or fiction.
Award: If lengthy, separate publication and percentage of royalties.
Information: "Looking for something that will reach the general audience. Left of Billy Carter. Urbane humor and biting insight into foibles. Heart, chutzpah . . . ."

SPUR AWARD CONTEST, Western Writers of America, 4316 Riverside Rd., S., Salem OR 97302. Contact: Kay L. McDonald, awards chairman. Estab. 1952. Annual award.
Purpose: To encourage excellence in western writing.
Requirements: Previously published submissions. Entries are accepted only from the current calendar year for each year's award; that is, books can only be entered in the year they are published. Deadline entry: December 31. Contest/award rules and entry forms available with SASE.
Award: A wooden plaque shaped like a W with a golden spur attached. No money is awarded.
Information: "Books must be of the traditional or historical western theme, set anywhere west of the Mississippi River before the 20th century, ideally from 1850 to 1900."

THE TREACLE FIRST BOOK AWARD, Treacle Press, Box 638, New Paltz NY 12561. Contact: Bruce McPherson, publisher. Estab. 1980. Biannual award.
Purpose: To acknowledge, encourage, and develop new talent in the novel.
Requirements: Unpublished submissions. Deadline entry: June 1. Contest/award rules and entry forms available with SASE.
Award: Book publication with advance against royalties, plus contract.
Information: Looking for experimental fiction.

MARK TWAIN AWARD, Missouri Library Association and Missouri Association of School Librarians, 402 S. 5th St., Columbia MO 65201. Contact: Frank Wranovix, executive coordinator. Estab. 1970. Annual award.
Purpose: To introduce children to the best of current literature for children and to stimulate reading.
Requirements: Previously published submissions. A committee selects the books nominat-

ed for the award; children throughout the state vote to choose a winner from the committee's list. Books must be published two years prior to nomination for the award list.
Award: A bronze bust of Mark Twain, created by Barbara Shanklin, a Missouri sculptor.
Information: 1) Books should be of interest to children in grades 3 through 8; 2) written by an author living in the US; 3) of literary value which may enrich children's personal lives.

UNIVERSITY OF MISSOURI BREAKTHROUGH COMPETITION, 107 Swallow Hall, Columbia MO 65211. Contact: Susan F. Kelpe, managing editor. Biannual award.
Requirements: Entry fee is $7.50. Mss are read only in odd numbered years.
Award: Publication in series.
Information: Looking for fiction, 96-124 pages. "In the past, most entries have been academics. Judges are professional writers."

EDWARD LEWIS WALLANT MEMORIAL BOOK AWARD, 3 Brighton Rd., West Hartford CT 06117. Sponsored by Dr. and Mrs. Irving Waltman in cooperation with the Hartford Jewish Community Center. Contact: Mrs. Irving Waltman. Estab. 1963. Annual award.
Purpose: Memorial to Edward Lewis Wallant which offers incentive and encouragement to beginning writers.
Requirements: Previously published submissions the year before the award is conferred in April. Deadline: Submission must be dated the previous year to the award ceremony in April—as early in the year as possible. There are no rules or forms. Books may be submitted for consideration to Dr. Lothar Kahn, one of the permanent judges. Address: Central Conn. State College, New Britain, CT.
Award: Cash plus award certificate.
Information: "Looking for creative work of fiction by an American Jew which has significance for the American Jew. The novel (or collection of short stories) should preferably bear a kinship to the writing of Wallant. The award will seek out the writer who has not yet achieved literary prominence when published."

WILLIAM ALLEN WHITE CHILDREN'S BOOK AWARD, Emporia State University, 1200 Commercial, Emporia KS 66801. Contact: Mary E. Bogan, executive secretary. Estab. 1952. Annual award.
Purpose: To honor the memory of one of the state's most distinguished citizens by encouraging the boys and girls of Kansas to read and enjoy good books.
Requirements: "We do not accept submissions from authors or publishers."
Award: Bronze medal.
Information: The White Award Book Selection Committee looks for excellence of literary quality in fiction, poetry and nonfiction appropriate for 4th through 8th graders. All nominations to the annual White Award master list must be made by a member of the White Award Book Selection Committee.

WRITER'S DIGEST ANNUAL WRITING COMPETITION (Short Story Division), *Writer's Digest*, *WD* Writing Competition, 9933 Alliance Rd., Cincinnati OH 45242. (513)984-0717.
Requirements: Unpublished submissions. Deadline entry: Midnight June 30. All entries must be original, unpublished, and not previously submitted to a *Writer's Digest* contest. Short story: 2,000 words maximum, one entry only. Entry form must accompany ms. No acknowledgment will be made of receipt of mss nor will mss be returned. Enclosure of SASE will disqualify entry.
Award: Cash ($500), electric typewriters, plaques, and certificates of recognition. Grand prize winner and top 10 entries are announced in *Writer's Digest*.
Information: Write to *WD* Writing Competition for rules and entry form.

Writers' organizations

Writing is a solitary business, but it need not always be lonely. Joining a writers' organization can offer a variety of benefits on a personal, financial and professional basis.

Membership in a writers' club allows access to specialized information about writing fellowships, grants, markets and agents through regular meetings and club publications. Schedules for writers' seminars, workshops and contests are made available, and these activities, in turn, offer new professional contacts and an exchange of ideas, in addition to opportunities for improving writing skills. And writers often need kindred spirits as well.

Joining a writing club can help you develop the professional image you are seeking. Inclusion in the membership directory increases your visibility and even credibility as an established writer, as does periodic contact with other writers and editors at meetings.

As an active member of a writing club you may find legal or moral support with publishing problems. Special club liaisons or legal representatives are often available to back a writer with a contract or copyright dispute.

Entrance requirements may range from a simple but sincere interest in the written word to the publication of a novel. There are local clubs and branches of national writers' organizations in many major cities (and some small towns). A list of national and regional organizations for the fiction writer follows:

AMERICAN ACADEMY AND INSTITUTE OF ARTS AND LETTERS, 633 W. 155th St., New York NY 10032. (212)368-5900. Executive Director: Margaret M. Mills. Estab. 1898. **Purpose:** "To foster, assist, and sustain an interest in literature, music and the fine arts. The goal is general, but the means are specific, aimed at singling out and encouraging individual artists and their work." Prospective members "must be native or naturalized citizens of the US, qualified by notable achievement in art, music or literature. In order to be eligible, the candidate's work must be essentially creative rather than interpretive. Candidates for membership can only be nominated by members and must qualify in their own department before their names are submitted for vote to the whole membership." 250 members.

AMERICAN TRANSLATORS ASSOCIATION, Box 129, Croton-on-Hudson NY 10520. Staff Administrator: Mrs. Rosemary Malia. Estab. 1959.
Purpose: As a national professional society to advance the standards of translation and to promote the intellectual and material interest of translators and interpreters in the United States. Welcomes to membership all those who are interested in the field as well as translators of foreign fiction and interpreters active in any branch of knowledge.

THE AUTHORS GUILD, INC., 234 W. 44th St., New York NY 10036. (212)398-0838. Executive Secretary: Peter Heggie. Estab. 1912.
Purpose: "To act and speak with the collective voice of 5,800 writers in matters of joint professional and business concern; to advise members on individual professional and business problems as far as possible. Those eligible for membership include any author who shall have had a book published by an established American publisher within 7 years prior to his application; any author who shall have had 3 works (fiction or nonfiction) published by magazines of general circulation within 18 months prior to application." Dues: $40/year.

THE AUTHORS INSTITUTE OF AMERICA, Box 9261, North Hollywood CA 91609. (213)985-2795. Vice President and Executive Director: Hamilton A. Stewart.
Purpose: To provide professional and financial assistance to deserving writers. "We do not accept unsolicited manuscripts, but everyone who writes is welcome to apply for assistance by submitting the first 3 chapters, an outline and a resume of his/her experience. After the application is completed and returned, we will judge whether to request samples of the writer's work." Members are mostly fiction writers from the Los Angeles area. Fees: $10/year for writers; and $5/year for students (no reading fees).

AUTHORS LEAGUE OF AMERICA, INC., 234 W. 44th St., New York NY 10036. Estab. 1912. Administrator: Shirley Salant Beck. The Authors League membership is restricted to authors and dramatists who are members of the Authors Guild, Inc., and the Dramatists Guild, Inc. Matters of joint concern to authors and dramatists, such as copyright and freedom of expression, are in the province of the league; other matters, such as contract terms and subsidiary rights, are in the province of the guilds.

CANADIAN AUTHORS ASSOCIATION, 22 Yorkville Ave., Toronto, Ontario, Canada M4W 1L4. Estab. 1921.
Purpose: To foster and develop a climate favorable to the creative arts and to promote recognition of Canadian writers and their work. Membership is divided into categories: active (regular) members who are engaged in writing (books, short stories, plays, articles, poetry, TV or radio scripts, etc.) and who have produced a sufficient body of work; and associate (non-voting) members who are interested in writing and have a sincere interest in Canadian Literature but have not yet written or published much. Branches are located all over Canada. Dues: $25/year.

FEMINIST WRITERS' GUILD, Box 9396, Berkeley CA 94709. (415)524-3692. Current Administrator: Laura Tow. Estab. 1977. 1,000 members.
Purpose: To act both as a service and political body for feminist writers. Publishes a national newsletter. Referrals to agents, to other useful publications, also to local chapters and contact people and to local support groups. Membership: $10 ($5 if unemployed), $20 to institutions.

INTERNATIONAL WOMEN'S WRITING GUILD, Box 810, Gracie Station, New York 10028. Executive Director: Hannelore Hahn.
Purpose: "Established in 1976 as an alliance open to all women connected to the written word who wish to use writing for personal growth and/or professionally. To facilitate these goals, the IWWG sponsors writing conferences and retreats, as well as regional year-round

writing workshops. It also publishes a bimonthly *Network* letter, operates a talent bank for job placements and refers members to New York literary agents." Dues: $15 annually.

MYSTERY WRITERS OF AMERICA, INC., 105 E. 19th St., New York NY 10003. Estab. 1945. Officers: President, William P. McGivern; Executive Vice-President, Hillary Waugh; Secretary, Lucy Freeman; Treasurer, Jay Bennett.
Purpose: "An organization dedicated to the proposition that the detective story is the noblest sport of man." Membership includes active members who have made at least one sale in mystery, crime, or suspense writing; associate members who are editors, publishers or non-writers allied to the field and affiliate members who are novices in the mystery writing field. Sponsors meetings, *The Third Degree* monthly publication, The MWA anthology, courses, library and awards. Annual dues: $35 for US members; $10 for Canadian and overseas members.

NATIONAL LEAGUE OF AMERICAN PEN WOMEN, INC., 1300 17th St. NW, Washington DC 20036. President: Maxine Lampshire. Estab. 1897. "Professionally qualified women engaged in creating and promoting letters, art, and music" are eligible for membership. Women interested in membership must qualify professionally and be presented for membership and endorsed by two active members in good standing in the league. The league holds branch, state and national meetings. Dues: Initiation fee: $5. Annual branch dues plus $15 national dues. For further information, write to national president at address given above.

NATIONAL WRITERS CLUB, INC., 1450 S. Havana, Suite 620, Aurora CO 80012. Estab. 1937. Executive Director: Donald E. Bower. "Founded for the purpose of informing, aiding and protecting freelance writers worldwide. Associate membership is available to anyone seriously interested in writing. Qualifications for professional membership are publication of a book by a recognized book publisher; or sales of at least three stories or articles to national or regional magazines; or a television, stage, or motion picture play professionally produced. Provides workshops and seminars nationwide (including seminar at sea). Majority of members are fiction writers." Annual dues: $27.50, associate membership; $32.50, professional membership; plus $12.50 initiation fee.

P.E.N., American Center, 47 5th Ave., New York NY 10003. (212)255-1977. Estab. 1921. Executive Secretary: Karen Kennerly. President: Bernard Malamud; Vice Presidents: E.L. Doctorow, Frances Fitzgerald, Richard Howard, Kirkpatrick Sale, Richard Sennett; Secretary: Grace Schulman; Treasurer: Joan Crowell. A world association of poets, playwrights, essayists, editors, and novelists.
Purpose: "To promote and maintain friendship and intellectual cooperation among men and women of letters in all countries, in the interests of literature, the exchange of ideas, freedom of expression, and good will. P.E.N. has more than 80 centers in Europe, Asia, Africa, Australia, and the Americas. Membership is open to all qualified writers, translators and editors who subscribe to the aims of International P.E.N." To qualify for membership, an applicant must have "acknowledged achievement in the literary field, which is generally interpreted as the publication by a recognized publisher of 2 books of literary merit. Membership is by invitation of the Admission Committee after nomination by a P.E.N. member."

POETS & WRITERS, INC., 201 W. 54th St., New York NY 10019. (212)757-1766. Information Coordinator: Victoria Brush. Estab. 1971.
Purpose: "To serve as an information clearinghouse and service organization for the nation's literary community. Anyone who needs help finding the current address of a writer listed with Poets & Writers, Inc., or has a question of a general literary nature should write or call the Information Center." Publishes *Coda: Poets & Writers Newsletter* 5 times/year.

Other Publications: *A Directory of American Poets and Fiction Writers, Literary Agents: A Complete Guide and Sponsors List, A Writer's Guide to Copyright.* "Anyone with an interest in contemporary literature may use our services, subscribe to our periodicals, or purchase our reference books and pamphlets. Writers who wish to be listed must meet publication requirements: for a poet—10 or more poems in 3 different US literary publicatons; for a fiction writer—1 book or 3 short works of fiction in 3 US periodicals. Work may be written in English, Spanish or Native American language. Some exceptions are made for performance poets who do not normally publish. No dues or listing fees at all. Writers listed with Poets and Writers are eligible for fees for reading or workshops in New York State."

SCIENCE FICTION WRITERS OF AMERICA, INC., Peter D. Pautz, Executive Secretary, 68 Countryside Apartments, Hackettstown NJ 07840. (201)852-8531. Membership is limited to established science fiction writers in the country.
Purpose: To inform writers of matters of professional benefit, to serve as an intermediary in disputes of a professional nature and to act as central clearinghouse for information on science fiction and science fiction writers. There are 3 classes of membership: active, for those who have had published or produced one long single-author work or 3 short works; affiliate, for those who have sold one work of any length to a professional market; institutional, for professionals in activities allied or associated with the writing of science fiction (agents, editors, artists). Publishes quarterly *Bulletin*. Membership includes access to a grievance committee. Also supports a publicity bureau for major PR regarding members and a speaker's bureau. Dues: $40 annually for active membership; $25 for affiliate plus installation fee of $7.50 for first year.

SOCIETY OF CHILDREN'S BOOK WRITERS, Box 296, Los Angeles CA 90066. President: Stephen Mooser.
Purpose: "The Society of Children's Book Writers is the only national organization designed to offer a variety of services to people who write or share a vital interest in children's literature. The SCBW acts as a network for the exchange of knowledge between children's writers, editors, publishers, illustrators and agents." Fees: $25/year.

WASHINGTON AREA WRITERS, 3100 S. Manchester St., Apt. 810, Falls Church VA 22044. President: Nancy L. Jorgensen. Estab. 1973. Approximately 75 members.
Purpose: "To share information about writing through year-round monthly meetings. Publishes monthly newsletter and a directory. Offers a library (including cassettes of speakers); monthly meetings on topics of interest to writers; legal insurance program; offshoot workshops meet regularly: poetry, fiction, speculative fiction and articles. Fees: $10 plus $5 initiation fee.

WASHINGTON INDEPENDENT WRITERS ASSOCIATION, INC., Terrace Level, Suite 13, National Press Building, Washington DC 20045. Executive Director: Judith Brody Saks. Estab. 1975.
Purpose: "To further the common goals of independent writers; to continue to raise the professional level of the independent writing craft; to combat unfair practices; to help establish ethical guidelines for the conduct of the profession; and to serve as a clearinghouse for the exchange of information and ideas. Full membership is open to persons who have written and published for compensation 5,000 words or its equivalent during the previous year or who have authored a book commercially published within the preceeding 5 years. Associate membership is open to anyone with serious interest in the independent writing profession. Offers monthly workshops and meetings; an annual directory of members; annual conferences; social events; a referral service; fundraisers; group legal services; a guide to local freelance markets; Legal Defense Fund; and three major medical plans. Its committees work on market information, problems of professional relations and development, and legislation.

WESTERN WRITERS OF AMERICA, INC., Rt. 1, Box 35H. Victor MT 59875. Contact: Rex Bundy. Writers eligible for membership in this organization are not restricted in their residence, "so long as their work, whether it be fiction, history, adult or juvenile, book-length or short material, movie or TV scripts, has the scene laid west of the Missouri River." Publishes *The Roundup* including the Western Ratings. "Established and beginning authors meet and exchange ideas with publishers, editors, agents, reviewers, motion picture and TV directors and producers. The annual convention offers unusual opportunities for authors and editors to meet informally." Dues $40/year.

Glossary

The following list of words, terms and phrases, found throughout the preceding text, pertain to fiction, and to the writing and publishing of short stories and novels.

Academic. Referring to a member of an association or institution for the advancement of learning; a follower of artistic or philosophic literary movements and traditions.

Action. An unfolding of events or series of real or imagined happenings which form the subject of a story.

Adaptation. A recasting of a work to fit another medium while retaining as much as possible of the original action, language and tone.

Advance. Payment by the publisher to the author before the book is published, to be deducted from future earnings (see **Royalties**).

Adventure. Genre in which action is more important than the characters, theme or setting; material in which the reader's goal is to find out what happens next.

Affiliate. A subsidiary (See **Subsidiary**).

All rights. Agreement between author and publisher whereby the writer forfeits the right to use his material in its present form elsewhere; publisher owns all rights to material.

Allegory. Work of fiction in which the author intends characters and their actions to be represented in terms other than their surface meanings and appearances; subsurface or extended meanings involving significant moral or spiritual concepts.

Allusion. A usually brief, casual or indirect reference to a person, event, or condition, presumably familiar (but sometimes obscure or unknown) to the reader.

Antagonist. The principal opponent, or foil, of the main character; one who contends with or opposes another in a conflict, fight.

Anthology. A collection of selected work by one or various authors.

Anti-climax. An action which is in disappointing contrast to a previous moment of intense interest; anything which follows the climax (the decisive, culminating struggle and resolution of conflict).

Anti-hero. A character lacking heroic qualities, a nobility of life or mind or lofty aims or moral purposes.

Avant-garde. That which is innovative in subject matter or style; often experimental or non-traditional.

Backlist. A publisher's list of all books not published during the current season but still in print.

Bestseller. A book having large sales during a given period; also applied to the author of such a work.

Bildungsroman. A novel concerning the youth and development of a major character (e.g., *David Copperfield*).

Bimonthly. Every two months.

Biography. A written account of history; a continuous, systematic narrative of past events relating to a particular people, country, period or person.

Biweekly. Every two weeks.

Catharsis. An emotional discharge which brings about a welcome moral or spiritual renewal from tension or anxiety; a purification of a character or reader.

CCLM. Coordinating Council of Literary Magazines (80 8th Ave., New York NY 10011).

Chapbook. A small booklet, usually paperback, of poetry, ballads or tales.

Characterization. Creation of images of credible imaginary persons, the major participants in the action of a story.

Clean copy. Material free of errors, cross-outs, wrinkles, smudges.

Clichés. Overused or trite words, phrases or expressions; ideas and plots lacking originality.

Cliff-hanger. Serial or fictional event in which the reader is left hanging in suspense so that interest in the outcome will be sustained.

Climax. The point in a story when the crisis reaches its greatest intensity and is resolved in some manner; a turning point in action.

Cloak-and-dagger. A highly dramatic and romantic novel dealing with espionage and intrigue.

Collective. A group of editors and authors who jointly publish books; an old-fashioned self-help club.

Color. Referring to a writing style that is vivid, fast moving, and filled with descriptive images; also refers to the slant or bias of a writer.

Column inch. All the type contained in one inch of a typeset column.

Commercial. Referring to those publishers and publications whose chief emphasis is on salability, profit or success.

Condensed novel. A shortened, capsulized account of a full-length novel.

Confession. Genre of formula love stories for (mostly) women; an autobiographical or third-person account told by a sympathetic narrator, usually a female from a blue collar family, in which she faces an emotional problem (with a lover, husband, or children) and subsequently solves it.

Conflict. Opposition of persons or forces upon which the action depends in fiction; the material from which a plot is constructed.

Contemporary. Referring to material with current trends, theme or subject matter.

Continuity. Unbroken, continuous, uninterrupted chain of events in a narrative which comprises the plot.

Contributor's copies. Copies of the issues of a magazine sent to an author in which his work appears; often a form of payment from literary/little magazines and small press.

Cooperative. Publishing arrangement within the small press; authors and editors work together to produce a book; a joint effort in writing, editing, printing.

Co-publishing. An arrangement (usually contractual) in which author and publisher share publication costs and profits.

Copy. Any material to be composed or photographed for printing.

Copy editing. Editing the manuscript for grammar, punctuation and printing style as opposed to subject content.

COSMEP. Committee of Small Magazine Editors and Publishers. (Box 703, San Francisco CA 94101)

Counterplot. Secondary theme; a variation of the principal theme; also subplot.

Crisis. A structural element of the plot; a positive or negative turning point in the action; a radical change of status in a character's life which may result in the climax.

Déja-vu. Refers to a trite, unoriginal story situation; the illusion of having previously experienced something encountered for the first time.

Deus ex machina. A literary device for resolving the problems in a plot; an often improbable and unexpected intervention of outside or supernatural forces; a forced or unprepared-for trick, a coincidence.

Dialogue. Conversation or speech exchanged between two characters; or the thoughts of a single character.

Division. An unincorporated branch of a company. (Penguin Books is a division of Viking Penguin, Inc.)

Dummy. Pages which show the shape, size, general appearance of a book; includes a rough layout with position of text and illustrations.

Denouement. The final outcome or result of a complex situation or sequence of events. (French term from the verb "to untie")

Eclectic. The choosing or selection of various types of material or genres; not following a particular system or format but using the best of several systems or elements.

Edition. All copies of a work printed from a single setting of type.

Epilogue. A concluding part of a literary work.

Episode. An incidental but related event or happening within the narrative or scene.

Epithet. A word or phrase to describe or show a characteristic.

Erotica. Fiction that is sexually oriented.

Escape literature. Writing which allows the reader to forget the realities of life and gratify his fantasies.

Esoteric. Refers to literary work that is understood by or intended for a select circle of readers with a special interest or knowledge.

Ethnic. A category of writing referring to the cultural, religious, racial or linguistic traditions of a people or country.

Euphony. Harmonious blend or combination of pleasant sounds.

Exegesis. Critical explanation and interpretation or analysis of a literary work.

Experimental. That which is innovative in subject matter and style; avant-garde or non-formula material.

Exposition. A form of discourse that explains, defines and interprets; also refers to the beginning portion of a plot in which background information is given.

Fable. A brief moral tale of no historical merit, often derived from folklore. Characters are usually animals with human characteristics.

Faction. A category; a combination of fact and fiction; fictional accounts of both depictions of real people under their own names and real people under fictitious names.

Fair use. A provision of the copyright law that says short passages from copyrighted material may be used without infringing on the owner's rights.

Fantasy. Literary work in which the action occurs in a non-existent and unreal world with incredible or fairy-like characters.

Feminist. Material pertaining to the needs, interests and equal rights of women, sometimes related to the lesbian category.

Fiction. From a Latin word meaning to "make" or "mold"; fiction is imagined and invented literary composition, fashioned to entertain and/or instruct.

First North American serial rights. The right to publish first in the United States and Canada. See **First serial rights.**

First serial rights. The right to publish material in a periodical prior to its appearance in book form.

Flashback. A narrative device inserted into a story to represent an earlier event; an incident prior to the opening scene (reverie, a recollection, a dream sequence or dialogue).

Flat character. A fictional person who is undeveloped, lacks complexity and never surprises the reader.

Foil. A contrasting person or thing that heightens another's characteristics or brings out the qualities of both.

Format. General physical appearance (size, shape, typeface, binding, etc.) of a book, magazine or newspaper.

Formula. A fixed and conventional method of developing a plot; pertaining to certain genres (western, gothic, etc.).

Freelance. An independent writer who prepares material without any advance guarantee of financial reward.

Galleys. The first paper proofs before the type has been divided into pages.

Gay/lesbian. A category of writing pertaining to or related to the needs and interests of homosexuals.

Genre. A category or class of artistic endeavor in a particular form, technique or content; a type or kind of fiction.

Gothic. A category in which the central character is usually a beautiful young girl, the setting is an old mansion or castle; there is a handsome hero and a real menace, either natural or supernatural.

Guidelines. A rulesheet for prospective contributors to a magazine or publishing house.

Historical novel. A combination of narrative fiction and history, characterized by an imaginative reconstruction of historical characters and events.

Historical romance. A specialized form of the gothic genre, a novel-length love story set in a specific historical period, such as Regency England (1800-1820) with a good story line and a "nice" romance with sex implied but usually never explicit.

Honorarium. A token payment, a very small amount of money, or simply a byline and copies of the publication in which published material appears.

Horror. A writing category stressing fears, death, reincarnation, the macabre.

Humor. A writing category in which there is recognition and expression of peculiarities, oddities and absurdities in a situation or action; a comic quality evoking amusement.

Hyperbole. Deliberate or obvious exaggeration for emphasis and effect. Opposite of understatement.

Imagery. The use of language to represent actions, persons, objects, ideas descriptively; making pictures with words.

Imprint. Name applied to a special line of books of a publisher. (MacFadden Paperback Romances is an imprint of Manor Books, Inc.)

Independent book packager/producer. An organization which draws all the elements of a book together, from the initial concept to writing and marketing strategies, then sells the book package to a book publisher and/or movie producer.

International reply coupons. To be purchased at a local post office and enclosed with the letter or manuscript to a foreign publisher to cover his postage costs when replying.

Intrigue. Crafty, secret dealings, deceitful and underhanded plans in an intricate plot.

Irony. A technique of indicating an intention or attitude opposed to what is actually stated.

Juvenile. Literary productions intended for young readers, 2-12 years.

Kill fee. A portion of the agreed-on price for a complete story that was assigned but which was subsequently cancelled.

Lead. An introduction to a story designated to hook the reader.

Libel. Written or printed words which defame, malign or damagingly misrepresent.

Literary. Engaged in or having the profession of writing; refers to the general category of serious quality writing, sometimes experimental.

Literary agent. A person who acts for an author in finding a publisher, arranging contract terms for a literary project.

Literary magazine. See **Little magazine**.

Little magazine. Literary journal and special interest publication of small circulation; usually underfinanced; often experimental in its prose. A term used interchangeably with literary magazine.

Macabre. Pertaining to or representing death (in horror fiction). Ghastly, grim, horrible.

Mainstream. Contemporary writing; subjects or trends which are current or traditional; that which is not category or genre fiction.

Manuscript. The author's unpublished copy of a work, in longhand or (usually) typewritten, used as the basis for typesetting.

Mass market paperbacks. Softcover books of popular subjects directed to a general audience.

Men's. Category for short stories (usually) in which erotica, suspense, adventure are the predominant fiction themes.

Mixed metaphors. Combination of two metaphors in one expression which are incongruous and often illogical. (ex. . . . when you boil it down to brass tacks . . .)

Mood. The prevailing atmosphere or tone.

Motivation. Psychological impulses and drives which impel a character in literature to act as he does.

Ms. Abbreviation for manuscript.

Mss. Abbreviation for more than one manuscript.

Multiple submissions. The sending of photocopies of the same ms to several editors or publishers at the same time. (Check individual listings in practicing this policy.)

Muse. The genius or powers which inspire or motivate a literary artist.

Mystery. A form (genre) of narration in which the methods, motives and details of a crime baffle and entertain the reader.

Narration. A form of discourse in which to relate an event or series of events in a story which appeal to the emotions of the reader.

Narrative hook. A device at the beginning of a novel or story used to arouse the reader's interest and make him eager to continue the story.

Narrator. One who tells the story, someone involved in the action or the writer himself.

Nom de plume. French phrase meaning "pen name"; a pseudonym.

Novel. Fictional prose narrative of substantial length involving conflict, characters, actions, settings, plot and theme.

Novelette. A short novel or a long short story, 7,000 to 15,000 words approximately.

Novella. A relatively short prose narrative, comparable in length to a short story or novelette.

Objectivity. A quality of impersonality, freedom from personal beliefs and emotions in a literary work.

One-time rights. Copyright arrangement by which the writer sells the right to use a piece of writing one time.

Outline. A general sketch, account indicating the main features and its related ideas or action of a book; the order and organization for developing a literary work; usually a one-page summary of its contents with chapter headings and a descriptive sentence or two under each.

Pace. Tempo, rate or flow of movement, varied to accommodate different moods and actions.

Page rate. A fixed rate per published page; a method of payment.

Parable. A story conveying a religious principle or moral lesson or a truth which teaches by comparison with actual events.

Paradox. An opinion or statement contrary to generally accepted ideas; a self-contradictory or absurd statement that contains a possible truth.

Payment on acceptance. Payment from the editor as soon as he decides to publish a story.

Payment on publication. Payment from the editor after the acceptance of a manuscript *and* its publication.

Pen name. A nom de plume, a pseudonym used by an author to conceal his real name.

Periodical. A publication released at regularly recurring intervals; referring to magazines and journals but not ordinarily newspapers.

Persona. (pl. personae) The character (or characters) in a literary piece.

Perspective. An author's mental view or facility for seeing his actions, ideas, and characters in meaningful relationships.

Photocopied submissions. An acceptable practice with many editors, in lieu of the original manuscript.

Picaresque. Humorous, satiric; a term applied to novels and tales that depict the adventures of a rogue in realistic detail.

Plagiarism. The passing off as one's own work, the expressions, ideas, words of another.

Plot. A carefully devised plan, with interrelated actions, that progresses through opposing forces to a climax.

Pornography. Obscene literature (or art or photography), usually possessing little literary merit.

Problem novel. A literary work dealing with a problem or thesis and the choices of action open to the characters in conflict or to society at large.

Proofreading. Close reading and corrections by authors and editors for errors in a manuscript.

Proofs. Trial impressions of composed type or illustrations for correcting errors and making changes.

Prose. Ordinary form of all spoken and written language that is not in a regular rhythmic pattern.

Prose poem. Short prose not in verse, with the language and expression of poetry.

Protagonist. The principal or leading character in a literary work with whom the reader can readily identify.

Pseudonym. Chosen fictitious name to conceal identity; also nom de plume, pen name.

Psychic/supernatural. A category involving that which is beyond what is natural or known, events which are unexplainable; explorations into the occult and infinity.

Psychological novel. A narrative emphasizing the interior and emotional aspects of characters and the motives resulting in exterior action.

Public domain. Material which was either never copyrighted or whose copyright term has expired.

Publication not copyrighted. An author's unprotected work which places it in the public domain. It cannot be subsequently copyrighted.

Pulp magazine. A periodical printed on low-quality paper made of wood pulp; usually containing lurid sensational stories or articles.

Purple prose. Ornate writing with exaggerated and excessive literary devices.

Query. A letter to an editor eliciting his interest in a story a writer wants to write.

Reader. A person hired by a publisher or magazine to read and sort through unsolicited manuscripts, usually from a slush pile.

Reader identification. The process by which a reader associates himself with the emotions and responses of the characters and the ultimate complete acceptance.

Reading fee. An arbitrary amount of money sometimes charged by an agent, magazine or publisher to read a submitted manuscript.

Religious/inspirational. Material characterized by an uplifting, upbeat tone or a moral message.

Reporting times. The number of days, weeks, etc. it takes an editor to report back to the author on his query or manuscript.

Reprint rights. Selling the right to reprint an already published work to other magazines or books.

Résumé. A summary or brief account of personal, educational and professional editorial (writing) experience and qualifications.

Rhythm. A uniform repetition of the beat or accent; the measured flow of words in prose.

Roman. The ordinary upright type style, as opposed to slanted italics.

Roman a clef. A novel that represents actual historical characters and events in fiction form. (French phrase meaning novel with a key.)

Romance. A genre, a fictional account of heroic achievements, colorful scenes and passionate love affairs; sometimes a fanciful or extravagant story or daydream.

Royalties. A percentage of the retail price on the first books sold, and a certain percentage thereafter. (Rates vary.)

SASE. Self-addressed stamped envelope.

Satire. A literary blend of humor and wit with a critical attitude toward human activities and institutions.

Scatology. Obscene literature; refers to a study of fossil excrement; closely related to pornography.

Scene. A unit of dramatic action in which a single point is made or one specific effect is reached.

Science fiction. Genre in which fantastic or scientific hypotheses form the basis for actions and events; imaginative narrative based on scientific knowledge and speculation.

Second serial rights. A term applied to the publication in other media after the first publication in book form.

Self-publishing. An independent effort, an alternative to small press or commercial publishing.

Semimonthly. Twice a month.

Semiweekly. Twice a week.

Sequel. A literary work that continues the narrative of a previous related work.

Serial rights. The rights (fees, payments, claims) of an author to anything that is published in installments.

Serialized novel. Sections of a book, published in a magazine in sequential form.

Setting. The environment or surroundings; the locale or period in which the action of a story takes place.

Shelf life. Projected length of selling time for a novel in a bookstore.

Short short story. A brief condensed piece of prose fiction, usually from 500 to 2000 words.

Short story. A relatively short piece of unified narrative prose, under 10,000 words, which contains all the dramatic elements of a story.

Simultaneous submissions. Submissions of the same story or novel to several publications at the same time.

Slice of life. A presentation of life the way it is. The novelist opens the door for a reader, permits him to see and hear a character and then closes the door without observation or comment.

Slick. Popular, usually non-literary publication. (Name derived from the appearance of the coated or polished stock on which it is printed.)

Slush pile. An accumulation of unsolicited, unwanted, sometimes worthless manuscripts in the editorial offices of a book or magazine publisher. (Slush refers to the sometimes silly emotional or sentimental tone in the mss.)

Small press. Independently owned and operated publishers of (usually serious) literary work.

Speculation. An editor's agreement to look at an author's manuscript, with no promise to buy.

Stet. Latin derivative meaning "Let it stand"; an editorial proofreader's mark.

Style. A mode or manner of writing construction; characteristics of a literary selection that concern the form of expression rather than the actual thought.

Subjectivity. The personal, reflective involvement of a writer with himself or his material; centering upon the author's experiences and reactions.

Subplot. A minor or secondary plot which may highlight, contrast or be totally unrelated to the principal plot.

Subsidiary. An incorporated branch of a company or conglomerate. (Alfred A. Knopf, Inc. is a subsidiary of Random House, Inc.)

Subsidiary rights. All rights other than book publishing rights included in a book contract, such as paperback, book club, movie rights, etc.

Subsidy publisher. A book publisher who charges the author for the cost to typeset and print his book, the jacket, etc., as opposed to a royalty publisher which pays the author.

Suspense. A quality of tension in a plot creating anticipation in the readers in regard to the outcome of events in a novel or story; also a genre, category novel.

Symbolism. A technique of representing objects or ideas by symbols or associated meanings.

Tabloid. Newspaper format publication on about half the size of the regular newspaper page (such as *The National Enquirer*).

Tearsheet. Pages from a magazine containing the printed story.

Theme. The dominating or central idea in a literary work; a message, moral or main thread of a story.

Tone. An author's attitude or point of view toward his characters in creating a mood or atmosphere.

Tour de force. An exceptional achievement, a stroke of genius by an author unlikely to be equaled; a particularly skillful technique in handling a difficult situation in writing.

Trade paperback. A softbound, over-sized volume published and designed for the general public, ordinarily available from a retail book dealer.

Transition. Movement from one scene or idea, topic, situation to another by using conjunctions, word repetition, linking phrases.

Uncopyrighted publication. The publishing of an author's work which puts it into the public domain.

Unity. Concept of organization in a story in which all parts are related to achieve an organic whole or oneness.

Unsolicited manuscript. A story that an editor did not specifically ask to see.

Vanity publishing. The publication of books by a printing house which diverts all or a high percentage of the costs and risks to the author; also subsidy publishing.

Viewpoint. First, third person or multiple observers who relate a story or tale; the narrating voice which records the subjective or objective thoughts or observations of the characters.

Vignette. A sketch or brief scene offering the reader a flash or illumination about a character as opposed to a more formal story with a beginning, middle and end.

Western. Genre with a traditional setting in the West and a formula plot with conflict (the good guys against the bad guys).

Whodunit. Informal term for a genre dealing with murder, suspense and the detection of criminals.

Women's. A category whose subjects are related to the needs and interests of the contemporary housewife and professional woman of the '80s.

Writer's block. An inability to begin or complete a work or project already planned in the writer's mind.

Yarn. An informal name for a tale, a western or adventure with long rambling often action-packed events.

Young adult. A category and general classification for readers 12 years through adolescence.

Category index

LITERARY/LITTLE MAGAZINES

Adventure. Alpha, The Argonaut, The Berkeley Monthly Magazine, Black Jack, Canadian Author & Bookman, Cedar Rock, Channel X, Coffee Break, Creative Pittsburgh Journal, Cross Currents, Cumberland Journal, Cumberlands, De Colores Journal, Descant, Dreams Unlimited, Dreamweaver Magazine, Earthwise Quarterly, Event, Fighting Woman News, Hob-Nob, The Icelandic Canadian, Image Literary Magazine, In a Nutshell, Inky Trails, John O'Hara Journal, "Joint" Conference, Juice, Kansas Quarterly, Lebeacon Review, Magical Blend, M'Godolim, The Missouri Review, Muscadine, New England Sampler, Nit & Wit, Phantasm, Pteranodon Magazine, The Pub, Ragged Readin', Raincoast Chronicles, RFD, Salome: A Literary Dance Magazine, Salt Lick, The Silver Unicorn, Sojourner, Straight Ahead International, Sunrise, Time to Pause, Urthkin, The Villager, Virginia Quarterly Review, Waves, Wildcat, Women: A Journal of Liberation.

Confession. Confrontation, Cross Currents, Cumberland Journal, Descant, Double Harness Magazine, Global Tapestry Journal, Kansas Quarterly, The Missouri Review, Some Other Magazine, Straight Ahead International, Sun & Moon: A Journal of Literature & Art.

Erotica. Albatross Magazine, The Alternate, The Bellingham Review, Blitz, Blue Horse, Boss, City Miner, Clifton Magazine, The Coe Review, Confrontation, Descant, Double Harness Magazine, Dreams Unlimited, Dreamweaver Magazine, Empty Window Review, Eureka Review, Exit, Fifth Sun, The Front Magazine, Gay Sunshine Journal, Global Tapestry Journal, Juice, Jump River Review, Lebeacon Review, Ludds Mill, Magic Changes, Maize: Notebooks of Xicano, Art and Literature, Mango, Mississippi Review, The Missouri Review, Not Guilty, Occident, The Pawn Review, Phantasm, Portico, Salt Lick, Samisdat, Some Other Magazine, Straight Ahead International, Total Abandon Modern Arts Magazine, Uroboros, Urthkin, Waves.

Ethnic. Arba Sicula, Aura Literary Arts Review, Bachy, The Bellingham Review, Black Forum Magazine, Black Jack, The Black Review, The Black Scholar, Boss, Box 749, Clifton Magazine, The Coe Review, The Coffeehouse, Confrontation/Change Review, Creacion, Creative Pittsburgh Journal, Cross Currents, De Colores Journal, Descant, Dreams Unlimited, Earthwise Quarterly, Epoch Magazine, Florida Arts Gazette, Inc., Gay Sunshine Journal, Global Tapestry Journal, Home Planet News, The Icelandic Canadian, "Joint" Conference, Jump River Review, Kansas Quarterly, Latin American Literary Review, Laurel Review, Lilith Magazine, Live Writers!

Bare Wires, The Bellingham Review, Black Maria, Blitz, Boss, Broadsheet Magazine, Clifton Magazine, The Coe Review, Confrontation, Cross Currents, Descant, Double Harness Magazine, Dreams Unlimited, Dreamweaver Magazine, Event, Feminist Studies, Fifth Sun, Focus: A Journal for Lesbians, The Front Magazine, Gay Community News, Gay Sunshine Journal, Harvard Advocate, Heresies, Home Planet News, John O'Hara Journal, "Joint" Conference, Juice, Kansas Quarterly, Letters Magazine, The Lilith Magazine, Ludds Mill, Mango, New America, Occident, Paragraph: A Quarterly of Gay Fiction, Phantasm, Primavera, Rara Avis Magazine, RFD, Room of One's Own, Salt Lick, Samisdat, Sez: A Multi-Racial Journal of Poetry & People's Culture, Sing Heavenly Muse!, Sojourner, Source, The Source, The Spirit That Moves Us, Straight Ahead International, Sun & Moon: A Journal of Literature & Art, 13th Moon, Women: A Journal of Liberation.

Gothic. Alpha, Aquila Magazine, The Bellingham Review, Blue Horse Publications, Canadian Author & Bookman, Confrontation, Cross Currents, Descant, Double Harness Magazine, Dreams Unlimited, Dreamweaver Magazine, Earthwise Quarterly, Eerie Country, Gothic, In a Nutshell, John O'Hara Journal, Kansas Quarterly, Karamu, The Missouri Review, New England Sampler, Pteranodon Magazine, Salome: A Literary Dance Magazine, Salt Lick, Samisdat, Sojourner, Sunrise, Waves, Weirdbook, Wildcat.

Historical. Alpha, The Berkeley Monthly Magazine, Florida Arts Gazette, Occasional Review, The Villager.

Horror. Afta, Albatross Magazine, Alpha, Aquila Magazine, The Argonaut, The Bellingham Review, Canadian Author & Bookman, Clifton Magazine, The Coe Review, Coffee Break, Compass Poetry, Confrontation, Creative Pittsburgh Journal, Cross Currents, Descant, Dreams Unlimited, Dreamweaver Magazine, Eerie Country, Empty Window Review, Fifth Sun, The Front Magazine, Golden Isis, Gothic, Hor-Tasy, The Hungry Years, Journal Fantome, Juice, Lebeacon Review, The Little Magazine, M'Godolim, The Missouri Review, North Country Anvil, The Pub, Ragged Readin', Salt Lick, The Silver Unicorn, Slick Press/Poetry Fiction Magazine, Umbral, Urthkin, Waves, Weirdbook, Whispers, Wildcat.

Humor. Afta, Albatross Magazine, Alpha, Another Chicago Magazine, Aquila Magazine, Bare Wires, The Bellingham Review, The Berkeley Monthly Magazine, Black Jack, Blitz, Blue Horse Publications, Box 749, Bug Tar, Calliope, Canadian Author & Bookman, Channel X, Chicago Review, Chunga Review, City Miner, Clifton Magazine, Coffee Break, Confrontation, Creative Pittsburgh Journal, Cross Currents, Cumberlands, De Colores Journal, Descant, Double Harness Magazine, Dreams Unlimited, Dreamweaver Magazine, Earthwise Quarterly, Eureka Review, Event, Fifth Sun, Florida Arts Gazette, Forms, The Front Magazine, Gargoyle Magazine, Gay Community News, Golden Isis, The Gramercy Review, Gusto Magazine, Hob-Nob, Home Planet News, The Icelandic Canadian, Illuminations, Image Literary Magazine, Impegno 80, In a Nutshell, Inky Trails, Inlet, Iron Magazine, "Joint" Conference, Juice, Kansas Quarterly, Karamu, Laurel Review, Lebeacon Review, Letters Magazine, Live Writers! Local on Tap, Lynn Voices, Maize: Notebooks of Xicano Art and Literature, M'Godolim, The Mississippi Review, The Missouri Review, The Moonshine Review, Muscadine, The Nantucket Review, New England Sampler, NIR/New Infinity Review, The New Renaissance, Nit & Wit, North Country Anvil, Old Hickory Review, The Pawn Review, Phantasm, Phoebe, Portico, Prairie Schooner, Primavera, Pteranodon Magazine, Purple Patch, Ragged Readin', Raincoast Chronicles, Salome: A Literary Dance Magazine, Salt Lick, Samisdat, San Jose Studies, Scholia Satyrica, Second Coming, Second Growth: Appalachian Nature & Culture, Sequoia Magazine, Sheba Review—The Literary Magazine for the Arts, Signals, Sojourner, The Source, South Carolina Review, Southern Humanities Review, The Spirit That Move Us, Story Quarterly, Straight Ahead International, Sunrise, Time to Pause, Touchstone Literary Quarterly, Two Worlds, Uncle Magazine, Uroboros, Urthkin, The Villager, Virginia Quarterly Review, Wascana Review, Western Humanities Review, Wildcat, The William and Mary Review, Women: A Journal of Liberation.

Juvenile. Albatross Magazine, The Black Scholar, Coffee Break, De Colores Journal, Inky Trails, Lilith Magazine, New England Sampler, Salt Lick, Sojourner, Stone Soup: The Magazine by Children, Straight Ahead International, Sunrise, Time to Pause, Wildcat.

Ragged Readin', Red Cedar Review, Salome: A Literary Dance Magazine, Salt Lick, Samisdat, Second Coming, The Second Wave, Sheba Review—The Literary Magazine for the Arts, The Silver Unicorn, Sojourner, Sorcerer's Apprentice, Sunrise, Tempest, Umbral, Urthkin, Waves, Wildcat.

Serialized, Condensed or Excerpted Works. The Alternate, The Bellingham Review, Black Jack, The Coe Review, Connecticut Artists Magazine, Cross Currents, De Colores Journal, Descant, Double Harness Magazine, Empty Window Review, Fiction International, Fifth Sun, Hob-Nob, The Hungry Years, Image Literary Magazine, Loonfeather: Minnesota North Country Art, Ludds Mill, The Massachusetts Review, The Missouri Review, The Newscribes Inc., The Phoenix, Portico, The Pub, Pulp, Salome: A Literary Dance Magazine, Salt Lick, The Source, Southern Humanities Review, Story Quarterly, Straight Ahead International, Sun Dog, Sunrise, Time to Pause, Waves, Western Humanities Review, Writ Magazine, Writers Forum.

Translations. The Alternate, American Literary Review, Another Chicago Magazine, The Antigonish Review, Antioch Review, Arba Sicula, Arizona Quarterly, Bachy, The Barat Review, The Bellingham Review, Boss, Box 749, The Chariton Review, Chelsea, Chock Magazine, The Coe Review, The Coffeehouse, Columbia: A Magazine of Poetry, Confrontation, Cottonwood Review, Cream City Review, Creative Pittsburgh Journal, Cross Currents, Cumberland Journal, De Colores Journal, Denver Quarterly, Descant, Double Harness Magazine, Dreamweaver Magazine, Empty Window Review, Exit, Fighting Woman News, Forms, Gargoyle Magazine, Gay Sunshine Journal, Global Tapestry Journal, Gothic, The Gramercy Review, Harvard Advocate, Heirs Magazine, The Icelandic Canadian, Impegno 80, Iron Magazine, John O'Hara Journal, Jump River Review, Latin American Literary Review, Lebeacon Review, Letters Magazine, Lilith Magazine, Live Writers! Local on Tap, The Malahat Review, Mango, Mati, M'Godolim, The Mississippi Review, The Missouri Review, The Moonshine Review, Moosehead Review, Mundus Artium, The Nantucket Review, New Edinburgh Review, New Laurel Review, New Orleans Review, The New Renaissance, Nit & Wit, Northwest Review, Occident, Parabola, The Pawn Review, Phantasm, The Phoenix, Portico, Prairie Schooner, Prism International, Prospice, Pulp, Quarterly West, Rara Avis Magazine, Rockbottom Magazine, Sackbut Review, Salome: A Literary Dance Magazine, Salt Lick, Sequoia Magazine, Sheba Review—The Literary Magazine for the Arts, Sing Heavenly Muse!, Snowy Egret, Sojourner, Some Other Magazine, Source, South Carolina Review, Southern Humanities Review, The Spirit That Moves Us, Stand, Stardancer, Straight Ahead International, Sun Dog, Sun & Moon: A Journal of Literature & Art, Sunrise, Thunder Mountain Review, Total Abandon, Translation, Triquarterly, Two Worlds, Virginia Quarterly Review, Waves, Webster Review, West Branch, Western Humanities Review, Wildcat, Writ Magazine.

War. Alpha, The Berkeley Monthly Magazine.

Western. Alpha, The Berkeley Monthly Review, Black Jack, Canadian Author & Bookman, Coffee Break, Creative Pittsburgh Journal, Cross Currents, De Colores Journal, Descant, Dreams Unlimited, Dreamweaver Magazine, Earthwise Quarterly, Empty Window Review, In a Nutshell, Inky Trails, John O'Hara Journal, "Joint" Conference, Juice, Kansas Quarterly, Lebeacon Review, The Missouri Review, Muscadine, Phantasm, Pteranodon Magazine, Samisdat, Sojourner, Straight Ahead International, Sunrise, Time to Pause, Valley Grapevine, Waves, Wildcat.

Women's. Afta, Aquila Magazine, Aura Literary Arts Review, The Barat Review, Bare Wires, The Berkeley Monthly Magazine, The Black Scholar, Blitz, Broadsheet Magazine, Calliope, Canadian Author & Bookman, The Coe Review, The Coffee Break, Confrontation, Cottonwood Review, Creative Pittsburgh Journal, Cross Currents, Croton Review, Cumberland Journal, Cumberlands, De Colores Journal, Descant, Double Harness Magazine, Feminist Studies, Fifth Sun, Heresies, Home Planet News, In a Nutshell, John O'Hara Journal, Juice, Kalliope: A Journal of Women's Arts, Kansas Quarterly, Lebeacon Review, Letters Magazine, Lilith Magazine, Maize: Notebooks of Xicano Art and Literature, The Malahat Review, Mango, The Missouri Review, Muscadine, New America, Occident, Parabola, Phantasm, Plains Woman, Rara Avis Magazine, Salome: A Literary Dance Magazine, Salt Lick, San Jose Studies, The Second Wave, Sequoia Magazine, Sez: A Multi-Racial Journal of Poetry & People's Culture, Signals, Sing Heavenly Muse!, Sojourner, The Source, The Spirit That Moves Us, Story Quarterly, Straight Ahead International, Syzygy, Virginia Quarterly Review, Wildcat, Women: A Journal of Liberation.

Young Adult. The Black Scholar, Channel X, Coffee Break, De Colores Journal, Descant, Hob-Nob, Inky Trails, Lilith Magazine, Ragged Readin', Salt Lick, Sojourner, Straight Ahead International, Sunrise, Time to Pause, Wildcat.

COMMERCIAL PERIODICALS

Adventure. The Augusta Spectator, Bread, Buffalo Spree, Canadian Skater, Chatelaine, Chesapeake Bay, Cosmopolitan, Dude, Easyriders, Essence, Gent, Good Housekeeping, Hustler, Messenger of the Sacred Heart, Mink, Ms., New Alaskan, Nugget, Orange Coast, Outside, Penthouse, Playboy, Players, Prime Times, Reflection, Road King, Rustler, RV'n On, San Gabriel Valley, Saturday Evening Post, Seventeen, Tar Heel, Venture, Western People, The Western Producer, The Wisconsin Restaurateur, Working for Boys.

Confession. Family Circle, Hers, Intimate Romances, Intimate Secrets, Intimate Story, The National Supermarket Shopper, Personal Romances, Secrets, True Love, True Secrets.

Erotica. Cavalier, Hustler, Playboy, Chic, Dude, Elite, Gallery, Gent, Harvey for Loving People, Hustler, Intimate Story, Mink, Nugget, Penthouse, Pillow Talk, Players, Prime Times, Rustler, Swank.

Ethnic. The American Mizrachi Woman, Ararat, Attenzione, Buffalo Spree, Chicago, The Deaf Canadian, Ebony Jr!, Family Circle, Hers, Mademoiselle, Ms., Players, Scandinavian Review, Scholastic Scope, Seventeen, Teens Today, World Over.

Experimental. Essence, Players.

Fantasy. Ares, Chesapeake Bay, Collage, Creative Computing, Elite, Essence, Gallery, Heavy Metal, Mink, Ms., National Doll World, The National Supermarket Shopper, Omni, Outside, Personal Romances, Playboy, Players, Reflection, Road King, Rustler, RV'n On, Seventeen, Starwind, Tar Heel, Western's World, Woman's Day.

Feminist. Buffalo Spree, Delaware Today, Mademoiselle, Ms., Personal Romances, Prime Times, Redbook, Seventeen, Woman's Day.

Gay/Lesbian. Harvey for Loving People, Mademoiselle, Ms.

Gothic. Good Housekeeping, Personal Romances, Romantic Times, RV'n On, Saturday Evening Post, Sunshine Magazine, True Secrets.

Historical. Players, Romantic Times, Tar Heel.

Horror. Cavalier, Collage, Dude, Gallery, Gent, Mink, Nugget, Penthouse, Playboy, Rustler, RV'n on, Starwind, Tar Heel.

Humor. The Augusta Spectator, Autosport Canada, Buffalo Spree, Canadian Driver/Owner, Chatelaine, Chesapeake Bay, Chicago, Collage, Contact, Creative Computing, Delaware Today, Dude, Elite, Essence, Family Circle, Farm Wife News, First Class, Gallery, Gent, Golf Journal, Harper's, Home Life, Ideals, Living Message, Mature Living, McCall's, Messenger of the Sacred Heart, Mink, Ms., The National Supermarket Shopper, New Alaskan, Nugget, Orange Coast, Outside, Personal Computing, Playboy, Players, Prime Times, Racquetball Illustrated, Reflection, Road King, Road Rider, Rustler, RV'n on, San Gabriel Valley, Saturday Evening Post, Seventeen, Smile and Chuckle, Sunshine, Swank, Tar Heel, 'Teen, Teens Today, Venture, Vista, Western People, The Western Producer, Western's World, The Wisconsin Restaurateur, Woman's Day, Working for Boys, Young Miss.

Juvenile. Beehive, Child Life, Children's Digest, Children's Playmate, The Church Herald, Cricket, Dash, Discoveries, Discovery, Ebony Jr!, The Friend, Highlights for Children, Humpty Dumpty's Magazine, Ideals, Jack and Jill, Junior Trails, Kindergartner, Magook, Ms., Prime

Times, R-A-D-A-R, Ranger Rick's Nature Magazine, RV'n On, Story Friend, Sunshine, Trails, Turtle Magazine, Venture, The Vine, The Western Producer, The Wisconsin Restaurateur, Woman's Day, Wonder Time, Working for Boys, Working Mother, World Over, The Young Crusader.

Men's. Buffalo Spree, Cavalier, Chicago, Cosmopolitan, Creative Computing, Dude, Easyriders, Elite, Esquire, Gent, Hers, Hustler, Ideals, Mademoiselle, Mink, Nugget, Penthouse, Playboy, Prime Times, Road King, Rustler, Sunshine, Swank, The Western Producer, The Wisconsin Restaurateur.

Mystery. Alfred Hitchcock's Mystery Magazine, The Augusta Spectator, Buffalo Spree, Chatelaine, Chesapeake Bay, Collage, Cosmopolitan, Delaware Today, Dude, Ellery Queen's Mystery Magazine, Family Circle, Gent, Grit, Jack and Jill, Messenger of the Sacred Heart, Mike Shayne Mystery Magazine, Mink, Ms., The National Supermarket Shopper, Nugget, Orange Coast Magazine, Playboy, Prime Times, Reflection, Road King Magazine, Rustler, RV'n On, Saturday Evening Post, Seventeen, Tar Heel, 'Teen, The Western Producer, The Wisconsin Restaurateur, Young Miss.

Psychic/Supernatural. Dude, Gent, Hers, Home Life, Hustler, Ideals, Intimate Story, Messenger of the Sacred Heart, Ms., National Doll World, Nugget, Penthouse, Personal Romances, Starwind.

Religious/Inspirational. Christian Living for Senior Highs, The Church Herald, Contact, Evangel, Face-to-Face, Family Circle, Hi-Call, In Touch, Insight, Junior Trails, Live, Living Message, Living with Teenagers, The Lookout, The Lutheran Journal, Mature Living, Mature Years, Messenger of the Sacred Heart, Reflection, St. Anthony Messenger, San Gabriel Valley, Saturday Evening Post, Seek, Seventeen, Sprint, Story Friend, Straight, Sunday Digest, Sunshine, Teens Today, Trails, Venture, Vista, Wind, Woman's Day, Wonder Time, Working for Boys, World Over, Young Ambassador, Young and Alive.

Romance. The Augusta Spectator, Chatelaine, Cosmopolitan, Essence, Family Circle, First Class, Good Housekeeping, Grit, Intimate Romances, Intimate Story, Messenger of the Sacred Heart, The National Supermarket Shopper, Orange Coast, Personal Romances, Prime Times, Reflection, Romantic Times, Saturday Evening Post, Seventeen, 'Teen Magazine, Teens Today, True Love, True Secrets, Western's World, Young Miss.

Science Fiction. Analog Science Fiction/Science Fact, Ares, Cavalier, Collage, Creative Computing, Dude, Gallery, Gent, Heavy Metal, Hustler, Isaac Asimov's Science Fiction Magazine, Jack and Jill, Messenger of the Sacred Heart, Ms., Nugget, Omni, Penthouse, Personal Computing, Playboy, Players, Reflection, Road King, RV'n On, Saturday Evening Post, Seventeen, Starwind, Tar Heel, The Wisconsin Restaurateur, Young Miss.

Senior Adults. Mature Living, Mature Years, Modern Maturity.

Serialized, Condensed or Excerpted Works. Analog Science Fiction/Science Fact, Capper's Weekly, Chicago, Ebony Jr!, Essence, Family Circle, Grit, Mademoiselle, McCall's, Penthouse, Redbook, Romantic Times, Western People, The Western Producer.

Translations. Hadassah Magazine, Scandanavian Review, World Over.

Western. Dude, Far West, Gent, Good Housekeeping, Grit, Messenger of the Sacred Heart, Nugget, Orange Coast, Penthouse, Playboy, Road King, RV'n On, San Gabriel Valley, Saturday Evening Post, Seventeen, The Western Producer, The Wisconsin Restaurateur.

Women's. Buffalo Spree, Chicago, Colorado Woman, Creative Computing, Delaware Today, Family Circle, Good Housekeeping, Hers, Ideals, Intimate Story, Mademoiselle, Ms., The National Supermarket Shopper, Personal Romances, Prime Times, Redbook, Secrets, Sunshine, The Western Producer, The Wisconsin Restaurateur, Woman's Day, Working Mother.

Young Adult. Alive! for Young Teens, Canadian Skater, Children's Digest, The Church Herald, Cobblestone, Contact, Dash, Evangel, Hers, Hi-Call, Home Life, Insight, Intimate Story, The Lookout, The Lutheran Journal, Ms., Reflection, RV'n On, Scholastic Scope, Seventeen, Sprint, 'Teen, Teens Today, Trails, Venture, The Wisconsin Restaurateur, World Over, Young and Alive, Young Miss.

SMALL PRESS

Adventure. Ariadne Press, Beninda Books, Bicentennial Era Enterprises, The Dragonsbreath Press, Fred A. Fleet, II, Gluxlit Press, J.C.R. Green, Ras Communications, Salt Lick Press, John Westburg.

Confession. Guernica Editions, Programmed Studies, Inc., R&M Publishing Company.

Erotica. Allegany Mountain Press, And Books, Angel Press, Applezaba Press, The Arcane Order, The Dragonsbreath Press, Fantome Press, Front Press, JCR Green, Guernica Editions, Noro Press, Peppermint Press, Perivale Press, Programmed Studies, Salt Lick Press, Surree Limited, Third Coast.

Ethnic. Challenge Press, Co-op Books, Cross-Cultural Communications, Curbstone Press, Gluxlit Press, Griffon House Publications, Holmgangers Press, House of Anansi Press, Liberator Press, Lynx House Press, Mountain State Press, New Seed Press, Nordic Books, Noro Press, Perivale Press, Pikeville College Press, Riversedge Press, R&M Publishing, Salt Lick Press, Story Press.

Experimental. Allegany Mountain Press, And Books, Applezaba Press, The Bieler Press, Broken Whisker Studio, Carpenter Press, Chock Publications, Chthon Press, Colorado State Review Press, Co-op Books, Cross-Cultural Communications, Curbstone Press, December Press, Dimensionist Press, The Dragonsbreath Press, Expanded Media Editions, Fiction Collective, Fred A. Fleet, Front Press, Gay Sunshine Press, Goethe's Press, J.C.R. Green, Griffon House Publications, Ground Under Press, Harian, Holmgangers Press, House of Anansi, Illuminations Press, Intermedia Press, Lapis Educational Association, Laughing Bear Press, Libra Press, Lintel, Lorien House, Mudborn Press, New Rivers Press, Ommation Press, Paycock Press, Perivale Press, Pig Iron Press, Pikestaff Publications, Poet Galley Press, Programmed Studies, Pulse-finger Press, Raccoon Books, Ras Communications, Riversedge Press, Salt Lick Press, School of Living Press, Small World Publications, Sono Nis Press, Third Coast, Thunder City Press, University of Illinois Press, John Westburg, Women's Educational Press, York Press.

Faction. Applezaba Press, Challenge Press, Curbstone Press, Expanded Media Editions, Mudborn Press, Ras Communications, Salt Lick Press.

Fantasy. And Books, Applezaba Press, The Arcane Order, The Bieler Press, Carpenter Press, Dimensionist Press, The Dragonsbreath Press, Fantome Press, Fred A. Fleet, Folden Editions, J.C.R. Green, Ground Under Press, Jelm Mountain Publishing, Harian, Lorien House, Noro Press, Peppermint Press, Perivale Press, Pig Iron Press, Ras Communications, Salt Lick Press, Seed Center, Third Coast, John Westburg, Women's Educational Press.

Feminist. Angel Press, Applezaba Press, Ariadne Press, Co-op Books, Crossing Press, Curbstone Press, Ground Under Press, Guernica Editions, Lakes and Prairies Press, Liberator Press, Metis Press, The Naiad Press, New Seed Press, Ommation Press, Perivale Press, Persephone Press, Press Gang Publishers, Programmed Studies, Riversedge Press, R&M Publishing, Salt Lick Press, Third Coast, Wim Publications, Women's Educational Press.

Gay/Lesbian. Angel Press, Applezaba Press, Calamus Books, Co-op Books, The Crossing Press, Curbstone Press, Gay Sunshine Press, Ground Under Press, Guernica Editions, Metis Press, The Naiad Press, New Seed Press, Noro Press, Programmed Studies, R&M Publishing Company, Salt Lick Press, Surree Limited, Third Coast, Wim Publications, Women's Educational Press.

Gothic. Fantome Press, Laughing Bear Press, Ras Communications, Salt Lick Press.

Historical. Ariadne Press, Challenge Press, Co-op Books, Curbstone Press, Gluxlit Press, JCR Green, Intermedia Press, Jelm Mountain Publishing, Lame Johnny Press, Liberator Press, Library Research Associates, Maine Writers Workshop, New Rivers Press, Ras Communications, Riversedge Press, Salt Lick Press, Shoal Creek Publishers, Sherry Urie, John Westburg.

Horror. And Books, The Bieler Press, The Dragonsbreath Press, Gluxlit Press, JCR Green, Noro Press, R&M Publishing Company, Salt Lick Press.

Humor. Allegany Mountain Press, Angel Press, Applezaba Press, Ariadne Press, Cheapo Press, Co-op Books, Cross-Cultural Communications, The Dragonsbreath Press, Fred A. Fleet, Front Press, Gluxlit Press, J.C.R. Green, Ground Under Press, Guernica Editions, Illuminations Press, Intermedia Press, Libra Press, Lorien House, Maine Writers Workshop, Paycock Press, Peppermint Press, Pig Iron Press, Programmed Studies, Ras Communications, Salt Lick Press, Seed Center, Small World Publications, Third Coast, John Westburg.

Juvenile. And Books, Cross-Cultural Communications, Dimensionist Press, Gluxlit Press, Guernica Editions, Holmgangers Press, In Between Books, Lollipop Power, Maine Writers Workshop, Masters Publications, New Seed Press, Peppermint Press, Press Gang Publishers, Ras Communications, R&M Publishing Company, Seed Center, Shoal Creek Publishers, Talespinner Publications, Walnut Press, Women's Educational Press.

Mystery. And Books, Ariadne Press, Beninda Books, Bicentennial Era Enterprises, Challenge Press, The Dragonsbreath Press, Gluxit Press, JCR Green, Laughing Bear Press, Maine Writers Workshop, Ras Communications, R&M Publishing Company, Salt Lick Press, Sherry Urie.

Psychic/Supernatural. The Arcane Order, Dimensionist Press, Fred A. Fleet, JCR Green, Guernica Editions, Lapis Educational Association, R&M Publishing Company, Salt Lick Press, Seed Center.

Religious/Inspirational. Angel Press, The Arcane Order, Guernica Editions, Lapis Educational Association, R&M Publishing Company, Seed Center, Small World Publications, Sherry Urie.

Romance. Fred A. Fleet, Gluxlit Press, Guernica Editions, Harian, R&M Publishing.

Science Fiction. The Bieler Press, Chthon Press, Dimensionist Press, The Dragonsbreath Press, Fantome Press, Front Press, Gluxlit Press, J.C.R. Green, Harian, Laughing Bear Press, Maine Writers Workshop, Noro Press, Peppermint Press, Pig Iron Press, R&M Publishing Company, Ras Communications, Salt Lick Press, Seed Center, Third Coast, John Westburg.

Serialized, Condensed or Excerpted Works. Cheapo Press, Lakes and Prairies Press, Noro Press.

Translations. And Books, Applezaba Press, Chock Publications, Cross-Cultural Communications, Curbstone Press, Folden Editions, Front Press, Gay Sunshine Press, J.C.R. Green, Griffon House Publications, Ground Under Press, Guernica Editions, Harian, Holmgangers Press, House of Anansi Press Limited, Intermedia Press, Mudborn Press, New Rivers Press, Nordic Books, Noro Press, Paycock Press, Perivale Press, Persephone Press, Riversedge Press, Salt Lick Press, Thunder City Press, York Press.

War. Ariadne Press, Gluxlit Press, Liberator Press, Ras Communications, Salt Lick Press, John Westburg.

Western. Beninda Books, The Dragonsbreath Press, Gluxlit Press, Holmgangers Press, Jelm Mountain Publishing, Lame Johnny Press, Laughing Bear Press, Perivale Press, Ras Communications, Salt Lick Press, John Westburg.

Women's. Ariadne Press, Co-op Books, The Crossing Press, Curbstone Press, Folden Editions, Ground Under Press, Guernica Editions, House of Anansi Press, Intermedia Press, Liberator Press, Metis Press, Perivale Press, Persephone Press, Press Gang Publishers, R&M Publishing Company, Salt Lick Press, Seed Center, Story Press, Third Coast, Sherry Urie, Women's Educational Press.

Young Adult. And Books, Cross-Cultural Communications, Gluxlit Press, Guernica Editions, Holmgangers Press, In Between Books, Lakes and Prairies Press, Maine Writers Workshop, Masters Publications, New Seed Press, Peppermint Press, Ras Communications, R&M Publishing Company, Seed Center, Walnut Press, Women's Educational Press.

COMMERCIAL PUBLISHERS

Adventure. Andrews and McMeel, Avon Books, Bantam Books, Beaufort Books, Bethany Fellowship, Borealis Press, Bradbury Press, Broadman Press, Celestial Arts, Clarke, Irwin & Co., Dell Publishing, The Dial Press, Dodd, Mead & Company, Elsevier/Nelson Books, Everest House Publishers, Fawcett Gold Medal, Fawcett Popular Library, Heian International, Holiday House, Holloway House Publishing, Leisure Books, Lester and Orpen Dennys, Little, Brown, Macmillan of Canada, Manor Books, Manyland Books, Methuen Publishers, Moody Press, William Morrow and Company, Mountaineers Books, New American Library, Nordon Publications, W.W. Norton, Peninsula Publishing, Pocket Books, Clarkson N. Potter, Red Dembner Enterprises, St. Martin's Press, Charles Scribner's Sons, Simon & Pierre Publishing, Thorndike Press, Tower Publications, University of Missouri Press, Vanguard Press, Western Publishing, Zebra Books.

Confession. Doubleday Canada, Manor Books, New American Library, Pan American Publishing, St. Martin's Press, Zebra Books.

Erotica. Celestial Arts, Eros Publishing, Greenleaf Classics, Grove Press, Manyland Books, Pocket Books, St. Martin's Press, Zebra Books.

Ethnic. Bantam Books, John F. Blair, Breakwater Books, Crown Publishers, Dodd, Mead, Doubleday Canada, David R. Godine, Grove Press, Harmony Books, Heian International, Hill Wang, Holiday House, Holloway House Publishing, Little, Brown, Manyland Books, Methuen Publishers, Pelican Publishing, Pocket Books, Ross-Erikson Publishers, St. Martin's Press, Seaview Books, Stemmer House Publishers, University of Missouri Press, Vesta Publications.

Experimental. Avalon Books, John F. Blair, Celestial Arts, Coker Publisher House, Columbia Publishing, Commoner's Publishing, Dodd, Mead, Elsevier/Nelson Books, Eros Publishing, Green Tiger Press, Grove Press, Lester and Orpen Dennys, Macmillan Canada, Manyland Books, Methuen Publishers, William Morrow, Pan American Publishing, Pelican Publishing, St. Martin's Press, Charles Scribner's Sons, Treacle Press, Urizen Books, Vesta Publications.

Faction. Beaufort Books, Bobbs-Merrill, Dell Publishing, Dodd, Mead, Doubleday Canada, E. P. Dutton Publishers, Harmony Books, Lester and Orpen Dennys, Little, Brown, Macmillan Canada, Manyland Books, Methuen Publishers, Pocket Books, Clarkson N. Potter, St. Martin's Press, Charles Scribner's Sons, Seaview Books, Vanguard Press.

Fantasy. Ace Science Fiction, Bantam Books, Beaufort Books, Clarke, Irwin, Coker Publisher House, The Donning Company/Publishers, Elsevier/Nelson Books, Eros Publishing, David R. Godine, Green Tiger Press, Leisure Books, Lester and Orpen Dennys, Manor Books, Methuen Publishers, Nordon Publications, Pan American Publishing, Playboy Press, Pocket Books, St. Martin's Press, Stemmer House Publishers, Tower Publications, University of Missouri Press.

Feminist. Academy Chicago Ltd., Bantam Books, John F. Blair, Celestial Arts, Dell Publishing,

Dial Press, Dodd, Mead, Doubleday Canada, Eros Publishing, Grove Press, Harmony Books, Lester and Orpen Dennys, Little, Brown, Macmillan Canada, Methuen, William Morrow & Company, Playboy Press, Pocket Books, Ross-Erikson, St. Martin's Press, Charles Scribner's Sons, Seaview Books, Talonbooks, Timely Books, Treacle Press, University of Missouri Press.

Gay/Lesbian. Bantam Books, Dell Publishing, Eros Publishing, Grove Press, Holiday House, Methuen Publishers, William Morrow, Ross-Erikson Publishers, St. Martin's Press, Talonbooks, Timely Books, University of Missouri Press, Urizen Books.

Gothic. Bantam Books, Beaufort Books, Bethany Fellowship, David C. Cook Publishing Company, Dodd, Mead, Donning Company/Publishers, Eros Publishing, Leisure Books, Manor Books, Nordon Publications, Pinnacle Books, Pocket Books, St. Martin's Press, Tandem Press Publishers, Tiara Books, Tower Publications, Vesta Publications, Zebra Books.

Historical. Andrews and McMeel, Bantam Books, Beaufort Books, Bethany Fellowship, John F. Blair, Bobbs-Merrill, Bookcraft, Borealis Press, Breakwater Books, Broadman Press, Celestial Arts, Clarke, Irwin, Columbia Publishing, Dell Publishing Co., Dial Press, Dodd, Mead, Donning Company/Publishers, Doubleday Canada, Elsevier/Nelson Books, Eros Publishing, Everest House Publishers, Fawcett Popular Library, Richard Gallen Books, David R. Godine, Grove Press, Harlequin Enterprises, Heian International, Holloway House, Icarus Press, Island Press, Leisure Books, Lester and Orpen Dennys, Little, Brown, Macmillan of Canada, Manor Books, Manyland Books, Moody Press, William Morrow, New American Library, Nordon Publications, W.W. Norton, Pan American Publishing, Pelican Publishing, Peninsula Publishing, Peregine Smith, Playboy Press, Pocket Books, Clarkson N. Potter, Red Dembner Enterprises, St. Martin's Press, Charles Scribner's Sons, Seaview Books, Simon & Pierre Publishing, Stemmer House Publishers, Tandem Press, Thorndike Press, Tiara Books, Times Books, Tower Publications, Vesta Publications, Zebra Books.

Horror. Bantam Books, Beaufort Books, Celestial Arts, Charter Books, Coward, McCann & Geoghegan, Dell Publishing, Donning Company/Publishers, Eros Publishing, Fawcett Popular Library, David R. Godine, Leisure Books, Lester and Orpen Dennys, Little, Brown, Manor Books, William Morrow, New American Library, Nordon Publications, Pan American Publishing, Pinnacle Books, Playboy Press, Pocket Books, St. Martin's Press, Charles Scribner's Sons, Tower Publications, Walker and Company, Zebra Books.

Humor. Alchemy Books, Bantam Books, Beaufort Books, John F. Blair, Bradbury Press, Broadman Press, Celestial Arts, Clarke, Irwin, Crown Publishers, Dodd, Mead, Donning Company/Publishers, Doubleday Canada, Elsevier/Nelson books, Eros Publishing, Everest House, David R. Godine, Grove Press, Holiday House, Leisure Books, Lester and Orpen Dennys Ltd., Little, Brown, Macmillan Canada, Methuen Publishers, William Morrow, Mountaineers Books, W. W. Norton, Pan American Publishing Company, Pelican Publishing, Pinnacle Books, Pocket Books, Clarkson N. Potter, Queenston House Publishing, St. Martin's Press, Charles Scribner's Sons, Simon & Pierre Publishing, That New Publishing Company, Thorndike Press, Times Books, University of Missouri Press, Vanguard Press, Western Publishing.

Juvenile. A&P Books, Addison-Wesley Publishing, Apple Press, Atlantic Monthly Press, Avon Books, Baker Book House, Beaufort Books, Bethany Fellowship, Bookcraft, Borealis Press, Bradbury Press, Breakwater Books, Broadman Press, Child's World, Clarion Books/Houghton Mifflin, Clarke, Irwin, David C. Cook Publishing, Coward, McCann & Geoghegan, Crowell and Lippincott Junior Books, Crown Publishers, Dawne-Leigh Publications, Dell Publishing, Dodd, Mead, E. P. Dutton Publishers, Eakin Publications, Farrar, Straus & Giroux, David R. Godine, Green Tiger Press, Greenwillow Books, Harcourt Brace Jovanovich, Harvey House Publishers, Heian International, Herald Press, Holloway House Publishing, Ideals Publishing, Lippincott Junior Books, Little, Brown, Margaret K. McElderry/Atheneum Publishers, Manyland Books, Methuen Publishers, William Morrow and Company, Oak Tree Publications, Oddo Publishing, Pan American Publishing, Parents Magazine Press, Pelican Publishing, Peninsula Publishing, Platt & Munk, Prentice-Hall, Rand McNally, Random House Juvenile Div., Scholastic-Tab Publications, Charles Scribner's Sons, Simon & Pierre Publishing Company, Standard Publishing, Stemmer House, Vanguard Press, Vesta Publications, Walker & Company, Frederick Warne and Co., Western Publishing, Westminster Press, Albert Whitman.

Mystery. Academy Chicago, Andrews and McMeel, Avon Books, Bantam Books, Beaufort Books, Bethany Fellowship, Charter Books, Clarke, Irwin, David C. Cook, Dell Publishing, Dial Press, Dodd, Mead, Doubleday Canada, Elsevier/Nelson Books, Eros Publishing, Everest House, Fawcett Gold Medal, Fawcett Popular Library, David R. Godine, Grove Press, Harlequin Enterprises, Alfred A. Knopf, Leisure Books, Lester and Orpen Dennys, Little, Brown, Macmillan of Canada, Manor Books, Manyland Books, Methuen Publishers, William Morrow, New American Library, Nordon Publications, W. W. Norton, Pan American Publishing, Pelican Publishing, Peninsula Publishing, Pinnacle Books, Pocket Books, Clarkson N. Potter, Red Dembner Enterprises, Ross-Erikson, St. Martin's Press, Charles Scribner's Sons, Simon & Pierre, Tandem Press Publishers, Times Books, Tower Publications, Vanguard Press, Walker and Company, Western Publishing.

Psychic/Supernatural. Alchemy Books, Bantam Books, Beaufort Books, Celestial Arts, Coward, McCann & Geoghegan, Dell Publishing, Dial Press, Donning Company/Publishers, Doubleday Canada, Eros Publishing, Leisure Books, Manor Books, New American Library, Pan American Publishing Company, Pocket Books, St. Martin's Press, Seaview Books, Tower Publications, Zebra Books.

Religious/Inspirational. Alchemy Books, Augsburg Publishing House, Bantam Books, Bethany Fellowship, Bookcraft, Broadman Press, Concordia Publishing House, David C. Cook, Dodd, Mead, Donning Company/Publisher, Heian International, Herald Press, Island Press, Manyland Books, Moody Press, Pan American Publishing, Pelican Publishing, Resource Publications, St. Martin's Press, Standard Publishing, Vesta Publications.

Romance. Ace/Tempo Books, Avalon Books, Bantam Books, Beaufort Books, John F. Blair, Bookcraft, David C. Cook, Dell Publishing, Richard Gallen Books, Harlequin Enterprises, Holiday House, Leisure Books, Manor Books, New American Library, Nordon Publications, Pan American Publishing, Peninsula Publishing, Playboy Press, Pocket Books, St. Martin's Press, Silhouette Romances, Tandem Press, Tiara Books, Tower Publications, Vesta Publications, Walker and Company, Zebra Books.

Science Fiction. Ace Science Fiction, Alchemy Books, Bantam Books, Beaufort Books, Bradbury Press, Celestial Arts, Clarke, Irwin, Donning Company/Publishers, Elsevier/Nelson Books, Fawcett Gold Medal, Grove Press, Harmony Books, Leisure Books, Lester and Orpen Dennys, Manor Books, Methuen Publishers, William Morrow, New American Library, Nordon Publications, Pan American Publishing, Pinnacle Books, Playboy Press, Pocket Books, St. Martin's Press, Charles Scribner's Sons, Sun Publishing, Tower Publications, Unity Press, Vesta Publications, Walker and Company.

Serialized, Condensed or Excerpted Works. A&P Books.

Translations. A&P Books, Academy Chicago, Columbia Publishing, Commoner's Publishing, E. P. Dutton Publishers, Grove Press, Heian International, Icarus Press, Lester and Orpen Dennys, Little, Brown, Manyland Books, Methuen Publishers, William Morrow, W. W. Norton, Pelican Publishing, Clarkson N. Potter, Charles Scribner's Sons, Simon & Pierre, Talonbooks, Times Books, Treacle Press, Urizen Books, Vesta Publications.

War. Bantam Books, Beaufort Books, Bobbs-Merrill, Clarke, Irwin, Ltd., Dell Publishing, Dodd, Mead, Doubleday Canada, Eros Publishing, Icarus Press, Leisure Books, Lester and Orpen Dennys, Little, Brown, Macmillan Canada, Manor Books, Manyland Books, Methuen Publishers, William Morrow, New American Library, Nordon Publications, W. W. Norton, Pelican Publishing, Pinnacle Books, Pocket Books, St. Martin's Press, Charles Scribner's Sons, Stemmer House, Times Books, Tower Publications, University of Missouri Press, Vanguard Press, Vesta Publications, Zebra Books.

Western. Avalon Books, Avon Books, Bantam Books, Bookcraft, Dell Publishing, Dial Press, Elsevier/Nelson Books, Eros Publishing, Leisure Books, Lester & Orpen Dennys, Macmillan Canada, Manor Books, Moody Press, William Morrow, Nordon Publications, W. W. Norton, Peninsula Publishing, Pocket Books, Ross-Erikson, St. Martin's Press, Seaview Books, Tower Publications, Zebra Books.

Women's. Bantam Books, Beaufort Books, Bobbs-Merrill, Bookcraft, Celestial Arts, Clarke, Irwin, Ltd., Dell Publishing, Dial Press, Dodd, Mead, Doubleday Canada, Everest House, Fawcett Popular Library, Grove Press, Harmony Books, Leisure Books, Lester and Orpen Dennys, Little, Brown, Macmillan Canada, Manor Books, William Morrow, New American Library, Nordon Publications, W. W. Norton, Pan American Publishing, Pinnacle Books, Playboy Press, Pocket Books, Clarkson N. Potter, Ross-Erikson Publishers, St. Martin's Press, Charles Scribner's Sons, Seaview Books, Talonbooks, Tandem Press, Tiara Books, Times Books, Tower Publications, Zebra Books.

Young Adult. A&P Books, Ace/Tempo Books, Addison-Wesley Publishing, Atlantic Monthly Press, Augsburg Publishing House, Avon Books, Baker Book House, Bantam Books, Beaufort Books, John F. Blair, Bookcraft, Borealis Press, Bradbury Press, Breakwater Books, Broadman Press, Clarion Books/Houghton Mifflin, Clarke, Irwin, Coward, McCann & Geoghegan, Crowell and Lippincott Junior Books, Crown Publishers, Dawne-Leigh Publications, Dodd, Mead, The Donning Company, Elsevier/Nelson Books, Farrar, Straus & Giroux, Fawcett Popular Library, David R. Godine, Greenwillow Books, Harcourt Brace Jovanovich, Harvey House, Heian International, Herald Press, Lippincott Junior Books, Little, Brown, Margaret K. Elderry/Atheneum Publishers, Manyland Books, Methuen Publishers, Moody Press, William Morrow, Oak Tree Publications, Oddo Publishing, Pan American Publishing, Pelican Publishing, Peninsula Publishing, Platt & Munk, Prentice-Hall, Charles Scribner's Sons, Simon & Pierre, Stemmer House Publishers, Vanguard Press, Vesta Publications, Walker and Company, Frederick Warne.

Index

O

P

Q

R

Other Writer's Digest Books

Market Books
Artist's Market, 474 pp. $11.95
Craftworker's Market, 570 pp. $12.95
Fiction Writer's Market, 504 pp. $15.95
Photographer's Market, 549 pp. $12.95
Songwriter's Market, 400 pp. $11.95
Writer's Market, 917 pp. $15.95

General Writing Books
Beginning Writer's Answer Book, 264 pp. $9.95
Law and the Writer, 240 pp. $9.95
Make Every Word Count, 256 pp. (cloth) $10.95; (paper) $6.95
Treasury of Tips for Writers, (paper), 174 pp. $6.95
Writer's Resource Guide, 488 pp. $12.95

Magazine/News Writing
Complete Guide to Marketing Magazine Articles, 248 pp. $9.95
Craft of Interviewing, 244 pp. $9.95
Magazine Writing: The Inside Angle, 256 pp. $10.95
Magazine Writing Today, 220 pp. $9.95
Newsthinking: The Secret of Great Newswriting, 204 pp. $11.95
1001 Article Ideas, 270 pp. $10.95
Stalking the Feature Story, 310 pp. $9.95
Writing and Selling Non-Fiction, 317 pp. $10.95

Fiction Writing
Creating Short Fiction, 228 pp. $11.95
Handbook of Short Story Writing, (paper), 238 pp. $6.95
How to Write Best-Selling Fiction, 300 pp. $13.95
How to Write Short Stories that Sell, 212 pp. $9.95
One Way to Write Your Novel, 138 pp. $8.95
Secrets of Successful Fiction, 119 pp. $8.95
Writing the Novel: From Plot to Print, 197 pp. $10.95

Category Writing Books
Cartoonist's and Gag Writer's Handbook, (paper), 157 pp. $9.95
Children's Picture Book: How to Write It, How to Sell It, 224 pp. $16.95
Confession Writer's Handbook, 173 pp. $9.95
Guide to Greeting Card Writing, 256 pp. $10.95
Guide to Writing History, 258 pp. $9.95
How to Write and Sell Your Personal Experiences, 226 pp. $10.95
Mystery Writer's Handbook, 273 pp. $9.95
The Poet and the Poem, 399 pp. $11.95
Poet's Handbook, 224 pp. $10.95
Sell Copy, 205 pp. $11.95
Successful Outdoor Writing, 244 pp. $11.95
Travel Writer's Handbook, 274 pp. $11.95
TV Scriptwriter's Handbook, 322 pp. $11.95
Writing and Selling Science Fiction, 191 pp. $8.95
Writing for Children & Teenagers, 269 pp. $9.95
Writing for Regional Publications, 203 pp. $11.95

The Writing Business
Complete Handbook for Freelance Writers, 400 pp. $14.95
How to Be a Successful Housewife/Writer, 254 pp. $10.95

How You Can Make $20,000 a Year Writing: No Matter Where You Live, 270 pp. (cloth) $10.95; (paper) $6.95
Jobs For Writers, 281 pp. $11.95
Profitable Part-time/Full-time Freelancing, 195 pp. $10.95
Writer's Digest Diary, 144 pp. $12.95

To order directly from the publisher, include $1.25 postage and handling for 1 book and 50¢ for each additional book. Allow 30 days for delivery.

For a current catalog of books for writers or information on *Writer's Digest* magazine, *Writer's Yearbook*, Writer's Digest School correspondence courses or manuscript criticism, write to:

Writer's Digest Books, Department B
9933 Alliance Road, Cincinnati OH 45242

Prices subject to change without notice.